Lecture Notes in Computer Science 4858

Commenced Publication in 1973
Founding and Former Series Editors:
Gerhard Goos, Juris Hartmanis, and Jan van Leeuwen

T0139930

Xiaotie Deng   Fan Chung Graham (Eds.)

Internet and Network Economics

Third International Workshop, WINE 2007
San Diego, CA, USA, December 12-14, 2007
Proceedings

 Springer

Volume Editors

Xiaotie Deng
City University of Hong Kong
Department of Computer Science
Tat Chee Avenue, Kowloon, Hong Kong, China
E-mail: csdeng@cityu.edu.hk

Fan Chung Graham
University of California at San Diego
Department of Mathematics
La Jolla, CA 92093-0112, USA
E-mail: fan@ucsd.edu

Library of Congress Control Number: Applied for

CR Subject Classification (1998): H.4, K.4.4, J.1, H.3, H.2, G.1.2

LNCS Sublibrary: SL 3 – Information Systems and Application, incl. Internet/Web
and HCI

ISSN   0302-9743
ISBN-10   3-540-77104-2 Springer Berlin Heidelberg New York
ISBN-13   978-3-540-77104-3 Springer Berlin Heidelberg New York

Springer is a part of Springer Science+Business Media

springer.com

© Springer-Verlag Berlin Heidelberg 2007
Printed in Germany

Typesetting: Camera-ready by author, data conversion by Scientific Publishing Services, Chennai, India
Printed on acid-free paper   SPIN: 12196593   06/3180   5 4 3 2 1 0

Preface

The Workshop on Internet and Network Economics (WINE 2007), held December 12–14, 2007 at San Diego for its third edition, provided a forum for researchers from different disciplines to communicate their research works in this emerging field.

We had four plenary speakers: Kenneth Arrow, Herbert Scarf, Vijay Vazirani, and Christos Papadimitriou, speaking on economic equilibrium and its history, its solution methodologies (the simplicial structure method and the primal dual method), as well as the computation of Nash equilibrium.

This final program included 61 peer-reviewed papers covering topics including equilibrium, information market, sponsored auction, network economics, mechanism design, social networks, advertisement pricing, computational general equilibrium, network games, algorithms and complexity for games.

December 2007
Xiaotie Deng
Fan Chung Graham

Organization

WINE'2007 was organized by the Department of Computer Science, Univeristy of California at San Diego.

Program Committee

Conference Chair	Ronald Graham (University of California, San Diego)
Local Arrangement Chair	Tara Javidi (University of California, San Diego)
Program Committee Co-chair	Xiaotie Deng (City University of Hong Kong)
Program Committee Co-chair	Fan Chung Graham (University of California, San Diego)
Plenary Speakers	Kenneth J. Arrow (Stanford University)
	Christos H. Papadimitriou (University of California, Berkeley)
	Herbert E. Scarf (Yale University)
	Vijay V. Vazirani (Georgia Institute of Technology)
Committee Members	Sushil Bikhchandani (University of California, Los Angeles)
	Samuel R. Buss (University of California, San Diego)
	Felix Brandt (University of Munich)
	Shuchi Chawla (University of Wisconsin-Madison)
	Xiaotie Deng (City University of Hong Kong)
	Andrew Goldberg (Microsoft Research, Silicon Valley)
	Paul Goldberg (University of Liverpool)
	Rica Gonen (Yahoo! Research)
	Fan Chung Graham (University of California, San Diego)
	Kamal Jain (Microsoft Research)
	Ehud Kalai (Northwestern University)
	Ming-Yang Kao (Northwestern University)
	Anna Karlin (University of Washington)
	Vangelis Markakis (The National Research Institute for Mathematics and Computer Science in The Netherlands)

Burkhard Monien (University of Paderborn)
Abraham Neyman (Hebrew University of
  Jerusalem)
Paul Spirakis (University of Patras, and
  Research Academic Computer Technology
  Institute)
David M. Pennock (Yahoo! Research)
Tim Roughgarden (Stanford University)
Amin Saberi (Stanford University)
Yoav Shoham (Stanford University)
Shanghua Teng (Boston University)
Vijay Vazirani (Georgia Institute of
  Technology)
Yinyu Ye (Stanford University)
Makoto Yokoo (Kyushu University)

Referees

Andrew Gilpin
Arash Rahimabadi
Arpita Ghosh
Ashok Kumar
  Ponnuswami
Atri Rudra
Atsushi Iwasaki
Bhaskar DasGupta
Chinmay Karande
Constantinos Daskalakis
Daniel Reeves
David Pennock
Deeparnab Chakrabarty
Dimitris Fotakis
Dominic Dumrauf
Edith Elkind
Enrico Gerding
Erik Vee
Eyal Even-Dar
Felix Fischer
Florian Schoppmann
Gagan Aggarwal
Gagan Goel
George Christodoulou

Hamid Nazerzadeh
Heiko Roeglin
Ian Kash
James Aspnes
Jaroslaw Byrka
Jenn Wortman
Kamal Jain
Karsten Tiemann
Konstantinos Daskalakis
Lance Fortnow
Liad Blumrosen
Mallesh Pai
Maria-Florina Balcan
Marios Mavronicolas
Markus Holzer
Martin Gairing
Ming-Yang Kao
Mira Gonen
Mohammad Mahdian
Moshe Babaioff
Moshe Tennenholtz
Mukund Sundararajan
Ning Chen
Panagiota Panagopoulou

Paul Harrenstein
Paul Spirakis
Petra Berenbrink
Qi Qi
Rainer Feldmann
Rakesh Vohra
Rica Gonen
Ron Lavi
Sam Buss
Seyed Omid Etesami
Shuchi Chawla
Spyros Kontogiannis
Susanne Albers
TianMing Bu
Uriel Feige
Vincent Conitzer
Xi Chen
Yan Chen
Yiling Chen
Yuko Sakurai
Yvonne Bleischwitz
Zoe Abrams

Sponsoring Institutions

California Institute for Telecommunications and Information Technology
Google Inc.
Yahoo! Research
National Science Foundation
Springer Lecture Notes in Computer Science
University of California, San Diego

Table of Contents

Sponsored Auction

Network Economics

Mechanism Design I

Social Networks

Advertisement Pricing I

Computational General Equilibrium

Network Games

Algorithmic Issues

Mechanism Design II

Advertisement Pricing II

Mechanism Design III

Getting to Economic Equilibrium:
A Problem and Its History
(Abstract)

Kenneth J. Arrow

Economics Department, Stanford University

The very concept of equilibrium, economic or otherwise, presupposes a dynamic system which determines change as a function of state variables. An equilibrium is a vector of state variables for which no change occurs. In economics, this is interpreted as a set of quantities and prices for which there is no incentive on anyone's part to change. The dynamics runs in terms of profit opportunities or incentives to outbid others for scarce commodities or for market opportunities. The idea that traders will respond to profit opportunities by increasing their activities and by, doing so, tend to wipe them out must have been recognized whenever there was trade. A 12th century rabbinical commentary argues that if someone charges "too high a price", others will offer the good at a lower price and thereby bring it down. Somewhat more systematic discussions of economic equilibrium are to be found in the founders of modern economic theory, Adam Smith and David Ricardo. Smith's principal emphasis was on the flow of capital from low-profit to high-opportunities, leading to a zero-profit equilibrium. Ricardo added the adjustment of population to wages and the setting of rents on scarce land.

The true complexity of the adjustment processes was not grasped until the formulation of general equilibrium theory. This introduced a formal element, the formulation of the market in terms of supply and demand, and an empirical element, the influence of the price on one market on the supplies and demands in other markets. Léon Walras recognized the need for an argument for stability (convergence of the dynamic system to an equilibrium ([8], pp. 84-86, 90-91, 105-106, 169-172, 243-254 and 284-295). He assumed crucially that the price for any given commodity increases proportionately to the difference between supply and demand on that market and used essentially a Gauss-Seidel argument, implicitly imposing the condition of a dominant diagonal on the excess demand functions. Walras introduced the term, "tatonnement" for the dynamic system, a term which has become standard. Despite casual references (e.g., Vilfredo Pareto's analogy between the market and the computer [5], pp. 233-234), the stability question was not addressed again until the magisterial work of John R. Hicks in 1939 [3]. In part by criticizing Hicks, Paul Samuelson (1941[6]) gave perhaps the first explicit formulation of a dynamic system based on supply and demand whose equilibrium was the competitive equilibrium. A subsequent literature (Metzler [4], Arrow, Block, and Hurwicz [2,1]) gave various sufficient conditions for the Samuelson system to be stable. These results could be used, when the conditions held, to actually calculate general equilibria. What started

X. Deng and F.C. Graham (Eds.): WINE 2007, LNCS 4858, pp. 1–2, 2007.

as a description of the economy could also be regarded as a way of computing its outcome. As computing power became available, this became a practicable possibility. However, Scarf (1960)[7] showed by example that the tatonnement process did not necessarily converge.

References

1. Arrow, K.J.: On the stability of competitive equilibrium ii. Econometrica 27, 82–109 (1959)
2. Arrow, K.J., Hurwicz, L.: On the stability of competitive equilibrium i. Econometrica 26, 522–532 (1958)
3. Hicks, J.R.: Value and capital. Oxford U. Press, Oxford (1939)
4. Metzler, L.A.: Stability of multiple markets: the Hicks conditions. Econometrica 13, 277–292 (1945)
5. Pareto, V.: Manuel déconomie politique. 2e ed., Paris: Marcel Giard, 1927 originally published in Italian in (1904)
6. Samuelson, P.A.: The stability of equilibrium: Comparative statics and dynamics. Econometrica 9, 97–120 (1941)
7. Scarf, H.E.: Some examples of global instability of the competitive equilibrium. International Economic Review 1, 157–172 (1960)
8. Walras, L.: Elements of pure economics. ed. and tr. by W. Jaffé, London: George Allen and Unwin, 1954 (originally published in 1874, 1877)

My Favorite Simplicial Complex and Some of Its Applications

Herbert E. Scarf

Yale University

I will discuss a specific class of simplicial complexes, $K(Y)$, whose vertices are contained in a set $Y \in R^n$. The vertex set is finite or denumerable and satisfies some *genericity* properties. The complex has been studied for many years under a variety of different names: ordinal bases, primitive sets, the complex of maximal lattice free bodies and most recently, Algebraic Geometers have used the name the Scarf Complex.

The complex has been applied in a number of different areas including:

game theory: (In particular the core of a balanced game), integer programming (including the Frobenius problem), fixed point computations, reliability theory, the stable paths problem and interdomain routing, multi-commodity network flows, graph theory (fractional kernels in digraphs) and resolutions of monomial ideals.

(The speaker does not understand many of these applications.)

The major problem is to be able to compute the simplicies, and faces, of $K(Y)$ in an effective way. In this talk I will restrict my attention to the case in which

$$Y = \left\{ y = Ah : h \in Z^{n-1} \right\}$$

and A is an $n \times (n-1)$ matrix with nice properties. I will discuss some features of the complex which may be useful in computing the complex by homotopy methods. A variety of other methods are known. There will be many examples to smooth our way.

X. Deng and F.C. Graham (Eds.): WINE 2007, LNCS 4858, p. 3, 2007.
© Springer-Verlag Berlin Heidelberg 2007

Markets and the Primal-Dual Paradigm

Vijay V. Vazirani

College of Computing, Georgia Institute of Technology, Atlanta, GA 30332–0280
vazirani@cc.gatech.edu

Abstract. The primal-dual paradigm was given by Kuhn in 1955. In the 1970's and 1980's, it yielded efficient exact algorithms for several fundamental problems in P. In the 1990's, this paradigm yielded algorithms, with good approximation factors and good running times, for several basic NP-hard optimization problems.

Interestingly enough, over the last five years, this paradigm has yielded combinatorial algorithms for finding equilibria in several natural market models. This has involved extending the paradigm from its original setting of LP-duality to the enhanced setting of nonlinear convex programs and KKT conditions. In this talk, I will survey this new and exciting development and present some of its challenging open problems.

X. Deng and F.C. Graham (Eds.): WINE 2007, LNCS 4858, p. 4, 2007.
© Springer-Verlag Berlin Heidelberg 2007

The Computation of Equilibria

Christos H. Papadimitriou

UC Berkeley, California
`christos@cs.berkeley.edu`*

Ever since Nash's existence theorem in 1951, the Nash equilibrium has been the standard solution concept in Game Theory, yet the issue of its computational complexity was resolved only recently by the proof that the problem is PPAD- complete [4], even in the two-player case [2]. In view of this result, research turned to several alternatives — an effect reminiscent of the reaction to NP-completeness in the 1970s: Approximation algorithms, special cases, and alternative equilibrium concepts.

Is there a polynomial-time approximation scheme (PTAS) for Nash equilibria in general games? (We know [3] that no *fully* PTAS is likely to exist, one whose exponent is independent of ϵ.) Progress in this front has been slow; even getting ϵ below $\frac{1}{2}$ has taken some time and effort [5]. However, it turns out that there is a PTAS for an important and broad class of games, *anonymous games*, as long as the number of strategies is kept a constant [6] (this reference settles the case of two strategies, but extension to any finite number of strategies seems plausible). The algorithm considers mixed strategies whose probabilities take on discrete values, and searches this space exhaustively, relying on a probabilistic lemma to establish approximation. The same exhaustive approach yields a quasi-PTAS (the exponent contains $\log \log n$, in addition to $-\log \epsilon$, where n is the length of the input) for general games, again for a constant number of strategies [7]. Exploring the limits of this exhaustive approach is an important problem.

Complexity considerations have in fact challenged some well accepted game-theoretic wisdom, regarding *repeated games*. Finding Nash equilibria in such games had been thought easy, through a protocol involving agreed play-cum-threat known as the *Folk Theorem;* this was indeed verified recently for two players in [9]. However, it was recently shown [1] that, for three or more players, finding a Nash equilibrium in a repeated game is as hard as doing so in a one-shot game — that is to say, PPAD-complete. Implementing the Folk Theorem is even more difficult, as finding the game's *threat point*, as required by the theorem, is NP-hard for three or more players.

Finally, the intractability results gave impetus to the search for alternative notions of equilibrium, such as the *sink equilibria* or *Nash dynamics* of the game (roughly, the best-response Markov chain). Another, related, refinement, called *unit recall equilibrium* [8], yields an equilibrium concept that is conjectured to be polynomially computable, and exists in almost all games.

---

* Research supported by an NSF grant, a MICRO grant, a France-Berkeley Fund grant, and a gift from Yahoo! Research.

X. Deng and F.C. Graham (Eds.): WINE 2007, LNCS 4858, pp. 5–6, 2007.

6   C.H. Papadimitriou

References

1. Borgs, C., Chayes, J., Immorlica, N., Kalai, A., Mirrokni, V., Papadimitriou, C.H.: The Myth of the Folk Theorem. ECCC TR07-82
2. Chen, X., Deng, X.: Settling the Complexity of 2-Player Nash-Equilibrium. In: Proceedings of FOCS (2006)
3. Chen, X., Deng, X., Teng, S.: Computing Nash Equilibria: Approximation and Smoothed Complexity. In: Proceedings of FOCS (2006)
4. Daskalakis, C., Goldberg, P.W., Papadimitriou, C.H.: The Complexity of Computing a Nash Equilibrium. In: Proceedings of STOC (2006)
5. Daskalakis, C., Mehta, A., Papadimitriou, C.H.: Progress in Approximate Nash equilibrium. In: 8th ACM Conference on Electronic Commerce (EC), ACM Press, New York (2007)
6. Daskalakis, C., Papadimitriou, C.H.: Computing Equilibria in Anonymous Games. In: proc. 2007 FOCS
7. Daskalakis, C., Papadimitriou, C.H.: In preparation
8. Fabrikant, A., Papadimitriou, C.H.: The Search for Equilibria: Sink Equilibria, Unit Recall Games, and BGP Oscillations in, SODA 2008 (to appear)
9. Littman, M., Stone, P.: A polynomial-time algorithm for repeated games. Decision Support Systems 31, 55–66 (2005)

A Note on Equilibrium Pricing as Convex Optimization

Lihua Chen[1], Yinyu Ye[2,*], and Jiawei Zhang[3]

[1] Guanghua School of Management, Peking University, Beijing 100871, P. R. China
chenlh@gsm.pku.edu.c
[2] Department of Management Science and Engineering and, by courtesy, Electrical Engineering, Stanford University, Stanford, CA 94305, USA
yinyu-ye@stanford.edu
[3] Department of Information, Operations, and Management Sciences, Stern School of Business, New York University, New York, NY 10012, USA
jzhang@stern.nyu.edu

Abstract. We study equilibrium computation for exchange markets. We show that the market equilibrium of either of the following two markets:
1. The Fisher market with several classes of concave non-homogeneous utility functions;
2. A mixed Fisher and Arrow-Debreu market with homogeneous and log-concave utility functions

can be computed as convex programming and by interior-point algorithms in polynomial time.

1 Introduction

The study of market equilibria occupies a central place in mathematical economics. This study was formally started by Walras [12] over a hundred years ago. In this problem everyone in a population of n players has an initial endowment of divisible goods and a utility function for consuming all goods—their own and others. Every player sells the entire initial endowment and then uses the revenue to buy a bundle of goods such that his or her utility function is maximized. Walras asked whether prices could be set for everyone's good such that this is possible. An answer was given by Arrow and Debreu in 1954 [1] who showed that such an equilibrium would exist, under very mild conditions, if the utility functions were concave. Their proof was non-constructive and did not offer any algorithm to find such equilibrium prices.

Fisher was the first to consider an algorithm to compute equilibrium prices for a related and different model where players are divided into two sets: producers and consumers; see Brainard and Scarf [2,11]. Consumers spend money only to buy goods and maximize their individual utility functions of goods; producers sell their goods only for money. The price equilibrium is an assignment of prices to goods so that when every consumer buys a maximal bundle of goods then the

---
* Research supported by NSF grant DMS-0604513.

X. Deng and F.C. Graham (Eds.): WINE 2007, LNCS 4858, pp. 7–16, 2007.
© Springer-Verlag Berlin Heidelberg 2007

market clears, meaning that all the money is spent and all the goods are sold. Fisher's model is a special case of Walras' model when money is also considered a good so that Arrow and Debreu's result applies.

In a remarkable piece of work, Eisenberg and Gale [6,9] give a convex programming (or optimization) formulation whose solution yields equilibrium allocations for the Fisher market with linear utility functions, and Eisenberg [7] extended this approach to derive a convex program for general concave and homogeneous functions of degree 1. Their program consists of maximizing an aggregate utility function of all consumers over a convex polyhedron defined by supply-demand linear constraints. The Lagrange or dual multipliers of these constraints yield equilibrium prices. Thus, finding a Fisher equilibrium becomes solving a convex optimization problem, and it could be computed by the Ellipsoid method or by efficient interior-point methods in polynomial time. Later, Codenotti et al. [4] rediscovered the convex programming formulation, and Jain et al. [10] generalized Eisenberg and Gale's convex model to handling homothetic and quasi-concave utilities introduced by Friedman [8]. Here, polynomial time means that one can compute an ϵ approximate equilibrium in a number of arithmetic operations bounded by polynomial in n and $\log \frac{1}{\epsilon}$; or, if there is a rational equilibrium solution, one can compute an *exact* equilibrium in a number of arithmetic operations bounded by polynomial in n and L, where L is the bit-length of the input data. When the utility functions are linear, the current best arithmetic operations complexity bound is $O(\sqrt{mn}(m+n)^3 L)$ given by [13].

Little is known on the computational complexity for computing market equilibria with non-homogeneous utility functions and for markets other than the Fisher and Arrow-Debreu settings. This note is to derive convex programs to solve several more general exchange market equilibrium problems. We show that the equilibrium of either of the following two markets:

1. The Fisher market with several classes of concave non-homogeneous utility functions;
2. A mixed Fisher and Arrow-Debreu market with homogeneous and log-concave utility functions

can be computed as convex programming and by interior-point algorithms in polynomial time.

First, a few mathematical notations. Let $\mathbb{R}^n$ denote the n-dimensional Euclidean space; $\mathbb{R}^n_+$ denote the subset of $\mathbb{R}^n$ where each coordinate is non-negative. $\mathbb{R}$ and $\mathbb{R}_+$ denote the set of real numbers and the set of non-negative real numbers, respectively.

A function $u : \mathbb{R}^n_+ \to \mathbb{R}_+$ is said to be *concave* if for any $\boldsymbol{x}, \boldsymbol{y} \in \mathbb{R}^n_+$ and any $0 \le \alpha \le 1$, we have $u(\alpha \boldsymbol{x} + (1-\alpha)\boldsymbol{y}) \ge \alpha u(\boldsymbol{x}) + (1-\alpha)u(\boldsymbol{y})$. It is *homothetic* if for any $\boldsymbol{x}, \boldsymbol{y} \in \mathbb{R}^n_+$ and any $\alpha > 0$, $u(\boldsymbol{x}) \ge u(\boldsymbol{y})$ iff $u(\alpha \boldsymbol{x}) \ge u(\alpha \boldsymbol{y})$. It is *monotone increasing* if for any $\boldsymbol{x}, \boldsymbol{y} \in \mathbb{R}^n_+$, $\boldsymbol{x} \ge \boldsymbol{y}$ implies that $u(\boldsymbol{x}) \ge u(\boldsymbol{y})$. It is *homogeneous* of degree d if for any $\boldsymbol{x} \in \mathbb{R}^n_+$ and any $\alpha > 0$, $u(\alpha \boldsymbol{x}) = \alpha^d u(\boldsymbol{x})$.

2 Convex Optimization for the Fisher Market with Non-homogeneous Utilities

Without loss of generality, assume that there is one unit of good for each type of good $j \in P$ with $|P| = n$. Let consumer $i \in C$ (with $|C| = m$) have an initial money endowment $w_i > 0$ to spend and buy goods to maximize his or her utility function for a given price vector $p \in \mathbb{R}^n_+$:

$$
\begin{aligned}
\text{maximize } \ & u_i(\boldsymbol{x}_i) \\
\text{subject to } \ & \boldsymbol{p}^T \boldsymbol{x}_i \leq w_i \\
& \boldsymbol{x}_i \geq \boldsymbol{0};
\end{aligned}
\tag{1}
$$

where variable $\boldsymbol{x}_i = (x_{i1}; ...; x_{in})$ is a column vector whose jth coordinates x_{ij} represents the amount of goods bought from producer j by consumer i, $j = 1, ..., n$. Let $u_i(\boldsymbol{x}_i)$ be concave and monotonically increasing. We also assume that every consumer is interested in buying at least one type of good and every type of good is sought by at least one consumer. Then, a price vector $\boldsymbol{p} \geq \boldsymbol{0}$, together with vectors $\boldsymbol{x}_i$, $i = 1, ..., m$ is called a Fisher equilibrium if $\boldsymbol{x}_i$ is optimal for (1) for the given $\boldsymbol{p}$, and $\sum_i \boldsymbol{x}_i = \boldsymbol{e}$ (the vector of all ones). The last condition requires that all the goods of the producers are sold.

2.1 Homogeneous and Log-Concave Utilities

If $u_i(\boldsymbol{x}_i)$ is homogeneous of degree 1 (this is without loss of generality since any homogeneous function with a positive degree can be monotonically transformed to a homogeneous function with degree 1) and $\log(u_i(\boldsymbol{x}_i))$ is concave in $\boldsymbol{x}_i \in \mathbb{R}^n_+$, the Fisher equilibrium problem can be solved as an aggregate social convex optimization problem (see Eisenberg and Gale [6,9,7]):

$$
\begin{aligned}
\text{maximize } \ & \textstyle\sum_i w_i \log(u_i(\boldsymbol{x}_i)) \\
\text{subject to } \ & \textstyle\sum_i \boldsymbol{x}_i = \boldsymbol{e}, \ \forall j, \\
& \boldsymbol{x}_i \geq \boldsymbol{0}, \ \forall i;
\end{aligned}
\tag{2}
$$

where the objective function may be interpreted as a socially aggregated utility. These homogeneous and log-concave functions include many classical utilities:

- All constant elasticity functions

$$
u_i(\boldsymbol{x}) = \left(\sum_{j=1}^{n} (a_j x_j)^{(\sigma-1)/\sigma} \right)^{\sigma/(\sigma-1)}, \ a_j \geq 0, \ 0 < \sigma < \infty;
$$

- Piece-wise concave linear function

$$
u_i(\boldsymbol{x}) = \min_k \{ (\boldsymbol{a}^k)^T \boldsymbol{x} \}, \ \boldsymbol{a}^k \geq \boldsymbol{0}, \ k = 1, ..., K;
$$

– The Cobb-Douglass utility function

$$u_i(\boldsymbol{x}) = \prod_{j=1}^{n} x_j^{a_j}, \ a_j \geq 0.$$

Jain et al. [10] showed how to transform a homothetic utility function into an equivalent homogeneous degree 1 and log-concave function. Thus, the Fisher equilibrium problem with homothetic utilities can be also solved as a convex optimization problem. A natural question arises: Does this approach apply to more general *non-homogeneous* utility functions?

2.2 Necessary and Sufficient Condition for a Fisher Equilibrium

Consider the optimality conditions of (1). Besides feasibility, they are

$$(\nabla u_i(\boldsymbol{x}_i)^T \boldsymbol{x}_i) \cdot \boldsymbol{p} \geq w_i \cdot \nabla u_i(\boldsymbol{x}_i),$$
$$\boldsymbol{p}^T \boldsymbol{x}_i = w_i, \quad (3)$$
$$\boldsymbol{x}_i \geq 0,$$

where $\nabla u(\boldsymbol{x})$ denotes any sub-gradient vector of $u(\boldsymbol{x})$ at $\boldsymbol{x}$.

Thus, the complete necessary and sufficient conditions for a Fisher equilibrium are the following:

$$(\nabla u_i(\boldsymbol{x}_i)^T \boldsymbol{x}_i) \cdot \boldsymbol{p} \geq w_i \cdot \nabla u_i(\boldsymbol{x}_i), \ \forall i$$
$$\boldsymbol{p}^T \boldsymbol{x}_i = w_i,$$
$$\sum_i \boldsymbol{x}_i \leq \boldsymbol{e}, \quad (4)$$
$$\boldsymbol{p}^T \boldsymbol{e} \leq \sum_i w_i,$$
$$\boldsymbol{x}_i, \boldsymbol{p} \geq 0, \ \forall i.$$

Note here that the condition $\boldsymbol{p}^T \boldsymbol{x}_i = w_i$ should be implied by the rest of conditions in (4): Multiplying $\boldsymbol{x}_i \geq 0$ to both sides of the first inequality in (4), we have $\boldsymbol{p}^T \boldsymbol{x}_i \geq w_i$ for all i, which, together with other inequality conditions in (4), imply

$$\sum_i w_i \geq \boldsymbol{p}^T \boldsymbol{e} \geq \boldsymbol{p}^T \left(\sum_i \boldsymbol{x}_i \right) = \sum_i \boldsymbol{p}^T \boldsymbol{x}_i \geq \sum_i w_i,$$

that is, every inequality in the sequence must be tight which implies $\boldsymbol{p}^T \boldsymbol{x}_i = w_i$ for all i. Thus, the reduced necessary and sufficient Fisher equilibrium conditions become

$$(\nabla u_i(\boldsymbol{x}_i)^T \boldsymbol{x}_i) \cdot \boldsymbol{p} \geq w_i \cdot \nabla u_i(\boldsymbol{x}_i), \ \forall i$$
$$\sum_i \boldsymbol{x}_i \leq \boldsymbol{e},$$
$$\boldsymbol{p}^T \boldsymbol{e} \leq \sum_i w_i, \quad (5)$$
$$\boldsymbol{x}_i, \boldsymbol{p} \geq 0, \ \forall i.$$

The inequalities and equalities in (5) are all linear, except the first

$$(\nabla u_i(\boldsymbol{x}_i)^T \boldsymbol{x}_i) \cdot \boldsymbol{p} \geq w_i \cdot \nabla u_i(\boldsymbol{x}_i).$$

An immediate observation is, if every consumer i is interested in exactly one type of good, that is, $u_i(\boldsymbol{x}_i)$ is a univariate concave function $u_i(x_{i\bar{j}_i})$ for some $\bar{j}_i \in P$, then the above condition becomes a single inequality:

$$(u_i'(x_{i\bar{j}_i}) \cdot x_{i\bar{j}_i}) \cdot p_{\bar{j}_i} \geq w_i \cdot u_i'(x_{i\bar{j}_i}),$$

or simply

$$x_{i\bar{j}_i} \cdot p_{\bar{j}_i} \geq w_i.$$

One can transfer this non-linear inequality to

$$\log(x_{i\bar{j}_i}) + \log(p_{\bar{j}_i}) \geq \log(w_i)$$

which is a convex inequality (meaning that the set of feasible solutions is convex). Thus, the Fisher equilibrium set is convex and can be found by solving a convex optimization problem. It turns out that this simple trick works for other utilities as well, as we shall present in the next subsection.

2.3 Concave and Non-homogeneous Utilities

Consider $u_i(\boldsymbol{x}_i)$ in the following additive or separable form:

$$u_i(\boldsymbol{x}_i) = \textstyle\sum_{j=1}^{n} a_{ij}(x_{ij} + b_{ij})^{d_{ij}},$$
$$\text{or} \qquad\qquad (6)$$
$$u_i(\boldsymbol{x}_i) = \textstyle\sum_{j=1}^{n} a_{ij} \log(x_{ij} + b_{ij}),$$

where $a_{ij}, b_{ij} \geq 0$, and $0 < d_{ij} \leq 1$, for all i and j, are given, and variable x_{ij} represents the amount of goods bought from good j by consumer i, $j = 1, ..., n$. One can see that $u_i(\boldsymbol{x}_i)$ is a concave and monotone increasing function in $\boldsymbol{x}_i = (x_{i1}; ...; x_{in}) \geq \boldsymbol{0}$.

This utility function (6) includes as special case several popular utilities:

- linear utility functions: $d_{ij} = 1$ for all j in the first form;
- certain constant elasticity functions: $b_{ij} = 0$ and $d_{ij} = d$, $0 \leq d \leq 1$, for all j in the first form;
- the Cobb-Douglas utility function: $b_{ij} = 0$ in the second form;
- a non-homogeneous Cobb-Douglas utility functions given by [3]: the second form.

Note that $u_i(\boldsymbol{x}_i)$ (6),can be non-homothetic; see, for example, $u(x, y) = \sqrt{x} + y$. Chen at al. [3] developed approximation algorithm with running time polynomial in n and $\frac{1}{\epsilon}$ for the utility function in the second form of (6).

Lemma 1. *Given $u_i(\boldsymbol{x}_i)$ in the forms of (6), $(\nabla u_i(\boldsymbol{x}_i)^T \boldsymbol{x}_i)$ is concave, and $\log(\nabla_j u_i(\boldsymbol{x}_i))$ is convex for every j, in $\boldsymbol{x}_i \in \mathbb{R}_+^n$.*

Proof. For simplicity, let us omit index i, so that

$$u(\boldsymbol{x}) = \sum_{j=1}^{n} a_j(x_j + b_j)^{d_j}$$

or

$$u(\boldsymbol{x}) = \sum_{j=1}^{n} a_j \log(x_j + b_j).$$

Thus, for the first form

$$\nabla u(\boldsymbol{x}) = (..., a_j d_j (x_j + b_j)^{d_j - 1}, ...),$$

so that

$$\nabla u(\boldsymbol{x})^T \boldsymbol{x} = \sum_{j} a_j d_j (x_j + b_j)^{d_j - 1} x_j.$$

It is easily see that each $(x_j + b_j)^{d_j-1}x_j$ is concave in $x_j \geq 0$ since $0 \leq d_j \leq 1$; therefore, so is the sum: $\sum_j a_j d_j (x_j + b_j)^{d_j-1}x_j$.

Furhtermore,

$$\log(\nabla_j u(\boldsymbol{x})) = (d_j - 1)\log(x_j + b_j) + \log(a_j d_j)$$

which is convex in $x_j > 0$ for every j.

Similarly, one can prove the lemma for the the second form. This completes the proof.   □

Thus, one can rewrite the nonlinear inequality in (5) as

$$\log(\nabla u_i(\boldsymbol{x}_i)^T \boldsymbol{x}_i) + \log(\boldsymbol{p}_j) \geq \log(w_i) + \log(\nabla_j u_i(\boldsymbol{x}_i)), \ \forall j,$$

which is a convex inequality (the set of feasible solutions is convex) by Lemma 1. Thus,

Theorem 1. *If utilities $u_i(\boldsymbol{x}_i)$ are given in the forms of (6), then the Fisher equilibrium set of (5) is convex and can be computed as a convex optimization problem; for example, by using polynomial-time interior-point methods.*

3   Convex Optimization for the Fisher Market Where Consumers May Retain Money

In the classical Fisher market, consumers spend money only to buy goods and maximize their individual utility functions of goods; producers sell their goods only for money. Now consider a market where each consumer can retain certain amount of money from his or her own budget, that is, his or her utility includes the amount of retained money:

$$\begin{aligned} \text{maximize} \quad & u_i(\boldsymbol{x}_i, s_i) \\ \text{subject to} \quad & \boldsymbol{p}^T \boldsymbol{x}_i + s_i \leq w_i \\ & \boldsymbol{x}_i, s_i \ \geq \mathbf{0}, \end{aligned} \qquad (7)$$

where again $\boldsymbol{x}_i = (x_{i1}; ...; x_{in})$ and its jth component x_{ij} represents the amount of good j bought by consumer i, and s_i denotes the retained money (e.g., deposited in a bank for a short-time interest gain). We assume that $u_i(\boldsymbol{x}_i, s_i)$ is a monotone increasing and concave function of $(\boldsymbol{x}_i, s_i) \geq \boldsymbol{0}$. This mixed market has a number of applications in managing supply chains and resource allocations.

3.1   The Mixed Market Equilibrium

In this mixed market, an equilibrium is defined as a non-negative price vector $\boldsymbol{p} \in \mathbb{R}^n_+$ at which there exist a bundle of goods $(\boldsymbol{x}_i \in \mathbb{R}^n_+, s_i \geq 0)$ for each consumer $i \in C$ such that the following conditions hold:

1. The vector $(\boldsymbol{x}_i; s_i)$ optimizes retailer i's utility (7) given her money budget w_i.
2. For each good j, the total amount available equals the total amount consumed by the consumers, that is, $\sum_{i \in C} x_{ij} = 1$.
3. The sum of the spending and retaining money equals the sum of the money possessed by all consumers, that is, $\sum_{j \in P} p_j + \sum_{i \in C} s_i = \sum_{i \in C} w_i$.

The existence of such an equilibrium is immediately implied by the existence of an Arrow-Debreu equilibrium by treating money as an additional "good". One may attempt to prove the existence using the Fisher equilibrium model. However, in such a Fisher equilibrium model the price for the money "good" (s_i) has to be fixed to 1 (the same as w_i), which is difficult to enforce. Thus, we need to invoke the Arrow-Debreu model by assigning price p_{n+1} to a unit of money. Then, each consumer's problem becomes

$$\begin{aligned} \text{maximize} \quad & u_i(\boldsymbol{x}_i, s_i) \\ \text{subject to} \quad & \boldsymbol{p}^T \boldsymbol{x}_i + p_{n+1} s_i \leq p_{n+1} w_i, \\ & \boldsymbol{x}_i, s_i \quad\quad \geq \boldsymbol{0}, \end{aligned}$$

where the total supply of money is $\sum_i w_i$. Therefore, the Arrow-Debreu theorem implies that an equilibrium price vector $(\boldsymbol{p}; p_{n+1}) \in \mathbb{R}^{n+1}_+$ exists. In particular, $p_{n+1} > 0$ at every Arrow-Debreu equilibrium since money has a value at least to every producer. By dividing $(\boldsymbol{p}; p_{n+1})$ by p_{n+1}, we have an equilibrium price for all goods, and the price for the money "good" equals 1:

Corollary 1. *An equilibrium always exists for the Fisher market where consumers may retain money.*

However, it was unknown if the mixed market admits a convex program for computing its equilibrium, or it has to use the more difficult Arrow-Debreu equilibrium framework to compute it, even the utility is homogeneous and log-concave. The computational complexity issue of the mixed market equilibrium problem is important, since there is a fundamental difference between the Fisher and Arrow-Debreu models with respect to computational complexity. For example, when the utility is Leontief

$$u_i(\boldsymbol{x}) = \min \left\{ \frac{x_j}{a_j} : a_j > 0 \right\},$$

a homogeneous of degree one and log-concave function, the Fisher market equilibrium can be computed as a convex program in polynomial time while the Arrow-Debreu market equilibrium is NP-hard to decide; see Ye [14] and Codenotti et al. [5].

We settle the computational complexity issue of the mixed market equilibrium problem in the next subsection by showing that any optimal solution to a convex program yields an equilibrium if the utility functions are log-concave and homogeneous of degree one.

3.2   Convex Optimization for Computing an Equilibrium

From (4), the necessary and sufficient conditions for the mixed market equilibrium are

$$(\boldsymbol{p};\ 1) \geq \frac{w_i}{\nabla u_i(\boldsymbol{x}_i,s_i)^T(x_i;s_i)} \cdot \nabla u_i(\boldsymbol{x}_i,s_i),\ \forall i$$
$$\sum_i \boldsymbol{x}_i \leq \boldsymbol{e},$$
$$\sum_j p_j + \sum_i s_i \leq \sum_i w_i,$$
$$\boldsymbol{x}_i, \boldsymbol{p} \geq \boldsymbol{0},\ \forall i; \tag{8}$$

where one can see that the price for the money good is set to 1.

Let $u_i(\boldsymbol{x}_i, s_i)$ be homogeneous of degree one and $\log(u_i(\boldsymbol{x}_i, s_i))$ be concave in $(\boldsymbol{x}_i; s)i) \in \mathbb{R}^{n+1}_+$. Recall that this function includes all constant elasticity, piecewise concave linear, the Cobb-Douglass utility, and the Leontief utility functions. Now consider the convex optimization problem

$$\begin{aligned}
\text{maximize } & \sum_i w_i \log(u_i(\boldsymbol{x}_i, s_i)) - s \\
\text{subject to } & \sum_i x_{ij} \leq 1,\ \forall j, \\
& \sum_i s_i - s = 0, \\
& (\boldsymbol{x}_i, s_i) \geq \boldsymbol{0},\ \forall i.
\end{aligned} \tag{9}$$

The first set of constraint inequalities indicates that the demand does not exceed the supply; the second simply records the total amount of money retained by all consumers as s. Then, the retained amount s is subtracted linearly from the aggregate social utility function. This makes economical sense since this amount has been withdrawn from the exchange market by the consumers so that one should extract them from the aggregated social utility for the exchange market.

We have

Theorem 2. *Let $(\bar{\boldsymbol{x}}_i, \bar{s}_i)$, $i = 1, ..., m$, be an optimal solution for convex program (9), and let p_j be an optimal Lagrange multiplier for each good j in the first constraint set of (9). Then, these solutions form an equilibrium for the mixed market (7).*

Proof. First, the feasible set of the optimization problem (9) is linear, compact and convex, the maximal solution exists and the maximum value is finite. Moreover, the objective function to be maximized is concave. Thus, the first-order optimality conditions are necessary and sufficient for an optimal solution $(\bar{\boldsymbol{x}}_i, \bar{s}_i)$. These optimality conditions can be written (using the fact that the optimal Lagrange multiplier for the second constraint automatically equals 1) as:

$$\frac{w_i}{u_i(\bar{\boldsymbol{x}}_i, \bar{s}_i)} \nabla_{\boldsymbol{x}_i} u_i(\bar{\boldsymbol{x}}_i, \bar{s}_i) \leq \boldsymbol{p}, \ \forall i$$

$$\frac{w_i}{u_i(\bar{\boldsymbol{x}}_i, \bar{s}_i)} \partial_{s_i} u_i(\bar{\boldsymbol{x}}_i, \bar{s}_i) \leq 1, \ \forall i \qquad (10)$$

$$\frac{w_i}{u_i(\bar{\boldsymbol{x}}_i, \bar{s}_i)} \left(\nabla_{\boldsymbol{x}_i} u_i(\bar{\boldsymbol{x}}_i, \bar{s}_i)^T \bar{\boldsymbol{x}}_i + \partial_{s_i} u_i(\bar{\boldsymbol{x}}_i, \bar{s}_i) \bar{s}_i \right) = \boldsymbol{p}^T \bar{\boldsymbol{x}}_i + \bar{s}_i,$$

where $\boldsymbol{p} = (p_1, ..., p_n)$ and p_j is the optimal Lagrange multiplier for each j in the first constraint set of (9). The third equality of condition (10) is called the complementarity condition, which, together with the fact that $u_i(\boldsymbol{x}_i, s_i)$ is homogeneous of degree one, namely $u_i(\bar{\boldsymbol{x}}_i, \bar{s}_i) = \nabla u_i(\bar{\boldsymbol{x}}_i, \bar{s}_i)^T (\bar{\boldsymbol{x}}_i; \bar{s}_i)$, imply

$$\begin{aligned}
\boldsymbol{p}^T \bar{\boldsymbol{x}}_i + \bar{s}_i &= \frac{w_i}{u_i(\bar{\boldsymbol{x}}_i, \bar{s}_i)} \left(\nabla_{\boldsymbol{x}_i} u_i(\bar{\boldsymbol{x}}_i, \bar{s}_i)^T \bar{\boldsymbol{x}}_i + \partial_{s_i} u_i(\bar{\boldsymbol{x}}_i, \bar{s}_i)\bar{s}_i \right) \\
&= \frac{w_i}{u_i(\bar{\boldsymbol{x}}_i, \bar{s}_i)} (\nabla u_i(\bar{\boldsymbol{x}}_i, \bar{s}_i)^T (\bar{\boldsymbol{x}}_i; \bar{s}_i)) \\
&= \frac{w_i}{u_i(\bar{\boldsymbol{x}}_i, \bar{s}_i)} \cdot u_i(\bar{\boldsymbol{x}}_i, \bar{s}_i) \\
&= w_i,
\end{aligned}$$

so that

$$\sum_i (\boldsymbol{p}^T \bar{\boldsymbol{x}}_i + \bar{s}_i) = \sum_i w_i.$$

Thus, $(\bar{\boldsymbol{x}}_i, \bar{s}_i)$, $i = 1, ..., m$, and $\boldsymbol{p}$ satisfy the equilibrium conditions of (8). □

It is well-known that one can use interior point methods to solve the linearly constrained convex program (9) to yield both primal and dual optimal solutions in polynomial time; see [13]. Therefore, an equilibrium for the mixed market (7) can be found in polynomial time.

References

1. Arrow, K.J., Debreu, G.: Existence of an Equilibrium for a Competitive Economy. Econometrica 22(3), 265–290 (1954)
2. Brainard, W.C., Scarf, H.: How to Compute Equilibrium Prices in 1891. Cowles Foundation Discussion Paper 1270 (2000)
3. Chen, N., Deng, X., Sun, X., Yao, A.C.: Fisher equilibrium price with a class of concave utility functions. In: Albers, S., Radzik, T. (eds.) ESA 2004. LNCS, vol. 3221, pp. 169–179. Springer, Heidelberg (2004)
4. Codenotti, B., Pemmaraju, S., Varadarajan, K.: On the polynomial time computation of equilibria for certain exchange economies. In: Proc. SODA 2005 (2005)
5. Codenotti, B., Saberi, A., Varadarajan, K., Ye, Y.: Leontief Economies Encode Nonzero Sum Two-Player Games. In: Proc. SODA 2006 (2006)
6. Eisenberg, E., Gale, D.: Consensus of Subjective Probabilities: The Pari-Mutuel Method. Annals of Mathematical Statistics 30, 165–168 (1959)
7. Eisenberg, E.: Aggregation of Utility Functions. Management Sciences 7(4), 337–350 (1961)
8. Friedman, J.W.: Concavity of Production Functions and Non-Increasing Returns to Scale. Econometrica 41(5), 981–984 (1973)
9. Gale, D.: The Theory of Linear Economic Models. McGraw-Hill, New York (1960)

10. Jain, K., Vazirani, V., Ye, Y.: Market equilibria for homothetic, quasi-concave utilities and economies of scale in production. In: Proc. SODA 2005 (2005)
11. Scarf, H.E.: The Computation of Economic Equilibria. With collaboration of T. Hansen, Cowles Foundation Monograph No. 24. New Haven: Yale University Press (1973)
12. Walras, L.: Elements d'economie politique pure; ou, Theorie de la richesse sociale. Elements of Pure Economics; Or the Theory of Social Wealth, Lausanne, Paris (1874)
13. Ye, Y.: A Path to the Arrow-Debreu Competitive Market Equilibrium. Math Programming (2006)
14. Ye, Y.: Exchange Market Equilibria with Leontief's Utility: Freedom of Pricing Leads to Rationality. In: Deng, X., Ye, Y. (eds.) WINE 2005. LNCS, vol. 3828, Springer, Heidelberg (2005)

New Algorithms for Approximate Nash Equilibria in Bimatrix Games[*]

Hartwig Bosse, Jaroslaw Byrka, and Evangelos Markakis

CWI (Center for Math and Computer Science)
Amsterdam, The Netherlands
{bosse, j.byrka, vangelis}@cwi.nl

Abstract. We consider the problem of computing additively approximate Nash equilibria in non-cooperative two-player games. We provide a new polynomial time algorithm that achieves an approximation guarantee of 0.36392. Our work improves the previously best known $(0.38197 + \epsilon)$-approximation algorithm of Daskalakis, Mehta and Papadimitriou [6].

First, we provide a simpler algorithm, which also achieves 0.38197. This algorithm is then tuned, improving the approximation error to 0.36392. Our method is relatively fast, as it requires solving only one linear program and it is based on using the solution of an auxiliary zero-sum game as a starting point.

1 Introduction

A Nash equilibrium of a bimatrix game is a pair of strategies, such that no player has an incentive to deviate (unilaterally). In a series of works [8,4,2], it was established that computing a Nash equilibrium is PPAD-complete even for two-player games. The focus has since then been on algorithms for approximate equilibria.

In this work we use the notion of *additive approximation* and consider the problem of computing approximate Nash equilibria in bimatrix games. Under the usual assumption that the payoff matrices are normalized to be in $[0,1]^{n \times n}$, we say that a pair of strategies is an ϵ-Nash equilibrium if no player can gain more than ϵ by unilaterally deviating to another strategy. In [3] it was proved that it is PPAD-complete to find an ϵ-Nash equilibrium when ϵ is of the order $\frac{1}{poly(n)}$. For constant ϵ however, the problem is still open. In [11], it was shown that for any constant $\epsilon > 0$, an ϵ-Nash equilibrium can be computed in subexponential time $(n^{O(\log n/\epsilon^2)})$. As for polynomial time algorithms, it is fairly simple to obtain a 3/4-approximation (see [9] for a slightly better result) and even better a 1/2-approximation [5]. Recently, an improved approximation for

---

[*] The first author was supported by NWO. The second and third author were supported by the EU Marie Curie Research Training Network, contract numbers MRTN-CT-2003-504438-ADONET and MRTN-CT-2004-504438-ADONET respectively.

X. Deng and F.C. Graham (Eds.): WINE 2007, LNCS 4858, pp. 17–29, 2007.

$\epsilon = \frac{3-\sqrt{5}}{2} + \zeta \approx 0.38197 + \zeta$ for any $\zeta > 0$ was obtained by Daskalakis, Mehta and Papadimitriou [6].

We provide two new algorithms for approximate Nash equilibria. The first one achieves exactly the same factor as [6] but with a simpler and faster technique. The second one, which is an extension of the first and has a more involved analysis, achieves an improved approximation of 0.36392. Both algorithms are based on solving a single linear program in contrast to [6], which may require to solve up to $n^{O(\frac{1}{\zeta^2})}$ linear programs for a $(0.38197 + \zeta)$-approximation.

The main idea of our algorithms is as follows: we first find an equilibrium (say x^*, y^*) in the zero-sum game $R - C$, where R and C are the payoff matrices of the two players. If x^*, y^* is not a good solution for the original game, then the players take turns and switch to appropriate strategies. Roughly speaking, the probabilities of switching are chosen such that the incentives to deviate become the same for both players. As a result, these probabilities are particular functions in the parameters of the underlying problem. The final part of the analysis then is to choose among these functions so as to minimize the approximation error. The intuition behind using the auxiliary zero-sum game $R - C$ is that a unilateral switch from x^*, y^* that improves the payoff of one player cannot hurt the other, as explained in the proof of Theorem 1. We should note that the use of certain zero-sum games has also been considered in [10] for obtaining *well-supported* approximate equilibria, which is a stronger notion of approximation.

In an independent work, Spirakis and Tsaknakis [13] have obtained another algorithm achieving an improved approximation of 0.3393. Their technique is also based on linear programming but seems unrelated to ours, and requires solving a polynomial number of linear programs.

2 Notation and Definitions

Consider a two person game G, where for simplicity the number of available (pure) strategies for each player is n. Our results still hold when the players do not have the same number of available strategies. We will refer to the two players as the row and the column player and we will denote their $n \times n$ payoff matrices by R, C respectively. Hence, if the row player chooses strategy i and the column player chooses strategy j, the payoffs are R_{ij} and C_{ij} respectively.

A *mixed strategy* for a player is a probability distribution over the set of his pure strategies and will be represented by a vector $x = (x_1, x_2, ..., x_n)^T$, where $x_i \geq 0$ and $\sum x_i = 1$. Here x_i is the probability that the player will choose his ith pure strategy. The ith pure strategy will be represented by the unit vector e_i, that has 1 in the ith coordinate and 0 elsewhere. For a mixed strategy pair x, y, the payoff to the row player is the expected value of a random variable which is equal to R_{ij} with probability $x_i y_j$. Therefore the payoff to the row player is $x^T R y$. Similarly the payoff to the column player is $x^T C y$.

A Nash equilibrium [12] is a pair of strategies x^*, y^* such that no player has an incentive to deviate unilaterally. Since mixed strategies are convex combinations of pure strategies, it suffices to consider only deviations to pure strategies:

Definition 1. *A pair of strategies* x^*, y^* *is a Nash equilibrium if:*

(i) For every pure strategy e_i *of the row player,* $e_i^T R y^* \leq (x^*)^T R y^*$, *and*
(ii) For every pure strategy e_i *of the column player,* $(x^*)^T C e_i \leq (x^*)^T C y^*$.

Assuming that we normalize the entries of the payoff matrices so that they all lie in $[0, 1]$, we can define the notion of an additive ϵ-approximate Nash equilibrium (or simply ϵ-Nash equilibrium) as follows:

Definition 2. *For any* $\epsilon > 0$, *a pair of strategies* x^*, y^* *is an* ϵ-*Nash equilibrium iff:*

(i) For every pure strategy e_i *of the row player,* $e_i^T R y^* \leq (x^*)^T R y^* + \epsilon$, *and*
(ii) For every pure strategy e_i *of the column player,* $(x^*)^T C e_i \leq (x^*)^T C y^* + \epsilon$.

In other words, no player will gain more than ϵ by unilaterally deviating to another strategy. A stronger notion of approximation was introduced in [4], namely ϵ-well-supported equilibria. We do not consider this approximation concept here. See [10] for new results on well-supported equilibria.

3 A $\left(\frac{3-\sqrt{5}}{2}\right)$-Approximation

In this section, we provide an algorithm that achieves exactly the same factor as in [6], which is $(3 - \sqrt{5})/2$, but by using a different and simpler method. In the next section we show how to modify our algorithm in order to improve the approximation.

Given a game $G = (R, C)$, where the entries of R and C are in $[0, 1]$, let $A = R - C$. Our algorithm is based on solving the zero-sum game $(A, -A)$ and then modifying appropriately the solution, if it does not provide a good approximation. It is well known that zero-sum games can be solved efficiently using linear programming. The decision on when to modify the zero-sum solution depends on a parameter of the algorithm $\alpha \in [0, 1]$. We first describe the algorithm parametrically and then show how to obtain the desired approximation.

Algorithm 1
Let $\alpha \in [0, 1]$ be a parameter of the algorithm.

1. Compute an equilibrium (x^*, y^*) for the zero-sum game defined by the matrix $A = R - C$.
2. Let g_1, g_2 be the incentives to deviate for the row and column player respectively if they play (x^*, y^*) in the game (R, C), i.e., $g_1 = \max_{i=1,\dots,n} e_i^T R y^* - (x^*)^T R y^*$ and $g_2 = \max_{i=1,\dots,n} (x^*)^T C e_i - (x^*)^T C y^*$. WLOG, assume, that $g_1 \geq g_2$ (the statement of the algorithm would be completely symmetrical if $g_1 < g_2$).
3. Let $r_1 \in \operatorname{argmax}_{e_i} e_i^T R y^*$ be an optimal response of the row player to the strategy y^*. Let $b_2 \in \operatorname{argmax}_{e_i} r_1^T C e_i$ be an optimal response of the column player to the strategy r_1.

4. Output the following pair of strategies, $(\hat{x}, \hat{y})$, depending on the value of g_1 with respect to the value of α:

$$(\hat{x}, \hat{y}) = \begin{cases} (x^*, y^*), & \text{if } g_1 \leq \alpha \\ (r_1, (1 - \delta_2) \cdot y^* + \delta_2 \cdot b_2), & \text{otherwise} \end{cases}$$

where $\delta_2 = \frac{1-g_1}{2-g_1}$.

Theorem 1. *Algorithm 1 outputs a* $\max\{\alpha, \frac{1-\alpha}{2-\alpha}\}$*-approximate Nash equilibrium.*

Proof. If $g_1 \leq \alpha$ (recall that we assumed $g_1 \geq g_2$), then clearly (x^*, y^*) is an α-approximate Nash equilibrium.

Suppose $g_1 > \alpha$. We will estimate the satisfaction of each player separately. Suppose b_1 is an optimal response for the row player to $\hat{y}$, i.e., $b_1 \in \text{argmax}_{e_i} e_i^T R \hat{y}$. The row player plays r_1, which is a best response to y^*. Hence b_1 can be better than r_1 only when the column player plays b_2, which happens with probability δ_2. Formally, the amount that the row player can earn by switching is at most:

$$b_1^T R \hat{y} - r_1^T R \hat{y} = (1 - \delta_2)(b_1^T R y^* - r_1^T R y^*) + \delta_2(b_1^T R b_2 - r_1^T R b_2)$$
$$\leq \delta_2 \cdot b_1^T R b_2 \leq \delta_2 = \frac{1-g_1}{2-g_1}$$

The first inequality above comes from the fact that r_1 is a best response to y^* and the second comes from our assumption that the entries of R and C are in $[0,1]$.

Consider the column player. The critical observation is that the column player also benefits (when he plays y^*) from the switch of the row player from x^* to r_1. In particular, since (x^*, y^*) is an equilibrium for the zero-sum game $(R - C, C - R)$, the following inequalities hold:

$$(x^*)^T R e_j - (x^*)^T C e_j \geq (x^*)^T R y^* - (x^*)^T C y^* \geq e_i^T R y^* - e_i^T C y^*, \forall\, i, j = 1, ..., n \tag{1}$$

If $e_i = r_1$, we get from (1) that $r_1^T C y^* \geq r_1^T R y^* - (x^*)^T R y^* + (x^*)^T C y^*$. But we know that $r_1^T R y^* - (x^*)^T R y^* = g_1$, which implies:

$$r_1^T C y^* \geq g_1 + (x^*)^T C y^* \geq g_1 \tag{2}$$

Inequality (2) shows that any deviation of the row player from x^*, y^*, that improves his payoff, guarantees at least the same gain to the column player as well. Now we can estimate the incentive of the column player to change his strategy. He plays $\hat{y}$ while he would prefer to play an optimal response to $\hat{x}$ which is b_2. Since b_2 is played with probability δ_2, by switching he could earn:

$$\hat{x}^T C b_2 - \hat{x}^T C \hat{y} = r_1^T C b_2 - r_1^T C \hat{y}$$
$$= r_1^T C b_2 - ((1 - \delta_2) r_1^T C y^* - \delta_2 \cdot r_1^T C b_2)$$
$$= (1 - \delta_2)(r_1^T C b_2 - r_1^T C y^*)$$
$$\leq (1 - \delta_2)(1 - g_1) = \delta_2 = \frac{1-g_1}{2-g_1}$$

The last inequality above follows from (2). The probability δ_2 was chosen so as to equalize the incentives of the two players to deviate in the case that $g_1 > \alpha$.

It is now easy to check that the function $(1 - g_1)/(2 - g_1)$ is decreasing, hence the incentive for both players to deviate is at most $(1 - \alpha)/(2 - \alpha)$. Combined with the case when $g_1 \leq \alpha$, we get a $\max\{\alpha, \frac{1-\alpha}{2-\alpha}\}$-approximate equilibrium.

In order to optimize the approximation factor of Algorithm 1, we only need to equate the two terms, α and $\frac{1-\alpha}{2-\alpha}$, which then gives:

$$\alpha^2 - 3\alpha + 1 = 0 \qquad (3)$$

The solution to (3) in the interval $[0, 1]$ is $\alpha = \frac{3-\sqrt{5}}{2} \approx 0.38197$. Note that $\alpha = 1 - 1/\phi$, where ϕ is the golden ratio. Since α is an irrational number, we need to ensure that we can still do the comparison $g_1 \leq \alpha$ to be able to run Algorithm 1 (note that this is the only point where the algorithm uses the value of α). But to test $g_1 \leq 3 - \sqrt{5}/2$, it suffices to test if $(3 - 2g_1)^2 \geq 5$ and clearly g_1 is a polynomially sized rational number. Concerning complexity, zero-sum games can be solved in polynomial time by linear programming. All the other steps of the algorithm require only polynomial time. Therefore, Theorem 1 implies:

Corollary 1. *We can compute in polynomial time a $\frac{3-\sqrt{5}}{2}$-approximate Nash equilibrium for bimatrix games.*

4   An Improved Approximation

In this section we obtain a better approximation of $1/2 - 1/(3\sqrt{6}) \approx 0.36392$ by essentially proposing a different solution in the cases where Algorithm 1 approaches its worst case guarantee. We first give some motivation for the new algorithm. From the analysis of Algorithm 1, one can easily check that as long as g_1 belongs to $[0, 1/3] \cup [1/2, 1]$, we can have a $1/3$-approximation if we run the algorithm with any $\alpha \in [1/3, 1/2)$. Therefore, the bottleneck for getting a better guarantee is when the maximum incentive to deviate is in $[1/3, 1/2]$. In this case, we will change the algorithm so that the row player will play a mix of r_1 and x^*. Note that in Algorithm 1, the probability of playing r_1 is either 0 or 1 depending on the value of g_1. This probability will now be a more complicated function of g_1, derived from a certain optimization problem. As for the column player, we again compute b_2 which is now the best response to the *mixture* of r_1 and x^*- not only to r_1. Then we compute an appropriate mixture of b_2 and y^*. Again, the probability of playing b_2 is chosen so as to equate the incentives of the two players to defect. Finally we should note that our modification will be not on $[1/3, 1/2]$ but instead on a subinterval of the form $[1/3, \beta]$, where β is derived from the optimization that we perform in our analysis.

Algorithm 2

1. Compute an equilibrium (x^*, y^*) for the zero-sum game defined by the matrix $A = R - C$.

2. As in Algorithm 1, let g_1, g_2 be the incentives to deviate for the row and column player respectively if they play (x^*, y^*) in the original game, i.e., $g_1 = \max_{i=1,\ldots,n} e_i^T R y^* - (x^*)^T R y^*$ and $g_2 = \max_{i=1,\ldots,n} (x^*)^T C e_i - (x^*)^T C y^*$. WLOG, assume, that $g_1 \geq g_2$.

3. Let $r_1 \in \operatorname{argmax}_{e_i} e_i^T R y^*$ be an optimal response of the row player to the strategy y^*.

4. The row player will play a mixture of r_1 and x^*, where the probability of playing r_1 is given by:

$$\delta_1 = \delta_1(g_1) = \begin{cases} 0, & \text{if } g_1 \in [0, 1/3] \\ \Delta_1(g_1), & \text{if } g_1 \in (1/3, \beta] \\ 1, & \text{otherwise} \end{cases}$$

where $\Delta_1(g_1) = (1 - g_1)\left(-1 + \sqrt{1 + \frac{1}{1-2g_1} - \frac{1}{g_1}}\right)$.

5. Let b_2 be an optimal response of the column player to $((1-\delta_1)x^* + \delta_1 r_1)$, i.e., $b_2 \in \operatorname{argmax}_{e_i} ((1-\delta_1)x^* + \delta_1 r_1)^T C e_i$. Let also $h_2 = (x^*)^T C b_2 - (x^*)^T C y^*$, i.e., the gain from switching to b_2 if the row player plays x^*.

6. The column player will play a mixture of b_2 and y^*, where the probability of playing b_2 is given by:

$$\delta_2 = \delta_2(\delta_1, g_1, h_2) = \begin{cases} 0, & \text{if } g_1 \in [0, 1/3] \\ \max\{0, \Delta_2(\delta_1, g_1, h_2)\}, & \text{if } g_1 \in (1/3, \beta] \\ \frac{1-g_1}{2-g_1}, & \text{otherwise} \end{cases}$$

where $\Delta_2(\delta_1, g_1, h_2) = \frac{\delta_1 - g_1 + (1-\delta_1)h_2}{1 + \delta_1 - g_1}$.

7. Output $(\hat{x}, \hat{y}) = ((1 - \delta_1)x^* + \delta_1 r_1, (1 - \delta_2)y^* + \delta_2 b_2)$.

In our analysis, we will take β to be the solution to $\Delta_1(g_1) = 1$ in $[1/3, 1/2]$, which coincides with the root of the polynomial $x^3 - x^2 - 2x + 1$ in that interval and it is:

$$\beta = \frac{1}{3} + \frac{\sqrt{7}}{3} \cos\left(\frac{1}{3} \tan^{-1}\left(3\sqrt{3}\right)\right) - \frac{\sqrt{21}}{3} \sin\left(\frac{1}{3} \tan^{-1}\left(3\sqrt{3}\right)\right) \quad (4)$$

Calculations show $0.445041 \leq \beta \leq 0.445042$. The emergence of β in our analysis arises in the proof of Lemma 1.

Remark 1. The actual probabilities δ_1 and δ_2 as well as the number β can be irrational numbers. However, for any constant $\epsilon > 0$, we can take approximations of high enough accuracy of all the square roots that are involved in the calculations so that the final loss in the approximation ratio will be at most ϵ. From now on, for ease of exposition, we will carry out the analysis of Algorithm 2, as if we can compute exactly all the expressions involved.

Note that for $g_1 \in [\frac{1}{3}, \frac{1}{2}]$ and $\delta_1 \in [0, 1]$ the denominators that appear in the functions Δ_1, Δ_2 do not vanish. The following lemma ensures that $\hat{x}$ is a valid strategy.

Lemma 1. *For $g_1 \in (1/3, \beta]$ we have $\Delta_1(g_1) \in [0,1]$.*

The proof of Lemma 1 is based on showing that the function Δ_1 is increasing in $[1/3, \beta]$ and that it maps $[1/3, \beta]$ to $[0,1]$. Due to lack of space we omit it in this version.

Now we bound the incentives of players to deviate. Let F be the following function:

$$F(\delta_1, g_1, h_2) := \frac{(\delta_1(1 - g_1 - h_2) + h_2)(1 - (1 - \delta_1)h_2)}{1 + \delta_1 - g_1} \tag{5}$$

Lemma 2. *The pair of strategies $(\hat{x}, \hat{y})$ is a λ-Nash equilibrium for game (R, C) with*

$$\lambda \leq \begin{cases} g_1 & \text{if } g_1 \leq 1/3 \\ \max_{h_2 \in [0, g1]} \begin{cases} F(\delta_1, g_1, h_2) & \text{if } \Delta_2(\delta_1, g_1, h_2) \geq 0 \\ (1 - \delta_1)g_1 & \text{if } \Delta_2(\delta_1, g_1, h_2) < 0 \end{cases} & \text{if } g_1 \in (1/3, \beta] \\ \frac{1 - g_1}{2 - g_1} & \text{if } g_1 > \beta \end{cases} \tag{6}$$

Proof. In the case that $g_1 \in [0, 1/3] \cup [\beta, 1]$, the answer follows from the proof of Theorem 1. The interesting case is when $g_1 \in [1/3, \beta]$.

Case 1: $g_1 \leq 1/3$
$(\hat{x}, \hat{y}) = (x^*, y^*)$ which is by definition a g_1-approximate Nash equilibrium.

Case 2a: $g_1 \in (1/3, \beta]$ and $\Delta_2(\delta_1, g_1, h_2) \geq 0$
Recall that Lemma 1 implies $\hat{x}$ is a valid strategy in Case 2. Observe, that $\delta_2(g_1, \delta_1, h_2) = \Delta_2(g_1, \delta_1, h_2) = \frac{\delta_1 - g_1 + (1 - \delta_1)h_2}{1 + \delta_1 - g_1} \leq 1$ is a valid probability, and therefore $\hat{y}$ is a valid mixed strategy too.

We estimate the incentive for the row player to deviate from $\hat{x}$. If b_1 is an optimal response to $\hat{y}$, then the gain from switching is at most:

$$b_1^T R\hat{y} - \hat{x}^T R\hat{y} = (b_1 - \hat{x})^T R\hat{y} =$$

$$
\begin{aligned}
&= \delta_2(b_1 - \hat{x})^T Rb_2 && +(1 - \delta_2)(b_1 - \hat{x})^T Ry^* \\
&\leq \delta_2(1 - \hat{x}^T Rb_2) && +(1 - \delta_2)(b_1 - \hat{x})^T Ry^* \\
&= \delta_2(1 - \delta_1 r_1^T Rb_2 - (1 - \delta_1)(x^*)^T Rb_2) && +(1 - \delta_2)(b_1 - \delta_1 r_1 - (1 - \delta_1)x^*)^T Ry^*
\end{aligned}
$$

By (1) we have $(x^*)^T Rb_2 \geq (x^*)^T Cb_2 - (x^*)^T Cy^* + (x^*)^T Ry^* \geq h_2$. Also r_1 is a best response to y^*, hence $(b_1 - r_1)^T Ry^* \leq 0$ and $(b_1 - x^*)^T Ry^* \leq g_1$. Therefore, the gain from deviating is at most:

$$b_1^T R\hat{y} - \hat{x}^T R\hat{y} \leq \delta_2(1 - (1 - \delta_1)h_2) + (1 - \delta_2)(1 - \delta_1)g_1 = \text{EST}_1.$$

We now estimate the incentive of the column player to switch. The best response to $\hat{x}$ for the column player is b_2, which is played with probability δ_2. Thus the incentive to deviate from $\hat{y}$ is:

$$
\begin{aligned}
\hat{x}^T Cb_2 - \hat{x}^T C\hat{y} &= (1 - \delta_2)(\hat{x}^T Cb_2 - \hat{x}^T Cy^*) \\
&= (1 - \delta_2)((1 - \delta_1)(x^{*T} Cb_2 - x^{*T} Cy^*) + \delta_1(r_1^T Cb_2 - r_1^T Cy^*)) \\
&\leq (1 - \delta_2)((1 - \delta_1)h_2 + \delta_1(1 - g_1)) = \text{EST}_2
\end{aligned}
$$

The last inequality follows from the definitions of g_1 and h_2. It remains to observe that our choice of $\delta_2(\delta_1, g_1, h_2) = \frac{\delta_1 - g_1 + (1 - \delta_1)h_2}{1 + \delta_1 - g_1}$ makes these estimates both equal to $F(\delta_1, g_1, h_2)$:

$$\text{EST}_1 = \text{EST}_2 = \frac{(\delta_1 (1 - g_1 - h_2) + h_2) (1 - (1 - \delta_1)h_2)}{\delta_1 + 1 - g_1} = F(\delta_1, g_1, h_2).$$

Case 2b: $g_1 \in (1/3, \beta]$ and $\Delta_2(\delta_1, g_1, h_2) < 0$
Then $\hat{y} = y^*$ and the best response of the row player is r_1. Hence he can improve his payoff by at most

$$r_1^T R y^* - \hat{x}^T R y^* = r_1^T R y^* - (\delta_1 \cdot r_1^T R y^* + (1 - \delta_1)((x^*)^T R y^*)) = (1 - \delta_1)g_1$$

while the column player can improve by at most

$$\hat{x}^T C b_2 - \hat{x}^T C y^* = \delta_1(r_1^T C b_2 - r_1^T C y^*) + (1 - \delta_1)((x^*)^T C b_2 - (x^*)^T C y^*)$$

By (1) we can see that $r_1^T C y^* \geq g_1$. Hence

$$\hat{x}^T C b_2 - \hat{x}^T C y^* \leq \delta_1(1 - g_1) + (1 - \delta_1)h_2$$

It is easy to check that $\Delta_2(g_1, \delta_1, h_2) < 0$ implies $\delta_1(1 - g_1) + (1 - \delta_1)h_2 < (1 - \delta_1)g_1$. Therefore the maximum incentive to deviate in this case is at most $(1 - \delta_1)g_1$. Combining Case 2a and Case 2b, and taking the worst possible case over the range of h_2 (recall that $h_2 \leq g_2 \leq g_1$), we get precisely the expression in the statement of Lemma 2.

Case 3: $g_1 > \beta$
Notice that in this case, the players are playing the same strategies as in Algorithm 1, when $g_1 \geq \alpha$. By the analysis in the proof of Theorem 1, we see that the maximum incentive is $(1 - g_1)/(2 - g_1)$. This completes the proof.

We will now argue that our choice of $\Delta_1(g_1)$ is optimal for any $g_1 \in (\frac{1}{3}, \beta]$ and that the expression (6) from Lemma 2 achieves an improvement over Algorithm 1. For this, we need to find the worst possible approximation in Case 2 of Lemma 2. In particular, we need to look at the maxima of the following function:

$$P(g_1) := \min_{\delta_1 \in [0,1]} \max_{h_2 \in [0,g_1]} \begin{cases} F(\delta_1, g_1, h_2) & \text{if } \Delta_2(\delta_1, g_1, h_2) \geq 0 \\ (1 - \delta_1)g_1 & \text{if } \Delta_2(\delta_1, g_1, h_2) < 0 \end{cases} \qquad (7)$$

Lemma 3. *The tuple* $(\delta_1, h_2) = (\Delta_1(g_1), g_1)$ *is an optimal solution for the expression* $P(g_1)$. *Furthermore, the maximum of* $P(g_1)$ *over* g_1 *is* $\frac{1}{2} - \frac{1}{3\sqrt{6}}$, *i.e., the following holds*

$$P(g_1) = F(\Delta_1(g_1), g_1, g_1) \quad \forall g_1 \in [\frac{1}{3}, \frac{1}{2}] \qquad (8)$$

$$\max_{g_1 \in [\frac{1}{3}, \beta]} P(g_1) = \frac{1}{2} - \frac{1}{3\sqrt{6}} \leq 0.36392. \qquad (9)$$

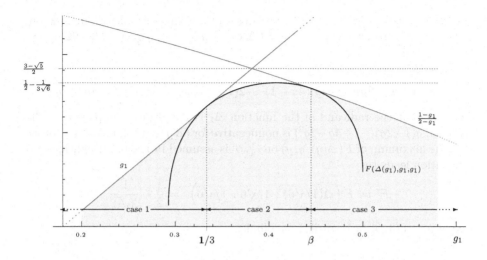

Fig. 1. How the approximation factor depends on g_1

The lemma will be proved in Section 5. Given Remark 1, we are now ready to conclude with the following:

Theorem 2. *For any $\epsilon > 0$, Algorithm 2 computes a $(0.36392 + \epsilon)$-approximate Nash equilibrium.*

Proof. By Lemma 2 the output of Algorithm 2, $(\hat{x}, \hat{y})$ is a pair of mixed strategies for players, such that the incentive of players to deviate is bounded by (6). By Lemma 3 we have that for $g_1 \in (1/3, \beta]$ the expression (6) is bounded by $\frac{1}{2} - \frac{1}{3\sqrt{6}} \leq 0.36392$. It is easy to observe, that for other values of g_1 the expression (6) takes only smaller values. In particular, it is at most $1/3$ when $g_1 \in [0, 1/3]$ and at most $\frac{1-\beta}{2-\beta} \approx 0.3569$ when $g_1 > \beta$. The dependence of the approximation on the variable g_1 is presented in Figure 1.

5   Proof of Lemma 3

Fact 3. *The square function is monotone increasing on the positive domain, i.e.,*

$$a - b \geq 0 \Leftrightarrow a^2 - b^2 \geq 0 \quad holds \ for \ all \ a, b \in \mathbb{R}, \ a, b \geq 0 \qquad (10)$$

We solved the optimization problem of Lemma 3 in the classic manner, eventually leading to the minimizer $\Delta_1(g)$. This procedure is lengthy, so here we give an uninspiring but short proof.

Proof of Lemma 3 :   Combining (11) and (12) from Lemma 4 below, we obtain:

$$F(\Delta_1(g_1), g_1, g_1) = \min_{\delta_1 \in [0,1]} \max_{h_2 \in [0,g_1]} \begin{cases} F(\delta_1, g_1, h_2) & \text{if } \Delta_2(\delta_1, g_1, h_2) \geq 0 \\ (1 - \delta_1)g_1 & \text{if } \Delta_2(\delta_1, g_1, h_2) < 0 \end{cases}$$

For ease of exposition, we drop the subscripts of the variables from now on. Hence we need to prove $\max_{g\in[\frac{1}{3},\beta]} F(\Delta_1(g),g,g) = \frac{1}{2} - \frac{1}{3\sqrt{6}} \le 0.36392$ where

$$F(\Delta_1(g),g,g) =$$
$$\tfrac{1}{4} - \tfrac{1}{4}(1-2g)(3-2g)(4g-1) + 2(1-g)\sqrt{g(1-2g)(-1+4g-2g^2)}$$

The fact that the radicand of the function Δ_1 is nonnegative implies that the radicand $g(1-2g)(-1+4g-2g^2)$ is nonnegative for all $g \in [1/3,\beta]$. We now prove that the maximum of $F(\Delta(g),g,g)$ on $[\frac{1}{3},\beta]$ is assumed in $1/\sqrt{6}$. Straightforward calculation leads to

$$\mathcal{F}^* := F\left(\Delta(1/\sqrt{6}),\, 1/\sqrt{6},\, 1/\sqrt{6}\right) = \frac{1}{2} - \frac{1}{3\sqrt{6}}$$

Fixing $g \in [1/3,\beta]$ (arbitrarily), one finds:

$$\mathcal{F}^* - F(\Delta_1(g),\, g,\, g) =$$
$$\underbrace{\tfrac{1}{4} - \tfrac{1}{3\sqrt{6}} + \tfrac{1}{4}(1-2g)(3-2g)(4g-1)}_{\ge 0\ (*)} - \underbrace{2(1-g)\sqrt{g(1-2g)(-1+4g-2g^2)}}_{\ge 0\ (**)}$$

Here $(*)$ and $(**)$ are implied by the choice of g, i.e., $(3-2g) \ge 2(1-g) \ge (1-2g) \ge 0$, and $4g-1 \ge 1/3 > 0$ hold. Finally since $\sqrt{6} > 2$ we have $\frac{1}{4} - \frac{1}{3\sqrt{6}} > \frac{1}{12} > 0$.

The inequalities in $(*)$ and $(**)$ together with (10) lead (after calculations which we omit due to lack of space) to the equivalence:

$$\mathcal{F}^* - F(\Delta_1(g),\, g,\, g) \ge 0 \quad \Leftrightarrow \quad \left(\tfrac{11}{18} + \tfrac{2}{3\sqrt{6}}(3-g) + (1-g)^2\right)\left(g - \tfrac{1}{\sqrt{6}}\right)^2 \ge 0$$

Here the second inequality trivially holds since $(3-g) > 0$ for $g \in [1/3,\beta]$.

Thus we showed $\mathcal{F}^* = F(\Delta_1(1/\sqrt{6}),1/\sqrt{6},1/\sqrt{6}) \ge F(\Delta_1(g),g,g)$, proving the lemma, since $g \in [1/3,\beta]$ was chosen arbitrarily and $1/\sqrt{6} \in [1/3,\beta]$ is implied by $0.40 \le 1/\sqrt{6} \le 0.41 < \beta$.   □

It now remains to prove the following Lemma:

Lemma 4. *For every pair* $(g,\delta) \in [1/3,\beta] \times [0,1]$ *we find*

$$F(\delta,g,g) = \max_{h\in[0,g]} \begin{cases} F(\delta,g,h) & \text{if } \Delta_2(\delta,g,h) \ge 0 \\ (1-\delta)g & \text{if } \Delta_2(\delta,g,h) < 0 \end{cases} \quad (11)$$

$$F(\Delta_1(g),g,g) = \min_{d\in[0,1]} F(d,g,g) \quad (12)$$

Proof. Fix some pair $(g,\delta) \in [1/3,\beta] \times [0,1]$. We rewrite (11) as

$$F(\delta,g,g) \le \left(\max_{h\in[0,g]} \begin{cases} F(\delta,g,h) & \text{if } \Delta_2(\delta,g,h) \ge 0 \\ (1-\delta)g & \text{if } \Delta_2(\delta,g,h) < 0 \end{cases}\right) \le \max_{h\in[0,g]} F(\delta,g,g)$$
$$(13)$$

and prove it as follows: Brief calculation together with $(1 - g) > 0$ lead to $\Delta_2(\delta, g, g) = (1 - g)\delta/(1 - g + \delta) \geq 0$. So there is a $h^* \in [0, g]$, namely $h^* := g$, such that $\Delta_2(\delta, g, h^*) \geq 0$. This implies the first inequality in (13).

Observe that to prove the second inequality in (13), it suffices to show that

$$F(\delta, g, g) \geq (1 - \delta)g \quad \text{and} \quad F(\delta, g, g) \geq F(\delta, g, h) \quad \text{for all } h \in [0, g] \quad (14)$$

both hold – independently of the value of Δ_2. Quick calculation proves the first inequality of (14): Recall that the choice on (g, δ) implies $(1 - g) \geq 0$, $2\delta g \geq 0$, and $(1 - 2g) \geq 0$, yielding

$$F(\delta, g, g) - (1 - \delta)g = \frac{(1 - g)\,\delta}{(1 - g) + \delta}\,(2\delta g + (1 - 2g)\,) \geq 0$$

To obtain the second inequality of (14), we show that for the chosen δ, g, the function $F(\delta, g, h)$ is monotone non-decreasing on $h \in [0, g]$: Recalling $h \leq g \leq 1/2$ we find $(1 - 2h) \geq 0$, implying

$$\frac{\mathrm{d}F(\delta, g, h)}{\mathrm{d}h} = \frac{(1 - 2h)(1 - \delta)^2 + g\delta(1 - \delta)}{(1 - g) + \delta} \geq 0$$

This finally proves (14), and thus the second inequality in (13), concluding the proof of (11). To prove (12) fix some $d \in [0, 1]$ arbitrarily and define $\mathfrak{p}(g) := g(1 - 2g)(-1 + 4g - 2g^2)$, which is the radicand appearing in $F(\Delta_1(g), g, g)$. Brief calculation leads to

$$(F(d, g, g) - F(\Delta_1(g), g, g))\ (1 - g + d) =$$

$$\underbrace{(4g - 1)(1 - g)^3 + 2g(1 - 2g)(1 - g)d + g(1 - 2g)d^2}_{\geq 0\ (\star)} - \underbrace{2(1 - g + d)(1 - g)\sqrt{\mathfrak{p}(g)}}_{\geq 0\ (\star\star)}$$

To obtain $(\star)$, recall $1/3 < \beta < 1/2$ and observe that the restrictions on g, d imply $g, d \geq 0$ as well as $(4g - 1) \geq 0$, $(1 - g) \geq 0$, and $(1 - 2g) \geq 0$. Moreover we have $(1 - g + d) > (1 - g) \geq 0$, showing $(\star\star)$. It can also be easily verified that $\mathfrak{p}(g) \geq 0$ for the chosen g. Hence exploiting $(1 - g + d) > 0$ and Fact 3 we obtain that $F(d, g, g) - F(\Delta_1(g), g, g)$ is nonnegative if and only if the following quantity is nonnegative:

$$\left((4g - 1)(1 - g)^3 + 2g(1 - 2g)(1 - g)d + g(1 - 2g)d^2\right)^2 - 4(1 - g + d)^2(1 - g)^2\mathfrak{p}(g)$$

This turns out to be equivalent to:

$$\left((1 - 3g)(1 - g)^2 + 2g(1 - 2g)(1 - g)d + g(1 - 2g)d^2\right)^2 \geq 0$$

The last inequality is trivially true, which finally proves (12) since $(g, d) \in [1/3, \beta] \times [0, 1]$ were chosen arbitrarily.

6 Discussion

It is worth noticing that the analysis of both presented algorithms is tight. Tracing all inequalities used, we constructed the following worst-case example, on which the second algorithm yields a 0.36392-approximation of the equilibrium:

$$R = \begin{pmatrix} 0 & \alpha & \alpha \\ \alpha & 0 & 1 \\ \alpha & 1 & 0 \end{pmatrix} \quad C = \begin{pmatrix} 0 & \alpha & \alpha \\ \alpha & 1 & 1/2 \\ \alpha & 1/2 & 1 \end{pmatrix} \quad \text{where } \alpha = 1/\sqrt{6}.$$

In general, our algorithms produce solutions with large support. This is to no surprise, as implied by negative results on the existence of approximate equilibrium strategies with small support [1,7].

The major open question remains whether a polynomial time algorithm for any constant $\epsilon > 0$ is possible. It would also be interesting to investigate if our methods can be modified to yield better approximations.

References

1. Althöfer, I.: On sparse approximations to randomized strategies and convex combinations. Linear Algebra and Applications 199, 339–355 (1994)
2. Chen, X., Deng, X.: Settling the complexity of 2-player Nash equilibrium. In: Annual IEEE Symposium on Foundations of Computer Science, pp. 261–272. IEEE Computer Society Press, Los Alamitos (2006)
3. Chen, X., Deng, X., Teng, S.: Computing Nash equilibria: Approximation and smoothed complexity. In: Annual IEEE Symposium on Foundations of Computer Science, pp. 603–612. IEEE Computer Society Press, Los Alamitos (2006)
4. Daskalakis, C., Goldberg, P., Papadimitriou, C.: The complexity of computing a Nash equilibrium. In: Annual ACM Symposium on Theory of Computing, pp. 71–78. ACM Press, New York (2006)
5. Daskalakis, C., Mehta, A., Papadimitriou, C.: A note on approximate Nash equilibria. In: Workshop on Internet and Network Economics, pp. 297–306 (2006)
6. Daskalakis, C., Mehta, A., Papadimitriou, C.: Progress on approximate Nash equilibria. In: ACM Conference on Electronic Commerce, ACM Press, New York (2007)
7. Feder, T., Nazerzadeh, H., Saberi, A.: Approximating Nash equilibria with small-support strategies. In: ACM Conference on Electronic Commerce, ACM Press, New York (2007)
8. Goldberg, P., Papadimitriou, C.: Reducibility among equilibrium problems. In: Annual ACM Symposium on Theory of Computing, pp. 61–70. ACM Press, New York (2006)
9. Kontogiannis, S., Panagopoulou, P., Spirakis, P.: Polynomial algorithms for approximating Nash equilibria of bimatrix games. In: Workshop on Internet and Network Economics (2006)
10. Kontogiannis, S., Spirakis, P.: Efficient algorithms for constant well supported approximate equilibria in bimatrix games. In: 34th International Colloquium on Automata, Languages and Programming (2007)

11. Lipton, R., Markakis, E., Mehta, A.: Playing large games using simple strategies. In: 4th ACM Conference on Electronic Commerce, pp. 36–41. ACM Press, New York (2003)
12. Nash, J.F.: Non-cooperative games. Annals of Mathematics 54, 286–295 (1951)
13. Spirakis, P., Tsaknakis, H.: An optimization approach for approximate Nash equilibria. In: Workshop on Internet and Network Economics (2007)

A Unified Approach to
Congestion Games and Two-Sided Markets[*]

Heiner Ackermann[1], Paul W. Goldberg[2],
Vahab S. Mirrokni[3], Heiko Röglin[1], and Berthold Vöcking[1]

[1] Department of Computer Science, RWTH Aachen, Germany
{ackermann,roeglin,voecking}@cs.rwth-aachen.de
[2] Department of Computer Science, University of Liverpool, U.K.
P.W.Goldberg@liverpool.ac.uk
[3] Microsoft Research, Redmond, WA, USA
mirrokni@microsoft.com

Abstract. Congestion games are a well-studied model for resource sharing among uncoordinated selfish agents. Usually, one assumes that the
resources in a congestion game do not have any preferences over the
players that can allocate them. In typical load balancing applications,
however, different jobs can have different priorities, and jobs with higher
priorities get, for example, larger shares of the processor time. We introduce a model in which each resource can assign priorities to the players
and players with higher priorities can displace players with lower priorities. Our model does not only extend standard congestion games, but it
can also be seen as a model of two-sided markets with ties. We prove that
singleton congestion games with priorities are potential games, and we
show that every player-specific singleton congestion game with priorities
possesses a pure Nash equilibrium that can be found in polynomial time.
Finally, we extend our results to matroid congestion games, in which the
strategy space of each player consists of the bases of a matroid over the
resources.

1 Introduction

In a *congestion game*, there is a set of players who compete for a set of resources.
Each player has to select a subset of resources that she wishes to allocate. The
delay of a resource depends on the number of players allocating that resource,
and every player is interested in allocating a subset of resources with small total delay. Congestion games are a well-studied model for resource sharing among
uncoordinated selfish agents. They are widely used to model routing, network design, and load balancing [4,5,11,3]. One appealing property of congestion games
is that they are *potential games* [21]. In particular, this implies that every congestion game possesses a *pure Nash equilibrium* and that myopic player eventually
reach a Nash equilibrium by iteratively playing better responses.

[*] This work was supported by DFG grant VO 889/2, EPSRC Grant GR/T07343/02,
and by the EU within the 6th Framework Programme under contract 001907
(DELIS).

X. Deng and F.C. Graham (Eds.): WINE 2007, LNCS 4858, pp. 30–41, 2007.
© Springer-Verlag Berlin Heidelberg 2007

One drawback of the standard model of congestion games is that resources do not have any preferences over the players. In typical load balancing applications, however, different jobs have different priorities, and depending on the policy, jobs with a low priority are stopped or slowed down when jobs with higher priorities are present. We introduce *congestion games with priorities* to model the scenario in which a job can prevent jobs with lower priorities from being processed. In our model, each resource can partition the set of players into classes of different priorities. As long as a resource is only allocated by players with the same priority, these players incur a delay depending on the congestion, as in standard congestion games. But if players with different priorities allocate a resource, only players with the highest priority incur a delay depending on the number of players with this priority, and players with lower priorities incur an infinite delay. Intuitively, they are displaced by the players with the highest priority. This model is applicable if every player controls a stream of jobs rather than only a single one. In the latter case, it might be more reasonable to assume that jobs with lower priorities incur a large but finite delay.

Motivated by the application of congestion games to load balancing, we mainly consider congestion games in which each player has to choose exactly one resource to allocate, namely one server on which her job is to be processed. Such *singleton congestion games* or congestion games on *parallel links* have been studied extensively in the literature [4,8,9,14]. Moreover, we show that singleton congestion games with priorities are potential games, implying that uncoordinated players who iteratively play better responses eventually reach a pure Nash equilibrium. If all resources have the same priorities, then we even obtain polynomial-time convergence to a Nash equilibrium. Milchtaich [19] introduces *player-specific congestion games* as an extended class of congestion games in which every player can have her own delay function for every resource. Milchtaich shows that player-specific singleton congestion games are not potential games anymore but that they possess pure Nash equilibria that can be computed in polynomial time. We show that also in player-specific singleton congestion games with priorities pure Nash equilibria exist that can be computed efficiently.

Interestingly, our model of player-specific congestion games with priorities does not only extend congestion games but also the well-known model of *two-sided markets*. This model was introduced by Gale and Shapley [10] to model markets on which different kinds of agents are matched to another, for example men and women, students and colleges [10], interns and hospitals [22], and firms and workers. Using the same terms as for congestion games, we say that the goal of a two-sided market is to match players and resources (or markets). In contrast to congestion games, each resource can only be matched to one player. With each pair of player and resource a payoff is associated, and players are interested in maximizing their payoffs. Hence, the payoffs implicitly define a preference list over the resources for each player. Additionally, each resource has a preference list over the players that is independent of the profits. Every player can *propose* to one resource and if several players propose to a resource, only the most preferred player is *assigned* to that resource and receives the corresponding payoff. This way, every set of proposals corresponds to a bipartite matching between players and resources. A matching is *stable* if no player can be assigned to a resource from which she receives a higher payoff than from her current resource given the current proposals of the other players. Gale and Shapley [10] show that stable matchings always exist and can be found in polynomial time. Since the seminal work of Gale and Shapley there has been a significant amount of work in studying two-sided markets. See for example, the book by Knuth [17], the book by Gusfield and Irving [12], or the book by Roth and Sotomayor [23].

In the same way as it is in many situations not realistic to assume that in congestion games the resources have no preferences over the players, it is in two-sided markets often unrealistic to assume that the preference lists of the resources are strict. Our model of player-specific congestion games with priorities can also be seen as a model of *two-sided markets with ties* in which several players can be assigned to one resource. If different players propose to a resource, only the most preferred ones are assigned to that resource. If the most preferred player is not unique, several players share the payoff of the market. Such two-sided markets correspond to our model of congestion games with priorities, except that players are now interested in maximizing their payoffs instead of minimizing their delays, which does not affect our results for congestion games with priorities. Two-sided markets with ties have been extensively studied in the literature [12,15]. In these models, ties are somehow broken, i. e., despite ties in the preference lists, every resource can be assigned to at most one player. Hence, these models differ significantly from our model. One application of our model are markets into which different companies can invest. As long as the investing companies are of comparable size, they share the payoff of the market, but large companies can utilize their market power to eliminate smaller companies completely from the market. Player-specific congestion games and two-sided markets are the special cases of our model in which all players have the same priority or distinct priorities, respectively. In the following, we use the terms *two-sided markets with ties* and *player-specific congestion games with priorities* interchangeably.

We also consider a special case of *correlated two-sided markets with ties* in which the payoffs of the players and the preference lists of the resources are correlated. In this model, every resource prefers to be assigned to players who receive the highest payoff when assigned to it. We show that this special case is a potential game. Variants of correlated two-sided markets without ties have been studied in the context of content distribution in networks and distributed caching problems [7,11,20]. These markets have also been considered for discovering stable geometric configurations with applications in VLSI design [13]. Our result implies that variants of the uniform distributed caching games with bandwidth constraints (defined by Mirrokni et. al [20,7]) are potential games.

Additionally, we consider player-specific congestion games with priorities in which the strategy space of each player consists of the bases of a matroid over the resources. For this case, we show that pure Nash equilibria exist that can be computed in polynomial time, extending a result for player-specific congestion games without priorities [2]. These games can also be seen as many-to-one two-sided markets with ties. Many-to-one two-sided markets are well studied in the economics literature [6,16,18]. Kelso and Crawford [16] show that if the preference list of every player satisfies a certain *substitutability property*, then stable matchings exist. Kojima and Ünver [18] prove that in this case, from every matching there exists a polynomially long better response sequence to a stable matching. This substitutability property is satisfied if the strategy spaces of the players are matroids. The crucial difference between our model of *many-to-one markets with ties* and the models considered in the economics literature is that in those models, every player specifies a ranking on the power set of the resources. This ranking is fixed and does not depend on the current matching. In our model with ties, however, players do not have fixed rankings but rankings that depend on the current matching.

2 Preliminaries

In this section, we define the problems and notations used throughout the paper.

Congestion Games. A *congestion game* Γ is a tuple $(\mathcal{N}, \mathcal{R}, (\Sigma_i)_{i \in \mathcal{N}}, (d_r)_{r \in \mathcal{R}})$ where $\mathcal{N} = \{1, \ldots, n\}$ denotes the set of players, $\mathcal{R}$ the set of resources, $\Sigma_i \subseteq 2^{\mathcal{R}}$ the strategy space of player i, and $d_r \colon \mathbb{N} \to \mathbb{N}$ a delay function associated with resource r. By m we denote $|\mathcal{R}|$, and we denote by $S = (S_1, \ldots, S_n)$ the *state of the game* where player i plays strategy $S_i \in \Sigma_i$. For a state S, we define the *congestion* $n_r(S)$ on resource r by $n_r(S) = |\{i \mid r \in S_i\}|$, that is, $n_r(S)$ is the number of players sharing resource r in state S. Every player i acts selfishly and wishes to play a strategy $S_i \in \Sigma_i$ that minimizes her individual delay, which is defined as $\sum_{r \in S_i} d_r(n_r(S))$. We call a state S a *Nash equilibrium* if, given the strategies of the others players, no player can decrease her delay by changing her strategy. Rosenthal [21] shows that every congestion game possesses at least one pure Nash equilibrium by considering the potential function $\phi \colon \Sigma_1 \times \cdots \times \Sigma_n \to \mathbb{N}$ with $\phi(S) = \sum_{r \in \mathcal{R}} \sum_{i=1}^{n_r(S)} d_r(i)$. A congestion game is called *singleton* if each strategy space Σ_i consists only of sets with cardinality one. The current state S of a singleton congestion game can be written as $S = (r_1, \ldots, r_n)$, meaning that player i currently allocates resource r_i.

Player-Specific Congestion Games. Player-specific congestion games are congestion games in which every player i has her own delay function $d_r^i \colon \mathbb{N} \to \mathbb{N}$ for each resource r. The delay of player i is then computed with respect to the functions d_r^i.

Player-Specific Congestion Games with Priorities. We define this model to be a generalization of player-specific congestion games in which each resource r assigns a *priority* or *rank* $\mathrm{rk}_r(i)$ to every player i. For a state S, let $\mathrm{rk}_r(S) = \max_{i \colon r \in S_i} \mathrm{rk}_r(i)$. We say that player i *allocates* resource r if $r \in S_i$, and we say that player i is *assigned* to resource r if $r \in S_i$ and $\mathrm{rk}_r(i) = \mathrm{rk}_r(S)$. We define $n_r^*(S)$ to be the number of players that are assigned to resource r, that is, the number of players i with $r \in S_i$ and $\mathrm{rk}_r(i) = \mathrm{rk}_r(S)$. The delay that an assigned player i incurs on r is $d_r^i(n_r^*(S))$. Players who allocate a resource r but are not assigned to it incur an infinite delay on resource r. Congestion games with priorities but without player-specific delay functions are defined in the same way, except that instead of player-specific delay functions d_r^i there is only one delay function d_r for each resource r. We say that the priorities are *consistent* if the priorities assigned to the players by different resources coincide.

Two-sided Markets. A *two-sided market* consists of two disjoint sets $\mathcal{N} = \{1,\ldots,n\}$ and $\mathcal{R}$ with $|\mathcal{R}| = m$. We use the terms *players* and *agents* to denote elements from $\mathcal{N}$, and we use the terms *resources* and *markets* to denote elements from $\mathcal{R}$. In a two-sided market, every player can be *matched* to one resource, and every resource can be matched to one player. We assume that with every pair $(i,r) \in \mathcal{N} \times \mathcal{R}$, a payoff $p_{i,r}$ is associated and that player i receives payoff $p_{i,r}$ if she is matched to resource r. Hence, the payoffs describe implicitly for each player a preference list over the resource. Additionally, we assume that every resource has a strict preference list over the players, which is independent of the payoffs. Each player $i \in \mathcal{N}$ can *propose* to a resource $r_i \in \mathcal{R}$. Given a state $S = (r_1,\ldots,r_n)$, each resource $r \in \mathcal{R}$ is matched to the *winner of* r, which is the player whom r ranks highest among all players $i \in \mathcal{N}$ with $r = r_i$. If i is the winner of r, she gets a payoff of $p_{i,r}$. If a player proposes to a resource won by another player, she receives no payoff at all. We say that S is a *stable matching* if none of the players can unilaterally increase her payoff by changing her proposal given the proposals of the other players. That is, for each player i who is assigned to a resource r_i, each resource r from which she receives a higher payoff than from r_i is matched to a player whom r prefers over i.

Two-sided Markets with Ties. We define a *two-sided market with ties* to be a two-sided market in which the preference lists of the resources can have ties. Given a vector of proposals $S = (r_1,\ldots,r_n)$, we say that a player $i \in \mathcal{N}$ is matched to resource $r \in \mathcal{R}$ if $r = r_i$ and if there is no player $j \in \mathcal{N}$ such that $r = r_j$ and j is strictly preferred to i by r. For a resource r, we denote by $n_r(S)$ the number of players proposing to r and by $n_r^*(S)$ the number of players that are matched to r. We assume that every player i has a non-increasing payoff function $p_r^i \colon \mathbb{N} \to \mathbb{N}$ for every resource r. A player i who is matched to resource r receives a payoff of $p_r^i(n_r^*(S))$. Also for two-sided markets with ties, we call a state S a stable matching if none of the players can increase her payoff given the proposals of the other players.

Correlated Two-sided Markets with Ties. In *correlated two-sided markets with ties*, the preferences of players and resources are correlated. We assume that also the preference lists of the resources are chosen according to the payoffs that are associated with the pairs from $\mathcal{N} \times \mathcal{R}$. That is, a player $i \in \mathcal{N}$ is preferred over a player $j \in \mathcal{N}$ by resource $r \in \mathcal{R}$ if and only if $p_{i,r} > p_{j,r}$. Due to this construction, if two players i and j are both matched to a resource r, then the payoffs $p_{i,r}$ and $p_{j,r}$ must be the same. We denote this payoff by $p_r(S)$, and we assume that it is split among the players that are matched to r.

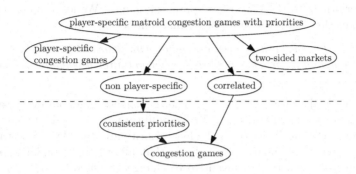

Fig. 1. For games on the upper level, equilibria can be computed in polynomial time, games on the mid-level are potential games, and games on the lower level converge in a polynomial number of rounds

The payoff that a player receives who is matched to r is specified by a function $q_r(p_r(S), n_r^*(S))$ with $q_r(p_r(S), 1) = p_r(S)$ that is non-increasing in the number of players matched to r.

Player-Specific Matroid Congestion Games with Priorities. In a player-specific *matroid* congestion game with priorities, each strategy space Σ_i must be the set of bases of a matroid over the set of resources. A set system $(\mathcal{R}, \mathcal{I})$ with $\mathcal{I} \subseteq 2^{\mathcal{R}}$ is said to be a matroid if $X \in \mathcal{I}$ implies $Y \in \mathcal{I}$ for all $Y \subseteq X$ and if for every $X, Y \in \mathcal{I}$ with $|Y| < |X|$ there exists an $x \in X$ with $Y \cup \{x\} \in \mathcal{I}$. A *basis* of a matroid $(\mathcal{R}, \mathcal{I})$ is a set $X \in \mathcal{I}$ with maximum cardinality. Every basis of a matroid has the same cardinality which is called the *rank* of the matroid. For a *matroid* congestion game Γ, we denote by $\mathrm{rk}(\Gamma)$ the maximal rank of one of the strategy spaces of the players. Examples of matroid congestion games are singleton games and games in which the resources are the edges of a graph and every player has to allocate a spanning tree. Again, these games can also be seen as an extension of two-sided markets in which each player can propose to a subset of resources instead of only one, so-called *many-to-one markets*, and in which the preference lists of the resources can have ties.

Figure 1 shows a summary of our results and the models we consider.

3   Singleton Congestion Games with Priorities

In this section, we consider singleton congestion games with priorities but without player-specific delay functions. For games with consistent priorities, we show that the better response dynamics reaches a Nash equilibrium after a polynomial number of *rounds*. We use the term round to denote a sequence of activations of players in which every player gets at least once the chance to improve. For example, our result implies that a polynomial (expected) number of better responses suffices if players are activated in a round-robin fashion or uniformly at random. We also prove that games in which different resources can assign different priorities to the players are potential games. We leave open the question whether they converge in a polynomial number of rounds.

Theorem 1. *In singleton congestion games with consistent priorities, the better response dynamics reaches a Nash equilibrium after a polynomial number of rounds.*

Proof. Ieong et al. [14] prove that in singleton congestion games every sequence of better responses terminates in a Nash equilibrium after a polynomial number of steps. Since the players with the highest priority are not affected by the other players, the result by Ieong et al. shows that after a polynomial number of rounds, none of them has an incentive to change her strategy anymore. From that point on, the strategies of these players are fixed and we can again apply the result by Ieong et al. to the players with the second highest priority. After a polynomially number of rounds, also none of them has an incentive to change her strategy anymore. After that, the argument can be applied to the players with the third highest priority and so on. □

Next we consider congestion games in which different resources can assign different priorities to the players.

Theorem 2. *Singleton congestion games with priorities are potential games.*

Proof. We set $\mathcal{D} = (\mathbb{N} \cup \{\infty\}) \times \mathbb{N}$ and for elements $x = (x_1, x_2) \in \mathcal{D}$ and $y = (y_1, y_2) \in \mathcal{D}$ we denote by "$<$" the lexicographic order on $\mathcal{D}$ in which the first component is to be minimized and the second component is to be maximized, i.e., we define $x < y$ if and only if $x_1 < y_1$ or if $x_1 = y_1$ and $x_2 > y_2$. We construct a potential function $\Phi \colon \Sigma_1 \times \cdots \times \Sigma_n \to \mathcal{D}^n$ that maps every state $S = (r_1, \ldots, r_n)$ to a vector of values from $\mathcal{D}$. In state S, every resource $r \in \mathcal{R}$ contributes $n_r(S)$ values to the vector $\Phi(S)$ and $\Phi(S)$ is obtained by sorting all values contributed by the resources in non-decreasing order according to the lexicographic order defined above. Resource r contributes the values $(d_r(1), \mathrm{rk}_r(S)), \ldots, (d_r(n_r^*(S)), \mathrm{rk}_r(S))$ to the vector $\Phi(S)$ and $n_r(S) - n_r^*(S)$ times the value $(\infty, 0)$. We claim that if state S' is obtained from S by letting one player play a better response, then $\Phi(S')$ is lexicographically smaller than $\Phi(S)$, i.e., there is a k with $\Phi_j(S) = \Phi_j(S')$ for all $j < k$ and $\Phi_k(S') < \Phi_k(S)$.

Assume that in state S player i plays a better response by changing her allocation from resource r_i to resource r_i'. We compare the two vectors $\Phi(S)$ and $\Phi(S')$, and we show that the smallest element added to the potential vector is smaller than the smallest element removed from the potential vector, showing that the potential decreases lexicographically. Due to the strategy change of player i, either the value $(d_{r_i}(n_{r_i}^*(S)), \mathrm{rk}_{r_i}(S))$ or the value $(\infty, 0)$ is replaced by the value $(d_{r_i'}(n_{r_i'}^*(S')), \mathrm{rk}_{r_i'}(S'))$. Since player i plays a better response, $d_{r_i'}(n_{r_i'}^*(S')) < d_{r_i}(n_{r_i}^*(S))$ or $d_{r_i'}(n_{r_i'}^*(S')) < \infty$, respectively, and hence the term added to the potential is smaller than the term removed from the potential. In the following we show that all values that are contained in $\Phi(S)$ but not in $\Phi(S')$ are larger than $(d_{r_i'}(n_{r_i'}^*(S')), \mathrm{rk}_{r_i'}(S'))$. Clearly, only terms for the resources r_i and r_i' change and we can restrict our considerations to these two resources.

Let us consider resource r_i first. If the rank of r_i does not decrease by the strategy change of player i or if no player allocates resource r_i in state S', then only the term $(d_{r_i}(n_{r_i}^*(S)), \mathrm{rk}_{r_i}(S))$ or $(\infty, 0)$ is not contained in the vector $\Phi(S')$ anymore. All other terms contributed by resource r_i do not change. If the rank of resource r_i is decreased by the strategy change of player i, then additionally some terms $(\infty, 0)$ in the potential are replaced by other terms. Obviously, the removed terms $(\infty, 0)$ are larger than $(d_{r_i'}(n_{r_i'}^*(S')), \mathrm{rk}_{r_i'}(S'))$.

Now we consider resource r_i'. If the rank of r_i' does not increase by the strategy change of player i or if no player allocates r_i' in state S, then only the term $(d_{r_i'}(n_{r_i'}^*(S')), \mathrm{rk}_{r_i'}(S'))$ is added to the potential. All other terms contributed by r_i' do not change. If the rank of r_i' is increased by the strategy change of player i, then additionally the terms $(d_{r_i'}(1), \mathrm{rk}_{r_i'}(S)), \ldots, (d_{r_i'}(n_{r_i'}^*(S)), \mathrm{rk}_{r_i'}(S))$ are replaced by $n_{r_i'}^*(S)$ terms $(\infty, 0)$. In this case, $n_{r_i'}^*(S') = 1$ and the smallest removed term, $(d_{r_i'}(1), \mathrm{rk}_{r_i'}(S))$, is larger than $(d_{r_i'}(1), \mathrm{rk}_{r_i'}(S')) = (d_{r_i'}(n_{r_i'}^*(S')), \mathrm{rk}_{r_i'}(S'))$ because $\mathrm{rk}_{r_i'}(S') > \mathrm{rk}_{r_i'}(S)$. □

4 Player-Specific Singleton Congestion Games with Priorities

In this section, we consider singleton congestion games with priorities and player-specific delay functions and we show that these games always possess Nash equilibria. Our proof also yields an efficient algorithm for finding an equilibrium.

Theorem 3. *Every player-specific singleton congestion game with priorities possesses a pure Nash equilibrium that can be computed in polynomial time by $O(m^2 \cdot n^3)$ strategy changes.*

Proof. In order to compute an equilibrium, we compute a sequence of states $S^0, \ldots, S^k$ such that S^0 is the state in which no player allocates a resource and S^k is a state in which every player allocates a resource. Remember that we distinguish between allocating a resource and being assigned to it. Our construction ensures the invariant that in each state S^a in this sequence, every player who allocates a resource has no incentive to change her strategy. Clearly, this invariant is true for S^0 and it implies that S^k is a pure Nash equilibrium.

In state S^a we pick an arbitrary player i who is allocating no resource and we let her play her best response. If in state S^a there is no resource to which i can be assigned, then i can allocate an arbitrary resource without affecting the players who are already allocating a resource and hence without affecting the invariant. It remains to consider the case that after her best response, player i is assigned to a resource r. If we leave the strategies of the other players unchanged, then the invariant may not be true anymore after the strategy change of player i. The invariant can, however, only be false for players who are assigned to resource r in state S^a. We distinguish between two cases in order to describe how the strategies of these players are modified in order to maintain the invariant.

First we consider the case that the rank of resource r does not change by the strategy change of player i. If there is a player j who is assigned to resource r in S^a and who can improve her strategy after i is also assigned to r, then we change the strategy of j to the empty set, i.e., in state S^{a+1} player j belongs to the set of players who do not allocate any resource. Besides this, no further modifications of the strategies are necessary because all other players are not affected by the replacement of j by i on resource r. In the case that the rank of resource r increases by the strategy change of player i, all players who are assigned to resource r in state S^a are set to their empty strategy in S^{a+1}.

It only remains to show that the described process terminates after a polynomial number of strategy changes in a stable state. We prove this by a potential function that is the lexicographic order of two components. The most important component is the sum of the ranks of the resources, i.e., $\sum_{r\in\mathcal{R}} \mathrm{rk}_r(S^a)$, which is to be maximized. Observe that this sum does not decrease in any of the two aforementioned cases, and that it increases strictly in the second case. Thus we need to show that after a polynomial number of consecutive occurrences of the first case, the second case must occur. Therefore, we need a second and less important component in our potential function. In order to define this component, we associate with every pair $(i,r) \in \mathcal{N} \times \mathcal{R}$ for which i is assigned to r in S^a a *tolerance* $\mathrm{tol}_a(i,r)$ that describes how many players (including i) can be assigned to r without changing the property that r is an optimal strategy for i, i.e.,

$$\min\{\max\{b \mid \text{in } S^a, r \text{ is best resp. for } i \text{ if } i \text{ shares } r \text{ with } b-1 \text{ players}\}, n\} \ .$$

The second component of the potential function is the sum of the tolerances of the assigned pairs in S^a, which is to be maximized. We denote the set of assignments in state S^a by $E^a \subseteq \mathcal{N} \times \mathcal{R}$ and define the potential function as

$$\Phi(S^a) = \left(\sum_{r\in\mathcal{R}} \mathrm{rk}_r(S^a), \sum_{(i,r)\in E^a} \mathrm{tol}_a(i,r) \right) \ .$$

In every occurrence of the first case, the second component increases by at least 1. Since the values of the components are bounded from above by $m \cdot n$ and $m \cdot n^2$ and bounded below from 0, the potential function implies that there can be at most $m^2 \cdot n^3$ strategy changes before an equilibrium is reached.

Let us remark that the potential function does not imply that the considered games are potential games because it increases only if the strategy changes are made according to the above described policy. □

5 Correlated Two-Sided Markets with Ties

In this section, we analyze the better response dynamics for correlated two-sided markets with ties and we show that these games are potential games.

Theorem 4. *Correlated two-sided markets with ties are potential games.*

Proof. We define a potential function $\Phi\colon \Sigma_1 \times \cdots \times \Sigma_n \to \mathbb{N}^n$ that is similar to the one used in the proof of Theorem 2, and we show that it increases strictly with every better response that is played. Again each resource r contributes $n_r(S)$ values to the potential, namely the values $q_r(p_r(S), 1), \ldots, q_r(p_r(S), n_r^*(S))$ and $n_r(S) - n_r^*(S)$ times the value 0. In the potential vector $\Phi(S)$, all these values are sorted in non-increasing order. A state S' has a higher potential than a state S if $\Phi(S')$ is lexicographically larger than $\Phi(S)$, i.e., if there exists an index k such that $\Phi_j(S) = \Phi_j(S')$ for all $j < k$ and $\Phi_k(S) < \Phi_k(S')$.

Let S denote the current state and assume that there exists one player $i \in \mathcal{N}$ who plays a better response, leading to state S'. We show that $\Phi(S')$ is lexicographically larger than $\Phi(S)$. Assume that i changes her proposal from r_i to r_i'. Since i plays a better response, she must be assigned to r_i' in state S'. That is, the value $q_{r_i'}(p_{i,r_i'}, n_{r_i'}^*(S'))$ is added to the potential. We show that only smaller values are removed from the potential, implying that the potential must lexicographically increase. If i is assigned to r_i in state S, then only the value $q_{r_i}(p_{r_i}(S), n_{r_i}^*(S))$ is removed from the vector and maybe, if $n_{r_i}^*(S) = 1$, some 0 values are replaced by larger values. Since player i plays a better response, $q_{r_i}(p_{r_i}(S), n_{r_i}^*(S)) < q_{r_i'}(p_{i,r_i'}, n_{r_i'}^*(S'))$. If $n_{r_i'}^*(S') = 1$ and there are players assigned to r_i' in state S, then also the values $q_{r_i'}(p_{r_i'}(S), 1), \ldots, q_{r_i'}(p_{r_i'}(S), n_{r_i'}^*(S))$ are removed from the potential vector. In this case, player i displaces the previously assigned players from resource r_i', which implies $q_{r_i'}(p_{i,r_i'}, n_{r_i'}^*(S')) = q_{r_i'}(p_{i,r_i'}, 1) > q_{r_i'}(p_{r_i'}(S), 1)$, as desired. □

6   Extensions to Matroid Strategy Spaces

In this section, we study player-specific congestion games with priorities in which each strategy space Σ_i consists of the bases of a matroid over the resources. For this setting, we generalize the results that we obtained for the singleton case. Due to space limitations, the proofs are omitted.

Theorem 5. *In matroid congestion games with consistent priorities, the best response dynamics reaches a Nash equilibrium after a polynomial number of rounds.*

For matroid congestion games, it is known that every sequence of best responses reaches a Nash equilibrium after a polynomial number of steps [1]. Using this result yields the theorem analogously to the proof of Theorem 1.

Theorem 6. *Matroid congestion games with priorities are potential games with respect to lazy better responses.*

Given a state S, we denote a better response of a player $i \in \mathcal{N}$ from S_i to S_i' *lazy* if it can be decomposed into a sequence of strategies $S_i = S_i^0, S_i^1, \ldots, S_i^k = S_i'$ such that $|S_i^{j+1} \setminus S_i^j| = 1$ and the delay of player i in state S_i^{j+1} is strictly smaller than her delay in state S_i^j for all $j \in \{0, \ldots, k-1\}$. That is, a lazy better response can be decomposed into a sequence of exchanges of single resources such that each step strictly decreases the delay of the corresponding player. In [2], it is observed that for matroid strategy spaces, there does always exist a best response that is lazy. In particular, the best response that exchanges the least number of resources is lazy, and in singleton games every better response is lazy. Since lazy best responses can be decomposed into exchanges of single resources, the same potential function as in the proof of Theorem 2 also works for the matroid case. The restriction to lazy better responses in Theorem 6 is necessary.

Remark 7. *The best response dynamics in matroid congestion games with priorities can cycle.*

Similar arguments as for Theorem 3 yield the following generalization.

Theorem 8. *Every player-specific matroid congestion game Γ with priorities possesses a pure Nash equilibrium that can be computed in polynomial time by $O(m^2 \cdot n^3 \cdot \mathrm{rk}(\Gamma))$ strategy changes.*

Since lazy better responses can be decomposed into exchanges of single resources, the potential function defined in the proof of Theorem 4 also works for matroid strategy sets if players play only lazy better responses.

Theorem 9. *Correlated two-sided matroid markets with ties are potential games with respect to lazy better responses.*

The restriction in Theorem 9 to lazy better responses is necessary.

Remark 10. *The best response dynamics in correlated two-sided matroid markets with ties can cycle.*

Acknowledgements. We thank Fuhito Kojima for pointing out related work and the reviewers for their helpful comments.

References

1. Ackermann, H., Röglin, H., Vöcking, B.: On the impact of combinatorial structure on congestion games. In: Proc. of the 47th Ann. IEEE Symp. on Foundations of Computer Science (FOCS), pp. 613–622 (2006)
2. Ackermann, H., Röglin, H., Vöcking, B.: Pure Nash equilibria in player-specific and weighted congestion games. In: Spirakis, P.G., Mavronicolas, M., Kontogiannis, S.C. (eds.) WINE 2006. LNCS, vol. 4286, pp. 50–61. Springer, Heidelberg (2006)
3. Anshelevich, E., Dasgupta, A., Kleinberg, J., Tardos, E., Wexler, T., Roughgarden, T.: The price of stability for network design with fair cost allocation. In: Proc. of the 45th Ann. IEEE Symp. on Foundations of Computer Science (FOCS), pp. 295–304 (2004)
4. Even-Dar, E., Kesselman, A., Mansour, Y.: Convergence time to nash equilibria. In: Baeten, J.C.M., Lenstra, J.K., Parrow, J., Woeginger, G.J. (eds.) ICALP 2003. LNCS, vol. 2719, pp. 502–513. Springer, Heidelberg (2003)
5. Fabrikant, A., Papadimitriou, C., Talwar, K.: The complexity of pure Nash equilibria. In: Proc. of the 36th Ann. ACM Symp. on Theory of Computing (STOC), pp. 604–612 (2004)

6. Fleiner, T.: A fixed-point approach to stable matchings and some applications. Mathematics of Operations Research 28(1), 103–126 (2003)
7. Fleischer, L., Goemans, M., Mirrokni, V.S., Sviridenko, M.: Tight approximation algorithms for maximum general assignment problems. In: Proc. of the 16th Ann. ACM–SIAM Symp. on Discrete Algorithms (SODA), pp. 611–620 (2006)
8. Fotakis, D., Kontogiannis, S.C., Koutsoupias, E., Mavronicolas, M., Spirakis, P.G.: The structure and complexity of Nash equilibria for a selfish routing game. In: Widmayer, P., Triguero, F., Morales, R., Hennessy, M., Eidenbenz, S., Conejo, R. (eds.) ICALP 2002. LNCS, vol. 2380, pp. 123–134. Springer, Heidelberg (2002)
9. Gairing, M., Lücking, T., Mavronicolas, M., Monien, B.: Computing Nash equilibria for scheduling on restricted parallel links. In: Proc. of the 36th Ann. ACM Symp. on Theory of Computing (STOC), pp. 613–622 (2004)
10. Gale, D., Shapley, L.S.: College admissions and the stability of marriage. American Mathematical Monthly 69, 9–15 (1962)
11. Goemans, M., Li, L., Mirrokni, V.S., Thottan, M.: Market sharing games applied to content distribution in ad-hoc networks. In: Proc. of the 5th ACM Int. Symp. on Mobile Ad Hoc Networking and Computing (MobiHoc), pp. 1020–1033 (2004)
12. Gusfield, D., Irving, R.: The stable Marriage Problem: Structure and Algorithms. MIT Press, Cambridge (1989)
13. Hoffman, C., Holroyd, A., Peres, Y.: A stable marriage of poisson and lebesgue. Annals of Probability 34(4), 1241–1272 (2006)
14. Ieong, S., McGrew, R., Nudelman, E., Shoham, Y., Sun, Q.: Fast and compact: A simple class of congestion games. In: Proc. of the 20th Nat. Conference on Artificial Intelligence (AAAI), pp. 489–494 (2005)
15. Iwama, K., Manlove, D., Miyazaki, S., Morita, Y.: Stable marriage with incomplete lists and ties. In: Wiedermann, J., van Emde Boas, P., Nielsen, M. (eds.) ICALP 1999. LNCS, vol. 1644, pp. 443–452. Springer, Heidelberg (1999)
16. Kelso, A., Crawford, V.: Job matchings, coalition formation, and gross substitute. Econometrica 50, 1483–1504 (1982)
17. Knuth, D.: Marriage Stables et leurs relations avec d'autres problèmes Combinatories. Les Presses de l'Université de Montréal (1976)
18. Kojima, F., Ünver, M.U.: Random paths to pairwise stability in many-to-many matching problems: a study on market equilibration. Int. Journal of Game Theory (2006)
19. Milchtaich, I.: Congestion games with player-specific payoff functions. Games and Economic Behavior 13(1), 111–124 (1996)
20. Mirrokni, V.S.: Approximation Algorithms for Distributed and Selfish Agents. PhD thesis, Massachusetts Institute of Technology (2005)
21. Rosenthal, R.W.: A class of games possessing pure-strategy Nash equilibria. Int. Journal of Game Theory 2, 65–67 (1973)
22. Roth, A.E.: The evolution of the labor market for medical interns and residents: A case study in game theory. Journal of Political Economy 92, 991–1016 (1984)
23. Roth, A.E., Sotomayor, M.A.O.: Two-sided Matching: A study in game-theoretic modeling and analysis. Cambridge University Press, Cambridge (1990)

An Optimization Approach for Approximate Nash Equilibria[*]

Haralampos Tsaknakis[1] and Paul G. Spirakis[1,2]

[1] Research Academic Computer Technology Institute (RACTI), Greece
{tsaknak,spirakis}@cti.gr
[2] Dept. of Computer Eng. and Informatics, Patras University, Patras Greece

Abstract. In this paper we propose a new methodology for determining approximate Nash equilibria of non-cooperative bimatrix games and, based on that, we provide an efficient algorithm that computes 0.3393-approximate equilibria, the best approximation till now. The methodology is based on the formulation of an appropriate function of pairs of mixed strategies reflecting the maximum deviation of the players' payoffs from the best payoff each player could achieve given the strategy chosen by the other. We then seek to minimize such a function using descent procedures. As it is unlikely to be able to find global minima in polynomial time, given the recently proven intractability of the problem, we concentrate on the computation of stationary points and prove that they can be approximated arbitrarily close in polynomial time and that they have the above mentioned approximation property. Our result provides the best ϵ till now for polynomially computable ϵ-approximate Nash equilibria of bimatrix games. Furthermore, our methodology for computing approximate Nash equilibria has not been used by others.

1 Introduction

Ever since it was proved that the problem of finding exact Nash equilibria is intractable in the sense that it is PPAD-complete even for 2-player games [2], attention has been focused on finding ϵ-approximate such equilibria for $\epsilon > 0$. In this respect, simple algorithms have recently been provided for finding approximate equilibria for constant $\epsilon = \frac{3}{4}$ and $\epsilon = \frac{1}{2}$ ([4], [5]) for general bimatrix games (and for positively normalized payoff matrices) based on examining small supports of 1 or 2 for either player. A well known result provides 0.38-approximate Nash equilibria of normalized bimatrix games in polynomial time ([3]). Concurrently with us , [1] gave an approach based on [7] that provides 0.36-approximate Nash equilibria of normalized bimatrix games. Furthermore, it has been shown ([6]) that the more general approximation problem of finding a fully polynomial time approximation scheme for any $\epsilon > 0$, has similar complexity with the problem of finding exact Nash equilibria.

[*] This work has been partially supported by the IST 6th Framework Programme of the European Union under contract 001907 DELIS.

X. Deng and F.C. Graham (Eds.): WINE 2007, LNCS 4858, pp. 42–56, 2007.
© Springer-Verlag Berlin Heidelberg 2007

For a different, stronger, notion of approximation, i.e. the well supported approximate Nash equilibria, the best known result so far provides 0.658-approximate well supported equilibria for normalized bimatrix games in polynomial time ([7]).

Most of the reported investigations of finding approximate equilibria for constant ϵ are based on the examination of small supports of the strategy sets of the players and the algorithms presented are based on brute force search over all such supports.

In this work we adopt a different approach that does not rely on any prespecified small supports neither on an indiscriminate search over all small support strategies. We define an equivalent optimization problem in the strategy spaces of both players and attempt to obtain a stationary point of a specific function that measures the maximum deviation of the players' payoffs from the best payoff each player could achieve given the strategy chosen by the other. We do so through a descent procedure along feasible directions in the strategy spaces of both players simultaneously. Feasible descent directions are computed by solving linear programming problems. Also, by solving similar linear programs we can determine whether or not there is a descent direction at any given point in the strategy spaces. If a descent direction does not exist, then we have reached a stationary point. We prove that at any stationary point of that function we obtain strategy pairs such that at least one of them is an 0.3393-approximate Nash equilibrium. We also prove that an almost stationary point of the function can be reached in polynomial time with respect to the input data of the game, and that point suffices to get arbitrarily close to 0.3393. Our work can be accessed as a full technical report (revised) also in [10].

2   Definitions and Notation

Let R, C denote the m by n row and column players' payoff matrices respectively, for m, n any positive integers. We assume that both payoff matrices are positively normalized, i.e. all their entries belong to $[0, 1]$ (without loss of generality any game can be equivalently transformed to a positively normalized game by appropriate shifting and scaling each one of the payoff matrices).

Let us denote by e_k the k-dimensional column vector having all its entries equal to 1 (for positive integer k). Let

$$\Delta_k = \{u : u \in R^k, u \geq 0, e_k^\tau u = 1\}$$

be the k-dimentional standard simplex (superscript τ denotes transpose).

Also, for any vector $u \in R^k$, we define the following :

$$supp(u) = \{i \in (1, k) : u_i \neq 0\}$$

being the support index subset of $u \in R^k$ and also

$$suppmax(u) = \{i \in (1, k) : u_i \geq u_j \; \forall j \in (1, k)\}$$

being the index subset where all entries are equal to the maximum entry of $u \in R^k$.

We also denote by
$$max(u) = \{u_i : u_i \geq u_j, \text{for all } j\}$$
the value of the maximum entry of the vector and by

$$max_S(u) = \{u_i, i \in S : u_i \geq u_j, \text{for all } j \in S\}$$

the value of the maximum entry of the vector within an index subset $S \subset (1, k)$.

Finally, we denote by $\overline{S}$ the complement of an index set S, i.e. $\overline{S} = \{i \in (1, k), i \notin S\}$.

The problem of finding an ϵ-approximate Nash equilibrium in the game (R, C), for some $\epsilon \geq 0$, is to compute a pair of strategies $\overline{x}$ in Δ_m and $\overline{y}$ in Δ_n such that the following relationships hold :

$$x^\tau R\overline{y} \leq \overline{x}^\tau R\overline{y} + \epsilon \text{ for all } x \in \Delta_m$$

and

$$\overline{x}^\tau Cy \leq \overline{x}^\tau C\overline{y} + \epsilon \text{ for all } y \in \Delta_n$$

3   Optimization Formulation

Key to our approach is the definition of the following continuous function mapping $\Delta_m \times \Delta_n$ into $[0, 1]$:

$$f(x, y) = max\{max(Ry) - x^\tau Ry, max(C^\tau x) - x^\tau Cy\} \qquad (1)$$

It is evident that $f(x, y) \geq 0$ for all $(x, y) \in \Delta_m \times \Delta_n$ and that exact Nash equilibria of (R, C) correspond to pairs of strategies such that $f(x, y) = 0$. Furthermore, ϵ- approximate equilibria correspond to strategy pairs that satisfy $f(x, y) \leq \epsilon$. This function represents the maximum deviation of the players' payoffs from the best payoff each player could achieve given the strategy chosen by the other.

An optimization formulation based on mixed integer programming methods was suggested in [9]. However, no approximation results were obtained there.

The function $f(x, y)$ is not jointly convex with respect to both x and y. However, it is convex in x alone, if y is kept fixed and vice versa.

Let us define the two ingredients of the function $f(x, y)$ as follows :
$f_R(x, y) = max(Ry) - x^\tau Ry$
and
$f_C(x, y) = max(C^\tau x) - x^\tau Cy$
From any point in $(x, y) \in \Delta_m \times \Delta_n$ we consider variations of $f(x, y)$ along feasible directions in both players' strategy spaces of the following form :

$$(1 - \epsilon) \begin{bmatrix} x \\ y \end{bmatrix} + \epsilon \begin{bmatrix} x' \\ y' \end{bmatrix}$$

where, $0 \le \epsilon \le 1, (x', y') \in \Delta_m \times \Delta_n$ (the vectors in brackets are $m + n$-dimensional column vectors).

The variation of the function along such a feasible direction is defined by the following relationship:

$$Df(x, y, x', y', \epsilon) = f(x + \epsilon(x' - x), y + \epsilon(y' - y)) - f(x, y)$$

We have derived an explicit formula for $Df(x, y, x', y', \epsilon)$ (see Appendix), which is a piecewise quadratic function of ϵ and the number of switches of the linear terms of the function is at most $m + n$. Therefore, for fixed (x', y') this function can be minimized with respect to ϵ in polynomial time. Furthermore, there always exists a positive number, say ϵ^*, such that for any $\epsilon \le \epsilon^*$ the coefficient of the linear term of this function of ϵ coincides with the gradient, as defined below. The number ϵ^* generally depends on both (x, y) and (x', y').(See Appendix A.3).

We define the gradient of f at the point (x, y) along an arbitrary feasible direction specified by another point (x', y') as follows:

$$Df(x, y, x', y') = \lim_{\epsilon \to 0} \frac{1}{\epsilon} Df(x, y, x', y', \epsilon)$$

The gradient $Df(x, y, x', y')$ of f at any point $(x, y) \in \Delta_m \times \Delta_n$ along a feasible direction (determined by another point $(x', y') \in \Delta_m \times \Delta_n$) provides the rate of decrease (or increase) of the function along that direction. For fixed (x, y), $Df(x, y, x', y')$ is a convex polyhedral function in (x', y'). In fact we have derived the explicit form of $Df(x, y, x', y')$ as the maximum of two linear forms in the (x', y') space (see the derivations below and in the Appendix A.1). At any point (x, y) we wish to minimize the gradient function with respect to (x', y') to find the steepest possible descent direction, or to determine that no such descent is possible.

Let us define the following index sets:

$$S_R(y) = suppmax(Ry) \ and \ S_C(x) = suppmax(C^\tau x)$$

By definition, $S_R(y) \subset (1, m)$ and $S_C(x) \subset (1, n)$.

From the Appendix A.1 we get :

(a) If $f_R(x, y) = f_C(x, y)$ then

$$Df(x, y, x', y') = max(T_1(x, y, x', y'), T_2(x, y, x', y')) - f(x, y)$$

where

$$m_1(y') = max(Ry') \ over \ the \ subset \ S_R(y)$$

and

$$m_2(x') = max(C^\tau x') \ over \ the \ subset \ S_C(x)$$

and

$$T_1(x, y, x', y') = m_1(y') - x^\tau Ry' - (x')^\tau Ry + x^\tau Ry$$

and

$$T_2(x, y, x', y') = m_2(x') - x^\tau C y' - (x\prime)^\tau C y + x^\tau C y$$

(b) If $f_R(x, y) > f_C(x, y)$ then
$Df(x, y, x', y') = T_1(x, y, x', y') - f(x, y)$
and
(c) If $f_R(x, y) < f_C(x, y)$ then
$Df(x, y, x', y') = T_2(x, y, x', y') - f(x, y)$. In the cases (b) and (c) the functions T_1 and T_2 are as defined in case (a).

The problem of finding $Df(x, y)$ as the minimum over all $(x', y') \in \Delta_m \times \Delta_n$ of the function $Df(x, y, x', y')$, is a linear programming problem.

This problem can be equivalently expressed as the following mini-max problem by introducing appropriate dual variables (we derive it for (x, y) such that $f_R(x, y) = f_C(x, y)$ since this is the most interestng case and the cases where the two terms are different can be reduced to this by solving an LP, as we shall see below) as follows :

Minimize (over x', y') the maximum (over w, z, ρ) of the function

$$[\rho w^\tau, (1 - \rho) z^\tau] G(x, y) \begin{bmatrix} y' \\ x' \end{bmatrix}$$

where :
(a) the maximum is taken with respect to dual variables w, z, ρ such that : $w \in \Delta_m, supp(w) \subset S_R(y)$ and $z \in \Delta_n, supp(z) \subset S_C(x)$ and $\rho \in [0, 1]$.
(b) The minimum is taken with respect to $(x', y') \in \Delta_m \times \Delta_n$, and
(c) the matrix $G(x, y)$ is the following $(m + n)$ by $(m + n)$ matrix :

$$G(x, y) = \begin{bmatrix} R - e_m x^\tau R & -e_m y^\tau R^\tau + e_m e_m{}^\tau x^\tau R y \\ -e_n x^\tau C + e_n e_n{}^\tau x^\tau C y & C^\tau - e_n y^\tau C^\tau \end{bmatrix}$$

The probability vectors w and z play the role of price vectors (or penalty vectors) for penalizing deviations from the support sets $S_R(y)$ and $S_C(x)$, and the parameter ρ plays the role of a trade-off parameter between the two parts of the function $f(x, y)$. In fact, the w, z and ρ are not independent variables but they are taken all together to represent a single $(m+n)$-dimensional probability vector on the left hand side (the maximizing term) of the linear mini-max problem.

Solving the above mini-max problem we obtain w, z, ρ, x' and y' that are all functions of the point (x, y) and take values in their respective domains of definition. Let us denote by $V(x, y)$ the value of the solution of the mini-max problem at the point (x, y). The solution of this problem yields a feasible descent direction (as a matter of fact the steepest feasible descent direction) for the function $f(x, y)$ if $Df(x, y) = V(x, y) - f(x, y) < 0$. Following such a descent direction we can perform an appropriate line search with respect to the parameter ϵ and find a new point that gives a lower value of the function $f(x, y)$. Applying repeatedly such a descent procedure we will eventually reach a point where no further reduction is possible. Such a point is a stationary point that satisfies $Df(x, y) \geq 0$.

In the next section we examine the approximation properties of stationary points. In fact, we prove that given any stationary point we can determine pairs of strategies such that at least one of them is a 0.3393-approximate Nash equilibrium.

4 Approximation Properties of Stationary Points

Let us assume that we have a stationary point $(x^\star, y^\star)$ of the function $f(x, y)$. Then, based on the above analysis and notation, the following relationship should be true :

$$Df(x^\star, y^\star) = V(x^\star, y^\star) - f(x^\star, y^\star) \geq 0$$

Let $(w^\star, z^\star) \in \Delta_m \times \Delta_n, \rho^\star \in [0,1]$ be a solution of the linear mini-max problem (with matrix $G(x^\star, y^\star)$) with respect to the dual variables corresponding to the pair $(x^\star, y^\star)$. Such a solution should satisfy the relations $supp(w^\star) \subset S_R(y^\star)$ and $supp(z^\star) \subset S_C(x^\star)$.

Let us define the following quantities:

$$\lambda = \min_{y':supp(y')\subset S_C(x^\star)} \{(w^\star - x^\star)^T Ry'\}$$

and

$$\mu = \min_{x':supp(x')\subset S_R(y^\star)} \{x'^T C(z^\star - y^\star)\}.$$

From the fact that R, C are positively normalized it follows that both λ and μ are less than or equal to 1.

At any point $(x^\star, y^\star)$ these quantities basically define the rates of decrease (or increase) of the function f along directions of the form $(1 - \epsilon)(x^\star, y^\star) + \epsilon(x^\star, y')$ and $(1-\epsilon)(x^\star, y^\star)+\epsilon(x', y^\star)$, i.e. the rates of decrease that are obtained when we keep one player's strategy fixed and move probability mass of the other player into his own maximum support, towards decreasing his own deviation from the maximum payoff he can achieve.

From the stationarity property of the point $(x^\star, y^\star)$ it follows that both λ and μ are nonnegative. Indeed, in the opposite case there would be a descent direction, which contradicts the stationarity condition.

Let us define a pair of strategies $(\hat{x}, \hat{y}) \in \Delta_m \times \Delta_n$ as follows:

$$(\hat{x}, \hat{y}) = \begin{cases} (x^\star, y^\star) & \text{,if } f(x^\star, y^\star) \leq f(\tilde{x}, \tilde{y}) \\ (\tilde{x}, \tilde{y}) & \text{,otherwise} \end{cases}$$

where

$$(\tilde{x}, \tilde{y}) = \begin{cases} \left(\frac{1}{1+\lambda-\mu}w^\star + \frac{\lambda-\mu}{1+\lambda-\mu}x^\star, z^\star\right) & \text{,if } \lambda \geq \mu \\ \left(w^\star, \frac{1}{1+\mu-\lambda}z^\star + \frac{\mu-\lambda}{1+\mu-\lambda}y^\star\right) & \text{,if } \lambda < \mu. \end{cases}$$

We now express the main result of this paper in the following theorem :

Theorem 1. *The pair of strategies* $(\hat{x}, \hat{y})$ *defined above, is a* 0.3393-*approximate Nash equilibrium.*

Proof. From the definition of $(\hat{x}, \hat{y})$ we have :

$$f(\hat{x}, \hat{y}) \leq min\{f(x^\star, y^\star), f(\tilde{x}, \tilde{y})\} \tag{2}$$

Using the stationarity condition for $(x^\star, y^\star)$ we obtain :

$$f(x^\star, y^\star) \leq V(x^\star, y^\star)$$

But $V(x^\star, y^\star)$ is less than or equal to

$$\rho^\star E_1 + (1 - \rho^\star)E_2$$

where

$$E_1 = (w^{\star T} Ry' - x^{\star T} Ry' - x'^T Ry^\star + x^{\star T} Ry^\star)$$

and

$$E_2 = (z^{\star T} C^T x' - x^{\star T} Cy' - x'^T Cy^\star + x^{\star T} Cy^\star)$$

and this holds $\forall (x', y') \in \Delta_m \times \Delta_n$

Setting $x' = x^\star$ and $y' : supp(y') \subset S_C(x^\star)$ in the above inequality we get :

$$f(x^\star, y^\star) \leq \rho^\star \lambda. \tag{3}$$

Next, setting $y' = y^\star$ and $x' : supp(x') \subset S_R(y^\star)$ in the same inequality, we get :

$$f(x^\star, y^\star) \leq (1 - \rho^\star)\mu. \tag{4}$$

Now using the definition of the strategy pair $(\tilde{x}, \tilde{y})$ above and exploiting the inequalities

$$(w^\star - x^\star)^T Rz^\star \geq \lambda, \text{since } supp(z^\star) \subset S_C(x^\star)$$
$$w^{\star T} C(z^\star - y^\star) \geq \mu, \text{since } supp(w^\star) \subset S_R(y^\star)$$

we obtain: (assume $\lambda \geq \mu$)

$$f_R(\tilde{x}, \tilde{y}) = max\{R\tilde{y}\} - \tilde{x}^T R\tilde{y} = max\{Rz^\star\} - \left(\frac{1}{1 + \lambda - \mu} w^\star + \frac{\lambda - \mu}{1 + \lambda - \mu} x^\star\right)^T Rz^\star$$

$$= max\{Rz^\star\} - \frac{1}{1 + \lambda - \mu} w^{\star T} Rz^\star - \frac{\lambda - \mu}{1 + \lambda - \mu} x^{\star T} Rz^\star$$

$$\leq max\{Rz^\star\} - x^{\star T} Rz^\star - \frac{\lambda}{1 + \lambda - \mu} \leq \frac{1 - \mu}{1 + \lambda - \mu}.$$

Similarly, setting $D = C^T$,

$$
\begin{aligned}
f_C(\tilde{x}, \tilde{y}) &= \max\{D\tilde{x}\} - \tilde{x}^T C\tilde{y} \\
&= \max\left\{\frac{1}{1+\lambda-\mu}Dw^* + \frac{\lambda-\mu}{1+\lambda-\mu}Dx^*\right\} - \frac{1}{1+\lambda-\mu}w^{*T}Cz^* - \frac{\lambda-\mu}{1+\lambda-\mu}x^{*T}Cz^* \\
&\leq \frac{1}{1+\lambda-\mu}\max\{Dw^*\} + \frac{\lambda-\mu}{1+\lambda-\mu}\max\{Dx^*\} - \frac{1}{1+\lambda-\mu}w^{*T}Cz^* - \\
&\quad - \frac{\lambda-\mu}{1+\lambda-\mu}\max\{Dx^*\} \\
&= \frac{1}{1+\lambda-\mu}(\max\{Dw^*\} - w^{*T}Cy^*) - \frac{1}{1+\lambda-\mu}(w^{*T}Cz^* - w^{*T}Cy^*) \\
&\leq \frac{1-\mu}{1+\lambda-\mu}.
\end{aligned}
$$

From the above relationships we obtain:

$$
f(\tilde{x}, \tilde{y}) \leq \frac{1-\mu}{1+\lambda-\mu} \qquad \text{for } \lambda \geq \mu \tag{5}
$$

(A similar inequality can be obtained if $\lambda < \mu$ and we interchange λ and μ)

In all cases, combining inequalities (3), (4), (5) and using the definition of $(\hat{x}, \hat{y})$ above, we get the following:

$$
f(\hat{x}, \hat{y}) \leq \min\left\{\rho^*\lambda, (1 - \rho^*)\mu, \frac{1 - \min\{\lambda, \mu\}}{1 + \max\{\lambda, \mu\} - \min\{\lambda, \mu\}}\right\}. \tag{6}
$$

We can prove that the quantity in (6) cannot exceed the number 0.3393 for any $\rho^*, \lambda, \mu \in [0, 1]$. For the proof see Appendix A.2.

This concludes the proof of our main Theorem.

5   Descent Procedure

A stationary point of any general Linear Complementarity problem can be approximated arbitrarily close **in polynomial time** via the method of Y. Ye [11]. We give here an alternative approach, directly applicable to our problem.

We present here an algorithm for finding a pair of stategies that achieve the 0.3393 approximation bound. The algorithm is based on a descent procedure of the function $f(x, y)$, $(x, y) \in \Delta_m \times \Delta_n$, and consists of the following steps: (set $b = 0.3393$)

1. Start with an arbitrary $(x, y) = (x_0, y_0)$ in $\Delta_m \times \Delta_n$ (e.g. the uniform distribution). Produce another pair (x, y) with lower value of $f(x, y)$ and for which $f_R(x, y) = f_C(x, y)$ as follows :

   (a) If $f_R(x_0, y_0) > f_C(x_0, y_0)$, keep y_0 fixed and solve the LP : minimize (over $x \in \Delta_m$) the

$$
max(Ry_0) - x^\tau Ry_0
$$

under the constraints :

$$max(C^T x) - x^T C y_0 \leq max(R y_0) - x^T R y_0$$

(b) If $f_R(x_0, y_0) < f_C(x_0, y_0)$, keep x_0 fixed and solve the LP :
minimize (over $y \in \Delta_n$) the

$$max(C^T x_0) - x_0{}^T C y$$

under the constraints :

$$max(Ry) - x_0{}^T R y \leq max(C^T x_0) - x_0{}^T R y$$

2. Solve the linear minimax problem with the matrix $G(x, y)$ as defined in section 3. Compute the value of $V(x, y)$, the pair of strategies (x', y'), the index sets $S_R(y) \subset (1, m)$, $S_C(x) \subset (1, n)$, the vectors w, z, the parameter ρ, and the values of λ, μ as defined in sections 3 and 4 for the current point (x, y). Also determine the pair of strategies $(\tilde{x}, \tilde{y})$ as defined in section 4.
3. If at least one of the following conditions is true, stop and exit – a pair of strategies achieving the approximation bound b has been found.
   (i) $V(x, y) - f(x, y) \geq 0$ (stationary condition: either $f(x, y)$ or $f(\tilde{x}, \tilde{y})$ is $\leq b$)
   (ii) $f(x, y) \leq b$
   (iii) $f(\tilde{x}, \tilde{y}) \leq b$
   (iv) $f(x', y') \leq b$
   (v) $f(x', y) \leq b$
   (vi) $f(x, y') \leq b$
4. If none of the conditions of step 3 is satisfied, compute the minimum with respect to ϵ of the function $f(x + \epsilon(x' - x), y + \epsilon(y' - y))$ along the direction specified by the pair (x', y') found in step 2, and set $(x, y) = (x + \epsilon(x' - x), y + \epsilon(y' - y))$ (such a minimization with respect to ϵ can be performed in polynomial time, as mentioned earlier, since the number of switches of the linear terms of the piecewise quadratic function cannot exceed $m + n$).
   Furthermore, if for the new pair (x, y) we have $f_R(x, y) \neq f_C(x, y)$, solve the LP specified in Step 1 and compute the new (x, y) with lower value of the function $f(x, y)$ and for which $f_R(x, y) = f_C(x, y)$.
   Go to Step 2.
   End of descent.

In regard to the number of steps that are required for convergence and exit, we provide a convergence analysis in Appendix A.3 that shows that the algorithm converges in a polynomial number of iterations.

6 The Complexity of Our Algorithm

Our algorithm is basically the procedure descent of the function $f(x, y)$. The number q of the descent steps for convergence, given any $\delta > 0$, is $O(\frac{1}{\delta^2})$ and that suffices to get an $0.3393 + \delta$-approximate equilibrium.

So, the total time complexity of our method is $O(\frac{1}{\delta^2})T_LP(n)$ time (when $n \geq m$) where $T_LP(n)$ is the time to solve a linear program of size n. Thus, our method is an FPTAS with respect to approximating a stationary point and hence an approximate equilibrium of the stated quality.

An arbitrary point $(x, y) \in \Delta_m \times \Delta_n$ can be used to initialize the algorithm.

7   Discussion and Future Work

It is known from Bellare and Rogaway ([8]) that (even in a weaker sense) there is no polynomial time μ - approximation of the optimal value of the problem $min\{x^\tau Qx, s.t.Bx = b, 0 \leq x \leq e\}$ for some $\mu \in (0, \frac{1}{3})$, unless $P = NP$. Of course, here μ is a multiplicative relative accuracy and the reduction that they use involves matrices that are different from the ones in our case. However, this gives evidence that going below $\frac{1}{3}$ in the approximation of equilibria will probably require a radically different approach (if any), perhaps probabilistic. We are currently working on this.

References

1. Boss, H., Byrka, J., Markakis, E.: New Algorithms for Approximate Nash Equilibria in Bimatrix Games. In: this volume of WINE (2007)
2. Chen, X., Deng, X.: Settling the complexity of 2-player Nash equilibrium. In: Proc. of the 47th IEEE Symp. on Foundations of Comp. Sci (FOCS 2006), pp. 261–272. IEEE Computer Society Press, Los Alamitos (2006)
3. Daskalakis, C., Mehta, A., Papadimitriou, C.: Progress in approximate Nash Equilibria. In: Proc. of the 8th ACM Conf. on Electronic Commerce (EC 2007), ACM Press, New York (2007)
4. Daskalakis, C., Mehta, A., Papadimitriou, C.: A note on approximate Nash equilibria. In: Spirakis, P.G., Mavronicolas, M., Kontogiannis, S.C. (eds.) WINE 2006. LNCS, vol. 4286, pp. 297–306. Springer, Heidelberg (2006)
5. Kontogiannis, S., Panagopoulou, P., Spirakis, P.G.: Polynomial algorithms for approximating Nash equilibria in bimatrix games. In: Spirakis, P.G., Mavronicolas, M., Kontogiannis, S.C. (eds.) WINE 2006. LNCS, vol. 4286, pp. 282–296. Springer, Heidelberg (2006)
6. Chen, X., Deng, X., Teng, S.: Computing Nash Equilibria: Approximation and smoothed complexity. In: Proc. of the 47th IEEE Symp. on Foundations of Comp. Sci (FOCS 2006), pp. 603–612. IEEE Press, New York (2006)
7. Kontogiannis, S., Spirakis, P.G.: Efficient algorithms for constant well supported approximate equilibria of bimatrix games. In: ICALP 2007 (2007)
8. Bellare, M., Rogaway, P.: The complexity of approximating a nonlinear program. Mathematical Programming 69, 429–441 (1995)
9. Sandholm, T., Gilpin, A., Conitzer, V.: Mixed-integer Programming Methods for Finding Nash Equilibria. In: Proceedings of the 20th National Conference on Artificial Intelligence (AAAI 2005), pp. 495–501 (2005)
10. Tsaknakis, H., Spirakis, P.G.: An Optimization Approach for Approximate Nash Equilibria. In: the Electronic Colloqium on Computational Complexity (ECCC), as a Technical Report with number TR07067

11. Ye, Y.: A fully polynomial time approximation algorithm for computing a stationary point of the general linear complementarity problem. Mathematics of Operations Research 18(2), 334–345 (1993)

A Appendix

A.1 Appendix A.1

Using the definitions for any $(x, y) \in \Delta_m \times \Delta_n$ i.e :

$$f_R(x, y) = max(Ry) - x^\tau Ry$$
$$f_C(x, y) = max(C^\tau x) - x^\tau Cy$$
$$f(x, y) = max\{f_R(x, y), f_C(x, y)\}$$

we have, for any $(x', y') \in \Delta_m \times \Delta_n$ and any $\epsilon \in [0, 1]$ that :

$$Df(x, y, x', y', \epsilon) = f(x + \epsilon(x' - x), y + \epsilon(y' - y)) - f(x, y)$$

This can be written as (analytically)

$$max\{f_R(x + \epsilon(x' - x), y + \epsilon(y' - y)), f_C(x + \epsilon(x' - x), y + \epsilon(y' - y))\} - max\{f_R(x, y), f_C(x, y)\}$$

and this is actually $max(K_1, K_2)$ where

$$K_1 = \epsilon Df_R + \Lambda f_R - \epsilon^2 Hf_R - (1 - \epsilon)max\{0, f_C(x, y) - f_R(x, y)\}$$

and also

$$K_2 = \epsilon Df_C + \Lambda f_C - \epsilon^2 Hf_C - (1 - \epsilon)max\{0, f_R(x, y) - f_C(x, y)\}$$

where now the functions $Df_R, \Lambda f_R, Hf_R, Df_C, \Lambda f_C, Hf_C$ are defined below.

$$Df_R(x, y, x', y') = \{max(Ry') over S_R(y)\} - x^\tau Ry' - x'^\tau Ry + x^\tau Ry - f(x, y)$$

$$and$$

$$Hf_R(x, y, x', y') = (x' - x)^\tau R(y' - y)$$

$$and$$

$$Df_C(x, y, x', y') = \{max(C^\tau x') over S_C(x)\} - x^\tau Cy' - x'^\tau Cy + x^\tau Cy - f(x, y)$$

$$and$$

$$Hf_C(x, y, x', y') = (x' - x)^\tau C(y' - y)$$

In order to define $\Lambda f_R, \Lambda f_C$ we remind the reader that $S_R(y) = suppmax(Ry)$ and that $S_C(x) = suppmax(C^\tau x)$ and we will also use their complements :

$\bar{S}_R(y)$ being the complement of $S_R(y)$ in the index set $\{1, m\}$ and

$\bar{S}_C(x)$ being the complement of $S_C(x)$ in the index set $\{1, n\}$

Let now

M_y be the maximum of Ry over $S_R(y)$

$M_{y'}$ be the maximum of Ry' over $S_R(y)$

and

M_x be the maximum of $C^\tau x$ over $S_C(x)$

$M_{x'}$ be the maximum of $C^\tau x'$ over $S_C(x)$

Finally $\Lambda f_R(x, y, x', y', \epsilon)$ is the maximum of $(0, \max$ over $\bar{S}_R(y)$ of $(I(y, y') + J(y)))$ where

$$I(y, y') = \epsilon((Ry' - e_m M_{y'}) + (M_y e_m - Ry))$$ and

$$J(y) = -(M_y e_m - Ry)$$

Also finally $\Lambda f_C(x, y, x', y', \epsilon)$ is also the maximum of $((0, \max$ over $\bar{S}_C(x)$ of $(I(x, x') + J(x)))$ where

$$I(x, x') = \epsilon((C^\tau x' - e_n M_{x'}) + (M_x e_n - C^\tau x))$$ and

$$J(x) = -(M_x e_n - C^\tau x)$$

From the above equations, the gradient at the point $(x, y) \in \Delta_m \times \Delta_n$ along a feasible direction specified by a $(x', y') \in \Delta_m \times \Delta_n$ can be determined by letting ϵ go to 0 and get finally :

$$Df(x, y, x', y') = \left\{ \begin{array}{ll} max(Df_R, Df_C) & \text{if } f_R(x,y) = f_C(x,y) \\ Df_R & \text{if } f_R(x,y) > f_C(x,y) \\ Df_C & \text{if } f_R(x,y) < f_C(x,y) \end{array} \right\}$$

A.2 Appendix A.2

We first notice that $\min\{\rho^*\lambda, (1 - \rho^*)\mu\} \le \frac{\lambda\mu}{\lambda+\mu}$. Indeed, if we assume that $\rho^*\lambda > \frac{\lambda\mu}{\lambda+\mu}$ and $(1 - \rho^*)\mu > \frac{\lambda\mu}{\lambda+\mu}$ for some $\rho^*, \lambda, \mu \in [0, 1]$, we would have $\rho^* > \frac{\mu}{\lambda+\mu}$ and $(1 - \rho^*) > \frac{\lambda}{\lambda+\mu}$, a contradiction. So

$$f(\hat{x}, \hat{y}) \le \min\left\{\frac{\lambda\mu}{\lambda+\mu}, \frac{1 - \min\{\lambda, \mu\}}{1 + \max\{\lambda, \mu\} - \min\{\lambda, \mu\}}\right\}.$$

Set $\mu = \min\{\lambda, \mu\}$. For $\mu \le \frac{1}{2}$ and since $\mu \le \lambda$, we have $\frac{\lambda\mu}{\lambda+\mu} \le \frac{\lambda\min\{1/2,\lambda\}}{\lambda+\min\{1/2,\lambda\}} \le \frac{1}{3} < 0.3393$. Also, for $\mu \ge \frac{2}{3}$ we have $1-\mu \le \frac{1}{3}$ and $\frac{1-\mu}{1+\lambda-\mu} \le 1-\mu \le \frac{1}{3} < 0.3393$, since $\lambda \ge \mu \ge \frac{2}{3}$.

Consider now cases for which $\frac{1}{2} < \mu < \frac{2}{3}$. If $\frac{1}{2} < \mu \le \lambda \le \frac{2}{3}$, then $\frac{\lambda\mu}{\lambda+\mu} \le \frac{\lambda}{2} \le \frac{1}{3} < 0.3393$.

For μ, λ such that $\frac{1}{2} < \mu < \frac{2}{3} < \lambda$, let us define $\xi = \frac{1-\mu}{\mu}$. Obviously, $\frac{1}{2} < \xi < 1$. Set $b = 0.3393$.

Let us assume that there are μ and λ satisfying the above relationships and also satisfy:

$$\frac{\lambda\mu}{\lambda+\mu} > b \quad \text{and} \quad \frac{1-\mu}{1+\lambda-\mu} > b.$$

Expressing these inequalities in terms of ξ and λ we get:

$$\frac{\xi(1-b)}{b(1+\xi)} > \lambda > \frac{b}{1-b(1+\xi)}.$$

Since $b < \frac{1}{2}$, the above inequality is equivalent to:

$$\xi(1-b)(1-b(1+\xi)) - b^2(1+\xi) > 0 \quad \Leftrightarrow \quad -\xi^2 b(1-b) + \xi(1-2b) - b^2 > 0.$$

It can be verified by direct calculation that the discriminant of the above quadratic is 0 for $b = 0.3393$ and the inequality becomes $-b(1-b)\left(\xi - \frac{1-2b}{2b(1-b)}\right)^2 > 0$, a contradiction.

Actually, the constant b is the smallest real solution of the equation

$$4b(1-b)(1+b^2) = 1.$$

The bound is attained at $\mu = 0.582523$ and $\lambda = 0.81281$.

A.3 Appendix A.3

Let (x, y) be the current pair of strategies obtained during the descent procedure, for which none of the conditions of step 3 of the algorithm is satisfied. Then, we should have:

$$V(x,y) < b < f(x,y)$$

Indeed, since $V(x, y)$ is always $\le \min\{\rho\lambda, (1-\rho)\mu\}$, if $V(x,y)$ was $\ge b$ we would also have $f(\tilde{x}, \tilde{y}) \le b$, since $f(\tilde{x}, \tilde{y})$ is always $\le \frac{1-\min(\lambda,\mu)}{1+\max(\lambda,\mu)-\min(\lambda,\mu)}$ and b is the maximum value for $\min\{\rho\lambda, (1-\rho)\mu, \frac{1-\min(\lambda,\mu)}{1+\max(\lambda,\mu)-\min(\lambda,\mu)}\}$ as proven before.

We also have:

$$f(x+\epsilon(x'-x), y+\epsilon(y'-y)) - f(x,y) = \epsilon(V(x,y) - f(x,y)) + \max\{\Lambda f_R - \epsilon^2 H f_R, \Lambda f_C - \epsilon^2 H f_C\}$$

where $H f_R, H f_C, \Lambda f_R, \Lambda f_C$ are as defined in appendix A.1.

The quantitites Λf_R, Λf_C are both piecewise linear convex functions of ϵ and are equal to 0 for $\epsilon \leq \epsilon^*$, where ϵ^* is given by $\epsilon^* = min\{\epsilon_1^*, \epsilon_2^*, 1\}$ and ϵ_1^* is the minimum over $i \in \overline{S}_R(y)$ of:

$$\frac{\max(Ry) - (Ry)_i}{\max(Ry) - (Ry)_i + (Ry')_i - \max_{S_R(y)}(Ry')} \text{ , for some } i \in \overline{S}_R(y)$$

and ϵ_2^* is the minimum over $j \in \overline{S}_C(x)$ of :

$$\frac{\max(C^T x) - (C^T x)_j}{\max(C^T x) - (C^T x)_j + (C^T x')_j - \max_{S_C(x)}(C^T x')} \text{ , for some } j \in \overline{S}_C(x)$$

It is pointed out that the terms $\max(Ry) - (Ry)_i$ for $i \in \overline{S}_R(y)$ are always positive and at least one of them is $\geq f(x, y)$, since $f(x, y) = \sum_{i \in \overline{S}_R(y)} x_i(\max(Ry) - (Ry)_i)$. The same is true for the terms $\max(C^T x) - (C^T x)_j$ for $j \in \overline{S}_C(x)$. Furthermore, the above expressions for ϵ^* are active only for those indices $i \in (1, m)$, $j \in (1, n)$, $i \in \overline{S}_R(y)$, $j \in \overline{S}_C(x)$ for which $(Ry')_i - \max_{S_R(y)}(Ry') \geq 0$ and $(C^T x')_j - \max_{S_C(x)}(C^T x') \geq 0$. If no such indices exist for the (x', y') pair of strategies, then the corresponding value of ϵ should be equal to 1.

The quantities Hf_R, Hf_C appearing in the quadratic terms of ϵ, are both bounded (in absolute value) by 2. So, the minimum possible descent that can be achieved is given by the following relationship :

$$f(x + \epsilon(x' - x), y + \epsilon(y' - y)) - f(x, y) = \epsilon(V(x, y) - f(x, y))$$
$$-\epsilon^2 \min(Hf_R, Hf_C) \leq \epsilon (V(x, y) - f(x, y)) + 2\epsilon^2, \ 0 \leq \epsilon \leq \epsilon^*$$

Defining the new value of f as f_{new} and dropping the arguments (for simplicity) we get

$$f_{new} - b \leq (1 - \epsilon)(f - b) + \epsilon(V - b) + 2\epsilon^2$$

Minimizing with respect to ϵ, for $\epsilon \leq \epsilon^*$, we get:

$$f_{new} - b \leq (f - b) \left(1 - \frac{b - V}{4}\right) - \frac{(f - b)^2 + (b - V)^2}{8}, \text{ if } \epsilon^* \geq \frac{f - V}{4}$$

$$f_{new} - b \leq (f - b)(1 - \epsilon^*) - (b - V)\epsilon^* + 2\epsilon^{*2}, \text{ if } \epsilon^* < \frac{f - V}{4}$$

In the first case above, we obtain a significant reduction of $f_{new} - b$ if ϵ^* is larger than $\frac{f-V}{4}$. In the second case, the reduction depends on how small ϵ^* is.

If the value of ϵ^* is small , then there is an index $i^* \in \overline{S}_R(y)$ or an index $j^* \in \overline{S}_C(x)$ such that the entry $(Ry)_{i^*}$ or $(C^T x)_{j^*}$, is close to the maximum support of the vector Ry , or $C^T x$. Such entries can be incorporated into the sets $S_R(y), S_C(x)$ by appropriately augmenting the supports of the vectors w, z in the formulation of the linear minimax problem described in Section 3.

Furthermore , it is not possible to encounter more than $m + n - 2$ such steps in a row without meeting one of the termination conditions of the algorithm , particularly the condition $f(x, y) \leq b$, since , if all the differences of the form $max(Ry) - (Ry)_i, i \in \overline{S}_R(y)$ are small , then $f(x, y)$ is also small.

From the above, we deduce that a termination condition of the algorithm can be approached as closely as desired , in polynomial time.

In fact, a detailed analysis of the number q of the steps needed , for any $\delta > 0$, in order to approximate a stationary point sufficiently close and find an $0.3393 + \delta$-approximate equilibrium, can show that q is $O(\frac{1}{\delta^2})$. A linear programming problem has to be solved in each such step.

Gradient-Based Algorithms for Finding Nash Equilibria in Extensive Form Games

Andrew Gilpin[1], Samid Hoda[2], Javier Peña[2], and Tuomas Sandholm[1]

[1] Computer Science Department, Carnegie Mellon University,
{gilpin,sandholm}@cs.cmu.edu
[2] Tepper School of Business, Carnegie Mellon University,
{shoda,jfp}@andrew.cmu.edu

Abstract. We present a computational approach to the saddle-point formulation for the Nash equilibria of two-person, zero-sum sequential games of imperfect information. The algorithm is a first-order gradient method based on modern smoothing techniques for non-smooth convex optimization. The algorithm requires $O(1/\epsilon)$ iterations to compute an ϵ-equilibrium, and the work per iteration is extremely low. These features enable us to find approximate Nash equilibria for sequential games with a tree representation of about 10^{10} nodes. This is three orders of magnitude larger than what previous algorithms can handle. We present two heuristic improvements to the basic algorithm and demonstrate their efficacy on a range of real-world games. Furthermore, we demonstrate how the algorithm can be customized to a specific class of problems with enormous memory savings.

1 Introduction

Extensive form games model the interaction of multiple, self-interested agents in stochastic environments with hidden information. The goal of each agent is to maximize its own utility. Since the outcome for a particular agent depends on the actions of the other agents, each agent must reason about the other agents' behavior before acting. A fundamental solution concept for these games is the *Nash equilibrium*, *i.e.* a specification of strategies for each agent such that no agent is better off by deviating from their prescribed equilibrium strategy. Generally, Nash equilibrium strategies involve randomized actions (called *mixed strategies*). For two-player zero-sum sequential games of imperfect information, the Nash equilibrium problem can be formulated using the sequence form representation [1,2,3] as the following saddle-point problem:

$$\max_{\mathbf{x} \in Q_1} \min_{\mathbf{y} \in Q_2} \langle A\mathbf{y}, \mathbf{x} \rangle = \min_{\mathbf{y} \in Q_2} \max_{\mathbf{x} \in Q_1} \langle A\mathbf{y}, \mathbf{x} \rangle. \tag{1}$$

In this formulation, $\mathbf{x}$ is player 1's strategy and $\mathbf{y}$ is player 2's strategy. The bilinear term $\langle A\mathbf{y}, \mathbf{x} \rangle$ is the payoff that player 1 receives from player 2 when the players play the strategies $\mathbf{x}$ and $\mathbf{y}$. The strategy spaces are represented by $Q_i \subseteq \mathbb{R}^{S_i}$, where S_i is the set of sequences of moves of player i, and Q_i is the *set of realization plans* of player i. Thus $\mathbf{x}$ ($\mathbf{y}$) encodes probability distributions over actions at each point in the game where player 1 (2) acts. The set Q_i has an explicit linear description of the form

X. Deng and F.C. Graham (Eds.): WINE 2007, LNCS 4858, pp. 57–69, 2007.
© Springer-Verlag Berlin Heidelberg 2007

$\{z \geq 0 : Ez = \mathbf{e}\}$. Consequently, problem (1) can be modeled as a linear program (see [3] for details).

The linear programs that result from this formulation have size linear in the size of the game tree. Thus, in principle, these linear programs can be solved using any algorithm for linear programming such as the simplex or interior-point methods. For some smaller games, this approach is successful [4]. However, for many games the size of the game tree and the corresponding linear program is enormous. For example, the Nash equilibrium problem for Rhode Island Hold'em poker [5], after a substantial reduction in size via the *GameShrink* lossless abstraction algorithm [6], leads to a linear program with about 10^6 variables and constraints, whose solution using the state-of-the-art CPLEX interior-point linear programming solver takes over one week on a 1.65 GHz IBM eServer p5 570, and consumes 25 GB of memory [6]. Prior to the work presented in this paper, this was the largest poker game instance solved to date. Recently there has been substantial interest in two-player limit Texas Hold'em poker, whose game tree has about 10^{18} variables and constraints. The latter problem is well beyond current computational technology.

A recent and fruitful approach to finding strategies for sequential games is to employ *lossy abstractions* [7,8,6,9,10] to approximate the Nash equilibrium. These abstractions yield smaller games that capture some of the main features of the full game. The quality of the approximate Nash equilibrium solution depends on the coarseness of the abstraction. The main current limitation on the degree of coarseness is the magnitude of the abstracted game that standard linear programming solvers can handle. With the current state-of-the art CPLEX solver the dimension is limited to games whose tree representation has about 10^7 nodes (the interior-point method is unusable primarily due to memory limitations and the simplex method is too slow [6]).

We propose a new approach to the approximation of Nash equilibria that directly tackles the saddle-point formulation of Equation 1. In particular, we compute, in $O(1/\epsilon)$ iterations, strategies $\mathbf{x}^* \in Q_1$ and $\mathbf{y}^* \in Q_2$ such that

$$\max_{\mathbf{x} \in Q_1} \langle A\mathbf{y}^*, \mathbf{x} \rangle - \min_{\mathbf{y} \in Q_2} \langle A\mathbf{y}, \mathbf{x}^* \rangle \leq \epsilon. \tag{2}$$

Strategies that satisfy this inequality are called ϵ-*equilibria*. This class of game-theoretic solution concepts encapsulates strategies in which either player can gain at most ϵ by deviating to another strategy. For most applications this type of approximation is acceptable if ϵ is small.[1] The algorithms of this paper are anytime algorithms and guarantee that ϵ approaches zero, and quickly find solutions that have a very small ϵ. In this respect, they are similar to other algorithms, such as fictitious play or multiplicative weighting [16]. Our algorithm differs from fictitious play in that the convergence of the algorithm is much faster, and it differs from the weighted-majority algorithm in that we assume that all aspects of the game are already known.

Our approach is based on modern smoothing techniques for saddle-point problems [17]. A particularly attractive feature of our approach is its simple work per

---

[1] There has been work on finding ϵ-equilibria in two-player normal-form games [11,12]. Other recent work has investigated the complexity of approximating Nash equilibria in non-zero-sum games [13,14,15].

iteration as well as the low cost per iteration: the most complicated operation is a matrix-vector multiplication involving the payoff matrix A. In addition, we can take advantage of the structure of the problem to improve the performance of this operation both in terms of time and memory requirements. As a result, we are able to handle games that are several orders of magnitude larger than games that can be solved using conventional linear programming solvers. For example, we compute approximate solutions to an abstracted version of Texas Hold'em poker whose LP formulation has 18,536,842 rows and 18,536,852 columns, and has 61,450,990,224 non-zeros in the payoff matrix. This is more than 1,200 times the number of non-zeros in the Rhode Island Hold'em problem mentioned above. Since conventional LP solvers require an explicit representation of the problem (in addition to their internal data structures), this would require such a solver to use more than 458 GB of memory *simply to represent the problem*. On the other hand, our algorithm only requires 2.49 GB of memory.

The algorithm we present herein can be seen as a primal-dual first-order algorithm applied to the pair of optimization problems

$$\max_{\mathbf{x} \in Q_1} f(\mathbf{x}) = \min_{\mathbf{y} \in Q_2} \phi(\mathbf{y})$$

where

$$f(\mathbf{x}) = \min_{\mathbf{y} \in Q_2} \langle A\mathbf{y}, \mathbf{x} \rangle \text{ and } \phi(\mathbf{y}) = \max_{\mathbf{x} \in Q_1} \langle A\mathbf{y}, \mathbf{x} \rangle.$$

It is easy to see that f and ϕ are respectively concave and convex non-smooth (*i.e.* not differentiable) functions. Our algorithm is based on a modern smoothing technique for non-smooth convex minimization [17]. This smoothing technique provides first-order algorithms whose theoretical iteration-complexity to find a feasible primal-dual solution with gap $\epsilon > 0$ is $O(1/\epsilon)$ iterations. We note that this is a substantial improvement to the black-box generic complexity bound $O(1/\epsilon^2)$ of general first-order methods for non-smooth convex minimization (concave maximization) [18].

Some recent work has applied smoothing techniques to the solution of large-scale semidefinite programming problems [19] and to large-scale linear programming problems [20]. However, our work appears to be the first application of smoothing techniques to Nash equilibrium computation in sequential games.

2   Nesterov's Excessive Gap Technique (EGT)

We next describe Nesterov's excessive gap smoothing technique [17], specialized to extensive form games. For $i = 1, 2$, assume that S_i is the set of sequences of moves of player i and $Q_i \subseteq \mathbb{R}^{S_i}$ is the *set of realization plans* of player i. For $i = 1, 2$, assume that d_i is a strongly convex function on Q_i, *i.e.* there exists $\rho_i > 0$ such that

$$d_i(\alpha \mathbf{z} + (1 - \alpha)\mathbf{w}) \leq \alpha d_i(\mathbf{z}) + (1 - \alpha)d_i(\mathbf{w}) - \frac{1}{2}\rho\alpha\|\mathbf{z} - \mathbf{w}\|^2 \qquad (3)$$

for all $\alpha \in [0, 1]$ and $\mathbf{z}, \mathbf{w} \in Q_i$. The largest ρ_i satisfying (3) is the *strong convexity parameter* of d_i. For convenience, we assume that $\min_{\mathbf{z} \in Q_i} d_i(\mathbf{z}) = 0$.

The *prox functions* d_1 and d_2 can be used to *smooth* the non-smooth functions f and ϕ as follows. For $\mu_1, \mu_2 > 0$ consider

$$f_{\mu_2}(\mathbf{x}) = \min_{\mathbf{y} \in Q_2} \{\langle A\mathbf{y}, \mathbf{x} \rangle + \mu_2 d_2(\mathbf{y})\}$$

and

$$\phi_{\mu_1}(\mathbf{y}) = \max_{\mathbf{x} \in Q_1} \{\langle A\mathbf{y}, \mathbf{x} \rangle - \mu_1 d_1(\mathbf{x})\}.$$

Because d_1 and d_2 are strongly convex, it follows [17] that f_{μ_2} and ϕ_{μ_1} are smooth (*i.e.* differentiable). Notice that $f(\mathbf{x}) \leq \phi(\mathbf{y})$ for all $\mathbf{x} \in Q_1, \mathbf{y} \in Q_2$. Consider the following related *excessive gap condition:*

$$f_{\mu_2}(\mathbf{x}) \geq \phi_{\mu_1}(\mathbf{y}). \tag{4}$$

Let $D_i := \max_{\mathbf{z} \in Q_i} d_i(\mathbf{z})$. If $\mu_1, \mu_2 > 0$, $\mathbf{x} \in Q_1, \mathbf{y} \in Q_2$ and $(\mu_1, \mu_2, \mathbf{x}, \mathbf{y})$ satisfies (4), then [17, Lemma 3.1] yields

$$0 \leq \phi(\mathbf{y}) - f(\mathbf{x}) \leq \mu_1 D_1 + \mu_2 D_2. \tag{5}$$

This suggests the following strategy to find an approximate solution to (1): generate a sequence $(\mu_1^k, \mu_2^k, \mathbf{x}^k, \mathbf{y}^k)$, $k = 0, 1, \ldots$, with μ_1^k and μ_2^k decreasing to zero as k increases, while $\mathbf{x}^k \in Q_1$, $\mathbf{y}^k \in Q_2$ and while maintaining the loop invariant that $(\mu_1^k, \mu_2^k, \mathbf{x}^k, \mathbf{y}^k)$ satisfies (4). This is the strategy underlying the EGT algorithms we present in this paper.

The building blocks of our algorithms are the mapping sargmax and the procedures initial and shrink. Let d be a strongly convex function with a convex, closed, and bounded domain $Q \subseteq \mathbb{R}^n$. Let $\text{sargmax}(d, \cdot) : \mathbb{R}^n \to Q$ be defined as

$$\text{sargmax}(d, \mathbf{g}) := \underset{\mathbf{x} \in Q}{\text{argmax}} \{\langle \mathbf{g}, \mathbf{x} \rangle - d(\mathbf{x})\}. \tag{6}$$

By [17, Lemma 5.1], the following procedure initial yields an initial point that satisfies the excessive gap condition (4). The notation $\|A\|$ indicates an appropriate operator norm (see [17] and Examples 1 and 2 for details), and $\nabla d_2(\hat{\mathbf{x}})$ is the gradient of d_2 at $\hat{\mathbf{x}}$.

initial(A, d_1, d_2)

1. $\mu_1^0 := \mu_2^0 := \frac{\|A\|}{\sqrt{\rho_1 \rho_2}}$
2. $\hat{\mathbf{y}} := \text{sargmax}(d_2, \mathbf{0})$
3. $\mathbf{x}^0 := \text{sargmax}\left(d_1, \frac{1}{\mu_1^0} A\hat{\mathbf{y}}\right)$
4. $\mathbf{y}^0 := \text{sargmax}\left(d_2, \nabla d_2(\hat{\mathbf{x}}) + \frac{1}{\mu_2^0} A^{\mathrm{T}} \mathbf{x}^0\right)$
5. return $(\mu_1^0, \mu_2^0, \mathbf{x}^0, \mathbf{y}^0)$

The following procedure shrink enables us to reduce μ_1 and μ_2 while maintaining (4).

shrink$(A, \mu_1, \mu_2, \tau, \mathbf{x}, \mathbf{y}, d_1, d_2)$

1. $\check{\mathbf{y}} := \text{sargmax}\left(d_2, -\frac{1}{\mu_2}A^T\mathbf{x}\right)$
2. $\hat{\mathbf{y}} := (1 - \tau)\mathbf{y} + \tau\check{\mathbf{y}}$
3. $\hat{\mathbf{x}} := \text{sargmax}\left(d_1, \frac{1}{\mu_1}A\hat{\mathbf{y}}\right)$
4. $\tilde{\mathbf{y}} := \text{sargmax}\left(d_2, \nabla d_2\left(\check{\mathbf{y}}\right) + \frac{\tau}{(1-\tau)\mu_2}A^T\hat{\mathbf{x}}\right)$
5. $\mathbf{x}^+ := (1 - \tau)\mathbf{x} + \tau\hat{\mathbf{x}}$
6. $\mathbf{y}^+ := (1 - \tau)\mathbf{y} + \tau\tilde{\mathbf{y}}$
7. $\mu_2^+ := (1 - \tau)\mu_2$
8. return $(\mu_2^+, \mathbf{x}^+, \mathbf{y}^+)$

By [17, Theorem 4.1], if the input $(\mu_1, \mu_2, \mathbf{x}, \mathbf{y})$ to shrink satisfies (4) then so does $(\mu_1, \mu_2^+, \mathbf{x}^+, \mathbf{y}^+)$ as long as τ satisfies $\tau^2/(1-\tau) \leq \mu_1\mu_2\rho_1\rho_2\|A\|^2$. Consequently, the iterates generated by procedure EGT below satisfy (4). In particular, after N iterations, Algorithm EGT yields points $\mathbf{x}^N \in Q_1$ and $\mathbf{y}^N \in Q_2$ with

$$0 \leq \max_{\mathbf{x}\in Q_1}\langle A\mathbf{y}^N, \mathbf{x}\rangle - \min_{\mathbf{y}\in Q_2}\langle A\mathbf{y}, \mathbf{x}^N\rangle \leq \frac{4\|A\|}{N}\sqrt{\frac{D_1 D_2}{\rho_1\rho_2}}.$$

EGT

1. $(\mu_1^0, \mu_2^0, \mathbf{x}^0, \mathbf{y}^0) = \text{initial}(A, d_1, d_2)$
2. For $k = 0, 1, \ldots$:
   (a) $\tau := \frac{2}{k+3}$
   (b) If k is even: // shrink μ_2
       i. $(\mu_2^{k+1}, \mathbf{x}^{k+1}, \mathbf{y}^{k+1}) := \text{shrink}(A, \mu_1^k, \mu_2^k, \tau, \mathbf{x}^k, \mathbf{y}^k, d_1, d_2)$
       ii. $\mu_1^{k+1} := \mu_1^k$
   (c) If k is odd: // shrink μ_1
       i. $(\mu_1^{k+1}, \mathbf{y}^{k+1}, \mathbf{x}^{k+1}) := \text{shrink}(A^T, -\mu_1^k, -\mu_2^k, \tau, \mathbf{y}^k, \mathbf{x}^k, d_2, d_1)$
       ii. $\mu_2^{k+1} := \mu_2^k$

Notice that Algorithm EGT is a *conceptual* algorithm that finds an ϵ-solution to (1). It is conceptual only because the algorithm requires that the mappings $\text{sargmax}(d_i, \cdot)$ be computed several times at each iteration. Consequently, a specific choice of the functions d_1 and d_2 is a critical step to convert Algorithm EGT into an actual algorithm.

2.1 Nice Prox Functions

Assume Q is a convex, closed, and bounded set. We say that a function $d : Q \to \mathbb{R}$ is a *nice prox function* for Q if it satisfies the following three conditions:

1. d is strongly convex and continuous everywhere in Q and is differentiable in the relative interior of Q;
2. $\min\{d(\mathbf{z}) : \mathbf{z} \in Q\} = 0$;
3. The mapping $\text{sargmax}(d, \cdot): \mathbb{R}^n \to Q$ is easily computable, *e.g.*, it has a closed-form expression.

We next provide two specific examples of nice prox functions for the simplex

$$\Delta_n = \{\mathbf{x} \in \mathbb{R}^n : \mathbf{x} \geq 0, \sum_{i=1}^{n} x_i = 1\}.$$

Example 1. Consider the *entropy* function $d(\mathbf{x}) = \ln n + \sum_{i=1}^{n} x_i \ln x_i$. The function d is strongly convex and continuous in Δ_n and $\min_{\mathbf{x} \in \Delta_n} d(\mathbf{x}) = 0$. It is also differentiable in the relative interior of Δ_n. It has strong convexity parameter $\rho = 1$ for the 1-norm in $\mathbb{R}^n$, namely, $\|\mathbf{x}\| = \sum_{i=1}^{n} |x_i|$. The corresponding operator norm, $\|A\|$, for this setting is simply the value of the largest entry in A in absolute value. Finally, the mapping sargmax$(d, \mathbf{g})$ has the easily computable expression

$$\text{sargmax}(d, \mathbf{g})_j = \frac{e^{g_j}}{\sum\limits_{i=1}^{n} e^{g_i}}.$$

Example 2. Consider the (squared) *Euclidean distance* to the center of Δ_n, that is, $d(\mathbf{x}) = \frac{1}{2} \sum_{i=1}^{n} \left(x_i - \frac{1}{n}\right)^2$. This function is strongly convex, continuous and differentiable in Δ_n, and $\min_{\mathbf{x} \in \Delta_n} d(\mathbf{x}) = 0$. It has strong convexity parameter $\rho = 1$ for the Euclidean norm, namely, $\|\mathbf{x}\| = \left(\sum_{i=1}^{n} |x_i|^2\right)^{1/2}$. The corresponding operator norm, $\|A\|$, for this setting is the spectral norm of A, *i.e.* the square root of the largest eigenvalue of $A^T A$. Although the mapping sargmax$(d, \mathbf{g})$ does not have a closed-form expression, it can easily be computed in $O(n \log n)$ steps [20].

In order to apply Algorithm EGT to problem (1) for sequential games we need nice prox-functions for the realization sets Q_1 and Q_2 (which are more complex than the simplex discussed above in Examples 1 and 2). This problem was recently solved [21]:

Theorem 1. *Any nice prox-function ψ for the simplex induces a nice prox-function for a set of realization plans Q. The mapping* sargmax$(d, \cdot)$ *can be computed by repeatedly applying* sargmax$(\psi, \cdot)$.

Figure 1 displays the relative performance of the entropy and Euclidean prox functions, described in Examples 1 and 2, respectively. (Heuristics 1 and 2 were enabled in this experiment.) In all of the figures, the units of the vertical axis are small bet sizes in the corresponding poker games.

The entropy prox function outperformed the Euclidean prox function on all four instances. Therefore, in the remaining experiments we use the entropy prox function.

3   Heuristics for Improving Speed of Convergence

While Algorithm EGT has theoretical iteration-complexity $O(1/\epsilon)$, and (as our experiments on EGT show later in this paper) EGT is already an improvement over the state of the art (in particular, the simplex method and standard interior point methods for solving the game modeled as a linear program), we introduce two heuristics for making EGT drastically faster. The heuristics attempt to speed up the decrease in μ_1 and μ_2, and thus the overall convergence time of the algorithm, while maintaining the excessive gap condition (4) as well as the guaranteed convergence of $O(1/\epsilon)$.

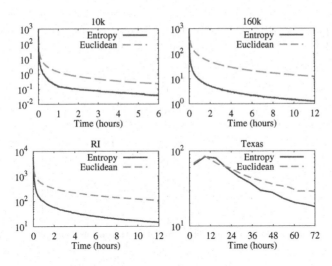

Fig. 1. Comparison of the entropy and Euclidean prox functions. The value axis is the gap ϵ (Equation 2).

3.1   Heuristic 1: Aggressive μ Reduction

The first heuristic is based on the following observation: although the value $\tau = 2/(k+3)$ computed in step 2(a) of EGT guarantees the excessive gap condition (4), computational experiments indicate that this is an overly conservative value, particularly during the first few iterations. Instead we can use an adaptive procedure to choose a larger value of τ. Since we now can no longer guarantee the excessive gap condition (4) *a priori*, we are required to do a *posterior* verification which occasionally leads to adjustments in the parameter τ. In order to check (4), we need to compute the values of f_{μ_2} and ϕ_{μ_1}. To that end, consider the following mapping smax, a variation of sargmax. Assume d is a prox-function with domain $Q \subseteq \mathbb{R}^n$. Let $\mathrm{smax}(d, \cdot) : \mathbb{R}^n \to \mathbb{R}$ be defined as

$$\mathrm{smax}(d, \mathbf{g}) := \max_{\mathbf{x} \in Q}\{\langle \mathbf{g}, \mathbf{x}\rangle - d(\mathbf{x})\}. \tag{7}$$

It is immediate that $\mathrm{smax}(d, \cdot)$ is easily computable provided $\mathrm{sargmax}(d, \cdot)$ is. Notice that $\phi_{\mu_1}(\mathbf{y}) = \mathrm{smax}(d_1, \frac{1}{\mu_1} A\mathbf{y})$ and $f_{\mu_2}(\mathbf{x}) = -\mathrm{smax}(d_2, -\frac{1}{\mu_2} A^{\mathrm{T}}\mathbf{x})$. To incorporate Heuristic 1 in Algorithm EGT we modify the procedure shrink as follows.

decrease$(A, \mu_1, \mu_2, \tau, \mathbf{x}, \mathbf{y}, d_1, d_2)$

1. $(\mu_2^+, \mathbf{x}^+, \mathbf{y}^+) := \mathrm{shrink}(A, \mu_1, \mu_2, \tau, \mathbf{x}, \mathbf{y}, d_1, d_2)$
2. while $\mathrm{smax}(d_1, \frac{1}{\mu_1} A\mathbf{y}^+) > -\mathrm{smax}(d_2, \frac{-1}{\mu_2^+} A^{\mathrm{T}}\mathbf{x}^+)$
   // reduced too much, τ is too big
   (a) $\tau := \tau/2$
   (b) $(\mu_2^+, \mathbf{x}^+, \mathbf{y}^+) := \mathrm{shrink}(A, \mu_1, \mu_2, \tau, \mathbf{x}, \mathbf{y}, d_1, d_2)$
3. return $(\mu_2^+, \mathbf{x}^+, \mathbf{y}^+)$

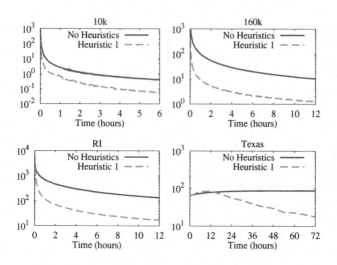

Fig. 2. Experimental evaluation of Heuristic 1

By [17, Theorem 4.1], when the input $(\mu_1, \mu_2, \mathbf{x}, \mathbf{y})$ to decrease satisfies (4), the procedure decrease will halt.

Figure 2 demonstrates the impact of applying Heuristic 1 only. On all four instances, Heuristic 1 reduced the gap significantly; on the larger instances, this reduction was an order of magnitude.

3.2 Heuristic 2: Balancing and Reduction of μ_1 and μ_2

Our second heuristic is motivated by the observation that after several calls of the decrease procedure, one of μ_1 and μ_2 may be much smaller than the other. This imbalance is undesirable because the larger one dominates in the bound given by (5). Hence after a certain number of iterations we perform a *balancing* step to bring these values closer together. The balancing consists of repeatedly shrinking the larger one of μ_1 and μ_2.

We also observed that after such balancing, the values of μ_1 and μ_2 can sometimes be further reduced without violating the excessive gap condition (4). We thus include a final reduction step in the balancing heuristic.

This balancing and reduction heuristic is incorporated via the following procedure.[2]

balance$(\mu_1, \mu_2, \mathbf{x}, \mathbf{y}, A)$

1. while $\mu_2 > 1.5\mu_1$ // shrink μ_2
   $(\mu_2, \mathbf{x}, \mathbf{y}) := \mathrm{decrease}(A, \mu_1, \mu_2, \tau, \mathbf{x}, \mathbf{y}, d_1, d_2)$
2. while $\mu_1 > 1.5\mu_2$ // shrink μ_1
   $(\mu_1, \mathbf{y}, \mathbf{x}) := \mathrm{decrease}(A^{\mathrm{T}}, -\mu_2, -\mu_1, \tau, \mathbf{y}, \mathbf{x}, d_2, d_1)$
3. while $\mathrm{smax}(d_1, \frac{1}{0.9\mu_1} A\mathbf{y}) \leq -\mathrm{smax}(d_2, \frac{-1}{0.9\mu_2} A^{\mathrm{T}}\mathbf{x})$
   // decrease μ_1 and μ_2 if possible

---

[2] We set the parameters (0.9 and 1.5) based on some initial experimentation.

$$\mu_1 := 0.9\mu_1$$
$$\mu_2 := 0.9\mu_2$$

We are now ready to describe the variant of EGT with Heuristics 1 and 2.

EGT-2

1. $(\mu_1^0, \mu_2^0, \mathbf{x}^0, \mathbf{y}^0) = \mathtt{initial}(A, Q_1, Q_2)$
2. $\tau := 0.5$
3. For $k = 0, 1, \ldots$:

    (a) If k is even: // Shrink μ_2
        i. $(\mu_1^{k+1}, \mathbf{x}^{k+1}, \mathbf{y}^{k+1}) := \mathtt{decrease}(A, \mu_1^k, \mu_2^k, \tau, \mathbf{x}^k, \mathbf{y}^k, d_1, d_2)$
        ii. $\mu_1^{k+1} = \mu_1^k$

    (b) If k is odd: // Shrink μ_1
        i. $(\mu_1^{k+1}, \mathbf{y}^{k+1}, \mathbf{x}^{k+1}) := \mathtt{decrease}(-A^{\mathrm{T}}, \mu_2^k, \mu_1^k, \tau, \mathbf{y}^k, \mathbf{x}^k, d_2, d_1)$
        ii. $\mu_2^{k+1} = \mu_2^k$

    (c) If $k \bmod 10 = 0$ // balance and reduce
        $\mathtt{balance}(\mu_1^k, \mu_2^k, \mathbf{x}^k, \mathbf{y}^k, A)$

Because Heuristic 2 takes more time to compute, we experimented with how often the algorithm should run it. (We did this by varying the constant in line 3(c) of Algorithm EGT-2. In this experiment, Heuristic 1 was turned off.) Figure 3 shows that it is better to run it than to not run it, and on most instances, it is better to run it every 100 iterations than every 10 iterations.

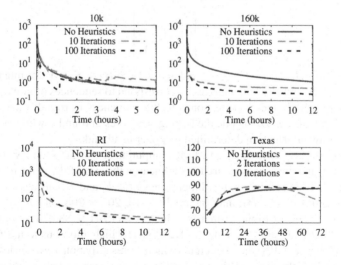

Fig. 3. Heuristic 2 applied at different intervals

4 Customizing the Algorithm for Poker Games

The bulk of the computational work at each iteration of Algorithms EGT and EGT-2 consists of matrix-vector multiplications $\mathbf{x} \mapsto A^{\mathrm{T}}\mathbf{x}$ and $\mathbf{y} \mapsto A\mathbf{y}$ in addition to calls to the mappings $\mathrm{smax}(d_i, \cdot)$ and $\mathrm{sargmax}(d_i, \cdot)$. Of these operations, the matrix-vector multiplications are by far the most expensive, both in terms of memory (for storing A) and time (for computing the product).

4.1 Addressing the Space Requirements

To address the memory requirements, we exploit the problem structure to obtain a concise representation for the payoff matrix A. This representation relies on a uniform structure that is present in poker games and many other games. For example, the betting sequences that can occur in most poker games are independent of the cards that are dealt. This conceptual separation of betting sequences and card deals is used by automated abstraction algorithms [6]. Analogously, we can decompose the payoff matrix based on these two aspects.

The basic operation we use in this decomposition is the *Kronecker product*, denoted by $\otimes$. Given two matrices $B \in \mathbb{R}^{m \times n}$ and $C \in \mathbb{R}^{p \times q}$, the Kronecker product is

$$B \otimes C = \begin{bmatrix} b_{11}C & \cdots & b_{1n}C \\ \vdots & \ddots & \vdots \\ b_{m1}C & \cdots & b_{mn}C \end{bmatrix} \in \mathbb{R}^{mp \times nq}.$$

For ease of exposition, we explain the concise representation in the context of Rhode Island Hold'em poker [5], although the general technique applies much more broadly. The payoff matrix A can be written as

$$A = \begin{bmatrix} A_1 & & \\ & A_2 & \\ & & A_3 \end{bmatrix}$$

where $A_1 = F_1 \otimes B_1$, $A_2 = F_2 \otimes B_2$, and $A_3 = F_3 \otimes B_3 + S \otimes W$ for much smaller matrices F_i, B_i, S, and W. The matrices F_i correspond to sequences of moves in round i that end with a fold, and S corresponds to the sequences in round 3 that end in a showdown. The matrices B_i encode the betting structures in round i, while W encodes the win/lose/draw information determined by poker hand ranks.

Given this concise representation of A, computing $\mathbf{x} \mapsto A^{\mathrm{T}}\mathbf{x}$ and $\mathbf{y} \mapsto A\mathbf{y}$ is straightforward, and the space required is sublinear in the size of the game tree. For example, in Rhode Island Hold'em, the dimensions of the F_i and S matrices are 10×10, and the dimensions of B_1, B_2, and B_3 are 13×13, 205×205, and $1,774 \times 1,774$, respectively—in contrast to the A-matrix, which is $883,741 \times 883,741$. Furthermore, the matrices F_i, B_i, S, and W are themselves sparse which allows us to use the Compressed Row Storage (CRS) data structure (which stores only non-zero entries).

Table 1 provides the sizes of the four test instances; each models some variant of poker, an important challenge problem in AI [22]. The first three instances, 10k, 160k, and RI, are abstractions of Rhode Island Hold'em [5] computed using the *GameShrink* automated abstraction algorithm [6]. The first two instances are lossy (non-equilibrium

Table 1. Problem sizes (when formulated as an LP) for the instances used in our experiments

Name	Rows	Columns	Non-zeros
10k	14,590	14,590	536,502
160k	226,074	226,074	9,238,993
RI	1,237,238	1,237,238	50,428,638
Texas	18,536,842	18,536,852	61,498,656,400

Table 2. Memory footprint in gigabytes of CPLEX interior-point method (IPM), CPLEX Simplex, and EGT algorithms. CPLEX requires more than 458 GB for the Texas instance.

Name	CPLEX IPM	CPLEX Simplex	EGT
10k	0.082 GB	> 0.051 GB	0.012 GB
160k	2.25 GB	> 0.664 GB	0.035 GB
RI	25.2 GB	> 3.45 GB	0.15 GB
Texas	> 458 GB	> 458 GB	2.49 GB

preserving) abstractions, while the RI instance is a lossless abstraction. The last instance, Texas, is a lossy abstraction of Texas Hold'em. A similar instance was used to generate the player *GS3*, one of the most competitive poker-playing programs [10]. We wanted to test the algorithms on problems of widely varying sizes, which is reflected by the data in Table 1. We also chose these four problems because we wanted to evaluate the algorithms on real-world instances, rather than on randomly generated games (which may not reflect any realistic setting).

Table 2 clearly demonstrates the extremely low memory requirements of the EGT algorithms. Most notably, on the Texas instance, both of the CPLEX algorithms require more than 458 GB simply to *represent* the problem. In contrast, using the decomposed payoff matrix representation, the EGT algorithms require only 2.49 GB. Furthermore, in order to solve the problem, both the simplex and interior-point algorithms would require additional memory for their internal data structures.[3] Therefore, the EGT family of algorithms is already an improvement over the state-of-the-art (even without the heuristics).

4.2 Speedup from Parallelizing the Matrix-Vector Product

To address the time requirements of the matrix-vector product, we can effectively parallelize the operation by simply partitioning the work into n pieces when n CPUs are available. The speedup we can achieve on parallel CPUs is demonstrated in Table 3. The instance used for this test is the Texas instance described above. The matrix-vector product operation scales linearly in the number of CPUs, and the time to perform one iteration of the algorithm (using the entropy prox function and including the time for applying Heuristic 1) scales nearly linearly, decreasing by a factor of 3.72 when using 4 CPUs.

---

[3] The memory usage for the CPLEX simplex algorithm reported in Table 2 is the memory used after 10 minutes of execution (except for the Texas instance which did not run at all as described above). This algorithm's memory requirements grow and shrink during the execution depending on its internal data structures. Therefore, the number reported is a lower bound on the maximum memory usage during execution.

Table 3. Effect of parallelization for the `Texas` instance

CPUs	matrix-vector product		EGT iteration	
	time (s)	speedup	time (s)	speedup
1	278.958	1.00x	1425.786	1.00x
2	140.579	1.98x	734.366	1.94x
3	92.851	3.00x	489.947	2.91x
4	68.831	4.05x	383.793	3.72x

5   Conclusions and Future Research

We applied Nesterov's excessive gap technique to extensive form games. We introduced two heuristics for improving convergence speed, and showed that each of them reduces the gap by an order of magnitude. Best results were achieved by using Heuristic 2 only every so often. It was best to use both heuristics together. We also observed that the entropy prox function yielded faster convergence than the Euclidean prox function. For poker games and similar games, we introduced a decomposed matrix representation that reduces storage requirements drastically. We also showed near-perfect efficacy of parallelization. Overall, our techniques enable one to solve orders of magnitude larger games than the prior state of the art.

Although current general-purpose simplex and interior-point solvers cannot handle problems of more than around 10^6 nodes [6], it is conceivable that specialized versions of these algorithms could be effective. However, taking advantage of the problem structure in these linear programming methods appears to be quite challenging. For example, a single interior-point iteration requires the solution of a symmetric non-definite system of equations whose matrix has the payoff matrix A and its transpose A^{T} in some blocks. Such a step is inherently far more complex than the simple matrix-vector multiplications required in EGT-2. On the upside, overcoming this obstacle would enable us to capitalize on the superb speed of convergence of interior-point methods. While first-order methods require $O(1/\epsilon)$ iterations to find an ϵ-solution, interior-point methods require only $O(\log(1/\epsilon))$ iterations. We leave the study of these alternative algorithms for Nash equilibrium finding as future work.

References

1. Romanovskii, I.: Reduction of a game with complete memory to a matrix game. Soviet Mathematics 3, 678–681 (1962)
2. Koller, D., Megiddo, N.: The complexity of two-person zero-sum games in extensive form. Games and Economic Behavior 4(4), 528–552 (1992)
3. von Stengel, B.: Efficient computation of behavior strategies. Games and Economic Behavior 14(2), 220–246 (1996)
4. Koller, D., Pfeffer, A.: Representations and solutions for game-theoretic problems. Artificial Intelligence 94(1), 167–215 (1997) (Early version appeared in IJCAI-95)
5. Shi, J., Littman, M.: Abstraction methods for game theoretic poker. In: Computers and Games, Springer-Verlag, pp. 333–345. Springer, Heidelberg (2001)

6. Gilpin, A., Sandholm, T.: Lossless abstraction method for sequential games of imperfect information. Journal of the ACM (to appear) Early version appeared as Finding equilibria in large sequential games of imperfect information. In: Proceedings of the ACM Conference on Electronic Commerce (ACM-EC), Ann Arbor, MI, 2006 (2007)

7. Billings, D., Burch, N., Davidson, A., Holte, R., Schaeffer, J., Schauenberg, T., Szafron, D.: Approximating game-theoretic optimal strategies for full-scale poker. In: Proceedings of the Eighteenth International Joint Conference on Artificial Intelligence (IJCAI), Acapulco, Mexico, pp. 661–668 (2003)

8. Gilpin, A., Sandholm, T.: A competitive Texas Hold'em poker player via automated abstraction and real-time equilibrium computation. In: Proceedings of the National Conference on Artificial Intelligence (AAAI), Boston, MA (2006)

9. Gilpin, A., Sandholm, T.: Better automated abstraction techniques for imperfect information games, with application to Texas Hold'em poker. In: International Joint Conference on Autonomous Agents and Multi-Agent Systems (AAMAS), Honolulu, HI (2007)

10. Gilpin, A., Sandholm, T., Sørensen, T.B.: Potential-aware automated abstraction of sequential games, and holistic equilibrium analysis of Texas Hold'em poker. In: Proceedings of the National Conference on Artificial Intelligence (AAAI), Vancouver, BC, Canada (2007)

11. Lipton, R.J., Young, N.E.: Simple strategies for large zero-sum games with applications to complexity theory. In: Proceedings of the Annual Symposium on Theory of Computing (STOC), Montreal, Quebec, Canada, pp. 734–740 (1994)

12. Lipton, R., Markakis, E., Mehta, A.: Playing large games using simple strategies. In: Proceedings of the ACM Conference on Electronic Commerce (ACM-EC), pp. 36–41. ACM Press, New York (2003)

13. Daskalakis, C., Mehta, A., Papadimitriou, C.: A note on approximate Nash equilibria. In: Spirakis, P.G., Mavronicolas, M., Kontogiannis, S.C. (eds.) WINE 2006. LNCS, vol. 4286, Springer, Heidelberg (2006)

14. Daskalakis, C., Mehta, A., Papadimitriou, C.: Progress in approximate Nash equilibria. In: Proceedings of the ACM Conference on Electronic Commerce (ACM-EC), pp. 355–358. ACM Press, New York (2007)

15. Feder, T., Nazerzadeh, H., Saberi, A.: Approximating Nash equilibria using small-support strategies. In: Proceedings of the ACM Conference on Electronic Commerce (ACM-EC), pp. 352–354. ACM Press, New York (2007)

16. Freund, Y., Schapire, R.: Adaptive game playing using multiplicative weights. Games and Economic Behavior 29, 79–103 (1999)

17. Nesterov, Y.: Excessive gap technique in nonsmooth convex minimization. SIAM Journal of Optimization 16(1), 235–249 (2005)

18. Nesterov, Y.: Introductory Lectures on Convex Optimization: A Basic Course. Kluwer Academic Publishers, Dordrecht (2004)

19. Lu, Z., Nemirovski, A., Monteiro, R.D.C.: Large-scale semidefinite programming via a saddle point mirror-prox algorithm. Mathematical Programming, Series B 109(2–3), 211–237 (2007)

20. Chudak, F.A., Eleutério, V.: Improved approximation schemes for linear programming relaxations of combinatorial optimization problems. In: Jünger, M., Kaibel, V. (eds.) Integer Programming and Combinatorial Optimization. LNCS, vol. 3509, pp. 81–96. Springer, Heidelberg (2005)

21. Hoda, S., Gilpin, A.: Peña, J.: A gradient-based approach for computing Nash equilibria of large sequential games (2007), Available at, http://www.optimization-online.org/

22. Billings, D., Davidson, A., Schaeffer, J., Szafron, D.: The challenge of poker. Artificial Intelligence 134(1-2), 201–240 (2002)

Bluffing and Strategic Reticence
in Prediction Markets*

Yiling Chen[1], Daniel M. Reeves[1], David M. Pennock[1],
Robin D. Hanson[2], Lance Fortnow[3], and Rica Gonen[1]

[1] Yahoo! Research
[2] George Mason University
[3] University of Chicago

Abstract. We study the equilibrium behavior of informed traders interacting with two types of automated market makers: market scoring rules (MSR) and dynamic parimutuel markets (DPM). Although both MSR and DPM subsidize trade to encourage information aggregation, and MSR is myopically incentive compatible, neither mechanism is incentive compatible in general. That is, there exist circumstances when traders can benefit by either hiding information (reticence) or lying about information (bluffing). We examine what information structures lead to straightforward play by traders, meaning that traders reveal all of their information truthfully as soon as they are able. Specifically, we analyze the behavior of risk-neutral traders with incomplete information playing in a finite-period dynamic game. We employ two different information structures for the logarithmic market scoring rule (LMSR): conditionally independent signals and conditionally dependent signals. When signals of traders are independent conditional on the state of the world, truthful betting is a Perfect Bayesian Equilibrium (PBE) for LMSR. However, when signals are conditionally dependent, there exist joint probability distributions on signals such that at a PBE in LMSR traders have an incentive to bet against their own information—strategically misleading other traders in order to later profit by correcting their errors. In DPM, we show that when traders anticipate sufficiently better-informed traders entering the market in the future, they have incentive to partially withhold their information by moving the market probability only partway toward their beliefs, or in some cases not participating in the market at all.

1   Introduction

The strongest form of the *efficient markets hypothesis* [1] posits that information is incorporated into prices fully and immediately, as soon as it becomes available to anyone. A *prediction market* is a financial market specifically designed to take advantage of this property. For example, to forecast whether a

---

* An early version of this paper appeared at the Second Workshop on Prediction Markets. This version is much improved thanks to the insightful comments by Stanko Dimitrov, Paul J. Healy, Mohammad Mahdian, Rahul Sami, and the anonymous reviewers.

X. Deng and F.C. Graham (Eds.): WINE 2007, LNCS 4858, pp. 70–81, 2007.

product will launch on time, a company might ask employees to trade a security that pays $1 if and only if the product launches by the planned date. Everyone from managers to developers to administrative assistants with different forms and amounts of information can bet on the outcome. The resulting price constitutes their collective probability estimate that the launch will occur on time. Empirically, prediction markets like this outperform experts, group consensus, and polls across a variety of settings [2,3,4,5,6,7,8,9,10].

Yet the double-sided auction at the heart of nearly every prediction market is *not* incentive compatible. Information holders do not necessarily have incentive to fully reveal all their information right away, as soon as they obtain it. The extreme case of this is captured by the so-called *no trade theorems* [11]: When rational, risk-neutral agents with common priors interact in an unsubsidized (zero-sum) market, *the agents will not trade at all*, even if they have vastly different information and posterier beliefs. The informal reason is that any offer by one trader is a signal to a potential trading partner that results in belief revision discouraging trade.

The classic *market microstructure* model of a financial market posits two types of traders: rational traders and noise traders [12]. The existence of noise traders turns the game among rational traders into a positive-sum game, thereby resolving the no-trade paradox. However, even in this setting, the mechanism is not incentive compatible. For example, monopolist information holders will not fully reveal their information right away: instead, they will leak their information into the market gradually over time and in doing so will obtain a greater profit [13].

Instead of assuming or subsidizing noise traders, a prediction market designer might choose to directly subsidize the market by employing an *automated market maker* that expects to lose some money on average. Hanson's *market scoring rule market maker* (MSR) is one example [14,15]. MSR requires a patron to subsidize the market, but guarantees that the patron cannot lose more than a fixed amount set in advance, regardless of how many shares are exchanged or what outcome eventually occurs. The greater the subsidy, the greater the effective liquidity of the market. Since traders face a positive-sum game, even rational risk-neutral agents have incentive to participate. In fact, even a single trader can be induced to reveal information, something impossible in a standard double auction with no market maker. Hanson proves that *myopic* risk-neutral traders have incentive to reveal all their information, however forward-looking traders may not.

Pennock's dynamic parimutuel market (DPM) [16,17] is another subsidized market game that functions much like a market maker. Players compete for shares of the total money wagered by all players, where the payoff of each share varies depending on the final state of the system. Whereas in a standard prediction market for a binary outcome the payoff of every winning share is exactly $1, the payoff in DPM is *at least* $1, but could be more.

Though subsidized market makers improve incentives for information revelation, the mechanisms are still not incentive compatible. Much of the allure of prediction markets is the promise to gather information from a distributed group quickly and accurately. However, if traders have demonstrable incentives to either hide or falsify information, the accuracy of the resulting forecast may be in question.

In this paper, we examine the strategic behavior of (non-myopic) risk-neutral agents participating in prediction markets using two-outcome MSR and DPM mechanisms. We model the market as a dynamic game and solve for equilibrium trading strategies. We employ two different information structures for LMSR with incomplete information: conditionally independent signals and conditionally dependent signals. The equilibrium concept that we use is the Perfect Bayesian Equilibrium (PBE) [18]. We prove that with conditionally independent signals, a PBE of LMSR with finite players and finite periods consists of all players truthfully revealing their private information at their first chance to bet. With conditionally dependent information, we show that in LMSR there exist joint probability distributions on signals such that traders have an incentive to bluff, or bet against their own information, strategically misleading other traders in order to later correct the price. DPM is shown, via a two-player, two-stage game, to face another problem: traders may have incentives to completely withhold their private information or only partially reveal their information when they anticipate sufficiently better-informed agents trading after them. Due to lack of space, we omit or abridge some proofs of lemmas and theorems in this paper; full proofs can be obtained as an Appendix by request.

Related Work. Theoretical work on price manipulation in financial markets [19,13,20] explains the logic of manipulation and indicates that double auctions are not incentive compatible. There are some experimental and empirical studies on price manipulation in prediction markets using double auction mechanisms; the results of which are mixed, some giving evidence for the success of price manipulation [21] and some showing the robustness of prediction markets to price manipulation [22,23,24,25]. The paper by Dimitrov and Sami [26], completed independently and first published simultaneously with an early version of this paper, is the most directly related work that we are aware of. Dimitro and Sami, with the aid of a projection game, study non-myopic strategies in LMSR with two players. By assuming signals of players are unconditionally independent and the LMSR market has infinite periods, they show that truthful betting is not an equilibrium strategy in general. Our study of LMSR with incomplete information in Sections 3 and 4 complements their work. Dimitro and Sami examine infinite periods of play, while we consider finite periods and finite players. On the one hand, the conditionally independent signals case that we examine directly implies that signals are unconditionally dependent unless they are not informative. On the other hand, the conditional dependence of signals assumption overlaps with Dimitro and Sami's unconditional independence of signals.

2   Background

Consider a discrete random variable X that has n mutually exclusive and exhaustive outcomes. Subsidizing a market to predict the likelihood of each outcome, two classes of mechanisms, MSR and DPM, are known to guarantee that the market maker's loss is bounded.

2.1 Marketing Scoring Rules

Hanson [14,15] shows how a proper scoring rule can be converted into a market maker mechanism, called market scoring rules (MSR). The market maker uses a proper scoring rule, $S = \{s_1(\boldsymbol{r}), \ldots, s_n(\boldsymbol{r})\}$, where $\boldsymbol{r} = \langle r_1, \ldots, r_n \rangle$ is a reported probability estimate for the random variable X. Conceptually, every trader in the market may change the current probability estimate to a new estimate of its choice at any time as long as it agrees to pay the scoring rule payment associated with the current probability estimate and receive the scoring rule payment associated with the new estimate. If outcome i is realized, a trader that changes the probability estimate from $\boldsymbol{r}^{\text{old}}$ to $\boldsymbol{r}^{\text{new}}$ pays $s_i(\boldsymbol{r}^{\text{old}})$ and receives $s_i(\boldsymbol{r}^{\text{new}})$.

Since a proper scoring rule is incentive compatible for a risk-neutral agents, if a trader can only change the probability estimate once, this modified proper scoring rule still incentivizes the trader to reveal its true probability estimate. However, when traders can participate multiple times, they might have incentives to manipulate information and mislead other traders.

Because traders change the probability estimate in sequence, MSR can be thought of as a sequential shared version of the scoring rule. The market maker pays the last trader and receives payment from the first trader. For a logarithmic market scoring rule market maker (LMSR) with the scoring function $s_i(\boldsymbol{r}) = b \log(r_i)$ and $b > 0$, the maximum amount the market maker can lose is $b \log n$.

An MSR market can be equivalently implemented as a market maker offering n securities, each corresponding to one outcome and paying \$1 if the outcome is realized [14,27]. Hence, changing the market probability of outcome i to some value r_i is the same as buying the security for outcome i until the market price of the security reaches r_i. Our analysis in this paper is facilitated by directly dealing with probabilities.

2.2 Dynamic Parimutuel Market

A dynamic parimutuel market (DPM) [16,17] is a dynamic-cost variant of a parimutuel market. There are n securities offered in the market, each corresponding to an outcome of X. As in a parimutuel market, traders who wager on the true outcome split the total pool of money at the end of the market. However, the price of a single share varies dynamically according to a price function, thus allowing traders to sell their shares prior to the determination of the outcome for profits or losses.

From a trader's perspective, DPM acts as a market maker. A particularly natural way for the market maker to set security prices is to equate the ratio of prices of any two securities by the ratio of number of shares outstanding for the two securities. Let $\boldsymbol{q} = \langle q_1, \ldots, q_n \rangle$ be the vector of shares outstanding for all securities. Then the total money wagered in the market is

$$C(\boldsymbol{q}) = \kappa \sqrt{\sum_{j=1}^{n} q_j^2}, \tag{1}$$

while the instantaneous price is

$$p_i(\boldsymbol{q}) = \frac{\kappa q_i}{\sqrt{\sum_{j=1}^{n} q_j^2}} \qquad \forall i, \tag{2}$$

where κ is a free parameter. When a trader buys or sells one or more securities, it changes the vector of outstanding shares from $\boldsymbol{q}^{\mathrm{old}}$ to $\boldsymbol{q}^{\mathrm{new}}$ and pays the market maker the amount $C(\boldsymbol{q}^{\mathrm{new}}) - C(\boldsymbol{q}^{\mathrm{old}})$, which equals the integral of the price functions from $\boldsymbol{q}^{\mathrm{old}}$ to $\boldsymbol{q}^{\mathrm{new}}$. If outcome i occurs and the quantity vector at the end of the market is $\boldsymbol{q}^f$, the payoff for each share of the winning security is

$$o_i = \frac{C(\boldsymbol{q}^f)}{q_i^f} = \frac{\kappa \sqrt{\sum_j (q_j^f)^2}}{q_i^f}. \tag{3}$$

Unlike LMSR where the market probability of an outcome is directly listed, the market probability of outcome i in DPM with the above described cost, price, and payoff functions is given by $\pi_i = \frac{p_i(\boldsymbol{q})}{C(\boldsymbol{q})/q_i}$ or, in terms of the shares directly,

$$\pi_i(\boldsymbol{q}) = \frac{q_i^2}{\sum_{j=1}^{n} q_j^2}. \tag{4}$$

For traders whose probabilities are the same as the market probabilities, they can not expect to profit from buying or selling securities if the DPM market liquidates in the current state.

A trader wagering on the correct outcome is guaranteed non-negative profit in DPM, because p_i is always less than or equal to κ and o_i is always greater than or equal to κ. Setting $\kappa = 1$ yields a natural version where prices are less than or equal to 1 and payoffs are greater than or equal to 1. Because the price functions are not well-defined when $\boldsymbol{q} = \boldsymbol{0}$, the market maker needs to initialize the market with a non-zero quantity vector $\boldsymbol{q}^0$ (which may be arbitrarily small). Hence, the market maker's loss is at most $C(\boldsymbol{q}^0)$ whichever outcome is realized.

Compared with a parimutuel market, where traders are never worse off for waiting until the last minute to put their money in, the advantage of DPM is that it provides some incentive for informed traders to reveal their information earlier, because the price of a security increases (decreases) when more people buy (sell) the security. But it is not clear whether traders are better off by always and completely revealing their information as soon as they can.

2.3   Terminology

Truthful betting (TB) for a player in MSR and DPM is the strategy of immediately changing market probabilities to the player's probabilities. In other words, it is the strategy of always buying immediately when the price is too low and selling when the price is too high according the the player's information. *Bluffing* is the strategy of betting contrary to one's information in order to deceive future traders, with the intent of capitalizing on their resultant misinformed trading. *Strategic reticence* means withholding one's information; that is, delaying or abstaining from trading, or moving the market probabilities only partway toward one's actual beliefs. This paper investigates scenarios where traders with incomplete information have an incentive to deviate from truthful betting.[1]

3   LMSR with Conditionally Independent Signals

In this part, we start with simple 2-player 3-stage games and move toward the general finite-player finite-stage games to gradually capture the strategic behavior in LMSR when players have conditionally independent signals.

3.1   General Settings

$\Omega = \{Y, N\}$ is the state space of the world. The true state, $\omega \in \Omega$, is picked by nature according to a prior $p^0 = \langle p_Y^0, p_N^0 \rangle = \langle \Pr(\omega = Y), \Pr(\omega = N) \rangle$. The prior is common knowledge to all players. A market, aiming at predicting the true state ω, uses a LMSR market maker with initial probability estimate $r^0 = \langle r_Y^0, r_N^0 \rangle$.

Players are risk neutral. Each player gets a private signal, $c_i \in \mathbf{C_i}$, about the state of the world at the beginning of the market. $\mathbf{C_i}$ is the signal space of player i with $|\mathbf{C_i}| = n_i$. Players' signals are independent conditional on the state of the world. In other words, player i's signal c_i is independently drawn by nature according to conditional probability distributions,

$$\Pr(c_i = \mathbf{C_i}\{1\} \mid Y), \ \Pr(c_i = \mathbf{C_i}\{2\} \mid Y), \ ..., \ \Pr(c_i = \mathbf{C_i}\{n_i\} \mid Y) \qquad (5)$$

if the true state is Y, and analogously if the true state in N. $\mathbf{C_i}\{1\}$ to $\mathbf{C_i}\{n_i\}$ are elements of $\mathbf{C_i}$. The signal distributions are common knowledge to all players. Based on their private signals, players update their beliefs. Then players trade in one or more rounds of LMSR.

3.2   Who Wants to Play First?

We first consider a simple 2-player sequence selection game. Suppose that Alice and Bob are the only players in the market. Alice independently gets a signal $c_A \in \mathbf{C_A}$. Similarly, Bob independently gets a signal $c_B \in \mathbf{C_B}$. Let $|\mathbf{C_A}| = n_A$ and $|\mathbf{C_B}| = n_B$.

In the first stage, Alice chooses who—herself or Bob—plays first. The selected player then changes the market probabilities as they see fit in the second stage. In the third stage, the other player gets the chance to change the market probabilities. Then, the market closes and the true state is revealed.

---

[1] With complete information, traders should reveal all information right away in both MSR and DPM, because the market degenerates to a race to capitalize on the shared information first.

Lemma 1. *In a LMSR market, if stage t is player i's last chance to play and μ_i is player i's belief over actions of previous players, player i's best response at stage t is to play truthfully by changing the market probabilities to $r^t = \langle \Pr(Y|c_i, r^{t-1}, \mu_i), \Pr(N|c_i, r^{t-1}, \mu_i) \rangle$, where r^{t-1} is the market probability vector before player i's action.*

Proof. When a player has its last chance to play in LMSR, it is the same as the player interacting with a logarithmic scoring rule. Because the logarithmic scoring rule is strictly proper, player i's expected utility is maximized by truthfully reporting its posterior probability estimate given the information it has. □

Lemma 2. *When players have conditionally independent signals, if player i knows player j's posterior probabilities $\langle \Pr(Y|c_j), \Pr(N|c_j) \rangle$, player i can infer the posterior probabilities conditionally on both signals. More specifically,*

$$\Pr(\omega|c_i, c_j) = \frac{\Pr(c_i|\omega)\Pr(\omega|c_j)}{\Pr(c_i|Y)\Pr(Y|c_j) + \Pr(c_i|N)\Pr(N|c_j)},$$

where $\omega \in \{Y, N\}$.

Lemma 2 is proved using Bayes rule. According to it, with conditionally independent signals, a player can make use of another player's information when knowing its posteriors, even if not knowing its signal distribution.

Let r be the posteriors of player j that player i observes. For simplicity, let $\mathbf{C_j}\{r\}$ be a fictitious signal that satisfies $\langle \Pr(Y|\mathbf{C_j}\{r\}), \Pr(N|\mathbf{C_j}\{r\}) \rangle = r$. $\mathbf{C_j}\{r\}$ does not necessarily belong to player j's signal space $\mathbf{C_j}$. When r is the true posteriors of player j, $\langle \Pr(Y|c_i, \mathbf{C_j}\{r\}), \Pr(N|c_i, \mathbf{C_j}\{r\}) \rangle$ is the same as $\langle \Pr(Y|c_i, c_j), \Pr(N|c_i, c_j) \rangle$. The following theorem gives a PBE of the sequence selection game.

Theorem 1. *When Alice and Bob have conditionally independent signals in LMSR, a PBE of the sequence selection game is a strategy-belief pair with strategies of (σ_A, σ_B) and belief μ_B, where*

- *Alice's strategy σ_A is (select herself to be the first player in the first stage, change the market probability to $\langle \Pr(Y|c_A), \Pr(N|c_A) \rangle$ in the second stage);*
- *Bob's strategy σ_B is (take current market prices r as Alice's posteriors and change the market probability to $\langle \Pr(Y|\mathbf{C_A}\{r\}, c_B), \Pr(N|\mathbf{C_A}\{r\}, c_B) \rangle$ when it's his turn to play);*
- *Bob's belief μ_B is that $\Pr$(in the second stage Alice changes market probabilities to $\langle \Pr(Y|c_A), \Pr(N|c_A) \rangle$)=1.*

Sketch of Proof: Let EU_A^I be Alice's expected utility conditional on her signal when she selects herself as the first player and EU_A^{II} be Alice's expected utility conditional on her signal when she selects Bob as the first player. The proof reduces $EU_A^I - EU_A^{II}$ to the Kullback-Leibler divergence (also called relative entropy or information divergence) [28] of two distributions, which is always non-negative.

3.3   The Alice-Bob-Alice Game

We now consider a 3-stage Alice-Bob-Alice game, where Alice plays in the first and third stages and Bob plays in the second stage. Alice may change the market probabilities however she wants in the first stage. Observing Alice's action, Bob may change the probabilities in the second stage. Alice can take another action in the third stage. Then, the market closes and the true state is revealed. We study the PBE of the game when Alice and Bob have conditionally independent signals.

Let $r^1 = \langle r_Y^1, r_N^1 \rangle$ be the market probabilities that Alice changes to in the first stage. Lemma 3 characterizes the equilibrium strategy of Alice in the third stage. Theorem 2 describes a PBE of the Alice-Bob-Alice game.

Lemma 3. *In a 3-stage Alice-Bob-Alice game in LMSR with conditionally independent signals, at a PBE Alice changes the market probabilities to $r^3 = \langle r_Y^3, r_N^3 \rangle = \langle \Pr(Y|\mathbf{C_A}\{k\}, \mathbf{C_B}\{l\}), \Pr(N|\mathbf{C_A}\{k\}, \mathbf{C_B}\{l\}) \rangle$ in the third stage, when Alice has signal $\mathbf{C_A}\{k\}$ and Bob has signal $\mathbf{C_B}\{l\}$.*

Theorem 2. *When Alice and Bob have conditionally independent signals in LMSR, a PBE of the 3-stage Alice-Bob-Alice game is a strategy-belief pair with strategies (σ_A, σ_B) and beliefs (μ_A, μ_B) where*

- *Alice's strategy σ_A is (change market probabilities to $r^1 = \langle \Pr(Y|c_A), \Pr(N|c_A) \rangle$ in the first stage, do nothing in the third stage);*
- *Bob's strategy σ_B is (take r^1 as Alice's posteriors and change market probabilities to $r^2 = \langle \Pr(Y|\mathbf{C_A}\{r^1\}, c_B), \Pr(N|\mathbf{C_A}\{r^1\}, c_B) \rangle$ in the second stage);*
- *Bob's belief of Alice's action in the first stage, μ_B, is (Pr(Alice changes market probabilities to $r^1 = \langle \Pr(Y|c_A), \Pr(N|c_A) \rangle$ in the first stage) = 1);*
- *Alice's belief of Bob's action in the second stage, μ_A, is (Pr(Bob changes market probabilities to $r^2 = \langle \Pr(Y|\mathbf{C_A}\{r^1\}, c_B), \Pr(N|\mathbf{C_A}\{r^1\}, c_B) \rangle$ in the second stage) = 1);*

Theorem 2 states that at a PBE of the Alice-Bob-Alice game, Alice truthfully reports her posterior probabilities in the first stage, Bob believes that Alice is truthful and reports his posterior probabilities based on both Alice's report and his private signal in the second stage, and Alice believes that Bob is truthful and does nothing in the third stage because all information has been revealed in the second stage. It's clear that Bob never wants to deviate from being truthful by Lemma 1. To prove that Alice does not want to deviate from being truthful either, we show that deviating is equivalent to selecting herself as the second player in a sequence selection game, while being truthful is equivalent to selecting herself as the first player in the sequence selection game. Alice is worse off by deviating.

3.4   Finite-Player Finite-Stage Game

We extend our results for the Alice-Bob-Alice game to games with a finite number of players and finite stages in LMSR. Each player can change the market probabilities multiple times and all changes happen in sequence.

Theorem 3. *In the finite-player, finite-stage game with LMSR, if players have conditionally independent signals, a PBE of the game is a strategy-belief pair where each player reports their posterior probabilities in their first stage of play and all players believe that other players are truthful.*

Proof. Given that every player believes that all players before it act truthfully, we prove the theorem recursively. If it's player i's last chance to play, it will truthfully report its posterior probabilities by Lemma 1. If it's player i's second to last chance to play, there are other players standing in between its second to last chance to play and its last chance to play. We can combine the signals of those players standing in between as one signal and treat those players as one composite player. Because signals are conditionally independent, the signal of the composite player is conditionally independent of the signal of player i. The game becomes an Alice-Bob-Alice game for player i and at the unique PBE player i reports truthfully at its second to last chance to play according to Theorem 2. Inferring recursively, any player should report truthfully at its first chance to play. □

4   LMSR with Conditionally Dependent Signals

We now introduce a simple model of conditionally dependent signals and show that bluffing can be an equilibrium. In our model, Alice and Bob each see an independent coin flip and then participate in an LMSR prediction market with outcomes corresponding to whether or not both coins came up heads. Thus $\omega \in \{HH, (HT|TH|TT)\}$. We again consider an Alice-Bob-Alice game structure.

Theorem 4. *In the Alice-Bob-Alice LMSR coin-flipping game, where the probability of heads is p, truthful betting (TB) is not a PBE. Now restrict Alice's first round strategies to either play TB or as if her coin is heads ($\hat{H}$). A PBE in this game has Alice play TB with probability $1 + \dfrac{p}{\left(1-(1-p)^{-1/p}\right)(1-p)}$, and otherwise play $\hat{H}$.*

Proof. TB cannot be an equilibrium because if Bob trusted Alice's move in the first round then her best response would be to pretend to have heads when she has tails. By doing so Bob would, when he has heads, move the probability of HH to 1. Alice would then move the probability to 0 in the last round and collect an infinite payout.

To show that bluffing is a PBE in the restricted game, we show that Bob's best response makes Alice indifferent between her pure strategies. Bob's best response is, if he has heads, to set the probability of HH to the probability that Alice has heads given that she plays $\hat{H}$, or $\Pr(HH \mid \hat{H}H)$. If Bob has tails he sets the probability of HH to zero. Assuming such a strategy for Bob, we can compute Alice's expected utility for playing TB and $\hat{H}$. It turns out that Alice's expected utility is the same whether she plays TB or $\hat{H}$. Thus in a PBE Alice should, with probability $\dfrac{p}{\left(1-(1-p)^{-1/p}\right)(1-p)}$, pretend to have seen heads regardless of her actual information. □

Note that conditional dependence of signals is not a sufficient condition for bluffing in LMSR. Taking an extreme example, suppose that Alice and Bob again predict whether or not two coins both come up heads. Alice observes the result of one coin flip, but Bob with probability $1/2$ observes the *same* coin flip as Alice and otherwise observes nothing. Then Alice will want to play truthfully and completely reveal her information in the first stage.

5   Withholding Information in DPM

Suppose Alice has the opportunity to trade in a two-outcome DPM with initial shares $q^0 = \langle 1, 1 \rangle$ for outcomes $\{Y, N\}$. According to equation (2), the initial market prices for the two outcomes are $\langle p_Y^0, p_N^0 \rangle = \langle \kappa/\sqrt{2}, \kappa/\sqrt{2} \rangle$. The initial market probabilities, according to equation (4), are $\langle \pi_Y^0, \pi_N^0 \rangle = \langle 1/2, 1/2 \rangle$.

Let p be Alice's posterior probability of outcome Y given her private information. If there are no other participants and $p > 1/2$ then Alice should buy shares in outcome Y until the market probability π_Y reaches p. Thus, Alice's best strategy is to change market probabilities to $\langle p, 1 - p \rangle$ when $p > 1/2$.

We now show that if Alice anticipates that a sufficiently better-informed player will bet *after* her, then she will not fully reveal her information.

Theorem 5. *Alice, believing that outcome Y will occur with probability $p > 1/2$, plays in a two-outcome DPM seeded with initial quantities $\langle 1, 1 \rangle$. If a perfectly-informed Oracle plays after her, Alice will move the market probability of outcome Y to $\max(p^2, 1/2)$.*

Proof. Alice's expected utility is:

$$\kappa \left(px \frac{\sqrt{(1+x+g)^2 + 1}}{1+x+g} - \left(\sqrt{(1+x)^2 + 1} - \sqrt{2} \right) \right). \tag{6}$$

where x and g are the quantities of shares of Y purchased by Alice and the Oracle, respectively. Without loss of generality, suppose the true outcome is Y. Since the Oracle knows the outcome with certainty, we take the limit of (6) as g approaches infinity, yielding: $\kappa(px - \sqrt{(1+x)^2 + 1} + \sqrt{2})$. We find the maximum using the first-order condition. This yields a function of p giving the optimal number of shares for Alice to purchase, $x^* = \max(0, \frac{p}{\sqrt{1-p^2}} - 1)$, which is greater than zero only when $p > 1/\sqrt{2} \approx 0.707$. The new numbers of shares are $q = \langle x^* + 1, 1 \rangle$, yielding the market probability of outcome Y equal to $\max(p^2, 1/2)$.   □

By assuming that the second player is perfectly informed, we mimic the scenario where a prediction market closes after the true outcome is revealed.

6   Conclusion

We have investigated the strategic behavior of traders in the MSR and DPM prediction markets using dynamic games. Specifically, we examine different scenarios where traders at equilibrium bet truthfully, bluff, or strategically delay.

Two different information structures, conditional independence and conditional dependence of signals, are considered for LMSR with incomplete information. We show that traders with conditionally independent signals may be worse off by either delaying trading or bluffing in LMSR. Moreover, truthful betting is a PBE strategy for all traders in LMSR with finite traders and finite periods. On the other hand, when the signals of traders are conditionally dependent there may exist probability distributions on signals such that truthful betting is not an equilibrium strategy; traders have an incentive to strategically mislead other traders with the intent of correcting the errors made by others in a later period; such bluffing can be a PBE strategy. DPM with incomplete information is shown to face another problem: traders may have an incentive to completely or partially withhold their private information if they anticipate sufficiently better-informed traders in later periods.

References

1. Fama, E.F.: Efficient capital market: A review of theory and empirical work. Journal of Finance 25, 383–417 (1970)
2. Forsythe, R., Nelson, F., Neumann, G.R., Wright, J.: Anatomy of an experimental political stock market. American Economic Review 82(5), 1142–1161 (1992)
3. Forsythe, R., Rietz, T.A., Ross, T.W.: Wishes, expectations, and actions: A survey on price formation in election stock markets. Journal of Economic Behavior and Organization 39, 83–110 (1999)
4. Oliven, K., Rietz, T.A.: Suckers are born, but markets are made: Individual rationality, arbitrage and market efficiency on an electronic futures market. Management Science 50(3), 336–351 (2004)
5. Berg, J.E., Forsythe, R., Nelson, F.D., Rietz, T.A.: Results from a dozen years of election futures markets research. In: Plott, C.A., Smith, V. (eds.) Handbook of Experimental Economic Results (forthcoming) (2001)
6. Berg, J.E., Rietz, T.A.: Prediction markets as decision support systems. Information Systems Frontier 5, 79–93 (2003)
7. Gandar, J.M., Dare, W.H., Brown, C.R., Zuber, R.A.: Informed traders and price variations in the betting market for professional basketball games. Journal of Finance LIII(1), 385–401 (1999)
8. Thaler, R.H., Ziemba, W.T.: Anomalies: Parimutuel betting markets: Racetracks and lotteries. Journal of Economic Perspectives 2(2), 161–174 (1988)
9. Debnath, S., Pennock, D.M., Giles, C.L., Lawrence, S.: Information incorporation in online in-game sports betting markets. In: Proceedings of the Fourth Annual ACM Conference on Electronic Commerce (EC 2003), San Diego, CA (2003)
10. Chen, K.Y., Plott, C.R.: Information aggregation mechanisms: Concept, design and implementation for a sales forecasting problem. Working paper No. 1131, California Institute of Technology, Division of the Humanities and Social Sciences (2002)
11. Milgrom, P., Stokey, N.L.: Information, trade and common knowledge. Journal of Economic Theory 26(1), 17–27 (1982)
12. Kyle, A.S.: Continuous auctions and insider trading. Econometrica 53(6), 1315–1336 (1985)
13. Chakraborty, A., Yilmaz, B.: Manipulation in market order models. Journal of Financial Markets 7(2), 187–206 (2004)

14. Hanson, R.D.: Combinatorial information market design. Information Systems Frontiers 5(1), 107–119 (2003)
15. Hanson, R.D.: Logarithmic market scoring rules for modular combinatorial information aggregation. Journal of Prediction Markets 1(1), 1–15 (2007)
16. Pennock, D.M.: A dynamic pari-mutuel market for hedging, wagering, and information aggregation. In: Proceedings of the Fifth ACM Conference on Electronic Commerce (EC 2004), ACM Press, New York (2004)
17. Mangold, B., Dooley, M., Dornfest, R., Flake, G.W., Hoffman, H., Kasturi, T., Pennock, D.M.: The tech buzz game. IEEE Computer 38(7), 94–97 (2005)
18. Mas-Colell, A., Whinston, M.D., Green, J.R.: Microeconomics Theory. Oxford University Press, New York (1995)
19. Allen, F., Gale, D.: Stock-price manipulation. The Review of Financial Studies 5, 503–529 (1992)
20. Kumar, P., Seppi, D.J.: Futures manipulation with cash settlement. Journal of Finance 47, 1485–1502 (1992)
21. Hansen, J., Schmidt, C., Strobel, M.: Manipulation in political stock markets - preconditions and evidence. Technical Report (2001)
22. Camerer, C.F.: Can asset markets be manipulated? A field experiment with race-track betting. Journal of Political Economy 106, 457–482 (1998)
23. Hanson, R.D., Oprea, R., Porter, D.: Information aggregation and manipulation in an experimental market. Journal of Economic Behavior and Organization 60(4), 449–459 (2007)
24. Rhode, P.W., Strumpf, K.S.: Historical presidential betting markets. Journal of Economic Perspectives 18(2), 127–142 (2004)
25. Rhode, P.W., Strumpf, K.S.: Manipulating political stock markets: A field experiment and a century of observational data. Working Paper (2007)
26. Dimitrov, S., Sami, R.: Non-myopic strategies in prediction markets. In: The Second Workshop on Prediction Markets, San Diego, CA (2007)
27. Chen, Y., Pennock, D.M.: A utility framework for bounded-loss market makers. In: Proceedings of the 23rd Conference on Uncertainty in Artificial Intelligence (UAI 2007), Vancouver, BC Canada, pp. 49–56 (2007)
28. Cover, T.M., Thomas, J.A.: Elements of Information Theory. John Wiley & Sons, Inc, West Sussex, England (1991)

Pari-Mutuel Markets: Mechanisms and Performance

Mark Peters[1], Anthony Man-Cho So[2], and Yinyu Ye[1]

[1] Stanford University, Stanford, CA
[2] Chinese University of Hong Kong, Hong Kong

Abstract. Recently, there has been an increase in the usage of centrally managed markets which are run by some form of pari-mutuel mechanism. A pari-mutuel mechanism is characterized by the ability to shield the market organizer from financial risk by paying the winners from the stakes of the losers. The recent introduction of new, modified pari-mutuel methods has spurred the growth of prediction markets as well as new financial derivative markets. Coinciding with this increased usage, there has been much work on the research front which has produced several mechanisms and a slew of interesting results. We will introduce a new pari-mutuel market-maker mechanism with many positive qualities including convexity, truthfulness and strong performance. Additionally, we will provide the first quantitative performance comparison of some of the existing pari-mutuel market-maker mechanisms.

1 Introduction

While pari-mutuel systems have long been one of the most popular means of organizing markets, recent innovations have created more applications for pari-mutuel market-making techniques. Lately, there has been a substantial increase in the number of markets being conducted by means of pari-mutuel techniques. It appears that this growth has been driven by the introduction of novel, non-standard pari-mutuel mechanisms that more easily facilitate the launch of a new market. While the mechanisms employed vary from market to market, they share the common bond of utilizing the pari-mutuel principle of paying the winners from the stakes collected from the losers.

The standard pari-mutuel market was developed in 1864 and is operated in a manner where market traders purchase shares for a specific possible outcome. When the outcome is determined, the money collected is paid out to the winners in proportion to the number of winning shares that they hold. This technique protects the market organizer from sustaining a loss under any circumstance. Some of the earliest work in the development of modified pari-mutuel techniques was done by Bossaerts et al. [2] where the authors study a continuous double auction where a thin market exists and the prices do not reach an equilibrium. They solved a contingent claim call auction market with a linear programming formulation that maintains the pari-mutuel property of paying the winners with the stakes of the losers.

Prediction Markets. Prediction markets are defined as speculative markets whose purpose is to create predictions for the outcome of a particular event. An important event in the growth of prediction markets was the development of the Logarithmic Market

X. Deng and F.C. Graham (Eds.): WINE 2007, LNCS 4858, pp. 82–95, 2007.

Scoring Rule (LMSR) by Hanson [6]. We will describe the mechanics of the LMSR in section 3 but one key point is that this mechanism serves as an automated market-maker. The market-maker will calculate and post prices for all possible states. This allows the market organizer to immediately post prices for all states - rather than waiting for traders to post orders as in a continuous double auction. While this mechanism is generally pari-mutuel (except for a controllable amount of seed money that the organizer must provide), it differs in an important manner from the standard pari-mutuel market. The value of a winning order is fixed in Hanson's mechanism.

In 2006, Pennock et al. [11] built upon some previous work to introduce another mechanism called the share-ratio Dynamic Pari-mutuel Market-Maker (DPM). Their mechanism also operates as an automated market-maker with controlled risk to the market organizer. Powered by these research innovations, many new prediction markets have been introduced in recent years. The Yahoo! Tech Buzz Game uses the DPM mechanism to set prices. Hanson's LMSR is being employed by many online prediction markets including the TheWSX and InklingMarkets.

Financial Markets. In 2002, Goldman Sachs and Deutsche Bank teamed up to create a market for their clients allowing them to trade claims over the potential values of economic indicators which would be announced in the future (Cass [3]). The technology for these markets is based on a call auction mechanism designed by a firm named Longitude (described in Baron and Lange [1] and Lange and Economides [7]). Since the market is conducted as a call auction, the organizer will collect all orders then close the market and determine which orders to accept and which to reject. The organizer has the advantage of seeing all the orders before needing to make commitments to accept any order. Therefore, the mechanism of Longitude is formulated as an optimization problem which the market organizer must solve. Constraints are used to ensure that the mechanism remains pari-mutuel. Fortnow et al. [4] have a linear programming formulation for this contingent claim call auction but it does not generate unique state prices. The mechanism developed by Bossaerts et al. [2] also addresses this auction but needs to be solved in multiple steps and also does not generate unique state prices. However, the call auction mechanism has one key disadvantage: the traders are not sure about the acceptance of their order until after the market is closed. Thus, if their order is rejected, there is no market to resubmit a modified order.

Let's pause to consider one key distinction between the mechanisms that we have discussed above. While these mechanisms are designed to be implemented in one of two different manners, we will show that it is possible to easily change the manner of implementation of these mechanisms. The mechanisms developed by Hanson and Pennock are designed to be implemented as posted price automated market-makers. On the other hand, the mechanism of Longitude must be implemented as a call auction. A fundamental difference in the posted price versus auction implementation is that the onus is placed on the trader to reveal a price for his order in the auction setting. Despite this difference, the posted price mechanisms can be implemented as an auction.

In Section 2, we will introduce a new mechanism which leverages the auction technology but is applied in a dynamic setting where the market organizer will make immediate, binding decisions about orders. A truthfulness property of the optimal bidding strategy in this auction setting will allow us to conduct a direct comparison with the posted price mechanisms. In Section 3, we will present an overview of the mechanisms developed by Hanson and Pennock plus some simulation results where we compare these mechanisms to the SCPM. We conclude with a discussion in Section 4.

2 The Sequential Convex Pari-Mutuel Mechanism (SCPM)

The development of the SCPM followed directly from earlier work of the authors (Peters et al. [12]). In this section, we will examine the predecessor of the SCPM and describe the modifications used to create the SCPM. Longitude had previously developed a mechanism named the Pari-mutuel Derivative Call Auction (PDCA). See Lange and Economides [7] for details of the PDCA. The PDCA has a number of desirable characteristics but is formulated as a non–convex program. Thus, a special solver is required to find global solutions. We have developed an alternative convex call auction mechanism which maintains all the positive characteristics of the PDCA. First, let's describe in detail the format of the market before explaining the details of the market-making mechanisms.

The primary motivation of these market-making mechanisms is to help generate liquidity in small or new markets without needing to expose the market organizer to financial risk. As shown by Bossaerts et al. [2], a call auction which receives limit orders can avoid some of the thin market problems suffered by a continuous double auction and help the market achieve substantially better liquidity. This approach allows the organizer to see the full set of orders before determining acceptances while the limit provisions allow the traders to express the bounds of their willingness to pay for claims.

Table 1. Notations Used in this Paper

Variable	Name	Description
$a_{i,j}$	State Order	Trader j's order on state i
q_j	Limit Quantity	Trader j's maximum number of orders requested
π_j	Limit Price	Trader j's maximum price for order
p_i	Price	Organizer's price level for state i
x_j	Order Fill	Number of trader j's orders accepted

Now, consider a market with one organizer and n traders. There are S states of the world in the future on which the market traders are submitting orders for contingent claims. For each order that is accepted by the organizer and contains the realized future state, the organizer will pay the trader some fixed amount of money w, which, without loss of generality, equals 1 in this paper. One caveat here is that one of the models which we will describe later in this paper, the Dynamic Pari-mutuel Market-Maker, does not pay a fixed amount to winners. The traders will submit orders to the organizer which specify the states which they want contingent claims over, the price at which they are willing to pay for the order, and the number of identical orders that they will buy. After all orders are submitted, the market is closed and the organizer will then decide whether to accept or reject each order. If the order is accepted, the organizer also decides the number of orders to accept and the price per order to be collected from the trader. As the reader might imagine, a wide range of markets from results of sporting events to elections can be organized in this manner. The challenge is to develop a mechanism for accepting and rejecting orders that doesn't expose the organizer to risk.

Throughout the analysis, we will use the notations in Table 1. The traders will supply the values of $a_{i,j}$, q_j and π_j for all i, j, which are denoted by the matrix A and vectors q and π. Thus, these data are considered given for the models. The market organizer will need to determine the decision variables p_i and x_j for all i, j.

2.1 Convex Pari-Mutuel Call Auction Mechanism (CPCAM)

In previous work [12], we have developed an alternative formulation of the PDCA which has similar constraints but is also a convex program. The primary constraints are to ensure that the market is self–funding and that the quantities granted to each trader are consistent based on the relationship of their limit price and the calculated state price of the order. Furthermore, it is valuable that the model has a unique optimum. Below is our alternative pari-mutuel formulation, again, with $w = 1$ where w is the value of the fixed payoff:

$$\begin{aligned}
\text{maximize} \quad & \pi^T x - M + \sum_i \theta_i \log(s_i) \\
\text{subject to} \quad & \sum_j a_{i,j} x_j + s_i = M \qquad \text{for } 1 \leq i \leq S \\
& 0 \leq x \leq q, \ s \geq 0
\end{aligned} \qquad (1)$$

In this formulation, θ represents a starting order needed to guarantee uniqueness of the state prices in the solution. The starting orders are not decision variables — in effect, the market organizer is seeding the market with this order. In some outcomes, the market organizer could actually lose some of this seed money. The objective function in this formulation has the following interpretation. The term $\pi^T x - M$ is the profit to the market organizer. On the other hand, the term $\sum_i \theta_i \log(s_i) = \sum_i \theta_i \log\left(M - \sum_j a_{i,j} x_j\right)$ can be viewed as a disutility function (or weighted logarithmic penalty function) for the market organizer that ensures she will find an allocation of accepted orders that is pari-mutuel. In our model, prices (p) are derived from the solution to the KKT conditions of the optimization model. They turn out to be the dual variables corresponding to the self-funding constraints. The KKT conditions also include the requirement that $\sum_i p_i = 1$.

Previous Results. It turns out that the CPCAM can be shown to have many valuable characteristics. In particular, our model yields the first fully polynomial–time approximation scheme (FPTAS) to the contingent claim call auction with unique prices problem. In prior work, we have established the following properties (see Peters et al. [12] for proofs):

- The CPCAM is a convex program that can be solved (up to any prescribed accuracy) in polynomial time using standard techniques.
- The market will be self-funding (other than the required starting orders).
- The optimal solution (x^*, p^*) from the CPCAM model would also be optimal if we replaced π_j with $(p^*)^T a_j$ in the objective function. Furthermore, the solution will remain optimal if we replace π_j with any c_j where $(p^*)^T a_j \leq c_j \leq \pi_j$.

- The state price vector p^* for any optimal solution to the CPCAM model is unique.
- As $\mu \searrow 0$, the solutions $p(\mu\theta)$ converge to the unique limit points $p(0) = p_\theta^*$.
- The set of feasible solutions of the PDCA model coincides with the set of optimal solutions of the CPCAM model (1) and they produce the identical state price vector. Furthermore, the PDCA model can be solved as a linear program after obtaining the state price vector p^*.

2.2   Sequential Convex Pari-Mutuel Mechanism (SCPM)

While the CPCAM possesses many powerful properties, the fact that it must be implemented in a call auction setting is limiting. Two fundamental drawbacks exist. First, market traders do not know whether their order is accepted until the conclusion of the auction. At this point, the market is closed and there is no longer a central platform with which traders can submit a new order. In many situations, they would prefer to have an immediate decision. Second, there is no ability for market traders to lock-in gains by trading accepted orders while the market is still open. This trading is important as it allows traders to hedge positions if there is a swing in the state prices.

Thus, we would like to utilize some of the powerful properties of the CPCAM but change the format of order placement from a call auction setting. We have developed a simple modification to the mechanism that allows us to run the mechanism each time a new order is received by the market organizer. We call this new mechanism the Sequential Convex Pari-mutuel Mechanism (SCPM). Essentially, we run a slightly modified version of the CPCAM where, after receiving each order, we add a constraint to the model to lock in optimal order fills from the previous solution of the model. Thus, when the first order is received, we just run the CPCAM as normal. Next, when the second order is received, we run the CPCAM but we add the constraint that the first order must be filled to the level dictated when we solved the model for only the first order. This process continues with new constraints added after each new order is processed.

Thus, the market organizer can immediately tell the trader whether or not his order was accepted. When the nth order is received, we can formulate the SCPM as follows:

$$
\begin{aligned}
\text{maximize} \quad & \pi^T x - M + \sum_i \theta_i \log(s_i) \\
\text{subject to} \quad & \sum_j a_{i,j} x_j + s_i = M && \text{for } 1 \leq i \leq S \\
& x_j = l_j && \text{for } 1 \leq j \leq n - 1 \qquad (2) \\
& 0 \leq x_n \leq q_n \\
& s \geq 0
\end{aligned}
$$

This model will determine the amount of the nth order that should be filled. Here, l_j represents the order quantities found from previous solutions of the model. The SCPM will produce state prices which can be used to charge the nth trader for his order.

Properties of the SCPM. Fortunately, the SCPM will preserve many of the positive properties of the CPCAM. First, the market organizer's risk will be bounded by the the starting orders. The maximum possible loss by the market organizer will never exceed $\left(\max_G \sum_{i \in G} \theta_i\right)$ where G represents a set of $S - 1$ states. It may be necessary to increase the magnitudes of each θ_i in comparison to the call auction setting since the dynamic setting will be more reliant on the seed money until a sufficient number of orders have been accepted.

In the CPCAM, the state prices would satisfy price consistency constraints for all orders whereby an order will only be accepted if its limit price is greater than or equal to the sum of p_i for all states included in the order. In the SCPM, we will find state prices but they will only satisfy price consistency for the current order. Thus, the prices are less useful in terms of providing information about all orders received previously. However, the current trader can be sure that his order will be accepted or rejected according to price consistency constraints based on the current price. The SCPM will also provide traders a certain payoff amount if one of their states is realized. The market organizer will pay each winning order a fixed amount w. Furthermore, the SCPM is easy to implement. As each order is received, we will be solving a slightly larger convex problem.

Truthfulness

In the call auction context, it is difficult to determine the optimal bidding strategy for the traders when the CPCAM is employed. However, the situation is different when we move to a sequential setting where the SCPM is implemented.

Theorem 1. *When the SCPM is operated in the purely pari-mutuel manner (in which traders are charged the calculated state price of their accepted orders), the optimal bidding strategy for traders in the SCPM is to bid their true valuations.*

Proof. Let's assume that trader j arrives at the market and seeks to submit an order. The states covered by this order can be represented by the vector a. We will assume that trader j seeks one order (so, his limit quantity is one). Finally, the trader j has a private valuation for his order of v_j. If the order is accepted, the trader will earn some surplus $(s = v_j - p)$ where p is the charged price of the order. We will assume that the trader has a utility function, $u(s)$, which is monotone non-decreasing in surplus.

If the trader decides not to bid his true valuation, let's inspect his possible alternative bidding strategies and check for optimality. There are two cases that we must evaluate: bidding less than his valuation and bidding more than his valuation. Remaining consistent with previous notation, we will use $\pi_j = v_j$ to represent the limit price of his truthful bid. Whenever the SCPM is solved for the new order, the model will calculate new state prices. From these prices p, we can obtain a calculated state price $p^T a$. This is the price that the trader will be charged if his order is accepted. Now, let's examine the two cases of bidding strategies.

Case 1 (Bidding less than his valuation): Let π'_j be the new limit price for the trader. We know that $\pi'_j < v_j$. When a truthful bid would be rejected since it is lower than the calculated order price, then the bid of π'_j will obviously also be rejected since $\pi'_j < \pi_j$. This outcome is equivalent in terms of surplus to the outcome in the truthful bidding strategy. Next, when the truthful bid would have been partially accepted when $p^T a = v_j$, the bid of π'_j would be rejected since $\pi'_j < v_j$. Finally, in the case where the truthful bid was fully accepted, we have two outcomes. The bid of π'_j could also be fully accepted. In that case, the trader will be charged $p^T a$ for his order and will have some positive surplus for the accepted order since $(v_j - p^T a)$ is positive. This is an identical outcome to the truthful bid case. However, there is a chance that $\pi'_j < p^T a < v_j$. In this case, the order will be rejected and the trader will receive no positive surplus. If he had bid truthfully, he would have had his order fully accepted and received positive surplus.

Thus, we can see that bidding truthfully weakly dominates bidding less than v_j.

Case 2 (Bidding more than his valuation): Next assume that the bid is π''_j where $\pi''_j > v_j$. When a truthful bid would be rejected since it is lower than the calculated order price, then we have two possibilities. The bid of π''_j could also be rejected if $\pi''_j < p^T a$. However, the bid could be accepted (partially or fully) if $\pi''_j \geq p^T a$. This is a bad outcome for the trader because there is a chance that $p^T a > v_j$. In this case, he actually receives negative surplus since the net value of the accepted order will be $z(v_j - p^T a)$ where z is the order fill amount. This quantity will be negative. If he had bid truthfully, the order would have been rejected. If $v_j > p^T a$, then he will earn positive surplus of $(v_j - p^T a)$ but he would have received this if he had bid truthfully. Thus, the trader can only do worse by bidding more than his valuation in this instance. In the case where the truthful bid is partially accepted, the bid of π''_j will be fully accepted. However, no positive surplus will be earned since $v_j = p^T a$. This is an equivalent outcome to bidding truthfully. In the case where the truthful bid is fully accepted, the bid of π''_j will clearly be fully accepted. However, the utility earned will be equivalent since in both cases, the trader will be charged $p^T a$.

So, bidding truthfully also weakly dominates bidding more than v_j. Therefore, we have shown that truthful bidding is the dominant strategy when the purely pari-mutuel version of the SCPM is implemented. Q.E.D.

Thus, the mechanism is truthful in a myopic sense since we are only considering the optimal bid for the current order of the trader. It should be noted that it is easy to construct an example where the the optimal bid is not truthful when the market organizer charges the trader his limit price instead of the calculated pari-mutuel price.

3   Performance Comparison

As we mentioned earlier, the SCPM can actually be designed to operate as a posted price market-maker. This involves some simple additional solves of the model by the market organizer to calculate the required prices for orders to be accepted. This flexibility allows us to apply the mechanism to any market which is operated by a market-maker who posts prices. In this section, we will compare the performance of the SCPM against two of the more interesting pari-mutuel posted price mechanisms: the Logarithmic Market Scoring Rule (LMSR) of Hanson [6] and the Dynamic Pari-mutuel Market-Maker (DPM) of Pennock et al. [11]. Two key properties that these mechanisms share are: 1) they allow the risk to the market organizer to be bounded and 2) they are based on pricing functions which allow the market to be priced up immediately. Both of these mechanisms are exceptionally easy to implement and are currently being used to operate various online prediction markets. We believe that our work is the first performance comparison testing that has been conducted amongst these mechanisms. Our initial results indicate that the optimal choice of mechanism depends on the objectives of the market organizer. Before we discuss results, we will quickly describe how these pari-mutuel mechanisms operate.

Logarithmic Market Scoring Rule (Hanson)

Hanson uses a market built on market scoring rules which avoid both thin and thick market problems. In particular, Hanson introduces a logarithmic market scoring rule in his work and we will focus on this rule. His market is organized as a market of contingent claims where claims are of the form "Pays $ 1 if the state is i". Pennock [10] has computed cost and pricing functions for Hanson's logarithmic market scoring rule mechanism. These cost and pricing functions allow the mechanism to be implemented as an automated market-maker where orders will be accepted or rejected based on these functions. Let's assume that there are S states over which contingent claims are traded. We will use the vector $q \in \mathbb{R}^S$ to represent the number of claims on each state that have already been accepted by the market organizer. The total cost of all the orders already accepted is calculated via the cost function $C(q)$. Now, let a new trader arrive and submit an order characterized by the vector $r \in \mathbb{R}^S$ where r_i reflects the number of claims over state i that the trader desires. The market organizer will charge the new trader $C(q + r) - C(q)$ for his order. The pricing function is simply the derivative of the cost function with respect to one of the states. It represents the instantaneous price for an order over one state.

Here are the cost and pricing functions for the Logarithmic Market Scoring Rule.

$$C(q) = b \log \left(\sum_j e^{q_j/b} \right) \text{ and } p_i(q) = \frac{e^{q_i/b}}{\sum_j e^{q_j/b}}$$

In this formulation, b is a parameter that must be chosen by the market organizer. It represents the risk that the organizer is willing to accept. The greater the value of b, the more orders the organizer is likely to accept. It turns out that the maximum possible loss to the market organizer is $(b \log S)$.

Share-Ratio DPM (Pennock)

Pennock et al. [11] have introduced a new market mechanism which combines some of the advantages of a traditional pari-mutuel market and a continuous double auction run by a market-maker. In this market, each dollar buys a variable share of the eventual payoff. The share is defined by a pricing function and the amount paid would be the integral of the pricing function over the number of shares purchased. In Pennock [9], the author explores several implementations of this market mechanism. Recently Pennock and his coauthors have introduced a modification where a share-ratio pricing function is used. We will now define P_i to be the current payoff to each holder of a share of state i if i is the eventual outcome. The following two relationships are required in this mechanism: $\frac{p_i}{p_k} = \frac{q_i}{q_k}$ and $P_i = \frac{M}{q_i}$, where M is the total money collected so far. The first ratio forces the states with more accepted shares to be more expensive. The second ratio calculates the pari-mutuel payoff for each state. From these, they derive a cost function which is the total cost of purchasing a vector q of shares. Additionally, p_i will be the instantaneous change in the cost function with respect to q_i. Thus we have:

$$C(q) = \kappa \sqrt{\sum_j q_j^2} \text{ and } p_i = \frac{\kappa q_i}{\sqrt{\sum_j q_j^2}}$$

Again, the market organizer must determine κ as well as an initial allocation of shares q^0. The market organizer will charge the new trader $C(q + r) - C(q)$ for his order. The maximum loss possible for the market organizer is $\kappa \sqrt{\sum_j (q_j^0)^2}$

These two pari-mutuel mechanisms share many of the same characteristics with the SCPM - the key difference from a trader's standpoint being that the payoffs of the DPM are uncertain (although they are bounded below by κ).

3.1   Sample Data Analysis

In order to compare the three mechanisms, we created some random orders and compared how the mechanisms handled the orders. In this analysis, we generated 10 datasets with 500 orders in each. These orders are constructed in the standard format for orders to the SCPM. For the DPM and LMSR which are based on a posted price mechanism, we will assume that the limit price and states indicated by the order dictate the rate of payoff required by the trader. Thus, we will use the pricing functions from the DPM or LMSR to determine the maximum order fill acceptable to the trader.

There are three possible states for these orders. For each order, the state which is covered by the order is equally likely to be any one of the three states. If the order covers the first or second state, the price limit is a random variable distributed uniformly over the interval [0.2, 0.6]. Otherwise, the price limit will be a random variable distributed uniformly over the interval [0.1, 0.3]. The quantity limit for all orders is 1.

In order to have a more fair comparison of these mechanisms, we would like to standardize the risk that each mechanism places on the market organizer. We have followed the approach of standardizing the worst case outcome for the market organizer of each mechanism. In Table 2, we describe the parameter settings used in our data analysis.

Table 2. Standardizing risk

Mechanism	Maximum Loss Formula	Parameter Values	Maximum Loss
SCPM	$\left(\max_G \sum_{i \in G} \theta_i \right)$	$\theta_i = 1$	2
LMSR	$(b \log S)$	$b \approx 1.82$	2
DPM	$\kappa \sqrt{\sum_j q_j^2}$	$\kappa = 1$ and $q_i^0 = \frac{2}{\sqrt{3}}$	2

In the SCPM, the risk assumed by the market organizer is controlled by the values of θ_i. These θ_i represent starting orders for the market or seed money inserted by the market organizer. In the calculation of the maximum possible loss, G represents a set of $S - 1$ states. In Pennock's share-ratio DPM, the choice of $\kappa = 1$ will guarantee that all orders will have an eventual payoff of at least 1.

3.2   Results

There are some challenges when implementing the DPM so that its results can be appropriately compared to those of the SCPM and LMSR. The primary difference is that the payoff for a winning order in the DPM is not guaranteed to be a fixed amount. In our implementation, we assume that the eventual payoff of an order will be equivalent to its current payoff. This is a slightly aggressive assumption as the lower bound for an order's payoff will be κ which is 1 in our case. By making our slightly more aggressive assumption, there is the possibility that the payoff will be lower than the current payoff. We'll see later that this doesn't appear to be a serious problem for our datasets.

Another issue is that the shares in the DPM are not necessarily equivalent to shares in the LMSR or SCPM since the current payoff for a DPM share will often be greater than one. While a share in the LMSR or SCPM will pay 1 if the correct state is realized, a share in the DPM will pay some amount greater than or equal to 1. Thus, shares in the DPM are actually worth more. Our traders have limit quantities of 1 for all orders, so we want to require that they are only allocated shares whose best case outcome would be a payment of 1. To achieve this goal, we must do two things. First, we must only fill DPM orders so that $xP(x) \leq 1$ where x is the number of DPM shares allocated and $P(x)$ is the current payoff for those shares. Second, for our comparison purposes, we must convert the number of shares allocated in the DPM into a number of shares which would have a payoff of 1 per share. We will use these converted share numbers when we compare the mechanisms below.

For our comparison, we have examined three situations with different profit implications for the market organizer.

1. **Purely pari-mutuel** - All monies collected are redistributed to winners. The market organizer will earn no profit.
2. **Full charge** - Each trader is charged his full limit price. The pricing functions from the DPM and LMSR will still determine if an order is to be accepted. However, after the order fill quantity is determined, the trader will be charged his limit price times the number of shares accepted.
3. **Tax penalty** - Each order is taxed at a certain percent which will guarantee the organizer a profit percentage. In essence we will divide each share that is bought by a trader into two portions. One portion of the share will be retained by the trader. The other portion (equivalent in size to the required profit percentage) will be retained by the market organizer. This profit percentage must be specified a priori.

Table 3 displays the performance data from our simulations under these profit settings. From the table, we see that the SCPM actually performs worse than the other mechanisms in the purely parimutuel and full charge settings in terms of revenue collected and orders accepted. However, it does outperform the LMSR in the tax penalty setting (where the profit percentage is set to the profit percentage of the SCPM in the full charge setting). Since they both offer certain payoffs to winners, the LMSR and SCPM are the most comparable mechanisms. Adoption of the DPM requires the market traders to accept uncertain payoffs. Thus, the market organizer will need to determine the importance of certain payoffs and organizer profitability when selecting the most appropriate mechanisms for his market.

It's not clear why the LMSR outperforms the DPM in the purely pari-mutuel setting. One hypothesis for the improved LMSR performance in comparison to the DPM is that the LMSR has a less stable pricing function which may allow it to accept more orders. Later, we will explore why the prices of the DPM demonstrate more stability.

Table 3. Performance comparison under different profit settings

Mechanism	Revenue Collected	Orders Accepted	Worst Case Profit	Profit Percentage
Purely Parimutuel				
SCPM	73.3	201	NA	NA
LMSR	86.8	254	NA	NA
DPM	81.6	240	NA	NA
Full Charge				
SCPM	84.5	201	15.9	18.9%
LMSR	99.3	254	14.0	14.1%
DPM	99.2	240	17.6	17.7%
Tax Penalty				
SCPM	84.5	201	15.9	18.9%
LMSR	69.7	168	13.2	18.9%
DPM	92.7	221	17.4	18.9%

In the full charge setting, we can see that the DPM and LMSR both collect significantly more revenue and orders than the SCPM. The LMSR actually accepts more orders than the DPM while still collecting similar amounts of revenue. Due to the fact that the LMSR accepts so many orders, its gross profit and profit percentage are actually the lowest of the three mechanisms. We believe that the volatility of the LMSR's prices is responsible for its acceptance of lower revenue orders.

In the tax penalty setting, the DPM continues to display strong performance. We see that the SCPM outperforms the LMSR in terms of orders accepted and revenue collected. This is not surprising since the SCPM is solving an optimization problem with an objective function that is partially geared towards maximizing worst case profitability. The LMSR is simply accepting orders in a manner consistent with its pricing function. Again, we believe that the rapid change of the LMSR's prices leads to lower levels of order acceptance when the tax is imposed.

We have also tested these mechanisms with random bids generated from a normal distribution. The results are very similar when the variance of the normal distribution is equivalent to the variance of the uniform. However, changing the variance has a substantial impact on the models' performance. The DPM tends to be less effective in the parimutuel and full charge settings when variance is reduced. In general, profits drop quickly as variance is reduced. Due to space constraints, we have omitted more details on this issue but we recognize this as an important consideration for mechanism selection.

Price Stability
One interesting feature of the mechanisms is that they provide updated state prices after each new order is accepted. In the DPM, the prices tend to stabilize to values close to the expected values of the limit prices for each state. However, the LMSR and SCPM both have prices that fluctuate greatly and don't appear to stabilize. Figure 1 shows the evolution of the state prices as orders were received in the first of our sample datasets.

The price of the SCPM is more volatile because it is only required to satisfy the price consistency constraints for the current order. Thus, its value is not tethered to

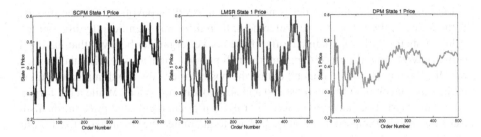

Fig. 1. State 1 Price Stability in the SCPM, LMSR and DPM

the previous orders. To gain a better estimate of overall demand for a state, the SCPM organizer could choose to solve the CPCAM model for the current orders. The prices in the CPCAM stabilize towards the mean order price. So, while the SCPM prices are not stable, there is a way to gain some further insight into the actual demand for the states. In contrast to the SCPM, the price of the LMSR is calculated by a formula that includes previous orders. To better understand the lack of stability in the LMSR's prices, we need to observe the derivative of its pricing function with respect to a new order being received in one state. From the LMSR pricing function, we have the following:

$$\frac{\partial p_i}{\partial q_i} = \frac{\frac{1}{b}e^{q_i/b}}{\sum_j e^{q_j/b}} - \frac{\frac{1}{b}e^{2q_i/b}}{(\sum_j e^{q_j/b})^2}$$

Now, we can also calculate the derivative of the DPM pricing function. We have:

$$\frac{\partial p_i}{\partial q_i} = \frac{\kappa}{(\sum_j e^{q_j/b})^{\frac{1}{2}}} - \frac{\kappa q_i^2}{(\sum_j e^{q_j/b})^{\frac{3}{2}}}$$

The value of the DPM price derivative will approach zero as the value of q, holding all q_j's in the same proportion, increases. Thus, as more orders are accepted, the price stabilizes. However, the derivative of the LMSR is actually independent of the number of orders received. It will remain constant if q increases as long as the proportion of the values of the q_j's is the same. This explains why the LMSR prices are so volatile. Given that the LMSR is widely used in prediction markets, it is surprising to find the lack of stability of its prices.

4   Discussion

We believe that the SCPM is a valuable and interesting new pari-mutuel mechanism for contingent claim markets. Our analysis indicates that the best choice of mechanism depends on the objectives of the market organizer. In prediction markets, the organizer is typically not interested in generating a profit but instead wants to maximize the number of orders accepted. Our results show that the LMSR will accept more orders and collect more revenue than the SCPM or DPM. In financial markets, the organizer may actually want to guarantee himself a certain profit level or even maximize his profit. The DPM or SCPM would seem to be the better choice in these cases. A second question that the market organizer should consider is how important certain payoffs are to the traders. If the traders exhibit risk averse preferences, then they may significantly discount the value of shares with uncertain payoffs. If the market organizer believes that having a certain payoff for a winning order is important for traders, then he will rule out the use of the DPM. It's important to remember that the posted price versus bid implementations of the mechanisms can be interchanged and are broadly equivalent. While a bid format allows the market organizer to charge the full limit price, the posted price mechanism can be adapted to impose a tax on each share to guarantee the organizer a fixed profit percentage.

One of the most interesting outputs from these market-makers are the state prices. In prediction markets, the generation of these prices is the raison d'être for the market. However, it is very interesting to discover that the LMSR actually doesn't produce very stable prices. The SCPM also suffers from less price stability when compared to the DPM. As a means for generating prices that are more representative of the entire market, one could take all the orders and solve the CPCAM. Since the limit prices on the orders should be truthful, the prices calculated by solving the CPCAM would most likely give a more accurate read of the demand for various states.

One assumption that we made when comparing the mechanisms was that traders would assume that the DPM eventual payoffs will be equal to the current payoffs. This might be an aggressive assumption since traders would probably want to discount the payoffs since there is some uncertainty in them. As a quick test, we also implemented the DPM in the conservative setting where the trader assumes that the actual payoff will be 1. However, this mechanism performed very poorly against our sample datasets - hardly any orders were accepted in this conservative setting. It would make sense that most traders would prefer certain payoffs but it is not clear that the traders would assume the worst case payoff when utilizing this mechanism. It would be interesting to see how the DPM performs under various levels of discounting.

References

[1] Baron, K., Lange, J.: From Horses to Hedging. Risk Magazine, vol. 16(2) (2003)
[2] Bossaerts, P., Fine, L., Ledyard, J.: Inducing Liquidity in Thin Financial Markets Through Combined–Value Trading Mechanisms. European Economic Review 46(9), 1671–1695 (2002)
[3] Cass, D.: Goldman and Deutsche to Launch Economic Data Options. Risk August 2002 (2002)
[4] Fortnow, L., Killian, J., Pennock, D., Wellman, M.: Betting Boolean-Style: A Framework for Trading in Securities Based on Logical Formulas. In: Proceedings of Electronic Commerce 2003 (2003)
[5] Goldman, A.J., Tucker, A.W.: Theory of linear programming. In: Kuhn, H.W., Tucker, A.W. (eds.) Linear Inequalities and Related Systems. Annals of Mathematical Studies, vol. 38, pp. 53–97 (1956)
[6] Hanson, R.: Combinatorial Information Market Design. Information Systems Frontiers 5(1), 107–119 (2003)
[7] Lange, J., Economides, N.: A Parimutuel Market Microstructure for Contingent Claims. European Financial Management 11(1), 25–49 (2005)

[8] Morrison, D.: Deutsche Bank adopts auction technology to trade economic statistics. Waters Magazine May 2002 (2002)

[9] Pennock, D.: A Dynamic pari-mutuel market for hedging, wagering, and information aggregation. In: Proceedings of Electronic Commerce 2004 (2004)

[10] Pennock, D.: Implementing Hanson's Market Maker (2006),
     http://blog.oddhead.com/2006/10/30/
     implementing-hansons-market-maker/

[11] Pennock, D., Chen, Y., Dooley, M.: Dynamic Pari-mutuel Market Working Paper (2006)

[12] Peters, M., So, A., Ye, Y.: A Convex Parimutuel Formulation for Contingent Claim Markets Working Paper (2005),
     http://www.stanford.edu/~yyye/cpcam-ec.pdf

[13] Ye, Y.: A Path to the Arrow–Debreu Competitive Market Equilibrium Mathematical Programming, Online (December 2006)

Information Sharing Communities

Gabrielle Demange

PSE, 48 Bd Jourdan Paris, 75014 France
demange@pse.ens.fr
http://www.pse.ens.fr/demange/index.html

Abstract. The paper investigates information sharing communities. The environment is characterized by the anonymity of the contributors and users, as on the Web. It is argued that a community may be worth forming because it facilitates the interpretation and understanding of the posted information. The admission criterion within a community is examined.

1 Introduction

Group structures on the Web such as peer-to-peer (P2P) systems aim at sharing various goods and disseminating information in a fully decentralized way. Quite often, information is non rivalrous and returns to scale are not decreasing. Why then do communities form with a free but restricted access? We provide an explanation based on the anonymity and preferences diversity of the participants, contributors and users. Consider individuals who regularly look for a piece of advice on a particular topic, on movies for instance. A tremendous quantity of information is posted on the Web. To be useful, Internet users must be able to find pages that are relevant to their queries. A ranking provided by a search engine may be of limited interest. Since the ranking results from the behaviors of the users who have experienced items in the topic, it is useful to other users only if they share similar tastes and know it. The diversity of preferences provides a rationale for the formation of communities.

The value of information as defined by Blackwell (1953) is our basic tool to investigate how communities form. The anonymity of contributors is shown to play a crucial role. More specifically, pieces of information posted by peers are valuable to other peers only if all share similar tastes. Furthermore, posted information without control on the contributors may not only be useless but also detrimental by introducing some noise in the information relevant to other peers. The admission rule in a community is therefore essential in determining the value that each peer derives from the information provided by the community's members. This leads us to analyze preferences over admission rules. Community's members do not fully agree on admission criteria owing to their differences in tastes, even if all of them benefit from the community. This divergence is analyzed. Then, assuming that a leader/initiator of a community chooses the admission rule, we perform comparative statics on the chosen community with respect the contribution rate, the cost and the probability of finding an answer to a query, the sharing of ads revenues.

X. Deng and F.C. Graham (Eds.): WINE 2007, LNCS 4858, pp. 96–107, 2007.

Related works. Dwork et al (2001) consider a search engine as an aggregator of preferences and study aggregation over different engines under a common underlying ranking. In our model instead, not only is there no common ranking, but also any anonymous aggregation of preferences over the whole population yields a completely flat ranking, i.e., the society is indifferent between any two objects. In such a situation, rankings provided by search engines can only be attributed to chance or to bias.

Various algorithms have been proposed for detecting communities through a link structure, as surveyed in Newman (2001). Here instead, we investigate in a specific context why a community forms in the first place.

"Bad" behavior due to the public good aspect of Internet -free riding and excessive overload of the platform on which peers operate- raises difficulties that may call for the implementation of incentives schemes (see e.g. Feldman et al. 2004 and Ng et al. 2005). Not surprisingly, the public good aspect is present in our analysis through the contribution rate within a community.

As here, collaborative filtering has value under diverse preferences. It is a system that aims at giving tailored recommendations to a user on the basis of his past behaviors and a collection of 'similar' user profiles (Hofmann and Puzicha 1999). But the system is centralized. Here instead, a peer voluntarily chooses a community and has access to the same recommendations, which allows to keep anonymity and privacy.

The plan of the paper is the following. Section 2 sets up the model, and Section 3 studies the design of a community. Proofs are gathered in the appendix.

2   The Model

Consider one category of 'objects', such as movies, or books, or restaurants for instance. Individuals widely differ in their tastes. The 'circle' model due to Salop (1979) is a stylized and parcimonious way to model these differences (results could be extended to more complex settings).[1] Individual's preferences over the objects are characterized by a single parameter, a point of a circle. An object, a movie or a restaurant for instance, is also characterized by a point on the same circle. An individual who buys an object derives a utility gain that is non increasing in his distance to the object. More precisely, an individual located at θ is called a θ-individual and similarly an object located at t is a t-object. The utility gain for a θ-individual who buys a t-object is given by $u(d(\theta, t))$ where $d(\theta, t)$ is the distance on the circle between θ and t and u is non increasing, identical for all individuals. To fix the idea, at most half of the objects are valuable to an individual: There is a threshold value d^*, $0 < d^* < \pi/2$ for which $u(d) > 0$ for $d < d^*$ and $u(d) < 0$ for $d > d^*$. Furthermore function u is continuous and derivable except possibly at d^*.

The society is uniformly distributed on the circle. New objects to buy are *a priori* uniformly distributed on the circle. If the characteristic of a particular

---

[1] Apart from the modeling of preferences, Salop's analysis widely differs since he studies competition between firms with differentiated products.

object is perfectly known, the set of individuals who benefit from buying it is given by those located at a distance smaller than d^*. Thus, under perfect information, whatever an object's location, the same proportion p of the people buy it, where $p = d^*/\pi$. Under imperfect information on objects' characteristics, an individual forms some assessment on the location and decides whether to buy a particular object by comparing the expected utility gain from buying it with 0. We assume a weak form of risk aversion: faced with the lottery of buying two objects with equal probability, a peer prefers not to buy if the sum of the distance is $2d^*$, i.e. $u(d) + u(2d^* - d) < 0$ for $d < d^*$. This implies that, under incomplete information, no one buys because its expected utility gain is negative.

As a simple example, consider the situation in which individuals either enjoy or not consuming the object. It is represented by a *binary* function[2] u: for some positive g and b, $u(d) = g, d < d^*, u(d) = -b, d > d^*$. Weak risk aversion is met for $b \geq g$.

Communities. Under incomplete information, there is some scope for information sharing. Individuals who have bought an object may post their opinion on it. Our aim is to study the value of a community in gathering and sharing such opinions. In a community, the role of contributors and users can *a priori* be distinguished. Contributors add to the content by providing information on the objects they have tested while users have access to the posted information. Here the set of contributors and users are identical. This is induced by the following assumptions. First we assume that there is no intrinsic motive to contribute such as altruism. Thus, for a community to be 'viable' as defined in the next section, contributors are also users so as to draw some benefit. Furthermore, even though there may be no direct cost (nor benefit) in allowing users not to contribute, it may be worth restricting access to contributors simply to encourage them to contribute. In that case users and contributors coincide.

Anonymity and restricted access can be implemented by a fully decentralized mechanism such as Gnutella and Freenet. These mechanisms propagate queries through a P2P network without the need of a server. A query is sent to neighbors who provide an answer if they have one or otherwise pass the query to their own neighbors and so on until an answer is reached.[3] The system can be anonymous by recognizing members by an address only. Records, which are not public, can keep track of peers' behavior. Sanctions such as exclusion are based on these records and automatic. Records on peers' contributions for instance allow the community to sustain some contribution level by excluding users who contribute too little.

Here, a community is composed of the set of individuals with characteristics in an arc. By convention, an arc $[\theta, \theta']$ designates the arc from θ to θ' going clockwise. The *size* of community $[\theta, \theta']$ is defined by $(\theta - \theta')/2$. and its *center*

---

[2] The utility level at d^* does not matter because the probability of an object being distant of d^* to a person is null.

[3] See for example Kleinberg and Raghavan (2005) for a description of decentralized mechanisms and an analysis of the incentives to pass the information.

is $(\theta + \theta')/2$. The technology is characterized by two data: the probability of success and an individual cost. In line with decentralized behavior, the size of a community determines the probability of finding a recommendation for a particular object in reasonable time. denoted by $P(\alpha)$ for a community of size α. P is assumed to be increasing and concave (as for a Poisson process as in the next section). The individual cost includes the cost for searching and contributing. Normalizing by the average number of requests, it is denoted by c. It is likely to be small and does not play an essential role in the analysis. The probability P and the cost c are assumed to be given except in Section 3.2.

Signals Opinions are described by signals. Stating a detailed judgment is difficult. To account for this, signals are assumed to be limited. A signal s on an object takes two values, *yes* or *no*, which are interpreted as a recommendation to buy or not to buy. Since there is no benefit from sending a false signal, signals are assumed to be truthful: a θ-individual having bought a t-object sends *yes* if $u(d(\theta, t)) \geq 0$ and *no* if the inequality is reversed.[4]

Let us consider a signal[5] $\tilde{s}$ on an object from a member of community $[\theta, \theta']$. As a result, the sender is considered as drawn at random from the community. In the sequel $s \in [\theta, \theta']$ refers to a signal sent by a member of community $[\theta, \theta']$. As defined by Blackwell (1953), signal $\tilde{s}$ is valuable to an individual if it enables him to make 'better' decisions in the sense that his expected payoff is increased. More precisely, the joint distribution of $(\tilde{t}, \tilde{s})$ for a signal $\tilde{s}$ sent by a member of community $[\theta, \theta']$ can be computed. After learning the realized value s, peers revise their prior on the characteristic t according to Bayes' formula and decide to buy or not. Clearly a signal that does not change the prior on the object's location is useless. The ignorance of the sender's location in the community has the following consequences.

- (i) A signal $\tilde{s}$ from the whole society is useless.
- (ii) A signal from a community smaller than the whole society may be useful: it changes the prior.
- (iii) Two simultaneous signals may convey less information than each one.

Point (i) is straightforward. A signal sent by an individual chosen at random in the whole group does not modify the prior, hence is not informative. Let us illustrate Point (ii) by Figure 1 for $d^* = \pi/2$. Each peer in community $[-\alpha, \alpha]$ sends *no* for an object located in $[\alpha + \pi/2, -\alpha - \pi/2]$. Thus the posterior density conditional on the signal being *yes* is null on that arc: the posterior clearly differs from the prior density. To show Point (iii), consider a signal from a community reduced to a point, say 0, so that the sender's preferences are known. The signal is informative: Conditional on a *yes* for example and taking again $d^* = \pi/2$, the posterior density on $[-\pi/2, \pi/2]$ is $1/\pi$, which is the double of the prior, and null elsewhere. Add a signal sent from $[\pi]$. The important point is that on the receipt of the two signals, it is not known which peer has sent which signal. The two

---

[4] Malicious individuals can be incorporated. Under some expectation on their distribution, their presence introduces additional noise in the information inferred by a signal. The same argument applies if individuals make error in their judgment.

[5] A random variable is denoted by $\tilde{x}$, and its realization (when observed) by x.

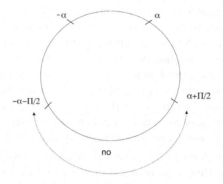

Fig. 1. $d^* = \pi/2$

signals, which are always opposite to each other, give no information because the prior is not changed. In this simple example, the new signal not only adds no information but also destroys the information conveyed by the first signal. The reason is that adding a signal introduces an additional source of randomness due to the anonymity of the sender. In contrast, in the standard framework, adding a signal is never harmful because it can simply be ignored.

The value of an informative signal to a person depends on his/her location and on the size of the community. The next proposition analyzes this further. Consider a community of size α and an individual whose distance to the center is θ. Let $U(\theta, \alpha)$ denote the expected utility per signal conditional on having an answer to a query. The utility is drawn by following the recommendation, that is from buying the object in the case of a positive signal and not buying it in the opposite case. The *a priori* probability for a positive signal is equal to p (which is $d^*/2\pi$), since, given an object at random, each individual says *yes* with probability p. Using that there is no purchase on the reception of a negative signal, this gives (since up to a rotation, we can consider arcs centered at zero):

$$U(\theta, \alpha) = pE[u(d(\theta, \tilde{t}))|yes \in [-\alpha, \alpha])]. \tag{1}$$

Proposition 1

- (i) Given α, $\alpha \leq d^*$, utility $U(\theta, \alpha)$ decreases with the distance θ to the center,[6] $\theta \leq d^*$.
- (ii) Given θ, $\theta \leq d^*$, utility $U(\theta, \alpha)$ decreases with α on $[0, d^*]$.

Point (i) is natural given the symmetry. It says that the expected benefits derived from following a signal decrease with the distance to the center. According to point (ii), the expected value per signal is greater the smaller the community, that is the less uncertain the sender. This is easy to understand for the center. As α increases, the objects that he dislikes (distant of more than d^*) are more likely to be recommended and those he likes get less recommended. For an individual

---

[6] Note that properties hold for individuals outside the community, i.e., for $\theta > \alpha$.

who is not at the center, the distribution of signals is 'biased' with respect to his own preferences and as α increases some objects that he likes get more recommended. Increasing α is however still harmful because the distribution of the distance to a peer of the recommended objects becomes riskier in the sense of first order stochastic dominance. An implication of property (ii) is the superiority of an expert 'everything else being equal'. More precisely, a system in which an expert sends as many signals as the communities' members at the same total cost makes every peer better off.

3   Community Choice

Our purpose is to analyze which community forms. A first requirement is that all community members benefit from it, a property that we call viability. There are however many viable communities, and members may have conflicting views about its scope, i.e., about the membership rule. In contrast to a setup in which a firm organizes the community, there is no unanimous criterion such as the maximization of profit. We shall analyze the choice of a 'leader'.

Viable community. Anybody is free not to join a community. A community is said to be *viable* if each of its members benefits from it, accounting for the failure of search and the participation cost. Specifically, an individual distant of θ from the center of a community of size α is indeed willing to participate if $P(\alpha)U(\theta,\alpha) \geq c$. To cover the cost, the utility from receiving a signal, U, must be positive. From point (i) of Proposition 1, the peers who achieve the lowest benefit are located at the extreme points of the community. Letting $V(\alpha)$ be the expected utility per signal for a peer located at an extreme point of a community of size α, the viability condition can be written simply as

$$P(\alpha)V(\alpha) \geq c \text{ where } V(\alpha) = U(\alpha,\alpha). \tag{2}$$

Note that V is positive for α small enough. Hence, under a small enough cost, the set of viable sizes is non empty. Also, viable communities are of size smaller than d^*.[7] Property (ii) points out a trade-off faced by peers: increasing the size increases the probability of getting an answer but decreases the value of an answer. To analyze this trade-off, we take the following assumptions throughout the paper.

   A0 (concavity assumption) For each θ, the functions $logU(\theta,\alpha)$ and $logV(\alpha)$ are concave with respect to α.

A1 (elasticity assumption) $$\frac{-V'}{V}(\alpha) \geq \frac{-U'_\alpha}{U}(0,\alpha) \geq \frac{-U'_\alpha}{U}(\theta,\alpha). \tag{3}$$

---

[7] Given two individuals distant of $2d^*$ or more, the sum of the distance of an object to these is at least $2d^*$, so that $u(d) + u(2d^* - d) < 0$. If the two individuals follow the same recommendations, taking expectation over objects, the sum of their utility levels is negative, in contradiction with viability (even for a null cost c).

Under A0, the set of viable sizes is a nonempty interval $[\underline{\alpha}, \overline{\alpha}]$ for a low enough cost c (because PV is log concave as a product of logconcave functions). Let us interpret the elasticity assumption. The second inequality of (3) says that the relative loss incurred by a peer due to an increase in the size is larger for the center. The first inequality says that these relative losses are all smaller than the relative decrease in the utility of an individual located at an extreme. Since this decrease includes not only the variation due to the size but also that due to the position $(V'(\alpha) = [U'_\alpha + U'_\theta](\alpha, \alpha)$ and U'_θ is negative because U decreases with the distance to the center) inequalities (3) are compatible. For example, assumptions A0 and A1 hold for a binary function.

3.1 Leaders' Choice

In practice, a 'leader' initiates a community and possibly defines criteria for accepting peers. The leader's optimal community size is given by the value α^0 that maximizes the payoff $P(\alpha)U(0, \alpha)$. This will be the leader's choice provided it is viable. Similarly let α^θ denote the value that maximizes the payoff $P(\alpha)U(\theta, \alpha)$, that is the preferred size of a θ-peer in a community centered at zero.

Proposition 2. *The leader's optimal size is less than the peers' optimal one:* $\alpha^0 \leq \alpha^\theta$. *The leader's choice is*

1. *either the leader's optimum α^0 if $P(\alpha^0)V(\alpha^0) > c$; in that case some outsiders would achieve a positive payoff by joining but the community is closed to them.*
2. *or the maximal viable size $\overline{\alpha}$.*

The first point makes precise the direction of possible disagreements with the leader: peers all prefer a larger size than the leader. Disagreement occurs in case *1* when the leader can choose his preferred size. By continuity of the payoffs, close enough outsiders would achieve a positive payoff by joining, but they are not allowed to do so: the community is closed. According to point *2*, it is never the case that the leader's optimum is not viable because it is too small. Instead all peers, including the leader, would benefit from an increase in the community size up to α^0. However no outsiders want to join and peers at the extreme of the community just cover their cost.

Comparative statics. Various policies can influence the probability of successful search. The next section studies the enforcement of a minimal contribution rate. Other factors, the efficiency of the technology or the number of Internet users for instance, result in an exogenous change of the probability of success. The impact of such a change is easily illustrated with a Poisson process $P(\alpha) = 1 - e^{-\lambda\alpha}$. An increase in the population of Internet users other things being equal is represented by an increase in the parameter λ. Figure 2 depicts the maximal viable size $\overline{\alpha}$ (the increasing line) and the leader's optimum α^0 (the decreasing line) as a function of λ for a binary function.[8] Since the leader's

---

[8] Easy computation gives $U(\theta, \alpha) = pg[1 - k(\alpha + \theta^2/\alpha)]$ with $k = \frac{(1+b/g)}{4d^*}$.

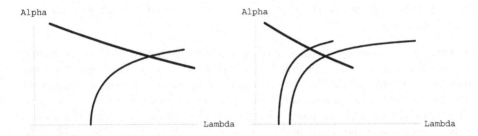

Fig. 2. $c = 0.1$, $b/g = 1.5$ **Fig. 3.** $c = 0.1$ and $c = 0.07$

choice is the minimum of these two values, increasing the population has different effects on the leader's choice depending on whether this choice is constrained
or not. The following configurations are obtained as λ increases: first there is no
viable community for λ low enough, second the leader's choice is constrained
equal to the maximal viable size, and third the leader can choose his optimum
value.

This can be explained as follows. Increasing the population within a community makes it more attractive to outsiders. When the community is constrained
by viability, for intermediate values of λ, these outsiders are welcome. As a result, the size is increased. Instead, when the community is closed, for a large
enough λ, increasing the population allows the leader to choose a community
restricted to peers whose tastes are more and more similar to his owns: the size
decreases. The impact of λ on the size directly translates into an impact on the
precision of information: as λ increases, information is first made less precise
(but the higher chance of getting some information compensates the loss) and
then more and more precise.

Advertising. Ads provide revenues that may change the leader's choice criteria.
To simplify, assume that peers do not mind ads and that ads do not influence
their preferences on the object on which they are searching information. Let the
revenues generated by ads be proportional to the number of peers and consider
two alternative ways of distributing them.

First, the leader captures all ad revenues. In that case he sets up a community
that maximizes a combination of his own interests and the revenues. His choice
is unchanged if the viability constraint binds. Otherwise, instead of choosing his
own optimum, α^0, he chooses a larger size (between α^0 and $\overline{\alpha}$). The more he
cares about revenues, the closer his choice to the maximal viable size. As a result,
information is less precise. The effect can be substantial for large λ because the
maximal viable size $\overline{\alpha}$ is large and α^0 is small. Whereas a community could be
tailored to his specific tastes, the leader may choose a loose criterion so as to
capture ad revenues.

Second, revenues are distributed equally among peers, which amounts to diminish cost c. This results in an increase in the maximal viable size and leaves
the optimal leader's size unchanged. Hence, the leader's choice is closer and more
often equal to his optimal value. In Figure 2, the maximal viable size is drawn

for two distinct values of the cost, $c = 0.1$ and $c = 0.07$, which give the two increasing lines.

Voting. In a community with size α^0, peers who are not located at the center would all like to increase the community (since $\alpha^\theta > \alpha^0$). This suggests some instability. To investigate this, let some peers propose to accept newcomers who are close to their own tastes, that is they propose to increase one boundary, say to increase α to $\alpha + d\alpha$ keeping $-\alpha$ fixed. (In view of the preceding discussion, only an increase of the community may be worth considering.) Then peers vote under the majority rule.

It is easy to see that the proposal is rejected if the community size is at the upper bound $\overline{\alpha}$. Increasing the community on one side implies that some individuals on the other side will leave: accepting the proposal can only result in a rotation of the community which becomes $[-\overline{\alpha}+d\alpha, \overline{\alpha}+d\alpha]$. Peers in $[-\overline{\alpha}, d\alpha/4[$ either leave or are further away from the center (with no change in size) and hence are made worse off (from Point (i) of Proposition 1): A strict majority of incumbents vote against the proposal.

If instead the community size is α^0, accepting the proposal results in $[-\alpha^0, \alpha^0 + d\alpha]$ (assuming $d\alpha$ small enough). Not only the community is enlarged but also the center is modified. Now the impact is unclear for individuals on the negative side because there are two opposite effects: a possible benefit from an increase in the size and a loss from being further away from the center. According to the following Proposition, the loss outweighs the benefit under the following assumption A2 (A2 is satisfied with a binary function for example).

A2 $[U_\alpha + U_\theta](\theta, \alpha^0)$ decreases with θ in $[0, \alpha^0]$

Proposition 3. *Assume A2. At the leader's choice, there is no strict majority for changing only one side of the community.*

3.2   Enticing Contribution

The success probability partly determines the viability and the choice of the size of a community. Instead of taking P as exogenous, it is assumed here to be influenced by the peers' contribution rates. A minimum rate is asked for, implemented through records on peers' contributions. The leader now chooses both the size and the minimal contribution rate.

We assume that the peer's participation cost c is an increasing function of his contributions. As a result, no peer will contribute more than the minimum required rate: his cost would increase with a null benefit since the impact of a single individual on the success probability is negligible. This is a standard effect in public good provision. Given the minimum required rate λ, let $P(\lambda, \alpha)$ and $c(\lambda)$ denote respectively the probability of success when *each* peer contributes λ and the incurred individual cost. P is non decreasing and concave in λ and c is non decreasing and convex.

Without constraint on viability, the leader's optimum is the value of (λ, α) that maximizes $P(\lambda, \alpha)U(0, \alpha) - c(\lambda)$. The maximal viable size now depends on λ; it is denoted by $\overline{\alpha}(\lambda)$.

Proposition 4. *The leader's choice is*

1. *the leader's optimum community if it is viable; the community is closed to outsiders. Other peers would prefer a larger size and a lower participation.*
2. *a community with maximal viable size $\overline{\alpha}(\lambda)$ for the chosen rate; the choice of λ trades off the benefits from increasing contribution and the loss due to a smaller community size (i.e. $\overline{\alpha}(\lambda)$ decreases at the chosen value of λ.)*

We find the two regimes in which, given the chosen contribution rate, the choice of the size is dictated by the same considerations as in the previous section. As for the contribution rate, note that the marginal benefit from increasing the contribution rate, $P_\lambda U(\theta, \alpha) - c'$, is decreasing with the distance to the center as U. Hence, surely, at the chosen contribution rate, the leader's marginal benefit is nonnegative: otherwise a Pareto improvement within the community would be found by reducing the rate. Thus, in case *1*, where the leader is not constrained by viability, all peers would prefer to increase the size and to decrease the contribution rate. In case *2*, the leader would benefit from an increase in the contribution rate and from an increase in size. He faces a trade-off because increasing contribution incites some peers at the extreme to leave thereby decreasing the size.

Concluding remarks. This paper considers a community as a cluster of individuals with similar preferences. The possible improvement in the value of information determines the scope of a community. A natural development is to allow signals to be aggregated in a community and to investigate how this would affect the value of information. Another direction is to analyze the coexistence of communities.

References

Blackwell, D.: Equivalent Comparison of Experiments. Annals of Mathematics and Statistics 24, 265–272 (1953)

Dwork, C., Kumar, R., Naor, M., Sivakumar, D.: Rank Aggregation Methods for the Web. In: Dwork, C. (ed.) Proceedings of the 10th international conference on World Wide Web, pp. 613–622 (2001)

Feldman, M., Papadimitriou, C., Chuang, J., Stoica, I.: Free-Riding and Whitewashing in Peer-to-Peer Systems. In: 3rd Annual Workshop on Economics and Information Security (WEIS 2004) (2004)

Hofmann, T., Puzicha, J.: Latent class models models for collaborative filtering. In: Proc. of IJCAI (1999)

Kleinberg, J., Raghavan, P.: Query Incentive Networks. In: Proc. 46th IEEE Symposium on Foundations of Computer Science, IEEE Computer Society Press, Los Alamitos (2005)

Newman, M.: Detecting community structures in networks. Physical Review E 69, 066133 (2001)

Ng, W.-Y, Chiu, D.M., Liu, W.K.: Club formation by rational sharing: Content, viability and community structure. LNCS. Springer, Heidelberg (2005)

Salop, S.C.: Monopolistic Competition with Outside Goods. The Bell Journal of Economics 10(1), 141–156 (1979)

4   Appendix: Proofs

PROOF OF PROPOSITION 1. By viability, we restrict to $\alpha \leq d^*$. From (1), we have $U(\theta, \alpha) = p \int_{-\pi}^{\pi} f^\alpha(t)u(d(\theta, t))dt$ where $f^\alpha(t)$ is the density of an object conditional on the receipt of a *yes* from $[-\alpha, \alpha]$. We can rewrite U as

$$U(\theta, \alpha) = p \int_{-\pi}^{\pi} u(\delta)dF(\theta, \alpha; \delta) \text{ where } F(\theta, \alpha; \delta) = \int_{-\pi}^{\pi} f^\alpha(t)1_{[\theta-\delta, \theta+\delta]}(t)dt \quad (4)$$

that is, $U(\theta, \alpha)$ is proportional to the expectation of $u(d)$ under the distribution $F(\theta, \alpha; .)$ of the distance to θ of the objects that are recommended by community $[-\alpha, \alpha]$. Since u is decreasing, the monotonicity properties of U (i) or (ii) follow if these distributions are ordered by first order stochastic dominance as θ or α varies. More specifically, U decreases with positive θ if for any $\delta, 0 \leq \delta \leq \pi$, any θ', θ with $\theta' \leq \theta$, then $F(\theta, \alpha; \delta) \leq F(\theta', \alpha; \delta)$, that is if F decreases with respect to α. Similarly, $U(\theta, \alpha)$ decreases with respect to α if F decreases with respect to α. These properties can be shown by computing the posterior density f^α. ∎

PROOF OF PROPOSITION 2. The size α^θ preferred by a θ-individual maximizes $P(\alpha)U(\theta, \alpha)$ with respect to α. Let α^{max} be the size for which $V(\alpha^{max}) = 0$. We may restrict to sizes smaller than α^{max}, and by symmetry, to positive θ, that is $0 \leq \theta \leq \alpha \leq \alpha^{max}$. Since U is positive, we consider instead the maximization of $logPU$. Under A0, the function is concave with respect to α, with a derivative given by $[\frac{P_\alpha}{P}(\alpha) + \frac{U_\alpha}{U}(\theta, \alpha)]$. Thus, $\alpha^0 \leq \alpha^\theta$ holds if this derivative is nonnegative at α^0. The derivative is null at $(\theta, \alpha) = (0, \alpha^0)$. From A1, it is increasing with respect to θ, which gives $\frac{P_\alpha}{P}(\alpha^0) + \frac{U_\alpha}{U}(\theta, \alpha^0) \geq 0$, the desired result.

The optimal choice of the leader is the value of α that maximizes $P(\alpha)U(0, \alpha)$ under the viability constraint $P(\alpha)V(\alpha) \geq c$. Let μ be the multiplier associated with the constraint. The first order condition is

$$P_\alpha U(0, \alpha) + PU_\alpha(0, \alpha) + \mu[P_\alpha V + PV'](\alpha) = 0. \quad (5)$$

If μ is null, the optimal choice is α^0 as expected. If μ is positive, the constraint binds: α^0 is not viable, i.e. outside the interval $[\underline{\alpha}, \overline{\alpha}]$. Furthermore the solution solves $P(\alpha)V(\alpha) = c$, hence is either $\underline{\alpha}$ or $\overline{\alpha}$. Note that PV increases at $\underline{\alpha}$ and decreases at $\overline{\alpha}$. From (5), the derivatives of PU and PV are of opposite sign. If the latter derivative is positive, PV increases: the solution is $\underline{\alpha}$. Since under A1, $P_\alpha V + PV' > 0$ implies $P_\alpha U(0, \alpha) + PU_\alpha(0, \alpha) > 0$, it must be that the derivative of PV is non positive: the solution is $\overline{\alpha}$.

PROOF OF PROPOSITION 3. The case where the community chosen by the leader is of size $\overline{\alpha}$ has been considered in the text. So let the optimal size be α^0 and assume that community $[-\alpha^0, \alpha^0]$ be changed into $[-\alpha^0 - d\alpha, \alpha^0]$. A θ-individual becomes distant of $\theta + d\alpha/2$ to the center; and the community size is increased to $\alpha^0 + d\alpha/2$. We show that all θ-peers with positive θ disapprove the change, that is

$$P(\alpha^0 + d\alpha/2)U(\theta + d\alpha/2, \alpha^0 + d\alpha/2) < P(\alpha^0)U(\theta, \alpha^0).$$

Let $G : G(\theta) = [P_\alpha U + PU_\alpha + PU_\theta](\theta, \alpha^0)$. By logconcavity of PU, the above inequality holds if $G(\theta) < 0$ for any positive θ. We have $G(0) = 0$, since by definition $[P_\alpha U + PU_\alpha](0, \alpha^0) = 0$ and by symmetry of U, $U_\theta(0, \alpha^0) = 0$. We have $G(\alpha^0) = (PV)'(\alpha^0)$. It is negative since by A1 it is smaller than $[P_\alpha U + PU_\alpha](0, \alpha^0)$, which is null. Hence $G(\theta) < 0$ for each $0 < \theta \le \alpha^0$ if G decreases with θ. This is true since U decreases with θ and A2 requires $U_\alpha + U_\theta$ to decrease as well. ∎

PROOF OF PROPOSITION 4. The optimal choice of the leader is the value that maximizes $P(\lambda, \alpha)U(0, \alpha) - c(\lambda)$ over (λ, α) subject to $P(\lambda, \alpha)V(\alpha) - c(\lambda) \ge 0$. Let μ be the multiplier associated with the constraint. The first order conditions are

$$P_\alpha U(0, \alpha) + PU_\alpha(0, \alpha) + \mu[P_\alpha V + PV'](\alpha) = 0 \tag{6}$$

$$P_\lambda U(0, \alpha) - c'(\lambda) + \mu[P_\lambda V(\alpha) - c'(\lambda)] = 0 \tag{7}$$

When μ is null, the viability constraint does not bind, and the leader can choose its optimal value. The same argument as in proposition 2 yields that for the chosen value of λ other peers would like the size to increase. As for the contribution rate, since $U(\theta, \alpha) \le U(0, \alpha)$, (7) yields $P_\lambda U(\theta, \alpha) - c'(\lambda) \le 0$: a θ-peer would prefer a smaller contribution rate.

When μ is positive, we know that (6) and A1 implies that α is set at the maximal viable size associated to the chosen λ, $\bar{\alpha}(\lambda)$. From the first order condition on λ (7), $P_\lambda U(0, \alpha) - c'(\lambda)$ and $P_\lambda V(\alpha) - c'(\lambda)$ are of opposite sign. Since $U(0, \alpha) > V(\alpha)$ it must be that the former is positive: the leader would prefer to increase the contribution rate. ∎

Competitive Safety Strategies in Position Auctions

Danny Kuminov and Moshe Tennenholtz

Technion – Israel Institute of Technology,
Haifa 32000, Israel
dannykv@tx.technion.ac.il
moshet@ie.technion.ac.il

Abstract. We attempt to address the challenge of suggesting a useful bidding strategy to an agent in the an ad auction setting. We explore the possibility of using competitive safety strategies in that context; a C-competitive strategy *guarantees* a payoff which is no less than $1/C$ of the payoff obtained in a best Nash equilibrium. We adopt the model of ad auctions suggested by Varian and provide analysis of competitive safety strategies in that context. We first show that no useful safety competitive strategies exist in a setting with complete information about the agents' valuations. Namely, in a setting with N bidders and exponential click-rate functions the ratio can be arbitrarily close to N. We also show that N is a general upper bound for any click-rates and valuations, while $\sum_{t=1}^{N} \frac{1}{t}$ is a tight bound for linear click-rates. However, in our main results we show that, surprisingly, useful C-competitive strategies do exist in the incomplete information setting. More specifically, we show that under the assumption that agents' valuations are uniformly distributed, an e-competitive strategy exists for the case of exponential click-rate functions, and a 2-competitive safety strategy exists for linear click-rate functions.

1 Introduction

One of the central challenges of game theory is to provide a decision maker with an advice about how he should choose his action in a given multi-agent encounter. This challenge, which falls under the so-called prescriptive agenda, has been left without a real answer. For example, the celebrated Nash equilibrium (NE), which is the basis for most game-theoretic analysis, suggests that a multi-agent behavior would be considered "rational" if no decision-maker would prefer to deviate from it, assuming the other decision-makers stick to it. However, while this is a very useful concept from a descriptive point of view, it does not address the question of how *should* a particular agent choose his action in a given game. A NE strategy can only be justified by assuming that the other agents are committed to a specific action profile, which is an unreasonably strong assumption regarding their rationality.

Only very few suggestions have been made in order to address the above challenge. One approach is to suggest to the agent a strategy which will be useful against an opponent taken from a particular class (see e.g. (Powers and Shoham2004)). A related idea is to try and learn the opponent model in a repeated interaction in order to optimize behavior against it (Carmel and Markovitch1999). Recently, the use of machine learning

X. Deng and F.C. Graham (Eds.): WINE 2007, LNCS 4858, pp. 108–118, 2007.

in order to predict opponent behavior in a game given his behavior in other games, has been shown to lead to significant success (Altman et al 2006). What is common to the above approaches is that there are no guarantees to our agent, unless we severely restrict the class of opponents he may face. An alternative approach, which is referred to as *competitive safety analysis* has been suggested in (Tennenholtz2002) motivated by an observation made by Aumann in (Aumann1985). This approach deals with guarantees the agent can be provided with, as discussed below.

It is well known that in a purely competitive setting, employing a safety level strategy, one that maximizes the agent's expected utility in the worst case, is the only reasonable mode of behavior. For partially cooperative settings, (Tennenholtz2002) justified the use of a safety-level strategy by introducing the notion of C-*competitive safety strategy* – a strategy that *guarantees* a payoff which is not less than $1/C$ of what is obtained in equilibrium. If there exists a C-competitive strategy for small C, then this strategy is a reasonable suggestion for the decision maker. However, the main challenge is whether, for interesting contexts, we do have such competitive safety strategies.

In this work we apply competitive safety analysis to the model of ad auctions, which are mechanisms for assigning online advertisement space to agents according to their (proclaimed) utility from using it. There has been only very limited study of bidding in ad auctions (see e.g. (Borgs et al 2005; Asdemir2005)). Moreover, we are not familiar with any work that deals with the challenging prescriptive problem of how should an agent choose his bids in that setting. The formal model that we use is based on (Varian2006), and will be described in the following section. Needless to say, if there exist useful C-competitive safety strategies in the ad auction setting, then they can provide useful means for bidders in such auctions.

The basic model of positions auctions assumes that the bidders' valuations for ad slots are common knowledge. In a more realistic model, each agent knows only his own valuation, while the valuations of all agents are assumed to be taken from some known distribution. We provide an analysis of competitive safety strategies for both the complete and the incomplete information settings. Interestingly, we obtain sharp difference between the usefulness of this approach in these settings. While in the complete information setting, it turns out that no general useful competitive safety strategies exist, they do exist in the (more realistic) incomplete information setting! Namely, we show that in the complete information setting with exponential click-rate functions, assuming N bidders, the competitive safety ratio can be arbitrarily close to N. We also show that N is a general upper bound. If we assume that the click-rates are linear, the ratio can not be greater than $\sum_{t=1}^{N} \frac{1}{t}$, and we show that this bound is tight. On the other hand, we show highly positive results in the incomplete information setting. We consider valuations which are taken from the uniform distribution, and two basic click-rate functions: the exponential and the linear click-rate functions. We show the existence of an e-competitive strategy for the case of exponential click-rate functions, and the existence of a 2-competitive safety strategy for linear click-rate functions.

In section 2 we present and discuss the basic model. In section 3 we provide the analysis of the complete information setting, and in section 4 we provide the analysis of the incomplete information setting.

All of our proofs appear in the full paper [1]. We include the proof of Theorem 1 in this version of the paper in order to illustrate our proof techniques. The proofs of our main theorems, Theorem 3 and Theorem 4, are lengthy, and make use of the notation presented in the proof of Theorem 1.

2   An Ad-Auction Setting

We now provide the model of ad auctions on which we will base our analysis. The formal model that we use is based on (Varian2006), with minor changes. The model has originally been presented for the complete information setting, but its adaptation to an incomplete information setting is immediate. The exact assumptions we take when computing safety-level strategies are discussed in sections 3 and 4, when we analyze the complete information and incomplete information settings, respectively.

The ad-auction setting:

- There are N players that compete for S ad slots. It is assumed that $N = S$.
- We denote the *clickthrough rate* (CTR) of a slot by $x_i, i \in \{1 \ldots N\}$. The CTR is a publicly known property of a slot, which does not depend on the player who is using it. The slots are numbered in decreasing order of CTR: $\forall i : x_i \geq x_{i+1}$. For ease of presentation, we define $x_i = 0$ for all $i > N$.
- The private value in this model is the utility that each agent derives from a single unit of CTR, which is assumed to be the same regardless of the slot from which it originates. We denote it by $v_i, i \in \{1 \ldots N\}$; naturally, $\forall i \in \{1 \ldots N\} : v_i > 0$. For ease of presentation, we define $v_i = 0$ for all $i > N$.
- The players' bids are interpreted as the maximal price per unit of CTR they are willing to pay to the CTR provider. We denote them by $\tilde{b}_i, i \in \{1 \ldots N\}$; w.l.o.g we assume that $\tilde{b}_i \geq \tilde{b}_{i+1}$; that is, the agents are ordered in decreasing order of bids. Naturally, $\forall i : \tilde{b}_i \geq 0$ by the rules of the auction. For ease of presentation, we define $\tilde{b}_i = 0$ for all $i > N$.
- The mechanism discussed by (Varian2006) assigns slots to users according to decreasing order of bids (the highest bidder gets the slot with the highest CTR, the second highest bidder – the second best slot, etc.). For ease of exposition, we assume that ties are broken according to some predefined ordering of the agents – it can be easily verified that our results hold for any other tie-breaking method as well. The price an agent has to pay per unit of CTR is the bid of the agent immediately below him in this ordering. We denote the price paid by agent i by p_i; since the agents are ordered in decreasing order of bids, $p_i = \tilde{b}_{i+1}$.
- The utility of agent i, which has private value v_i, when the agents' bids are $\tilde{b}_1 \geq \tilde{b}_2 \geq \ldots \tilde{b}_i \geq \tilde{b}_{i+1} \ldots \geq \tilde{b}_N$ is $(v_i - \tilde{b}_{i+1})x_i$.

A Nash equilibrium is a bidding profile in which each agent prefers his current slot to any alternative slot. Formally:

Definition 1 (A (pure) Nash equilibrium). *A Nash equilibrium (NE) is a set of bids* $\tilde{b}_1 > \tilde{b}_2 \ldots > \tilde{b}_N$ *such that:*

---

[1] Available at http://www.technion.ac.il/~dannykv/csad-full.pdf.

1. *No agent strictly benefits by decreasing his bid and getting a lesser slot:*

$$\forall s, t > s : (v_s - p_s)x_s \geq (v_s - p_t)x_t$$

2. *No agent strictly benefits by increasing his bid and getting a better slot:*

$$\forall s, t < s : (v_s - p_s)x_s \geq (v_s - p_{t-1})x_t$$

where $p_i = \tilde{b}_{i+1}$.

(Varian2006) defined *Symmetric Nash Equilibrium* (SNE) as a bidding profile that satisfies the following:

Definition 2 (SNE). *A SNE is a set of bids $\tilde{b}_1 > \tilde{b}_2 \ldots > \tilde{b}_N$ such that:*

$$\forall s, t : (v_s - p_s)x_s \geq (v_s - p_t)x_t$$

where $p_i = \tilde{b}_{i+1}$.

Note that the above definitions assume fixed valuations and therefore the game is essentially a *complete information game*.

As shown in (Varian2006), SNE has several nice properties:

1. In a SNE, $\forall s : v_s > v_{s+1}$ (i.e. agent i bids higher than agent k iff i's true type is indeed higher than that of k). This observation is important, since from now on we will assume that agents are indexed in decreasing order of *valuations* and use this property to assert that this order is also the order of their bids in a SNE.
2. If an ordered sequence of bids is a SNE, then it satisfies

$$\tilde{b}_s x_{s-1} \geq v_s(x_{s-1} - x_s) + \tilde{b}_{s+1}x_s$$

3. The latter implies that the bid of agent i in a SNE is bounded as follows:

$$\tilde{b}_i \geq \frac{1}{x_{i-1}} \sum_{t=i}^{N+1} v_t(x_{t-1} - x_t)$$

Note that a bidding profile in which all bids are equal to their respective lower bounds shown above is a SNE; we will use the term *the best SNE* to refer to this bidding profile (the term refers to the players' utility; the "best" SNE actually yields the lowest revenue for the auctioneer). Also, it is a simple observation that in the best SNE, agents never overbid (but there may exist equilibria in which they do so). Finally, it is important to note that the payoff of agent i in the best SNE is $v_i x_i - \sum_{t=i+1}^{N+1} v_t(x_{t-1} - x_t)$, which equals to what his payoff would be in the dominant strategies equilibrium of a VCG auction with the same valuations (his payment is exactly the externality that he imposes on the other players).

Note that it can be helpful to rewrite the expressions (due to (Varian2006)) for the bid of agent i ($\tilde{b}_i$) and the utility of agent i ($\tilde{U}_i$) in the best SNE as follows:

$$\tilde{b}_i = \frac{1}{x_{i-1}} \sum_{t=i}^{N+1} v_t(x_{t-1} - x_t) =$$

$$= \frac{1}{x_{i-1}} [v_i x_{i-1} - v_i x_i + v_{i+1} x_i - v_{i+1} x_{i+1} + \dots$$

$$\dots + v_N x_{N-1} - v_N x_N + v_{N+1} x_N - v_{N+1} \cdot 0] =$$

$$= \frac{1}{x_{i-1}} \left[v_i x_{i-1} - \sum_{t=i}^{N} x_t (v_t - v_{t+1}) \right]$$

$$\tilde{U}_i = (v_i - \tilde{b}_{i+1}) x_i = v_i x_i - v_{i+1} x_i + \sum_{t=i+1}^{N} x_t (v_t - v_{t+1}) = \sum_{t=i}^{N} x_t (v_t - v_{t+1})$$

It is important to note that our model slightly differs from that of (Varian2006); namely, while the previous work assumes $N > S$, we assume that $N = S$. This models a situation in which the auctioneer has enough ad slots for all the agents, and the only motivation for agents' bidding is the desire to get a higher (better) slot. We think that this is a reasonable model for the online ad auction setting – by the nature of online advertisement, there is no practical limit on the number of ad slots, and therefore the auctioneer has no real reason to deny agents' requests for slots. For the sake of simplicity, we also assume that there is no reserve price, and therefore the agent with the lowest bid gets the N'th slot for free. While this is definitely not the case in reality, the results presented here are a good approximation as long as the reserve price is negligible compared to the agents' valuations. Note that although the formulae for the bid and the utility in the *best* equilibrium that are quoted above come from (Varian2006), they are true in our model as well (by assuming $v_{N+1} = 0$). This is true since our model can be reduced to that of (Varian2006) by adding a fictitious player with fixed valuation 0 – in the best equilibrium, this player always bids truthfully and therefore does not affect slot allocation and expected utility. Note that the reduction does not work for other equilibria, because then the fictitious agent may overbid.

3   Competitive Safety Analysis in the Complete Information Model

Let us consider now the safety level of an agent in the *complete information game* that is induced by the ad-auction presented in the previous section. That is, we assume that the agents' valuations are fixed and are common knowledge, and we want to explore what is the payoff that an agent can guarantee to himself regardless of the other agents' behavior. Naturally, if we make no assumptions regarding the rationality of the other agents, they can always force the agent to take the N'th slot (by bidding higher than the agent's valuation). In this case, it can be easily seen that the payoff loss that the agent suffers relative to his payoff in an equilibrium is unbounded. Even if we limit the other agents not to bid above their valuation[2], the agent's payoff in best SNE can be $N - \epsilon$ times bigger than his safety level (for any $0 < \epsilon \ll 1$), as can be seen from the following example:

---

[2] This seems a most natural requirement, although there exist Nash equilibria in which agents overbid. It is useful to remember that the rules of ad auction effectively interpret the bid of an agent as the maximal price he is willing to pay per unit of CTR, so by overbidding the agent risks getting negative payoff. Agents do not overbid in the best SNE we compare to.

Example 1. Let there be N agents and N slots, let $0 < q < 1$, $x_1 > 0$ be parameters and let the valuations be

$$v_i = \sum_{t=i}^{N} q^{N-t} = \frac{1 - q^{N-i+1}}{1-q}$$

and CTR's be

$$x_i = x_1 q^{i-1}$$

Then for any N and ϵ, there exists $0 < q < 1$ so that the competitive safety ratio is at least $N - \epsilon$.

The analysis of the example can be found in the full paper. In fact, N is an upper bound on the competitive safety ratio, as shown by the following theorem:

Theorem 1. *In the complete information ad auction setting with N slots and N players, the competitive safety ratio (the ratio between an agent's payoff in a best SNE and the payoff guaranteed by a safety level strategy, under the assumption that the agents do not overbid) is at most N.*

Proof. When computing the (pure) safety level of an agent, it is assumed that the other agents know the bid of the agent under consideration (from now on, we will simply refer to him as *the* agent) and all the valuations, and they seek to minimize the utility of the agent. We will us the following notation:

- v_i is the i'th valuation in the ordered sequence of *all agents'* valuations (including the agent).
- $\hat{b}_i$ is the i'th bid in the ordered sequence of *all agents'* bids (including the agent).
- v' is the valuation of the agent.
- $\hat{b}'$ is the bid of the agent.
- $v\text{-}index(x) : [0,1] \to \{0\dots N-1\}$ is the number of adversarial agents with valuations that are strictly higher than x (for example, the valuation of the agent under consideration is $v_{v\text{-}index(v')+1}$, the valuation of the adversarial agent immediately below the agent under consideration in the ordering of valuations is $v_{v\text{-}index(v')+2}$, etc.).
- $b\text{-}index(x) : [0,1] \to \{0\dots N-1\}$ is the number of adversarial agents with bids that are strictly higher than x (for example, the bid of the adversarial agent immediately below the agent under consideration in the ordering of bids is $v_{b\text{-}index(b')+2}$).

The utility of the agent is $(v' - \hat{b}_{b\text{-}index(\hat{b}')+2})x_{b\text{-}index(\hat{b}')+1}$. Therefore, in order to minimize our agent's payoff, the other agents should choose their bids so that they maximize $\hat{b}_{b\text{-}index(\hat{b}')+2}$ and $b\text{-}index(\hat{b}') + 1$; those are conflicting goals, since the agents cannot overbid and therefore in order to maximize the price that the agent pays some of the agents with valuation higher than his bid might have to bid lower than him, letting him to get a better slot. It can be easily seen that there is no need to let the agent go up more than one slot and therefore the following is an optimal adversarial strategy:[3]

---

[3] The strategy described here is not unique - we chose the strategy with the most concise description.

- All adversarial agents that have valuations smaller than the agent's bid should bid truthfully.
- All adversarial agents that have valuations higher than the agent's bid, *except one*, should bid truthfully.
- One of the players that have higher valuation has to choose whether to bid truthfully or submit the same bid as the agent (which raises the agent's position by one slot but forces him to pay his bid, instead of the valuation of the player below him). Note that we assume here, for ease of exposition, that in the case of a tie the agent under consideration is given the higher slot.[4]

Therefore:

- The agent's utility when all adversarial players bid truthfully is $x_{v\text{-}index(\hat{b}')+1}(v' - v_{v\text{-}index(\hat{b}')+2})$.
- The agent's utility when one of the adversarial players with higher valuation bids the same as he is $x_{v\text{-}index(\hat{b}')}(v' - \hat{b}')$.
- Therefore, the utility of an agent given all valuations and his bid $\hat{b}$ is

$$\min\{x_{v\text{-}index(\hat{b}')+1}(v' - v_{v\text{-}index(\hat{b}')+2}), x_{v\text{-}index(\hat{b}')}(v' - \hat{b}')\}$$

Given that the adversarial agents use the strategy described above and the fact that in the complete information setting all the valuations are known to the agent, it can be easily seen that between all the bids that guarantee slot k (i.e. all $\hat{b}'$ so that $v\text{-}index(\hat{b}') = k - 1$), the agent weakly prefers to submit the smallest bid possible. Recall that we assume that ties are decided in favor of the agent[5], in which case the above observation means that the agent can, without loss of utility, consider only $N - v\text{-}index(v') + 1$ strategies – the valuations $\{v_i : i > v\text{-}index(v') + 1\}$ of the adversarial agents with valuations smaller than his valuation (note that these strategies include 0 as a possible bid which gives the agent the lowest possible slot). Therefore, his safety level payoff is:

$$\hat{U} = \max_{0 \le \hat{b}'} \min\{x_{v\text{-}index(\hat{b}')+1}(v' - v_{v\text{-}index(\hat{b}')+2}), x_{v\text{-}index(\hat{b}')}(v' - \hat{b}')\} =$$

$$= \max_{i:v\text{-}index(v')+1 < i \le N+1} \min\{x_{i-1}(v' - v_i), x_{i-2}(v' - v_i)\} =$$

$$= \max_{i:v\text{-}index(v')+1 < i \le N+1} x_{i-1}(v' - v_i) =$$

$$= \max_{i:v\text{-}index(v')+1 \le i \le N} x_i(v' - v_{i+1})$$

This implies that for any index j such that $v\text{-}index(v') + 1 \le j \le N$:

$$\frac{x_j}{\hat{U}} \le \frac{1}{v' - v_{j+1}}$$

---

[4] If that is not the case, an approximately equivalent strategy would be to submit a bid that is ϵ-smaller than that of the agent and force him to pay a price that is ϵ-close to his bid.

[5] Otherwise, we would have to consider the set of strategies $\{v_i + \epsilon : i > v\text{-}index(v') + 1\}$ for some small ϵ. It would not affect the nature of the results, but would make the exposition somewhat cumbersome.

Therefore, the competitive safety ratio is:

$$\frac{\tilde{U}}{\hat{U}} = \frac{\sum_{t=v\text{-}index(v')+1}^{N} x_t(v_t - v_{t+1})}{\hat{U}} \leq \sum_{t=v\text{-}index(v')+1}^{N} \frac{v_t - v_{t+1}}{v' - v_{t+1}} \leq N$$

The latter inequality is due to the fact that $\forall t \geq v\text{-}index(v') + 1 : v_t \leq v'$. □

For the special case when the CTR's are linear, the worst-case bound is given by the following theorem:

Theorem 2. *In the complete information ad auction setting with N slots and N players, when the CTR's are given by $x_i = d(N - i + 1)$ for some $d > 0$, the competitive safety ratio is at most $\sum_{t=1}^{N} \frac{1}{t} < 1 + \ln N$.*

The proof of the theorem, together with an example that demonstrates that this bound is tight, can be found in the full paper.

4 Competitive Safety Strategies for the Incomplete Information Setting

Now we want to consider the incomplete information setting. Specifically, we want to consider the following decision problem of an agent in this auction:

- The agent under consideration has valuation $v' \in [0, 1]$ which is known to him.
- The agent assumes that the other agents' valuations are distributed according to some known distribution.
- The agent is risk-neutral.
- The agent has two possible courses of action:
  1. To select to "play for the best SNE". This may mean, for example, that the auction is repeated with the same agents (and the same valuations), and the play sequence is assumed to converge to the best SNE. Alternatively, there may exist a central entity (a "mediator") that offers a course of action that is guaranteed to lead to the best SNE. In any case, the value that the agent assigns to this action is his expected payoff in the best SNE that is induced by the realizations of the players' valuations, where expectation is taken w.r.t the distribution of the other agents' valuations. It is important to note that this is also his expected payoff, given his valuation, in the corresponding Bayes-Nash equilibrium of this auction.[6]

---

[6] To see why, consider the following sequence of equalities. The allocation and payments are the same, for any tuple of valuations, in the best SNE and in the corresponding VCG auction (under complete information). However, assuming the incomplete information setup, the VCG auction is truthful, and therefore for any given valuation, the expected payoff of the agent in the incomplete information setting equals its expected payoff in the corresponding equilibrium of the complete information setting, where the expectation is taken over all possible instantiations of other agents' valuations. This implies that the expected payoff of our agent in the best SNE, computed according to the realizations of the agents' valuations, equals its expected payoff in the VCG ad auction with incomplete information. Finally, using the payoff equivalence theorem (Krishna and Perry1998) we get that this payoff equals the agent's payoff, for the given valuation, in the corresponding Bayes-Nash equilibrium of Varian's mechanism.

2. To use a "safety level strategy". This means that the agent selects an action that guarantees him the best expected payoff in the auction, against any *reasonable* action by the other players (where the expectation is taken w.r.t the distribution of the other agents' valuations). The value that the agent assigns to this action is the guaranteed expected payoff. Specifically, the following model of interaction is assumed:
    - All agents are assigned with their private values. Those values are fixed.
    - The agent under consideration selects his bid $\hat{b}'$, based on his valuation only (he does not know the realizations of other agents' valuations - he only knows their distribution).
    - The other agents select their bids based on the bid $\hat{b}'$ and the realizations of *all* valuations (including the agent's). It is assumed that they can communicate freely. They cannot overbid (i.e. each of them has to submit a bid that is less or equal to his valuation). It is assumed that they select the joint action that minimizes the agent's utility.

    It can be easily seen that in this model of interaction, agents can not gain by using mixed strategies and therefore we can consider, w.l.o.g, only pure strategies.
  - Intuitively, all things being equal, action 2 is preferred to action 1, since it does not require elaborate and hard-to-justify assumptions about the rationality of other agents, neither does it require any additional structure on top of the basic auction.
  - Therefore, the agent would like to know how much utility he loses by selecting action 2 instead of 1.

Naturally, the answer to the question formulated above depends on the distribution of valuations and the CTR values of the ad slots. We consider uniformly distributed valuations, and two central types of CTRs : exponentially decreasing CTRs, and linearly decreasing CTRs.

4.1   Exponentially Decreasing CTRs

For the case of uniformly distributed valuations and exponentially decreasing CTR's, the answer is given by the following theorem:

Theorem 3. *In the incomplete information ad auction setting with the following parameters:*

  - *the agents' valuations are distributed independently and uniformly over* $[0, 1]$,
  - *the CTR's are given by* $x_k = x_1 q^{k-1}$ *for* $0 < q < 1$ *and* $x_1 > 0$,

the ratio between

  - *the expected payoff in the best SNE that is induced by the valuations' realizations and*
  - *the expected payoff guaranteed by the safety level strategy, under the assumption that other agents do not overbid*

is at most e.

The proof of this theorem can be found in the full paper.

4.2   Linearly Decreasing CTRs

For the case of uniformly distributed valuations and linearly decreasing CTR's, the answer is given by the following theorem:

Theorem 4. *In the incomplete information ad auction setting with the following parameters:*

- *the agents' valuations are distributed independently and uniformly over* $[0, 1]$,
- *the CTR's are given by* $x_k = d(N - k + 1)$ *for* $d > 0$,

the ratio between

- *the expected payoff in the best SNE that is induced by the valuations' realizations and*
- *the expected payoff guaranteed by the safety level strategy, under the assumption that other agents do not overbid*

is at most 2.

The proof of this theorem can be found in the full paper.

5   Conclusions and Future Work

In this work, we have investigated whether useful C-competitive strategies exist in the setting of ad auctions, both in the complete and the incomplete information models. We have focused in our work on a model in which the slot values are decreasing exponentially or linearly, which we believe to be realistic assumptions. For these settings, we have shown by examples that in the complete information model there is no hope of achieving constant competitive safety ratio. On the other hand, in the incomplete information model with uniformly distributed valuations a competitive safety ratio of e can be achieved for exponentially decreasing CTRs, and a competitive safety ratio of 2 can be achieved for linearly decreasing CTRs. The intuition behind the difference in the results for the complete and incomplete information settings, is that while we can show a specific profile of valuations that is arbitrarily bad for the agent, the probability that "bad" profiles actually occur is negligible, and the profiles that do occur with high probability exhibit constant competitive safety ratio.

We see two conceptually different directions for future work:

- Investigate the existence of C-competitive strategies in other models of ad auctions. Those may include non-uniform distributions of valuations, other models of slot values or refinement of auction rules (such as introducing the quality factor parameter (Varian2006)).
- Investigating the existence of C-competitive strategies in other interesting subclasses of games, such as congestion games (Rosenthal1973), other non-VCG auctions, etc.

References

[Altman et al 2006] Altman, A., Boden-Bercovici, A., Tennenholtz, M.: Learning in one-shot strategic form games. In: Fürnkranz, J., Scheffer, T., Spiliopoulou, M. (eds.) ECML 2006. LNCS (LNAI), vol. 4212, Springer, Heidelberg (2006)

[Asdemir2005] Asdemir, K.: Bidding Patterns in Search Engine Auctions. Working Paper, University of Alberta School of Business (2005), Available at: http://www.business.ualberta.ca/kasdemir/biddingWARS.PDF

[Aumann1985] Aumann, R.J.: On the Non-Transferable Utility Value: A Comment on the Roth-Shaper Examples. Econometrica 53(3), 667–677 (1985)

[Borgs et al 2005] Borgs, C., Chayes, J., Etesami, O., Immorlica, N., Jain, K., Mahdian, M.: Bid Optimization in Online Advertisement Auctions. manuscript (2005)

[Carmel and Markovitch1999] Carmel, D., Markovitch, S.: Exploration strategies for model-based learning in multiagent systems. Autonomous Agents and Multi-agent Systems 2(2), 141–172 (1999)

[Krishna and Perry1998] Krishna, V., Perry, M.: Efficient Mechanism Design. Technical report, Pennsylvania State University (1998), Available at: http://econ.la.psu.edu/~vkrishna/papers/vcg20.pdf

[Powers and Shoham2004] Powers, R., Shoham, Y.: New criteria and a new algorithm for learning in multi-agent systems. In: Proceedings of NIPS 2004 (2004)

[Rosenthal1973] Rosenthal, R.W.: A Class of Games Possessing Pure-Strategy Nash Equilibria. International Journal of Game Theory 2, 65–67 (1973)

[Tennenholtz2002] Tennenholtz, M.: Competitive Safety Analysis: Robust Decision-Making in Multi-Agent Systems. Journal of Artificial Intelligence Research 17, 363–378 (2002)

[Varian2006] Varian, H.R.: Position auctions. Technical Report, UC Berkeley (2006), Available at: http://www.sims.berkeley.edu/~hal/Papers/2006/

Maintaining Equilibria During Exploration in Sponsored Search Auctions

Jennifer Wortman[1], Yevgeniy Vorobeychik[2],
Lihong Li[3], and John Langford[4]

[1] Computer and Information Science, University of Pennsylvania
wortmanj@seas.upenn.edu*
[2] Computer Science & Engineering, University of Michigan
yvorobey@umich.edu*
[3] Computer Science, Rutgers University
lihong@cs.rutgers.edu*
[4] Yahoo! Research
jl@yahoo-inc.com

Abstract. We introduce an exploration scheme aimed at learning advertiser click-through rates in sponsored search auctions with minimal effect on advertiser incentives. The scheme preserves both the current ranking and pricing policies of the search engine and only introduces one parameter which controls the rate of exploration. This parameter can be set so as to allow enough exploration to learn advertiser click-through rates over time, but also eliminate incentives for advertisers to alter their currently submitted bids. When advertisers have much more information than the search engine, we show that although this goal is not achievable, incentives to deviate can be made arbitrarily small by appropriately setting the exploration rate. Given that advertisers do not alter their bids, we bound revenue loss due to exploration.

1   Introduction

Recent years have seen an explosion of interest in sponsored search auctions, due in large part to the unique opportunity for targeted advertising and the resulting billions of dollars in revenue. Most sponsored search auctions display a list of advertisements on the sidebar or other sections of a search engine's results page, ranked by some function of advertisers' revealed willingness-to-pay for every click on their ad. The advertisers in turn pay the search engine for every click their ad receives. While several pricing schemes have been circulated in the literature [7], by far the most popular is a generalization of second-price auctions, under which each advertiser pays the lowest bid that is sufficient to ensure that the ad remain in its current slot. Typically the number of available slots for advertisements on the first search page is fixed, and thus only high ranking advertisements are displayed.

---

* This work was done while J. Wortman, Y. Vorobeychik, and L. Li were at Yahoo! Research, New York.

X. Deng and F.C. Graham (Eds.): WINE 2007, LNCS 4858, pp. 119–130, 2007.
© Springer-Verlag Berlin Heidelberg 2007

An essential part of both designing sponsored search auction mechanisms and bidding in them is the knowledge of the probability that a given ad is clicked each time it is displayed in a particular slot for a particular search query or keyword. This probability is known as the *click-through rate* or *CTR* of the ad. Knowledge of these click-through rates helps advertisers determine optimal bidding behavior. CTRs can also be an integral part of the ad ranking policy. For example, it is common for policies to rank bidders by the product of their bid and some function of their *relevance*, a slot-independent measure of CTR. Throughout the paper, we assume that CTRs do not change over time.

Most of the existing literature on sponsored search auctions treats CTRs as known. When advertisers first enter the system, however, their CTRs are not yet known either by the search engine or even by the advertisers themselves, and can only be estimated over time based on the observed clicks. Observations are inherently limited to slots in which ads appear, and estimates are generally poor for advertisers with low rank that do not usually appear at all. Furthermore, without the assumption of factorable CTRs, little can be said about CTRs of an ad in slots in which it has not previously appeared (or has appeared only a small number of times). Thus there is a need for an exploration policy that periodically perturbs the current slate of displayed ads, showing some in alternate slots and occasionally displaying those ads that are ranked below the last slot. Ideally, this exploration policy should not be difficult to incorporate into the current sponsored search mechanisms. Additionally, if the advertisers' bids have reached an equilibrium, the exploration policy should, when possible, eliminate the incentives for bidders to change their bids, thereby destabilizing the auction. Such destabilization can result in negative user and advertiser experience, as well as unnecessary loss in revenue to the search engine, and can make exploration harder to control.

In this paper, we address the problem of learning the click-through rates for each ad in every slot. Our primary goal is to maintain an equilibrium bid configuration if the bidders did indeed play according to an equilibrium prior to exploration. When this is not possible, we provide bounds on the amount that any advertiser could gain by deviating. This incentive to deviate can be minimized by reducing exploration, at the cost of slowing down the process of learning the CTRs. Additionally, we bound the revenue loss that the search engine incurs due to exploration, as compared to maintaining a policy based on current estimates of CTRs.

A similar problem has been addressed by Pandey and Olston [9] and Gonen and Pavlov [5]. The former work addresses the learning problem without considering advertiser incentives. The latter addresses both. Our model differs from existing ones in three primary ways:

1. We avoid imposing a particular ranking policy or introducing a new pricing scheme so that changes to existing systems are minimal.
2. The data gathered by our approach can be incorporated into general learning algorithms using sample selection debiasing techniques.[6]
3. We avoid the standard but unrealistic assumption that click-through rates can be factored into advertiser- and slot-specific components.

2 Notation and Definitions

We consider an auction for a particular keyword in which there are N advertisers (alternately called bidders or players) placing bids.[1] We assume that the search engine has K slots with non-negligible CTRs. Throughout the discussion on incentives, we assume that the CTRs depend only on the ad being displayed and the slot in which it is shown. Thus, we use c_i^s to denote the true CTR of player i in slot s. We assume that for each player i, $c_i^s > c_i^t$ whenever $1 \le s < t \le K$. For convenience, we define $c_i^s = 0$ for $s > K$ and $s < 1$. In most of our analysis we deal explicitly with estimated click-through rates; the search engine estimates are denoted by $\hat{c}_i^s$, whereas the advertiser i's estimates are denoted by $\tilde{c}_i^s$. Finally, we let v_i denote the value of a click to player i.

For now we assume that throughout the exploration process, advertisers are ranked according to their bid b_i multiplied by a weight w_i which is an increasing function of their estimated relevance scores for the particular keyword. Setting this weight equal to relevance recovers the standard rank-by-revenue model. Without loss of generality, assume that advertisers are indexed in the order in which they are ranked when playing equilibrium, i.e. advertiser i is in slot i in the ranking. Each advertiser pays a price per click equal to the lowest bid that maintains his current position; thus the price paid by bidder i in rank s is $p_i^s = w_{s+1} b_{s+1} / w_i$.

The relevance score of an advertiser, which we denote by e_i, can be thought of as an average CTR over all slots for the given keyword. We might choose to define this relevance as $\sum_{s=1}^{K} c_i^s$ or alternately as $\sum_{s=1}^{K} c_i^s / c_s$ where c_s is the "average" CTR that any ad might expect to receive on slot s.[2] We can fix the weights for each advertiser prior to (each phase of) exploration and reveal the new estimates of CTRs at the end of the exploration period only, allowing greater control of exploration.

We assume that prior to exploration the advertisers converge to a symmetric Nash equilibrium, a variant of Nash equilibrium introduced simultaneously by Varian [10] and Edelman et al.[3]. We slightly alter the standard definition to take into account CTR estimates as follows.

Definition 1. *A* symmetric Nash equilibrium (SNE) *is an ordering and a set of bids such that for every player i and for every slot s, $\tilde{c}_i^i (v_i - p_i^i) \ge \tilde{c}_i^s (v_i - p_i^s)$, where $\tilde{c}_i^s$ denotes advertiser i's CTR estimate at slot s.*

Existence of at least one symmetric Nash Equilibrium was proved in a slightly different setting than ours by Börgers et al. [1]. Their proof applies essentially without change to our setting.

---

[1] Since our analysis can be repeated for each keyword, the restriction to a single keyword is without loss of generality. Indeed, the analysis can even be generalized to incorporate arbitrary context information, as long as the number of contexts is finite and advertisers may submit separate bids for each. [4]

[2] Observe that when c_i^s is factorable into the product $e_i c_s$, both of these relevance scores are proportional to e_i.

3   An Algorithm for Exploration

We begin by describing a simple algorithm for learning click-through rates. Below (in Section 4) we show that we can set parameters of this algorithm in such a way as to minimize or entirely eliminate incentives for advertisers to deviate from a pre-exploration SNE. Our key condition will be that throughout the entire run of the algorithm the prices which the advertisers pay are fixed to their pre-exploration equilibrium prices.

The algorithm, which we call k-swap (Algorithm 1), starts by ranking ads by the product of bid and weight as usual, and repeatedly chooses pairs of ads to swap in order to explore. In particular, each time the given keyword receives an *impression* (i.e. each time a query is made on the keyword), a swapping distance $k \in \{1, \cdots, K\}$ is chosen from some distribution (e.g. uniformly at random). The algorithm calculates or looks up a swapping probability for each pair of slots s and $s + k$ that are a distance k apart. (The method for choosing these probabilities will be discussed in Section 4.) Finally, the algorithm uses this set of swapping probabilities to decide which (if any) pair of ads to swap.

We must be careful about how pairs of ads are chosen to be swapped so we can avoid swapping the same ad more than once on a single query. Let S_i denote the event that the ads in slots i and $i + k$ are swapped and let $r_i^k = \Pr(S_i)$ be the probability that this event occurs. We have

$$\Pr(S_i) = \Pr(S_i|S_{i-k})\Pr(S_{i-k}) + \Pr(S_i|\neg S_{i-k})\Pr(\neg S_{i-k}).$$

To avoid conflicting swaps, we can set $\Pr(S_i|S_{i-k}) = 0$, which implies that $\Pr(S_i|\neg S_{i-k}) = \Pr(S_i)/\Pr(\neg S_{i-k}) = r_i^k/(1 - r_{i-k}^k)$, which is no greater than one as long as we enforce that $r_{i-1}^k + r_i^k \leq 1$.

For the sake of this algorithm, all ads with rank $K + 1, \cdots, N$ can be thought of as sharing slot $K + 1$. Thus whenever an ad in slot $s \leq K$ is chosen to swap with slot $K + 1$, any ad with rank $K + 1, \cdots, N$ could be displayed in slot s. Due to lack of space, we do not discuss how the algorithm might decide which losing ad to display, but one could imagine giving preference to ads that have not often been displayed in the past.

4   Maintaining Equilibrium During Pairwise Swapping

In this section, we consider the effect on advertiser incentives of implementing an exploration policy that occasionally chooses pairs of ads that are k slots apart to swap or moves an undisplayed ad into slot $K - k + 1$ for some *fixed* value of k. By ensuring that advertisers do not have incentives to deviate from equilibrium bids for any fixed k, we ensure that the advertisers do not deviate throughout the entire run of k-swap.

We assume that the search engine bases the weights w_i on the CTR estimates $\hat{c}_i^s$, and fix the prices paid by the advertisers through the entire run of k-swap. The updated CTR estimates obtained during exploration are only reported to advertisers after the algorithm completes. In practice, the algorithm may need

---

Algorithm 1. The `k-swap` algorithm.

Calculate all swapping probabilities r_i^k
for all queries on the given keyword **do**
    Randomly select a $k \in \{1, \cdots, K\}$
    for $i = 1$ to $\min\{k, K - k + 1\}$ **do**
        Set $S_i \leftarrow 1$ with probability r_i^k, $S_i \leftarrow 0$ otherwise
    end for
    for $i = k + 1$ to $K - k + 1$ **do** {Note that this statement is null if $2k > K$}
        if $S_{i-k} = 1$ **then**
            Set $S_i \leftarrow 0$
        else
            Set $S_i \leftarrow 1$ with probability $r_i^k/(1 - r_{i-k}^k)$, $S_i \leftarrow 0$ otherwise
        end if
    end for
    for $i = 1$ to $K - k$ **do**
        Swap the ads in slots i and $i + k$ if $S_i = 1$
    end for
    if $S_{K-k+1} = 1$ **then**
        Choose an $i \in \{K + 1, \cdots, N\}$ to display in slot $K - k + 1$
    end if
end for

---

to be run in multiple phases, interleaving exploration with updates of CTR estimates, and allowing sufficient time for advertisers to reach a new equilibrium after each phase.

Our assumptions raise a conceptual question: if the advertisers care about the *real* CTRs, how can we maintain incentives given only estimates? We posit that often advertisers do not know the CTRs any better than the search engine and formulate their own optimization problem (at least approximately) in terms of the estimates provided by the search engine; that is, we assume that $\tilde{c}_i^s = \hat{c}_i^s \, \forall i, s$. We consider the case in which advertisers have additional information about their CTRs in Section 6.

For the analysis that follows, we assume that the search engine knows (or can obtain good estimates of) each advertiser's value per click. If we assume that a SNE is played prior to exploration, we can derive bounds on advertiser values [10] and base our estimates on these bounds. In practice, this assumption will not be necessary; we do not actually advocate setting the swapping probabilities separately for each individual auction, but rather fixing probabilities in such a way that the guarantees will hold for most typical auctions.

Since all analysis in this section is for a fixed value of k, we drop the superscript and use r_i in place of r_i^k to denote be the probability that ads i and $i + k$ are swapped. These probabilities can be represented as multiples of r_1, i.e. $r_i = \alpha_i r_1$. Then, if α_i are set exogenously (for example, $\alpha_i = 1$ for all $1 \leq i \leq K$), `k-swap` has only one tunable parameter, r_1, for a fixed value of k. For convenience of notation, we define $\alpha_i = 0$ for all $i < 1$ and $i > K - k + 1$. In order to allow exploration of CTRs of all bidders, we let r_{K-k+1} designate the total probability that *any* losing bidder is swapped into slot $K - k + 1$. Let q_s denote the probability that a losing bidder with rank $K + 1 \leq s \leq N$ is displayed *conditional* on *some* losing ad being displayed.[3] We have that $\sum_{s=K+1}^{N} q_s = 1$. Finally, define $q_{max} = \max_{K+1 \leq s \leq N} q_s$.

Once we add exploration, the *effective* estimate of CTR for advertiser i in slot s is no longer $\hat{c}_i^s$. Rather, now with some probability r_{s-k} the ad in slot s is moved to slot $s - k$, and with some probability r_s the ad is moved to slot $s + k$. Then the new effective estimate of CTR of player i for rank s is $\hat{c}_i'^s = (1 - r_{s-k} - r_s)\hat{c}_i^s + r_{s-k}\hat{c}_i^{s-k} + r_s\hat{c}_i^{s+k}$.[4]

Let $D_{i,s} = \alpha_s(\hat{c}_i^s - \hat{c}_i^{s+k}) - \alpha_{s-k}(\hat{c}_i^{s-k} - \hat{c}_i^s)$. Observe that $r_1 D_{i,s}$ is the marginal CTR loss of advertiser i in slot s when exploration is allowed. We now define the quantities $J_{i,j}$ and Z_i which are used in Theorem 1:

$$J_{i,j} = (v_i - p_i^i)D_{i,i} - (v_i - p_i^j)D_{i,j} \tag{1}$$

$$Z_i = (v_i - p_i^i)D_{i,i} + \alpha_{K-k+1}q_{max}\hat{c}_i^{K-k+1}v_i. \tag{2}$$

To get some intuition about what these mean, note that $r_1 J_{i,j}$ is the difference between the marginal loss in expected payoff due to exploration that the advertiser i receives in slot j and the marginal loss in expected payoff due to exploration in slot i. Similarly, $r_1 Z_i$ is the difference between the marginal loss in payoff due to exploration that the advertiser i receives by switching to rank above $K + 1$ (and thereby not occupying any slot) and the marginal loss due to exploration in slot i.

The following result gives the conditions under which exploration does not incent advertisers to change their bids and characterizes the settings in which this is not possible. The proof of this theorem and others can be found in the appendix of the extended version of this paper.[5]

Theorem 1. *Assume that each advertiser* $i \in \{1, \cdots, K\}$ *strictly prefers his current slot to all others in equilibrium, i.e. the condition* $(v_i - p_i^i)\hat{c}_i^i > (v_i - p_i^j)\hat{c}_i^j$ *holds for all* $1 \leq i, j \leq K, i \neq j$ *whenever* $J_{i,j} > 0$ *and* $v_i - p_i^i > 0$ $\forall i$ *whenever* $Z_i > 0$. *Then for generic valuations and relevances there exists an* $r_1 > 0$ *such that no advertiser has incentive to deviate from the pre-exploration SNE bids once exploration is added. In particular, any* r_1 *satisfying the following set of conditions is sufficient:*

$$r_1 \leq \min \left\{ \min_{2 \leq i \leq K} \frac{1}{\alpha_i + \alpha_{i-k}}, \quad \min_{1 \leq i \leq K; Z_i > 0} \frac{1}{Z_i}(v_i - p_i^i)\hat{c}_i^i, \right.$$

$$\left. \min_{1 \leq i,j \leq K; i \neq j; J_{i,j} > 0} \frac{1}{J_{i,j}}\left((v_i - p_i^i)\hat{c}_i^i - (v_i - p_i^j)\hat{c}_i^j \right) \right\}.$$

---

[3] Thus, the probability that a particular losing bidder s gets selected is $q_s r_{K-k+1}$.

[4] Recall that $r_s = 0$ and $\hat{c}_i^s = 0$ for $s < 1$ and $s > K - k + 1$. We can replace CTR with effective CTR because the prices paid by all advertisers remain fixed for the duration of exploration.

[5] The extended version is available on the authors' websites.

To get some intuition about how the theorem can be applied and about the magnitude of r_1, consider the following example.

Example 1. Suppose that there are 3 advertisers bidding on 2 slots. Let $\hat{c}_i^j = \hat{c}_j$ for all players $i \in \{1, 2, 3\}$ and slots $j \in \{1, 2\}$ where $\hat{c}_1 = 1$ and $\hat{c}_2 = 0.5$. Let $v_1 = v_2 = 3$, and $v_3 = 1$. Suppose that prior to exploration each advertiser bids his value per click and pays the next highest bid. One can easily verify that this configuration constitutes a SNE in which player 1 gets slot 1, player 2 gets slot 2, and player 3 gets no slot, and that in this equilibrium, player 1 is indifferent between slots 1 and 2.

Let us fix $\alpha_2 = 3/2$. Now we can determine the setting of r_1 that allows us to swap neighboring ads ($k = 1$) without introducing incentives to deviate during exploration. Applying the first constraint, we find the condition that $r_1 \leq 1/(1 + 3/2) = 2/5$ must hold. By the second constraint, since $Z_1 = 11/4$, we must have $r_1 \leq 4/11$, and since $Z_2 = 7/4$, we must have $r_1 \leq 2/7$. With our setting of α_2, $J_{1,2} = 0$ and $J_{2,1} = -1/4 < 0$. Consequently, the third constraint on r_1 has no effect. Combining the effects of these constraints, we see that we can set the swapping probabilities as high as $r_1 = 2/7$ and $r_2 = 3/7$ without giving any of the advertisers incentive to deviate during exploration.

Suppose we want to increase r_1 to $2/7 + \epsilon$ and thereby learn a little bit faster. Consider the incentives of the second bidder to switch to rank 3 (i.e., receive no slot). The utility from being ranked third is $3/7 + 3\epsilon/2 > 3/7$, while the utility from remaining in slot two is $3/7 - \epsilon/4 < 3/7$. Consequently, for any $\epsilon > 0$ (and, thus, for any $r_1 > 2/7$) the second bidder wants to deviate from his equilibrium bid.

A similar analysis of constraints and incentives shows that we cannot increase α_2 without decreasing r_1 or altering advertiser incentives. Similarly, any attempt to decrease α_2 can destabilize the equilibrium.

As the example suggests, the bounds in Theorem 1 are close to tight. In fact, the bounds can be made tight simply by replacing q_{max} with the conditional probability with which ad i would be selected if it were not in one of the top K ranks.

Note that we would not expect a search engine to calculate a distinct set of swapping probabilities using Theorem 1 for each individual auction in practice. Indeed it may not be possible for the search engine to estimate advertiser values accurately in all cases. We instead advocate using the theorem to find a single fixed set of swapping probabilities such that advertisers will not wish to deviate when k-swap is run for *most* or *all typical* auctions.

5   Learning Bounds

In this section, we bound the error of our estimated click-through rates for each advertiser in each slot after Q queries have been made on the given keyword. Let $n_{i,s}$ denote the number of times we have observed advertiser i in slot s, and let $z_{i,s,j}$ be the indicator random variable which is 1 if ad i is clicked the jth time it appears in slot s, and 0 otherwise. Finally, let $\pi_{i,s}^k$ be the probability that ad i is displayed at slot s when we are swapping ads that are k slots apart, as discussed in Section 4.

To simplify the presentation of results, we assume that the swapping distance k is drawn uniformly at random from $\{1, \cdots, K\}$ for each query, but the extension to arbitrary distributions is straight-forward.

Theorem 2. *Suppose the k-swap algorithm has been run for Q queries with a fixed set of broadcasted CTR estimates. Let $\hat{c}_i^s$ be our new estimate of CTR, defined as $\hat{c}_i^s = (1/n_{i,s}) \sum_{j=1}^{n_{i,s}} z_{i,s,j}$ for all advertisers i and slots s such that $n_{i,s} \geq 1$. Then for any $\delta \in (0,1)$, with probability $1 - \delta$, the following holds for all i and s for which we have made at least one observation:*

$$|\hat{c}_i^s - c_i^s| \leq \sqrt{\frac{\ln(2KN/\delta)}{2n_{i,s}}}.$$

Furthermore, with probability $1 - \delta$, for all i and s, we have that $n_{i,s} \geq \max\{(Q/K) \sum_{k=1}^{K} \pi_{i,s}^k - \sqrt{Q \ln(2KN/\delta)/2}, 0\}$.

Thus as the number of queries Q grows, our estimates of the CTR vectors for each advertiser grow arbitrarily close to the true CTR vectors.

6   Bounds on the Incentives of "Omniscient" Advertisers

If players have much more information about the actual click-through rates than the search engine, it is unlikely that we can entirely eliminate incentives of advertisers to change their bids during exploration. However, if we can bound the error in our estimates of the click-through rates, we can also bound how much advertisers can gain by deviating. When incentives to deviate are small, we may reasonably expect advertisers to maintain their equilibrium bids, since computing the new optimal bids may be costly. The search engine may further dull benefits from deviation by charging a small fee to advertisers when they change their bids.

From this point on, we assume that the error in search engine estimates of the CTRs is uniformly bounded by ϵ; that is, $|c_i^s - \hat{c}_i^s| \leq \epsilon$ for every i and s.

Assume that r_1^k were set such that the bidders have no incentive to change their bids if they use $\hat{c}_i^s$ as their CTR estimates. We now establish how much incentive they have to deviate if they know their *actual* CTR c_i^s, that is, $\tilde{c}_i^s = c_i^s$; we call such advertisers "omniscient".

Theorem 3. *The most that any omniscient advertiser can gain by deviating in expectation per impression is $\max_{1 \leq i \leq K} 2\epsilon(v_i - p_i^K)$.*

This bound has the intuitive property that as our CTR estimates improve, the bound on incentives to deviate from equilibrium bids improves as well.[6] It is also

---

[6] Note that given r_1^k the actual payoffs to deviation are not affected as we learn unless we also publicize the learned information.

intuitive, however, that incentives diminish if the exploration probabilities fall. This motivates the following alternate bound which shows that we can make the incentives to deviate arbitrarily small even for omniscient advertisers by appropriately setting r_1^k.

Theorem 4. *The most that any omniscient advertiser can gain by deviating in expectation per impression is*

$$\max_{1 \leq i,j,k \leq K} \left\{ r_1^k \left(\alpha_i(\hat{c}_i^i - \hat{c}_i^{i+k}) + \alpha_{j-k}(\hat{c}_i^{j-k} - \hat{c}_i^j) + 2\epsilon(\alpha_i + \alpha_{j-k}) \right) \left(v_i - p_i^K \right) \right\}.$$

7 Bounds on Revenue Loss Due to Exploration

We now assume that the advertisers play according to the symmetric Nash equilibrium that was played prior to exploration and, as in the previous section, assume that the errors of the search engine's estimates of CTRs are uniformly bounded by ϵ with high probability. Given these assumptions, the theorem that follows bounds the loss in revenue due entirely to exploration.

Theorem 5. *The maximum expected loss to the search engine revenue per impression due to exploration is bounded by*

$$\max_{1 \leq k \leq K} \left\{ r_1^k \sum_{i=2}^{K} p_i^i \left(\alpha_i(\hat{c}_i^i - \hat{c}_i^{i+k}) - \alpha_{i-k}(\hat{c}_i^{i-k} - \hat{c}_i^i) + 2\epsilon \right) \right\}.$$

8 Special Cases

In this section we study the problem of exploration while maintaining a pre-exploration symmetric Nash equilibrium in two special cases. In both cases, it is only necessary to swap adjacent pairs of ads in order to learn reasonable estimates of advertiser CTRs.

8.1 Factorable Click-Through Rates

The first special case we consider is the commonly studied setting where $c_i^s = e_i c_s$; that is, CTRs are factored into a product of advertiser relevance and slot-specific factors. Since there are far more data for estimating c_s than e_i, we assume c_s is known and e_i is to be learned for all advertisers. Under these assumptions, using k-swap may seem strange; after all, we can learn e_i for all advertisers $i \leq K$ just as well by leaving them in their current slots! The only problem to be addressed then is to learn CTRs of losing bidders. Consequently, if we truly believe that CTRs are factorable, we need only do adjacent-ad swapping ($k = 1$) and can set $r_1 = \cdots = r_{K-1} = 0$ and only allow $r_K > 0$. In this case, we need not worry about deviations by advertisers in slots $1, \ldots, K - 1$ to alternative slots $1, \ldots, K - 1$, since the effective CTRs for these deviations are unchanged.

Additionally, no advertiser wants to deviate to slot K, since the CTR in this slot is strictly lower than it was before exploration, and no advertiser ranked $K+1, \ldots, N$ wants a higher slot, since their effective CTRs increase. Thus we need only consider the incentives of the advertiser in slot K. It is not difficult to verify that the condition under which exploration does not affect advertiser K's incentives is

$$
r_K \leq \min \left\{ \min_{1 \leq j \leq K-1} \frac{c_K \left(v_K - p_K^K \right) - c_j \left(v_K - p_K^j \right)}{c_K (v_K - p_K^K)}, \frac{v_K - p_K^K}{v_K (q_{max} + 1) - p_K^K} \right\},
$$

and we can find an $r_K > 0$ when $c_K(v_K - p_K^K) > c_j(v_K - p_K^j)$ for $j < K$.

There is, however, another possible scenario in which exploration might be useful under the factorable CTR assumption. Suppose that we initially posit the factorable CTR model, but want to verify whether this is really the case. To do so, we can use adjacent-ad swapping to form multiple estimates of e_i using data from multiple adjacent slots. By comparing these estimates, we can vet our current model while also improving our CTR estimates for losing bidders.

Since CTR is factorable, our analysis need only consider the effective slot-specific CTRs, which we assume are known, $c_s' = (1 - r_{s-1} - r_s)c_s + r_{s-1}c_{s-1} + r_s c_{s+1}$. Set $\alpha_i = \prod_{j=2}^{i} [(c_{j-1} - c_j)/(c_j - c_{j+1})]$. By setting the swapping probabilities in this manner, the effective CTRs in slots $2, \cdots, K-1$ are unchanged when exploration is added. We can now simplify the bounds and characterization of Theorem 1. In particular, the precondition of the theorem and the second bound on r_1 need only to hold for $i = 1$. Furthermore, it can be shown that in the factorable setting, the necessary precondition $(v_1 - p_1^1)c_1 > (v_1 - p_1^j)c_j$ always holds in the minimum revenue SNE [10,8,2] for generic valuations and relevances. Formal statements and proofs of these results are in the appendix of the extended version.

As in the general setting, it is possible to derive learning bounds that show that as the number of observed queries grow, our estimates of the advertiser CTR vectors grow arbitrarily close to the true CTRs with high probability. Here our estimates of CTR are simply $\hat{c}_i^s = (c_s/c_{s_i} n_{i,s_i}) \sum_{j=1}^{n_{i,s_i}} z_{i,s_i,j}$ for all i and s, where $s_i = \arg\max_s c_s \sqrt{n_{i,s}}$. We once again defer the theorem statement and proof to the appendix of the extended version due to lack of space.

8.2 Click-Through Rates with Constant Slot Ratios

In this section, we consider adjacent-ad swapping ($k = 1$) for the case in which for each player i, the click-through rates have constant ratios for adjacent slots. That is, for all i and all $1 \leq s \leq K-1$, we assume that $c_i^{s+1}/c_i^s = \gamma_i \leq 1$ where γ_i is advertiser-dependent and unknown. Let $\hat{\gamma}_i$ denote the search engine estimate of γ_i and suppose as before that advertisers use these as their own estimates. Let $\alpha_j = 1$ for every $j \in \{2, \ldots, K-1\}$, so $r_1 = r_2 = \cdots = r_{K-1}$. Additionally, let $\alpha_K = \min\{(\hat{\gamma}_i - 1)^2/q_{max}, 1\}$.

As in the previous section, we can considerably simplify the bounds and characterization of Theorem 1 in this special case. In particular, the first and second bounds on r_1 must hold, but the third bound on r_1 and the precondition need only to hold for $i = 1$ and $i = K$.

We can also prove analogous learning bounds in this setting that show that it is only necessary to explore via adjacent-ad swapping in order to obtain CTR estimates for all advertisers at all slots. This can be accomplished by estimating γ_i for each i as

$$\hat{\gamma}_i = \frac{(1/n_{i,s_i+1}) \sum_{j=1}^{n_{i,s_i+1}} z_{i,s_i+1,j}}{(1/n_{i,s_i}) \sum_{j=1}^{n_{i,s_i}} z_{i,s_i,j}}$$

for a chosen slot s_i at which there is a sufficient amount of data available. The CTR at each slot is then estimated using $\hat{\gamma}_i$ and the estimate of the CTR at the designated slot s_i.

Formal theorems describing the conditions on r_1 necessary to maintain equilibrium in this setting and the corresponding learning bounds can be found in the appendix of the extended version, along with their proofs.

9 Conclusion

We have introduced an exploration scheme which allows search engines to learn click-through rates for advertisements. We showed how, when possible, to set the exploration parameters in order to eliminate the incentives for advertisers to deviate from a pre-exploration symmetric Nash equilibrium. In situations in which we cannot entirely eliminate incentives to change bids, we can make returns to changing bids arbitrarily small. Particularly, we can make these small enough to ensure that bid manipulation is hardly worth advertisers' time. Finally, we derived a bound on worst-case expected per-impression revenue loss due to exploration. Since this loss is zero in the limit of no exploration, we can set exploration parameters in order to make it arbitrarily small, while still ensuring that we eventually learn click-through rates.

Acknowledgements

The authors thank Alexander Strehl and Yiling Chen for insightful comments on early drafts of this paper.

References

1. Börgers, T., Cox, I., Pesendorfer, M., Petricek, V.: Equilibrium bids in auctions of sponsored links: theory and evidence. Technical report, University of Michigan (2007)
2. Cary, M., Das, A., Edelman, B., Giotis, I., Heimerl, K., Karlin, A.R., Mathieu, C., Schwarz, M.: Greedy bidding strategies for keyword auctions. In: Eighth ACM Conference on Electronic Commerce (2007)
3. Edelman, B., Ostrovsky, M., Schwarz, M.: Internet advertising and the generalized second price auction: Selling billions of dollars worth of keywords. American Economic Review 9(1), 242–259 (2007)

4. Even-Dar, E., Kearns, M., Wortman, J.: Sponsored search with contexts. In: 3rd International Workshop on Internet and Network Economics (2007)
5. Gonen, R., Pavlov, E.: An incentive-compatible multi-armed bandit mechanism. In: 26th Annual ACM Symp. on Principles of Distributed Computing (2007)
6. Heckman, J.: Sample selection bias as a specification error. Econometrica 47, 153–161 (1979)
7. Lahaie, S.: An analysis of alternative slot auction designs for sponsored search. In: ACM Conference on Electronic Commerce, pp. 218–227 (2006)
8. Lahaie, S., Pennock, D.M.: Revenue analysis of a family of ranking rules for keyword auctions. In: ACM Conference on Electronic Commerce (2007)
9. Pandey, S., Olston, C.: Handling advertisements of unknown quality in search advertising. In: Neural Information and Processing Systems (2006)
10. Varian, H.: Position auctions. Int'l Journal of Industrial Organization (to appear)

Stochastic Models for Budget Optimization in Search-Based Advertising*

S. Muthukrishnan[1], Martin Pál[1], and Zoya Svitkina[2,**]

[1] Google, Inc., New York, NY
muthu@google.com, mpal@google.com
[2] Department of Computer Science, Dartmouth College
zoya@cs.dartmouth.edu

Abstract. Internet search companies sell advertisement slots based on users' search queries via an auction. Advertisers have to determine how to place bids on the keywords of their interest in order to maximize their return for a given budget: this is the *budget optimization* problem. The solution depends on the distribution of future queries. In this paper, we formulate *stochastic* versions of the budget optimization problem based on natural probabilistic models of distribution over future queries, and address two questions that arise.

Evaluation. Given a solution, can we evaluate the expected value of the objective function?

Optimization. Can we find a solution that maximizes the objective function in expectation?

Our main results are approximation and complexity results for these two problems in our three stochastic models. In particular, our algorithmic results show that simple *prefix* strategies that bid on all cheap keywords up to some level are either optimal or good approximations for many cases; we show other cases to be NP-hard.

1 Introduction

Internet search companies use auctions to sell advertising slots in response to users' search queries. To participate in these auctions, an advertiser selects a set of keywords that are relevant or descriptive of her business, and submits a bid for each of them. Upon seeing a user's query, the search company runs an auction among the advertisers who have placed bids for keywords matching the query and arranges the winners in slots. The advertiser pays only if a user clicks on her ad. Advertiser's bid affects the position of the ad, which in turn affects the number of clicks received and the cost incurred. In addition to the bids, the advertiser specifies a daily budget. When the cost charged for the clicks reaches the budget, the advertiser's ads stop participating in the auctions.

---

* A preliminary announcement of these results appears in the WWW Workshop on Sponsored Search, 2007.

** This work was done while visiting Google, Inc., New York, NY.

X. Deng and F.C. Graham (Eds.): WINE 2007, LNCS 4858, pp. 131–142, 2007.
© Springer-Verlag Berlin Heidelberg 2007

In what follows, we first model and abstract the budget optimization problem, and then present our stochastic versions, before describing our results.

1.1   Advertiser's Budget Optimization Problem

We adopt the viewpoint of an advertiser and study the optimization problem she faces. The advertiser has to determine the daily budget, a good set of keywords, and bids for these keywords so as to maximize the effectiveness of her campaign. The daily budget and the choice of keywords are business-specific, so they are assumed to be given in our problem formulation. Effectiveness of a campaign is difficult to quantify since clicks resulting from some keywords may be more desirable than others, and in some cases, just appearing on the results page for a user's query may have some utility. We adopt a common measure of the effectiveness of a campaign, namely, the *number of clicks*[1] obtained. Further, seen from an individual advertiser's point of view, the budgets and bids of other advertisers are fixed for the day. We model a single-slot auction, and disregard the possibility of other advertisers changing their bids or running out of budget. Under these assumptions, each keyword i has a single threshold bid amount, such that any bid below this amount loses the auction and does not get any clicks. Any bid above the threshold wins the auction, and gets clicks with cost per click equal to the threshold bid amount[2]. In this case the advertiser's decision for each keyword becomes binary: whether or not to bid on it above its threshold. We use decision variables b_i, which can be integral ($b_i \in \{0,1\}$) or fractional ($b_i \in [0,1]$), to indicate whether or not there is a bid on keyword i. A fractional bid represents bidding for b_i fraction of the queries that correspond to keyword i, or equivalently bids on each such query with probability b_i. Integer bid solutions are slightly simpler to implement and are more desirable when they exist.

Finally, consider the effect of user behavior on the advertiser. We abstract it using the function $\mathbf{clicks}_i$, which is the number of clicks the advertiser gets for queries corresponding to keyword i. Each such click entails a cost $\mathbf{cpc}_i$, which is assumed to be known. Now, the advertiser is *budget-constrained*, and some solutions may run out of budget, which decreases the total number of clicks obtained. In particular, the advertiser has a global daily budget B, which is used to get clicks for all of the keywords. When the budget is spent, the ads stop being shown, and no more clicks can be bought. We model the limited budget as follows. Consider a solution $\mathbf{b}$ that bids on some keywords. With unlimited budget, bidding on those keywords would bring $\mathbf{clicks}(\mathbf{b})$ clicks, which together would cost $\mathbf{cost}(\mathbf{b})$. But when the budget B is smaller than $\mathbf{cost}(\mathbf{b})$, this solution runs out of money before the end of the day, and misses the clicks that come after that point. If we assume that the queries and clicks for all keywords are distributed uniformly throughout the day and are well-mixed, then this solution reaches the budget after $B/\mathbf{cost}(\mathbf{b})$ fraction of the day passes,

---

[1] An easy extension allows clicks for different keywords to have different values.

[2] This assumes *second price* auctions, where the winner's cost is the highest bid of others. All results also apply to weighted second price auctions.

missing $(1 - B/\mathbf{cost}(b))$ fraction of the possible clicks for each keyword. As a result, the number of clicks collected before the budget is exceeded is $\frac{\mathbf{clicks}(b)}{\mathbf{cost}(b)/B}$ in expectation.

Based on the discussion so far, we can now state the optimization problem an advertiser faces.

Definition 1. BUDGET OPTIMIZATION PROBLEM *(BO). An advertiser has a set T of keywords, with $|T| = n$, and a budget B. For each keyword $i \in T$, we are given $\mathbf{clicks}_i$, the number of clicks that correspond to i, and $\mathbf{cpc}_i$, the cost per click of these clicks. We define $\mathbf{cost}_i = \mathbf{cpc}_i \cdot \mathbf{clicks}_i$. The objective is to find a solution $b = (b_1, ..., b_n)$ with a bid $0 \le b_i \le 1$ for each $i \in T$ to maximize*

$$\mathbf{value}(b) = \frac{\sum_{i \in T} b_i \mathbf{clicks}_i}{\max\left(1, \sum_{i \in T} b_i \mathbf{cost}_i / B\right)}. \tag{1}$$

The numerator of the objective function is the number of clicks available to b, and the denominator scales it down in the case that the budget is exceeded. If we define $\mathbf{clicks}(b) = \sum_{i \in T} b_i \mathbf{clicks}_i$, $\mathbf{cost}(b) = \sum_{i \in T} b_i \mathbf{cost}_i$, and the average cost per click of solution b as $\mathbf{cpc}(b) = \frac{\mathbf{cost}(b)}{\mathbf{clicks}(b)}$, then

$$\mathbf{value}(b) = \begin{cases} \mathbf{clicks}(b) & \text{if } \mathbf{cost}(b) \le B \\ B/\mathbf{cpc}(b) & \text{if } \mathbf{cost}(b) > B \end{cases} \tag{2}$$

So maximizing $\mathbf{value}(b)$ is equivalent to maximizing the number of clicks in case that we are under budget, and minimizing the average cost per click if we are over budget. We always assume that the keywords are numbered in the order of non-decreasing $\mathbf{cpc}_i$, i.e. $\mathbf{cpc}_1 \le \mathbf{cpc}_2 \le \cdots \le \mathbf{cpc}_n$.

1.2 Stochastic Versions

Many variables affect the number of clicks that an advertiser receives in a day. Besides the advertiser's choice of her own budget and keywords which we take to be given, and the choices of other advertisers which remain fixed, the main *variable* in our problem is the number of queries of relevance that users issue on that day, and the frequency with which the ads are clicked.[3] These quantities are not known precisely in advance. Our premise is that Internet search companies can analyze past data and provide probability distributions for parameters of interest. They currently do provide limited amount of information about the range of values taken by these parameters.[4] This motivates us to study the problem in the *stochastic* setting where the goal is to maximize the *expected* value of the objective under such probability distributions.

---

[3] The nature and number of queries vary significantly. An example in Google Trends shows the spikes in searches for shoes, flowers and chocolate:
http://www.google.com/trends?q=shoes,flowers,chocolate.

[4] See for example the information provided to any AdWords advertiser. See also
https://adwords.google.com/support.

In the stochastic versions of our problem, the set of keywords T, the budget B, and the cost per click $\mathbf{cpc}_i$ for each keyword are fixed and given, just like in the BO problem of Definition 1. What is different is that the numbers of clicks $\mathbf{clicks}_i$ corresponding to different keywords are random variables having some joint probability distribution. But because general joint probability distributions are difficult to represent and to work with, we formulate the following natural stochastic models. (In contrast, the problem where $\mathbf{clicks}_i$ are known precisely for all i is called the *fixed* model from here on.)

Proportional Model. The relative proportions of clicks for different keywords remain constant. This is modeled by one global random variable for the total number of clicks in the day, and a fixed known multiplier for each keyword that represents that keyword's share of the clicks.

Independent Keywords Model. Each keyword comes with its own probability distribution for the number of clicks, and the samples are drawn from these distributions independently.

Scenario Model. There is an explicit list of N *scenarios*. Each scenario specifies the number of clicks for each keyword, and has a probability of occurring. We think of N as reasonably small, and allow the running time of our algorithms to depend (polynomially) on N.

The scenario model is important for two reasons. For one, market analysts often think of uncertainty by explicitly creating a set of a few model scenarios, possibly attaching a weight to each scenario. The second reason is that the scenario model gives us an important segue into understanding the fully general problem with arbitrary joint distributions. Allowing the full generality of an arbitrary joint distribution gives us significant modeling power, but poses challenges to the algorithm designer. Since a naive explicit representation of the joint distribution requires space exponential in the number of random variables, one often represents the distribution implicitly by a sampling oracle. A common technique, Sampled Average Approximation (SAA), is to replace the true distribution $\mathcal{D}$ by a uniform or non-uniform distribution $\hat{\mathcal{D}}$ over a set of samples drawn by some process from the sampling oracle, effectively reducing the problem to the scenario model. For some classes of problems, see e.g. [13,7,20], it is known that SAA approximates the original distribution to within an arbitrarily small error using polynomially many samples. While we are not aware of such bounds applicable to the budget optimization problem, understanding the scenario model is still an important step in understanding the general problem.

There are two issues that arise in each of the three stochastic models.

– STOCHASTIC EVALUATION PROBLEM (SE). Given a solution $\boldsymbol{b}$, can we evaluate $E[\mathbf{value}(\boldsymbol{b})]$ for the three models above? Even this is nontrivial as is typical in stochastic optimization problems. It is also of interest in solving the budget optimization problem below.
– STOCHASTIC BUDGET OPTIMIZATION PROBLEM (SBO). This is the Budget Optimization problem with one of the stochastic models above determining $\mathbf{clicks}_i$ for each i, with the objective to maximize

$$E[\textbf{value}(b)] = E\left[\frac{\sum_{i \in T} b_i \textbf{clicks}_i}{\max\left(1, \sum_{i \in T} b_i \textbf{cost}_i / B\right)}\right]. \tag{3}$$

The expectation is taken over the joint distribution of $\textbf{clicks}_i$ for all $i \in T$.

1.3 Our Results

Our results for SE and SBO problems are algorithmic and complexity-theoretic.

For SE problems, our results are as follows. The problem is straight-forward to solve for the fixed and scenario models since the expression for the expected value of the objective can be explicitly written in polynomial time. For the proportional model, we give an exact algorithm to evaluate a solution, assuming that some elementary quantities (such as probability of a range of values) can be extracted from the given probability distribution in polynomial time. For the independent model, the number of possibilities for different click quantities may be exponential in the number of keywords, and the problem of evaluating a solution is likely to be #P-hard. We give a PTAS for this case. These evaluation results are used to derive algorithms for the SBO problem, though they may be of independent interest.

Our main results are for the SBO problem. In fact, all our algorithms produce a special kind of solutions called *prefix solutions*. A prefix solution bids on some prefix of the list of keywords sorted in the increasing order of cost per click ($\textbf{cpc}_i$), i.e., on the cheap ones. Formally, an *integer prefix solution* with bids b_i has the property that there exists some i^* such that $b_i = 1$ for all $i \leq i^*$, and $b_i = 0$ for $i > i^*$. For a *fractional prefix solution*, there exists an i^* such that $b_i = 1$ for $i < i^*$, $b_i = 0$ for $i > i^*$, and $b_{i^*} \in [0, 1]$. We show:

- For the proportional model, we can find an optimal fractional solution in polynomial time if the distribution of clicks can be described using polynomial number of points; else, we obtain a PTAS. We get this result by showing that the optimal fractional solution in this case is a prefix solution and giving an algorithm to find the best prefix.
- Our main technical contribution is the result for the independent model, where we prove that every integer solution can be transformed to a prefix solution by removing a set of expensive keywords and adding a set of cheap ones, while losing at most half of the value of the solution. Thus, some integer prefix is always a 2-approximate integer solution. When combined with our PTAS for the evaluation problem, this leads to a $2 + \varepsilon$ approximation algorithm. We also show that the best fractional prefix is not in general the optimal fractional solution in this case.
- For the scenario model, we show a negative result that finding the optimum, fractional or integer, is NP-hard. In this case, the best prefix solution is arbitrarily far from the optimum.

1.4 Related Work

Together, our results represent a new theoretical study of stochastic versions of budget optimization problems in search-related advertising. The budget optimization problem was studied recently [9] in the fixed model, when **clicks**$_i$'s are known. On one hand, our study is more general, with the emphasis on the uncertainty in modeling **clicks**$_i$'s and the stochastic models we have formulated. We do not know of prior work in this area that formulates and uses our stochastic models. On the other hand, our study is less general as it does not consider the interaction between keywords that occurs when a user's search query matches two or more keywords, which is studied in [9].

Stochastic versions of many optimization problems have been considered, such as facility location, Steiner trees, bin-packing and LP (see, for example, the survey [20]). Perhaps the most relevant to our setting is the work on the stochastic knapsack problem, of which several versions have been studied. Dean et al. [8] consider a version of the problem in which item values are fixed, and item sizes are independent random variables. The realization of an item's size becomes known as soon as it is placed in the knapsack, so an algorithm has to select the items one at a time, until the knapsack capacity is exceeded. In [12] and [10], a version of the problem with fixed item values and random sizes is considered as well, but there the goal is to choose a valuable set of items whose probability of exceeding the knapsack capacity is small. Other authors [5,11,18,19] have studied versions with fixed item sizes but random values. If viewed as a version of stochastic knapsack, our problem is different from all of these in several respects. First, there is no hard capacity constraint, but instead the objective function decreases continuously if the cost of the keywords (which is analogous to the size of the items) exceeds the budget (the analog of the knapsack capacity). The second difference is that in our model, both the number of clicks and the cost of the keywords (i.e. item values and sizes, respectively) are random, but their ratio for each particular keyword (item) is fixed and known. Another difference is that previous work on stochastic knapsack considers independent distributions of item parameters, whereas two of our models (proportional and scenario) have correlated variables. Furthermore, although the greedy algorithm which takes items in the order of their value-to-size ratio is well-known and variations of it have been applied to knapsack-like problems, our analysis proving the 2-approximation result is new.

Recently, Chakrabarty et al. [6] considered an online knapsack problem with the assumption of small element sizes, and Babaioff et al. [2] considered an online knapsack problem with a random order of element arrival, both motivated by bidding in advertising auctions. The difference with our work is that these authors consider the problem in the online algorithms framework, and analyze the competitive ratios of the obtained algorithms. In contrast, our algorithms make decisions offline, and we analyze the obtained approximation ratios for the expected value of the objective. Also, our algorithms base their decisions on the probability distributions of the clicks, whereas the authors of [2] and [6] do not assume any advance knowledge of these distributions. The two approaches are in some sense complementary: online algorithms have the disadvantage that in practice it may not be possible to make new decisions about bidding every time that a query arrives, and stochastic optimization has the disadvantage of requiring the knowledge of the probability distributions.

Also motivated by advertising in search-based auctions, Rusmevichientong and Williamson [17] have studied the *keyword selection* problem, where the goal is to select a subset of keywords from a large pool for the advertiser to choose to bid. Their model is similar to our proportional model, but the proportions of clicks for different keywords are unknown. An adaptive algorithm is developed that learns the proportions by bidding on different prefix solutions, and eventually converges to near-optimal profits [17], assuming that various parameters are concentrated around their means. The difference with our work is that we consider algorithms that solve the problem in advance, and not by adaptive learning, and work for any arbitrary (but pre-specified) probability distributions.

There has been a lot of other work on search-related auctions in the presence of budgets, but it has primarily focused on the game-theoretic aspects [16,1], strategy-proof mechanisms [4,3], and revenue maximization [15,14].

We discuss the fixed case first, and focus on the three stochastic models in the following sections; in each case, we solve both evaluation and BO problems.

2   Fixed Model

For the BO problem in the fixed model, a certain fractional prefix, which is easy to find, is the optimal solution. The algorithm is analogous to that for the fractional knapsack problem. We find the maximum index i^* such that $\sum_{i \le i^*} \text{cost}_i \le B$. If i^* is the last index in T, we set $b_i = 1$ for all keywords i. Otherwise find a fraction $\alpha \in [0, 1)$ such that $\sum_{i \le i^*} \text{cost}_i + \alpha \cdot \text{cost}_{i^*+1} = B$, and set $b_i = 1$ for $i \le i^*$, $b_{i^*+1} = \alpha$, and $b_i = 0$ for $i > i^* + 1$.

Theorem 1. *In the fixed model, the optimal fractional solution for the BO problem is the maximal prefix whose cost does not exceed the budget, which can be found in linear time.*

The integer version of this problem is NP-hard by reduction from KNAPSACK.

3   Proportional Model

In the proportional model of SBO, we are given q_i, the *click frequency* for each keyword $i \in T$, with $\sum_{i \in T} q_i = 1$. The total number of clicks is denoted by a random variable C, and has a known probability distribution p. The number of clicks for a keyword i is then determined as $\text{clicks}_i = q_i \cdot C$. For a specific value c of C, let $\text{clicks}_i^c = q_i c$ and $\text{cost}_i^c = \text{cpc}_i \text{clicks}_i^c$. The objective is to maximize the expected number of clicks, given by expression (3).

Theorem 2. *The optimal fractional solution for the SBO problem in the proportional model is a fractional prefix solution.*

The proof is by an interchange argument and is omitted. We now show how to solve the SE problem efficiently in the proportional model, and then use it to find the best prefix, which by Theorem 2 is the optimal fractional solution.

3.1   Evaluating a Solution

Assuming that the distribution for C is given in such a way that it is easy to evaluate $\Pr[C > c^*]$ and $\sum_{c \leq c^*} c \cdot p(c)$ for any c^*, we show how to find $E[\mathbf{value}(b)]$ for any given solution b without explicitly going through all possible values of C and evaluating the objective function for each one.

The solution b may be under or over budget depending on the value of C. Define a threshold $c^* = B/\sum_{i \in T} b_i q_i \mathbf{cpc}_i$, so that for $c \leq c^*$, $\mathbf{cost}^c(b) \leq B$, and for $c > c^*$, $\mathbf{cost}^c(b) > B$. Notice that in the proportional model, $\mathbf{cpc}(b)$ is independent of C, as both $\mathbf{clicks}(b)$ and $\mathbf{cost}(b)$ are proportional to C. Then using expression (2) for $\mathbf{value}(b)$, the objective becomes easy to evaluate:

$$E[\mathbf{value}(b)] = \sum_{i \in T} b_i q_i \sum_{c \leq c^*} c\, p(c) + \frac{B}{\mathbf{cpc}(b)} \Pr[C > c^*]. \tag{4}$$

3.2   Finding the Optimal Prefix

It is nontrivial to find the best fractional prefix solution for the proportional case, and we mention two approaches that do not work. One of them is to set the number of clicks for a keyword to its expectation. Another approach is some greedy procedure that lengthens the prefix while the solution improves. This does not work because the expected value of the solution as a function of the length of the prefix can have multiple local maxima.

The best prefix can be found by producing a list of $O(n + t)$ prefixes (out of uncountably many possible ones) containing the optimum. Here t is the number of possible values of C. If t is not polynomial in n, then the probability distribution for C can be partitioned into buckets, yielding a PTAS for the problem. The list of prefixes to evaluate includes all the integer prefixes, as well as a threshold prefix that exactly spends the budget for each possible value of C. This partitions the space of possible prefixes into intervals, and the optimal prefix solution inside each interval, which is also added to the list, can be found by writing an expression for its value as a function of its length and taking a derivative.

Theorem 3. *The optimal fractional solution to SBO problem in the proportional model can be found exactly in time $O(n + t)$, where t is the number of possible values of C, or approximated by a PTAS.*

4   Independent Model

In the independent model of SBO, the number of clicks for keyword $i \in T$, $\mathbf{clicks}_i$, has a probability distribution p_i (which can be different for different keywords). The key distinguishing feature of this model is that for $i \neq j$, the variables $\mathbf{clicks}_i$ and $\mathbf{clicks}_j$ are independent. This model is more complex than the ones discussed so far. A three-keyword example shows the following.

Theorem 4. *In the independent model of the SBO problem, the optimal fractional solution may not be a prefix solution.*

However, in Section 4.1 we prove that some integer prefix solution is a 2-approximate integer solution. But finding the best integer prefix requires the ability to evaluate a given solution, which in this model is likely to be #P-hard. We develop a PTAS, based on dynamic programming, for evaluating a solution (the algorithm is omitted). Combined, these two results imply a $(2+\varepsilon)$-approximation for the SBO problem in the independent model.

4.1 Prefix is a 2-Approximation

In this section we show that for any instance of the SBO problem in the independent model, there exists an integer prefix solution whose expected value is at least half that of the optimal integer solution. In particular, any integer solution $\boldsymbol{b}$ can be transformed into a prefix solution $\boldsymbol{b}_V$ without losing more than half of its value. Let $S = \{i \mid b_i = 1\}$ be the set of keywords that $\boldsymbol{b}$ bids on.

We make some definitions that allow us to specify the prefix solution $\boldsymbol{b}_V$ precisely in Theorem 5. Let σ be the event that clicks for each keyword $i \in T$ come in quantity $\mathbf{clicks}^{\sigma}(i)$. Then its probability is $p(\sigma) = \prod_{i \in T} p_i(\mathbf{clicks}^{\sigma}(i))$. Define the number of clicks available to solution $\boldsymbol{b}$ in the event σ as $\mathbf{clicks}^{\sigma}(\boldsymbol{b}) = \sum_{i \in S} \mathbf{clicks}^{\sigma}(i)$, corresponding cost per keyword $\mathbf{cost}^{\sigma}(i) = \mathbf{cpc}_i \cdot \mathbf{clicks}^{\sigma}(i)$, and total cost $\mathbf{cost}^{\sigma}(\boldsymbol{b}) = \sum_{i \in S} \mathbf{cost}^{\sigma}(i)$. The effective number of clicks (taking budget into account) that solution $\boldsymbol{b}$ gets from keyword i in the event σ is

$$\overline{\mathbf{clicks}}^{\sigma}_S(i) = \frac{\mathbf{clicks}^{\sigma}(i)}{\max(1, \mathbf{cost}^{\sigma}(\boldsymbol{b})/B)},$$

and the total effective number of clicks is $\overline{\mathbf{clicks}}^{\sigma}(\boldsymbol{b}) = \sum_{i \in S} \overline{\mathbf{clicks}}^{\sigma}_S(i)$. Then the objective becomes the sum of effective number of clicks in each scenario, weighted by that scenario's probability: $E[\mathbf{value}(\boldsymbol{b})] = \sum_{\sigma} p(\sigma) \overline{\mathbf{clicks}}^{\sigma}(\boldsymbol{b})$.

Let $i^*(\boldsymbol{b})$ be the minimum index i^* such that keywords up to i^* account for half the clicks:

$$\sum_{\sigma} p(\sigma) \sum_{i \in S, i \leq i^*} \overline{\mathbf{clicks}}^{\sigma}_S(i) \geq \frac{1}{2} E[\mathbf{value}(\boldsymbol{b})].$$

Theorem 5. *For any integer solution $\boldsymbol{b}$ to the SBO problem with independent keywords, there exists an integer prefix solution $\boldsymbol{b}_V$ such that $E[\mathbf{value}(\boldsymbol{b}_V)] \geq \frac{1}{2} E[\mathbf{value}(\boldsymbol{b})]$. In particular, the solution $\boldsymbol{b}_V$ bidding on the set $V = \{i \mid i \leq i^*(\boldsymbol{b})\}$ has this property.*

The idea of the proof is to think of the above prefix solution as obtained in two steps from the original solution $\boldsymbol{b}$. First, we truncate $\boldsymbol{b}$ by discarding all keywords after i^*. Then we fill in the gaps in the resulting solution to make it into a prefix. To analyze the result, we first show that all keywords up to i^* are relatively cheap, and that the truncated solution (called $\boldsymbol{b}_U$) retains at least half the value of the original one (Proposition 1). Then we show that filling in the gaps preserves this guarantee. Intuitively, two good things may happen: either clicks for new keywords don't come, and we get all the clicks we had before; or many of them come, spending the budget, which is good because they are cheap. Lemma 1 analyzes what happens if new clicks spend α^σ fraction of the budget.

Let $i^* = i^*(b)$. To analyze our proposed prefix solution b_V, we break the set V into two disjoint sets U and N. $U = V \cap S = \{i \le i^* \mid i \in S\}$ is the set of cheapest keywords that get half the clicks of b. The new set $N = V \setminus S = \{i \le i^* \mid i \notin S\}$ fills in the gaps in U. Let b_U and b_N be the solutions that bid on keywords in U and N respectively.

Define the average cost per click of solution b as

$$\mathbf{cpc}^* = \frac{\sum_\sigma p(\sigma) \sum_{i \in S} \mathbf{cpc}_i \, \overline{\mathbf{clicks}}_S^\sigma(i)}{\sum_\sigma p(\sigma) \, \overline{\mathbf{clicks}}^\sigma(b)},$$

where the numerator is the average amount of money spent by b, and the denominator is the average number of clicks obtained. Since the numerator of this expression never exceeds the budget, and the denominator is equal to $E[\mathbf{value}(b)]$,

$$E[\mathbf{value}(b)] \le \frac{B}{\mathbf{cpc}^*}. \tag{5}$$

We make two observations about b_U and i^*, and then state the main lemma.

Proposition 1. $E[\mathbf{value}(b_U)] \ge \frac{1}{2}E[\mathbf{value}(b)]$ and $\mathbf{cpc}_{i^*} \le 2\mathbf{cpc}^*$.

Lemma 1. For any σ, let $\alpha^\sigma = \min(B, \mathbf{cost}^\sigma(b_N))/B$. Then

$$\overline{\mathbf{clicks}}^\sigma(b_V) \ge \alpha^\sigma \frac{B}{2\mathbf{cpc}^*} + (1 - \alpha^\sigma) \, \overline{\mathbf{clicks}}^\sigma(b_U).$$

The idea here is that α^σ is the fraction of the budget spent by the new keywords (ones from set N) in the event σ. So $(1 - \alpha^\sigma)$ fraction of the budget can be used to buy $(1 - \alpha^\sigma)$ fraction of clicks that b_U was getting, and α^σ fraction is spent on keywords (whether from U or N) that cost at most $2\mathbf{cpc}^*$.

Proof of Theorem 5. We now use the above results to prove the theorem. Let σ_U be the event that clicks for each keyword $i \in U$ come in quantity $\mathbf{clicks}^{\sigma_U}(i)$, whose probability is $p(\sigma_U) = \prod_{i \in U} p_i(\mathbf{clicks}^{\sigma_U}(i))$. Here the independence of keywords becomes crucial. In particular, what we need is that the number of clicks that come for keywords in U is independent of the number of clicks for keywords in N. So the probability of σ_V is the product of $p(\sigma_U)$ and $p(\sigma_N)$, where σ_V is the event that both σ_U and σ_N happen. Notice that α^σ of Lemma 1 depends only on keywords in N, and is independent of what happens with keywords in U. So here we call it α^{σ_N}. We have $E[\mathbf{value}(b_V)] =$

$$\sum_{\sigma_V} p(\sigma_V)\overline{\mathbf{clicks}}^{\sigma_V}(b_V) \ge \sum_{\sigma_N}\sum_{\sigma_U} p(\sigma_N)p(\sigma_U)\left[\frac{\alpha^{\sigma_N} B}{2\mathbf{cpc}^*} + (1-\alpha^{\sigma_N})\overline{\mathbf{clicks}}^{\sigma_V}(b_U)\right] =$$

$$\sum_{\sigma_N} p(\sigma_N)\left[\frac{\alpha^{\sigma_N} B}{2\mathbf{cpc}^*} + (1-\alpha^{\sigma_N})\sum_{\sigma_U} p(\sigma_U)\overline{\mathbf{clicks}}^{\sigma_V}(b_U)\right] \ge \sum_{\sigma_N} p(\sigma_N)\frac{1}{2}E[\mathbf{value}(b)]$$

$= \frac{1}{2} E[\mathbf{value}(b)]$, bounding both $\frac{B}{2\mathbf{cpc}^*}$ and $E[\mathbf{value}(b_U)]$ by $\frac{1}{2} E[\mathbf{value}(b)]$ using inequality (5) and Proposition 1.   □

Combining Theorem 5 with PTAS for the SE problem, we get

Theorem 6. *There is a $(2 + \varepsilon)$-approximation algorithm for the SBO problem in the independent model, which runs in time polynomial in n, $\frac{1}{\varepsilon}$, and $\log M$, where M is the maximum possible cost of all clicks.*

5 Scenario Model

In the scenario model, we are given T, B and costs $\mathbf{cpc}_i$ as usual. The numbers of clicks are determined by a set of scenarios Σ and a probability distribution p over it, so that a scenario $\sigma \in \Sigma$ materializes with probability $p(\sigma)$, in which case each keyword i gets $\mathbf{clicks}_i^\sigma$ clicks. The scenarios are disjoint and $\sum_{\sigma \in \Sigma} p(\sigma) = 1$. The reason this model does not capture the full generality of arbitrary distributions is that we assume that the number of scenarios, $|\Sigma|$, is relatively small, in the sense that algorithms are allowed to run in time polynomial in $|\Sigma|$. This is the most difficult model for SBO that we consider. We give two negative results.

Theorem 7. *The SBO problem is NP-hard in the scenario model.*

Theorem 8. *The gap between the optimal fractional prefix solution and the optimal (integer or fractional) solution to the SBO problem in the scenario model can be arbitrarily large.*

6 Concluding Remarks

We have initiated the study of stochastic version of budget optimization. We obtained approximation results via prefix bids and showed hardness results for other cases. A lot remains to be done, both technically and conceptually. Technically, we need to extend the results to the case when there are interactions between keywords, that is, two or more of them apply to a user query and some resolution is needed. Also, we need to study online algorithms, including online budget optimization. Further, we would like to obtain some positive approximation results for the scenario model, which seems quite intriguing from an application point of view. The conceptual challenge is one of modeling. Are there other suitable stochastic models for search-related advertising, that are both expressive, physically realistic and computationally feasible?

References

1. Aggarwal, G., Goel, A., Motwani, R.: Truthful auctions for pricing search keywords. In: Proc. 8th ACM Conf. on Electronic Commerce, pp. 1–7 (2006)
2. Babaioff, M., Immorlica, N., Kempe, D., Kleinberg, R.: A knapsack secretary problem with applications. In: Proc. 10th APPROX (2007)

3. Borgs, C., Chayes, J., Etesami, O., Immorlica, N., Jain, K., Mahdian, M.: Bid optimization in online advertisement auctions. In: 16th International World Wide Web Conference (2007)
4. Borgs, C., Chayes, J., Immorlica, N., Mahdian, M., Saberi, A.: Multi-unit auctions with budget-constrained bidders. In: Proc. 7th ACM Conf. on Electronic Commerce, pp. 44–51 (2005)
5. Carraway, R.L., Schmidt, R.L., Weatherford, L.R.: An algorithm for maximizing target achievement in the stochastic knapsack problem with normal returns. Naval Research Logistics 40, 161–173 (1993)
6. Chakrabarty, D., Zhou, Y., Lukose, R.: Budget constrained bidding in keyword auctions and online knapsack problems. In: WWW 2007 Workshop on Sponsored Search Auctions (2007)
7. Charikar, M., Chekuri, C., Pal, M.: Sampling bounds for stochastic optimization. In: Proc. 9th International Workshop on Randomization and Computation (2005)
8. Dean, B.C., Goemans, M.X., Vondrak, J.: Approximating the stochastic knapsack problem: The benefit of adaptivity. In: Proc. 45th IEEE Symp. on Foundations of Computer Science, pp. 208–217 (2004)
9. Feldman, J., Muthukrishnan, S., Pal, M., Stein, C.: Budget optimization in search-based advertising auctions. In: Proc. 9th ACM Conf. on Electronic Commerce (2007)
10. Goel, A., Indyk, P.: Stochastic load balancing and related problems. In: Proc. 40th IEEE Symp. on Foundations of Computer Science (1999)
11. Henig, M.I.: Risk criteria in a stochastic knapsack problem. Oper. Res. 38(5), 820–825 (1990)
12. Kleinberg, J., Rabani, Y., Tardos, E.: Allocating bandwidth for bursty connections. SIAM Journal on Computing 30(1), 191–217 (2000)
13. Kleywegt, A.J., Shapiro, A., Homem-de-Mello, T.: The sample average approximation method for stochastic discrete optimization. SIAM J. on Optimization 12, 479–502 (2002)
14. Mahdian, M., Nazerzadeh, H., Saberi, A.: Allocating online advertisement space with unreliable estimates. In: Proc. 9th ACM Conf. on Electronic Commerce (2007)
15. Mehta, A., Saberi, A., Vazirani, U., Vazirani, V.: Adwords and generalized on-line matching. In: Proc. 46th IEEE Symp. on Foundations of Computer Science, pp. 264–273 (2005)
16. Ostrovsky, M., Edelman, B., Schwarz, M.: Internet advertising and the generalized second price auction: Selling billions of dollars worth of keywords (forthcoming). American Economic Review (2006)
17. Rusmevichientong, P., Williamson, D.P.: An adaptive algorithm for selecting profitable keywords for search-based advertising services. In: Proc. 8th ACM Conf. on Electronic Commerce, pp. 260–269 (2006)
18. Sniedovich, M.: Preference order stochastic knapsack problems: Methodological issues. The Journal of the Operational Research Society 31, 1025–1032 (1980)
19. Steinberg, E., Parks, M.: A preference order dynamic program for a knapsack problem with stochastic rewards. The Journal of the Operational Research Society 30(2), 141–147 (1979)
20. Swamy, C., Shmoys, D.B.: Approximation algorithms for 2-stage stochastic optimization problems. SIGACT News 37(1), 33–46 (2006)

Auctions with Revenue Guarantees
for Sponsored Search

Zoë Abrams and Arpita Ghosh

Yahoo!, Inc. and Yahoo! Research
{za,arpita}@yahoo-inc.com

Abstract. We consider the problem of designing auctions with worst case revenue guarantees for sponsored search. In contrast with other settings, ad dependent clickthrough rates lead to *two* natural posted-price benchmarks. In one benchmark, winning advertisers are charged the same price per click, and in the other, the product of the price per click and the advertiser clickability (which can be thought of as the probability an advertisement is clicked if it has been seen) is the same for all winning advertisers. We adapt the random sampling auction from [9] to the sponsored search setting and improve the analysis from [1], to show a high competitive ratio for two truthful auctions, each with respect to one of the two described benchmarks. However, the two posted price benchmarks (and therefore the revenue guarantees from the corresponding random sampling auctions) can each be larger than the other; further, which is the larger cannot be determined without knowing the private values of the advertisers. We design a new auction, that incorporates these two random sampling auctions, with the following property: the auction has a Nash equilibrium, and *every* equilibrium has revenue at least the larger of the revenues raised by running each of the two auctions individually (assuming bidders bid truthfully when doing so is a utility maximizing strategy). Finally, we perform simulations which indicate that the revenue from our auction outperforms that from the VCG auction in less competitive markets.

1 Introduction

We address the problem of designing auctions with revenue guarantees in the sponsored search setting. This problem is crucial for search engines, most of which rely heavily on sponsored search for revenue. The efficient auction in this setting, namely VCG [21,5,10,6,15], and the current mechanism used for sponsored search, namely GSP [6,20] (of which the VCG outcome is an equilibrium [6]), do not provide revenue guarantees. In fact, the revenue from VCG can be arbitrarily bad compared to the optimal revenue with full knowledge of bidder valuations, as the footnote shows[1]. Our simulations indicate that the revenue

---

[1] This is shown by the following (extreme) example. Suppose there are k slots and $k + 1$ bidders, where k of these bidders have value per click 1, and one bidder has a value per click of ϵ. Each of these ads has a clickthrough rate of c in every slot. Under VCG, the k bidders with the highest values are assigned slots, and every bidder pays his negative externality, which in this case is ϵc. So the revenue extracted by VCG is $\epsilon c k$, which can be arbitrarily small compared to the optimal revenue which is ck.

X. Deng and F.C. Graham (Eds.): WINE 2007, LNCS 4858, pp. 143–154, 2007.

from the VCG outcome can be particularly small in less competitive yet realistic markets, where there are not many bidders with similar values for the keyword.

Can we ensure revenue guarantees even in markets with less competition? The metric we use to gauge the performance of an auction is the revenue that could be raised by an *optimal omniscient posted price auction* (the auction that raises the optimal revenue if the auctioneer knows the true valuations of all bidders and charges every winner the same price). The *competitive ratio* is the worst case ratio, over all possible inputs, between the revenue of an optimal omniscient posted price auction and the revenue of the proposed auction.

The main challenge in applying competitive analysis to our setting is to incorporate the existence of multiple posted price benchmarks arising from the structure of clickthrough rates. As in [6,2], we model clickthrough rates as *separable*, *i.e.*, the probability that a particular ad in a particular slot is clicked can be broken down into two probabilities. First is the slot-clickability, which can be thought of as the probability that the user will look at the displayed advertisement (the higher the slot placement, the more likely it is that the user will see the ad). The second is the ad-clickability, which can be thought of as the bidder dependent probability that the advertisement will be clicked, given that it has been seen. While the basic component of our mechanism is a random sampling auction as in [9], there are now *two* natural posted-price benchmarks depending on whether or not advertisers are discounted for their clickabilities: the optimal omniscient single-price revenue where all winning advertisers must be charged the same price per click, and the optimal omniscient 'weighted-price' revenue, where all winning advertisers are charged the same price per sighting, *i.e.*, the product of price per click and ad-clickability is the same for all winning advertisers. These two benchmarks are the natural posted-price analogs of two charging schemes that have been used in practice: charge an advertiser the bid-per-click of the bidder below him, or discount the bidder proportional to his ad-clickability, *i.e.*, divide the bid per click of the advertiser below by the ad-clickability of the bidder being charged.

Although our work is motivated by sponsored search, it is also applicable in other settings where the probability of a successful event is the product of the probability of two separate events: one event based on factors that depend on the allocation, and the other event based on bidder dependent factors. For example, an airport manager may want to auction off a set of vendor sites. One event is that a potential customer walks past a site, and this event depends on the particular location of the site within the airport (i.e. the allocation). The other event is that the potential customer walking past the site will actually enter the site, and this event depends on factors related to the bidder occupying the site such as attractiveness of the site and brand familiarity.

The main contribution of our paper is a mechanism with a Nash equilibrium that raises revenue competitive against both the single price and weighted price benchmarks. To do this, we first adapt the random sampling auction to obtain two auctions, each with revenue guarantees against one of the two benchmarks. The contribution here is improving an existing analysis of the random sampling auction by a factor 2, in addition to an analysis of the random sampling approach in the sponsored setting, accounting for advertiser and slot clickabilities.

The two random sampling auctions are then used as building blocks for a single auction with Nash equilibria that raises revenue at least as large as that raised by each of the two random sampling auctions independently; further, if bidders bid their true value whenever that belongs to the set of utility maximizing strategies, *every* Nash equilibrium of the auction raises this high revenue. This is significant for the following reason. As we show in Section 2, either of these two benchmarks can be larger than the other: the optimal weighted price revenue can be as small as a factor $O(\log k)$ of the optimal single price revenue, and the optimal single price revenue can be as small as a factor $1/k$ of the optimal weighted price revenue. In addition, which benchmark is larger cannot be determined *without knowing the private values of the bidders*. One significant challenge in designing an auction competitive against both benchmarks is that the same bidders participate in both auctions and can have higher utility in one or the other. Despite the presence of such bidders, we find that there is a way to *always* raise revenue competitive with both benchmarks. While the auction is no longer truthful, every Nash equilibrium of the auction has this competitive property.

We also perform numerical simulations to compare the performance of our auction against that of the VCG auction. In crowded markets with a large amount of competition, both auctions achieve a large fraction of the optimal revenue, and the VCG auction obtains more revenue than the competitive auction. However, as the market becomes less competitive and both auctions achieve a smaller fraction of the optimal revenue, the competitive auction overtakes the VCG auction. Our findings that the competitive auction produces more revenue than the VCG alternative in more challenging situations (*i.e.*, less competitive markets) is in keeping with our analytical framework, as competitive auctions are designed to perform well in worst case settings.

Related work: The classical work of Myerson [17,15] discusses the design of revenue-maximizing auctions in the Bayesian setting. Roughgarden and Sundararajan [19] show that in the Bayesian setting, the VCG mechanism applied to sponsored search auctions obtains higher revenue in more competitive markets. Edelman and Schwarz [7] explore setting reserve prices to increase revenues. The authors in [13] study how to use ad-clickabilities in ranking and pricing to improve revenue. In terms of competitive analysis for auctions, the random sampling approach was first proposed in [9], and has since been used in several problems and contexts, see for example [14,4,11]. Finally, there are several papers that combine multiple auctions into a single auction [3,16,1]. In [3], the generalized auction uses two successive auctions to create an auction that is truthful while maintaining the competitive ratio; this composition does not apply in our context.

1.1 Model

Our model is the following. There are n bidders competing for k slots. Each bidder has a private valuation for a click, v_i. We order bidders by value, *i.e.*,

$v_1 \geq \ldots \geq v_n$. Every slot-bidder pair has a clickthrough rate c_{ij} associated with it, which is the probability that the advertisement of bidder i in slot j is clicked. We assume that this clickthrough rate is *separable*, *i.e.*, $c_{ij} = \mu_i \theta_j$, where we refer to μ_i as the ad-clickability of bidder i, and θ_j as the slot-clickability of slot j. The separability assumption is equivalent to saying that the events of clicking on a particular ad (regardless of which slot it is displayed in) and a particular slot (regardless of which ad is displayed in it) are independent. Although this assumption is not always entirely accurate, analysis shows it is often reasonable [22], and it has been widely adopted in the literature [2,6,18,12]. We assume that the ad-clickabilities μ_i and slot-clickabilities θ_i are public knowledge (for our results in §3, we only need μ_i and θ_i to be known to the seller). We assume that the clickabilities of the slots decrease with position, *i.e.*, $\theta_1 \geq \theta_2 \geq \ldots \geq \theta_k$. We define Θ_i to be the sum of the clickabilities of the top i slots. Precisely, $\Theta_i = \sum_{j=1}^{i} \theta_j$. We denote by b_i the bid of bidder i, and the price charged to bidder i in an allocation by p_i. The auction mechanism takes the bids b_i, and computes an allocation x and pricing p, where $x_i = j$ if bidder i is assigned to slot j, and is 0 if bidder i is not assigned a slot; p_i is the price that bidder i pays for every click he receives in his slot. For a bidder i, we define $w_i = v_i \mu_i$, which is the expected value to the bidder from a slot with clickability $\theta_j = 1$. By the separability assumption, the expected value to bidder i in a slot with clickability θ_j is $w_i \theta_j$.

2   Optimum Pricing Solutions

The previous work on digital goods auctions uses as a benchmark the optimal multi-price and optimal single price revenues [11,9,1]. In this section, we extend these concepts to our problem, introducing a new benchmark, optimal weighted price revenue, and bound these benchmarks against each other. While current auctions do not sell clicks in different slots at the same price, a single price (or single weighted price) per click is still meaningful when interpreted as a common reserve price for all slots.

Definition 1. *Multi-price optimal (OPT_{MP}): The multi-price optimal revenue, OPT_{MP}, is the maximum possible revenue that can be extracted with k slots, when the true values of all bidders are known. Let $w_{i(j)}$ denote the jth largest value in w, then*

$$OPT_{MP} = \sum_{j=1}^{\min(n,k)} w_{i(j)} \theta_j. \qquad (1)$$

We denote by O_M the set of bidders that are assigned slots in this allocation.

Definition 2. *Single price optimal (OPT_{SP}): The single price optimal revenue OPT_{SP} is the maximum revenue that can be extracted with k slots, when the true values of all bidders are known, and every bidder assigned to a slot must be charged the same price per click. Here $p \leq k$ items are sold at a single price v_p,* *where the single price is chosen to maximize revenue. Let $\mu_{i(j)}^p$ be the jth largest μ_i of bidders with values $v_i \geq v_p$. Then, OPT_{SP} is computed as*

$$OPT_{SP} = \max_{p=1,\ldots,\min(n,k)} v_p \sum_{j=1}^{p} \mu_{i(j)}^p \theta_j. \tag{2}$$

We denote the set of bidders contributing positive revenue to OPT_{SP} as O_S.

Unlike in settings without ad-clickabilities, the optimal single price here is not necessarily limited to one of the values $v_1, \ldots, v_k$ – the optimal single price can be any of the values $v_1, \ldots, v_n$. (If $v_i \geq v_j$ implies $\mu_i \geq \mu_j$, however, v_p is clearly greater equal v_k).

Definition 3. *Weighted price optimal (OPT_{WP}): The weighted price optimal revenue OPT_{WP} is the maximum revenue that can be extracted with k slots, when the true values of all bidders are known, and every bidder assigned to a slot is charged a price inversely proportional to his clickability, i.e., such that $p_i \mu_i$ is constant. OPT_{WP} is computed as follows: sort the w in decreasing order, and choose an index $r \leq k$ that maximizes the revenue when every bidder with $w_i \geq w_r$ contributes w_r to the revenue, i.e.,*

$$OPT_{WP} = w_r \Theta_r = \max_{j=1,\ldots,\min(k,n)} w_{i(j)} \Theta_j. \tag{3}$$

Every bidder who is allocated a slot pays a price $p_i = \frac{w_r}{\mu_i} \leq \frac{w_i}{\mu_i} = v_i$. We denote the set of bidders contributing positive revenue to OPT_{WP} as O_W.

Note that when all ad-clickabilities μ_i are equal, the weighted price and single price revenues are exactly the same. We will sometimes use $OPT_{WP}(S)$ and $OPT_{SP}(S)$ to denote the optimal weighted price and single price revenues for a set of bidders S.

The OPT_{WP} benchmark is attractive for several reasons. It seems natural to give a discount to bidders that bring the auction most value; this is the prominent framework in both theory (VCG, and GSP) and in practice (Google and Yahoo! charge bidders proportional to ad-clickabilities). In addition, Theorems 4 and 5 show that OPT_{MP} is at most H_k times as large as OPT_{WP}, as opposed to k times as large as OPT_{SP}. We also point out that when $|O_S| = |O_W|$, then the competitive ratio against OPT_{SP} is worse than the competitive ratio against OPT_{WP}.

But a further examination of Theorem 2 below will indicate that, in fact, weighted prices are not clearly superior to charging a single price. As we would anticipate, in practice it is often the case that value and ad-clickability are correlated, since the ultimate goal is to match the user with a relevant advertisement. We can think of the ad-clickability and the value as both being increasing functions of the quality of the user-advertisement match. Since in this case we always have $OPT_{SP} \geq OPT_{WP}$, it is quite common for single prices to provide better revenue than weighted prices.

The following example shows how OPT_{SP} or OPT_{WP} can be larger: suppose $\theta_i = 1$ for all slots, and ad-clickabilities are $\mu_1 = 12, \mu_2 = 6, \mu_3 = 4, \mu_4 = 3$. If the bidders valuations are $v = (1,1,1,1)$, then $OPT_{SP} = 25$, and $OPT_{WP} = 12$. However if the values are $v = (1/12, 1/6, 1/4, 1/3)$, then $OPT_{SP} = 13/6$ which is less than $OPT_{WP} = 4$. Notice that which of OPT_{SP} and OPT_{WP} has larger revenue cannot be determined without knowing the true valuations of the bidders. We now show some theoretical results about how OPT_{SP} and OPT_{WP} are related.

Theorem 1. *The optimal single price and weighted price revenue are related as follows:* $\frac{1}{k}OPT_{WP} \le OPT_{SP} \le H_k OPT_{WP}$.

Theorem 2. *Suppose clickabilities decrease with values, i.e.,* $v_i \ge v_j$ *implies* $\mu_i \ge \mu_j$. *Then, the optimal single price revenue is greater equal the optimal weighted price revenue.*

Finally we show that OPT_{SP} and OPT_{WP} are close to each other when the clickabilities of winning bidders are not very different.

Theorem 3. *Let* μ_{max} *and* μ_{min} *be the largest and smallest clickabilities of bidders in* $O_S \cup O_W$. *Then* $\frac{\mu_{min}}{\mu_{max}}OPT_{WP} \le OPT_{SP} \le \frac{\mu_{max}}{\mu_{min}}OPT_{WP}$.

Bounding Against OPT_{MP}: We now relate OPT_{WP} and OPT_{SP} to OPT_{MP}. Note that while the worst case bounds for both benchmarks are large, the results in Theorem 3 and 4 show that when the top k bidders values for slots is not very widely different, these benchmarks are quite close to OPT_{MP}.

Theorem 4. $OPT_{MP} \le kOPT_{SP}$, *and this bound is tight.*

However, when clickthrough rates are bidder independent (*i.e.,* $\mu_i = 1$), the optimal single-price revenue can be no smaller than a factor $O(\log k)$ of the optimal multi-price revenue. This follows directly from the next result since in this case $OPT_{WP} = OPT_{SP}$.

Theorem 5. $OPT_{MP} \le H_k OPT_{WP}$, *where* $H_k = 1 + \frac{1}{2} + \ldots + \frac{1}{k}$. *This bound is tight.*

While these theorems show that OPT_{SP} and OPT_{WP} can be quite small compared to the multiprice optimal, when bidders' valuations are more consistent, OPT_{SP} and OPT_{WP} are quite close to OPT_{MP}, as shown in the following theorems.

Theorem 6. *Let* $v_{\max}$ *be the largest, and* $v_{\min}$ *be the smallest value of the bidders contributing to* OPT_{MP}. *Then* $OPT_{MP} \le (v_{\max}/v_{\min})OPT_{SP}$.

Note here that $v_{\max}$ and $v_{\min}$ are values from OPT_{MP}, and need not be the largest and smallest values from the entire set of bidders (*i.e.,* not necessarily v_1 and v_n). A nearly identical argument can be used to show

Theorem 7. *Let* $w_{\max}$ *be the largest, and* $w_{\min}$ *be the smallest revenues of the bidders contributing to* OPT_{MP}. *Then* $OPT_{MP} \le (w_{\max}/w_{\min})OPT_{WP}$.

3   Auctions Competitive Against a Single Benchmark

In this section we describe two truthful auctions that are competitive against the optimal single price and weighted price revenues. The two competitive auctions use versions of $ProfitExtract$ from [9]. Given a set of bidders S and a revenue R, $ProfitExtract_{WP}^{R}$ is an incentive compatible auction that extracts revenue R using *weighted* pricing, if $OPT_{WP}(S) \geq R$. Given a set of bidders S and a revenue R, $ProfitExtract_{SP}^{R}$ is an incentive compatible auction that extracts revenue R using *single* pricing, when possible.

Mechanism competitive with OPT_{WP}: An auction mechanism M_{WP} which has high competitive ratio with respect to OPT_{WP} follows. We assume revenues are calculated to some finite precision, and choose $\epsilon > 0$ to be small compared with this precision.

Mechanism M_{WP}

---

1. Partition bidders independently and uniformly at random into subsets S_1 and S_2.
2. Compute $R_1 = OPT_{WP}(S_1) - \epsilon$, and $R_2 = OPT_{WP}(S_2) + \epsilon$.
3. Run $ProfitExtract_{WP}^{R_1}$ on the bidders in S_2, and $ProfitExtract_{WP}^{R_2}$ with the bidders in S_1.

A straightforward application of the analysis from [9] provides at most a guarantee of two, because the revenue extracted is the lesser of the random division of contributions to the optimum. Our setting has a unique structure which allows us to improve upon this guarantee: clickthrough rates are decreasing with respect to rank. The performance of M_{WP} depends on the bidder dominance with respect to participants (*i.e.*, the inverse of the number of participants), and the drop-off rate of the slot-clickabilities. We show that the revenue from M_{WP} is at least a factor $1/4$ of OPT_{WP}, and approaches optimal as the bidder dominance decreases *and* the drop-off in slot-clickabilities becomes steep:

Theorem 8. *M_{WP} is truthful, and has competitive ratio $\beta_{WP} = \dfrac{\bar{\theta}_r}{g(\alpha_{WP})\bar{\theta}_{\lfloor r/2 \rfloor}}$ with respect to OPT_{WP}^{2} (the optimal weighted price auction selling at least two items), where $g(\alpha_{WP}) \geq 1/4$, and $g(\alpha_{WP}) \to 1/2$ as $\alpha_{WP} \to 0$.*

Here $\bar{\theta}_m = \Theta_m / m$ is the average clickability for the top m slots. (Since the θ are decreasing, $\bar{\theta}_m$ decreases as m increases, *i.e.*, as we average over more slots.) The bidder dominance, α_{WP}, is defined as $\alpha_{WP} = 1/r$ where $r = |O_W|$ is the number of slots sold in OPT_{WP}. The function $g(x) = x\lfloor \frac{1}{x} \rfloor \left(\frac{1}{2} - \binom{\lfloor \frac{1}{x} \rfloor - 1}{\lfloor \frac{1}{2x} \rfloor} 2^{-\lfloor \frac{1}{x} \rfloor} \right)$, and lies between $1/4$ and $1/2$ for $x \leq 1/2$. That is, the value of β_{WP} is roughly the product of two values: one value starts at 2 and tends to 1 as the number of bidders in the optimum solution increases, the other value is the sum of all slot clickabilities, divided by the sum of the largest half of the slot clickabilities, and always lies between 1 and 2.

Mechanism competitive with OPT_{SP}: Next we describe and analyze a mechanism which is competitive with respect to OPT_{SP}. An application of previous results [1,9] gives an auction that approaches a competitive ratio of 4 as the bidder dominance decreases. We give a new proof that tightens previous analysis and allows us to achieve a competitive ratio of 2 (this also improves on the results in [1]). We define bidder dominance in the context of single price, to be the largest advertiser clickability in the optimum solution divided by the sum of advertiser clickabilities in the optimum solution. Then, we provide an analysis showing that as the CTRs become more steep, and the bidder dominance approaches 0, the competitive ratio approaches 1.

Recall that O_S is the set of bidders contributing positive revenue to OPT_{SP}, $p = |O_S|$ and the optimal single price is v_p. Define the average clickability of bidders in O_S as $\bar{\mu} = \sum_{i \in O_S} \mu_i / p$, and the bidder dominance $\alpha_{SP} = \mu_{\max} / \sum_{i \in O_S} \mu_i$ where $\mu_{\max}$ is the largest clickability of bidders in O_S. The smallest value of α_{SP} with p bidders in the optimal single price solution is $1/p$, when all bidders have the same clickability. (Note that this bidder dominance depends both on bidders' values (which are implicitly present in α_{SP} through p), and the clickabilities of the bidders in O_S.) Define a second bidder dominance parameter $\alpha'_{SP} = \theta_1 \mu_{\max} / \sum_{i \in O_S} \theta_j \mu_{i(j)}$. Observe that since the θ are decreasing, $\alpha_{SP} \leq \alpha'_{SP}$, with equality when all the θ_i are equal.

We prove that the mechanism below achieves near optimal revenue as $\alpha_{SP} \to 0$, and the slot clickabilities decrease steeply enough. The competitive ratio also shows that the revenue is always greater than $\frac{1}{4}$ when at least two items are sold.

Mechanism M_{SP}

---

1. Partition bidders independently and uniformly at random into subsets S_1 and S_2.
2. Compute $R_1 = OPT_{SP}(S_1) - \epsilon$ and $R_2 = OPT_{SP}(S_2) + \epsilon$.
3. Run $ProfitExtract_{SP}^{R_1}$ on the bidders in S_2, and $ProfitExtract_{SP}^{R_2}$ with the bidders in S_1.

Theorem 9. *M_{SP} is truthful, and has competitive ratio*

$$\beta_{SP} = \max \left(\frac{p \bar{\theta}_p \alpha_{SP}}{g(\alpha_{SP}) \bar{\theta}_{p - \frac{1}{2\alpha_{SP}}}}, \frac{1}{g(\alpha'_{SP})} \right),$$

against OPT_{SP} when $\alpha_{SP} \leq 1/2$, where $\frac{1}{2} \leq \frac{1}{2\alpha_{SP}} \leq \frac{p}{2}$, and $g(x)$ is as defined earlier.

The first term in the max is the product of three values. The first is the largest ad clickability divided by the average ad clickability. The second is the average slot clickability, divided by the average slot clickability of a portion of the largest slot clickabilities (at least the half largest). The last value is at least $1/4$ and approaches $1/2$ as the bidder dominance decreases (here, bidder dominance is measured by ad-clickabilities and is assumed to be at most $1/2$).

4 An Auction Competitive Against Multiple Benchmarks

In this section, we describe a mechanism with high revenue guarantees against both the single price and weighted price benchmarks. To do this, we use the two random-sampling auctions from §3 that have high competitive ratio against OPT_{SP} and OPT_{WP} respectively. We combine these two auctions to derive a single auction with a Nash equilibrium that raises revenue at least that raised by each of the individual random-sampling auctions.

As we saw in §2, for a particular set of values and clickabilities (v_i, μ_i), either the optimum weighted price revenue OPT_{WP} or optimum single price revenue OPT_{SP} could be larger. However, which of the two is actually larger cannot be determined without knowing the true values of the bidders. Of course, we can combine the two auctions using randomization into a single truthful auction that raises expected revenue $\frac{1}{2}(OPT_{SP}/\beta_{SP} + OPT_{WP}/\beta_{WP})$. To achieve a revenue that is the better of the two auctions, we break from truthful mechanism design and instead design an auction with equilibria (which we show always exist) such that the revenue raised is at least the larger of the revenues that would be raised by the auctions M_{WP} and M_{SP}. The resulting equilibrium analysis framework for the random sampling approach is more robust and malleable. (We point out that the revelation principle does not apply in our setting; also, bidding truthfully is not necessarily an equilibrium strategy.)

Mechanism M_C

---

1. Partition the bidders randomly into two sets A and B, announce the partition, and collect bids from all bidders.
2. Compute $R^A = \max(OPT^A_{SP}, OPT^A_{WP})$, and
   $R^B = \max(OPT^B_{SP}, OPT^B_{WP})$ using the reported bids.
3. Run $ProfitExtract^{R^B}_{SP}$ on the bidders in A; if the auction fails to raise revenue R^B, run $ProfitExtract^{R^B}_{WP}$. Do the same for the bidders in B.
4. If $R^A = R^B$, then items are only assigned to bidders in partition A.

In what follows, we will use R^{A^*} to denote the value of R^A when every bidder bids his true value (similarly for R^B, OPT^A_{SP}, OPT^A_{WP}, OPT^B_{SP}, and OPT^B_{WP}).

Theorem 10. *There always exists an equilibrium solution with revenue at least*

$$R = \min(\max(OPT^{A^*}_{SP}, OPT^{A^*}_{WP}), \max(OPT^{B^*}_{SP}, OPT^{B^*}_{WP})).$$

Further, if bidders bid their true value whenever bidding truthfully belongs to the set of utility maximizing strategies, every Nash equilibrium of M_C has this property.

For a particular partition of the bidders into A and B, the revenue extracted by M_{SP} is $R_{SP} = \min(OPT^{A^*}_{SP}, OPT^{B^*}_{SP})$, and the revenue extracted by M_{WP} is $R_{WP} = \min(OPT^{A^*}_{WP}, OPT^{B^*}_{WP})$. From Theorem 10, the revenue extracted by the auction M_C is greater equal $\max(R_{WP}, R_{SP})$. Taking the expectation over random partitions, we see that the expected revenue from M_C is max($\beta_p OPT_{SP}, \beta_r OPT_{WP}$). (Note that M_C is actually stronger, since we obtain the larger revenue of M_{WP} and M_{SP} for *every* partition, not just in expectation over partitions.)

5   Simulation Results

In this section we discuss our simulation results. We draw bidder valuations from a lognormal distribution with increasing variance and unit mean. This distribution has been used previously [7] and also fits the distribution observed in practice. For our simulations, we used $n = 50$ bidders, $k = 12$ slots, and ad-clickabilities μ_i proportional to v_i. Each point plotted in a figure is obtained by averaging over 800 draws of bidder valuations from a lognormal distribution of the corresponding variance and unit mean. We use two sets of vectors for the slot clickabilities θ. We call slot clickabilities with $\theta_i = 0.7^i$ *Geometric Slot-clickabilities*. This distribution for slot clickabilites is in keeping with [8]. When several advertisements are shown at the top of the page and others shown along the right hand side, the slot clickabilities tend to be significantly larger for advertisements shown along the top. To model this situation, we use a set of *Sharp Geometric Slot-clickabilities*, where the first four slots (presumably shown along the top), decrease by a factor of .85, starting from .85, and the remaining slots along the east, starting from .4, decrease by a factor of .4. We also point out that because ad-clickabilities have the same ordering as the bid values, due to Theorem 2, the revenue of a Nash equlibria using Mechanism M_C equals the revenue extracted using Mechanism M_{SP}.

The general shape of the two graphs in Figure 1 follow a similar pattern. For $\sigma = 0$, there is no variance in the bids and both algorithms achieve the revenue of the optimal multi-price solution. Initially, the variance of the bids is small, and the VCG auction outperforms the combined auction. As the variance in the bid values begin to diverge more sharply, the combined mechanism outperforms VCG. VCG revenue decreases dramatically as the bid values become more varied and every individual's bid value more distinctive, since the externalities a bidder imposes on others decreases (externalities measure, to some degree, how 'replaceable' a bidder is). We can also think of highly varied bid values as a less

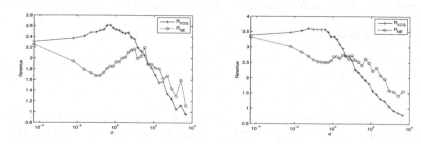

Fig. 1. Revenue versus Variance of Bidder Valuations Drawn from a Log-normal Distribution: Geometric (Left) and Sharp Geometric (Right) Clickabilities

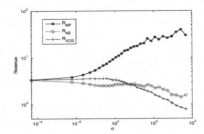

Fig. 2. Revenue versus Variance Including OPT_{MP}

competitive market. If a single bidder's value lies far away from others, it does not have to fight other contenders off for his position: it is clear who the winners should be and there is not much competition for the clicks.

It is often difficult to design incentive compatible auctions for markets with little competition. Truthful auctions rely on bids other than b_i to set values for bidder i. When there is a lot of variance in the bids, choosing a reasonable price is more challenging. This can be seen by observing Figure 2. The multiprice optimum shoots up, relative to both algorithms, as the bidder variance increases. This suggests that both algorithms have difficulty obtaining revenue in these situations. The simulations corroborate the findings in Theorem 6, which prove analytically that the tighter the range of bidder vales, the higher the performance guarantee. Since the combined mechanism is designed to do well in a worst case setting, it is not surprising that its performance improves relative to VCG exactly when maintaining a minimal amount of revenue in the face of a challenging situation (*i.e.*, non-competitive market) is encountered.

Figure 1 highlights how the steepness of slot-clickabilities impacts the algorithms' revenues. There is very little difference in the curve for the VCG mechanism when the slot clickabilities are steeper. However, the improvement for the combined mechanism is more noticeable, outperforming VCG earlier and by a larger margin. This is consistent with our analysis, which indicates that the auction will perform better as the steepness in slot clickabilities increases.

Acknowledgements. We are very grateful to Andrei Broder, Ravi Kumar, Ofer Mendelevitch and Michael Schwarz for helpful discussions.

References

1. Abrams, Z.: Revenue maximization when bidders have budgets. In: Proc. Symposium on Discrete Algorithms, pp. 1074–1082 (2006)
2. Aggarwal, G., Goel, A., Motwani, R.: Truthful auctions for pricing search keywords. In: Proc. 7th ACM conference on Electronic Commerce, pp. 1–7. ACM Press, New York (2006)
3. Aggarwal, G., Hartline, J.: Knapsack auctions. Symposium on Discrete Algorithms (2006)

4. Borgs, C., Chayes, J., Immorlica, N., Mahdian, M., Saberi, A.: Multi-unit auctions with budget-constrained bidders. In: Proc. 6th ACM Conference on Electronic Commerce, pp. 44–51. ACM Press, New York (2005)
5. Clarke, E.H.: Multipart pricing of public goods. Public Choice 11, 17–33 (1971)
6. Edelman, B., Ostrovsky, M., Schwarz, M.: Internet advertising and the generalizaed second price auction: Selling billions of dollars worth of keywords. American Economic Review 97(1), 242–259 (2007)
7. Edelman, B., Schwarz, M.: Optimal auction design in a multi-unit environment: The case of sponsored search auctions. ACM Conference on Electronic Commerce (2007)
8. Feng, J., Bhargava, H., Pennock, D.M.: Implementing sponsored search in web search engines: Computational evaluation of alternative mechanisms. INFORMS Journal on Computing (2006)
9. Goldberg, A., Hartline, J., Wright, A.: Competitive auctions and digital goods. Proc. Symposium on Discrete Algorithms (2001)
10. Groves, T.: Incentives in teams. Econometrica 41, 617–631 (1973)
11. Hartline, J.: Optimization in the private value model: Competitive analysis applied to auction design. PhD Thesis (2003)
12. Immorlica, N., Jain, K., Mahdian, M., Talwar, K.: Click fraud resistant methods for learning click-through rates. Workshop on Internet and Network Economics (2005)
13. Lahaie, S., Pennock, D.M.: Revenue analysis of a family of ranking rules for keyword auctions. ACM Conference on Electronic Commerce (2007)
14. Mahdian, M., Saberi, A.: Multi-unit auctions with unknown supply. ACM Conference on Electronic Commerce (2006)
15. Milgrom, P.: Putting Auction Theory to Work. something, 9999
16. Mu'alem, A., Nisan, N.: Truthful approximation mechanisms for restricted combinatorial auctions. AAAI (2002)
17. Myerson, R.: Optimal auction design. Mathematics of Operations Research 6(1), 58–73 (1981)
18. Pandey, S., Olston, C.: Handling advertisements of uknown quality in search advertising. Neural Information Processing Systems Conference (2006)
19. Roughgarden, T., Sundararajan, M.: Is efficiency expensive? Third Workshop on Sponsored Search Auctions (2007)
20. Varian, H.R.: Position auctions. International Journal of Industrial Organization (2005)
21. Vickrey, W.: Counterspeculation, auctions, and competitive sealed tenders. Journal of Finance 16, 8–37 (1961)
22. Zhang, T.: Clickthrough-rates positional effect and calibration model. Manuscript in preparation (2006)

Equilibrium Analysis of Dynamic Bidding in Sponsored Search Auctions

Yevgeniy Vorobeychik[1] and Daniel M. Reeves[2]

[1] Computer Science & Engineering, University of Michigan
yvorobey@umich.edu*
[2] Yahoo! Research
dreeves@yahoo-inc.com

Abstract. We analyze symmetric pure strategy equilibria in dynamic sponsored search auction games using simulations by restricting the strategies to several in a class introduced by Cary et al. [1]. We show that a particular convergent strategy also exhibits high stability to deviations. On the other hand, a strategy which yields high payoffs to all players is not sustainable in equilibrium play. Additionally, we analyze a repeated game in which each stage is a static complete-information sponsored search game. In this setting, we demonstrate a collusion strategy which yields high payoffs to all players and empirically show it to be sustainable over a range of settings.

1 Motivation

Much progress has been made in modeling sponsored search auctions as one-shot games of complete information, in which the players' values per click and click-through-rates are common knowledge. A typical justification for such an approach is the abundance of information in the system, since the advertisers have ample opportunity to explore, submitting and resubmitting bids at will. As the complexity of modeling the full dynamic game between advertisers that is actually taking place is quite intractable, static models provide a good first approximation. However, it ultimately pays to understand how relevant the dynamics really are to strategic choices of players.

One question which has been addressed in the dynamic setting is whether it is reasonable to expect simple dynamic strategies to converge to Nash equilibria. Cary et al. [1] explored several *greedy bidding strategies*, that is, strategies under which players submit bids with the goal of obtaining the most profitable slot given that other players bids are fixed. One of these strategies, *balanced bidding*, was shown to provably converge to a minimum revenue symmetric Nash equilibrium of the static game of complete information, which happens to be particularly analytically tractable and has therefore received special attention

---

* This work was done while the author was at Yahoo! Research.

X. Deng and F.C. Graham (Eds.): WINE 2007, LNCS 4858, pp. 155–166, 2007.

in the literature [9,6,2]. Similar questions, particularly in the context of pools of vindictive agents, have been studied by Liang and Qi [7].[1]

Convergence of dynamic bidding strategies is only one of many relevant questions that arise if we try to account for the dynamic nature of the sponsored search game. Another significant aspect is whether we can identify Nash equilibrium strategies in the dynamic game. This problem in general is, of course, quite hard, as there are many possible actions and ways to account for the changing information structure. One approach, taken by Feng and Zhang [3], is to model the dynamic process using Markovian framework. Our own approach focuses on a set of greedy bidding strategies studied by Cary et al. [1]. In motivating greedy bidding strategies, Cary et al. have argued that advertisers are unlikely to engage in highly fine-grained strategic reasoning and will rather prefer to follow relatively straightforward strategies. This motivation, however, only restricts attention to a set of plausible candidates. To identify which are likely to be selected by advertisers, we need to assess their relative stability to profitable deviations. For example, while we would perhaps like advertisers to follow a convergent strategy like balanced bidding, it is unclear whether the players would perhaps find it more profitable to follow a non-convergent strategy.

Our goal is to provide some initial information about equilibrium stability of a small set of greedy bidding strategies under incomplete information. Specifically, we use simulations to estimate the gain any advertiser can accrue by deviating from pure strategy symmetric equilibria in greedy bidding strategies. The results are promising: the convergent *balanced bidding* is typically the most stable of the set of strategies we study.

To complement the analysis above, we examine the incentives when joint valuations are common knowledge, but the game is repeated indefinitely. Folk theorems [8] suggest that players may be able to increase individual profits (and decrease search engine revenue) by colluding. We demonstrate one such collusion strategy and show it to be effective over a range of sponsored search auction environments. Our analysis complements other approaches to study collusion in auctions, in a dynamic context in sponsored search auctions [3], as well as in a general one-shot context [4].

2   Game Theoretic Preliminaries

2.1   One-Shot Games of Incomplete Information

In much of this work we analyze *one-shot games of incomplete information* [8], denoted by $[I, \{R_i\}, \{T_i\}, F(\cdot), \{u_i(r,t)\}]$[2], where I refers to the set of players

---

[1] Some of the motivation and questions raised and addressed in this work have considerable similarity with our own work below.

[2] Although strategies are dynamic in that players choose their *actions* as a function of history, our model of the meta-level strategic interaction is one-shot in that players choose the dynamic strategies (which dictate actions in specific states) once and follow these throughout.

and $m = |I|$ is the number of players. R_i is the set of actions available to player $i \in I$, and $R_1 \times \cdots \times R_m$ is the joint action space. T_i is the set of types (private information) of player i, with $T = T_1 \times \cdots \times T_m$ representing the joint type space. Since we presume that a player knows its type prior to taking an action, but does not know types of others, we allow it to condition its action on own type. Thus, we define a strategy of a player i to be a function $s_i : T_i \to \mathbb{R}$, and use $s(t)$ to denote the vector $(s_1(t_1), \ldots, s_m(t_m))$. $F(\cdot)$ is the distribution over the joint type space.

We use s_{-i} to denote the joint strategy of all players other than player i. Similarly, t_{-i} designates the joint type of all players other than i. We define the payoff (utility) function of each player i by $u_i : R \times T \to \mathbb{R}$, where $u_i(r_i, r_{-i}, t_i, t_{-i})$ indicates the payoff to player i with type t_i for playing action $r_i \in R_i$ when the remaining players with joint types t_{-i} play r_{-i}. Given a strategy profile $s \in S$, the expected payoff of player i is $\tilde{u}_i(s) = E_t[u_i(s(t), t)]$.

Given a known strategy profile of players other than i, we define the best response of player i to s_{-i} to be the strategy s_i^* that maximizes expected utility $\tilde{u}_i(s_i, s_{-i})$. If we know the best response of every player to a strategy profile s, we can evaluate the maximum amount that any player can gain by deviating from s. Such an amount, which we also call *regret*, we denote by $\epsilon(s) = \max_{i \in I}[\tilde{u}_i(s_i^*, s_{-i}) - \tilde{u}_i(s_i, s_{-i})]$, where s_i^* is the best response to s_{-i}. Henceforth, when we use the term "stability", it is in the sense of low *regret*. Faced with a one-shot game of incomplete information, an agent would ideally play a strategy that is a best response to strategies of others. A joint strategy s where all agents play best responses to each other constitutes a *Nash equilibrium* ($\epsilon(s) = 0$); when applied to games of incomplete information, it is called a *Bayes-Nash equilibrium*.

2.2 Complete Information Infinitely Repeated Games

The second model we use is an *infinitely repeated game* [8]. The model divides time into an infinite number of discrete stages and presumes that at each stage players interact strategically in a one-shot fashion (that is, no one agent can observe actions of others until the next stage). Naturally, all players care not just about the payoffs they receive in one stage, but all the payoffs in past and subsequent stages of the dynamic interaction. We assume that their total utility from playing the repeated game is a discounted sum of stage utilities. Formally, it can be described by the tuple $[I, \{R_i\}, u_i(r), \gamma_i]$, where I, R_i and $u_i(r)$ are as before, and γ_i is the amount by which each player discounts utility at each stage. That is, if we let $\bar{r} = \{r_1, r_2, \ldots, r_i, \ldots\}, r_j \in R$ be a sequence of choices by players indexed by the chronological sequence of stages, $U_i(\bar{r}) = \sum_{t=1}^{\infty} \gamma_i^{t-1} u_i(r_t)$.

Define a stage-k *subgame* of a repeated game as a restricted repeated game which begins at stage k rather than at stage 1. The solution concept that we will use for infinitely repeated games is a *subgame perfect Nash equilibrium* [8], which obtains when the players have no incentive to deviate from their sequence of strategic choices in any stage of the interaction.

3 Modeling Sponsored Search Auctions

A traditional model of sponsored search auctions specifies a ranking rule, which ranks advertisers based on their bid and some information about their relevance to the user query, click-through-rates for each player and slot, and players' valuations or distributions of valuations per click. Let a player i's click-through-rate in slot s be denoted by c_s^i and its value per click by v_i. Like many models in the literature (e.g., [5,6]) we assume that click-through-rate can be factored into $e_i c_s$ for every player i and every slot s. If player i pays p_i^s in slot s, then its utility is $u_i = e_i c_s (v_i - p_i^s)$. The parameter e_i is often referred to as *relevance* of the advertiser i, and c_s is the slot-specific click-through-rate. We assume that the search engine has the number of slots denoted by K with slot-specific click-through-rates $c_1 > c_2 > \ldots > c_K$.

Lahaie and Pennock [6] discuss a family of ranking strategies which rank bidders in order of the product of their bid b_i and some weight function w_i. They study in some depth a particular weight function $w(e_i) = e_i^q$, where q is a real number. In the analysis below, we consider two settings of q: 0 and 1. The former corresponds to rank-by-bid, b_i, whereas the latter is typically called rank-by-revenue, $e_i b_i$.

When players are ranked by their bids, two alternative pricing schemes have been studied: first-price (set price equal to player's bid) and generalized second-price (set price equal to next highest bid). As is well-known, neither is incentive compatible. However, stability issues have induced the major search engines to use generalized second-price auctions. These have been generalized further to ranking by weighted bid schemes by using the price rule $p_i^s = \frac{w_{s+1} b_{s+1}}{w_i}$. The interpretation is that the bidder i pays the amount of the lowest bid sufficient to win slot s.

4 Dynamic Bidding Strategies

In much of this work we restrict the strategy space of players to four dynamic strategies. While this is a dramatic restriction, it allows me to gain some insight into the stability properties of the dynamic game and to identify particularly interesting candidates for further analysis in the future. Additionally, it has been argued as unlikely that players will engage in full-fledged strategic reasoning and will rather follow relatively straightforward dynamic strategies [1], such as the ones we consider. We now give the definition of a class of "simple" strategies.

Definition 1 (Greedy Bidding Strategies). *A greedy bidding strategy [1] for a player i is to choose a bid for the next round of a repeated keyword auction that obtains a slot which maximizes its utility u_i assuming the bids of all other players remain fixed.*

If the player bids so as to win slot s which it is selecting according to a greedy bidding strategy, any bid in the interval (p_i^{s-1}, p_i^s), will win that slot at the same price. The particular rule which chooses a bid in this interval defines a member of a class of greedy bidding strategies. We analyze strategic behavior of agents who can select from four greedy bidding strategies specified below. For all of these, let s^* designate the slot which myopically maximizes player i's utility as long as other players' bids are fixed.

Definition 2 (Balanced Bidding). *The* Balanced Bidding [1] *strategy* BB *chooses the bid* b *which solves* $c_{s^*}(v_i - p_i^{s^*}) = c_{s^*-1}(v_i - b)$. *If* s^* *is the top slot, choose* $b = (v_i + p_i^1)/2$.

Definition 3 (Random Bidding). *The* Random *strategy* RAND *selects the bid* b *uniformly randomly in the interval* (p_i^{s-1}, p_i^s).

Definition 4 (Competitor Busting). *The* Competitor Busting [1] *strategy* CB *selects the bid* $b = \min\{v_i, p_i^{s^*-1} - \epsilon\}$.

Thus, the CB strategy tries to cause the player that receives slot immediately above s^* to pay as much as possible.

Definition 5 (Altruistic Bidding). *The* Altruistic Bidding [1] *strategy* AB *chooses the bid* $b = \min\{v_i, p_i^{s^*} + \epsilon\}$.

This strategy, ensures the highest payoff (lowest price) of the player receiving the slot immediately above s^*.

5   Empirical Bayesian Meta-game Analysis

In this section we construct and analyze a Bayesian meta-game played between advertisers (alternatively, bidders or players) who may choose one of four greedy bidding strategies described above. As is typical in a one-shot game of incomplete information, the bidders are allowed to condition their strategic choices on their own valuations, but not those of other players. However, we do not allow conditioning based on relevances, as these are assumed to be a priori unknown both to the search engine and to the bidders. The reason we refer to the model as a meta-game is that we abstract away the dynamic nature of the game by enforcing a one-shot choice of a dynamic strategy, that is, once the strategy is chosen, the player must follow it forever after. While this is a strong assumption given the restriction of the strategy space, it is without loss of generality when no such restriction is imposed, since an optimal dynamic strategy is optimal in any subgame along the played path.

In order to construct the meta-game, we need to define player payoffs for every joint realization of values and relevances, as well as the corresponding choice of dynamic strategies. As is common for dynamic interactions, we define the payoff in the meta-game as the discounted sum of stage payoffs. In each stage, exactly one bidder, selected uniformly randomly, is allowed to modify its bid according to its choice of dynamic bidding strategy.[3] The corresponding stage payoff is an expected payoff given the ranking and payments of players as a function

---

[3] This condition ensures the convergence of *balanced bidding* dynamics.

of joint bids, as defined in Section 3. We model the entire dynamic process—once relevances, values, and strategies are determined—using a simulator, which outputs a sample payoff at the end of a run of 100 stages. The discount factor is set to 0.95. With this discount factor, the total contribution from stage 101 to infinity is 0.006, and we thus presume that the history thereafter is negligible.

Expected payoff to a particular player for a fixed value per click, relevance, and strategy is estimated using a sample average of payoffs based on 1000 draws from the distribution of valuations and relevances of other players. The metric for quality with which a particular strategy profile s approximates a Bayes-Nash equilibrium is the estimate of $\epsilon(s)$, which is the sample average gain from playing a best response to s over 100 draws from the players value and relevance distributions. For each of these 100 draws, the gain from playing a best response to s is computed as the difference between the highest expected payoff for any strategy in the restricted set and the expected payoff from s_i, estimated as described above.

Since the meta-game is constructed numerically for every choice of values, relevances, and strategies of all players, an in-depth analysis of all strategies in the game is hopeless. Instead, we focus much of our attention on four pure symmetric strategy profiles, in which each player chooses the same dynamic strategy for any valuation. While this seems an enormous restriction, it turns out to be sufficient for our purposes, as these happen to contain near-equilibria.

5.1   Equal Relevances

In this section we focus on the setting in which all players' relevances are equal and assume that values per click are distributed normally with mean 500 and standard deviation 200.Three sponsored search auction games are considered: in one, 5 advertisers compete for 2 slots; in the others, 20 and 50 advertisers respectively compete for 8 slots.

Figure 1 presents average $\epsilon(s)$ and payoffs for all four pure symmetric profiles in strategies which are constant functions of player values per click. The first observation we can make is that BB has a very low $\epsilon(s)$ in every case, suggesting that it has considerable strategic stability in the restricted strategy space. This result can also be claimed with high statistical confidence, as 99% confidence intervals are so small that they are not visible in the figure. In contrast, AB manifests very high $\epsilon(s)$ in the plot and we can be reasonably certain that it is not sustainable as an equilibrium. The picture that emerges is most appealing to the search engine: AB, which is unlikely to be played, yields the greatest payoffs to players (and least to the auctioneer), whereas BB yields the lowest player payoffs in the restricted strategy space.

5.2   Independently Distributed Values and Relevances

We now consider the setting in which relevances of players are not identical, but are rather identically distributed—and independently from values per click—according to a uniform distribution on the interval [0,1]. Since now the particulars of the bid ranking scheme come into play, we present results for the two schemes

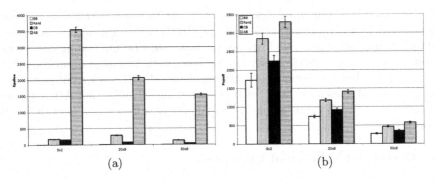

Fig. 1. (a) Experimental $\epsilon(s)$ and (b) symmetric payoff for every pure symmetric profile in constant strategies with associated 99% confidence bounds

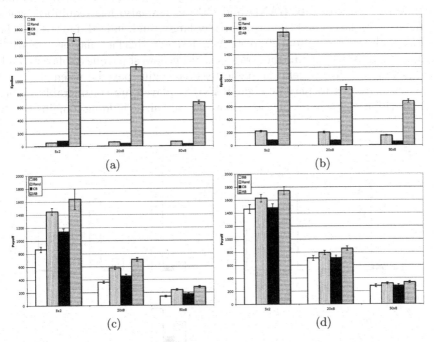

Fig. 2. Experimental $\epsilon(s)$ (a) when $q = 0$ (b) when $q = 1$ for every pure symmetric profile; experimental payoff (c) when $q = 0$ (d) when $q = 1$ for every pure symmetric profile

that have received the most attention: rank-by-bid ($q = 0$) and rank-by-revenue ($q = 1$).

Figures 2a and b present the results on stability of each symmetric pure strategy profile to deviations for $q = 0$ and $q = 1$ respectively. We can see that there are really no significant qualitative differences between the two settings, and indeed between the setting of independently distributed values and relevances and the previous one in which relevances were set to a constant for all players. Perhaps a slight difference is that RAND and CB strategies appear to have better stability properties when $q = 0$. However, this could be misleading, since the payoffs to players are also generally lower when $q = 0$. The most notable quality we previously observed however, remains unchanged: BB is an equilibrium (or nearly so) in all games for both advertiser ranking schemes, and AB is highly unstable, whereas BB yields a considerably lower payoff to advertisers than AB in all settings.

5.3   Correlated Values and Relevances

In the final set of experiments we draw values and relevances from a joint distribution with a correlation coefficient of 0.5. As may by now be expected, BB remains a near-equilibrium both when we set $q = 0$ and $q = 1$ (Figures 3a and b). However, when $q = 0$, RAND and CB are now also near-equilibria when the number of players and slots is relatively large—and, indeed, more so as the number of players grows from 20 to 50. As a designer, this fact may be somewhat disconcerting, as BB remains the strategy with the lowest payoffs to players (and, consequently, will likely yield the highest search engine payoffs) when $q = 0$; by comparison, payoffs to players when RAND is played are considerably higher than BB (Figure 3c). In all the cases, however, altruistic bidding remains highly

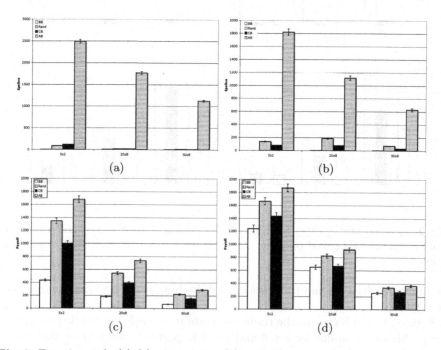

Fig. 3. Experimental $\epsilon(s)$ (a) when $q = 0$ (b) when $q = 1$ for every pure symmetric profile; experimental payoff (c) when $q = 0$ (d) when $q = 1$ for every pure symmetric profile

unstable, to the bidders' great chagrin, as it is uniformly more advantageous in terms of payoffs (Figures 3c and d).

6 Repeated Game with Common Knowledge of Values

It is common in the sponsored search auction literature to assume that the player valuations and click-through-rates are common knowledge, suggesting that the resulting equilibria are rest points of natural bidder adjustment dynamics. The justification offered alludes to the repeated nature of the agent interactions. Yet, the equilibrium concept used is a static one. If a game is infinitely repeated, the space of Nash equilibrium strategies expands considerably [8]. Thus, if we take the dynamic story seriously, it pays to seek subgame perfect equilibria in the repeated game, particularly if they may offer considerably better payoffs to players than the corresponding static Nash equilibria.

As typical analysis of repeated interactions goes, our subgame perfect equilibrium consists of two parts: the main path, and the deviation-punishment path. The main path has players jointly follow an agreed-upon profitable strategy profile, whereas the deviation path punishes any deviant. The trick, of course, is that for the equilibrium to be subgame perfect, the punishment subgame must itself be in equilibrium, yet must be sufficiently bad to discourage deviation.

A natural candidate for punishment is the worst (in terms of player payoffs) Nash equilibrium in the static game. Clearly, such a path would be in equilibrium, and is likely to offer considerable discouragement to deviants. A desirable main path would have players pay as little as possible, but needs to nevertheless discourage bidders who receive no slots from outbidding those who do. Furthermore, all "slotless" bidders should remain slotless in the deviation subgame, since it is then clear that no incentives to deviate exist among such bidders, and we need only consider bidders who occupy some slot.

For the remainder of this section, we assume that the valuations are generic and bidders are indexed by the number of the slot they obtain in a symmetric Nash equilibrium.[4] Define the dynamic strategy profile $COLLUSION$ as follows:

- *main path*: $\forall s > K$, $b_s = v_s$. For all others, $b_s = \frac{w_{K+1}}{w_s}v_{K+1} + (K - s + 1)\epsilon$, where ϵ is some very small (negligible) number. Note that this yields the same ordering of bidders who receive slots as any symmetric Nash equilibrium of the game.
- *deviation path*: play the maximum revenue symmetric Nash equilibrium strategies in every stage game. This yields the maximum revenue to the auctioneer and the lowest utilities to the players of any Nash equilibrium in the stage game [9].

Whether the delineated strategy constitutes a subgame perfect Nash equilibrium depends on the magnitude of the discount factor, γ_i, of every player i. The

---

[4] Via a simple extension of the results by Varian [9] we can show that in a symmetric Nash equilibrium, bidders are ranked by $w_s b_s$.

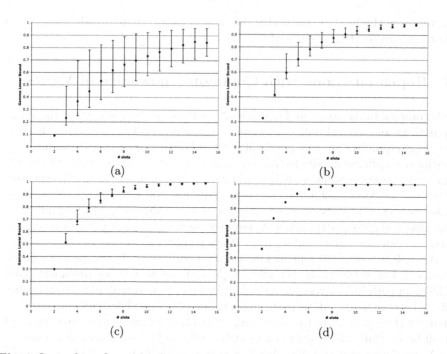

Fig. 4. Lower bounds on the discount factor as the number of available slots varies when (a) $\delta = 1.1$, (b) $\delta = 1.3$, (c) $\delta = 1.428$, and (d) $\delta = 1.9$

relevant question is then how large does γ need to be to enable enforcement of *COLLUSION*. Clearly, $\gamma_i = 0$ will deter nothing, since there are no consequences (and the game is effectively a one-stage game). Below, we give the general result to this effect.

Theorem 1. *The* COLLUSION *strategy profile is a subgame perfect Nash equilibrium if, for all players i,*

$$\gamma_i \geq \max_{s \leq K, t \leq s} \frac{(c_t - c_s)(v_s - \frac{w_{K+1}v_{K+1}}{w_s}) - (c_t \frac{w_t}{w_s}(K - t + 1) - c_s(K - s))\epsilon}{c_t(v_s - \frac{w_{K+1}v_{K+1}}{w_s}) - c_s v_s - c_t \frac{w_t}{w_s}(K - t + 1)\epsilon + V_{sum}}, \quad (1)$$

where $V_{sum} = \sum_{t=s+1}^{K} w_{t-1}v_{t-1}(c_{t-1} - c_t) + w_K v_K c_K$

The lower bound on the discount factor in Equation 1 depends on the particular valuation vector, the relative merits of slots, and the total number of slots, and it is not immediately clear whether there actually are reasonable discount factors for which deviations can be discouraged. To get a sense of how sustainable such an equilibrium could be, we study the effect of these parameters on the lower bound of the discount factor. To do this, we let the relevances of all players be constant, fix the number of players at 20 and take 100 draws of their valuations from the normal distribution with mean 500 and standard deviation 200. We vary the number of slots between 2 and 15, recording the average, minimum, and maximum values of the lower bound. Furthermore, we normalize c_1 to 1 and let $\frac{c_s}{c_{s+1}} = \delta$ for all $s \leq K - 1$. The results are displayed in Figure 4 for different values of δ.

First, focus on Figure 4c which shows the results for $\delta = 1.428$, an empirically observed click-through-rate ratio. As the figure suggests, when the number of slots is between 0 and 5, it seems likely that *COLLUSION* can obtain as a subgame perfect equilibrium, as the requirements on the discount factor are not too strong. When the number of slots grows, however, the incentives to deviate increase, and when the number of slots is above 10, such a collusive equilibrium no longer seems likely.

Figures 4a, b, and d display similar plots for other settings of δ. These suggest that as δ rises, incentives to deviate rise, since when there is a greater dropoff in slot quality for lower slots, players have more to gain by moving to a higher slot even for a one-shot payoff.

7 Conclusion

This paper presents some initial results on equilibrium stability of dynamic bidding strategies in sponsored search auctions. Many of the results are less favorable to players: a high-payoff strategy profile is not sustainable in equilibrium, whereas a low-payoff profile is reasonably stable. On the other hand, when complete information about valuations and click-through-rates is available, there are possibilities for collusion that yield high payoffs to players which are sustainable over a range of settings.

References

1. Cary, M., Das, A., Edelman, B., Giotis, I., Heimerl, K., Karlin, A.R., Mathieu, C., Schwarz, M.: Greedy bidding strategies for keyword auctions. In: Eighth ACM Conference on Electronic Commerce (2007)
2. Edelman, B., Ostrovsky, M., Schwarz, M.: Internet advertising and the generalized second price auction: Selling billions of dollars worth of keywords. American Economic Review 9(1), 242–259 (2007)
3. Feng, J., Zhang, X.: Dynamic price competition on the internet: advertising auctions. In: Eighth ACM Conference on Electronic Commerce, pp. 57–58 (2007)
4. Krishna, V.: Auction Theory, 1st edn. Academic Press, San Diego (2002)
5. Lahaie, S.: An analysis of alternative slot auction designs for sponsored search. In: Seventh ACM Conference on Electronic Commerce (2006)
6. Lahaie, S., Pennock, D.M.: Revenue analysis of a family of ranking rules for keyword auctions. In: Eighth ACM Conference on Electronic Commerce (2007)
7. Liang, L., Qi, Q.: Cooperative or vindictive: bidding strategies in sponsored search auctions. In: Third International Workshop on Internet and Network Economics. LNCS, Springer, Heidelberg (2007)
8. Mas-Colell, A., Whinston, M.D., Green, J.R.: Microeconomic Theory. Oxford University Press, Oxford (1995)
9. Varian, H.: Position auctions. International Journal of Industrial Organization (to appear)

Appendix

A   Proof of Theorem 1

Take a player s (recall that players are indexed according to the slots they occupy) and let the discount factor of that player be γ. First, note that if $s \geq K + 1$, the player can only win a slot by paying more than v_s, and thus has no incentive to deviate.

Suppose that $s \leq K$. If the player s never deviates, it will accrue the payoff of $u_s = c_s(v_s - (K-s)\epsilon - \frac{w_{K+1}v_{K+1}}{w_s})$ at every stage. With γ as the discount factor, the resulting total payoff would be $\sum_{i=0}^{\infty} \gamma^i u_s = \frac{u_s}{1-\gamma}$. For ϵ sufficiently small, there will be no incentive to deviate to an inferior slot, since it offers a strictly lower click-through-rate with negligible difference in payment. The one-shot payoff for deviating to $t \leq s$ is $u'_s = c_t(v_s - \frac{w_t}{w_s}(K - t + 1)\epsilon - \frac{w_{K+1}v_{K+1}}{w_s})$. For all stages thereafter, the utility will be $u_s^p = c_s(v_s - \sum_{t=s+1}^{K+1} w_{t-1}v_{t-1}\frac{c_{t-1}-c_t}{c_s}) = c_s v_s - \sum_{t=s+1}^{K+1} w_{t-1}v_{t-1}(c_{t-1} - c_t) = c_s v_s - \sum_{t=s+1}^{K} w_{t-1}v_{t-1}(c_{t-1} - c_t) - w_K v_K c_K$. Since this utility will be played starting at the second stage, the total utility from deviating is $u'_s + \frac{\gamma u_s^p}{1-\gamma}$. For deviations to be unprofitable, it must be that for every $s \leq K$ and every $t \leq s$, $\frac{u_s}{1-\gamma} \geq u'_s + \frac{\gamma u_s^p}{1-\gamma}$, or, alternatively, $u_s \geq (1-\gamma)u'_s + \gamma u_s^p$. Plugging in the expressions for utilities and rearranging gives us the result. $\square$

Cooperative or Vindictive: Bidding Strategies in Sponsored Search Auction

Li Liang and Qi Qi*

Department of Computer Science, City University of Hong Kong
{chris.liangli,qi.qi}@student.cityu.edu.hk

Abstract. We analyze the economic stability and dynamic manipulation of vindictive strategies in conjunction with forward-looking cooperative bidders in Sponsored Search Auction. We investigate different vindictive strategies of different rationalities : malicious, conservative and selective. In a malicious vindictive strategy, the bidder forces his competitors to pay more by bidding just one cent lower of his competitor's bid. We show that Nash Equilibrium is vulnerable even there is one malicious vindictive bidder. However, on bidder's perspective, he has not much incentive to use a malicious vindictive strategy. A conservative vindictive bidding strategy makes a bidder never sacrifices his own benefit to take revenge on his competitor. Under this strategy, we prove that there always exists an output truthful Nash Equilibrium. However, it may not always be the unique equilibrium. Lastly, we investigate a selective vindictive strategy that a bidder rationally chooses to bid cooperatively or vindictively. The bidder takes a vindictive strategy only if the bidder who gets one position higher has a larger private value. We prove that selective vindictive strategy always results in a unique truthful Nash Equilibrium in conjunction with forward looking cooperative bidders. Interestingly, forward looking strategy gives the same payment as VCG mechanism if all the bidders takes it. However, the bidder prefers selective vindictive strategy while the auctioneer's revenue reach maximum when all the bidders takes the selective vindictive strategy.

1 Introduction

Sponsored Search Auction has been one of the most indispensable economic mechanisms in the online advertising industry. Based on products, advertisers choose a set of keywords and compete for advertising slots on the search results pages to display their own advertisements. They are charged only if their advertisements are shown to the users who click the advertisement, which is known as "Pay-Per-Click". Due to the limited budget of each advertiser, strategic bidding behavior plays a crucial role in Sponsored Search Auction. In advertisers' perspective, a good strategy not only prevents the advertiser from overbidding for

---

* The work described in this paper was supported by a grant from the Research Grants Council of the Hong Kong Special Administrative Region, China [Project No. CityU 112707].

his preferred position but also guarantees his favorite position beating his competitors. In auctioneer's point of view, strategic behaviors severely affect both the stability of the auction and his own revenue. Thus, it raises many interesting problems how advertisers compete for their advertising slots.

In a fair competitive mechanism, the bidder who has a higher private value deserves to get a higher slot, which is referred as *output truthful* [4,3,9]. On the other hand, a rational bidder intuitively wants to maximize his own benefits. Bu et al.[3] proposes a forward looking response function which results in the same allocation and payment as the the celebrated VCG mechanism[12] which justifies the fairness of mechanism design of sponsored search auction. To achieve such a result, everyone must follow the forward-looking response function - being cooperative in the auction. We regard such kind of bidders as *forward looking cooperative bidders*. However, in the competitive sponsored search market, maximizing the benefit might not be enough. Bidder could play the game more aggressively. In an aggressive strategy, beating competitors may be as important as maximizing the benefits in the design of bidding strategy. A bidder would bid higher than the bid in the cooperative case in order to force the bidders who get higher slots to pay more and use up their budget faster. On the other hand, they raise their bid rationally as long as his own benefit is preserved. We regard such kind of aggressive strategy as *vindictive bidding strategies*.

In this paper, we investigate sponsored search auctions composed of arbitrary potion of forward-looking rational bidders and different kinds of vindictive bidders. First of all, we study a *malicious* vindictive bidding strategy [13]. Each vindictive bidder picks his favorite position and bids one cent lower than the bid which gets one slot higher than him. However, the occurrence of malicious vindictive bidders would make the market extremely unstable. We show that there may not always exist an equilibrium even if there is only one malicious vindictive bidder. Besides, bidders mostly do not have incentive to take this strategy. We give empirical evidence that a malicious vindictive bidder cannot preserve its own benefit if he chooses to be forward looking cooperative in most of the cases. Meanwhile, the auctioneer's revenue increases with the growth of number of malicious vindictive bidders. The instability of malicious vindictive strategy is because it bids too much that will immediately force his competitors to choose other slots. It neither effectively takes revenge on his competitors nor preserves his own benefit. Secondly, we propose and study a *conservative* vindictive strategy. It bids as high as possible that his competitors do not want to choose any slot that is lower than his, thus he preserves his current benefit. We prove that there always exists an *output truthful* [4,3,9] Nash Equilibrium regardless of the number of such vindictive bidders. However, the *output truthful* equilibrium may not always be the unique Nash equilibrium. A vindictive bidder may stuck in a lower slot than a bidder whose private value is smaller than his. This is because that the bidder bids vindictively all the time without considering the competitive relation between his competitors. To avoid this phenomenon, we investigate a more rational vindictive strategy: *selective* vindictive strategy, that a bidder takes a conservative vindictive strategy only if his private value is larger than his. Otherwise, he will play the forward-looking strategy. We show that there always exists a unique Nash Equilibrium which is output truthful for Sponsored Search Auction. The bidder still preserves his preferred position and payment while all his competitors pays more than the case he plays the forward looking cooperative strategy. However, auctioneer's revenue keeps increasing with the growth of number of vindictive bidders. And the revenue reaches theoretical maximum Nash Equilibrium yields. In a global view, the benefits the by taking a forward looking cooperative strategies is much better than the benefits they take vindictive strategies.

1.1 Related Work

Equilibrium solutions are interesting and widely studied of the auction model. Edelman et al. [6] focused on *locally envy-free equilibrium(LEFE)* where any bidder cannot improve his own benefit by switching position with the bidder who is one position higher than him. Varian [11] studied a subset of Nash Equilibrium: *Symmetric Nash Equilibrium(SNE)* which is well formulated with nice properties. Indeed, it is public known that the two equilibria are the same with different definitions. The maximum revenue of both equilibria yield are the same as Nash Equilibrium's maximum revenue.

In [3], the authors studied the strategic behaviors and dynamic manipulations of the game. The strategy they proposed, named *forward looking* strategy, yields a unique Nash Equilibrium whose revenue is the same as the one under VCG mechanism ([12], [5] and [8]). Actually, it is the same as the lower bound of SNE [11] and LEFE [6]. The authors also show that the strategy always converges in finite steps with probability one. Interestingly, the *conservative* vindictive strategy we studied in this paper is the same as the upper bound of SNE and LEFE. But using it as a strategy does not always result in an output truthful equilibrium, which does not belong to SNE or LEFE.

Brandt and Weiß [2] proposed the concept "antisocial behavior" which investigated the strategic behaviors of decreasing competitors' benefits, namely vindictive strategies. Feng and Zhang discussed interesting bidding wars in [7]. Zhou et al. [13] studied a vindictive strategies which bids one cent lower than the bid one position higher than his. They showed the non-existence of Nash Equilibrium with *three* consecutive players using this strategy. The strategy they studied is referred as *malicious* vindictive strategy in this paper.

There are also other interesting studies of strategic behaviors concerning Sponsored Search Auction as dynamic systems. Borgs et al. [1] study a heuristic based optimal strategy and its stability. Kitts et al. [10] make use of a trading agent to assist bidding in Sponsored Search Auction.

1.2 Organization

The rest of the paper is organized as follows. In section 2, we present the auction model and other preliminaries. Section 3 elaborates the existence of Nash Equilibrium and its properties in our model. We discuss different vindictive strategies and give both theoretical and empirical evidence of our result. Lastly, we summaries and concludes in section 4.

2   Preliminaries

Considering a single auction for a specific keyword, there are N bidders competing for K slots to display their advertisements. We denote the set $\mathbf{b}=\{b_1, b_2, ...b_n\}$, to be the set of bids where the $\mathbf{b}$ is sorted in descending order, i.e., $b_1 > b_2 > ... > b_n$. To display an advertisement, usually, the higher you get, more clicks you would receive. We denote a set $\mathbf{c}=\{c_1, c_2, ...c_K\}$ representing the popularity of each slot which is also referred as *click-through-rate* (CTR). In set $\mathbf{c}$, c_i represents CTR of the i-th slot in a descending order, thus, $c_1 > c_2 > ... > c_K$. Moreover, for each bidder i, there is a private value, v^i, representing his own return-on-investment (ROI) for each click of his advertisement. We also denote v_k as the private value of the bidder who gets the k-th slot. For simplicity, we say each bidder can only bid for one value and each of the bidder has a unique private value.

The winners of the auction are the bidders who bids for the highest K values, namely, $b_1, b_2, ...b_K$. Each winner is assigned a slot to display their advertisement. The bidder who bids b_i gets the i-th slot whose CTR is c_i. The payment scheme used is the generalized second price auction. The bidder assigned the i-th slot pays for b_{i+1}, which is the bid value that the winner of $i + 1$-th slot bids for $i + 1$-th slot. For the bidder who gets K-th slot pays for the highest bid value among all the losing bidders. Hence, for each bidder i, $i \in N$, who gets the k-th slot, $k \in K$, his payoff (utility) function is represented as

$$u_k^i = (v^i - b_{k+1}) \cdot c_k \tag{1}$$

Definition 1. *Nash Equilibrium of Sponsored Search Auction* [11] *For each bidder $i \in N$ who gets slot k, the following equation satisfies*

$$(v^i - b_{k+1})c_k \geq (v^i - b_t)c_t, \ for \ \forall t < k$$
$$(v^i - b_{k+1})c_k \geq (v^i - b_{t+1})c_t, \ for \ \forall t > k$$

In a Nash Equilibrium, no one can improve their payoff by choosing other position in the game. All of them will prefer his current position.

In [3], the authors proposed a well defined response function: *Forward Looking Response Function* that as long as everyone plays cooperatively, they will result in a unique Nash Equilibrium and have a revenue which is the same as VCG mechanism.

Definition 2. *Output Truthful* [4,3,9] *For any instance of ad-words auction and the corresponding equilibrium set $\mathcal{E}$, if $\forall e \in \mathcal{E}$ and $\forall i \in \mathcal{N}$, $\mathcal{O}^i(\mathbf{e}) = \mathcal{O}^i(v^1, ..., v^N)$, then we say ad-words auction is output truthful on $\mathcal{E}$.*

where $\mathcal{O}^i(\mathbf{b})$ denotes the rank of bidder i's bid in the descending bidding profile.

Definition 3. *Myopic Best Response Function* [3] *Given* $\mathbf{b}^{-i}$, *bidder i's myopic best-response function* $\mathcal{M}^i(\mathbf{b}^{-i})$ *returns a set defined as*

$$\mathcal{M}^i(\mathbf{b}^{-i}) = \arg \max_{b^i \in [0,v^i]} \{u^i \mathcal{O}^i(b^i, \mathbf{b}^{-i})\} \qquad (2)$$

Definition 4. *Forward Looking Response Function* [3] *Given* $\mathbf{b}^{-i}$, *suppose* $\mathcal{O}^i(\mathcal{M}^i(\mathbf{b}^{-i}), \mathbf{b}^{-i}) = k$, *then bidder i's forward-looking response function* $\mathcal{F}^i(\mathbf{b}^{-i})$ *is defined as*

$$\mathcal{F}^i(\mathbf{b}^{-i}) = \begin{cases} v^i - \frac{c_k}{c_{k-1}}(v^i - b_{k+1}) & 2 \leq k \leq K \\ v^i & k = 1 \ or \ k > K \end{cases}$$

Throughout the paper, we assume all the forward looking cooperative bidders follows the forward looking response function.

3 Nash Equilibrium for Sponsored Search Auction with Forward Looking Cooperative Bidders and Vindictive Bidders

In this section, we discuss Nash Equilibrium and its properties of Sponsored Search Auction with forward looking cooperative bidders and different kinds of vindictive bidders. For a vindictive bidder, he takes a strategy that forces other bidders paying more without sacrificing his myopic benefits. Formally, there exists a vindictive bidder set $\Psi = \{i|i \in [1, N]\}$ where all the vindictive bidders take a uniform vindictive strategy.

3.1 Malicious Vindictive Strategy

In a malicious vindictive strategy, a bidder tries to raise his competitors' payment as much as possible at the current step. First, he picks his favorite slot and bids one cent lower than the bid one slot higher. Formally,

Definition 5. *(Malicious Vindictive Response Function)* *If $i \in \Psi$ given* $\mathbf{b}^{-i}$, *Suppose* $O^i(M^i(\mathbf{b}^{-i}), \mathbf{b}^{-i}) = k$,

$$\mathcal{V}^i(\mathbf{b}^{-i}) = \begin{cases} v^i, & k = 1; \\ b_{k-1} - 0.01, & otherwise \end{cases}$$

However, this strategy results in an unstable situation even if there is only one such kind of bidder. Concerning an auction with three bidders competing for two slots, the click-through-rates are 20 and 10 respectively. The private values are 5, 2 and 1 and the initial bids are 5, 4.99, 1. Let the second bidder whose private value is 2 be the malicious vindictive bidder. In this simple example, we can see that after the vindictive bidder bids for 4.99, the first bidder will choose the second slot and bids for 3. Since the vindictive bidder's private value is less than 3, he will never prefer the first slot. Then he changes his bid to be 2.99. Then the first bidder again chooses the first slot and bids for 5. In the whole process, the last bidder is not vindictive and never prefer a higher slot. So his bid always remains 1. Thus we get a loop here.

Theorem 1. *There does not always exist a Nash Equilibrium for Sponsored Search Auction with one malicious Vindictive Bidder*

Besides the unstable result, in long term, the bidder mostly sacrifices his own benefits to follow this malicious strategy in the dynamic process. On the other hand, the auctioneer's revenue increases with the number of malicious vindictive bidders increases. However, there also exists exceptional cases that the a bidder improves his benefits by taking the malicious strategy or the auctioneer's revenue decreases. To show this result, we design a simulation on different sets of data. We take randomized adjustment scheme to simulate all the intermediate steps and record every bidder's payoff and the auctioneer's revenue. According to the number of bidders, we set the number of adjustment rounds larger than the factorial of the number of bidders to ensure the accuracy of the simulation. Due to the limit of the space, we illustrate a representative example to show the irrationality of malicious vindictive strategy and the increasing trend of the auctioneer's revenue. We consider a sponsor auction game with 7 advertisers competing for 6 slots. Both CTR and private value are chosen uniformly random within a given range. The detail information about are shown in Table 1.

Table 1. Click-Through-Rates and Private Values of the sample auction

CTR	191.35	171.28	87.16	82.74	59.67	55.98	
Private Value	89.41	71.98	67.09	75.40	59.49	58.97	73.02

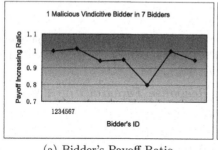
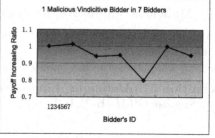

(a) Bidder's Payoff Ratio   (b) Auctioneer's Revenue Ratio

Fig. 1. Sample Example with 6 slots and 7 bidders

Figure 1(a) shows a payoff increasing ratio when there is only one malicious vindictive bidder. Each bidder was set to be malicious vindictive in turn. The horizontal axis shows the index of the vindictive bidder while the vertical axis shows the payoff increasing ratio which is calculated as payoff when the bidder takes the malicious vindictive strategy divided by the payoff he takes the Forward Looking strategy. When the ratio is less than one, its payoff decreases. From the figure, we could see that, most of the bidders reduce their payoff by taking the vindictive strategy. However, there also exists one bidder who increases his payoff by taking the malicious vindictive strategy. This is because after he takes revenge on his competitors, some of them prefer a lower position than the vindictive bidders so that the vindictive bidder benefits from this period. However, this is quite sensitive to the private values and click-through-rate. There is no certain assertion whether a bidder will benefit or not if he migrates from Forward-Looking strategy into a malicious vindictive strategy.

Figure 1(b), on the other hand, shows the revenue in the auctioneer's point of view. The revenue increasing ratio is the revenue when there are n malicious vindictive bidders divides the revenue there is no vindictive bidders where n varies from 1 to N. From the figure, the auctioneer will benefit when the number of vindictive bidder increases. However, the ratio illustrates an increasing but not monotone increasing function which means when given a constant number of malicious vindictive bidders c participates in the auction, the auctioneer cannot tell whether one more malicious vindictive bidder will give him more benefit or not.

3.2   Conservative Vindictive Strategy

In a conservative strategy, a bidder bids vindictively so that he never sacrifices his own payoff. The amount he raises his bid will not affect the stability of the whole auction. In other words, after he changes his bid, no bidder in the auction will prefer other position other than his current position.

Definition 6. *(Conservative Vindictive Response Function)* If $i \in \Psi$, given $\mathbf{b}^{-i}$. Suppose $O^i(M^i(\mathbf{b}^{-i}), \mathbf{b}^{-i}) = k$,

$$\mathcal{V}^i(\mathbf{b}^{-i}) = \begin{cases} v^i, & k \geq K \ or \ k = 1; \\ v_{k-1} - \frac{c_k}{c_{k-1}}(v_{k-1} - b_{k+1}), & 2 \leq k < K \end{cases}$$

3.2.1 The Existence of Output Truthful Nash Equilibrium in Sponsored Search Auction with Conservative Vindictive Bids

To prove the existence of such equilibrium, we first give a specified bidding profile construction, then we show that the construction is indeed the same equilibrium as we claim. Here we assume $v^1, v^2, ..., v^N$ are sorted in descending order.

Construction 1. Construction$(\mathbf{b}, v^1, v^2, ..., v^N, c_1, c_2, ..., c_K, \Psi)$

1: **for** $i = N \rightarrow 1$
2:    **if** $(i > K)$ or $(i = 1)$ **then**
3:       $b_i = v^i$
4:    **else if** $(i \in \Psi)$ **then**
5:       $b_i = v^{i-1} - \frac{c_i}{c_{i-1}}(v^{i-1} - b_{i+1})$
6:    **else**
7:       $b_i = v^i - \frac{c_i}{c_{i-1}}(v^i - b_{i+1})$
8:    **end if**
9: **end for**

Lemma 1. *A bidder never prefers a slot whose private value is smaller than his private value in Construction 1.*

Proof. First, we prove that if a bidder prefers slot c_k to slot c_{k+1} whose owner's private value is smaller than his. Supposing v^i is the bidder's private value. His payoff is $(v^i - b_{k+1})c_k$. Since b_{k+1} follows either Forward-Looking Response Function or conservative Vindictive Response function, we could rewrite it as $(v^i - (v^j - \frac{c_{k+1}}{c_k}(v^j - b_{k+2})))c_k$. From the construction, we could see that the private values are sorted in descending order. If b_{k+1} is calculated by a Forward-Looking Response function, then $v^i > v^j$, otherwise $v^i = v^j$. Thus v^i is no less than v^j.

$$(v^i - (v^j - \frac{c_{k+1}}{c_k}(v^j - b_{k+2})))c_k$$
$$= (v^i - v^j)c_k + (v^j - b_{k+2})c_{k+1}$$
$$\geq (v^i - v^j)c_{k+1} + (v^j - b_{k+2})c_{k+1}$$
$$= (v^i - b_{k+2})c_{k+1}$$

We can see the payoff bidder i gets c_k is no less than the payoff he gets c_{k+1}. Secondly, we show that there is a transition property hold for the claim above. Namely, if a bidder prefers slot c_k to c_{k+1}, he also prefers slot c_{k+1} to c_{k+2} and he prefers slot c_k to c_{k+2}. The mathematical prove is exactly the same as the previous one. To space the limited space, we omit the proof here. Combining two points above, the claim follows.

Lemma 2. *A bidder never prefers a slot whose private value is bigger than his private value in Construction 1.*

Proof. We first prove that if a bidder prefers slot c_k to slot c_{k-1} whose owner's private value is bigger than his. Supposing v^i is the bidder's private value. His payoff of getting slot c_{k-1} is $(v^i - b_{k-1})c_{k-1}$ where $b_{k-1} = v^j - \frac{c_{k-1}}{c_{k-2}}(v^j - b_k)$ and $b_k = \hat{v} - \frac{c_k}{c_{k-1}}(\hat{v} - b_{k+1})$. Since both b_{k-1} and b_k follows either Forward-Looking Response Function or conservative Vindictive Response function, we have $v^j \geq \hat{v} \geq v^i$.

$$(v^i - b_{k-1})c_{k-1}$$
$$= (v^i - (v^j - \frac{c_{k-1}}{c_{k-2}}(v^j - b_k)))c_{k-1}$$
$$= (v^i - v^j)c_{k-1} + \frac{c_{k-1}^2}{c_{k-2}}(v^j - b_k)$$
$$= (v^i - v^j)c_{k-1} + \frac{c_{k-1}^2}{c_{k-2}}(v^j - (\hat{v} - \frac{c_k}{c_{k-1}}(\hat{v} - b_{k+1})))$$

$$= (v^i - v^j)c_{k-1} - \frac{c_{k-1}^2}{c_{k-2}}(\hat{v} - v^j) + \frac{c_k c_{k-1}}{c_{k-2}}(\hat{v} - b_{k+1})$$

$$= (v^i - v^j)c_{k-1} + \frac{c_{k-1}^2}{c_{k-2}}v^i - \frac{c_{k-1}^2}{c_{k-2}}v^i - \frac{c_{k-1}^2}{c_{k-2}}(\hat{v} - v^j) + \frac{c_k c_{k-1}}{c_{k-2}}(\hat{v} - b_{k+1})$$

$$= (v^i - v^j)(c_{k-1} - \frac{c_{k-1}^2}{c_{k-2}}) + \frac{c_{k-1}^2}{c_{k-2}}(v^i - \hat{v}) + \frac{c_k c_{k-1}}{c_{k-2}}(\hat{v} - b_{k+1})$$

$$\leq \frac{c_{k-1}^2}{c_{k-2}}(v^i - \hat{v}) + \frac{c_k c_{k-1}}{c_{k-2}}(\hat{v} - b_{k+1})$$

$$= \frac{c_{k-1}^2}{c_{k-2}}(v^i - \hat{v}) + \frac{c_k c_{k-1}}{c_{k-2}}v^i - \frac{c_k c_{k-1}}{c_{k-2}}v^i + \frac{c_k c_{k-1}}{c_{k-2}}(\hat{v} - b_{k+1})$$

$$= \frac{c_{k-1}^2}{c_{k-2}}(v^i - \hat{v}) - \frac{c_k c_{k-1}}{c_{k-2}}(v^i - \hat{v}) + \frac{c_k c_{k-1}}{c_{k-2}}(v^i - b_{k+1})$$

$$= (\frac{c_{k-1}^2}{c_{k-2}} - \frac{c_k c_{k-1}}{c_{k-2}})(v^i - \hat{v}) + \frac{c_k c_{k-1}}{c_{k-2}}(v^i - b_{k+1})$$

$$\leq (v^i - b_{k+1})\frac{c_k c_{k-1}}{c_{k-2}}$$

$$\leq (v^i - b_{k+1})c_k$$

We can see the payoff bidder i gets c_k is no less than the payoff he gets c_{k-1}. For any slot which is higher, we could derive similar prove that the bidder would prefer c_k. To save the space, we omit it here. So we conclude that a bidder never prefers a higher slot in Construction 1.

Theorem 2. *There always exists an output truthful Nash Equilibrium for Sponsored Search Auction with Vindictive Bidders*

Proof. Based on the construction we have, every bidder in the construction follows either Forward-Looking Response function or conservative Vindictive Response function. For every bidder, all the bidders who get higher positions have higher private values and those who get lower positions have lower values. From *Lemma 1* and *2*, we could conclude for every bidder in the construction does not prefer any slot higher or lower than his. Thus the resulting construction is a Nash Equilibrium. Moreover, the position thats the bidders get are sorted in descending order. Indeed, it is an output truthful Nash Equilibrium.

3.2.2 (Non)Uniqueness of Nash Equilibrium in Sponsored Search Auction with Conservative Vindictive Bidders

Even though there always exists an output truthful Forward-Looking Equilibrium in Sponsored Search Auction with conservative Vindictive Bidders, different from previous results, there may also exist other Nash Equilibrium which is not output truthful.

From Table 2, we can see that both the second and third bidder bids vindictively and all the bidders prefer his current slot. However, the third bidder's

Table 2. Example of a non-output truthful Nash Equilibrium

(a) The click-through rate

slot	1	2	3
CTR	20	16	10

(b) The Nash Equilibrium

true value	5	4	4.1	1
vindictive	No	Yes	Yes	No
bids	5	2.7	2.125	1

private value is higher than the second bidder. This is because the third bidder's bid under vindictive strategy is smaller than his forward-looking cooperative strategy. The competitor whose private value is lower than his will enjoy this underestimated bid and result in non-truthful equilibrium.

Theorem 3. *The output truthful Nash Equilibrium may not always be the unique Nash Equilibrium of Sponsored Search Auction with conservative Vindictive Bidders.*

3.3 Selective Vindictive Bidding Strategy

In real world, bidder bids vindictively only if he cannot get that position to improve his utility. Otherwise, he would compete for the position he deserves to get. In a selective strategy, the bidder only bids vindictively on his potential competitors whose private value is larger than his.

Definition 7. *(Selective Vindictive Response Function)* *If* $i \in \Psi$, *given* $\mathbf{b}^{-i}$, *Suppose* $O^i(M^i(\mathbf{b}^{-i}), \mathbf{b}^{-i}) = k$,

$$V^i(\mathbf{b}^{-i}) = \begin{cases} v^i, & k \geq K \text{ or } k = 1; \\ v_{k-1} - \frac{c_k}{c_{k-1}}(v_{k-1} - b_{k+1}), & 2 \leq k < K \text{ and } v^{i-1} > v^i \\ v^i - \frac{c_k}{c_{k-1}}(v^i - b_{k+1}), & 2 \leq k < K \text{ and } v^{i-1} < v^i \end{cases} \quad (3)$$

3.3.1 The Existence of Nash Equilibrium in Sponsored Search Auction with *Selective* Vindictive Bidders

Theorem 4. *There always exists an output truthful Nash Equilibrium for Sponsored Search Auction with Selective Vindictive Bidders*

Proof. To prove the existence, we first use the same construction algorithm as Construction 1. All the bids in the bid profile is sorted in descending order according to their private values. So in this construction, Sponsored Search Auction with Selective Vindictive Bidders is the same as the one with Conservative Vindictive Bidders. From Lemma 1 and Lemma 2, the claim follows.

Theorem 5. *Sponsored Search Auction with Selective Vindictive Bidders has a unique Nash Equilibrium*

Proof. Suppose there exists another instance of Forward Looking Nash Equilibrium **e** which must not be an output truthful one. In such an Equilibrium **e**, there must be a pair of adjacent slots k and $k + 1$, where bidder i gets slot k and j gets slot $k + 1$ and $v^i < v^j$. The case is trivial when $k > K$ since every one bids their private value. When $k < K$, since $v^i < v^j$, bidder j must use the Forward Looking Bidding strategy. Bidder i's payoff on slot k is

$$(v^i - b_{k+1})c_k$$
$$= (v^i - (v^j - \frac{c_{k+1}}{c_k}(v^j - b_{k+2})))c_k$$
$$= (v^i - v^j)c_k + (v^j - b_{k+2})c_{k+1}$$
$$= (v^i - v^j)(c_k - c_{k+1}) + (v^i - b_{k+2})c_{k+1}$$
$$< (v^i - b_{k+2})c_{k+1}$$

So bidder i will prefer slot $k + 1$ to slot k which contradicts **e** is already a Nash Equilibrium.

Selective vindictive strategy perfectly preserves bidders' own utilities while all his competitors have to pay more to get their position. Taking this strategy does no harm to the bidder as well as all the bidders who gets lower positions but increases his competitors budget. On the other hand, he does not increase his utility by taking vindictive strategy, either. In a global view, the summation of bidders's utilities keeps deceasing and the revenue of the auctioneer keeps increasing. Interestingly, when all the bidders becomes selective vindictive, the revenue of the auctioneer becomes the maximum among all possible Nash Equilibrium [11] and if all of them use forward looking strategy, their payment is the same as VCG [3].

4   Conclusion

In this paper, we investigate the effectiveness of vindictive strategies in different rationalities in conjunction with forward-looking cooperative strategies. We gave both theoretical and empirical evidences to the intriguing decision whether a bidder bids vindictively or cooperatively. A malicious vindictive strategy gave an unstable situation which mostly hurt their own benefit. Conservative strategy gives better result in terms of stability but may hurt his benefit by irrationally take revenge on everyone. Selective vindictive strategy ensures both the stability and the bidders' utilities. The bidder may have more incentive to play vindictively. However, comparing to forward looking strategy, this strategy results in an internecine result in terms of revenue for all the bidders.

References

1. Borgs, C., Chayes, J., Etesami, O., Immorlica, N., Jain, K., Mahdian, M.: Bid optimization in online advertisement auctions. In: Second Workshop on Sponsored Search Auctions, in conjunction with the ACM Conference on Electronic Commerce (EC 2006), Ann Arbor, Michigan, ACM Press, New York (2006)
2. Brandt, F., Weiß, G.: Antisocial agents and vickrey auctions. In: Meyer, J.-J., Tambe, M. (eds.) Pre-proceedings of the Eighth International Workshop on Agent Theories, Architectures, and Languages (ATAL-2001), pp. 120–132 (August 2001)
3. Bu, T.-M., Deng, X., Qi, Q.: Dynamic of strategic manipulation in ad-wordss auction. In: Workshop on Sponsered Search Auctions, in conjuction with the 16th International World Wide Web Conference, Banff, Alberta, Canada (May 11, 2007)
4. Chen, X., Deng, X., Liu, B.J.: On incentive compatible competitive selection protocol. In: Chen, D.Z., Lee, D.T. (eds.) COCOON 2006. LNCS, vol. 4112, pp. 13–22. Springer, Heidelberg (2006)
5. Clarke, E.H.: Multipart pricing of public goods. Public Choice 11, 11–33 (1971)
6. Edelman, B., Ostrovsky, M., Schwarz, M.: Internet advertising and the generalized second price auction: Selling billions of dollars worth of dollars worth of keywords. In: Second Workshop on Sponsored Search Auctions, in conjunction with the ACM Conference on Electronic Commerce (EC 2006), Ann Arbor, Michigan, ACM Press, New York (2006)
7. Feng, J., Zhang, X.M.: Dynamic price competition on the internet: advertising auctions. In: EC 2007: Proceedings of the 8th ACM conference on Electronic commerce, pp. 57–58. ACM Press, New York (2007)
8. Groves, T.: Incentives in teams. Econometrica 41, 617–631 (1973)
9. Kao, M.-Y., Li, X.-Y., Wang, W.: Output truthful versus input truthful: A new concept for algorithmic mechanism design (2006)
10. Kitts, B., Leblanc, B.: Optimal bidding on keyword auctions. Electronic Markets, Sepcial issue: Innovative Auction Markets 14(3), 186–201 (2004)
11. Varian, H.R.: Position auctions. To appear in International Journal of Industrial Organization
12. Vickrey, W.: Counterspeculation, auctions, and competitive sealed tenders. Journal of Finance XVI, 8–37 (1961)
13. Zhou, Y., Lukose, R.: Vindictive bidding in keyword auctions. In: Second Workshop on Sponsored Search Auctions, in conjunction with the ACM Conference on Electronic Commerce (EC 2006), Ann Arbor, Michigan, ACM Press, New York (2006)

Cost-Balancing Tolls for
Atomic Network Congestion Games[*]

Dimitris Fotakis[1] and Paul G. Spirakis[2]

[1] Dept. of Information and Communication Systems Engineering,
University of the Aegean, 83200 Samos, Greece
`fotakis@aegean.gr`
[2] Research Academic Computer Technology Institute,
P.O. Box 1382, N. Kazantzaki Str., Rion, 26500 Patras, Greece
`spirakis@cti.gr`

Abstract. We investigate the existence of optimal tolls for atomic symmetric network congestion games with unsplittable traffic and arbitrary non-negative and non-decreasing latency functions. We focus on pure Nash equilibria and a natural toll mechanism, which we call *cost-balancing tolls*. A set of cost-balancing tolls turns every path with positive traffic on its edges into a minimum cost path. Hence any given configuration is induced as a pure Nash equilibrium of the modified game with the corresponding cost-balancing tolls. We show how to compute in linear time a set of cost-balancing tolls for the optimal solution such that the total amount of tolls paid by any player in any pure Nash equilibrium of the modified game does not exceed the latency on the maximum latency path in the optimal solution. Our main result is that for congestion games on series-parallel networks with increasing latencies, the optimal solution is induced as the *unique* pure Nash equilibrium of the game with the corresponding cost-balancing tolls. To the best of our knowledge, only linear congestion games on parallel links were known to admit optimal tolls prior to this work. To demonstrate the difficulty of computing a better set of optimal tolls, we show that even for 2-player linear congestion games on series-parallel networks, it is NP-hard to decide whether the optimal solution is the unique pure Nash equilibrium or there is another equilibrium of total cost at least $6/5$ times the optimal cost.

1 Introduction

Congestion games provide a natural model for non-cooperative resource allocation in large-scale communication networks and have been the subject of intensive research in algorithmic game theory. In an (atomic) *congestion game* [19], a finite set of non-cooperative players, each controlling an unsplittable unit of traffic, compete over a finite set of resources. All players using a resource experience a latency given by a non-negative and non-decreasing function of the resource's traffic (or congestion). Among a given set of resource subsets (or strategies), each player selects one selfishly trying to minimize her *individual cost*, that is the sum of the latencies on the resources in the chosen strategy. A natural solution concept is that of a *pure Nash equilibrium*, a configuration where no player can decrease her individual cost by unilaterally changing her strategy.

---

[*] Partially supported by EU / 6th Framework Programme, contract 001907 (DELIS).

At the other end, the network manager seeks to minimize the *social cost* measured by the total cost incurred by all players. It is well known that a Nash equilibrium does not need to optimize the social cost. To mitigate the performance degradation due to the players' non-cooperative and selfish behaviour, the network manager can introduce economic incentives that influence the players' selfish choices and hopefully induce an optimal network configuration.

Economic incentives can be naturally modelled by non-negative per-unit-of-traffic *tolls* (aka taxes or prices) assigned to the resources. The tolls are levied by the network manager and comprise an additional cost factor which the players should take into account. In the modified congestion game with tolls, a player's cost for using a resource is equal to the latency due to the resource's congestion plus the toll for using the resource. The player's individual cost for adopting a strategy is equal to the sum of the latencies and the tolls for the resources in the chosen strategy. Although tolls increase the players' individual cost, they do not affect the social cost because they are payments inside the system and can be feasibly refunded to the players. The goal is to find a set of moderate and efficiently computable *optimal tolls*, which make the Nash equilibria of the modified game coincide with the optimal solution.

Related Work. In the non-atomic setting, where there is an infinite number of players each controlling an infinitesimal amount of traffic, the existence and the efficiency of optimal tolls has been investigated extensively (see e.g. [7,6] and references therein). A classical result is that the optimal solution is realized as the Nash equilibrium of a non-atomic congestion game with *marginal cost tolls* [2]. In simple words, the performance degradation due to the selfish and non-cooperative behaviour of non-atomic players can be eliminated by an appropriate set of tolls. Unfortunately, marginal cost tolls fail to induce the optimal solution even for simple congestion games with unsplittable traffic[1].

Recent work on tolls for non-atomic congestion games was motivated by the limitations of marginal cost tolls. Cole *et al.* [7] were the first to consider *heterogeneous* players, who may have a different valuation of time (latency) in terms of money (toll), and established the existence of optimal tolls for non-atomic symmetric network congestion games. Their proof was based on Brouwer's fixed point theorem and was non-constructive. In addition, Cole *et al.* showed how to compute a set of optimal tolls efficiently if the number of player types is finite and the latency functions are convex. Fleischer [11] extended the results of [7] and proved that the optimal toll on each edge need not exceed the latency of the maximum latency path in the optimal solution times the maximum valuation of time. For series-parallel networks, Fleischer showed how to compute a set of optimal tolls efficiently even if there are infinitely many player types. Subsequently, Fleischer *et al.* [12] and Karakostas and Kolliopoulos [16] independently

---

[1] Let $d_e(x)$ be the (differentiable) latency function of a resource e, let $d'_e(x)$ denote the first derivative of $d_e(x)$, and let o_e be the traffic of e in the optimal solution. Then the marginal cost toll of e is $o_e d'_e(o_e)$. For a congestion game with unsplittable traffic where marginal cost tolls fail to induce the optimal solution, consider two players and two parallel links with latency functions $d_1(x) = x/2$ and $d_2(x) = (1+\varepsilon)x$, $\varepsilon > 0$. In the optimal configuration, there is one player on every link, while in the unique pure Nash equilibrium, both players choose the first link. The latter configuration remains the unique pure Nash equilibrium of the modified game with marginal cost tolls.

proved that the existence of optimal tolls for non-atomic congestion games with heterogeneous players and arbitrary strategies follows from Linear Programming duality. Therefore, optimal tolls can be computed efficiently by solving a Linear Program.

For non-atomic congestion games, the Nash equilibrium is essentially unique (under mild assumptions on the latency functions, see e.g. [20]). Hence the tolls of [2,7,11,12,16] induce the optimal solution as the unique equilibrium of the game with tolls[2]. On the other hand, atomic congestion games (even with splittable traffic) may admit many different Nash equilibria. Therefore, when considering atomic games, one has to distinguish between the case where a set of tolls *weakly enforces* the optimal solution, in the sense that the optimal solution is realized as some equilibrium of the game with tolls, and the case where a set of tolls *strongly enforces* the optimal solution, in the sense that the optimal solution is realized as the unique equilibrium of the game with tolls.

For atomic congestion games with splittable traffic and heterogeneous players, Swamy [21] proved that a set of tolls that weakly enforce the optimal solution can be computed efficiently by solving a Convex Program. For homogeneous players with splittable traffic, Cominetti *et al.* [8] presented a toll mechanism that reduces the price of anarchy[3] though it is not known whether it weakly enforces the optimal solution.

To the best of our knowledge, the only work prior to ours that investigates the efficiency of toll mechanisms for atomic congestion games with unsplittable traffic is [4]. Caragiannis *et al.* considered games with linear latency functions and homogeneous players, and investigated how much tolls can improve the price of anarchy. On the negative side, they presented a simple non-symmetric game for which the price of anarchy remains at least 1.2 under any toll mechanism. Therefore, non-symmetric congestion games do not necessarily admit tolls that strongly enforce the optimal solution. On the positive side, Caragiannis *et al.* presented a set of tolls strongly enforcing the optimal solution for linear congestion games on parallel links. In addition, they presented two efficiently computable toll mechanisms that improve the price of anarchy of linear games with arbitrary strategies. The first mechanism [4, Theorem 3] is simple and improves the pure price of anarchy to 2.155 (from 2.5 [1,5]). The second mechanism [4, Theorem 5] applies to the more general setting of mixed equilibria and weighted players, and improves the price of anarchy to 2 (from 2.618 [1,5]). However, the former mechanism may not weakly enforce the optimal solution even for linear games on parallel links, while the latter mechanism may not strongly enforce the optimal solution even for linear games on series-parallel networks[4].

---

[2] The uniqueness of Nash equilibrium in non-atomic games is also exploited by the algorithm of [15], which computes the smallest fraction of coordinated players required by a Stackelberg routing strategy to induce the optimal solution.

[3] The *price of anarchy* [17] is a widely accepted measure of the performance degradation due to the players' non-cooperative and selfish behaviour. The (pure) price of anarchy is the worst-case ratio of the total cost of a (pure) Nash equilibrium to the optimal total cost. For a survey on the price of anarchy of congestion games, see e.g. [13].

[4] For a game where the tolls of [4, Theorem 3] do not weakly enforce the optimal solution, consider 2 players and two parallel links with latency functions $d_1(x) = x/2$ and $d_2(x) = x$. For a game on a series-parallel network where the tolls of [4, Theorem 5] do not strongly enforce the optimal solution, consider the instance of Fig. 1.b with $k = 2$, $q_1 = q_2 = 2$, and latency function $d_{(s,t)}(x) = (3 + \varepsilon)x, \varepsilon \in (0, 1)$, for the direct (s, t) edge.

Contribution. Despite the considerable interest in optimal toll mechanisms for atomic and non-atomic congestion games, it is still unknown whether there is an optimal toll mechanism for symmetric games with unsplittable traffic. This is true even for relatively simple symmetric network congestion games, such as games on series-parallel networks and games on parallel links with non-linear latencies.

In this work, we investigate the existence of optimal tolls for symmetric network congestion games with unsplittable traffic, homogeneous players, and arbitrary non-negative and non-decreasing latency functions. We focus on pure Nash equilibria and consider a natural toll mechanism, which we call *cost-balancing tolls*. Cost balancing-tolls are motivated by the optimal toll mechanisms for non-atomic games [7,11,12,16]. A set of cost-balancing tolls turns every path with positive traffic on its edges into a minimum cost path (the optimal tolls for linear congestion games on parallel links [4] are also based on the same principle). Hence any given configuration is induced as a pure Nash equilibrium of the game with the corresponding cost-balancing tolls. We show how to compute in linear time a set of cost-balancing tolls for the optimal configuration such that the total amount of tolls paid by any player in any pure Nash equilibrium of the modified game does not exceed the latency on the maximum latency path in the optimal configuration. Roughly speaking, we prove that the optimal solution is weakly enforceable by a set of moderate cost-balancing tolls computable in linear time. Moreover, we give a simple example where the optimal solution cannot be weakly enforced by tolls substantially smaller than the cost-balancing tolls.

Motivated by the recent interest in analyzing toll mechanisms (e.g. [11]) and Stackel-berg routing strategies (e.g. [10,21]) for games on series-parallel networks, we study the efficiency of cost-balancing tolls for such games. Our main result is that for congestion games on series-parallel networks with strictly increasing latencies, the optimal solution is *strongly enforceable* by the corresponding cost-balancing tolls. Therefore, congestion games on series-parallel networks with increasing latencies admit a set of moderate optimal tolls computable in linear time. To the best of our knowledge, only linear congestion games on parallel links were known to admit optimal tolls [4, Theorem 1] prior to this work. Our result is considerably stronger, since it applies to arbitrary increasing latency functions and to series-parallel networks, which are significantly more complex than parallel-link networks. On the negative side, we show that if the network is not series-parallel, the cost-balancing tolls may not strongly enforce the optimal solution even for linear latency functions.

To highlight the difficulty of computing a better set of optimal tolls, we prove that even for 2-player linear congestion games on series-parallel networks, it is NP-hard to distinguish between the case where the optimal solution is the unique pure Nash equilibrium (thus any positive tolls only serve to increase the players' disutility) and the case where there is another equilibrium of total cost at least $6/5$ times the optimal cost (and hence some positive tolls are required to strongly enforce the optimal solution).

2   Model, Definitions, and Notation

Congestion Games. A *congestion game* is a tuple $\Gamma(N, E, (\Sigma_i)_{i \in N}, (d_e)_{e \in E})$, where N denotes the set of players, E denotes the set of resources, $\Sigma_i \subseteq 2^E$ denotes the strategy space of each player i, and $d_e : \mathbb{N} \mapsto \mathbb{R}_{\geq 0}$ is a non-negative and non-decreasing latency function associated with each resource $e \in E$. A congestion game is *symmetric* if all players share the same strategy space. A congestion game is *linear* if the latency function of each resource e is $d_e(x) = a_e x + b_e$, $a_e, b_e \geq 0$.

A *configuration* is a vector $\sigma = (\sigma_1, \ldots, \sigma_n)$ consisting of a strategy $\sigma_i \in \Sigma_i$ for each player $i \in N$. For each resource e, $\sigma_e = |\{i \in N : e \in \sigma_i\}|$ denotes the congestion induced on e by σ. The individual cost of player i in the configuration σ is $c_i(\sigma) = \sum_{e \in \sigma_i} d_e(\sigma_e)$. A configuration σ is a *pure Nash equilibrium* if no player can improve his individual cost by unilaterally changing his strategy. Formally, σ is a Nash equilibrium if for every player i and every strategy $s_i \in \Sigma_i$, $c_i(\sigma) \leq c_i(\sigma_{-i}, s_i)$ [5].

We say that a congestion game Γ admits a *unique* pure Nash equilibrium if all pure Nash equilibria of Γ induce the same congestion on every resource. Rosenthal [19] proved that the pure Nash equilibria of a congestion game correspond to the local optima of a natural potential function. Therefore, every congestion game admits a pure Nash equilibrium, which is not necessarily unique.

In the following, we let n denote the number of players and m denote the number of resources. We restrict our attention to *symmetric network* congestion games, where the players' strategies are determined by a directed network $G(V, E)$ with a distinguished source s and destination t. The network edges play the role of the resources and the common strategy space of all players is the set of simple $s - t$ paths in G, denoted $\mathcal{P}$.

Flows and Configurations. Let $G(V, E)$ be a directed network with source s and destination t. An $s - t$ *flow* f is a vector $(f_e)_{e \in E} \in \mathbb{R}_{\geq 0}^m$ that satisfies the flow conservation at all vertices other than s and t. The *volume* of an $s - t$ flow is the total flow leaving s. A flow is *acyclic* if there is no directed cycle in G with positive flow on all its edges. For a flow f and a path $p \in \mathcal{P}$, we let $f_p^{\min} = \min_{e \in p}\{f_e\}$.

Given a configuration σ for a symmetric network congestion game, we refer to the congestion vector $(\sigma_e)_{e \in E}$ as the *flow* induced by σ. We say that a flow σ is *feasible* if there is a configuration inducing congestion σ_e on every edge e. We slightly abuse the notation by letting the same symbol denote both a configuration and the feasible flow induced by it.

Social Cost. We evaluate configurations and the corresponding feasible flows using the objective of *total cost*. The total cost $C(\sigma)$ of a configuration σ is the sum of players' costs in σ. Formally, $C(\sigma) = \sum_{i=1}^{n} c_i(\sigma) = \sum_{e \in E} \sigma_e d_e(\sigma_e)$. The optimal configuration, usually denoted o, minimizes the total cost $C(o)$ among all configurations in $\mathcal{P}^n$. In the following, we let o denote both the optimal configuration and the optimal flow induced by it.

Every $s - t$ network with non-negative and non-decreasing latency functions admits an integral acyclic min-cost flow of volume n computable in polynomial time if $x d_e(x)$ are convex. Therefore, if $x d_e(x)$ are convex, an optimal configuration for a symmetric network congestion game can be computed in polynomial time by a min-cost flow computation followed by a flow decomposition in n $s - t$ paths. For series-parallel networks with arbitrary non-negative and non-decreasing latencies, an optimal configuration can be computed in $O(m + n \log m)$ time by the greedy algorithm [3].

---

[5] For a vector $x = (x_1, \ldots, x_n)$, $(x_{-i}, x_i') \equiv (x_1, \ldots, x_{i-1}, x_i', x_{i+1}, \ldots, x_n)$.

Tolls. We consider a scenario where the network manager levies tolls on the edges
of the network trying to influence the players' selfish choices and induce an optimal
configuration. A set of *tolls* is a function $\tau : E \mapsto \mathbb{R}_{\geq 0}$ that assigns a non-negative
per-unit-of-traffic toll τ_e to each resource e. The modified congestion game induced by
τ is $\bar{\Gamma}_\tau(N, E, (\Sigma_i)_{i \in N}, (\bar{d}_e)_{e \in E})$, where $\bar{d}_e(x) = d_e(x) + \tau_e$ for all $e \in E$. In $\bar{\Gamma}_\tau$, the
players have the same strategy space as in the original game. The cost of each player
i in a configuration σ increases by the total amount of tolls on the resources in σ_i and
becomes:

$$\bar{c}_i(\sigma) = \sum_{e \in \sigma_i} \bar{d}_e(\sigma_e) = \sum_{e \in \sigma_i} (d_e(\sigma_e) + \tau_e) = c_i(\sigma) + \sum_{e \in \sigma_i} \tau_e$$

The selfish players reach a pure Nash equilibrium of $\bar{\Gamma}_\tau$. Since the tolls are payments
inside the network, a common assumption is that the tolls can be feasibly refunded to
the players and thus do not affect the social cost (see e.g. [7,12,16], and the case of
refundable tolls in [4]). Hence the social cost of a configuration σ remains $C(\sigma) = \sum_{e \in E} \sigma_e d_e(\sigma_e)$ as in the original congestion game Γ.

The goal is to compute a set of tolls τ that motivate the selfish players to induce
a given feasible flow f (in particular, the optimal flow). A first natural requirement is
that every configuration corresponding to f should be a pure Nash equilibrium of $\bar{\Gamma}_\tau$.
Namely if the players take the tolls into account and adopt an arbitrary configuration
inducing congestion f_e on each edge e, they should not have an incentive to deviate.
Formally, a feasible flow f is *weakly enforceable* by tolls τ if every configuration inducing congestion f_e on each edge e is a Nash equilibrium of $\bar{\Gamma}_\tau$. By definition, if a
feasible flow f is weakly enforceable, there is at least one pure Nash equilibrium of $\bar{\Gamma}_\tau$
with congestion f_e on all $e \in E$.

Since $\bar{\Gamma}_\tau$ does not need to admit a unique pure Nash equilibrium, some equilibria
of $\bar{\Gamma}_\tau$ may induce flows quite different from f. To exclude this possibility, we require
that f should be not only weakly enforceable by τ, but also the unique pure Nash
equilibrium of $\bar{\Gamma}_\tau$. Formally, a feasible flow f is *strongly enforceable* by tolls τ when a
configuration σ is a Nash equilibrium of $\bar{\Gamma}_\tau$ if and only if $\sigma_e = f_e$ for all $e \in E$. A set
of tolls τ is *optimal* if the optimal flow is strongly enforceable by τ.

Series-Parallel Networks. A directed $s{-}t$ network is *series-parallel* if it either consists
of a single edge (s, t) or can be obtained from two series-parallel graphs with terminals
(s_1, t_1) and (s_2, t_2) composed either in series or in parallel. In a *series composition*,
t_1 is identified with s_2, s_1 becomes s, and t_2 becomes t. In a *parallel composition*,
s_1 is identified with s_2 and becomes s, and t_1 is identified with t_2 and becomes t. A
maximal set of contiguous series compositions is a *series component*, and a maximal
set of parallel compositions is a *parallel component*.

A series-parallel network can be completely specified by its *decomposition tree*,
which is a rooted tree with a leaf for each edge. Each internal node of the decomposition tree represents either a series or a parallel component obtained from series
(resp. parallel) compositions of the networks represented by its subtrees. The root of
the tree represents the entire network. The decomposition tree of a series-parallel net-
work $G(V, E)$ can be computed in $O(|V| + |E|)$ time (see e.g. [22] for more details).

3 Cost-Balancing Tolls

A set of tolls τ is *cost-balancing* for a feasible flow f if for every path $p \in \mathcal{P}$ with $f_p^{\min} > 0$ and every path $p' \in \mathcal{P}$,

$$\sum_{e \in p} \bar{d}_e(f_e) = \sum_{e \in p} (d_e(f_e) + \tau_e) \leq \sum_{e \in p'} (d_e(f_e) + \tau_e) = \sum_{e \in p'} \bar{d}_e(f_e) \qquad (1)$$

Proposition 1. *Let f be a feasible flow that admits a set of cost-balancing tolls τ. Then f is weakly enforceable by τ.*

Proof. We prove that any configuration σ with $\sigma_e = f_e$ on each edge e is a pure Nash equilibrium of the congestion game $\bar{\Gamma}_\tau$. In particular, for every player i and every path $p \in \mathcal{P}$, the individual cost of i (in $\bar{\Gamma}_\tau$) does not decrease if i switches from σ_i to p:

$$\bar{c}_i(\sigma) = \sum_{e \in \sigma_i} \bar{d}_e(f_e) \leq \sum_{e \in p} \bar{d}_e(f_e) \leq \bar{c}_i(\sigma_{-i}, p),$$

where the first inequality follows from the definition of cost-balancing tolls. $\square$

We present a simple linear-time algorithm, called BALANCE, that computes a set of cost-balancing tolls for any acyclic $s - t$ flow f. The input of BALANCE consists of a $s - t$ network $G(V, E)$ and an acyclic $s - t$ flow f. BALANCE works as follows:

1. Let $E_f = \{e \in E : f_e > 0\}$, and let $G_f(V, E_f)$ be the spanning subgraph of G consisting of the edges with positive flow in f.
2. BALANCE assigns a non-negative length $d_e(f_e)$ to each edge $e \in E_f$ and computes the longest path from s to any vertex in G_f reachable from s. Let $\ell_s = 0$, and for every vertex $u \in V \setminus \{s\}$ reachable from s, let ℓ_u be the length of the longest $s - u$ path in G_f.
3. The toll of every edge $e = (u, v) \in E_f$ is $\tau_e = \ell_v - (\ell_u + d_e(f_e))$. The toll of every edge $e \notin E_f$ is $\tau_e = \tau^{\max}$, where $\tau^{\max} = \delta + \max_{p \in \mathcal{P}} \sum_{e \in p} d_e(n)$, with $\delta > 0$ chosen arbitrarily small.

If f is acyclic, G_f is a directed acyclic graph (DAG). Therefore, the longest paths from s can be computed in $O(|V| + |E_f|)$ time by negating the edge lengths and solving the corresponding single-source shortest path problem (see e.g. [9, Section 24.2]). Hence BALANCE can be implemented in time linear in the size of the network.

Lemma 1. *For any acyclic $s - t$ flow f, the tolls τ computed by BALANCE are cost-balancing for f.*

Proof. We first show that $\tau_e \geq 0$ for all $e \in E$. The claim is trivial for the edges not in E_f. For the edges in E_f, we recall that a longest path in a DAG becomes a shortest path if we negate the edge lengths. Therefore, for every vertex v reachable from s, $-\ell_v$ is the length of the shortest $s - v$ path in $G_f(V, E_f, (-d_e(f_e))_{e \in E_f})$. Hence, for every edge $e = (u, v) \in E_f$, $-\ell_v \leq -\ell_u - d_e(f_e)$, which implies that $\tau_e = \ell_v - (\ell_u + d_e(f_e)) \geq 0$. By the same reasoning, if an edge $e \in E_f$ lies on some longest path, then $\tau_e = 0$.

We have also to show that for every $s - t$ path p with $f_p^{\min} > 0$, and every $s - t$ path p', $\sum_{e \in p} (d_e(f_e) + \tau_e) \leq \sum_{e \in p'} (d_e(f_e) + \tau_e)$. Let $p = (s = u_0, u_1, \ldots u_k = t)$ be an $s - t$ path with positive flow on all edges. Since for every edge $e = (u_i, u_{i+1}) \in p$, $\tau_e = \ell_{u_{i+1}} - (\ell_{u_i} + d_e(f_e))$, $\sum_{e \in p} (d_e(f_e) + \tau_e) = \ell_t$. On the other hand, the cost on every $s - t$ path p' containing an edge e with $f_e = 0$ is at least $\tau^{\max} \geq \ell_t$.   □

In the following, we refer to the tolls computed by BALANCE for an acyclic flow f as *the cost-balancing tolls for f*.

Theorem 1. *For every symmetric network congestion game Γ, the optimal flow o is weakly enforceable by the cost-balancing tolls τ for o, which have the following properties:*

(a) *Given the optimal flow o, τ is computed in time linear in the size of the network.*
(b) *The maximum toll on any edge is at most $\tau^{\max} = \delta + \max_{p \in \mathcal{P}} \sum_{e \in p} d_e(n)$, for any $\delta > 0$. No edge with toll $\tau^{\max}$ is used in any pure Nash equilibrium of $\bar{\Gamma}_\tau$.*
(c) *The total amount of tolls paid by any player in any pure Nash equilibrium of $\bar{\Gamma}_\tau$ does not exceed $\ell_t = \max_{p:o_p^{\min} > 0} \sum_{e \in p} d_e(o_e)$.*

Proof. (a). Every symmetric network congestion game with non-negative and non-decreasing latency functions admits an optimal configuration that corresponds to a feasible integral acyclic flow o. The linear-time algorithm BALANCE computes the cost-balancing tolls τ for o (Lemma 1) and o is weakly enforceable by τ (Proposition 1).

(b). Let $G(V, E)$ be the $s - t$ network determining the strategy space of Γ. Since o is an acyclic $s - t$ flow, $\ell_v \leq \ell_t$ for all vertices v reachable from s in G_o. Therefore, every edge with positive flow in o is assigned a toll no greater than ℓ_t. The remaining edges are assigned a toll equal to $\tau^{\max}$.

We then prove that all edges with toll $\tau^{\max}$ remain unused in any pure Nash equilibrium of $\bar{\Gamma}_\tau$. To reach a contradiction, we assume that there is a pure Nash equilibrium σ of $\bar{\Gamma}_\tau$ in which some player i uses an edge e with $o_e = 0$. Then, $\bar{c}_i(\sigma) \geq \tau^{\max}$. Let p_t be the longest $s - t$ path in G_o. In the proof of Lemma 1, we show that for every edge e lying on some longest path in G_o, $\tau_e = 0$. Therefore, if player i switches to p_t, her cost becomes at most $\max_{p:o_p^{\min} > 0} \sum_{e \in p} d_e(n) < \tau^{\max} \leq \bar{c}_i(\sigma)$, a contradiction.

(c). By (b), every Nash equilibrium σ of $\bar{\Gamma}_\tau$ induces congestion $\sigma_e = 0$ on every edge e with $o_e = 0$. Hence the strategy σ_i of each player i entirely consists of edges with positive flow in o. In the proof of Lemma 1, we show that for every $s - t$ path p with $o_p^{\min} > 0$, $\sum_{e \in p} (d_e(o_e) + \tau_e) = \ell_t$. Consequently, the total amount of tolls paid by player i in σ is at most $\ell_t = \max_{p:o_p^{\min} > 0} \sum_{e \in p} d_e(o_e)$.   □

Remark 1. There are symmetric network games for which the optimal solution cannot be weakly enforced by tolls substantially smaller than the cost-balancing tolls. For instance, let us consider the discrete version of Pigou's example with an even number n of players and two parallel links with latencies $d_1(x) = x/n$ and $d_2(x) = 1$. In the optimal solution, there are $n/2$ players on each link. For this example, the cost balancing tolls coincide with the marginal cost tolls and are $\tau_1 = 1/2$ and $\tau_2 = 0$. The optimal solution is weakly enforced by τ (note that it is not strongly enforced by τ because the latency of the second link is constant). On the other hand, for any set of tolls τ', either $\frac{1}{2} - \frac{1}{n} \leq \tau_1' - \tau_2' \leq \frac{1}{2}$, or the optimal solution is not weakly enforced by τ'.

3.1 Optimality of Cost-Balancing Tolls for Series-Parallel Networks

It is not hard to prove that if the latency functions are increasing, the optimal solution is strongly enforceable by the cost-balancing tolls for *networks with linearly independent routes* (e.g. [18]), an interesting class of $s - t$ networks including parallel-link networks. Next we generalize this result to series-parallel networks, an important class of networks considerably more complex than networks with linearly independent routes. This generalization is particularly interesting because in a series-parallel network, an $s - t$ flow may be realized by many different configurations (see e.g. the proof of Theorem 3).

Lemma 2. *Let Γ be a symmetric congestion game on a series-parallel network $G(V, E)$ with increasing latency functions, and let f be any feasible acyclic flow that admits a set of cost-balancing tolls τ. Then every pure Nash equilibrium σ of the congestion game $\bar{\Gamma}_\tau$ induces congestion $\sigma_e = f_e$ on each edge e.*

Proof. To reach a contradiction, we assume that there is a pure Nash equilibrium σ of $\bar{\Gamma}_\tau$ that induces congestion $\sigma_e \neq f_e$ on some edge e. The corresponding flow σ is acyclic because the network is series-parallel, the latency functions are non-negative and increasing, and σ is a Nash equilibrium of $\bar{\Gamma}_\tau$. Hence both f and σ are integral acyclic $s - t$ flows of volume n.

We refer to an edge e as a *forward* edge if $\sigma_e > f_e$, and as a *backward* edge if $\sigma_e < f_e$. Since σ_e's and f_e's are integral, $\sigma_e \geq f_e + 1$ for all forward edges e and $f_{e'} \geq \sigma_{e'} + 1$ for all backward edges e'. Since σ and f are different acyclic flows of the same volume, there is at least one forward edge and at least one backward edge.

Let H be a component in the series-parallel decomposition of G (H is the induced subgraph of G determined by the vertices in the corresponding component) such that H contains both forward and backward edges and none of H's subcomponents $H_1, \ldots, H_k$ has this property. In other words, H corresponds to the entire subtree of an internal node u_H in G's decomposition tree, and $H_1, \ldots, H_k$ correspond to the entire subtrees of u_H's children (an H_i may consist of a single edge and correspond to a leaf of the decomposition tree). H is a *minimal* component in the series-parallel decomposition of G wrt the property that it contains both forward and backward edges. Such a component exists and can be found by traversing G's decomposition tree bottom-up because every edge e with $\sigma_e \neq f_e$ is either a forward or a backward edge but not both.

Let H_1 be a component of H that contains at least one forward edge and no backward edges, and let H_2 be a component of H that contains at least one backward edge and no forward edges (their existence is guaranteed by the definition of H). Since σ is acyclic and H_1 does not contain any backward edges, by flow conservation, the number of players going through H_1 in σ is greater than the number of players going through H_1 in f. Similarly, since f is acyclic and H_2 does not contain any forward edges, the number of players going through H_2 in σ is less than the number of players going through H_2 in f. Hence, by flow conservation, H_1 and H_2 are not connected in series. Therefore, H is formed by a parallel composition of $H_1, \ldots, H_k$. Let s_H and t_H be the common endpoints of H and its components $H_1, \ldots, H_k$.

Let e^+ be a forward edge in H_1, let i be any player with $e^+ \in \sigma_i$ (such a player exists because e^+ is a forward edge and thus $\sigma_{e^+} \geq 1$), and let p^+ denote the restriction of σ_i to H_1 (i.e. p^+ is the part of σ_i between s_H and t_H). Since H_1 does not contain any backward edges, $\sigma_e \geq f_e$ and $\bar{d}_e(\sigma_e) \geq \bar{d}_e(f_e)$ for all $e \in p^+$. Moreover, for the forward edge e^+, $\bar{d}_{e^+}(\sigma_e) > \bar{d}_{e^+}(f_e)$ because the latency functions $d_e(x)$ (and thus the functions $\bar{d}_e(x)$) are increasing. Therefore, the individual cost of player i on p^+ is:

$$\sum_{e \in p^+} \bar{d}_e(\sigma_e) > \sum_{e \in p^+} \bar{d}_e(f_e) \tag{2}$$

On the other hand, since f is acyclic and H_2 does not contain any forward edges, H_2 contains an $s_H - t_H$ path p^- entirely consisting of backward edges. Therefore $\sigma_e + 1 \leq f_e$ for all $e \in p^-$, which implies that:

$$\sum_{e \in p^-} \bar{d}_e(\sigma_e + 1) \leq \sum_{e \in p^-} \bar{d}_e(f_e) \leq \sum_{e \in p^+} \bar{d}_e(f_e) \tag{3}$$

For the last inequality, we observe that $f_{p^-}^{\min} \geq 1$ and that (1) holds for p^- and p^+, since they are segments of $s - t$ paths with common endpoints s_H and t_H.

Combining (2) and (3), we conclude that $\sum_{e \in p^+} \bar{d}_e(\sigma_e) > \sum_{e \in p^-} \bar{d}_e(\sigma_e + 1)$. Therefore player i can decrease her cost by changing her path between s_H and t_H from p^+ to p^-. This contradicts the assumption that σ is a Nash equilibrium of $\bar{\Gamma}_\tau$. □

Theorem 1 and Lemma 2 immediately imply the following:

Theorem 2. *Every symmetric congestion game on a series-parallel network with increasing latency functions admits a set of optimal tolls with the properties (a), (b), and (c) in Theorem 1.*

Remark 2. If the network is not series parallel, the optimal flow may not be strongly enforceable by the cost-balancing tolls even for linear latencies $d_e(x) = a_e x$, $a_e > 0$. For example, consider the 4-player game in Fig. 1.a. The set of $s - t$ paths consists of $p^u = (e_1, e_3, e_7, e_{11})$ (upper path), $p_1^m = (e_1, e_4, e_8, e_{11})$ (upper middle path), $p_2^m = (e_2, e_5, e_9, e_{12})$ (lower middle path), $p^l = (e_2, e_6, e_{10}, e_{12})$ (lower path), $p_1^c = (e_1, e_4, e_9, e_{12})$ (first cross path), and $p_2^c = (e_2, e_5, e_8, e_{11})$ (second cross path).

An optimal configuration is $o = (p^u, p_1^m, p_2^m, p^l)$ and has cost 92. The longest $s - t$ path in o is p_2^c and has length 24. The cost-balancing tolls assign a toll of 1 to e_4, e_7, and e_{12}, and no tolls to the remaining edges. The configuration $\sigma = (p_1^c, p_1^c, p_2^c, p_2^c)$ has cost 104 and is a pure Nash equilibrium of the modified game with cost-balancing tolls.

4   Hardness of Deciding the Necessity of Tolls

To highlight the difficulty of computing a better set of optimal tolls, we prove that even for simple games on series-parallel networks, it is NP-hard to decide whether the use of tolls is really necessary to strongly enforce the optimal flow.

Theorem 3. *Given a 2-player linear congestion game Γ on a series-parallel network for which the optimal configuration o is Nash equilibrium, it is NP-hard to distinguish between the case where o is the unique pure Nash equilibrium of Γ, and the case where Γ admits another pure Nash equilibrium of cost at least $\frac{6}{5}C(o)$.*

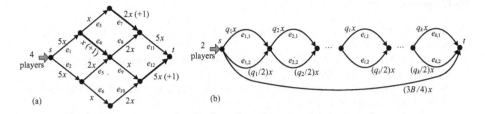

Fig. 1. (a). A symmetric network congestion game with (increasing) linear latency functions for which the cost-balancing tolls do not strongly enforce the optimal flow. Each edge is labeled with its latency function and its identifier. The edges with positive cost-balancing tolls are bold and the tolls appear in parenthesis next to the original latency functions. (b). The series-parallel network used in the proof of Theorem 3.

Proof. We use a reduction from Partition, which is weakly NP-complete [14, Problem SP12]. Let $q_1, \ldots, q_k$ be positive integers such that $\sum_{i=1}^{k} q_i = B$, with B even. Partition asks whether there is a set $A^* \subseteq [k]$ such that $\sum_{i \in A^*} q_i = \sum_{i \notin A^*} q_i = B/2$.

Given $q_1, \ldots, q_k$, we construct a 2-player game Γ on the series-parallel network in Fig. 1.b. The latency functions are $d_{e_{i,1}}(x) = q_i x$, $d_{e_{i,2}}(x) = (q_i/2)x$, $i \in [k]$, and $d_{(s,t)}(x) = (3B/4)x$. In the optimal configuration o, one player uses path $p_2 = (e_{i,j_i})_{i \in [k]}$ and has cost $B/2$ and the other player uses the direct edge from s to t and has cost $3B/4$. The optimal configuration has cost $C(o) = 5B/4$ and is a Nash equilibrium of Γ (in fact, o is weakly enforceable by the trivial tolls $\tau_e = 0$ for all $e \in E$).

We prove that Γ admits a pure Nash equilibrium of cost $3B/2$ iff there exists a set $A^* \subseteq [k]$ such that $\sum_{i \in A^*} q_i = B/2$. For every set $A \subseteq [k]$, we define a configuration $\sigma_A = (p_A, p_{\bar{A}})$ consisting of a pair of complementary paths $p_A = (e_{i,j_i})_{i \in [k]}$, and $p_{\bar{A}} = (e_{i,3-j_i})_{i \in [k]}$, where $j_i = 1$ if $i \in A$ and $j_i = 2$ otherwise. Let $S_A = \sum_{i \in A} q_i$. The cost of the player on p_A is $(B + S_A)/2$ and the cost of the player on $p_{\bar{A}}$ is $B - S_A/2$. The total cost of σ_A is $C(\sigma_A) = 3B/2$. We prove that σ_A is a Nash equilibrium iff $S_A = B/2$. If $S_A = B/2$, the cost of both players is $3B/4$ and none of them has an incentive to deviate to the direct edge (s, t). Hence the configuration σ_A is Nash equilibrium. If $S_A > B/2$ (resp. $S_A < B/2$), the player on p_A (resp. $p_{\bar{A}}$) has cost greater than $3B/4$ and can decrease her cost by switching to the direct edge (s, t).

To conclude the proof, we show that Γ does not admit any pure Nash equilibrium other than the optimal configuration and the configurations σ_A corresponding to sets $A \subseteq [k]$ with $S_A = B/2$. First we observe that in any pure Nash equilibrium of Γ, at most one player uses the direct edge (s, t). If one player uses (s, t), the other player uses p_2, and we have the optimal configuration. If no player uses (s, t), there is one player on every edge $e_{i,j}$, $i \in [k]$, $j \in \{1, 2\}$. If there are two players on some edge $e_{i,2}$, the total cost is greater than $3B/2$. Hence, some player has cost greater than $3B/4$ and can decrease her cost by switching to (s, t). If both players use some edge $e_{i,1}$, one of them can decrease her cost by switching to $e_{i,2}$. Every configuration with one player on every edge $e_{i,j}$, $i \in [k]$, $j \in \{1, 2\}$, corresponds to a configuration σ_A for an appropriate $A \subseteq [k]$. □

References

1. Awerbuch, B., Azar, Y., Epstein, A.: The Price of Routing Unsplittable Flow. In: Proc. of STOC 2005, pp. 57–66 (2005)
2. Beckmann, M., McGuire, C.B., Winsten, C.B.: Studies in the Economics of Transportation. Yale University Press (1956)
3. Bein, W., Brucker, P., Tamir, A.: Minimum Cost Flow Algorithms for Series-Parallel Networks. Discrete Applied Mathematics 10, 117–124 (1985)
4. Caragiannis, I., Kaklamanis, C., Kanellopoulos, P.: Taxes for Linear Atomic Congestion Games. In: Azar, Y., Erlebach, T. (eds.) ESA 2006. LNCS, vol. 4168, pp. 184–195. Springer, Heidelberg (2006)
5. Christodoulou, G., Koutsoupias, E.: The Price of Anarchy of Finite Congestion Games. In: Proc. of STOC 2005, pp. 67–73 (2005)
6. Cole, R., Dodis, Y., Roughgarden, T.: How Much Can Taxes Help Selfish Routing. In: Proc. of EC 2003, pp. 98–107 (2003)
7. Cole, R., Dodis, Y., Roughgarden, T.: Pricing Network Edges for Heterogeneous Selfish Users. In: Proc. of STOC 2003, pp. 521–530 (2003)
8. Cominetti, R., Correa, J.R., Stier-Moses, N.E.: The Impact of Oligopolistic Competition in Networks. DRO-2006-03, Columbia Business School (2006)
9. Cormen, T.H., Leiserson, C.E., Rivest, R.L., Stein, C.: Introduction to Algorithms, 2nd edn. McGraw-Hill, New York (2001)
10. Correa, J.R., Stier-Moses, N.E.: Stackelberg Routing in Atomic Network Games. DRO-2007-03, Columbia Business School (2007)
11. Fleischer, L.: Linear Tolls Suffice: New Bounds and Algorithms for Tolls in Single Source Networks. Theoretical Computer Science 348, 217–225 (2005)
12. Fleischer, L., Jain, K., Mahdian, M.: Tolls for Heterogeneous Selfish Users in Multicommodity Networks and Generalized Congestion Games. In: Proc. of FOCS 2004, pp. 277–285 (2004)
13. Gairing, M., Lücking, T., Monien, B., Tiemann, K.: Nash Equilibria, the Price of Anarchy and the Fully Mixed Nash Equilibrium Conjecture. In: Caires, L., Italiano, G.F., Monteiro, L., Palamidessi, C., Yung, M. (eds.) ICALP 2005. LNCS, vol. 3580, pp. 51–65. Springer, Heidelberg (2005)
14. Garey, M.R., Johnson, D.S.: Computers and Intractability: A Guide to the Theory of NP-Completeness. W.H. Freeman, New York (1979)
15. Kaporis, A.C., Spirakis, P.G.: The Price of Optimum in Stackelberg Games on Arbitrary Single Commodity Networks and Latency Functions. In: Proc. of SPAA 2006, pp. 19–28 (2006)
16. Karakostas, G., Kolliopoulos, S.: Edge Pricing of Multicommodity Networks for Heterogeneous Users. In: Proc. of FOCS 2004, pp. 268–276 (2004)
17. Koutsoupias, E., Papadimitriou, C.: Worst-case Equilibria. In: Meinel, C., Tison, S. (eds.) STACS 99. LNCS, vol. 1563, pp. 404–413. Springer, Heidelberg (1999)
18. Milchtaich, I.: Network Topology and the Efficiency of Equilibrium. Games and Economic Behaviour 57, 321–346 (2006)
19. Rosenthal, R.W.: A Class of Games Possessing Pure-Strategy Nash Equilibria. International Journal of Game Theory 2, 65–67 (1973)
20. Roughdarden, T., Tardos, É.: How Bad is Selfish Routing? Journal of the ACM 49(2), 236–259 (2002)
21. Swamy, C.: The Effectiveness of Stackelberg Strategies and Tolls for Network Congestion Games. In: Proc. of SODA 2007, pp. 1133–1142 (2007)
22. Valdez, J., Tarjan, R.E., Lawler, E.L.: The Recognition of Series-Parallel Digraphs. SIAM Journal on Computing 11(2), 298–313 (1982)

Network Formation: Bilateral Contracting and Myopic Dynamics

Esteban Arcaute[1], Ramesh Johari[2], and Shie Mannor[3]

[1] Institute for Computational and Mathematical Engineering, Stanford University
arcaute@stanford.edu
[2] Department of Management Science and Engineering, Stanford University
rjohari@stanford.edu
[3] Department of Electrical and Computer Engineering, McGill University
shie@ece.mcgill.ca

Abstract. We consider a network formation game where a finite number of nodes wish to send traffic to each other. Nodes contract bilaterally with each other to form bidirectional communication links; once the network is formed, traffic is routed along shortest paths (if possible). Cost is incurred to a node from four sources: (1) routing traffic; (2) maintaining links to other nodes; (3) disconnection from destinations the node wishes to reach; and (4) payments made to other nodes. We assume that a network is stable if no single node wishes to unilaterally deviate, and no pair of nodes can profitably deviate together (a variation on the notion of pairwise stability). We study such a game under a form of *myopic best response dynamics*. In choosing their best strategy, nodes optimize their single period payoff only. We characterize a simple set of assumptions under which these dynamics will converge to a pairwise stable network topology; we also characterize an important special case, where the dynamics converge to a star centered at a node with minimum cost for routing traffic. In this sense, our dynamics naturally *select* an efficient equilibrium. Further, we show that these assumptions are satisfied by a contractual model motivated by bilateral Rubinstein bargaining with infinitely patient players.

1 Introduction

Given the reliance of modern society on data networks, it is remarkable that such networks — particularly the Internet — are in fact "networks of networks". They are held together through a federation of independently owned and operated service providers, that compete and cooperate to provide service. If we wish to understand how the network will evolve under decisions made by independent self-interested network operators, then we must turn our attention to the strategic analysis of *network formation games* (NFGs).

NFGs describe the interaction between a collection of nodes that wish to form a graph. Such models have been introduced and studied in the economics literature; see, e.g., [1, 2, 3]. We consider a game theoretic model where each of the nodes in the network is a different player, and a network is formed through interaction between the players. We are interested in understanding and characterizing the networks that result

X. Deng and F.C. Graham (Eds.): WINE 2007, LNCS 4858, pp. 191–207, 2007.

when individuals interact to choose their connections. In particular, we will focus on the role of bilateral contracting and the dynamic process of network formation in shaping the eventual network structure. As a specific example, we are motivated by the interaction between Internet service providers (ISPs) to form connections that yield the fabric of the global Internet. Most contractual relationships between ISPs may be classified into one of two types: *transit*, and *peer*. Provider A provides transit service to provider B if B pays A to carry traffic originating within B and destined elsewhere in the Internet (either inside or outside A's network). In such an agreement, provider A accepts the responsibility of carrying any traffic entering from B across their interconnection link. In peering agreements, one or more bidirectional links are established between two providers A and B. In contrast to transit service, where traffic is accepted regardless of the destination, in a peering relationship provider B will only accept traffic from A that is destined for points *within* B, and vice versa. (For details on Internet contracting, see [4, 5, 6].)

We highlight several key points about the contracting between ISPs that motivates the high level questions addressed in this paper. First, notice that although any given end-to-end path in the Internet may involve multiple ISPs, the network is connected only thanks to *bilateral contracts* between the different providers. Second, the ISPs use (by and large) a relatively limited set of contracts in forming connections with each other. At a high level, this motivates an important question: what contracting structures are likely to lead to "good" network topologies?

In this paper, we study this high level question through a particular network formation model. We assume that each node in the network represents a selfish agent. Motivated by data networks where links are physically present, we assume that each node participating in a link incurs a fixed maintenance cost per link. We further assume that every node is interested in sending traffic to every other node. Thus we assume that they incur a disconnectivity cost per unit of traffic they do not successfully transmit, and that nodes' experience a per-unit routing cost when forwarding or terminating traffic.

We assume that a link in the network is formed as the result of a *contract* the two nodes participating in the link at some point agreed upon. It is natural to assume that such contract induces a transfer of utility between the two nodes, and that the amount transferred is a function of the topology of the network *when the contract was formed*. We view contracting from a design perspective: what types of contracts lead to good eventual outcomes? To abstract this notion, we define a *contracting function*. If two nodes decide to form a link in a given network topology, the contracting function gives the value of the contract: both direction and amount of payment between the nodes. Given our cost structure and this notion of contracting, a given network topology together with the associated set of contracts defines the utility of an agent in the network.

Given the NFGs, we define pairwise stability of an outcome in the spirit of [3]. However, networks are not static objects; agents might negotiate a contract at a given time, but that contract might become unattractive as the structure of the network evolves. We consider dynamics that account for bilateral deviations of nodes that are assumed to be selfish and myopic. The main questions our paper answers are the following: under what conditions *on the contracting function* do the dynamics converge? When the dynamics converge, are the limiting networks pairwise stable? Are they Pareto efficient? We will find a remarkably simple set of conditions under which a form of myopic best response dynamics converge to efficient pairwise stable equilibria. Note that the dynamics we consider differ significantly from that of [7, 8] in that they account separately for both unilateral and bilateral deviations.

We also note that several other papers have also considered bilateral network formation games with transfers among the agents, including [9, 10, 1, 11, 12]. Our work differs from these earlier works by combining a network formation model where cost is incurred due to routing of traffic as well as link formation and maintenance, with the question of characterization of contracting functions that yield good limiting network topologies dynamically.

The remainder of the paper is organized as follows. We first define the class of network formation games considered in Section 2; in particular, we develop the notion of contracting in such games. In Section 3, we define *pairwise stable equilibrium*, and highlight the potential tension between pairwise stability and Pareto efficiency. In Section 4 we define and discuss the dynamics studied. Section 5 specializes our model to a particular case of interest: a network formation game with traffic routing. In Section 6 we establish the main convergence results for our myopic dynamics, in the network formation game with traffic routing.

2   The Game and Contracting

In this section, we present a network formation game where agents are the set of nodes of the network. Nodes receive value that depends on the network topology that arises. We model a scenario where each link in the network is the result of bilateral "contracting" between nodes. Each contract carries with it some utility transfer from the node seeking the agreement, to the node accepting it; we assume that the value of the utility transfers depends only on the network topology realized after agreement. We assume this contracting function satisfies certain natural properties.

We use the notation $G = (V, E)$ to denote a graph, or *network topology*, consisting of a set of n nodes V and edges E; the nodes will be the players in our network formation game. We assume throughout that all edges in G are *undirected*; we use ij to denote an undirected edge between i and j. As all models in the paper address only a fixed set of nodes V, we will typically use the shorthand $ij \in G$ when the edge ij is present in E. We use $G + ij$ and $G - ij$ to denote, respectively, adding and subtracting the link ij to the graph G.

For a node $i \in V$, let $v_i(G)$ be the monetary value to node i of network topology G. Let P_{ij} denote a payment from i to j; we assume that if no undirected link ij exists, or if $i = j$, then $P_{ij} = 0$. We refer to $\mathbf{P} = (P_{ij}, i, j \in V)$ as the *payment matrix*. Given a payment matrix P, the total transfer of utility to node i is $TU_i(\mathbf{P}) = \sum_j P_{ji} - P_{ij}$; the first term is the sum of payments received by i, while the second term is the sum of payments made by i. Thus the total utility of node i in graph G is $U_i(\mathbf{P}, G) = TU_i(\mathbf{P}) + v_i(G)$.

We consider a network formation game in which each node selects nodes it wishes to connect to, as well as nodes it is willing to accept connections from. Formally, each node i simultaneously selects a subset $F_i \subseteq V$ of nodes i is willing to accept connections from, and a subset $T_i \subseteq V$ of nodes i wishes to connect to. We let $\mathbf{T} = (T_i, i \in V)$ and $\mathbf{F} = (F_i, i \in V)$ denote the composite strategy vectors.

An undirected link is formed between two nodes i and j if i wishes to connect to j (i.e., $j \in T_i$), and j is willing to accept a connection from i (i.e., $i \in F_j$). All edges that are formed in this way define the network topology $G(\mathbf{T}, \mathbf{F})$ realized by the strategy vectors $\mathbf{T}$ and $\mathbf{F}$; i.e., $j \in T_i, i \in F_j$ implies that $ij \in G(\mathbf{T}, \mathbf{F})$.

In our model of network formation, we also assume that if $i \in F_j$ and $j \in T_i$, then a *binding contract* is formed from i to j; we denote this contract by (i, j), and refer to the *directed* graph $\Gamma(\mathbf{T}, \mathbf{F})$ as the *contracting graph*. The contracting graph captures the inherent directionality of link formation: in our model a link is only formed if one node asks for the link, and the target of the request accepts.

The contracting graph and the network topology together determine the transfers between the nodes. Formally, we assume the existence of a *contracting function* $Q(i, j; G)$ that gives the payment in a contract from i to j when the network topology is G; note that if $Q(i, j; G)$ is negative, then j pays i. Thus given the strategy vectors $\mathbf{T}$ and $\mathbf{F}$, the payment matrix $\mathbf{P}(\mathbf{T}, \mathbf{F})$ at the outcome of the game is given by:

$$P_{ij}(\mathbf{T}, \mathbf{F}) = \begin{cases} Q(i, j; G(\mathbf{T}, \mathbf{F})), & \text{if } (i, j) \in \Gamma(\mathbf{T}, \mathbf{F}); \\ 0, & \text{otherwise.} \end{cases} \tag{1}$$

Thus given strategy vectors $\mathbf{T}$ and $\mathbf{F}$, the payoff to node i is $U_i(G(\mathbf{T}, \mathbf{F}), \mathbf{P}(\mathbf{T}, \mathbf{F}))$. By an abuse of notation, and where clear from context, we will often use the shorthand $G = G(\mathbf{T}, \mathbf{F})$, $\Gamma = \Gamma(\mathbf{T}, \mathbf{F})$, and $\mathbf{P} = \mathbf{P}(\mathbf{T}, \mathbf{F})$ to represent specific instantiations of the network topology, contracting graph, and payment matrix, respectively, arising from strategy vectors $\mathbf{T}$ and $\mathbf{F}$. We refer to a triple $(G, \Gamma, \mathbf{P})$ arising from strategic decisions of the nodes as a *feasible outcome* if there are strategy vectors $\mathbf{T}$ and $\mathbf{F}$ that give rise to $(G, \Gamma, \mathbf{P})$.

We believe two interpretations of the contracting function are reasonable. First, we might imagine that an external regulator has dictated that contracts between nodes must have pre-negotiated tariffs associated with them; these tariffs are encoded in the contracting function. Note that the regulator in this case dictates changes in the value of the contract as the surrounding network topology changes.

A second interpretation of the contracting function does not assume the existence of the regulator; instead, we presume that the value of the contracting function is the outcome of bilateral negotiation between the nodes in the contract. Note that the structure of our game assumes that this negotiation takes place *holding the network topology fixed*; i.e., the negotiation is used to determine the value of the contract, given the topology that is in place. One example is simply that $Q(i, j; G)$ is the result of a Rubinstein bargaining game of alternating offers between i and j, where i makes the first offer [13]. We investigate this example in further detail in Appendix A.

We will be interested in contracting functions exhibiting two natural properties: *monotonicity* and *anti-symmetry*. We start with some additional notation: given $j \neq i$, let the cost to node i in network topology G be defined as $C_i(G) = -v_i(G)$. We define the *difference* in cost to node i between graph G and graph $G + ij$ as $\Delta C_i(G, ij) = C_i(G + ij) - C_i(G)$. (Note that if $ij \in G$, then $\Delta C_i(G, ij) = 0$.)

We first define monotonicity.

Property 1 (Monotonicity). Let G be a graph such that $ij \notin G$ and $ik \notin G$. We say that the contracting function is monotone if $\Delta C_j(G, ij) > \Delta C_k(G, ik)$ if and only if $Q(i, j; G + ij) > Q(i, k; G + ik)$.

(Note that since j and k are interchangeable, if the differences on the left hand side of the previous definition are equal, then the contract values on the right hand side must be equal as well.) Informally, monotonicity requires that the payment to form a link must increase as the burden of forming that link increases on the accepting node.

Our second property is inspired by the observation that, in general, $Q(i, j; G)$ is not related to $Q(j, i; G)$; anti-symmetry asserts these values must be equal.

Property 2 (Anti-symmetry). We say that the contracting function Q is *anti-symmetric* if, for all nodes i and j, and for all graphs G, we have $Q(i, j; G) = -Q(j, i; G)$.

Note that in the game we are considering, a contracting function that is anti-symmetric has the property that at any feasible outcome of the game, the payment for a link ij does not depend on which node asked for the connection.

3 Stability and Efficiency

We study our game through two complementary notions. First, because nodes act as self-interested players, we define a reasonable game-theoretic notion of equilibrium for our model, called *pairwise stability* (first introduced by Jackson and Wolinsky [3]). Informally, pairwise stability requires that no unilateral deviations by a single node are profitable, and that no bilateral deviations by any pair of nodes are profitable. However, we are also interested in system-wide performance from a global perspective, and for this purpose we must study the *efficiency* of the network as well; we measure the efficiency of a network topology via the total value obtained by all nodes using that topology.

We start by considering game theoretic notions of equilibrium for our model. The simplest notion of equilibrium is *Nash equilibrium*. However, as is commonly observed, Nash equilibrium lacks sufficient predictive power in many network formation games due to the presence of trivial equilibria.

The problem with Nash equilibrium is that link formation is inherently *bilateral*: the consent of two nodes is required to form a single link. For this reason we consider a notion of stability that is robust to *both* unilateral and *bilateral* deviations. This notion is known as *pairwise stability*. It follows that any pairwise stable outcome is a Nash Equilibrium.

Formally, suppose that the current strategy vectors are $\mathbf{T}$ and $\mathbf{F}$, and the current network topology and contract graph are $G = G(\mathbf{T}, \mathbf{F})$ and $\Gamma = \Gamma(\mathbf{T}, \mathbf{F})$ respectively. Suppose that two nodes i and j attempt to bilaterally deviate; this involves changing the pair of strategies (T_i, F_i) and (T_j, F_j) together. Any deviation will of course change both the network topology, as well as the contract graph.

However, we assume that any contracts present both before and after the deviation *retain the same payment*. This is consistent with the notion of a contract: unless the deviation by i and j entails either breaking an existing contract or forming a new contract, there is no reason that the payment associated to a contract should change. With this caveat in mind, we formalize our definition of pairwise stability as follows; note that it is similar in spirit to the definition of Jackson and Wolinsky [3].

Definition 1. *Assume Q is a contracting function. Given strategy vectors* $\mathbf{T}$ *and* $\mathbf{F}$, *let* $G = G(\mathbf{T}, \mathbf{F})$, $\Gamma = \Gamma(\mathbf{T}, \mathbf{F})$, *and* $\mathbf{P} = \mathbf{P}(\mathbf{T}, \mathbf{F})$. *Given strategy vectors* $\mathbf{T}'$ *and* $\mathbf{F}'$, *define* $G' = G(\mathbf{T}', \mathbf{F}')$ *and* $\Gamma' = \Gamma(\mathbf{T}', \mathbf{F}')$. *Define* $\mathbf{P}'$ *according to:*

$$
P'_{k\ell} = \begin{cases} P_{k\ell}, & \text{if } (k, \ell) \in \Gamma' \text{ and } (k, \ell) \in \Gamma; \\ Q(k, \ell; G'), & \text{if } (k, \ell) \in \Gamma' \text{ and } (k, \ell) \notin \Gamma; \\ 0, & \text{otherwise.} \end{cases} \tag{2}
$$

Then $(\mathbf{T}, \mathbf{F})$ *is a* pairwise stable equilibrium *if: (1) No unilateral deviation is profitable, i.e., for all i, and for all* $\mathbf{T}'$ *and* $\mathbf{F}'$ *that differ from* $\mathbf{T}$ *and* $\mathbf{F}$ *(respectively) only in the i'th components,*

$$
U_i(\mathbf{P}, G) \geq U_i(\mathbf{P}', G');
$$

and (2) no bilateral deviation is profitable, i.e., for all pairs i and j, and for all $\mathbf{T}'$ *and* $\mathbf{F}'$ *that differ from* $\mathbf{T}$ *and* $\mathbf{F}$ *only in the i'th and j'th components,*

$$
U_i(\mathbf{P}, G) < U_i(\mathbf{P}', G') \implies U_j(\mathbf{P}, G) > U_j(\mathbf{P}', G').
$$

Notice that (2) is a formalization of the discussion above.

When nodes i and j deviate to the strategy vectors $\mathbf{T}'$ and $\mathbf{F}'$, all payments associated to preexisting contracts remain the same. If a contract is formed, the payment becomes the value of the contracting function given the new graph. Finally, if a contract is broken, the payment of course becomes zero. These conditions give rise to the new payment matrix $\mathbf{P}'$. Nodes then evaluate their payoffs before and after a deviation. The first condition in the definition ensures no unilateral deviation is profitable, and the second condition ensures that if node i benefits from a bilateral deviation with j, then node j must be strictly worse off.

We will typically be interested in pairwise stability of the network topology and contracting graph, rather than pairwise stability of strategy vectors. We will thus say that a feasible outcome $(G, \Gamma, \mathbf{P})$ is a *pairwise stable outcome* if there exists a pair of strategy vectors $\mathbf{T}$ and $\mathbf{F}$ such that (1) $(\mathbf{T}, \mathbf{F})$ is a pairwise stable equilibrium; and (2) $(\mathbf{T}, \mathbf{F})$ give rise to $(G, \Gamma, \mathbf{P})$. Note that by our definition of the game, for all i and j such that $(i, j) \in \Gamma$ we must have $P_{ij} = Q(i, j; G)$ in a pairwise stable outcome.

The following lemma yields a useful property of pairwise stable outcomes; for the proof, see [14].

Lemma 1. *Let $(G, \Gamma, \mathbf{P})$ be a pairwise stable outcome. Then for all nodes i and j, if $(i, j) \in \Gamma$ and $(j, i) \in \Gamma$, then $Q(i, j; G) = 0$ and $Q(j, i; G) = 0$.*

We will investigate the *efficiency* of pairwise stable equilibria.

Let $(G, \Gamma, \mathbf{P})$ and $(G', \Gamma', \mathbf{P}')$ be two feasible outcomes. We say that $(G, \Gamma, \mathbf{P})$ Pareto dominates $(G', \Gamma', \mathbf{P}')$ if all players are better off in $(G, \Gamma, \mathbf{P})$ than in $(G', \Gamma', \mathbf{P}')$, and at least one is strictly better off. A feasible outcome is *Pareto efficient* if it is not Pareto dominated by any other feasible outcome. Since payoffs to nodes are *quasilinear* in our model, i.e., utility is measured in monetary units [15], it is not hard to show that a feasible outcome $(G, \Gamma, \mathbf{P})$ is Pareto efficient if and only if $G \in \arg\min_{G'} S(G')$, where $S(G)$ is the *social cost function*:

$$S(G) = \sum_{i \in V} C_i(G).$$

(Note that, in particular, the preceding condition does not involve the contracting function; contracts induce zero-sum monetary transfers among nodes, and do not affect global efficiency.)

Given a graph G, we define the *efficiency* of G as the ratio $S(G)/S(G_{\text{eff}})$, where G_{eff} is the network topology in a Pareto efficient outcome.

4   Dynamics

This section proposes a *myopic best response dynamic* for our network formation game. Myopic dynamics refer to the fact that at any given round, nodes update their strategic decisions only to optimize their current payoff. We have two complementary objectives in the dynamics we propose. First, we would like our dynamics to be consistent with the potential for *bilateral* deviations by pairs of nodes. Ultimately, our goal is to ensure that our dynamics always converge to a pairwise stable equilibrium. Our second objective involves efficiency: we aim to ensure that such dynamics lead to *desirable* pairwise stable equilibria. Note that this is a significant departure from the usual approach in the literature on learning in games (see, e.g., [16]), which is typically focused on ensuring convergence to some equilibrium without regard to efficiency. The remainder of our paper presents a simple set of conditions on the contracting function that ensure precisely the desired convergence results on the dynamics, in the case of a network formation game with routing.

Informally we consider a discrete-time myopic dynamic that includes two stages at every round. At round k, both a node u_k and an edge $u_k v_k$ are *activated*. At the first stage of the round, with probability $p_d \in [0, 1]$, node u_k can choose to unilaterally break the edge $u_k v_k$ if it is profitable to do so; and, with probability $1 - p_d$, the link (and thus all contracts associated with) $u_k v_k$ is broken, regardless of node u_k's preference. In the second stage, u_k selects a node w and proposes to form the contract (u_k, w) to w, with associated payment given by the contracting function. (Although the second stage appears to be a restricted form of bilateral deviation, we will later see that in the cost model we consider, it is sufficient to restrict to bilateral deviations this form.) Node w then decides whether to accept or reject, and play then continues to the next round given the new triple of network topology, contracting graph, and payment matrix. It is crucial to note that u_k's strategic decisions are made so that its utility is maximized *at the end of the round*. We contrast this with w's strategic decision, which is made to maximize its utility at the end of the second stage *given* its utility at the end of the first stage.

We consider two variations on our basic model of dynamics: either $p_d = 1$, or $p_d < 1$. When $p_d = 1$, node u_k can choose to break either or both of the contracts associated with $u_k v_k$ (if they exist). When $p_d < 1$, provided all links are activated infinitely often, all links are broken infinitely often *regardless of the activated node's best interest*. For ease of exposition, unless otherwise stated, all the subsequent discussion will be made assuming $p_d = 1$.

This informal discussion leads to the following definitions. We call an *activation process* any discrete-time stochastic process $\{(u_k, v_k)\}_{k \in \mathbb{N}}$ where the pairs (u_k, v_k) are i.i.d. random pairs of distinct nodes from V drawn with full support. A realization of an activation process is called an *activation sequence*. (In fact, all results in this paper can be proved under the following generalization of an activation process. Let u, v, w and x be four nodes from V such that $u \neq v$ and $w \neq x$. We can define an activation process to be any sequence of pairs of nodes such that, almost surely, all two pairs of nodes (u, v) and (w, x) are activated successively infinitely often.)

The next example considers a natural activation process.

Example 1 (Uniform Activation Process). The activation process is said to be *uniform* if, for all k, u and v, $u \neq v$, the probability that $(u_k, v_k) = (u, v)$ is uniform over all ordered pairs. Thus $\mathbb{P}\left[(u_k, v_k) = (u, v)\right] = 1/(n(n-1))$.

Let (u_k, v_k) be the pair selected at the beginning of round k. Let $\left(G^{(k)}, \Gamma^{(k)}, \mathbf{P}^{(k)}\right)$ be the state at the beginning of the round. In a single round k, our dynamics consist of two sequential stages, as follows:

1. *Stage 1:* If $u_k v_k \in G^{(k)}$, then node u_k decides whether to break the contract (u_k, v_k) (if it exists), the contract (v_k, u_k) (if it exists), or both.
2. *Stage 2:* Node u_k decides if it wishes to form a contract with another w_k. If it chooses to do so, then u_k asks to form the contract (u_k, w_k), and w_k can accept or reject. The contract is added to the contracting graph if w_k accepts the contract.

Node u_k takes actions in stages 1 and 2 that maximize its utility in the state *at the end of the round*; in the event no action can strictly improve node u_k's utility in a stage, we assume that u_k takes no action at that stage. Note, in particular, that at stage 1 node u_k only breaks (u_k, v_k) and/or (v_k, u_k) if a profitable deviation is anticipated to be possible at stage 2. At stage 2, node w_k accepts u_k's offer if this yields a higher utility to w_k than the state *at the beginning of stage 2*. (Tie-breaking is discussed at the end of the section.)

The rules for updating the contracting graph $\Gamma^{(k+1)}$, at the end of round k, are summarized in Table 1. The first three actions described in table 1 are the basic actions the first node of the selected pair can do during a round. The last two actions are compositions of two of the basic actions.

We define $G^{(k+1)}$ to be the associated network topology: i.e., $ij \in G^{(k+1)}$ if and only if either $(i, j) \in \Gamma^{(k+1)}$ or $(j, i) \in \Gamma^{(k+1)}$ (or both). In all cases, the payment vector $\mathbf{P}^{(k+1)}$ is updated as in (2), first after stage 1, and then after stage 2.

It is critical to observe that the *state* of the dynamics at round k, $\left(G^{(k)}, \Gamma^{(k)}, \mathbf{P}^{(k)}\right)$, need not be a *feasible outcome*. This follows because the payment matrix may not be consistent with the current contracting graph: when contracts are updated, only payments associated to the added or deleted contracts are updated—all other payments remain the same (cf. (2)). This motivates the following definition.

Definition 2 (Adaptedness). *Let $(G, \Gamma, \mathbf{P})$ be a triple consisting of a (undirected) network topology, a (directed) contracting graph, and a payment matrix. We say that the*

Table 1. Updating the contracting graph

Action(s) selected by u_k	$\Gamma^{(k+1)}$
Breaks (u_k, v_k)	$\Gamma^{(k)} \setminus \{(u_k, v_k)\}$
Breaks (v_k, u_k)	$\Gamma^{(k)} \setminus \{(v_k, u_k)\}$
Adds (u_k, w_k)	$\Gamma^{(k)} \bigcup \{(u_k, w_k)\}$
Breaks (u_k, v_k) and (v_k, u_k)	$\Gamma^{(k)} \setminus \{(u_k, v_k), (v_k, u_k)\}$
Breaks (u_k, v_k) and adds (u_k, w_k)	$\left(\Gamma^{(k)} \setminus \{(u_k, v_k)\}\right) \bigcup \{(u_k, w_k)\}$

edge ij is adapted in $(G, \Gamma, \mathbf{P})$ if (1) if $(i, j) \in \Gamma$, then $P_{ij} = Q(i, j; G)$; otherwise $P_{ij} = 0$; if (2) if $(j, i) \in \Gamma$, then $P_{ji} = Q(j, i; G)$; otherwise $P_{ji} = 0$; and (3) $ij \in G$ if and only if $(i, j) \in \Gamma$ or $(j, i) \in \Gamma$.

Note that if every edge ij is adapted to $(G, \Gamma, \mathbf{P})$, then $(G, \Gamma, \mathbf{P})$ must be a feasible outcome. Further, note that if the initial state of our dynamics was a feasible outcome, then condition 3 of the preceding definition is satisfied in every round.

The following definition captures convergence.

Definition 3 (Convergence). *Given any initial feasible outcome* $\left(G^{(0)}, \Gamma^{(0)}, \mathbf{P}^{(0)}\right)$ *and an activation process AP, we say the dynamics* converge *if, almost surely, there exists K such that, for $k > K$,*

$$\left(G^{(k+1)}, \Gamma^{(k+1)}, \mathbf{P}^{(k+1)}\right) = \left(G^{(k)}, \Gamma^{(k)}, \mathbf{P}^{(k)}\right).$$

For a given activation sequence and initial feasible outcome, we call the limiting state $(G, \Gamma, \mathbf{P})$.

(We say that *the network topology converges* if the preceding condition is only satisfied by $G^{(k)}$.) Note that in our definition of convergence, we do not require that the payments between nodes in the limiting state have any relation to the contracting function; we will establish such a connection in our convergence results.

As noted above, the active node at a round, say u, may not have a unique utility-maximizing choice of a "partner" node at stage 2. To avoid oscillations induced by the possibility of multiple optimal choices, we introduce the following assumption of *inertia*. Let u_k be the node activated at round k, and suppose that at the start of stage 2 in round k, u_k has multiple utility-maximizing choices of nodes w_k. Then we assume that among such utility-maximizing nodes, u_k chooses the node w_k *it was connected to most recently*, or at random if no such node exists; *this assumption remains in force throughout the paper*. While we have chosen a specific notion of inertia, we emphasize that many other assumptions can also lead to convergent dynamics. For instance, among utility-maximizing choices of w_k, if node u_k always chooses the node w_k with the highest degree, our convergence results remain valid.

We emphasize that the dynamics we have defined here address an inherent tension. On one hand, any dynamic process must allow sufficient exploration of bilateral deviations to have any hope of converging to a pairwise stable equilibrium. On the other hand, if the dynamics are completely unconstrained—for example, if nodes can choose any bilateral or unilateral deviation they wish—then we have little hope of converging to an efficient pairwise stable equilibrium. Our dynamics are designed to allow sufficient exploration without sacrificing efficiency, under reasonable assumptions on the contracting function and the cost model.

The remainder of the paper formalizes the claim of the preceding paragraph, in a specific cost model motivated by network routing. We define our model in the next section, and study stability and efficiency in the context of this model. We then show in Section 6 that weak assumptions on the contracting function are sufficient to establish that the dynamics presented in this section always converge to a desirable pairwise stable equilibrium. In particular, when $p_d = 1$, we show that anti-symmetry and monotonicity of the contracting function suffice to establish convergence. If $p_d < 1$, then we do not need the assumption of anti-symmetry: monotonicity of the contracting function alone suffices to establish convergence.

5   A Traffic Routing Utility Model

In this section we define a network formation game where nodes extract some utility per unit of data they successfully send through the network, and study pairwise stability and efficiency in the context of this model. However, nodes experience per-unit routing costs when in the data network, as well as maintenance costs per adjacent link. Our motivation is the formation of networks in data communication settings, such as wireless ad hoc networks. Such networks are typically highly reconfigurable, with a tradeoff between costs for both link maintenance and disconnectivity.

We start by describing our traffic routing model. Formally, we suppose that each user i wants to send one unit of traffic to each node in the network; we refer to this as a *uniform all-to-all* traffic matrix. We assume that given a network topology, traffic is routed along shortest paths, where the length of a path is measured by the number of hops. Further, we assume that in case of multiple shortest paths of equal length, traffic is split equally among all available paths. We let $f_i(G)$ be the total traffic that transits through i plus the total traffic received by i. We assume that node i experiences a positive routing cost of c_i per unit of traffic. Thus given a graph G, the total routing cost experienced by node i is $R_i(G) = c_i f_i(G)$.

We next turn our attention to network maintenance costs. We assume that each node experiences a maintenance cost $\pi > 0$ per link incident to it. Note that this maintenance cost is incurred by both endpoints of a link, so that the effective cost of a single link is 2π. Further, note that the link maintenance cost does not depend on the identities of the endpoints of the link; this homogeneity assumption is made for technical simplicity. Thus given a graph $G = (V, E)$, the total link maintenance cost incurred by node i is $M_i(G) = \pi d_i(G)$, where $d_i(G)$ is the degree of node i in the graph G.

Finally, nodes' experience a disconnection cost that is decreasing in the amount of traffic successfully sent. An equivalent way to view this cost is to assume that links receive an increasing utility in the amount traffic sent. Formally, we assume that each node experiences a cost of $\lambda > 0$ per unit of traffic not sent. Note that λ is identical for all nodes; again, this homogeneity assumption simplifies the technical development.

Thus given a graph G, the cost to a node i from incomplete connectivity, or disconnection cost, is $D_i = \lambda(n - n_i(G))$, where $n_i(G)$ is the number of nodes i can reach in the graph G.

Thus the total cost to a node i in a graph G is:

$$C_i(G) = R_i(G) + M_i(G) + D_i(G). \tag{3}$$

5.1 Pairwise Stability

We now characterize pairwise stable outcomes, given the cost model (3). We start with the following structural characterization; the proof can be found in [14].

Proposition 1. *Let $(G, \Gamma, \mathbf{P})$ be a pairwise stable outcome. Then G is a forest (i.e., all connected components of G are trees).*

The preceding proposition shows the "minimality" of pairwise stable graphs: since our payoff model does not include any value for redundant links, any pairwise stable equilibria must be forests. An interesting open direction for our model includes the addition of a utility for redundancy (e.g., for robustness to failures).

Most of the pairwise stable equilibria we discuss are framed under the following assumption on the disconnectivity cost λ.

Assumption 1 (Disconnection Cost). *Given a contracting function Q, the disconnectivity cost $\lambda > 0$ is such that for all disconnected graphs G and for all pairs i and j that are disconnected in G, there holds $\Delta C_i(G, ij) + Q(i, j; G + ij) < 0$ and $\Delta C_i(G, ij) - Q(j, i; G + ij) < 0$.*

This implies that if nodes i and j are not connected in G, then both are better off by forming the link ij using either the contract (i, j) or (j, i). (Note that if Q is anti-symmetric the second condition is trivially satisfied.)

The preceding assumption is meant to ensure that we can restrict attention to connected graphs in our analysis. From our utility structure, it is easy to see that only the payments and disconnectivity costs act as incentives to nodes to build a connected network topology. But payments alone are not enough to induce connectivity, since of course the node paying for a link feels a negative incentive due to the payment. We emphasize that the preceding assumption is made assuming that *the contracting function and all other model parameters are given*, so that the threshold value of λ necessary to satisfy the preceding assumption may depend on these other parameters. Nevertheless, as we will see this assumption has interesting implications for our model. It is clear from our model that if all other model parameters are fixed, then a λ satisfying the preceding assumption must exist. Examples where λ scales as $O(n)$ can be found in [14].

If Assumption 1 holds, we have the following corollary about pairwise stable outcomes; the proof is immediate.

Corollary 1. *If Assumption 1 holds, all pairwise stable outcomes are trees.*

From the preceding corollary, we can prove the following simple characterization of pairwise stable outcomes; see [14] for the proof.

Proposition 2. *Suppose that Assumption 1 holds, and that Q is monotone. Let* $(G, \Gamma, \mathbf{P})$ *be a feasible outcome where G is a tree. Then* $(G, \Gamma, \mathbf{P})$ *is pairwise stable if and only if no pair of nodes can profitably deviate by simultaneously breaking one link and forming another, i.e.: given nodes i and j and any link* $ik \in G$, *let* $G = G - ik + ij$, $\Gamma' = (\Gamma \setminus \{(i,k),(k,i)\}) \bigcup \{(i,j)\}$, *and define* $\mathbf{P}'$ *as in (2). Then:*

$$U_i(\mathbf{P}, G) < U_i(\mathbf{P}', G') \implies U_j(\mathbf{P}, G) > U_j(\mathbf{P}', G').$$

5.2   Efficiency of Equilibria

Pairwise stable equilibria will typically be inefficient (see [14] for explicit constructions of an arbitrarily inefficient equilibrium). If we restrict our attention to minimally connected pairwise stable equilibria, one can see that a star centered at $u_{\min}$ would generate lower social cost than any other minimally connected network topology.

As long as the contracting function is monotone, it is possible to show that any tree where non-leaf nodes have minimum routing cost can be sustained as pairwise stable equilibrium. This is the result of the next proposition.

Proposition 3. *Suppose that Assumption 1 holds. Let* $(G, \Gamma, \mathbf{P})$ *be a feasible outcome such that G is a tree, and any non-leaf node i has* $c_i = \min_j c_j$; *i.e., all internal nodes of G have minimum per-unit routing cost. Then* $(G, \Gamma, \mathbf{P})$ *is pairwise stable.*

The key result we require is the following.

Lemma 2. *Suppose that G is a tree, and u, v, and w are distinct nodes such that* $G - uv + uw$ *is a tree. Then the cost to u is the same in both graphs.*

The preceding proposition shows that although inefficient pairwise stable equilibria may exist, any tree where only minimum routing cost nodes appear in the interior is also sustainable as a pairwise stable equilibrium. This is of critical importance: in particular, any star centered at a node u with $c_u \leq c_v$ for all v can thus be sustained as a pairwise stable equilibrium. It is not difficult to establish that among all forests, such a star has the lowest social cost, i.e., the highest efficiency. (See [14] for details.) In particular, we obtain the important conclusion that *the most efficient minimally connected topology can be sustained as a pairwise stable equilibrium.* We will establish in Section 6 that our dynamics *always* converge to a topology of the form assumed in the preceding proposition. Thus our dynamics select a "good" equilibrium from the set of pairwise stable equilibria.

6   Convergence Results

In this section we prove that, under an anti-symmetric and monotone contracting function, the dynamics previously defined converge to a pairwise stable outcome where the network topology is a tree, and where non-leaf nodes have minimum per-unit routing cost. In the special case where there exists a unique minimum per-unit routing cost node $u_{\min}$, our result implies that the dynamics always converge to a star centered at $u_{\min}$.

Note that other, less efficient pairwise stable outcomes may exist; thus in this special case, our dynamics converge to a feasible outcome that minimizes the price of stability. Further, we prove that, if $p_d < 1$ (i.e. if all links are broken exogenously infinitely often), then the results still hold even when the contracting function is only monotone. In all that follows let $V_{\min} = \{i \in V : c_i \leq c_j \text{ for all } j \in V\}$. Thus $V_{\min}$ is the set of all nodes with minimum per-unit routing cost.

We begin by relating the cost model of (3) to the dynamics proposed in Section 4. We consider a model where λ satisfies Assumption 1; as a result, as suggested by Corollary 1 and Proposition 2, we can expect two implications. First, nodes will break links until the graph is minimally connected. Second, if the graph is minimally connected at the beginning of a round, then it must remain so at the end of the round; thus, if u_k's action breaks the link $u_k v_k$ at the first stage of round k, then the bilateral deviation at the second stage must involve formation of exactly one link. Note that this observation serves as justification of the bilateral deviation considered at stage 2 of our dynamics for, at the second stage, we need only to consider deviations where u_k either identifies a node w_k with which to establish the contract (u_k, w_k), or does nothing.[1]

The following theorems are the central results of this paper. Our first result establishes convergence of our dynamics when the contracting function is anti-symmetric and monotone, and $p_d = 1$.

Theorem 2. *Suppose Assumption 1 holds, and that the contracting function is monotone and anti-symmetric. Let $\left(G^{(0)}, \Gamma^{(0)}, \mathbf{P}^{(0)}\right)$ be a feasible outcome. Then for any activation process, the dynamics initiated at $\left(G^{(0)}, \Gamma^{(0)}, \mathbf{P}^{(0)}\right)$ converge. Further, if the activation process is a uniform activation process, then the expected number of rounds to convergence is $O(n^5)$.*

For a given activation sequence, let the limiting state be $(G, \Gamma, \mathbf{P})$. Then: (1) G is a tree where any node that is not a leaf is in $V_{\min}$; and (2) $(G, \Gamma, \mathbf{P})$ is a pairwise stable outcome.

As the proof is somewhat lengthy, we only sketch it here. Details can be found in [14].

Proof sketch. The proof proceeds in three main steps.

(1) *Convergence to a tree.* We first show that the network topology converges to a tree. More precisely we show that in expectation, after $O(n^4)$ rounds, $G^{(k)}$ is a tree; and, if (u, v) and (v, u) are both in $\Gamma^{(k)}$, then $P_{uv}^{(k)} = P_{vu}^{(k)} = 0$. (2) *Convergence of the network topology.* Next, we show that the network topology converges. In particular, we show that in expectation, after an additional $O(n^5)$ rounds, the network topology converges to a tree where all non-leaf nodes are in $V_{\min}$. (3) *Convergence of the contracting graph.* The remainder of the proof establishes that the contracting graph converges: in expectation, after an additional $O(n^3)$ rounds, the contracting graph remains constant, and all edges are adapted (and remain so). □

---

[1] In general, the directionality of the contract may affect the payment; however, in the case of anti-symmetric contracting functions, whether (u_k, w_k) or (w_k, u_k) is formed will not impact the payment made across the contract.

When $p_d < 1$, we get an even stronger result regarding dynamics: we can prove that monotonicity of the contracting function suffices to establish convergence; anti-symmetry is no longer required.

Theorem 3. *Suppose Assumption 1 holds, and that the contracting function is monotone. Further, assume that $p_d < 1$. Let $\left(G^{(0)}, \Gamma^{(0)}, \mathbf{P}^{(0)}\right)$ be a feasible outcome. Then the dynamics initiated at $\left(G^{(0)}, \Gamma^{(0)}, \mathbf{P}^{(0)}\right)$ are such that, for any activation process, the network topology converges.*

For a given activation sequence, let the limiting network topology be G. Also, let K be such that, $G^k = G$ for all $k > K$. Then, for $k > K$ sufficiently large: (1) G is a tree where any node that is not a leaf is in $V_{\min}$; and (2) $(G, \Gamma^k, \mathbf{P}^k)$ is a pairwise stable outcome.

The proof of this second theorem requires some mild modifications to the proof of Theorem 2. It is important to note that, if the contracting function is not anti-symmetric, convergence of the network topology does not imply convergence of the contracting graph. Nevertheless, our result is very surprising as it states that, although the contracting graph might not converge, the network topology always converges. Further, after a finite time, all outcomes exhibited are pairwise stable. If p_d is inversely polynomial in n, then the expected time to convergence is polynomial as well. Details can be found in [14].

The following corollary addresses an important special case; it follows from Theorems 2 and 3.

Corollary 4. *Suppose Assumption 1 holds and the contracting function is monotone. Suppose in addition that either: (1) $p_d = 1$ and the contracting function is anti-symmetric; or (2) that $p_d < 1$. Suppose in addition that $V_{\min}$ consists of only a single node $u_{\min}$. Given $\left(G^{(0)}, \Gamma^{(0)}, \mathbf{P}^{(0)}\right)$ and an activation sequence, let $(G, \Gamma, \mathbf{P})$ be the limiting pairwise stable outcome. Then G is the unique minimally connected efficient network topology: a star centered at $u_{\min}$.*

The preceding results demonstrate the power of the dynamics we have defined, as well as the importance of the assumptions made on the contracting functions. Despite the fact that our model may have many pairwise stable equilibria, our dynamics select "good" network topologies as their limit points *regardless of the initial state*. At the very least, only nodes with minimum per-unit routing cost are responsible for forwarding traffic (cf. Theorems 2 and 3); and at best, when only a single node has minimum per-unit routing cost, our dynamics select the network topology that minimizes social cost among all forests. This result suggests that from a regulatory or design perspective, monotone anti-symmetric contracting functions have significant efficiency benefits.

7 Conclusion

There are several natural open directions suggested by this paper. The most obvious one is to expand the strategy space considered by each node in our dynamics. More precisely, it would be interesting to analyze the robustness of the results when the active node *can select which link to break* during phase 1. Though our proofs rely on each link being broken infinitely often, it seems natural to believe that the results can be extended to the case where such a property is not de-facto assumed.

Finally, while our model is entirely heterogeneous in the assumptions made about the routing costs of nodes, we require the traffic matrix to be uniform all-to-all, and all links to have the same formation cost π. We intend to study the extension of the model defined here to such settings.

Acknowledgments

The authors benefited from helpful conversations with Eric Dallal, John N. Tsitsiklis and Matthew O. Jackson. This work was supported by DARPA under the Information Theory for Mobile Ad Hoc Networks Program, by the Media X Program at Stanford, by the Canada Research Chairs Program, by the NSERC, and by the NSF under grant CMMI-0620811.

References

[1] Bala, V., Goyal, S.: A noncooperative model of network formation. Econometrica 68(5), 1181–1230 (2000), available at: http://ideas.repec.org/a/ecm/emetrp/v68y2000i5p1181-1230.html

[2] Jackson, M.O.: A survey of models of network formation: Stability and efficiency. Working Paper, 1161California Institute of Technology, Division of the Humanities and Social Sciences (2003) Available at: http://ideas.repec.org/p/clt/sswopa/1161.html

[3] Jackson, M.O., Wolinsky, A.: A strategic model of social and economic networks. Journal of Economic Theory 71(1), 44–74 (1996), available at: http://ideas.repec.org/a/eee/jetheo/v71y1996i1p44-74.html

[4] Gao, L., Rexford, J.: Stable Internet routing without global coordination. IEEE/ACM Transactions on Networking 9(6), 681–692 (2001)

[5] Norton, W.: A business case for peering. Available on request from (2002), http://www.equinix.com/resources/whitepapers

[6] Norton, W.: Evolution of the U.S. Internet peering ecosystem. Available on request from (2003), http://www.equinix.com/resources/whitepapers

[7] Jackson, M.O., Watts, A.: The existence of pairwise stable networks. Seoul Journal of Economics 14(3), 299–321 (2001)

[8] Jackson, M.O., Watts, A.: The evolution of social and economic networks. Journal of Economic Theory 106(2), 265–295 (2002)

[9] Anshelevich, E., Dasgupta, A., Kleinberg, J., Tardos, E., Wexler, T., Roughgarden, T.: The price of stability for network design with fair cost allocation (2004)

[10] Anshelevich, E., Dasgupta, A., Tardos, É., Wexler, T.: Near-optimal network design with selfish agents. In: Proceedings of ACM Symposium on the Theory of Computing, pp. 511–520 (2003)

[11] Bloch, F., Jackson, M.O.: The formation of networks with transfers among players. Working Papers, 2004.80, Fondazione Eni Enrico Mattei (May 2004), Available at: http://ideas.repec.org/p/fem/femwpa/2004.80.html

[12] Johari, R., Mannor, S., Tsitsiklis, J.N.: A contract-based model for directed network formation. Games and Economic Behavior 56(2), 201–224 (2006), available at: http://ideas.repec.org/a/eee/gamebe/v56y2006i2p201-224.html

[13] Osborne, M.J., Rubinstein, A.: Bargaining and Markets. Academic Press, San Diego, California (1990)

[14] Arcaute, E., Johari, R., Mannor, S.: Network formation: Bilateral contracting and myopic dynamics. Technical report, Stanford University Management Science and Engineering (2007)

[15] Mas-Colell, A., Whinston, M.D., Green, J.R.: Microeconomic Theory. Oxford University Press, Oxford, United Kingdom (1995)

[16] Fudenberg, D., Levine, D.K.: The Theory of Learning in Games. MIT Press, Cambridge, Massachusetts (1998)

[17] Muthoo, A.: Bargaining Theory with Applications. Cambridge University Press, Cambridge, United Kingdom (1999)

A   Rubinstein Bargaining and Contracting

In this appendix we derive the contracting functions associated to solutions of a *two player Rubinstein Bargaining game of alternating offers*. We first derive the contracting function when players are infinitely patient. This corresponds to the *cost sharing* case. We then derive the contracting function for the general case.

We begin with the *Cost Sharing Contracting Function*. The cost sharing contracting function is defined by:

$$Q(i,j;G) = \begin{cases} \dfrac{1}{2}\left(\Delta C_j(G - ij, ij) - \Delta C_i(G - ij, ij)\right), & \text{if } ij \in G; \\ \\ 0, & \text{otherwise.} \end{cases}$$

The cost sharing contracting function has the property that if a link ij is added to the network topology, the resulting total change in utility to i and j is equally shared between them. Formally, suppose $ij \notin G$, and that the contract (i,j) is formed. Then the total change in the utility of node i is:

$$-\Delta C_i(G, ij) - Q(i,j;G + ij) = -\frac{1}{2}\left(\Delta C_i(G, ij) + \Delta C_j(G, ij)\right).$$

Similarly, the total change in the utility of node j is:

$$-\Delta C_j(G, ij) + Q(i,j;G + ij) = -\frac{1}{2}\left(\Delta C_i(G, ij) + \Delta C_j(G, ij)\right).$$

Thus both i and j experience the same change in utility; note that identical expressions emerge if the contract (j,i) is formed instead. We conclude *the net change in utility to i and j is identical, and independent of the direction of the contract formed.*

We now consider the general solution of the two player Rubinstein Bargaining game of alternating offers. We call the corresponding contracting function the *Bilateral Bargaining* contracting function.

Consider a graph G containing the link ij. The *bilateral bargaining* contracting function value $Q(i,j;G)$ is based on the outcome of a Rubinstein bilateral bargaining game of alternating offers (see [17] for more details), with the following properties:

1. Node i (resp, j) has discount factor $\delta_i \in [0, 1)$ (resp., $\delta_j \in [0, 1)$);
2. Node i makes the first offer in the bargaining game; and
3. The players are bargaining to split a common "pie," where the size of the pie is the total difference in cost to both players between the graph G and the graph $G - ij$ G, i.e., $\Delta C_i(G - ij, ij) + \Delta C_j(G - ij, ij)$.

Thus the players i and j are bargaining to split any increase or decrease in utility that accrues to the pair as a result of the formation of the link ij. The directionality in the contract corresponds to the fact that one players leads in the bargaining game. It is well known that this game has a unique subgame perfect equilibrium, in which node i makes the first offer and j immediately accepts.

The contracting function value $Q(i, j; G)$ corresponds to the payment i must make to j so that the total difference in the utilities of nodes i and j between the network topologies G and $G - ij$ matches the unique subgame perfect equilibrium of the game of alternating offers described above. Thus we wish to ensure that:

$$-\Delta C_i(G - ij; ij) - Q(i, j; G) = -\left(\frac{1 - \delta_j}{1 - \delta_i \delta_j}\right)(\Delta C_i(G - ij, ij) + \Delta C_j(G - ij, ij)).$$

Rearranging terms yields:

$$Q(i, j; G) = \left(\frac{1 - \delta_j}{1 - \delta_i \delta_j}\right)\Delta C_j(G - ij, ij) - \left(\frac{\delta_j - \delta_i \delta_j}{1 - \delta_i \delta_j}\right)\Delta C_i(G - ij, ij).$$

Note that if $\delta_i \to 1$ and $\delta_j \to 1$, then the preceding expression converges to the cost sharing contracting function described in the preceding example. Thus we can view cost sharing as the outcome of a Rubinstein bilateral bargaining game where players are infinitely patient.

Who Should Pay for Forwarding Packets?*

Heiner Ackermann[1], Patrick Briest[2],
Alexander Fanghänel[1], and Berthold Vöcking[1]

[1] Department of Computer Science, RWTH Aachen, Germany
{ackermann,fanghaenel,voecking}@cs.rwth-aachen.de
[2] Department of Computer Science, University of Liverpool, UK
patrick.briest@liverpool.ac.uk

Abstract. We present a game theoretic study of hybrid communication networks in which mobile devices can connect in an ad hoc fashion to a base station, possibly via a few hops using other mobile devices as intermediate nodes. The maximal number of allowed hops might be bounded with the motivation to guarantee small latency. We introduce *hybrid connectivity games* to study the impact of selfishness on this kind of infrastructure.

Mobile devices are represented by selfish players, each of which aims at establishing an uplink path to the base station minimizing its individual cost. Our model assumes that intermediate nodes on an uplink path are reimbursed for transmitting the packets of other devices. The reimbursements can be paid either by a benevolent network operator or by the senders of the packets using micropayments via a clearing agency that possibly collects a small percentage as commission. These different ways to implement the payments lead to different variants of the hybrid connectivity game. Our main findings are: (1) If there is no constraint on the number of allowed hops on the path to the base station, then the existence of equilibria is guaranteed regardless of whether the network operator or the senders pay for forwarding packets. (2) If the network operator pays, then the existence of equilibria is guaranteed only if at most one intermediate node is allowed, i.e., for at most two hops on the uplink path of a device, but not if the maximal number of allowed hops is three or larger. (3) In contrast, if the senders pay for forwarding their packets, then equilibria are guaranteed to exist given any bound on the number of allowed hops.

The equilibrium analysis presented in this paper gives a first game theoretical motivation for the implementation of micropayment schemes in which senders pay for forwarding their packets. We further support this evidence by giving an upper bound on the Price of Anarchy for this kind of hybrid connectivity games that is independent of the number of nodes, but only depends on the number of hops and the power gradient.

* This work was supported in part by the EU within the 6th Framework Programme under contract 001907 (DELIS), by Ultra High-Speed Mobile Information and Communication Research cluster (UMIC) established under the excellence initiative of the German government, and by the DFG under grant Kr 2332/1-2 within the Emmy Noether program.

X. Deng and F.C. Graham (Eds.): WINE 2007, LNCS 4858, pp. 208–219, 2007.
© Springer-Verlag Berlin Heidelberg 2007

1   Introduction

Hybrid communication networks are a promising direction to combine the features of wireless ad hoc networks with the advantages of wired networks guaranteeing flexible connectivity at low cost in combination with a high throughput close to the standards as encountered in wired networks. In such an infrastructure mobile devices connect in an ad hoc fashion to a base station, i.e., an access point to the wired part of the network, possibly via a few hops using other mobile devices as relay stations [11,15,16]. Since energy requirements increase super-linear in the distance between two devices, the usage of intermediate nodes can significantly reduce the energy consumption in comparison to directly connecting to the base station. This is of particular importance for up-link connections from the mobile devices to the base stations as mobile devices have rather limited energy resources. Using mobile devices as relay stations, on the one hand, might also increase the Quality of Service (QoS) due to a reduction of interference. On the other hand, however, the QoS suffers from an increase in latency if packages need to be forwarded several times until they reach the wired part of the network. For this reason only a relatively small number of hops seems to be acceptable.

Although the benefits of using multihop connections are convincing from a global point of view, one might ask why participants in a commercially operated network should forward packets of other participants, as this only drains the battery of the forwarding node, thus, bringing a negative utility to that participant. The usual response to this objection is that the forwarding nodes should receive a payment for forwarding packets. Let us simplify and assume that there is perfect information about the cost of forwarding packets. More specifically, we assume that the energy consumption for sending packets between any pair of nodes is publicly known and there is a common valuation per unit energy among the players, so that intermediate nodes can, in principle, get reimbursed for forwarding packets. Additionally, we assume that payments exactly compensate the cost players suffer in the case of forwarding packets. Thus, there exists no overpayments which could give an incentive to forward as many packets as possible.

In this paper we study the effects different payments have on the scenario that arises when selfish players aim at connecting to an access point. We introduce *hybrid connectivity games* as a game theoretic model for hybrid communication networks and study the existence, structure, and complexity of Nash equilibria in these games. Mobile devices are represented by players that aim at minimizing their individual cost. We assume that nodes get reimbursed for forwarding packets either by the network operator or by the senders of the packet. In our study, we focus on energy consumption while neglecting aspects of efficient frequency assignment and interference. The aspect of keeping the latency at a reasonable level is modeled by introducing *hop constraints*, which ensure that uplink paths are not too long.

The games that we study are variants of the connectivity games introduced by Eidenbenz et al. [9]. However, there are various technical differences between our model and their models. For example, the networks considered in [9] are assumed to be completely wireless rather than hybrid and nodes want to be connected to all other nodes or, alternatively, to a specified subset of the other nodes. Another difference is that their analysis does not consider hop constraints. The main conceptual difference, however, is that the study in [9] does not explicitly take into account that somebody has to pay for reimbursing the intermediate nodes. The justification that is given for neglecting this aspect is that the payments are made on the network layer, whereas the decisions relevant for the topology are made on the data link layer. It is pointed out in [9], however, that "the ultimate goal of this line of research would be to combine the notion of selfishness such that it stretches across all protocol stack layers".

In this paper, we study the effects of payments on the equilibrium topologies in hybrid connectivity games depending on who is paying for reimbursing the intermediate nodes for forwarding packets. Essentially, there are two possibilities: either, the network operator pays for all reimbursements, or the senders of the forwarded packets pay. One can imagine that the first variant can be implemented internally within the accounting system of the network operator/provider. The second variant suggests itself for an implementation using micropayments as elucidated, e.g., in [13]. A clearing agency realizing the micropayments possibly collects a small additional percentage as commission from the senders. We will incorporate these different variants into our model in form of a parameter α describing the fraction of payments made by the senders. Here, $\alpha = 0$ means that the network operator completely pays for the reimbursements, whereas $\alpha \geq 1$ means that the senders reimburse the nodes forwarding their packets and the additional payment, i.e., a fraction of $\alpha - 1$, goes to the clearing agency.

1.1 The Model

A hybrid connectivity game consists of a complete, edge-weighted graph $G = (V, E)$ with $V = P \dot\cup A$ and two parameters $\alpha \geq 0$ and $h \in \mathbb{N}$. We denote by P the set of players, and by A the set of access points. In the following, let $n = |P|$. The edge weights are assumed to be positive, and weight $w(i, j)$ of edge $\{i, j\}$ describes the cost of transmitting a unit of data from i to j or vice versa.

Each player aims to establish an uplink path to an access point. Towards this end, player i chooses a gateway $g_i \in V$. The idea is that i sends its own packets and all other packets that it receives to g_i. Then this node forwards these packets to its gateway and so on until the packets reach an access point unless there is a cycle. The path followed by the packets to the access point is called i's *uplink path*.

In the following, we call a vector $s = (g_1, \ldots, g_n) \in V^n$ a state of the game and assume that player i chooses g_i as gateway. The cost $c_i(s)$ of player i in state s is defined as follows. If i is connected via the uplink path $i = p_0, p_1, \ldots, p_{l-1}, p_l = a$ to the access point a and this route has at most h hops, i.e., $l \leq h$, then the cost of i is

$$c_i(s) = w(p_0, p_1) + \alpha \cdot \sum_{j=1}^{l-1} w(p_j, p_{j+1}) \ . \tag{1}$$

Otherwise, the cost of i is assumed to be infinitely large. We assume that each player selfishly aims at minimizing its cost. A state s is called a *Nash equilibrium* if no player has an incentive to change its gateway.

In the following, we assume w. l. o. g. that there exists a single access point only, that is $|A| = 1$. In the case of multiple access points we can always merge them into a single one and choose for every player the weight of the edge between the player and the new access point as the minimum over all weights between the player and each access point from the set A.

1.2 Our Contribution

First, we consider the case that the network operator pays for reimbursing the intermediate nodes, i.e., we assume $\alpha = 0$. In this case nodes can forward packets along intermediate nodes for free so that they solely aim at minimizing the energy requirement for the first link on their path. Let us remark that this is the general assumption in the work by Eidenbenz et al. [9].

We show that if there is no hop constraint (i.e., $h = n$), then hybrid connectivity games with $\alpha = 0$ always have pure equilibria. The situation changes, however, when introducing hop constraints. We prove that the existence of equilibria is guaranteed only for $h \in \{1, 2\}$. For any $h \geq 3$, there is an instance of the hybrid connectivity game with $\alpha = 0$ that does not have an equilibrium. Let us remark that both existence proofs are constructive and yield algorithms computing equilibria efficiently. Second, we study the case that intermediate nodes are reimbursed for forwarding packets by the senders of the packets via an agency that might collect a small percentage as commission, that is, we assume $\alpha \geq 1$. In this case, our analysis shows that these games always have pure equilibria. Again our proof is constructive and yields an efficient algorithm computing an equilibrium.

We view our result as the first game theoretical evidence that senders rather than a benevolent network operator should pay for forwarding their packets. This is true even if this causes some overhead for implementing the accounting and payment, as our positive results about the existence of equilibria hold even if there is a clearing agency taking some percentage as commission.

We complete our analysis by studying the Price of Anarchy (PoA) for hybrid connectivity games. We start by presenting examples for different variants of hybrid connectivity games showing that the PoA is unbounded for general cost matrices. For this reason, we restrict ourselves to cost matrices generated by power graphs with an underlying Euclidean embedding. Assuming that senders pay for forwarding their packets – as suggested by our preceding equilibrium analysis – we obtain an upper bound of $h^{\beta-1}$ for the PoA with h denoting the hop constraint and β the power gradient. Thus, the PoA is independent of the size of the network.

1.3   Related Work

In recent years various papers have studied wireless networks from a game theoretic perspective. Among others, Altman and Altman [2], Krishnaswamy [14],
and Heikkinen [12] observe that due to the increased complexity of modern
wireless networks resource management tasks should be shifted from the wired
part of the infrastructure to the mobile devices. Such management tasks include
power assignments to and channel allocation of mobile devices. They propose to
study these problems in the framework of potential games, and present potential
functions showing that best response dynamics converge to stable assignments.

Most closely related to our work is the work of Eidenbenz et al. [9], who introduce several topology control games. In such games selfish mobile devices aim to
be connected to specified sets of others devices at the lowest cost. Although they
suggest that senders should pay for forwarding their packets, they do not take
into account the effects of these payments on the preferences of the players. In
our notation, they assume $\alpha = 0$. They show that the connectivity games they
consider do no not possess Nash equilibria in general. However, if each device
would like to be connected to every other device, then the existence of equilibria
is guaranteed. Hop constraints are not taken into account.

Different approaches encouraging mobile devices to forward packets are presented, e.g., in [3,8,13,17]. Jakobsson et al. [13] present a micro-payment scheme,
whereas others discuss incentive compatible payment schemes [3,8,17].

Another branches of research related to our work are network design and
network formation games [1,4,5,7,10]. Anshelevich et al. [4] consider a network
creation game in which players represent subsets of nodes of a graph and can
contribute towards the purchase of fixed price edges. Among other results they
show that if each player wants to connect a single node to some common source,
there exist socially optimal Nash equilibria, or, more formally, the *price of stability* in this game is 1.

Fabrikant et al. [10] introduce another basic model of network formation, in
which each node is represented by a selfish agent. Every player can create incident
links to other nodes and incurs a cost that equals α times the number of created
links plus the sum of distances to all other nodes. Fabrikant et al. [10] presented
first results on the Price of Anarchy in these games. Corbo and Parkes [6], Albers
et al. [1], and Demaine et al. [7] present several extentions and improvements on
these results.

2   Payments by the Network Operator

In this section, we consider hybrid connectivity games with $\alpha = 0$, that is, we
consider games in which the network operator reimburses players forwarding
packets. First we consider games without hop constraint.

Theorem 1. *Every hybrid connectivity game with $\alpha = 0$ and without hop constraint possesses a Nash equilibrium which can be computed efficiently.*

Proof. The potential function $\phi(s) = \sum_{i \in P} c_i(s)$, which maps a state s to the sum of all players' costs in this state. Suppose now that player i chooses a new gateway in order to decrease its cost. In the following, we denote by s' the state obtained after its strategy change. It is not difficult to verify that $\phi(s') < \phi(s)$ since only the cost of player i decreases, whereas the costs of all other players remain unchanged.

In order to prove that an equilibrium can be computed efficiently, observe that a player can choose at most n different gateways. Since a player's best response does not decrease any other players costs, each player chooses a gateway at most once. Therefore, after at most n^2 best responses an equilibrium is reached. □

We now turn our attention to hybrid connectivity games with $\alpha = 0$ and hop constraint. Recall that in this case an uplink path is only feasible if the number of hops on this path does not exceed the hop constraint h. First, note that we cannot apply the potential function introduced in the previous proof to games with hop constraints. This is essentially true since a best response of a single player may violate the hop constraints of other players and, thus, the costs of other players may increase to infinity.

In the following, we prove that every such game with hop constraint $h \in \{1, 2\}$ possesses a Nash equilibrium. In case of h=1 all players connect to the access point which is obviously a Nash equilibrium. In case of $h = 2$ we present an efficient algorithm. Additionally, we observe that for every hop constraint $h \geq 3$ there exists a game which does not possess a Nash equilibrium.

Theorem 2. *Every hybrid connectivity game with $\alpha = 0$ and hop constraint $h = 2$ possesses a Nash equilibrium, which can be computed efficiently.*

Proof. In the following, we present an efficient algorithm computing a Nash equilibrium of such a game. The algorithm proceeds in two phases. Without loss of generality, assume that $w(1, a) \leq w(2, a) \leq \ldots \leq w(n, a)$ holds.

Phase 1: Initially, all players are unconnected. The algorithm then processes the players $1, \ldots, n$ in that order and connects player i to the access point if there exists no player $j < i$ with the following properties. Player j has already been connected to the access point, and $w(i, j) < w(i, a)$. If such a player j exists, player i remains unconnected.

Phase 2: All players who have not been connected in the first phase are connected to their best response.

Obviously, all players who were connected in the second phase do not have an incentive to change their gateways. Thus, it remains to show that none of the players who were connected in the first phase have an incentive to change their gateways. Towards a contradiction, assume that player i has an incentive to choose a new gateway g_i. Note, that g_i was connected in the first phase, too. Thus, $g_i > i$ since otherwise i would not have been connected in the first phase. We conclude

$$w(i, a) \leq w(g_i, a) \quad \text{since } i \text{ was connected before } g_i,$$
$$w(g_i, a) \leq w(i, g_i) \quad \text{since } g_i \text{ connected to the access point, and}$$
$$w(i, g_i) < w(i, a) \quad \text{since } i \text{ wants to connect to } g_i.$$

Finally, we obtain a contradiction, since the inequalities imply that it holds that $w(i, g_i) < w(i, g_i)$. $\qquad\qquad\qquad\qquad\qquad\qquad\qquad\qquad\qquad\qquad\qquad\qquad$ □

Next, we show that, in general, the existence of Nash equilibria cannot be extended towards games with hop constraint $h \geq 3$.

Observation 1. *For every integer $h \geq 3$, there exists a hybrid connectivity game with $\alpha = 0$ and hop constraint h that does not possess a Nash equilibrium.*

Proof. First, we present such a game with hop constraint $h = 3$. In this game there are 5 devices and a single access point. Edge weights are defined according to Figure 1. Exhaustive search shows that this game does not possess a Nash equilibrium.

	a	p_1	p_2	p_3	p_4	p_5
a	-	20	58	60	97	85
p_1	20	-	65	46	33	82
p_2	58	65	-	48	71	15
p_3	60	46	48	-	34	72
p_4	97	33	71	34	-	18
p_5	85	82	15	72	18	-

Fig. 1. A counter-example with $h = 3$

In order to extend the example towards arbitrary hop constraints $h > 3$ one simply replaces the former access point by a sequence of $h - 3$ players and attaches a new access point to this sequence. The weights are chosen in such a way that the new players always line up, and such that none of the old players ever connect to a new one. $\qquad\qquad\qquad\qquad\qquad\qquad\qquad\qquad\qquad\qquad\qquad\qquad$ □

3 Payments by the Senders

In this section, we consider hybrid connectivity games with $\alpha \geq 1$ and prove that every such game possesses a Nash equilibrium even in the presence of a hop constraint. In the following, we assume that players have strict preferences in the case of two or more alternatives with the same cost. One way to achieve this is to assume that all paths have pairwise disjoint cost.

Theorem 3. *Every hybrid connectivity game with $\alpha \geq 1$ and hop constraint h possesses a Nash equilibrium, which can be computed efficiently. Moreover, this equilibrium is unique.*

Proof. First, we present an efficient iterative algorithm computing an equilibrium. We then show that the computed equilibrium is unique. The algorithm works as follows. Initially, no player is connected. The algorithm then selects player i, such that $i = \operatorname{argmin}_{j \in P}\{w(j, a)\}$ and connects it to the access point a.

Without loss of generality, assume that $i = 1$. Obviously, this state corresponds to an equilibrium if we ignore all unconnected players.

The algorithm then proceeds as follows. By induction hypothesis we may assume that the algorithm already connected the players $1, \ldots, i - 1$ via paths to the access point, such that none of them have an incentive to change their gateways. For every unconnected player j, let $C_j(i-1)$ be the cost of a shortest uplink path via players $1, \ldots, i - 1$ which does not violate the hop constraint. Without loss of generality, let i be the player such that $C_i(i-1)$ is minimal. The algorithm then connects i to the first player on this path. In order to prove that we obtain a Nash equilibrium with i players, we claim that $C_i(i-1)$ is larger than the cost of every uplink path of one of the players $1, \ldots, i - 1$.

We first prove that the claim is true for player $i - 1$. Let $C_k(i-2)$ be the cost of player k's shortest uplink path via players $1, \ldots, i - 2$. Since the algorithm connected player $i - 1$ before player i, $C_{i-1}(i-2) < C_i(i-2)$ holds. Strict inequality holds due to our assumption that all paths have pairwise disjoint cost. Now, we distinguish between the following two cases. In the first case, player i chooses $i-1$ as gateway. In the second case, it chooses one of the devices $1, \ldots, i - 2$ or the access point itself as gateway. In the first case, $C_{i-1}(i-1) < C_i(i-1)$ since i pays at least $w(i, i-1) + C_{i-1}(i-1)$. This is true since $\alpha \geq 1$. In the second case, $C_i(i-1) = C_i(i-2) > C_{i-1}(i-2) = C_{i-1}(i-1)$. By the same arguments the cost of player $i-1$'s uplink path is also larger than the cost of the paths of the players $1, \ldots, i - 2$ our claim follows.

Thus, we conclude that no player $j < i$ has an incentive to choose player i as gateway, since in this case its cost would increase to at least $w(j, i) + C_i(i-1)$. Again, this is true since $\alpha \geq 1$.

In order to prove uniqueness, suppose that there exists at least one additional equilibrium s' besides the previously computed one s^*. In the following, we denote the gateway of player i in state s by $g_i(s)$. Without loss of generality assume that

$$c_1(s^*) \leq c_2(s^*) \leq \ldots \leq c_n(s^*) \ . \tag{2}$$

Since $s^* \neq s'$ and due to our assumption that all paths have pairwise disjoint cost, there exists at least one player i such that $c_i(s^*) \neq c_i(s')$. Among all such players let player k be the one with smallest index. Thus, due to our assumption players $1, \ldots, k - 1$ are connected in the same manner in both equilibria. Now, we distinguish between the following two cases both leading to a contradiction:

$c_k(s^*) < c_k(s')$: If k is connected to the access point in s^*, then k could obviously decrease its cost in s' by directly connecting to the access point. Thus, assume that k is not directly connected to the access point in s^*. By Equation 2, $g_k(s^*) < k$. We conclude that $c_{g_k(s^*)}(s^*) = c_{g_k(s^*)}(s')$ holds due to our choice of k. Thus, k could decrease its cost in state s' by choosing $g_k(s^*)$ as gateway, since players $1, \ldots, k - 1$ are connected in the same manner in both states. We conclude that s' is not an equilibrium.

$c_k(s^*) > c_k(s')$: If k is connected to the access point in s', then k could obviously decrease its cost in s^* by directly connecting to the access point. Thus, assume that k is not directly connected to the access point in s'. In this case, let k' be the last player on the path from k to the access point in s', who does not belong to the set $\{1, \ldots, k-1\}$. We observe that such a player always exists. Assume towards a contradiction that such a player does not exists. Since the players $1, \ldots, k-1$ are connected in the same manner in both equilibria, k could obviously decrease its cost in s^* by connecting to the same gateway as in s'. Now, observe that the following inequalities are true:

$$c_{k'}(s') < c_k(s') \text{ by the choice of } k' \text{ and since } \alpha \geq 1,$$
$$c_k(s') < c_k(s^*) \text{ by our assumption, and}$$
$$c_k(s^*) < c_{k'}(s^*) \text{ by the choice of } k \text{ and since k' } \notin \{1, \ldots, k-1\} \text{ .}$$

Thus, $c_{k'}(s') < c_{k'}(s^*)$. Finally, by the same arguments as in the previous case k' has an incentive to change its gateway in state s^*. We conclude that s^* is not an equilibrium.

It follows that the equilibrium is unique.   □

From a theoretical point of view, it would also be interesting to consider games with $\alpha \in {]0,1[}$. In this case reimbursements would be shared among the sender and the network operator. However, we conjecture that for every $\alpha \in {]0,1[}$, there exists a hybrid connectivity game that does not have an equilibrium.

4   Price of Anarchy

In this section, we provide some results on the Price of Anarchy (PoA) in hybrid connectivity games. As usually, the PoA upper bounds the increase of the sum of the players' cost due to their selfish behavior. First, we present examples for $\alpha \in \{0, 1\}$ showing that, in general, the PoA cannot be bounded by any constant. In the case of games with $\alpha = 0$ this is already true without hop constraint.

Observation 2. *The Price of Anarchy in hybrid connectivity games with $\alpha = 0$ is unbounded.*

Proof. Consider the example depicted in Figure 2(a). In the socially optimal state player 1 connects to the access point, and player 2 connects to player 1. In the worst Nash equilibrium player 2 connects to the access point, and player 1 connects to player 2. In this case, the Price of Anarchy equals $(M+1)/3$. Since M can be chosen arbitrarily, the observation follows.   □

Next, we consider hybrid connectivity games with $\alpha = 1$. In the case of games without hop constraint, the Price of Anarchy is trivially 1. This is true, since each player is connected to the access point via a globally shortest path. Unfortunately, this positive result does no hold any longer in games with hop constraint.

Observation 3. *The Price of Anarchy in hybrid connectivity games with $\alpha = 1$ and hop constraint is unbounded.*

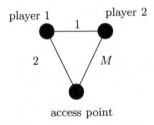

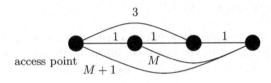

(a) The Price of Anarchy is unbounded in hybrid connectivity games with $\alpha = 0$.

(b) The Price of Anarchy in hybrid connectivity games with $\alpha = 1$ and hop constraint is unbounded.

Fig. 2. Worst Case Instances

Proof. Consider the example depicted in Figure 2(b), and assume that the hop constraint equals 2. Then, in the only equilibrium player 1 connects to the access point, and player 2 and 3 to player 1. In contrast to this, in the socially optimal state player 2 connects to the access point, and player 3 to player 2. In this case, the Price of Anarchy equals $(M+4)/8$. Since M can be chosen arbitrarily the observation follows. □

In the aforementioned examples we did not make any assumptions on the cost function. However, in real world wireless networks devices are embedded into the Euclidean space $\mathbb{R}^2$ or $\mathbb{R}^3$ and costs depend on the Euclidean distance and the path-loss or distance power gradient $\beta \geq 1$. To be precise, the cost for a successful transmission of a data packet between two players p_1 and p_2 equals $w(p_1, p_2)^\beta$, where $w(p_1, p_2)$ denotes the Euclidean distance between the two players. The distance power gradient usually ranges from 2 to 6.

Next, we consider the Price of Anarchy in hybrid connectivity games with $\alpha = 1$, which are embedded into the Euclidean space. Given the distance power gradient β, we call these games β-*embedded*. We show that for such β-embedded games the PoA is upper bounded by $h^{\beta-1}$. In real world wireless networks the distance power gradient β and the hop constraint are expected to be small constants. Thus, in real world networks the impact of selfish players is not too big and especially does not depend on the number of players.

Theorem 4. *The Price of Anarchy in β-embedded hybrid connectivity games with $\alpha = 1$ and hop constraint h is upper bounded by $h^{\beta-1}$.*

Proof. In the Nash equilibrium s of a β-embedded hybrid connectivity game with $\alpha = 1$ and hop constraint the cost of player i is trivially upper bounded by $w(i, a)^\beta$. Additionally, in a socially optimal state s^* the cost of i is lower bounded by $h \cdot (w(i, a)/h)^\beta$. Thus, in every Nash equilibrium each player pays at most

$$\frac{w(i, a)^\beta}{h \cdot (w(i, a)/h)^\beta} = h^{\beta-1} \qquad (3)$$

times more than in a socially optimal state. Therefore, the Price of Anarchy is upper bounded by $h^{\beta-1}$.   □

Examples show that games exist where a single player actually pays $O(h^{\beta-1})$ times more in the Nash equilibrium, than in the socially optimal state. This shows that our analysis is essentially tight.

5   Conclusion

By taking into account different kinds of payments, our analysis is a first step towards studying the impacts of selfishness stretching across the network and the data link layer. The major simplifying assumption in our model is that, that the energy consumption for sending packets between any pair of players is public knowledge and that there is a common valuation per unit of energy. Because of this assumption, reimbursements can be chosen in such a way that they precisely cover the cost for forwarding a packet.

One way to get rid of the assumption of global knowledge about the cost matrix, might be to simply set a fixed price for forwarding packets, regardless of the required energy. In this case, only those nodes participate as relay stations, that can forward packets along edges whose energy cost is not larger than the fixed price per packet. An alternative approach could be to use mechanisms like VCG to let the players truthfully report their cost values as described, e. g., in [3,8].

Both approaches have the problem that players might have an incentive to increase the number of packets they have to forward, because the payment that they receive is larger than the cost for forwarding a packet. For example, they might decrease the number of hops on their path to the base station in order to get more attractive to serve as a gateway for other nodes. That is, overpayments change the strategic behavior of the players and, hence, are not covered by our analysis.

We think that it is an important step towards more practical models and a challenging open problem to investigate the effects of different payment schemes in a game theoretical study.

References

1. Albers, S., Eilts, S., Even-Dar, E., Mansour, Y., Roditty, L.: On Nash equilibria for a network creation game. In: Proc. of 17th Ann. ACM–SIAM Symposium on Discrete Algorithms (SODA), pp. 89–98. ACM Press, New York (2006)
2. Altman, E., Altman, Z.: S-modular games and power control in wireless networks. IEEE Transactions on Automatic Control 48(5), 839–842 (2003)
3. Anderegg, L., Eidenbenz, S.: Ad hoc-VCG: a truthful and cost-efficient routing protocol for mobile ad hoc networks with selfish agents. In: Proc. of the 9th Ann. international conference on Mobile computing and networking (MobiCom), pp. 245–259 (2003)

4. Anshelevich, E., Dasgupta, A., Tardos, E., Wexler, T.: Near-optimal network design with selfish agents. In: Proc. of 35th Ann. ACM Symposium on Theory of Computing (STOC), pp. 511–520. ACM Press, New York (2003)
5. Bala, V., Goyal, S.: A non-cooperative theory of network formation. Econometrica 68(5), 1181–1229 (2000)
6. Corbo, J., Parkes, D.: The price of selfish behavior in bilateral network formation. In: Proc. of 24th Ann. ACM SIGACT-SIGOPS Symposium on Principles of Distributed Computing (PODC), pp. 99–107. ACM Press, New York (2005)
7. Demaine, E.D., Hajiaghayi, M., Mahini, H., Zadimoghaddam, M.: The price of anarchy in network creation games. In: Proc. of 26th Ann. ACM SIGACT-SIGOPS Symposium on Principles of Distributed Computing (PODC), ACM Press, New York (2007)
8. Eidenbenz, S., Anderegg, L., Wattenhofer, R.: Incentive-compatible, energy-optimal, and efficient ad hoc networking in a selfish milieu. In: Proc. of the 40th Ann. Hawaii International Conference on System Sciences (HICSS), p. 293 (2007)
9. Eidenbenz, S., Kumar, V.S.A., Zust, S.: Equilibria in topology control games for ad hoc networks. In: Proc. of the 3rd joint workshop on Foundations of mobile computing (DIALM-POMC), pp. 2–11 (2003)
10. Fabrikant, A., Luthra, A., Maneva, E., Papadimitriou, C.H., Shenker, S.: On a network creation game. In: Proc. of 22th Ann. ACM SIGACT-SIGOPS Symposium on Principles of Distributed Computing (PODC), pp. 347–351. ACM Press, New York (2003)
11. Frodigh, M., Parkvall, S., Roobol, C., Johansson, P., Larsson, P.: Future-generation wireless networks. IEEE Personal Communications 8(5) (2001)
12. Heikkinen, T.: A potential game approach to distributed power control and scheduling. Computer Networks 50(13), 2295–2311 (2006)
13. Jakobsson, M., Hubaux, J.P., Buttyán, L.: A micro-payment scheme encouraging collaboration in multi-hop cellular networks. Financial Cryptography, 15–33 (2003)
14. Krishnaswamy, D.: Game theoretic formulations for network-assisted resource management in wireless networks. In: Proc. of 56th IEEE Vehicular Technology Conference (VTC), pp. 1312–1316. IEEE Computer Society Press, Los Alamitos (2002)
15. Singh, S., Woo, M., Raghavendra, C.S.: Power-aware routing in mobile ad hoc networks. In: Proc. of the 4th Ann. ACM/IEEE international conference on Mobile computing and networking (MobiCom), pp. 181–190. IEEE Computer Society Press, Los Alamitos (1998)
16. Tang, J., Xue, G., Zhang, W.: Interference-aware topology control and QoS routing in multi-channel wireless mesh networks. In: Proc. of the 6th ACM international symposium on Mobile ad hoc networking and computing (MobiHoC), pp. 68–77. ACM Press, New York (2005)
17. Zhong, S., Li, E.L., Liu, Y.G., Yang, Y.: On designing incentive-compatible routing and forwarding protocols in wireless ad-hoc networks: an integrated approach using game theoretical and cryptographic techniques. In: Proc. of the 11th Ann. International Conference on Mobile Computing and Networking (MOBICOM), pp. 117–131 (2005)

On the Performance of Congestion Games for Optimum Satisfiability Problems

Aristotelis Giannakos, Laurent Gourvès, Jérôme Monnot,
and Vangelis Th. Paschos

LAMSADE, CNRS UMR 7024, Université de Paris-Dauphine, Paris, France
{aristotelis.giannakos, laurent.gourves, monnot,
paschos}@lamsade.dauphine.fr

Abstract. We introduce and study a congestion game having MAX SAT as an underlying structure and show that its price of anarchy is 1/2. The main result is a redesign of the game leading to an improved price of anarchy of 2/3 from which we derive a non oblivious local search algorithm for MAX SAT with locality gap 2/3. A similar congestion MIN SAT game is also studied.

Keywords: price of anarchy, non oblivious local search, approximation algorithm, MAX SAT.

1 Introduction

Starting from the seminal articles [12,14,15], a lot of attention is paid to the performance of decentralized systems involving selfish users. Probably, the most extensively studied ones are *congestion games* [13,16] because they model central issues in networks. At the same time, the *price of anarchy* (PoA) and the *price of stability* (PoS) are certainly the most employed tools to analyze the performance of these games [3,12,14].

A congestion game is a tuple $\langle N, M, (A_i)_{i \in N}, (c_j)_{j \in M} \rangle$ where N is the set of players, M is the set of facilities, $A_i \subseteq 2^M$ is the set of strategies of player i and c_j is a cost function associated to facility j. In congestion games, a player's cost for using a facility depends only on the total number of players using this facility, and is independent of the player herself. A player's *total cost* is defined as the sum of the single costs over all facilities.

The PoA and the PoS are dominant tools to study the performance of decentralized systems [3,12,14]. In minimization problems, the PoA (resp., the PoS) is the maximum (resp., the minimum) value that the ratio of the overall optimum to the cost of a Nash equilibrium (NE) can take over the set of all Nash equilibria. A NE is a combination of strategies, one for each agent, in which no agent has an incentive to unilaterally move away. Because Nash equilibria are known to deviate from the optimum in many optimization situations, the PoA captures the lack of coordination between independent agents while the PoS indicates how good a solution from which no agent will defect is.

X. Deng and F.C. Graham (Eds.): WINE 2007, LNCS 4858, pp. 220–231, 2007.
© Springer-Verlag Berlin Heidelberg 2007

General congestion games make no particular assumption on the set of facilities; however, an extensive part of the literature deals with congestion games whose facilities sets are the edge sets of graphs (see for example [12,15] on selfish routing in networks). In this paper, we introduce and study a congestion game associated to MAX SAT. The importance of this underlying structure does not need to be emphasized, since it is involved in numerous combinatorial optimization problems. Each clause is a facility and the players are the variables with strategy set {true, false} (playing true means selecting the clauses where her corresponding variable occurs unnegated, playing false means selecting the clauses where her corresponding variable occurs negated). Moreover, every clause/facility pays the variables/players a fraction $f(j)$ of its weight where j denotes the number of players who satisfy it. Players rationally act in order to maximize their payments.

First, we discuss the question *What is the price of anarchy and price of stability of the game?* The next step is *How can we reduce the price of anarchy?* To do so, we use a powerful technique known as *non oblivious local search* [1,11] which consists in using a specific cost function (i.e. different from the weight of all satisfied clauses which is the classical economic function) in a local search algorithm.

Related Work

Articles on selfish routing in networks have mushroomed since the papers by [12,15]. Interestingly, congestion games provide the following unifying framework for such problems (often called *network congestion games*): we are given a graph $G = (V, E)$ where E is the set of facilities. Each player chooses a path between a given source-destination pair of nodes in V. Each edge has a cost/latency function which depends on the number of players who use it. Each player selfishly selects her path in order to minimize her total cost/latency, i.e. the sum over all edges. The performance of the system is often measured by the average or maximum total cost/latency experimented by the players when they are at a Nash equilibrium.

In [12,8], the network consists of m parallel links between a single source-destination couple of nodes. Players are weighted and the latency function associated to an edge is the sum of player's weights using it. The performance of the system is measured by the maximum total latency over all players. In [5,6], the authors study *linear general* congestion games (not necessarily defined over a graph) with cost function of the form $c_e = a_e k + b_e$ where k denotes the number of players using e while a_e and b_e are positive coefficients. The performance of the system is both measured by the maximum and average total latency. In [3], Anshelevich et al. study a network design game where each edge is assigned a fixed cost. Each player buys/selects a path between her source and destination nodes. The cost of an edge is distributed over the players who select it. The social function is what the players collectively pay.

Bilò [4] independently introduced satisfiability games in an effort to classify non-cooperative games according to three aspects: expressiveness, complexity of computing their Nash equilibria and the quality of these equilibria. His definition of the game differs on our since not only disjunctive clauses are considered, a player may control several variables and her payoff is the weight of the clauses she satisfies. He mainly proves that satisifability games, according to his definition are equivalent to congestion games.

Algorithmic game theory and *local search theory* have several common points (see [9,10]). The *locality gap* (or approximation ratio) for a problem can be viewed as the PoA of a specific associated game. The well known fact that every congestion game admits a pure NE [13,16] can be interpreted in terms of local search theory: players, though separately guided by their self-interest follow a *potential function* and converge to a NE as a local search algorithm, following an *economic function*, converges to a *local optimum*.

A survey on MAX SAT, including local search algorithms, can be found in [2]. The most intuitive economic function, termed oblivious objective function, is the number of satisifed clauses: $\sum_i cov_i$ where cov_i denotes the number of clauses satisfied by exactly i variables. Nevertheless, less intuitive (termed non oblivious) functions can be used. In particular, we can cite Khanna et al. [11] who obtain a $(1 - \frac{1}{2^k})$-approximate algorithm for MAX E k−SAT (the restriction of MAX SAT to clauses with exactly k literals). They use a 1-neighborhood (at most one variable is modified at a time) and the function $\sum_i \alpha_i cov_i$ where α_i's are real constants. Remark that it generalizes the oblivious function. When $k = 2$, this non oblivious function is $\frac{3}{2} cov_1 + 2 cov_2$. With the classical (oblivious) function $cov_1 + cov_2$, the locality gap is 2/3 while the non oblivious function gives a 3/4-approximation algorithm. Unfortunately, Khanna et al. crucially use the fact that all clauses have exactly k literals. Up to our knowledge, no extension of this approach to the MAX k−SAT problem (the restriction of MAX SAT to clauses with at most k literals) is known.[1]

Changing the rule of a game in order to improve its PoA is not a new approach. In [7], Christodoulou et al., introduce the notion of *coordination mechanism* which attempts to redesign the system to reduce the PoA.

Contribution and Organization of the Paper
We introduce a congestion game (defined formally in Section 2) associated to the weighted MAX SAT problem where every clause/facility pays the variables/players a fraction $f(j)$ of its weight where j denotes the number of players who satisfy it. We first analyze the natural, so called *fair*, *payment scheme* where $f(j) = 1/j$ (the weight of a clause is evenly distributed to the variables who satisfy it) in Section 3. We undertake the same analysis in Section 4, using redesigned, in fact *non oblivious*, payment schemes and prove that the system shows improved performances. Our results on the PoA are summarized in the following table.

	MAX E k−SAT	MAX k−SAT
Fair	$\frac{k}{k+1}$	$\frac{k}{2k-1}$
Non oblivious	$1 - \frac{1}{2^k}$	$2/3$

Note that the given ratios cannot be improved under the considered payment scheme. Interestingly, we derive a 2/3-approximate non oblivious local search

---

[1] It is not difficult to see that the locality gap of the MAX k−SAT problem is 1/2 if we use the 1-neighborhood and the classical economic function, even for $k = 2$.

algorithm using the 1-neighborhood for the MAX $k-$ SAT problem. Some particular instances state in Section 5 that PoA=PoS. Finally, Section 6 is devoted to a game associated to MIN $k-$SAT. We prove that its PoA, under the fair payment scheme, is equal to k and that no non oblivious payment scheme can reduce it. Nevertheless, the PoS is equal to the kth harmonic number $H(k)$ (even for MIN E $k-$SAT).

As done in [3,5,6,7] we only consider pure strategy Nash equilibria (all players deterministically choose between *true* or *false*). Thus, we restrict our analysis to the pure PoA and pure PoS of the MAX SAT and MIN SAT games. Proofs are sometimes omitted due to space limitation.

2   Definitions

2.1   MAX $k-$ SAT and MIN $k-$ SAT

Let $X = \{x_1, \ldots, x_n\}$ be a set of boolean variables. A *literal* in X is either a boolean variable x_i, or its negation $\overline{x_i}$, for some $1 \leq i \leq n$. A *clause* on X is a disjunction of literals in X. The size of a clause C, i.e., the number of literals that C contains, is denoted by $\sigma(C)$. An instance $I = (X, \mathcal{C}, w)$ of SAT consists of a set of variables $X = \{x_1, \ldots, x_n\}$, a set of clauses $\mathcal{C} = \{C_1, \ldots, C_m\}$, and a non-negative weight $w(C) \geq 0$ for each clause $C \in \mathcal{C}$. A *truth assignment* d is an assignment of the value *true* or *false* to each variable in X, that is $\forall x \in X, d(x) \in \{true, false\}$. The well known **NP**-hard MAX SAT (resp., MIN SAT) problem is to find an assignment d^* that maximizes (resp., minimizes) the total weight of satisfied clauses $W(d^*)$ where $W(d) = \sum_{\{C \mid d \text{ satisfies } C\}} w(C)$. The MAX $k-$SAT (resp., MIN $k-$SAT) problem is the restriction to instances where $\sigma(C) \leq k, \forall C \in \mathcal{C}$. The MAX E $k-$SAT (resp., MIN E $k-$SAT) problem is the restriction to instances where $\sigma(C) = k, \forall C \in \mathcal{C}$. In the unweighted version, every clause C has a weight $w(C) = 1$. W.l.o.g., we assume that instances are "simple": a variable occurs at most once in a clause and no couple $C = x, C' = \overline{x}$ exists. We also note $W(\mathcal{C}') = \sum_{C \in \mathcal{C}'} w(C)$ for any $\mathcal{C}' \subseteq \mathcal{C}$.

2.2   A MAX $k-$SAT Congestion Game

The system is given by an instance of the weighted MAX $k-$SAT problem where every clause $C \in \mathcal{C}$ is a facility and every variable $x_i \in \{x_1, \ldots, x_n\}$ is controlled by an independent and selfish player $i \in \{1, \ldots, n\}$. Player i has strategy set

$$A_i = \{\{C \in \mathcal{C} \mid x_i \text{ occurs unnegated in } C\}, \{C \in \mathcal{C} \mid x_i \text{ occurs negated in } C\}\}$$

or equivalently, $A_i = \{true, false\}$. The system's state (a strategy profile or truth assignment) is denoted by $d = (d_1, d_2, \ldots, d_n) \in \{true, false\}^n$, where d_i is i's strategy. As in the classical MAX SAT problem, the quality is measured by the total weight of the set of satisfied clauses. The above model is not yet a game because the players have no preference between *true* and *false*. We suppose then that the system also guides the players in their choice by giving rewards. To do so, it uses a payment scheme $\mathcal{P} : \{true, false\}^n \to R^n$ where $\mathcal{P}_i(d)$ is what i receives when d is the strategy profile. Then, every player i rationally acts in order to maximize $\mathcal{P}_i(d)$.

We focus on decentralized payment schemes where $\mathcal{P}_i(d)$ is defined as a sum of atomic rewards over the set of facilities, i.e., $\mathcal{P}_i(d) = \sum_{C \in \mathcal{C}} \pi(x_i, C, d)$ with $\pi(x_i, C, d)$, denoting what i receives from C when d is the system's state, does not depend on the other clauses $\mathcal{C} \setminus C$. The motivation is that such a scheme can be easily implemented in a distributed system since it does not require communication between facilities.

2.3   Payments and Potential Functions

We consider general payment schemes such that $\pi(x_i, C, d)$ is proportional to $w(C)$: a player satisfying a clause C with $j - 1$ others receives $f(j) w(C)$ from C where $f(j) \geq 0$; she receives nothing from C if she does not satisfy it. Here, f is called the *payment function*. Since $f()$ and $cf()$ lead to equivalent payment schemes if c is a positive constant, we fix $f(1) = 1$.

As it is defined, the MAX $k-$SAT game is a congestion game. We know from [13,16] that it always has a pure Nash equilibrium. Indeed, the game admits a *potential function*

$$\Phi(d) = \sum_{C \in \mathcal{C}} \sum_{l=1}^{\nu(d,C)} f(l) w(C)$$

where $\nu(d, C)$ denotes the number of players satisfying C when d is the strategy profile.

A natural way to share the weight of a clause is to cut it evenly, i.e., $f(j) = 1/j$. As in [3], we will call it the *fair payment scheme*. Every player i maximizes

$$\mathcal{P}_i(d) = \sum_{C \in \mathcal{C}} \pi(x_i, C, d) = \sum_{j=1}^{k} \frac{1}{j} W(cov_j(i, d))$$

where $cov_j(i, d)$ denotes the set of clauses satisfied by player i and exactly $j - 1$ other players. This payment has the following nice property: $\sum_{i=1}^{n} \mathcal{P}_i(d) = W(d)$.

In that case, the potential function is

$$\Phi(d) = \sum_{C \in \mathcal{C}} \sum_{l=1}^{\nu(d,C)} \frac{w(C)}{l} = \sum_{j=1}^{k} H(j) W(cov_j(d))$$

where $H(j) = 1 + \frac{1}{2} + \frac{1}{3} + \cdots + \frac{1}{j}$ and $cov_j(d)$ denotes the set of clauses satisfied by exactly j variables. Hence, the Nash equilibria of the MAX SAT game with the fair payment function are different from the local optima of the local search algorithm with the 1-neighborhood and the classical economic function $\sum_{j=1}^{k} W(cov_j(d))$.

2.4   Generalities

W.l.o.g. we will assume along the paper that $d = \{true\}^n$ is the worst Nash equilibrium[2] and d^* is an optimal truth assignment. Moreover, S (resp., S^*) will be the set of clauses that d (resp., d^*) satisfies. Thus, PoA= $W(S)/W(S^*)$ (resp., PoA= $W(S)/W(S^*)$) for the MAX $k-$SAT game (resp., MIN $k-$SAT game). We can write $\pi(x_i, C)$ instead of $\pi(x_i, C, d)$ since $d = \{true\}^n$.

Now, we define the notion of *atomic gain* which will be useful in the proofs.

Definition 1. *Given a variable $x \in X$ and a clause $C \in \mathcal{C}$, the atomic gain of x in C under the payment function f is denoted by $\gamma(x, C)$ and defined as follows:*

$$\gamma(x, C) = \begin{cases} 0 & \text{when } x \text{ does not occur in } C \\ f(j)\, w(C) & \text{when } C \text{ contains the unnegated variable } x \\ & \text{and exactly } j - 1 \text{ other unnegated variables} \\ -f(j)\, w(C) & \text{when } C \text{ contains } \bar{x} \text{ and exactly } j - 1 \text{ unnegated variables} \end{cases}$$

Actually, $\gamma(x, C)$ is x's reward when she satisfies C, otherwise this is the negative of what she would get if she changed her strategy.

3   The PoA of the MAX $k-$SAT Game

In this section, we consider the MAX $k-$SAT game with the fair payment scheme.

Theorem 1. *The PoA of the MAX E $k-$SAT game is $k/(k + 1)$, even in the unweighted case.*

Proof. Since $d = \{true\}^n$ is a NE we have $\sum_{C \in \mathcal{C}} \gamma(x, C) \geq 0$ for any $x \in X$. Summing these inequalities over all variables, we get $\sum_{C \in \mathcal{C}} \sum_{x \in X} \gamma(x, C) \geq 0$ or equivalently,

$$\sum_{C \in S} \sum_{x \in X} \gamma(x, C) \geq - \sum_{C \in S^* \setminus S} \sum_{x \in X} \gamma(x, C) - \sum_{C \in \mathcal{C} \setminus (S^* \cup S)} \sum_{x \in X} \gamma(x, C)$$

We remark that $-\sum_{C \in \mathcal{C} \setminus (S^* \cup S)} \sum_{x \in X} \gamma(x, C) \geq 0$ since each clause $C \notin S^* \cup S$ is only composed of negated variables. Thus, we get

$$\sum_{C \in S} \sum_{x \in X} \gamma(x, C) \geq - \sum_{C \in S^* \setminus S} \sum_{x \in X} \gamma(x, C) \tag{1}$$

Take any clause $C \in S^* \setminus S$. We know that C is composed of k negated variables. We have $\gamma(x, C) = -w(C)$ if $x \in C$ and $\gamma(x, C) = 0$ otherwise. Then, $\sum_{x \in X} \gamma(x, C) = -k\, w(C)$ and the following equality holds.

$$-\sum_{C \in S^* \setminus S} \sum_{x \in X} \gamma(x, C) = \sum_{C \in S^* \setminus S} k\, w(C) = k\, W(S^* \setminus S) \tag{2}$$

---

[2] One can always replace $\bar{x}$ by x and x by $\bar{x}$ in the instance if $d(x) = false$.

Now, take any clause $C \in S$. We know that C is composed of j unnegated variables $(1 \leq j \leq k)$ and $k - j$ negated variables. We have $\gamma(x, C) = \frac{1}{j}w(C)$ if x occurs unnegated in C, $\gamma(x, C) = \frac{-1}{j+1}w(C)$ if x occurs negated in C and $\gamma(x, C) = 0$ otherwise. Thus, $\sum_{x \in X} \gamma(x, C) = \left(1 - \frac{k-j}{j+1}\right)w(C) \leq w(C)$ and the following inequality holds.

$$\sum_{C \in S} \sum_{x \in X} \gamma(x, C) \leq \sum_{C \in S} w(C) = W(S) \tag{3}$$

Using (1), (2) and (3) we get $W(S) \geq kW(S^* \setminus S)$ and thus $W(S)/W(S^*) \geq k/(k+1)$.

Theorem 2. *The PoA of the* MAX k-SAT *game is* $k/(2k - 1)$, *even in the unweighted case.*

Proof. Before getting started, we modify the instance in order to characterize d^*. More precisely, if $X^+ \subseteq X$ denotes the set of variables appearing only unnegated in C, then we will prove that $d^*(x_i) = true$ if $x_i \in X^+$ and $d^*(x_i) = false$ otherwise. Moreover, we can suppose that $C = S \cup S^*$.

The transformation is the following: for all $x_i \in X$ such that $d^*(x_i) = true$, remove every occurrence of $\overline{x_i}$. It is not difficult to see that $d = \{true\}^n$ remains a NE. Moreover $W(S)$ and $W(S^*)$ are unchanged. Actually, S^* may not be optimal anymore but the PoA can only be worse. Note that by this process we will get $C \setminus (S \cup S^*) = \emptyset$. Finally, we always assume that a clause cannot be only composed of unnegated variables of X^+ (the PoA can only be worse if we delete those clauses). Let κ be a function defined as follows.

$$\kappa(x, C) = \begin{cases} \gamma(x, C) - w(C)/k & \text{when } x \in X^+ \text{ and } x \text{ occurs in } C \\ \gamma(x, C) & \text{otherwise} \end{cases}$$

We have

$$\forall x \in X, \quad \sum_{C \in S^* \cup S} \kappa(x, C) \geq 0 \tag{4}$$

Actually, it holds for any variable $x \in X \setminus X^+$ because d is a NE. Now, every $x \in X^+$ rationally plays strategy $true$ and her atomic gain is at least $w(C)/k$ in any clause C where she occurs. Summing inequalities (4) over all $x \in X$, we obtain

$$\sum_{C \in S} \sum_{x \in X} \kappa(x, C) \geq - \sum_{C \in S^* \setminus S} \sum_{x \in X} \kappa(x, C) \tag{5}$$

Let C be a clause of $S^* \setminus S$. We know that C is only composed of negated variables belonging to $X \setminus X^+$. For every variable x appearing in C, we have $\kappa(x, C) = \gamma(x, C) = -w(C)$. Hence, we have $\sum_{x \in X} \kappa(x, C) = -\sigma(C)w(C) \leq -w(C)$ from which we obtain

$$- \sum_{C \in S^* \setminus S} \sum_{x \in X} \kappa(x, C) \geq W(S^* \setminus S) \tag{6}$$

Now, we prove the following inequality.

$$\sum_{C \in S} \sum_{x \in X} \kappa(x, C) \le \frac{k-1}{k} W(S \cap S^*) + W(S \setminus S^*) \tag{7}$$

Let C be a clause of S. If C only contains unnegated variables, i.e., $C = x_1 \vee \cdots \vee x_p$ for some $p \le k$, then we consider two cases:

- $C \in S \setminus S^*$. All variables in C are set to *false* by d^*. Then, they all belong to $X \setminus X^+$ and $\sum_{x \in X} \kappa(x, C) = \sum_{x \in X} \gamma(x, C) = w(C)$.

- $C \in S \cap S^*$. At least one variable in C, say x_1 w.l.o.g., is set to *true* by d^*. Then, $x_1 \in X^+$ and $\sum_{x \in X} \kappa(x, C) \le \sum_{x \in X \setminus \{x_1\}} \gamma(x, C) + \kappa(x_1, C) \le \sum_{x \in X} \gamma(x, C) - \frac{w(C)}{k} = \frac{k-1}{k} w(C)$.

If C contains both unnegated and negated variables, i.e., $C = x_1 \vee \cdots \vee x_j \vee \overline{x}_{j+1} \vee \cdots \vee \overline{x}_p$ with $1 \le j \le p-1 \le k-1$, then $\{x_{j+1}, \ldots, x_p\} \subseteq X \setminus X^+$. We have $C \in S \cap S^*$ and
$\sum_{x \in X} \kappa(x, C) \le \sum_{i=1}^{p} \gamma(x_i, C) - \frac{p-j}{j+1} w(C) = w(C) - \frac{p-j}{j+1} w(C) \le \frac{k-1}{k} w(C)$.

Inequality (7) holds because $\sum_{x \in X} \kappa(x, C) \le w(C)$ for all $C \in S \setminus S^*$ and $\sum_{x \in X} \kappa(x, C) \le \frac{k-1}{k} w(C)$ for all $C \in S \cap S^*$. Using inequalities (5), (6) and (7), we get $W(S^* \setminus S) \le \frac{k-1}{k} W(S \cap S^*) + W(S \setminus S^*)$. Thus, $k\, W(S^*) \le (2k-1) W(S)$. The following instance of the unweighted case shows the tightness of the analysis: $C_i = y_i \vee x_1 \vee x_2 \vee \ldots \vee x_{k-1}$ for $i = 1, \ldots, k$, and $C_{k+i} = \overline{x_i}$ for $i = 1, \ldots, k-1$.

Corollary 1. *The price of anarchy of the* MAX SAT *game is* $1/2$ *with the fair payment scheme, even in the unweighted case.*

4 The PoA with Non Oblivious Payment Functions

First, we analyze a parameterized payment function for the MAX E 2− SAT game where $f(1) = 1$ and $f(2) = \varepsilon$.[3]

Theorem 3. *The PoA of the* MAX E 2− SAT *game is* $\frac{2}{3-\varepsilon}$ *if* $\varepsilon \in [0; 1/3]$ *and* $\frac{1}{1+\varepsilon}$ *if* $\varepsilon \in [1/3; 1]$. *Moreover, these ratios are tight even in the unweighted case.*

Using Theorem 3, we deduce that $\varepsilon = 1/3$ gives the best payment scheme for the MAX E 2− SAT game and the corresponding PoA is $3/4$. The potential function of the game is $\Phi(d) = W(S_1) + \frac{4}{3} W(S_2)$ where $W(S_i)$ is the weight of clauses satisfied by i literals, $i = 1, 2$. The correspondence with non oblivious local search is now clear since Khanna et al [11] use $\frac{3}{2} W(S_1) + 2 W(S_2) = \frac{3}{2} \Phi(d)$ to guide their local search procedure.

We can undertake the same analysis for the MAX E $k-$ SAT game but the resulting expression is not simple. Thus, we directly propose the function leading

---

[3] We restrict ourselves to $0 \le \varepsilon \le 1$ because a simple instance shows that the PoA$\le$ $1/2$ if $\varepsilon \ge 1$: $x \vee y$ and $\overline{x} \vee \overline{y}$.

to the best PoA: when exactly j variables satisfy a clause C, each of them receives $\alpha_j^{\sigma(C)} w(C)$ where $\sigma(C)$ is the size of C. Here, $(\alpha_j^k)_{j=1..k}$ is a sequence defined by $\alpha_j^k = \frac{k}{j(2^k-1)} + \frac{(k-j)}{j}\alpha_{j+1}^k$ which satisfies $\alpha_k^k = \frac{1}{2^k-1}$ and $\alpha_1^k = 1$. The atomic gain $\gamma(x,C)$ is 0 when x does not appear in C, $\alpha_j^{\sigma(C)} w(C)$ when C contains the unnegated variable x and exactly $j-1$ other unnegated variables, and $-\alpha_j^{\sigma(C)} w(C)$ when C contains $\overline{x}$ and exactly $j-1$ unnegated variables.

Theorem 4. *The PoA of the* MAX E $k-$ SAT *game with the non oblivious payment scheme is* $1 - 1/2^k$, *even in the unweighted case.*

Interestingly, the proposed non oblivious payment scheme gives the best possible PoA for the MAX E $k-$ SAT game since there exists a family of instances of the (unweighted) MAX E $k-$ SAT game such that PoA= $1 - 1/2^k$.

We now propose a sequence $\widetilde{\alpha}_j^k$ leading to the best possible payment scheme (according to the definition of Subsection 2.2) for the MAX $k-$SAT game: $\widetilde{\alpha}_1^k = 1$ and $\widetilde{\alpha}_j^k = \frac{1}{2(\sigma(C)-1)}$ for $j = 2, \ldots, k$.

Theorem 5. *The PoA of the* MAX $k-$ SAT *game with payment function* $f(j) = \widetilde{\alpha}_j^k$ *is* $2/3$, *even in the unweighted case.*

Proof. We first modify the instance as done in the proof of Theorem 2 and use a function κ defined as follows:

$$\kappa(x,C) = \begin{cases} \gamma(x,C) - \frac{1}{2(\sigma(C)-1)} & \text{when } x \in X^+ \text{ and } x \text{ occurs in } C \\ \gamma(x,C) & \text{otherwise} \end{cases}$$

We remark that inequalities (5) and (6) still hold. Now, we prove the following inequality:

$$\sum_{C \in S} \sum_{x \in X} \kappa(x,C) \le \frac{1}{2}W(S \cap S^*) + W(S \setminus S^*) \tag{8}$$

Let C be a clause of S. If C only contains unnegated variables, i.e., $C = x_1 \vee \cdots \vee x_p$ for some $p \le k$, then we consider two cases:

- $C \in S \setminus S^*$. All variables in C are set to *false* by d^*. Then, they all belong to $X \setminus X^+$ and $\sum_{x \in X} \kappa(x,C) = \sum_{x \in X} \gamma(x,C) \le w(C)$.

- $C \in S \cap S^*$. At least one variable in C, say x_1 w.l.o.g., is set to *true* by d^*. This means $x_1 \in X^+$. Moreover, we know that $p \ge 2$ (otherwise, C will be only composed of variables of X^+). We have $\sum_{x \in X} \kappa(x,C) \le \frac{p}{2(p-1)} w(C) - \frac{1}{2(p-1)}w(C) = \frac{1}{2}w(C)$.

If C contains both unnegated and negated variables, i.e., $C = x_1 \vee \cdots \vee x_j \vee \overline{x}_{j+1} \vee \cdots \vee \overline{x}_p$ with $1 \le j \le p-1 \le k-1$, then $\{x_{j+1}, \ldots, x_p\} \subseteq X \setminus X^+$. Thus, we have $C \in S \cap S^*$.

If $j = 1$, then $\sum_{x \in X} \kappa(x, C) = (1 - \frac{p-1}{2(p-1)})w(C) = \frac{1}{2}w(C)$. Otherwise, $j \geq 2$ and then $p \geq 3$. We have $\sum_{x \in X} \kappa(x, C) = (\frac{j}{2(p-1)} - \frac{p-j}{2(p-1)})w(C) \leq \frac{p-2}{2(p-1)}w(C) \leq \frac{1}{2}w(C)$.

Inequality (8) holds because $\sum_{x \in X} \kappa(x, C) \leq w(C)$ whenever $C \in S \setminus S^*$ and $\sum_{x \in X} \kappa(x, C) \leq \frac{1}{2}w(C)$ whenever $C \in S \cap S^*$.

Using inequalities (5), (6) and (8), we get $W(S^* \setminus S) \leq \frac{1}{2}W(S \cap S^*) + W(S \setminus S^*)$ which, with simple calculus, gives $2\,W(S^*) \leq 3\,W(S)$.

Finally, consider the following instance of the unweighted MAX $k-$ SAT problem: $C_1 = \overline{x}$, $C_2 = x \vee \overline{y}$ and $C_3 = y \vee z$. When each variable plays *true* then they are at a NE satisfying two clauses, whatever how f is defined. If x and y play *false* while z plays *true*, three clauses are satisfied. Thus, the non oblivious payment function given here is the best possible.

Corollary 2. *The PoA of the* MAX SAT *game is 2/3 with the non oblivious payment scheme, even in the unweighted case.*

Corollary 3. *There exists a polynomial time local search algorithm with locality gap 2/3 for the unweighted* MAX $-k$ SAT *problem.*

Proof. Use the potential function w.r.t. the non oblivious payment $\widetilde{\alpha}_j^k$ as economic function and the 1-neighborhood: $\Phi(\tau) = \sum_{j=1}^{m} \frac{2k + j - 3}{2k - 2} cov_j(\tau).$

5   The PoS of the MAX $k-$SAT Game

We investigate the price of stability [3] of the MAX SAT game. We were able to present non trivial instances in which each player possesses a *strictly dominant strategy* (a strategy strictly better than the others, whatever the other players choose). In such instances, only one NE exists, hence PoA=PoS. We restrict ourselves to the fair and non oblivious payment schemes; however there exists a payment scheme with PoS= 1.[4]

Theorem 6. *The PoS of the* MAX E $k-$ SAT *game with the fair payment scheme is $k/(k + 1)$ for large enough instances. It is $1 - 1/2^k$ with the non oblivious payment scheme using $f(j) = \alpha_j^k$.*

One can remark that the PoS of the MAX $k-$ SAT game is 2/3 when $k = 2$ by Theorem 6.

Theorem 7. *The PoS of the* MAX $k-$ SAT *game with the fair payment scheme is at most $\frac{k+1}{2k}$.*

Since $\widetilde{\alpha}_j^k$ corresponds to the fair payment scheme when $k = 2$ and MAX E $2-$ SAT is a particular case of MAX $k-$ SAT, Theorem 6 gives the following result.

---

[4] Set $f(1) = 1$ and $f(i) = 0$, for $i \neq 1$. The potential function $\Phi(d)$ is $\sum_{j=1}^{m} W(cov_j(d))$. Hence, any NE – a local optimum w.r.t. Φ – is a global optimum.

Corollary 4. *The price of stability of the* MAX $k-$ SAT *game with the non oblivious payment scheme using* $f(j) = \tilde{\alpha}_j^k$ *is* 2/3 *for large enough instances.*

6   On a MIN $k-$ SAT Game

We consider the minimization version of the SAT game. Instead of giving rewards, the system uses penalties proportionnal to the weight of the clauses. All variables satisfying a clause evenly share its price/weight. Now, each variable x_i tries to minimize $\mathcal{P}_i(d) = \sum_{j=1}^{k} \frac{1}{j} W(cov_j(i,d))$. We call it the *fair penalty scheme.*

Any instance with at most k literals per clause can be turned into a new one with exactly k literals per clause such that a NE remains a NE and an optimum remains optimal: just add $k - j$ new negated variables to each clause with j literals. These new variables only appear negated so they must be set to *true* in any truth assignment at NE. Thus, the MIN $k-$ SAT and the MIN E $k-$ SAT games have the same PoA and PoS.

Let I be the following (unweighted) instance of the MIN $k-$ SAT game: $C_0 = \overline{x}_1 \vee \cdots \vee \overline{x}_k$ and $C_i = x_i$ for $i = 1, \ldots, k$. The truth assignment $\{true\}^n$ is a NE with total weight k while $\{false\}^n$ satisfies only one clause. It shows that the PoA is a least k. In fact, PoA= k.

Theorem 8. *The PoA of the* MIN $k-$ SAT *and the* MIN E $k-$ SAT *games with the fair penalty scheme is* k, *even in the unweighted case.*

Using I, it is not difficult to see that no penalty scheme, as defined in Subsection 2.2, can improve the PoA of the MIN $k-$ SAT game since when players are at NE $d = \{true\}^k$, we have $\forall i \ \mathcal{P}_i(d) = \mathcal{P}_i(d_{-i}, false) = f(1)$.

Let I' be the following weighted instance of the MIN $k-$ SAT game (an equivalent unweighted instance exists) and consider the fair penalty scheme: $C_0 = \overline{x}_1 \vee \cdots \vee \overline{x}_k$ with $w(C_0) = 1 + \varepsilon$ and $C_i = x_i$ with $w(C_i) = 1/i$ for $i = 1, \ldots, k$. If $H(k) > \varepsilon > 0$, it is not difficult to see that $d^* = \{false\}^k$ is optimal but not at NE. Indeed, if $d = \{false\}^k$ then x_k will change her strategy and improve her utility (from $(1+\varepsilon)/k$ to $1/k$). After, x_{k-1} will also change her strategy and improve her utility (from $(1 + \varepsilon)/(k - 1)$ to $1/(k - 1)$) and so on. Actually, $d = \{true\}^k$ is the only NE; its total weight is $1 + 1/2 + \cdots + 1/k$. As ε tends to 0, the PoS is at best $H(k)$. In fact, PoS= $H(k)$.

Theorem 9. *The PoS of the* MIN $k-$ SAT *game with the fair penalty scheme is* $H(k) = 1 + \frac{1}{2} + \frac{1}{3} + \ldots + \frac{1}{k}$.

7   Concluding Remarks

We focused on pure strategies but it would be interesting to extend the results to mixed Nash equilibria. Remark that we were not able to build an instance where mixed strategies yield a worse PoA. It would also be interesting to state if the PoA remains unchanged if some sets of agents (a coalition), controlling their variable, could cooperate to improve their payoff.

References

1. Alimonti, P.: New Local Search Approximation Techniques for Maximum Generalized Satisfiability Problems. In: Bonuccelli, M.A., Crescenzi, P.P., Petreschi, R. (eds.) CIAC 1994. LNCS, vol. 778, pp. 40–53. Springer, Heidelberg (1994)
2. Battiti, R., Protasi, M.: Approximate Algorithms and Heuristics for MAX-SAT. In: Du, D.-Z., Pardalos, P.M. (eds.) Handbook of combinatorial optimization, vol. 1, pp. 77–148. Kluwer Academic Publishers, Dordrecht (1998)
3. Anshelevich, E., Dasgupta, A., Kleinberg, J.M., Tardos, É., Wexler, T., Roughgarden, T.: The Price of Stability for Network Design with Fair Cost Allocation. In: Proc. of FOCS 2004, pp. 295–304 (2004)
4. Bilò, V.: On Satisfiability Games and the Power of Congestion Games. In: Proc. of AAIM 2007. LNCS, vol. 4508, pp. 231–240 (2007)
5. Christodoulou, G., Koutsoupias, E.: On the Price of Anarchy and Stability of Correlated Equilibria of Linear Congestion Games. In: Brodal, G.S., Leonardi, S. (eds.) ESA 2005. LNCS, vol. 3669, pp. 59–70. Springer, Heidelberg (2005)
6. Christodoulou, G., Koutsoupias, E.: The Price of Anarchy of Finite Congestion Games. In: Proc. of STOC 2005, pp. 67–73 (2005)
7. Christodoulou, G., Koutsoupias, E., Nanavati, A.: Coordination Mechanisms. In: Díaz, J., Karhumäki, J., Lepistö, A., Sannella, D. (eds.) ICALP 2004. LNCS, vol. 3142, pp. 345–357. Springer, Heidelberg (2004)
8. Czumaj, A., Vöcking, B.: Tight bounds for worst-case equilibria. In: Proc. of SODA 2002, pp. 413–420 (2002)
9. Devanur, N.R., Garg, N., Khandekar, R., Pandit, V., Saberi, A., Vazirani, V.V.: Price of Anarchy, Locality Gap, and a Network Service Provider Game. In: Deng, X., Ye, Y. (eds.) WINE 2005. LNCS, vol. 3828, pp. 1046–1055. Springer, Heidelberg (2005)
10. Fabrikant, A., Papadimitriou, C.H., Talwar, K.: The complexity of pure Nash equilibria. In: Proc. of STOC 2004, pp. 604–612 (2004)
11. Khanna, S., Motwani, R., Sudan, M., Vazirani, U.V.: On Syntactic versus Computational Views of Approximability. SIAM Journal on Computing 28(1), 164–191 (1998)
12. Koutsoupias, E., Papadimitriou, C.: Worst Case Equilibria. In: Meinel, C., Tison, S. (eds.) STACS 1999. LNCS, vol. 1563, pp. 404–413. Springer, Heidelberg (1999)
13. Monderer, D., Shapley, L.S.: Potential Games. Games and Economic Behavior 14, 124–143 (1996)
14. Papadimitriou, C.H.: Algorithms, games, and the internet. In: Proc. of STOC 2001, pp. 749–753 (2001)
15. Roughgarden, T., Tardos, É.: How bad is selfish routing? In: Proc. of FOCS 2000, pp. 93–102 (2000)
16. Rosenthal, R.W.: A class of games possessing pure-strategy Nash equilibria. International Journal of Game Theory 2(1), 65–67 (1973)

Incentive-Compatible Interdomain Routing with Linear Utilities*

Alexander Hall[1], Evdokia Nikolova[2], and Christos Papadimitriou[1]

[1] UC Berkeley, USA
alex.hall@gmail.com, christos@cs.berkeley.edu
[2] MIT CSAIL, USA
nikolova@mit.edu

Abstract. We revisit the problem of incentive-compatible interdomain routing, examining the, quite realistic, special case in which the autonomous systems' (ASes') utilities are linear functions of the traffic in the incident links, and the traffic leaving each AS. We show that incentive-compatibility towards maximizing total welfare is achievable efficiently, and, in the uncapacitated case, by an algorithm that can be implemented by BGP, the standard protocol for interdomain routing.

1 Introduction

The Internet is in many ways a mysterious object, a complex wonder which we must approach with the same puzzled humility with which neuroscientists approach the brain and biologists the cell. Even at the most basic level of routing, for example, it is not clear at all how and why the approximately 20,000 independent, and presumably selfish, autonomous systems (ASes) cooperate to provide connectivity between any two of them. The problem is quintessentially economic. ASes are known to have confidential financial agreements on how traffic between them is to be handled and paid for, and such agreements are reflected in the ways in which each AS routes traffic. We can think of the ASes as nodes of an undirected graph, with edges signifying the existence of such an agreement between the two endpoints (equivalently, the possibility of traffic routed directly between the two). In particular, ASes communicate in terms of the border gateway protocol (BGP), a flexible protocol allowing them to implement routing decisions of arbitrary complexity, by "advertising" paths to adjacent ASes, and selecting among the paths advertised by their neighbors. Hence, the Internet is in its essence an economy, a game, an arena where agents act selfishly and are affected by everybody's decisions; consequently, one can ask of it the questions we usually ask of such systems, for example the price of anarchy, or the possibility of incentive-compatible maximization of social welfare (questions typically studied by algorithmic mechanism design [18]); in this paper we address the latter.

* The authors were supported through: NSF grant CCF - 0635319, a gift from Yahoo! Research, a MICRO grant, the American Foundation for Bulgaria Fellowship, and a fellowship by the Swiss National Science Foundation PA002 - 113170 / 1.

X. Deng and F.C. Graham (Eds.): WINE 2007, LNCS 4858, pp. 232–244, 2007.
© Springer-Verlag Berlin Heidelberg 2007

Indeed, starting with Feigenbaum *et al.* [10], BGP has been studied in the past under the lens of algorithmic mechanism design, and in particular in terms of the Vickrey-Clarke-Groves (VCG) mechanism (see, e.g., [17] for an introduction to mechanism design). It was noticed [10] that social welfare can be optimized in routing, if one assumes that each AS has a fixed per packet cost, via the VCG mechanism with payments; and in fact, that this can be achieved in a way that is very "BGP-friendly," i.e., can be implemented by minimal disruption of BGP's ordinary operation. Furthermore, it was observed that in the real Internet VCG would result in relatively very small overpayments.

In a subsequent paper [12], the problem of more realistic BGP routing was addressed in the same spirit. Each AS was assumed to have a utility for each path to the destination (assumed in this literature to be a fixed node 0), and the goal is to maximize total utility. It was shown that the problem is too hard to solve in general even with no consideration to incentive compatibility, while a special case, in which the utility of a path only depends on the next hop, is easy to solve in an incentive-compatible way, but hard to implement on BGP. To show this latter negative result, the authors of [12] formalize what it means for an algorithm to be "BGP-friendly": roughly speaking, a local distributed algorithm with quick convergence, small storage needs, and no rippling updates in case of small parameter changes. All said, the message of Feigenbaum, Shenker and Sami [12] was that, if one models BGP routing a little more realistically, incentive compatibility becomes problematic. This negative message was ameliorated in [11], where it was pointed out that, if one further restricts the special case of next-hop utilities so that paths are required to be of a particular kind mandated by the kinds of inter-AS agreements seen in practice, called *valley-free* in this paper, BGP-friendly incentive compatibility is restored.

There is an extensive literature on BGP (see, e.g., [9,14,16,20,21,22]). The protocol has also been examined within other game-theoretic contexts, such as with respect to network creation games, e.g., [2,7], cooperative game theory [19], and BGP oscillation prediction [8].

In this paper we present an elementary model of BGP routing. The key feature of our model is that *path preferences are based exclusively on per packet costs and per packet agreed-upon compensation* between *adjacent* nodes. In other words, we look into the utilities of each path to each AS, taken as raw data in previous literature, and postulate that they are linear functions of the traffic, depending on two factors: Objective per packet costs to each AS for each incoming or outgoing link, and agreed per packet payment, positive or negative, to the AS for this link and direction. As a result, social welfare optimization becomes a min-cost flow problem, and incentive-compatibility can always be achieved in polynomial time. If there are no capacity constraints, we show (Theorem 1) that the resulting algorithm is BGP-friendly, essentially because the BGP-friendly version of the Bellman-Ford algorithm in [10] can be extended to cover this case. When capacities are present, the algorithm becomes a more generic min-cost flow computation (Theorem 2), and, as we show by a counterexample, does not adhere to the criteria of BGP-friendliness (it may not converge fast enough), even though it is still a local, distributed algorithm with modest memory requirements and no need for global data. If, on top of this, we also require that the paths be of the "valley-free" kind suggested by the kinds of agreements between ASes one sees in practice (that is, the kind of restriction which led to tractability in [11]), the resulting algorithm solves a rather generic linear program (Theorem 3), and so local, distributed computation appears to be impossible.

2 Basic Model and the VCG Mechanism

We model interdomain routing as a symmetric directed network with node set $V = \{0, 1, ..., n\}$ and edges E, where node 0 is the given destination, assumed unique as is common in this literature. Note that we postulate that the network is symmetric, in that if $(i, j) \in E$ then also $(j, i) \in E$. There are no self-loops. Each node i has a *demand* of k_i packets it wants to send to the destination. In addition, each node i has a *per packet value* $v_{i,e}$ (sometimes also denoted as $v_i(e)$) for each of its incident edges e, and a value π_i for each of its packets that gets delivered. The *cost* of an edge $e = (i, j) \in E$ is the negative of the sum of values of i and j for it, $p_e = -(v_{i,e} + v_{j,e})$.

We denote by θ_i the *type* of node i, that is the collection of values for its incident edges and its value per packet delivery. Denote by θ the vector of all node types and by θ_{-i} the vector of all node types except that of node i.

If F is an integer-valued flow through this network, with sink 0 and sources at all other nodes with the given demands, then the utility of each node $i \neq 0$ from this flow is $v_i(F, \theta_i) = \sum_j v_i(i, j)F(i, j) + \sum_j v_i(j, i)F(j, i) + \pi_i F_i$, where by $F_i = \sum_j F(i, j) - \sum_j F(j, i)$ we denote the flow out of i, assumed to be at most k_i. The total welfare of F is $W(F) = \sum_{i \in V \setminus \{0\}} \pi_i F_i - \sum_{e \in E} p_e F(e)$. Let $F^*(\theta)$ be the optimum, with respect to W, flow for types θ; we denote $W(F^*(\theta))$ simply by $W^*(\theta)$; $W^*(\theta_{-i})$ is the welfare of the optimum flow when node i is deleted from the network. We assume initially that all capacities are infinite, which implies that the optimum flow is the union of n or fewer flow-weighted source-to-sink shortest paths; this assumption is removed in Section 2.2.

2.1 VCG Mechanism

Notice that in order to compute the optimum flow we need to know the types of all players; the difficulty is, of course, that the type of player $i > 0$ is known only to player i, who is not inclined to publicize it in the absence of appropriate incentives. The *VCG mechanism* for this problem incentivizes the players to reveal their true types, and thus participate in a socially optimum flow, by making payments to them. Let $|a|_{[b \geq 0]} = a$ for $b \geq 0$ and $|a|_{[b \geq 0]} = 0$ otherwise. Consider in particular the following transfers for each node (negative for payments made by the node and positive for payments received by the node).

$$t_i(\theta) = \left[\sum_{j\neq i} v_j(F^*(\theta), \theta_j)\right] - \left[\sum_{j\neq i} v_j(F^*(\theta_{-i}), \theta_j)\right]$$

$$= \sum_{j\neq i} k_j \cdot \left(|\pi_j - P_j^{-i}|_{[\pi_j - P_j \geq 0]} - |\pi_j - P_{j,-i}|_{[\pi_j - P_{j,-i} \geq 0]}\right),$$

where $P_{j,-i}$ is the cost of the cheapest path from j to 0 which does not go through node i. P_j^{-i} is the cost of the cheapest path p_j from j to 0 without taking costs potentially incurred by i into account: if $i \notin p_j$, $P_j^{-i} = P_j$, otherwise $P_j^{-i} = P_j + (v_{i,e_1} + v_{i,e_2})$ with $e_1, e_2 \in p_j$ denoting the edges incident to i.

The proof that these transfers lead to truthful reporting is the corresponding proof about the Groves mechanism in [17] specialized to the current situation. We repeat it here for completeness:

Proof. Suppose truth is not a dominant strategy for some node i, that is the node gets higher utility by reporting a collection of values $\hat{\theta}_i$ different from his true values θ_i when the other nodes report θ_{-i}. The utility of the node is its welfare plus the transfer imposed by the mechanism: $v_i(F^*(\hat{\theta}_i, \theta_{-i}), \theta_i) + t_i(\hat{\theta}_i, \theta_{-i}) > v_i(F^*(\theta), \theta_i) + t_i(\theta_i, \theta_{-i})$.

Substituting the form of the transfer on both sides and canceling identical terms, we get $v_i(F^*(\hat{\theta}_i, \theta_{-i}), \theta_i) + \left[\sum_{j\neq i} v_j(F^*(\hat{\theta}_i, \theta_{-i}), \theta_j)\right] > v_i(F^*(\theta), \theta_i) + \left[\sum_{j\neq i} v_j(F^*(\theta), \theta_j)\right] \Leftrightarrow W(F^*(\hat{\theta}_i, \theta_{-i}), \theta) > W(F^*(\theta), \theta)$. The last inequality contradicts the fact that $F^*(\theta)$ is the welfare maximizing choice of paths (*i.e.,* the least cost paths) for node types θ.   □

2.2   The Model with Capacities

In this subsection we consider the same basic model, with the addition that each edge e has a corresponding capacity c_e. We would like to find a min-cost (multicommodity) flow from all nodes to the sink 0, satisfying the demands of the nodes. We can transform the problem to an equivalent one by adding a new node—a supersource, which is connected to each node j via an edge of cost $-\pi_j$ and capacity equal to the demand k_j at node j.

Call the resulting min-cost flow with known types θ by $F^*(\theta)$, and denote the min-cost flow in the graph with node i removed as $F^*(\theta_{-i})$. We can now get a VCG mechanism similar to the one in the basic model above. As before, the total welfare is $W(F^*(\theta), \theta) = \sum_i v_i(F^*(\theta), \theta_i)$, where $v_i(F^*(\theta), \theta_i)$ is the value of the flow from i (more precisely, from the supersource through i) to 0. Similarly, the VCG mechanism is specified by the transfers

$$t_i(\theta) = \left[\sum_{j\neq i} v_j(F^*(\theta), \theta_j)\right] - \left[\sum_{j\neq i} v_j(F^*_{-i}(\theta_{-i}), \theta_j)\right]$$

and a proof of truthfulness of the mechanism follows as before.

3   Economic Relationships

The economic relationships between individual ASes in the Internet severely influence the paths which can be taken in the BGP graph. So far we assumed that all paths which are present in the underlying undirected graph (there is an edge between two ASes, if they are connected by a physical link) are valid. In reality this is not the case. Routing policies which are based on the economic relationships between ASes forbid many paths which theoretically exist. Inferring these economic relationships and investigating the resulting consequences for the connectivity of the BGP graph have attracted a large amount of scientific interest recently, see, e.g., [1,3,4,6,14,15,22].

Below we will give a detailed description of the valley-free path model which classifies the prohibited paths in the BGP graph.

The Valley-Free Path Model. In this model there are basically three different types of relationships a pair of connected ASes can be in: either *customer-provider*, in which the customer pays the provider to obtain access to the Internet, or *peer-peer*, in which both peers agree on mutually routing traffic of their customers for each other free of charge, or *sibling*, in which both siblings agree on mutually routing any traffic for each other free of charge. Note that an individual AS may take several roles—as customer, provider, sibling, or peer—simultaneously; it can for instance be a customer of one AS and at the same time a provider for another AS.

In the following for ease of exposition we will focus on customer-provider relationships only. The other types of relationships (peer-peer, sibling) can be incorporated easily, as we will note in Section 4.3.

We call a directed graph $G = (V, E)$ a *ToR graph*, if it contains no self loops and the edge directions describe the economic relationships. If the AS v is a customer of a provider AS w, we direct the edge between v and w towards w. This follows the terminology of [22].

In practice routing is done in the following way. If AS w is a provider of v (i.e. $(v, w) \in E$) it announces all its routes to v, but AS v on the other hand only announces its own routes and the routes of its customers to w. In other words, the customer v essentially advertizes only its incomming links to the provider w. The idea behind this is that v pays w for the connection and thus is not inclined to take over "work" for w. This would happen if v also announced the routes it has from other providers. Then it would potentially have to donate bandwidth to packets that arrive from the provider w, only to proceed to another provider.

This leads to the model proposed in [22] that a path p is *valid* if and only if it consists of a sequence of customer-provider edges (●—▶●) followed by a sequence of provider-customer edges (●◀—●). The first part, containing only customer-provider edges, is also called the *forward part* of p. The last part, containing only provider-customer edges, is called the *backward part* of p. It is easy to see that the following is an equivalent definition of the validity of a path:

A path $p = v_1, e_1, v_2, e_2, \cdots, e_{r-1}, v_r$ in the ToR graph G is a *valid v_1-v_r-path* in G, if and only if there is no inner node v_i of p for which e_{i-1} and e_i are outgoing edges of v_i.

If such an inner node—one which does have this property—exists, it is called a *valley*. The intuition behind this name is that outgoing edges point "upwards", out of the valley. In the literature the situation that a path contains a valley is also called an *anomaly*. A flow which only uses valley-free paths we call a *valid* or *valley-free* flow.

The VCG mechanism. The transfers can be specified as in Section 2.2 for the model with capacities. The only difference is that all flows (i.e., F^* and F^*_{-i} for all i) must be valley-free (and may be fractional).

4 Distributed Computation of VCG Payments

It is of great interest to determine to what extent the payments $t_i(\theta)$ can be computed not only efficiently, but in a distributed manner which is "BGP-friendly," that is, compatible with current usage of the BGP protocol. In [12] this concept of "BGP-friendliness" was formalized as three requirements:

1. The algorithm should converge in a number of rounds that is proportional to the diameter of the graph, and not its size.
2. Only local data should be needed.
3. No rippling updates should be needed as data changes.

Here we relax requirement (1) to a number of rounds that is proportional to the diameter times R, where R is the ratio between the largest and smallest edge cost. This is necessary (also in [12], where the stricter version is used by oversight) because the computed shortest path, whose length is the upper bound on convergence time, may be longer than the diameter. We do not bother to formalize here the second and third requirement (the reader is referred to [12]) because our algorithms either trivially satisfy any conceivable version, or fail to satisfy (1). As it turns out, this important aspect of BGP-friendliness sets the basic model apart from the model with capacities. In both cases the implementation is quite simple and makes only modest use of local resources. But only in the former case the strict conditions on the convergence time are fulfilled.

4.1 Basic Model

For the basic model it is easy to adapt the approach presented by Feigenbaum et al. [10]. BGP is a *path-vector* protocol which computes the lowest-cost paths (LCPs) in a sequence of stages. In a stage each node in the network sends all the LCPs it knows of to its neighbors. It also receives LCPs from its neighbors. If these contain shorter paths than the ones it has currently stored, it updates the list of its own LCPs. This basically corresponds to a distributed computation of all shortest paths via the Bellman-Ford algorithm. The computation terminates after d stages and involves $O(nd)$ communication on any edge, where d denotes the maximum number of edges on an LCP.

Feigenbaum et al. give an interesting and easy to implement extension of the path-vector protocol which computes not only the lowest cost paths, but at the same time the lowest cost paths which do not traverse a given node i. These two quantities are then used to compute the payments for node i. This increases the number of stages and communication needed to d' and $O(nd')$, respectively. Here d' denotes the maximum number of edges on an LCP avoiding node i, over all nodes i for which $G \setminus \{i\}$ is still connected. Feigenbaum et al. argue that this is still an acceptable convergence time.

The only difference of the approach in [10] to ours is that the per packet values in our model are given individually for each edge and node, i.e., as $v_{i,e}$, and not only as one total value per node.[1] Hence, it is easy to adapt their method to compute the values P_j and $P_{j,-i}$, for $j, i \in \{1, \ldots, n\}$, which is all we need to compute $t_i(\theta) = \sum_{j \neq i} (P_{j,-i} - P_j^{-i}) k_j$. Note that the partial path cost P_j^{-i} can be easily derived from the cost P_j of the cheapest path from j to the sink.

Let $\mathrm{diam}'(G)$ denote the maximum diameter of $G \setminus \{i\}$ (as d', measured in number of edges) over all nodes i for which $G \setminus \{i\}$ is still connected. Since $d' \leq \mathrm{diam}'(G) \cdot R$, where R is the ratio between the largest and smallest edge cost, we obtain the following theorem.

Theorem 1. *In the basic per packet utility model without capacity constraints (described in Section 2) the Vickrey-Clarke-Groves allocation and payments can be computed in a distributed, BGP-friendly manner. The computation converges in $O(\mathrm{diam}'(G) \cdot R)$ rounds of communication.*

4.2 Model with Capacities

Instead of lowest cost paths and lowest cost paths avoiding node i, we now need to know a min-cost flow $F(\theta)$ and a min-cost flow $F_{-i}(\theta)$ avoiding node i for each of the payments $t_i(\theta)$, $i \in \{1, \ldots, n\}$. In the following we will explain how to compute $F(\theta)$ in a distributed fashion. The flow $F_{-i}(\theta)$ can be computed correspondingly by blocking node i. Therefore, altogether $(n+1)$ flow computations are performed, one for $F(\theta)$ and n for the $F_{-i}(\theta)$, $i \in V \setminus \{0\}$.

We assume the sink 0 controls all the computations: it chooses which node is blocked (in the $F_{-i}(\theta)$ case), it selects paths to send flow along together with the corresponding amounts, and it recognizes when a min-cost flow computation is finished. These all are computationally simple tasks. The only intensive computations needed will be those to obtain the shortest paths with respect to certain costs and where certain edges may be blocked. These will be done in a distributed manner applying the standard distributed Bellman-Ford algorithm, which is used by BGP as mentioned above.

---

[1] This allows for more fine-granular and thus more realistic modeling.

Distributed Computation of $F(\theta)$. We start with a description of a simple Ford-Fulkerson approach [13] of computing a min-cost flow from the supersource to the sink via augmenting shortest paths. Then we explain how to modify it to use the Edmonds-Karp scaling technique [5].

A virtual residual graph is overlayed over the given network. The residual edge capacities and costs are derived from the original graph. The residual capacities depend on the flow present on the corresponding residual edges and thus may change during the computation of the flow. Each node keeps track of flow values on residual edges incident to it.

Consider an original pair of directed edges (i,j) and (j,i) with costs $p_{(i,j)}$ and $p_{(j,i)}$. We assume the costs to be greater or equal to 0. Let $f_{(i,j)}$ and $f_{(j,i)}$ denote the flow amounts on these edges, only one of which may be greater 0. Otherwise, a circular flow of $\min(f_{(i,j)}, f_{(j,i)})$ is subtracted from both without increasing the costs. The residual capacities are set to $c'_{(i,j)} = c_{(i,j)} - f_{(i,j)}$ and $c'_{(j,i)} = c_{(j,i)} - f_{(j,i)}$. Additionally, we add the virtual edges $\overline{(i,j)}$ and $\overline{(j,i)}$ with capacities $c_{\overline{(i,j)}} = f_{(j,i)}$ and $c_{\overline{(j,i)}} = f_{(i,j)}$ and costs $p_{\overline{(i,j)}} = -p_{(i,j)}$ and $p_{\overline{(j,i)}} = -p_{(j,i)}$. Flow sent onto these edges is subtracted from the corresponding flow on the edge in the opposite direction. Finally, for each $i \in V \setminus \{0\}$ a virtual edge is added from the supersource to node i with cost $-\pi_i$.

The algorithm now proceeds as follows, steps 2-4 comprise a phase.

1. For each node $i \in V$ initialize the flow values $f_{(i,j)} = f_{(j,i)} = 0$ of all incident residual edges. Update the local capacities as described above.
2. Compute the shortest paths in the current residual graph only considering edges with capacities greater than 0. Do this with the distributed Bellman-Ford algorithm, adapting the BGP implementation. Modify the algorithm to also forward the bottleneck capacity of each path.
3. The sink checks the min-cost path to the supersource. If the cost is ≥ 0, we are done. Otherwise send a flow corresponding to the bottleneck capacity along the path. This is done by sending a message along the path, which notifies the contained nodes to update their local flow values (and thus capacities).
4. Continue at step 2 with the updated residual graph.

Time to Converge, Improvements. Each phase consists of a (re)computation of the shortest paths in Step 2. Unfortunately, in the capacitated case the rounds of communication for a shortest paths computation is not bounded by d or d' anymore. It may actually take up to n rounds of communication, as the example at the end of this subsection shows.

Let $C = \max\{c_e | e \in E\}$ be the maximum capacity. The algorithm finishes in $O(|E| \cdot C)$ phases. This can be improved to $O(n \cdot \log C)$ by applying the following well-known scaling technique. A variable Δ is introduced and initialized to $2^{\lceil \log C \rceil - 1}$ in step 1. In step 2 only edges with capacity $\geq \Delta$ are considered. In step 3, Δ is updated to $\Delta/2$, if no more negative cost paths are found (unless $\Delta = 1$, then we are done). The updated Δ is broadcast to all nodes.

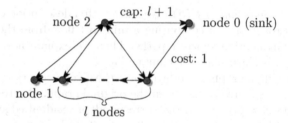

Fig. 1. All edges have capacity 1, except the top edge with capacity $l + 1$. The edge costs are all 0, except the rightmost edge with cost 1. All nodes have a demand of 1 to be sent to node 0.

As mentioned, with $(n + 1)$ such flow computations we can compute all node payments $t_i(\theta)$. Altogether this yields the following theorem.

Theorem 2. *In the per packet utility model with capacity constraints (described in Section 2.2) the VCG allocation and payments can be computed in a distributed manner. The computation converges in $O(n^3 \cdot \log C)$ rounds of communication.*

Shortest Paths Computation. Unfortunately, the number of rounds of communication to compute the shortest path cannot be bound by d (or d') anymore. Figure 1 shows an example where the shortest path in the residual graph has length $n - 2$, whereas the number of hops in the corresponding LCP in the original graph is 2. Assume that all nodes have already (virtually) sent their flow through the residual graph except node 1 which is selected last. Since the nodes are indistinguishable, we may assume this. The only path remaining in the residual graph is the one at the bottom of length $n - 2$, since the capacities of all other edges (expect $(1, 2)$) are fully saturated by flow sent to the sink via node 2. This compares to the LCP from node 1 over node 2 directly to node 0 with only two edges.

4.3 Model with Economic Relationships

In the following we will explain the two-layer graph, a helpful notion which was originally suggested in [6]. With the help of the two-layer model it will be easy to see that one can compute min-cost valley-free flows as needed in our model with capacities introduced in Section 2.2.

The Two-Layer Model. From a ToR graph $G = (V, E)$ and source, sink $s, t \in V$ we construct a *two-layer model* H, which is a directed graph, in the following way (see Figure 2 for an example). Two copies of the graph G are made, called the *lower* and the *upper layer*. In the upper layer all edge-directions are reversed. Every node v in the lower layer is connected with an edge to the corresponding copy of v, denoted v', in the upper layer. The edge is directed from v to v'. Finally, we obtain the two-layer model H by identifying the two s-nodes (of lower and upper layer) and also the two t-nodes, and by removing the incoming edges of s and the outgoing edges of t.

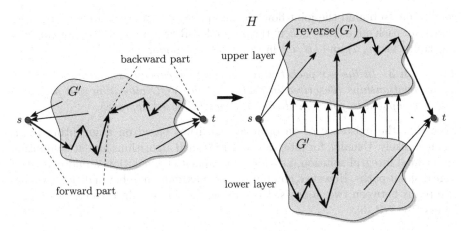

Fig. 2. A path in the ToR graph G and the corresponding path in the two-layer model H. (G' is G, excluding s and t.).

A valid path $p = v_1 \cdots v_r$ in G with $v_1 = s$ and $v_r = t$ is equivalent to a directed path in H in the following way. The forward part of p, that is the part containing all edges $(v_i, v_{i+1}) \in p$, is routed in the lower layer. Then there is a possible switch to the upper layer with a (v, v')-type edge (there can be at most one such switch for each path). The backward part of p is routed in the upper layer. In other words for each original edge $(v_{i+1}, v_i) \in p$ the corresponding edge (v_i', v_{i+1}') of the upper layer is traversed. If there is only a forward (respectively backward) part of p, then the corresponding path in H is only in the lower (respectively upper) layer.

This definition of the two-layer model can easily be extended to the case of multiple sources. Note that a peer-peer relationship between two nodes $v, u \in V$ can be incorporated by adding the edges (v, u') and (u, v') from lower to upper layer (reflecting that at most one peer-peer edge is allowed between the forward and the backward part of a path). Similarly, a sibling relationship between two nodes $v, u \in V$ can be incorporated by adding the symmetric edges (v, u), (u, v), (v', u'), and (u', v') in both layers (reflecting that sibling edges are allowed at arbitrary points in a path).

Min-Cost Valley-Free Flows. By simply computing a min-cost flow in the two-layer graph it is easy to derive a valley-free flow which will have at most the cost of an optimum min-cost valley-free flow. The edge capacities may be violated by at most a factor of two though, since each edge may be used twice: once in the upper and once in the lower layer. Note that such a min-cost flow could be computed in a distributed fashion by slightly modifying the approach described in Section 4.2.

This approximate solution cannot be used to compute the VCG allocation and payments though. To this end, we need the optimal solution. The latter can be computed with the help of a standard LP flow formulation with added constraints to bound the joint flow on the upper and lower layer edges. In other words, for each edge $(v, u) \in E$ in the original ToR graph, we add a joint capacity constraint for (v, u) and (u', v') in the two-layer model.

Theorem 3. *In the per packet utility model with capacity constraints and economic relationships (described in Section 3) the VCG allocation and payments can be computed in polynomial time with an LP based approach.*

Note that the existence of an optimal algorithm based on augmenting paths seems unlikely. Usually, for integral capacities such algorithms aim at computing an optimal integral solution, i.e., for unit capacities a solution would consist of edge disjoint paths. However, computing the maximum number of disjoint valley-free paths between two nodes s, t is inapproximable within a factor of $(2 - \varepsilon)$, unless P = NP [6].

5   Conclusions and Open Problems

Despite the fact that incentive compatibility for BGP routing had been known to be problematic in general, as well as for several apparently realistic special cases, we have identified one important special case of practical importance, namely the one in which path utilities depend on local per packet costs as well as delivery values. In this case incentive compatibility is achievable through payments which can be computed efficiently and in a BGP-compatible way; adding capacities and the "valley-free" constraint for paths makes incentives harder to compute in a BGP-compatible way, but still tractable.

Regarding the latter point, in this work we have simply pointed out that the algorithms we devised for VCG incentive computation are not implementable in a BGP-compatible way; it would be interesting to actually prove that this is inherent to the problem, i.e., to prove a lower bound on the convergence time of any algorithm for the min-cost flow problem and its valley-free constrained case.

Our model for path utilities is suggestive of a more general project for understanding BGP routing: We postulate that each directed edge in and out of every node has a value for this node, depending on the cost to this node, as well as agreed upon payments to or from its neighbors, for each packet sent or received along this edge. Suppose that the graph, as well as the demand, and per packet cost and delivery value of each node, are given. A game is thus defined in which strategies are payment agreements between neighbors, and the utility to each node is the one obtained by our model of BGP min-cost routing. This game is thus a very realistic network creation game, with special emphasis on BGP routing. The quality of equilibria compared to the social optimum (i.e., the price of anarchy and its variants) for this game would be a most interesting research direction. The social optimum is, of course, the min-cost flow with only costs and delivery values taken into account. Further, such a model would allow one to study how inter-AS agreements can depend on the underlying fundamentals of each AS, such as costs, delivery value, demand, and position in the network.

References

1. Achlioptas, D., Clauset, A., Kempe, D., Moore, C.: On the bias of traceroute sampling; or, power-law degree distributions in regular graphs. In: STOC 2005, pp. 694–703 (2005)
2. Anshelevich, E., Shepherd, B., Wilfong, G.: Strategic network formation through peering and service agreements. In: FOCS 2006, Washington, DC, USA, pp. 77–86. IEEE Computer Society Press, Los Alamitos (2006)
3. Barford, P., Bestavros, A., Byers, J., Crovella, M.: On the marginal utility of deploying measurement infrastructure. In: ACM SIGCOMM Internet Measurement Workshop, November 2001, ACM Press, New York (2001)
4. Di Battista, G., Erlebach, T., Hall, A., Patrignani, M., Pizzonia, M., Schank, T.: Computing the types of the relationships between autonomous systems. IEEE/ACM Transactions on Networking 15, 267–280 (2007)
5. Edmonds, J., Karp, R.M.: Theoretical improvements in algorithmic efficiency for network flow problems. J. ACM 19(2), 248–264 (1972)
6. Erlebach, T., Hall, A., Panconesi, A., Vukadinovic, D.: Cuts and disjoint paths in the valley-free path model of Internet BGP routing. In: CAAN, pp. 49–62 (2004)
7. Fabrikant, A., Luthra, A., Maneva, E., Papadimitriou, C.H., Shenker, S.: On a network creation game. In: PODC 2003, pp. 347–351. ACM Press, New York (2003)
8. Fabrikant, A., Papadimitriou, C.H.: The search for equilibria: Sink equilibria, unit recall games, and BGP oscillations. In: submitted manuscript (2007)
9. Feamster, N., Winick, J., Rexford, J.: A model of BGP routing for network engineering. In: SIGMETRICS 2004/Performance 2004, pp. 331–342. ACM Press, New York (2004)
10. Feigenbaum, J., Papadimitriou, C.H., Sami, R., Shenker, S.: A BGP-based mechanism for lowest-cost routing. In: PODC 2002, pp. 173–182 (2002)
11. Feigenbaum, J., Ramachandran, V., Schapira, M.: Incentive-compatible interdomain routing. In: EC 2006, pp. 130–139. ACM Press, New York (2006)
12. Feigenbaum, J., Sami, R., Shenker, S.: Mechanism design for policy routing. Distrib. Comput. 18(4), 293–305 (2006)
13. Ford, L.R., Fulkerson, D.R.: Constructing maximal dynamic flows from static flows. Operations Research 6, 419–433 (1958)
14. Gao, L.: On inferring autonomous system relationships in the Internet. IEEE/ACM Trans. Networking 9(6), 733–745 (2001)
15. Govindan, R., Reddy, A.: An analysis of Internet inter-domain topology and route stability. In: IEEE INFOCOM 1997, April 1997, pp. 850–857. IEEE Computer Society Press, Los Alamitos (1997)
16. Griffin, T.G., Wilfong, G.: An analysis of BGP convergence properties. In: SIGCOMM 1999, pp. 277–288. ACM Press, New York (1999)
17. Mas-Colell, A., Whinston, M.D., Green, J.R.: Microeconomic Theory. Oxford University Press, New York (1995)
18. Nisan, N., Ronen, A.: Algorithmic mechanism design. In: STOC'99, pp. 129–140. ACM Press, New York (1999)
19. Papadimitriou, C.H.: Algorithms, games, and the Internet. In: STOC 2001, pp. 749–753 (2001)

20. Rekhter, Y., Li, T.: A border gateway protocol 4 (bgp-4) (1995)
21. Stewart, J.W.: BGP4: Inter-Domain Routing in the Internet. Addison-Wesley, London, UK (1998)
22. Subramanian, L., Agarwal, S., Rexford, J., Katz, R.: Characterizing the Internet hierarchy from multiple vantage points. In: IEEE INFOCOM 2002, IEEE Computer Society Press, Los Alamitos (2002)

False-Name-Proof Mechanisms for Hiring a Team

Atsushi Iwasaki[1], David Kempe[2], Yasumasa Saito[1],
Mahyar Salek[2], and Makoto Yokoo[1]

[1] Department of ISEE, Kyushu University, Fukuoka 819-0395, Japan
{iwasaki@, saito@agent, yokoo@}is.kyushu-u.ac.jp
[2] Department of Computer Science, University of Southern California, CA
90089-0781, USA
{dkempe, salek}@usc.edu

Abstract. We study the problem of hiring a team of selfish agents to
perform a task. Each agent is assumed to own one or more elements of
a set system, and the auctioneer is trying to purchase a feasible solution
by conducting an auction. Our goal is to design auctions that are truthful and false-name-proof, meaning that it is in the agents' best interest
to reveal ownership of all elements (which may not be known to the
auctioneer a priori) as well as their true incurred costs. We first propose
and analyze a false-name-proof mechanism for the special cases where
each agent owns only one element in reality. We prove that its frugality
ratio is bounded by $n2^n$, which nearly matches a lower bound of $\Omega(2^n)$
for all false-name-proof mechanisms in this scenario. We then propose
a second mechanism. It requires the auctioneer to choose a reserve cost
a priori, and thus does not always purchase a solution. In return, it is
false-name-proof even when agents own multiple elements. We experimentally evaluate the payment (as well as social surplus) of the second
mechanism through simulation.

1   Introduction

In the problem of *hiring a team of agents* [1,2,3], an auctioneer knows which
subsets of agents can perform a complex task together, and needs to hire such
a team (called a *feasible set* of agents). Since the auctioneer does not know the
true costs incurred by agents, we assume that the auctioneer will use an auction
to elicit bids. A particularly well-studied special case of this problem is that of a
path auction [1,4,5,6]: the agents own edges of a known graph, and the auctioneer
wants to purchase an *s-t* path.

Selfish agents will try to maximize their profit, even if it requires misrepresenting their incurred cost or their identity. Thus, the auctioneer should design
the auction to be *truthful*, i.e., making it in agents' best interest to reveal actual
costs and ownership. The area of designing such auctions is known as *mechanism
design* [6,7,8]. Most recent results on truthful mechanism design have focused on
discouraging misrepresentation of costs. However, as recently pointed out by
Yokoo et al. in the context of combinatorial auctions [9,10], a second threat is

X. Deng and F.C. Graham (Eds.): WINE 2007, LNCS 4858, pp. 245–256, 2007.

that of *false-name manipulations*, in which agents owning multiple elements of the underlying set system invent "pseudo-agents" in order to pretend that all these agents must be paid, leading to higher total payments.

1.1   Our Contributions

We introduce a model of false-name manipulation in auctions for hiring a team, such as *s-t* path auctions. In this model, the set system structure and element ownership are not completely known to the auctioneer. Thus, in order to increase profit, an agent who owns an element can pretend that the element is in fact a set consisting of multiple elements owned by different agents. Similarly, an agent owning multiple elements can submit bids for these elements under different identities. We call a mechanism *false-name-proof* if it is truthful, and a dominant strategy is for each agent to reveal ownership of all elements.

Our first main contribution is a false-name-proof mechanism MP for the special case in which each agent owns exactly one element. This mechanism introduces an exponential multiplicative penalty against sets in the number of participating agents. We show that its frugality ratio (according to the definition of Karlin et al. [5]) is at most $n2^n$ for all set systems of n elements, which nearly matches a worst-case lower bound of $\Omega(2^n)$ we establish for *every* false-name-proof mechanism.

When agents may own multiple elements, we present an alternative mechanism AP, based on an a priori chosen reserve cost r and additive penalties. The mechanism is false-name-proof in the general setting, but depends crucially on the choice of r, as it will not purchase a solution unless there is one whose cost (including the penalty) is at most r. We investigate the AP mechanism experimentally for *s-t* path auctions on random graphs, observing that AP provides social surplus not too far from a Pareto-efficient one at an appropriate reserve cost.

1.2   Related Work

If false-name bids are not a concern, then it has long been known that the VCG mechanism gives a truthful mechanism and identifies the Pareto optimal solution. As the payments of VCG can be significantly higher than the cheapest alternative solution, several papers [1,3,4,5] have investigated the *frugality* of mechanisms: the overpayment compared to a natural lower bound. In particular, [5] presents a mechanism called the $\sqrt{}$ mechanism achieving frugality ratio within a constant factor of optimal for *s-t* path auctions in graphs.

The issue of false-name bids was recently studied in combinatorial auctions and several special cases by Yokoo et al. [11,12,13,14,9], who developed false-name-proof mechanisms in those scenarios, but also proved that no mechanism can be both false-name-proof and Pareto efficient. Notice that the false-name-proof mechanisms for combinatorial procurement auctions given in [12,13] cannot be applied in our setting, as they assume additive valuations on the part of the auctioneer, i.e., that the auctioneer derives partial utility from partial solutions. A somewhat similar scenario arises in job scheduling, where users may split or merge jobs to obtain earlier assignments. Moulin [15] gives a mechanism that is strategy-proof against both merges and splits and achieves efficiency within a constant factor of optimum. However, when agents can exchange money, no such mechanism is possible [15].

For the specific case of path auctions, the impact of false-name bids was recently studied by Du et al. [16]. They showed that if agents can own multiple edges, then there is no false-name-proof and efficient mechanism. Furthermore, if bids are anonymous, i.e., agents do not report any identity for edge ownership, then no mechanism can be strategy-proof. Notice that this does not preclude false-name-proof and truthful mechanisms in which the auctioneer takes ownership of multiple edge by the same agent into account, and rewards the agent accordingly.

2   Preliminaries

Our framework is based on that of [1,17,5,3]. A *set system* $(E, \mathcal{F})$ is specified by a set E of n *elements* and a collection $\mathcal{F} \subseteq 2^E$ of *feasible sets*. For instance, in the important special case of an *s-t path auction*, $S \in \mathcal{F}$ if and only if S is an *s-t path*.

Agents can own multiple elements, and A^i denotes an element of a partition $\mathcal{A}$ of E and the set of elements owned by agent i. An *owned set system*, i.e., a set system with ownership structure, is specified by $((E, \mathcal{F}), \mathcal{A})$. Each element e has an associated *cost* c_e, the true cost that its owner $o(e)$ will incur if e is selected by the mechanism.[1] This cost is *private*, i.e., known only to $o(e)$. An *auction* consists of two steps:

1. Each agent i submits sealed bids $(b_e, \tilde{o}(e))$ for elements e, where $\tilde{o}(e)$ denotes the identifier of e's purported owner (which need not be the actual owner).
2. Based on the bids, the auctioneer uses an algorithm that is common knowledge among the agents in order to select a feasible set $S^* \in \mathcal{F}$ as the winner and compute a payment p_i for each agent i with an element e such that $i = \tilde{o}(e)$. We say that the elements $e \in S^*$ *win*, and all other elements *lose*.

The *profit* of an agent i is the sum of all payments she receives, minus the incurred cost $c(S^* \cap A^i)$. Each agent is only interested in maximizing her profit, and might choose to misrepresent ownership or costs to this end. However, we assume that agents do not collude. If agents report correct ownership for all $e \in A^i$, then a mechanism is truthful by definition if for any fixed vector b^{-i} of bids by all agents other than i, it is in agents i's best interest to bid $b_e = c_e$ for all $e \in A^i$, i.e., agent e's profit is maximized by bidding $b_e = c_e$ for all these elements e.

In this paper, we extend the study of truthful mechanisms to take into account *false-name manipulation*: agents claiming ownership of non-existent elements

---

[1] For costs, bids, etc., we extend the notation by writing $c(S) = \sum_{e \in S} c_e$ and $b(S) = \sum_{e \in S} b_e$, etc.

(which we call *self-division*) or choosing not to disclose ownership of elements (which we call *identifier splitting*).

Definition 1 (Identifier Splitting [9,10]). *An agent i owning a set A^i may choose to use different identifiers in her bid for some or all of the elements. Formally, the owned set system $((E, \mathcal{F}), \mathcal{A})$ is replaced by $((E, \mathcal{F}), \mathcal{A}')$, where $\mathcal{A}' = \mathcal{A} \setminus \{A^i\} \cup \{A^{i'}\} \cup \{A^{i''}\}$, and $A^i = A^{i'} \cup A^{i''}$.*

Definition 2 (Self-Division). *An agent i owning element e is said to self-divide e if e is replaced by two or more elements $e_1, \ldots, e_k$, and different owners are reported for the e_i. Formally, the owned set system $((E, \mathcal{F}), \mathcal{A})$ is replaced by $((E', \mathcal{F}'), \mathcal{A}')$, whose elements are $E' = E \setminus \{e\} \cup \{e_1, \ldots, e_k\}$, such that the feasible sets $\mathcal{F}'$ are exactly those sets S not containing e, as well as sets $S \setminus \{e\} \cup \{e_1, \ldots, e_k\}$ for all feasible sets $S \in \mathcal{F}$ containing e. The ownership structure is $A^{i_j} = \{e_j\}$ for $j = 1, \ldots, k$, where each i_j is a new agent.*

Intuitively, self-division allows an agent to pretend that multiple distinct agents are involved in doing the work of element e, and that each of them must be paid separately. For self-division to be a threat, there must be uncertainty on the part of the auctioneer about the true set system $(E, \mathcal{F})$. In particular, it is meaningless to talk about a mechanism for an individual set system, as the auctioneer does not know a priori what the set system is. Hence, we define *classes of set systems closed under subdivision*, as the candidate classes on which mechanisms must operate.

Definition 3. *1. For two set systems $(E, \mathcal{F})$ and $(E', \mathcal{F}')$, we say $(E', \mathcal{F}')$ is reachable from $(E, \mathcal{F})$ by subdivisions if $(E', \mathcal{F}')$ is obtained by (repeatedly) replacing individual elements $e \in E$ with $\{e_1, \ldots, e_k\}$, such that the feasible sets $\mathcal{F}'$ are exactly those sets S not containing e, as well as sets $S \setminus \{e\} \cup \{e_1, \ldots, e_k\}$ for all feasible sets $S \in \mathcal{F}$ containing e.*
2. A class $\mathcal{C}$ of set systems is closed under subdivisions iff with $(E, \mathcal{F})$, all set systems reachable from $(E, \mathcal{F})$ by subdivisions are also in $\mathcal{C}$.

For example, s-t path auction set systems are closed under subdivisions, whereas minimum spanning tree set systems are not (because subdivisions would introduce new nodes that must be spanned).

In both identifier splitting and self-division, we will sometimes refer to the new agents i' whose existence i invents as *pseudo-agents*. A mechanism is *false-name-proof* if it is a dominant strategy for each agent i to simply report the pair (c_e, i) as a bid for each element $e \in A^i$. Thus, neither identifier splitting nor self-division nor bids $b_e \neq c_e$ can increase the agent's profit. Among other things, this allows us to use b_e and c_e interchangeably when discussing false-name-proof mechanisms. Notice that we explicitly define the concept of false-name-proof mechanisms to imply that the mechanism is also truthful when each agent i owns only one element.

Efficiency and Frugality

A mechanism is *Pareto efficient* if it always maximizes the sum of all participants' utilities (including that of the auctioneer). While it is well known that the VCG mechanism is truthful and Pareto efficient, Du et al. [16] show that there is no Pareto efficient and false-name-proof mechanism, even for s-t path auctions. Yokoo et al. [10] showed the same for combinatorial auctions.

While Pareto efficient mechanisms maximize social welfare, they can significantly overpay compared to other mechanisms [5]. In order to analyze the overpayment, we use the definition of *frugality ratio* from [5].

Definition 4 ([5]). *Let $(E, \mathcal{F})$ be a set system, and S the cheapest feasible set with respect to the true costs c_e (where ties are broken lexicographically). For any vector of costs $\mathbf{c}$ for elements, we define $\nu(\mathbf{c})$ to be the solution to the following optimization problem.*

Minimize $\sum_{e \in S} b_e$ subject to

(1) $b_e \geq c_e$ for all e

(2) $b(S \setminus T) \leq c(T \setminus S)$ for all $T \in \mathcal{F}$

(3) For every $e \in S$, there is a $T_e \in \mathcal{F}$ such that $e \notin T_e$ and $b(S \setminus T_e) = c(T_e \setminus S)$

This definition essentially captures the payments in a "cheapest Nash Equilibrium" of a first-price auction, and gives a natural lower bound generalizing second-lowest cost for comparison purposes.

Definition 5. *The frugality of a mechanism $\mathcal{M}$ for a set system $(E, \mathcal{F})$ is*

$$\phi_{\mathcal{M}} = \sup_{\mathbf{c}} \frac{p_{\mathcal{M}}(\mathbf{c})}{\nu(\mathbf{c})},$$

i.e., the worst case, over all cost vectors $\mathbf{c}$, of the overpayment compared to the "first-price" payments. Here, $p_{\mathcal{M}}(\mathbf{c})$ denotes the total payments made by $\mathcal{M}$ when the cost vector is $\mathbf{c}$.

3   A Multiplicative Penalty Mechanism

We present a mechanism MP based on exponential multiplicative penalties. It is false-name-proof for arbitrary classes of set systems closed under subdivisions, *so long as each agent only owns one element.* We can therefore identify elements e with agents. Since we assume each agent owns exactly one element, $\mathcal{A}$ is automatically determined by E, so we can focus on set systems instead of owned set systems. After the agents submit bids b_e for elements, MP chooses the set S^* minimizing $b(S) \cdot 2^{|S|-1}$, among all feasible sets $S \in \mathcal{F}$. Each agent $e \in S^*$ is then paid her threshold bid $2^{|S^{-e}| - |S^*|} b(S^{-e}) - b(S^* \setminus \{e\})$, where S^{-e} denote the best solution (with respect to the objective function $b(S) \cdot 2^{|S|-1}$) among feasible sets S not containing e. Notice that while this selection may be NP-hard in general, it can be accomplished in polynomial time for path auctions, by using the Bellman/Ford algorithm to compute the shortest path for each number of hops, and then comparing among the at most n such shortest paths.

Theorem 1. *For all classes of set systems closed under subdivision, MP is false-name-proof, so long as each agent only owns one element. Furthermore, it has frugality ratio $O(n \cdot 2^n)$, where $n = |E|$.*

Proof. If an agent $e = e_0$ self-divides into $k+1$ elements $e_0, \ldots, e_k$, then either all of the e_i or none of them are included in any feasible set S. Thus, we can always think of just one threshold $\tau_k(e)$ for the self-divided agent e: if the sum of the bids of all the new elements e_j exceeds $\tau_k(e)$, then e loses; otherwise, it is paid at most $(k+1)\tau_k(e)$. The original threshold of agent e is $\tau(e) = \tau_0(e)$.

The definition of the MP mechanism implies $\tau_k(e) \le 2^{-k}\tau(e)$. If e still wins after self-division (otherwise, there clearly is no incentive to self-divide), the total payment to e is at most $(k+1)2^{-k}\tau(e)$. The alternative of not self-dividing, and submitting a bid of 0, yields a payment of $\tau(e) \ge (k+1)2^{-k}\tau(e)$. Thus, refraining from self-division is a dominant strategy. Given that no agent will submit false-name bids, the monotonicity of the selection rule implies that the mechanism is incentive compatible, and we can assume that $b_e = c_e$ for all agents e.

To prove the upper bound on the frugality ratio, consider again any winning agent $e \in S^*$. Her threshold bid is $\tau(e) = \min_{T \in \mathcal{F}: e \notin T} 2^{|T|-|S^*|} c(T) - c(S^* \setminus \{e\})$, and the total payment is the sum of individual thresholds for S^*,

$$p_{\mathrm{MP}}(\mathbf{c}) = \sum_{e \in S^*} \min_{T \in \mathcal{F}: e \notin T} 2^{|T|-|S^*|} c(T) - c(S^* \setminus \{e\})$$
$$\le 2^n \sum_{e \in S^*} \min_{T \in \mathcal{F}: e \notin T} c(T).$$

Let S be the cheapest solution with respect to the c_e, i.e., without regard to the sizes of the sets. By Definition 4, $\nu(\mathbf{c}) = \sum_{e \in S} b_e$, subject to the constraints of the mathematical program given. Focusing on any fixed agent e', we let $T_{e'}$ denote the set from the third constraint of Definition 4, and can rewrite

$$\nu(\mathbf{c}) = \sum_{e \in S-T_{e'}} b_e + \sum_{e \in S \cap T_{e'}} b_e = \sum_{e \in T_{e'}-S} c_e + \sum_{e \in T_{e'} \cap S} b_e \ge c(T_{e'}).$$

Since this inequality holds for all e', we have proved that $\nu(\mathbf{c}) \ge \max_{e \in S} c(T_e)$. On the other hand we can further bound the payments by

$$2^n \sum_{e \in S^*} \min_{T \in \mathcal{F}: e \notin T} c(T) \le n2^n \max_{e \in S^*} \min_{T \in \mathcal{F}: e \notin T} c(T)$$
$$\le n2^n \max_{e \in S} \min_{T \in \mathcal{F}: e \notin T} c(T)$$
$$\le n2^n \max_{e \in S} c(T_e).$$

Here, the second-to-last inequality followed because for all $e \in S^* \setminus S$, the minimizing set T is actually equal to S, and therefore cannot have larger cost than $c(T_e)$ for any $e \in S$, by definition of S. Thus, the frugality ratio of MP is

$$\phi_{\mathrm{MP}} = \sup_{\mathbf{c}} \frac{p_{\mathrm{MP}}(\mathbf{c})}{\nu(\mathbf{c})} \le \frac{n2^n \max_{e \in S} c(T_e)}{\max_{e \in S} c(T_e)} = n2^n. \qquad \blacksquare$$

3.1   An Exponential Lower Bound

An exponentially large frugality ratio is not desirable. Unfortunately, any mechanism which is false-name-proof will have to incur such a penalty, as shown by the following theorem.

Theorem 2. *Let $\mathcal{C}$ be any class of monopoly free set systems closed under subdivisions, and $\mathcal{M}$ be any truthful and false-name-proof mechanism for $\mathcal{C}$. Then, the frugality ratio of $\mathcal{M}$ on $\mathcal{C}$ is $\Omega(2^n)$ for set systems with $|E| = n$.*

Proof. Let $(E_0, F_0) \in \mathcal{C}$ be a set system minimizing $|E_0|$. Let $S^* \in F_0$ be the winning set under $\mathcal{M}$ winning when all agents $e \in E_0$ bid 0, and let $e \in S^*$ be arbitrary, but fixed. Because (E_0, F_0) is monopoly free, there must be a feasible set $T \in F_0$ with $e \notin T$ and $T \not\subseteq S^*$. Among all such sets T, let T_e be the one minimizing $|S^* \cup T|$, and let $\hat{e}$ in T_e be arbitrary. Define $Z = T_e \cup S^* \setminus \{e, \hat{e}\}$ (the "zero bidders"), and $I = E_0 \setminus (T_e \cup S^*)$ (the "infinity bidders"). Consider the following bid vector: both e and $\hat{e}$ bid 1, all agents $e' \in Z$ bid 0, and all agents $e' \in I$ bid ∞. Let W be the winning set. We claim that W must contain at least one of e and $\hat{e}$ (w.l.o.g., assume that $e \in W$). For W cannot contain any of the infinity bidders. And if it contained neither e nor $\hat{e}$, then W would have been a candidate for T_e with smaller $|W \cup S^*|$, which would contradict the choice of T_e.

Now, let (E_k, F_k) be the set system resulting if agent e self-divides into new agents $e_0, \ldots, e_k$, for $k \geq 0$. Define $\tau(j, k)$, for $j = 0, \ldots, k$, to be the threshold bid under $\mathcal{M}$ for agent e_j in the set system (E_k, F_k), given that all $e' \in Z$ bid 0, all $e' \in I$ bid ∞, and all e_i for $i \neq j$ also bid 0, while $\hat{e}$ bids 1. Above, we thus showed that $1 \leq \tau(0, 0) < \infty$. We now show by induction on d that for all d, there exists an $h \leq d$ such that

$$2^{-d} \sum_{i=0}^{k} \tau(i, k) \geq \sum_{i=h}^{k+h} \tau(i, k+d).$$

The base case $d = 0$ is trivial. For the inductive step, assume that we have proved the statement for d. Because $\mathcal{M}$ is truthful, the payment of an agent is exactly equal to the threshold bid, so each agent i is paid $\tau(i, k+d)$ in the auction on the set system (E_{k+d}, F_{k+d}) with the bids as given above. If agent i were to self-divide into two new agents, the new set system would be (E_{k+d+1}, F_{k+d+1}), and the payment of agent i (who is now getting paid as two pseudo-agents i and $i+1$) would be $\tau(i, k+d+1) + \tau(i+1, k+d+1)$. Because $\mathcal{M}$ was assumed to be false-name-proof, it is not in the agent's best interest to self-divide in such a way, i.e., $\tau(i, k+d) \geq \tau(i, k+d+1) + \tau(i+1, k+d+1)$. Summing this inequality over all agents $i = h, \ldots, h+k$, we obtain

$$\sum_{i=h}^{h+k} \tau(i, k+d) \geq \sum_{i=h}^{h+k} (\tau(i, k+d+1) + \tau(i+1, k+d+1))$$
$$= \sum_{i=h}^{h+k} \tau(i, k+d+1) + \sum_{i=h+1}^{h+k+1} \tau(i, k+d+1).$$

Define $\ell = 0$ if $\sum_{i=h}^{h+k} \tau(i, k+d+1) \leq \sum_{i=h+1}^{h+k+1} \tau(i, k+d+1)$; otherwise, let $\ell = 1$. Then, the above inequality implies that

$$\sum_{i=h}^{h+k} \tau(i, k+d) \geq 2 \sum_{i=h+\ell}^{h+k+\ell} \tau(i, k+d+1).$$

Finally, setting $h' := h + \ell$, we can combine this inequality with the induction hypothesis to obtain that

$$2^{-(d+1)} \sum_{i=0}^{k} \tau(i, k) \geq \sum_{i=h'}^{k+h'} \tau(i, k+d+1),$$

which completes the inductive proof.

Applying this equation with $k = 0$, we obtain that for each $d \geq 0$, there exists an $h \leq d$ such that $\tau(h, d) \leq 2^{-d} \cdot \tau(0, 0)$. Thus, in the set system (E_d, F_d), if all infinity bidders have cost ∞, agent h has cost just above $2^{-d}\tau(0,0)$, and all other agents have cost 0, then agent $\hat{e}$ must be in the winning set, and must be paid at least 1. But it is easy to see that in this case, $\nu(c) = 2^{-d}\tau(0,0)$, and the frugality ratio is thus at least $2^d/\tau(0,0) = \Omega(2^d)$ (since $\tau(0,0)$ is a constant independent of d). Finally, $|E_d| = |Z| + |I| + d + 1$, and because Z and I are constant for our class of examples, the frugality ratio is $2^{-(|Z|+|I|-1)} \cdot 2^n/\tau(0,0) = \Omega(2^n)$. ■

4   An Additive Penalty Mechanism with Reserve Cost

We next propose and analyze a mechanism called AP, based on additive penalties and a reserve cost. It will only purchase a solution when the total cost (including penalties) does not exceed the a priori chosen reserve cost r, and thus requires a judicious choice of r by the auctioneer. In return, AP is false-name-proof even when agents own multiple elements.

For any set $S \in \mathcal{F}$, let $w(S)$ denote the number of (pseudo-)agents owning one or more elements of S, called the *width* of the set S. The width-based *penalty* for a set S of width w is $D_r(w) = \frac{2^{w-1}-1}{2^{w-1}} \cdot r$. Based on the actual costs and the penalty, we define the *adjusted cost* of a set S to be $\beta(S) = b(S) + D_r(w(S))$.

The AP mechanism first determines the set S^* minimizing the adjusted cost $\beta(S)$, among all feasible sets $S \in \mathcal{F}$. If its adjusted cost exceeds the reserve cost r, then AP does not purchase any set, and does not pay any agents. Otherwise, it chooses S^*, and pays each winning agent (i.e., each agent i with $S^* \cap A^i \neq \emptyset$) her threshold bid $p_i = \min(r, \beta(S^{-i})) - (b(S^* \setminus A^i) + D_r(w(S^*)))$ with respect to $\beta(S)$. Here, S^{-i} denotes the best solution with respect to $\beta(S)$ such that S^{-i} contains no elements from A^i.

4.1   Analysis of AP

In this section, we prove that simply submitting the pair (b_e, i) for each element $e \in A^i$ is a dominant strategy for each agent i under the mechanism AP. Furthermore, we prove that the payments of the AP mechanism never exceed r. As a first step, we prove that it never increases an agent's profit to engage in identifier splitting.

Lemma 1. *Suppose that agent i owns elements A^i, and splits identifiers into i', i'', with sets $A^{i'}, A^{i''}$, such that $A^{i'} \cup A^{i''} = A^i$. Then, the profit agent i obtains after splitting is no larger than that obtained before splitting.*

Proof. Let $S^* \in \mathcal{F}$ be the winning set prior to agent i's identifier split. We first consider the case when the winning set does not change due to the identifier split. If only one of the new pseudo-agents i', i'' wins (say, i'), then $\beta(S^{-i'}) \leq \beta(S^{-i})$, because every feasible set not using elements from A^i also does not use elements from $A^{i'}$. Hence, the payment of i could only decrease, and we may henceforth assume that both i' and i'' win, which means that the width of the winning set S^* increases from w to $w + 1$.

For simplicity, we write $B^{-i} = \min(r, \beta(S^{-i}))$, and similarly for i' and i''. The payment to i before the split is $B^{-i} - (b(S^* \setminus A^i) + D_r(w))$, whereas the new payment after the split is

$$B^{-i'} - (b(S^* \setminus A^{i'}) + D_r(w+1)) + B^{-i''} - (b(S^* \setminus A^{i''}) + D_r(w+1))$$
$$= B^{-i'} + B^{-i''} - 2b(S^*) + b(S^* \cap A^i) - 2D_r(w+1).$$

As argued above, we have that $B^{-i''} \leq B^{-i}$, and by definition of $B^{-i'}$, we also know that $B^{-i'} \leq r$. Thus, canceling out penalty terms, the increase in payment to agent i is bounded from above by

$$B^{-i'} + B^{-i''} - B^{-i} - b(S^*) - r \leq r + B^{-i} - B^{-i} - b(S^*) - r = -b(S^*) \leq 0.$$

Hence, identifier splitting can only lower the payment of agent i. Since the total cost incurred by agent i stays the same, this proves that there is no benefit in identifier splitting.

Next, suppose that the winning set after the split changes to $S'^* \neq S^*$. Clearly, if i does not win at all after the split, i.e., $S'^* \cap A^i = \emptyset$, then i has no incentive to split identifiers. Otherwise, if i does win after the split, then i must also win before the split. For the split can only increase $D_r(w(S))$ for all sets S containing any of i's elements, while not affecting $D_r(w(S))$ for other sets. We can assume w.l.o.g. that agent i bids ∞ on all elements $e \in A^i \setminus S'^*$. For the winning set will stay the same, because $\beta(S'^*)$ stays the same, and $\beta(S)$ can only increase for other sets S, and the payments can only increase.

But then, S'^* will also be the winning set if i does not split identifiers (the adjusted cost $\beta(S'^*)$ decreases, while all other adjusted costs stay the same). Now, we can apply the argument from above to show that the payments to agent i do not increase as a result of splitting identifiers. Thus, so long as an agent can submit bids of false cost instead, it is never a dominant strategy to split identifiers.   ∎

Theorem 3. *For all classes of set systems closed under subdivision, AP is false-name-proof, even if agents can own multiple elements and split identifiers. Thus, for each agent i, submitting bids (c_e, i) for each element $e \in A^i$ is a dominant strategy.*

Proof. First, notice that if an agent owns two elements in the winning solution, AP does not treat the agent differently from if she only owned one element. Thus, the proof of Lemma 1 also shows that self-division can never be beneficial for an agent, and we can assume from now on that no agent will self-divide or split identifiers. Thus, each agent i submits bids (b_e, i) for all elements $e \in A^i$. If the set $S^* \in \mathcal{F}$ wins under AP, agent i's utility is

$$p_i - c(S^* \cap A^i) = B^{-i} - (b(S^* \setminus A^i) + D_r(w(S^*)) + c(S^* \cap A^i)).$$

Since B^{-i} is a constant independent of the bids $b(e)$ by agent i, agent i's utility is maximized when $(b(S^* \setminus A^i) + D_r(w(S^*)) + c(S^* \cap A^i))$ is minimized. But this is exactly the quantity that AP will minimize when agent i submits truthful bids for all her elements; hence, truthfulness is a dominant strategy.   ∎

The next theorem proves that an auctioneer with a reserve cost of r faces no loss.

Theorem 4. *The sum of the payments made by AP to agents never exceeds r.*

Proof. Because we already proved that AP is false-name-proof, we can without loss of generality identify $c(e)$ and $b(e)$ for each element e. When w agents are part of the winning set S^*, the payment to agent i is

$$p_i = B^{-i} - (c(S^* \setminus A^i) + D_r(w)) \leq r - (c(S^* \setminus A^i) + r - \tfrac{r}{2^{w-1}}) = \tfrac{r}{2^{w-1}}$$

Thus, the sum of all payments to agents i is at most $w \cdot \tfrac{r}{2^{w-1}} \leq r$.   ∎

4.2   Experiments

Since the AP mechanism does not always purchase a feasible set, we cannot analyze its frugality ratio in the sense of Definition 5. (The definition is based on the assumption that the mechanism always purchases a set.) Instead, we complement the analysis of the previous section with experiments for shortest s-t path auctions on random graphs. Our simulation compares the payments of the AP mechanism with VCG, under the assumption that there is in fact no false-name manipulation and each agent owns one edge. Thus, we evaluate the overpayment caused by preventing false-name manipulation.

Since some of our graphs have monopolies, we modify VCG by introducing a reserve cost r. Thus, if S^* is the cheapest solution with respect to the cost, the reserve-cost VCG mechanism (RVCG) only purchases a path when $c(S^*) \leq r$. In that case, the payment to each edge $e \in S^*$ is $p_e = \min(r, c(S^{-e})) - c(S^* \setminus \{e\})$, where S^{-e} is the cheapest solution not containing e.

Our generation process for random graphs is as follows: 40 nodes are placed independently and uniformly at random in the unit square $[0, 1]^2$. Then, 200 independent and uniformly random node pairs are connected with edges.[2] The cost of each edge e is its Euclidean length. We evaluate 100 random trials; in each, we seek to buy a path between two randomly chosen nodes. While the number of nodes is rather small compared to the real-world networks on which one would like to run auctions, it is dictated by the computational complexity of the mechanisms we study. Larger-scale experiments are a fruitful direction for future work.

Figure 1 shows the average social surplus (the difference between the reserve cost and the true cost incurred by edges on the chosen path, $r - \sum_{e \in S^*} c_e$) in AP and RVCG, as well as the ratio between the two, when varying the reserve cost $r \in [0, 3.5]$. The social surplus for both increases roughly linearly under both mechanisms. While the plot shows some efficiency loss by using AP, it is always within a factor of about 60% for our instances, and on average around 80%.

Figure 2 illustrates the average payments of the auctioneer. Clearly, small reserve costs lead to small payments, and when the reserve costs are less than

---

[2] We also ran simulations on random small-world networks [18]. Our results for small-world networks are qualitatively similar, and we therefore focus on the case of uniformly random networks here.

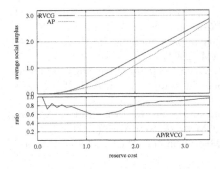 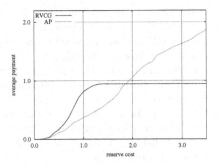

Fig. 1. The evaluation results of social surplus

Fig. 2. The evaluation results of payments

1.8, the payment of AP is in fact smaller than that of RVCG. As the reserve cost r increases, RVCG's payments converge, while those of AP keep increasing almost linearly. The reason is that the winning path in AP tends to have fewer edges than other competing paths, and is thus paid an increased bonus as r increases. We would expect such behavior to subside as there are more competing paths with the same number of edges.

5 Open Questions

It remains open whether there is a mechanism which always purchases a solution, and is false-name-proof even when each agent has multiple elements. This holds even for such seemingly simple cases as s-t path auctions. It may be possible that no such mechanism exists, which would be an interesting result in its own right. The difficulty of designing false-name-proof mechanisms for hiring a team is mainly due to a lack of useful characterization results for incentive-compatible mechanisms when agents have multiple parameters. While a characterization of truthful mechanisms has been given by Rochet [19], this condition is difficult to apply in practice.

It would also be desirable to get the bounds in Section 3 to match asymptotically, i.e., to either remove the factor n from the upper bound, or tighten the lower bound accordingly. The latter may be difficult, as it is likely at least as difficult as designing a truthful mechanism for all set systems with frugality ratio within a constant factor of optimum. Thus, even progress on this question for specific classes of set systems would be desirable.

References

1. Archer, A., Tardos, E.: Frugal path mechanisms. In: Proc. 13th ACM Symp. on Discrete Algorithms, ACM/SIAM, pp. 991–999. ACM Press, New York (2002)
2. Garg, R., Kumar, V., Rudra, A., Verma, A.: Coalitional games on graphs: core structures, substitutes and frugality. Technical Report TR-02-60, UTCS (2002)

3. Talwar, K.: The price of truth: Frugality in truthful mechanisms. In: Proc. 21st Annual Symp. on Theoretical Aspects of Computer Science (2003)
4. Elkind, E., Sahai, A., Steiglitz, K.: Frugality in path auctions. In: Proc. 15th ACM Symp. on Discrete Algorithms, ACM/SIAM (2004)
5. Karlin, A., Kempe, D., Tamir, T.: Beyond VCG: Frugality of truthful mechanisms. In: Proc. 46th IEEE Symp. on Foundations of Computer Science, IEEE Computer Society Press, Los Alamitos (2005)
6. Nisan, N., Ronen, A.: Algorithmic mechanism design. In: Proc. 31st ACM Symp. on Theory of Computing, pp. 129–140. ACM Press, New York (1999)
7. Mas-Collel, A., Whinston, W., Green, J.: Microeconomic Theory. Oxford University Press, Oxford (1995)
8. Papadimitriou, C.: Algorithms, games and the internet. In: Proc. 33rd ACM Symp. on Theory of Computing, pp. 749–752. ACM Press, New York (2001)
9. Yokoo, M., Sakurai, Y., Matsubara, S.: Robust Combinatorial Auction Protocol against False-name Bids. Artificial Intelligence 130(2), 167–181 (2001)
10. Yokoo, M., Sakurai, Y., Matsubara, S.: The effect of false-name bids in combinatorial auctions: New fraud in Internet auctions. Games and Economic Behavior 46(1), 174–188 (2004)
11. Iwasaki, A., Yokoo, M., Terada, K.: A Robust Open Ascending-price Multi-unit Auction Protocol against False-name bids. Decision Support Systems 39(1), 23–39 (2005)
12. Suyama, T., Yokoo, M.: Strategy/false-name proof protocols for combinatorial multi-attribute procurement auction. Autonomous Agents and Multi-Agent Systems 11(1), 7–21 (2005)
13. Suyama, T., Yokoo, M.: Strategy/false-name proof protocols for combinatorial multi-attribute procurement auction: Handling arbitrary utility of the buyer. In: Deng, X., Ye, Y. (eds.) WINE 2005. LNCS, vol. 3828, Springer, Heidelberg (2005)
14. Yokoo, M.: The characterization of strategy/false-name proof combinatorial auction protocols: Price-oriented, rationing-free protocol. In: Proceedings of the 18th International Joint Conference on Artificial Intelligence, pp. 733–739 (2003)
15. Moulin, H.: Proportional scheduling, split-proofness, and merge-proofness. Games and Economic Behavior
16. Du, Y., Sami, R., Shi, Y.: Path Auction Games When an Agent Can Own Multiple Edges. In: Proc. 1st Workshop on the Economics of Networked Systems (NetEcon06), pp. 48–55 (2006)
17. Bikhchandani, S., de Vries, S., Schummer, J., Vohra, R.: Linear programming and vickrey auctions. IMA Volume in Mathematics and its Applications, Mathematics of the Internet: E-auction and Markets 127, 75–116 (2001)
18. Watts, D.J., Strogatz, S.H.: Collective dynamics of 'small-world' networks. Nature 393(6684), 440–442 (1998)
19. Rochet, J.C.: A necessary and sufficient condition for rationalizability in a quasi-linear context. Journal of Mathematical Economics 16, 191–200 (1987)

Mechanism Design on Trust Networks

Arpita Ghosh[1], Mohammad Mahdian[1], Daniel M. Reeves[1],
David M. Pennock[1], and Ryan Fugger[2]

[1] Yahoo! Research
{arpita,mahdian,dreeves,pennockd}@yahoo-inc.com
[2] RipplePay.com
rfugger@gmail.com

Abstract. We introduce the concept of a trust network—a decentralized payment infrastructure in which payments are routed as IOUs between trusted entities. The trust network has directed links between pairs of agents, with capacities that are related to the credit an agent is willing to extend another; payments may be routed between any two agents that are connected by a path in the network. The network structure introduces *group budget constraints* on the payments from a subset of agents to another on the trust network: this generalizes the notion of individually budget constrained bidders.

We consider a multi-unit auction of identical items among bidders with unit demand, when the auctioneer and bidders are all nodes on a trust network. We define a generalized notion of social welfare for such budget-constrained bidders, and show that the winner determination problem under this notion of social welfare is NP-hard; however the flow structure in a trust network can be exploited to approximate the solution with a factor of $1 - 1/e$. We then present a pricing scheme that leads to an incentive compatible, individually rational mechanism with feasible payments that respect the trust network's payment constraints and that maximizes the modified social welfare to within a factor $1 - 1/e$.

1 Introduction

Consider an auction where payments take the form of IOUs. That is, the winning buyer(s) do not immediately pay with dollars or other standardized currency, but instead commit to compensate the seller appropriately at some later date. In this setting, the seller must consider not only the magnitude of a buyer's bid, but also the risk of the buyers defaulting on their commitments. Naturally the seller may not wish to accept a large IOU from an unknown or untrustworthy bidder.

Now suppose the seller will not accept an IOU from buyer Alice. Alice might still be able to compete in the auction if someone that the seller does trust, say Bob, in turn trusts Alice. Then Alice can pass an IOU to Bob who can pass an IOU to the seller. The seller is paid with a commitment from Bob, someone the seller trusts, and Bob receives a commitment from Alice, someone he trusts.

In Section 3, we formalize this notion of a payment infrastructure based on a trust network. The trust network induces pairwise (directed) limits on how

X. Deng and F.C. Graham (Eds.): WINE 2007, LNCS 4858, pp. 257–268, 2007.
© Springer-Verlag Berlin Heidelberg 2007

much compensation can flow from any one agent to another. In this way, trust networks generalize the notion of budget constraints where, instead of a single budget per agent denominated in a common currency, there may exist different budgets for every subset of agents. Note that it is not enough to consider budget limits on how much individual agents can pay the seller since there may be multiple buyers whose payments Bob needs to vouch for. Thus, the amount that a buyer can pay the seller depends on the degree to which other buyers have exhausted the Bob link.

We examine the problem of mechanism design in trust networks, specifically, a multi-item auction of identical items. The auctioneer is a node in the network, and payments to the auctioneer are constrained by link capacities: The payments from a subset of bidders cannot exceed the maximum flow from these nodes to the auctioneer on the trust network. It is not possible to design incentive compatible mechanisms to maximize social welfare in this setting so we define a modified notion of social welfare based on budget-capped values. In Section 4, we show that the winner determination problem—choosing the set of winners that maximizes this modified notion of welfare—is NP-hard. We present an algorithm for this problem in Section 4.2 that exploits the the flow structure in the trust network to approximate the solution within a factor $1 - 1/e$. Using this, in Section 5, we present a pricing scheme that leads to an incentive compatible, individually rational mechanism with feasible payments that respect the group budgets and that approximately maximizes the modified social welfare to within a factor $1 - 1/e$.

The next section compares trust networks with more traditional payment infrastructures and describes the existing trust network implementations that motivate our research.

2   Payment as a Routing Problem

Currencies can in fact operate as abstract IOUs, or obligations. Modern currencies are issued in the form of abstract obligations to provide value of some form, be it banks' obligations to redeem account balances for government notes, governments' obligations to redeem those notes as credit toward taxes due, or e-gold's obligations to store gold in trust for account holders. A decision to accept a certain currency[1] is a decision to trust the issuer to fulfill its obligations. From this perspective, a loan repayment agreement is currency issued by the borrower and accepted by the lender.

Payment is the transfer of obligations from one entity, the payer, to another, the recipient, in a form the recipient will accept. In other words, to make payment, the payer must present obligations from a currency issuer that is trusted by the recipient. The payer is faced with the problem of how to route the payment: how to convert obligations that it holds or can readily obtain (for example, via a line of credit) into obligations from an issuer that the recipient considers

---

[1] Currency here is defined as obligations from a certain issuer, as considered separately from the units of value in which those obligations are accounted.

trustworthy. This routing takes place in a trust network. The most ubiquitous routable financial trust network is the banking system. At the national level this is essentially a tree, with the central bank at the root, regular banks as children of the central bank, and bank customers as the leaves. This arrangement makes it feasible to route payments manually, since there is only one path between any two nodes in a tree.

Analogy to computer networks. Computer networks are built to route information from one computer to another. The evolution of computer networks follows a similar course to that of currency networks. For a small network, computers can be directly connected to each other as needed using wires. As the number of computers grows, this soon becomes unwieldy, and it is easier to connect all the computers to a special intermediary computer (a router), which relays information between computers in the network. Routers accept and transmit data like any other computer, but act as hubs for transferring messages between computers because they are highly connected in the computer network, just as banks act as hubs for transferring obligations between people because they are highly connected in the financial trust network. Eventually, it is desirable to send information between networks, and to accomplish this, several routers can be connected to a super-router, and these in turn can be connected to an even higher router, and so on in a hierarchical fashion as needed. Since there is only a single route between any two points, routing messages in strictly hierarchical networks is simple.

The designers of the Internet did not build it as a strict hierarchical network—primarily because to withstand a nuclear attack, it could not have any single points of failure. As a side effect, the Internet can operate as the most democratic forum for communication ever known, because it does not require, and is in fact resistant to, control by special groups. A non-hierarchical financial network can have similar advantages. Two systems recently implemented by the authors—first Ripple [7] and then Yootles [12]—demonstrate this powerful generalization of the usual financial trust tree. These systems route payments through arbitrary financial trust networks much like the internet routes data through arbitrary computer networks, demonstrating how advances in routing enable the formation of decentralized routable payments. The Yootles system allows its users to conduct auctions of a variety of types [12]. This paper formally defines the concept of a trust network, and describes how auction design is impacted by the payment constraints implied by the network.

3   The Model

We first define our proposed decentralized payment infrastructure. We denominate the hypothetical currency in utils, representing an abstract measure of utility [12], but this choice is orthogonal to our results.

Trust networks.   A trust network, or decentralized ledger, consists of two directed graphs defined on a set of vertices $V = \{0, \ldots, m\}$ representing entities, or agents. (Vertex 0 will be treated specially in the next section.) A set of edges E_O gives the pairwise account balances between nodes. The weight o_{ij} on an edge $(i, j) \in E_O$ quantifies the obligations that i has to j, that is, i is committed to increasing j's utility by o_{ij} utils or, if $o_{ij} < 0$ then j owes $-o_{ij}$ utils to i. By definition, $o_{ij} = -o_{ji}$ for all i, j and $o_{ii} \equiv 0$.

A set of edges E_T gives pairwise credit limits between agents. The weights on these edges quantify the trust in the trust network. An edge $(i, j) \in E_T$ with weight t_{ij} specifies that i has extended j a credit line of t_{ij} utils. In practice these edges may have concomitant interest rates and there may be multiple lines of credit issued between agents at different interest rates. In this paper we ignore interest and assume that every directed pair of agents has exactly one credit limit, possibly zero.

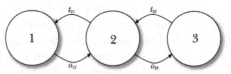

Fig. 1. A trust network with three agents. Credit extended from 1 to 2 and from 2 to 3 are not shown.

The power of a trust network defined above is that arbitrary payments can be made by passing obligations between agents that explicitly trust each other if the network is sufficiently well-connected. For example, in Figure 1 agent 1 can make a payment of x utils to agent 3 by issuing an obligation of x utils to agent 2 and agent 2 issuing an obligation for the same amount to agent 3, increasing both o_{12} and o_{23} by x utils. (Note that agent 2's net balance remains unchanged.) The payment is feasible as long as both 1's remaining credit with 2 (i.e., $t_{21} - o_{12}$) and 2's remaining credit with 3 (i.e., $t_{32} - o_{23}$) are greater than or equal to the payment amount of x utils. This generalizes to arbitrarily long payment chains in the obvious way. The maximum x satisfying the credit constraints along a path from i to j is the *payment capacity* of that path. The overall payment capacity for (i, j) is the amount that could be paid from i to j if each path from i to j was maxed out in sequence—that is, the *maximum flow* [1] from i to j.[2]

Auctions on trust networks. We consider multi-unit auctions of k identical items among n bidders on the trust network. We label the nodes $V = \{0, \ldots, m\}$ so that auctioneer is node 0, and the bidders are $\mathcal{A} = \{1, \ldots, n\}$. (The remaining nodes $\{n + 1, \ldots, m\}$ may be used for routing payments, but do not participate in the auction.) Every bidder i has a private value v_i for the item. Bidders have unit demand—that is, they want no more than one unit of the item.

---

[2] In practice, the system may limit routing, for example by only considering paths up to a certain length or only considering a subset of all paths. If so, the system will be computing lower bounds on the true payment capacities. Payment feasibility thus degrades gracefully with computational restrictions on payment routing.

To study this problem, we do not need to consider the account balances and credit limits on the edges of the trust network separately—all that matters is the remaining credit on a link. The trust network can therefore be defined by a single graph G comprising the same set of vertices V and a set of edges E representing the payment capacities of edges, where an edge $(i,j) \in E$ has capacity $c_{ij} = t_{ji} - o_{ij}$. We assume that the network structure and link capacities c_{ij} are publicly known: bidders cannot strategically report link capacities to the auctioneer.

The link capacities limit the maximum payment that can be made by any subset of bidders $S \subseteq A$ to the auctioneer. We denote by $c(S)$ the maximum flow that can be routed from S to 0 on the graph with link capacities c_{ij}; $c(S)$ is a *group budget*, or combined budget, for the nodes in S. This generalizes the notion of individually budget-constrained bidders [3]. (However, note that our setting is a special case of combined budgets: not all values for combined budgets can be derived from maximum flow constraints on a network with link capacities.) We will refer to payments that can be routed along the trust network without violating any link capacity constraints as *feasible payments*. Feasible payments correspond exactly to those where the total payment from every subset of nodes is less than or equal to the budget constraint for that subset.

Due to the budget constraints, it is not possible to design an incentive compatible mechanism to maximize social welfare, or the sum of private values of winning bidders.[3] Instead we define a modified notion of welfare. For any subset of bidders $S \subseteq A$, let $v(S)$ denote the budget-capped value of this set, defined as the optimal value of the linear program with variables x_i:

$$\text{maximize} \quad \sum_{i \in S} x_i$$
$$\text{s.t.} \quad \sum_{i \in T} x_i \leq c(T) \quad \forall T \subseteq S \qquad (1)$$
$$0 \leq x_i \leq v_i.$$

In a regular auction, a bidder's private value can be thought of as the maximum individually rational payment the bidder is willing to make to the auctioneer; here the budget-capped value of a set of bidders is the maximum individually rational payment from this set of bidders that are feasible on the trust network. When the group budgets, $c(T)$, are sufficiently large, that is, $c(T) \geq \sum_{i \in T} v_i$ for all T, then the modified welfare is exactly the sum of the valuations of the bidders: $v(S) = \sum_{i \in S} v_i$. We define $v(S, b)$ as the value of (1) with v_i replaced by b_i (i.e., with the constraint $0 \leq x_i \leq b_i$). As usual, we will use b_{-i} to denote the vector b with the ith component removed.

---

[3] To see why, consider a mechanism that tries to maximize welfare in the face of budget-constrained bidders. The mechanism would have to base allocation decisions on agents' reported values—values that can be greater than what the agents could pay. But then low valuation agents with the same ability to pay would report valuations that made them appear identical to the high-valuation agents.

4   Complexity of Winner Determination

In this section we study the winner determination problem in a k-unit auction on a trust network, *i.e.*, to select a set of at most k bidders on a trust network to maximize the budget-capped social welfare defined in §3. This is essentially equivalent to the problem of selecting k sources in a graph that can send the maximum amount of flow to a given destination (the auctioneer). The problem can be studied in two models: one where ex-post individual rationality is required (the ex-post IR model), and another where it is enough to satisfy ex-ante individual rationality (the ex-ante IR model).

Problem Formulation.   We start by formulating the problem in the ex-post IR model as the mathematical program (2) below. The binary variable y_i in the program indicates whether the bidder i is selected as a winner. The variable x_i is the amount of "value" extracted from bidder i. The constraints (2c)–(2e) guarantee that these amounts are routable through the trust network. The variable $z_{u,w}$ in these constraints corresponds to the amount of flow routed through the directed edge (u, w) in the graph.

The ex-ante IR problem can be formulated similarly, except the constraint (2g) is relaxed to $0 \le y_i \le 1$. The value of y_i means that the bidder i receives a unit of the good with probability y_i. Note that the ex-ante IR property allows us to charge a bidder, who (due to the outcome of the coin flip) does not receive any item, as long as the expected value the bidder receives is not more than the expected amount she pays. The winner determination problem in the ex-ante IR case can thus be solved exactly by solving a linear program. For the rest of this section, we will focus on the winner determination problem in the ex-post IR model, and show tight hardness and approximability results.

$$\text{maximize} \quad \sum_{i \in A} x_i \tag{2a}$$

$$\text{s.t.} \quad \forall i \in A : x_i \le v_i y_i \tag{2b}$$

$$\forall u \in \{n+1, \ldots, m\} : \sum_{(u,w) \in E} z_{u,w} = \sum_{(w,u) \in E} z_{w,u} \tag{2c}$$

$$\forall u \in A : \sum_{(u,w) \in E} z_{u,w} - \sum_{(w,u) \in E} z_{w,u} \ge x_i \tag{2d}$$

$$\forall (u,w) \in E : 0 \le z_{u,w} \le c_{u,w} \tag{2e}$$

$$\sum_{i \in A} y_i \le k \tag{2f}$$

$$\forall i \in A : y_i \in \{0, 1\} \tag{2g}$$

4.1   Hardness of the Ex-post Problem

The following theorem shows that the winner determination problem is hard to approximate within any factor better than $1 - 1/e$, even if all edges of the trust network have capacity 1.

Theorem 1. *If the winner determination problem for ex-post IR multi-unit auctions on trust networks can be approximated within a factor of $1 - 1/e + \varepsilon$ for any $\varepsilon > 0$, then $NP \subseteq TIME(n^{O(\log \log n)})$.*

Proof. We reduce the problem of maximum k-coverage to this problem. An instance of the max k-coverage problem consists of a number k and a collection of subsets $S_1, S_2, \ldots, S_p$ of a universe $\mathcal{U}$. The goal is to find a subcollection $S_{i_1}, \ldots, S_{i_k}$ of size k whose union has the maximum size. Given such an instance, we construct an instance of the winner determination problem as follows: the parameter k corresponds to the number of items available for sale, each set S_i corresponds to a bidder i, and each element of $\mathcal{U}$ corresponds to a non-bidder node in the trust network. The only other node in the trust network corresponds to the auctioneer, which is denoted by 0. For every element $j \in \mathcal{U}$, there is an edge from j to 0, and for every $i \in \{1, \ldots, p\}$ and $j \in S_i$, there is an edge from the vertex i to the vertex j. The capacity of all edges are 1. The value of each bidder $i \in \{1, \ldots, p\}$ is $|S_i|$. It is easy to see that the budget-capped value of a collection of bidders is equal to the size of the union of the corresponding sets. Therefore the solution of the winner determination problem is precisely equal to the solution of the max k-coverage problem. The hardness result follows from a theorem of [6], who show that the max k-coverage problem is hard to approximate within any factor better than $1 - 1/e$, unless $NP \subseteq TIME(n^{O(\log \log n)})$.

4.2   Approximation Algorithm

The above theorem shows that the ex-post IR winner determination problem is at least as hard as the max k-coverage problem. For the max k-coverage problem, there is a well-known greedy algorithm that achieves an approximation factor of $1 - 1/e$. Using this algorithm, and a lemma proved in [4] for a different problem, we can show that the ex-post IR winner determination problem can be approximated within a factor of $1 - 1/e$.

The algorithm, which is a natural generalization of the greedy algorithm for max k-coverage, is as follows. Start with $S = \emptyset$. In every iteration, select a bidder that maximizes the *marginal value* $\mathrm{v}(S \cup \{i\}) - \mathrm{v}(S)$, and add this bidder to S. Continue this for k iterations, until $|S| = k$. To prove the approximation factor of this algorithm, we need the following lemma, which is an adaptation of Lemma 3 in [4].

Lemma 1. *Let G be a directed graph with capacities on the edges, and S_1 and S_2 be two subsets of vertices of G. Consider a maximum flow f from the vertices in S_1 to a special vertex $0 \notin S_1 \cup S_2$, and let f_i denote the amount of flow originating from the vertex $i \in S_1$ in this solution. Then there is a solution to the maximum flow problem from vertices in $S_1 \cup S_2$ to the vertex 0, in which the amount of flow originating from every vertex $i \in S_1$ is precisely f_i.*

Proof (sketch). We use the Ford-Fulkerson [1] algorithm for solving the maximum flow problem from $S_1 \cup S_2$ to 0. In each iteration of the algorithm, an augmenting path is found, with respect to the current feasible flow, to increase the total flow sent from $S_1 \cup S_2$ to 0: the Ford-Fulkerson theorem guarantees that such an augmenting path can be found in any non-optimal flow. To prove the lemma, we apply this algorithm starting from the flow f. If in each iteration we find the shortest augmenting path from $S_1 \cup S_2$ to 0, the path cannot contain any vertex of $S_1 \cup S_2$ as an interior vertex, and therefore it will never change the amount of flow originating from a vertex in S_1. Hence, in the final maximum flow computed by this algorithm, the amount of flow originating from every $i \in S_1$ is f_i.

Theorem 2. *The greedy algorithm achieves an approximation ratio of $1 - 1/e$ for the winner determination problem in ex-post IR multi-unit auctions on trust networks.*

Proof. Consider an instance of the problem, and let OPT denote the value of the optimal solution on this instance, and S^* denote the set of winners in this solution. Let T_i denote the value of the solution found at the end of the i'th iteration of the greedy algorithm, and set $T_0 = 0$. The main ingredient of the proof is the following inequality, which bounds the amount of marginal value in iteration r:

$$T_r - T_{r-1} \geq \frac{\text{OPT} - T_{r-1}}{k} \qquad (3)$$

To prove this, we construct the graph G' from the trust network by adding a *shadow* vertex i' for every bidder i, and connecting i' to i with an edge of capacity v_i. Clearly, the budget-capped value of any set S of bidders is equal to the maximum amount of flow that can be sent from the set of shadow vertices of bidders in S to the vertex 0. Let S_1 denote the set of shadow vertices corresponding to the bidders selected in the first $i - 1$ iterations of the greedy algorithm, and S_2 denote the shadow vertices for bidders in S^*. Consider a solution to the maximum flow problem from the vertices in S_1 to 0, and denote by f_i the amount of flow originating from $i \in S_1$ in this solution. By Lemma 1, there is a maximum flow $\tilde{f}$ from the vertices of $S_1 \cup S_2$ to 0 in which the flow originating from any vertex $i \in S_1$ is precisely f_1. On the other hand, since the amount of flow that can be sent from S_2 to 0 is OPT, the value of the flow $\tilde{f}$ is also at least OPT. Therefore in $\tilde{f}$, vertices in $S_2 \setminus S_1$ send at least $\text{OPT} - \sum_{i \in S_1} f_i = \text{OPT} - T_{r-1}$. Since there are at most k vertices in $S_2 \setminus S_1$, there must be a vertex i' in this set (corresponding to the bidder i), which sends at least $(\text{OPT} - T_{r-1})/k$ units of flow to 0. This implies that the marginal value resulting from adding the vertex i in the r'th iteration of the algorithm is at least $(\text{OPT} - T_{r-1})/k$. Since the algorithm always adds a vertex with the highest marginal value, the inequality (3) follows. Inequality (3) can be re-arranged as follows:

$$\left(1 - \frac{1}{k}\right)^{-r} T_r \geq \frac{\text{OPT}}{k}\left(1 - \frac{1}{k}\right)^{-r} + \left(1 - \frac{1}{k}\right)^{-(r-1)} T_{r-1}.$$

By adding these inequalities for $r = 1, \ldots, k$ and simplifying, we obtain

$$T_k \geq \text{OPT}\left(1 - \left(1 - \frac{1}{k}\right)^k\right) \geq \left(1 - \frac{1}{e}\right)\text{OPT}.$$

This completes the proof of the theorem, as T_k is the value of the greedy solution.

The above proof heavily uses the combinatorial structure of the budgets imposed by the trust network, and therefore does not generalize to the more abstract model of collective budgets. In fact, the winner determination problem in the abstract model cannot be approximated to within any factor better than $n^{1-\varepsilon}$ even if all subsets that have a budget are of size two, as shown by the following reduction from the maximum independent set problem. Each node of the given graph G corresponds to a bidder of value 1, and the collective budget of any pair of bidders connected by an edge in G is 1. No other subset of bidders has a collective budget. It is clear that the solution of the winner determination problem in this instance corresponds to a maximum independent set in G. By the hardness of the maximum independent set problem [8], the winner determination problem in this case is hard to approximate.

4.3   Algorithms for Special Cases

Despite the hardness result in Theorem 1, the winner determination problem can be solved exactly in some special cases, most notably in the case that the trust network is hierarchical, as for a national banking system.

Theorem 3. *If the underlying undirected graph of the trust network G is a tree, the winner determination problem for ex-post IR multi-unit auctions on G can be solved in polynomial time.*

Proof (sketch). First, we show that without changing the value of the solution, we may transform the trust network into an (incomplete) binary tree T with bidders as leaf nodes. Also, for every bidder i, add a shadow node i', and add a link from i' to i with capacity v_i. Let $\mathcal{U}$ denote the set of shadow nodes. Define $V[v, l]$ as the maximum flow that can be routed to an internal node v from at most l nodes in $\mathcal{U}$ that are in the subtree rooted at v. Then

$$V[v, l] = \max_{l_1+l_2=l} (\min(V[v_1, l_1], c_{v_1,v}) + \min(V[v_2, l_2], c_{v_2,v})),$$

where v_1 and v_2 are the children of v. It is not hard to see that values of $V[v, l]$ can be computed efficiently using dynamic programming given the above recursive formula. The solution to the winner determination problem is $V[0, k]$.

5   Mechanism Design

In this section, we discuss the question of designing an incentive compatible mechanism that maximizes the modified welfare. The solution to the winner determination problem specifies the allocation of items amongst bidders that maximizes, or approximately maximizes, modified welfare; the pricing scheme must be chosen to ensure incentive compatibility, as well as feasible payments.

We show that mechanisms $\mathcal{M}$ and $\mathcal{M}'$, stated below, are incentive compatible, individually rational mechanisms with feasible payments, that respectively maximize and approximately maximize modified welfare: $\mathcal{M}$ assumes that the winner determination problem can be solved exactly, and allocates items according to this solution, while $\mathcal{M}'$ allocates items according to the greedy algorithm in the previous section. (Although the mechanisms look very similar, the proofs for feasibility of payments are different, so we present them separately.)

Mechanism $\mathcal{M}$: Every bidder submits a bid b_i to the auctioneer.

- *Allocation*: The *winning* set is the lexicographically first subset S^* of bidders that maximizes $\mathrm{v}(S, b)$ over all subsets with $|S| \leq k$. Assign the k items to bidders in the winning set S^*.
- *Pricing*: Charge bidder $i \in S$ the smallest value $p_i \leq b_i$ such that i would still belong to the winning set with bids (b_{-i}, p_i).[4]

Note that the winning set need not be S^* with input b_j for $j \neq i$ and p_i—we only require that the winning set contains i.

Theorem 4. *The mechanism $\mathcal{M}$ is incentive compatible, ex-post individually rational, maximizes modified social welfare, and leads to payments that are feasible on the trust network.*

Proof. Incentive compatibility follows from the results in [2]; a direct proof can also be found in the full version of this paper. The main component of the proof is showing that these payments are feasible, *i.e.*, they can be routed to the auctioneer along the network. For this, we need to show that the payments p_i satisfy the first set of constraints in (1).

Let $w^* = \mathrm{v}(S^*)$ denote the value of the winning set, when $b_j = v_j$ for all bidders j. Abusing notation slightly, let $\mathrm{v}(S, b_i)$ denote the value of set S when bidder i bids b_i and all other bidders continue to bid v_j. For $i \in S^*$, let v_i' be the smallest value such that $v(S^*, v_i')$ is still w^*. In fact, $v_i' = x_i^*$, where x_i^* is the smallest value of x_i amongst all optimal solution vectors x for the linear program (1) (with the true values v_i as input).

With $b_i = v_i'$, S^* is still the winning set: $\mathrm{v}(S)$ is unchanged for sets not containing i, and $\mathrm{v}(S, v_i') \leq \mathrm{v}(S, v_i)$ for sets containing i, since $v_i' \leq v_i$ (the feasible set in (1) with $b_i = v_i'$ is a subset of the feasible set with $b_i = v_i$, so the optimal value cannot increase). Since S^* was the lexicographically first set with $b_i = v_i$, and the value of no set increases when b_i decreases to v_i', S^* is still the lexicographically first set with the highest value when $b_i = v_i'$. Thus the bid at which i still belongs to the winning set is at least as small as v_i', *i.e.*, $p_i \leq v_i' = x_i^*$. Since x (the optimal solution to 1 with entry x_i^* for bidder i) is feasible, we have

$$x_i^* + \sum_{j \neq i, j \in T} x_j \leq \mathrm{c}(T) \quad \forall\, T,$$

---

[4] Note that this price p_i need not be the same as the smallest report p_i' at which i still belongs to some set with the highest value (*i.e.*, not necessarily the lexicographically first set): clearly $p_i \geq p_i'$; p_i can in fact be strictly larger.

Using identical arguments for all other winners j, $p_j \leq x_j^* \leq x_j$, and substituting above, we get

$$\sum_{i \in T} p_i \leq \sum_{i \in T} x_i^* \leq c(T) \quad \forall\, T,$$

i.e., the payments are feasible. Individual rationality follows from the fact that $p_i \leq v_i' \leq v_i$ if the bidder wins an item, and is 0 otherwise.

The greedy algorithm in Section 4.2 can be used to design a mechanism $\mathcal{M}'$ that approximates modified social welfare to a factor $1 - 1/e$, when the winner determination problem cannot be solved exactly:

- *Allocation in $\mathcal{M}'$*: Choose the set of winning bidders according to the greedy algorithm in Theorem 2, breaking all ties in favor of the bidder with the lower index.
- *Pricing in $\mathcal{M}'$* : Charge bidder $i \in S$ the smallest value $p_i \leq b_i$, such that i would still be chosen by the greedy algorithm when all bidders $j \neq i$ report b_j, and bidder i reports p_i.

Theorem 5. *The mechanism $\mathcal{M}'$ approximates modified social welfare by a factor $1 - 1/e$, is incentive compatible, ex-post individually rational, and results in feasible payments.*

The proof of feasibility of payments relies on Lemma 1, and can be found in the full version of this paper.

6   Discussion

There are myriad additional mechanism design problems that can be studied in the context of trust networks. For instance, we might have multiple sellers, heterogeneous goods, the auctioneer may prefer to maximize revenue instead of welfare and so on [5]. However, the impossibility result in [3] shows that in many of these cases achieving incentive compatibility in dominant strategies is impossible. A natural extension to consider, particularly for the case of repeated auctions, is interest rates on the credit links Interest causes positive balances to become more positive over time and negative balances to become more negative. Not only does this complicate the payment routing problem (unless a single universal interest rate is used) but it means link capacities decrease over time, impacting the mechanism design problem. Other mechanisms besides auctions are also affected by the constraints inherent in a trust network. For example, betting games like poker become complicated when not every bet is honored by every player and if the degree to which a bet is honored depends on how other players—intermediate nodes in the trust network—fare in the game. Other mechanisms of interest to study in this setting include decision auctions, prediction markets [13] (with and without automated market makers [9,10,11]), and various incentive schemes for participation in the trust network itself.

The continued growth and development of online services and protocols for building decentralized financial trust networks will also pose questions and challenges in areas such as routing, distributed transactions, online identity verification, reputation systems, and spam prevention. Both in terms of design and analysis of trust networks and in terms of mechanism design problems on trust networks, we hope that this paper opens a number of interesting research avenues.

Acknowledgments.   We thank Varsha Dani and Lance Fortnow helping to clarify the mechanism design problem in this paper. We thank Bethany Soule for valuable suggestions and for (yootling us for) creating the figure.

References

1. Ahuja, R.K., Magnanti, T.L., Orlin, J.B.: Network Flows: Theory, Algorithms, and Applications. Prentice-Hall, Englewood Cliffs (1993)
2. Archer, A., Tardos, E.: Truthful mechanisms for one-parameter agents. In: IEEE Symposium on Foundations of Computer Science, pp. 482–491 (2001)
3. Borgs, C., Chayes, J., Immorlica, N., Mahdian, M., Saberi, A.: Multi-unit auctions with budget-constrained bidders. In: Proceedings of the 6th ACM Conference on Electronic Commerce (EC), pp. 44–51 (2005)
4. Chandra, R., Qiu, L., Jain, K., Mahdian, M.: Optimizing the placement of integration points in multi-hop wireless networks. In: Proceedings of the 12th IEEE International Conference on Network Protocols (ICNP) (2004)
5. Dash, R.K., Jennings, N.R., Parkes, D.C.: Computational mechanism design: A call to arms. IEEE Intelligent Systems 18, 40–47 (2003)
6. Feige, U.: A threshold of $\ln n$ for approximating set cover. J.ACM 45, 634–652 (1998)
7. Fugger, R.: The ripple project (2004), http://ripple.sourceforge.net
8. Håstad, J.: Clique is hard to approximate within $n^{1-\epsilon}$. Acta Mathematica 182, 105–142 (1999)
9. Hanson, R.D.: Combinatorial information market design. Information Systems Frontiers 5(1), 107–119 (2003)
10. Hanson, R.D.: Logarithmic market scoring rules for modular combinatorial information aggregation. Journal of Prediction Markets 1(1), 1–15 (2007)
11. Pennock, D.M.: A dynamic pari-mutuel market for hedging, wagering, and information aggregation. In: David, M. (ed.) Proceedings of the Fifth ACM Conference on Electronic Commerce (EC 2004) (May 2004)
12. Reeves, D.M., Soule, B.M., Kasturi, T.: Yootopia! SIGecom Exchanges 6, 1–26 (2006)
13. Wolfers, J., Zitzewitz, E.: Prediction markets. Journal of Economic Perspective 18(2), 107–126 (2004)

Stochastic Mechanism Design

(Extended Abstract)*

Samuel Ieong[1], Anthony Man-Cho So[2], and Mukund Sundararajan[1]

[1] Department of Computer Science, Stanford University
[2] Department of Sys. Eng. & Eng. Mgmt., The Chinese University of Hong Kong
{sieong,manchoso,mukunds}@cs.stanford.edu

Abstract. We study the problem of welfare maximization in a novel setting motivated by the standard stochastic two-stage optimization with
recourse model. We identify and address algorithmic and game-theoretic
challenges that arise from this framework. In contrast, prior work in algorithmic mechanism design has focused almost exclusively on optimization
problems without uncertainty. We make two kinds of contributions.

First, we introduce a family of mechanisms that induce truth-telling
in general two-stage stochastic settings. These mechanisms are *not* simple extensions of VCG mechanisms, as the latter do not readily address incentive issues in multi-stage settings. Our mechanisms implement
the welfare maximizer in *sequential ex post* equilibrium for risk-neutral
agents. We provide formal evidence that this is the strongest implementation one can expect.

Next, we investigate algorithmic issues by studying a novel combinatorial optimization problem called the *Coverage Cost* problem, which
includes the well-studied Fixed-Tree Multicast problem as a special case.
We note that even simple instances of the stochastic variant of this problem are $\#P$-Hard. We propose an algorithm that approximates optimal
welfare with high probability, using a combination of sampling and supermodular set function maximization—the techniques may be of independent interest. To the best of our knowledge, our work is the first to
address both game-theoretic *and* algorithmic challenges of mechanism
design in multi-stage settings with data uncertainty.

1   Introduction

Welfare maximization has been a central problem in both computer science and
economics research. Much work to-date, especially in algorithmic mechanism
design, has focused on welfare maximization in deterministic settings [11,14,15].
In this paper, we identify and address new challenges that arise in stochastic
optimization frameworks. In particular, we consider both algorithmic and incentive issues motivated by the *two-stage stochastic optimization with recourse*

---

* A journal version of the paper is under preparation and a draft can be found at the
authors' websites. Samuel Ieong is funded by a Stanford Graduate Fellowship and
NSF ITR-0205633.

model, a model that has been studied extensively in both the operations research community [5], and the computer science community [9,16,17].

Roughly speaking, two-stage optimization requires a decision maker (the *center*) to make sequential decisions. In the first stage, given a probability distribution over possible problem instances (called *scenarios*), the center deploys some resources and incurs some cost. Typically, such an initial deployment is not a feasible solution to every possible scenario, but represents a *hedge* on the center's part. In the second stage, once a specific scenario is realized, the center may take *recourse* actions to augment its initial solution to ensure feasibility, and incurs an additional cost for doing so. The goal of the center is to minimize its *expected* cost (or maximize its expected profit).

In this paper, we are interested in situations where the uncertainty is initially unknown to the center, and it needs to learn this information from *selfish agents* in order to maximize social welfare. However, an agent may lie about its private information to improve its utility. To solve this informational problem, the center has to interleave elicitation and optimization. In order to appreciate the challenges that arise from the stochastic setting, let us first consider a stochastic variant of the well-studied *Fixed Tree Multicast (FTM)* problem [1,6,13].

Recall that an FTM instance consists of a tree T with undirected edges and a designated node called the *root*. A set of players, $U = \{1, 2, \ldots, n\}$, are located at the nodes of the tree. Each player $i \in U$ is interested in a service provided by the root and has a private value θ_i for being *served*. Serving a user involves building the path from the root to the node at which the user is located. The center serves a set $S \subseteq U$ of users by building edges in the union of paths that correspond to the serviced nodes, and pays the costs of the edges built.

In our stochastic two-stage formulation, there is initially some uncertainty regarding the values of players being served. This uncertainty is modeled as a distribution over values for each player, and is resolved in the second stage when each learns of its value. Both the distribution and the value are private to the player. Edges can be built in either the first or the second stage, with the costs being higher in the second stage for the corresponding edge. Such an increase in costs can be viewed as a premium for the extra information obtained in the second stage. A precise formulation is given in Section 4.

Our objective is to maximize expected social welfare — the sum of the values of the players served less the cost incurred. *What are the challenges introduced by the two-stage stochastic setting?*

The first challenge is game-theoretic. While Vickrey-Clarke-Groves (VCG) mechanisms can induce players to report their true information in single-shot settings [8], they do not apply directly to the two-stage setting. We demonstrate that it is possible to induce truth-telling behavior in *sequential ex post* equilibrium via an explicit construction of a two-stage mechanism. This solution concept is different from classical ex post implementation, and will be further explained in Section 4. We also formally argue that this is the strongest implementation one can expect, by showing that it is impossible to construct a mechanism that implements the social objective in dominant strategies.

The second challenge is algorithmic. We consider a novel combinatorial optimization problem called the *Coverage Cost* problem (see Section 5 for the precise formulation) to investigate algorithmic issues that arise in such settings. The Coverage Cost (CC) problem contains FTM as a special case. We find that maximizing welfare can be difficult even when the deterministic version is easy to solve. For instance, maximizing welfare in a deterministic, single-shot version of FTM can be solved by a linear time algorithm [6]. On the other hand, maximizing welfare for a stochastic version of FTM is #P-hard (Theorem 5). We then develop an algorithm for stochastic CC problems that yields an additive approximation to the optimal expected welfare with high probability. Our solution is based on a combination of sampling techniques (see, e.g., [12]) and supermodular function maximization [10] (Theorem 6), and may be of independent interest.

Due to space constraints, most proofs have been omitted in this extended abstract. Readers interested in more details can find the proofs in the full paper.

2 Related Work

A few recent papers have focused on *dynamic mechanisms*, under the setting of Markov Decision Processes [2,3]. Our work differs from these in three respects. First, to the best of our knowledge, this is the first time an algorithmic aspect of a two-stage mechanism has been studied. The computational hardness leads to the use of a sampling-based approximation algorithm, and we describe the precise trade-off between incentive compatibility and computational efficiency (Theorem 4). Second, by application of backward induction, we identify a *family* of incentive compatible mechanisms, rather than a single mechanism. Finally, we introduce the *sequential* generalization of classical solution concepts, and formally argue why a stronger incentive guarantee — namely an implementation in dominant strategies — is impossible to achieve (Theorem 3). We expect our impossibility result to be applicable to the works mentioned above.

To the best of our knowledge, our algorithmic result, i.e. approximating maximum welfare for a stochastic coverage cost instance, is not obtainable via current techniques. For instance, the technique in [4] requires the objective function to be non-negative for all possible actions and scenarios. This condition does not hold in our problem. The technique in [12] does not address how the underlying problem is to be solved, and yields a different bound that depends on the variance of a certain quantity.

3 Stochastic Welfare Maximization

In this section, we define stochastic welfare maximization in a general setting. The terminology and the general definition introduced in this section are motivated by mechanism design. We review two-stage stochastic optimization in the appendix and refer the interested readers to the survey [17].

Informally, in a two-stage stochastic welfare maximization problem, the center decides on the eventual social outcome in two stages. In the first stage, with less information available, the center commits some resources, at a cost. In the second stage, with additional, precise information available, it augments initial allocation by performing (typically more expensive) *recourse* actions.

Formally, in the first stage the center picks an outcome from the set of feasible outcomes $\mathcal{O}^1$, incurring a first-stage cost $c^1 : \mathcal{O}^1 \mapsto \mathbb{R}$. In the second stage, the center may augment the first stage allocation by picking an outcome from the set $\mathcal{O}^2$, incurring an additional cost $c^2 : \mathcal{O}^1 \times \mathcal{O}^2 \mapsto \mathbb{R}$. Note that the second-stage cost depends on both the first and second-stage choices.

Next, we describe the relationship between agent types and their valuations.[1] Let Θ_i be the (ground) type space of agent i, for $i = 1, \ldots, n$. Let $v_i : \Theta_i \times \mathcal{O}^1 \times \mathcal{O}^2 \mapsto \mathbb{R}$ denote i's *valuation*. In other words, an agent's valuation depends on its realized type and the outcomes of both stages.

The ground type of an agent is revealed in two stages. In the first stage, an agent i only learns of a *probability distribution* δ_i over its ground types. We call this distribution the agent's *supertype*, and denote the supertype space of agent i by Δ_i. Its elements, $\delta_i \in \Delta_i$, are distributions on Θ_i. In the second stage, agent i learns of its *ground type* (or *type* for short), realized according to the distribution δ_i that is *independent* of other agents' type realizations. We call the collective realized types of all agents in the system a *scenario*, corresponding to a scenario in two-stage stochastic optimization.

Most work on two-stage stochastic optimization focus on minimizing cost. In contrast, we are interested in maximizing *social welfare* as defined below:

Definition 1. *The social welfare of outcomes* $x^1 \in \mathcal{O}^1$ *and* $x^2 \in \mathcal{O}^2$ *in scenario* $\theta = (\theta_1, \ldots, \theta_n)$ *is:*

$$SW(\theta, x^1, x^2) = \sum_{i=1}^{n} v_i(\theta_i, x^1, x^2) - c^1(x^1) - c^2(x^1, x^2) \qquad (1)$$

As first-stage outcomes are picked without precise information on agent types, we focus on maximizing *expected* social welfare, i.e.

$$\max \mathbb{E}_{\theta \sim \delta} \left[SW(\theta, x^1, x^2) \right] \qquad (2)$$

where $\theta \sim \delta$ means that the scenario vector θ is distributed according to δ.

4   Mechanism Design Formulation

We now address the first challenge in stochastic welfare maximization, that of eliciting the supertypes and the realized types from selfish agents. Our treatment is fully general, and applies to any two-stage stochastic optimization problems.

First, let us define agents' utility functions. We assume that agents have *quasi-linear* utilities. If t is the transfer to agent i, then he has utility:

$$u_i(\theta_i, x^1, x^2, t) = v_i(\theta_i, x^1, x^2) + t \qquad (3)$$

---

[1] For notation, when a type/supertype (space) is subscripted, it refers to that of a particular agent; when it is not, it refers to the Cartesian product over the agents.

We also assume that agents are *risk-neutral* in the first stage, i.e., they look to maximize their expected utility over the distribution of scenarios.

The mechanism design framework is as follows:

Definition 2. *A two-stage stochastic mechanism* is *parametrized by a pair of mechanisms,* $(\langle f^1, \{t_i^1\}_{i=1}^n \rangle, \langle f^2, \{t_i^2\}_{i=1}^n \rangle)$, *where:*

1. Initially, each agent i has a supertype $\delta_i \in \Delta_i$. The first-stage mechanism accepts "supertype" bids from agents.
2. The mechanism applies the decision rule, $f^1 : \Delta \mapsto \mathcal{O}^1$ to pick a first-stage outcome as a function of declared supertypes. It applies the transfer functions $t_i^1 : \Delta \mapsto \mathbb{R}$ to determine first-stage transfers for each agent i.
3. Each agent i now realizes its type θ_i according to the distribution specified by the supertype δ_i. The mechanism accepts "type" bids from each agent.
4. The second-stage mechanism applies the decision rule, $f^2 : \Delta \times \mathcal{O}^1 \times \Theta \mapsto \mathcal{O}^2$ and picks a second-stage outcome as a function of the declared types, the declared supertypes, and the first-stage outcome. It applies the transfer functions $t_i^2 : \Delta \times \mathcal{O}^1 \times \Theta \mapsto \mathbb{R}$ to determine second-stage transfers for each agent i. At this stage the utility of each agent i, $u_i(\theta_i, x^1, x^2, t_i^1 + t_i^2)$, is determined based on its true type, the two outcomes, and the two transfers.

We model the game induced by the two-stage stochastic mechanism among the agents as a *dynamic game of incomplete information*. The strategy of each agent specifies its actions for each of its information sets. Note that an agent's second-stage action may depend on the first stage outcome, the agent's supertype and the agent's realized type. Thus, we define the strategy of agent i with supertype δ_i and type θ_i to be $s_i(\delta_i, \theta_i) = \langle s_i^1(\delta_i), s_i^2(\delta_i, x^1, \theta_i) \rangle$, where x^1 is the (publicly observable) first-stage decision made by the center, and s_i^1 and s_i^2 are the strategy mappings of agent i in the two stages.

4.1 *Sequential* Solution Concepts

Before explaining our mechanism, let us first consider what solution concept is appropriate for our setting. Classical solution concepts, including dominant-strategy (DS), ex post (EP), and Bayes-Nash (BN) equilibrium, all focus on whether an agent has incentive to deviate from truth-telling *knowing its own type*. For example, in the classical BN equilibrium, an agent cannot deviate from its strategy and improve its expected utility, where the expectation is taken over the distribution of the other agent's types. In contrast, in our two-stage setting, an agent is also uncertain about its own realized type in the first stage. The uncertainty about an agent's own type makes these classical concepts inappropriate for our setting. Formally,

Theorem 1. *For general two-stage stochastic optimization problems, if the outcomes picked by the mechanism depend on both the supertype and ground type of an agent, then there exists a supertype space for which the agent may have incentive to lie about its supertype if he foresees its realized type. This holds even if the agent is the only participant in the mechanism.*

The impossibility result is based on a public-good problem where the center can decide to serve the agent in either the first stage, the second stage, or not at all, and the agents may have a high or low type realization.

In order to match the flow of the information in the execution of the mechanism with the timing of agents' reports, we introduce a *sequential* generalization of the classical solution concepts. Informally, a sequential solution is one where agents have no incentive to deviate from their equilibrium strategy given the information available up to the time they take an action. Applied to our setting, a set of strategies is in sequential EP equilibrium if an agent

- cannot improve its *expected utility* by lying in the first stage, where the expectation is taken over the scenarios, even if he knows the other agents' true supertype, provided the other agents are truthful; and
- cannot improve its utility by lying in the second stage[2].

4.2   A *Sequential Ex Post* Implementation of Welfare Maximizer

Since we are interested in implementing the welfare maximizer, the decision rules for both stages are fixed, and our goal is to find transfer functions such that truth-telling by all agents constitutes a sequential EP equilibrium.

We start by noting that once first-stage decisions have been made, the situation resembles a standard one-shot VCG setting. Hence, we have:

Lemma 1. *For any first-stage decisions $\overline{x}^1 \in \mathcal{O}^1$, first-stage payments t^1, realization of types θ, the family of Groves mechanism implements the social welfare maximizer, conditional on the first-stage decisions, in dominant strategies.*

Henceforth, we set the second-stage transfer function to be:

$$t_i^{2*}(\delta, \overline{x}^1, \hat{\theta}) = \sum_{j \neq i} v(\hat{\theta}_j, \overline{x}^1, x^{2*}) - c^2(\overline{x}^1, x^{2*}) + g_i^2(\delta_{-i}, \theta_{-i}) + h_i^2(\delta, \hat{\theta}_{-i})$$

where $g_i^2(\cdot, \cdot)$ is an arbitrary function that does not dependent on either δ_i or θ_i, and $h_i^2(\cdot, \cdot)$ is an arbitrary function that does not depend on θ_i.

We next apply the technique of *backward induction* to analyze the first stage of the dynamic game. Suppose that we fix our second-stage mechanism to be a Groves mechanism $\langle f^{2*}, \{t_i^{2*}\}_{i=1}^n \rangle$. When we evaluate the expected utility of an agent's first-stage strategy, we can assume that all agents will truthfully report their second-stage realized types. By propagating the expected transfers in the second stage to the first stage, we find the following family of transfer functions that helps to implement the first-stage decision rule truthfully. The proof can be found in the full paper.

Theorem 2. *Let x^{1*} be the optimal first-stage decisions based on the declared supertypes $\hat{\delta}$. Let the first-stage transfers be given by:*

$$t_i^{1*}(\hat{\delta}) = -c^1(x^{1*}) + h_i^1(\hat{\delta}_{-i}) - \mathbb{E}_{\theta_{-i} \sim \delta_{-i}}[h_i^2(\hat{\delta}, \theta_{-i})]$$

---

[2] In fact, in our mechanism, truth-telling is weakly dominant in the second stage.

where $h_i^1(\cdot)$ is an arbitrary function that does not depend on the declaration $\hat{\delta}_i$ of agent i. Then, together with any Groves mechanism in the second stage, the two-stage mechanism implements the expected social welfare maximizer in sequential ex post equilibrium.

For a concrete application of this theorem, we consider the problem of implementing the social welfare maximizer for a class of problems known as the stochastic two-stage *coverage cost* problems in Section 5, which includes (stochastic) public goods and FTM problems as special cases.

Similar mechanisms have been proposed in [2,3]. Our results differ in that our proof is based on an explicit backward induction analysis. As a result, we obtain a family of incentive compatible mechanisms, of which the mechanisms in [2,3], when specialized to a two-stage setting, are members of the family.

4.3 Impossibility of Sequential Dominant Strategy Implementation

A stronger form of incentive compatibility than sequential EP equilibrium is that of sequential DS equilibrium. This asserts that truth-telling is a weakly dominant strategy regardless of the other agents' strategies, provided that an agent does not know the future realization. We now show that under mild restrictions on the transfer functions, no mechanism can achieve welfare maximization in DS.

Definition 3. *A mechanism satisfies* No Positive Transfers *(NPT) if for all players i, the first and second-stage payments t_i^1, t_i^2 are non-positive.*

Definition 4. *A mechanism satisfies* Voluntary Participation *(VP) if all truthful players are guaranteed non-negative expected utility and non-negative marginal second-stage utility.*

The definition of NPT asserts that all payments flow from the players to the mechanism. The VP condition requires that it is in the agents' interest to participate in the mechanism in both stages. We now state our main theorem.

Theorem 3. *There exists an instance of the two-stage stochastic public goods problem with two players for which no mechanism satisfying VP, NPT can implement the expected welfare maximizer (WLF) in DS.*

Thus, subject to the conditions of NPT and VP, we have shown that our implementation in the previous section is the strongest possible.

Informally, one cannot implement the socially efficient outcome in dominant strategies because when certain agents in the mechanism lie *inconsistently* — for example, by first declaring a "low" distribution in the first stage, followed by a "high" valuation in the second stage — other agents may benefit from misrepresenting their distributions. We now formalize this intuition.

Consider an instance of a two-stage stochastic public goods problem with two players, A and B, with some distributions δ_A, δ_B on their respective values of being served by a public good e. The cost of the public good is $c^1 \gg 0$ in the first stage and $c^2 = 2c^1$ in the second stage. Let h be some value $> c^2$. We now define distributions that play a role in the proof. Let $\hat{H}$ be a degenerate distribution localized at h, H denote a full-support distribution[3] with most of its mass at h, L denote a full-support distribution with most of its mass at 0, and $\hat{M}$ denote the degenerate distribution localized at $c^1/2$.

For notation, let $\langle D^1, D^2 \rangle$ denote the strategy of a player that reports D^1 as its supertype and reports $v \sim D^2$ as its type. When we consider only the first-stage strategy, we may write $\langle D, \cdot \rangle$ instead. A strategy is consistent if it is of the form $\langle D, D \rangle$, and truthful if it is consistent and $D = \delta_i$ for agent i.

The following lemmas are simple consequences of VP, NPT, DS, and WLF.

Lemma 2. *If player A and player B both play $\langle L, \cdot \rangle$, then $t_B^1 \to 0$.*

Lemma 3. *Suppose that player B plays $\langle D, \cdot \rangle$ and then reports b in the second stage, where $0 < b \leq h$ and D is a full-support distribution. If either one of the following conditions holds, then player B is serviced and $t_B^2 = 0$:*

1. $x^1 = 1$
2. *Player A plays $\langle D', \hat{H} \rangle$, where D' is a full-support distribution.*

We now establish our main lemma: because of the possibility of inconsistent lies, the mechanism cannot charge players with high supertypes. The proof of the main theorem follows from this lemma and details are in the full paper.

Lemma 4. *If player A plays $\langle L, \cdot \rangle$ and B plays $\langle H, \cdot \rangle$, then $t_B^1 \to 0$.*

4.4   Incentive Compatibility and Sampling-Based Solutions

As we will see in Section 5, even for simple stochastic welfare maximization problems, there may exist no efficient solutions. To algorithmically implement the desired objective, one may have to approximate the optimal value via sampling, a technique commonly employed in stochastic optimization. In this section, we discuss the impact of such approximation on incentive compatibility.

Theorem 4. *For a given two-stage stochastic optimization problem, suppose that:*

- *there exists a sample average approximation algorithm that finds an ϵ-optimal first-stage decision with prob. $\geq (1 - \xi)$ for any $\epsilon > 0$ and $\xi \in (0, 1)$ in polynomial time;*
- *the exact second-stage optimal decision can be found in polynomial time; and*
- *the worst-case error can be bounded,*

then an ϵ^*-approximate sequential ex post equilibrium can be algorithmically implemented for any $\epsilon^* \equiv \epsilon^*(\epsilon, \xi) > 0$.

---

[3] A distribution D is a *full-support* distribution if it has support $(0, h]$ and a cumulative density function that is strictly increasing at every point in its support. Full support distributions play the following role in the proofs: When players report full-support distributions in the first stage, reporting any bid in $(0, h]$ in the second stage is consistent with the behavior of a truthful player.

The key idea in the proof is that sampling is required only in the first stage. Hence, to the agents, this additional source of uncertainty only happens in the first stage, when they are interested in maximizing expected utilities. Therefore, the sampling required can be factored into the agents' expected utilities.

Note that the above theorem applies to both multiplicative and additive approximation, with corresponding changes in the incentive guarantees. It demonstrates a trade-off between stronger incentive guarantees and the running time of the sampling-based algorithm. As stochastic welfare maximization involves a mixed-sign objective, in our following result, we focus on additive approximation.

5   A Polynomial Time Implementation for a Class of Stochastic Coverage Cost Problems

To better appreciate the algorithmic challenge posed by stochastic welfare maximization, we now examine the class of stochastic CC (Coverage Cost) problems. This class of problems includes FTM as a special case.

Our approach is based on a combination of the Sample Average Approximation (SAA) method (see, e.g, [12,17]) and supermodular set function maximization. However, our analysis differs from those found in recent work (e.g. [16,4]), as we are faced with a mixed-sign objective. To begin, let us first define a single-shot version of the *coverage-cost* problem.

Definition 5. *A* coverage cost problem *(CC) consists of three components:*

- *a set of players $U = \{1, 2, \ldots, n\}$ and a universe of elements E;*
- *a cost function $c : E \mapsto \mathbb{R}^+$ that assigns a non-negative cost to each element $e \in E$; (we let $c(S) = \sum_{e \in S} c(e)$ for $S \subseteq E$)*
- *a service set $P_s \subseteq E$ for each player s that needs to be constructed in order to serve s, and a value of θ_s of serving s.*

The objective is to find $P \subseteq E$ that maximizes welfare: $\sum_{s:P_s \subseteq P} \theta_s - c(P)$.

Stochastic CC is defined by extending the CC problem to have two cost functions, c^1 and c^2, for the respective stages. Also, instead of a precise value θ_s of serving agent $s \in U$, in the first stage, only a distribution δ_s is known. The objective is to maximize expected welfare.

By interpreting the universe of elements E as the set of edges in the fixed tree, and the service sets P_s as the (unique) path connecting a node s to the root r of the tree, we see that CC is a generalization of FTM. The following example shows that the generalization is strict:

Example 1. *Consider an instance with three players: $U = \{1, 2, 3\}$ and three elements $E = \{a, b, c\}$. Let $P_1 = \{a, b\}$, $P_2 = \{b, c\}$, $P_3 = \{a, c\}$. The cyclic structure entails that this cannot be a FTM instance.*

It is formally hard to solve two-stage stochastic CC. The difficulty is not due to a lack of combinatorial structure, as we will show that deterministic CC can

indeed be solved in polynomial time. The difficulty is due to the uncertainty
in the optimization parameters. We show that it is difficult to solve optimally
a stochastic CC instance with only one element (a single-edge FTM instance),
even when the distributions are discrete and communicated explicitly as tables
of probabilities. The theorem is by reduction from PARTITION ([7]).

Theorem 5. *Maximizing expected welfare for stochastic CC is #P-hard.*

5.1   A Probabilistic Approximation

In view of the above hardness result, we propose a sampling-based solution that
approximates the expected welfare with high probability. Our algorithm achieves
an additive approximation, as multiplicative approximation is unachievable with
a polynomial number of samples (due to the mixed-sign objective; example in
full paper). The main theorem of this section is as follows:

Theorem 6. *The two-stage stochastic CC problem can be approximated to within
an additive error of ϵ in time polynomial in M, $|E|$, and $\frac{1}{\epsilon}$, for all $\epsilon > 0$, where
$M = \max_\theta \sum_{s \in U} \theta_s$.*

We now describe the framework for solving two-stage stochastic CC problems.
The key structure we will establish and exploit is that optimizations at both
stages involve supermodular functions. Recall that a set function $f : 2^N \mapsto \mathbb{R}$ is
supermodular if for all $S, T \subseteq N$, $f(S) + f(T) \leq f(S \cup T) + f(S \cap T)$. We will
show that the expected welfare is supermodular in the set of elements bought in
the first stage (see Corollary 1), and that the welfare in the second stage, given
the elements bought in the first stage, is also supermodular in the remaining
elements. Once these results are established, it is natural to consider the following
algorithm:

1. Use the algorithm for supermodular function maximization of [10] to find
   the optimal first-stage elements to buy. Note that the algorithm needs a
   value oracle that cannot be implemented in polynomial time. We instead
   use sampling to approximate the solution value.
2. Given the realized values, use the algorithm of [10] to find the optimal second-
   stage elements to buy. In this case, the exact value for the value oracle can
   be found in polynomial time.

In Lemmas 5–8 and Corollary 1, we establish that both the first-stage optimization problem, denoted by $\bar{w}(\cdot)$, and the second-stage optimization problem,
denoted by $f_\theta(\cdot)$, involve supermodular functions.

Lemma 5. *For any valuation θ, the function $V_\theta(\cdot)$ defined via:*

$$V_\theta(E') = \sum_{s:P_s \subseteq E'} \theta_s$$

is supermodular in E'.

Lemma 6. *For any valuation θ and any set E_1 of elements bought in the first stage, the second-stage objective $f_\theta(\cdot)$ given by:*

$$f_\theta(E') = V_\theta(E_1 \cup E') - c^2(E')$$

is supermodular in E'.

Lemma 7. *Given any realization θ, the optimal value of the second-stage objective $f_\theta^*(\cdot)$ given by:*

$$f_\theta^*(P) = \max_{F \subseteq E \backslash P} V_\theta(F \cup P) - c^2(F)$$

is supermodular in the set P of elements bought in the first stage.

Lemma 8. *Given any realization θ, the welfare function $w_\theta(\cdot)$ defined via:*

$$w_\theta(P) = f_\theta^*(P) - c^1(P)$$

is supermodular in the set P of elements bought in the first stage.

Corollary 1 *The function $\overline{w}(\cdot) = \mathbb{E}_{\theta \sim \delta}[w_\theta(\cdot)]$ is supermodular.*

Armed with Lemma 8 and Corollary 1, we now address the algorithmic issues of the stochastic CC problem. In the proof of Theorem 5, we have shown that evaluating $\overline{w}(\cdot)$ exactly is #P-hard in general. Fortunately, we can approximate its value in polynomial time, while preserving supermodularity.

Lemma 9. *Let S be a size $\mathcal{O}(\frac{M^2}{\epsilon^2}|E|)$ set of scenarios drawn from the universe. Let $\hat{w}(\cdot)$ be the sample average approximation of $\overline{w}(\cdot)$ constructed using the samples in S. Then,*

1. *$\hat{w}(\cdot)$ is supermodular;*
2. *for all $F \subseteq E$, $\mathbb{P}\left[\left|\hat{w}(F) - \overline{w}(F)\right| > \epsilon\right] \leq o(e^{-|E|})$.*

The proof of Lemma 9 is in the full paper. We now prove Theorem 6.

Proof (Theorem 6). For running time, by using the strongly polynomial-time algorithm of Iwata et al. [10] to perform maximization of supermodular function, the number of function evaluation is bounded by $\mathcal{O}(|E|^5 \log |E|)$. Each function evaluation requires, for each of the $\mathcal{O}((\frac{M^2}{\epsilon^2}|E|))$ samples, finding the second-stage optimal solution given a first-stage solution. The second-stage optimal solution is solved again using supermodular function maximization, and hence each function evaluation takes $\mathcal{O}(|E|^5 \log |E| \times (\frac{M^2}{\epsilon^2}|E|))$ time.

For correctness, by Lemma 9, we can approximate the function $\overline{w}(\cdot)$ by $\hat{w}(\cdot)$ to within an additive error of ϵ' with probability at least $(1 - o(e^{-|E|}))$. As $\hat{w}(\cdot)$ is supermodular by construction, the algorithm of [10] applies.

Given this algorithm, the fact that the second-stage optimization can be solved efficiently using supermodular function maximization, and that the worst-case error of any stochastic CC problem is bounded by $\max\{\max_\theta \sum_{i \in U} \theta_i, c^1(E)\}$, we see that Theorem 4 applies. Thus, the welfare maximizer of stochastic CC problem can be implemented in ϵ-approximate sequential EP equilibrium for any desired $\epsilon > 0$.

Acknowledgments

We thank Kevin Leyton-Brown, David Parkes, and Bob Wilson for fruitful discussion, and especially to Bob for suggesting the term *sequential EP equilibrium*.

References

1. Archer, A., Feigenbaum, J., Krishnamurthy, A., Sami, R., Shenker, S.: Approximation and collusion in multicast cost sharing. Games and Economic Behavior 47, 36–71 (2004)
2. Bergemann, D., Välimäki, J.: Efficient dynamic auctions. Working paper (2006)
3. Cavallo, R., Parkes, D.C., Singh, S.: Optimal coordinated planning amongst self-interested agents with private state. In: Proc. UAI 2006 (2006)
4. Charikar, M., Chekuri, C., Pál, M.: Sampling bounds for stochastic optimization. In: Chekuri, C., Jansen, K., Rolim, J.D.P., Trevisan, L. (eds.) APPROX 2005 and RANDOM 2005. LNCS, vol. 3624, pp. 257–269. Springer, Heidelberg (2005)
5. Dantzig, G.B.: Linear programming under uncertainty. Management Science 1(3/4), 197–206 (1955)
6. Feigenbaum, J., Papadimitriou, C.H., Shenker, S.: Sharing the cost of multicast transmissions. JCSS 63(1), 21–41 (2001)
7. Garey, M.R., Johnson, D.S.: Computers and Intractability. W. H. Freeman and Co., New York (1979)
8. Groves, T.: Incentives in teams. Econometrica 41(4), 617–631 (1973)
9. Immorlica, N., Karger, D., Minkoff, M., Mirrokni, V.S.: On the costs and benefits of procrastination: approximation algorithms for stochastic combinatorial optimization problems. In: SODA 2004, pp. 691–700 (2004)
10. Iwata, S., Fleischer, L., Fujishige, S.: A combinatorial strongly polynomial algorithm for minimizing submodular functions. JACM 48, 761–777 (2001)
11. Jackson, M.: Mechanism theory. In: Derigs, U. (ed.) Encyclopedia of Life Support Systems, EOLSS Publishers, Oxford, UK (2003)
12. Anton, J., Kleywegt, A.J., Shapiro, A., de Mello, T.H.: The sample average approximation method for stochastic discrete optimization. SIAM Journal on Optimization 12(1), 479–502 (2001)
13. Mehta, A., Shenker, S., Vazirani, V.: Profit-maximizing multicast pricing by approximating fixed points. J. Algorithms 58(2), 150–164 (2006)
14. Nisan, N., Ronen, A.: Algorithmic mechanism design (extended abstract). In: Proc. 31st STOC, pp. 129–140 (1999)
15. Nisan, N., Ronen, A.: Computationally feasible VCG mechanisms. In: Proc. 1st EC, pp. 242–252 (2000)
16. David, B., Shmoys, D.B., Swamy, C.: An approximation scheme for stochastic linear programming and its application to stochastic integer programs. JACM 53(6), 978–1012 (2006)
17. Swamy, C., Shmoys, D.B.: Approximation algorithms for 2-stage stochastic optimization problems. SIGACT News 37(1), 33–46 (2006)

A Note on Maximizing the Spread of Influence in Social Networks

Eyal Even-Dar[1] and Asaf Shapira[2]

[1] Google Research
evendar@google.com
[2] Microsoft Research
asafico@microsoft.com

Abstract. We consider the *spread maximization* problem that was defined by Domingos and Richardson [6,15]. In this problem, we are given
a social network represented as a graph and are required to find the set
of the most "influential" individuals that by introducing them with a
new technology, we maximize the expected number of individuals in the
network, later in time, that adopt the new technology. This problem has
applications in viral marketing, where a company may wish to spread the
rumor of a new product via the most influential individuals in popular
social networks such as Myspace and Blogsphere.

The spread maximization problem was recently studied in several
models of social networks [10,11,13]. In this short paper we study this
problem in the context of the well studied probabilistic *voter model*. We
provide very simple and efficient algorithms for solving this problem. An
interesting special case of our result is that the most natural heuristic
solution, which picks the nodes in the network with the highest degree,
is indeed the optimal solution.

1 Introduction

With the emerging Web 2.0, the importance of social networks as a marketing
tool is growing rapidly and the use of social networks as a marketing tool spans
diverse areas, and has even been recently used by the campaigns of presidential
candidates in the United States. Social networks are networks (i.e. graphs) in
which the nodes represent individuals and the edges represent relations between
them. To illustrate the viral marketing channel (see [2,3,6]), consider a new
company that wishes to promote its new specialized search engine. A promising way these days would be through popular social network such as Myspace,
Blogsphere etc, rather than using classical advertising channels. By convincing
several key persons in each network to adopt (or even to try) the new search
engine, the company can obtain an effective marketing campaign and to enjoy
the diffusion effect over the network. If we assume that "convincing" each key
person to "spread" the rumor on the new product costs money, then a natural
problem is the following: given a social network, how can we detect the players through which we can spread, or "diffuse", the new technology in the most
effective way.

X. Deng and F.C. Graham (Eds.): WINE 2007, LNCS 4858, pp. 281–286, 2007.

Diffusion processes in social network have been studied for a long time in social sciences, see e.g. [5,8,3,16]. The algorithmic aspect of marketing in social networks was introduced by Domingos and Richardson [6,15] and can be formulated as follows. Given a social network structure and a diffusion dynamics (i.e. how the individuals influence each other), find a set S of nodes of cost at most K that by introducing them with a new technology/product, the spread of the technology/product will be maximized. We refer to the problem of finding such a maximizing set S as the *Spread maximization set problem*. The work of Domingos and Richardson [6,15] studied this problem in a probabilistic setting and mainly provided heuristics to compute a maximizing set. Following [6,15], Kempe et al. [10,11] and Mossel and Roch [13] considered a threshold network, in which users adopt a new technology only if a fixed fraction of their neighbors have already adopted this new technology. Their results show that finding the optimal subset of size K is NP-Hard to approximate within a factor smaller than $1 - 1/e$ and also show that a greedy algorithm achieves this ratio.

Our contribution: In this paper we consider the Spread maximization set problem, in the case where the underlying social network behaves like the *voter model*. The voter model, which was introduced by Clifford and Sudbury [4] and Holley and Liggett [9], is probably one of the most basic and natural probabilistic models to represent the diffusion of opinions in a social network; it models the diffusion of opinions in a network as follows: in each step, each person changes his opinion by choosing one of his neighbors at random and adopting the neighbor's opinion. The model has been studied extensively in the field of interacting particle systems [12,1].

While the voter model is different from the threshold models that were studied in [10,11,13], it still has the same key property that a person is more likely to change his opinion to the one held by most of his neighbors. In fact, the threshold models of [10,11,13] are monotone in the sense that once a vertex becomes "activated" it stays activated forever. This makes these models suitable for studying phenomena such as infection processes. However, some process, such as which product a user is currently using, are not monotone in this sense. Therefore, the voter model, which allows to deactivate vertices, may be more suitable for studying non monotone processes.

Our main contributions are an exact solution to the spread maximization set problem in the voter model, when all nodes have the same cost (the cost of a node is the cost of introducing the person with a new technology/product), and providing an FPTAS [1] for the more general case in which different nodes may have different costs. In contrast to most of the previous results, which considered only the status of the network in the "limit", that is, when the network converges to a steady state, our algorithms easily adopt to the case of different target

---

[1] An FPTAS, short for Fully Polynomial Time Approximation Scheme, is an algorithm that for any ϵ approximates the optimal solution up to an error $(1 + \epsilon)$ in time poly(n/ϵ).

times.[2] An interesting special case of our result is that the most natural heuristic solution, which picks the nodes in the network with the highest degree, is indeed the optimal solution, when all nodes have the same cost. We show that the optimal set for the long term is the set that maximizes the chances of reaching consensus with new technology/product.

2   The Voter Model

We start by providing a formal definition of the voter model (see [4,9] for more details).

Definition 1. *Let $G = G(V, E)$ be an undirected graph with self loops. For a node $v \in V$, we denote by $N(v)$ the set of neighbors of v in G. Starting from an arbitrary initial 0/1 assignment to the vertices of G, at each time $t \geq 1$, each node picks uniformly at random one of its neighbors and adopts its opinion. More formally, starting from any assignment $f_0 : V \to \{0, 1\}$, we inductively define*

$$f_{t+1}(v) = \begin{cases} 1, & \text{with probability } \frac{|\{u \in N(v) : f_t(u) = 1\}|}{|N(v)|} \\ 0, & \text{with probability } \frac{|\{u \in N(v) : f_t(u) = 0\}|}{|N(v)|} \end{cases}$$

Note that the voter model is a random process whose behavior depends on the initial assignment f_0. If we think of $f_t(v) = 1$ as indicating whether v is using the product we wish to advertise, then a natural quantity we wish to study is the expected number of nodes satisfying $f_t(v) = 1$ at any given time t. Of course, a simple way to maximize the number of such nodes is to start from an initial assignment f_0 in which $f_0(v) = 1$ for all v. However, in reality we may not be able to start from such an assignment as there is a cost c_v for setting $f_0(v) = 1$ and we have a limited budget B. For example, c_v can be the cost of "convincing" a website to use a certain application we want other websites to use as well. This is the main motivation for the spread maximization set problem that is defined below in the context of the voter model. As we have previous mentioned, this (meta) problem was first defined by Domingos and Richardson [6,15] and was studied by [15,10,11,13] in other models of social networks.

Definition 2 (The spread maximization set problem). *Let G be a graph representing a social network, $\bar{c} \in \mathbb{R}^n$ a vector of costs indicating the cost c_v of setting $f_0(v) = 1$, B a budget, and t a target time. The spread maximization set problem is the problem of finding an assignment $f_0 : V \to \{0, 1\}$ that will maximize the expectation $\mathbb{E}\left[\sum_{v \in V} f_t(v)\right]$ subject to the budget constraint $\sum_{\{v : f_0(v) = 1\}} c_v \leq B$.*

---

[2] Kempe et al. [10] considered also finite horizon but under different objective function, i.e. for every individual how many timesteps she held the desired opinion until the target time. Furthermore, their approach required maintaining a graph whose size is proportional to the original graph size times the target time.

3   Solving the Spread Maximization Set Problem

Our algorithms for solving the spread maximization set problem all rely on the well known fact that the voter model can be analyzed using *graphical models* (see [7] for more details). Let us state a very simple yet crucial fact regarding the voter model that follows from this perspective. Recall that in the voter model, the probability that node v adopts the opinion of one of its neighbors u is precisely $1/N(v)$. Stated equivalently, this is the probability that a random walk of length 1 that starts at v ends up in u. Generalizing this observation to more than one step, one can easily prove the following by induction on t.

Proposition 1. *Let $p_{u,v}^t$ denote the probability that a random walk of length t starting at node u stops at node v. Then the probability that after t iterations of the voter model, node u will adopt the opinion that node v had at time $t = 0$ is precisely $p_{u,v}^t$.*

We thus get the following corollary.

Corollary 1. *Let $S = \{u : f_0(u) = 1\}$. The probability that $f_t(v) = 1$ is the probability that a random walk of length t starting at v ends in S.*

Equipped with the above facts we can now turn to describe the simple algorithms for the spread maximization set problem.

The case of short term:
We start by showing how to solve the problem for the case of the short term, that is when t is (any) polynomial in n. We note that studying the spread maximization problem for short time term is crucial to the early stages of introducing a new technology into the market. As usual, let M be the normalized transition matrix of G, i.e. $M(v, u) = 1/|N(v)|$. For a subset $S \subseteq \{1, \ldots, n\}$ we will denote by 1_S the 0/1 vector, whose i^{th} entry is 1 iff $i \in S$. The following lemma gives a characterization of the spread maximizing set.

Lemma 1. *For any graph G with transition matrix M, the spread maximizing set S is the set which maximizes $1_S M^t$ subject to $\sum_{v \in S} c_v \leq B$.*

Proof. Recall the well known fact that $p_{u,v}^t$, which is the probability that a random walk of length t starting at u ends in v, is given by the (u, v) entry of the matrix M^t. The spread maximizing set problem asks for maximizing $\mathbb{E}\left[\sum_{v \in V} f_t(v)\right]$ subject to $\sum_{v \in S} c_v \leq B$. By linearity of expectation, we have that $\mathbb{E}\left[\sum_{v \in V} f_t(v)\right] = \sum_{v \in V} Prob[f_t(v) = 1]$. By Corollary 1 we have that if we set $f_0(v) = 1$ for any $v \in S$ then $Prob[f_t(v) = 1] = 1_S M^t 1_{\{v\}}^T$. Therefore, $\mathbb{E}\left[\sum_{v \in V} f_t(v)\right] = \sum_{v \in V} 1_S M^t 1_{\{v\}}^T = 1_S M^t$, and we conclude that the optimal set S is indeed the one maximizing $1_S M^t$ subject to $\sum_{v \in S} c_v \leq B$.   ∎

Using this formulation we can obtain the following theorems that shed light on how well can be the maximizing spread set problem solved.

Theorem 1. *If the vector cost $\bar{c}$ is uniform, that is, if for all v we have $c_v = c$, then the spread maximization set problem can be solved exactly in polynomial time for any $t = poly(n)$.*

Proof. First note the entries of M^t can be computed efficiently for any $t = poly(n)$. For any t to compute M^t we need to preform $O(\log t)$ matrix multiplication which can be done efficiently. For every node v denote $g_v = 1_{\{v\}}M^t$. By Lemma 1 we have that the problem is equivalent to the problem of maximizing $1_S M^t$ subject to $\sum_{v \in S} c_v \leq B$. As $1_S M^t = \sum_{v \in S} g_v$ and the cost of every node is identical, we get that for every budget B, the optimal set is the first $\lfloor B/c \rfloor$ nodes when sorted according to g_v. ∎

Theorem 2. *There exists an FPTAS to the spread maximization set problem for any $t = poly(n)$.*

Observe that in general we can cannot expect to be able to solve the spread maximization set problem exactly because when $t = 0$ this problem is equivalent to the Knapsack problem, which is NP-hard.

The case of long term:
Let us consider now the case of large t, where by large we mean $t \geq n^5$. Recall the well known fact that for any graph G with self loops, a random walk starting from *any* node v, converges to the steady state distribution after $O(n^3)$ steps (see [14]). Furthermore, if we set $d_v = |N(v)|$ then the (unique) steady state distribution is that the probability of being at node u is $d_u/2|E|$. In other words, if $t \gg n^3$ then $M^t_{u,v} = (1 + o(1))d_u/2|E|$. [3] Once again, using Lemma 1 we can obtain the following theorem.

Theorem 3. *There exists a linear time FPTAS to the spread maximization set problem when $t \geq n^5$.*

An interesting special case of Theorem 3 is when all nodes have the same cost c. Observe that in this case we get that the optimal solution is simply to pick the $\lfloor B/c \rfloor$ vertices of G of highest degree. This gives a formal justification for the "heuristic" approach of picking the nodes in the social network with the largest number of acquaintances, e.g. [17,6,15].

Maximizing the probability of consensus:
It is a well known fact that after $O(n^3 \log n)$ time the voter model reaches a consensus with high probability, that is, when $t \geq n^3 \log n$ either $f_t(v) = 1$ for all v or $f_t(v) = 1$ for all v.

Theorem 4. *With probability $1 - o(1)$, the voter model converges to consensus after $O(n^3 \log n)$ steps .*

By Theorems 3 and 4 we derive the following corollary,

Corollary 2. *For any $t \geq n^3 \log n$ and $\epsilon > 0$, there is a linear time algorithm for maximizing, up to an additive error of ϵ, the probability that the voter model reaches an all-ones consensus after $t \geq n^3 \log n$ steps.*

---

[3] More precisely, the smaller we want the $o(1)$ term to be the larger we need t to be.

Acknowledgments. The authors would like to thank Michael Kearns and Yuval Peres for valuable discussions concerning the voter model.

References

1. Aldous, D., Fill, J.: Reversible Markov Chains and Random Walks on Graphs (Draft). Draft (2007)
2. Bass, F.M.: A new product growth model for consumer durables. Management Science 15, 215–227 (1969)
3. Brown, J.J., Reinegen, P.H.: Social ties and word-of-mouth referral behavior. Journal of Consumer Research
4. Clifford, P., Sudbury, A.: A model for spatial conflict. Biometrika 60(3), 581–588 (1973)
5. Coleman, J.S., Katz, E., Menzel, H.: Medical Innovations: A Diffusion Study. Bobbs Merrill (1966)
6. Domingos, P., Richardson, M.: Miningthe network value of customers. In: KDD, pp. 57–66 (2001)
7. Durrrett, R.: Lecture Notes on Particle Systems and Percolation. Wadsworth (1988)
8. Granovetter, M.: Threshold models of collective behavior. American Journal of Sociology 83(6), 1420–1443 (1978)
9. Holley, R.A., Liggett, T.M.: Ergodic theorems for weakly interacting infinite. systems and the voter model. Annals of Probability 3, 643–663 (1975)
10. Kempe, D., Kleinberg, J.M., Tardos, E.: Maximizing the spread of influence through a social network. In: KDD, pp. 137–146 (2003)
11. Kempe, D., Kleinberg, J.M., Tardos, E.: Influential nodes in a diffusion model for social networks. In: Caires, L., Italiano, G.F., Monteiro, L., Palamidessi, C., Yung, M. (eds.) ICALP 2005. LNCS, vol. 3580, pp. 1127–1138. Springer, Heidelberg (2005)
12. Liggett, T.M.: Stochastic Interacting Systems: Contact, Voter and Exclusion Processes. Springer, Heidelberg (1999)
13. Mossel, E., Roch, S.: On the submodularity of influence in social networks. In: STOC, pp. 128–134 (2007)
14. Motwani, R., Raghavan, P.: Randomized Algorithms. Cambridge University Press, Cambridge (1996)
15. Richardson, M., Domingos, P.: Mining knowledge-sharing sites for viral marketing. In: KDD, pp. 61–70 (2002)
16. Valente, T.: Network Models of the Diffusion of Innovations. Hampton Press (1995)
17. Wasserman, S., Faust, K.: Social Network Analysis. Cambridge University Press, Cambridge (1994)

A Network Creation Game with Nonuniform Interests*

Yair Halevi and Yishay Mansour**

School of Computer Science, Tel Aviv University
{yairhale,mansour}@tau.ac.il

Abstract. In a network creation game, initially proposed by Fabrikant et al. [11], selfish players build a network by buying links to each other. Each player pays a fixed price per link $\alpha > 0$, and suffers an additional cost that is the sum of distances to all other players. We study an extension of this game where each player is only interested in its distances to a certain subset of players, called its friends. We study the social optima and Nash equilibria of our game, and prove upper and lower bounds for the "Price of Anarchy", the ratio between the social cost of the worst Nash equilibria and the optimal social cost. Our upper bound on the Price of Anarchy is

$$O\left(1 + \min\left(\alpha, \bar{d}, \log n + \sqrt{n\alpha/\bar{d}}, \sqrt{n\bar{d}/\alpha}\right)\right) = O(\sqrt{n}),$$

where n is the number of players, α is the edge building price, and $\bar{d}$ is the average number of friends per player. We derive a lower bound of $\Omega(\log n / \log \log n)$ on the Price of Anarchy.

1 Introduction

In many natural settings entities form connections to other entities, in a distributed and selfish manner, in order to increase their utility. A few examples include social networks, trade networks and most importantly communication networks such as the Internet. The structure of such networks, and in particular the Internet, has been recently of prime research interest. In this work we will focus primarily on the loss of efficiency due to the distributed and selfish behavior of the entities.

We model the network creation as a game between selfish players and focus on networks that are in equilibrium (no player can benefit by unilaterally deviating). Our measure of the "loss of efficiency" is the *Price of Anarchy*, which is the worse ratio between the social cost of a Nash equilibrium and that of the socially optimal solution. The concept of the Price of Anarchy was introduced by Koutsoupias and Papadimitriou [15], and has been successfully studied for

---

* Research partially supported by a grant of the Israel Science Foundation, BSF, and an IBM faculty award. A complete version of the paper can be found at [13].
** The author is currently visiting Google, Inc.

X. Deng and F.C. Graham (Eds.): WINE 2007, LNCS 4858, pp. 287–292, 2007.
© Springer-Verlag Berlin Heidelberg 2007

a wide range of settings including job scheduling, routing, facility location and network design (see e.g. [6, 14, 10, 12, 16, 5, 4, 9]).

We study an extension of the network creation game proposed by Fabrikant et al. [11], where n players form a network by building edges to other players, and edges may be used by any player in either directions. The player's cost models both the "infrastructure cost" (of building the edges) and the "communication cost" (of reaching the other players). Formally, each player pays a fixed price $\alpha > 0$ for each edge it builds, and suffers an additional distance cost, which is the sum of distances to all other players in the resulting network. The social cost is the sum of the players' costs. This basic game and several extensions were studied in [11, 8, 1, 3].

By focusing on the distance to **all** players for the distance cost, the model implicitly assumes that the communication needs of every player are uniformly distributed over all other players. This may be far from true in most real world networks. For instance, Autonomous Systems in the Internet rarely communicate equally with every other Autonomous System. Our model extends the original game by specifying which pairs of players have non-negligible communication needs. We call such pairs of players *friends*, and model this new information using an undirected graph called the *friendship graph*, whose vertices are the players and edges connect pairs of friends. We assume that friendship is symmetric, hence our use of an undirected graph. Players, as before, build an edge to any other player (friend or non-friend) at a cost of α, however, their distance cost now includes only the distance to their friends (rather than the distance to all the players). The social cost, as before, is the sum of the players' costs. We call our game a *network creation game with nonuniform interests* (NI-NCG), which generalizes the network creation game of [11] (which we refer to as *complete interest network creation game*).

Our contributions: We first prove the existence of pure Nash equilibria for most values of α (specifically for $\alpha \leq 1$ and $\alpha \geq 2$). Our main result is an upper bound of $O\left(1 + \min\left(\alpha, \bar{d}, \log n + \sqrt{n\alpha/\bar{d}}, \sqrt{n\bar{d}/\alpha}\right)\right) = O(\sqrt{n})$ on the Price of Anarchy of any NI-NCG, where n is the number of players and $\bar{d}$ is the average degree of the friendship graph H, i.e., the average number of friends per player. For either $\alpha = O(1)$, $\bar{d} = O(1)$, or $\alpha = \Omega(n\bar{d})$, this upper bound is a constant.[1] An important part of our proof is bounding the ratio of the edge building cost and the social optimum cost to be at most $O(\log n)$.[2]

For a lower bound, based on cage graphs, we construct a family of games for which the Price of Anarchy is $\Omega(\log n/\log \log n)$. The resulting games have $\alpha = \Theta(\log n/\log \log n)$ and $\bar{d} = \Omega(\log n)$, and they have the special property that some Nash equilibrium is achieved when players build exactly the friendship graph, i.e., every pair of friends has an edge connecting them. Our lower bound

---

[1] By comparison, Albers et al. [1] show that for the complete interest game, the Price of Anarchy is a constant for $\alpha = O(\sqrt{n})$ and $\alpha \geq 12n\log n$, and is at most $O\left(1 + \left(\min\left(\frac{\alpha^2}{n}, \frac{n^2}{\alpha}\right)\right)^{1/3}\right) = O(n^{1/3})$ for any α.

[2] In contrast, [1] show that for the complete interest game this ratio is only a constant.

construction also gives a lower bound of $\Omega(\log n / \log \log n)$ on the ratio of the edge building cost to the social optimum. Hence, our upper and lower bounds for this ratio are almost tight. We remark that no non-constant lower bound for the Price of Anarchy in the complete interest game is known.

The full version of the paper [13] contains several additional results as well as the proofs. Specifically, we provide bounds on the *Price of Stability* (the social cost ratio between the best Nash equilibrium and the social optimum), and show that it is at most 2. We analyze specific friendship structures such as a forest and a cycle. We study a weighted extension of our game, where each player has a non-negative friendship weight assigned to every other player, and the distance cost for the player is the weighted sum of distances to all other players, and we show an $O(\sqrt{n})$ upper bound on the Price of Anarchy.

2   The Model

A *network creation game with nonuniform interests* (NI-NCG), is a tuple $\mathcal{N} = \langle V, H, \alpha \rangle$ where $V = \{1 \ldots n\}$ is the set of players, $H = (V, E_H)$ is an undirected graph whose vertices are V and edges are E_H (H is called the *friendship graph*) and $\alpha \in \mathbb{R}^+$ is an *edge building price*. We say that players v and u are *friends* iff $(v, u) \in E_H$, and player's v neighborhood in H, denoted $N(v) = \{u : (v, u) \in E_H\}$, is also called the *friend set* of v. A strategy s_v for a player v is a subset of the other players $s_v \subseteq V - \{v\}$ (these are the players to which v builds an edge). A *joint strategy* s is an n-tuple of player strategies, i.e., $s = (s_1, s_2, \ldots, s_n)$. We define the *network* created by a joint strategy s, denoted $G = \mathcal{G}(s) = (V, E)$, as the undirected graph of built links, i.e., $E = \{(v, u) : u \in s_v \vee v \in s_u\}$. We limit our discussion to NI-NCGs for which H has no isolated vertices. The special case $H = K_n$ (the complete graph over n vertices) is called the *complete interest network creation game*, and was extensively studied in [11, 1, 3].

The *cost* of a player $v \in V$ in s is $C(s, v)$ and it is the sum of two components: (1) an *edge building cost* $B(s, v) = \alpha|s_v|$, which implies a cost of α per edge bought, and (2) a *distance cost* which is $Dist(s, v) = \sum_{u \in N(v)} \delta(v, u)$, where $\delta(v, u)$ is the distance between v and u in $G = \mathcal{G}(s)$ (if there is no path in G between v and u then $\delta(v, u) = \infty$). We define the *social cost* of a joint strategy s as the sum of the player costs, i.e., $C(s) = \sum_{v \in V} C(s, v)$, and the *social edge building cost* and *social distance cost* are defined similarly. The minimal social cost for an NI-NCG $\mathcal{N}$ is denoted by $OPT_\mathcal{N}$, and any joint strategy s that yields this cost is a *social optimum* for $\mathcal{N}$.

A joint strategy s is a Nash equilibrium (NE) for the game $\mathcal{N}$ if no player v can benefit by unilaterally deviating. The Price of Anarchy of $\mathcal{N}$, denoted $PoA_\mathcal{N}$, is the ratio between the maximal social cost of a NE and the cost of a social optimum, i.e., $PoA_\mathcal{N} = \max_{s \in \Phi_\mathcal{N}} C(s)/OPT_\mathcal{N}$ where $\Phi_\mathcal{N}$ is the set of Nash equilibria of an NI-NCG. (If $\Phi_\mathcal{N} = \emptyset$ then the Price of Anarchy is not defined.) The Price of Anarchy for a nonempty set of games $\mathcal{N}'$ is $PoA = \max_{\mathcal{N} \in \mathcal{N}'} PoA_\mathcal{N}$.

We denote by $d(v) = |N(v)|$ the degree of v in H (the number of friends of v) and by $\bar{d} = \sum_{v \in V} d(v)/|V|$ the average vertex degree of H.

3   Basic Results

We start by bounding the social optimum.

Theorem 1. *Let* $\mathcal{N} = \langle V, H, \alpha \rangle$ *be an NI-NCG. Then* $n(\alpha/2 + \bar{d}) \leq OPT_{\mathcal{N}} < 2n(\alpha/2 + \bar{d})$, *hence* $OPT_{\mathcal{N}} = \Theta(n(\alpha + \bar{d}))$.

The lower bound follows from the fact that any social optimum cannot have less than $n/2$ edges, and has distance at least 1 between any two friends. The upper bound follows from an analysis of the social cost of a star network.

Next we prove the existence of Nash equilibria.

Theorem 2. *Let* $\mathcal{N} = \langle V, H, \alpha \rangle$ *be an NI-NCG. For any* $\alpha \geq 2$ *there exists a NE for* $\mathcal{N}$ *whose cost is at most* $n(\alpha + 2\bar{d})$, *and for any* $\alpha \leq 1$ *there exists a NE for* $\mathcal{N}$ *which achieves the social optimum.*

Our proof constructs a specific NE for $\alpha \geq 2$, where the distance between any two friends is at most 2 and the resulting network is a forest.

4   Upper Bounds on the Price of Anarchy

In this section we derive our main result, an upper bound of:

$$O\left(1 + \min\left(\alpha, \bar{d}, \log n + \sqrt{n\alpha/\bar{d}}, \sqrt{n\bar{d}/\alpha}\right)\right) = O(\sqrt{n}).$$

We first show a simple upper bound. In any NE, the cost of no player can be greater than its cost if it were to buy an edge to every friend. Therefore we must have that $C(s) \leq (\alpha + 1)n\bar{d}$. Using Theorem 1, we have,

Theorem 3. *Let* $\mathcal{N} = \langle V, H, \alpha \rangle$ *be an NI-NCG, and assume that a NE exists. Then* $PoA_{\mathcal{N}} = O(1 + \min(\alpha, \bar{d}))$.

This result already provides us with some basic insights. In particular, if either α or $\bar{d}$ are constant, then the Price of Anarchy is constant.

We proceed by showing an improved bound on the social edge building cost. For the complete interest game, the contribution of the edge building cost to the Price of Anarchy was shown to be at most a constant (see [1]). We show a similar (but weaker) result for a general NI-NCG. Specifically we show an upper bound of $O\left(1 + \min(1, \bar{d}/\alpha)\log n\right) = O(\log n)$. A proof sketch is as follows: for any edge (v, u) built from v to u in a NE, we assign a weight $w(v, u)$ that is the number of friends x of v, for which removal of this edge would result in an increase in distance between v and x (this weight is a measure of the "effectiveness" of the edge). We then notice that for any threshold $\beta > 0$: (1) the number of edges built, for which $w(v, u) \geq \beta$, is at most $2|E_H|/\beta$, since the sum of all edge weights is at most twice the number of friendship edges, and (2) the length of any cycle C consisting only of edges with weights $w(v, u) < \beta$ must be at least $2 + \alpha/\beta$. We now use a bound (see [2]) on the average degree of a graph given its number of vertices and girth (the *girth* of an undirected graph is the minimal length of a cycle in it). By selecting an appropriate β, we derive,

Theorem 4. *Let $\mathcal{N} = \langle V, H, \alpha \rangle$ be an NI-NCG, and s a NE of $\mathcal{N}$. Then:*
$B(s)/OPT_{\mathcal{N}} = O\left(1 + \min\left(1, \bar{d}/\alpha\right)\log n\right) = O(\log n)$.

Next we show an upper bound of $O\left(1 + \min\left(1, \frac{\bar{d}}{\alpha}\right)\min\left(n, \sqrt{n\alpha/\bar{d}}\right)\right) = O(\sqrt{n})$
on the contribution of the distance cost to the Price of Anarchy. We use the
following lemma, due to the fact that in a NE, no player may benefit from
adding an edge:

Lemma 5. *Let $\mathcal{N} = \langle V, H, \alpha \rangle$ be an NI-NCG, s a NE, $G = \mathcal{G}(s)$, and $v \in V$
a player. Let T be a shortest path tree of v in G. For any vertex $u \in V(T)$,
denote by k_u the number of friends of v that are in u's subtree in T. Then
$\alpha \geq (\delta(v, u) - 1)k_u$.*

Using Lemma 5 we bound the distance cost for a single player as follows. Fix
a player $v \in V$, a shortest path tree T of v in G, and a parameter $h \geq 1$.
We split the distance cost of v into two sums D_1 and D_2. Let the sum D_1
be the distance cost "up to depth h", consisting of the distances between v
and all its friends, taking a maximum of h of distance per friend, i.e., $D_1 = \sum_{x \in N(v)} \max(\delta(v, x), h) \leq d(v)h$. The sum D_2 is the distance cost "from depth
h", containing, for all friends x of v of depth greater than h in T, the distance
from depth h to x in T, i.e., $D_2 = \sum_{x \in N(v):\delta(v,x)>h} \delta(v, x) - h$. Lemma 5 yields
an upper bound of $(n - 2)\alpha/h$ on D_2. Optimizing over h we derive,

Theorem 6. *Let $\mathcal{N} = \langle V, H, \alpha \rangle$ be an NI-NCG and s a NE for $\mathcal{N}$. Then:*
$Dist(s)/OPT_{\mathcal{N}} = O\left(1 + \min\left(1, \bar{d}/\alpha\right)\min\left(n, \sqrt{n\alpha/\bar{d}}\right)\right) = O(\sqrt{n})$

Combining Theorem 3, 4 and 6, we obtain our main upper bound:

Theorem 7. *Let $\mathcal{N} = \langle V, H, \alpha \rangle$ be an NI-NCG, and assume that a NE exists.
Then: $PoA_{\mathcal{N}} = O\left(1 + \min\left(\alpha, \bar{d}, \log n + \sqrt{n\alpha/\bar{d}}, \sqrt{n\bar{d}/\alpha}\right)\right) = O(\sqrt{n})$.*

As stated in the theorem, in all cases we have an upper bound of $O(\sqrt{n})$ on the
Price of Anarchy, however, for many combinations of n, α and $\bar{d}$ we get a better
bound.

5   Lower Bound: NI-NCG with $PoA = \Omega(\log n/\log\log n)$

In this section we show that there is an NI-NCG with n players for which the
Price of Anarchy is bounded from below by $\Omega(\log n/\log\log n)$. Our construction
is based on the observation that if the friendship graph of the game has large
enough girth, then it is a NE network itself.

Lemma 8. *Let $\mathcal{N} = \langle V, H, \alpha \rangle$ be an NI-NCG, such that $0 < \alpha < \frac{g(H)}{2} - 1$. Then
H is a NE network.*

This implies that for the lower bound we need to construct a graph with both large girth and large average degree. Using the well known constructions of cage graphs - regular graphs of a given girth and degree with a minimal number of vertices (see [7]), we derive,

Theorem 9. *For any integer $n \geq 64$ there is an NI-NCG $\mathcal{N} = \langle V, H, \alpha \rangle$ with n players, $\alpha = \Theta(\log n / \log \log n)$, and $\bar{d} = \Omega(\log n)$, whose Price of Anarchy is $\Omega(\log n / \log \log n)$.*

Our proof also implicitly shows that the contribution of the edge building cost to the Price of Anarchy for the construction is $\Omega(\log n / \log \log n)$. This is almost tight to our upper bound from Theorem 4.

References

[1] Albers, S., Eilts, S., Even-Dar, E., Mansour, Y., Roditty, L.: On nash equilibria for a network creation game. In: SODA, pp. 89–98 (2006)
[2] Alon, N., Hoory, S., Linial, N.: The Moore Bound for Irregular Graphs. Graphs and Combinatorics 18(1), 53–57 (2002)
[3] Andelman, N., Feldman, M., Mansour, Y.: Strong Price of Anarchy. In: SODA (2007)
[4] Anshelevich, E., Dasgupta, A., Kleinberg, J., Tardos, E., Wexler, T., Roughgarden, T.: The price of stability for network design with fair cost allocation. In: FOCS, pp. 295–304 (2004)
[5] Anshelevich, E., Dasgupta, A., Tardos, E., Wexler, T.: Near-optimal network design with selfish agents. In: STOC, pp. 511–520 (2003)
[6] Bala, V., Goyal, S.: A Noncooperative Model of Network Formation. Econometrica 68(5), 1181–1229 (2000)
[7] Bollobas, B.: Extremal graph theory. Academic Press, London (1978)
[8] Corbo, J., Parkes, D.: The price of selfish behavior in bilateral network formation. In: PODC, pp. 99–107 (2005)
[9] Correa, J.R., Schulz, A.S., Stier-Moses, N.E.: Selfish Routing in Capacitated Networks. Mathematics of Operations Research 29(4), 961–976 (2004)
[10] Czumaj, A., Krysta, P., Vocking, B.: Selfish traffic allocation for server farms. In: STOC, pp. 287–296 (2002)
[11] Fabrikant, A., Luthra, A., Maneva, E., Papadimitriou, C.H., Shenker, S.: On a network creation game. In: PODC, pp. 347–351 (2003)
[12] Fotakis, D., Kontogiannis, S., Koutsoupias, E., Mavronicolas, M., Spirakis, P.: The Structure and Complexity of Nash Equilibria for a Selfish Routing Game. In: Widmayer, P., Triguero, F., Morales, R., Hennessy, M., Eidenbenz, S., Conejo, R. (eds.) ICALP 2002. LNCS, vol. 2380, pp. 123–134. Springer, Heidelberg (2002)
[13] Halevi, Y.: A Network Creation Game with Nonuniform Interests. Master's thesis, School of Computer Science, Tel Aviv University (2007), http://www.tau.ac.il/~yairhale/publish/halevi_nincg_thesis.pdf
[14] Jain, K., Vazirani, V.: Applications of approximation algorithms to cooperative games. In: STOC, pp. 364–372 (2001)
[15] Koutsoupias, E., Papadimitriou, C.: Worst-case equilibria. In: Meinel, C., Tison, S. (eds.) STACS 1999. LNCS, vol. 1563, pp. 404–413. Springer, Heidelberg (1999)
[16] Roughgarden, T., Tardos, É.: How bad is selfish routing?. Journal of the ACM (JACM) 49(2), 236–259 (2002)

A Theory of Loss-Leaders:
Making Money by Pricing Below Cost

Maria-Florina Balcan, Avrim Blum, T-H. Hubert Chan,
and MohammadTaghi Hajiaghayi

Computer Science Department, Carnegie Mellon University
{ninamf,avrim,hubert,hajiagha}@cs.cmu.edu

Abstract. We consider the problem of assigning prices to goods of fixed marginal cost in order to maximize revenue in the presence of single-minded customers. We focus in particular on the question of how pricing certain items below their marginal costs can lead to an improvement in overall profit, even when customers behave in a fully rational manner. We develop two frameworks for analyzing this issue that we call the *discount* and the *coupon* models, and examine both fundamental "profitability gaps" (to what extent can pricing below cost help to improve profit) as well as algorithms for pricing in these models in a number of settings considered previously in the literature.

1 Introduction

The notion of *loss-leaders*, namely pricing certain items below cost in a way that increases profit overall from the sales of other items, is a common technique in marketing. For example, a hamburger chain might price its burgers below production cost but then have a large profit margin on sodas. Grocery stores often give discounts that reduce the cost of certain items even to zero, making money from other items the customers will buy while in the store.

Such "loss leaders" are often viewed as motivated by psychology: producing extra profit from the emotional behavior of customers who are attracted by the good deals and then do not fully account for their total spending. Alternatively, they are also often discussed in the context of selling goods of decreasing marginal cost (so the loss-leader of today will be a profit center tomorrow once sales have risen). However, even for items of fixed marginal cost, with fully rational customers who have valuations on different bundles of items and act to maximize utility, pricing certain items below cost can produce an increase in profit. For example, DeGraba [5] analyzes equilibria in a 2-firm, 2-good Hotelling market, and argues that the power of loss leaders is that they provide a method for focusing on high-profit customers: "a product could be priced as a loss leader if, in a market in which some customers purchase bundles of products that are more profitable than bundles purchased by others, the product is purchased primarily by customers that purchase more profitable bundles." Balcan and Blum [1] give an example, in the context of pricing n items of fixed marginal cost to a set

X. Deng and F.C. Graham (Eds.): WINE 2007, LNCS 4858, pp. 293–299, 2007.

of single-minded customers, where allowing items to be priced below cost can produce an $\Omega(\log n)$ factor more than the maximum possible profit obtained by pricing all items above cost. However, the problem of developing algorithms taking advantage of this idea was left as an open question.

In this paper we consider this problem more formally, introducing two theoretical models which we call the *coupon model* and the *discount model* for analyzing the profit that can be obtained by pricing below cost. These models are motivated by two different types of settings in which such pricing schemes can naturally arise. We then develop algorithms for several problems studied in the literature, including the "highway problem" [8] and problems of pricing vertices in graphs, as well as analyze fundamental gaps between the profit obtainable under the different models. It is worth noting that the algorithmic problem becomes much more difficult in these settings than in the setting where pricing below cost is not allowed.

The two models we introduce are motivated by two types of scenarios. In the *discount model*, we imagine a retailer (say a supermarket or a hamburger chain) selling n different types of items, where each item i has some fixed marginal (production) cost c_i to the retailer. The retailer needs to assign a sales price s_i to each item, which could potentially be less than c_i. That is, the profit margin $p_i = s_i - c_i$ for item i could be positive or negative. The goal of the retailer is to assign these prices so as make as much profit as possible from the customers. We will be considering the case of single-minded customers, meaning that each customer j has some set S_j of items he is interested in and will purchase the entire set (one unit of each item $i \in S_j$) if its total cost is at most his valuation v_j, else nothing. As an example, suppose we have two items $\{1, 2\}$, each with production cost $c_i = 10$ and two customers, one interested in item 1 only and willing to pay 20, and the other interested in both and willing to pay 25. In this case, by setting $s_1 = 20$ and $s_2 = 5$ (which correspond to profit margins $p_1 = 10$ and $p_2 = -5$, and hence the second item is priced below cost) the retailer can make a total profit of 15. This is greater than the maximum profit (10) obtainable from these customers if pricing below cost were not allowed.

One thing that makes the discount model especially challenging is that profit is not necessarily monotone in the customers' valuations. For instance, in the above example, if we add a new customer with $S_j = \{2\}$ and $v_j = 3$ then the solution above still yields profit 15 (because the new customer does not buy), but if we increase v_j to 10, then any solution will make profit at most 10.

The second model we introduce, the *coupon model*, is designed to at least satisfy monotonicity. This model is motivated by the case of goods with zero marginal cost (such as airport taxes or highway tolls). However, rather than setting actual negative prices, we instead will allow the retailer to give credit that can be used towards other purchases. Formally, each item i has marginal cost $c_i = 0$ and is assigned a sales price p_i which can be positive or negative, and the price of a bundle S is $\max(\sum_{i \in S} p_i, 0)$, which is also the profit for selling this bundle. We again consider single-minded customers. A customer j will purchase his desired bundle S_j iff its price is at most his valuation v_j. Note that in this model we are assuming *no free disposal*: the customer is only interested in a particular set of items and will not purchase a superset even if cheaper (e.g., in the case of highway tolls, we assume a driver would either use the highway to go from his source to his destination or not, but would not travel additional stretches of highway just to save on tolls). As an example of the coupon model, consider a highway with three toll portions (items) 1, 2, and 3. Assume there are four drivers (customers) A, B, C, and D as follows: A, B, and C each only use portions 1, 2, and 3 respectively, but D uses all three portions. Assume that A, C, and D each are willing to pay 10 while B is wiling to pay only 1. In this case, by setting $p_1 = p_3 = 10$ and $p_2 = -10$, we have a solution with profit of 30 (driver B gets to travel for free, but is not actually paid for using the highway). This is larger than the maximum profit possible (21) in the discount model or if we are not allowed to assign negative prices. Note that unlike the discount model, the coupon model does satisfy monotonicity.

We can make the discount model look syntactically more like the coupon model by subtracting production costs from the valuations. In this view, $w_j := v_j - \sum_{i \in S_j} c_i$ represents the amount *above production cost* that customer j is willing to pay for S_j, and our goal is to assign positive or negative profit margins p_i to each item i to maximize the total profit $\sum_{j:w_j \geq p(S_j)} p(S_j)$ where $p(S_j) = \sum_{i \in S_j} p_i$. It is interesting in this context to consider two versions: in the *unbounded discount* model we allow the p_i to be as large or as small as desired, ignoring the implicit constraint that $p_i \geq -c_i$, whereas in the *bounded discount* model we impose those constraints. Note that in this view, the only difference between the unbounded discount model and the coupon model is that in the coupon model we redefine $p(S_j)$ as $\max(\sum_{i \in S_j} p_i, 0)$.

We primarily focus on two well-studied problems first introduced formally by Guruswami et al. [8]: the *highway tollbooth* problem and the *graph vertex pricing* problem. In the highway tollbooth problem, we have n items (highway segments) $1, \ldots, n$, and each customer (driver) has a desired bundle that consists of some interval $[i, i']$ of items (consecutive segments of the highway). The seller is the owner of the highway system, and would like to choose tolls on the segments (and possibly also coupons in the coupon model) so as to maximize profits. Even if all customers have the same valuation for their desired bundles, we show that there are $\log(n)$-sized gaps between the profit obtainable in the different models. In the graph vertex pricing problem, we instead have the constraint that all desired bundles S_j have size at most 2. Thus, we can consider the input as a multi-graph whose vertex set represent the set of items and whose edges represent the costumers who want end-points of the edges. We show that if this graph is *planar* then one can in fact achieve a PTAS for profit in each model.

It is worth mentioning we do not focus on *incentive-compatibility* aspects in this paper since one can use the generic reductions in [3] to convert our approximations algorithms into good truthful mechanisms. In this version, we only state the results and the reader is referred to the full version [2] for the proofs.

2   Notation, Definitions, and Gaps Between the Models

We assume we have m customers and n items (or "products"). We are in an *unlimited supply* setting, meaning that the seller is able to sell any number of units of each item. We consider *single-minded customers*, which means that each customer is interested in only a single bundle of items and has valuation 0 on all other bundles. Therefore, valuations can be summarized by a set of pairs (e, v_e) indicating that a customer is interested in bundle (hyperedge) e and values it at v_e. Given the hyperedges e and valuations v_e, we wish to compute a pricing of the items that maximizes the seller's profit. We assume that if the total price of the items in e is at most v_e, then the customer (e, v_e) will purchase all of the items in e, and otherwise the customer will purchase nothing. Given a price vector $\mathbf{p}$ over the n items, it will be convenient to define $p(e) = \sum_{i \in e} p_i$.

Let us denote by E the set of customers, and V the set of items, and let h be $\max_{e \in E} v_e$. Let $G = (V, E, v)$ be the induced hypergraph, whose vertices represent the set of items, and whose hyperedges represent the customers. Notice that G might contain self-loops (since a customer might be interested in only a single item) and multi-edges (several customers might want the same subset of items). The special case that all customers want at most two items, so G is a graph, is known as the *graph vertex pricing* problem [1]. Another interesting case considered in previous work [1,8] is the *highway* problem. In this problem we think of the items as segments of a highway, and each desired subset e is required to be an interval $[i, j]$ of the highway.

Reduced Instance: In many of our algorithms, it is convenient to think about the *reduced instance* $\tilde{G} = (V, E, w)$ of the problem which is defined as follows. Let b_i denote the marginal cost of item i. Suppose customer e has valuation v_e. Then, in the reduced instance, its valuation becomes $w_e := v_e - \sum_{i \in e} b_i$. Now, if we give item i a price p_i in the reduced instance, then its real selling price would be $s_i := p_i + b_i$. In previous work [1,8,4], the focus was on pricing above cost, which in our notation, corresponds to the case where $p_i \geq 0$, for every item i. However, as mentioned in the introduction, in many natural cases, we can potentially extract more profit by pricing certain items below cost (which corresponds to the case where $p_i < 0$).

From now on, we always think in terms of the reduced instance. We formally define all the *pricing models* we consider as follows:

Positive Price Model: In this model, we require the selling price of an item to be at or above its production cost. Hence, in the reduced instance, we want the price vector $\mathbf{p}$ with positive components $p_i \geq 0$ that maximizes $\text{Profit}_{pos}(\mathbf{p}) = \sum_{e : w_e \geq p(e)} p(e)$. Let $\mathbf{p}^*_{pos}$ be the price vector with the maximum profit under positive prices and let $\text{OPT}_{pos} = \text{Profit}_{pos}(\mathbf{p}^*_{pos})$.

Discount Model: In this model, the selling price of an item can be arbitrary. In particular, the price can be below the cost, or even below zero. We want the price vector $\mathbf{p}$ that maximizes $\text{Profit}_{disc}(\mathbf{p}) = \sum_{e : w_e \geq p(e)} p(e)$. Let $\mathbf{p}^*_{disc}$ be the price vector with the maximum profit and let $\text{OPT}_{disc} = \text{Profit}_{disc}(\mathbf{p}^*_{disc})$.

B-**Bounded Discount Model:** In this model, the selling price of an item i can be below its production cost b_i, but cannot be below zero. This corresponds to a negative price in the reduced instance, but it is bounded below by $-b_i$. For simplicity, we assume that the production costs of all items are each B. We want the price vector $\mathbf{p}$ with components $p_i \geq -B$ that maximizes $\text{Profit}_B(\mathbf{p}) = \sum_{e:w_e \geq p(e)} p(e)$. Let $\mathbf{p}_B^*$ be the price vector with the maximum profit and let $\text{OPT}_B = \text{Profit}_B(\mathbf{p}_B^*)$. Observe that $\text{OPT}_{pos} \leq \text{OPT}_B \leq \text{OPT}_{disc}$.

Coupon Model: This model makes most sense in which the items have zero marginal cost, such as airport taxes or highway tolls. In this model, the selling price of an item can actually be negative. However, we impose the condition that the seller not make a loss in any transaction with any customer. We want the price vector $\mathbf{p}$ that maximizes $\text{Profit}_{coup}(\mathbf{p}) = \sum_{e:w_e \geq p(e)} \max(p(e), 0)$. Let $\mathbf{p}_{coup}^*$ be the price vector with the maximum coupon profit and let $\text{OPT}_{coup} = \text{Profit}_{coup}(\mathbf{p}_{coup}^*)$. From the definition, it is immediate that $\text{OPT}_{pos} \leq \text{OPT}_{coup}$.

Gaps between the Models. We state below a few fundamental gaps between the profits obtainable in these models.

Theorem 1. *For the highway problem, there exists an $\Omega(\log n)$ gap between the positive price model and the (B-bounded) discount model, even for $B = 1$. Moreover, there exists an $\Omega(\log n)$ gap between the coupon model and the (B-bounded) discount model.*

Theorem 2. *For the graph vertex pricing problem[1], there exists an $\Omega(\log B)$ gap between the positive price model and the B-bounded discount model, even for a bipartite graph.*

3   Main Tools and Main Results

We describe now the main tools used in the paper. These tools allow us to give bounds on the prices of items in an optimal solution in each of the pricing models.

DAG Representation of the Highway Problem: We describe here an alternative representation of the Highway Problem. This representation proves to be extremely convenient both for the analysis and for the design of algorithms.

Suppose the n items are in the order $l_1, l_2, \ldots, l_n$, with corresponding prices $p_1, p_2, \ldots, p_n$. Then, for each $0 \leq i \leq n$, we have a node v_i labelled with the partial sum $s_i := \sum_{j=1}^{i} p_j$, where $s_0 = 0$. A customer corresponds to a subset of the form $\{l_i, \ldots, l_j\}$, which is represented by a directed arc from v_{i-1} to v_j.

Lemma 1. *Under all pricing models (positive price model, (bounded) discount model, coupon model), there is always an optimal solution such that $s_{max} - s_{min} \leq nh$, where $s_M := \max\{s_i : 0 \leq i \leq n\}$ and $s_m := \min\{s_i : 0 \leq i \leq n\}$, and h is the maximum valuation.*

---

[1] The graph vertex pricing problem is APX-hard under all our models. One can easily extend the result in [8] to our setting too.

Existence of Bounded Solution for Graph Vertex Pricing: Recall that in the graph setting, we denote the set of items by V, and each customer is interested in at most two items. We represent the set of customers interested in exactly two items by the set of (multi) edges E, and the set of customers interested in exactly one item by the (multi) set N, where for each $e \in E \cup N$, $w_e \in \mathbb{Z}$ is customer e's valuation.

Lemma 2. *Under all the pricing models (the coupon model and (bounded) discount model), there is an optimal price vector $\mathbf{p}^* \in \mathbb{R}^V$ that is half-integral if all customers' valuations are integral. Moreover, if all valuations are at most h, then $\mathbf{p}^*$ can be chosen to be bounded in the sense that for all $v \in V$, $|\mathbf{p}^*(v)| \leq 2nh$.*

3.1   Coupon Model

The main feature of the coupon model is that even when the sum of the prices for the items that a customer wants is negative, the net profit obtained from that customer is zero.

A Constant Factor Approximation for the Highway Problem: We show here a constant factor approximation algorithm for the highway problem under the coupon model, in the case where all the customers' valuations are identical.

Theorem 3. *There is a 2.33-approximation algorithm under the coupon model for the highway problem in the case when all all customers' valuations are all 1.*

Proof. First, we represent the problem as a DAG as described above: each node corresponds to a partial sum and each customer is represented as a directed edge from its left node to its right node. We then use the approximation algorithm presented in [7] for the MAX DICUT problem to get a $\frac{1}{0.859}$-approximation for OPT that uses no more than two levels, i.e., the partial sums are either 0 or 1. Hence, in order to show the result, it suffices[2] to show that there exists a solution in which the partial sums are either 0 or 1 and has profit at least $\frac{1}{2}$OPT$_{coup}$. Consider the partial sums in an optimal solution. Observe that for each customer from which we get a profit (of 1), we still obtain a profit for that customer after modifying the solution in exactly one of the following ways: If a partial sum is even, set it to 0, otherwise set it to 1. If a partial sum is even, set it to 1, otherwise set it to 0. Hence, by choosing the modification that yields higher profit, the claim follows.   □

Theorem 4. *Under the coupon model we have a fully polynomial time approximation scheme for the case that the desired subsets of different customers form a hierarchy.*

Planar and Minor-free Graph Vertex Pricing Problem: We give a PTAS that uses negative prices to obtain $(1 + \epsilon)$-approximation, using decomposition techniques for H-minor-free graphs by Demaine et al. [6]

---

[2] If all the valuations are integral, then there exists an optimal solution with all prices integral, under all our models (positive, coupon, and (B-bounded) discount models).

Theorem 5. *There exists a PTAS for minor-free instances of the graph vertex pricing problem under the coupon model.*

3.2 *B*-Bounded Discount Model

The main feature is that the net profit we obtain from a customer is exactly the sum of the prices of the items in the bundle of that customer, and hence can be negative. As explained in the introduction, the extra condition that the price of an item must be at least $-B$ corresponds to the real life situation in which the selling price of an item can be below its cost, but not negative.

Theorem 6. *There exists an $O(B)$ approximation algorithm for the vertex pricing problem under the B-bounded discount model.*

There exists an PTAS for minor-free instances of the graph vertex pricing problem under the B-bounded discount model for fixed B under either one of the following assumptions: (1) All customers have valuations at least 1, or (2) There is no multi-edge in the graph.

Theorem 7. *There exists an FPTAS for the case that the desired subsets of different customers form a hierarchy under both the discount and the B-bounded discount models.*

References

1. Balcan, M.-F., Blum, A.: Approximation Algorithms and Online Mechanisms for Item Pricing. In: ACM Conference on Electronic Commerce (2006)
2. Balcan, M.-F., Blum, A., Chan, T.-H.H., Hajiaghai, M.T.: A theory of loss-leaders: Making money by pricing below cost. Technical Report, CMU-CS-07-142 (July 2007)
3. Balcan, M.-F., Blum, A., Hartline, J., Mansour, Y.: Mechanism Design via Machine Learning. In: 46th Annual IEEE Symposium on Foundations of Computer Science, pp. 605–614. IEEE Computer Society Press, Los Alamitos (2005)
4. Briest, P., Krysta, P.: Single-Minded Unlimited Supply Pricing on Sparse Instances. In: Proceedings of the 17th ACM-SIAM Symposium on Discrete Algorithms, ACM Press, New York (2006)
5. DeGraba, P.: Volume discounts, loss leaders, and competition for more profitable customers. Federal Trade Commission Bureau of Economics, Working Paper 260 (February 2003)
6. Demaine, E.D., Hajiaghayi, M., Kawarabayashi, K.: Algorithmic Graph Minor Theory: Decomposition, Approximation, and Coloring. In: 46th Annual IEEE Symposium on Foundations of Computer Science, pp. 637–646. IEEE Computer Society Press, Los Alamitos (2005)
7. Feige, U., Goemans, M.X.: Approximating the Value of Two Prover Proof Systems, with Applications to MaxtwoSat and MaxDicut. In: Proceedings of the Third Israel Symposium on Theory of Computing and Systems, pp. 182–189 (1995)
8. Guruswami, V., Hartline, J., Karlin, A., Kempe, D., Kenyon, C., McSherry, F.: On Profit-Maximizing Envy-Free Pricing. In: Proceedings of the 16th Annual ACM-SIAM Symposium on Discrete Algorithms, pp. 1164–1173. ACM Press, New York (2005)

PageRank as a Weak Tournament Solution[*]

Felix Brandt and Felix Fischer

Institut für Informatik, Universität München
80538 München, Germany
{brandtf,fischerf}@tcs.ifi.lmu.de

Abstract. We observe that ranking systems—a theoretical framework for web page ranking and collaborative filtering introduced by Altman and Tennenholtz—and tournament solutions—a well-studied area of social choice theory—are strongly related. This relationship permits a mutual transfer of axioms and solution concepts. As a first step, we formally analyze a tournament solution that is based on Google's PageRank algorithm and study its interrelationships with common tournament solutions. It turns out that the PageRank set is always contained in both the Schwartz set and the uncovered set, but may be disjoint from most other tournament solutions. While PageRank does not satisfy various standard properties from the tournament literature, it can be much more discriminatory than established tournament solutions.

1 Introduction

The central problem of the literature on tournament solutions is as appealing as it is simple: Given an irreflexive, asymmetric, and complete binary relation over a set, find the "maximal" elements of this set. As the standard notion of maximality is not well-defined in the presence of cycles, numerous alternative solution concepts have been devised and axiomatized [see, *e.g.*, 14, 12]. In social choice theory, the base relation, which we call dominance relation, is usually defined via pairwise majority voting, and many well-known tournament solutions yield attractive social choice correspondences. Recently, a number of concepts have been extended to the more general setting of *incomplete* dominance relations [9, 17, 6, 5]. These generalized dominance relations are commonly referred to as *weak tournaments*.

Motivated by the problem of ranking web pages based solely on the structure of the underlying link graph, Altman and Tennenholtz [3] introduced the notion of a *ranking system*, which maps each (strongly connected) directed graph to a complete preorder on the set of vertices. Obviously, this notion is strongly related to that of a tournament solution. In fact, Moulin [14] identifies "ranking the participants of a given tournament" as an important open problem. While little effort has been made so far to solve this problem, this is precisely what *ranking systems* achieve for strongly connected weak tournaments.

---

[*] This material is based upon work supported by the Deutsche Forschungsgemeinschaft under grant BR 2312/3-1.

Altman and Tennenholtz do not refer to the vast literature on tournament solutions, and their recent work on ranking systems does not seem to be well known in the tournament community. This is regrettable for two reasons. For one, ranking systems address a problem that has long been neglected in social choice theory. Secondly, both research areas could benefit from a mutual transfer of concepts and axioms. We take a first step in this direction by formally analyzing a tournament solution that is based on Google's PageRank ranking system.

2 The PageRank Set

Fix an infinite set $\mathcal{A}$. A *weak tournament* is a pair $G = (A, \succ)$ of a finite set $A \subseteq \mathcal{A}$ of *alternatives* and an irreflexive and asymmetric *dominance relation* $\succ \subseteq A \times A$. Intuitively, $a \succ b$ means that a "beats" b in a pairwise comparison. We write $\mathcal{T}$ for the set of all weak tournaments, $\mathcal{T}(A)$ for the set of all weak tournaments on A, and $G|_{A'} = (A', A' \times A' \cap \succ)$ for the restriction of $G \in \mathcal{T}(A)$ to a subset $A' \subseteq A$ of the alternatives. A weak tournament is also called a *dominance graph*, and a weak tournament $(A, \succ)$ is a *tournament* if $\succ$ is complete. In the presence of (directed) cycles in the dominance relation, the concept of "best" or *maximal* elements is no longer well-defined, and various solution concepts that take over the role of maximality have been suggested. Some of these will be considered in Section 3. Formally, a *weak tournament solution* is a total function $S : \mathcal{T} \to 2^{\mathcal{A}} \setminus \{\emptyset\}$ such that for all $G \in \mathcal{T}(A)$, $S(G) \subseteq A$. We further require S to commute with any automorphism of $\mathcal{A}$, and to select the *maximum*, i.e., an alternative that dominates any other alternative, whenever it exists.

PageRank assigns scores to pages on the Web based on the frequency with which they are visited by a "random surfer" [7, 15]. Pages are then ranked in accordance with these scores. It is straightforward to apply a similar idea to dominance graphs, starting at some alternative and then randomly moving to one of the alternatives that dominate the current one. Intuitively, this corresponds to a contestation process where the status quo is constantly being replaced by some dominating alternative. Arguably, alternatives that are chosen more frequently according to this process are more desirable than alternatives that are chosen less frequently.[1] A tournament solution based on PageRank should thus choose the alternatives visited most often by an infinite random walk on the dominance graph.[2]

More formally, let $G = (A, \succ) \in \mathcal{T}(A)$ be a dominance graph, and let $d(a, G) = \{\, b \in A \mid a \succ b \,\}$ denote the dominion and $\overline{d}(a, G) = \{\, b \in A \mid b \succ a \,\}$ the dominators of alternative $a \in A$. Further let $\alpha \in [0, 1]$ be a parameter called the *damping factor*. Applying the original definition of Page et al. [15] to dominance graphs, the *PageRank score* $pr_\alpha(a, G)$ of alternative a in G is given by

---

[1] The key idea of this procedure is much older than PageRank and goes back to work by Daniels [8] and Moon and Pullman [13].

[2] It should be noted that transitions take place in the *reverse* direction of the dominance relation, from a dominated to a dominating alternative.

$$pr_\alpha(a, G) = \alpha \left(\sum_{b \in d(a, G)} \frac{pr(b, G)}{|\overline{d}(b, G)|} \right) + \frac{(1 - \alpha)}{|A|} .$$

That is, the score of a is determined by the scores of the alternatives it dominates, normalized by the number of alternatives dominating these, plus a constant.

It is well known that a solution to this system of equations such that $\sum_{a \in A} pr_\alpha(a, G) = 1$ corresponds to a stationary distribution of a Markov chain, and that a unique stationary distribution exists if the chain is irreducible, *i.e.*, if the dominance graph is strongly connected [see, *e.g.*, 11]. Undominated alternatives in the dominance graph lead to sinks in the Markov chain, thus making it irreducible. This problem can be handled by attaching either a self-loop or (uniform) transitions to all other states in the Markov chain to these sinks. The latter method, being the one commonly used in web page ranking, is clearly undesirable in the context of tournament solutions: For example, an undominated alternative that dominates some alternative inside a strongly connected subgraph would no longer be selected. Instead, we obtain the transition matrix of the Markov chain by transposing the adjacency matrix of the dominance graph, changing the diagonal entry to 1 in every row with sum 0, and row-normalizing the resulting matrix.

In the absence of sinks, pr_α is well-defined for every $\alpha < 1$. In the context of web page ranking, α has to be chosen carefully to accurately model the probability that a human user surfing the Web will stop following links and instead move to a random page [see, *e.g.*, 18]. Furthermore, the ability to differentiate between elements with lower scores is lost as α increases. The situation is different when PageRank is to be used as a tournament solution. In this case we want the solution to depend entirely on the dominance relation, and we are only interested in the best alternatives rather than a complete ranking. We thus want to compute pr_α for α as close to 1 as possible. It turns out that $\lim_{\alpha \to 1} pr_\alpha(a, G)$ is always well-defined [4], and we arrive at the following definition.

Definition 1. *Let $G \in \mathcal{T}(A)$ be a weak tournament. The PageRank score of an alternative $a \in A$ is defined as $pr(a, G) = \lim_{\alpha \to 1} pr_\alpha(a, G)$ where $\sum_{a \in A} pr_\alpha(a, G) = 1$. The PageRank set of G is given by $PR(G) = \{ a \in A \mid pr(a, G) = \max_{b \in A} pr(b, G) \}$.*[3]

Boldi et al. [4] further observe that $\lim_{\alpha \to 1} pr_\alpha$ must equal one of the (possibly infinitely many) solutions of the system of equations for pr_1. This can be used to relate the PageRank set to a well-known tournament solution called the Schwartz set. Given a weak tournament $G \in \mathcal{T}(A)$, a set $X \subseteq A$ has the *Schwartz property* if no alternative in X is dominated by some alternative *not* in X. The *Schwartz set* $T(G)$ is then defined as the union of all sets with the Schwartz property that are minimal w.r.t. set inclusion. We further write $\overline{T}(G)$ for the set of weak tournaments induced by the minimal subsets of A with the Schwartz property.

---

[3] Another tournament solution based on random walks in tournaments, called the *Markov set*, is described by Laslier [12]. While their definitions are similar, there exists a tournament with five alternatives for which the two solutions are disjoint.

It is well known from the theory of Markov chains that *every* solution of the system of equations for $\alpha = 1$ must satisfy $pr_1(a, G) = 0$ for all $a \notin T(G)$, and $pr_1(a, H)/pr_1(b, H) = pr_1(a, G)/pr_1(b, G)$ if $a, b \in A'$ for some $H = (A', \succ') \in \overline{T}(G)$ [see, *e.g.*, 11]. We thus have the following.

Fact 1. *Let $G \in T(A)$ be a weak tournament. Then, for all $a \in A \setminus T(G)$, $pr(a, G) = 0$, and for all $H = (A', \succ') \in \overline{T}(G)$ and $a, b \in A'$, $pr(a, H)/pr(b, H) = pr(a, G)/pr(b, G)$.*

In particular, $PR(G)$ can be determined by directly computing pr_1 for the (strongly connected) graph $G|_{T(G)}$ if $|\overline{T}(G)| = 1$, a property that always holds in tournaments. If there is more than one minimal set with the Schwartz property, relative scores of alternatives in *different* elements of $\overline{T}(G)$ may very well depend on the dominance structure outside the Schwartz set, and it is not obvious that scores can be computed directly in this case.

3   Set-Theoretic Relationships

It follows directly from Fact 1 that the PageRank set is always contained in the Schwartz set. We will now investigate its relationship to various other tournament solutions considered in the literature [see, *e.g.*, 12, 6, 5]. In particular, we look at the uncovered set and three other solutions that are always contained in the uncovered set. The *uncovered set* $UC(G)$ of a weak tournament $G \in T(A)$ consists of all alternatives that are not covered, where $a \in A$ is said to *cover* $b \in A$ if $a \succ b$, every alternative that dominates a also dominates b, and every alternative dominated by b is also dominated by a. The *Banks set* $B(G)$ consists of those elements that are maximal in some complete and transitive subgraph of G that is itself maximal w.r.t. set inclusion. The *Slater set* $SL(G)$ consists of the maximal alternatives of those acyclic relations that disagree with a minimal number of elements of the dominance relation. Finally, the *Copeland set* $C(G)$ is the set of alternatives for which the difference between the number of alternatives it dominates and the number of alternatives it is dominated by is maximal. We further write $UC^k(G) = UC^{k-1}(G|_{UC(G)})$ for the kth iteration of the uncovered set. It is known that the Banks set intersects with all of these iterations, whereas $SL(G)$ may have an empty intersection with $UC^2(G)$.

The main result of this section is stated next. We omit all proofs in this paper due to space restrictions.

Theorem 1. *$PR(G)$ is always contained in $UC(G)$. $PR(G)$ may have an empty intersection with $UC^2(G)$, $B(G)$, $SL(G)$, and $C(G)$.*

4   Properties

In this section, we evaluate PageRank using standard properties. Definitions of these properties can be found in texts on social choice theory and tournament solutions [see, *e.g.*, 9, 12]. Although some of the properties were originally introduced in the context of complete dominance relations, they naturally extend to the incomplete case. We now state the main result of this section.

Theorem 2. *PR satisfies monotonicity. PR does* not *satisfy SSP, idempotency, Aïzerman, independence of the losers, weak composition-consistency, and γ^*.*

Let us now consider a property of tournament solutions that is in some sense orthogonal to the ones considered so far, namely *discriminatory power*. Indeed, the above properties describe which elements should be chosen given that some other elements are chosen as well, or should still be chosen as the overall set of alternatives changes. As we have shown, the PageRank set is uniformly smaller than both the Schwartz set and the uncovered set. We further establish that PageRank can be arbitrarily more discriminatory than every composition-consistent solution (*e.g.*, UC, UC^2, or B) in the sense that there exist instances where PageRank yields a singleton and any composition-consistent solution does not discriminate at all.

Theorem 3. *For any composition-consistent solution concept S and any set A of alternatives with $|A| \geq 5$, there exists a dominance graph $G \in T(A)$ such that $|PR(G)| = 1$ and $S(G) = A$.*

Similar properties, although less severe, can also be shown individually for solutions that are not composition-consistent, like the Slater set. We leave it as an open problem whether there exist dominance graphs in which PageRank yields a significantly larger choice than any of these sets.

It should finally be noted that PageRank has the advantage of being efficiently computable (if $|\overline{T}(G)| = 1$), whereas determining the Banks or the Slater set is NP-hard even in tournaments [20, 1].

5 Conclusion

The contribution of this paper is twofold. First, we identified a strong relationship between ranking systems and tournament solutions. Secondly, we formally analyzed PageRank using properties and solution concepts defined in the literature on tournament solutions. PageRank fails to satisfy a number of these properties, but on the other hand is very discriminatory—a well-known issue of most established tournament solutions [10]. It is open to debate whether these results cast doubt upon the significance of PageRank as a tournament solution, or the usefulness of some of the axiomatic properties used in the tournament literature.

An interesting problem for future work is to unify axioms in the literature on ranking systems [3, 2, 16, 19] and tournament solutions [*e.g.*, 12]. Some of these axioms are apparently based on very similar ideas.

Acknowledgements. We thank Markus Holzer for helpful discussions and Paul Harrenstein for comments on a draft of this paper.

References

1. Alon, N.: Ranking tournaments. SIAM Journal of Discrete Mathematics 20(1), 137–142 (2006)
2. Altman, A., Tennenholtz, M.: On the axiomatic foundations of ranking systems. In: Proc. of 19th IJCAI, pp. 917–922 (2005) (Professional Book Center)
3. Altman, A., Tennenholtz, M.: Ranking systems: The PageRank axioms. In: Proc. of 6th ACM-EC Conference, pp. 1–8. ACM Press, New York (2005)
4. Boldi, P., Santini, M., Vigna, S.: A deeper investigation of PageRank as a function of the damping factor. In: Web Information Retrieval and Linear Algebra Algorithms, number 07071 in Dagstuhl Seminar Proceedings (2007)
5. Brandt, F., Fischer, F.: Computational aspects of covering in dominance graphs. In: Holte, R.C., Howe, A. (eds.) Proc. of 22nd AAAI Conference, pp. 694–699. AAAI Press, Stanford, California, USA (2007)
6. Brandt, F., Fischer, F., Harrenstein, P.: The computational complexity of choice sets. In: Samet, D. (ed.) Proc. of 11th TARK Conference, pp. 82–91. Presses Universitaires de Louvain (2007)
7. Brin, S., Page, L.: The anatomy of a large-scale hypertextual web search engine. Computer Networks 30(1-7), 107–117 (1998)
8. Daniels, H.E.: Round-robin tournament scores. Biometrika 56(2), 295–299 (1969)
9. Dutta, B., Laslier, J.-F.: Comparison functions and choice correspondences. Social Choice and Welfare 16(4), 513–532 (1999)
10. Fey, M.: Choosing form a large tournament. Mimeographed, University of Rochester (2002)
11. Kemeny, J.G., Snell, J.L.: Finite Markov Chains. Springer, Heidelberg (1976)
12. Laslier, J.-F.: Tournament Solutions and Majority Voting. Springer, Heidelberg (1997)
13. Moon, J.W., Pullman, N.K.: On generalized tournament matrics. SIAM Review 12(3), 384–399 (1970)
14. Moulin, H.: Choosing from a tournament. Social Choice and Welfare 3, 271–291 (1986)
15. Page, L., Brin, S., Motwani, R., Winograd, T.: The PageRank citation ranking: Bringing order to the Web. Technical Report 1999–66, Stanford University (1999)
16. Palacios-Huerta, I., Volij, O.: The measurement of intellectual influence. Econometrica 72(3), 963–977 (2004)
17. Peris, J.E., Subiza, B.: Condorcet choice correspondences for weak tournaments. Social Choice and Welfare 16(2), 217–231 (1999)
18. Pretto, L.: A theoretical analysis of Google's PageRank. In: Laender, A.H.F., Oliveira, A.L. (eds.) SPIRE 2002. LNCS, vol. 2476, pp. 131–144. Springer, Heidelberg (2002)
19. Slutzki, G., Volij, O.: Scoring of web pages and tournaments—axiomatizations. Social Choice and Welfare 26, 75–92 (2006)
20. Woeginger, G.J.: Banks winners in tournaments are difficult to recognize. Social Choice and Welfare 20, 523–528 (2003)

Competitive Influence Maximization in Social Networks

Shishir Bharathi, David Kempe, and Mahyar Salek

Department of Computer Science, University of Southern California

Abstract. Social networks often serve as a medium for the diffusion of ideas or innovations. An individual's decision whether to adopt a product or innovation will be highly dependent on the choices made by the individual's peers or neighbors in the social network. In this work, we study the game of innovation diffusion with multiple competing innovations such as when multiple companies market competing products using viral marketing. Our first contribution is a natural and mathematically tractable model for the diffusion of multiple innovations in a network. We give a $(1-1/e)$ approximation algorithm for computing the best response to an opponent's strategy, and prove that the "price of competition" of this game is at most 2. We also discuss "first mover" strategies which try to maximize the expected diffusion against perfect competition. Finally, we give an FPTAS for the problem of maximizing the influence of a single player when the underlying graph is a tree.

1 Introduction

Social networks are graphs of individuals and their relationships, such as friendships, collaborations, or advice seeking relationships. In deciding whether to adopt an innovation (such as a political idea or product), individuals will frequently be influenced, explicitly or implicitly, by their social contacts. In order to effectively employ *viral marketing* [1,2], i.e., marketing via "word-of-mouth" recommendations, it is thus essential for companies to identify "opinion leaders" to target, in the hopes that influencing them will lead to a large cascade of further recommendations. More formally, the *influence maximization problem* is the following: Given a probabilistic model for influence, determine a set A of k individuals yielding the largest expected cascade.[1] The formalization of influence maximization as an optimization problem is due to Domingos and Richardson [1], who modeled influence by an arbitrary Markov random field, and gave heuristics for maximization. The first provable approximation guarantees are given in [3,4,5].

In this paper, we extend past work by focusing on the case when multiple innovations are competing within a social network. This scenario will frequently arise in the real world: multiple companies with comparable products will vie for

---

[1] More realistic models considering different marketing actions which affect multiple individuals can usually be reduced to the problem as described here (see [3]).

X. Deng and F.C. Graham (Eds.): WINE 2007, LNCS 4858, pp. 306–311, 2007.

sales with competing word-of-mouth cascades; similarly, many innovations face active opposition also spreading by word of mouth. We propose a natural generalization of the *independent cascade model* [2] to multiple competing influences. Our model extends Hotelling's model of competition [6], and is related to competitive facility location and Voronoi games [7,8]. Similar models have also been considered recently by Lotker et al. [9] (who study mixed Nash Equilibria of the Voronoi game on the line), and Dubey et al. [10], who focus on Nash Equilibria for the (simpler) case of quasi-linear influence. We first study second-mover strategies and equilibria of the resulting activation game and show that:

Theorem 1. *The last agent i to commit to a set S_i for initial activation can efficiently find a $(1 - 1/e)$ approximation to the optimal S_i.*

Theorem 2. *The price of competition of the game (resulting from lack of coordination among the agents) is at most a factor of 2.*

We give exact algorithms for first-mover strategies in the two-player game on simple graph structures in Section 4. Finally, we give an FPTAS for maximizing the influence of a single player on bidirected trees, even when the edges in opposite directions have different probabilities.

2   Models and Preliminaries

The social network is represented as a directed graph $G = (V, E)$. Following the independent cascade model [2,3], each edge $e = (u, v) \in E$ has an activation probability p_e. Each node can be either *inactive* or *active*; in the latter case, it has a color denoting the influence for which it is active (intuitively, the product the node has adopted). We augment the model by a notion of *activation time* for each activation attempt. When node u becomes active at time t, it attempts to activate each currently inactive neighbor v. If the activation attempt from u on v succeeds, v will become active, of the same color as u, at time $t + T_{uv}$. The T_{uv} are independent and exponentially distributed continuous random variables. Subsequently, v will try to activate inactive neighbors, and so forth. Thus, a node always has the color of the first neighbor succeeding in activating it.

In the influence maximization game, each of b players selects a set S_i of at most k_i nodes. A node selected by multiple players will take the color of one of the players uniformly at random. Then, with S_i being active for influence i, the process unfolds as described above until no new activations occur. Letting $T_1, \ldots, T_b$ be the active sets at that point, the goal of each player i is to maximize $E[|T_i|]$. Player i is indifferent between strategies S_i and S_i' if their expected gain is the same. Simple examples show that in general, this game has no pure strategy Nash Equilibria; however, it does have mixed-strategy Nash Equilibria.

3   Best Response Strategies

In order to gain a better understanding of the influence maximization game, we first focus on best response strategies for players.

Lemma 1. *Suppose that the strategies $S_j, j \neq i$ for other players are fixed. Then, player i's payoff $\mathrm{E}\left[|T_i| \mid S_1, \ldots, S_b\right]$ from the strategy S_i is a monotone and submodular function of S_i.*

Proof. We obtain a deterministic equivalent of the activation process by choosing independently if each edge $e = (u, v)$ will constitute a successful activation attempt by u on v (a biased coin flip with probability p_e), as well as the activation time T_e, beforehand. Then, we consider running the (now deterministic) activation process using these outcomes and delays.

If node u has color j, and activates node v successfully, we color the edge (u, v) with color j. A path P is called a color-j path if all its edges have color j. Then, a node u ends up colored with color j iff there is a color-j path from some node in S_j to u.

Conditioned on any outcome of all random choices as well as all $S_j, j \neq i$, the set of nodes reachable along color-i paths from S_i is the union of all nodes reachable from any one node of S_i. Thus, if $S_i \subseteq S_i'$, the set of nodes reachable from $S_i + v$, but not from S_i, is a superset of those reachable from $S_i' + v$, but not from S_i' (by monotonicity). Thus, given fixed outcomes of all random choices and $S_j, j \neq i$, the number of nodes reachable from S_i is a monotone and submodular function of S_i. Being a non-negative linear combination of submodular functions (with coefficients equal to the probabilities of the outcomes of the random choices), the objective function of player i is thus also monotone and submodular. ∎

The above lemma implies that for the last player to commit to a strategy, the greedy algorithm of iteratively adding a node with largest marginal gain is within a factor $(1 - 1/e)$ of the best response (see [3]), thus proving Theorem 1. Second, as the expected total number of active nodes at the end is also a monotone submodular function of $S := \bigcup_j S_j$, the game meets the requirements of a *valid utility system* as defined by Vetta [11]. We can apply Theorem 3.4 of [11] to obtain that the expected total number of nodes activated in any Nash Equilibrium is at least half the number activated by the best solution with a single player controlling all of the $\sum_i b_i$ initial activations. This proves Theorem 2.

4   First Mover Strategies

We now consider first mover strategies in a duopoly, with 2 players called "red" and "blue". The following variant of the competitive influence maximization problem is motivated by its similarity both to the case of multiple disjoint directed lines (discussed briefly below) and to a fair division problem: Given n lines of lengths $\ell_1, \ldots, \ell_n$, the red player first gets to make any k cuts, creating $k + n$ pieces whose lengths sum up to the original lengths. The blue player picks the k largest segments ("blue pieces") and the red player gets the next-largest $\min(n, k)$ segments ("red pieces").

Assume for now that we know a "cutoff point" c such that all blue pieces have size at least c, and all red pieces have size at most c. Let $F(i, r, b, c)$ denote the maximum total size of r red pieces in the ith line, subject to the constraint that it must be cut into b blue segments of size at least c and r red segments of size at most c. Let $G(i, r, b, c)$ be the maximum total size of r red pieces in the first i lines combined, subject to having r red and b blue pieces, with a cutoff of c. Then, we obtain the following recurrence relation, which turns into a dynamic program in the standard way.

$$G(i, r, b, c) = \max_{r'=0...r} \max_{b'=0...b} F(i, r', b', c) + G(i-1, r-r', b-b', c)$$
$$G(0, r, b, c) = -\infty \text{ (or 0)} \qquad \text{whenever } b > 0 \text{ (or } b = 0).$$

Notice that we do indeed take a maximum over values of b', as the red player can decide how many "large" pieces to make available on each line for the blue player. The final answer we are interested in is then $G(n, \min(n, k), k, c)$. The main issue is how to reduce the candidates for the cutoff point c to a strongly polynomial number. The following lemma shows that we only need to try out nk candidate values $\ell_i/j, i = 1, \ldots, n, j = 1, \ldots, k$ for c (retaining the best solution found by the dynamic program), making the algorithm strongly polynomial.

Lemma 2. *The optimal solution cuts each line segment into equal-sized pieces.*

Proof. First, we can remove unused line segments from the problem instance. Second, partially used line segments can be converted to completely used line segments by adding the unused part to an existing blue segment (if it exists) or to an existing red segment (if no blue piece exists). The latter may entice the blue player to take a red piece. But this frees up a formerly blue piece (of size at least c) to be picked up by the red player.

W.l.o.g., all pieces of the same color on a line segment are of the same size. If the optimal solution contains an unevenly cut line with red and blue pieces, we increase the sizes of all red pieces and decrease the sizes of all blue pieces until the line is cut evenly. As before, the red player's gain cannot be reduced by the blue player switching to a different piece, because any new piece the red player may obtain after the blue player switches will have size at least c. ∎

The above algorithm can be extended to deal with directed lines and even out-directed arborescences. In the former case, the slight difference is that the "leftmost" piece of any line is not available to the red player. These extensions are deferred to the full version due to space constraints.

5 Influence Maximization on Bidirected Trees

While the single-player influence maximization problem is APX-hard in general [3], special cases of graph structures are more amenable to approximation. Here, we will give an FPTAS for the influence maximization problem for bi-directed trees. (This FPTAS can be extended to bounded treewidth graphs with a significant increase in complexity.) Given a target ε, we will give a $1 - \varepsilon$ approximation based on a combination of dynamic programming and rounding of probabilities.

For the subtree rooted at node v, let $G(v, k, q^+, q^-)$ denote the expected number of nodes that will be activated by an optimum strategy, provided that

(1) v is activated by its parent with probability at most q^-, and (2) v has to be activated by its subtree with probability at least q^+.

Let v be a node of degree d with children $v_1, \ldots v_d$. Then, for the respective subproblems, we can choose arbitrary $k_1, \ldots, k_d,\ q_1^+, \ldots, q_d^+,\ q_1^-, \ldots, q_d^-$, such that (1) $\sum_i k_i = k$, $q^+ \leq 1 - \prod_i (1 - q_i^+ p_{v_i,v})$ and $q_i^- \leq p_{v,v_i}(1 - (1 - q^-)\prod_{j \neq i}(1 - q_j^+ p_{v_j,v}))$ if v is selected, or (2) $\sum_i k_i = k - 1$, $q^+ \leq 1$ and $q_i^- \leq p_{v,v_i}$ if v is not selected. If (1) or (2) is satisfied, we call the values *consistent*. For consistent values, the optimum can be characterized as:

$$G(v, k, q^+, q^-) = \max_{(k_i),(q_i^+),(q_i^-)} \sum_{i=1}^{m} G(v_i, k_i, q_i^+, q_i^-) + 1 - (1 - q^+)(1 - q^-). \quad (1)$$

As discussed above, the maximum is over both the case that v is selected, and that it is not. It can be computed via a nested dynamic program over the values of i. In this form, $G(v, k, q^+, q^-)$ may have to be calculated for exponentially many values of q^+ and q^-. To deal with this problem, we define $\delta = \varepsilon/n^3$, and compute (and store) the values $G(v, k, q^+, q^-)$ only for q^+ and q^- which are multiples of δ between 0 and 1. The number of computed entries is then polynomial in n and $1/\varepsilon$. Let $G'(v, k, q^+, q^-)$ denote the gain obtained by the best consistent solution to the rounding version of the dynamic program, and $\lfloor q \rfloor_\delta$ the value of q rounded down to the nearest multiple of δ. Then, for the rounding version, we have

Theorem 3. *For all v, k, q^+, q^-, there exists a value $r^+ \leq q^+$ with $q^+ - r^+ \leq \delta |T_v|$, such that $G(v, k, q^+, q^-) - G'(v, k, r^+, \lfloor q^- \rfloor_\delta) \leq \delta |T_v|^3$, where $|T_v|$ is the number of nodes in the subtree rooted at v.*

Applying the theorem at the root of the tree, we obtain that the rounding dynamic program will find a solution differing from the optimum by at most an additive $\delta n^3 \leq \varepsilon \leq \varepsilon \cdot \text{OPT}$, proving that the algorithm is an FPTAS.

Proof. We will prove the theorem by induction on the tree structure. It clearly holds for all leaves, by choosing $r^+ = \lfloor q^+ \rfloor_\delta$. Let v be an internal node of degree d, with children $v_1, \ldots, v_d$. Let $(k_i), (q_i^+), (q_i^-)$ be the arguments for the optimum subproblems of $G(v, k, q^+, q^-)$. By induction hypothesis, applied to each of the subtrees, there are values $r_i^+ \leq q_i^+$ with $q_i^+ - r_i^+ \leq \delta |T_{v_i}|$, such that $G(v_i, k_i, q_i^+, q_i^-) - G'(v_i, k_i, r_i^+, \lfloor q_i^- \rfloor_\delta) \leq \delta |T_{v_i}|^3$.

Define $r^+ := \lfloor 1 - \prod_i (1 - r_i^+ p_{v_i,v}) \rfloor_\delta$, (or $r^+ = 1$, if the optimum solution included node v). By definition, r^+ is consistent with the r_i^+. Using Lemma 4 below and the inductive guarantee on the r_i^+ values, we obtain directly that $q^+ - r^+ \leq \delta |T_v|$ (where we used the fact that $\sum_i |T_{v_i}| + 1 = |T_v|$). Next, we define $r_i^- = \lfloor p_{v,v_i}(1 - (1 - \lfloor q^- \rfloor_\delta) \prod_{j \neq i}(1 - r_j^+ p_{v_j,v})) \rfloor_\delta$ for all i. Again, the r_i^- are consistent by definition, and by using the inductively guaranteed bounds on $q_j^+ - r_j^+$ as well as Lemma 4, we obtain that $q_i^- - r_i^- \leq \delta(|T_v| + 1)$ for all i.

Now, applying Lemma 3, we obtain that $G'(v_i, k_i, r_i^+, q_i^-) - G'(v_i, k_i, r_i^+, r_i^-) \leq \delta |T_{v_i}|(|T_v| + 1)$, for all i. In other words, because the input values to the subproblems did not need to be perturbed significantly to make the r_i^- consistent, the value of the rounding dynamic program cannot have changed too much. Combining these bounds with the inductive assumption for each subproblem, we have:

$$
\begin{aligned}
G'(v, k, r^+, \lfloor q^- \rfloor_\delta) &\geq \sum_i G'(v_i, k_i, r_i^+, r_i^-) + 1 - (1 - r^+)(1 - \lfloor q^- \rfloor_\delta) \\
&\geq \sum_i (G'(v_i, k_i, r_i^+, \lfloor q_i^- \rfloor_\delta) - \delta |T_{v_i}|(|T_v| + 1)) \\
&\quad + 1 - (1 - q^+ + \delta |T_v|)(1 - q^- + \delta) \\
&\overset{IH}{\geq} \sum_i (G(v_i, k_i, q_i^+, q_i^-) - \delta(|T_{v_i}|^3 + (|T_v| + 1)|T_{v_i}|)) \\
&\quad + 1 - (1 - q^+)(1 - q^-) - \delta(1 + |T_v|) \\
&\geq G(v, k, q^+, q^-) - \delta |T_v|^3.
\end{aligned}
$$
■

The following two lemmas are proved by induction; their proofs are deferred to the full version due to space constraints.

Lemma 3. *If $r^- \leq q^-$, then $G'(v, k, q^+, q^-) - G'(v, k, q^+, r^-) \leq |T_v|(q^- - r^-)$.*

Lemma 4. *For any $a_1, \ldots, a_n$ and $b_1, \ldots, b_n$,*

$$
\prod_{i=1}^n a_i - \prod_{i=1}^n b_i = \sum_{i=1}^n (a_i - b_i) \cdot \prod_{j=1}^{i-1} a_j \cdot \prod_{j=i+1}^n b_j
$$

Acknowledgments. We would like to thank Bobby Kleinberg and Ranjit Raveendran for useful discussions, and anonymous reviewers for helpful feedback.

References

1. Domingos, P., Richardson, M.: Mining the network value of customers. In: Proc. 7th KDD, pp. 57–66 (2001)
2. Goldenberg, J., Libai, B., Muller, E.: Talk of the network: A complex systems look at the underlying process of word-of-mouth. Marketing Letters 12, 211–223 (2001)
3. Kempe, D., Kleinberg, J., Tardos, E.: Maximizing the spread of influence in a social network. In: Proc. 9th KDD, pp. 137–146 (2003)
4. Kempe, D., Kleinberg, J., Tardos, E.: Influential nodes in a diffusion model for social networks. In: Proc. 32nd ICALP (2005)
5. Mossel, E., Roch, S.: On the submodularity of influence in social networks. In: Proc. 38th ACM STOC (2007)
6. Hotelling, H.: Stability in competition. The Economic Journal 39, 41–57 (1929)
7. Ahn, H., Cheng, S., Cheong, O., Golin, M., van Oostrom, R.: Competitive facility location along a highway. In: Wang, J. (ed.) COCOON 2001. LNCS, vol. 2108, pp. 237–246. Springer, Heidelberg (2001)
8. Cheong, O., Har-Peled, S., Linial, N., Matoušek, J.: The one-round voronoi game. Discrete And Computational Geometry 31, 125–138 (2004)
9. Lotker, Z., Patt-Shamir, B., M.R.T.: Publish and perish: definition and analysis of an n-person publication impact game. In: Proc. 18th ACM SPAA, pp. 11–18 (2006)
10. Dubey, P., Garg, R., de Meyer, B.: Competing for customers in a social network: The quasi-linear case. In: Spirakis, P.G., Mavronicolas, M., Kontogiannis, S.C. (eds.) WINE 2006. LNCS, vol. 4286, Springer, Heidelberg (2006)
11. Vetta, A.: Nash equlibria in competitive societies with applications to facility location, traffic routing and auctions. In: Proc. 43rd IEEE FOCS, pp. 416–425 (2002)

Sponsored Search with Contexts*

Eyal Even-Dar[1,**], Michael Kearns[2], and Jennifer Wortman[2]

[1] Google Research
[2] Dept. of Computer and Information Science, University of Pennsylvania

Abstract. We examine a formal model of sponsored search in which advertisers can bid not only on search terms, but on search terms under specific *contexts*. A context is any auxiliary information that might accompany a search, and might include information that is factual, estimated or inferred. Natural examples of contexts include the zip code, gender, or abstract "intentions" (such as researching a vacation) of the searcher. After introducing a natural probabilistic model for context-based auctions, we provide several theoretical results, including the fact that under general circumstances, the overall social welfare of the advertisers and auctioneer together can only increase when moving from standard to context-based mechanisms. In contrast, we provide and discuss specific examples in which only one party (advertisers or auctioneer) benefits at the expense of the other in moving to context-based search.

1   Introduction

In the standard model of sponsored search, advertisers place bids on individual terms or keywords. When a query is made on a given keyword, an auction is held to determine which advertisers' ads will appear on the search results page presented to the user and in what order. Generally the auction mechanism used is a generalized second-price (or *next-price*) mechanism [2] in which advertisers are ranked either by bid alone (the so-called "Rank By Bid" allocation, or RBB) or by the product of bid and a numerical measure of the quality of the ad ("Rank By Revenue," or RBR) [4]. An advertiser pays a fee to the auctioneer (in this case, the search engine) only when the search results in a click on the ad.

In this paper we investigate the extension of this standard model to incorporate what we shall call *contexts*. A context is any piece of auxiliary information that might modify the interpretation or expected value of a specific search query. Contexts may be "factual" information, or may be based on (possibly noisy) inferences. For example, it is often possible to infer a user's zip code from their IP address. Advertisers providing only local services (such as dentistry or child care) might value searches originating from certain zip codes much more highly than others. Similarly, an online retailer specializing in maternity clothing might place a high value on clicks from women in their twenties and thirties, while a

---

* An extended version of this paper including a more detailed analysis and simulations can be found at http://www.cis.upenn.edu/~mkearns/papers/contexts.pdf.
** This work was done while the author was a postdoctoral researcher at UPenn.

X. Deng and F.C. Graham (Eds.): WINE 2007, LNCS 4858, pp. 312–317, 2007.

website selling dorm room supplies might prefer clicks from teenagers of either gender. Search engines are often able to collect such demographic information about searchers directly via site accounts and could potentially use this information to select more relevant ads. Additionally, it may be possible to estimate a user's abstract "intention" from recent web activity. We might infer a user's interest in planning a vacation from a series of searches for travel web sites. A hotel in Istanbul would probably be willing to pay more per click for the keyword "turkey" if it were *more likely* that the searcher was planning a vacation than a home-cooked meal.

Search engines already include limited abilities for advertisers to modify bids based on searcher context. Both Google's AdWords program and Yahoo!'s Search Marketing program allow advertisers to bid on searches limited to specified geographic areas. Microsoft's adCenter allows bidders to target searchers by location, age, or gender by specifying an additional bid amount for targeted searches on top of a base keyword bid. Aside from these formal context-based mechanisms, advertisers may informally implement their own by bidding on more specific search terms (e.g. "Philadelphia dentist" rather than "dentist" alone).

Despite these various existing forms of context-based bidding, no formal study has been published showing that these additional bidding capabilities are beneficial either to the advertisers or to the search engines themselves. The closest existing work is the economic literature on *bundling*, the strategy of offering multiple distinct goods for sale together as a single item. (In our setting, these goods are clicks from searches on the same keyword in different contexts, and we are interested in what happens when they are *unbundled*.) Palfrey first analyzed the effects of bundling on bidder and auctioneer welfare in VCG auctions [5]. While these results do not carry over directly to the more complex multiple-slot sponsored search auction setting, the underlying intuition is similar.

The idea of allowing increased expressiveness in sponsored search auctions, including context-specific bidding, has also been suggested by Parkes and Sandholm in the context of efficient solutions for the winner determination problem [6]. However, their work does not address the effects of this increased expressiveness on revenue. Here we examine sponsored search auctions in which advertisers may place explicit bids on pairs of keywords and contexts, and compare the welfare of both the advertisers and the search engines in this setting to the welfare when bids are restricted to words alone.

2   Preliminaries

Without loss of generality we will limit our analysis to auctions on a single fixed keyword (or search term) w. We assume that there exists a fixed and known distribution P over the set of user contexts C for searches on w, and that for all $c \in C$, each advertiser $a \in \{1, \cdots, A\}$ has a known (expected) value $v_{a,c}$ for a click from a user with context c.

For each query, we assume there are S advertiser slots available. We make the standard assumption [7,1] that the click-through rate (CTR) of an ad shown in slot s can be factored into two parts, a slot-specific base click-through rate x_s that is monotonically decreasing in the s, and a quality effect $e_{a,c}$ that can depend on the advertiser a and context c in an arbitrary way. We can then write the click-through rate of advertiser a in slot s for context c as the product $e_{a,c}x_s$, and the expected click-through rate over all contexts as $e_a x_s$ where $e_a = \sum_{c \in C} P(c)e_{a,c}$. For convenience, we define $x_s = 0$ for $s > S$.

In order to compute the expected value over all contexts of a click to an advertiser, we must take into account the advertiser's quality since the distribution of clicks that an advertiser receives will be affected by his quality scores. We can compute the expected value of a click to advertiser a as $v_a = \sum_{c \in C} P(c)v_{a,c}e_{a,c}/e_a$. Note that if the quality of the advertiser is constant over all contexts then $v_a = \sum_{c \in C} P(c)v_{a,c}$ as expected.

We examine both the standard VCG mechanism (see, for example, Edelman et al. [2]) and the generalized second-price auction mechanism using a rank by revenue (RBR) allocation scheme [4]. Under RBR, advertisers are ranked by the product of their quality effect ($e_{a,c}$ or e_a) and their bid ($b_{a,c}$ or b_a) rather than bid alone. This approximately models the allocation methods currently used by both Yahoo! and Google. In the RBR generalized second-price auction, the payment of advertiser i for a click in slot s is calculated as $b_j e_j / e_i$ (or $b_{j,c}e_{j,c}/e_{i,c}$ in a context-based model) where j is the advertiser in slot $s+1$. Notice that this payment is the minimum amount that advertiser i must bid to remain in slot i, i.e. the minimum value of b_i for which $b_i e_i \geq b_j e_j$.

We will analyze three quantities of interest: advertiser profit, auctioneer revenue, and social welfare. We define the advertiser profit as the sum over all advertisers of the expected value received from clicks on a given user search minus the expected price paid. The social welfare is simply the advertiser profit plus the expected revenue of a user search to the auctioneer, i.e. the social welfare if we think of the search engine as a player. Intuitively, this can be thought of as a measure of the economic efficiency of the auction. Note that since the revenue of the auctioneer is by definition equal to the total amount paid by all bidders, the social welfare is equivalent to the sum over all advertisers of the expected value of a search.

We will examine sponsored search mechanisms under various equilibrium concepts. For next-price auctions, it is appropriate to consider the concept of symmetric Nash equilibrium (SNE) introduced simultaneously by Edelman et al. [2] and Varian [7]. While the SNE was originally defined in the RBB setting, it can naturally be extended to the RBR setting. For example, letting v_s and e_s denote the value and quality of the bidder in slot s, we can express the bids under the so-called *low SNE* as $b_s = \frac{1}{e_s x_{s-1}} \sum_{t=s}^{S+1} (x_{t-1} - x_t)e_t v_t$ where $b_{S+1} = v_{S+1}$. For VCG, it is appropriate to examine the dominant-strategy truthful equilibrium. Here we simply have $b_s = v_s$ for all s.

Given a sponsored search mechanism and an equilibrium concept (such as Nash, symmetric Nash, or dominant strategy equilibria), we will say that the mechanism is *efficient at equilibrium* under the specified equilibrium concept if the mechanism maximizes social welfare any time such an equilibrium is played.

It is easy to see that an RBR generalized second-price auction is efficient under symmetric Nash equilibria. (The proof, which is similar to Varian's "monotone values" proof for SNE of next-price auctions without quality scores [7], relies on the fact that in sponsored search auctions, social welfare is always maximized when ads are ranked in decreasing order by the product of value and quality.) Additionally, VCG is efficient under the dominant-strategy equilibrium.

3   Social Welfare

We begin by examining the shift in social welfare that occurs when we move from the standard keyword auction to a context-based auction. We show that under a variety of conditions, the social welfare can only increase when context-based bidding is introduced. This is not surprising given similar results from bundling theory (see, for example, Theorem 4 of Palfrey [5]), but is nice in its generality; our result generalizes Palfrey's to the multiple-slot auction setting. We state the conditions of the next theorem as generally as possible. The proof appears in the extended version of this paper [3].

Theorem 1. *Consider any sponsored search mechanism that is efficient at equilibrium for a given equilibrium concept. For this mechanism, the social welfare at equilibrium under context-based bidding is at least as high as the social welfare at equilibrium under standard keyword bidding.*

The following corollaries illustrate cases in which Theorem 1 applies.

Corollary 1. *In a RBR generalized second-price auction, the social welfare at any symmetric Nash equilibrium under context-based bidding is at least as high as the social welfare at any SNE under keyword bidding.*

Corollary 2. *In a VCG auction, the social welfare at the dominant-strategy truthful equilibrium under context-based bidding is at least as high as the social welfare at the dominant-strategy truthful equilibrium under keyword bidding.*

4   Trade-Offs in Revenue

In the previous section, we saw that under a wide variety of auction mechanisms and bidding assumptions, it will always be more efficient in terms of social welfare to allow context-based bidding. However, this does not necessarily imply that context-based bidding always produces higher revenue for the auctioneer or that it always increases the total revenue of the advertisers. Indeed there are situations in which context-based auctions result in lower revenue for the auctioneer or for the bidders as a whole. In this section we examine scenarios in which decreases in revenue might occur and analyze why this is the case. The full details of the examples can be found in a the long version [3].

For simplicity, we consider next-price auctions over a single ad slot and assume that all advertisers bid truthfully.[1] Similar examples can be shown in multiple-slot models. In each example, the word w will have two possible contexts, c_1 and c_2, with $P(c_1) = P(c_2) = 0.5$, and all advertisers will have a uniform quality effect of 1.

A Decrease in Auctioneer Revenue. It is possible to construct an example with only two bidders in which auctioneer revenue decreases when context-based bidding is allowed. Suppose the value of advertiser 1 for context 1 is 10 and for context 2 is 1, while the value for advertiser 2 is 1 for context 1 and 10 for context 2. Clearly both value the word at 5.5 on expectation. Under standard word-based bidding, the expected auctioneer revenue is $5.5x_1$ while under context-based bidding, the expected auctioneer revenue is x_1. The problem that arises in this simple example is the general problem of splitting the competition. When the advertisers are forced to bid on both contexts of w, they are placed in direct competition with each other. Because of the nature of second-price auctions, this competition is enough to drive up the price per click. However, when the advertisers are free to bid separately for each context, they are not in direct competition for the contexts they each prefer most and are thus able to pay less per click, reducing the revenue to the auctioneer.

Such a situation might occur when advertisers are cable service providers and zip code-based bidding is introduced. While all cable providers are likely to value clicks from sponsored ads on keywords like "cable tv", there is typically only one cable provider available in a given zip code. It is likely that context-based bidding would thus reduce competition between cable providers, lowering prices per click which would in turn lower the revenue to the auctioneer. In this case, it would be in the search engine's best interest to stick with standard keyword bidding.

A Decrease in Advertiser Profit. Context-based bidding can also lead to a *concentration* of competition, yielding higher revenue for the auctioneer at the expense of the advertisers. Suppose there are three advertisers with values as follows. Advertiser 1 has a constant value of 10. Advertiser 2 values context c_1 at 9 and context c_2 at 1, while advertiser 3 values context c_1 as 1 and context c_2 as 9. Advertiser 1 will be the high bidder for both the word- and context-based auctions. Because advertisers 2 and 3 value only one context, advertiser 1 can pay a low price in the word-based auction. Context-based bidding will increase competition for each context, raising the price.

In the word-based auction, the advertiser profit can be calculated as

$$x_1 e_{r(1)} \left(v_{r(1)} - (b_{r(2)} e_{r(2)} / e_{r(1)}) \right) = x_1 (10 - 5) = 5x_1,$$

while in the context-based auction, the advertiser profit will be

$$\sum_{c \in C} P(c) x_1 e_{r_c(1),c} \left(v_{r_c(1),c} - (b_{r_c(2),c} e_{r_c(2),c} / e_{r_c(1),c}) \right) = x_1 .$$

---

[1] With only one slot, the next-price auction mechanism is equivalent to VCG. Truthful bidding is thus a dominant-strategy equilibrium that maximizes social welfare.

This example is especially striking because the allocation of clicks is the same under both models; only the payment scheme has changed. The introduction of contexts has concentrated the competition forcing advertiser 1 to pay a higher price per click.

Such phenomenon can occur when there is a mix of large corporations and smaller local services in competition a keyword. Consider the market for the term "pizza." Most local pizzerias would not bother to place ads on this term in a word-based setting as the majority of their clicks would have no value. This would allow nationwide pizza chains to purchase these ads at moderate prices. However, adding zip code-based bidding could motivate smaller chains to begin placing ads to attract locals, driving up the prices of ads for the large chains and increasing the revenue to the auctioneer.

Increased Revenue for Everyone. Finally, it is often the case that context-based bidding will simultaneously allow advertisers to reach their target audience while still allowing enough competition for the auctioneer to benefit. In this scenario, advertisers can focus ads on their target audiences, raising advertiser profit, but without completely splitting up the competition, enabling the auctioneer to profit as well. This could happen when contexts are again zip codes and advertisers are competing local businesses. Consider a set of dentist offices bidding on ads for the keyword "dentist." Each dentist office would be interested only in local clicks and would be happy to have the option to bid by context. However, since there are multiple dentists servicing patients in any zip code, there would still be enough competition that the search engine would profit. We suspect that this scenario is likely to fit the bidding patterns of advertisers on most common keywords.

References

1. Borgs, C., Chayes, J., Etesami, O., Immorlica, N., Jain, K., Mahdian, M.: Dynamics of bid optimization in online advertisement auctions. In: WWW (2007)
2. Edelman, B., Ostrovsky, M., Schwarz, M.: Internet advertising and the generalized second price auction: Selling billions of dollars worth of keywords. American Economic Review 97(1), 242–259 (2007)
3. Even-Dar, E., Kearns, M., Wortman, J.: Sponsored search with contexts (2007), Available at: http://www.cis.upenn.edu/~mkearns/papers/contexts.pdf
4. Lahaie, S.: An analysis of alternative slot auction designs for sponsored search. In: Proceedings of the 7th ACM Conference on Electronic Commerce, ACM Press, New York (2006)
5. Palfrey, T.: Bundling decisions by a multiproduct monopolist with incomplete information. Econometrica 51(2), 463–483 (1983)
6. Parkes, D., Sandholm, T.: Optimize-and-dispatch architecture for expressive ad auctions. Paper presented at the First Workshop on Sponsored Search Auctions, Vancouver, Canada (June 2005)
7. Varian, H.: Position auctions (Forthcoming). International Journal of Industrial Organization (2006)

Capacity Constraints and the Inevitability of Mediators in Adword Auctions

Sudhir Kumar Singh[1,*], Vwani P. Roychowdhury[1,2], Himawan Gunadhi[2], and Behnam A. Rezaei[2]

[1] Department of Electrical Engineering, University of California, Los Angeles, CA 90095
[2] Ilial Inc., 11943 Montana Ave. Suite 200, Los Angeles, CA 90049
{sudhir,vwani,gunadhi,behnam}@ilial.com

Abstract. One natural constraint in the sponsored search advertising framework arises from the fact that there is a limit on the number of available slots, especially for the popular keywords, and as a result, a significant pool of advertisers are left out. We study the emergence of diversification in the adword market triggered by such capacity constraints in the sense that new market mechanisms, as well as, new for-profit agents are likely to emerge to combat or to make profit from the opportunities created by shortages in ad-space inventory. We propose a model where the additional capacity is provided by for-profit agents (or, mediators), who compete for slots in the original auction, draw traffic, and run their own sub-auctions. The quality of the additional capacity provided by a mediator is measured by its *fitness* factor. We compute revenues and payoffs for all the different parties at a *symmetric Nash equilibrium* (SNE) when the mediator-based model is operated by a mechanism currently being used by Google and Yahoo!, and then compare these numbers with those obtained at a corresponding SNE for the same mechanism, but without any mediators involved in the auctions. Such calculations allow us to determine the value of the additional capacity. Our results show that the revenue of the auctioneer, as well as the social value (i.e. efficiency), always increase when mediators are involved; moreover even the payoffs of *all* the bidders will increase if the mediator has a high enough fitness. Thus, our analysis indicates that there are significant opportunities for diversification in the internet economy and we should expect it to continue to develop richer structure, with room for different types of agents and mechanisms to coexist.

1 Introduction

Sponsored search advertising is a significant growth market and is witnessing rapid growth and evolution. The analysis of the underlying models has so far primarily focused on the scenario, where advertisers/bidders interact directly with the auctioneers, i.e., the Search Engines and publishers. However, the market is already witnessing the spontaneous emergence of several categories of companies who are trying to mediate or facilitate the auction process. For example, a number of different AdNetworks have started proliferating, and so have companies who specialize in reselling ad inventories.

---

* This work was done while the author was working for Ilial Inc.. The financial support from Ilial Inc. is highly acknowledged.

X. Deng and F.C. Graham (Eds.): WINE 2007, LNCS 4858, pp. 318–325, 2007.

Hence, there is a need for analyzing the impact of such incentive driven and for-profit agents, especially as they become more sophisticated in playing the game. In the present work, our focus is on the emergence of market mechanisms and for-profit agents motivated by capacity constraint inherent to the present models.

For instance, one natural constraint comes from the fact that there is a limit on the number of slots available for putting ads, especially for the popular keywords, and a significant pool of advertisers are left out due to this capacity constraint. We ask whether there are sustainable market constructs and mechanisms, where new players interact with the existing auction mechanisms to increase the overall capacity. In particular, lead-generation companies who bid for keywords, draw traffic from search pages and then redirect such traffic to service/product providers, have spontaneously emerged. However, the incentive and equilibria properties of paid-search auctions in the presence of such profit-driven players have not been explored. We investigate key questions, including what happens to the overall revenue of the auctioneer when such mediators participate, what is the payoff of a mediator and how does it depend on her quality, how are the payoffs of the bidders affected, and is there an overall value that is generated by such mechanisms.

Formally, in the current models, there are K slots to be allocated among N ($\geq K$) bidders (i.e. the advertisers). A bidder i has a true valuation v_i (known only to the bidder i) for the specific keyword and she bids b_i. The expected *click through rate* (CTR) of an ad put by bidder i when allocated slot j has the form $\gamma_j e_i$ i.e. separable in to a position effect and an advertiser effect. γ_j's can be interpreted as the probability that an ad will be noticed when put in slot j and it is assumed that $\gamma_1 > \gamma_2 > \cdots > \gamma_K > \gamma_{K+1} = \gamma_{K+2} = \ldots \gamma_N = 0$. e_i can be interpreted as the probability that an ad put by bidder i will be clicked on if noticed and is referred to as the *relevance* of bidder i. The payoff/utility of bidder i when given slot j at a price of p per click is given by $e_i \gamma_j (v_i - p)$ and they are assumed to be rational agents trying to maximize their payoffs. As of now, Google as well as Yahoo! uses schemes closely modeled as RBR(rank by revenue) with GSP(generalized second pricing). The bidders are ranked according to $e_i v_i$ and the slots are allocated as per this ranks. For simplicity of notation, assume that the ith bidder is the one allocated slot i according to this ranking rule, then i is charged an amount equal to $\frac{e_{i+1} v_{i+1}}{e_i}$. Formal analysis of such sponsored search advertising model has been done extensively in recent years, from algorithmic as well as from game theoretic perspective[2,6,3,1,7,4,5].

In the following section, we propose and study a model wherein the additional capacity is provided by a for-profit agent who competes for a slot in the original auction, draws traffic and runs its own sub-auction for the added slots. We discuss the cost or the value of capacity by analyzing the change in the revenues due to added capacity as compared to the ones without added capacity.

2 The Model

In this section, we discuss our model motivated by the capacity constraint, which can be formally described as follows:

- **Primary Auction (p-auction)** : Mediators participate in the original auction run by the search engine (called *p-auction*) and compete with advertisers for slots (called *primary slots*). For the ith agent (an advertiser or a mediator), let v_i^p and b_i^p denote her true valuation and the bid for the p-auction respectively. Further, let us denote $v_i^p e_i^p$ by s_i^p where e_i^p is the relevance score of ith agent for p-auction. Let there are κ mediators and there indices are $M_1, M_2, \ldots, M_\kappa$ respectively.

- **Secondary auctions (s-auctions):**
  - **Secondary slots:** Suppose that in the primary auction, the slots assigned to the mediators are $l_1, l_2, \ldots, l_\kappa$ respectively, then effectively, the additional slots are obtained by forking these *primary slots* in to $L_1, L_2, \ldots, L_\kappa$ additional slots respectively, where $L_i \leq K$ for all $i = 1, 2, \ldots, \kappa$. By forking we mean the following: on the associated landing page the mediator puts some information relevant to the specific keyword associated with the p-auction along with the space for additional slots. Let us call these additional slots as *secondary slots*.
  - **Properties of secondary slots and *fitness* of the mediators:** For the ith mediator, there will be a probability associated with her ad to be clicked if noticed, which is actually her relevence score $e_{M_i}^p$ and the position based CTRs might actually improve say by a factor of α_i. This means that the position based CTR for the jth secondary slot of ith mediator is modeled as $\alpha_i \gamma_j$ for $1 \leq j \leq L_i$ and 0 otherwise. Therefore, we can define a *fitness* f_i for the ith mediator, which is equal to $e_{M_i}^p \alpha_i$. Thus corresponding to the l_ith primary slot (the one being forked by the ith mediator), the *effective* position based CTR for the jth secondary slot obtained is $\tilde{\gamma}_{i,j}$ where

$$\tilde{\gamma}_{i,j} = \begin{cases} \gamma_{l_i} f_i \gamma_j & \text{for } j = 1, 2, \ldots, L_i, \\ 0 & \text{otherwise.} \end{cases} \tag{1}$$

  Note that $f_i \gamma_1 < 1$, however f_i could be greater than 1.
  - **s-auctions:** Mediators run their individual sub-auctions (called *s-auctions*) for the secondary slots provided by them. For an advertiser there is another type of valuations and bids, the ones associated with s-auctions. For the ith agent, let $v_{i,j}^s$ and $b_{i,j}^s$ denote her true valuation and the bid for the s-auction of jth mediator respectively. In general, the two types of valuations or bids corresponding to p-auction and the s-auctions might differ a lot. We also assume that $v_{i,j}^s = 0$ and $b_{i,j}^s = 0$ whenever i is a mediator. Further, for the advertisers who do not participate in one auction (p-auction or s-auction), the corresponding true valuation and the bid are assumed to be zero. Also, for notational convenience let us denote $v_{i,j}^s e_{i,j}^s$ by $s_{i,j}^s$ where $e_{i,j}^s$ is the relevance score of ith agent for the s-auction of jth mediator.
  - **Payment models for s-auctions:** Mediators could sell their secondary slots by impression (PPM), by pay-per-click (PPC) or pay-per-conversion(PPA). In the following analysis, we consider PPC.

- **Freedom of participation:** Advertisers are free to bid for primary as well as secondary slots.

- **True valuations of the mediators:** The true valuation of the mediators are derived from the expected revenue (total payments from advertisers) they obtain from the corresponding s-auctions[1] *ex ante*.

3 Bid Profiles at SNE

For simplicity, let us assume participation of a single mediator and the analysis involving several mediators can be done in a similar fashion. For notational convenience let

$$f = f_1, \text{ the fitness of the mediator}$$
$$l = l_1, \text{ the position of the primary slot assigned to the mediator}$$
$$L = L_1, \text{ the number of secondary slots provided by the mediator in her } s\text{-auction}$$
$$M = M_1, \text{ the index of the mediator i.e. } M\text{th agent is the mediator}$$
$$\tilde{\gamma}_j = \tilde{\gamma}_{1,j}, \text{ is the } \textit{effective} \text{ position based CTR of the } j\text{th secondary slot provided by the mediator}$$
$$v^s_{i,1} = v^s_i, \text{ is the true valuation of the agent } i \text{ for the } s\text{-auction}$$
$$b^s_{i,1} = b^s_i, \text{ is the bid of the agent } i \text{ for the } s\text{-auction, and}$$
$$s^s_{i,1} = s^s_i = v^s_i e^s_i, \text{ where } e^s_i = e^s_{i,1} \text{ is the relevance score of } i\text{th agent for the } s\text{-auction.}$$

The p-auction as well as the s-auction is done via *RBR* with *GSP*, i.e. the mechanism currently being used by Google and Yahoo!, and the solution concept we use is *Symmetric Nash Equilibria(SNE)*[2,7]. Suppose the allocations for the p-auction and s-auction are $\sigma : \{1, 2, \ldots, N\} \longrightarrow \{1, 2, \ldots, N\}$ and $\tau : \{1, 2, \ldots, N\} \longrightarrow \{1, 2, \ldots, N\}$ respectively. Then the payoff of the ith agent from the combined auction (p-auction and s-auction together) is

$$u_i = \gamma_{\sigma^{-1}(i)}\left(s^p_i - r^p_{\sigma^{-1}(i)+1}\right) + \tilde{\gamma}_{\tau^{-1}(i)}\left(s^s_i - r^s_{\tau^{-1}(i)+1}\right)$$

where

$$r^p_j = b^p_{\sigma(j)} e^p_{\sigma(j)},$$
$$r^s_j = b^s_{\tau(j)} e^s_{\tau(j)}.$$

From the mathematical structure of payoffs and strategies available to the bidders wherein two different uncorrelated values can be reported as bids in the two types of auctions independently of each other[2], it is clear that the equilibrium of the combined auction game is the one obtained from the equilibria of the p-auction game and the s-auction game each played in isolation. In particular at *SNE*[2,7],

$$\gamma_i r^p_{i+1} = \sum_{j=i}^{K}(\gamma_j - \gamma_{j+1})s^p_{\sigma(j+1)} \text{ for all } i = 1, 2, \ldots, K$$

and

---

[1] This way of deriving the true valuation for the mediator is reasonable for the mediator can participate in the p-auction several times and run her corresponding s-auction and can estimate the revenue she is deriving from the s-auction.

[2] This assumption was motivated by some mathematical examples from Google Adword[3].

$$\tilde{\gamma}_i r^s_{i+1} = \sum_{j=i}^{L} (\tilde{\gamma}_j - \tilde{\gamma}_{j+1}) s^s_{\tau(j+1)} \text{ for all } i = 1, 2, \ldots, L$$

which implies that (see Eq. (1))

$$\gamma_i r^s_{i+1} = \sum_{j=i}^{L-1} (\gamma_j - \gamma_{j+1}) s^s_{\tau(j+1)} + \gamma_L s^s_{\tau(L+1)} \text{ for all } i = 1, 2, \ldots, L$$

where

$$s^p_{\sigma(l)} = s^p_M = f \sum_{j=1}^{L} \gamma_j r^s_{j+1} = f \left(\sum_{j=1}^{L-1} (\gamma_j - \gamma_{j+1}) j s^s_{\tau(j+1)} + \gamma_L L s^s_{\tau(L+1)} \right)$$

is the true valuation of the mediator multiplied by her relevance score as per our definition[1], which is the expected revenue she derives from her s-auction *ex ante* given a slot in the p-auction and therefore the mediator's payoff at SNE is

$$u_M = \gamma_l f \left(\sum_{j=1}^{L-1} (\gamma_j - \gamma_{j+1}) j s^s_{\tau(j+1)} + \gamma_L L s^s_{\tau(L+1)} \right) - \sum_{j=l}^{K} (\gamma_j - \gamma_{j+1}) s^p_{\sigma(j+1)}.$$

4   Revenue of the Auctioneer

In this section, we discuss the change in the revenue of the auctioneer due to the involvement of the mediator. The revenue of the auctioneer with the participation of the mediator is

$$R = \sum_{j=1}^{K} \gamma_j r^p_{j+1} = \sum_{j=1}^{K} (\gamma_j - \gamma_{j+1}) j s^p_{\sigma(j+1)}$$

and similarly, the revenue of the auctioneer without the participation of the mediator is

$$R_0 = \sum_{j=1}^{K} (\gamma_j - \gamma_{j+1}) j s^p_{\tilde{\sigma}(j+1)} \text{ where } \tilde{\sigma}(j) = \sigma(j) \text{ for } j < l \text{ and } \tilde{\sigma}(j) = \sigma(j+1) \text{ for } j \geq l$$

$$= \sum_{j=1}^{l-2} (\gamma_j - \gamma_{j+1}) j s^p_{\sigma(j+1)} + \sum_{j=l-1}^{K} (\gamma_j - \gamma_{j+1}) j s^p_{\sigma(j+2)}.$$

Therefore,

$$R - R_0 = \sum_{j=max\{1,l-1\}}^{K} (\gamma_j - \gamma_{j+1}) j (s^p_{\sigma(j+1)} - s^p_{\sigma(j+2)})$$

$$\geq 0 \text{ as } s^p_{\sigma(i)} \geq s^p_{\sigma(i+1)} \forall i = 1, 2, \ldots, K+1 \text{ at } SNE.$$

Thus revenue of the auctioneer always increases by the involvement of the mediator. As we can note from the above expression, smaller the l better the improvement in the revenue of the auctioneer. To ensure a smaller value of l, the mediator's valuation which is the expected payments that she obtains from the s-auction should be better, therefore fitness factor f should be very good. There is another way to improve her true valuation. The mediator could actually run many subauctions related to the specific keyword in question. This can be done as follows: besides providing the additional slots on the landing page, the information section of the page could contain links to other pages wherein further additional slots associated with a related keyword could be provided[3]. With this variation of the model, a better value of l could possibly be ensured leading to a win-win situation for everyone.

Theorem 1. *Increasing the capacity via mediator improves the revenue of auctioneer.*

5   Efficiency

Now let us turn our attention to the change in the efficiency and as we will prove below, the efficiency always improves by the participation of the mediator.

$$E_0 = \sum_{j=1}^{K} \gamma_j s_{\hat{\sigma}(j)}^p = \sum_{j=1}^{l-1} \gamma_j s_{\sigma(j)}^p + \sum_{j=l}^{K} \gamma_j s_{\sigma(j+1)}^p \text{ and}$$

$$E = \sum_{j=1}^{l-1} \gamma_j s_{\sigma(j)}^p + \sum_{j=l+1}^{K} \gamma_j s_{\sigma(j)}^p + \gamma_l f \sum_{j=1}^{L} \gamma_j s_{\tau(j)}^s$$

$$\therefore E - E_0 = \gamma_l f \sum_{j=1}^{L} \gamma_j s_{\tau(j)}^s - \sum_{l}^{K} (\gamma_j - \gamma_{j+1}) s_{\sigma(j+1)}^p$$

$$= \gamma_l f \sum_{j=1}^{L} \gamma_j s_{\tau(j)}^s - \gamma_l r_{l+1}^p$$

$$\geq 0$$

$$\text{as } \gamma_l f \sum_{j=1}^{L} \gamma_j s_{\tau(j)}^s \geq \gamma_l f \sum_{j=1}^{L} \gamma_j r_{j+1}^s = \gamma_l s_{\sigma(l)}^p \geq \gamma_l r_{l+1}^p \text{ at } SNE.$$

Theorem 2. *Increasing the capacity via mediator improves the efficiency.*

6   Advertisers' Payoffs

Clearly, for the newly accommodated advertisers, that is the ones who lost in the p-auction but win a slot in s-auction, the payoffs increase from zero to a postitive number.

---

[3] For example, the keyword "personal loans" or "easy loans" and the mediator "personal-loans.com".

Now let us see where do these improvements in the revenue of the auctioneer, in payoffs of newly accommodated advertisers, and in the efficiency come from? Only thing left to look at is the change in the payoffs for the advertisers who originally won in the p-auction, that is the winners when there was no mediator. The new payoff for jth ranked advertiser in p-auction is

$$u_{\sigma(j)} = \gamma_j s^p_{\sigma(j)} - \sum_{i=j}^{K}(\gamma_i - \gamma_{i+1})s^p_{\sigma(i+1)} + u^s_{\sigma(j)}$$

where

$$u^s_{\sigma(j)} = \gamma_l f \gamma_{\tau^{-1}(\sigma(j))}\left(s^s_{\sigma(j)} - r^s_{\tau^{-1}(\sigma(j))+1}\right)$$

is her payoff from the s-auction. Also, for $j \leq l - 1$, her payoff when there was no mediator is

$$u^0_{\sigma(j)} = \gamma_j s^p_{\sigma(j)} - \sum_{i=j}^{K}(\gamma_i - \gamma_{i+1})s^p_{\tilde{\sigma}(i+1)}$$

$$= \gamma_j s^p_{\sigma(j)} - \sum_{i=j}^{l-2}(\gamma_i - \gamma_{i+1})s^p_{\sigma(i+1)} - \sum_{i=l-1}^{K}(\gamma_i - \gamma_{i+1})s^p_{\sigma(i+2)}.$$

$$\therefore u_{\sigma(j)} - u^0_{\sigma(j)} = u^s_{\sigma(j)} - \sum_{i=l-1}^{K}(\gamma_i - \gamma_{i+1})(s^p_{\sigma(i+1)} - s^p_{\sigma(i+2)})$$

Similarly, for $j \geq l + 1$, her payoff when there was no mediator is

$$u^0_{\sigma(j)} = \gamma_{j-1} s^p_{\sigma(j)} - \sum_{i=j-1}^{K}(\gamma_i - \gamma_{i+1})s^p_{\sigma(i+2)}$$

$$\therefore u_{\sigma(j)} - u^0_{\sigma(j)} = u^s_{\sigma(j)} - \sum_{i=j-1}^{K}(\gamma_i - \gamma_{i+1})(s^p_{\sigma(i+1)} - s^p_{\sigma(i+2)})$$

Therefore, in general we have,

$$u_{\sigma(j)} - u^0_{\sigma(j)} = u^s_{\sigma(j)} - \sum_{i=max\{l-1,j-1\}}^{K}(\gamma_i - \gamma_{i+1})(s^p_{\sigma(i+1)} - s^p_{\sigma(i+2)}).$$

Thus, for the jth ranked winning advertiser from the auction without mediation, the revenue from the p-auction decreases by $\sum_{i=max\{l-1,j-1\}}^{K}(\gamma_i - \gamma_{i+1})(s^p_{\sigma(i+1)} - s^p_{\sigma(i+2)})$ and she faces a loss unless compensated for by her payoffs in s-auction. Further, this payoff loss will be visible only to the advertisers who joined the auction game before the mediator and they are likely to participate in the s-auction so as to make up for this loss. Thus, via the mediator, a part of the payoffs of the originally winning advertisers essentially gets distributed among the newly accommodated advertisers. However, when the mediator's fitness factor f is very good, it might be a win-win situation for everyone. Depending on how good the fitness factor f is, sometimes the payoff from the s-auction might be enough to compensate for any loss by accommodating new advertisers. Let us consider an extreme situation when $L = K$ and $\tau = \tilde{\sigma}$. The *gain* in payoff for the advertiser $\sigma(j), j \leq l - 1$ is

$$\gamma_l f \sum_{i=j}^{K}(\gamma_i - \gamma_{i+1})(s^s_{\sigma(j)} - s^s_{\tau(i+1)}) - \sum_{i=l-1}^{K}(\gamma_i - \gamma_{i+1})(s^p_{\sigma(i+1)} - s^p_{\sigma(i+2)})$$

Therefore as long as

$$f \geq \frac{\sum_{i=l-1}^{K}(\gamma_i - \gamma_{i+1})(s^p_{\sigma(i+1)} - s^p_{\sigma(i+2)})}{\gamma_l \sum_{i=j}^{K}(\gamma_i - \gamma_{i+1})(s^s_{\sigma(j)} - s^s_{\tau(i+1)})}$$

$$= \frac{\sum_{i=l-1}^{K}(\gamma_i - \gamma_{i+1})(s^p_{\sigma(i+1)} - s^p_{\sigma(i+2)})}{\gamma_l \left(\sum_{i=j}^{l-2}(\gamma_i - \gamma_{i+1})(s^s_{\sigma(j)} - s^s_{\sigma(i+1)}) + \sum_{i=l-1}^{K}(\gamma_i - \gamma_{i+1})(s^s_{\sigma(j)} - s^s_{\sigma(i+2)}) \right)}$$

the advertiser $\sigma(j)$ faces no net loss in payoff and might actually gain and similarly for the advertisers $\sigma(j)$ for $j \geq l+1$.

7 Concluding Remarks

In the present work, we have studied the emergence of diversification in the adword market triggered by the inherent capacity constraint. We proposed and analyzed a model where additional capacity is created by a for-profit agent who compete for a slot in the original auction, draws traffic and runs its own sub-auction. Our study potentially indicate a 3-fold diversification in the adword market in terms of (i) the emergence of new market mechanisms, (ii) emergence of new for-profit agents, and (iii) involvement of a wider pool of advertisers. Therefore, we should expect the internet economy to continue to develop richer structure, with room for different types of agents and mechanisms to coexist. In particular, the capacity constraint motivates the study of yet another model where the additional capacity is created by the search engine itself, essentially acting as a mediator itself and running a single combined auction. This study will be presented in an extended version of the present work.

References

1. Aggarwal, G., Goel, A., Motwani, R.: Truthful Auctions for Pricing Search Keywords, EC (2006)
2. Edelman, B., Ostrovsky, M., Schwarz, M.: Internet Advertising and the Generalized Second Price Auction: Selling Billions of Dollars Worth of Keywords. American Economic Review (2007)
3. Lahaie, S.: An Analysis of Alternative Slot Auction Designs for Sponsored Search, EC (2006)
4. Lahaie, S., Pennock, D.: Revenue Analysis of a Family of Ranking Rules for Keyword Auctions, EC (2007)
5. Mahdian, M., Nazerzadeh, H., Saberi, A.: Allocating online advertisement space with unreliable estimates, EC (2007)
6. Mehta, A., Saberi, A., Vazirani, U., Vazirani, V.: AdWords and generalized on-line matching. In: FOCS 2005 (2005)
7. Varian, H.: Position Auctions. To appear in International Journal of Industrial Organization

Cost of Conciseness in Sponsored Search Auctions

Zoë Abrams, Arpita Ghosh, and Erik Vee

Yahoo! Inc., Yahoo! Research, Yahoo! Research
2821 Mission College Blvd.
Santa Clara, CA, USA
{za,arpita,erikvee}@yahoo-inc.com

Abstract. The generalized second price auction used in sponsored search has been analyzed for models where bidders value clicks on ads. However, advertisers do not derive value only from clicks, nor do they value clicks in all slots equally. There is a need to understand sponsored search auctions in a setting with more general bidder valuations, in order to encompass realistic advertising objectives such as branding and conversions.

We investigate the practical scenario where bidders have a full spectrum of values for slots, which are not necessarily proportional to the expected number of clicks received, and report a single scalar bid to the generalized second price auction. We show that there always exists an equilibrium corresponding to the VCG outcome using these full vector values, under monotonicity conditions on the valuations of bidders and clickthrough rates. Further, we discuss the problem of bidding strategies leading to such efficient equilibria: contrary to the case when bidders have one-dimensional types, bidding strategies with reasonable restrictions on bid values do not exist.

1 Introduction and Related Work

Internet advertisers spend billions of dollars every year, and internet-search companies run keyword auctions millions of times a day. Despite this, our understanding of these auctions is built on incredibly simple assumptions. One striking assumption is that advertisers derive their value solely from users clicking on their ads. In reality, many advertisers care about *conversions* (that is, users actually completing some desired action such as buying items from their websites), while others care about *branding* (that is, simply familiarizing users with the name of the advertiser). Not all of these forms of deriving value from sponsored search advertisements can be mapped to a value per click, or the same value-per-click for all slots. Thus, while the value-per-click model is a reasonable first step, it leaves open many questions. In this paper, we embark on the study of keyword auctions in which the value-per-click assumption is removed. Rather than modeling advertisers as having some fixed value per click, we allow them to have a full spectrum of values for slots, which are not necessarily proportional to the expected number of clicks received. This allows modeling, for example, advertisers who value slots based on some combination of factors including conversions, branding, and of course, clicks. Our main focus in this paper is to understand

X. Deng and F.C. Graham (Eds.): WINE 2007, LNCS 4858, pp. 326–334, 2007.

the implications of using a *single-bid* system when bidders actually have a full spectrum of values for slots. While the VCG mechanism [7,2,4] applies to this setting and has the advantage of being a truthful mechanism and maximizing total efficiency (i.e. social welfare), it requires every advertiser to report a vector of bids rather than just one single bid. In addition to placing an extra burden on advertisers and the system infrastructure, reporting a vector of bids is a significant departure from current bidding systems. And, how much would be gained? In particular, when the bidding system is a generalized second price auction (essentially the mechanism used in most sponsored search auctions), what can we say about efficiency and equilibria?

If advertisers only derive value from clicks and value clicks in all slots equally, and if the clickthrough rate of slots are advertiser-independent, the full spectrum of private values is the vector of clickthrough rates for the slots multiplied by the advertiser's value per click. The authors in [3,6] show that under these assumptions, the generalized second price auction (GSP) does have at least one equilibrium corresponding to the VCG outcome. Although the techniques used to prove these results can be generalized somewhat, e.g. to allow separable advertiser-dependent clickabilities, they cannot handle the more general case when the value-per-click assumption is removed. More general in terms of modeling bidder preferences, [1] considers a *thresholded* value-per-click assumption: each advertiser has a threshold t such that she has value-per-click v for slots 1 through t, and value-per-click 0 for slots below t. In addition to capturing the normal value-per-click model, this model also allows some notion of branding. The authors propose a new auction mechanism which has the VCG outcome as an equilibrium. However, this work is quite different from ours: an advertiser is still assumed to derive positive value from clicks only, while our work allows any ranking of slots (specifically, an advertiser's value for an impression can be higher for a slot with a lower clickthrough rate). Second, the authors do not address the question of equilibria in the current GSP model; *i.e.*, the question of whether there are single bids corresponding to value vectors of this form that lead to efficient equilibria under GSP.

To the best of our knowledge, our work is the first to consider such a general form of advertiser valuations, and the effect of using a GSP auction with a single report from each advertiser. We address the following question: Can the VCG outcome with vector inputs be achieved as an equilibrium of the GSP auction when bidders report a single value? In the full version of our paper, we show that for any (reasonable) oblivious bidding strategy, there is always a set of valuations that lead to $\frac{1}{k}$ of the optimal efficiency, where k is the number of slots, even when all advertiser agree on the relative ranking of the slots. In §3, we show the surprising result that when advertisers report a single bid per impression and all agree on the ordering of the slots' values, *there exists a set of single bids for the GSP auction that leads to the efficient VCG outcome*. The same result holds, when bids and prices are per-click (even though values need not be per-click), and all bidders agree on the ordering of the slots' values, in terms of value-per-click, and this ordering agrees with the clickthrough rate ordering.

Note that this result is more surprising than the corresponding results in
[3,6] where bidders have one-dimensional types and report a single scalar to the
system; a similar situation exists in [1] where bidders have two-dimensional types,
and are allowed to report two values to a modified GSP-like auction. In contrast,
bidders in our model have vector valuations and yet the VCG outcome can be
achieved with just a one-dimensional report to a GSP auction. In our proof of
this result, we additionally give a new, direct proof that the VCG outcome of
any auction in which every bidder wants at most one item must be envy-free.
Although this was shown in [5], we present a simpler, more accessible argument.

Our assumptions on bidders' valuations for our equilibrium results, although
reasonable, may not always hold. In the full version of the paper, we give examples showing that without these assumptions, there exist scenarios where no
equilibrium solution exists. Finally, we address the question of whether there is
a natural bidding strategy that leads to the VCG outcome, and present some
negative results in §4.

2   Model and Problem Statement

We study a single instance of an auction for slots of a single keyword. There are n
bidders (advertisers) competing in this auction, and k slots being auctioned. Each
bidder has a vector of private values for the k slots, $\vec{v}_i = (v_i^1, \ldots, v_i^k)$, where v_i^j is
bidder i's value for being shown in the jth slot (v_i^j is the value-per-impression in
slot j, not the value-per-click in slot j). We define $\vec{\theta} = (\theta_1, \ldots, \theta_k)$ as the vector
of (ad-independent) *clickthrough rates* in the k slots, and use these to define the
value-per-click for bidder i at slot j to be v_i^j/θ_j. These values-per-click may be
meaningless quantities, such as for bidders who value impressions. This model
is the most general model of private bidder valuations for the sponsored search
setting. Specifically, it subsumes two important models used in prior work:

- $v_i^j = \theta_j v_{ii}$: This is the model used in [3,6], and says that bidder i has a
  value-per-click v_{ii}, and her value (per impression) for slot j is the expected
  clickthrough rate of slot j times her value-per-click. It is easy to see that
  advertiser-dependent clickthrough rates, which we denote by μ_i, can be accounted for by multiplying it by the value-per-click.
- $v_i^j = \theta_j v_{ii}$ for $j \le t_i$, and $v_i^j = 0$ otherwise: This is the thresholded value
  model studied in the work on position auctions in [1], and says that advertiser
  i has a uniform value-per-click v_{ii} *until position* t_i; his value for clicks in slots
  beyond t_i is 0.

There are two important kinds of bidder valuations not covered in previous
models: (1) Bidders may have different per-click values in different slots, (for
example, due to different conversion rates). (2) Bidders may have values not
based on the number of clicks received; for example, advertisers concerned only
with branding may not have a value proportional to the number of clicks received
at all, but rather simply to the position in which they are displayed. Our model
allows for both these kinds of bidder valuations.

Advertisers' private values are *monotone* if they all agree on the ordering of the slots' values. That is, there is an ordering of the slots $1, 2, \ldots, k$ such that every bidder values slot i at least as much as slot j for $i \leq j$, i.e., $v_\ell^i \geq v_\ell^j$ for all $\ell = 1, \ldots, n$, $1 \leq i \leq j \leq k$. Private values are *strictly monotone* if in addition to being monotone, for all ℓ and $i \neq j$, $v_\ell^i \neq v_\ell^j$ unless $v_\ell^j = 0$. In other words, each advertiser's values for slots 1,2,...,k are *strictly* decreasing, until the value becomes 0, at which point the values remain 0. Advertisers' private values are *click-monotone* if they all agree on the ordering of the slots' values, in terms of value-per-click, and this ordering agrees with the clickthrough rate. That is, there is an ordering of the slots such that $\theta_1 \geq \theta_2 \geq \ldots \geq \theta_k$ and for all $i \leq j$ and for every bidder ℓ, bidder ℓ's value-per-click for slot i is at least as high as her value-per-click for slot j, i.e., $v_\ell^i/\theta_i \geq v_\ell^j/\theta_j$. These values are *strictly click-monotone* if in addition to being click-monotone, for all ℓ and $i \neq j$, $v_\ell^i/\theta_i \neq v_\ell^j/\theta_j$ unless $v_\ell^j/\theta_j = 0$.

Auction Model: We consider two auction models. The first is based on bidding and paying per impression. This is preferable for a few reasons: first, advertisers' values need not be click-based at all; a per-impression bid simply says how much the advertiser values winning a slot in that auction, without saying that the value comes from clicks. The VCG mechanism computes allocations based on per-impression values. Also, the per-impression bid model makes no assumptions about the clickability of ads or slots. However, real internet auctions require bidders to report a value-per-click, not a value per impression; the value-per-impression is assumed to be the product of the value-per-click times the clickthrough rate. Hence, we consider this auction as well, giving analogous results for both auctions throughout. We now describe both models, which we refer to as *single-bid auctions* to emphasize that they require bidders to use a single bid to represent a full spectrum of private values.

We refer to the pay-per-impression auction as $\text{GSP}_{\vec{v}}$, since it is the standard generalized second price (GSP) auction in which bidders pay for impressions. We assume that the auctioneer knows the ranking of the slots according to the monotone bidder values, and we assume that slots are numbered $1, \ldots, k$, in this order. In $\text{GSP}_{\vec{v}}$, every bidder submits a *single* bid b_i to the auctioneer, despite having a vector of values that may not be possible to represent with a single value (here, b_i is a bid-per-impression). Bidders are assigned to slots in decreasing order of bids b_i, i.e., the bidder with the highest b_i is assigned slot 1, and so on. Slots are priced according to the generalized second price auction (GSP), i.e., a bidder in slot j pays $b_{[j+1]}$ (where $b_{[j]}$ denotes the jth largest b_i), which is the bid of the bidder in the slot below. In the case of ties, we assume that the auctioneer is allowed to break ties in whatever way he chooses; generally, this will be at random. If the number of bidders is not greater than the number of slots, we will simply insert imaginary bidders, each bidding 0. So we may assume that $n > k$. Any bidder not assigned to one of the first k slots is simply not shown. For convenience, we allow bidders to be "assigned" to slots beyond the k-th— this is equivalent to not being shown.

We refer to the pay-per-click auction as $\text{GSP}_{\vec{c}}$ (see [3]). In $\text{GSP}_{\vec{c}}$, each bidder submits a bid per-click, which the auctioneer puts in order. The ith-place bidder then pays a price equal to $b_{[i+1]}$ every time a user *clicks* on her ad. In line with previous work, we assume that each slot has a fixed clickthrough rate, θ_j (for slot j). We say the clickthrough rates are *independent* if any advertiser placed in slot j will receive, in expectation, precisely θ_j clicks. Thus, if advertiser i is the j-th place bidder, she will be placed in slot j and pay a total of $\theta_j b_{[j+1]}$, netting a utility of $v_i^j - \theta_j b_{[j+1]}$.

VCG allocation and pricing: When bidders are allowed to report their full vector of valuations, the VCG mechanism can be applied to truthfully produce an efficient allocation. Let G be a bipartite graph with advertisers on one side and slots on the other. The weight of edge (i, j) between bidder i and slot j has weight v_i^j. The VCG allocation computes the maximum weight matching on this graph, and assigns advertisers to slots according to this matching. We will use $\mathcal{M}$ to denote the maximum matching on G, M to denote the weight of matching $\mathcal{M}$, and number advertisers so that bidder i is assigned to slot i. Let M_{-i} denote the weight of the maximum weight matching on G when all edges incident to bidder i are removed. Then p_i, the VCG price for bidder i, is $p_i = M_{-i} + v_i^i - M$.

3   Equilibrium with Single Bids

We prove the following surprising result: the (full-spectrum) VCG outcome is also an envy-free equilibrium of $\text{GSP}_{\vec{c}}$ [and of $\text{GSP}_{\vec{v}}$] so long as the values are strictly click-monotone [respectively, strictly monotone]. An envy-free outcome is an outcome where for every bidder i, $v_i^i - p_i \geq 0$, and for every slot j, $v_i^i - p_i \geq v_i^j - p_j$, where p_j is the (current) price for slot j. That is, bidder i (weakly) prefers slot i at price p_i to slot j at price p_j, for all $j \neq i$.

Our proof is comprised of two main parts. In the first part, we show that when the values are strictly click-monotone [respectively, strictly monotone], any envy-free outcome is a realizable equilibrium in $\text{GSP}_{\vec{c}}$ [resp., $\text{GSP}_{\vec{v}}$]. The second part gives a direct proof that the VCG outcome is always envy-free in auctions that match bidders to at most one item each (this proof holds even when the spectrum of values are not monotone).

Theorem 1. *Any envy-free outcome on k slots and $n > k$ bidders in which prices are nonnegative and values are strictly click-monotone [resp., strictly monotone] is a realizable equilibrium in $\text{GSP}_{\vec{c}}$ [resp., $\text{GSP}_{\vec{v}}$].*[1]

Proof. We give the proof for the $\text{GSP}_{\vec{c}}$ auction. The proof for the $\text{GSP}_{\vec{v}}$ follows by setting $\theta_j = 1$ for all slots j. As above, label bidders so that the envy-free outcome we consider assigns bidder i to slot i, at price p_i (p_i is a price per-impression, or simply the cost of slot i). We construct an equilibrium in $\text{GSP}_{\vec{c}}$

---

[1] For technical reasons, we say an envy-free outcome is a realizable equilibrium so long as there is a set of bids leading to an equilibrium that agrees with the outcome for every bidder having nonzero value for her slot.

as follows: bidder j bids p_{j-1}/θ_{j-1} for all j (for convenience, we set $p_0 > p_1$, $\theta_0 > \theta_1$, and for all $j > k$, $p_j = 0, \theta_j = 1$).

First, we show that the ranking according to the bids assigns bidders the same position as in the envy-free outcome. Precisely, the jth largest bid is indeed b_j. ; however, there may be ties. Hence, according to $\text{GSP}_{\vec{c}}$, bidder j is assigned slot j at a price $b_{j+1}\theta_j = p_j$, for $j = 1, \ldots, k$, assuming that the auctioneer breaks ties in the "right" way. We now appeal to the fact that values are strictly click-monotone to remove this assumption.

Further, recall that $p_i = b_{i+1}\theta_i$. We first show that $p_i/\theta_i \geq p_j/\theta_j$ for all $i < j$ (which shows that $b_{i+1} \geq b_{j+1}$). Suppose $i < j$. By definition of an envy-free outcome, $v_j^j - p_j \geq v_j^i - p_i$, which implies $\theta_j \left(\frac{v_j^j}{\theta_j} - \frac{p_j}{\theta_j} \right) \geq \theta_i \left(\frac{v_j^i}{\theta_i} - \frac{p_i}{\theta_i} \right)$

$\geq \theta_j \left(\frac{v_j^i}{\theta_i} - \frac{p_i}{\theta_i} \right) \geq \theta_j \left(\frac{v_j^j}{\theta_j} - \frac{p_i}{\theta_i} \right)$. This implies $\frac{p_i}{\theta_i} \geq \frac{p_j}{\theta_j}$. We see equality can occur only if $v_j^j = 0$.

We now show that bidding ties occur only when both bids are 0, and the bidders have no value for the slots they are tied for. To see this, first note that if $v_j^j = 0$, then $p_j = 0$, by the envy-free condition, hence $p_j/\theta_j = 0$. Hence, if $i < j$ and $p_i/\theta_i = p_j/\theta_j$, it must be the case that $v_j^j = 0$, implying $p_i/\theta_i = p_j/\theta_j = 0$. That is, bids are tied only when both bids are 0. Suppose bidder j bids 0. We will show that $v_j^j = 0$. To this end, notice that bidder j bids $p_{j-1}/\theta_{j-1} = 0$, which implies $p_j/\theta_j = 0$, from the above argument. So $p_{j-1} = p_j = 0$. By the envy-free condition, $v_j^{j-1} - p_{j-1} \leq v_j^j - p_j$, hence $v_j^{j-1} \leq v_j^j$. But this violates strict click-monotonicity, unless $v_j^{j-1} = v_j^j = 0$. Hence, bidder j has value 0 for slot j. Putting this together, we see that the auctioneer only breaks ties between bidders that bid 0, and have no value for any slot they are tied for. (Hence, these ties may be broken arbitrarily and still satisfy our goal.)

We finish by showing that this envy-free outcome is indeed an equilibrium. Suppose bidder i bids lower, so she gets slot $j > i$ rather than i. She then pays p_j, and by definition of envy-free, does not increase her utility. On the other hand, if bidder i bids higher, getting slot $j < i$, then she pays p_{j-1}, with utility $v_i^j - p_{j-1} \leq v_i^j - p_j \leq v_i^i - p_i$, since prices decrease with slot rankings.

Next we show that the VCG outcome is envy-free in auctions that match each bidder to at most one item, even when the values are not monotone. We do not need clickthrough rates here at all, since the VCG price is simply a price per slot, or per-impression.

Lemma 1. *If advertiser j is assigned to slot j in a maximum matching, $M_{-j} \geq M_{-i} + v_i^j - v_j^j$.*

Proof. The proof of the lemma takes a maximum matching of G with i removed, and uses it to produce a matching of G with only j removed. This new matching will have weight at least $M_{-i} + v_i^j - v_j^j$, showing that M_{-j} must also be at least this large.

Fix a maximum matching of G with i removed, call it $\mathcal{M}_{-i}$. If there is more than one such maximum matching, we will take $\mathcal{M}_{-i}$ to be one in which advertiser j is matched to slot j, if such a maximum matching exists. Either advertiser j is matched to slot j in $\mathcal{M}_{-i}$ or not. We consider each case in turn. **Case I:** Bidder j is assigned to slot j in $\mathcal{M}_{-i}$. In this case, simply remove the edge from advertiser j to slot j in $\mathcal{M}_{-i}$, and add the edge from advertiser i to slot j. This is now a matching on G without j, and its total weight is $M_{-i} + v_i^j - v_j^j$. Hence, $M_{-j} \geq M_{-j} + v_i^j - v_j^j$. **Case II:** Bidder j is not assigned to slot j in $\mathcal{M}_{-i}$. Again, we will construct a matching for G without j, in a somewhat more complicated way. We first observe that removing advertiser i from a maximum matching on G creates a "chain of replacements." More precisely, let i_1 be the advertiser that is matched to slot i in $\mathcal{M}_{-i}$. Notice that $i_1 \neq i$. If $i_1 \leq k$, then let i_2 be the advertiser matched to slot i_1 in $\mathcal{M}_{-i}$. And in general, if $i_\ell \leq k$, let $i_{\ell+1}$ be the advertiser matched to slot i_ℓ in $\mathcal{M}_{-i}$. Let t be the smallest index such that advertiser $i_t > k$. Clearly, for some $s < t$, $j = i_s$ (otherwise we would be in Case I).

So, $j = i_s$ for some $s < t$. For convenience, let $i_0 = i$. Change $\mathcal{M}_{-i}$ as follows: for each $\ell = 1, 2, ..., s$, remove the edge from advertiser i_ℓ to slot $i_{\ell-1}$, and replace it with the edge from $i_{\ell-1}$ to $i_{\ell-1}$. Notice that in this new matching, advertiser $i_s = j$ is matched to no one. It is easy to see that its weight is $M_{-i} + \sum_{\ell=1}^s v_{i_{\ell-1}}^{i_{\ell-1}} - \sum_{\ell=1}^s v_{i_\ell}^{i_{\ell-1}}$. Since $\mathcal{M}$ is a maximum matching, we see $\sum_{\ell=1}^s v_{i_{\ell-1}}^{i_{\ell-1}} + v_{i_s}^{i_s} \geq \sum_{\ell=1}^s v_{i_\ell}^{i_{\ell-1}} + v_{i_0}^{i_s}$ which implies $\sum_{\ell=1}^s v_{i_{\ell-1}}^{i_{\ell-1}} - \sum_{\ell=1}^s v_{i_\ell}^{i_{\ell-1}} \geq v_i^j - v_j^j$. Substituting, we have that $M_{-j} \geq M_{-i} + v_i^j - v_j^j$.   □

Theorem 2. *The VCG outcome is envy-free, even when bidder values are not monotone.*

Proof. As always, we assume without loss of generality that bidder i is assigned to slot i in the VCG outcome, for $i = 1, \ldots, k$. Recall that the price set in the VCG outcome for bidder j is $p_j = M_{-j} - M + v_j^j$. Hence, from our lemma above, we have that for all i, j, $v_i^j - p_j = v_i^j - M_{-j} + M - v_j^j \leq v_i^j - (M_{-i} + v_i^j - v_j^j) + M - v_j^j = M - M_{-i} = v_i^i - p_i$. Furthermore, $v_i^i - p_i = M - M_{-i} \geq 0$. That is, the VCG outcome is envy-free.   □

Theorem 3. *When bidder values are strictly click-monotone [resp., strictly monotone], there exists an equilibrium of $GSP_{\bar{c}}$ [resp., $GSP_{\bar{v}}$] that corresponds to the welfare-maximizing outcome, i.e., the VCG outcome.*

4   Bidding Strategies

We consider the following question: while the VCG outcome is indeed realizable as an efficient equilibrium of single-bid auctions, is there a natural bidding strategy for bidders, such that when all bidders bid according to this strategy in repeated auctions for the same keyword, they converge to this efficient outcome?

We define an *history-independent bidding strategy*, g, to be a set of functions $g_1, ..., g_n$, one for each bidder i, where g_i takes the bids $\vec{b}$ from the previous round of the auction, together with the vector of private values $\vec{v}_i$, and outputs a nonnegative real number, which is the bid of player i.[2] We call the history-independent strategy *myopic* if the value of g_i does not depend on the bid of player i from the last round. Finally, we say a vector of bids $\vec{b}$ is a *fixed point* for history-independent strategy g, if after bidding $\vec{b}$, the bidding strategy continues to output that same vector of bids $\vec{b}$, *i.e.*, $g_i(\vec{b}; \vec{v}_i) = \vec{b}$. Throughout this section, we will focus primarily on $\mathrm{GSP}_{\vec{v}}$ for clarity, although the results also hold for $\mathrm{GSP}_{\vec{c}}$.

First, we show that for any bidding strategy that always has an envy-free fixed point, there are value vectors where bidders must bid more than their maximum value over all slots. This puts them at risk to lose money (*i.e.*, have negative utility) if other bidders change their bids, or new bidders join the auction. We call a strategy *safe* if it never require bidders to bid beyond their maximum value. Although it would not be surprising to see bidders occasionally bid values that are not safe, it seems questionable whether they would continue to bid this way repeatedly. The proof appears in the full version of this paper.

Theorem 4. *There is no safe, history-independent bidding strategy that always has an envy-free fixed point whenever the private values are strictly monotonic.*

We further show that no bidding strategy has the VCG outcome as a fixed point, under a few minor assumptions that stem from our need to stop bidders from encoding information in their bids, artificially allowing the players to calculate the fixed point and bid accordingly. Recall that when the values are strictly monotone, all non-zero VCG bids are distinct and determined. Further, the highest bidder is free to bid any value larger than some quantity (determined by the VCG prices).

Theorem 5. *There is no myopic bidding strategy that always attains the VCG outcome as a fixed point, even if that VCG outcome does not require bidders to bid above their maximum value over all slots.*

5   Discussion

This work raises several questions. First, what are bidder values really like? How much do they deviate from the one-dimensional assumption? And, do they satisfy the conditions under which we show $\mathrm{GSP}_{\vec{c}}$ to have an efficient equilibrium? Note also that our conditions for existence of efficient equilibria are sufficient, but not necessary: the question of necessary conditions for the existence of efficient equilibria in $\mathrm{GSP}_{\vec{c}}$ is open. Also, under what conditions on bidder values do there exist simple bidding strategies that converge to the efficient outcome? There is a tradeoff between expressiveness, and the overhead imposed on bidders and the

---

[2] Notice that our definition actually allows a kind of collaboration between bidders, despite the fact that in practice, we do not expect this to happen.

mechanism: at one extreme, a full vector of bids can be accepted, but this imposes a severe burden on both bidders, and the bidding system, which must compute allocations and prices for millions of auctions everyday. At the other extreme is the current system, which arguably is not expressive enough- bidders with widely varying types might be forced to report a single number to the system, leading to possible instability and inefficiency. The question of choosing the right tradeoff is a problem ripe with opportunity for experimental and theoretical research.

References

1. Aggarwal, G., Feldman, J., Muthukrishnan, S.: Bidding to the top: VCG and equilibria of position-based auctions. Workshop on Approximation and Online Algorithms (2006)
2. Clarke, E.H.: Multipart pricing of public goods. Public Choice 11, 17–33 (1971)
3. Edelman, B., Ostrovsky, M., Schwarz, M.: Internet advertising and the generalizaed second price auction: Selling billions of dollars worth of keywords. In: Second Workshop on Sponsored Search Auctions, Ann Arbor, MI (June 2006)
4. Groves, T.: Incentives in teams. Econometrica 41, 617–631 (1973)
5. Leonard, H.: Elicitation of honest preferences for the assignment of individuals to positions. the Journal of Political Economy 91(3), 461–479 (1983)
6. Varian, H.R.: Position auctions. To appear in International Journal of Industrial Organization (2006)
7. Vickrey, W.: Counterspeculation, auctions, and competitive sealed tenders. Journal of Finance 16, 8–37 (1961)

Adwords Auctions with Decreasing Valuation Bids

Gagan Goel[1] and Aranyak Mehta[2,*]

[1] Georgia Institute of Technology, Atlanta, GA
gagang@cc.gatech.edu
[2] Google, Inc., Mountain View, CA
aranyak@google.com

Abstract. The choice of a bidding language is crucial in auction design in order to correctly capture bidder utilities. We propose a new bidding model for the Adwords auctions of search engine advertisement – *decreasing valuation bids*. This provides a richer language than the current model for advertisers to convey their preferences. Besides providing more expressivity, our bidding model has two additional advantages: It is an *add-on* to the standard model, and retains its simplicity of expression. Furthermore, it allows efficient algorithms – we show that the greedy (highest bid) algorithm retains its factor of 1/2 from the standard bidding model, and also provide an optimal allocation algorithm with a factor of 1-1/e (as is case in the standard bidding model).

We also show how these bidding languages achieve a good trade-off between expressivity and complexity – we demonstrate a slight generalization of these models for which the greedy allocation algorithm has an arbitrarily bad competitive ratio.

1 Introduction

One of the most important design parameters in auction design is the choice of a bidding language. This is the *interface* provided to the bidders by the seller, which allows them to express their preferences to the seller. There is always a trade-off in this choice. The more complex a bidding language is, the better can it capture bidder preferences, and indirectly, the better it is for the seller. But at the same time, it is essential to have a simple bidding language, so that the bidders will be able to translate their innate preferences into the language in the first place. Simplicity of expression is not the only reason preventing us from choosing highly complex bidding languages. A second reason is *computational*: Even if the bidders express their preferences in a complex bidding language, it may be impossible for the seller to process such complex preferences and decide on an optimal (or even a good) outcome efficiently. Such a trade-off becomes apparent in the design of complex auctions, and has been studied in detail, for example, in the case of combinatorial auctions [4].

In this paper we are interested in the study of the Adwords auctions of search engines such as Google, Yahoo! and MSN with respect to the issue of bidding

---

* Work done while the author was at IBM Almaden Research Center, San Jose, CA.

X. Deng and F.C. Graham (Eds.): WINE 2007, LNCS 4858, pp. 335–340, 2007.

languages. These auctions, which account for a large portion of the extremely high revenues of these companies, sell keyword search queries to interested advertisers. These are online auctions, in which the bidders (advertisers) express their preferences to the search engines in advance, and as users enter keyword queries, the search engine decides whose ad to display with the search results.

The bidding languages currently provided by the search engines are of the following form: A bidder i can bid, for each keyword q he is interested in, a monetary bid b_{iq}, expressing the value he gets if his ad is displayed with search results for queries of type q. Together with the bids, the bidder is also allowed to report a *daily global budget* B_i, which means that over all the keywords, he is not willing to spend more than B_i.

While this bidding model does capture the essential features of advertiser preferences, namely, the individual bids and a global budget, it fails to express more complex constraints that the advertisers may have. For example, the advertiser may not want to be in a situation in which he wins many ad slots, but all of them for queries of the same single keyword. He would prefer to have diversity, in the sense of winning a reasonable amount of ad slots for several different keywords of his choice. There are two reasons to expect real advertisers to have such preferences: firstly, advertisers may wish to make their presence felt in several different sub-markets at the same time, and sell different products at comparable rates. Secondly, there are situations in which advertisers have decreasing marginal utility from subsequent advertisements, e.g., once the ad reaches a certain fraction of the target audience.

It is important to find expressive, yet simple and practically implementable bidding languages which would provide bidders with more control to express such preferences. Note that it is not even possible to simulate such preferences in the current bidding model, say by splitting into several different accounts. We stress the following four **properties of our model**: *Firstly*, our bidding model is an *add-on* to the current model, and hence can be gradually introduced on top of the current model. Bidders may choose to continue bidding as they did in the current model if they prefer. *Secondly*, as our results show, there may be no need to change the allocation algorithms used by the search engine, even upon introducing the new bidding model. *Thirdly*, the better expressivity will, in our opinion, allow the bidders to bid with more control and less risk, and therefore more aggressively, indirectly improving the revenue of the search engine. *Finally*, we believe that this model may lead to less fluctuations in the bids, as opposed to the current model in which bidders may dynamically change their bids as they win certain number of queries.

We note that the importance of expressiveness to achieve efficiency and increased revenue has been studied earlier in the context of Ad auctions [5]. A notion of *spending constraints* was introduced in [1] in the context market equilibrium. There the utility of a bidder for the next item of a good depended on how much *money* he had already spent on that good. In the first price auction setting, spending constraints would translate to the constraints used in our setting.

2   A New Bidding Language: Decreasing Valuation Bids

In this paper we propose a new bidding language for the Adwords auctions, designed to express the type of preferences outlined above. We state the model in full generality, but also specify an important special case which is practical, simple to use (e.g. via a simple GUI), and has low communication overhead.

In the *decreasing valuations bid* model, bidder i bids the following:

- A global daily budget B_i.
- For each keyword w he is interested in, a *decreasing function* $f_{i,w} : Z^+ \rightarrow \mathbf{R}$, which is to be interpreted as follows: If bidder i has already been allocated x number of queries of keyword w, then his bid for the next query of keyword w is $f_{iw}(x)$.

Note that the current model only allows constant functions $f_{iw}(x) = b_{iw}, \forall x$. A simple and practical special case of our model is one which allows only functions of the form

$$f_{iw}(x) = \begin{cases} b_{iw} & \text{if } x \leq t_{iw} \\ 0 & \text{otherwise} \end{cases}$$

This special case means that bidder i values each of the first t_{iw} queries of keyword w at b_{iw} each, but does not want more than t_{iw} of w's . We shall call this special case the case of *keyword*-budgets.

3   Results in the New Models

Better expressivity is clearly better for the bidder (as long as the language remains simple enough to understand). So with the introduction of this new models of bidding languages, the question which arises naturally is: How does this affect the search engine's profits?

Intuitively, it is clear that the bidders will now be able to bid with more control and therefore face less risk, and will bid more aggressively. This is clearly better for the search engine, in terms of the optimal profit (OPT) derivable from the bidders. But what if the bidding language introduces computationally difficult problems for the search engine? Then it will not be able to efficiently extract a good portion of the OPT as profit. We show that our models do not introduce such computational difficulties, by describing optimal algorithms in the first price setting, whose competitive ratio (in an online competitive analysis model) is $1 - 1/e$, as good as that of the optimal algorithm [3] in the standard model. We also show that the natural greedy algorithm retains its competitive ratio of $1/2$.

We also show that our bidding language is at the correct trade-off point between expressivity, simplicity and computational efficiency. Simple generalizations of our bidding model (by adding more expressivity) result in computational problems for which no algorithms can perform better than a factor of $1/2$, and for which the natural Greedy algorithm has an arbitrarily bad factor.

3.1   Our Techniques

The algorithm we analyze in the new model is precisely the algorithm from [3] for the standard bidding model. For each arriving query, this algorithm (which we will call MSVV) determines the *effective bid* of each bidder as his bid for the query scaled by a function ψ of the fraction of budget that the bidder has spent so far (the function is $\psi(x) = 1 - e^{-(1-x)}$). Then the algorithm awards the query to the bidder with maximum effective bid. It is shown in [3] that this algorithm has a competitive ratio of $1 - 1/e$ in the standard bidding model, and that this is optimal (even over randomized algorithms). We show that the same algorithm has the same factor even in our generalized bidding models. Clearly it is optimal since our models are more general than the standard model.

Our proof technique follows the proofs in [3]. In that proof, the main idea was to show that for each query q, the algorithm gets some effective amount of money (which is the real money scaled by some factor depending on ψ) which is comparable to an effective amount that OPT gains for q. This kind of query-by-query analysis is not possible here, since the bid of a bidder i for a query q itself depends on how many other queries of that type have already been allocated to him. Thus the bid depends on the *context* in which q arrives with respect to the previous choices of the algorithm. We take care of this by a careful charging argument: we demonstrate the existence of a map between the queries that OPT assigns and the queries that ALG assigns (not necessarily to the same bidder). This helps us show sufficient profit for ALG. The analysis in [3] can be thought of as the special case when this map is the identity map.

4   Analysis of Greedy and MSVV

We show that the Greedy algorithm, which assigns a query to the bidder with current highest bid retains its competitive ratio of $1/2$ (Proof in the full version).

Theorem 1. *The competitive ratio of Greedy algorithm in the decreasing valuation bid model is $1/2$.*

Now we will analyze the performance of the MSVV algorithm in the decreasing bids model. Let us recall the algorithm in the standard model (without decreasing bids). For clarification, we will use w to name a keyword, and q to name a query – a query q can be of type w.

The Algorithm: For the next query q (of type w) compute the *effective bid* of bidder i as: $b_{iw}\psi(y)$ where y is the fraction of budget spent by i, and $\psi(y) = 1 - e^{-(1-y)}$. Award q to the bidder with the highest effective bid.

In the decreasing bids model, the *effective bid* becomes: $f_{iw}(x)\psi(y)$. where x is the number of queries of keyword w already allocated to i.

We will prove the following theorem:

Theorem 2. *MSVV achieves a factor of $1 - 1/e$.*

We will follow the proof structure as in [3]. The crucial difference in the proof is in a careful charging via a well-chosen map between queries. We start with some preliminary notation from [3].

Start by picking a large integer parameter k. Define the *type* of a bidder according to the fraction of budget spent by that bidder at the end of the algorithm MSVV: say that the bidder is of type j if the fraction of his budget spent at the end of the algorithm lies in the range $((j-1)/k, j/k]$. Slab i of a bidder is the portion of money spent in $[(i-1)/k, i/k]$ fraction of his budget.

As in [3], Wlog we can assume that budgets of all the bidders are same (say N). Also, let α_j denote the number of bidders of type j. Let β_i denote the total money spent by the bidders from slab i in the run of the algorithm. It is easy to see that $\beta_1 = N/k$, and

$$\forall\, 2 \leq i \leq k, \quad \beta_i = N/k - (\alpha_1 + \ldots + \alpha_{i-1})/k \tag{1}$$

Let $ALG(q)$ $(OPT(q))$ denote the revenue earned by the algorithm (OPT) for query q. Say that a query q is of *type* i if OPT assigns it to a bidder of type i, and say that q lies in *slab* i if the algorithm pays for it from slab i.

This concludes the notation from [3]. Fix a keyword w, and let Q_w be the set of all queries of keyword w, and let Q_w^{OPT} be the set of queries of keyword w assigned by OPT to all the bidders of type *strictly less* than k (these are the bidders who haven't spent all their money). We will drop the subscript w when it is clear by context. We will use subscript i to denote the restriction of any variable to bidder i.

Lemma 1. *For each keyword w, there exists a injective map $\sigma : Q_w^{OPT} \to Q_w$ s.t. $\forall q \in Q_w^{OPT}: OPT(q)\psi(type(q)) \leq ALG(\sigma(q))\psi(slab(\sigma(q)))$*

Proof. In the full version.

Now we will aggregate the above result to prove the following corollary(proof given in the full version).

Corollary 1. $\sum_{i=1}^{k-1} \psi(i)(\alpha_i - \beta_i) \leq 0$

Now, the calculations follow as in [3]: Using Corollary 1, Equation 1 and the definition of the trade-off function ψ, we get that the loss of the algorithm is at most OPT/e, hence proving the theorem.

5   Discussions

5.1   The Difficulty with More Expressive Models

We show that providing even slightly more (non-trivial) expressiveness leads to computational issues. Consider the case of *Group Budgets*: Instead of restricting to local budget constraints on a single keyword, the bidders are allowed to set a local budget on a group of keywords.

Suppose that the set of keywords is $\{w_0, w_1, .., w_k\}$. Let c_w represent the number of queries of keyword w. Consider the following instance: There is a single bidder and his bid on all the keywords is one dollar. His budget is $t * k$, and has following k constraints on group of keywords:

$\forall i \in [1, k]$, $c_{w_0} + c_{w_i} \leq t$

Now consider the two sequence of queries (w_0 t *times*) and (w_0 t *times*, w_1 t *times*, .., w_k t *times*). Its easy to see that: No randomized algorithm can do better than $1/2$ on both the sequences. Also Greedy has a factor $1/k$ on the second sequence. Thus the extension to group budgets loses the computational possibilities available in our decreasing bids model. We believe that our bidding model achieves the correct trade-off between simplicity, expressivity and computational complexity.

5.2 Beyond the Factor $1 - 1/e$ When Bids Are Strictly Decreasing

We now show how tightening Corollary 1 helps in getting bounds better than 1-1/e. Later we will try to see the conditions which tighten the Corollary 1.

Suppose we had that $\sum_{i=1}^{k-1} \psi(i)(\alpha_i - \beta_i) \leq -x$. This $(-x)$ goes directly to the objective function of the dual LP considered in the analysis of MSVV (see[3] for details). Since the objective function of the dual represents the maximum loss of the algorithm as compared to OPT, hence the total loss becomes $\frac{OPT}{e} - x$, and the competive ratio of the algorithm will be $(1 - \frac{1}{e} + \frac{x}{OPT})$.

What are the cases when the x value is substantial? We believe that one case is when the bid curves decrease rapidly. The intuition is that if for a bidder i and keyword w, the seemingly bad case in which algorithm allocates less queries of type w to i than OPT does, is actually a good case. This is so because OPT derives much lesser profit for the extra queries (since they are farther in the bid-curve), while ALG allocates these elsewhere, more profitably. Characterizing this gain over $1 - 1/e$ in terms of input parameters (such as the derivative of the bid-curves) remains an open question. Similarly, we expect the performance of Greedy to be better than $1/2$ in such cases.

References

1. Devanur, N., Vazirani, V.: The spending constraint model for market equilibrium: Algorithmic, existence and uniqueness results. In: STOC (2004)
2. Kalyanasundaram, B., Pruhs, K.R.: An optimal deterministic algorithm for online b -matching. Theoretical Computer Science 233(1–2), 319–325 (2000)
3. Mehta, A., Saberi, A., Vazirani, U., Vazirani, V.: Adwords and generalized online matching. In: FOCS (2005)
4. Nisan, N.: Bidding languages for combinatorial auctions. In: Shoham, Steinberg (eds.) Combinatorial Auctions by Cramton (2005)
5. Parkes, D., Sandholm, T.: Optimize-and-Dispatch Architecture for Expressive Ad Auctions. In: EC (2005)
6. Vazirani, V.: Spending constraint utilities, with applications to the adwords market. Manuscript (2006)

An Adaptive Sponsored Search Mechanism δ-Gain Truthful in Valuation, Time, and Budget

Rica Gonen[1] and Elan Pavlov[2]

[1] Yahoo! Research Labs, 701 First Street, Sunnyvale, CA 94089
gonenr@yahoo-inc.com
[2] Media Lab, MIT, Cambridge MA, 02149
elan@mit.edu

Abstract. This paper presents an online sponsored search auction that motivates advertisers to report their true budget, arrival time, departure time, and value per click. The auction is based on a modified *Multi-Armed Bandit (MAB)* mechanism that allows for advertisers who arrive and depart in an online fashion, have a value per click, and are budget constrained.

In tackling the problem of truthful budget, arrival and departure times, it turns out that it is not possible to achieve truthfulness in the classical sense (which we show in a companion paper). As such, we define a new concept called δ-*gain*. δ-gain bounds the utility a player can gain by lying as opposed to his utility when telling the truth. Building on the δ-gain concept we define another new concept called *relative ϵ-gain*, which bounds the relative ratio of the gain a player can achieve by lying with respect to his true utility. We argue that for many practical applications if the δ-gain and or the relative ϵ-gain are small, then players will not invest time and effort in making strategic choices but will truthtell as a default strategy. These concepts capture the essence of dominant strategy mechanisms as they lead the advertiser to choose truthtelling over other strategies.

In order to achieve δ-gain truthful mechanism this paper also presents a new payment scheme, Time series Truthful Payment Scheme (TTPS), for an online budget-constrained auction mechanism. The payment scheme is a generalization of the VCG principles for an online scheduling environment with budgeted players.

Using the concepts of δ-gain truthful we present the only known budget-constrained sponsored search auction with truthful guarantees on budget, arrivals, departures, and valuations. Previous works that deal with advertiser budgets only deal with the non-strategic case.

1 Introduction

With the advent of advertising as a pillar [7] of Internet commerce, there is an acute need for improved means of increasing the value achieved by advertising agencies. In the increasingly competitive and high stakes duel between the main advertising search engines (Google, Microsoft and Yahoo!) every bit of advantage is important.

In this competition mechanism design is an important part of optimizing the monetization of search advertising. Mechanism design allows us to define allocations and

X. Deng and F.C. Graham (Eds.): WINE 2007, LNCS 4858, pp. 341–346, 2007.

payments that maximize the welfare of participants. In doing so search engines can attract advertisers who have a strong interest (high valuation) in users interacting with their ad placements.

1.1 Problem Setting Considerations

The main tool that a mechanism designer can bring to the table is *preference elicitation* which essentially means finding incentives (via payment rules) that motivate the participants to honestly report their valuations for any possible allocation.

Indeed, in assuming that advertisers have a known valuation per click as well as a bounded budget, many authors have suggested algorithms that increase welfare for the search engine e.g., [1]. Some authors have even suggested mechanisms which do not assume the knowledge of CTRs but learn them while running the algorithm [17].

However we argue that the assumption of known valuations is unrealistic. In practice advertisers' values are *private information* and hence advertisers might be motivated to act strategically to increase their utility. In [11] we suggest a truthful multi-armed bandit (MAB) mechanism for the case where advertisers have no budget and are always available to show an ad. Furthermore, [11] allows the different slots (possible places to display an ad) to be of different quality (although the slot quality ratio is unrelated to the advertiser).

In this paper we make the restricting assumption that the slots are of equal quality. This assumption is not necessary other than to manage the complexity of the algorithm's presentation and allows us to express the essential elements of the model where advertisers have budget constraints as well as time constraints. We believe that this scenario captures the core nature of advertising. For example, advertisers commonly value a click through more highly in the pre-Christmas gift season than during the rest of the year.

Our follow-on paper [13] creates an auction that is truthful in budget, arrival, departure, and valuation while recognizing that slots are not of equal quality.

The budget constraint is harder to justify theoretically, inasmuch as what is important is the marginal utility from additional clicks. However, budgets decrease advertiser risk and are a standard assumption in the theory as well as a standard assumption in practice. Advertiser budgets cause a theoretical difficulty in that it is well known [6] that it is impossible to maximize welfare given the existence of budget constraints. Even when advertisers are time constrained in addition to being budget constrained [10]. Hence, we define our approximation relative to the optimal allocation under budget constraints.

Four parameters are assigned to each participant; arrival time, departure time, value per click, and budget. These parameters are private information that must be reported to the mechanism. Our results take another step toward capturing reality by allowing advertisers multiple arrivals and departures to and from the system.

Some of these parameters pose special challenges. For instance the arrival and departure times pose a challenge as [16] showed in a different context that it is impossible to achieve a truthful scheduling mechanism. [16]'s scheduling problem can hint that in our setting, there exists an impossibility of scheduling advertisers who desire a single impression with a value per click that is identical to their budget.

Fortunately, in our setting, it is quite sensible to assume, as in [15], that the budget is much larger than the value for a single click. In [10] we extended [16]'s impossibility to apply to budget-constrained sponsored search auctions and to apply even when the above assumption is made. Nevertheless assuming that the budget is much larger than the value per click allows us, together with the new payment scheme (TTPS), to bound the number of "free" clicks a player can receive by lying.

In order to formalize this intuition we define two new concepts which we call δ-gain and relative ϵ-gain. δ-gain is a bound on the utility gain that a player can achieve by lying independent of the lie's size. In contrast to prior work which bounded the size of a lie, δ-gain allows lies to be arbitrarily large. We argue that if the maximum utility gain from a lie is small (in our case $O(value)$) then players will forgo this risky gain in favor of the simplicity of truthtelling. Our mechanism has the additional property that this gain can only be achieved at the risk of hazarding the entire budget. To express this we define the relative ϵ-gain concept which not only ensures a small additive gain in utility but also ensures that the relative gain is small with respect to the total utility achieved when acting truthfully. We believe that the above definitions are of independent interest and can be applied to a range of other mechanism design problems.

We assume throughout this paper that an advertiser has zero value if his ad is not clicked on[1]. Under this assumption the value to the advertiser is the *value per click* × CTR.

1.2   Selection of Underlying Bandit Algorithm

Since the advertising search engine is assumed to be interested in maximizing welfare, which depends on the CTR as well as on the private values of the advertisers, it is natural to cast the problem as a multi armed bandit.

The multi-armed bandit is a well-studied problem [3] which deals with the balancing of exploration and exploitation in online problems with multiple possible solutions. In the simplest version of the MAB problem a user must choose at each stage (the number of stages is known in advance) a single bandit/arm. This bandit will yield a reward which depends on some *hidden* distribution. The user must then choose whether to exploit the currently best known distribution or to attempt to gather more information on a distribution that currently appears suboptimal. The MAB is known to be solvable via the Gittins [9] index and there are solutions which approximate the optimal expected payoff. We choose to generalize the MAB solution in [8] dues to its simplicity and optimal sampling complexity. Our solution retains the sample complexity of [8] (what we call the suboptimal exposure complexity) and hence is sample complexity optimal.

Since we want to elicit the private information of the advertisers we must design a MAB which is truthful. Models of imperfect and symmetric information for prices have been extensively studied recently, e.g., [4]. The MAB has been recently studied in a more general setting by [5] but using a weaker notion of truthfulness.

Although the MAB has been extensively studied it has generally been studied in the context of a single user choosing from non-strategic arms [14] even when studied in the context of slot auctions [17]. In [11] we constructed a truthful MAB under the

---

[1] In practice some advertisers are interested in rasing visibility.

assumption that the only private valuation was the value of an advertiser (although in contrast to the current work we allowed slots of different quality). The mechanism was called the **M**ulti-**A**rmed truth**F**ul band**I**t **A**uction *(MAFIA)* and hence the current mechanism is called **B**udgeted **M**ulti-**A**rmed truth**F**ul band**I**t **A**uction *(B-MAFIA)*.

In the context of an online keyword auction the arms/advertisers will act as strategic utility maximizing agents who will be the slots for the MAB. Our mechanism will also achieve a good approximation of the optimal welfare (under budget constraints) and hence improves over current methods of sampling and/or heuristic-based modeling.

2   The Model

In our model a set N of risk neutral, utility-maximizing advertisers bid for advertising slots based on a keyword ($|N| = n$). This paper focuses on the bidding process for a single keyword, as multiple keywords are analogous in current mechanisms. It is therefore supposed w.l.o.g. that the keyword appears at every time t. Whenever that keyword appears in the search at time t, K_t[2] slots of advertisements appear in the results.

The advertisers arrive and depart the system in an online manner and may arrive and depart several times. S_t denotes the set of advertisers present in the system at time t. Each advertiser i has a private value for each click through (independent of the slot the ad originally appeared in) which is denoted by v_i. For every arrival and departure each advertiser i also has a privately known arrival and departure times, denoted a_i and l_i respectively, and a privately known budget denoted b_i.

The algorithm runs from time starting at $t = 1$ and ending at $t = T$. Each time period is called a round. During each round, the algorithm allocates advertisers to the K_t slots (or if there are too many slots to some portion of the slots). When advertiser i appears in a slot during some time period t we say that i received an impression. We denote the number of impressions (plus 1) that advertiser i receives from i's first arrival by e_i. We also denote the number of clicks that advertiser i received during his current stay in the system by ω_i.

In this paper it is assumed that the "quality" of each slot (which is essentially the probability of a click though if an advertisement appears in that slot) is identical in all K_t slots and is independent of the advertisers. In our paper [11] it is assumed that the "quality" of each slot is monotonically decreasing and is independent of the advertisers. In our working paper [13] we show that the common assumption of that the quality of a slot is independent of the advertiser can be relaxed.

Each advertiser i has a *click through rate* α_i which is the probability of a click on the advertisement given that the advertiser was allotted an impression. The value α_i is unknown to i as well as to the mechanism. Since α_i is unknown to i as well as to the mechanism, we must estimate it at each time t and denote the observed probability at time t by α_i^t. We denote the payoff of advertiser i by $x_i^t = v_i \cdot \alpha_i^t$

Finally, by $\overline{v}_i$ we denote the bid for each click-through stated by advertiser i to the mechanism. $\overline{a}_i, \overline{l}_i$, and $\overline{b}_i$ respectively denote the arrival time, the departure time, and

---

[2] We assume for the ease of exposition that $K_t = K_{t+1} = K$ for all time period t. We also assume without the loss of generality that $K \leq |N| = n$, since superfluous slots can remain blank.

the budget stated by advertiser i to the mechanism when advertiser i enters the system. (a_i and l_i may be reported multiple times with multiple entries).

To achieve this paper's main claim of a truthful report of budget, time, and value, we make the natural assumption that advertiser i's reported budget, b_i is significantly larger than his value, i.e., $\bar{b}_i >> v_i$ for every advertiser. In practice this is indeed the case for the keywords auctions currently in use[3]. This assumption is commonly made even in non-strategic settings (e.g., [15]).

For ease of exposition $\overline{X}_i$ denotes the vector of parameters stated by advertiser i in a single arrival, i.e., $(\bar{a}_i, \bar{l}_i, \bar{v}_i, \bar{b}_i)$. The mechanism charges advertiser i a price denoted p^{l_i} every time i departs. At every round we charge advertiser i an "interim price' (This price can decrease as time goes on as well as increase.) $p_i^t \leq \omega_i \cdot \bar{v}_i$, where ω_i is the number of clicks i received during his current sojourn in the system, i.e., from $\bar{a}_i$ to time t. Since our advertisers are budget constrained we denote the budget i has remaining at time t as $B_i^t \geq 0$. It is assumed that advertisers have quasi-linear utility functions[4] and consequently at each departure time advertiser i obtains utility of $\alpha_i^{l_i} \cdot (\omega_i \cdot v_i - p^{l_i})$.

2.1 Illustration of the Protocol for the Single-Slot Case

We illustrate the main idea behind our protocol for the simple case where there is only a single slot available at any given time. In this case for each time period t we can look at the set of available advertisers S_t (note that since advertisers enter and depart the system this set might increase or decrease). For each advertiser $i \in S_t$ we have an estimation of i's click through rate α_i^t as well as an estimate of how accurate our estimation is, i.e., a bound on $|\alpha_i^t - \alpha_i|$ which depends on the number of impressions e_i that advertiser i received. We will denote this bound by γ_{e_i} (the definition of γ_{e_i} is elaborated on below).

Consider the set S_t. Naturally, this set has an i such that $v_i * \alpha_i^t$ is maximal.(In practice we have to ensure that there is sufficient remaining budget. Details appear in the technical part of the paper.) Suppose w.l.o.g. that the maximal element is the first element that our bandit algorithm explores (i.e., allocates a slot to). If the algorithm merely chooses to exploit then it could just allocate the slot to the first advertiser. However, there are other possible advertisers that are worthy of consideration. These are the advertisers j s.t. $v_i \alpha_i^t - \gamma_{e_i} < v_j \alpha_j^t + \gamma_{e_j}$ since the errors of i and j overlap. Therefore the algorithm allocates the slot to a random advertiser whose slot overlaps with the maximal element.

This generalization of [8] works (in a PAC sense) if the advertisers are non-strategic (but arrive in an online fashion). Of course, if the advertisers are strategic we have to motivate them to give the correct values. If advertisers' arrival and departure times are public knowledge and advertisers are not budget constrained then one could set prices of allocated advertisers to be defined as the critical values at each time to receive the slot, (i.e., the minimum value advertiser i can report and still be allocated to the slot) and extract true reported values from the advertisers. However, since we do not assume that arrival and departure times are public knowledge and our advertisers are budgeted the incentive solution has to take a more subtle approach.

---

[3] Typical valuations for click through are several cents while the budgets for those click throughs are on the order of hundreds of dollars.

[4] As long as their budget constrained is maintained.

An example of the incentive problem with the naive pricing scheme and our new pricing scheme as well as all technical details of the theorems, claims, proofs and additional references can be found in the full version of the paper at [12].

Acknowledgements

The authors would like to thank Uri Feige, Chris Meek, and Seffi Naor for helpful comments.

References

1. Aggarwal, G., Goel, A., Motwani, R.: Truthful Auctions for Pricing Search Keywords. In: Proceding of EC 2006 (2006)
2. Archer, A., Papadimitriou, C., Talwar, K., Tardos, E.: An approximate truthful mechanism for combinatorial auctions with single parameter agents. In: Proc. of the 14th SODA (2003)
3. Berry, D.A., Fristedt, B.: Bandit problems. Sequential allocation of experiments. Chapman and Hall (1985)
4. Bergemann, D., Valimaki, J.: Learning and Strategic Pricing. Econometrica, Econometric Society 64(5), 1125–1149 (1996)
5. Bergemann and Valimaki   Efficient Auctions, Available at: http://papers.ssrn.com/sol3/papers.cfm?abstract_id=936633
6. Borgs, C., Chayes, J., Immorlica, N., Mahdian, M., Saberi, A.: Multi-unit auctions with budget-constrained bidders. In: ACMConference on Electronic Commerce (EC 2005), 2005
7. Edelman, B., Ostrovsky, M., Schwarz, M.: Internet Advertising and the Generalized Second Price Auction: Selling Billions of Dollars Worth of Keywords. Working paper (2005)
8. Even-Dar, E., Manor, S., Mansour, Y.: PAC Bounds for Multi-Armed Bandit and Markov Decision Processes. In: The Fifthteenth Annual Conference on Computational Learning Theory 2002 (2002)
9. Gittins, J.C.: Multi-armed Bandit Allocation Indices. In: Mathematical Reviews: MR90e:62113, Wiley, New York (1989)
10. Gonen, R.: On the Hardness of Truthful Online Auctions with Multidimensional Constraints Submitted (2007)
11. Gonen, R., Pavlov, E.: An Incentive-Compatible Multi Armed Bandit Mechanism. In: Third Workshop on Sponsored Search Auctions WWW2007, PODC 2007 (2007)
12. Gonen, R., Pavlov, E.: An Adaptive Sponsored Search Mechanism δ-Gain Truthful in Valuation, Time, and Budget, http://www.cs.huji.ac.il/~rgonen or http://www.ricagonen.com
13. Gonen, R., Pavlov, E.: An Incentive Compatible Budgete constraind sponsored search auction with monotonicaly decreasing slots. Working paper (2007)
14. Kleinberg, R.: Anytime Algorithms for Multi-Armed Bandit Problems. In: Proceedings of the 17th ACM-SIAM Symposium on Discrete Algorithms (SODA 2006) (2006)
15. Mehta, A., Saberi, A., Vazirani, U., Vazirani, V.: Adwords and Generalized Online Matching. In: Proceedings of the 46th Annual IEEE Symposium on Foundations of Computer Science (FOCS), pp. 264–273. IEEE Computer Society, Los Alamitos (2005)
16. Lavi, R., Nisan, N.: Online Ascending Auctions for Gradually Expiring Items. In: Proceedings of SODA 2005 (2005)
17. Pandey, S., Olston, C.: Handling Advertisements of Unknown Quality in Search Advertising. In: the proceedings of NIPS 2006

Extending Polynomial Time Computability to Markets with Demand Correspondences

Benton McCune*

University of Iowa
bmccune@cs.uiowa.edu

Abstract. We present a polynomial time algorithm that computes an approximate equilibrium for any exchange economy with a demand correspondence satisfying gross substitutability. Such a result was previously known only for the case where the demand is a function, that is, at any price, there is only one demand vector. The case of multi valued demands that is dealt with here arises in many settings, notably when the traders have linear utilities.

We also show that exchange markets in the spending constraint model have demand correspodences satisfying gross substitutability and that they always have an equilibrium price vector with rational numbers. As a consequence, the framework considered here leads to the first exact polynomial time algorithm for this model.

1 Introduction

The study of market equilibria is central to microeconomic theory . Though long serving as a cornerstone in the foundation of microeconomic theory, in the past few decades economists have increasingly come to rely on general equilibrium models to model real world problems [22]. General equilibrium analysis has been applied to areas such as income tax reform and international trade policy.

Efficient algorithms for computing market equilibria would be helpful when analyzing models with many variables. The problem of finding efficient algorithms for computing market equilibria has elicited a great deal of interest from computer scientists in recent years. In a short span of time, there has been a good deal of progress.

In order to outline the contributions of this article to this line of work, I will begin by providing the necessary definitions and concepts needed to discuss the market equilibrium problem.

Definitions We consider the exchange model in detail. We are given m economic agents or traders who trade in n goods. Let R^n_+ be the subset of R^n where each vector has only nonnegative components. Each trader will have a concave, typically continuous, utility function $u_i : \mathbf{R}^n_+ \to \mathbf{R}_+$ that induces a preference ordering on bundles of goods which are represented by vectors in $\mathbf{R}^n_+$.

---

* The author was supported by NSF CAREER award CCR 0237431.

X. Deng and F.C. Graham (Eds.): WINE 2007, LNCS 4858, pp. 347–355, 2007.
© Springer-Verlag Berlin Heidelberg 2007

Traders enter the market with an initial endowment of goods represented by $w_i = (w_{i1}, \ldots, w_{in}) \in \mathbf{R}_+^n$. All traders then sell all their goods at the market price and buy the most favorable bundle of goods they can afford. If all traders do this and demand does not exceed supply, we are at an equilibrium.

More formally, a price is represented by a vector $\pi = (\pi_1, \ldots, \pi_n) \in R_+^n$ with π_j signifying the price of the jth good. The bundle of goods purchased by the ith trader is given by $x_i = (x_{i1}, \ldots, x_{in}) \in \mathbf{R}_+^n$. We have an equilibrium price and allocation if each trader maximizes utility subject to their budget constraints and aggregate demand does not exceed initial endowments.

For any price vector π, not necessarily an equilibrium price, we call an $x_i(\pi)$ that maximizes utility subject to budjet constraints a *demand* of trader i at price π. *Market or Aggregate Demand* of good j at price π is defined to be $X_j(\pi) = \sum_{i=1}^m x_{ij}$. We call $Z_j(\pi) = X_j(\pi) - \sum_{i=1}^m w_{ij}$ the *market excess demand* of good j at price π. The collections $\mathcal{X}(\pi) = \{X(\pi) | X(\pi) = (X_1(\pi), \ldots, X_n(\pi))\}$ and $\mathcal{Z}(\pi) = \{Z(\pi) = Z(\pi) = (Z_1(\pi), \ldots, Z_n(\pi))\}$ are simply called *market demand* and *market excess demand*. Note that $\mathcal{X}$ and $\mathcal{Z}$ are both mappings from $\mathbf{R}_+^n$ to $2^{\mathbf{R}^n}$.

We can now simply express what it means for a price π to be an equilibrium for a market with excess demand $\mathcal{Z}$. π is an equilibrium if there exist $z \in \mathcal{Z}(\pi)$ such that $z \leq 0$.

The property of gross substitutability has an important effect on the structure of price equilibria and the possibility of computing market equilibria. Roughly speaking, a market possesses the gross substitutability property if when the prices on one set of goods are raised, demand does not decrease for the other goods. A formal definition is provided below.

Following Polterovich and Spivak [20], we define gross substitutability (GS) correspondences. Let π^1 and π^2 be price vectors for a market with n goods. We denote $I(\pi^1, \pi^2) = \{i | \pi_i^1 = \pi_i^2\}$.

We say that gross substitutability prevails for $\mathcal{Z}$, or $\mathcal{Z}$ is a GS correspondence, if for all π^1, π^2 such that $\pi^1 \leq \pi^2$ and $I(\pi^1, \pi^2) \neq \emptyset$, and for any $z \in \mathcal{Z}(\pi^1), y \in \mathcal{Z}(\pi^2)$, the following relation holds

$$min_{i \in I(\pi^1, \pi^2)}(z_i - y_i) \leq 0.$$

That is, at least one good that has its price unchanged does not have its demand decreased. This is an extremely mild definition for gross subsitutability. Other definitions that one might come across (typically in cases where the demand is assumed to be a function) are stronger and imply this one.

When equilibrium prices are irrational, algorithms cannot compute exact equilibria. We therefore need precise definitions of approximate equilibria which can be computed. Roughly speaking, weak approximate equilibria occur when traders get bundles near their optimal utility whenever the traders come close to staying within their budget constraints.

More precisely, we say that a bundle $x_i \in \mathbf{R}_+^n$ is a μ-approximate demand of trader i at price π if for $\mu \geq 1$ (this restriction on μ holds in all definitions that follow), if $u_i(x_i) \geq \frac{1}{\mu}u_i^*$ and $\pi \cdot x_i \leq \mu\pi \cdot w_i$ where u_i^* is the trader's optimal utility subject to the budget constraint.

Prices π and allocations x form a weak μ-approximate equlibrium if x_i is a μ-approximate demand of trader i at prices π and $\sum_{i=1}^{m} x_{ij} \leq \mu \sum_{i=1}^{m} w_{ij}$ for each good j. A price π is considered a weak μ-approximate equlibrium price if if there exists x such that π and x form a weak μ-approximate equlibrium.

We call an algorithm a polynomial time algorithm if it computes a $(1 + \epsilon)$-approximate equilibrium for any $\epsilon > 0$ in time that is polynomial in the input parameters and $\log(\frac{1}{\epsilon})$.

1.1 Results

We show that when an excess demand correspondence satisfies gross subsitutability, a weak approximate equiilibrium can be computed in polynomial time using the ellipsoid method. Such a result had been previously established only when the demand was single valued. The exchange market where traders have linear utilities is the most prominent market where the demand need not be single-valued. Previously, this linear utilities market had to be treated as a special case [17], but in the framework provided by this paper it is solved naturally as merely one case of a market with a demand correspondence satisfying gross substitutability.

The previous result on the single valued case [5] was obtained by extending an important separation lemma [2] due to Arrow, Block, and Hurwicz. The main techinical contribution of our result is an extension of the separation lemma of Polterovich and Spivak [20] for the case of correspondences. This then allows the ellipsoid method to be used to compute approximate equilibria in polynomial time.

We also consider the spending constraint model of Vazirani and Devanur [11] and it is shown that the demand in this model is a GS correspondence. This gives a prominent example of a market that did not naturally fit into any other general framework. We also show that price equilibria for the spending constraint model are rational and can be computed exactly in polynomial time.

1.2 Related Work

In 2001, Christos Papadimitriou gave a lecture that initiated the recent computer science research on computing market equilibria [19]. It has recently been shown that in general, the problem of computing an equilibrium is quite thorny. Codenotti, Saberi, Varadarajan and Ye [8] show that it is NP-hard to decide whether a Leontief exchange economy even has an equilibrium. (For some classes of exchange economies, such as CES markets, it can be determined whether or not an equilibrium exists in polynomial time [4].) Chen and Deng [9] made a major breakthrough in algorithmic game theory when they demonstrated that finding a Nash equilibrium in a two player game is PPAD complete. When this result is combined with the result from [8] that reduces two-player games to a special type of Leontief Exchange economy, we see that it is PPAD-complete to compute an equilibrium for markets even when they are known to exist. Huang and Teng [16] show that the polynomial time computation of an approximate equilibrium is not possible unless $PPAD \subset P$.

Codenotti, Pemmaraju, and Varadarajan [5] were able to expand upon the Separation Lemma of Arrow, Block, Hurwicz [2] to compute a polynomial time algorithm for markets where the aggregate excess demand function satisfies weak gross subsitutability and you have the ability to efficiently compute an approximate demand. This result thus includes many of the important special cases such as the Cobb-Douglas, and CES functions with elasticity $\sigma \geq 1$. The framework can be used to generate polynomial time algorithms without assuming anything about the precise form of the utility functions other than that the excess demand function will satisfy weak gross substitutability (and a few other weak assumptions).

For a more thorough review of the literature on market equilibirum computation, see [6].

2   Preliminaries

Some more extensive definitions and basic lemmas are needed in order to proceed to the main results of the paper. This is followed by an important market transformation which leads to the main technical contribution of the paper, a strong separation lemma for correspondences. With this lemma, the ellipsoid method can be used to compute approximate equilibria in polynomial time. We then introduce the spending constraint model and show that markets in this model fit within the framework of this paper. The final section shows that equilibria for markets in the spending constraint model can be computed exactly in polynomial time.

2.1   Polterovich-Spivak Separation Lemma

Following Polterovich and Spivak [20], there are some mild, elementary assumptions regarding the excess demand correspondences in this paper. They can be seen in [18]. Polterovich and Spivak [20] prove a separation lemma for correspondences (that satisfy the assumptions listed above) that generalizes the important lemma from Arrow, Block and Hurwicz [2]. The lemma is as follows

Lemma 1. *Let $\mathcal{Z}$ be a GS correspondence. If $\hat{\pi}$ is an equilibrium, π a price, and $z \in \mathcal{Z}(\pi)$, then $\hat{\pi} \cdot z \geq 0$. If, moreover, π is not an equilibrium price, then $\hat{\pi} \cdot z > 0$.*

2.2   Demand Oracle

We say that an exchange market M is equipped with a *demand oracle* if there is an algorithm that takes a rational price vector π and returns a vector $Y \in \mathbf{Q^n}$ such that there is a $Z(\pi) \in \mathcal{Z}(\pi)$, with $|Y_j - Z_j(\pi)| \leq \sigma$ for all j. The algorithm is required to run in polynomial time in the input size and $log(1/\sigma)$.

2.3   A Market Transformation

Let M be an exchange market with m traders and n goods. We then transform market M into market $\hat{M}$ by adding a phantom trader that will give us an equilibrium price vector with a reasonably bounded price ratio. Let $0 < \eta \leq 1$ be a parameter. For each trader i, the new utility functions and initial endowments are the same as in M' except that there is one additional trader $m + 1$. We set $\hat{w}_{m+1} = (\eta W_1, \dots, \eta W_n)$ for the initial endowment while the trader's utility function is the Cobb-Douglas function $\hat{u}_{m+1}(x) = \prod_{j=1}^{n} x_j^{1/n}$. This trader will spend $1/n$-th of her budget on each good. Notice that the total amount of each good j in the market $\hat{M}$ is now $\hat{W}_j = \sum_{i=1}^{m+1} \hat{w}_{ij} = W_j(1 + \eta)$.

The following lemma contains various useful results:

Lemma 2. $-$ *The market $\hat{M}$ has an equilibrium.*
  - *Every equilibrium π of $\hat{M}$ satisfies the condition $\frac{max_j \pi_j}{min_j \pi_j} \leq 2^L$, where L is bounded by a polynomial in the input size of M and $log(\frac{1}{\epsilon})$.*
  - *For any $\mu \geq 1$, a weak μ-approx equilibrium for $\hat{M}$ is a a weak $\mu(1+\eta)$-approx equilibrium for M.*
  - *$\hat{M}$ has a demand oracle if M does.*
  - *Let π and π' be two sets of prices in $\mathbf{R}_+^n$ such that $|\pi_j - \pi_j'| \leq \epsilon \cdot min\{\pi_j, \pi_j'\}$ for each j, where $\epsilon > 0$. Let x_i be a $(1 + \delta)$-approximate demand for trader i at prices π. Then x_i is a $(1 + \epsilon)^2(1 + \delta)$-approximate demand for trader i at prices π'*

The ratios of largest price to smallest price must be bounded and we define some regions where this is the case. We define the region $\Delta = \{\pi \in \mathbf{R}_+^n | 2^{-L} \leq \pi_j \leq 1\}$. Here, L is given by the second item in lemma 2 and bounded by a polynomial in the input size of M and $log(1/\epsilon)$. We note that a normalized equilibrium price for $\hat{M}$ lies in Δ. Also, $\Delta^+ = \{\pi \in \mathbf{R}_+^n | 2^{-L} - \frac{2^{-L}}{2} \leq \pi_j \leq 1 + \frac{2^{-L}}{2}\}$.

3   Strong Separation Lemma for Correspondences

In this section, we present the main technical contribution of the paper, a strong separation lemma for correspondences. This lemma strengthens Theorem 3 from [20] in a way that is similar to how the separation lemma 3.2 in [5] strengthens the celebrated lemma from [2]. Once this strong separation lemma is established, the ellipsoid method will be able to produce an approximate equilibrium in polynomial time whenever the demand is a GS correspondence.

Lemma 3. *Let M be an exchange market with an excess demand $\mathcal{Z}$ that is a GS correspondence and let $\hat{M}$ with excess demand $\mathcal{Z}'$ be the market M with the special Cobb-Douglas trader added. If $\hat{\pi}$ is an equilibrium for $\hat{M}$ and $\hat{\pi} \in \Delta$, $z' \in \mathcal{Z}'(\pi)$, $\pi \in \Delta^+$, and π is not a $(1 + \epsilon)$-approximate equilibrium price for $\hat{M}$. then $\hat{\pi} \cdot z' \geq \delta$ where $\delta \geq 2^{-E}$ and E is bounded by a polynomial in the input size of $\hat{M}$ and $log(\frac{1}{\epsilon})$.*

For a proof of this and other theorems, see [18].

The separation lemma allows us to use the ellipsoid method to construct a polynomial time algorithm. As stated previously, this approach follows the work of [5] and utilizes the central-cut ellipsoid method.

The following theorem is the algorithmic result of the strong separation lemma for correspondences.

Theorem 4. *Let M be an exchange market where the excess demand is a GS correspondence. Assume that M is equipped with a demand oracle. A polynomial-time algorithm that given any $\pi \in \mathbf{R}_+^n$ and $\mu > 0$, asserts that π is a weak $(1+\mu)$-approximate equilibrium or that π is not a weak $(1+\mu/2)$-approximate equilibrium is also assumed to exist. There then exists an algorithm that takes M, a rational $\epsilon > 0$ and returns a weak $(1+\epsilon)$-approximate equilibrium price vector in time that is polynomial in the input size of M and in $\log(\frac{1}{\epsilon})$.*

For a thorough discussion of the central-cut ellipsoid method, see [15].

4   The Spending Constraint Model

Nikhil Devanur and Vijay Vazirani have introduced a new market model which they call the "Spending Constraint Model" [11,12]. Their purpose in introducing their new model is to retain weak gross substitutability, but present an efficient algorithm for a wide class of concave utility functions. We present the spending constraint model for the Exchange or Arrow-Debreu Market and show that our techniques can compute equilibria for these markets in polynomial time.

There are n goods and n' traders. Each agent i has an endowment of $e_i \in [0,1]^n$. The income of the trader will be represented by $m_i = \sum_{1 \le i \le n} e_{ij}\pi_j$. There is one unit of each good in the market. For $i \in 1,2,\ldots n$ and $j \in 1,2,\ldots n'$, let $f_j^i : [0,m_i] \to \mathbf{R}^+$ be the *rate function* of trader i for good j; the rate at which i derives utility per unit of j received as a function of the amount of her budget spent on j. Define $g_j^i : [0,m_i] \to \mathbf{R}^+$ to be:

$$g_j^i = \int_o^x \frac{f_j^i(y)}{\pi_j} dy.$$

This function give the utility derived by trader i spending x dollars on good j at price π_j. We let $j = 0$ represent money, thus f_0^i and g_0^i will be used to determine the utility of unspent money. The price of money, π_o, is assumed to be 1. Devanur and Vazirani provide a further restriction that the f_j^i's be decreasing step functions. In this case, the g_j^i's will then be piecewise-linear concave functions.

Each step of f_j^i is called a *segment*. The set of segments defined by function f_j^i is denoted by $\text{seg}(f_j^i)$. Suppose one of these segments, s has range $[a,b] \subseteq [0,m_i]$, and $f_j^i = c$, for $x \in [a,b]$. Then we define $\text{value}(s) = b-a$, $\text{rate}(s) = c$, and $\text{good}(s) = j$ ($\text{good}(0) = \text{money}$.) Let $\text{segments}(i)$ be the union of all the segments of buyer i.

Devanur and Vazirani also add the two following assumptions. For each good, there is a buyer who desires it. That is, For all $j \in 1, 2, \ldots n$, there is $i \in 1, 2, \ldots n'$ such that there is $s \in seg(f_j^i) : rate(s) > 0$. Also, each buyer i wishes to use all of her money: $\sum_{s \in segments(i), rate(s) > 0} value(s) \geq m_i$. These assumptions will ensure that an equilibrium exists and that all equilibrium prices are positive.

With all these assumptions in place, optimal baskets for traders are easily characterized. *Bang for the Buck* relative to prices π for segment $s \in seg(f_j^i)$, is defined as $rate(s)/\pi_j$ (or just $rate(s)$ if $j = 0$). Sort all segments $s \in segments(i)$ by decreasing bang per buck, and partition by equality into classes: $Q_1, Q_2, \ldots$. For a class Q_l, value(Q_l) is defined to be the sum of the values of segments in it. At prices p, goods corresponding to any segment in Q_l make i equally happy, and those in Q_l are desired strictly more by i than those in Q_{l+1}. There is k such that

$$\sum_{1 \leq l \leq k-1} value(Q_l) < e(i) \leq \sum_{1 \leq l \leq k} value(Q_l).$$

Clearly, i's optimal allocation, that is i's demand, must contain all goods corresponding to segments in $Q_1, \ldots, Q_{k-1}$, and a bundle of goods worth $m_i - (\sum_{1 \leq l \leq k-1} value(Q_l))$ from segments in Q_k. It is said that for buyer i, at prices p, $Q_1, \ldots, Q_{k-1}$ are *forced partitions*, Q_k is the *flexible partition*, and $Q_{k+1}, \ldots$ are the undesirable partitions.

Note that the possibility of a flexible partition implies that the demand of this market need not be single-valued, it is a correspondence. It is reasonably straightforward to show spending constraint formulation provides us with a well defined demand correspondence with the appropriate properties[18]. We can then prove the following lemma.

Lemma 5. *A Spending constraint model exchange market M has a demand $\mathcal{Z}$ that is a GS correspondence.*

The proof of this lemma is similar to Vazarani's demonstration of weak gross subsitutability for the Fisher market with spending constraint utilities [12].

4.1   Rationality of Prices in the Spending Constraint Model

This section demonstrates that when the Spending Constraint Model has rational input parameters, equilibirum prices will also be rational. The existence of a rational price equilibrium along with lemma 5, lemma 1 and an extension of the ellipsoid method due to Jain [17] will allow the computation of an exact equilibria in polynomial time.

Lemma 6. *Let M be an Spending Constraint Exchange Market with rational input parameters. There is a rational equilibrium price vector for M. The binary represenation of the numerator and denominator of this vector is bounded by a polynomial in the input size.*

Vazarani [12] has proven a similar lemma for the Spending Constraint Fisher market.

Theorem 7. *Exact equilibrium prices for Spending Constraint Markets can be computed in polynomial time.*

The theorem follows from lemma 6, lemma 5, lemma 1 and a straightforward application of Theorem 12 in [17].

Acknowledgements. I would like to acknowledge valuable and extensive discussions with Kasturi Varadarajan.

References

1. Arrow, K.J., Debreu, G.: Existence of an equilibrium for a eompetitive economy. Econometrica 22(3), 265–290 (1954)
2. Arrow, K.J., Block, H.D., Hurwicz, L.: On the stability of the competitive equilibrium, II. Econometrica 27, 82–109 (1959)
3. Codenotti, B., McCune, B., Varadarajan, K.: Market equilibrium via the excess eemand function. In: STOC 2005 (2005)
4. Codenotti, B., McCune, B., Penumatcha, S., Varadarajan, K.: Market equilibirum for CES exchange economies: existence, multiplicity, and computation. In: Ramanujam, R., Sen, S. (eds.) FSTTCS 2005. LNCS, vol. 3821, Springer, Heidelberg (2005)
5. Codenotti, B., Pemmaraju, S., Varadarajan, K.: On the polynomial time computation of equilibria for certain exchange economies. In: SODA 2005 (2005)
6. Codenotti, B., Pemmaraju, S., Varadarajan, K.: Algorithms column: the computation of market equilibria. ACM SIGACT News 35(4) (December 2004)
7. Codenotti, B., Varadarajan, K.: Efficient computation of equilibrium prices for markets with leontief utilities. In: Díaz, J., Karhumäki, J., Lepistö, A., Sannella, D. (eds.) ICALP 2004. LNCS, vol. 3142, Springer, Heidelberg (2004)
8. Codenotti, B., Saberi, A., Varadarajan, K., Ye, Y.: Leontief economies encode nonzero sum two-player Games. In: SODA 2006 (2006)
9. Chen, X., Deng, X.: Settling the complexity of 2-Player nash-equilibrium, FOCS (2006)
10. Devanur, N.R., Papadimitriou, C.H., Saberi, A., Vazirani, V.V.: Market equilibrium via a primal-dual-type algorithm. In: FOCS, pp. 389–395 (2002) (Revised version available online)
11. Devanur, N., Vazirani, V.V.: The spending constraint model for market equilibrium: algorithmic, existence and uniqueness results. In: STOC 2004 (2004)
12. Vazirani, V.V.: Spending Constriant Utilities, with Applications to the Adwords Market Market, http://www-static.cc.gatech.edu/~vazirani/spending.pdf
13. Eisenberg, E.: Aggregation of utility functions. Management Sciences 7(4), 337–350 (1961)
14. Eisenberg, E., Gale, D.: Consensus of subjective probabilities: the pari-mutuel method. Annals of Mathematical Statistics 30, 165–168 (1959)
15. Grotschel, M., Lovasz, L., Schrijver, A.: Geometric Algorithms and Combinatorial Optimization, 2nd edn. Springer, Heidelberg (1993)

16. Huang, L., Teng, S.: On the approximation and smoothed complexity of leontief market equilibria. ECCC Report TR06-031 (2006)
17. Jain, K.: A polynomial time algorithm for computing the Arrow-Debreu market equilibrium for linear utilities. In: FOCS 2004 (2004)
18. McCune, B.: Extending polynomial time computability to markets with demand correspondences - full version (2006), http://www.cs.uiowa.edu/~bmccune/correspondence.pdf
19. Papadimitriou, C.H.: Algorithms, games, and the internet. In: STOC 2001 (2001)
20. Polterovich, V.M., Spivak, V.A.: Gross-substitutability of point-to-set correspondences. Journal of Mathematical Economics 11, 117–140 (1983)
21. Scarf, H.: The computation of equilibrium prices. In: Scarf, Shove (eds.) Applied General Equilibrium Analysis (1984)
22. Shoven, J.B., Whalley, J.: Applying General Equilibrium. Cambridge University Press, Cambridge (1992)
23. Ye, Y.: A Path to the Arrow-Debreu Competitive Market Equilibrium, Discussion Paper, Stanford University, February 2004 Updated (April 2005)

Market Equilibrium Using Auctions for a Class of Gross-Substitute Utilities

Rahul Garg[1] and Sanjiv Kapoor[2]

[1] IBM T.J. Watson Research Center, USA
[2] Illinois Institute of Technology, Chicago, USA

Abstract. In addition to useful Economic interpretation, auction based algorithms are generally found to be efficient. In this note, we observe that the auction-based mechanism can also be used to efficiently compute market equilibrium for a large class of utility functions satisfying gross substitutability, including a range of CES (constant elasticity of substitution) and Cobb-Douglas functions.

1 Introduction

The Market Equilibrium model is a classical problem in micro-economics. In the late nineteenth century two market models have been studied, termed the Fisher model [2] and the more general Walrasian model [14]. Given a set of goods and a set of buyers who have utility for the goods, the problem is to determine prices and allocation of the goods such that no buyer is induced to switch his allocation. An initial endowment is provided for the buyers. In the Fisher case it is money and in the case of the Walrasian model it is a portfolio of goods (which may include money as a special case).

The existence of such equilibrium prices has been shown by Arrow and Debreau, under some mild assumptions. The proof is existential, however. Since then, there has been considerable interest in the computation of market equilibria in economic models. The utility of buyer i for the goods is given by $u_i(X_i)$ where X_i is the vector of allocation $\{x_{i1}, x_{i2} \ldots x_{im}\}$. A number of utility functions have been used in this context, which include linear functions, the *Cobb-Douglas functions* of the form $u_i(x) = \prod_j (x_{ij})^{a_{ij}}$ for constants a_{ij} such that $\sum_j a_{ij} = 1$. Another class of functions which is useful is the *CES* function which is $u_i(x) = (\sum_j (c_{ij} x_{ij})^\rho)^{1/\rho}$ where $-\infty \leq \rho \leq 1, \rho \neq 0$. c_{ij} are constants.

The market equilibrium problem has been solved for a number of special cases using a variety of algorithmic techniques. The combinatorial techniques are : (a) primal-dual techniques algorithms based on maximum flows [4,5] and (b) the auction based approaches [8] (c) Other classes of iterative procedures termed tâtonnement processes. Non-linear or convex programming techniques, which express the equilibrium problem as a convex programming problem, may be found in a variety of works starting from the works of Eisenberg and Gale [7,6] in 1959 to the works (in Russian) of Primak et al. [11–13]. . Polynomial time approximation schemes which use a tâtonnement process was recently established in exchange economies with *weak gross substitutes* (WGS) utilities [3].

X. Deng and F.C. Graham (Eds.): WINE 2007, LNCS 4858, pp. 356–361, 2007.

Auction based approaches have been shown to efficiently find (approximate) solutions to a wide class of problems [1]. In the context of the market equilibrium problem, auction based approaches are a subset of *tâtonnement* processes suggested in the economics literature, in fact by Walras himself. Such techniques may be very insightful in practice. It is very desirable to design markets where interaction of self-motivated trading agents provably leads to a market equilibrium in a reasonable amount of time. Auction based approaches may indeed help in designing such markets.

The auction based approach for the market equilibrium problem presented in [8] found an approximate solution for a market with linear utilities. Using price-rollback, the auction approach finds an exact solution to the problem [9]. Further, path auctions improve the complexity of the algorithm to the best known bound [9]. Auction algorithms has also been extended to non-linear case where the utilities are separable gross substitute [10]. In this paper we show that the basic auction mechanism of [10], can also find $(1 + \epsilon)$ approximate market equilibrium for a larger class of utility function which includes CES, in the range that CES is WGS, and Cobb-Douglas utility functions. This is significant since this class includes functions widely used in economic models. The algorithm has a complexity which is a function of $O(1/\epsilon)$.

In Section 2 we define the market model and provide a characterization of utility functions. In Section 3 we outline our algorithm. The proof of correctness and complexity is similar to that in [10] and is skipped.

2 Market Model

Consider a market consisting of a set of n buyers and a set of m divisible goods. Buyer i has, initially, an amount of money equal to e_i. The amount of good j available in the market is a_j. Buyer i has a utility function, $U_i : R_+^M \rightarrow R_+$ which is non-decreasing, concave and differentiable in the range $0 \leq X_i \leq A$ where $A = (a_1, a_2, \ldots, a_m)$. Given prices $P = \{p_1, p_2, \ldots, p_m\}$ of these m goods, a buyer uses its money to purchase goods that maximize its total utility subject to its budget constraint. Thus a buyer i will choose an allocation $X_i \equiv (x_{i1}, x_{i2}, \ldots, x_{im})$ that solves the following buyer program $B_i(P)$:

$$\text{Maximize} : U_i(X_i) \tag{1}$$
$$\text{Subject to:} \sum_{1 \leq j \leq m} x_{ij} p_j \leq e_i \tag{2}$$

and $\forall j : x_{ij} \geq 0$.

We say that the pair (X, P), $X = (X_1, X_2 \ldots X_n)$ forms a market equilibrium if (a) the vector $X_i \in R_+^n$ solves the problem $B_i(P)$ for all users i and (b) there is neither a surplus or a deficiency of any good i.e., $\forall j : \sum_{1 \leq i \leq n} x_{ij} = a_j$.

The prices P are called market clearing prices and the allocation X is called an equilibrium allocation at price P. Let $v_{ij} : R_+^m \rightarrow R_+$ be equal to $\frac{\partial U_i(X_i)}{\partial x_{ij}}$. Since U_i is assumed to be differentiable for all i, v_{ij} is well defined for all i, j.

Using the theory of duality it can be shown that the optimal solution X_i to $B_i(P)$ will satisfy the following:

$$\forall i : \sum_{1 \leq j \leq m} x_{ij} p_j = e_i \tag{3}$$

$$\forall j : \alpha_i p_j \geq v_{ij}(X_i) \tag{4}$$

$$\forall j : x_{ij} > 0 \Rightarrow \alpha_i p_j = v_{ij}(X_i) \tag{5}$$

and $\forall i : \alpha_i \geq 0, \forall i, j : x_{ij} \geq 0$. The equations (3) imply that all the buyers have exhausted their budget. Equations (4) and (5) imply that (a) that every buyer has the same marginal utility per unit price on the goods it gets and (b) every good that a buyer is not allocated provides less marginal utility.

2.1   Uniformly Separable Utilities

We say that a utility function U_i is *uniformly separable* iff $v_{ij} \equiv \frac{\partial U_i(X_i)}{\partial x_{ij}}$ can be factored as: $v_{ij}(X_i) = f_{ij}(x_{ij}) g_i(X_i)$ such that f_{ij} is a strictly decreasing function. The following utility functions can be verified to be uniformly separable and gross substitute:

- CES (constant elasticity of substitution $u(X_i) = (\sum_i (w_{ij} x_{ij})^\rho)^{1/\rho}$, where $0 < \rho < 1$;
- Cobb-Douglas utility $u(X_i) = \Pi_j (x_{ij})^{a_{ij}}$ where $a_{ij} \geq 0$ and $\sum_j a_{ij} = 1$.

A buyer is said to have *gross substitute* demand for goods iff increasing the price of a good does not decrease the buyer's demand for other goods. Similarly, an economy is said to have gross substitutes demand iff increasing the price of a good does not decrease the total demand of other goods. Clearly, if every buyer has gross substitute demand then so does the economy. The following result characterizes the class of uniformly separable concave gross substitute utility functions.

Lemma 1. *Let U_i be a concave, strictly monotone, uniformly separable function $(\frac{\partial U_i(X_i)}{\partial x_{ij}} = f_{ij}(x_{ij}) g_i(X_i))$. U_i is gross substitute iff for all j, $y f_{ij}(y)$ is a non-decreasing function of the scalar y.*

Proof. We first prove that if U_i is a gross substitute function then $y f_{ij}(y)$ is non-decreasing. Assume, for contradiction, that there are scalars y and y' such that $y' < y$ and $y' f_{ij}(y') > y f_{ij}(y)$. Choose a price P and an optimal solution X_i of $B_i(P)$ such that $x_{ij} = y$ (it is always possible to do so because of strict monotonicity of U_i). Let α_i be the optimal dual solution of $B_i(P)$. The optimality conditions (4) and (5) for the dual of the program $B_i(P)$ can be rewritten as:

$$\forall j : x_{ij} > 0 \Rightarrow f_{ij}(x_{ij}) g_i(X_i) = \alpha_i p_j \tag{6}$$

$$\forall j : \alpha_i p_j \geq f_{ij}(x_{ij}) g_i(X_i) \tag{7}$$

Construct a corresponding (P', X'_i, α'_i) such that $x'_{ik} = x_{ik}$, $p'_k = p_k$ for all $k \neq j$, $x'_{ij} = y'$, $p'_j = p_j f_{ij}(x'_{ij})/f_{ij}(x_{ij}) = p_j f_{ij}(y')/f_{ij}(y)$ and $\alpha'_i = \alpha_i g_i(X'_i)/g_i(X_i)$. Note that the solution (X'_i, α'_i, P') satisfies (6) and (7). Now,

$$x'_{ij}p'_j = y'p'_j = p_j y' f_{ij}(y')/f_{ij}(y) > p_j y f_{ij}(y)/f_{ij}(y) = yp_j = x_{ij}p_j$$

Thus, $\sum_{j=1}^m x'_{ij}p'_j > \sum_{j=1}^m x_{ij}p_j = e_i$, implying that the solution X'_i violates the optimality condition (3) of program $B_i(P')$. Therefore, the optimal solution (X''_i, α''_i) of $B_i(P')$ must have $x''_{ij} < x'_{ij}$ for some j. Since (X'_i, α'_i) and (X''_i, α''_i) satisfy (6) and (7) for the same price P' and f_{ij} is strictly decreasing for all j, we must also have $x''_{ij} < x'_{ij}$ for all j. From the definition of X'_i, it is clear that this violates the gross substitutability condition.

We next show that if $yf_{ij}(y)$ is non-decreasing then the goods satisfy gross-substitutability. Consider an optimal solution X_i of $B_i(P)$. If $x_{ij} > 0$, equation (6) gives $x_{ij}p_j = x_{ij}f_{ij}(x_{ij})g_i(X_i)/\alpha_i$. Consider $P' > P$. For this price vector we construct a feasible solution X'_i satisfying (6) and (7) as follows: If $p'_j = p_j$ then $x'_{ij} = x_{ij}, \forall i$. Alternately, if $f_{ij}(0)g_i(X_i) < \alpha_i p'_j$ then set x'_{ij} to zero, else choose x'_{ij} such that $f_{ij}(x'_{ij})g_i(X_i) = \alpha_i p'_j$. Set $\alpha'_i = \alpha_i(g_i(X'_i)/g_i(X_i))$. By definition, the solution X'_i satisfies the complementary slackness conditions (6). Since $P' > P$, X'_i also satisfies (7). Also since f_{ij} is a strictly decreasing function $p'_j > p_j \Rightarrow x'_{ij} < x_{ij}$. Now, if $x'_{ij} > 0$ then

$$x'_{ij}p'_j = x'_{ij}f_{ij}(x'_{ij})g_i(X'_i)/\alpha'_i \leq x_{ij}f_{ij}(x_{ij})g_i(X_i)/\alpha_i = x_{ij}p_j$$

If $x'_{ij} = 0$ then also we have $x'_{ij}p'_j \leq x_{ij}p_j$ The above equations give

$$\sum_{j=1}^m x'_{ij}p'_j \leq \sum_{j=1}^m x_{ij}p_j = e_i$$

Therefore, any optimal solution (X''_i, α''_i) of the program $B_i(P')$ should have $x''_{ij} > x'_{ij}$ for some j. Since (X''_i, α''_i) and (X'_i, α'_i) both satisfy (6) and (7) for the same price P' and f_{ij} is strictly decreasing, we must have $x''_{ij} \geq x'_{ij}$ for all j. Gross substitutability now follows from the definition of X'_i.

3   An Auction Algorithm for Market Clearing

An auction algorithm similar to that in [10] solves the market equilibrium problem for the uniformly separable gross substitute utility functions. For the sake of completeness we give a brief description of the algorithm.

The algorithm (formally presented in Figure 1) begins with assigning all the goods to one buyer (say buyer 1) and adjusting the prices such that (a) all the money of the buyer is exhausted and (b) the initial allocation is optimal for the buyer. During the course of the algorithm, goods may be allocated at two prices, p_j and $p_j/(1 + \epsilon)$. The allocation of good j to buyer i at price p_j is represented by h_{ij} and the allocation at price $p_{ij}/(1 + \epsilon)$ is represented by y_{ij}. The total allocation of good j to buyer i is given by $x_{ij} = h_{ij} + y_{ij}$. Define

```
algorithm main                              procedure initialize
   initialize                                  ∀i, ∀j : h_ij = 0
   while ∃i : r_i > εe_i                       ∀i ≠ 1, ∀j : y_ij = 0
      while (r_i > 0) and                      ∀j : y_1j = a_j ;  a = (a_1, ..., a_n);
         (∃j : α_ij p_j < f_ij(x_ij)g_i(X_i))  ∀j : α_1j = (Σ_j a_j f_1j(a_j)g_1(a))/e_i
         if ∃k : y_kj > 0 then                 ∀j : p_j = f_1j(a_j)g_1(a)/α_1
            outbid(i, k, j, α_ij)              ∀i ≠ 1 : α_i = f_ij(0)g_i(0̂)/p_j ;  r_i = e_i
         else raise_price(j)                   ∀i ≠ 1, ∀j : α_ij = f_ij(x_ij)g_i(X_i)/p_j
      end while                                r_1 = 0
      j = arg max_l α_il                    end procedure initialize
      if ∃k : y_kj > 0
         outbid(i, k, j, α_ij/(1 + ε))      procedure outbid(i, k, j, α)
         α_ij = f_ij(x_ij)g_i(X_i)/p_j         t_1 = y_kj
      else raise_price(j)                      t_2 = r_i/p_j
   end while                                   if (f_ij(a_j)g_i(X_i) ≥ αp_j) then
end algorithm main                               t_3 = a_j  (x'_ik = x_ik, k ≠ j;  x'_ij = a_j)
                                               else
                                                 t_3 = min δ : f_ij(x_ij + δ)g_i(X_i) = αp_j
procedure raise_price(j)                       t = min(t_1, t_2, t_3)
   ∀i : y_ij = h_ij; h_ij = 0;                 h_ij = h_ij + t
   p_j = (1 + ε)p_j                            r_i = r_i - tp_j
end procedure raise_price                      y_kj = y_kj - t
                                               r_k = r_k + tp_j/(1 + ε)
                                            end procedure outbid
```

Fig. 1. The auction algorithm

the surplus of a buyer i as $r_i = \sum_{j=1}^{m}(h_{ij}p_j + y_{ij}p_j/(1 + \epsilon))$. Define the total surplus in the system as $r = \sum_{i=1}^{n} r_i$. The parameter ϵ is called the minimum bid increment and determines the accuracy of the final solution obtained. Now buyers with unspent money try to acquire items that give them the maximum utility per unit money, by outbidding other buyers and raising the price of items. The bidding is carried out till all the buyers have little unspent money.

Note this algorithm is very characteristic of a typical auction market. The bidding is asynchronous, decentralized and local. The buyers do not have to coordinate their actions. Any buyer with surplus money can place a bid on an item that maximizes the value of the buyer, this outbidding other buyers. The process stops when the unspent money with every buyer is sufficiently small.

To show convergence of the algorithm, the bidding may be organized in rounds. In each round every buyer (i) is picked once and reduces his surplus to 0, i.e. $r_i = 0$. Now it can be shown that in every round of bidding, the total unspent money decreases by a factor of $(1 + \epsilon)$. This gives the following bound on the time complexity of the algorithm ($v_{max} = \max_{ij} v_{ij}(0)$) (see [10]).

Theorem 1. *The auction algorithm terminates in* $O((E/\epsilon) \log((ev v_{max})/(\epsilon e_{min} v_{min})) \log n)$ *steps,*

4   Conclusions

Naive auction algorithms give approximate market equilibrium. The approximation is related to the minimum bid increment parameter ϵ used in the algorithm. It was shown that for linear utility functions, auctions with suitable price-rollbacks and modifications to ϵ lead to exact market equilibrium. It will be interesting to see if any such approach may also work for the general class of gross substitute utilities.

References

1. Bertsekas, D.P.: Auction Algorithms for Network Flow Problems: A Tutorial Introduction. Computational Optimization and Applications 1, 7–66 (1992)
2. Brainard, W.C., Scarf, H.E.: How to Compute Equilibrium Prices in 1891. Cowles Foundation Discussion Paper (1272) (2000)
3. Codenotti, B., McCune, B., Varadarajan, K.: Market equilibrium via the excess demand function. In: STOC 2005: Proceedings of the thirty-seventh annual ACM symposium on Theory of computing, pp. 74–83. ACM Press, New York (2005)
4. Devanur, N., Papadimitriou, C., Saberi, A., Vazirani, V.: Market Equilibrium via a Primal-Dual-Type Algorithm. In: 43rd Symposium on Foundations of Computer Science (FOCS 2002), November 2002, pp. 389–395 (2002)
5. Devanur, N.R., Vazirani, V.V.: The Spending Constraint Model for Market Equilibrium: Algorithmic, Existence and Uniqueness Results. In: Proceedings of the 36th Annual ACM Symposium on the Theory of Computing, ACM Press, New York (2004)
6. Eisenberg, E.: Aggregation of utility functions. Management Sciences 7(4), 337–350 (1961)
7. Eisenberg, E., Gale, D.: Consensus of Subjective Probabilities: The Pari-Mutuel Method. Annals of Mathematical Statistics 30, 165–168 (1959)
8. Garg, R., Kapoor, S.: Auction algorithms for market equilibrium. Math. Oper. Res. 31(4), 714–729 (2006)
9. Garg, R., Kapoor, S.: Price roll-backs and path auctions: An approximation scheme for computing the market equilibrium. In: Spirakis, P.G., Mavronicolas, M., Kontogiannis, S.C. (eds.) WINE 2006. LNCS, vol. 4286, pp. 225–238. Springer, Heidelberg (2006)
10. Garg, R., Kapoor, S., Vazirani, V.: An Auction-Based Market Equilbrium Algorithm for the Separable Gross Substitutibility Case. In: Jansen, K., Khanna, S., Rolim, J.D.P., Ron, D. (eds.) RANDOM 2004 and APPROX 2004. LNCS, vol. 3122, Springer, Heidelberg (2004)
11. Nenakov, E.I., Primak, M.E.: One algorithm for finding solutions of the Arrow-Debreu model. Kibernetica 3, 127–128 (1983)
12. Newman, D.J., Primak, M.E.: Complexity of Circumscribed and Inscribed Ellipsod Methods for Solving Equilibrium Economical Models. Applied Mathematics and Computations 52, 223–231 (1992)
13. Primak, M.E.: A Converging Algorithm for a Linear Exchange Model. Applied Mathematics and Computations 52, 223–231 (1992)
14. Walras, L.: Elements of Pure Economics, or the Theory of Social Wealth (in French). Lausanne, Paris (1874)

Continuity Properties of Equilibrium Prices and Allocations in Linear Fisher Markets

Nimrod Megiddo and Vijay V. Vazirani

[1] IBM Almaden Research Center, 650 Harry Road, San Jose, CA 95120
megiddo@us.ibm.com
[2] College of Computing, Georgia Institute of Technology, Atlanta, GA 30332–0280
vazirani@cc.gatech.edu

Abstract. Continuity of the mapping from initial endowments and utilities to equilibria is an essential property for a desirable model of an economy – without continuity, small errors in the observation of parameters of the economy may lead to entirely different predicted equilibria.

We show that for the linear case of Fisher's market model, the (unique) vector of equilibrium prices, $\mathbf{p} = \mathbf{p}(\mathbf{m}, \mathbf{U})$ is a continuous function of the initial amounts of money held by the agents, $\mathbf{m}$, and their utility functions, $\mathbf{U}$. Furthermore, the correspondence $X(\mathbf{m}, \mathbf{U})$, giving the set of equilibrium allocations for any specified $\mathbf{m}$ and $\mathbf{U}$, is upper hemicontinuous, but not lower hemicontinuous. However, for a fixed $\mathbf{U}$, this correspondence is lower hemicontinuous in $\mathbf{m}$.

1   Introduction

Mathematical economists have studied extensively three basic properties that a desirable model of an economy should possess: existence, uniqueness, and continuity of equilibria.[1] An equilibrium operating point ensures parity between demand and supply, uniqueness of the equilibrium ensures stability, and continuity is essential for this theory to have predictive value – without continuity, small errors in the observation of parameters of an economy may lead to entirely different predicted equilibria.

The questions of existence and uniqueness (or its relaxation to local uniqueness) were studied for several concrete and realistic models. However, to the best of our knowledge, the question of continuity was studied only in an abstract setting; for example, demand functions of agents were assumed to be continuously differentiable and, using differential topology, the set of "bad" economies was shown to be "negligible" (of Lebesgue measure zero if the set of economies is finite-dimensional).[2]

In this paper, we study continuity of equilibrium prices and allocations for perhaps the simplest market model – the linear case of Fisher's model. It is

---

[1] See [3], Chapter 15, "Smooth preferences".
[2] See [3], Chapter 19, "The application to economies of differential topology and global analysis: regular differentiable economies".

X. Deng and F.C. Graham (Eds.): WINE 2007, LNCS 4858, pp. 362–367, 2007.
© Springer-Verlag Berlin Heidelberg 2007

well known that equilibrium prices are unique for this case [5]. An instance of this market is specified by $\mathbf{m}$ and $\mathbf{U}$, the initial amounts of money held by the agents and their utility functions, respectively. We denote by $\mathbf{p} = \mathbf{p}(\mathbf{m}, \mathbf{U})$ be the corresponding (unique) vector of equilibrium prices. In Section 3 we prove that the equilibrium utility values are continuous functions of the unit utility values and the initial amounts of money. In Section 4 we prove that $\mathbf{p}(\mathbf{m}, \mathbf{U})$ is a continuous mapping.

Such linear markets can, however, have more than one equilibrium allocation of goods; let $X(\mathbf{m}, \mathbf{U})$ denote the correspondence giving the set of equilibrium allocations. In Section 5 we prove that this correspondence is upper hemicontinuous, but not lower hemicontinuous. For a fixed $\mathbf{U}$, however, this correspondence turns out to be lower hemicontinuous in $\mathbf{m}$ as well.

2   Fisher's Linear Case and Some Basic Polyhedra

Fisher's linear market model (see [2]) consists of N *buyers* and n divisible *goods*; without loss of generality, the amount of each good may be assumed to be unity. Let u_{ij} denote the utility derived by i on obtaining a unit amount of good j. Thus, the utility of buyer i from receiving x_{ij} units of good j, $j = 1, \ldots, n$, is equal to $\sum_{j=1}^{n} u_{ij} x_{ij}$. Let m_i, $i = 1, \ldots, N$, denote the initial amount of money of buyer i. Unit prices, $p_1, \ldots, p_n$, of the goods are said to be *equilibrium prices* if there exists an allocation $\mathbf{x} = (x_{ij})$ of all the goods to the buyers so that each buyer receives a bundle of maximum utility value among all bundles that the buyer can afford, given these prices; in this case $\mathbf{x}$ is called an *equilibrium allocation*.

Denote by P_X the polytope of feasible allocations, i.e.,

$$P_X \equiv \left\{ \mathbf{x} = (x_{ij}) \in \mathbb{R}^{Nn} : \sum_{i=1}^{N} x_{ij} \leq 1 \ (j = 1, \ldots, n), \ \mathbf{x} \geq \mathbf{0} \right\}.$$

Obviously, $\mathbf{x}$ is a vertex of P_X if and only if for all i and j, $x_{ij} \in \{0, 1\}$, and for each j, there is at most one i such that $x_{ij} = 1$. In other words, an allocation $\mathbf{x}$ is a vertex of P_X if and only if in $\mathbf{x}$ each good is given in its entirety to one agent. Denote by $\mathbf{U}$ the $(N \times (Nn))$-matrix that maps a vector $\mathbf{x}$ to the associated vector $\mathbf{y} = (y_1, \ldots, y_N)$ of utilities, where $y_i = \sum_{j=1}^{n} u_{ij} x_{ij}$, i.e., $\mathbf{y} = \mathbf{U}\mathbf{x}$. Uniqueness of equilibrium prices implies uniqueness of $\mathbf{y}$ at equilibrium.

Denote by $P_Y = P_Y(\mathbf{U})$ the polytope of feasible N-tuples of utility values, i.e., $P_Y = \mathbf{U} P_X$. Obviously, $\mathbf{y} \geq \mathbf{0}$ for every $\mathbf{y} \in P_Y$. It follows that for every vertex $\mathbf{y}$ of P_Y, there exists a vertex $\mathbf{x}$ of P_X such that $\mathbf{y} = \mathbf{U}\mathbf{x}$. Denote by S_i the set of goods that i receives under vertex allocation $\mathbf{x}$. Then, $y_i = \sum_{j \in S_i} u_{ij}$, $i = 1, \ldots, N$.[3]

---

[3] The converse is not true in general. In fact, in the case of $N = n = 2$, if $u_{ij} = 1$ for all i and j, then the allocation $(1, 0, 0, 1)$, where good 1 is allocated to agent 1 and good 2 is allocated to agent 2, is a vertex of P_X but the associated vector of utilities $(1, 1)$ is not a vertex because it is a convex combination of the feasible vectors of utilities $(2, 0)$ and $(0, 2)$.

3   Continuity of Equilibrium Utility Values

Denote $G(\mathbf{y}, \mathbf{U}, \mathbf{x}) \equiv \|\mathbf{y} - \mathbf{U}\mathbf{x}\|^2$. Obviously,

(i) G is continuous,
(ii) $G(\mathbf{y}, \mathbf{U}, \mathbf{x}) \geq 0$ for all $\mathbf{y}$, $\mathbf{U}$, and $\mathbf{x}$,
(iii) $G(\mathbf{y}, \mathbf{U}, \mathbf{x}) = 0$ if and only if $\mathbf{y} = \mathbf{U}\mathbf{x}$, and
(iv) for every $\mathbf{y}$ and $\mathbf{U}$, the function $g(\mathbf{x}) \equiv G(\mathbf{y}, \mathbf{U}, \mathbf{x})$ has a minimum over P_X.

Denote by $F(\mathbf{y}, \mathbf{U})$ the minimum of $G(\mathbf{y}, \mathbf{U}, \mathbf{x})$ over $\mathbf{x} \in P_X$. It is easy to verify the following:

(i) F is continuous, because G is continuous and P_X is compact,
(ii) $F(\mathbf{y}, \mathbf{U}) \geq 0$ for all $\mathbf{y}$ and $\mathbf{U}$, and
(iii) $F(\mathbf{y}, \mathbf{U}) = 0$ if and only if $\mathbf{y} \in P_Y(\mathbf{U})$.

For $\mathbf{y} \geq 0$, $\mathbf{m} > 0$ and $\mathbf{U} \geq 0$, denote

$$f(\mathbf{y}; \mathbf{m}, \mathbf{U}) \equiv \sum_{i=1}^{n} m_i \cdot \log y_i - M \cdot F(\mathbf{y}, \mathbf{U}) , \tag{1}$$

where M is a sufficiently large scalar. By definition, $P_Y(\mathbf{U}) \neq \emptyset$ for every $\mathbf{U} \geq 0$. For $\mathbf{m} > 0$, f is strictly concave in $\mathbf{y}$ over $P_Y(\mathbf{U})$, and hence has a unique maximizer over $P_Y(\mathbf{U})$. For M sufficiently large, this is also a maximizer over all $\mathbf{y} \geq 0$. Thus, for $\mathbf{m} > 0$ and $\mathbf{U} \geq 0$, denote by $\mathbf{y}^* = \mathbf{y}^*(\mathbf{m}, \mathbf{U})$ that unique maximizer.

Theorem 1. *The mapping $\mathbf{y}^*(\mathbf{m}, \mathbf{U})$ is continuous.*

Proof. Suppose $\{(\mathbf{m}^k, \mathbf{U}^k)\}_{k=1}^{\infty}$ is a sequence that converges to $(\mathbf{m}^0, \mathbf{U}^0)$, where for every $k \geq 0$, $\mathbf{m}^k > 0$ and $\mathbf{U}^k \geq 0$. Denote $\mathbf{y}^k = \mathbf{y}^*(\mathbf{m}^k, \mathbf{U}^k)$, $k = 0, 1, \dots$ By continuity of f as a function of $(\mathbf{y}; \mathbf{m}, \mathbf{U})$, $\{f(\mathbf{y}^0; \mathbf{m}^k, \mathbf{U}^k)\}$ converges to $f(\mathbf{y}^0; \mathbf{m}^0, \mathbf{U}^0)$. Since $\mathbf{y}^k \in P_Y(\mathbf{U}^k)$ and $\{\mathbf{U}^k\}$ converges, there exists a bound u such that $\|\mathbf{y}^k\| \leq u$ for every k. Thus, we may assume without loss of generality that $\mathbf{y}$ is restricted to a compact set. Let $\{\mathbf{y}^{k_j}\}_{j=1}^{\infty}$ be any convergent subsequence, and denote its limit by $\overline{\mathbf{y}}$. By continuity of f, $\{f(\mathbf{y}^{k_j}; \mathbf{m}^{k_j}, \mathbf{U}^{k_j})\}$ converges to $f(\overline{\mathbf{y}}; \mathbf{m}^0, \mathbf{U}^0)$. Since $f(\mathbf{y}^{k_j}; \mathbf{m}^{k_j}, \mathbf{U}^{k_j}) \geq f(\mathbf{y}^0; \mathbf{m}^{k_j}, \mathbf{U}^{k_j})$, it follows that $f(\overline{\mathbf{y}}; \mathbf{m}^0, \mathbf{U}^0) \geq f(\mathbf{y}^0; \mathbf{m}^0, \mathbf{U}^0)$. Since $\mathbf{y}^0$ maximizes $f(\mathbf{y}; \mathbf{m}^0, \mathbf{U}^0)$ and the maximum is unique, it follows that $\overline{\mathbf{y}} = \mathbf{y}^0$. This implies that $\{\mathbf{y}^k\}$ converges to $\mathbf{y}^0$.

4   Continuity of Equilibrium Prices

Denote by $\mathbf{p} = \mathbf{p}(\mathbf{m}, \mathbf{U}) = (p_1(\mathbf{m}, \mathbf{U}), \dots, p_n(\mathbf{m}, \mathbf{U}))$ the prices that are generated as dual variables in the Eisenberg-Gale convex program, whose optimal solutions give equilibrium allocations and dual variables give equilibrium prices [4]:[4]

$$\text{Maximize} \sum_{i=1}^{n} m_i \cdot \log \left(\sum_{j=1}^{n} u_{ij} x_{ij} \right) \tag{2}$$

$$\text{subject to } \mathbf{x} = (x_{ij}) \in P_X \ ,$$

i.e., given an optimal solution $\mathbf{x} = (x_{ij})$ of (2),

$$p_j(\mathbf{m}, \mathbf{U}) = \max \left\{ \frac{m_i \cdot u_{ij}}{\sum_{k=1}^{n} u_{ik} x_{ik}} \ : \ i = 1, \ldots, n \right\} \ . \tag{3}$$

The vector $\mathbf{y} = \mathbf{U}\mathbf{x}$ of utilities is the same for all optimal solutions $\mathbf{x}$, and hence $\mathbf{p}$ is unique. The problem can alternately be formulated in terms of the vector of utilities:

$$\text{Maximize} \sum_{i=1}^{n} m_i \cdot \log y_i \tag{4}$$

$$\text{subject to } \mathbf{y} = (y_1, \ldots, y_n) \in P_Y$$

and the prices can be represented as

$$p_j(\mathbf{m}, \mathbf{U}) = \max \left\{ \frac{m_i \cdot u_{ij}}{y_i} \ : \ i = 1, \ldots, n \right\} \ . \tag{5}$$

The latter, together with Theorem 1 gives:

Theorem 2. *The mapping* $\mathbf{p}(\mathbf{m}, \mathbf{U})$ *is continuous.*

5   Hemicontinuity of Equilibrium Allocations

5.1   Upper Hemicontinuity

For every $\mathbf{m} > \mathbf{0}$ and $\mathbf{U} \geq \mathbf{0}$, denote

$$g(\mathbf{x}) = g(\mathbf{x}; \mathbf{m}, \mathbf{U}) \equiv \sum_{i=1}^{n} m_i \cdot \log \left(\sum_{j=1}^{n} u_{ij} x_{ij} \right) \ .$$

Denote by $X(\mathbf{m}, \mathbf{U})$ the set of optimal solutions of (2). Obviously, $X(\mathbf{m}, \mathbf{U})$ is compact and nonempty for every $\mathbf{m}$ and $\mathbf{U}$. Denote by $v(\mathbf{m}, \mathbf{U})$ the maximum of $g(\mathbf{x})$ over P_X.

Theorem 3. *The correspondence* $X(\mathbf{m}, \mathbf{U})$ *is upper hemicontinuous.*

Proof. To prove that X is upper hemicontinuous at $(\mathbf{m}^0, \mathbf{U}^0)$, one has to show the following: *for every sequence* $\{\mathbf{m}^k, \mathbf{U}^k\}_{k=1}^{\infty}$ *that converges to* $(\mathbf{m}^0, \mathbf{U}^0)$, *and every sequence* $\{\mathbf{x}^k\}_{k=1}^{\infty}$ *such that* $\mathbf{x}^k \in X(\mathbf{m}^k, \mathbf{U}^k)$, *there exists a convergent subsequence* $\{\mathbf{x}^{k_j}\}_{j=1}^{\infty}$, *whose limit* $\mathbf{x}^0$ *belongs to* $X(\mathbf{m}^0, \mathbf{U}^0)$.

---

[4] We use the convention that $\log 0 = -\infty$.

Suppose $\{\mathbf{m}^k, \mathbf{U}^k\}_{k=1}^{\infty}$ converges to $(\mathbf{m}^0, \mathbf{U}^0)$, and $\{\mathbf{x}^k\}_{k=1}^{\infty}$ is a sequence such that $\mathbf{x}^k \in X(\mathbf{m}^k, \mathbf{U}^k)$. Since $\mathbf{x}^k \in P_X$ for every k, there exists a subsequence $\{\mathbf{x}^{k_j}\}_{j=1}^{\infty}$ that converges to a point $\mathbf{x}^0$. Since g is a continuous function of $(\mathbf{x}; \mathbf{m}, \mathbf{U})$, it follows that the sequence $\{g(\mathbf{x}^{k_j}; \mathbf{m}^{k_j}, \mathbf{U}^{k_j})\}$ converges to $g(\mathbf{x}^0; \mathbf{m}^0, \mathbf{U}^0)$. On the other hand, $g(\mathbf{x}^k; \mathbf{m}^k, \mathbf{U}^k) = v(\mathbf{m}^k, \mathbf{U}^k)$. By Theorem 1, $\{\mathbf{y}^k \equiv \mathbf{U}^k \mathbf{x}^k\}$ converges to an optimal $\mathbf{y}$ with respect to $(\mathbf{m}^0, \mathbf{U}^0)$, so that $\{v(\mathbf{m}^k, \mathbf{U}^k)\}$ converges to $v(\mathbf{m}^0, \mathbf{U}^0)$. Thus, $g(\mathbf{x}^0; \mathbf{m}^0, \mathbf{U}^0) = v(\mathbf{m}^0, \mathbf{U}^0)$, which means $\mathbf{x}^0 \in X(\mathbf{m}^0, \mathbf{U}^0)$.

5.2   Lower Hemicontinuity

Proposition 1. *There exist* $\mathbf{m}$ *and* $\mathbf{U}^0$ *such that the correspondence* $\Xi(\mathbf{U}) \equiv X(\mathbf{m}, \mathbf{U})$ *is not lower hemicontinuous at* $\mathbf{U}^0$.

Proof. To prove that $\Xi(\mathbf{U})$ is lower hemicontinuous at $\mathbf{U}^0$, one has to show the following: *for every sequence* $\{\mathbf{U}^k\}_{k=1}^{\infty}$ *that converges to* $\mathbf{U}^0$, *and every* $\mathbf{x}^0 \in X(\mathbf{U}^0)$, *there exists a sequence* $\{\mathbf{x}^k \in X(\mathbf{U}^k)\}$ *that converges to* $\mathbf{x}^0$.

Consider a linear Fisher market with two goods and two buyers, each having one unit of money ($\mathbf{m} = (1, 1)$), and the utilities per unit $\mathbf{U}$ are: $u_{11} = u_{12} = u_{21} = 1$ and $u_{22} = u$, where $0 < u \leq 1$. Under these circumstances, the equilibrium prices are $(1, 1)$ for every u. If $u < 1$, there is only one equilibrium allocation: Buyer 1 gets Good 2 and Buyer 2 gets Good 1. However, if $u = 1$, there are infinitely many equilibrium allocations: Buyer 1 gets x units of Good 1 and $1 - x$ units of Good 2, and Buyer 2 gets $1 - x$ units of Good 1 and x units of Good 2, for $0 \leq x \leq 1$. This implies that the correspondence $\Xi(\mathbf{U})$ is not lower hemicontinuous at the point $\mathbf{U}^0$ where $u = 1$.

To prove that X is lower hemicontinuous in $\mathbf{m}$ we need the following lemmas:

Lemma 1. *Let* $\mathbf{A} \in \mathbb{R}^{m \times n}$ *and let* $\mathbf{x}^0 \in \mathbb{R}^n$. *For every* $\mathbf{y}$ *in the column space of* $\mathbf{A}$, *denote by* $\mathbf{x}^*(\mathbf{y})$ *the closest[5] point to* $\mathbf{x}^0$ *among all points* $\mathbf{x}$ *such that* $\mathbf{A}\mathbf{x} = \mathbf{y}$. *Under these conditions, the mapping* $\mathbf{x}^*(\mathbf{y})$ *is affine.*

Proof. Since we consider only vectors $\mathbf{y}$ in the column space of $\mathbf{A}$, we may assume, without loss of generality, that the rows of $\mathbf{A}$ are linearly independent; otherwise, we may drop dependent rows. Thus, $\mathbf{A}\mathbf{A}^T$ is nonsingular. Let $\mathbf{y}^0 = \mathbf{A}\mathbf{x}^0$. Obviously, $\mathbf{x}^0 = \mathbf{x}^*(\mathbf{y}^0)$. Let $\mathbf{y}$ in the column space of $\mathbf{A}$ be fixed, and consider the problem of minimizing $\frac{1}{2}\|\mathbf{x} - \mathbf{x}^0\|^2$ subject to $\mathbf{A}\mathbf{x} = \mathbf{y}$. It follows that there exists a vector of Lagrange multipliers $\mathbf{z} \in \mathbb{R}^m$ such that $\mathbf{x}^*(\mathbf{y}) - \mathbf{x}^0 = \mathbf{A}^T \mathbf{z}$. Thus, $\mathbf{A}\mathbf{x}^*(\mathbf{y}) - \mathbf{A}\mathbf{x}^0 = \mathbf{A}\mathbf{A}^T\mathbf{z}$, and hence $\mathbf{z} = (\mathbf{A}\mathbf{A}^T)^{-1}(\mathbf{y} - \mathbf{y}^0)$. It follows that $\mathbf{x}^*(\mathbf{y}) = \mathbf{x}^0 + \mathbf{A}^T\mathbf{z} = \mathbf{x}^0 + \mathbf{A}^T(\mathbf{A}\mathbf{A}^T)^{-1}(\mathbf{y} - \mathbf{y}^0)$.

Lemma 2. *Let* $\mathbf{A} \in \mathbb{R}^{m \times n}$ *be a matrix whose columns are linearly independent. Let* $\mathbf{x}^0 \in \mathbb{R}^n$ *and* $\mathbf{y}^0 \in \mathbb{R}^m$ *be such that* $\mathbf{A}\mathbf{x}^0 \leq \mathbf{y}^0$. *For every* $\mathbf{y} \in \mathbb{R}^m$ *such that* $\{\mathbf{x} \mid \mathbf{A}\mathbf{x} \leq \mathbf{y}\} \neq \varnothing$, *denote by* $\mathbf{x}^*(\mathbf{y})$ *the closest point to* $\mathbf{x}^0$ *among all points* $\mathbf{x}$ *such that* $\mathbf{A}\mathbf{x} \leq \mathbf{y}$. *Under these conditions, the mapping* $\mathbf{x}^*(\mathbf{y})$ *is continuous at* $\mathbf{y}^0$.

---

[5] We use the Euclidean norm throughout; thus the, closest point is unique.

Proof. For every $S \subseteq M \equiv \{1, \ldots, m\}$, denote $\overline{S} \equiv M \setminus S$. Denote by $\mathbf{A}_S$ the matrix consisting of the rows of $\mathbf{A}$ whose indices i belong to S. Similarly, let $\mathbf{y}_S$ denote the projection of $\mathbf{y}$ on the coordinates in S. Denote $F_S(\mathbf{y}) = F_S(\mathbf{y}_S) \equiv \{\mathbf{x} : \mathbf{A}_S \mathbf{x} = \mathbf{y}_S\}$. Let $\mathbf{x}_S^*(\mathbf{y})$ be the point in $F_S(\mathbf{y})$ that is closest to $\mathbf{x}^0$. By Lemma 1, $\mathbf{x}_S^*(\mathbf{y})$ is an affine transformation of $\mathbf{y}_S$. It follows that there exists an $\alpha > 0$ such that for every $\mathbf{y}$, $\|\mathbf{x}_S^*(\mathbf{y}) - \mathbf{x}_S^*(\mathbf{y}^0)\| \leq \alpha \cdot \|\mathbf{y} - \mathbf{y}^0\|$. Let $\epsilon > 0$ be any number. Fix $S \equiv \{i : (\mathbf{A}\mathbf{x}^0)_i = y_i^0\}$. Obviously, $\mathbf{x}^0 = \mathbf{x}_S^*(\mathbf{y}^0)$ and $\mathbf{A}_{\overline{S}} \mathbf{x}^0 < \mathbf{y}_{\overline{S}}^0$. Let $0 < \delta < \epsilon/\alpha$ be sufficiently small so that $\|\mathbf{y} - \mathbf{y}^0\| < \delta$ implies $\mathbf{A}_{\overline{S}} \mathbf{x}_S^*(\mathbf{y}) < \mathbf{y}_{\overline{S}}$. It follows that $\|\mathbf{y} - \mathbf{y}^0\| < \delta$ implies $\|\mathbf{x}^*(\mathbf{y}) - \mathbf{x}^0\| \leq \|\mathbf{x}_S^*(\mathbf{y}) - \mathbf{x}^0\| < \alpha\delta < \epsilon$.

Theorem 4. *For every fixed* $\mathbf{U}$, *the correspondence* $\Xi(\mathbf{m}) = X(\mathbf{m}, \mathbf{U})$ *is lower hemicontinuous at every* $\mathbf{m}^0 > 0$.

Proof. To prove that $\Xi(\mathbf{m})$ is lower hemicontinuous at $\mathbf{m}^0 > 0$, one has to show the following: *for every sequence* $\{\mathbf{m}^k\}_{k=1}^{\infty}$ *that converges to* $\mathbf{m}^0$, *and every* $\mathbf{x}^0 \in \Xi(\mathbf{m}^0)$, *there exists a sequence* $\{\mathbf{x}^k \in \Xi(\mathbf{m}^k)\}$ *that converges to* $\mathbf{x}^0$.

Suppose $\{\mathbf{m}^k\}_{k=1}^{\infty}$ converges to $\mathbf{m}^0$, and let $\mathbf{x}^0 \in \Xi(\mathbf{m}^0)$ be any point. Let $\mathbf{y}^k = \mathbf{y}^*(\mathbf{m}^k)$, $k = 0, 1, \ldots$, i.e., $\mathbf{y}^k$ is the unique maximizer of $f(\mathbf{y}; \mathbf{m}^k, \mathbf{U})$ (see (1)) or, equivalently, the optimal solution of (4). By Theorem 1, $\{\mathbf{y}^k\}$ converges to $\mathbf{y}^0$. Thus, $\Xi(\mathbf{m}^k)$ is the set of all vectors $\mathbf{x} \in P_X$ such that $\mathbf{U}\mathbf{x} = \mathbf{y}^k$. In particular, $\mathbf{x}^0 \in P_X$ and $\mathbf{U}\mathbf{x}^0 = \mathbf{y}^0$. Let $\mathbf{x}^k$ denote the minimizer of $\|\mathbf{x} - \mathbf{x}^0\|$ subject to $\mathbf{x} \in P_X$ and $\mathbf{U}\mathbf{x} = \mathbf{y}^k$. Denote by $\mathbf{x}^* = \mathbf{x}^*(\mathbf{y})$ the optimal solution of the following optimization problem:

$$\text{Minimize}_{\mathbf{x}} \ \|\mathbf{x} - \mathbf{x}^0\|$$
$$\text{subject to} \ \mathbf{U}\mathbf{x} = \mathbf{y}$$
$$\sum_i x_{ij} \leq 1 \quad (\forall j)$$
$$x_{ij} \geq 0 \quad (\forall i)(\forall j) .$$

Thus, $\mathbf{x}^k = \mathbf{x}^*(\mathbf{y}^k)$. By Lemma 2, the mapping $\mathbf{x}^*(\mathbf{y})$ is continuous. Since $\{\mathbf{y}^k\}$ converges to $\mathbf{y}^0$, $\{\mathbf{x}^k\}$ converges to $\mathbf{x}^0$.

Acknowledgements. We wish to thank Kenneth Arrow and Michel Goemans for valuable discussions.

References

1. Arrow, K.J., Debreu, G.: Existence of an equilibrium for a competitive economy. Econometrica 22, 265–290 (1954)
2. Brainard, W.C., Scarf, H.E.: How to compute equilibrium prices in 1891. Cowles Foundation Discussion Paper 1270 (2000)
3. Debreu, G.: Mathematical Economics: Twenty papers of Gerard Debreu. Cambridge University Press, Cambridge (1986)
4. Eisenberg, E., Gale, D.: Consensus of subjective probabilities: the Pari-Mutuel method. The Annals of Mathematical Statistics 30, 165–168 (1959)
5. Gale, D.: Theory of Linear Economic Models. McGraw-Hill, New York (1960)

Computing Market Equilibrium: Beyond Weak Gross Substitutes

Chinmay Karande and Nikhil Devanur

Georgia Institute of Technology, Atlanta, GA 30318, USA
ckarande@cc.gatech.edu, nikhil@cc.gatech.edu

Abstract. The property of Weak Gross Substitutibility (WGS) of goods in a market has been found to be conducive to efficient algorithms for finding equilibria. In this paper, we give a natural definition of a δ-approximate WGS property, and show that the auction algorithm of [GK04][GKV04] can be extended to give an $(\epsilon + \delta)$-approximate equilibrium for markets with this property.

1 Introduction

The computational complexity of finding a market equilibrium has recieved a lot of interest lately [DPS02][DPSV02][Jai04][DV04][GK04][CSVY06][CMV05] (also see [CPV04] for a survey). A key property that has been used in designing some of these algorithms is that of Weak Gross Substitutibility (WGS). A market satisfies WGS if an increase in price of one good does not lead to a decrease in demand of any other good. Markets with WGS have been well studied in both the economics and the algorithmic game theory literature. It has been shown, for instance, [ABH59] that the *tatonnement* process converges for all markets satisfying WGS.

In this paper we extend the definition of WGS to approximate WGS and design algorithms for the same. We formulate the following alternate definition of WGS: the monetary demand for any good, which is the demand for the good times the price, is a decreasing function of its price, given that all the other prices are fixed. Our definition of an approximate WGS now follows from bounding the increase in the monetary demand for a good with an increase in its price.

2 Preliminaries

In this section, we define the Fisher market model which we refer to throughout this paper. Consider a market with n buyers and m goods. The goods are assumed to be perfectly divisible, and w.l.o.g. a unit amount of each good is available as supply. Each buyer i has an intial endowment e_i of money, and utility functions u_{ij}: $u_{ij}(x_{ij})$ gives the utility gained by her for having bought (consumed) x_{ij} units of good j. Given prices $P = (p_1, ..., p_m)$, a buyer uses her money to buy a bundle of goods $X_i = (x_{i1}, ..., x_{im})$, called the *demand vector* for

X. Deng and F.C. Graham (Eds.): WINE 2007, LNCS 4858, pp. 368–373, 2007.
© Springer-Verlag Berlin Heidelberg 2007

buyer i, such that her total utility $U_i(X_i) = \sum_j u_{ij}(x_{ij})$ is maximized, subject to the budget constraint: $\sum_j x_{ij} p_j \leq e_i$. Equilibrium prices are such that the market clears, that is, total demand for every good is equal to the supply: for all goods j, $\sum_i x_{ij} = 1$.

Let v_{ij} be $\frac{dU_i}{dx_{ij}}$. We assume that for all i and j, U_i is non-negative, non-decreasing, differentiable and concave. These constraints translate into v_{ij} being non-negative, non-increasing and well defined. From the KKT conditions on the buyers' optimization program, it follows that $v_{ij}(x_{ij})/p_j$ is equalized over all goods for which $x_{ij} > 0$. So for any optimal bundle of goods X_i for buyer i, there exists α such that $x_{ij} > 0 \Rightarrow \frac{v_{ij}(x_{ij})}{p_j} = \alpha$, and $x_{ij} = 0 \Rightarrow \frac{v_{ij}(x_{ij})}{p_j} \leq \alpha$.

Definition 1. *For any $\epsilon > 0$, a price vector P is an ϵ-approximate market equilibrium if each buyer can be allocated a bundle X_i such that $U_i(X_i)$ is at least the optimal utility times $(1 - \epsilon)$ and the market clears exactly.*

Definition 2. *A market satisfies WGS if for two price vectors P and P', such that $p_j = p'_j$ for all goods $j \neq k$ and $p_k < p'_k$, the demand of good j at P' is at least its demand at P.*

[GKV04] gave the following equivalent condition for WGS, when the utilities are separable.

Lemma 1. *([GKV04]) A market satsfies WGS if and only if the function $x_{ij} v_{ij}(x_{ij})$ is non-decreasing for all i and j.*

3 Extending WGS

3.1 An Alternate Definition of WGS

Let the monetary demand for a good be its demand times its price. We motivate our alternate definition of WGS by analysing how the monetary demand for a good changes as its price goes up.

Consider a buyer i who has an optimal bundle of goods $(x_{i1}, ..., x_{im})$. For any good j such that $x_{ij} > 0$, $\frac{v_{ij}(x_{ij})}{p_j} = \alpha$. Now suppose price of good k is driven up to $p'_k > p_k$, rest of the prices being unchanged. In this case, clearly the current allocation no more represents an optimal bundle for the buyer. We now describe a way for the buyer to adjust her allocation in order to attain the new optimum. This is done in two stages.

In the first stage, she sells some of good k to equalize the marginal rate of utility of good k with that of other goods. Let x'_{ik} be such that $v_{ik}(x'_{ik}) = \alpha p'_k$. The difference between the values of the new and original holdings is $x'_{ik} p'_k - x_{ik} p_k$. This is the amount of money she will have to pay as a result of the increase in price. From Lemma 1,

$$x'_{ij} p'_j - x_{ij} p_j = \frac{1}{\alpha}(x'_{ij} v_{ij}(x'_{ij}) - x_{ij} v_{ij}(x_{ij}))$$
$$\leq 0$$

This means that she has some money left over at the end of the first stage. In the second stage, she splits the left over money among all goods in such a way that $\frac{v_{ij}(x_{ij})}{p_j}$ remains the same for all goods with $x_{ij} > 0$. Two things are worth noting: the monetary demand for good k and the value of α both decrease as a result. This leads us to an alternate formulation of WGS.

Lemma 2. *A market satisfies WGS if and only if for two price vectors P and P', such that $p_j = p'_j$ for all goods $j \neq k$ and $p_k < p'_k$, the monetary demand for good k at P' is smaller than that at P.*

Proof. Suppose that the market is WGS. Let the demand at P and P' be X and X' respectively. Then WGS implies that $x'_j \geq x_j$ for all $j \neq k$. Therefore $p'_j x'_j \geq p_j x_j$ for all $j \neq k$. Since $\sum_j p'_j x'_j = \sum_j p_j x_j$, it follows that $p'_k x'_k \leq p_k x_k$.

Now assume that $p'_k x'_k \leq p_k x_k$. We need to prove that $x'_j \geq x_j$. We can ignore those j for which $x_j = 0$. Again, since $\sum_j p'_j x'_j = \sum_j p_j x_j$, there exists some $j \neq k$ such that $p'_j x'_j \geq p_j x_j$, and in turn $x'_j \geq x_j$. Therefore $\alpha' = \frac{v_{ij}(x'_j)}{p'_j} \leq \frac{v_{ij}(x_j)}{p_j} = \alpha$. Hence for all $j \neq k$ such that $x_j > 0, x'_j \geq x_j$. $\square$

3.2   Approximate-WGS Utility Functions

We have seen how WGS can be interpreted from the demand perspective as well as the revenue perspective. Extending the revenue interpretation from Lemma 2, we say that a market satisfies δ-approximate WGS if increasing the price of a good does not cause its monetary demand to increase by more than a factor of $(1 + \delta)$.

Definition 3. *For any $\delta \geq 0$, a market satisfies δ-approximate WGS if for two price vectors P and P', such that $p_j = p'_j$ for all goods $j \neq k$ and $p_k < p'_k$, the monetary demand for good k at P' is at most $(1 + \delta)$ times that at P.*

In the next section, we will prove that this definition allows us to design efficient approximation algorithms for these markets. Henceforth we will refer to definition 3 as δ-approximate weak gross substitutability.

The above definition gives the following necessary condition on a δ-approximate WGS market, which is proved in [KD07]:

Lemma 3. *If a market satisfies δ-approximate WGS, then*

$$\forall i, j, \forall x > x' \Rightarrow x v_{ij}(x) \geq \frac{x' v_{ij}(x')}{(1 + \delta)}$$

4   Auction Algorithm

In this section we show that by slightly modifying the auction algorithm in [GKV04], we can compute an $(\epsilon + \delta)$-approximate equilibrium for a market exhibiting δ-approximate WGS property. This result shows that WGS is not a hard threshold: Markets do not suddenly become intractable if they slightly violate the WGS property.

We will use the auction algorithm of [GKV04] as the starting point. This algorithm computes ϵ-approximate equilibrium when the market satisfies WGS. We only modify the buy-back step of this algorithm. An outline of the modified auction algorithm is as follows: (For pseudocode, refer to [KD07])

- **Ascending prices:** Prices start out at suitably low values and are raised in multiplicative steps. At any stage, some buyers may have an allocation of good j at price p_j, where as others may have bought the same good at price $\frac{p_j}{(1+\epsilon)}$. Buyer i's holding of good j at price p_j is denoted by h_{ij} and that at price $p_j/(1+\epsilon)$ is denoted by y_{ij}. Total allocation of good j to buyer i is $x_{ij} = h_{ij} + y_{ij}$.
- **Decreasing surplus:** A buyer's surplus is the money she hasn't spent. It is denoted by $r_i = e_i - \sum_j h_{ij} p_j - \sum_j y_{ij} p_j/(1+\epsilon)$. Each buyer exhausts her surplus by buying goods at price p_j from others whose allocation of good j is at price $p_j/(1+\epsilon)$. If no other buyer has the good at lower price, the price is raised from p_j to $(1+\epsilon)p_j$. Finally due to rising prices, total surplus of all buyers $r = \sum_i r_i$ approaches zero.
- **Buy-back:** We split the buy-back step into two rounds: (Let X_i' and P' denote the allocation and price vectors at the begining of each round)
    1. **First round:** For each good j such that $\frac{v_{ij}(x_{ij}')}{p_j'} > (1+\delta)\alpha_{ij}$, buyer i buys it back to an amount x_{ij}^* such that $(1+\delta)\alpha_{ij} = \frac{v_{ij}(x_{ij}^*)}{p_j^*}$. (As opposed to buy back until $\alpha_{ij} = \frac{v_{ij}(x_{ij}^*)}{p_j^*}$ in the original algorithm). If buyer i has to raise price of good j in this process, p_j^* may be strictly higher than p_j'. As we shall see, this ensures that the buyer does not spend more on any good than she originally had when the value of α_{ij} was set. Therefore, the buy-back **is** possible for all goods.
    2. **Second round:** For each good j such that $\frac{v_{ij}(x_{ij}')}{p_j'} > \alpha_{ij}$, buyer i buys it back to an amount x_{ij}^* such that $\alpha_{ij} = \frac{v_{ij}(x_{ij}^*)}{p_j^*}$, until she has surplus money left. This round is identical to the buy-back step in the original algorithm.
- **Near-Optimality:** ϵ-approximate optimality of the partial bundle of goods is maintained for each buyer throughout the algorithm. Therefore, when the total surplus tends to zero, the current price and allocation vectors represent ϵ-approximate equilibrium.

Lemma 4. *First buy-back round finishes with each good j considered having* $\alpha_{ij} = \frac{v_{ij}(x_{ij}^*)}{(1+\delta)p_j^*}$.

Proof. Consider a situation when buyer i has x_{ij}' amount of good j when her turn arrives to spend her surplus. Let p_j' be the current price and $\alpha_{ij} < \frac{v_{ij}(x_{ij}')}{(1+\delta)p_j'}$. Let x_{ij}^* be the amount and p_j^* be the price such that

$$x_{ij}^* \leq x_{ij}' < x_{ij} \text{ AND } p_j^* \geq p_j' > p_j \text{ AND } \alpha_{ij} = \frac{v_{ij}(x_{ij}^*)}{(1+\delta)p_j^*}$$

where x_{ij} and p_j is the endowment and price of good j respectively when α_{ij} was set, *i.e.* $\alpha_{ij} = \frac{v_{ij}(x_{ij})}{p_j}$. Then using property of the market from lemma 3, we get:

$$\frac{v_{ij}(x_{ij}^*)}{(1+\delta)p_j^*} = \alpha_{ij} = \frac{v_{ij}(x_{ij})}{p_j} \geq \frac{x_{ij}^* v_{ij}(x_{ij}^*)}{(1+\delta)x_{ij}p_j}$$
$$\Rightarrow x_{ij}p_j \geq x_{ij}^* p_j^*$$

The above equation certifies that the value of good j held by buyer i at the end of the first buy-back round is at most the value of her holding at original price p_j. When competing buyers reduced x_{ij} to x_{ij}', the value was returned to buyer i in dollars. The above equation says that she can safely buy back upto x_{ij}^* of good j, using up **only** the surplus value returned to her for good j. The same is true for all such goods, hence buyer i can buy all goods considered in the first buy-back round upto x_{ij}^* such that $\alpha_{ij} = \frac{v_{ij}(x_{ij}^*)}{(1+\delta)p_j^*}$. □

Correctness and convergence of the algorithm can be proved along the lines of [GKV04], by showing that the algorithm maintains following invariants at the start of each iteration of the outer *while* loop in **procedure main** (Refer to the psudocode in [KD07]:

I1: $\forall j,$ $\sum_i x_{ij} = a_j$	**I4**: $\forall i,j,\ x_{ij} > 0 \Rightarrow \frac{(1+\epsilon)v_{ij}(x_{ij})}{p_j} \geq \alpha_{ij}$	
I2: $\forall i,$ $\sum_j x_{ij}p_j \leq e_i$	**I5**: $\forall j,$ p_j does not fall	
I3: $\forall i,j,\ r_i = 0 \Rightarrow \alpha_{ij} \geq \frac{v_{ij}(x_{ij})}{(1+\delta)p_j}$	**I6**: r does not increase	

Invariant I1 says that all goods are fully sold at any stage. Invariant I2 conveys the fact the buyers never exceed their budget — the initial endowment. Invariants I3 and I4 together guarantee the optimality of the bundle each buyer has after she has exhausted her surplus. Only I3 is different from the earlier auction algorithm. By invariants I3 and I4, as well as the manner in which α_{ij}'s are modified in the algorithm, we have the following at the termination for all buyers i and goods j, k:

$$\frac{(1+\epsilon)v_{ij}(x_{ij})}{p_j} \geq \alpha_{ij} \geq \frac{v_{ij}(x_{ij})}{(1+\delta)p_j}$$
$$\alpha_{ij} \leq (1+\epsilon)\alpha_{ik}$$

Above constraints imply that all the bang-per-buck values for a buyer $\left(\frac{v_{ij}(x_{ij})}{p_j}\right)$ are within a factor $(1+\epsilon)^2(1+\delta)$ of each other at termination. Therefore, the modified algorithm terminates with $(\epsilon + \delta)$-approximate equilibrium, ignoring the higher order terms. The analysis of the running time is similar to that in [GKV04]:

Lemma 5. *If bidding is organized in rounds, i.e. if each buyer is chosen once in a round to exhaust his surplus in* **procedure main**, *the total unspent surplus money* $r = \sum_i r_i$ *decreases by a factor of* $(1+\epsilon)$.

5   Open Problems

Our result holds for separable utility functions. Clearly, definition 3 makes sense in the non-separable setting as well. An important open problem therefore is to devise an algorithm that finds approximate equilibrium for non-separable utility markets. Alternatively, it will be interesting to see if other algorithms that solve WGS markets extend to approximate-WGS markets.

References

[ABH59]   Arrow, K., Block, H., Hurwicz, L.: On the stability of the competitive equilibrium: II. Econometrica 27(1), 82–109 (1959)

[CMV05]   Codenotti, B., McCune, B., Varadarajan, K.: Market equilibrium via the excess demand function. In: Proceedings of ACM Symposium on Theory of Computing, ACM Press, New York (2005)

[CPV04]   Codenotti, B., Pemmaraju, S., Varadarajan, K.: Algorithms column: The computation of market equilibria. In: ACM SIGACT News, vol. 35(4), ACM Press, New York (2004)

[CSVY06]   Codenotti, B., Saberi, A., Varadarajan, K., Ye, Y.: Leontief economies encode nonzero sum two-player games. In: Proceedings of ACM Symposium on Discrete Algorithms, ACM Press, New York (2006)

[DPS02]   Deng, X., Papadimitriou, C., Safra, S.: On the complexity of equilibria. In: Proceedings of ACM Symposium on Theory of Computing, ACM Press, New York (2002)

[DPSV02]   Devanur, N.R., Papadimitriou, C.H., Saberi, A., Vazirani, V.V.: Market equilibrium via a primal-dual-type algorithm. In: Proceedings of IEEE Annual Symposium on Foundations of Computer Science, Journal version (2002), available at: http://www-static.cc.gatech.edu/~nikhil/pubs/AD/market-full.ps

[DV04]   Devanur, N.R., Vazirani, V.V.: The spending constraint model for market equilibrium: Algorithmic, existence and uniqueness results. In: Proceedings of 36th STOC (2004)

[GK04]   Garg, R., Kapoor, S.: Auction algorithms for market equilibrium. In: Proceedings of 36th STOC (2004)

[GKV04]   Garg, R., Kapoor, S., Vazirani, V.V.: An auction-based market equilibrium algorithm for the separable gross substitutibility case. In: Jansen, K., Khanna, S., Rolim, J.D.P., Ron, D. (eds.) RANDOM 2004 and APPROX 2004. LNCS, vol. 3122, Springer, Heidelberg (2004)

[Jai04]   Jain, K.: A polynomial time algorithm for computing the Arrow-Debreu market equilibrium for linear utilities. In: Proc. of the IEEE Annual Symposium on Foundations of Computer Science FOCS, IEEE Computer Society Press, Los Alamitos (2004)

[KD07]   Karande, C., Devanur, N.: Approximate market equilibrium for near gross substitutes. Technical report (July 2007), http://www.cc.gatech.edu/~ckarande/kd-approx-wgs.pdf

On Competitiveness in Uniform Utility Allocation Markets*

Deeparnab Chakrabarty and Nikhil Devanur

College of Computing, Georgia Institute of Technology, Atlanta, GA 30332–0280.
{deepc,nikhil}@cc.gatech.edu

Abstract. In this paper, we study competitive markets - a market is competitive if increasing the endowment of any one buyer does not increase the equilibrium utility of any other buyer. In the Fisher setting, competitive markets contain all markets with weak gross substitutability (WGS), a property which enable efficient algorithms for equilibrium computation. We show that every uniform utility allocation (UUA) market which is competitive, is a submodular utility allocation (SUA) market. Our result provides evidence for the existence of efficient algorithms for the class of competitive markets.

1 Introduction

In the past few years, there has been a surge of activity to design efficient algorithms for computation of market equilibrium. These include the linear utilities case in the Fisher model [8,10] and the Arrow-Debreu model [12], the spending constraint model [9], Leontief utility functions in the Fisher model [7] and so on. Interestingly, almost all of these markets for which efficient equilibrium computation algorithms are known, satisfy the property of *weak gross substitutability* (WGS). A market is WGS if raising the price of any good does not lead to the decrease in the demand of some other good. This property has extensively been studied in mathematical economics, [1,15,2] and recently Codenotti et.al. [6] gave polytime algorithms to compute equilibriums in WGS markets, under fairly general assumptions.

WGS relates how one good's price influences the demands for other goods. Analogously, competitiveness relates how one person's assets influence the returns to others. A market is called competitive if increasing the money of one agent cannot lead to increase in the equilibrium utility of some other agent. This notion was introduced by Jain and Vazirani [13] [1], who showed that in the Fisher setting any WGS market is competitive. In this paper, we provide a characterization of competitive markets in a class of Eisenberg-Gale markets, introduced by [13]. Combined with results of [13], our result provides some evidence that competitive markets, like WGS markets, might also be amenable to efficient algorithms. In particular, [11,13] gave combinatorial polynomial time algorithms for some markets that were not WGS; our result shows that these markets are competitive.

---

* Work supported by NSF Grants 0311541, 0220343 and 0515186.
[1] They used the term *competition monotonicity* instead.

X. Deng and F.C. Graham (Eds.): WINE 2007, LNCS 4858, pp. 374–380, 2007.

Recently, Jain and Vazirani [13] proposed a new class of markets called *Eisenberg-Gale markets* or simply EG markets. In 1959, Eisenberg and Gale [10] gave a convex program for obtaining the equilibrium in the linear utilities case of the Fisher model. An EG market is any market whose equilibrium is captured by a similar convex program. Thus, the linear utilities case of Fisher is an example of an EG market. [13] showed that this class captured many other interesting markets including several variants of resource allocation markets defined by Kelly [14] to model TCP congestion control.

The convex program capturing equilibria of EG markets maximizes the money weighted geometric mean of the utilities of buyers over all *feasible* utilities, which form a convex set. For instance, in the program of Eisenberg and Gale [10], the set of feasible utilities are those implied by the condition that no good is over-sold. Thus EG markets do away with the concept of goods and deal only with allocations of utility and one can think of EG markets as *utility allocation markets*.

If the constraints on feasible utilities are just those which limit the total utility obtainable by any set of agents, the EG market so obtained is called an *uniform utility allocation (UUA) market*. The linear utilities case of Fisher with the utility of each unit of good for each agent being either 0 or 1 is a UUA market. UUA markets can be represented via a set-function called the *valuation function*, where the value of any subset of agents denotes the maximum utility obtainable by that set. If the valuation function is submodular, the market is called a *submodular utility allocation (SUA) market*. In fact, the Fisher example above turns out to be a SUA market.

[13] define the notion of *competition monotonicity* which we call *competitiveness* in this paper. In their paper, [13] prove that every SUA market is competitive. They also give an algorithm for computing equilibrium in SUA markets. The paper also asks if there exist competitive UUA markets which are not SUA.

Our results: Our main result, proved in Section 3, answers the question asked in [13]. We show that *any* UUA market which is competitive must be an SUA market. Our characterization of competitive markets in UUA markets shows that the algorithm of [13] works for *all* competitive UUA markets. A natural question is whether there are efficient algorithms for all competitive markets. [13] showed that all WGS markets are competitive and [6] gave efficient algorithms for all WGS markets; this probably gives evidence in favor of existence of algorithms for competitive markets. Competitiveness seems to be a natural property for markets, but a lot remains to understand it clearly. A first step might be investigating competitiveness in EG markets alone. We do not know of any EG markets which are competitive and have irrational equilibria. Apart from SUA markets, the other large class of competitive markets are EG[2] markets [5]: EG markets with only two agents. [5] showed recently that these markets also have rational equilibria. Are all competitive EG markets rational? Settling these questions seems to be an important avenue for research.

Our techniques: We prove all competitive UUA markets are SUA by proving the contrapositive: For *every* UUA market which is not an SUA market, we construct money vectors such that on increasing the money of one particular buyer, the equilibrium utility of some other buyer increases. The main difficulty in constructing these money vectors is that the equilibrium utilities are obtained via solving a convex program with the money as parameters. A change in the money of even one buyer, in general, can change the utilities of all agents.

To argue about the equilibrium utilities, as we see in Section 2, we deal with dual variables, the prices for various subsets of agents, which act as a certificates to equilibrium utility allocations. We use the *non-submodularity* of the valuation function to identify the precise set of agents having money, and the precise amount of money to be given to them. As we see, this construction is delicate, and in particular requires proving the following fact about non-submodular functions which might be of independent interest.

Given an allocation, call a set of agents *tight* (w.r.t the allocation) if the total utility of agents in that set equals the maximum allowed by the valuation function. If a valuation function v is not submodular, then there exists a set of agents T, agents $i, j \notin T$, and a feasible utility allocation so that

1. $T, T \cup i, T \cup j$ are tight.
2. *No set* containing both i and j are tight.
3. *All* tight sets containing i or j also contain a common agent l.

The correctness of the algorithm of [13] for finding equilibria in SUA markets and the proof that SUA markets are competitive use crucially the fact that if v is submodular, tight sets formed are closed under taking unions or intersections. Note that this implies if v is submodular, conditions 1 and 2 cannot hold simultaneously.

2   Preliminaries

Definition 1. *An EG market $\mathcal{M}$ with agents $[n]$ is one where the feasible utilities $u \in \mathbf{R}_+^n$ of the agents can be captured by a polytope*

$$\mathcal{P} = \{\forall j \in J : \quad \sum_{i \in [n]} a_{ij} u(i) \leq b_j \qquad u(i) \geq 0\}$$

with the following free disposal *property: If u is a feasible utility allocation, then so is any u' dominated by u.*

An instance of an EG market $\mathcal{M}$ is given by the money of the agents $m \in \mathbf{R}_+^n$. The equilibrium utility allocation of an EG market is captured by the following convex program similar to the one considered by Eisenberg and Gale [10] for the Fisher market with linear utilities.

$$\max \sum_{i=1}^{n} m_i \log u(i) \quad \text{s.t.} \quad u \in \mathcal{P}$$

Since the objective function is strictly concave and $\mathcal{P}$ is non-empty, the equilibrium always exists and is unique. Applying the Karash-Kuhn-Tucker (KKT) conditions (see e.g. [3]) characterizing optima of convex programs, for each constraint we have a Lagrangean variable p_j which we think of as *price* of the constraint, and we have the following equivalent definition of equilibrium allocations in EG markets.

Definition 2. *Given a market instance* $m \in \mathbf{R}_+^n$ *of an EG market* $\mathcal{M}$, *a feasible utility allocation* $u \in \mathbf{R}_+^n$ *is an* equilibrium allocation *iff there exists prices* $p \in \mathbf{R}_+^{|J|}$ *satisfying*

- *For all agents* $i \in [n]$, $m_i = u(i) \cdot rate(i)$ *where* $rate(i) = (\sum_{j \in J} a_{ij} p(j))$, *the money spent by agent* i *to get unit utility.*
- $\forall j \in J : p(j) > 0$, $\quad \sum_{i \in [n]} a_{ij} u(i) = b_j$

Thus, in the equilibrium allocation, only those constraints are priced which are satisfied with equality (these constraints are called tight constraints), and each agent exhausts his or her money paying for the utility he obtains.

We now consider the case when each a_{ij} above is either 0 or 1.

Definition 3. *An EG market* $\mathcal{M}$ *is a UUA market if the feasible region* $\mathcal{P}$ *of utilities can be encoded via a valuation function* $v : 2^{[n]} \to \mathbf{R}$ *as follows*

$$\mathcal{P} = \{\forall S \subseteq [n] \quad \sum_{i \in S} u(i) \le v(S)\}$$

Such an EG market will be denoted as $\mathcal{M}(v)$, *as the market constraints is completely described by* v.

Definition 4. *If the valuation function* v *in Definition 3 is a submodular function, then the market is called a* Submodular Utility Allocation *(SUA) market. To remind, a function* $v : 2^{[n]} \to \mathbf{R}$ *is submodular if for all sets* $S, T \subseteq [n]$, $v(S \cup T) + v(S \cap T) \le v(S) + v(T)$.

For UUA (and SUA) markets, as in Definition 2 the following gives a characterization of the equilibrium allocation. Given a feasible utility allocation u, a set S is called *tight* if $u(S) \equiv \sum_{i \in S} u(i) = v(S)$.

Definition 5. *For a UUA market, an utility allocation* u *is the equilibrium allocation iff there exists prices for each subset* $S \subseteq [n]$ *such that*

- $\forall S \subseteq [n], p(S) > 0 \Rightarrow S$ *is tight.*
- *For all* $i \in [n]$, $m_i = u(i) \cdot rate(i)$ *where* $rate(i) = \sum_{i \in S} p(S)$.

Given a UUA market, the following observation of [13] shows assumptions we can make on the valuation function.

Lemma 1. *The valuation function* v *of UUA markets can be assumed to have the following properties*

- *Non degeneracy:* $v(\varnothing) = 0$
- *Monotonicity:* $S \subseteq T \Rightarrow v(S) \le v(T)$

- Non redundancy of sets: *For any subset of agents $T \subseteq [n]$, there exists a feasible utility allocation u such that $\sum_{i \in T} u(i) = v(T)$.*
- Complement free: $v(S \cup T) \leq v(S) + v(T)$.

Definition 6. ([13]) *An EG market $\mathcal{M}$ is* competitive *(competition monotone in [13]) if for any money vector m, any agent $i \in [n]$ and all $\epsilon > 0$, let u, u' be the equilibrium allocations with money m and m', where $m'(j) = m(j)$ for all $j \neq i$ and $m'(i) = m(i) + \epsilon$, we have $u'(j) \leq u(j)$ for all $j \neq i$.*

In Section 3, we prove the main result of this paper.

Theorem 1. *If a UUA market is competitive, then it is an SUA market.*

3   Competitive *UUA* Markets Are *SUA* Markets

In this section we prove Theorem 1. Let $\mathcal{M}$ be any UUA market which is not an SUA market. We construct money vectors m_1 and m_2 along with the respective equilibrium utility allocations u_1 and u_2, with the following properties:

- $m_2(i) \geq m_1(i)$ for all $i \in [n]$
- There exists j with $m_2(j) = m_1(j)$ and $u_2(j) > u_1(j)$

We first show the above contradicts competitiveness. Since m_2 is greater than m_1 in each coordinate, we can construct vectors $m'_1, m'_2, \cdots, m'_k$ for some k, such that $m'_1 = m_1$, $m'_k = m_2$ and each consecutive m'_i, m'_{i+1} differ in exactly one coordinate j' with $m'_{i+1}(j') > m'_i(j')$. Note that $m'_i(j) = m_1(j) = m_2(j)$.

Let $u'_1, u'_2, \cdots, u'_k$ be the equilibrium allocations corresponding to the money vectors. We have $u_1 = u'_1$ and $u_2 = u'_k$. $u_2(j) > u_1(j)$ implies for some consecutive $i, i+1$ also $u'_{i+1}(j) > u'_i(j)$. Since $m'_{i+1}(j) = m'_i(j)$, we get the contradiction.

To construct the vectors m_1, m_2, we need the following structural theorem about set-valued functions.

Theorem 2. *Given any valuation function v satisfying the conditions of Lemma 1 which is not submodular, there exists set T, i, j and a feasible utility allocation u such that*

1. *$T, T \cup i, T \cup j$ are tight.*
2. *No set containing both i and j is tight*
3. *All tight sets containing either i or j contain a common element l with $u(l) > 0$.*

The proof of the theorem is technical and we do not provide it in this abstract. We refer the interested reader to the full version of this paper [4].

Let T, i, j, l, u be as in the theorem above. To construct both the instances, we first construct feasible utilities and then derive the money vectors such that the utilities are indeed equilibrium utility allocations.

Let $u_1 := u$ except $u_1(i) = 0$. Define $m_1(k) = u_1(k)$ for all k. By condition 1 in Theorem 2, we get $T \cup j$ is tight. Pricing $p(T \cup j) = 1$ shows u_1 is the equilibrium allocation with respect to m_1.

Let $u_2 := u$ except $u_2(i) = u(i) + \epsilon$, $u_2(j) = u(j) + \epsilon$ and $u_2(l) = u(l) - \epsilon$ for some $\epsilon > 0$. ϵ is picked to satisfy two properties: $(a)\epsilon \leq u(l)/2$ and $(b)u_2$ is feasible. We show later how to pick ϵ. Construct m_2 as follows. Define $p' := u_1(j)/u_2(j)$. $m_2(j) = m_1(j)$, $m_2(k) = (2 + p')u_2(k)$ for all $k \in T$, and $m_2(i) = u_2(i)$. Check that m_2 dominates m_1 in each coordinate and $m_2(j) = m_1(j)$.

To see u_2 is an equilibrium allocation w.r.t m_2, note that $T \cup i$, $T \cup j$ remain tight. Let $p(T \cup i) = 2$, $p(T \cup j) = p'$. Check all the conditions of Definition 5 are satisfied.

The proof is complete via the definition of ϵ. Note that in the allocation u_2, the sets which have more utility than in u are ones which contain i or j. By conditions 2,3 of Theorem 2, one can choose ϵ small enough so that u_2 doesn't make any new set tight and is smaller than $u(l)/2$. This completes the proof of Theorem 1.

References

1. Arrow, K., Block, H., Hurwicz, L.: On the stability of the competitive equilibrium: II. Econometrica 27(1), 82–109 (1959)
2. Arrow, K., Hurwicz, L.: Weak gross substitutability and the existence of competitive equilibria. International Economic Review 33, 38–49 (1965)
3. Boyd, S., Vandenberghe, L.: Convex Optimization. Cambridge University Press, Cambridge (2004)
4. Chakrabarty, D., Devanur, N.: On competitiveness in uniform utility allocation markets. Available online, http://www.cc.gatech.edu/~deepc/
5. Chakrabarty, D., Devanur, N.R., Vazirani, V.V.: New results on rationality and strongly polynomial time solvability in Eisenberg-Gale markets. In: Spirakis, P.G., Mavronicolas, M., Kontogiannis, S.C. (eds.) WINE 2006. LNCS, vol. 4286, Springer, Heidelberg (2006)
6. Codenotti, B., Pemmaraju, S., Varadarajan, K.: On the polynomial time computation of equilibria for certain exchange economies. In: Proceedings of ACM Symposium on Discrete Algorithms, ACM Press, New York (2005)
7. Codenotti, B., Varadarajan, K.: Efficient computation of equilibrium prices for markets with Leontief utilities. In: Díaz, J., Karhumäki, J., Lepistö, A., Sannella, D. (eds.) ICALP 2004. LNCS, vol. 3142, Springer, Heidelberg (2004)
8. Devanur, N., Papadimitriou, C.H., Saberi, A., Vazirani, V.V.: Market equilibrium via a primal-dual-type algorithm. In: Proceedings of IEEE Annual Symposium on Foundations of Computer Science, IEEE Computer Society Press, Los Alamitos (2002)
9. Devanur, N., Vazirani, V.V.: The spending constraint model for market equilibrium: Algorithmic, existence and uniqueness results. In: Proceedings of 36th STOC (2004)
10. Eisenberg, E., Gale, D.: Consensus of subjective probabilities: the Pari-Mutuel method. The Annals of Mathematical Statistics 30, 165–168 (1959)
11. Garg, D., Jain, K., Talwar, K., Vazirani, V.: A primal-dual algorithm for computing Fisher equilibrium in absence of gross substitutability property. In: Deng, X., Ye, Y. (eds.) WINE 2005. LNCS, vol. 3828, Springer, Heidelberg (2005)

12. Jain, K.: A polynomial time algorithm for computing the Arrow-Debreu market equilibrium for linear utilities. In: FOCS (2004)
13. Jain, K., Vazirani, V.V.: Eisenberg-Gale markets: Algorithms and structural properties. In: STOC (2007)
14. Kelly, F.P.: Charging and rate control for elastic traffic. European Transactions on Telecommunications 8, 33–37 (1997)
15. Kuga, K.: Competitive stability under weak gross substitutability: The euclidean distance approach. Internation Economic Review 1, 593–599 (1960)

Total Latency in Singleton Congestion Games[*]

Martin Gairing[1] and Florian Schoppmann[2]

[1] International Computer Science Institute, Berkeley, CA, USA
gairing@icsi.berkeley.edu
[2] International Graduate School of Dynamic Intelligent Systems,
University of Paderborn, Paderborn, Germany
fschopp@uni-paderborn.de

Abstract. We provide a collection of new upper and lower bounds on the *price of anarchy* for *singleton congestion games*. In our study, we distinguish between restricted and unrestricted strategy sets, between weighted and unweighted player weights, and between linear and polynomial latency functions.

1 Introduction

Congestion games [19] and variants thereof [17] have long been used to model non-cooperative resource sharing among selfish players. Examples include traffic behavior in road or communication networks or competition among firms for production processes. In this work, we study *singleton congestion games* where each player's *strategy* consists only of a single resource. A sample application for these modified games is load balancing [3].

The focal point of our work is determining the *price of anarchy* [15], a measure of the extent to which competition approximates the global objective, e.g., the minimum total travel time (latency) in the case of road networks. Typically, the price of anarchy is the worst-case ratio between the value of an objective function in some state where no *player* can *unilaterally* improve its situation, and that of some optimum. As such, the price of anarchy represents a rendezvous of *Nash equilibrium* [18], a concept fundamental to Game Theory, with *approximation*, an omnipresent concept in Theoretical Computer Science today.

1.1 Preliminaries and Model

Notation. For all $d \in \mathbb{N}$, let $[d] := \{1, \ldots, d\}$ and $[d]_0 := [d] \cup \{0\}$. For a vector $\mathsf{v} = (v_1, \ldots, v_n)$, let $(\mathsf{v}_{-i}, v_i') := (v_1, \ldots, v_{i-1}, v_i', v_{i+1}, \ldots, v_n)$. Moreover, we denote by B_d the d-th Bell Number and by Φ_d a natural generalization of the golden ratio such that Φ_d is the (only) positive real solution to $(x+1)^d = x^{d+1}$.

---

[*] Work partially supported by the European Union within the Integrated Project IST-15964 "Algorithmic Principles for Building Efficient Overlay Computers" (AEOLUS). Research for this work was done while the first author was at the University of Paderborn.

X. Deng and F.C. Graham (Eds.): WINE 2007, LNCS 4858, pp. 381–387, 2007.

Instance. A (weighted) *singleton congestion game* is a tuple $\Gamma = \left(n, m, (w_i)_{i \in [n]}, (S_i)_{i \in [n]}, (f_e)_{e \in [m]}\right)$. Here, n is the number of *players* and m is the number of *resources*. For every player $i \in [n]$, $w_i \in \mathbb{R}_{>0}$ is its *weight* (w.l.o.g., $w_i = 1$ if Γ is *unweighted*) and $S_i \subseteq [m]$ its *pure strategy set*. Denote by $W := \sum_{i \in [n]} w_i$ the *total weight* of the players. Strategy sets are *unrestricted* if $S_i = [m]$ for all $i \in [n]$ and *restricted* otherwise. Denote $S := S_1 \times \dots \times S_n$. For every resource $e \in [m]$, the *latency function* $f_e : \mathbb{R}_{\geq 0} \to \mathbb{R}_{\geq 0}$ defines the *latency* on resource e. We consider *polynomial latency functions* with maximum degree d and non-negative coefficients, i.e., for each $e \in [m]$, the latency function is of the form $f_e(x) = \sum_{j=0}^{d} a_{e,j} \cdot x^j$ with $a_{e,j} \geq 0$ for all $j \in [d]_0$. For the special case of *affine latency functions*, we let $a_e := a_{e,1}$ and $b_e := a_{e,0}$, i.e., for any $e \in [m]$ we have $f_e(x) = a_e \cdot x + b_e$. Affine latency functions are *linear* if $b_e = 0$ for all $e \in [m]$.

Strategies and Strategy Profiles. A *mixed* strategy $P_i = (P_{i,e})_{e \in S_i}$ of player $i \in [n]$ is a probability distribution over S_i. For a pair of pure and mixed *strategy profiles* $\boldsymbol{s} = (s_1, \dots, s_n)$ and $\mathbf{P} = (P_1, \dots, P_n)$, we denote by $\mathbf{P}(\boldsymbol{s}) := \prod_{i \in [n]} P_{i,s_i}$ the probability that the players choose $\boldsymbol{s}$. Throughout the paper, we identify any pure strategy (profile) with the respective degenerate mixed strategy (profile).

Load and Private Cost. Denote by $\delta_e(\mathbf{P}) = \sum_{i \in [n]} P_{i,e} \cdot w_i$ the (expected) *load* on resource $e \in [m]$ under profile $\mathbf{P}$. The *private cost* of a player $i \in [n]$ is $\mathsf{PC}_i(\mathbf{P}) := \sum_{\boldsymbol{s} \in S} \mathbf{P}(\boldsymbol{s}) \cdot f_{s_i}(\delta_{s_i}(\boldsymbol{s}))$.

Nash Equilibria. A profile $\mathbf{P}$ is a *Nash equilibrium* if no player $i \in [n]$ could unilaterally improve its private cost; i.e., $\mathsf{PC}_i(\mathbf{P}) \leq \mathsf{PC}_i(\mathbf{P}_{-i}, e)$ for all $i \in [n]$ and $e \in S_i$. Depending on the profile, we distinguish *pure* and *mixed* Nash equilibria. $\mathcal{NE}(\Gamma)$ and $\mathcal{NE}_{\mathsf{pure}}(\Gamma)$ are the sets of all mixed (resp. pure) Nash equilibria.

Social Cost. *Social cost* $\mathsf{SC}(\Gamma, \mathbf{P})$ is defined as the (expected) *total latency* [20], i.e., $\mathsf{SC}(\Gamma, \mathbf{P}) := \sum_{\boldsymbol{s} \in S} \mathbf{P}(\boldsymbol{s}) \sum_{e \in [m]} \delta_e(\boldsymbol{s}) \cdot f_e(\delta_e(\boldsymbol{s})) = \sum_{i \in [n]} w_i \cdot \mathsf{PC}_i(\mathbf{P})$. The *optimum total latency* is $\mathsf{OPT}(\Gamma) := \min_{\boldsymbol{s} \in S} \mathsf{SC}(\Gamma, \boldsymbol{s})$.

Price of Anarchy. Let $\mathcal{G}$ be a class of weighted singleton congestion games. The *mixed price of anarchy* is defined as $\mathsf{PoA}(\mathcal{G}) := \sup_{\Gamma \in \mathcal{G}, \mathbf{P} \in \mathcal{NE}(\Gamma)} \frac{\mathsf{SC}(\Gamma, \mathbf{P})}{\mathsf{OPT}(\Gamma)}$. For the definition of the *pure price of anarchy* $\mathsf{PoA}_{\mathsf{pure}}$ replace $\mathcal{NE}$ with $\mathcal{NE}_{\mathsf{pure}}$.

1.2   Previous Work and Our Contribution

The price of anarchy was first introduced and studied by Koutsoupias and Papadimitriou [15] for weighted singleton congestion games with unrestricted strategy sets and linear latency functions, yet social cost defined as the expected maximum latency on a resource. Their setting became known as the *KP-model* and initiated a sequence of papers determining the price of anarchy both for the KP-model and generalizations thereof; see, e.g., [14,9,12,10,13,6].

For general (weighted) congestion games and social cost defined as the total latency, exact values for the price of anarchy have been given in [2,5,1]. In particular, Aland et al. [1] proved that for identical players the price of anarchy for polynomial latency functions (of maximum degree d and with non-negative

Table 1. Lower/upper bounds on the price of anarchy for singleton congestion games. Terms $o(1)$ are in m.

	$f_e(x) =$	player	PoA$_{\text{pure}}$ LB	PoA$_{\text{pure}}$ UP	PoA LB	PoA UP
unrestricted strategies	x	ident.	1		$2 - \frac{1}{m}$ [16]	
	x	arb.	$\frac{9}{8}$ [16]		$2 - \frac{1}{m}$ [16,12]	
	$a_e x$	ident.	$\frac{4}{3}$ [16]		$2 - \frac{1}{m}$ (T.1)	
	$a_e x$	arb.	$2 - o(1)$ (T.2)	$1 + \Phi$ [2]	2.036 (T.3)	$1 + \Phi$ [2]
	x^d	ident.	1		$B_{d+1} - o(1)$ [11]	B_{d+1} [11]
	$\sum_{j=0}^{d} a_{e,j} x^j$	arb.	$B_{d+1} - o(1)$ (T.2)	Φ_d^{d+1} [1]		
restricted strategies	x	ident.	2.012 [21]	2.012 [3]		
	$a_e x$	ident.	$\frac{5}{2} - o(1)$ [3]	$\frac{5}{2}$ [21]	$\frac{5}{2} - o(1)$ [3]	$\frac{5}{2}$ [4]
	$\sum_{j=0}^{d} a_{e,j} x^j$	ident.	$\Upsilon(d) - o(1)$ (T.5)	$\Upsilon(d)$ [1]	$\Upsilon(d) - o(1)$ (T.5)	$\Upsilon(d)$ [1]
	$a_e x$	arb.	$1 + \Phi - o(1)$ [3]	$1 + \Phi$ [2]	$1 + \Phi - o(1)$ [3]	$1 + \Phi$ [2]
	$\sum_{j=0}^{d} a_{e,j} x^j$	arb.	$\Phi_d^{d+1} - o(1)$ (T.4)	Φ_d^{d+1} [1]	$\Phi_d^{d+1} - o(1)$ (T.4)	Φ_d^{d+1} [1]

coefficients) is exactly $\Upsilon(d) := \frac{(\lambda+1)^{2d+1} - \lambda^{d+1}(\lambda+2)^d}{(\lambda+1)^{d+1} - (\lambda+2)^d + (\lambda+1)^d - \lambda^{d+1}}$, where $\lambda = \lfloor \Phi_d \rfloor$. For weighted players the price of anarchy increases slightly to Φ_d^{d+1} [1].

Finally, singleton congestion games with social cost defined as the total latency have been studied in [3,11,16,21]; see Table 1 for a comparison. Since such games always possess a pure Nash equilibrium (if latency functions are non-decreasing [8]), also the *pure* price of anarchy is of interest. In this work, we prove a collection of new bounds on the price of anarchy for multiple interesting classes of singleton congestion games, as shown (and highlighted by a gray background) in Table 1. Surprisingly, the upper bounds from [1] – proved for general congestion games with polynomial latency functions – are already exact for the case of singleton strategy sets and pure Nash equilibria.

2   Unrestricted Strategy Sets

Proposition 1. *Let Γ be a weighted singleton congestion game with unrestricted strategy sets, affine latency functions and associated Nash equilibrium* **P**. *Then, for all nonempty subsets* $\mathcal{M} \subseteq [m]$, $SC(\Gamma, \mathbf{P}) \leq \sum_{i \in [n]} w_i \cdot \frac{W + (|\mathcal{M}| - 1)w_i + \sum_{j \in \mathcal{M}} \frac{b_j}{a_j}}{\sum_{j \in \mathcal{M}} \frac{1}{a_j}}$.

Proposition 2. *Let Γ be a weighted singleton congestion game with unrestricted strategy sets and affine latency functions. Let* $\mathbf{s}$ *be an associated pure strategy profile with optimum total latency and let* $\mathcal{M} = \{e : \delta_e(\mathbf{s}) > 0\}$. *Define* $X = \{\mathbf{x} \in \mathbb{R}_{\geq 0}^{\mathcal{M}} : \sum_{j \in \mathcal{M}} x_j = W\}$ *and let* $\mathbf{x}^* \in \arg\min_{\mathbf{x} \in X} \{\sum_{j \in \mathcal{M}} x_j \cdot f_j(x_j)\}$. *Denote* $\mathcal{M}^* = \{j \in \mathcal{M} : x_j^* > 0\}$. *Then,* $OPT(\Gamma) = SC(\Gamma, \mathbf{s}) \geq \frac{W^2 + \frac{W}{2} \cdot \sum_{j \in \mathcal{M}^*} \frac{b_j}{a_j}}{\sum_{j \in \mathcal{M}^*} \frac{1}{a_j}}$.

We are now equipped with all tools to prove the following upper bounds:

Theorem 1. *Let $\mathcal{G}_a$ be the class of unweighted singleton congestion games with at most m resources, unrestricted strategy sets and affine latency functions and $\mathcal{G}_b$ be the subset of $\mathcal{G}_a$ with linear latency functions. Then (a) $\mathsf{PoA}(\mathcal{G}_a) < 2$ and (b) $\mathsf{PoA}(\mathcal{G}_b) \leq 2 - \frac{1}{m}$.*

Theorem 2. *Let $\mathcal{G}$ be the class of weighted singleton congestion games with unrestricted strategy sets and polynomial latency functions of maximum degree d. Then $\mathsf{PoA}_{\mathsf{pure}}(\mathcal{G}) \geq B_{d+1}$.*

Proof. For some parameter $k \in \mathbb{N}$ define the following weighted singleton congestion game $\Gamma(k)$ with unrestricted strategy sets and polynomial latency functions:

- There are $k + 1$ disjoint sets $\mathcal{M}_0, \ldots, \mathcal{M}_k$ of resources. Set $\mathcal{M}_j, j \in [k]_0$, consists of $|\mathcal{M}_j| = 2^{k-j} \cdot \frac{k!}{j!}$ resources sharing the polynomial latency function $f_e(x) = 2^{-jd} \cdot x^d$ for all resources $e \in \mathcal{M}_j$.
- There are k disjoint sets of players $\mathcal{N}_1, \ldots, \mathcal{N}_k$. Set $\mathcal{N}_j, j \in [k]$, consists of $|\mathcal{N}_j| = |\mathcal{M}_{j-1}| = 2^{k-(j-1)} \cdot \frac{k!}{(j-1)!}$ players with weight $w_i = 2^{j-1}$ for all players $i \in \mathcal{N}_j$.

Observe that $|\mathcal{M}_j| = 2^{k-j} \cdot \frac{k!}{j!} = 2^{k-(j+1)} \cdot \frac{k!}{(j+1)!} \cdot 2(j+1) = |\mathcal{M}_{j+1}| \cdot 2(j+1)$.

Let s be a pure strategy profile that assigns exactly $2j$ players from $\mathcal{N}_j$ to each resource in $\mathcal{M}_j$ for $j \in [k]_0$. Then, for all resources $e \in \mathcal{M}_j, j \in [k]$, we have $\delta_e(s) = 2j \cdot 2^{j-1} = j \cdot 2^j$ and $f_e(\delta_e(s)) = 2^{-jd} \cdot (j \cdot 2^j)^d = j^d$. It is now easy to check that s is a Nash equilibrium for $\Gamma(k)$ with $\mathsf{SC}(\Gamma(k), s) = 2^k \cdot k! \cdot \sum_{j \in [k]_0} \frac{j^{d+1}}{j!}$. Now let s^* be a strategy profile that assigns each player $\mathcal{N}_j$ to a separate resource in $\mathcal{M}_{j-1}$. Then, for all resources $e \in \mathcal{M}_j, j \in [k-1]_0$, we have $\delta_e(s^*) = 2^j$ and $f_e(\delta_e(s^*)) = 2^{-jd} \cdot (2^j)^d = 1$. So $\mathsf{SC}(\Gamma(k), s^*) = 2^k \cdot k! \sum_{j \in [k-1]_0} \frac{1}{j!}$. Hence,

$$\mathsf{PoA}_{\mathsf{pure}}(\mathcal{G}) \geq \lim_{k \to \infty} \frac{\mathsf{SC}(\Gamma(k), s)}{\mathsf{SC}(\Gamma(k), s^*)} = \frac{\sum_{j=1}^{\infty} \frac{j^{d+1}}{j!}}{\sum_{j=0}^{\infty} \frac{1}{j!}} = \frac{1}{e} \sum_{j=1}^{\infty} \frac{j^{d+1}}{j!} = B_{d+1}. \qquad \square$$

Theorem 3. *Let $\mathcal{G}$ be the class of weighted singleton congestion games with unrestricted strategy sets and linear latency functions. Then $\mathsf{PoA}(\mathcal{G}) > 2.036$.*

Proof. For $w \in \mathbb{R}_{>0}$, define the singleton congestion game $\Gamma(w)$ with 5 players of weights $w_1 = w$ and $w_i = 1$ for $i \in \{2, \ldots, 5\}$ and 5 resources with latency functions $f_1(x) = \frac{w}{w+4} \cdot x$ and $f_e(x) = x$ for $e \in \{2, \ldots, 5\}$.

Let $s := (i)_{i=1}^n \in S$ and let $\mathbf{P}$ be the mixed strategy profile where $P_{1,1} = p$, $P_{1,e} = \frac{1-p}{4}$ for $e \in \{2, \ldots, 5\}$, and $P_{i,1} = 1$ for $i \in \{2, \ldots, 5\}$. It is easy to check that $\mathbf{P}$ is a Nash equilibrium for $p \leq \frac{w^2 - 8w + 16}{5w^2 + 4w}$. Since $\mathsf{SC}(\Gamma(w), \mathbf{P}) = p\frac{4w^2}{w+4} + \frac{16w}{w+4} + w^2$ is monotonically increasing in p, choose $p = \frac{w^2 - 8w + 16}{5w^2 + 4w}$. Clearly, $\mathsf{PoA}(\mathcal{G}) \geq \frac{\mathsf{SC}(\Gamma(w), \mathbf{P})}{\mathsf{SC}(\Gamma(w), s)}$. Setting $w = 3.258$ yields the claimed lower bound. $\square$

3   Restricted Strategy Sets

Theorem 4. *Let $\mathcal{G}$ be the class of weighted singleton congestion games with restricted strategy sets and polynomial latency functions of maximum degree d. Then $\mathsf{PoA}(\mathcal{G}) = \mathsf{PoA}_{\mathsf{pure}}(\mathcal{G}) = \Phi_d^{d+1}$.*

Proof. Due to [1], we only need to show the lower bound. For $n \in \mathbb{N}$, define the singleton congestion game $\Gamma(n)$ with n players and $n + 1$ resources. The weight of player $i \in [n]$ is $w_i = \Phi_d^i$ and the latency functions are $f_{n+1}(x) = \Phi_d^{-(d+1)\cdot(n-1)} \cdot x^d$ for resource $n + 1$ and $f_e(x) = \Phi_d^{-(d+1)\cdot e} \cdot x^d$ for resources $e \in [n]$. Each player $i \in [n]$ only has two available resources: $S_i = \{i, i+1\}$.

Let $s := (i)_{i=1}^n \in S$. One can verify that s is a Nash Equilibrium and $\mathsf{SC}(\Gamma(n), s) = n$. Now let $s^* := (i + 1)_{i=1}^n \in S$. Then, $\mathsf{SC}(\Gamma(n), s^*) = (n - 1) \cdot \frac{1}{\Phi_d^{d+1}} + 1$, so $\sup_{n \in \mathbb{N}} \left\{ \frac{\mathsf{SC}(\Gamma(n), s)}{\mathsf{SC}(\Gamma(n), s^*)} \right\} = \Phi_d^{d+1}$. $\square$

Theorem 5. *Let $\mathcal{G}$ be the class of unweighted singleton congestion games with restricted strategy sets and polynomial latency functions of maximum degree d. Then $\mathsf{PoA}(\mathcal{G}) = \mathsf{PoA}_{\mathsf{pure}}(\mathcal{G}) = \Upsilon(d)$.*

Proof (Sketch). For $k \in \mathbb{N}$, define an unweighted singleton congestion game $\Gamma(k)$. We borrow the representation introduced by [7] which makes use of an "interaction graph" $G = (N, A)$: Resources correspond to nodes and players correspond to arcs. Every player has exactly two strategies, namely choosing one or the other of its adjacent nodes.

The interaction graph is a tree which is constructed as follows: At the root there is a complete $(d+1)$-ary tree with $k + 1$ levels. Each leaf of this tree is then the root of a complete d-ary tree the leafs of which are again the root of a complete $(d - 1)$-ary tree; and so on. 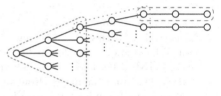 This recursive definition stops with the unary trees. For an example of this construction, see Figure 1.

Fig. 1. The game graph for $d = k = 2$

Altogether, the game graph consists of $(d + 1) \cdot k + 1$ levels. We let level 0 denote the root level. Thus, clearly, the nodes on level $i \cdot k$, where $i \in [d]_0$, are the root of a complete $(d + 1 - i)$-ary subtree (as indicated by the hatched shapes).

For any resource on level $(d+1-i)\cdot k+j$, where $i \in [d+1]$ and $j \in [k-1]_0$, let the latency function be $f_{i,j} : \mathbb{R}_{\geq 0} \to \mathbb{R}_{\geq 0}$, $f_{i,j}(x) := \left[\prod_{l=i+1}^{d+1} \frac{l}{l+1} \right]^{d\cdot(k-1)} \cdot \left(\frac{i}{i+1} \right)^{dj} \cdot x^d$. The resources on level $(d + 1) \cdot k$ have the same latency function $f_{0,0} := f_{1,k-1}$ as those on level $(d + 1) \cdot k - 1$.

Let s denote the strategy profile in $\Gamma(k)$ where each player uses the resource which is closer to the root. Similarly, let s^* be the profile where players us the resources farther away from the root. One can verify that s is a Nash equilibrium and the quotient $\frac{\mathsf{SC}(\Gamma(k), s)}{\mathsf{SC}(\Gamma(k), s^*)}$ can be written in the form $\frac{\sum_{i=0}^{d+1} \beta_i \cdot \alpha_i^{k-1}}{\sum_{i=0}^{d+1} \gamma_i \cdot \alpha_i^{k-1}}$ where $\beta_i, \gamma_i \in \mathbb{Q}$, $\alpha_0 = 1$, and $\alpha_i = \prod_{l=i}^{d+1} \frac{l^{d+1}}{(l+1)^d} = \frac{i^{d+1}}{(d+2)^d} \cdot \prod_{l=i+1}^{d+1} l$ for all $i \in [d+1]$.

Now let $\lambda := \lfloor \Phi_d \rfloor$. Then, $(\lambda + 1)^d > \lambda^{d+1}$ but $(\lambda + 2)^d < (\lambda + 1)^{d+1}$, so $\lambda \in [d]$. It holds that $\alpha_{\lambda+1} > \alpha_i$ for all $i \in [d + 1]_0 \setminus \{\lambda + 1\}$ because, for all $i \in [d]$, $\alpha_{i+1} > \alpha_i$ if and only if $(i + 1)^d > i^{d+1}$ and $\alpha_1 = \frac{(d+1)!}{(d+2)^d} < 1$

386   M. Gairing and F. Schoppmann

and $\alpha_{d+1} = \frac{(d+1)^{d+1}}{(d+2)^d} > 1$. Using standard calculus we therefore get $\lim_{k\to\infty} \frac{SC(\Gamma(k),s)}{SC(\Gamma(k),s^*)} = \frac{\beta_{\lambda+1}}{\gamma_{\lambda+1}} = \frac{(\lambda+1)^{2d+1}-\lambda^{d+1}\cdot(\lambda+2)^d}{(\lambda+1)^{d+1}-(\lambda+2)^d+(\lambda+1)^d-\lambda^{d+1}}$. $\square$

References

1. Aland, S., Dumrauf, D., Gairing, M., Monien, B., Schoppmann, F.: Exact Price of Anarchy for Polynomial Congestion Games. In: Durand, B., Thomas, W. (eds.) STACS 2006. LNCS, vol. 3884, pp. 218–229. Springer, Heidelberg (2006)
2. Awerbuch, B., Azar, Y., Epstein, A.: The Price of Routing Unsplittable Flow. In: Proc. of 37th STOC, pp. 57–66 (2005)
3. Caragiannis, I., Flammini, M., Kaklamanis, C., Kanellopoulos, P., Moscardelli, L.: Tight Bounds for Selfish and Greedy Load Balancing. In: Bugliesi, M., Preneel, B., Sassone, V., Wegener, I. (eds.) ICALP 2006. LNCS, vol. 4051, pp. 311–322. Springer, Heidelberg (2006)
4. Christodoulou, G., Koutsoupias, E.: On The Price of Anarchy and Stability of Correlated Equilibria of Linear Congestion Games. In: Brodal, G.S., Leonardi, S. (eds.) ESA 2005. LNCS, vol. 3669, pp. 59–70. Springer, Heidelberg (2005)
5. Christodoulou, G., Koutsoupias, E.: The Price of Anarchy of Finite Congestion Games. In: Proc. of 37th STOC, pp. 67–73 (2005)
6. Czumaj, A., Vöcking, B.: Tight Bounds for Worst-Case Equilibria. ACM Transactions on Algorithms 3(1) (2007) (Article No. 4)
7. Elsässer, R., Gairing, M., Lücking, T., Mavronicolas, M., Monien, B.: A Simple Graph-Theoretic Model for Selfish Restricted Scheduling. In: Deng, X., Ye, Y. (eds.) WINE 2005. LNCS, vol. 3828, pp. 195–209. Springer, Heidelberg (2005)
8. Fotakis, D., Kontogiannis, S., Koutsoupias, E., Mavronicolas, M., Spirakis, P.: The Structure and Complexity of Nash Equilibria for a Selfish Routing Game. In: Widmayer, P., Triguero, F., Morales, R., Hennessy, M., Eidenbenz, S., Conejo, R. (eds.) ICALP 2002. LNCS, vol. 2380, pp. 123–134. Springer, Heidelberg (2002)
9. Gairing, M., Lücking, T., Mavronicolas, M., Monien, B.: Computing Nash Equilibria for Scheduling on Restricted Parallel Links. In: Proc. of 36th STOC, pp. 613–622 (2004)
10. Gairing, M., Lücking, T., Mavronicolas, M., Monien, B.: The Price of Anarchy for Restricted Parallel Links. Parallel Processing Letters 16(1), 117–131 (2006)
11. Gairing, M., Lücking, T., Mavronicolas, M., Monien, B., Rode, M.: Nash Equilibria in Discrete Routing Games with Convex Latency Functions. In: Díaz, J., Karhumäki, J., Lepistö, A., Sannella, D. (eds.) ICALP 2004. LNCS, vol. 3142, pp. 645–657. Springer, Heidelberg (2004)
12. Gairing, M., Monien, B., Tiemann, K.: Selfish Routing with Incomplete Information. In: Proc. of 17th SPAA, pp. 203–212 (2005)
13. Gairing, M., Monien, B., Tiemann, K.: Routing (Un-) Splittable Flow in Games with Player-Specific Linear Latency Functions. In: Bugliesi, M., Preneel, B., Sassone, V., Wegener, I. (eds.) ICALP 2006. LNCS, vol. 4051, pp. 501–512. Springer, Heidelberg (2006)
14. Koutsoupias, E., Mavronicolas, M., Spirakis, P.: Approximate Equilibria and Ball Fusion. Theory of Computing Systems 36(6), 683–693 (2003)
15. Koutsoupias, E., Papadimitriou, C.H.: Worst-Case Equilibria. In: Meinel, C., Tison, S. (eds.) STACS 99. LNCS, vol. 1563, pp. 404–413. Springer, Heidelberg (1999)

16. Lücking, T., Mavronicolas, M., Monien, B., Rode, M.: A New Model for Selfish Routing. In: Diekert, V., Habib, M. (eds.) STACS 2004. LNCS, vol. 2996, pp. 547–558. Springer, Heidelberg (2004)
17. Milchtaich, I.: Congestion Games with Player-Specific Payoff Functions. Games and Economic Behavior 13(1), 111–124 (1996)
18. Nash, J.F.: Non-Cooperative Games. Annals of Mathematics 54(2), 286–295 (1951)
19. Rosenthal, R.W.: A Class of Games Possessing Pure-Strategy Nash Equilibria. International Journal of Game Theory 2, 65–67 (1973)
20. Roughgarden, T., Tardos, E.: How Bad Is Selfish Routing? Journal of the ACM 49(2), 236–259 (2002)
21. Suri, S., Tóth, C.D., Zhou, Y.: Selfish Load Balancing and Atomic Congestion Games. In: Proc. of 16th SPAA, pp. 188–195 (2004)

The Importance of Network Topology in Local Contribution Games

Jacomo Corbo[1], Antoni Calvó-Armengol[2], and David C. Parkes[1]

[1] School of Engineering and Applied Sciences
Harvard University, Cambridge MA 02138, USA
{jacomo,parkes}@eecs.harvard.edu
[2] ICREA, Universitat Autònoma de Barcelona
Barcelona, Spain
antoni.calvo@uab.es

Abstract. We consider a model of content contribution in peer-to-peer networks with linear quadratic payoffs and very general interaction patterns. We find that Nash equilibria of this game always exist; moreover, they are computable by solving a linear complementarity problem. The equilibrium is unique when goods are strategic complements or weak substitutes and contributions are proportional to a network centrality measure called the Bonacich index. In the case of public goods, the equilibrium is non-unique and characterized by k-order maximal independent sets. The structure of optimal networks is always star-like when the game exhibits strict or weak complements. Under public good scenarios, while star-like networks remain optimal in the best case, they also yield the worst-performing equilibria. We also discuss a network-based policy for improving the equilibrium performance of networks by the exclusion of a single player.

1 Introduction

Peer effects, or the dependence of individual outcomes on group behaviour, is a characterizing feature of peer-to-peer systems. File-sharing systems rely on participants to provision the network with content. Participants can experience a marginal increase or decrease in utility from the kind of content contributed by others. We call such goods strategic complements and strategic substitutes, respectively. Following Ballester et al. (2006), we adopt a simple model for a contribution game in this paper. A player is modeled with a *linear-quadratic* utility function, that allows for utility-dependence on the contribution by other players. The utility structure provides for an individualized component, reflecting decreasing marginal-returns for a player's own contribution, in addition to a term that reflects *local interaction* that varies across pairs of players, meaning pairs of players can affect each other differently.

The model is appealing because Nash equilibria are always computable by solving a linear complementarity problem. Moreover, a unique Nash equilibrium of the contribution game can be readily computed as a metric of network centrality when the network exhibits complementarities. When substitutabilities are

X. Deng and F.C. Graham (Eds.): WINE 2007, LNCS 4858, pp. 388–395, 2007.

strong, equilibria are non-unique and the only stable equilibria are characterized by k-order maximal independent sets of optimally-contributing players, with the rest of the population free-riding completely.

We consider the problems of designing networks that maximize aggregate contribution and welfare, and find that the structure of optimal networks is star-like when the game exhibits strict or weak complements. Under public good scenarios, while star-like networks remain optimal in the best case, they also yield the worst-performing equilibria. We discuss a network-based policy aimed at improving the equilibrium performance of networks by the removal of a single *key* player.

This paper situates itself in a growing body of literature interested in games where endogenous play is susceptible to externalities passed along or represented by network links. Jackson (2008) and Kearns (2007) provide a good survey of the area. Demange (2007) and Bramoulle and Kranton (2006) study equilibrium profiles in a game with public (*substitutable*) good provisioning. Johari and Tsitsiklis (2005) and Roughgarden and Tardos (2004) investigate the effects of network architecture on the worst-case efficiency *(the price of anarchy)* of equilibria in routing games. Our model deals with a different payoff structure and allows for externalities to be either complementary or substitutable. We provide a partial characterization of equilibria in our game and relate a network's efficiency, in both the best and worst case, to its geometric properties.

2   The Model

Let $\mathcal{G}(v, e)$ denote the set of undirected and unweighted connected graphs without loops with v vertices and e edges.

Players are connected by a network $\mathbf{g} \in \mathcal{G}(v, e)$ with adjacency matrix $\mathbf{G} = [g_{ij}]$. This is a zero diagonal and non-negative square matrix, with $g_{ij} \in \{0, 1\}$ for all $i \neq j$.

Each player $i = 1, ..., n$ selects a contribution $x_i \geq 0$, and gets a payoff $u_i(x_1, \ldots, x_n)$. Letting $\mathbf{x} = (x_1, \ldots, x_n)$, we focus on *bilinear* utility functions of the form:

$$u_i(\mathbf{x}, \mathbf{g}) = x_i - \frac{1}{2}x_i^2 + a \sum_{j=1}^{n} g_{ij} x_i x_j, \tag{1}$$

The external effect of another agent on the utility of agent i is captured by the cross-derivatives $\frac{\partial^2 u_i}{\partial x_i x_j} = ag_{ij}$, for $i \neq j$. When $a > 0$, the effect on agent i of agent j's contribution is marginal-increasing if and only if i and j are connected in $\mathbf{g}$; when $a < 0$, the effect is marginal-decreasing. The network $\mathbf{g}$ reflects the pattern of existing payoff complementarities when a is positive, and substitutabilities, when a is negative, across all pairs of players. We use Σ to refer to the n-player game with payoffs given by Equation 1 and strategy space, the non-negative real line.

2.1   The Linear Complementarity Problem

We analyze the set of pure strategy Nash equilibria of the game introduced above. We note that an equilibrium exists if and only if $\frac{\partial u_i}{\partial x_i}(x^*) \leq 0, \forall i \in N$. In matrix notation, this necessary and sufficient condition for a Nash equilibrium becomes:

$$\mathbf{x}^* >= \mathbf{0}, \tag{2}$$
$$-\mathbf{a} + \Sigma \mathbf{x}^* >= \mathbf{0},$$
$$-\mathbf{x}^{t*}(-a + \Sigma \mathbf{x}^*) = \mathbf{0}.$$

The problem of finding a vector $\mathbf{x}^*$ such that the above conditions hold is known as the linear complementarity problem $LCP(-a, -\Sigma)$. We can therefore state the following:

Theorem 1. *The set of pure strategy Nash equilibria of the contribution game with parameters α and Σ are given by the set of solutions to $LCP(-\alpha, -\Sigma)$.*

The linear complementarity problem is a well-studied problem and we borrow from this literature to address existence of the Nash equilibrium in our game, as well as in our empirical studies to characterize optimally-designed networks. In the next sections we study the current model under strict complementarities, when $a > 0$, and under substitutabilities, when $a < 0$. The local interaction graph connecting agents becomes irrelevent when $a = 0$, as the contribution levels of other agents does not impact an agent's utility. In this case, the network-independent optimal contribution level for each agent is 1.

3   Complementary Goods

We first study the game under local complementarities, i.e. $a > 0$. Before turning to the equilibrium analysis, we define a network centrality measure due to Bonacich (1987) that proves useful for this analysis.

3.1   The Bonacich Network Centrality Measure

Given the network $\mathbf{g} \in \mathcal{G}(v, e)$, denote by $\lambda_1(\mathbf{g})$ its largest eigenvalue, also called the *index* of $\mathbf{g}$. This index is always well-defined and $\lambda_1(\mathbf{g}) > 0$.

Definition 1. *Let $\mathbf{B}(\mathbf{g}, a) = [\mathbf{I} - a\mathbf{G}]^{-1}$, which is well-defined and non-negative if and only if $a\lambda_1(\mathbf{G}) < 1$. The vector of Bonacich centralities of parameter a in $\mathbf{g}$ is $\mathbf{b}(\mathbf{g}, a) = \mathbf{B}(\mathbf{g}, a) \cdot \mathbf{1}$.*

Since $\mathbf{B}(\mathbf{g}, a) = \sum_{k=0}^{+\infty} a^k \mathbf{G}^k$, its coefficients $b_{ij}(\mathbf{g}, a)$ count the number of paths in $\mathbf{g}$ starting at i and ending at j, where paths of length k are weighted by a^k.

Theorem 2. *For $a\lambda_1(\mathbf{G}) < 1$, the game Σ has a unique Nash equilibrium $\mathbf{x}^*(\Sigma)$ given by $\mathbf{x}^*(\Sigma) = \mathbf{b}(\mathbf{g}, a)$, where the utility of player i at equilibrium is $u_i(\mathbf{x}^*, \mathbf{g}) = \frac{1}{2}x_i^{*2} = \frac{1}{2}b_i(\mathbf{g}, a)^2$.*

The correspondence between the Bonacich centrality indices of a graph and its equilibrium when $a > 0$ establishes the uniqueness and interiority of equilibria when $a\lambda_1(\mathbf{G}) < 1$. When $a\lambda_1(\mathbf{G}) > 1$, an equilibrium fails to exist because the positive feedback from other agents' contributions is too high and contributions increase without bound.

4 Substitutable Goods

When $a < 0$ we have a substitutability effect between players' contributions, i.e. we have a public good game. Contrary to the case when $a > 0$, an equilibrium now always exists. The best-response function is continuous from the compact convex set $\{x \in \mathcal{R}^n : \forall i, 0 \leq x_i \leq x^*\}$ to itself and so Brouwer's Fixed Point Theorem applies. We study the game under two separate conditions: when subtitutabilities are weak and when they are strong, i.e. the case of pure public goods.

4.1 Weak Substitutes

We define the complement network $\overline{\mathbf{G}} = \mathbf{J} - \mathbf{I} - \mathbf{G}$, where $\mathbf{J}$ is the all-ones matrix, i.e., $\overline{g_{ij}} = 1 - g_{ij}$, for all $i \neq j$. In words, two vertices are linked in $\overline{\mathbf{G}}$ if and only if they are not linked in $\mathbf{G}$. We write:

$$\Sigma = (1 + a)\mathbf{I} + a\overline{\mathbf{G}} - a\mathbf{J}.$$

Suppose first that $-1 < a < 0$. Solving for the Nash equilibrium is then equivalent to solving $LCP(-\frac{1}{1+a}\mathbf{e}, \mathbf{I} + \frac{a}{1+a}\overline{\mathbf{G}} - \frac{a}{1+a}\mathbf{J})$. The solution can be equivalently written in terms of the Bonacich index of nodes on the complement network.

Theorem 3. *Consider a game on G where $a < 0$ and let $\overline{\mathbf{G}} = \mathbf{J} - \mathbf{I} - \mathbf{G}$ as before. There exists a unique equilibrium if and only if $-a\lambda_1\left(\overline{\mathbf{G}}\right) < 1 + a$. Then, the equilibrium is unique, interior and proportional to Bonacich, that is,*

$$x_i^* = \frac{1}{1 + a + a\sum_{j=1}^n b_j\left(\frac{-a}{1+a}, \overline{\mathbf{G}}\right)} b_i\left(\frac{-a}{1+a}, \overline{\mathbf{G}}\right), \text{ for all } i = 1, ..., n$$

Recall that we are dealing with the case $-1 < a < 0$. Notice that $-a\lambda_1\left(\overline{\mathbf{G}}\right) < 1 + a$ is equivalent to $-\frac{1}{1+\lambda_1(\overline{\mathbf{G}})} < a$. Therefore, the interior unique equilibrium is obtained on $-\frac{1}{1+\lambda_1(\overline{\mathbf{G}})} < a < 0$.

4.2 Pure Public Goods

When substitutabilities are large, i.e. when $a < -\frac{1}{1+\lambda_1(\overline{\mathbf{G}})}$, the above transformations fail to work. In these circumstances, agents' free-riding on others' contributions is severe enough that some agents do not contribute at all. Agents whose equilibrium contribution levels are non-zero either contribute the optimum (i.e. in this case 1) or some value less than optimum.

Partially Corner Equilibria. Precisely, a partially corner equilibrium profile $\mathbf{x}^*$ on the network $\mathbf{G}(\mathbf{v}, \mathbf{e})$ is one such that there exists some $i, j \in v$ such that $x_i = 0$ and $0 < x_j < 1$. We remark that equilibrium contributions of non-corner agents, i.e. all agents $j \in v$ such that $0 < x_j < 1$, are related to the Bonacich centrality index on the subnetwork joining them.

Lemma 1. *Let $a < 0$. Given a partially corner equilibrium profile $\mathbf{x}$ on the network $\mathbf{G}(\mathbf{v}, \mathbf{e})$, the contribution levels of all nodes i such that $0 < x_i < 1$ is given by the expression in Theorem 3.*

Corner Equilibria. As mentioned earlier, when local substitutabilities are large, corner equilibria, with agents either free-riding completely or contributing optimally, also exist. For such a situation to be an equilibrium, both free-riders and contributors must gain by doing so. Given the graph $\mathbf{G} = (v, e)$, let $N_G(v')$ designate the set of neighbors of node $v' \in v$. We find that all corner equilibria for $a \leq -1$ are described by maximal independent sets of contributors.

Definition 2. *A set $S \subseteq v$ is called a k-order maximal independent set if and only if it is a maximal independent set such that each node not in the set is connected to at least k nodes in the set, i.e. $\forall v' \notin S, |N_G(v') \cap S| \geq k$.*

Theorem 4. *Let $\lceil 1/a \rceil$ be the smallest integer greater than or equal to $|1/a|$. For $a \leq -\frac{1}{1+\lambda_1(\overline{\mathbf{G}})}$, a corner profile is a Nash equilibrium if and only if the set of contributing players, i.e. $\{i \in v : x_i = 1\}$, is a $\lceil 1/a \rceil$-order maximal independent set of the graph $\mathbf{G}$.*

Maximal independent sets correspond to maximal independent sets of order 1. Every graph has a maximal independent set, therefore there always exists a corner equilibrium for $a \leq -1$. However, for $k \geq 2$, k-order maximal independent sets need not always exist. Therefore, when $-1 < a \leq -\frac{1}{1+\lambda_1(\overline{\mathbf{G}})}$, we may not have a corner equilibrium, though we may still have a partially corner equilibrium. Recall that an equilibrium is guaranteed to exist for all $a \leq 0$.

Stable Equilibria. We use a simple notion of stability based on Nash tâtonnement (e.g. Fudenberg 1991). We find that corner equilibria are the only stable equilibria to this perturbed best-response procedure.

Theorem 5. *For any network $\mathbf{G}$, an equilibrium is stable if and only if it is a corner equilibrium.*

The result is convenient because it helps to mitigate the problem of multiple equilibria when $a \leq -\frac{1}{1+\lambda_1(\overline{\mathbf{G}})}$, where $\overline{\mathbf{G}}$ is given as the complement of the network $\mathbf{G}$, as before. The correspondence of corner equilibria to maximal independent sets of order k also gives us insight into the computational complexity of computing equilibria under substitutabilities. These results are discussed in the full paper (Corbo et al. 2007) and are leveraged in this paper's empirical studies to solve for a graph's contribution-maximizing (best-case) and contribution-minimizing (worst-case) equilibria, across all a when equilibria are non-unique.

5   Optimal Network Design

The problem of optimal network design consists of arranging a network's v vertices and e edges in such a way that some objective function is maximized. In the first problem, the social planner wants to maximize aggregate activity (or contribution) at equilibrium. In the second problem, the social planner wants

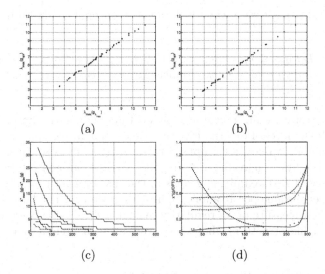

(a)   (b)

(c)   (d)

Fig. 1. (a) shows that the first eigenvalue of aggregate contribution- and utility-maximizing equilibrium graphs corresponds to the largest first eigenvalue possible for v, e. When equilibria are non-unique, (a) includes the best case equilibrium performance of the graph, while (b) plots the first eigenvalue of networks with best worst-case stable equilibrium performance (against the smallest first eigenvalue possible for v, e). (a), (b) refer to networks with varying number of edges while keeping $v = 12$ and $-3 < a < 0.5$. (c) shows the difference in aggregate contribution for the best- and worst-case equilibria, for graphs with the best best-case and best worst-case performance, fixing $a = -1$. $v = 15$ **(dash blue)**, 25 **(dot-dash blue)**, 35 **(solid red)**. (d) shows the best-case and worst-case equilibrium performance of graphs with best worst-case performance **(dot-dash blue)** compared to graphs with best best-case performance **(solid red)**, for $v = 12$, $a = -1$. The best best-case performing graphs have worse worst-case performance. The **dash black** curve in (d) gives the worst-case performance of graphs with the *key player* removed, starting from the best best-case performing graphs **(solid red)**.

to maximize aggregate equilibrium welfare. When equilibria are non-unique, we consider both the best case and worst case, respectively contribution- or utility-maximizing and contribution- or utility-minimizing, equilibria of networks. We study the relationship between the best-case and worst-case equilibria of a given network, and particularly how contribution- or utility-maximizing networks in the best case perform in the worst case, as well as how contribution- or utility-maximizing networks in the worst case perform in the best case.

5.1   Optimizing Under Complementarities

Let $a > 0$. We observe that contribution- and welfare-maximization correspond to maximizing the L_1 and L_2 norms of the Bonacich index vector, i.e. $\max_g\{\mathbf{b}(\mathbf{g}, a) \cdot \mathbf{1} : \mathbf{g} \in \mathcal{G}(v, e)\}$ and $\max_g\{\mathbf{u}(\mathbf{x}^*(\mathbf{g}, a)) : g \in \mathcal{G}(v, e)\}$, respectively.

The relationship suggests a way to characterize optimal equilibria using spectral graph theory.

Lemma 2. *Let* $\mathbf{g} \in \mathcal{G}(v, e)$, *and* $\lambda_1(\mathbf{G})$ *its index. As* $a \uparrow \frac{1}{\lambda_1 \mathbf{G}}$, *the welfare- and contribution-maximizing graphs problems are equivalent and reduce to* $\max\{\lambda_1(\mathbf{g}) : \mathbf{g} \in \mathcal{G}(v, e)\}$.

These asymptotic results reveal a great deal about how the optimal networks change with the level of externalities. Figure (a) illustrates precisely this across a large range of a values, for graphs with varying numbers of edges. The graph shows that the first eigenvalue of aggregate contribution- and utility-maximizing graphs (L_1- and L_2-maximizing graphs in the case of $a > 0$) corresponds to the largest first eigenvalue possible for graphs with given v, e. The largest eigenvalue of a graph is a measure of its regularity. A higher eigenvalue corresponds to an irregular star-like structure, whereas a lower eigenvalue refers to a more regular network.

5.2   Optimizing Under Substitutabilities

While equilibria are interior, aggregate contribution- and utility-maximizing graphs still coincide; these networks are maximal index graphs. When substitutabilities are strong enough, we lose interiority and have both partially corner and corner equilibria. Corner equilibria being the only stable equilibria, we only consider these.

Figures (c), (d) illustrate the tension between optimal networks in the best and worst cases. Networks that yield the highest contribution in the best case also exhibit worse worst case performance. These networks are maximal index graphs. Networks that yield the best worst case performance are minimal index graphs, as shown in Figure (b). Minimal index graphs also exhibit the smallest spread between best and worst case equilibrium performance, as illustrated in Figure (d).

5.3   Excluding the Key Player: A Network-Based Policy

We investigate a policy aimed at mitigating the discrepancy between best- and worst-case equilibrium performance. We denote by $\mathbf{G}^{-i}$ (respectively $\mathbf{\Sigma}^{-i}$) the new adjacency matrix (respectively the matrix of cross-effects), obtained from $\mathbf{G}$ (respectively from Σ) by setting to zero all of its i-th row and column coefficients. The resulting network is $\mathbf{g}^{-i}$. We want to solve $\max_{i \in N}\{\mathbf{x}^*(\mathbf{\Sigma}^{-i}) - \mathbf{x}^*(\mathbf{\Sigma})\}$

This is a finite optimization problem, that admits at least one solution. A good heuristic for the solution of this problem is the the removal of the highest degree node, since a node with highest degree imposes the largest number of constraints on the independent set construction. Figure (d) illustrates the policy's effectiveness in reconciling best- and worst- case equilibrium performance. Worst-case performance of graphs can be dramatically improved and even match best-case performance when the network graph is sparse. Figure (d) also shows that the policy becomes less effective as graphs grow dense.

References

1. Ballester, C., Calvó-Armengol, A., Zenou, Y.: Who's Who in Crime Networks. Wanted: The Key Player. Econometrica, 1403–1418 (2006)
2. Bonacich, P.: Power and Centrality: A Family of Measures. American Journal of Sociology 92, 1170–1182 (1987)
3. Bramoulle, Y., Kranton, R.: Public Goods in Networks. Journal of Economic Theory 135, 478–494 (2007)
4. Corbo, J., Calvó-Armengol, A., Parkes, D.C.: The Importance of Network Topology in Local Contribution Games: Full Version, Harvard Computer Science Working Paper Series (2007)
5. Cvetković, D., Rowlinson, P., Simić, S.: Eigenspaces of Graphs. Cambridge University Press, Cambridge (1997)
6. Demange, G.: Information sharing communities. In: Deng, X., Graham, F.C. (eds.) WINE 2007. LNCS, vol. 4858, pp. 96–107. Springer, Heidelberg (2007)
7. Fudenberg, D., Tirole, J.: Game Theory, pp. 23–25. MIT Press, Cambridge (1991)
8. Jackson, M.O.: Social and Economic Networks (Forthcoming Print). Princeton University Press
9. Johari, R., Tsitsiklis, J.: Efficiency Loss in a Network Resource Allocation Game. Mathematics of Operations Research 29(3), 407–435 (2004)
10. Kearns, M.: Graphical Games. In: Nisan, N., Roughgarden, T., Tardos, E., Vazirani, V. (eds.) Algorithmic Game Theory, Cambridge University Press, Cambridge (2007)
11. Roughgarden, T., Tardos, E.: Bounding the Inefficiency of Equilibria in Nonatomic Congestion Games. Games and Economic Behavior 47(2), 389–403 (2004)

Secure Relative Performance Scheme

Kurt Nielsen[1] and Tomas Toft[2]

[1] Inst. of Food and Resource Economics, University of Copenhagen,
kun@life.ku.dk
[2] Dept. of Computer Science, University of Aarhus,
tomas@daimi.au.dk

Abstract. We suggest a relative performance scheme that provides incentives for e.g. a manager to strive for the firm's strategy. A number of comparable firms submit private performance data to a trusted third party and receive a single number reflecting the firm's relative catch up with the frontier evaluated with the shadow prices associated with a tailored benchmark. The distributed information avoid signaling among the firms by revealing no recognizable information about the other firms performances. To enhance the applicability the computation of the required linear programming problems is based on distributed cryptography. Preliminary results on the computation time is provided.

1 Introduction

In this paper we consider the owner's (Principal's) classical problem of motivating the manager or employees (Agents) to put the optimal effort into the realization of the firm's strategy. The central issue is the asymmetric distribution of information which makes it impossible for the owner to contract directly on the manager's or employees' privately selected effort. One of the central results in this field is that sufficient external statistics from comparable firms minimizes the information rent, see e.g. (Holmstrom [5]).

We suggest a secure relative performance scheme that implement the desired motivation based on secure coordination and benchmarking of possibly competing firms. The paper treats three central issues. First, we suggest a performance scheme based on directional distance functions and Data Envelopment Analysis (DEA). This approach makes it possible to direct the incentives towards the firm's strategy with respect to an unknown best practice. Second, we address misuse of the suggested performance scheme for signaling between the firms. Third, we discuss how the required trusted third party can be replaced by distributed cryptography, in particular Secure Multiparty Computation (SMC). Preliminary results on the computation time for the required Linear Programming (LP) problems is provided.

The outline of the paper is as follows. Section 2 provides a relative performance scheme and discuss possible signaling. Section 3 discusses how distributed cryptography may replace the trusted third party and concluding remarks are provided in Sect. 4.

X. Deng and F.C. Graham (Eds.): WINE 2007, LNCS 4858, pp. 396–403, 2007.

2   A Relative Performance Scheme

The crux is to design a performance scheme based on peer performance that provides the right incentives without revealing any sensitive peer information. The related problem of handling the submitted private information is discussed in Sect. 3.

A failure to address this problem may cause signaling of higher or lower performance to be the optimal behavior in order to influence the behavior of competing firms. E.g. to intimidate competitors in tenders for future contracts or location of future stores. Also firms that are not engaged in direct competition (public administrations, sub-branches within a large firm or small firms in large branches) may also signal e.g. to show off.

2.1   The Individual Benchmark

Consider a group of N firms that in different ways use the same K inputs to produce the same L outputs. All firms are assumed to belong to the same production possibility set, which describes various relationships between the applied inputs and the produced outputs. The production possibility set is estimated by the non-parametric Data Envelopment Analysis (DEA), which provides a benchmark used for incentive provision within each firm.

Let $x^i = (x^i_1, \ldots, x^i_K) \in \mathbb{R}^K_0$ be the inputs consumed and $y^i = (y^i_1, \ldots, y^i_L) \in \mathbb{R}^L_0$ the outputs produced by firm i, $i = 1, 2, \ldots, N$. The production possibility set is given by:

$$\mathbb{T} = \left\{ (x, y) \in \mathbb{R}^{K+L}_0 \mid x \text{ can produce } y \right\} \tag{1}$$

In the directional approach, the user expresses his preferences by specifying a direction, $d = (d_x, d_y) \in \mathbb{R}^{K+L}$, for the firm to move in. Here d^i is based on the firms operational goal $z^i_g = (x^i_g, y^i_g)$ and the actual performance $z^i = (x^i, y^i)$ by $d^i = z^i_g - z^i$. Firm i's benchmark $\bar{z}^i = (\bar{x}^i, \bar{y}^i)$ is given as $z^{i,DEA}(x, y) = (x^i, y^i) + d^i \cdot \sigma$, where σ is:

$$\sigma = \max \left\{ \sigma \mid (x^i, y^i) + d^i \cdot \sigma \in \mathbb{T} \right\} \tag{2}$$

σ is computed by the following LP-problem:

$$\sigma^i = \max_{\sigma, \lambda} \sigma$$

$$\text{s.t.} \quad \sum_{j=1}^{N} \lambda^j x^j_k \leq x^i_k - \sigma d^x_k, \quad k = 1, \ldots, K$$

$$\sum_{j=1}^{N} \lambda^j y^j_l \geq y^i_l + \sigma d^y_l, \quad l = 1, \ldots, L \tag{3}$$

$$\lambda^j \in \Lambda, \quad j = 1, \ldots, N$$

where Λ defines the overall assumption about the envelopment i.e. the underlying technology $\mathbb{T}$. There is a large literature that discuss various restrictions on $\mathbb{T}$, see e.g. (Cooper et al. [3]). We will limit our attention to cases where $\mathbb{T}$ is defined as a convex hull. Figure 1 in Sect. 2.2 illustrates how the benchmark is constructed.

In terms of incentive provision Bogetoft ([1]) shows that DEA estimates may provide sufficient statistics as defined in (Holmstrom [5]).

2.2   The Suggested Performance Scheme

We suggest a relative performance scheme that returns a *relative deduction* to each firm which is minimized by striving directly for the individual firm's operational strategy. The *relative deduction* is designed to avoid signaling.

The suggested relative performance scheme is based on each participant's performance and goal ex ante (period $t = 0$) and $\mathbb{T}$ is defined by the others' production ex post (period $t = 1$)[1]. This is illustrated in Fig. 1 and the LP problem in Sect. 2.1 compute the benchmark[2]. The performance pay (b) is defined on a predetermined interval by a minimum and a maximum payment ($Q^{\text{low}}, Q^{\text{high}}$) as:

$$b^i(z, d^i) = \max \left\{ Q^{\text{low}}, Q^{\text{high}} + \underbrace{\min\{\alpha[(z^{i,DEA}(z^{-i}, d^i) - z^i) \cdot p^*], 0\}}_{\text{Relative deduction}} \right\} \qquad (4)$$

The *relative deduction* is less than or equal to 0 and defined as a fraction of the difference between the desired benchmark $z^{i,DEA}(z^{-i}, d^i)$ and the actual performance z^i valued with the prices p^* (with negative prices on inputs)[3]. p^* is the so-called shadow prices which is the solution to the dual of the LP problem given in Sect. 2.1. The shadow prices are defined as the prices that makes any further use of input and production of output unprofitable. The shadow prices[4] is simply the tangent of the frontier at the computed benchmark as illustrated in Fig. 1.

Clearly the performance scheme is individual rational by setting Q^{low} equal to the agent minimum required salary. Also, the scheme is incentive compatible since it is optimal for the agent to maximize the performance along the line $\sigma \cdot d^i$ from $z^i_{t=0}$ towards z^i_g. To see this note that an efficient point along this line will be an allocative efficient point with certainty and that any other efficient points will be allocative efficient with a probability less than 1 due to the unknown but convex $\mathbb{T}$. An allocative efficient point will result in the smallest relative deduction (0) and thereby the largest payment.

---

[1] To simplify we focus on the agent's incentives to select the optimal effort by assuming that the performance z^i is observable ex post by both the agent and the principal.

[2] The relative performance scheme is not applicable for firm i if the line $\sigma \cdot d^i$ is outside $\mathbb{T}$.

[3] Written out the relative deduction is: $(\bar{x}^i_1 - x^i_1) \cdot -p^i_{x_1} + \ldots + (\bar{x}^i_K - x^i_K) \cdot -p^i_{x_K} + (\bar{y}^i_1 - y^i_1) \cdot p^i_{y_1} + \ldots + (\bar{y}^i_L - y^i_L) \cdot p^i_{y_L}$

[4] The linearity causes two problems: A risk of extreme shadow prices and corner solutions with shadow prices associated with multiple adjacent hyperplans. Since the shadow prices are computed on z^{-i} the chance of reaching a corner solution is small. In practice one may decide on a policy to handle these problems e.g. by predetermined limits on the shadow prices and a selection mechanism in case of a corner solution.

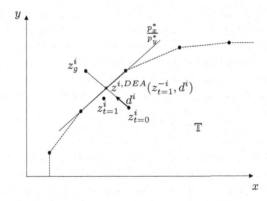

Fig. 1. The relative performance scheme

Signaling is addressed by lowering the expected value of a signal and increasing the expected cost of sending a signal.

The value of a signal is essentially limited by limiting the information revealed. The participants receive the number: $\min\{\alpha[z^{i,DEA}(z^{-i},d^i) - z^i) \cdot p^*], 0\}$ (*the relative deduction*), which is constructed by two unknown vectors with $K + L$ elements each: The benchmark $(z^{i,DEA}(z^{-i},d^i))$ and the associated shadow prices (p^*). The received number indicates if z^i is above or below the hyperplan constructed by p^* and $z^{i,DEA}(z^{-i},d^i)$. If a participant receives a 0 (above the hyperplan) he only knows that no other firms dominates him. A negative number does not have the same unambiguous interpretation. Furthermore the actual number may be supported by an infinite number of hyperplans. It is therefore impossible for a receiver to identify the peer information behind the received number. Also, the sender of a possible manipulated performance can not identify the receiver since the receiver's performance and goal (the chosen direction d^i) is private information.

The cost of sending the signal may come directly from a participation fee. Since the value of a well received signal is private but most likely correlated with the size of the firm, the participation fee should depend on the size of the firm. Also, there is an indirect cost from not receiving useful benchmarks if deviating from truth-telling. Since either the benchmark or the associated shadow prices are known, the received number is useless if based on biased performances.

Therefore, since the received number (*the relative deduction*) does not identify either the benchmark, the shadow prices or peers, the value of signaling is disappearing and even a small participation fee may avoid any signaling.

3   Secure Implementation

The system relies heavily on central coordination by a trusted third party. Paying a third party (e.g. a consultancy house) to truthfully handle the data is not only expensive but also prone to human mistakes. Moreover, it may be impossible to find a single entity that all firms are willing to entrust their data, which may skew incentives to provide truthful information. However, cryptography provides a solution to this through secure multiparty computation, which allows a number of parties to jointly perform a computation on private inputs releasing no other information than the final result. Assuming that sufficiently few collude, no parties learn anything except the final result, allowing trust to be distributed between multiple entities, potentially the firms themselves.

SMC often finds its basis in secret sharing: A dealer may distribute a secret between many parties; this may only be reconstructed if sufficiently many agree, fewer parties obtain no information at all. This allows the firms to distribute their information among multiple entities, who then perform the desired computation. The trusted third party is emulated by these, and each firm must only trust a subset.

3.1   Solving Linear Programs Using SMC

Toft ([7]) describes a protocol for securely solving LP's. Based on secret shared constraints and objective function, a secret sharing of an optimal solution may be determined using only secure arithmetic and a protocol for comparison. The solution uses secure modulo computation to simulate integer arithmetic, the modulus is simply chosen sufficiently large such that no reductions occur. Privacy is not fully ensured, however, the amount of information disclosed is minor and deemed acceptable in the present context.

The protocol is a variation of simplex based on SMC-primitives. Starting from an initial (sub-optimal) solution, the optimal one is determined through repeated refinement. Though simplex requires an exponential number of iterations in the worst case, in practice very few are needed. It therefore forms a good basis, and provides a complexity essentially equivalent to that of running the computation on known data, though naturally computation is replaced by protocol executions.

Performing an iteration discloses no information at all, however, after each iteration the termination condition is revealed. Overall, this leaks the number of iterations performed, but no more. If this is not acceptable, a likely upper bound may be chosen. Performing this many iterations (with dummy-computation once the solution is found) hides the actual number of iterations. A second disclosure comes from the solution itself. The values are rational, each represented by two integers, numerator and denominator, and unless these fractions are reduced, a minor amount of information on the final iteration is disclosed. While reducing such fractions is possible[5] this leak is disregarded, as it is not believed to provide useful information on the initial values or distort incentives.

The focus of (Toft [7]) was theoretic in nature, for efficiency reasons a few changes are made, these are described further in (Toft [8]). Sketching the main differences, first, issues with simplex rarely encountered in practice – such as cycling – are disregarded. This allows changes to the overall computation, which

---

[5] Toft ([7]) computes the GCD and divides, however, this computation is comparable to multiple iterations.

generally result in fewer iterations. Second, theoretically efficient secure computations is not always the best choice in practice. Expensive tricks are employed to obtain desirable properties, where a simpler solution may be better on "small" inputs. An example is comparison: This work prefers a sub-protocol with round-complexity logarithmic in the bit-length of the inputs rather than constant. For the input-sizes considered, simplicity seems a better strategy than current state of the art constant rounds comparison protocols.

One final comment is that this work requires not only the solution to the LP, but also the solution to the dual, the shadow prices. This is immediately obtainable from the final state of the computation, thus no additional secure computation is needed. The concluding computation is easily performed.

3.2   A Performance Estimate

At present, the full secure computation has not been implemented, however, initial timing results for arithmetic provide an estimate for solving LP's – the remaining computation is marginal and therefore disregarded. This timing data is based on an implementation of Shamir sharings over $\mathbb{Z}_p$ for prime p and the protocols of Gennaro et al., (Shamir [6]; Gennaro et al. [4]).[6] The basic measure of complexity is secure multiplication. Linear combinations do not require interaction and are considered costless.

Initial timing data on multiplications suggest that the desired computation is feasible, though more thorough tests need to be performed. The test setup consists of three computers connected by a fast, low-latency LAN, the secret sharing scheme is used with a threshold of one. Multiplying 2000 elements of a 1500 bit prime field (log-rounds solution) requires roughly three seconds. The average time per multiplication is not affected by the number of terms, except when quite few are considered. Decreasing the bit-length decreases average time per multiplication, though no further than approximately 1 ms. For moduli less than 5000 bits, the resulting increase appears linear.

Secure comparisons of values will be performed using a protocol to appear in (Toft [8]), it is essentially a combination of ideas from multiple previous works. The complexity of comparing ℓ-bit values is comparable to multiplying 2ℓ field elements. Half of these multiplications are independent of the actual inputs and may be performed in advance resulting in a better online running time.

The overall complexity depends on the complexity of an iteration and the number of these performed. Letting $M = K + L + 1$ be the number of constraints of the LP, Chvátal ([2]) comments that the latter is generally between $3M/2$ and $3M$ when the greatest coefficient rule is used. The dependency on N is lesser (often stated as logarithmic), thus varying the number of firms does not affect the number of iterations to a high degree.

Regarding the performance of a single iteration, approximately $3(N + M + 1)(M + 1) + 2N + 5M$ multiplications and $N + 3M$ comparisons are needed to improve the solution. The complexity of state of the art comparison protocols

---

[6] Only passive adversaries are considered, i.e. it is assumed that parties do not deviate from the protocol.

402   K. Nielsen and T. Toft

depends on the bit-length of the inputs, which in turn depends on the LP. Toft ([7]) provides a broad upper bound on this:

$$(M \cdot (2B + \log(M)))/2 + 2B + M + N + 1 \qquad (5)$$

where B is the bit-length of the initial values.

An estimate using a concrete problem size demonstrates feasibility. Consider a case of $N = 200$ firms with five inputs and outputs, i.e. $M = 6$. Assuming that all initial values are 32 bits long, approximately 500 bits are needed to represent intermediate and final values – for technical reasons the bit-length of the modulus must be bigger, 1500 bits suffices. This implies 1.5 seconds per comparisons, with an online requirement of half of that. Additional optimizations suggest that the latter may be reduced to 1/2 second, though at the cost of slightly more preprocessing.

Each iteration requires around 4800 multiplications and $N + 3M = 218$ comparisons. The latter is dominating, 1/2 second per comparison results in approximately two minutes of processing time. With $3M = 18$ iterations a result is expected in about half an hour. Solving one LP per firm implies half a week of computation time – this is of course in addition to the preprocessing required.

4   Concluding Remarks

We suggest a secure relative performance scheme that provides proper incentives for the agent to strive for the principal's strategy. The principal's strategy and the agent's performance provides the direction in a non-parametric directional distance function based on the other participating firms' performances. The resulting benchmark and the associated shadow prices construct a *relative deduction* that provides proper incentives and address potential signaling. The computation is entirely based on secure multiparty computation allowing trust to be distributed among multiple third parties, none of which learn any significant information. Though the time requirements are relatively large, they are manageable – at least for the problem size suggested – and the technique definitely applicable. Future work will attempt to verify that timings of the full protocol agree with the current extrapolated ones.

References

1. Bogetoft, P.: Incentive efficient production frontiers: An agency perspective in DEA. Management Science 40, 959–968 (1994)
2. Chvátal, V.: Linear Programming. W. H. FREEMAN, New York (1983)
3. Cooper, W.W., Seiford, L.M., Tone, K.: Data Envelopment Analysis. Kluwer Academic Publishers, Dordrecht (2000)
4. Gennaro, R., Rabin, M., Rabin, T.: Simplified VSS and fast-track multiparty computations with applications to threshold cryptography. In: PODC 1998: Proceedings of the seventeenth annual ACM symposium on Principles of distributed computing, pp. 101–111. ACM Press, New York (1998)

5. Holmstrom, B.: Moral hazard in teams. Bell Journal of Economics 13, 324–340 (1982)
6. Shamir, A.: How to share a secret. Communications of the ACM 22(11), 612–613 (1979)
7. Toft, T.: Primitives and Applications for Multi-party Computation. PhD thesis, University of Aarhus (2007), Available at http://www.daimi.au.dk/~tomas/publications/dissertation.pdf
8. Toft, T.: An implementation of an MPC LP-solver. Work in progress (n.d.)

Selfishness, Collusion and Power of Local Search for the ADMs Minimization Problem[*]

(Extended Abstract)

Stefania Di Giannantonio[1], Michele Flammini[1], Gianpiero Monaco[1],
Luca Moscardelli[1], Mordechai Shalom[2], and Shmuel Zaks[3]

[1] Dipartmento di Informatica, Università degli Studi dell'Aquila, L'Aquila, Italy
{stefania.digiannantonio,flammini,
gianpiero.monaco,moscardelli}@di.univaq.it
[2] TelHai Academic College, Upper Galilee, 12210, Israel
cmshalom@telhai.ac.il
[3] Department of Computer Science, Technion, Haifa, Israel
zaks@cs.technion.ac.il

Abstract. We consider non cooperative games in all-optical networks where users share the cost of the used ADM switches for realizing given communication patterns. We show that the two fundamental cost sharing methods, Shapley and Egalitarian, induce polynomial converging games with price of anarchy at most 5/3, regardless of the network topology. Such a bound is tight even for rings. Then, we show that if collusion of at most k players is allowed, the Egalitarian method yields polynomially converging games with price of collusion between $\frac{3}{2}$ and $\frac{3}{2} + \frac{1}{k}$. This result is very interesting and quite surprising, as the best known approximation ratio, that is $\frac{3}{2} + \epsilon$, can be achieved in polynomial time by uncoordinated evolutions of collusion games with coalitions of increasing size. Finally, the Shapley method does not induce well defined collusion games, but can be exploited in the definition of local search algorithms with local optima arbitrarily close to optimal solutions. This would potentially generate PTAS, but unfortunately the arising algorithm might not converge. The determination of new cost sharing methods or local search algorithms reaching a compromise between Shapley and Egalitarian is thus outlined as being a promising and worth pursuing investigating direction.

Keywords: Optical Networks, Wavelength Division Multiplexing (WDM), Add-Drop Multiplexer (ADM), Game Theory, Nash Equilibria, Price of Anarchy, Price of Collusion.

1 Introduction

All-optical networks have been largely investigated in recent years due to the promise of data transmission rates several orders of magnitudes higher than

[*] This research was partly supported by the EU Project "Graphs and Algorithms in Communication Networks (GRAAL)" - COST Action TIST 293.

current networks [2,3,15,17]. Major applications are in video conferencing, scientific visualization and real-time medical imaging, high-speed supercomputing and distributed computing [7,15].

A large portion of research concentrates with the total hardware cost. This is modelled by considering the basic electronic switching units of the electronic Add-Drop Multiplexer (ADM) and focusing on the total number of these hardware components. Each lightpath uses two ADMs, one at each endpoint. If two non-overlapping lightpaths are assigned the same wavelength and are incident to the same node, then they can use the same ADM. Thus, an ADM may be shared by at most two lightpaths. The problem of minimizing the number of ADMs was introduced in [14] for ring networks. For such a topology it was shown to be NP-complete in [9] and an approximation algorithm with approximation ratio 3/2 was presented in [5] and improved in [21,10] to 10/7 + ϵ and 10/7 respectively. For general topologies [9] provided an algorithm with approximation ratio 8/5. The same problem was studied in [4,12], where algorithms with approximation ratio 3/2 + ϵ were presented.

In a distributed and decentralized environment characterizing an optical communication network, besides the classical design of centralized algorithms optimizing the resources utilization, the analysis of the uncooperative interaction between the network users and the design of distributed algorithms call for more research effort. On this respect, Game Theory and the associated concept of Nash equilibria [19] have recently emerged as a powerful tool for modelling and analyzing such a lack of coordination. In this setting, each communication request is handled by an agent (or player) selfishly performing *moves*, i.e. changing her routing strategy in order to maximize her own benefit. A Nash equilibrium is a solution of the game in which no agent gains by unilaterally changing her routing strategy. Nash equilibria are known not to always optimize the overall performance. Such a loss in [6,1] has been formalized by the so-called *price of anarchy* (resp. *optimistic price of anarchy*), defined as the ratio between the cost of the worst (resp. best) Nash equilibrium and the one of an optimal centralized solution. There exists a vast literature on Nash Equilibria in communication networks (see for instance [18,20]).

Even if in non-cooperative games players are usually considered to act selfishly and independently, an interesting investigated issue is the one of collusion. Roughly speaking, collusion allows two or more players forming a coalition to come to an agreement in order to obtain a gain by changing at the same time their strategies. In this framework, a Nash equilibrium is a solution in which there exists no coalition of players having convenience in changing their strategies. The lack of performance with respect to the optimal solution has been measured by the *price of collusion* introduced in [13] and [16], where the authors focused on a particular class of games, the congestion games, assuming the players partitioned into sets of coalitions.

Following the research direction outlined in [11], in this paper we are interested in analyzing the non-cooperative scenario in which the users of an optical network interact sharing the cost of the used hardware components. More precisely, we focus on ADM switches, considering the game in which their total cost is divided between the users according to two fundamental cost sharing methods: the Shapley [22] method, in which the agents using an ADM pay for it by equally splitting its cost, and the Egalitarian one, where the whole hardware cost is equally split among all the players.

The paper is organized as follows. In the next section we give the basic notation and definitions and show some preliminary results. In Section 3 we focus on the ADM minimization, and we show the results concerning Nash equilibria without and with collusion. Finally, in Section 4 we discuss the power of local search algorithm, give some conclusive remarks and discuss some open questions.

2   Model and Preliminary Results

An instance of the ADMs minimization problem is a pair (G, P), where G is an undirected graph and $P = \{p_1, \ldots, p_n\}$ is a multi-set of n simple paths in G, also called lightpaths or requests.

A coloring (or wavelength assignment) of (G, P) is a function $w : P \mapsto \mathbb{N}^+ = \{1, 2, \ldots\}$ such that $w(p_i) \neq w(p_j)$ for any pair of paths $p_i, p_j \in P$ sharing an edge in G.

Given a coloring function w, a valid cycle (resp. chain) is a cycle (resp. chain) formed by the concatenation of distinct paths in P of the same color.

A solution s of the problem consists of a set of valid chains and cycles partitioning the paths in P, expressing the particular sharing of ADMs.

More precisely, we say that two paths are adjacent if they have a common endpoint. Each path uses two ADMs, one at each endpoint; if two adjacent paths are assigned the same wavelength, then they can use the same ADM. Thus, an ADM may be shared by at most two lightpaths. In this way each valid cycle of k paths in s uses k ADMs, because every ADM is shared by exactly two paths. Similarly, each chain of k paths uses $k + 1$ ADMs, as the initial and final ADMs in the chain are used only by the initial and the final path of the chain, respectively.

We are interested in finding a solution s such that the total number of used ADMs, denoted as $ADM(s)$, is minimized.

We assume that every path $p_i \in P$, $i = 1, \ldots, n$, is issued and handled by a player α_i, that for the sake of simplicity in the sequel we will often identify with p_i. At every given step a single agent α_i, by performing a selfish move, can decide whether and with whom to share the cost of the ADMs at the endpoints of p_i. Hence, her strategy set is the collection of all the possible subsets of at most two other adjacent (not overlapping) paths, one per endpoint. A given strategy is feasible if and only if (i) the chosen paths are not already sharing the involved ADMs with some other path and (ii) the new created chain or ring of requests induces a valid coloring, that is no two paths have an edge in common.

Clearly, a strategy profile $(s_1, \ldots, s_n)$ defines a solution $s \in S$ of the game. A non-cooperative game $\mathcal{G}$ is defined by a tuple (G, P, f, k) where (G, P) is an optical network instance, f is a cost sharing method inducing a cost sharing function $c : S \times P \to \Re$ distributing the whole hardware cost among the players and k is the maximum size of a coalition of players that can collude (notice that if $k = 1$ no collusion is allowed and thus $\mathcal{G}$ is a "classical" non-cooperative game).

We consider two fundamental cost sharing methods: the Shapley [22] ($f =$ SHAPLEY) and the Egalitarian ($f =$ EGALITARIAN) ones.

In the Shapley cost sharing method, the agents sharing an ADM pay for it by equally splitting its cost. Thus, recalling that each requests needs exactly 2 ADMs, and that each ADM can be shared at most by 2 agents, the cost $c_i(s)$ charged to player α_i in the strategy profile s can be 1 (if she shares both her ADMs with other requests), $\frac{3}{2}$ (if she shares only an ADM with another request), or 2 (if she does not share any ADM with other requests).

In the Egalitarian cost sharing method, the whole hardware cost corresponding to a strategy profile s is divided between all the players in an egalitarian way, i.e. $c_i(s) = \frac{ADM(s)}{n}$ for every $i = 1, \ldots, n$.

Clearly in both cases, given a strategy profile s, $\sum_{i=1}^{n} c_i(s) = ADM(s)$.

If the parameter k of the game (G, P, f, k) is equal to 1, no coalition can be constituted and each player acts independently. In such a setting, a *Nash equilibrium* is a strategy profile such that no player can reduce her cost by seceding in favor of a better strategy, given the strategies of the other players. Denoting by $\mathcal{N}$ the set of all the possible Nash equilibria, the *price of anarchy* (*PoA*) of a game $\mathcal{G}$ is defined as the worst case ratio among the Nash versus optimal performance, i.e., $PoA(\mathcal{G}) = \frac{\max_{s \in \mathcal{N}} ADM(s)}{ADM(s^*)}$, where s^* is the strategy profile corresponding to the optimal solution. Moreover, the *optimistic price of anarchy* (*OPoA*) of $\mathcal{G}$ is defined as the best case ratio among the Nash versus the optimal performance, i.e., $OPoA(\mathcal{G}) = \frac{\min_{s \in \mathcal{N}} ADM(s)}{ADM(s^*)}$.

If the parameter k of the game (G, P, f, k) is greater than 1, a *Nash equilibrium* is a strategy profile such that no coalition of k player can reduce its whole cost (sum of single costs) by seceding in favor of a better strategy, given the strategies of the other $n - k$ players. In such a setting, denoting by $\mathcal{N}_k$ the set of all the possible Nash equilibria with coalitions of size at most k, the *price of collusion* (*PoC*) of a game $\mathcal{G}$ is defined as the worst case ratio among the Nash versus optimal performance, i.e., $PoC_k(\mathcal{G}) = \frac{\max_{s \in \mathcal{N}_k} ADM(s)}{ADM(s^*)}$, where s^* is the strategy profile corresponding to the optimal solution. Moreover, the *optimistic price of collusion* (*OPoC*) of $\mathcal{G}$ is defined as the best case ratio among the Nash versus the optimal performance, i.e., $OPoC_k(\mathcal{G}) = \frac{\min_{s \in \mathcal{N}_k} ADM(s)}{ADM(s^*)}$. Notice that, since the coalitions can dynamically change, in this case the Shapley cost sharing method is not well defined. Thus, for $k > 1$ we will focus only on the games induced by the egalitarian cost sharing method.

Let us now present some preliminary results about the existence and convergence to Nash Equilibria. In particular, we show that every game always converges to a Nash equilibrium in a linear number of moves.

Proposition 1. *In every game* $\mathcal{G} = (G, P, f, k)$, *where* $f \in$ {SHAPLEY, EGALITARIAN} *and* $k = 1$ *or* $f =$ EGALITARIAN *and* $k \geq 2$, *the social function ADM is a potential function, i.e. if s' is the strategy profile* *resulting from the strategy profile* s *after the selfish moves of the colluding players* $\alpha_{i_1}, \ldots, \alpha_{i_h}$, *with* $h \leq k$, $ADM(s') < ADM(s)$.

As a direct consequence of the previous propositions, since the social function, that is a potential function for the game, can assume at most $n + 1$ different values, it holds that every game always converges to a Nash equilibrium in at most n selfish moves.

Moreover, since the optimal solution is a minimum of the defined potential functions, it follows that the optimal solution is also an equilibrium. Therefore, given any game $\mathcal{G}$, the *optimistic* price of anarchy is the best possible one, i.e. $OPoA(\mathcal{G}) = 1$, and, for every integer $k > 1$, the same holds for the *optimistic* price of collusion, i.e. $OPoC_k(\mathcal{G}) = 1$. Therefore, in the remaining part of the paper we will focus on the price of anarchy (for $k = 1$) and price of collusion (for $k > 1$).

3 Price of Anarchy and Price of Collusion

If no collusion between players is allowed, and thus each selfish player acts independently, we prove that the price of anarchy is at most $\frac{5}{3}$ regardless of the network topology. This result is very interesting, as it matches the performance of three different algorithms presented in [9] and [4].

Theorem 1. *For any game* $\mathcal{G} = (G, P, f, 1)$, *with* $f \in \{$SHAPLEY, EGALITARIAN$\}$, $PoA(\mathcal{G}) \leq \frac{5}{3}$.

Now we provide a matching lower bound, holding for a network having ring topology. The following theorem proves that the previous upper bound is tight even for ring networks, and thus the price of anarchy is equal to $\frac{5}{3}$.

Theorem 2. *For any* $\epsilon > 0$, *there exists an instance of the ADM minimization game* $\mathcal{G} = (G, P, f, 1)$, *where* $f \in \{$SHAPLEY, EGALITARIAN$\}$ *and* G *is a ring network, such that* $PoA(\mathcal{G}) \geq \frac{5}{3} - \epsilon$.

Now we turn our attention on games in which coalitions of at most k players can collude. We prove that the price of collusion is between $\frac{3}{2}$ and $\frac{3}{2} + \frac{1}{k}$, with $\frac{3}{2} + \epsilon$ being the approximation guaranteed by the best know approximation algorithms [4,12] for this problem on general network topologies.

Theorem 3. *For every* $k = 2, 3, \ldots$, *any game* $\mathcal{G} = (G, P, $EGALITARIAN$, k)$ *is such that* $PoC_k(\mathcal{G}) \leq \frac{3}{2} + \frac{1}{k}$.

The following theorem provides an almost matching lower bound.

Theorem 4. *For every* $k = 2, 3, \ldots$, *there exists an instance of the ADM minimization game* $\mathcal{G} = (G, P, $EGALITARIAN$, k)$ *such that* $PoC_k(\mathcal{G}) \geq \frac{3}{2}$.

4   Local Search and Concluding Remarks

In this section we show some basic results emphasizing that local search is a promising approach for possibly improving the achievable approximation ratio of the ADMs minimization problem.

As already remarked, under the assumption of collusion of at most k players, the Shapley method does not induce well defined games. This stems on the fact that the payment of a player is not solely a function of the current strategy profile, but is also affected by the history of the past coalitions. However, Shapley naturally yields local search schema with the induced definition of neighborhood of a current solution s. Namely, any solution s' that can be obtained from s by modifying the strategy of at most k players is a neighbor of s; such a solution is an improving one with respect to s and the fixed coalition if it reduces the sum of the Shapley costs of the involved players, that is it increases the sum of their degrees in the saving graph.

The following proposition characterizes the performance of local optima according to such a neighborhood definition.

Proposition 2. *For every* $k = 2, 3, \ldots,$ *any local optimum solution* s *in the schema induced by the above definition of neighborhood has total cost* $ADM(s) \leq \left(1 + \frac{2}{k}\right) ADM(s^*)$, *where* s^* *is an optimal solution.*

Unfortunately, such a neighbor definition for increasing values of k does not induce a PTAS, since the schema not only does not converge in a polynomial number of steps, might not converge at all and local optima may even not exist.

Proposition 3. *The local search schema induced by the above definition of neighborhood may posses no local optimum.*

The above results on local search emphasize that the determination of new cost sharing methods reaching a compromise between the Shapley and Egalitarian ones in terms of optimization and performance is a promising and worth investigating issue. To this aim we observe that a linear combination of the two criteria is affected by the same unconvergence behavior. In fact, in the instance shown in the proof of Proposition 3, the solutions in which two requests connect can be involved in a cycle of improving steps and have the same total cost: since the Egalitarian contribution in the linear combination is fixed, the Shapley part causes exactly the same behavior. Nevertheless, the determination of other intermediate methods combining both the Shapley and Egalitarian advantages is an important left open question.

Besides the above mentioned results for general topologies, it would be also nice to determine specific collusion results for ring networks, possibly improving the related approximation ratios.

Finally, a last interesting issue is that of extending our results to the grooming case in which up to a certain number of paths g of the same color can share the same physical links and the same ADMs [8].

References

1. Anshelevich, E., Dasgupta, A., Tardos, E., Wexler, T.: Near-optimal network design with selfish agents. In: STOC 2003: Proceedings of the thirty-fifth annual ACM symposium on Theory of computing, pp. 511–520. ACM Press, New York (2003)
2. Brackett, C.A.: Dense wavelength division multiplexing networks: principles and applications. IEEE Journal on Selected Areas in Communications 8, 948–964 (1990)
3. Chung, N.K., Nosu, K., Winzer, G.: Special issue on dense wdm networks. IEEE Journal on Selected Areas in Communications 8 (1990)
4. Călinescu, G., Frieder, O., Wan, P.-J.: Minimizing electronic line terminals for automatic ring protection in general wdm optical networks. IEEE Journal of Selected Area on Communications 20(1), 183–189 (2002)
5. Călinescu, G., Wan, P.-J.: Traffic partition in wdm/sonet rings to minimize sonet adms. Journal of Combinatorial Optimization 6(4), 425–453 (2002)
6. Czumaj, A., Vocking, B.: Tight bound for the worst-case equilibria. In: Proceedings of the 13th Annual ACM-SIAM Symposium on Discrete Mathematics (SODA), pp. 413–420. SIAM (2002)
7. Du, D.H.C., Vetter, R.J.: Distributed computing with high-speed optical networks. Proceeding of IEEE Computer 26, 8–18 (1993)
8. Dutta, R., Rouskas, G.N.: Traffic grooming in wdm networks: past and future. IEEE Network, 44–56, November-December (2002)
9. Eilam, T., Moran, S., Zaks, S.: Lightpath arrangement in survivable rings to minimize the switching cost. IEEE Journal of Selected Area on Communications 20(1), 172–182 (2002)
10. Epstein, L., Levin, A.: Better bounds for minimizing sonet adms. In: 2nd Workshop on Approximation and Online Algorithms, Bergen, Norway (September 2004)
11. Fanelli, A., Flammini, M., Melideo, G., Moscardelli, L.: Game theoretical issues in optical networks. In: Proceedings of the 8th International Conference on Transparent Optical Networks (ICTON), Nottingham, United Kingdom, IEEE, Los Alamitos (2006)
12. Flammini, M., Shalom, M., Zaks, S.: On minimizing the number of adms in a general topology optical network. In: Dolev, S. (ed.) DISC 2006. LNCS, vol. 4167, pp. 459–473. Springer, Heidelberg (2006)
13. Fotakis, D., Kontogiannis, S.C., Spirakis, P.G.: Atomic congestion games among coalitions. In: Bugliesi, M., Preneel, B., Sassone, V., Wegener, I. (eds.) ICALP 2006. LNCS, vol. 4051, pp. 572–583. Springer, Heidelberg (2006)
14. Gerstel, O., Lin, P., Sasaki, G.: Wavelength assignment in a wdm ring to minimize cost of embedded sonet rings. In: INFOCOM 1998, Seventeenth Annual Joint Conference of the IEEE Computer and Communications Societies (1998)
15. Green, P.E.: Fiber-Optic Communication Networks. Prentice Hall, Englewood Cliffs (1992)
16. Hayrapetyan, A., Tardos, É., Wexler, T.: The effect of collusion in congestion games. In: Kleinberg, J.M. (ed.) STOC, pp. 89–98. ACM, New York (2006)
17. Klasing, R.: Methods and problems of wavelength-routing in all-optical networks. In: Brim, L., Gruska, J., Zlatuška, J. (eds.) MFCS 1998. LNCS, vol. 1450, pp. 1–9. Springer, Heidelberg (1998)
18. Mavronicolas, M., Spirakis, P.: The price of selfish routing. In: Proceedings of the 33rd Annual ACM Symposium on the Theory of Computing (STOC), pp. 510–519 (2001)

19. Nash, J.F.: Equilibrium points in n-person games. Proceedings of the National Academy of Sciences 36, 48–49 (1950)
20. Roughgarden, T., Tardos, E.: How bad is selfish routing? Journal of ACM 49(2), 236–259 (2002)
21. Shalom, M., Zaks, S.: A $10/7 + \epsilon$ approximation scheme for minimizing the number of adms in sonet rings. In: First Annual International Conference on Broadband Networks, San-José, California, USA (October 2004)
22. Shapley, L.S.: The value of n-person games. Contributions to the theory of games, pp. 31–40, Princeton University Press (1953)

The Wi-Fi Roaming Game

Hossein Falaki

David R. Cheriton School of Computer Science,
University of Waterloo
mhfalaki@uwaterloo.ca

Abstract. We propose an extensive-form game as a model for pricing roaming charges in 802.11 wireless data networks. We specify utility functions for the three agents involved in the game: the wireless user and the visited and home operators. With realistic assumptions, we use the model to find optimal roaming prices for delay insensitive users.

1   Introduction

In wireless telecommunications, *roaming* refers to the provision of service in a location other than the home location of the service subscriber. The economic aspects of roaming in cellular voice networks have been studied in the literature [1,2,3]. In such networks, supporting roaming is a static decision which is enforced by a "roaming agreement" between the operators. However, new wireless networks with different properties, such as 802.11, are growing in ubiquity. In 802.11 wireless networks, user accounting and incentives of operators for providing roaming are different from cellular voice networks. In addition to geographical coverage, 802.11 network operators are interested in supporting roaming for better quality of service and load balancing. In these networks, the decision of whether to provide service to a roaming user or not should be made dynamically, especially considering that 802.11 is an open system [4] and users can easily switch between networks.

In this paper, we propose an extensive-form game as a model for users' roaming between multiple 802.11 wireless data networks. we specify the utility functions of the agents involved in the game according to the network properties of the 802.11 protocol. We then examine a specific version of the game to find the behavior of the network operators when charging delay insensitive users for roaming.

In the next section we present the model and specify the utility functions. We will then outline a simplified version of the game in section 3 to gain insight into the properties of the game equilibrium. Finally, section 4 concludes the paper and presents some future work.

2   Modeling

Assume two operators, A and B, have installed infrastructure for wireless mesh [5] networks in an urban area. In some areas their network coverage is exclusive

X. Deng and F.C. Graham (Eds.): WINE 2007, LNCS 4858, pp. 412–418, 2007.

and in other parts, such as heavily crowded malls, their coverage overlaps[1]. Two extensive-form games for roaming users can be envisioned:

1. **User initiated hand-off**: A subscriber to A proposes to connect to an access point belonging to B. B is called the *visited operator* and A is the *home operator*. The visited operator has two choices: *admit* or *reject*. If B decides to admit, the home operator may *agree* or *disagree* with the hand-off[2].

2. **Operator initiated hand-off**: As the home operator, A may instruct a subscriber to *switch* to the other operator. If the subscriber decides to switch, the visited operator may *admit* or *reject* the request. The open nature of 802.11 networks and the limited control of the operators over the users, make the *operator initiated* hand-off scenario impractical.

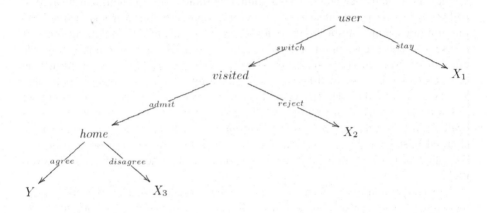

Fig. 1. User-initiated roaming game

In this paper we will focus on the first scenario because the technical properties of the 802.11 standard [4] suggest that *user initiated* hand-off is more realistic. As demonstrated in Figure 1, the user initiated hand-off is a *perfect information extensive-form game* $G = (N, A, Z, u)$ where:

- The set of agents is $N = \{user, home, visited\}$.
- The set of actions available to agents is $A = \{A_{user}, A_{home}, A_{visited}\}$ where $A_{user} = \{switch, stay\}, A_{home} = \{admit, reject\}$ and $A_{visited} = \{agree, disagree\}$.
- The set of terminal choice nodes is $Z = \{X_1, X_2, X_3, Y\}$.
- The utility function, u, of each agent in each terminal node is defined in section 2.1.

---

[1] Mesh network deployments are not planned, therefore each operator may suffer from bad signal quality in some locations.

[2] The home operator can enforce its decision, if it does not agree, by denying to pay the charges to the visited operator.

2.1   Utility Functions

In this section we introduce the utility functions of the agents participating in the roaming game. Throughout this paper we use the v subscript for the visited operator and the h subscript for the home operator.

Visited Operator Utility Function. The visited operator's decision to admit or reject a visitor connection request depends on the cost and benefit of providing the service. The cost consists of the *basic service cost* (C_v) and the cost incurred by the risk of potential congestion in the network $(C_{congestion})$. The benefit to the visited operator is the revenue from the home operator. This revenue may be either fixed for every hand-off instance or dynamic. For simplicity, we consider the fixed revenue and denote it by R_v.

In 802.11 data networks, as a result of contention, if the number of users trying to use an access point crosses some threshold, none of them will be able to utilize the access point effectively. We assume that the operator has decided the maximum possible number of users for an access point, M. If the current number of users of the access point, N_v, plus one exceeds M_v (the maximum possible number of users in the visited access point), the *congestion cost* of admitting the extra roaming user will be too high and admission is effectively impossible.. However, if $N_v + 1 < M_v$ the visited operator will evaluate the congestion cost based on the congestion risk of admitting the visitor to the network. This cost evaluation is similar to *congestion pricing* [6]. Although the user will not be charged based on the congestion cost (this has been proved to be impractical [7]), she will not be admitted if her congestion cost for the visited network is too high.

The congestion cost of the visitor can be modeled by the expected delay incurred by the visitor. We assume adequate resources in the network core, therefore, we only consider delay at an access point based on an $M/M/1$ queueing model [8]:

$$C_{congestion} = k \times \frac{1}{M_v - N_v - 1}$$

where k is the congestion cost coefficient that is determined by the operator. The visited operator would evaluate the following utility function. If the outcome is positive, it would admit the user and otherwise will reject it.

$$U_{visited} = \begin{cases} R_v - C_{congestion} - C_v & \text{if } N_v + 1 < M_v \text{ and } R_v > C_{congestion} + C_v \\ 0 & \text{otherwise} \end{cases}$$

Home Operator Utility Function. If hand-off takes place, the home operator charges the user an extra switching cost, S, (i.e. if the normal service charge is R, the use is charged $R + S$). If hand-off does not take place, then the utility of the home operator would be similar to the utility of the visited operator:

$$U_{home} = \begin{cases} R + S - R_v & \text{if hand-off takes place} \\ R - C_{congestion} - C_h & \text{if hand-off does not take place} \end{cases}$$

Where $C_{congestion}$ is evaluated similar to the visited operator.

User Utility Function. The user utility depends on the *bandwidth*, B, and *delay*, D, that she experiences [6], plus the service charge. We assume a linear function to evaluate a user's utility:

$$U_{user} = \begin{cases} \alpha B_h - \beta D_h - R & \text{if hand-off does not take place} \\ \alpha B_v - \beta D_v - R - S & \text{if hand-off takes place} \end{cases}$$

where α and β determine the user's sensitivity to bandwidth and delay.

Agent Utilities in Each Game State. In 3 of the 4 possible outcomes of the game, no hand-off takes place and the utilities of the agents are as follows:

$$X_1, X_2, X_3 : \begin{cases} U_{user} &= \alpha B_h - \beta D_h - R \\ U_{home} &= R - C_{congestion} - C_h \\ U_{visited} &= 0 \end{cases}$$

If the hand-off takes place (Y) the utility of the agents would be:

$$Y : \begin{cases} U_{user} &= \alpha B_v - \beta D_v - R - S \\ U_{home} &= R + S - R_v \\ U_{visited} &= R_v - C_{congestion} - C_v \end{cases}$$

3   Roaming Prices for Delay Insensitive Users

To find the optimal pricing strategies for roaming charges for delay insensitive users (i.e. $\beta = 0$) we examine the conditions under which the *sub-game perfect equilibrium* for these users is switching. We assume that congestion costs are negligible ($C_{congestion} \approx 0$). This is a valid assumption for any lightly loaded network. With these assumptions the hand-off takes place if:

$$\alpha B_v - \alpha B_h > S$$
$$R_v - C_h < S$$
$$R_v - C_v > 0$$

In the absence of any congestion cost, the last inequality will always hold. That is, the visited operator will always charge more than its cost of service. For now, assume that $R_v - C_h < S$ (we will re-consider this assumption later). The hand-off will take place if:

$$\alpha B_v - \alpha B_h > S$$

The bandwidth available to a user would only be limited by other users in the same access point. We assume that the bandwidth available to any user is a linear function of the number of active users of the same access point, N_h and N_v for the home and the visited operator respectively:

$$B_v(N_v) = (1 - \tfrac{N_v}{M_v})B_v^m$$
$$B_h(N_h) = (1 - \tfrac{N_h}{M_h})B_h^m$$

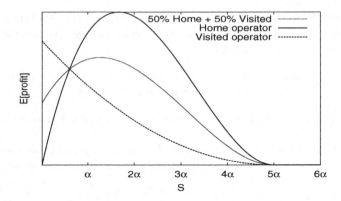

Fig. 2. Expected roaming profit of operators vs. switching cost

where B_v^m and B_h^m are the maximum available bandwidth of the visited and home access points respectively. Assuming a uniform distribution for users, the probability of hand-off is:

$$Pr(B_v(N_v) - B_h(N_h) > \frac{S}{\alpha}) = \int\int_{\text{where } (B_v(N_v)-B_h(N_h))>\frac{S}{\alpha}} \frac{1}{M_v \times M_h} \, dN_v \, dN_h$$

$$= \begin{cases} \frac{2S/\alpha + B_h^m}{2B_v^m} & \text{if } S/\alpha < B_v^m - B_h^m \\ \frac{(B_v^m - S/\alpha)^2}{2B_v^m B_h^m} & \text{if } S/\alpha > B_v^m - B_h^m \text{ and } S/\alpha < B_v^m \\ 0 & \text{if } S/\alpha > B_v^m \end{cases}$$

Figure 2 illustrates the expected value of the roaming profit of each of the operators versus the switching cost. In this figure, the values of S that satisfy $S > R_v - C_h$ are valid. If $R_v < C_h$, then the highest expected value of profit for the visited operator is when $S = 0$. The expected value of profit for the home operator is maximized for a non-zero value of S.

In practice, each operator will play both visited and home roles in the roaming game. If the value of S is the same for both operators in the "roaming agreement," then the optimal pricing strategy depends on how often each operator will play each of the two roles. In Figure 2, the profit of an operator that plays each role 50% of the time is plotted. In such a scenario the operators can easily agree on the switching cost. But if one operator has a priori knowledge that the other operator will take home role more often, then, as illustrated in Figure 3, the optimal value of S for them will be different. The extreme case of such asymmetry in roles is a Mobile Virtual Network Operator (MVNO) [9]. An MVNO always plays the role of a home operator and can never be visited, because it does not own any infrastructure.

If the "roaming agreement" has distinct values for the switching cost between operators then each operator would try to set its subscribers' switching cost to the optimal value of itself, as a home operator. At the same time it would try to reduce the switching cost of the other operator's subscribers to get higher revenue as a visited operator.

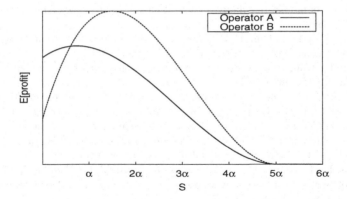

Fig. 3. Expected roaming profit of two operators vs. switching cost. Operator A is 20% of the time visited while operator B is visited 80% of the time.

4   Conclusion and Future Work

In this paper we presented a model for the 802.11 roaming game and constructed the generalized utility functions of the agents involved in the game. The proposed model is rich enough to account for different network aspects of real-world Wi-Fi roaming situations.

To find the optimal pricing strategies of the operators regarding delay insensitive users, we studied the sub-game perfect equilibrium in a congestion-free network and found the optimal value of the switching cost for each of the operators. The results suggest that arbitrarily increasing the roaming charges is not the best strategy for either of the operators.

We believe that Wi-Fi network providers can use the proposed model along with specific field and user behavior information to find optimal pricing strategies. The impact of the relative size of the operators on roaming charges can be studied through service costs. The economic model of mobile virtual network operators (MVNO) [9] for Wi-Fi networks can be studied as a special case of a home operator in the proposed roaming game.

Acknowledgements

I would like to acknowledge my supervisor Prof. Keshav, Prof. Larson, Earl Oliver, Nabeel Ahmed and Mohammad Derakhshani for their comments.

References

1. R.Salsas, C.K.: Roaming free? roaming network selection and inter-operator tariffs. Information Economics and Policy (2004)
2. Valletti, T.: A model of competition in mobile communications. Information Economics and Policy (1999)

3. Valletti, T.: Is mobile telephony a natural oligopoly? Review of Industrial Organization (2003)
4. Crow, B., Widjaja, I., Kim, L., Sakai, P.: IEEE 802.11 Wireless Local Area Networks. Communications Magazine, IEEE 35(9), 116–126 (1997)
5. Akyildiz, I., Wang, X., Wang, W.: Wireless mesh networks: a survey. Computer Networks 47, 445–487 (2005)
6. Keshav, S.: An Engineering Approach to Computer Networking: ATM Networks, the Internet, and the Telephone Network. Addison-Wesley, Reading (1997)
7. Shenker, S., Clark, D., Estrin, D., Herzog, S.: Pricing in computer networks: reshaping the research agenda. SIGCOMM Comput. Commun. Rev. 26, 19–43 (1996)
8. Kleinrock, L.: Queueing Systems, vol. I Theory (New York)
9. Varoutas, D., Katsianis, D., Sphicopoulos, T., Stordahl, K., Welling, I.: On the economics of 3g mobile virtual network operators (mvnos). Wirel. Pers. Commun. 36(2), 129–142 (2006)

On the Complexity of Pure Nash Equilibria in Player-Specific Network Congestion Games*

Heiner Ackermann and Alexander Skopalik

Department of Computer Science
RWTH Aachen, D-52056 Aachen, Germany
{ackermann, skopalik}@cs.rwth-aachen.de

Abstract. Network congestion games with player-specific delay functions do not necessarily possess pure Nash equilibria. We therefore address the computational complexity of the corresponding decision problem, and show that it is NP-complete to decide whether such games possess pure Nash equilibria. This negative result still holds in the case of games with two players only. In contrast, we show that one can decide in polynomial time whether an equilibrium exists if the number of resources is constant.

In addition, we introduce a family of player-specific network congestion games which are guaranteed to possess equilibria. In these games players have identical delay functions, however, each player may only use a certain subset of the edges. For this class of games we prove that finding a pure Nash equilibrium is PLS-complete even in the case of three players. Again, in the case of a constant number of edges an equilibrium can be computed in polynomial time.

We conclude that the number of resources has a bigger impact on the computation complexity of certain problems related to network congestion games than the number of players.

1 Introduction

Network congestion games are a well-known and generally accepted approach to model resource allocation among selfish agents in large-scale networks like the internet. In these games agents share a network and each of them selects a path with minimum delay (cost, payoff) that connects an individual pair of nodes. The delay of a path equals the sum of delays of the edges in that path, and the delay of an edge depends on the number of players currently using that edge. In recent years network congestion games have been considered in various occurrences and with respect to different questions like the price of anarchy, the computational complexity of finding Nash equilibria[1], or certain network design

---

* This work was supported in part by the EU within the 6th Framework Programme under contract 001907 (DELIS) and the German Israeli Foundation (GIF) under contract 877/05.
[1] In this paper, the term *Nash equilibrium* always refers to a pure Nash equilibrium.

X. Deng and F.C. Graham (Eds.): WINE 2007, LNCS 4858, pp. 419–430, 2007.
© Springer-Verlag Berlin Heidelberg 2007

problems. For an introduction into many of these questions we refer the reader to the forthcoming book of Nisan, Tardos, Roughgarden, and Vazirani [12].

In this paper we are interested in *player-specific network congestion games*. In such games we consider a finite set of players and assume that each of them is equipped with a set of player-specific delay functions. This is in contrast to the previously mentioned games in which all players sharing an edge observe the same delay. Player-specific network congestion games naturally arise when different players have different preferences on the edges of the network. Some players might prefer to use motor-ways, others might prefer to use scenic roads. It is well known that player-specific network congestion games do not necessarily possess Nash equilibria [11]. We therefore investigate the computational complexity of deciding whether such a game possesses a Nash equilibrium. We prove by a reduction from the problem NODE-DISJOINT PATH that this problem is NP-complete. We also consider games with constant number of players or resources. In the first case the decision problem remains NP-complete even in the case of two players, whereas in the second case we present a polynomial time algorithm.

In order to bypass the limitations of general player-specific congestion games, we introduce a family of games for which the existence of a Nash equilibrium is guaranteed by Rosenthal's potential function [13]. We assume that all players sharing an edge observe the same delay, however, each player may only use a certain subset of the edges. Such games naturally arise when drivers are prohibited to use certain roads, e. g., trucks may be prohibited to use narrows roads, slow vehicles may be prohibited to use motor-ways. These games – in the following called *restricted network congestion games* – are closely related to standard network congestion games in which players compute their delays with respect to common delay functions and in which each player may use every edge. Fabrikant, Papadimitriou, and Talwar [6] introduce standard network congestion games and show that computing an equilibrium is PLS-complete, that is, computing a Nash equilibrium is "as hard to compute as any object whose existence is guaranteed by a potential function" [6]. Ackermann, Röglin, and Vöcking [1] present a simplified proof for this. Thus, computing a Nash equilibrium of a restricted network congestion game is PLS-complete, too. However, the previously mentioned proofs require an arbitrary number of players and resources. In this paper we consider games in which one of these two parameters is kept constant. In the case of a constant number of player we prove that computing a Nash equilibrium remains PLS-complete, whereas it is polynomial time solvable in the case of constant number of resources. The later result follows easily by a potential function argument and applies to every congestion game with common delay functions and with a constant number of resources. Unfortunately, we failed to prove PLS-completeness for computing Nash equilibria in standard network congestion games with a constant number of players. This question was our primary motivation and remains a challenging open problem.

To the best of our knowledge, this is the first paper systematically comparing the impact of the number of player and of the resources on the computational complexity of certain problems related to player-specific network congestion games. From our results we conclude that the impact of the number of resources is much bigger than the impact of the number of players.

Player-specific Network Congestion Games. A player-specific network congestion game Γ consists of four components: (1) a network $G = (V, E)$ with m directed edges, (2) a set $\mathcal{N} = \{1, \ldots n\}$ of n players, (3) for every player i a source-sink pair $(s_i, t_i) \in V \times V$, and (4) for every player i and every edge $e \in E$ a non-decreasing delay function $d_i^e \colon \mathbb{N} \to \mathbb{N}$. The *strategy space* of player i equals the set of paths connecting source s_i with target t_i. We denote by $S = (P_1, \ldots, P_n)$ a *state of the game* where player i chooses path P_i. Furthermore, we denote by $n_e(S) = |\{i \in \mathcal{N} \mid e \in P_i\}|$ the congestion on edge e in state S, that is, $n_e(S)$ equals the number of players sharing edge e in state S. Players act selfishly and choose paths with minimum delay given fixed choices of the other players. The delay $\delta_i(S)$ of player i in state S equals $\sum_{e \in P_i} d_i^e(n_e(S))$. Finally, we call a state S a *Nash equilibrium* if no player has an incentive to change her strategy.

It is well know that, in general, a pure Nash equilibrium is not guaranteed to exist. However, if the network consists of parallel links only or if for every edge e the player-specific delay functions d_i^e are identical, then a Nash equilibrium is guaranteed to exist [10,13]. In the following, we consider also network congestion games with common delay functions and assume that each player is restricted to a certain subset of the edges. We call such a game a *restricted network congestion game*. Such a game can easily be interpreted as a player-specific game by defining player-specific delay functions in the following way. If a player is allowed to use an edge, her delay functions equals the common one, if a player is not allowed to use an edge, she observes delay ∞ for every congestion on that edge. By Rosenthal's potential function argument [13], every restricted network congestion games possess a Nash equilibrium.

The Complexity Class PLS. A local search problem Π is given by its set of instances $\mathcal{I}_\Pi$. For every instance $I \in \mathcal{I}_\Pi$, we are given a finite set of feasible solutions $\mathcal{F}(I) \subseteq \{0, 1\}^*$, an objective function $c \colon \mathcal{F}(I) \to \mathbb{N}$, and for every feasible solution $S \in \mathcal{F}(I)$ a neighborhood $\mathcal{N}(S, I) \subseteq \mathcal{F}(I)$. Given an instance I of a local search problem, we seek for a *locally optimal solution* S^*, i. e., a solution which does not have a strictly better neighbor with respect to the objective function c.

A local search problem Π belongs to PLS if the following polynomial time algorithms exist: an algorithm A which computes for every instance I of Π an initial feasible solution $S_0 \in \mathcal{F}(I)$, an algorithm B which computes for every instance I of Π and every feasible solution $S \in \mathcal{F}(I)$ the objective value $c(S)$, and an algorithm C which determines for every instance I of Π and every feasible solution $S \in \mathcal{F}(I)$ whether S is locally optimal or not, and finds a better solution in the neighborhood of S in the latter case.

Johnson et al. [8] introduce the notion of a PLS-*reduction*. A problem Π_1 in PLS is PLS-reducible to a problem Π_2 in PLS if there exist polynomial-time computable functions f and g such that f maps instances I of Π_1 to instances

$f(I)$ of Π_2, g maps pairs (S_2, I) where S_2 denotes a solution of $f(I)$ to solutions S_1 of I, and for all instances I of Π_1, if S_2 is a local optimum of instance $f(I)$, then $g(S_2, I)$ is a local optimum of I. A local search problem Π in PLS is PLS-*complete* if every problem in PLS is PLS-reducible to Π. PLS-completeness results for various local search problems can be found in [8,14].

Related Work. Most closely related to our work is the work of Milchtaich [10,11] and the work of Dunkel and Schulz [5]. Milchtaich [10] introduces player-specific network congestion games on parallel links and proves that every such game possesses a Nash equilibrium if the player-specific delay functions are non-decreasing. In [11] he presents some network topologies such that every player-specific network congestion game on such a topology possesses an equilibrium without any assumption on the delay functions except monotonicity. Dunkel and Schulz [5] consider the computational complexity of deciding whether a weighted network congestion games possesses a Nash equilibrium. In such games players sharing an edge observe the same delay, however, the congestion on an edge depends on the weighted number of players. They prove that this decision problem is NP-complete. Ackermann, Röglin, and Vöcking [2] prove that every player-specific matroid congestion game possesses a Nash equilibrium. In such games the players' strategy spaces are the sets of bases of a matroid on the resources. Additionally, they show that the matroid property is the maximal property on the strategy spaces guaranteeing the existence of equilibria. Chakrabarty, Mehta, and Nagarajan [4] consider player-specific network congestion games on (a constant number of) parallel links from a global optimization perspective, and investigate whether one can compute social optimal states of such games efficiently. Anshelevich et al. [3] and Meyers [9] consider several problem involving congestion games with a constant number of players.

2   General Player-Specific Network Games

In this section, we consider the complexity of deciding whether a general player-specific network congestion game possesses a Nash equilibrium.

Theorem 1. *It is* NP-*complete to decide whether a player-specific network congestion game with* two players *possesses a Nash equilibrium.*

Proof. Obviously, the decision problem belongs to NP as one can decide in polynomial time whether a given state S of such a game is a Nash equilibrium. In order to prove that the problem is complete, we present a polynomial time reduction from the NODE-DISJOINT PATH problem. An instance of the NODE-DISJOINT PATH problem consists of a directed graph $G = (V, E)$ and two pairwise disjoint node pairs (s_1, t_1) and (s_2, t_2). Given such an instance, we like to decide whether there exist node-disjoint paths from s_1 to t_1 and from s_2 to t_2. It is well know that this problem is NP-complete [7].

Given an instance $(G, (s_1, t_1), (s_2, t_2))$ of the problem NODE-DISJOINT PATH we construct a player-specific network congestion game with two players as follows. Given $G = (V, E)$ we substitute every node $v \in V$ by the gadget G_v

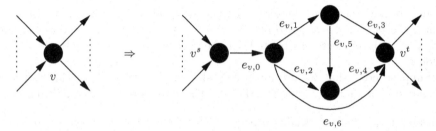

Fig. 1. The gadget G_v of a node v

presented in Figure 1 in order to obtain the network $G_\Gamma = (V_\Gamma, E_\Gamma)$ on which the game is played. Player $i \in \{1, 2\}$ wants to allocate a path between the nodes s_i^s and t_i^t in G_Γ. Observe that this construction ensures a one-to-one corresponds between the paths in G and in G_Γ in the natural way if we ignore the precise subpaths through every gadget. The player-specific delay functions are chosen as follows. For every edge $e = (v_i^t, v_j^s)$, i. e., for edges that represent edges from the original graph G, we assume that for each player and every congestion the delay on such an edge equals 0. In the following, let M be a sufficiently large number. Then, the player-specific delay functions of edges $e_{v,i}$, $i \in \{0, \dots, 6\}$, are defined as presented in Figure 2. Observe that every gadget G_v implements a subgame that is played by the players if both want to allocate a path connecting the nodes v^s and v^t. If only one player wants to allocate such a path, then she allocates a player-specific shortest path from v^s to v^t. If we choose M sufficiently large, such that the second player will never allocate one of the edges $e_{v,5}$ or $e_{v,6}$, then the cost of these shortest path are 56 and 62. Suppose now, that the two players play such a subgame. In this case, it is not difficult to verify that the subgame possesses no Nash equilibrium. Note that a game that is similar to the gadgets presented here can be found in [11].

	$e_{v,0}$		$e_{v,1}$		$e_{v,2}$		$e_{v,3}$		$e_{v,4}$		$e_{v,5}$		$e_{v,6}$	
congestion	1	2	1	2	1	2	1	2	1	2	1	2	1	2
player 1	0	M	20	28	45	45	48	48	20	30	16	16	65	65
player 2	0	M	14	18	45	45	48	48	20	30	M	M	M	M

Fig. 2. The player-specific delay functions of the edges e_v, i

Suppose now, that we are given two node-disjoint paths P_1 and P_2 in G connecting s_1 and t_1, and s_2 and t_2. We map these paths to paths in G_Γ in the natural way, and choose player-specific shortest paths through every gadget. Let $n(P_i)$ be the number of nodes on the path P_i. Thus, player 1 has delay $56 \cdot n(P_1)$, and player 2 has delay $62 \cdot n(P_2)$. If one of the players had an incentive to change her strategy, then she will only choose a path in which she shares no gadget with the other player, as otherwise her delay would increase to at least M. This is true as in this case the players would share at least one edge $e_{v,0}$. This also implies that the delay of the other player does not increase due to the strategy change of the first player. Observe that this holds for any further best response. Thus, the players converge to an equilibrium after $O(n)$ best responses as the delay of a player decreases by at least the cost of the shortest path through a gadget.

Suppose now, that we are given a Nash equilibrium of Γ. In this case the players do not share a gadget as otherwise the state is no Nash equilibrium.   □

Theorem 2. *One can decide in polynomial time whether a player-specific network congestion game Γ with a constant number of resources possesses a Nash equilibrium.*

In order to prove Theorem 2, we generalize an algorithm introduced by Chakrabarty et al. [4] that computes a social optimal state of a player-specific network congestion game with a constant number of parallel links. Details of this approach can be found in a full version of this paper.

3   Restricted Network Congestion Games

In this section, we analyze the complexity of computing Nash equilibria of restricted network congestion games with a constant number of players or resources.

Theorem 3. *Computing a Nash equilibrium of a restricted network congestion games with k players is PLS-complete for any $k \geq 3$.*

Proof. We prove the theorem by a reduction from the local search problem *positive not-all-equal 2-satisfiability* POSNAE2SAT which is known to be PLS-complete [14]. Let $x_1, \ldots, x_n$ be boolean variables. An instance φ of POSNAE2SAT consists of a set of m weighted clauses C_j over the variables x_i which contain two positive literals each. We denote by w_j the (integer) weight of clause C_j. A clause is satisfied if and only if the two variables it contains have different values. By $\bar{X} = (X_1, \ldots, X_n) \in \{0, 1\}^n$ we denote a bit assignment to the variables $x_1, \ldots, x_n$. The weight $w(\bar{X})$ of a bit assignment $\bar{X}$ is defined as the sum of the weights of all satisfied clauses. We denote the maximum weight by $W = \sum_{j=1}^{m} w_j$. By $\bar{X}_{X_i=b}$, we denote the bit vector $(X_1, \ldots, X_{i-1}, b, X_{i+1}, \ldots, X_n)$. A local optimum of φ is a bit assignment $\bar{X}$ whose weight cannot be increased by flipping a single variable x_i, i.e., $w(\bar{X}) \geq w(\bar{X}_{X_i=b})$ for all $1 \leq i \leq n$ and $b \in \{0, 1\}$. Therefore, the neighborhood of an assignment is defined as the set of assignments with Hamming distance one.

Given an instance φ, we construct a restricted network congestion game Γ_φ such that one can easily construct a local optimum of φ given a Nash equilibrium of Γ_φ. Γ_φ simulates two copies of φ, which we call φ_A and φ_B, in parallel. Furthermore, the game consists of three players, a *bit player* and two *clause players*.

Every path the bit player can choose determines assignments $\bar{X}_A$ and $\bar{X}_B$ for φ_A and φ_B, respectively. The set of paths the bit player can choose from can be divided into two disjoint sets $\mathcal{P}_1$ and $\mathcal{P}_2$. If she chooses a path from $\mathcal{P}_1$, $\bar{X}_A$ is the actual assignment for φ and $\bar{X}_B$ is a (probably better) neighboring assignment. For every path in $\mathcal{P}_2$ it is the other way round. The bit player switches between paths in $\mathcal{P}_1$ and $\mathcal{P}_2$ as long as she can switch to a better neighboring assignment.

The paths of the clause players lead through $2m$ gadgets. For both copies of φ there is one gadget for every clause. The two clause players simulate a clause by choosing paths through the corresponding gadget. We ensure that they always have an incentive to correctly simulate the clauses according to the assignments determined by the bit player.

To implement this, we introduce four levels of delays: large, medium, small, and tiny. If the bit player is on a path in $\mathcal{P}_1$ ($\mathcal{P}_2$) and the clause players do not correctly simulate the clauses of φ_A (φ_B) according to the assignment $\bar{X}_A$ ($\bar{X}_B$), at least one of them has large delay. If the bit player is on a path in $\mathcal{P}_1$ ($\mathcal{P}_2$) and the clause players simulate φ_A (φ_B) correctly, she observes medium delay proportional to the weight of the unsatisfied clauses according to the actual assignment $\bar{X}_A$ ($\bar{X}_B$). Furthermore, she has additionally small delay that is proportional to the weight of the unsatisfied clauses of the neighboring assignment $\bar{X}_B$ ($\bar{X}_A$). If the bit player is on a path in $\mathcal{P}_1$ ($\mathcal{P}_2$) and the clause players do not correctly simulate φ_B (φ_A), they additionally have tiny delays. This ensures that the clause players have an incentive to correctly simulate the clauses and that the bit player has an incentive to choose the best neighboring assignment.

As long as there is a better neighboring assignment, the bit player can change from a path from $\mathcal{P}_1$ ($\mathcal{P}_2$) to a path from $\mathcal{P}_2$ ($\mathcal{P}_1$) by adopting the neighboring assignment as the actual assignment and by choosing a new neighboring assignment.

We are now ready to describe our construction in detail. We present the network of Γ_φ as two subnetworks. One subnetwork contains the edges the bit player is allowed to choose, the other subnetwork contains the edges the two clause players are allowed to choose. The edges that are contained in both networks are called *connection edges*. The connection edges are almost the only edges that cause delay to the players. Almost all other edges have delay 0 regardless of the number of players using it. To further simplify the presentation, we merge path segments into sets of edges and use dashed edges to indicate these path segments in Figure 3 and 4. The precise network can be constructed by concatenating the edges from a set in arbitrary order while adding an edge that is not contained in the other subnetwork between every pair of consecutive edges with constant delay 0.

The subnetwork of the bit player is depicted in Figure 3. We now define the corresponding sets of edges and the delays on the edges. Let $M \gg \alpha W \gg \alpha \gg \beta W \gg \beta \geq 4m$.

- $\mathcal{P}^A_{x_i=b} := \{u^A_{j,x_i=b}, t^B_{j,x_i=b}|$ for all clauses C_j with $x_i \in C_j\}$. Such a path segment corresponds to the fact that bit $x_i = b$ in the assignment $\bar{X}_A$. It also corresponds to the fact that $x_i = b$ in the assignment $\bar{X}_B$, unless the bit player chooses to flip this bit (see below). The u-edges have delay 0 for one player and delay M for two or more players. They induce large delay to clause players if they do not correctly simulate this bit assignment φ_A. The

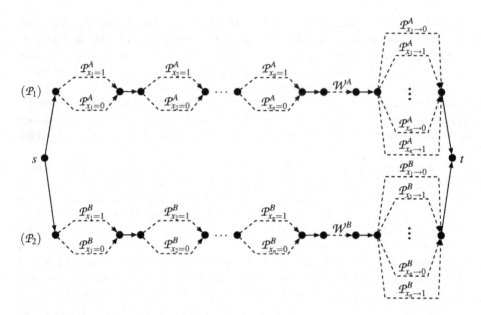

Fig. 3. The subnetwork of the bit player. The dashed edges correspond to set of edges.

t-edges have delay 0 for one player and delay 1 for two or more players. They induce tiny delay to the clause players if they do not correctly simulate the bit assignment φ_B.

- $\mathcal{W}^A := \{w_{j,0}^A, w_{j,1}^A |$ for all $1 \leq j \leq m\}$. If the clause players correctly simulate φ_A, this path segment induces medium delay proportional to the weight of the unsatisfied clauses of $\bar{X}_A$ to the bit player. The edges $w_{j,0}^A$ and $w_{j,1}^A$ have delay 0 for one or two players and delay αw_j for three players.

- $\mathcal{P}_{x_i \to b}^A := \{w_{j,0,x_i \to b}^A, w_{j,1,x_i \to b}^A |$ for all $1 \leq j \leq m$ with $x_i \notin C_j\} \cup \{t_{j,x_i \to b}^B, w_{j,x_i \to b}^A |$ for all $1 \leq j \leq m$ with $x_i \in C_j\}$. If the bit player chooses such a path segment, then she determines the neighboring assignment $\bar{X}_B$ to be obtained from $\bar{X}_A$ by flipping bit x_i to b. If the clause players correctly simulate φ_A, this path segment induces small delay proportional to the weight of the unsatisfied clauses of that neighboring assignment. For each $1 \leq j \leq m$ with $x_i \notin C_j$, the edges $w_{j,0,x_i \to b}^A$ and $w_{j,1,x_i \to b}^A$ have delay 0 for at most two players and delay βw_j for three. For each $1 \leq j \leq m$ with $x_i \in C_j$, the edge $w_{j,x_i \to b}^A$ has delay 0 for one player and delay βw_j for two or more players. The t-edges have delay 0 for one player and delay 2 for two or more players. They induce tiny delay to the clause players if they do not simulate this bit flip in φ_B.

Additionally, there are sets $\mathcal{P}_{x_i=b}^B$, $\mathcal{W}^B$, and $\mathcal{P}_{x_i \to b}^B$ which are defined in the same manner.

The two clause players are symmetric in the sense that they play on the same subnetwork and have the same source and target node. Their subnetwork is a concatenation of m A-gadgets and m B-gadgets. Figure 4 depicts such a pair of

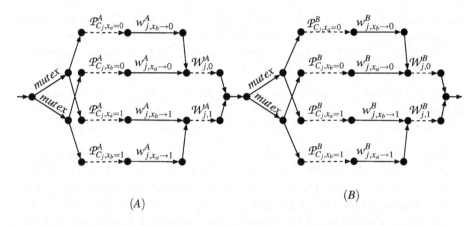

$$(A) \qquad\qquad\qquad\qquad (B)$$

Fig. 4. This figure shows an A-gadget and a B-gadget for a clause $C_j = \{x_a, x_b\}$. There are four paths through each gadget. From top to bottom, we denote the paths with $x_a = 0$, $x_b = 0$, $x_a = 1$, and $x_b = 1$. The subnetwork of the two clause players is a concatenations of the A- and B-gadgets for all clauses.

gadgets. Their source-sink paths lead through all $2m$ gadgets. The edges labeled with *mutex* have delay 0 for one player and delay M^2 for two or more players. The dashed edges correspond to the following sets of connection edges:

- $\mathcal{P}^A_{C_j, x_i = b} := \{u^A_{j, x_i = 1-b}, t^A_{j, x_i = 1-b}, t^A_{j, x_i \to 1-b}\}$. A clause player using such a path segment simulates the assignment of b to x_i of $\bar{X}_A$ in the clause C_j of φ_A. In the following, we say she sets $x_i = b$ in this gadget. If this is not a correct simulation and the bit player is on a path from $\mathcal{P}_1$, then a u-edge induces large delay. If this is not a correct simulation and the bit player is on a path from $\mathcal{P}_2$, then a t-edge induces tiny delay.
- For each $d \in \{0, 1\}$, $\mathcal{W}^A_{j,d} := \{w^A_{j,d}\} \cup \{w^A_{j,d,x_i \to b} | \text{ for all } b \in \{0, 1\} \text{ and } 1 \le i \le n \text{ with } x_i \notin C_j\}$. If and only if both players use the same $\mathcal{W}^A_{j,d}$ path segment, they simulate an unsatisfying assignment for C_j. If, additionally, the bit player chooses a path from $\mathcal{P}_1$, the edge $w^A_{j,d}$ has medium delay proportional to w_j. Furthermore, one of the edges $w^A_{j,d,x_i \to b}$ induces small delay if x_i is not in clause C_j. Note, that in the case that x_i is in the clause C_j, there are extra edges in the gadget.

The sets $\mathcal{P}^B_{C_j, x_i = b}$ and $\mathcal{W}^B_{j,d}$ are defined analogously.

We now prove that every Nash equilibrium of Γ_φ corresponds to a locally optimal assignment of φ. Consider a Nash equilibrium of Γ_φ and assume that the bit player chooses a path from the set $\mathcal{P}_1$. Let $\mathcal{P}^A_{x_1 = X_1}, \dots, \mathcal{P}^A_{x_n = X_n}$, $\mathcal{W}^A$, and $\mathcal{P}^A_{x_{i^*} \to b}$ be the path segments she chooses. Then the following properties hold.

Lemma 4.

a) *In every A-gadget for every clause $C_j = \{x_a, x_b\}$ one clause player sets $x_a = X_a$ and the other player sets $x_b = X_b$.*

b) In every *B*-gadget for every clause $C_j = \{x_a, x_b\}$ with $a, b \neq i^*$ one clause player sets $x_a = X_a$ and the other player sets $x_b = X_b$.

c) In every *B*-gadget for every clause $C_j = \{x_{i^*}, x_c\}$ one clause player sets $x_c = X_c$ and the other player sets $x_{i^*} = b$.

Proof. Observe that in any gadget for any clause $C_j = \{x_a, x_b\}$ one of the clause players chooses $x_a = 0$ or $x_a = 1$ whereas the other player chooses $x_b = 0$ or $x_b = 1$. Otherwise both have delay M^2 and, thus, an incentive to change.

a) Consider the *A*-gadget of a clause $C_j = \{x_a, x_b\}$. Due to our assumptions, all edges of the path segment $\mathcal{P}^A_{C_j, x_a = X_a}$ are not used by the bit player and therefore have delay 0 for a single clause player, whereas the edge $u^A_{j, x_a = X_a}$ that is contained in the path segment $\mathcal{P}^A_{C_j, x_a = (1 - X_a)}$ is used by the bit player and therefore causes delay M to a clause player. The same is true for the path segments $\mathcal{P}^A_{C_j, x_b = X_b}$ and $\mathcal{P}^A_{C_j, x_b = (1 - X_b)}$, respectively. The delay of all other edges in the gadget sums up to less than M. Thus, in every Nash equilibrium, one of the clause players chooses $x_a = X_a$ and the other player chooses $x_b = X_b$.

b) In the *B*-gadgets all w^B-edges and all edges in the $\mathcal{W}^B$-sets are not used by the bit player and therefore have delay 0. Consider the *B*-gadget for a clause $C_j = \{x_a, x_b\}$ with $a, b \neq i^*$. All edges of the path segment $\mathcal{P}^B_{C_j, x_a = X_a}$ are not used by the bit player and therefore have delay 0 for a single clause player, whereas the edge $t^B_{j, x_a = X_a}$ that is contained in the path segment $\mathcal{P}^B_{C_j, x_a = (1 - X_a)}$ is used by the bit player and therefore has delay 1 for a clause player. The same is true for the path segments $\mathcal{P}^B_{C_j, x_b = X_b}$ and $\mathcal{P}^B_{C_j, x_b = (1 - X_b)}$, respectively.

c) Let $C_j = \{x_{i^*}, x_c\}$ be a clause that contains x_{i^*}. In the *B*-gadgets of clause C_j one clause player sets $x_c = X_c$ which has delay 0. The other clause player sets $x_{i^*} = b$ which has delay of at most 1. The path $x_{i^*} = 1 - b$ has delay of at least 2 due to the edge $t^B_{j, x_i \to b}$ which is currently used by the bit player. □

Note that an equivalent version of Lemma 4 holds for Nash equilibria in which the bit player chooses a path from the set $\mathcal{P}_2$. The following corollary follows directly from Lemma 4.

Corollary 5. *In every Nash equilibrium the path segment $\mathcal{W}^A$ has delay $\alpha(W - w(\bar{X}))$ for the bit player. Furthermore, the delay on the path segment $\mathcal{P}^A_{x_{i^*} \to b}$ equals $\beta(W - w(\bar{X}_{x_{i^*} = b}))$ plus an additive term of at most $2m$ for the bit player.*

Lemma 6. *Every Nash equilibrium of Γ_φ corresponds to a local optimum of φ.*

Proof. For the purpose of contradiction, consider a Nash equilibrium that does not correspond to a local optimum of φ. Let $\mathcal{P}^A_{x_1 = X_1}, \ldots, \mathcal{P}^A_{x_n = X_n}, \mathcal{W}^A$, and $\mathcal{P}^A_{x_{i^*} \to b}$ be the path segments used by the bit player. By Corollary 5, we can conclude that $\bar{X}_{X_{i^*} = b}$ is the best neighboring assignment, otherwise the path segment $\mathcal{P}^A_{x_{i^*} \to b}$ has more delay then another path segment $\mathcal{P}^A_{x_{i^{**}} \to b^{**}}$ for the bit player. We show that this implies that the bit player can improve her delay by choosing another path. The delays of all edges in the set $\mathcal{W}^A$ sum up to $\alpha(W - w(\bar{X}))$. Thus, the bit player has at least this amount of delay.

Now, observe that each path segment $\mathcal{P}^B_{x_i=X_1}$ with $i \neq i^*$ has delay 0 for the bit player since the clause players correctly simulate φ_B with the assignment $\bar{X}_{X_{i^*}=b}$. The path segment $\mathcal{P}^B_{x_{i^*}=b}$ has delay of at most m. The delays of all edges in the set $\mathcal{W}^B$ sum up to $\alpha(W - w(\bar{X}_{x_{i^*}=b}))$. The delay of any path $\mathcal{P}^B_{x_{i'}\to b'}$ is at most $\beta W + 2m$. Note that $\beta W + 3m < \alpha$. Thus, the bit player could decrease her delay by changing to such a path. This is a contradiction to the assumption that this is a Nash equilibrium.   □

We conclude that every Nash equilibrium of G_φ corresponds to a locally optimal assignment of φ. Obviously, the construction of G_φ and the mapping of an equilibrium to a assignment of φ can be done in polynomial time. This conclude the proof of Theorem 3   □

It is an interesting open problem whether computing Nash equilibria for restricted network congestion games with two players remains PLS-complete. Moreover, it is an challenging open problem to prove any results in standard congestion games with a constant number of players.

Theorem 7. *One can compute a Nash equilibrium of a restricted network congestion game Γ with a constant number of resources in polynomial time.*

Theorem 7 is a consequence of the simple observation that there are only polynomial many different possible values for Rosenthal's potential functions. Again, details can be found in a full version of this paper.

Acknowledgment

The authors wish to thank Matthias Englert and Berthold Vöcking for helpful discussions.

References

1. Ackermann, H., Röglin, H., Vöcking, B.: On the impact of combinatorial structure on congestion games. In: Proc. of the 47th Annual IEEE Symposium on Foundations of Computer Science (FOCS), pp. 613–622 (2006)
2. Ackermann, H., Röglin, H., Vöcking, B.: Pure Nash equilibria in player-specific and weighted congestion games. In: Spirakis, P.G., Mavronicolas, M., Kontogiannis, S.C. (eds.) WINE 2006. LNCS, vol. 4286, pp. 50–61. Springer, Heidelberg (2006)
3. Anshelevich, E., Dasgupta, A., Kleinberg, J.M., Tardos, É., Wexler, T., Roughgarden, T.: The price of stability for network design with fair cost allocation. In: Proc. of the 45th Annual IEEE Symposium on Foundations of Computer Science (FOCS), pp. 295–304 (2004)
4. Chakrabarty, D., Mehta, A., Nagarajan, V.: Fairness and optimality in congestion games. In: Proc. of the 6th ACM conference on Electronic Commerce (EC), pp. 52–57. ACM Press, New York (2005)

5. Dunkel, J., Schulz, A.S.: On the complexity of pure-strategy Nash equilibria in congestion and local-effect games. In: Spirakis, P.G., Mavronicolas, M., Kontogiannis, S.C. (eds.) WINE 2006. LNCS, vol. 4286, pp. 62–73. Springer, Heidelberg (2006)
6. Fabrikant, A., Papadimitriou, C., Talwar, K.: The complexity of pure Nash equilibria. In: Proc. of the 36th Annual ACM Symposium on Theory of Computing (STOC), pp. 604–612 (2004)
7. Garey, M.R., Johnson, D.S.: Computers and Intractability: A Guide to the Theory of NP-Completeness. W. H. Freeman & Co., New York (1979)
8. Johnson, D.S., Papadimtriou, C.H., Yannakakis, M.: How easy is local search? Journal on Computer and System Sciences 37(1), 79–100 (1988)
9. Meyers, C.: Network Flow Problems and Congestion Games: Complexitiy and Approximation. Massachusetts Institute of Technology (2006)
10. Milchtaich, I.: Congestion games with player-specific payoff functions. Games and Economic Behavior 13(1), 111–124 (1996)
11. Milchtaich, I.: The equilibrium existence problem in finite network congestion games. In: Spirakis, P.G., Mavronicolas, M., Kontogiannis, S.C. (eds.) WINE 2006. LNCS, vol. 4286, pp. 87–98. Springer, Heidelberg (2006)
12. Nisan, N., Roughgarden, T., Tardos, E., Vazirani, V.: Algorithmic Game Theory. Cambridge University Press, Cambridge (forthcoming)
13. Rosenthal, R.W.: A class of games possessing pure-strategy Nash equilibria. Int. Journal of Game Theory 2, 65–67 (1973)
14. Schäffer, A.A., Yannakakis, M.: Simple local search problems that are hard to solve. SIAM Journal on Computing 20(1), 56–87 (1991)

The Stable Roommates Problem with Globally-Ranked Pairs

David J. Abraham[1,*], Ariel Levavi[1],
David F. Manlove[2,**], and Gregg O'Malley[2]

[1] Computer Science Department, Carnegie Mellon University, USA
dabraham@cs.cmu.edu, alevavi@andrew.cmu.edu
[2] Department of Computing Science, University of Glasgow, UK
davidm@dcs.gla.ac.uk, gregg@dcs.gla.ac.uk

Abstract. We introduce a restriction of the stable roommates problem in which roommate pairs are ranked globally. In contrast to the unrestricted problem, weakly stable matchings are guaranteed to exist, and additionally, can be found in polynomial time. However, it is still the case that strongly stable matchings may not exist, and so we consider the complexity of finding weakly stable matchings with various desirable properties. In particular, we present a polynomial-time algorithm to find a rank-maximal (weakly stable) matching. This is the first generalization of the algorithm due to Irving et al. [18] to a non-bipartite setting. Also, we prove several hardness results in an even more restricted setting for each of the problems of finding weakly stable matchings that are of maximum size, are egalitarian, have minimum regret, and admit the minimum number of weakly blocking pairs.

1 Introduction

The STABLE ROOMMATES problem (SR) [11,16,15,17] involves pairing-up a set of *agents*, each of whom ranks the others in (not necessarily strict) order of preference. Agents can declare each other *unacceptable*, in which case they cannot be paired together. Our task is to find a pairing of mutually acceptable agents such that no two agents would prefer to partner each other over those that we prescribed for them.

We represent acceptable pairs by a graph $G = (V, E)$, with one vertex $u \in V$ for each agent, and an edge $\{u, v\} \in E$ whenever agents u and v are mutually acceptable. A pairing is just a *matching* M of G, i.e. a subset of edges in E, no two of which share a vertex. If $\{u, v\} \in M$, we say that u is *matched* in M and $M(u)$ denotes v, otherwise u is *unmatched* in M. An agent u prefers one matching M' over another M if i) u is matched in M' and unmatched in M, or ii) u prefers $M'(u)$ to $M(u)$. Similarly, u is indifferent between M' and M if i) u is unmatched in M' and M, or ii) u is indifferent between $M'(u)$ and $M(u)$.

* Research supported in part by NSF grants IIS-0427858 and CCF-0514922IIS-0427858. Part of this work completed while visiting Microsoft Research, Redmond.
** Supported by EPSRC grant EP/E011993/1.

A matching M is *weakly stable* if it admits no *strongly blocking pair*, which is an edge $\{u, v\} \in E \backslash M$ such that u and v prefer $\{\{u, v\}\}$ to M. A matching M is *strongly stable* if it admits no *weakly blocking pair*, which is an edge $\{u, v\} \in E \backslash M$ such that u prefers $\{\{u, v\}\}$ to M, while v either prefers $\{\{u, v\}\}$ to M, or is indifferent between them.

In this paper, we introduce and study the STABLE ROOMMATES WITH GLOB-ALLY-RANKED PAIRS problem (SR-GRP). An instance of SR-GRP is a restriction of SR in which preferences may be derived from a ranking function $rank : E \to \mathbb{N}$. An agent u prefers v to w if $e = \{u, v\}$, $e' = \{u, w\}$ and $rank(e) < rank(e')$, and u is indifferent between them if $rank(e) = rank(e')$.

Before giving our motivation for studying this restriction, we introduce some notation. We define E_i to be the set of edges with rank i, and $E_{\leq i}$ to be the set $E_1 \cup E_2 \cup \ldots \cup E_i$. Additionally, let $n = |V|$ be the number of agents, $m = |E|$ be the number of mutually acceptable pairs. Without loss of generality, we assume the maximum edge rank is at most m. Also, we make the standard assumption in stable marriage problems that the adjacency list for a vertex is given in order of preference/rank.

Motivation. In several real-world settings, agents have restricted preferences that can be represented by the SR-GRP model. A pairwise kidney exchange market [26,25,1] is one such setting. Here, patients with terminal kidney-disease obtain compatible donors by swapping their own willing but incompatible donors. We can model the basic market by constructing one vertex for each patient, and an undirected edge between any two patients where the incompatible donor for one patient is compatible with the other patient, and vice versa. Of course, patients may have different preferences over donors. However, since the expected years of life gained from a transplant is similar amongst all compatible kidneys, the medical community has suggested that patient preferences should be *binary/dichotomous* [14,7] – i.e., patients are indifferent between all compatible donors. Binary preferences are easily modelled in SR-GRP by giving all edges the same rank.

A second example also comes from pairwise kidney exchange markets. When two (patient,donor) pairs are matched with each other (in order to swap donors), we are not certain if the swap can occur until expensive last-minute compatibility tests are performed on the donors and patients. If either potential transplant in the swap is incompatible, the swap is cancelled and the two patients must wait for a future match run. Since doctors can rank potential swaps by their chance of success, and patients prefer swaps with better chances of success, this generalizes the binary preference model above, and can clearly still be modelled by SR-GRP.

One final real-world setting is described in [4]. When colleges pair-up freshmen roommates, it is not feasible for students to rank each other explicitly. Instead, each student submits a form which describes him/herself in several different dimensions (e.g. bedtime preference, cleanliness preference etc). Students can then be represented as points in a multidimensional space, and preferences over other students can be inferred by a distance function. Note that this model [4] is a restriction of SR-GRP in that it is not possible to declare another student unacceptable.

In order to highlight the generality of the SR-GRP model, we introduce a second restriction of SR called STABLE ROOMMATES WITH GLOBALLY-ACYCLIC PREFERENCES (SR-GAP). Instances of SR-GAP satisfy the following characterization test: given an arbitrary instance I of SR with $G = (V, E)$, construct a digraph $P(G)$, containing one vertex e for each edge in $e \in E$, and an arc from $e = \{u, v\} \in E$ to $e' = \{u, w\} \in E$ if u prefers w to v. Now, for each $e = \{u, v\}$ and $e' = \{u, w\}$ in E, if u is indifferent between v and w, merge vertices e and e'. Note that a merged vertex may contain several original edge-vertices and have self-loops. Instance I belongs to SR-GAP iff $P(G)$ is acyclic.

Instances of SR-GRP satisfy the SR-GAP test, since any directed path in $P(G)$ consists of arcs with monotonically improving ranks, and so no cycles are possible. In the reverse direction, given any instance of SR-GAP, we can derive a suitable rank function from a reverse topological sort on $P(G)$, i.e. $rank(e) < rank(e')$ iff e appears before e'. The following proposition is clear:

Proposition 1. *Let I be an instance of* SR. *Then I is an instance of* SR-GRP *if and only if I is an instance of* SR-GAP.

As well as modelling real-world problems, SR-GRP is an important theoretical restriction of SR. It is well-known that SR has two key undesirable properties. First, some instances of SR admit no weakly stable matchings (see, for example, [15, page 164]). And second, the problem of finding a weakly stable matching, or proving that no such matching exists, is NP-hard [24,17]. It turns out that SR-GRP has neither of these undesirable properties [4] [1].

Lemma 1. *Let $G = (V, E_1 \cup \ldots \cup E_m)$ be an instance of* SR-GRP. *Then M is a weakly stable matching of G if and only if $M \cap E_{\leq i}$ is a maximal matching of $E_{\leq i}$, for all i.*

So we can construct a weakly stable matching in $O(n + m)$ time by finding a maximal matching on rank-1 edges, removing the matched vertices, finding a maximal matching on rank-2 edges, and so on.

Strongly stable matchings are also easy to characterize in SR-GRP [4].

Lemma 2. *Let $G = (V, E_1 \cup \ldots \cup E_m)$ be an instance of* SR-GRP. *Then M is a strongly stable matching of G if and only if $M \cap E_i$ is a perfect matching of $\{e \in E_i : e$ is not adjacent to any $e' \in E_{<i}\}$, for all i.*

Of course, even E_1 may not admit a perfect matching, and so strongly stable matchings may not exist. However, we can find a strongly stable matching, or prove that no such matching exists in $O(m\sqrt{n})$ time by using the maximum matching algorithm of Micali and Vazirani for non-bipartite graphs [23]. This improves on the best known running time of $O(m^2)$ for general SR [27].

These observations show that SR-GRP can be far simpler than SR. In this paper, we are interested in which problems become more tractable in SR-GRP, and which problems maintain their hardness. Work along these lines has been done before

---

[1] Lemmas 1 and 2 are proved by [4] in a restricted setting. However, their extensions to SR-GRP are straightforward.

[5,28,6,4]. For example, Chung [6] shows that the "no odd ring" condition on preferences is sufficient for the existence of a weakly stable matching. The SR-GAP acyclic condition is a restriction of the "no odd ring" condition, in that neither odd nor even rings are permitted.

The possible non-existence of a strongly stable matching motivates the search for weakly stable matchings with desirable properties. A *rank-maximal* matching [18,29] includes the maximum possible number of rank-1 edges, and subject to this, the maximum possible number of rank-2 edges, and so on. More formally, define the *signature* of a matching M as $\langle s_1, s_2, \ldots, s_m \rangle$, where s_i is the number of rank-i edges in M. Then a matching is rank-maximal iff it has the lexicographic-maximal signature amongst all matchings.

Recall from Lemma 2 that a strongly stable matching is perfect on rank-1 edges, and subject to this, perfect on rank-2 edges, and so on. It is clear that a rank-maximal matching is strongly stable, when strong stability is possible. If no strongly stable matching exists, then a rank-maximal matching, which by Lemma 1 is always weakly stable, seems a natural substitute. Irving et al. [18] gave an $O(\min(n + R, R\sqrt{n})m)$ algorithm for the problem of finding a rank-maximal matching in a bipartite graph, where R is the rank of the worst-ranked edge in the matching.

Other desirable types of weakly stable matchings may be those that have maximum cardinality, are *egalitarian*, are of *minimum regret*, or admit the fewest number of weakly blocking pairs. An egalitarian (respectively minimum regret) weakly stable matching satisfies the property that the sum of the ranks (respectively the maximum rank) of the edges is minimised, taken over all weakly stable matchings. Given a general SR instance I, each of the problems of finding an egalitarian and a minimum regret weakly stable matching is NP-hard [9,20] (in the former case, even if the preference lists are complete and strictly-ordered, and in the latter case, even if the underlying graph is bipartite). However the complexity of the problem of finding a weakly stable matching with the minimum number of weakly blocking pairs in I has, until now, been open.

Paper outline and summary of contribution. In Section 2, we consider rank-maximal matchings, and present the first generalization of Irving et al.'s [18] algorithm to a non-bipartite setting. In Section 3, we prove hardness results for for each of the problems of finding weakly stable matchings that are of maximum size, are egalitarian, have minimum regret, and admit the minimum number of weakly blocking pairs. We also show that this last problem is inapproximable within a factor of $n^{1-\varepsilon}$, for any $\varepsilon > 0$, unless P = NP. These hardness results apply even in a restricted version of SR-GRP in which the graph G is bipartite, and (in the first three cases) if an agent v is incident to an edge of rank k, then v is incident to an edge of rank k', for $1 \leq k' \leq k$. Finally, Section 4 contains concluding remarks.

2   Rank-Maximal Matching

One obvious way to construct a rank-maximal matching is to find a maximum-weight matching using edge weights that increase exponentially with improving rank. However, with K distinct rank values, Gabow and Tarjan's matching algorithm [10] takes $O(K^2 \sqrt{n} \alpha(m,n) \lg nm \lg n)$ time[2], where α is the inverse Ackermann function. As in the bipartite restriction [18], our combinatorial algorithm avoids the problem of exponential-sized edge weights, leading to an improved runtime of $O(\min\{n + R, R\sqrt{n}\}m)$, where $R \leq K$ is the rank of the worst-ranked edge in the matching.

Let $G_i = (V, E_{\leq i})$. Our algorithm begins by constructing a maximum matching M_1 on G_1. Note that M_1 is rank-maximal on G_1 by definition. Then inductively, given a rank-maximal matching M_{i-1} on G_{i-1}, the algorithm exhaustively augments M_{i-1} with edges from E_i to construct a rank-maximal matching M_i on G_i. In order to ensure rank-maximality, certain types of edges are deleted before augmenting. With these edges deleted, it becomes possible to augment M_{i-1} *arbitrarily*, while still guaranteeing rank-maximality. Hence, we can perform the augmentations using Micali and Vazirani's fast maximum matching algorithm [23]. In the non-bipartite setting, we perform one additional type of edge deletion beyond the bipartite setting. Additionally, we shrink certain components into *supervertices*. Note that this shrinking is separate from any blossom-shrinking [8] that might occur in the maximum matching subroutine.

In order to understand the edge deletions and component shrinking, recall the Gallai-Edmonds decomposition lemma [19]: Let $G = (V, E)$ be an arbitrary undirected graph. Then V can be partitioned into the following three sets, namely GED-U[G], GED-O[G] and GED-P[G]. Vertices in GED-U[G] are *underdemanded*, since they are unmatched in some maximum matching of G. All other vertices that are adjacent to one in GED-U[G] are *overdemanded* and belong to GED-O[G]. Finally, all remaining vertices are *perfectly demanded* and belong to GED-P[G]. The decomposition lemma gives many useful structural properties of maximum matchings. For example, in every maximum matching, vertices in GED-O[G] are always matched, and their partner is in GED-U[G]. Similarly, vertices in GED-P[G] are always matched, though their partners are also in GED-P[G]. We will use the properties given in Lemma 3.

Lemma 3 (Gallai-Edmonds Decomposition). *In any maximum matching M of G,*

1. *For all u in GED-O[G], $M(u)$ is in GED-U[G]*
2. *For all even (cardinality) components C of $G \setminus$ GED-O[G], i) $C \subseteq$ GED-P[G], and ii) $M(u)$ is in C, for all u in C*
3. *For all odd (cardinality) components C of $G \setminus$ GED-O[G], i) $C \subseteq$ GED-U[G], ii) $M(u)$ is in C, for all u in C except one, say v, and iii) either v is unmatched in M, or $M(v)$ is in GED-O[G]*

Consider the first inductive step of the algorithm, in which we are trying to construct a rank-maximal matching M_2 of $G_2 = (V, E_{\leq 2})$, given a maximum matching M_1 of $G_1 = (V, E_1)$. We do not want to *commit* to edges in M_1 at this point, because perhaps no rank-maximal matching on G_2 contains these edges.

---

[2] See [22] for an explanation of the K^2 factor.

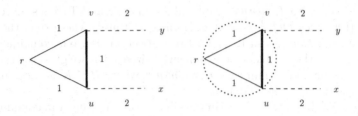

Fig. 1. Example of shrinking operation

However, according to the decomposition lemma, we can safely *delete* any edge $e = \{u, v\}$ such that:

(i) $u \in$ GED-O$[G_1]$ and $v \in$ GED-O$[G_1] \cup$ GED-P$[G_1]$
(ii) $e \in E_{\geq 2}$, and $u \in$ GED-O$[G_1] \cup$ GED-P$[G_1]$
(iii) $e \in E_{\geq 2}$, and both u and v belong to the same odd component of G_1

We delete all such edges to ensure they are not subsequently added to the matching when we augment. Note that the third deletion type is required for non-bipartite graphs, since only one vertex in each odd component C is unmatched internally.

After deleting edges in G_1, we *shrink* each odd component C into a supervertex. We define the *root* r of C as the one vertex in C that is unmatched within C. Note that C's supervertex is matched iff r is matched. Now, when we add in undeleted edges from $e = \{u, v\} \in E_{\geq 2}$ into the graph, if $u \in C$ and $v \notin C$, we replace e with an edge between v and C's supervertex. Note that during the course of the algorithm, we will be dealing with graphs containing supervertices, which themselves, recursively contain supervertices. In such graphs, we define a *legal* matching to be any collection of independent edges such that in every supervertex, all top-level vertices but the root are matched internally.

To give some intuition for why we shrink odd components, consider the graph in Figure 1. The triangle of rank-1 edges is an odd component (with $\{u, v\}$ matched), and so neither rank-2 edges are deleted. One way to augment this graph is to include the two rank-2 edges and take out the rank-1 $\{u, v\}$ edge. This destroys the rank-maximal matching on G_1. If we shrink the triangle however, the supervertex is unmatched, and so $\{x, u\}$ and $\{y, v\}$ are both valid augmenting paths. Note how these augmenting paths can be expanded *inside* the supervertex by removing and adding one rank-1 edge to end at the root r. This expansion makes the augmenting path legal in the original graph, while not changing the number of matching edges internal to the supervertex.

Figure 2 contains pseudocode for our non-bipartite rank-maximal matching algorithm. One aspect that requires more explanation is how we augment M_i in G_i'. The overall approach is to find an augmenting path P while regarding each top-level supervertex in G_i' as a regular vertex. Then for each supervertex C in P, we expand P through C in the following way. Let u be the vertex in C that P enters along an unmatched edge. If u is the root r of C, then C is unmatched, and we can replace C by u in P. Otherwise, $u \neq r$, and either C is unmatched or

Rank-Maximal-Matching$(G = (V, E_1 \cup E_2 \cup \ldots \cup E_m))$
    Set G'_1 to G_1;
    Let M_1 be any maximum matching of G_1;
    For $i = 2$ to m:
        Set G'_i to G'_{i-1}, and M_i to M_{i-1};
        Compute the GED of G'_{i-1} using M_{i-1};
        Delete edges in G'_i between two vertices in GED-O$[G'_{i-1}]$;
        Delete edges in G'_i between vertices in GED-O$[G'_{i-1}]$ and GED-P$[G'_{i-1}]$;
        Delete any edge e in $E_{\geq i}$ where:
            i) e is incident on a GED-O$[G'_{i-1}]$ or GED-P$[G'_{i-1}]$ vertex, or
            ii) e is incident on two vertices in the same odd component of G_{i-1};
        Shrink each odd component of G_{i-1} in the graph G'_i;
        Add undeleted edges in E_i to G'_i;
        Augment M_i in G'_i until it is a maximum matching;
    End For
    Return M_m;

Fig. 2. Non-bipartite rank-maximal matching algorithm

P leaves C via the matched edge incident on r. In the next lemma, we show that there is an even-length alternating path from u to r, beginning with a matched edge. We can expand P by replacing C with this even-length alternating path.

Lemma 4. *Let M be a legal matching on some supervertex C with root r. Let u be any other node in C. Then there is an even-length alternating path from u to r beginning with a matched edge.*

Proof. Let M' be a legal matching of C in which u is unmatched (such a matching is guaranteed by the decomposition lemma). Consider the symmetric difference of M and M'. Since every vertex besides u and r is matched in both matchings, there must be an even-length alternating path consisting of M and M' edges from u to r. □

In all cases of P and C, note that C has the same number of internally matched edges before and after augmentation by P, and so the matching remains legal. Also, if r was matched prior to augmentation, then it is still matched afterwards.

    The next three lemmas, which generalize those in [18], establish the correctness of the algorithm. Lemma 5 proves that no rank-maximal matching contains a deleted edge. Lemma 6 proves that augmenting a rank-maximal matching M_{i-1} of G_{i-1} does not change its signature up to rank $(i-1)$. And finally, Lemma 7 proves that the final matching is rank-maximal on the original graph G.

Lemma 5. *Suppose that every rank-maximal matching of G_{i-1} is a maximum legal matching on G'_{i-1}. Then every rank-maximal matching of G_i is contained in G'_i.*

Proof. Let M be an arbitrary rank-maximal matching of G_i. Then $M \cap E_{\leq i-1}$ is a rank-maximal matching of G_{i-1}, and by assumption, a maximum legal matching of G'_{i-1}. By Lemma 3, the edges we delete when constructing G'_i belong to no maximum matching of G'_{i-1}, in particular $M \cap E_{\leq i-1}$. So $M \cap E_{\leq i-1}$ is contained in G'_i. Furthermore, since M is a matching and $M \supseteq M \cap E_{\leq i-1}$, it follows that M contains no deleted edges, and therefore must be contained in G'_i. □

Lemma 6. *Let M_i and M_j be the matchings produced by the algorithm, where $i < j$. Then M_i and M_j have the same number of edges with rank at most i.*

Proof. M_i consists of edges contained within top-level supervertices of G'_i, and edges between top-level (super)vertices of G'_i. We have already shown that augmenting through a supervertex does not change the number of matching edges internal to the supervertex. Hence, M_j contains the same number of such edges as M_i.

By Lemma 3, the remaining edges of M_i are all be incident on some GED-O$[G'_i]$ or GED-P$[G'_i]$ (super)vertex. Since these vertices are matched in M_i, they are also matched in M_j, as augmenting does not affect the matched status of a vertex. Also, no edges of rank worse than i are incident on such vertices, due to deletions, and so each must be matched along a rank-i edge or better in M_j. Hence $|M_i| \leq |M_j \cap E_{\leq i}|$. Of course, $|M_j \cap E_{\leq i}| \leq |M_i|$, since all edges from $E_{\leq i}$ in G'_j are also in G'_i, and M_i is a maximum legal matching of G'_i. □

Lemma 7. *For every i, the following statements hold: 1) Every rank-maximal matching of G_i is a maximum legal matching of G'_i, and 2) M_i is a rank-maximal matching of G_i.*

Proof. For the base case, rank-maximal matchings are maximum matchings on rank-1 edges, and so both statements hold for $i = 1$. Now, by Lemma 5 and the inductive hypothesis, every rank-maximal matching of G_i is contained in G'_i. Let $\langle s_1, s_2, .., s_i \rangle$ be the signature of such a matching. By Lemma 6, M_i has the same signature as M_{i-1} up to rank-$(i-1)$. Hence, M_i's signature is $\langle s_1, s_2, .., t_i \rangle$ for some $t_i \leq s_i$, since M_{i-1} is a rank-maximal matching of G_{i-1}. However, M_i is a maximum legal matching of G'_i, hence $t_i = s_i$ and M_i is rank-maximal matching of G_i. This proves the second statement.

Now, for the first statement, let N_i be any rank-maximal matching of G_i. By Lemma 5 and the inductive hypothesis, we know that N_i is contained in G'_i. N_i has signature $\langle s_1, s_2, ..., s_i \rangle$, which is the same signature as M_i. Hence, N_i is also a maximum legal matching of G'_i. □

We now comment on the runtime of the algorithm. In each iteration i, it is clear that computing the decomposition (given a maximum matching), deleting edges and shrinking components all take $O(m)$ time. Constructing M_i from M_{i-1} requires $|M_i| - |M_{i-1}| + 1$ augmentations. At the top-level of augmenting (when supervertices are regarded as vertices), we can use the Micali and Vazirani nonbipartite matching algorithm, which runs in time $O(min(\sqrt{n}, |M_{i+1}| - |M_i| + 1)m)$. Next, we have to expand each augmenting path P through its incident supervertices. Let u be the first vertex of some supervertex C that P enters along an unmatched edge. It is clear that we can do this expansion in time linear in the size of C by appending a dummy unmatched vertex d to u, and then looking for an augmenting path from d to r in C. Since each supervertex belongs to at most one augmenting path in each round of the Micali and Vazirani algorithm, this does not affect the asymptotic runtime. It follows that after R iterations, the running time is at most $O(\min(n+R, R\sqrt{n})m)$. Using the idea in [18], we can stop once R is the rank of the worst-ranked edge in a rank-maximal matching, because we can test in $O(m)$ time if M_R is a maximum matching of G_R together with all undeleted edges of rank worse than R (in which case M_R is rank-maximal).

Theorem 1. *Let R be the rank of the worst-ranked edge in a rank-maximal matching of $G = (V, E_1 \cup \ldots \cup E_m)$. Then a rank-maximal matching of G can be found in time $O(\min(n + R, R\sqrt{n})m)$.*

3 Hardness Results

In this section we establish several NP-hardness results for a special case of SR-GRP. We refer to this restriction as STABLE MARRIAGE WITH SYMMETRIC PREFERENCES (SM-SYM). An instance of SM-SYM is an instance of SR in which the underlying graph is bipartite (with *men* and *women* representing the two sets of agents in the bipartition) subject to the restriction that a woman w_j appears in the kth tie in a man m_i's list if and only if m_i appears in the kth tie in w_j's list. Clearly an instance of SM-SYM is a bipartite instance of SR-GRP in which $rank(\{m_i, w_j\}) = k$ if and only if w_j appears in the kth tie in m_i's preference list, for any man m_i and woman w_j. Indeed it will be helpful to assume subsequently that $rank$ is defined implicitly in this way, given an instance of SM-SYM.

   Our first result demonstrates the NP-completeness of COM-SM-SYM, which is the problem of deciding whether a complete weakly stable matching (i.e. a weakly stable matching in which everyone is matched) exists, given an instance of SM-SYM. Our transformation begins from EXACT-MM, which is the problem of deciding, given a graph G and an integer K, whether G admits a maximal matching of size K.

Theorem 2. COM-SM-SYM *is NP-complete.*

Proof. Clearly COM-SM-SYM is in NP. To show NP-hardness, we reduce from EXACT-MM in subdivision graphs, which is NP-complete [21]. Let $G = (V, E)$, a subdivision graph of some graph G', and K, a positive integer, be an instance of EXACT-MM. Suppose that $V = U \cup W$ is a bipartition of G, where $U = \{m_1, m_2, \ldots, m_{n_1}\}$ and $W = \{w_1, w_2, \ldots, w_{n_2}\}$. Then we denote the set of vertices adjacent to a vertex $m_i \in U$ in G by W_i and similarly the set of vertices adjacent to $w_j \in W$ in G by U_j.

   We construct an instance I of COM-SM-SYM as follows: let $U \cup X \cup A \cup B$ be the set of men and $W \cup Y \cup A' \cup B'$ be the set of women, where $X = \{x_1, x_2, \ldots, x_{n_2 - K}\}, Y = \{y_1, y_2, \ldots, y_{n_1 - K}\}, A = \{a_1, a_2, \ldots, a_K\}, B = \{b_1, b_2, \ldots, b_K\}, A' = \{a'_1, a'_2, \ldots, a'_K\}$ and $B' = \{b'_1, b'_2, \ldots, b'_K\}$. The preference lists of I are shown in Figure 3 (entries in round brackets are tied). It may be verified

Men's preferences

$m_i : (W_i) \ (y_1 \ y_2 \ \ldots \ y_{n_1-K})$ $\qquad (1 \le i \le n_1)$

$x_i : \ a'_i \ (W)$ $\qquad\qquad\qquad\quad (1 \le i \le n_2 - K)$

$a_i : \ (y_i \ b'_i)$ $\qquad\qquad\qquad\quad (1 \le i \le K)$

$b_i : \ a'_i$ $\qquad\qquad\qquad\qquad\quad (1 \le i \le K)$

Women's preferences

$w_j : (U_j) \ (x_1 \ x_2 \ \ldots \ x_{n_2-K})$ $\qquad (1 \le j \le n_2)$

$y_j : \ a_j \ (U)$ $\qquad\qquad\qquad\quad (1 \le j \le n_1 - K)$

$a'_j : \ (x_j \ b_j)$ $\qquad\qquad\qquad\quad (1 \le j \le K)$

$b'_j : \ a_j$ $\qquad\qquad\qquad\qquad\quad (1 \le j \le K)$

Fig. 3. Preference lists for the constructed instance of COM-SM-SYM

that I is an instance of SM-SYM. We claim that G has an exact maximal matching of size K if and only if I admits a complete weakly stable matching.

Suppose G has a maximal matching M, where $|M| = K$. We construct a matching M' in I as follows. Initially let $M' = M$. There remain $n_1 - K$ men in U that are not assigned to women in W; denote these men by m_{k_i} $(1 \le i \le n_1 - K)$ and add (m_{k_i}, y_i) to M'. Similarly there remain $n_2 - K$ women in W that are not assigned to men in U; denote these women by w_{l_j} $(1 \le j \le n_2 - K)$, and add (x_j, w_{l_j}) to M'. Finally we add (a_i, b'_i) and (b_i, a'_i) $(1 \le i \le K)$ to M'. It may then be verified that M' is a complete weakly stable matching in I.

Conversely suppose that M' is a complete weakly stable matching in I. Let $M = M' \cap E$. We now show that $|M| = K$. First suppose that $|M| < K$. Then since M' is a complete weakly stable matching, at least $n_1 - K + 1$ men in U must be assigned in M' to women in Y, which is impossible as there are only $n_1 - K$ women in Y. Now suppose $|M| > K$. Hence at most $n_1 - K - 1$ women in Y are assigned in M' to men in U. Then since M' is complete, there exists at least one women in Y assigned in M' to a man in A. Thus at most $K - 1$ men in A are assigned in M' to women in B'. Hence only $K - 1$ women in B' are assigned in M', contradicting the fact that M' is a compete weakly stable matching. Finally, it is straightforward to verify that M is maximal in G. $\qquad \square$

The following corollary (see [3] for the proof) will be useful for establishing subsequent results.

Corollary 1. *COM-SM-SYM is NP-complete, even if each preference list comprises exactly two ties (where a tie can be of length 1).*

We next consider *minimum regret* and *egalitarian* weakly stable matchings, given an instance I of SMC-SYM, which is the restriction of SM-SYM in which each person finds all members of the opposite sex acceptable. Let U and W be the set of men and women in I respectively, let M be a weakly stable matching in I, and let p be some agent in I. Then we define the *cost* of p with respect to M, denoted by $cost_M(p)$, to be $rank(p, M(p))$. Furthermore we define the *regret* of M, denoted by $r(M)$ to be $\max_{p \in U \cup W} cost_M(p)$. M has *minimum regret* if

$r(M)$ is minimised over all weakly stable matchings in I. Similarly we define the *cost* of M, denoted by $c(M)$, to be $\sum_{p \in U \cup W} cost_M(p)$. M is *egalitarian* if $c(M)$ is minimised over all weakly stable matchings in I.

We define REGRET-SMC-SYM (respectively EGAL-SMC-SYM) to be the problem of deciding, given an instance I of SMC-SYM and a positive integer K, whether I admits a weakly stable matching such that $r(M) \leq K$ (respectively $c(M) \leq K$). We now show that REGRET-SMC-SYM is NP-complete.

Theorem 3. REGRET-SMC-SYM *is NP-complete.*

Proof. Clearly the problem belongs to NP. To show NP-hardness, we reduce from the restriction of COM-SM-SYM in which each person's list has exactly two ties, which is NP-complete by Corollary 1. Let I be such an instance of this problem. We form an instance I' of REGRET-SMC-SYM as follows. Initially the people and preference lists in I and I' are identical. Next, in I', each person adds a third tie in their preference list containing all members of the opposite sex that are not already contained in their first two ties. It is not difficult to verify that I admits a complete weakly stable matching if and only if I' admits a weakly stable matching M such that $r(M) \leq 2$. $\square$

We next prove that EGAL-SMC-SYM is NP-complete, using a result of Gergely [13], shown in Theorem 4, relating to *diagonalized* Latin squares. A *transversal* of an order-n Latin square is a set S of n distinct-valued cells, no two of which are in the same row or column. A Latin square is said to be diagonalized if the main diagonal is a transversal.

Theorem 4 (Gergely [13]). *For any integer $n \geq 3$, there exists a diagonalized Latin square of order n having a transversal which has no common entry with the main diagonal.*

Theorem 5. EGAL-SMC-SYM *is NP-complete.*

Proof. Clearly EGAL-SMC-SYM is in NP. To show NP-hardness, we reduce from the restriction of COM-SM-SYM in which each person's list has exactly two ties, which is NP-complete by Corollary 1. Let I be such an instance of this problem, where $U = \{m_1, m_2, \ldots, m_n\}$ is the set of men and $W = \{w_1, w_2, \ldots, w_n\}$ is the set of women. For each man $m_i \in U$ ($1 \leq i \leq n$) we denote the women in the first and second ties on m_i's preference list in I by $W_{i,1}$ and $W_{i,2}$ respectively, and let $W_i = W_{i,1} \cup W_{i,2}$. Similarly for each woman $w_j \in W$ ($1 \leq j \leq n$) we denote the men in the first and second ties on w_j's preference list in I by $U_{j,1}$ and $U_{j,2}$ respectively, and let $U_j = U_{j,1} \cup U_{j,2}$.

We construct an instance I' of EGAL-SMC-SYM as follows: let $U \cup X \cup \{p\}$ be the set of men and let $W \cup Y \cup \{q\}$ be the set of women, where $X = \{x_1, x_2, \ldots, x_n\}$ and $Y = \{y_1, y_2, \ldots, y_n\}$. Then we construct the preference lists in I' by considering the diagonalized Latin square $S = (s_{i,j})$ of order n, as constructed using Gergely's method [13] (we note that Gergely's method is polynomial-time computable). Without loss of generality we may assume that the entries in the main diagonal are in the order $1, 2, \ldots, n$ (this can be achieved by simply permuting

442   D.J. Abraham et al.

Men's preferences

$m_i : W_{i,1} \ W_{i,2} \ (y_1 \ q) \ y_2 \ \dots \ y_n \ (W \setminus W_i) \quad (1 \le i \le n)$

$x_1 : y_1 \ q \ (W) \ y_{s_{1,2}} \ y_{s_{1,3}} \ y_{s_{1,4}} \ \cdots \ y_{s_{1,n}}$

$x_2 : y_2 \ q \ y_{s_{2,1}} \ (W) \ y_{s_{2,3}} \ y_{s_{2,4}} \ \cdots \ y_{s_{2,n}}$

$x_3 : y_3 \ q \ y_{s_{3,1}} \ y_{s_{3,2}} \ (W) \ y_{s_{3,4}} \ \cdots \ y_{s_{3,n}}$

$\vdots$

$x_n : y_n \ q \ y_{s_{n,1}} \ y_{s_{n,2}} \ y_{s_{n,3}} \ y_{s_{n,4}} \ \cdots \ (W)$

$p : \ q \ (Y) \ (W)$

Women's preferences

$w_j : U_{j,1} \ U_{j,2} \ (x_1 \ p) \ x_2 \ \dots \ x_n \ (U \setminus U_j) \quad (1 \le j \le n)$

$y_1 : x_1 \ p \ (U) \ x_{t_{1,2}} \ x_{t_{1,3}} \ x_{t_{1,4}} \ \cdots \ x_{t_{1,n}}$

$y_2 : x_2 \ p \ x_{t_{2,1}} \ (U) \ x_{t_{2,3}} \ x_{t_{2,4}} \ \cdots \ x_{t_{2,n}}$

$y_3 : x_3 \ p \ x_{t_{3,1}} \ x_{t_{3,2}} \ (U) \ x_{t_{3,4}} \ \cdots \ x_{t_{3,n}}$

$\vdots$

$y_n : x_n \ p \ x_{t_{n,1}} \ x_{t_{n,2}} \ x_{t_{n,3}} \ x_{t_{n,4}} \ \cdots \ (U)$

$q : \ p \ (X) \ (U)$

Fig. 4. Preference lists for the constructed instance of EGAL-SMC-SYM

symbols in S if necessary). Next we construct a matrix $T = (t_{i,j})$ from S as follows: for each i and j $(1 \le i, j \le n)$, if $s_{i,j} = k$ then $t_{k,j} = i$. We claim that T is a Latin square.

For, suppose not. First suppose $t_{i,j} = t_{i,k} = l$, for some $j \ne k$. Thus it follows that $s_{l,j} = s_{l,k} = i$, contradicting the fact that S is a Latin square. Now suppose $t_{i,j} = t_{k,j} = l$, for some $i \ne k$. Therefore $s_{l,j} = i$ and $s_{l,j} = k$, which is impossible. Hence T is a Latin square. Moreover the elements $1, 2, \dots, n$ appear in order on the main diagonal of T.

We then use S and T to constructed the preference lists as shown in Figure 4. By the construction of T from S and by inspection of the remaining preference list entries, we observe that I' is an instance of EGAL-SMC-SYM. Let $K = 2(3n + 1)$. It may be verified (see [3] for the proof) that I has a complete weakly stable matching M if and only if I' has a weakly stable matching M' such that $c(M') \le K$.

$\square$

Our final hardness result (whose proof appears in [3]) applies to SM-GRP, which is the restriction of SR-GRP to bipartite graphs. Recall that a strongly stable matching has no weakly blocking pairs. MIN-BP-SM-GRP is the problem of finding a weakly stable matching (which by definition has no strongly blocking pairs) with the minimum number of weakly blocking pairs, given an instance of SM-GRP.

Theorem 6. MIN-BP-SM-GRP *is not approximate within a factor of* $n^{1-\varepsilon}$, *for any* $\varepsilon > 0$, *unless P=NP, where n is the number of men and women.*

4   Future Work

We conclude with an open problem. A matching M' is *more popular than* another M if more agents prefer M' to M than M to M'. A matching M is *popular* if there is no matching M' that is more popular than it. Because the *more popular than* relation is not acyclic, popular matchings may not exist. As with rank-maximality, the problem of finding popular matchings (or proving no such matching exists) has been solved in the bipartite setting [2]. This setting involves allocating items to agents, when only agents have preferences. However, the original popular matching problem, as proposed by Gärdenfors [12], applied to the stable marriage setting (with preferences on both sides). We believe that SR-GRP, and its bipartite restriction, are promising models in which to begin to solve Gärdenfors' original problem.

Acknowledgement

We would like to thank Péter Biró and Utku Ünver for helpful remarks concerning relationships between SR-GRP and SR-GAP.

References

1. Abraham, D.J., Blum, A., Sandholm, T.: Clearing algorithms for barter exchange markets: enabling nationwide kidney exchanges. In: EC 2007: Proceedings of the 8th ACM Conference on Electronic Commerce, pp. 295–304. ACM Press, New York (2007)
2. Abraham, D.J., Irving, R.W., Telikepalli, K., Mehlhorn, K.: Popular matchings. In: Proceedings of SODA 2005 the 16th ACM-SIAM Symposium on Discrete Algorithms, pp. 424–432. ACM Press, New York (2005)
3. Abraham, D.J., Levavi, A., Manlove, D.F., O'Malley, G.: The stable roommates problem with globally-ranked pairs. Technical Report TR-2007-257, University of Glasgow, Department of Computing Science (September 2007)
4. Arkin, E.M., Efrat, A., Mitchell, J.S.B., Polishchuk, V.: Geometric Stable Roommates. Manuscript (2007), http://www.ams.sunysb.edu/~kotya/ pages/ geomSR.pdf
5. Bartholdi, J.J., Trick, M.A.: Stable matchings with preferences derived from a psychological model. Operations Research Letters 5, 165–169 (1986)
6. Chung, K.S.: On the existence of stable roommate matchings. Games and Economic Behavior 33(2), 206–230 (2000)
7. Delmonico, F.L.: Exchanging kidneys - advances in living-donor transplantation. New England Journal of Medicine 350, 1812–1814 (2004)
8. Edmonds, J.: Path, trees, and flowers. Canadian Journal of Mathematics 17, 449–467 (1965)
9. Feder, T.: A new fixed point approach for stable networks and stable marriages. Journal of Computer and System Sciences 45, 233–284 (1992)
10. Gabow, H.N., Tarjan, R.E.: Faster scaling algorithms for general graph matching problems. Journal of the ACM 38(4), 815–853 (1991)

11. Gale, D., Shapley, L.S.: College admissions and the stability of marriage. American Mathematical Monthly 69, 9–15 (1962)
12. Gärdenfors, P.: Match making: assignments based on bilateral preferences. Behavioural Sciences 20, 166–173 (1975)
13. Gergely, E.: A simple method for constructing doubly diagonalized latin squares. Journal of Combinatorial Theory, Series A 16(2), 266–272 (1974)
14. Gjertson, D.W., Cecka, J.M.: Living unrelated donor kidney transplantation. Kidney International 58, 491–499 (2000)
15. Gusfield, D., Irving, R.W.: The Stable Marriage Problem: Structure and Algorithms. MIT Press, Cambridge (1989)
16. Irving, R.W.: An efficient algorithm for the stable roommates problem. Journal of Algorithms 6, 577–595 (1985)
17. Irving, R.W., Manlove, D.F.: The Stable Roommates Problem with Ties. Journal of Algorithms 43, 85–105 (2002)
18. Irving, R.W., Michail, D., Mehlhorn, K., Paluch, K., Telikepalli, K.: Rank-maximal matchings. ACM Transactions on Algorithms 2(4), 602–610 (2006)
19. Lovász, L., Plummer, M.D.: Matching Theory. No. 29 in Annals of Discrete Mathematics. North-Holland (1986)
20. Manlove, D.F., Irving, R.W., Iwama, K., Miyazaki, S., Morita, Y.: Hard variants of stable marriage. Theoretical Computer Science 276(1-2), 261–279 (2002)
21. Manlove, D.F., O'Malley, G.: Student project allocation with preferences over projects. In: Proceedings of ACiD 2005 the 1st Algorithms and Complexity in Durham workshop. Texts in Algorithmics, vol. 4, pp. 69–80. KCL Publications (2005)
22. Mehlhorn, K., Michail, D.: Network problems with non-polynomial weights and applications (Unpublished manuscript)
23. Micali, S., Vazirani, V.V.: An O(—V—. —E—) algorithm for finding maximum matching in general graphs. In: Proceedings of FOCS 1980 the 21st Annual IEEE Symposium on Foundations of Computer Science, pp. 17–27. IEEE Computer Society Press, Los Alamitos (1980)
24. Ronn, E.: NP-complete stable matching problems. Journal of Algorithms 11, 285–304 (1990)
25. Roth, A.E., Sönmez, T., Ünver, M.U.: Pairwise kidney exchange. Journal of Economic Theory 125(2), 151–188 (2005)
26. Roth, A.E., Sönmez, T., Ünver, M.U.: Kidney exchange. Quarterly Journal of Economics 119(2), 457–488 (2004)
27. Scott, S.: A study of stable marriage problems with ties. PhD thesis, University of Glasgow, Department of Computing Science (2005)
28. Tan, J.J.M.: A necessary and sufficient condition for the existence of a complete stable matching. J. Algorithms 12(1), 154–178 (1991)
29. Telikepalli, K., Shah, C.: Efficient algorithms for weighted rank-maximal matchings and related problems. In: Asano, T. (ed.) ISAAC 2006. LNCS, vol. 4288, pp. 153–162. Springer, Heidelberg (2006)

A PSPACE-complete Sperner Triangle Game

Kyle W. Burke[1,*] and Shang-Hua Teng[2,**]

Boston University
paithan@cs.bu.edu, steng@cs.bu.edu

Abstract. We create a new two-player game on the Sperner Triangle based on Sperner's lemma. Our game has simple rules and several desirable properties. First, the game is always certain to have a winner. Second, like many other interesting games such as Hex and Geography, we prove that deciding whether one can win our game is a *PSPACE*-complete problem. Third, there is an elegant balance in the game such that neither the first nor the second player always has a decisive advantage. We provide a web-based version of the game, playable at: *http://cs-people.bu.edu/paithan/spernerGame/*. In addition we propose other games, also based on fixed-point theorems.

1 Introduction

The relationship between computational complexity and game strategies has encouraged the development of both of these fields. Games, due to their enjoyable and competetive nature, create a breeding pool for analysis as strategies are discussed and revised. The ability to express strategies using computational complexity allows us to categorize them based on concrete classes of difficulty. Inversely, the ability to express complexity classes in terms of finding game strategies motivates the study of these classes.

Many two-player games can employ simple rules yet still resist simple methods to efficiently produce winning strategies. Games such as Geography, Hex and Go all require *PSPACE* computational capability to always deduce these winning strategies [9,10,7]. For these games, the simplicity of the rules often masks the mathematical intricacies of the underlying structure. In Hex, for instance, the existence of a winner has been shown to be equivalent [6] to Brouwer's fixed-point theorem [1].

Motivated by the equivalence of the fixed-point theorem to another result, namely Sperner's Lemma [11], we present a new two-player game, designed to attain some hardness result. As Eppstein argues, games with polynomial strategies lose their fun once players learn "the trick" [5]. This concern might be amplified in this day and age when we encourage the most talented human game players to compete with highly optimized machines. If polynomial strategies for a game exists, these machines can efficiently implement the strategies, and

---

[*] This material partially supported by the National Science Foundation under Grant No. DGE-0221680.

[**] Partly supported by NSF ITR grant CCR-0325630.

X. Deng and F.C. Graham (Eds.): WINE 2007, LNCS 4858, pp. 445–456, 2007.

Fig. 1. A triangular array of size 5 (left) next to our Sperner Triangle gameboard, also of size 5, with added functional boundaries (right)

the game play becomes trivial. Thus, we continue by proving that our game is *PSPACE*-complete.

Luckily, the rules of the game are very simple, and a player does not require any mathematical background to be a fierce contender[1]. Before we define the rules of the game, we discuss the Sperner Triangle and the Lemma which ensures that exactly one of the players has won at the end of the game.

2   The Sperner Triangle

Sperner's Triangle is simply a triangular array of nodes (see the left half of Figure 1) each colored in one of three colors with a simple boundary condition: each side of the outer triangle is assigned a different color, and nodes along that edge may not be given that color [11]. Along each axis of the array, each node has two natural neighbors, aside from the boundary nodes, which may not have a second neighbor along some axes. Since the triangular array has three axes, each interior node of the triangle has exactly six neighbors.

Fig. 2. From left to right: A barred node, a shaded node and a filled node

Here, in lieu of colors, we use three different symbols: bars, shading and filled-in, as demonstrated in Figure 2. We will often use the verbs *barring*, *shading* and *filling* to describe the action of assigning the relative symbol to a node.

Our games are inspired by the following brilliant result of Sperner [11]:

Lemma 1 (Sperner's Lemma). *On any sized Sperner Triangle, if all the nodes are colored, there will exist a triangle of three neighboring nodes, each of which has a different color. In fact, there will be an odd number of these triangles.*

---

[1] During a Thanksgiving break, the first author played against his mother, who is not a mathematician, and was often beaten in a short span of games.

3   Playing Games on the Sperner Triangle

Given the challenge of attempting to avoid tri-colored triangles, natural games emerge in which players take turns coloring empty nodes on an initially-uncolored Sperner Triangle. In these games, a player loses when their play creates a tri-colored triangle. Because of this, we refer to triangles with three colors as "bad" triangles. In addition, open circles at which any color played would result in a bad triangle are called "doomed" circles. Although playing at one of them is legal, it results immediatley in a loss, and thus we often refer to them with the "unplayable" misnomer. Also, we often speak of playable circles as not including those which are doomed. When we want to include doomed circles, we will use the term "open".

3.1   The Game Board

In order to elegantly enforce the border restrictions, we enhance the triangle by adding an alternating series of the other two colors to each side, as shown in the right-hand side of Figure 1. Thus, if a player plays the forbidden color along one of those sides, they immediately create a bad triangle and lose the game.

Since it is often helpful to focus on one player whilst analyzing two-player games, we will often refer to one player as the hero and their opponent as the adversary.

3.2   Sperner Rules

1. On their turn, each player colors a circle on the triangle one of the three colors.
2. The first player may choose any uncolored circle at which to play for the first move.
3. If any circles adjacent to the last-colored circle are uncolored, the current player must choose one of them to color. Otherwise, they may choose to play at any uncolored circle on the board.
4. The first player to color a circle which creates a tri-colored triangle loses the game.

We call this game *Sperner*. *Atropos*, the Java applet version, is playable at:

http://cs-people.bu.edu/paithan/spernerGame/

4   On the Complexity of Sperner

Our central complexity question concerns the following decision problem:

SPERNER: Given a legal *Sperner* state, determine whether the current player has a winning strategy.

Before analyzing the complexity of this problem, we must comment on the phrase "legal *Sperner* state". A legal state of the game is one which can be realized from any legal sequence of plays from an initial game board. A game state then consists of either:

1. An initial game board, or
2. A game board attainable from some legal sequence of moves on an initial game board, with the last move identified.

As our main complexity result, we prove:

Theorem 1 (Main). *SPERNER is PSPACE-complete.*

4.1   SPERNER is in *PSPACE*

Lemma 2. *SPERNER is in PSPACE.*

Proof. Since the number of plays is at most the number of nodes in the game-board, the depth of every branch of the game tree is linear in the size of the input. Thus, in polynomial space we can determine the result of following one path of the game tree. In order to search for a winning result, we can systematically try each possible game branch. Thus, we require only space enough to evaluate one branch at a time, as well as some bookkeeping to recall which branches we have already visited. This bookkeeping will require at most only $O(m^2)$ space, where m is the number of nodes on the board. Thus, in polynomial space, we can evaluate all the possible outcomes of the game tree until we either find a winning strategy or determine that none exists.

4.2   Outline of the Reduction

It remains to be shown that strategies for the Sperner Game are $PSPACE$-hard.

Classically, we show that problems are $PSPACE$-hard by reducing TQBF to them [8]. In general, TQBF is the problem of determining whether a quantified boolean formula—a formula of the form $\exists x_1 : \forall x_2 : \exists x_3 : \forall x_4 : \ldots : Q_n x_n : \phi(x_1, x_2, \ldots, x_n)$—is true. In our notation here, $\phi(x_1, \ldots, x_n)$ is a conjunctive normal form formula using the literals x_1 through x_n, while Q_n is a quantifier (either $\forall$ or $\exists$).

Because of the inherent alternation in quantified boolean formulae, many games with non-obvious strategies for two players have been shown to be $PSPACE$-hard [8]. Indeed, we see that fulfilling a TQBF instance is much like playing a game. The hero will choose a variable assignment for x_1, then the adversary will choose for x_2. The hero responds by choosing x_3, and so on.

Our reduction will model this behavior. We will create a legal Sperner game state from a TQBF instance such that a winning strategy in the game exists for the hero if and only if the formula is true. The game will proceed by letting the appropriate players make moves corresponding to the assignment of values to the variables x_i. Each player will then make one further choice and one of the literals

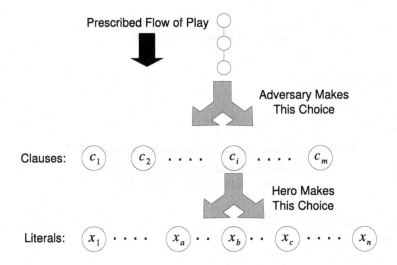

Fig. 3. Construction Sketch: End of the Game. Clause c_i contains the literals x_a, x_b, x_c.

in one of the clauses will be selected. We will "investigate" the literal through its interpretation in the game state and force an end of the game with it.

In our resulting game boards, most of the moves players make will be very restrictive. In our construction, there is a resulting "prescribed flow of play" directing players to make choices in the order we described above. Our reduction provides punishment strategies such that any player violating the prescribed flow of play will lose in a constant number of turns. We describe these punishment strategies, ensuring that players must follow the prescribed flow in order to have a chance of winning the game.

Using our construction, each player's last choice is easily described: the adversary will choose a clause to investigate, and the hero will choose one of the literals in that clause. That literal will be evaluated, according to the assignment it received. If the literal is true, the hero should win, otherwise the adversary should win.

We give the adversary the power to pick a clause because, in the case where the formula is true, all the clauses must be true; the adversary will have no power. However, if at least one of the clauses is false, the formula will be false, and the adversary should be able to select one of these false clauses in order to discredit the correctness. Conversely, inside each clause we will give the hero the ability to choose between literals. Thus, if at least one of those literals is true, the hero will be able to choose and identify it. Figure 3 illustrates the layout style we desire.

Before the flow of play reaches this point, we must have already set all of the variables. In order to accomplish this, the path of play must first pass by each of the variable settings, as showing in Figure 4, forcing the appropriate player to make a decision at each variable. Once the settings have been accomplished, we can move to the investigation procedure, as portrayed back in Figure 3.

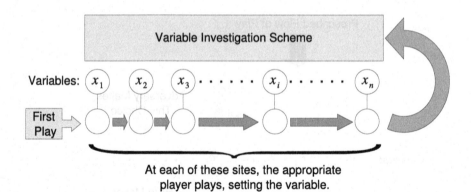

Fig. 4. Construction Sketch: Setting the Variables. The Variable Investigation Scheme is laid out in Figure 3.

Overall, this plan is very reminiscent of the reduction from GEOGRAPHY. In addition, our topology meets some similar hurdles that must be overcome in that construction. For instance, our plan has a non-planar design (paths must often intersect between the selection of a clause and the selection of a literal during investigation). Thus, we will need to produce widgets which allow for these logical crossovers to occur, as we do in the following section.

Our blueprints also seem to defy the rigid structure of the gameboard we are operating on. We require widgets which provide pathways for our prescribed flow of play. GEOGRAPHY is played on a directed graph, so enforcing the flow of play is somewhat more simple. We will need to be very careful that players cannot subjugate design plans by moving in unexpected directions. Also, we need widgets to handle variable assignment, path splitting, and other obstacles to realizing our layout on a Sperner Board. We continue by exhaustively describing these widgets.

5   Reduction Widgets

Our reduction requires widgets to enforce various moves and allow for appropriate decisions to be made through others. In addition, the widgets must be able to connect, allowing us to build the overlying structure by fitting them together. In this section, we describe each of the widgets and specify how they are used.

Many of the widgets are simple and are only pathways to guide the flow of play. For more complex widgets, however, we need to be able to ensure that plays not following this flow correspond to losing choices. This means that any player attempting to go against the prescribed pathway will be vulnerable to an optimal opposing winning strategy which is easily computable (here in constant time).

5.1   Paths

Paths are the most simple of the widgets in our construction, although we have two different versions for different circumstances. Players should not make

 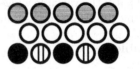

Fig. 5. Left: a Single-Symbol Path. Right: a Two-Symbol Path.

non-trivial decisions along paths, thus we build them to strongly restrict playing options.

The first of our two versions is a path in which on any move a player has the option of playing exactly one symbol without immediately losing. On the left side of Figure 5, assuming the flow of play comes in from the left, the leftmost circle can and must be filled. Then, the next player is forced to fill the circle to the right, and so on. This path pattern can be extended to any length. Turning widgets for these paths also exist as we describe later.

The other type of path supports a chain of one of two different symbols. In this type of path, shown on the right side of Figure 5, whichever symbol is initially played between barred and filled forces the next plays to follow suit. If a space is barred, the next play must also be bars. The same is true for filled (we assume again that the flow of play is going from left to right).

This type of path is often the by-product of play leaving other widgets. Since all our widgets use single-symbol paths leading in, it is vital to be able to force the path to switch from a two-symbol path to a single-symbol path. Although such a widget exists, we omit it here for brevity.

Fig. 6. Two 60 degree turns in a One-Symbol Path

We must also be able to turn our paths in order to have them line up with other widgets. Figure 6 reveals 60-degree turning options. In order to turn further than 60-degrees, we can just pair two or three of these together to attain 120 or 180 degree rotations. Note that in the second example there are two possibilities for playing at the "elbow" of the turn. This does not affect the overall restriction; further plays after the elbow must return to the original symbol.

Unfortunately for fans of two-symbol paths, we do not bother to create turning widgets for them. Instead, whenever we are presented with a situation where a two-symbol path occurs, we will immediately switch it to a one-symbol path. This does not present a problem, as only one of our widgets results in an out-going two-symbol path: the variable widget. The out-going paths for these widgets will be followed by the two-to-one symbol switch widget (not given here).

5.2   Variables

Having described these devices, we are prepared to reveal the widget for modelling variables, presented in Figure 7.

Here the flow of play enters initially from the bottom left and exits through the lower right path. During this time, the "playability" of the circle corresponding to some boolean variable x_i is determined. If that variable is investigated at the end of the game, then the flow of play will enter through the entrance in the upper right corner, and will terminate inside the widget.

The choice of symbol played in the space directly below x_i determines the playability of x_i (and corresponds to the assignment of true or false). Since the plays up to that point must all either be fills, or—in the case of the last space— bars, the deciding play must also either be a fill or bars, and can be either, independent of what the previous play was. Notice now that if a fill is made, the location x_i will be playable later, whereas a play of bars means that x_i is unplayable. Thus, we associate a play of fill as setting x_i to true, while a play of bars sets x_i to false.

After this choice is made, the prescribed flow of play continues rightward, which is clearly forced in the case that x_i is made unplayable. We now must describe a winning response strategy to a player deviating from the play flow, which occurs when x_i is played prematurely.

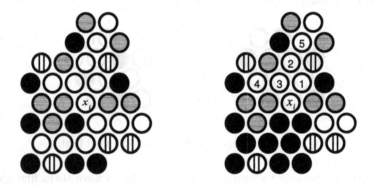

Fig. 7. An untouched Variable Widget (left) and a partly-played widget (right). Numbers on the right side are used to describe blocking premature plays at x_i and explain what happens at the end of the game.

Lemma 3. *Prematurely playing at x_i is suboptimal.*

Proof. In order to prove this lemma, we must show a winning counter-strategy to a premature play in x_i. We use the numbers from Figure 7 to refer to play locations in this strategy.

Assume that an offending player played prematurely at x_i. If they have not already lost, then they must have either shaded or filled x_i. In either case, the winning punishment strategy begins by filling location 1. The offending player will have to respond by either

a) Filling location 2. A winning response to this play consists of filling 3. Now, the offending player must play at the unplayable location 4.
b) Filling or shading location 3. The winning response to this is to fill 2. Now, the offending player can only play at 5, which is unplayable.

Thus, playing at x_i prematurely is a losing strategy, and is suboptimal.

Now, assuming the players follow the prescribed flow, the parity of playable spaces in the upper portion of the widget is defined by the playability of x_i. If x_i is investigated, then the flow of play will enter at the upper right from a single-symbol shading path. Notice that these incoming plays cause location 1 in Figure 7 to be unplayable. Thus, the following sequence of non-suicidal plays is at locations 2, 3, then—if it is playable—x_i.

Thus, if x_i is playable, the play at 3 loses (a play at x_i forces the loss at 1). Otherwise, the play at 3 wins, because all three neighboring spaces are unplayable.

5.3   Splitting and Rejoining Paths

When determining which variable to investigate, players need to be able to make choices to follow different paths. In turn, multiple paths must converge towards the same variable, as multiple clauses can contain the same literal from our instance of QSAT. Thus, we require widgets for splitting and rejoining paths.

In the course of any game, exactly one path through the variable investigation process will be used. We will enforce this through the design of these splitting and rejoining widgets.

 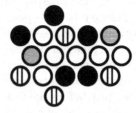

Fig. 8. Left: This widget splits a path. Right: This widget joins two paths.

The splitter (Figure 8), with play flowing from left to right, gives the second player the ability to choose between the two paths. (A One-Symbol path leads into the widget; the first play must be a fill.)

Joiner widgets (in Figure 8) have the additional responsibility of protecting the flow of play (again, left to right) to prevent a player from "going" backwards. The widget performs this automatically. Independent of which path is taken from the left, the play at the intersection prevents plays through the other left path.

5.4   Path Crossing

The graph of paths in our model is not necessarily planar, meaning that we have to be able to handle paths which cross. We use the crossover widget (Figure 9) to accomplish this. Regardless of the flow of play, any series of plays entering this widget must exit from the opposite side. For example, entering from the upper-left path will result in play continuing out through the lower-right path (the careful reader can verify this for all entrance options). Since any game will use exactly one path to investigate a variable, each crossover will be used at most once.

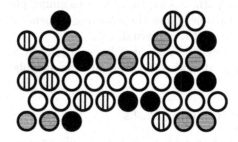

Fig. 9. This widget crosses two paths

6   An Open Question and a Conjecture

The unrestricted Sperner game could be an interesting variation of Sperner for beginners. It is an amusing game and can be useful to gain intuition about the parity underlying the Sperner's Lemma without a topology background. Although its complexity is still open, we conjecture that this parity structure will lead to a polynomial-time solution.

We would like conclude our discussion about Sperner by outlining a possible approach to solve this open question. Recall that Sperner's Lemma dictates that there will be an odd number of triangles if the board is filled up. At the end of an unrestricted game, just before the last player makes a losing play, only doomed circles remain. Coloring any of these will create either an odd or even number of bad triangles (regardless of which color is chosen).

It turns out that the structure required to force a doomed circle to represent an even number of bad triangles is very fragile. As a piece of the game board approaches such a circle, it is very simple for a player to break the pattern, and ensure that only odd-weighted doomed circles will appear. Unfortunately, this approach is not quite as simple when dealing with many connected and possibly overlapping such structures.

If one of the players can either influence or predict the number of doomed circles representing an even number of bad triangles, then they can determine the number of doomed circles at the end of the game. With this knowledge, the number of non-losing plays is apparent, and it will be clear which player will be the last to make a non-losing play. Although it is not yet fully understood, we believe that correct predictions can be made in polynomial time.

7 Conclusion

With the recent amount of attention paid to the implications of Sperner's Lemma in the theoretical computer science community, the study of Sperner and other similar fixed-point games might enhance our understanding of the complexity of fixed-point computation. Indeed, with the newfound relationship between the complexity class $PPAD$, fixed points and Nash equilibria [9,4,3,2], this is a promising avenue for continuing study.

Assuming our conjecture for the unrestricted version of Sperner holds, we would have already generated an environment which somehow contains the boundary between P and $PSPACE$ (should one exist). The solution of our open question could lead immediately to another: How much distance do we allow between plays before the game is no longer $PSPACE$-complete? For example, what happens to the complexity if we allow one player to color in a circle with distance *two* from the last-colored circle? What if we allow a non-constant amount of space between plays? Answers to these questions may reveal additional information about the divisive properties of complexity classes.

Aside from the ramifications of our conjecture, Sperner is a simple, $PSPACE$-complete game rising from a mathematically-significant construct. It inherently carries a fixed-point awareness (a loss in the game corresponds to the creation of a fixed-point) and simultaneously avoids the first-player-wins dilemma faced by similar games. Most exciting, perhaps, is that it accomplishes both these benchmarks without sacrificing any elegance.

Acknowledgments

Kyle wishes to thanks all his friends at Boston University, his mother Janelle, Silvia Montarani and Katelyn Mann for being good initial *Sperner* opponents, as well as everyone who has played with him since. We also thank Xi Chen for teaching us many cool fixed-point theorems and Scott Russell for proofreading our paper.

References

1. Brouwer, L.: Über Abbildung von Mannigfaltigkeiten. Mathematische Annalen 71, 97–115 (1910)
2. Chen, X., Deng, X.: Settling the complexity of two-player Nash equilibrium. In: Proceedings of the 47th Annual IEEE Symposium on Foundations of Computer Science (FOCS), IEEE Computer Society Press, Los Alamitos (2006)

3. Chen, X., Deng, X., Teng, S.-H.: Computing Nash equilibria: Approximation and smoothed complexity. In: Proceedings of the 47th Annual IEEE Symposium on Foundations of Computer Science (FOCS), IEEE Computer Society Press, Los Alamitos (2006)
4. Daskalakis, C., Goldberg, P.W., Papadimitriou, C.H.: The complexity of computing a Nash equilibrium. In: Proceedings of the 38th Annual ACM Symposium on Theory of computing (STOC), IEEE Computer Society Press, Los Alamitos (2006)
5. Eppstein, D.: Computational complexity of games and puzzles (2006), http://www.ics.uci.edu/~eppstein/cgt/hard.html
6. Gale, D.: The game of Hex and the Brouwer fixed-point theorem. American Mathematical Monthly, 818–827 (1979)
7. Lichtenstein, D., Sipser, M.: Go is polynomial-space hard. J. ACM 27(2), 393–401 (1980)
8. Papadimitriou, C.H.: Computational Complexity. Addison Wesley, Reading, Massachsetts (1994)
9. Papadimitriou, C.H.: On the complexity of the parity argument and other inefficient proofs of existence. Journal of Computer and System Sciences, 498–532 (1994)
10. Reisch, S.: Hex ist PSPACE-vollständig. Acta Inf. 15, 167–191 (1981)
11. Sperner, E.: Neuer Beweis für die Invarianz der Dimensionszahl und des Gebietes. Abhandlungen aus dem Mathematischen Seminar Universitat Hamburg 6, 265–272 (1928)

Group Dominant Strategies

(Extended Abstract)

Ola Rozenfeld[1] and Moshe Tennenholtz[2]

Technion – Israel Institute of Technology, Haifa 32000, Israel
ola.rozenfeld@gmail.com, moshet@ie.technion.ac.il

Abstract. We introduce a new solution concept for complete information games, which we call equilibrium in group dominant strategies. This concept is the strongest of all known solution concepts so far, since it encompasses both the ideas behind the concepts of dominant strategies and strong equilibrium. Because of its strength, a solution in group dominant strategies does not exist in any interesting game; however, as we show, such solutions can be achieved in various rich settings with the use of mediators.

1 Introduction

A *finite game in strategic form* is a tuple $\Gamma = \langle N, \{A_i\}_{i \in N}, \{u_i\}_{i \in N} \rangle$ where:

- $N = \{1, \ldots, n\}$ is a finite set of players.
- For each player $i \in N$, A_i is a finite non-empty set of actions (or strategies, we use the terms interchangeably) available to player i.
- For $S \subseteq N$, A_S denotes $\prod_{i \in S} A_i$, and A_{-S} denotes $\prod_{i \in N \setminus S} A_i$. A_N is denoted by A.
- For each player $i \in N$, $u_i : A \rightarrow \Re$ is a utility function, which represents the "contentment" of the player with each specific strategy profile.
- Let $a \in A$. We will sometimes write a as (a_i, a_{-i}) for $i \in N$ and as (a_S, a_{-S}) for $S \subseteq N$.

One of the most basic questions of game theory is: given a game in strategic form, what is the solution of the game? Basically, by a "solution" we mean a *stable* strategy profile which can be proposed to all agents, in a sense that no rational agent would want to deviate from it. Many solution concepts for games have been studied, differing mainly by the assumptions that a rational agent would have to make about the rationality of other agents. For example, probably the most well known solution concept for games is the Nash equilibrium:

A profile of actions $a \in A$ is a *Nash equilibrium* (NE) if

$$\forall i \in N \ a_i \in br_i(a_{-i})$$

Here, $br_i(a_{-i})$ for $i \in N$, $a_{-i} \in A_{-i}$ denotes $\arg \max_{a_i \in A_i} \{u_i(a_i, a_{-i})\}$ (the set of *best responses* of i to a_{-i}).

There are two basic problems with the Nash equilibrium as a solution concept for games:

X. Deng and F.C. Graham (Eds.): WINE 2007, LNCS 4858, pp. 457–468, 2007.

<u>Problem 1:</u> A NE guarantees absence of profitable deviations to a player only in the case that all the other players play according to the suggested profile; in the case where even one of the other players deviates, we have no such guarantees. So, the assumption that this concept requires about the rationality of other players is: all the other players will stick to their prescribed strategies. But why should a rational player make that assumption?

The following stability concept takes this problem into account: A profile of actions $a \in A$ is an *equilibrium in weakly dominant strategies* if

$$\forall i \in N, b_{-i} \in A_{-i} \quad a_i \in br_i(b_{-i})$$

The above definition strengthens the concept of NE by taking care of the aforementioned problem: no unilateral deviation *can ever be* beneficial, no matter what other players do; in other words, it requires no assumptions on the rationality of other players.

<u>Problem 2:</u> A NE does not take into account joint deviations by coalitions of players. We usually assume that an individual will deviate from a profile if she has an available strategy that strictly increases her income. In some settings it would be natural to assume also that a group of individuals will deviate if they have an available joint strategy that strictly increases the income of each group member. For example, consider the famous Prisoner's Dilemma game:

	C	D
C	4,4	0,6
D	6,0	1,1

The strategy profile (D, D) is a NE and even an equilibrium in weakly dominant strategies; however, it is not stable in the sense that if both players deviate to (C, C), the income of each one of them will increase. The following stability concept by (Aumann1959) deals with this problem:

A profile of actions $a \in A$ is a *strong equilibrium* (SE) if

$$\forall S \subseteq N \quad a_S \in br_S(a_{-S})$$

Here, the concept of best response strategy is extended to multiple players as follows: for $S \subseteq N$ and $a_{-S} \in A_{-S}$, $br_S(a_{-S})$ denotes the set of best responses of S to a_{-S}:

$$br_S(a_{-S}) = \{a_S \in A_S | \forall b_S \in A_S \; \exists i \in S \quad u_i(b_S, a_{-S}) \leq u_i(a_S, a_{-S})\}$$

The concept of strong equilibrium indeed takes care of Problem 2; however, it again does not take Problem 1 into account. What we would ideally like to have is a solution concept that has neither of these problems: we would like to assume that players are able to cooperate for mutual benefit, and on the other hand we would also like to assume nothing about the actions of the other players. These requirements may seem conflicting. Note that simply saying that we are interested in a profile $a \in A$ that is both a SE and an equilibrium in weakly dominant strategies is not enough: for games with more than 2 players, we would have no guarantees about the absence of joint deviations for players 1 and 2, in the case that player 3 deviated.

This brings us to the stability concept that we wish to present: a profile of actions $a \in A$ is an *equilibrium in group (weakly) dominant strategies* (GDS) if

$$\forall S \subseteq N, b_{-S} \in A_{-S} \quad a_S \in br_S(b_{-S})$$

Existence of a GDS implies, for each player, that no matter what the other players choose, and no matter with whom can she unite in making her decision, they will not find a joint strategy that will be better to all of them than the proposed one. And thus, if a GDS exists in a given game, we can safely declare it to be the solution of the game. However, a GDS does not exist in any game that has ever been a subject of interest. This is not surprising, since the concept is so strong that its mere existence renders any game not interesting. For this reason, the concept was never a subject of exploration in complete information games. In incomplete information games the concept is known under the name of *group strategy proofness* and is widely studied, because in some cases such solutions can be indeed implemented by mechanism design. However, the whole approach of mechanism design is not applicable to complete information games – although we would indeed want to assume the existence of an interested party, we don't want to give it the power to design the game.

An interested party who wishes to influence the behavior of agents in a (complete information) game, which is not under his control, will be called a mediator. This concept is highly natural; in many systems there is some form of reliable party or administrator who is interested in a "good" behavior of the system. Many kinds of mediators have been studied in the literature, differing by their power in influencing the game (see e.g.(Mas-Colell et al. 1995; Jackson2001; Aumann1974; Myerson1986)). The less power we assume on the mediator, the more applicable the positive results will be to the real world. For example, if we assume that a mediator is able to observe the chosen strategies of the players and issue arbitrarily large fines for deviating from a proposed strategy profile, then, on one hand, such mediator will trivially be able to implement any profile as a very stable solution (e.g. GDS); on the other hand, though, this model will not be applicable to almost any real life multi-agent encounter. For this reason, as the focus of this paper is to study the power of mediators in establishing equilibrium in group dominant strategies, we make some restricting assumptions: the mediator cannot design a new game, cannot enforce agents' behavior, cannot enforce payments by the agents, and cannot prohibit strategies available to the agents.

In the rich literature about mediators, two different kinds of mediators exist that adhere to our restricting assumptions: *routing mediators* and *k-implementation*. K-implementation was introduced by (Monderer and Tennenholtz2004). There, a mediator is a reliable authority who can observe the strategies selected by the players and commit to non-negative monetary payments based on the selected profile. Obviously, by making sufficiently big payments one can implement any desirable outcome. The question is: what is the cost of implementation? A major point in k-implementation is that monetary offers need not necessarily materialize when following desired behaviors; the promise itself might suffice. In particular, (Monderer and Tennenholtz2004) show that any NE of a game can be implemented as an equilibrium in dominant strategies with 0-cost.

Routing mediators were introduced by (Rozenfeld and Tennenholtz2007), continuing the work of (Monderer and Tennenholtz2006). A routing mediator is a reliable authority which can play the game on behalf of players who give it such right. Such mediator devises a conditional contract that he proposes to all players to sign: in this contract, the mediator specifies exactly which actions he will take on behalf of the players who sign the contract, given every possible combination of actions by players who do not sign it. If a player signs the contract, the mediator is then committed to playing the game on behalf of that player by the contract specifications. So, in essence, the mediator adds a new strategy that is available to each player – to sign the contract; the payoffs of this new game are specified exactly by the contract he offers. Note that no matter which players sign the contract, in the end a strategy profile from the original game is played, and the payoffs are not altered.[1] For example, consider such a mediator in the Prisoner's Dilemma game. The mediator offers the agents the following protocol: if both agents agree to use his services then he will play C on behalf of both agents. However, if only one agent agrees to use his services then he will play D on behalf of that agent. The mediator's protocol generates a new game, where a new strategy M is available for using the mediator services:

	C	D	M
C	4,4	0,6	0,6
D	6,0	1,1	1,1
M	6,0	1,1	4,4

Note that the mediated game has a most desirable property: in this game jointly delegating the right of play to the mediator is an equilibrium in group dominant strategies! We can also note that in this example the mediator did not, in fact, require to be informed of the player's chosen strategy – it sufficed for him to know which agents agreed to delegate him their right of play. However, as we will show (in the full paper), in general such mediators will be too weak for implementing GDS; the Prisoner's Dilemma is, in a way, the only example. Therefore, in this paper we will concentrate on fully informed mediators, i.e. ones who can observe the entire action profile selected by the agents and condition their action on it.

Our results: In this paper we explore how different mediators can implement GDS. Most proofs are omitted due to lack of space. Section 2 deals with routing mediators. In subsection 2.2 we present a general sufficient condition for the existence of GDS. We show two natural classes of games that satisfy this condition; both of them are subclasses of ID-congestion games, defined in (Monderer2006). We show that simple monotone increasing identity-dependent [MIID] congestion games satisfy our positive criterion, and hence have a solution in GDS using a routing mediator; we show that this also holds for quasi-symmetric MIID-congestion games. Our results also imply that such implementation can be efficiently computed for these classes of games, even when the input representation is succinct.

---

[1] Similar ideas are explored in the extensive literature on commitments and conditional commitments. In particular, (Kalai et al.2007) shows a folk theorem result for two-player games, using a completely different model of interaction.

In subsection 2.3 we aim to characterize the games which have a solution in GDS using an informed routing mediator. Our goal is a polynomial algorithm that gets a game in strategic form as input, and outputs a routing mediator which implements a solution in GDS, if such exists. We present a polynomial algorithm for this problem for games with 2 and 3 players.

Section 3 deals with k-implementation. Extending the results of (Monderer and Tennenholtz2004), we show that a profile can be implemented as GDS with 0 cost if and only if it is a strong equilibrium. In particular, this result implies that we can implement GDS with 0 cost in all settings where SE is known to always exist, such as job scheduling, network design and certain forms of monotone congestion games (see e.g. (Andelman et al. 2007; Holzman and Law-Yone1997)). We also observe that the minimal-cost implementation of a given strategy profile can be computed in polynomial time, given an explicit representation of the game, if we assume that either the number of players or the number of distinct payoffs for each player are constant. Note that an explicit representation of a game takes exponential space in the amount of players, therefore these simplifying assumptions can be justified.

In section 4 we investigate what happens when our mediator has the power of both routing mediators and of k-implementation; i.e. he can both play on behalf of players who give him such right and commit to non-negative payments. There, we derive our main result: the max-min fair outcome of any minimally fair game can be implemented as GDS with 0 cost. Minimally fair games are a generalization of symmetric games: a game is minimally fair if the agents have the same strategy space and, in addition, in every strategy profile agents who chose the same strategy receive the same payoff. This setting applies to many situations where the users are not identical, for example job scheduling (where users may have tasks of different sizes) or certain forms of ID-congestion games.

(Rozenfeld and Tennenholtz2007) showed that the max-min fair outcome of any minimally fair game can be implemented as a strong equilibrium with the aid of an informed routing mediator; therefore, our current result can be simply derived from the combination of the result of (Rozenfeld and Tennenholtz2007) and our result in section 3. Nevertheless, we consider it to be the main positive result of the paper, because of its importance: we show that a socially optimal profile of a very large class of games can be implemented as an equilibrium in group dominant strategies with 0 cost.

2   Routing Mediators

2.1   Preliminaries

Recall our intuition on routing mediators: a mediator is a party who can offer agents to play the game on their behalf, and whose behavior on behalf of the agents who agreed to use his services is specified by a contract. This contract can be conditioned on the choices of all other agents. Hence, in this setting, we assume that the original game can be played, in a sense, only through the mediator – for example, the mediator sits on a router that receives all messages about the actions chosen by the players. The mediator cannot alter these messages, but he can observe them; this observability can serve him as a critical tool in establishing his chosen actions on behalf of the players who delegated him their right of play.

First, we formally define routing mediators. We simplify the definitions given in (Rozenfeld and Tennenholtz2007), for the following two reasons: first, in this work we consider only pure strategies, and secondly, we restrict ourselves to fully informed mediators (in the notation of (Rozenfeld and Tennenholtz2007), we fix $\Omega = \Omega_{full}$).

Let $\Gamma = \langle N, \{A_i\}_{i \in N}, \{u_i\}_{i \in N} \rangle$ be a game in strategic form. A *(fully informed) routing mediator for* Γ is a tuple $\mathcal{M} = \langle m, (\mathbf{c}_z)_{z \in Z} \rangle$, where the following holds:

- $m \notin A_i$ for all $i \in N$. m denotes the new strategy that is now available to each player: to send a message to the mediator, indicating that the player agrees to give the mediator the right of play for him.
- $Z_i = A_i \cup \{m\}$, and $Z = \times_{i \in N} Z_i$. Given $z \in Z$, let $T(z)$ denote $\{j \in N | z_j = m\}$. That is, $T(z)$ denotes the players who agree to give the mediator the right of play for them in z.
- For every $z \in Z$, $\mathbf{c}_z \in A_{T(z)}$. That is, $\mathbf{c}$ is the conditional contract that is offered by the mediator: it specifies exactly which actions the mediator will perform on behalf of the players who agree to use his services, as a function of the strategy profile chosen by all agents.

Every mediator $\mathcal{M}$ for Γ induces a new game $\Gamma(\mathcal{M})$ in strategic form in which the strategy set of player i is Z_i. The payoff function of i is defined for every $z \in Z$ as follows: $u_i^{\mathcal{M}}(z) = u_i(\mathbf{c}_z, z_{-T(z)})$. For $S \subseteq N$ we denote by m^S the strategy profile $(m, \ldots, m) \in Z_S$. We say that a mediator $\mathcal{M}$ implements a profile a in GDS (resp., SE), if $c_{m^N} = a$ and m^N is a GDS (resp., SE) in $\Gamma(\mathcal{M})$.

Note that when informed mediators are considered, the requirement on the implemented profile to be a GDS (and not some weaker solution concept, such as SE) makes even more sense: the mediator is able, indeed, to observe all the players' actions, so a group of players will want to sign the contract only if the mediator commits to always play in their best interests, according to how the other players play.

Before we proceed with our results, we show an alternative definition of implementing a profile in GDS with the use of a routing mediator; this version is easier to work with and it will serve us in our proofs.

Let $S \subseteq N$, $a_S \in A_S$. We define a game $\Gamma' = (\Gamma \uparrow a_S)$ (the *subgame of Γ induced by* a_S) as follows: $\Gamma' = \langle N', \{A_i\}_{i \in N'}, \{u_i'\}_{i \in N'} \rangle$ where $N' = N \setminus S$ and $u_i' : A_{N'} \to \Re$ is defined as follows: for any $a_{N \setminus S} \in A_{N'}$, $u_i'(a_{N \setminus S}) = u_i(a_S, a_{N \setminus S})$.

We say that Γ' is a *subgame of* Γ if there exist $S \subseteq N$, $a_S \in A_S$ so that $\Gamma' = (\Gamma \uparrow a_S)$. In particular, Γ is a subgame of itself (we call it the *full subgame*).

Let $a, b \in A$ be two strategy profiles. We say that a *strictly dominates* b (or b is *strictly dominated by* a) if $\forall i \in N$ $u_i(a) > u_i(b)$. We say that $b \in A$ is *strictly dominated* if there exists $a \in A$ that strictly dominates b.

Note that for any $S \subseteq N, a_S \in A_S, b_{-S} \in A_{-S}$, a_S is not strictly dominated in the subgame $(\Gamma \uparrow b_{-S})$ if and only if $a_S \in br(b_{-S})$.

Let Γ be a game and $\mathcal{M} = \langle m, (\mathbf{c}_z)_{z \in Z} \rangle$ a mediator for Γ. We say that $\mathcal{M}$ implements a profile a in GDS if and only if for any $S \subseteq N, a_{-S} \in A_{-S}$, m^S is a SE in $(\Gamma(\mathcal{M}) \uparrow a_{-S})$. Note the equivalence to the original definition; note also that when checking the requirements for SE it will be enough to check that no profile $b_T \in A_T$ for $T \subseteq S$ strictly dominates m^T in $\left(\Gamma(\mathcal{M}) \upharpoonright (a_{-S}, m^{S \setminus T})\right)$.

2.2 Positive Results

Now we begin our exploration of the power of informed routing mediators in establishing GDS. The following theorem presents a sufficient condition for existence of GDS with the aid of a fully informed mediator:

Theorem 1. *Let Γ be a game which satisfies the following property: in any subgame Γ' of Γ there exists a non-empty $S \subseteq N'$ and a profile $a_S \in A_S$, such that for each $i \in S$ and every $b_{-S} \in A_{N' \setminus S}, c \in A_{N'}$ $u_i'(a_S, b_{-S}) \geq u_i'(c)$. In words, the profile a_S guarantees each member of S the highest possible payoff for her in the subgame Γ', no matter what the remaining players in $N' \setminus S$ do. Then:*

1. *There exists a profile $a^* \in A$ that is a SE.*
2. *An informed routing mediator can implement a^* as a GDS.*

Proof. 1. Suppose that the game Γ satisfies the above property. Then, we iteratively define the profile a^* as follows: Γ is in particular a subgame of Γ, therefore there exists a non-empty $S^0 \subseteq N$ and a profile $a_{S^0} \in A_{S^0}$ that satisfies the requirements of the theorem: a_{S^0} guarantees all players in S^0 the highest payoff in Γ. We take $a^*_{S^0} = a_{S^0}$, and consider the subgame $\Gamma' = (\Gamma \upharpoonright a^*_{S^0})$. By the conditions of the theorem, there exists a non-empty $S^1 \subseteq N \setminus S^0$ and a profile $a_{S^1} \in A_{S^1}$ that satisfies the requirements. We take $a^*_{S^1} = a_{S^1}$. We continue in the same manner until the profile a^* is fully defined. Since in every step k the subset S^k is non empty, we need at most $|N|$ steps to define the profile.

   Now we must show that a^* is a strong equilibrium. We show by induction on k that no $i \in S^k$ can be a member of a deviating coalition. It is clear that no member of S^0 will want to deviate, since by playing a^* they guarantee themselves the highest possible payoff in the game. From the definition of a^* we see that the same logic can be used for the induction step: no player in S^{k+1} will want to deviate, since a^* was chosen so that all players in S^{k+1} guarantee themselves the best payoff in the subgame where players in $S^0 \cup \ldots \cup S^k$ play according to a^*.

2. We have to fully define the conditional contract that the mediator offers; in other words, for every $z \in Z$ we have to define the profile $c_z \in A_{T(z)}$ that the mediator commits to playing on behalf of $T(z)$. We define this profile iteratively, in the similar manner that we defined a^*: we start with the subgame of Γ induced by $z_{-T(z)}$, and fix the action of the set S^0 of players who can guarantee the highest payoff in the subgame; then we fix the action of the set S^1 of players who can guarantee themselves the highest possible payoff in the resulting new subgame; etc. Now the game $\Gamma(\mathcal{M})$ is defined, it remains to verify that in every subgame $\Gamma(\mathcal{M}) \upharpoonright a_{-S}$, playing m^S is a SE. This can be proved in the same manner as (1): by induction on k we can show that no member of S^k will participate in a deviating coalition. We show the induction step: suppose in a profile z players in $S^0 \cup \ldots \cup S^k$ choose m; we must prove that no member of S^{k+1} will want to join a deviating coalition T and play according to some $w_T \in A_T$. Let us denote

$z' = (w_T, z_{-T})$ (the profile after the deviation of T). The important thing to notice here is that $(c_z)_i = (c_{z'})_i$ for all $i \in S^0 \cup \ldots \cup S^k$ – this follows from our definition of c_z and the induction hypothesis. Then we can use the same logic as in the proof of (1) to derive the result.   □

The proof has certain computational implications that might be of interest: suppose we have a game which satisfies the conditions of Thm. 1, and we want to implement a solution in GDS efficiently. We can treat the mediator as a kind of oracle: given a profile z, we want to be able to compute c_z efficiently. It follows from the proof of Thm. 1 that all that we need in order to achieve this goal is the ability to efficiently compute, for any given subgame Γ', the $S \subseteq N'$ and $a_S \in A_S$ whose existence is guaranteed by the theorem. As we will see, in some natural classes of games such computation can be done efficiently, even when the game is given in a succinct representation.

Now we will show two classes of games which satisfy the condition of Thm. 1.

A *monotone increasing identity-dependent [MIID]-congestion game* is defined as follows:

- A finite set of players, $N = \{1, \ldots, n\}$.
- A finite non-empty set of facilities, M.
- For each player $i \in N$ a non-empty set $A_i \subseteq 2^M$, which is the set of actions available to player i (an action is a subset of the facilities).
- With every facility $m \in M$ and set of players $S \subseteq N$ a real number $v_m(S)$ is associated, having the following interpretation: $v_m(S)$ is the payoff to each user of m when the set of users of m equals S.
- For each $m \in M, S \subseteq N, T \subseteq S :\ v_m(T) \le v_m(S)$, meaning that the payoff from a resource is non-decreasing with its the users.

The utility function of player i, $u_i : A \to \Re$, is then defined as follows:

$$u_i(a) = \sum_{m \in a_i} v_m(\{i | m \in a_i\})$$

MIID-congestion games are not congestion games in the original sense of (Rosenthal1973), since we allow the payoff from a resource to depend on the identity of its users. It is a particular subclass of ID-congestion games, defined in (Monderer2006), with the restrictions to non-player-specific version (users occupying the same resource get the same payoff) and monotone-increasing payoffs. MIID-congestion games can be used to model situations such as buyers clubs, where players choose providers and get discounts based on the group of people they buy with; also they can be used in various situations of non-symmetric sharing of the cost of a resource by the occupying players.

We say that a MIID-congestion game is *simple* if $\forall i \in N, a \in A_i : |a| = 1$.

We say that a MIID-congestion game is *quasi symmetric* if $\forall i, j \in N, A_i = A_j = A$.

Proposition 1. *Let Γ be a MIID-congestion game. Then, Γ satisfies the conditions of Thm. 1 if either one of the following holds:*

1. *Γ is quasi symmetric.*
2. *Γ is simple.*

Note that in both simple and quasi symmetric MIID-congestion games the $S \subseteq N, a_S \in A_S$ of Thm. 1 can be efficiently computed, even if the games are given in a succinct representation; this implies, as we showed, that a solution in GDS can be implemented efficiently.

We have to remark that quasi-symmetric MIID-congestion games would usually be considered trivial – the symmetric socially optimal outcome where each player gets the highest possible payoff in the game is a SE, so where is the problem? The problem is that SE is not GDS. The simplest example of such apparently "trivial" game is the coordination game:

	A	B
A	1,1	0,0
B	0,0	1,1

Obviously, (A, A) and (B, B) are both SE, but what would be a good advice to play? A routing mediator will be able to solve this game by the following contract: if both players cooperate, the mediator plays (A, A), and if one deviates, the mediator will copy her action on behalf of the cooperating player. This solution is more than SE – it is GDS, and it is non-achievable here without a mediator.

Note also that the condition of Thm. 1 is sufficient for being able to implement GDS with an informed mediator, but it is not necessary: the Prisoner's Dilemma game does not satisfy this condition, however the profile (C, C) is implementable as GDS by an informed mediator, as we saw in the introduction. In the next section we will attempt to derive a necessary and sufficient condition for existence of GDS with an informed mediator.

2.3   Characterization for $n = 2$ and $n = 3$

Our goal is to characterize all the games in which a GDS is implementable using an informed mediator. We begin with the simple case $n = 2$:

Proposition 2. *Let Γ be a 2 player game, and let a be a strategy profile. a is implementable as GDS using an informed mediator if and only if a is not strictly dominated and*

$$\forall i \in N \ u_i(a) \geq \max_{b_i \in A_i} \{ \min_{b_{3-i} \in br_{3-i}(b_i)} \{ u_i(b) \} \} \qquad (*)$$

Proposition 3. *There exists a polynomial algorithm that accepts as input a 3 player game Γ in explicit form and a strategy profile a, and if a is implementable in GDS by an informed mediator, outputs such a mediator.*

For non-constant number of players, the explicit representation of a game is infeasible; so, in a sense, it would not help us much to find an algorithm for general n whose running time is polynomial in the size of the input. We conjecture that even for $n = 4$, the decision problem of whether a given profile can be implemented as GDS by an informed mediator is NP-hard.

3   K-Implementation

In this section we turn to a different kind of mediators, introduced by (Monderer and Tennenholtz2004). We assume that the mediator is an interested party who has the power to alter the game by committing to non-negative monetary transfers to the players, conditioned on the outcome of the game. Formally, given a game $\Gamma = \langle N, A, U \rangle$, such a mediator is defined by a payoff function vector $V = \{v_i\}_{i \in N}$, where each $v_i : A \to \Re$ is non-negative. Given a mediator a game Γ and a mediator V, the mediated game $\Gamma(V)$ is simply $\langle N, A, U + V \rangle$.

Note that the above definition implicitly makes two important assumptions:

- Output observability: The interested party can observe the actions chosen by the players.
- Commitment power: The interested party is reliable in the sense that the players believe that he will indeed pay the additional payoff defined by V.

Note also that unlike routing mediators discussed in the previous section, here the mediator does not play the game on behalf of the agents. Similarly to routing mediators, though, he observes players actions and offers a reliable contract conditioned on these actions; he also does not restrict the players' actions in any way, and does not enforce behavior.

Given a game Γ and a profile $a \in A$, we say that a *has a k-implementation in weakly dominant strategies* if there exists a V such that:

1. a is an equilibrium in weakly dominant strategies in $\Gamma(V)$
2. $\sum_{i \in N} v_i(a) \le k$

Similarly, we define a *k-implementation in group dominant strategies*. It is easy to see that a k-implementation of any profile always exists; in particular, if we denote the maximal difference of payoffs in the game matrix by D, it is easy to see that an $D \cdot n$ implementation of any profile always exists. Obviously, our goal is to find *cheap* implementations; in particular, we are interested in 0-implementation.

Theorem 2. *(Monderer and Tennenholtz2004) Let Γ be a game and a a strategy profile. Then, a has a 0-implementation in weakly dominant strategies if and only if a is a NE.*

The above result can be extended into the following:

Theorem 3. *Let Γ be a game and a a strategy profile. Then, a has a 0-implementation in GDS if and only if a is a SE.*

This result implies that we can implement GDS with 0 cost in all settings where SE is known to always exist, e.g.: job scheduling, network design (Andelman et al. 2007) and certain forms of monotone congestion games (Holzman and Law-Yone1997; Rozenfeld and Tennenholtz2006).

Now we turn to the computational question of finding the optimal k-implementation. (Monderer and Tennenholtz2004) showed a polynomial algorithm for finding the optimal k-implementation in dominant strategies; now we would like to extend their results to implementation in GDS.

It is easy to observe that:

Proposition 4. *Let* $\Gamma = \langle N, \{A_i\}_{i \in N}, \{u_i\}_{i \in N} \rangle$ *be a game, with* $|N| = n$, $|A_i| \leq m$, *and* $|\{u_i(a)|a \in A\}| \leq p$ *for all* $i \in N$. *Then, an exhaustive brute-force algorithm for finding an optimal k-implementation in GDS of a given profile* $a \in A$ *runs in* $O(p^n \cdot n \cdot m^n)$.

In general, p is bounded by m^n; note that if the game is given explicitly, p is at most polynomial in the size of the input, and n is at most logarithmic in the size of the input. Therefore, in the case where either n or p are constant, the brute-force algorithm that checks all the possibilities is polynomial in the size of the input[2].

4 Combining Routing Mediators with K-Implementation

In this section we consider mediators who combine the power of routing mediators and k-implementation. Our goal is to implement a good solution in GDS in an interesting class of games. First, we formally define combined mediators:

Let Γ be a game in strategic form. A *combined mediator for* Γ is a tuple $(\mathcal{M}, V)$, where $\mathcal{M}$ is a routing mediator for Γ and V is a payoff function vector for $\Gamma(\mathcal{M})$ (as defined in the previous section).

We say that a combined mediator $(\mathcal{M}, V)$, where $\mathcal{M} = \langle m, (\mathbf{c}_z)_{z \in Z} \rangle$, implements a profile a in GDS with cost k, if:

- $c_{m^N} = a$
- V is a k-implementation in GDS of m^N in the game $\Gamma(\mathcal{M})$

Let Γ be a game in strategic form. Γ is a *minimally fair game* (Rozenfeld and Tennenholtz2007) if for all $i, j \in N$, $X_i = X_j$ and for every action profile $x \in X$, $x_i = x_j$ implies that $u_i(x) = u_j(x)$. That is, a game is minimally fair if players who play the same strategy get the same payoff. The exact value of the received payoff may depend on the identities of the players who chose the strategy, as well as on the rest of the profile. In particular, every symmetric game is a minimally fair game; however, minimally fair games capture a much wider class of settings. For example, typical job-shop scheduling games are minimally fair games.

In order to define what solution is considered "good", we employ the standard model of max-min fairness (Kleinberg et al.1999; Kumar and Kleinberg2000). We call an allocation of strategies to players max-min fair if the utility of any player cannot be increased without decreasing the utility of a player who was facing an already lower utility. In many settings max-min fairness is a natural social optimality criterion.

Now we are ready to state our main result:

Theorem 4. *Let* Γ *be a minimally fair game and let* a *be a max-min fair profile of the game. Then,* a *can be implemented in GDS by combined routing mediator with 0 cost.*

---

[2] It is an interesting question to consider the computational complexity of finding the optimal k-implementation for non-constant n and p, when the game is given explicitly. It is very unlikely that the problem is NP-hard, since, as we saw, the size of the witness is $O(t^{\log t})$ (where t represents the input size). In fact, several complexity classes have been defined that are good candidates for this problem (Papadimitriou and Yannakakis1996); we conjecture that finding the optimal k-implementation in GDS is LOGSNP-complete.

References

[Andelman et al. 2007] Andelman, N., Feldman, M., Mansour, Y.: Strong price of anarchy. In: SODA (2007)

[Aumann1959] Aumann, R.J.: Acceptable points in general cooperative n-person games. In: Tucker, A.W., Luce, R.D. (eds.) Contribution to the Theory of Games. Annals of Mathematics Studies, 40, vol. IV, pp. 287–324 (1959)

[Aumann1974] Aumann, R.J.: Subjectivity and correlation in randomized strategies. Journal of Mathematical Economics 1, 67–96 (1974)

[Holzman and Law-Yone1997] Holzman, R., Law.-Yone, N.: Strong equilibrium in congestion games. Games and Economic Behavior 21, 85–101 (1997)

[Jackson2001] Jackson, M.O.: A crash course in implementation theory. Social Choice and Welfare 18(4), 655–708 (2001)

[Kalai et al.2007] Kalai, A.T. Kalai, E., Lehrer, E., Samet, D.: Voluntary commitments lead to efficiency. Discussion Papers, Northwestern University, Center for Mathematical Studies in Economics and Management Science (April 2007), available at: http://ideas.repec.org/p/nwu/cmsems/1444.html

[Kleinberg et al.1999] Kleinberg, J.M., Rabani, Y., Tardos, E.: Fairness in routing and load balancing. In: IEEE Symposium on Foundations of Computer Science, pp. 568–578. IEEE Computer Society Press, Los Alamitos (1999)

[Kumar and Kleinberg2000] Kumar, A., Kleinberg, J.: Fairness measures for resource allocation. In: Proc. 41th IEEE Symp. on Foundations of Computer Science, IEEE Computer Society Press, Los Alamitos (2000)

[Mas-Colell et al. 1995] Mas-Colell, A., Whinston, M.D., Green, J.R.: Microeconomic Theory. Oxford University Press, Oxford (1995)

[Monderer and Tennenholtz2004] Monderer, D., Tennenholtz, M.: K-Implementation. Journal of Artificial Intelligence Research 21, 37–62 (2004)

[Monderer and Tennenholtz2006] Monderer, D., Tennenholtz, M.: Strong Mediated Equilibrium. In: Proceedings of AAAI 2006 (2006)

[Monderer2006] Monderer, D.: Solution-based congestion games. 8, 397–409 (2006)

[Myerson1986] Myerson, R.B.: Multistage games with communication. Econometrica 54(2), 323–358 (1986)

[Papadimitriou and Yannakakis1996] Papadimitriou, C.H., Yannakakis, M.: On limited nondeterminism and the complexity of the v-c dimension. Journal of Computer and System Sciences 53(2), 161–170 (1996)

[Rosenthal1973] Rosenthal, R.W.: A class of games possessing pure-strategy nash equilibria. International Journal of Game Theory 2, 65–67 (1973)

[Rozenfeld and Tennenholtz2006] Rozenfeld, O., Tennenholtz, M.: Strong and Correlated Strong Equilibria in Monotone Congestion Games. In: Proc. of 2nd international Workshop on Internet & Network Economics (2006)

[Rozenfeld and Tennenholtz2007] Rozenfeld, O., Tennenholtz, M.: Routing Mediators. In: Proc. 20th International Joint Conference on Artificial Intelligence (2007)

Weighted Boolean Formula Games[*]

Marios Mavronicolas[1], Burkhard Monien[2], and Klaus W. Wagner[3]

[1] Department of Computer Science, University of Cyprus, Nicosia CY-1678, Cyprus.
Currently visiting Faculty of Computer Science, Electrical Engineering and
Mathematics, University of Paderborn, 33102 Paderborn, Germany
mavronic@cs.ucy.ac.cy
[2] Faculty of Computer Science, Electrical Engineering and Mathematics, University
of Paderborn, 33102 Paderborn, Germany
bm@upb.de
[3] Lehrstuhl für Theoretische Informatik, Institut für Informatik,
Julius-Maximilians-Universität Würzburg, 97074 Würzburg, Germany
wagner@informatik.uni-wuerzburg.de

Abstract. We introduce a new class of *succinct games,* called *weighted boolean formula games.* Here, each player has a set of boolean formulas he wants to get satisfied. The boolean formulas of all players involve a ground set of boolean *variables,* and every player controls some of these variables. The *payoff* of a player is the *weighted* sum of the values of his boolean formulas. We consider *pure Nash equilibria* [18] and their well-studied refinement of *payoff-dominant equilibria* [12], where every player is no-worse-off than in any other pure Nash equilibrium. We study both structural and complexity properties for both *decision* and *search* problems.

– We consider a subclass of weighted boolean formula games, called *mutual weighted boolean formula games,* which make a natural *mutuality* assumption. We present a very simple *exact potential* for mutual weighted boolean formula games. We also prove that each *weighted, linear-affine (network) congestion game with player-specific constants* is *polynomial, sound monomorphic* to a mutual weighted boolean formula game. In a general way, we prove that each *weighted, linear-affine (network) congestion game with player-specific coefficients and constants* is polynomial, sound monomorphic to a weighted boolean formula game.
– We present a comprehensive collection of high intractability results. These results show that the computational complexity of decision (and search) problems for both payoff-dominant and pure Nash equilibria in weighted boolean formula games depends in a crucial way on five parameters: *(i)* the number of players; *(ii)* the number of variables per player; *(iii)* the number of boolean formulas per player; *(iv)* the *weights* in the payoff functions (whether *identical* or *non-identical*), and *(v)* the syntax of the boolean formulas. These results show that decision problems for payoff-dominant equilibria are considerably harder than for pure Nash equilibria (unless the *polynomial hierarchy* collapses).

[*] This work has been partially supported by the IST Program of the European Union under contract numbers IST-2004-001907 (DELIS) and 15964 (AEOLUS).

X. Deng and F.C. Graham (Eds.): WINE 2007, LNCS 4858, pp. 469–481, 2007.
© Springer-Verlag Berlin Heidelberg 2007

1   Introduction

Motivation and Framework. Deciding the existence of and finding *Nash equilibria* [18] for a *strategic game* are among the most important problems studied in *Algorithmic Game Theory* today. When the players' *strategy spaces* and *payoffs* are presented explicitly, there is a straightforward polynomial time algorithm to decide the existence of and compute a pure Nash equilibrium. More interesting are the cases where the strategy spaces and the payoffs are presented in a *succinct* way. Interesting examples of *succinct games* include *(unweighted) congestion games* [20], where the payoffs are represented by *payoff functions,* and their even more succinct subclass of *network congestion games* where, in addition, strategy spaces are described succinctly by a graph. The complexity of Nash equilibria for succinct games has been studied in [1,8,10,15,21].

We introduce *weighted boolean formula games,* abbreviated as WBFG, as an adequate and very general form of succinct games. The idea is that each player controls a set of *boolean variables*; different players control disjoint sets of variables. A *strategy* of a player is a truth assignment to his boolean variables. Each player targets a set of constraints expressed by *boolean formulas,* which he wants to get satisfied; naturally, his formulas depend also on variables of other players.[1] For each formula, there is an (integer) *weight,* expressing the relative priority of the constraint (for the player). The *payoff* for a player is the *weighted* sum of his satisfied constraints. In an *unweighted boolean formula game,* all weights are 1.

We shall especially consider a subclass of WBFG, called *mutual weighted boolean formula games* and abbreviated as MWBFG; these add a natural *mutuality* assumption on the constraints targeted by different players: whenever some formula of a player involves a boolean variable of a second player, then the same formula is a constraint for the second player with the *same* weight.

In a (pure) Nash equilibrium [18], no player can increase his payoff by changing the values of his variables. A *payoff-dominant equilibrium* [12] is a Nash equilibrium where every player is *no-worse-off* than in any other Nash equilibrium; so, this is a stable outcome that *payoff-dominates* all other stable outcomes. Payoff-dominance is a well-know refinement of Nash equilibrium that has been studied extensively in Game Theory. Games admitting payoff-dominance have been intuitively called *games of common interests* (cf. [2]); Colman and Bacharach [7, Section 1] mention the abstract classes of *unanimity games* [13] and *matching games* [3] as the simplest exemplars of them. We shall study the structure and complexity of payoff-dominant and pure Nash equilibria in WBFG.

State-of-the-Art. Studied in the literature have been three formalisms of succinct games similar to (but different than) WBFGs:

- (Boolean) Circuit games: Those were introduced in [21]. In a *circuit game,* players still control disjoint sets of *variables,* but each player's payoff is given by a **single** boolean circuit and there are **no** weights. Note that a WBFG can

---

[1] A boolean formula is the special case of a *(boolean) circuit* where every *boolean gate* has *fan-out* one; so, a boolean formula is a circuit whose underlying graph is a tree.

be encoded as a circuit game since our utility functions can be evaluated by a *single* boolean circuit. Hence, WBFG make a **restricted** subclass of circuit games. *Boolean circuit games* are the special case where each player controls a **single** boolean variable.

Recall that the best-known upper bound for the *formula size* $\mathsf{L}(f)$ of a Boolean function f in terms of its *(boolean) circuit size* $\mathsf{C}(f)$ is $\mathsf{L}(f) = \mathcal{O}(2^{\mathsf{C}(f)})$ [14,19]. So, there is no known polynomial time transformation of a circuit game into a boolean formula game where each player has a **single** formula. It is nevertheless possible to transform a boolean circuit into a polynomial size set of boolean *clauses*; this requires introducing new (polynomially many) boolean variables which express the correctness of the computations by the gates. Hence, there is a polynomial time transformation of a circuit game into a boolean formula game where each player has a polynomial number of clauses. Nevertheless, we aim at WBFG where the number of boolean formulas (in particular, clauses) per player is a (small) constant.

– Turing machine games: Álvarez *et al.* [1] study three different levels (*forms*) of succinct representations of strategic games. In the *implicit form,* payoff functions are represented by a deterministic Turing Machine (DTM) computing the payoffs, and strategies are described succinctly. In the *general form,* payoff functions are represented by a DTM and strategy spaces are listed explicitly. For each form, there are two cases: in the *non-uniform* case, the payoff functions are represented by a tuple $\langle M, 1^t \rangle$, where M is a DTM and t is a natural number bounding its computation time; in the *uniform* case, the payoff functions are represented by a (polynomial time) DTM M. Álvarez *et al.* [1] present completeness results on the decision problem for pure Nash equilibria. Their proofs are based on a simple construction of a *gadget game* [1, Section 2]; the payoff functions of the gadget game may be expressed as an instance of a WBFG with $r = 5$. Recall the folklore facts that Turing machine computations with t steps can be encoded as a boolean circuit of size $\mathcal{O}(t^2)$, and that boolean circuits can be evaluated by Turing machines in polynomial time. Hence, Turing machine games in implicit form and circuit games are *equivalent*. It follows from our previous discussion on the relation of WBFG to circuit games that there holds an identical relation of WBFG to Turing machine games in implicit form. In the *explicit form,* payoffs are explicitly listed and the decision problem for Nash equilibria is $\mathcal{P}$-complete [1, Theorem 3]. However, it is *not* possible to obtain from a succinct WBFG such an explicit form in polynomial time.

– Boolean games: Those were introduced in [11] in the context of a logical consequence relation defined in terms of Nash equilibrium; they were further extended and studied in [5,6]. The formulation of boolean games in [6] is very similar to WBFG: each player still wishes to satisfy a particular set of boolean formulas, but the preferences of each player over his formulas were not defined by means of weights attached to the formulas.

The problem of singling out some "best" Nash equilibrium is probably as old as the concept of Nash equilibrium itself [18]. The corresponding stream of game-theoretic research is called *equilibrium selection* (cf. [12]). Besides payoff-dominance, there are several, well-studied refinements of pure Nash equilibria, such as *dominating equilibrium, Pareto-optimality,* and *risk-dominance* [12]. Due to their strength, such refinements are usually unlikely to exist.

Concurrent Work. Independently and concurrently to our work, Biló [4] introduced and studied *satisfiability games*; these are *almost identical* to our MWBFG, except that associated with each player i is some integer $l_i \geq 1$ such that his strategy set is contained in $\{0,1\}^{l_i}$, while it is equal to $\{0,1\}^{l_i}$ in WBFG; however, this difference is *not* essential in general. Their restricted subclass of *unconstrained satisfiability problems* [4] coincides with the class of MWBFG. Studied by Biló [4] are also the so called *satisfiability games with player-specific payoffs*; these correspond to WBFG with the additional *semi-mutuality* assumption: whenever some function of a player involves a variable of another player, the same function is a constraint for the other player as well, but with possibly different weight.

Summary of Results and Significance. We present two types of results. First, we identify structural properties for both WBFG and its rich subclass of MWBFG. Second, we present a collection of complexity results about payoff-dominant and pure Nash equilibria. More specifically, we investigate how the complexity of their decision and search problems depends on five natural parameters: *(i)* the number of players m; *(ii)* the (maximum) number of variables per player k; *(iii)* the (maximum) number of boolean formulas r weight-summed into each payoff function; *(iv)* the *weights* for the payoff functions (that is, whether *weighted* or *unweighted*), and *(v)* the syntax of the boolean formulas. Each of the parameters m, k, and r can be chosen to be fixed as a specific natural number or can be chosen to be not fixed. We discover that the choice of these parameters may have a crucial impact on complexity. In all cases, corresponding results for the search problem follow from those for the decision problem.

Structural results: We prove that MWBFG is an *exact potential* game [17]; so, the decision problem about pure Nash equilibria for these games is trivial and the search problem is in $\mathcal{PLS}$. We next consider the relation between (mutual) WBFG and another class of succinct games, namely *weighted, linear-affine congestion games with player-specific (coefficients and) constants* [15]. We prove that every weighted, linear-affine congestion game with player-specific coefficients and constants is *polynomial, sound monomorphic* to a WBFG. This implies that every weighted, linear-affine congestion game with player-specific constants is polynomial, sound monomorphic to a MWBFG. We also prove that the same hold for weighted, linear-affine *network* congestion games with player-specific constants. Since the search problem for Nash equilibria is $\mathcal{PLS}$-complete for weighted, asymmetric network congestion games (with player-specific constants) [15, Theorem 5], it follows that the search problem for Nash equilibria in MWBFG is $\mathcal{PLS}$-complete.

Complexity results for payoff-dominant equilibria (Theorem 5:): We present the *first* complexity results about payoff-dominant equilibria. We first consider the case where m is not fixed and $k \geq 1$ is fixed. For unweighted formulas with $r \geq 1$ fixed or not fixed, the problem is Θ_2^P-complete (Case (2)); for weighted formulas with r not fixed, the problem is Δ_2^P-complete (Case (1)). We next consider the case where k is not fixed and $m \geq 4$ is fixed or not fixed. For unweighted formulas with r not fixed, the problem is Θ_3^P-complete (Case (4)); for weighted formulas with r not fixed, the problem is Δ_3^P-complete (Case (3)). These complexity results about payoff-dominant equilibria in WBFG indicate that allowing an arbitrary number of variables per player has a stronger impact on their complexity than allowing an arbitrary number of players.

Complexity results for pure Nash equilibria (Theorem 6): We first consider the case where m is not fixed and $k \geq 1$ is fixed. For (weighted) formulas with $r \geq 1$ fixed or not fixed, the problem is $\mathcal{NP}$-complete (Case (1)); for (weighted) clauses with $r \geq 2$ fixed or not fixed, the problem is $\mathcal{NP}$-complete (Case (2)); for (weighted) clauses with $r = 1$, it is in $\mathcal{P}$ (Case (3)). We next consider the case that k is not fixed and $m \geq 2$ is fixed or not fixed. For (weighted) formulas with $r \geq 1$ fixed or not fixed, the problem is Σ_2^P-complete (Case (4)).

Related Work. Since WBFG have a restricted structure, our completeness proofs have required more detailed arguments than the ones in [1,21].

- (Boolean) Circuit games: Recall that boolean formula games form a restricted subclass of boolean circuit games. Observe that all upper bounds established in this paper for boolean formula games are obviously also valid for circuit games. It is shown [21, Theorem 6.1] that the decision problem in *two-player* circuit games is Σ_2^P-complete; this follows from Theorem 6 (Case (4)). It is shown [21, Theorem 6.2] that the decision problem in boolean circuit games is $\mathcal{NP}$-complete; this follows from Theorem 6 (Case (1)).
- Turing machine games: Álvarez *et al.* [1] prove that the problem is $\mathcal{NP}$-complete for strategic games in general form for both the non-uniform [1, Theorem 2] and the uniform [1, Theorem 5] cases. It follows from either [1, Theorem 2] or [1, Theorem 5] that if m is not fixed, then the problem for (weighted) boolean formulas is $\mathcal{NP}$-complete when $k \geq 1$ is fixed and $r \geq 5$ is fixed or not fixed. This implied result is *weaker* than Theorem 6. (Case (1)). Furthermore, Álvarez *et al.* [1] prove that the problem is Σ_2^P-complete for strategic games in implicit form for both the non-uniform [1, Theorem 1 and Corollary 1] and the uniform [1, Theorem 4] cases. It follows from [1, Corollary 1] that if k is not fixed, then the problem for (weighted) boolean formulas is Σ_2^P-complete when $m \geq 3$ is fixed or not fixed and $r \geq 5$ is fixed or not fixed. This implied result is *incomparable* to Theorem 6 (Case (4)).
- Boolean games: Bonzon *et al.* [6, Proposition 5] had *independently* proved a stronger version of Case (4) in Theorem 6 (which holds for $m \geq 3$ fixed or not fixed) with $m \geq 2$ (fixed or not fixed); furthermore, their result applies to *zero-sum* (two-player) games. Bonzon *et al.* [6, Proposition 6] prove that in the case where k is not fixed, the decision problem for boolean formula games with $m \geq 2$ fixed or not fixed is $\mathcal{NP}$-complete when all formulas are in DNF. This is an interesting complement to Theorem 6 (Case (2)).
- Satisfiability games: Bilò [4] considers *restricted satisfiability games,* where the strategy set of each player is the set of strategies in which the player is allowed

to set to 1 one and only one of his variables. It is proved [4, Theorem 3] that the class of restricted satisfiability games with player specific payoffs where all functions are conjunctive encompasses *all* strategic games. Furthermore, Biló [4, Theorem 1] proves that every satisfiability game is an unweighted congestion game. Since every unweighted congestion game is (isomorphic to) an exact potential game and vice versa [17,20], this result is equivalent to Theorem 1. However, Theorem 1 provides an exact potential for a MWBFG, which is very simple and intuitive, and it may have further applications.

2   Background and Framework

Notation and Preliminaries. A *strategic game* (or *game* for short) is a triple $\Gamma = \langle m, (S_i)_{i \in [m]}, (u_i)_{i \in [m]} \rangle$, where m is the number of players, S_i is the *strategy space* of player $i \in [m]$, and $u_i : S_1 \times \ldots \times S_m \to \mathbb{R}$ is the *payoff function* of player $i \in [m]$. The game Γ is *finite* if all strategy spaces are finite; all games considered in this paper will be assumed to be finite. For the game Γ, denote $S = S_1 \times \ldots \times S_m$. A *profile* is a tuple of strategies $\mathbf{s} = \langle s_1, \ldots, s_m \rangle$, one for each player; denote as $\mathbf{s}_{-i}$ the partial profile resulting from eliminating the strategy of player i from $\mathbf{s}$. Given a profile $\mathbf{s}$, a player $i \in [m]$ and a strategy $t \in S_i$, denote as $(\mathbf{s}_{-i}, t) = \langle s_1, \ldots, s_{i-1}, t, s_{i+1}, \ldots, s_m \rangle$; so, $(\mathbf{s}_{-i}, t)$ results by substituting in the profile $\mathbf{s}$ the strategy s_i of player i with t.

A profile $\mathbf{s} \in S$ is a *(pure) Nash equilibrium* [18] if for each player $i \in [m]$, for each strategy $t \in S_i$, $u_i(\mathbf{s}) \geq u_i(\mathbf{s}_{-i}, t)$. Denote as $\mathsf{NE}(\Gamma)$ the set of Nash equilibria of Γ. A Nash equilibrium $\mathbf{s}$ is called a *payoff-dominant equilibrium* for Γ if for each (pure) Nash equilibrium $\mathbf{s}'$, for each player $i \in [m]$, $u_i(\mathbf{s}) \geq u_i(\mathbf{s}')$. Denote as $\mathsf{PD}(\Gamma)$ the set of payoff-dominant equilibria for Γ.

Maps. Consider two strategic games $\Gamma = \langle m, (S_i)_{i \in [m]}, (u_i)_{i \in [m]} \rangle$ and $\Gamma' = \langle m, (S'_i)_{i \in [m]}, (u'_i)_{i \in [m]} \rangle$ with the same number of players. A *player map* (or *player bijection*) $\pi : [m] \to [m]$ identifies player $i \in [m]$ for Γ with player $\pi(i) \in [m]$ for Γ'. An *action map* is an m-tuple of *action bijections* $\phi = (\phi_i)_{i \in [m]}$ such that each ϕ_i is a bijection $\phi_i : S_i \to S'_{\pi(i)}$; so, the bijection ϕ_i identifies action $s_i \in S_i$ with action $\phi_i(s_i) \in S'_{\pi(i)}$. A *bijection pair* from Γ to Γ' is a pair $\langle \pi, \phi \rangle$ of a player map and an action map. The map $\langle \pi, \phi \rangle$ maps profiles from S to profiles in S' in the natural way; that is, for a profile $\mathbf{s} \in S$, $\langle \pi, \phi \rangle(\mathbf{s}) = \mathbf{s}'$ where for each $i \in [m]$, $s'_{\pi(i)} = \phi_i(s_i)$. A *Harsanyi-Selten isomorphism* [12] (from Γ to Γ') is a map $\langle \pi, \phi \rangle$ such that for each player $i \in [m]$, there are constants $\gamma_i > 0$ and δ_i such that for each profile $\mathbf{s} \in S$, $u_{\pi(i)}(\langle \pi, \phi \rangle(\mathbf{s})) = \gamma_i u_i(\mathbf{s}) + \delta_i$; then, say that Γ is *Harsanyi-Selten isomorphic* to Γ'. Defined earlier by Nash [18], a *strong isomorphism* is the special case of a Harsanyi-Selten isomorphism where for each player $i \in [m]$, $\delta_i = 0$. We shall use a relaxation of the Harsanyi-Selten isomorphism which we call a *Harsanyi-Selten monomorphism*; there, the action map is relaxed to be an m-tuple of *action injections* (which need not be surjective), and the bijection pair $\langle \pi, \phi \rangle$ becomes a *monomorphism*.

Consider two classes of strategic games $\mathcal{C}$ and $\mathcal{C}'$. Say that the class $\mathcal{C}$ is **Harsanyi-Selten monomorphic** to the class $\mathcal{C}'$ if every game $\Gamma \in \mathcal{C}$ is Harsanyi-Selten monomorphic to some game $\Gamma' \in \mathcal{C}'$, which can be computed from Γ via a map $\lambda : \mathcal{C} \to \mathcal{C}'$. (For each particular game $\Gamma \in \mathcal{C}$, λ and $\langle \pi, \phi \rangle$ induce together a corresponding map, denoted as $\lambda \circ \langle \pi, \phi \rangle$ by abuse of notation, which maps each profile $\mathbf{s} \in S(\Gamma)$ to the profile $\langle \pi, \phi \rangle(\mathbf{s}) \in S(\lambda(\Gamma))$; denote as $\lambda \circ \langle \pi, \phi \rangle(S(\Gamma))$ the resulting set of images of profiles in $S(\Gamma)$.) Say that the class $\mathcal{C}$ is **polynomial Harsanyi-Selten monomorphic** to the class $\mathcal{C}'$ if *(i)* $\mathcal{C}$ is Harsanyi-Selten monomorphic to $\mathcal{C}'$, *(ii)* the map $\lambda : \mathcal{C} \to \mathcal{C}$ is polynomial time, and *(iii)* for each pair of a game $\Gamma \in \mathcal{C}$ and its image $\lambda(\Gamma) \in \mathcal{C}'$, the map $\langle \pi, \phi \rangle$ can be computed in polynomial time. Clearly, a Harsanyi-Selten isomorphism from Γ to Γ' induces a bijection from $\mathsf{NE}(\Gamma)$ to $\mathsf{NE}(\Gamma')$; a Harsanyi-Selten monomorphism from Γ to Γ' induces an injection from $\mathsf{NE}(\Gamma)$ to $\mathsf{NE}(\Gamma')$.

Definition 1 (Polynomial Sound Monomorphism). *A **polynomial sound monomorphism** from $\mathcal{C}$ to $\mathcal{C}'$ is a triple $\langle \lambda, \langle \pi, \phi \rangle, \psi \rangle$ where:*

(1) *The class $\mathcal{C}$ is polynomial Harsanyi-Selten monomorphic to the class $\mathcal{C}'$ via the map $\lambda : \mathcal{C} \to \mathcal{C}'$ and the (Harsanyi-Selten) monomorphism $\langle \pi, \phi \rangle$.*
(2) *For each game $\Gamma \in \mathcal{C}$, ψ_Γ is a function $\psi_\Gamma : \mathsf{NE}(\lambda((\Gamma))) \to \mathsf{NE}(\Gamma)$; that is, ψ_Γ maps a Nash equilibrium for the game $\lambda(\Gamma) \in \mathcal{C}'$ to a Nash equilibrium for Γ. Then, $\psi := \bigcup_{\Gamma \in \mathcal{C}} \psi_\Gamma$, Furthermore, ψ is a polynomial time map.*
(3) *(Soundness Condition) For each game $\Gamma \in \mathcal{C}$, $\mathsf{NE}(\lambda(\Gamma)) \subseteq \lambda \circ \langle \pi, \phi \rangle(S(\Gamma))$; that is, a Nash equilibrium for the image game $\lambda(\Gamma)$ is necessarily the image (under $\lambda \circ \langle \pi, \phi \rangle$) of some profile of Γ.*

Note that Condition (3) requires that that for any game $\Gamma \in \mathcal{C}$, the Harsanyi-Selten monomorphism $\langle \pi, \phi \rangle$ from Γ to Γ' (from Condition (1)) induces indeed a bijection from $\mathsf{NE}(\Gamma)$ to $\mathsf{NE}(\Gamma')$.

Potential and Congestion Games. Fix a positive vector $\mathbf{b} = \langle b_1, \ldots, b_n \rangle$. Then, a $\mathbf{b}$-**potential** for the game Γ is a function $\Phi : S \to \mathbb{R}$ such that for each profile $\mathbf{s} \in S$, for each player $i \in [m]$ and strategy $s_i' \in S_i$, $u_i(\mathbf{s}_{-i}, s_i') - u_i(\mathbf{s}) = b_i(\Phi(\mathbf{s}_{-i}, s_i') - \Phi(\mathbf{s}))$. A **vector potential game** is a game that admits a $\mathbf{w}$-potential for some (non-negative) vector $\mathbf{w}$. A finite vector potential game has a pure Nash equilibrium [17], which is a local maximizer of the vector potential. An **exact potential game** (or **potential game** for short) is a $\mathbf{b}$-potential game for some constant vector $\mathbf{b}$; such a $\mathbf{b}$-potential is called an **exact potential** (or **potential** for short).. Note that if a game Γ is Harsanyi-Selten monomorphic to a (vector) potential game Γ', then Γ is a vector potential game; hence, to prove that a game is vector potential, it suffices to provide a Harsanyi-Selten monomorphism (from it) to a (vector) potential game.

A *weighted, linear-affine congestion game with player-specific constants* [15] is a game $\Gamma = \langle m, (S_i)_{i \in [m]}, (u_i)_{i \in [m]} \rangle$ such that: (1) There is an integer $k \geq 2$ such that for each player $i \in [m]$, $S_i \subseteq \mathcal{P}(\{1, 2, \ldots, k\})$. (Equivalently, $S_i \subseteq \{0, 1\}^k$.) (2) There exist families of integers $(\beta_e)_{e \in [k]}$ with $\beta_e \geq 0$ (the *coefficients*), $(\gamma_{ie})_{i \in [m], e \in [k]}$ with $\gamma_{ie} \geq 0$ (the *constants*), and $(w_i)_{i \in [m]}$ with

$w_i \geq 1$ (the *weights*) such that for each profile $\mathbf{s} = \langle s_1, \dots, s_m \rangle$, for each player $i \in [m]$, $u_i(\mathbf{s}) = -\sum_{e \in s_i} \left(\beta_e \cdot \sum_{j \in [m] | e \in s_j} w_j + \gamma_{ie} \right)$. Denote as WLACGwPSC the class of weighted, linear-affine congestion games with player-specific constants. Clearly, WLACGwPSC contains the class of *weighted, linear-affine congestion games* [9] where the constants $(\gamma_e)_{e \in [k]}$ are no more player-specific; it is also contained in the class WLACGwPSC^2 of *weighted, linear-affine congestion games with player-specific coefficients and constants* [10], which, in turn, is contained in the general class of *weighted congestion games with player-specific payoff functions* [16]. It is known that WLACGwPSC admit a vector potential and a pure Nash equilibrium [15, Theorem 6 and Corollary 7]; in contrast, WLACGwPSC^2 do *not* necessarily admit a pure Nash equilibrium [10, Theorem 2].

Weighted Boolean Formula Games. We now provide our main definition.

Definition 2 (Weighted Boolean Formula Game). *Fix a triple of integers* $m \geq 2$, $k \geq 1$ *and* $r \geq 1$. *A game* $\Gamma = \langle m, (S_i)_{i \in [m]}, (u_i)_{i \in [m]} \rangle$, *is called a* **weighted** (m, k, r)-**boolean formula game** (*or* **weighted boolean formula game** *for short*) *if* (1) *for each player* $i \in [m]$, $S_i = \{0, 1\}^k$; (2) *there is a set* $F_i = \{(f, \alpha) \mid f$ *is a* (km)-*ary boolean formula and* $\alpha \in \mathbb{N}\}$ *with* $|F_i| \leq r$ *such that for each* $\langle s_1, \dots, s_m \rangle \in S$, $u_i(s_1, \dots, s_m) = \sum_{(f, \alpha) \in F_i} \alpha \cdot f(s_1, \dots, s_m)$.

We also write $\Gamma = \langle m, k, r, (F_i)_{i \in [m]} \rangle$. Denote $F = \bigcup_{i \in [m]} F_i$. We use WBFG as an abbreviation for a weighted boolean formula game. An (m, k, r)-**boolean formula game** is the special case of a weighted (m, k, r)-boolean formula game $\Gamma = \langle m, k, r, (F_i)_{i \in [m]} \rangle$ such that for each pair $(f, \alpha) \in F$, $\alpha = 1$. A **(weighted)** (m, k, r)-**boolean clause game** is the special case of a (weighted) (m, k, r)-boolean formula game $\Gamma = \langle m, k, r, (F_i)_{i \in [m]} \rangle$ such that for each pair $(f, \alpha) \in F$, f is a *clause*. We formulate a restricted class of WBFG, denoted as MWBFG.

Definition 3. *A weighted boolean formula game* $\Gamma = \langle m, k, r, (F_i)_{i \in [m]} \rangle$, *is called* **mutual** *if the following holds: For each pair* $(f, \alpha) \in F$, *if* f *depends on a variable of player* $i \in [m]$, *then* $(f, \alpha) \in F_i$.

Decision and Search Problems. Let $m \in \{2, 3, \dots\}$, $k \in \{1, 2, \dots\}$ and $r \in \{1, 2, \dots\}$. We formulate and study the following decision problems:

PROBLEM:	PROBLEM:	GIVEN a Γ which is:
WBF-PD$_d(m, k, r)$	WBF-NASH$_d(m, k, r)$	Weighted (m, k, r)-boolean formula game.
BF-PD$_d(m, k, r)$	BF-NASH$_d(m, k, r)$	(m, k, r)-boolean formula game.
WBC-PD$_d(m, k, r)$	WBC-NASH$_d(m, k, r)$	Weighted (m, k, r)-boolean clause game.
BC-PD$_d(m, k, r)$	BC-NASH$_d(m, k, r)$	(m, k, r)-boolean clause game.
QUESTION:	QUESTION:	
Is PD$(\Gamma) \neq \emptyset$?	Is NASH$(\Gamma) \neq \emptyset$?	

We shall often consider the case where some of the parameters m, k, and r are not restricted to a fixed value. In this case, such a parameter gets the value $*$. For example, for $k \in \{1, 2, \dots\}$ and $r \in \{1, 2, \dots\}$, we define $\mathsf{BF\text{-}NASH}_d(*, k, r) = \bigcup_{m \geq 2} \mathsf{BF\text{-}NASH}_d(m, k, r)$. Denote as $\mathsf{MWBF\text{-}NASH}_s(*, *, *)$ the search problem for pure Nash equilibria in MWBFG.

3   Structure

Theorem 1. *Consider the MWBFG* $\Gamma = \langle m, k, r, (F_i)_{i \in [m]} \rangle$. *Then, the function* $\Phi : (\{0, 1\}^k)^m \to \mathbb{R}$ *with* $\Phi(\mathbf{s}) = \sum_{\langle f, \alpha \rangle \in F} \alpha \cdot f(\mathbf{s})$ *is an exact potential for* Γ.

Proof. Consider a profile $\mathbf{s} \in S$ and a strategy $t_i \in \{0, 1\}^k$ of player $i \in [m]$. Then,

$$\Phi(\mathbf{s}_{-i}, t_i) - \Phi(\mathbf{s})$$
$$= \sum_{\langle f, \alpha \rangle \in F} \alpha \cdot f(\mathbf{s}_{-i}, t_i) - \sum_{\langle f, \alpha \rangle \in F} \alpha \cdot f(\mathbf{s})$$
$$= \sum_{\langle f, \alpha \rangle \in F_i} \alpha \cdot f(\mathbf{s}_{-i}, t_i) + \sum_{\langle f, \alpha \rangle \in F \setminus F_i} \alpha \cdot f(\mathbf{s}_{-i}, t_i) - \sum_{\langle f, \alpha \rangle \in F_i} \alpha \cdot f(\mathbf{s}) - \sum_{\langle f, \alpha \rangle \in F \setminus F_i} \alpha \cdot f(\mathbf{s})$$
$$= \sum_{\langle f, \alpha \rangle \in F_i} \alpha \cdot f(\mathbf{s}_{-i}, t_i) - \sum_{\langle f, \alpha \rangle \in F_i} \alpha \cdot f(\mathbf{s}) + \sum_{\langle f, \alpha \rangle \in F \setminus F_i} \alpha \cdot (f(\mathbf{s}_{-i}, t_i) - f(\mathbf{s})).$$

Since Γ is a MWBFG, it follows that for each pair $\langle f, \alpha \rangle \in F \setminus F_i$, $f(s_1, \dots, s_m)$ does *not* depend on s_i; hence, for each pair $\langle f, \alpha \rangle \in F \setminus F_i$, $f(\mathbf{s}_{-i}, t_i) = f(\mathbf{s})$. It follows that

$$\Phi(\mathbf{s}_{-i}, t_i) - \Phi(\mathbf{s}) = \sum_{\langle f, \alpha \rangle \in F_i} \alpha \cdot f(\mathbf{s}_{-i}, t_i) - \sum_{\langle f, \alpha \rangle \in F_i} \alpha \cdot f(\mathbf{s}) \quad = \quad u_i(\mathbf{s}_{-i}, t_i) - u_i(\mathbf{s});$$

hence, Φ is an exact potential for Γ, as needed.   □

An inspection to the proof reveals that the assumption that player variables and formulas are boolean is *not* essential: mutuality alone suffices for the existence of an exact potential. Theorem 1 implies that every MWBFG has a pure Nash equilibrium and $\mathsf{MWBF\text{-}NASH}_d(*, *, *) \in \mathcal{PLS}$. We now prove:

Theorem 2. *The class of weighted, linear-affine congestion games with player-specific coefficients and constants is polynomial, sound monomorphic to the class of weighted boolean formula games.*

We will identify a set $t \subseteq \{1, \dots, k\}$ with the *characteristic vector* $\langle \chi_t(1), \dots, \chi_t(k) \rangle$, where χ_t is the *characteristic function* for t: for $e \in [k]$, $\chi_t(e) = 1$ if $e \in t$ and 0 otherwise. For a boolean x, set $x^{\chi_t(e)} = x$ if $\chi_t(e) = 1$ and $\overline{x}$ otherwise.

Proof. Here is a polynomial, sound monomorphism $\langle \lambda, \langle \pi, \phi \rangle, \psi \rangle$ from $\mathsf{WLACGwPSC}^2$ to WBFG. The action of λ on any $\mathsf{WLACGwPSC}^2$ $\Gamma = \langle m, (S_i)_{i \in [m]}, (u_i)_{i \in [m]} \rangle$, with $S_i \subseteq \{0, 1\}^k$ for each $i \in [m]$, is defined as follows:

Each player $i \in [n]$ has variables $x_i = \langle x_{i1}, \ldots, x_{ik} \rangle$; so, $S'_i = \{0,1\}^k$. F_i consists of:

	Boolean formula	Weight
For $e \in [k]$:	$f_{ie}(x_1, \ldots, x_m) = \overline{x_{ie}}$	$\alpha_{ie} = \delta_{ie} \cdot w_i$
For $j \in [m]$ and $e \in [k]$:	$f_{ije}(x_1, \ldots, x_m) = \overline{x_{ie}} \bigvee \overline{x_{je}}$	$\alpha_{ije} = \beta_{ie} \cdot w_i \cdot w_j$
For $t \in S_i$:	$f_{it}(x_1, \ldots, x_m) = \bigwedge_{e \in [k]} x_{ie}^{\chi_t(e)}$	$\alpha_{it} = w_i \cdot \sum_{e \in [k]} (\beta_{ie} \cdot \sum_{j \in [m]} w_j + \delta_{ie}) + 1$

Set π and ϕ to be the identity maps, respectively. Furthermore, set ψ_Γ to be the identity map; so, ψ_Γ maps a Nash equilibrium $\mathbf{s}'$ (for Γ') to itself. We now show Conditions (1), (2) and (3) in Definition 1. Clearly, both maps λ and $\langle \pi, \phi \rangle$ are polynomial. Furthermore, since for each player $i \in [m]$, $S_i \subseteq S'_i$, the map $\langle \pi, \phi \rangle$ is a homomorphism. For Condition (1), we proceed to show that $\langle \pi, \phi \rangle$ is Harsanyi-Selten. Fix any profile $\mathbf{s}' = \langle s'_1, \ldots, s'_m \rangle$ (for Γ'), where for each player $i \in [m]$, $s_i = \langle s'_{i1}, \ldots, s'_{ik} \rangle$. (Note that it need not be the case that $\mathbf{s}'$ is a profile for Γ.) Note that for each player $i \in [m]$,

$$u_{\pi(i)}(\mathbf{s}') = u'_i(\mathbf{s}')$$
$$= \underbrace{\sum_{e \in [k]} \alpha_{ie} \cdot (1 - \overline{f_{ie}(\mathbf{s}')})}_{\Sigma_1(\mathbf{s}')} + \underbrace{\sum_{j \in [m]} \sum_{e \in [k]} \alpha_{ije} \cdot (1 - \overline{f_{ije}(\mathbf{s}')})}_{\Sigma_2(\mathbf{s}')} + \underbrace{\sum_{t \in S_i} \alpha_{it} \cdot f_{it}(\mathbf{s}')}_{\Sigma_3(\mathbf{s}')} .$$

We establish that

$$\Sigma_1(\mathbf{s}') + \Sigma_2(\mathbf{s}') = w_i \sum_{e \in [k]} \left(\beta_{ie} \cdot \sum_{j \in [m]} w_j + \delta_{ie} \right) - w_i \sum_{e \in s'_i} \left(\beta_{ie} \cdot \sum_{j | e \in s'_j} w_j + \delta_{ie} \right) .$$

$$\Sigma_3(\mathbf{s}') = \left(w_i \cdot \sum_{e \in [k]} \left(\beta_{ie} \cdot \sum_{j \in [m]} w_j + \delta_{ie} \right) + 1 \right) \cdot \chi_{S_i}(s'_i) .$$

We next prove that $\langle \pi, \phi \rangle$ is Harsanyi-Selten and sound. This completes the proof for Condition (1) and Condition (3). To prove Condition (2), note that the map $\langle \pi, \phi \rangle$ induces a Harsanyi-Selten bijection from $\mathsf{NE}(\Gamma)$ to $\mathsf{NE}(\Gamma')$. Since both π and ϕ are identity, this bijection is also identity as well as its inverse. So, the identity map is a bijection from $\mathsf{NE}(\Gamma')$ to $\mathsf{NE}(\Gamma)$. Since Ψ_Γ is this identity map, Condition (2) follows.   □

An inspection to the proof of Theorem 2 reveals that if we had *player-independent* coefficients $(\beta_e)_{e \in [k]}$ in the original game Γ, the resulting WBFG $\lambda(\Gamma)$ would be mutual. Hence, Theorem 2 implies:

Corollary 1. *The class of weighted, linear-affine congestion games with player-specific constants is polynomial, sound monomorphic to the class of mutual weighted boolean formula games.*

We continue to prove in a similar way:

Theorem 3. *The class of weighted, linear-affine network congestion games with player-specific coefficients and constants is polynomial, sound monomorphic to the class of weighted boolean formula games.*

Similar to Corollary 1, we obtain:

Corollary 2. *The class of weighted, linear-affine network congestion games with player-specific constants is polynomial, sound monomorphic to the class of mutual weighted boolean formula games.*

Since the search problem for pure Nash equilibria in weighted, asymmetric network congestion games with player-specific constants is $\mathcal{PLS}$-complete [15, Theorem 5], Corollary 1 and Corollary 2 immediately imply:

Corollary 3. MWBF-NASH$_s(*,*,*)$ *is $\mathcal{PLS}$-complete.*

4 Complexity

For payoff-dominant equilibria, we first show:

Theorem 4. *Let $m \in \{2,3,\ldots\}$, $k \in \{1,2,\ldots\}$ and $r \in \{1,2,\ldots,*\}$. Then:* (1) WBF-PD$_d(m,k,r) \in \mathcal{P}$. (2) BF-PD$_d(*,k,r) \in \Theta_2^P$. (3) WBF-PD$_d(*,k,r) \in \Delta_2^P$. (4) BF-PD$_d(*,*,r) \in \Theta_3^P$. (5) WBF-PD$_d(*,*,r) \in \Delta_3^P$.

We finally show:

Theorem 5. *We have:*
(1) WBF-PD$_d(*,k,*)$ *is Δ_2^P-complete for $k \in \{1,2,\ldots\}$.*
(2) BF-PD$_d(*,k,r)$ *is Θ_2^P-complete for $k \in \{1,2,\ldots\}$ and $r \in \{1,2,\ldots,*\}$.*
(3) WBF-PD$_d(m,*,*)$ *is Δ_3^P-complete for $m \in \{4,5,\ldots,*\}$.*
(4) BF-PD$_d(m,*,*)$ *is Θ_3^P-complete for $m \in \{4,5,\ldots,*\}$.*

For pure Nash equilibria, we first observe:

Proposition 1. *Let $m \in \{2,3,\ldots\}$, $k \in \{1,2,\ldots\}$ and $r \in \{1,2,\ldots,*\}$. Then:*
(1) WBF-NASH$_d(m,k,r) \in \mathcal{P}$ *(and WBF-NASH$_s(m,k,r) \in$ F$\mathcal{P}$).*
(2) WBF-NASH$_d(*,k,r) \in \mathcal{NP}$ *(and WBF-NASH$_s(*,k,r) \in$ F$\mathcal{NP}$).*
(3) WBF-NASH$_d(m,*,r) \in \Sigma_2^P$ *(and WBF-NASH$_s(m,*,r) \in$ FΣ_2^P).*
(4) WBF-NASH$_d(*,*,r) \in \Sigma_2^P$ *(and WBF-NASH$_s(*,*,r) \in$ FΣ_2^P).*

We finally show:

Theorem 6. *We have:*
(1) *For $k \in \{1,2,\ldots\}$ and $r \in \{1,2,\ldots,*\}$, BF-NASH$_d(*,k,r)$ is $\mathcal{NP}$-complete.*
(2) *For $k \in \{1,2,\ldots\}$ and $r \in \{2,3,\ldots,*\}$, BC-NASH$_d(*,k,r)$ is $\mathcal{NP}$-complete.*
(3) *For $k \in \{1,2,\ldots,*\}$, WBC-NASH$_d(*,k,1) \in \mathcal{P}$. In fact, every weighted $(*,k,1)$-boolean clause game has a pure Nash equilibrium.*
(4) *For $m \in \{3,4,\ldots,*\}$ and $r \in \{1,2,\ldots,*\}$, BF-NASH$_d(m,*,r)$ is Σ_2^P-complete*

References

1. Álvarez, C., Gabarró, J., Serna, M.: Pure Nash Equilibria in Games with a Large Number of Actions. In: Jedrzejowicz, J., Szepietowski, A. (eds.) MFCS 2005. LNCS, vol. 3618, pp. 95–106. Springer, Heidelberg (2005)
2. Aumann, R.J., Sorin, S.: Cooperation and Bounded Recall. Games and Economic Behavior 1, 5–39 (1989)
3. Bacharach, M., Bernasconi, M.: An Experimental Study of the Variable Frame Theory of Focal Points. Games and Economic Behavior 19, 1–45 (1997)
4. Biló, V.: On Satisfiability Games and the Power of Congestion Games. In: Biló, V. (ed.) AAIM 2007. LNCS, vol. 4508, pp. 231–240. Springer, Heidelberg (2007)
5. Bonzon, E., Lagasquie-Schiex, M.-C., Lang, J.: Compact Preference Representation for Boolean Games. In: Yang, Q., Webb, G. (eds.) PRICAI 2006. LNCS (LNAI), vol. 4099, pp. 41–50. Springer, Heidelberg (2006)
6. Bonzon, E., Lagasquie-Schiex, M.-C., Lang, J., Zanuttini, B.: Boolean Games Revisited. In: Proceedings of the 17th European Conference on Artificial Intelligence, pp. 265–269 (2006)
7. Colman, A.M., Bacharach, M.: Payoff Dominance and the Stackelberg Heuristic. Theory and Decision 43, 1–19 (1997)
8. Fabrikant, A., Papadimitriou, C.H., Talwar, K.: The Complexity of Pure Nash Equilibria. In: Proceedings of the 36th Annual ACM Symposium on Theory of Computing, pp. 604–612 (2004)
9. Fotakis, D., Kontogiannis, S., Spirakis, P.: Selfish Unsplittable Flows. Theoretical Computer Science 348, 226–239 (2005)
10. Gairing, M., Monien, B., Tiemann, K.: Routing (Un-)Splittable Flow in Games with Player-Specific Linear Latency Functions. In: Bugliesi, M., Preneel, B., Sassone, V., Wegener, I. (eds.) ICALP 2006. LNCS, vol. 4051, pp. 501–512. Springer, Heidelberg (2006)
11. Harrenstein, P., van der Hoek, W., Meyer, J.-J., Witteveen, C.: Boolean Games. In: Proceedings of the 8th Conference on Theoretical Aspects of Rationality and Knowledge, pp. 287–298 (2001)
12. Harsanyi, J.C., Selten, R.: A General Theory of Equilibrium Selection in Games. MIT Press, Cambridge (1988)
13. Kalai, E., Samet, D.: Unanimity Games and Pareto Optimality. International Journal of Game Theory 14, 41–50 (1985)
14. Krapchenko, V.M.: Complexity of the Realization of a Linear Function in the Class of π-Circuits. Mathematical Notes of the Academy of Sciences USSR 11, 70–76 (1971)
15. Mavronicolas, M., Milchtaich, I., Monien, B., Tiemann, K.: Congestion Games with Player-Specific Constants. In: Proceedings of the 32nd International Symposium on Mathematical Foundations of Computer Science (August 2007)
16. Milchtaich, I.: Congestion Games with Player-Specific Payoff Functions. Games and Economic Behavior 13, 111–124 (1996)
17. Monderer, D., Shapley, L.S.: Potential Games. Games and Economic Behavior 14, 124–143 (1996)
18. Nash, J.F.: Non-Cooperative Games. Annals of Mathematics 54, 286–295 (1951)

19. Paterson, M., Valiant, L.G.: Circuit Size is Nonlinear in Depth. Theoretical Computer Science 2, 397–400 (1976)
20. Rosenthal, R.W.: A Class of Games Possessing Pure Strategy Nash Equilibria. International Journal on Game Theory 2, 65–67 (1973)
21. Schoenebeck, G., Vadhan, S.: The Computational Complexity of Nash Equilibria in Concisely Represented Games. In: Proceedings of the 7th ACM Conference on Electronic Commerce, pp. 270–279 (2006)

Core Stability of Vertex Cover Games*

Qizhi Fang and Liang Kong

Department of Mathematics, Ocean University of China
Qingdao 266071, P.R. China
qfang@ouc.edu.cn

Abstract. In this paper, we focus on the core stability of vertex cover games, which arise from vertex cover problems on graphs. Based on duality theory of linear programming, we first prove that a balanced vertex cover game has the stable core if and only if every edge belongs to a maximum matching in the corresponding graph. We also show that for a totally balanced vertex cover game, the core largeness, extendability and exactness are all equivalent, which imply the core stability.

Keywords: Vertex cover game, balanced, stable core, largeness, exactness, extendability.

1 Introduction

A transferable cooperative game $\Gamma = (N, \gamma)$ consists of a player set $N = \{1, 2, \cdots, n\}$ and a characteristic function $\gamma : 2^N \to R$, where for each subset $S \subseteq N$ of players, $\gamma(S)$ represents the revenue or cost achieved by the players in S without assistance of other players. One of the scopes of cooperative game theory is to study how to distribute the total revenue or cost $\gamma(N)$ among the participants in a fair way. Different philosophies result in different solution concepts, *e.g.*, the core, the Shapley value, the Nucleolus and the stable set. Von Neumann and Morgenstern [11] first introduce the concept of the stable set and claimed that it is very useful in the analysis of a lot of bargaining situations. However, it seems difficult to investigate the properties of the stable set because of the complexity of its definition. Moreover, Deng and Papadimitriou [4] pointed out that determining the existence of the stable set for a given cooperative game is not known to be computable, and it is still unsolved.

While the core and the stable set are different, Shapley [7] has shown that for convex games, the core is the unique stable set. This result motivated researchers to study the problem: when do the core and the stable set coincide, that is, when is the core stable? As far as the core stability for concrete cooperative game model is concerned, only a few results have been obtained. Solymosi and Raghavan [9] studied the core stability for assignment games, Bietenhader and Okamoto [1] studied it for minimum coloring games defined on perfect graphs, and Sun and Fang [12] studied it for simple flow games.

* This work is supported by NCET (No.05-0598) and NSFC (No.10771200).

X. Deng and F.C. Graham (Eds.): WINE 2007, LNCS 4858, pp. 482–490, 2007.

In this paper, we focus on core stability of vertex cover games introduced by Deng, Ibaraki and Nagamochi [2], which arise from the cost allocation problems related to vertex covers on graphs. We show that a vertex cover game has the stable core if and only if every edge belongs to a maximum matching in the corresponding graph. We also consider the problems on the core largeness, the extendability and the exactness of the game, which are closely related to core stability. We prove that all the three properties are equivalent for vertex cover games defined on bipartite graphs, and also equivalent to that every matching is contained in a maximum matching. Finally, we conclude with extensions of above results to general covering games.

2   Definitions and Preliminaries

Throughout this paper, all the games concerned are cost game, that is, the characteristic function specifies the cost of every coalitions. Let $\Gamma = (N, \gamma)$ be a cooperative game. A vector $x = (x_1, x_2, \cdots, x_n)$ is called an *imputation* if $\sum_{i \in N} x_i = \gamma(N)$ and $\forall\, i \in N$: $x_i \leq \gamma(\{i\})$. The set of imputations is denoted by $I(\Gamma)$. The *core* is defined as:

$$C(\Gamma) = \{x \in R^n : x(N) = \gamma(N) \text{ and } x(S) \leq \gamma(S), \forall S \subseteq N\},$$

where $x(S) = \sum_{i \in S} x_i$. The game $\Gamma = (N, v)$ is *balanced* if $C(\Gamma)$ is nonempty; and *totally balanced*, if every subgame (i.e., the game obtained by restricting the player set to a coalition and the characteristic function to the power set of that coalition) is balanced.

The concept of stability is due to von Neumann and Morgenstern [11]. Given a game $\Gamma = (N, \gamma)$ and $x, y \in I(\Gamma)$. We say that x *dominates* y if there is a coalition S such that $x(S) \geq \gamma(S)$ and $\forall\, i \in S$, $x_i < y_i$. A set $\mathcal{F} \subseteq I(\Gamma)$ is *stable* if any two imputations in $\mathcal{F}$ do not dominate each other and any imputation not in $\mathcal{F}$ can be dominated by an imputation in $\mathcal{F}$. Since the core allocations do not dominate each other, the core is stable simply means that any imputation not in the core can be dominated by a core imputation. Formally, the core of a balanced game Γ is *stable*, if for every $y \in I(\Gamma) \setminus C(\Gamma)$, there exists an $x \in C(\Gamma)$ and a nonempty coalition $S \subset N$ such that $x(S) = \gamma(S)$ and $x_i < y_i$ for each $i \in S$.

Now let us give the definition of a vertex cover game. Given an undirected graph $G = (V, E)$ with vertex set V and edge set E, the corresponding *vertex cover game* $\Gamma_G = (E, \gamma)$ is defined by:

1. The player set is $E = \{e_1, e_2, \cdots, e_n\}$;
2. For each coalition $S \subseteq E$, $\gamma(S)$ is the size of a minimum vertex cover in the edge induced subgraph $G[S] = (V, S)$.

The vertex cover game falls into the scope of the class of combinatorial cooperative games studied in Deng, Ibaraki and Nagamochi [2]. With the technique of integer programming and duality theory of linear programming, Deng, Ibaraki and Nagamochi [2] presented a necessary and sufficient condition for a vertex cover game being balanced.

Theorem 2.1 [2]. *Give a graph $G = (V, E)$, the vertex cover game defined on G is balanced if and only if the size of a maximum matching is equal to the size of a minimum vertex cover on G. In such case, an imputation is in the core if and only if it is a convex combination of the indicator vectors of maximum matchings of G.*

3   Vertex Cover Game with Stable Core

In the rest of the paper, we assume that all the graphs concerned are undirected graph with nonempty edge set. Let $\Gamma_G = (E, \gamma)$ be the vertex cover game defined on graph $G = (V, E)$. For $v \in V$, the set of edges incident to v is denoted by $E(v)$. A matching of G is called *maximal* if adding any other edge to it makes it no longer a matching, called *maximum* if it has the maximum size among all the matchings. Before discussing the core stability, we need the following lemmas.

Lemma 3.1 [2]. $x \in C(\Gamma_G)$ *if and only if*
1) $x \geq 0$; *2)* $x(E) = \gamma(E)$ *and 3)* $x(E(v)) \leq 1$ *for each $v \in V$.*

Lemma 3.2. *Let the vertex cover game $\Gamma_G = (E, \gamma)$ be balanced. If Γ_G has the stable core, then for every $e \in E$, there exists a core allocation x such that $x(e) > 0$.*

Proof. Suppose that there exists an edge $e_0 \in E$ such that $x(e_0) = 0$ for all $x \in C(\Gamma_G)$. Since $\gamma(E) > 0$, there exists $e_1 \in E$ and $\hat{x} \in C(\Gamma_G)$ such that $\hat{x}(e_1) > 0$. Construct a vector $y : E \to R^+$ based on $\hat{x}$ as follows:

$$y(e) = \begin{cases} \hat{x}(e) & \text{if } e \notin \{e_0, e_1\} \\ \hat{x}(e_1) & \text{if } e = e_0 \\ 0 & \text{if } e = e_1 \end{cases}$$

Obviously, $y \in I(\Gamma_G) \setminus C(\Gamma_G)$. Since $C(\Gamma_G)$ is stable, there exists $x^* \in C(\Gamma_G)$ and a nonempty set $S \subseteq E$ such that x^* dominates y on S.

Note that it must be the case $e_0 \in S$. Otherwise, we can distinguish in two cases:

(a) $e_1 \in S$. Since $y(e_1) = 0$, each core allocation can not dominate y on S;

(b) $e_1 \notin S$. Since $\hat{x} \in C(\Gamma_G)$ and $y(e) = \hat{x}(e)$ for each $e \in S$, x^* can not dominate y on S either.

Therefore, we have $\gamma(S) = x^*(S) = x^*(S \setminus \{e_0\}) < y(S \setminus \{e_0\}) = \hat{x}(S \setminus \{e_0\}) \leq \gamma(S \setminus \{e_0\}) \leq \gamma(S)$, which is a contradiction. ∎

The following theorem is the main result of this section.

Theorem 3.3. *Let $\Gamma_G = (E, \gamma)$ be a balanced vertex cover game defined on graph $G = (V, E)$. Then Γ_G has the stable core if and only if every edge $e \in E$ belongs to a maximum matching of G.*

Proof. Necessity. Assume that $\Gamma_G = (E, \gamma)$ has the stable core. By Lemma 3.2, for every $e \in E$, there exists a core allocation x such that $x(e) > 0$. Also followed from Theorem 2.1, x is a convex combination of the indicator vectors of the maximum matchings. Hence, e belongs to at least one maximum matching of G.

Sufficiency. Given $y \in I(\Gamma_G) \setminus C(\Gamma_G)$. According to Lemma 3.1, there exists a vertex $v \in V$ such that $y(E(v)) > 1$. Let $S = E(v) \setminus \{e \in E(v) : y(e) \le 0\}$, which is denoted as $S = \{e_1, e_2, \cdots, e_k\}$. It is easy to see that $S \ne \emptyset$, $y(S) > 1$ and $y(e_i) > 0$ $(i = 1, 2, \cdots, k)$. By our assumption, each edge e_i belongs to a maximum matching of G, namely M_i $(\forall i = 1, 2, \cdots, k)$. Since S is a subset of $E(v)$ and M_i is a matching, $M_i \cap S$ must contain the unique element e_i in $E(v)$, $(i = 1, 2, \cdots, k)$.

Denoted by $\mathbb{I}_1, \mathbb{I}_2, \cdots, \mathbb{I}_k$ the indicator vectors of $M_1, M_2, \cdots, M_k$, respectively. Define $x \in R^{|E|}$ as follows:

$$x = \lambda_1 \mathbb{I}_1 + \lambda_2 \mathbb{I}_2 + \cdots + \lambda_k \mathbb{I}_k,$$

where $\lambda_i = \frac{y(e_i)}{y(S)}$ $(i = 1, 2, \cdots, k)$. Obviously, $\lambda_i > 0$ and $\sum_{i=1}^{k} \lambda_i = 1$. Following from Theorem 2.1, we conclude that $x \in C(\Gamma_G)$, and

$$x(S) = \sum_{i=1}^{k} \lambda_i \mathbb{I}_i(S) = \sum_{i=1}^{k} \lambda_i |M_i \cap S| = 1 = \gamma(S),$$
$$x(e_i) = \lambda_i = \frac{y(e_i)}{y(S)} < y(e_i), \quad \forall e_i \in S.$$

That is, x dominates y on S. Therefore, $C(\Gamma_G)$ is stable. ∎

Now we consider the algorithmic issue of checking whether a vertex cover game possesses the stable core. The problem is stated as:

Problem A: Checking Core Stability of Vertex Cover Game

Instance: The vertex cover game Γ_G defined on a graph G

Question: Does Γ_G possess a stable core?

In Deng, Ibaraki and Nagamochi [2], it was shown that testing nonemptiness of the core of a vertex cover game can be done in polynomial time. Again, Theorem 3.3 yields that Problem A is equivalent to the problem of checking whether every edge belongs to a maximum matching of G. And this can be solved as follows:

Denote the size of a maximum matching by m_0. For each $e \in E$, we define an edge weight function $\beta^e : E \to Z^+$ such that $\beta^e(e) = L$ and $\beta^e(e') = 1$ for $e' \in E \setminus \{e\}$, where L is an integer large enough. We compute the maximum weighted matching in G with respect to β^e, and denote the weight by $m(e)$. It is easy to see that if there exists an edge $e^* \in E$ such that $m(e^*) - m_0 < L - 1$, then e^* is not contained in any maximum matching of G; otherwise, every edge belongs to a maximum matching of G. Since both the problems of maximum matching and maximum weighted matching can be solved in polynomial time, we have

Theorem 3.4. *The problem of Checking Core Stability of Vertex Cover Game can be solved in polynomial time.*

4   Exactness, Extendability and Core Largeness

In this section, we discuss three properties closely related to the core stability: the core largeness, the game exactness and extendability. Given a cooperative game $\Gamma = (N, \gamma)$ with $|N| = n$. Γ is said to have a *large core* if for every $y \in R^n$ satisfying that $y(S) \leq \gamma(S)$ ($\forall S \subseteq N$), there exists $x \in C(\Gamma)$ such that $x \geq y$. Γ is called *extendable* if for every nonempty set $S \subset N$ and every core allocation y of the subgame (S, γ_S), there exists $x \in C(\Gamma)$ such that $x_i = y_i$ for all $i \in S$. Γ is called *exact* if for every $S \subset N$ there exists $x \in C(\Gamma)$ such that $x(S) = \gamma(S)$.

Kikuta and Shapley [6] showed that if a balanced game has a large core, then it is extendable; and if a balanced game is extendable, then it has the stable core. Sharkey [8] showed that if a totally balanced game has large core, then it must be exact. We summarize these results in the following theorem.

Theorem 4.1 [6,8]. *Let* $\Gamma = (N, \gamma)$ *be a totally balanced game. Then*
    (1) Γ *has a large core implies that* Γ *is extendable;*
    (2) Γ *is extendable implies that* Γ *is exact and has the stable core.*

Since for bipartite graphs, the size of a maximum matching equals the size of a minimum vertex cover, it follows from Theorem 2.1 that the corresponding vertex cover game is balanced. Furthermore, Deng, Ibaraki, Nagamochi and Zang [3] presented a necessary and sufficient condition for a vertex cover game being totally balanced.

Theorem 4.2 [3]. *Let* $\Gamma_G = (E, \gamma)$ *be the vertex cover game defined on graph* $G = (V, E)$. *Then* Γ_G *is totally balanced if and only if* G *is a bipartite graph.*

Therefore, in the following we will focus on bipartite graphs. We will show that the three properties: exactness, extendability and core largeness, are equivalent for the vertex cover games defined on bipartite graphs.

Theorem 4.3. *Let* $\Gamma_H = (E, \gamma)$ *be the vertex cover game defined on bipartite graph* $H = (V_1, V_2; E)$. *Then the following conditions are equivalent:*
    (1) $C(\Gamma_H)$ *is large;*
    (2) Γ_H *is extendable;*
    (3) Γ_H *is exact;*
    (4) Every matching is contained in a maximum matching in graph H.

By Theorem 4.1, "(1) $\Rightarrow$ (2) $\Rightarrow$ (3)" is true. It remains to prove "(3) $\Rightarrow$ (4)" and "(4) $\Rightarrow$ (1)".

Proof of "(3) $\Rightarrow$ (4)". Suppose that $\Gamma_H = (E, \gamma)$ is exact. Let M^* be a matching of H. By the definition of the exactness, there exists $x^* \in C(\Gamma_H)$ such that $x^*(M^*) = \gamma(M^*) = |M^*|$. Let $\mathcal{M} = \{M_1, M_2, \cdots, M_k\}$ be the set of maximum matchings of H. Followed from Theorem 2.1, x^* can be expressed as $x^* = \sum_{i=1}^{k} \lambda_i \mathbb{I}_i$, where $\mathbb{I}_i$ is the indicator vector of the matching M_i, $\lambda_i \geq 0$ ($i = 1, 2, \cdots, k$) and $\sum_{i=1}^{k} \lambda_i = 1$. Then we have

$$x^*(M^*) = \sum_{i=1}^{k} \lambda_i \mathbb{I}_i(M^*) = \sum_{i=1}^{k} \lambda_i |M^* \cap M_i| \leq \sum_{i=1}^{k} \lambda_i |M^*| = |M^*|.$$

Therefore, "$\leq$" holds for "=" in above formula, which implies that $M^* \cap M_i = M^*$ for any M_i with $\lambda_i > 0$. That is, M^* is contained in at least one maximum matching of H. ∎

To show "(4) $\Rightarrow$ (1)", we need some more facts. The first one is due to van Gellekom, et al. [10]. For game $\Gamma = (N, \gamma)$ with $|N| = n$, the set of lower vectors is defined as:

$$L(\Gamma) = \{y \in R^n : y(S) \leq \gamma(S), \ \forall S \subseteq N\}.$$

Lemma 4.4 [10]. *Let $\Gamma = (N, \gamma)$ be a balanced game. Then $\Gamma = (N, \gamma)$ has a large core if and only if $y(N) \geq \gamma(N)$ for each extreme point y of $L(\Gamma)$.*

In order to show the core largeness of Γ_H, we need to characterize the extreme points of $L(\Gamma_H)$. For this purpose, we give an alternative description of $L(\Gamma_H)$. Let $\mathcal{S} = \{T : T \subseteq E(v), v \in V_1 \cup V_2\}$, and

$$L'(\Gamma_H) = \{y \in R^n : y(S) \leq 1, \ \forall \ S \in \mathcal{S}\}.$$

Lemma 4.5. *Let $\Gamma_H = (E, \gamma)$ be the vertex cover game defined on bipartite graph $H = (V_1, V_2; E)$. Then*
(1) $L(\Gamma_H) = L'(\Gamma_H)$;
(2) each extreme point of $L'(\Gamma_H)$ is the indicator vector of a maximal matching of H.

Proof. (1) It is easy to verify that $L(\Gamma_H) \subseteq L'(\Gamma_H)$. Then we prove the other direction. Given $y \in L'(\Gamma_H)$, we have to check that $y(S) \leq \gamma(S)$ for every $S \subseteq E$. Assume that $\gamma(S) = k$. Then S can be divided into k disjoint sets, namely, $S_1, S_2, \cdots, S_k$, such that $S_i \in \mathcal{S}$ ($i = 1, 2, \cdots, k$). Since $y \in L'(\Gamma_H)$, $y(S_i) \leq 1$ for each $i = 1, 2, \cdots, k$. Therefore, $y(S) = \sum_{i=1}^{k} y(S_i) \leq k = \gamma(S)$. That is, $y \in L(\Gamma_H)$. Hence, $L(\Gamma_H) = L'(\Gamma_H)$.

(2) First, we prove that the extreme points of $L'(\Gamma_H)$ are non-negative. Suppose that y is an extreme point of $L'(\Gamma_H)$ with at least one negative component. Then define two vectors y^1 and y^2 as follows:

$$y_i^1 = \begin{cases} y_i & \text{if } y_i \geq 0 \\ 0 & \text{if } y_i < 0 \end{cases} \ ; \ y_i^2 = \begin{cases} y_i & \text{if } y_i \geq 0 \\ 2y_i & \text{if } y_i < 0 \end{cases}$$

It is easy to see that $y^1, y^2 \in L'(\Gamma_H)$. Since $y \neq y^1, y \neq y^2$ and $y = \frac{y^1 + y^2}{2}$, y is not an extreme point of $L'(\Gamma_H)$.

Secondly, we show the correctness of the statement (2) of this lemma. Consider the following polyhedron:

$$\begin{aligned} L''(\Gamma_H) &= \{y \in R^n : y(S) \leq 1, \forall S \in \mathcal{S}; \ y \geq 0\} \\ &= \{y \in R^n : y(E(v)) \leq 1, \forall v \in V; \ y \geq 0\}, \end{aligned}$$

where the second equality follows from the definition of $\mathcal{S}$. Since the extreme points of $L'(\Gamma_H)$ are non-negative, each extreme point of $L'(\Gamma_H)$ is also an extreme point of $L''(\Gamma_H)$. Let y^* be an extreme point of $L''(\Gamma_H)$. Based on the linear programming theory, there exists a non-negative function ω, such that y^* is the unique optimal solution of the following linear program:

$$\text{LP}^* : \quad \max\{\omega^t y : y(E(v)) \le 1, \ \forall v \in V; \ y \ge 0\}.$$

Since H is a bipartite graph, the coefficient matrix of the constraints in (LP*) is totally balanced. Hence, y^* must be an integer vector, i.e., a $\{0,1\}$-vector, which is the indicator vector of a matching M of H.

Assume that M is not a maximal matching, then there exists a matching M' with $M \subset M'$. It follows that the indicator vector of M' is also an optimal solution of (LP*), contradicting to the fact that y^* is the unique optimal solution. Therefore, M is a maximal matching. ∎

With Lemma 4.4 and 4.5, we are ready to show "(4) $\Rightarrow$ (3)".

Proof of "(4) $\Rightarrow$ (3)". Let $H = (V_1, V_2; E)$ satisfy condition (4), and y be an extreme point of $L(\Gamma_H)$. Followed from Lemma 4.5, y is the indicator vector of a maximal matching M. By condition (4), M is certainly a maximum matching of H. Hence, $y(E) = |M| = \gamma(E)$. Followed by Lemma 4.4, Γ_H has large core. ∎

There are also algorithmic issues related to the core largeness, exactness and extendability for vertex cover game:

Problem B: Checking Extendability, Exactness and Core Largeness of Vertex Cover Game on Bipartite Graph

Instance: The vertex cover game Γ_H defined on bipartite graph H

Question: Is Γ_H extendable, exact and with large core?

Thanks to Theorem 4.3, these problems are equivalent to determining whether every matching is contained in a maximum matching of H.

5 Further Discussions

The vertex cover game is an example of the class of covering games introduced in Deng, Ibaraki and Nagamochi [2]. In fact, there are many game models can be formulated as covering games, such as the minimum coloring game [1] and dominating set game [13]. In this section, we show that some of the results given in above sections can be generalized to general covering games.

Let $U = \{u_1, u_2, \cdots, u_n\}$ be the universe set and $\Phi = \{S_1, S_2, \cdots, S_m\}$ be a collection of subsets of U. A covering of U is a sub-collection of Φ' of Φ such that each element of U occurs in at least one subset in Φ'. A covering Φ' is called *minimum* if the number of subsets contained in Φ' is minimum among all the coverings. On the other hand, a *packing* of Φ is a subset $U' \subseteq U$ such that $|S_i \cap U'| \le 1$ for each $i = 1, 2, \cdots, m$. A packing is called *maximum* if it has the maximum size among all the packings. The *covering game* $\Gamma = (U, \gamma)$ corresponding to (U, Φ) is defined as:

1. The player set is U;
2. For each coalition $S \subseteq U$, $\gamma(S)$ is the minimum size of a sub-collection of Φ that covers all elements in S.

Let $A = [a_{ij}]_{n \times m}$ be the universe-subset incident matrix, where $a_{ij} = 1$ if the element u_i is in the subset S_j; $a_{ij} = 0$, otherwise. The covering problem related to U can be formulated as a 0-1 program (P):

$$\text{P}: \quad \min\{\textstyle\sum_{i=1}^{m} x_i : Ax \geq 1, x \in \{0,1\}^m\}.$$

Its linear program relaxation (LP) and the dual (DP) are as follows:

$$\text{LP}: \quad \min\{\textstyle\sum_{i=1}^{m} x_i : Ax \geq 1, x \geq 0\};$$
$$\text{DP}: \quad \max\{\textstyle\sum_{i=1}^{n} y_i : y^t A \leq 1, y \geq 0\}.$$

Deng Ibaraki and Nagamochi [2] showed that the covering game $\Gamma = (U, \gamma)$ is balanced if and only if (LP) has an integer optimal solution. In such case, $x \in C(\Gamma)$ if and only if it is an optimal solution to (DP). Based on their result, we consider one kind of balanced covering games for which the universe-subset incident matrix is balanced.

A $\{0,1\}$-matrix M is called *balanced* if M has no square submatrix of odd order, with in each row and in each column exactly two 1's. It was shown in [5] that if the universe-subset incident matrix A is balanced, then both polyhedrons of feasible solutions of (LP) and (DP) are integral. That is, this kind of covering games have nonempty cores. Also since the balanced matrices are closed under taking sub-matrices, the corresponding covering games are totally balanced. With similar techniques used in previous sections, the results on core stability and other related properties for general covering games can be obtained.

Theorem 5.1 *Let $\Gamma = (U, \gamma)$ be the covering game corresponding to (U, Φ) and the universe-subset incident matrix be balanced. Then Γ has the stable core if and only if each element $u \in U$ belongs to a maximum packing of (U, Φ).*

Theorem 5.2 *Let $\Gamma = (U, \gamma)$ be the covering game corresponding to (U, Φ) and the universe-subset incident matrix be balanced. Then the following conditions are equivalent:*
   (1) $C(\Gamma)$ is large;
   (2) Γ is extendable;
   (3) Γ is exact;
   (4) Every packing is contained in a maximum packing for (U, Φ).

References

1. Bietenhader, T., Okamoto, Y.: Core Stability of Minimum Coloring Games. In: Hromkovič, J., Nagl, M., Westfechtel, B. (eds.) WG 2004. LNCS, vol. 3353, pp. 389–401. Springer, Heidelberg (2004)
2. Deng, X., Ibaraki, T., Nagamochi, H.: Algorithmic Aspects of The Core of Combinatorial Optimization Games. Mathematics of Operations Research 24, 751–766 (1999)
3. Deng, X., Ibaraki, T., Nagamochi, H., Zang, W.: Totally Balanced Combinatorial Optimization Games. Mathematical Programming (Ser. A) 87, 441–452 (2000)

4. Deng, X., Papadimitriou, C.H.: On The Complexity of Cooperative Solution Concepts. Mathematics of Operations Research 19, 257–266 (1994)
5. Fulkerson, D., Hoffman, A., Oppenheim, R.: On Balanced Matrices. Math. Programming Study 1, 120–132 (1974)
6. Kikuta, K., Shapley, L.S.: Core Stability in n-person Games (Manuscript) (1986)
7. Shapley, L.S.: Cores and Convex Games. International Journal of Game Theory 1, 11–26 (1971)
8. Sharkey, W.W.: Cooperative Games with Large Cores. International Journal of Game Theory 11, 175–182 (1982)
9. Solymosi, T., Raghavan, T.E.S.: Assignment Games with Stable Cores. International Journal of Game Theory 30, 177–185 (2001)
10. van Gellekom, J.R.G., Potters, J.A.M., Reijnierse, J.H.: Prosperity Properties of TU-games. International Journal of Game Theory 28, 211–277 (1999)
11. von Neumann, J., Morgenstern, O.: Theory of Games and Economic Behaviour. Prinseton University Press, Princeton (1944)
12. Sun, X., Fang, Q.: Core Stability of Flow Games. In: Akiyama, J., Chen, W.Y.C., Kano, M., Li, X., Yu, Q. (eds.) CJCDGCGT 2005. LNCS, vol. 4381, pp. 189–199. Springer, Heidelberg (2007)
13. Velzen, B.V.: Dominating Set Game. Operations Research Letters 32, 565–573 (2004)

Maximizing Revenue in Sequential Auctions

Edith Elkind[1] and Shaheen Fatima[2,*]

[1] School of Electronics and Computer Science, University of Southampton,
SO17 1BJ, United Kingdom
[2] Department of Computer Science, Loughborough University, Loughborough,
LE11 3TU, United Kingdom

Abstract. We study sequential auctions for private value objects and unit-demand bidders using second-price sealed-bid rules. We analyze this scenario from the seller's perspective and consider several approaches to increasing the total revenue. We derive the equilibrium bidding strategies for each individual auction. We then study the problem of selecting an optimal agenda, i.e., a revenue-maximizing ordering of the auctions. We describe an efficient algorithm that finds an optimal agenda in the important special case when the revenue of each auction is guaranteed to be strictly positive. We also show that the seller can increase his revenue by canceling one or more auctions, even if the number of bidders exceeds the number of objects for sale, and analyze the bidders' behavior and the seller's profit for different cancellation rules.

1 Introduction

Market-based mechanisms such as auctions are now being widely studied as a means of allocating resources in multiagent systems. There are several reasons for their popularity: auctions are simple to implement and can also have desirable economic properties, probably the most important of which are their ability to generate high revenues to the seller and also allocate resources efficiently [8,2,9]. In many practical applications, the number of objects for sale is large, and the seller has to choose a suitable auction format, such as a *combinatorial* [7], *simultaneous*, or *sequential* [5,1] auction. Each of these formats has unique advantages, and selecting the best mechanism for a given setting can be a challenging task. For example, while a combinatorial auction is a good choice when it is imperative to allocate the objects efficiently, simultaneous or sequential auctions are easier to implement, as one can use off-the-shelf systems for single-item auctions.

In this paper, we study sequential auctions, i.e., mechanisms in which objects are sold consecutively one at a time. Even though at any given moment there is only one item being auctioned, the bidders' behavior in any individual auction strongly depends on the auctions that are yet to be conducted [5,1]. In particular, even if the auctions are run using second-price rules, the bidders are not likely to bid their true value for the item if they expect to profit from subsequent auctions. Moreover, the bidding strategies for an auction strongly depend on the agenda (i.e., the order in which the objects are

---

* The work was done when both authors were at University of Liverpool. The first author was supported by the EPSRC grant GR/T07343/01 "Algorithmics of Network-sharing Games".

X. Deng and F.C. Graham (Eds.): WINE 2007, LNCS 4858, pp. 491–502, 2007.

auctioned); if we change the agenda, then the bidding strategies and consequently the equilibrium outcome changes [5].

The model considered in this paper is motivated by the following scenario. Suppose that we are selling advertising space in a recurring event, such as several episodes of a TV show or all football games in a given season. Assume for simplicity that each event is associated with a single advertising slot, and all bidders are ex ante symmetric and have unit demand, i.e., each of them only needs one slot. Consequently, if a bidder wins an auction, he does not participate in the future auctions. Clearly, some games or episodes of the show will be more attractive to the advertisers than others: a game between top teams will have a larger audience than a game between less successful teams, some episodes of the show may include appearances by celebrities, etc. In the beginning of the season, the seller and the advertisers have some estimates of the value of advertising in each slot, which, as argued above, can be different for different slots. One can associate such an estimate with a probability distribution over possible values. In the symmetric setting, it is natural to assume that these distributions are publicly known.

If the slots are to be auctioned off in the beginning of the season, the advertisers will have to bid based on these imprecise value estimates. However, it is possible to postpone selling each slot till the respective episode or game is about to be shown. At this point the bidders are likely to have a better understanding of how much this slot is worth to them, based on their current stock, existing orders, etc. Therefore, we can treat their value for a slot just before the screening as their actual value for this slot, i.e., a random variable drawn from the initial distribution associated with this slot.

In this situation, the seller may have (partial) control over the order of individual auctions. Indeed, in many TV shows, the order in which some (or all) of the episodes are shown is flexible. It is also possible to take into account revenue considerations when scheduling football games. Therefore, it is natural to ask whether the seller can order the individual auctions to optimize his revenue. An alternative approach to maximizing the total revenue, which is also feasible in the above-described scenario, is canceling some of the auctions. In this paper, we study both of these revenue maximization techniques.

We describe our formal model in Section 2. Note that we assume that the bidders can commit to participating in the entire series of auctions, i.e., they take part in all auctions until they win an object. We believe that in the above-described setting, this assumption can be justified. Also, in most of the paper we restrict ourselves to the case where all bidders are symmetric and the seller has full control over the ordering of individual auctions. In the end of the paper, we briefly discuss relaxing some of these assumptions.

We consider several approaches to increasing the total revenue. We assume that each auction is run using second-price rules, and compute the participants' equilibrium bids. Using this result as a starting point, we study the problem of selecting the optimal agenda, i.e., a revenue-maximizing ordering of the auctions. We describe an efficient algorithm that finds the optimal agenda whenever the revenue of each auction is guaranteed to be strictly positive. While the latter condition does not always hold, it is likely to be satisfied when the number of bidders is large; also, our approach may provide a reasonable heuristic in the general case.

We then study the complementary case when in some of the auctions there is at most one bidder who submits a non-zero bid. The second-price auction rules allocates the object to one of the highest bidders and charges him the second-highest bid. This means that when all bids are zero, we will give the object to an arbitrary bidder (e.g., one chosen at random) for free. Similarly, if there is exactly one bidder with a non-zero bid, he will get the item and pay nothing. Intuitively, in this situation we are better off canceling the auction altogether: it brings in no revenue anyway, and by allocating the object we eliminate one of the bidders who could otherwise submit a high bid in a future auction. However, to formalize this intuition we have to take into account the ripple effect of this decision, i.e., its influence on bidders' behavior in other auctions. We study the changes in the bidders' strategies under the new rules. We also sketch an efficient algorithm that chooses in advance which auctions to cancel based on the respective value distributions rather than actual bids.

2 The Auction Setting

There are m private value objects for sale. Each object is sold in a separate auction using the second-price sealed-bid rules, and the auctions are held sequentially. Initially, there are n risk-neutral bidders. For each object j, $j = 1, \ldots, m$, the bidders' valuations are drawn independently from a distribution with a cumulative density function $V_j : R_+ \rightarrow [0, 1]$. Consequently, any bidder's valuations for different objects are independent random variables. However, each bidder only needs one object. Therefore, if he wins an auction, he does not participate in subsequent auctions.

The number of objects m, the initial number of bidders n, and the functions $V_j :$ $R_+ \rightarrow [0, 1]$ are common knowledge to all bidders. However, each bidder draws his private value signal for auction j after the end of auction $j - 1$. This model was introduced in [1] in the context of sequential auctions for two private value objects. Here, we generalize the approach of [1] to $m > 2$ objects.

The sequential auctions are conducted as follows. The first object is sold in a second-price sealed bid auction. There are n bidders for this auction. The winner is announced at the end of the auction. He receives the object and leaves. All other bidders then draw their values for the second object and take part in the second auction. The process repeats until all objects are sold (if $n > m$) or until there are no more bidders (if $n \leq m$); without loss of generality we can assume $n \geq m$. Note that there are $n - j + 1$ bidders for auction j.

Note that in our model the private values are not correlated across the m objects. While in general this may not be the case, the special case of uncorrelated values captures the real-life scenarios in which the objects are sufficiently dissimilar, and also provides an interesting technical challenge.

3 Equilibrium Bids

In this section, we find the equilibrium bids for our setting. Since there is more than one auction, a bidder's behavior in an auction depends not only on that auction but also on the profit he expects to get from the future auctions. We first determine this profit and then find the equilibrium bids.

For a series of m auctions with n bidders in the first one, let $EP(j, m, n)$ denote the winner's expected profit for the jth auction, let $ER(j, m, n)$ denote the expected revenue of the jth auction, and let $ES(j, m, n) = ER(j, m, n) + EP(j, m, n)$ be the expected surplus from the jth auction, i.e., the total increase in social welfare that results from allocating the jth object. In what follows, we express these quantities as certain functions of the parameters of the problem and use them to derive an explicit expression for each bidder's bidding strategy.

Let $E(f_i^n)$ and $E(s_i^n)$ denote the expected first and second order statistics for n draws from the distribution V_i, i.e., set $X_i^n = \{x^1, \ldots, x^n \mid x^j \sim V_i\}$ and let $f_i^n = \max X_i^n$, $s_i^n = \max X \setminus \{f_i^n\}$.

For any $1 \le j \le y \le m$, let $\beta(y, j, m, n)$ denote a bidder's ex-ante probability of winning the yth auction in the series from the jth to the mth one before the jth auction begins. For instance, $\beta(1, 1, m, n)$ is the probability of winning the first auction in the series of auctions from the first to the mth one. When the number of bidders and objects is fixed, we sometimes write $\beta(y, j)$ instead of $\beta(y, j, m, n)$. As we assume that all bidders are ex ante symmetric, we have

$$\beta(y, 1) = \frac{1}{n - y + 1} \prod_{k=1}^{y-1}\left(1 - \frac{1}{n - k + 1}\right) = \frac{1}{n}.$$

In general, for $j \le y \le m$, $\beta(y, j)$ is given by

$$\beta(y, j) = \frac{1}{n - y + 1} \prod_{k=j}^{y-1}\left(1 - \frac{1}{n - k + 1}\right) = \frac{1}{n - j + 1}.$$

Note that $\beta(y, j, m, n)$ does not depend on y. Intuitively, before the beginning of the jth auction, all bidders are symmetric with respect to winning the yth auction, and there are $n - j + 1$ bidders left at that point. Hence, each bidder's probability of winning the yth auction is $1/(n - j + 1)$.

Let $\alpha(j, m, n)$ denote a bidder's ex-ante expected profit from winning any one auction in the series of auctions from the jth (for $1 \le j \le m$) to the mth one. We have

$$\alpha(j, m, n) = \sum_{y=j}^{m} \beta(y, j) EP(y, m, n) = \frac{1}{n - j + 1} \sum_{y=j}^{m} EP(y, m, n). \qquad (1)$$

Note that by definition, $\alpha(m + 1, m, n) = 0$ for any $n > 0$.

Theorem 1. *If each auction in a series is conducted using the second price rules, then the equilibrium bidding strategy for a bidder whose value in auction j is v is given by*

$$B_j(v) = \max\{0, v - \alpha(j + 1, m, n)\}. \qquad (2)$$

Proof. In order to find the equilibrium strategies, we begin with the last auction and then reason backwards. Recall that a bidder comes to know his valuation v just before auction j begins (i.e., after the previous $j - 1$ auctions are over).

Consider auction m. The number of bidders for this auction is $n - m + 1$. Since this is the last auction, the bidding strategies for it are the same as those for a single object auction [8], i.e., each bidder's equilibrium strategy is to bid his true value $v = v - \alpha(m + 1, m, n)$.

Now consider auction j ($1 \leq j < m$). Consider bidder 1 whose value is v and set $x = v - \alpha(j + 1, m, n)$. Let $b^* = max_{j \neq 1} b_j$ be the highest competing bid. Assume for simplicity that the draw resolution rule is lexicographic, i.e., bidder 1 wins as long as $x \geq b^*$; the analysis for other draw resolution rules is similar.

If $x < 0$, it means that the bidder's expected profit from the future auctions exceeds his valuation for the object that is being auctioned, so he prefers not to win the object. Therefore, bidder 1's equilibrium strategy is to make the lowest possible bid, i.e., 0.

Otherwise, if $x \geq b^*$, then by bidding $z = x$ bidder 1 wins and his profit from the current auction is $v - b^*$. As $x = v - \alpha(j + 1, m, n) \geq b^*$, we have $v - b^* \geq \alpha(j + 1, m, n)$, i.e., the bidder weakly prefers winning this auction to participating in the future auctions. Now, if bidder 1 bids any other amount $z > b^*$, he still wins and his profit does not change, whereas if he bids $z < b^*$, he loses the auction, so his expected profit is $\alpha(j + 1, m, n) \leq v - b^*$.

If $x < b^*$, then by bidding $z = x$ or, in fact, any $z < b^*$, bidder 1 loses the auction, so his total profit from the entire series is $\alpha(j + 1, m, n)$. If he bids $z \geq b^*$, he wins, but his total profit is $v - b^* < \alpha(j + 1, m, n)$, i.e., this outcome is less preferable than losing the current auction. In all cases, bidding $z \neq x$ may decrease the bidder's profit, but cannot increase it, i.e., bidding $\max\{x, 0\}$ is an equilibrium strategy.   □

To characterize the bidding strategies, it remains to show how to compute $\alpha(j, m, n)$. For $j = m$ we have

$$ES(m, m, n) = E(f_m^{n-m+1})$$
$$ER(m, m, n) = E(s_m^{n-m+1})$$
$$EP(m, m, n) = E(f_m^{n-m+1}) - E(s_m^{n-m+1}).$$

For $j < m$, the value of $\alpha(j, m, n)$ can be computed inductively: in what follows, we describe how to compute $\alpha(j, m, n)$ given $\alpha(y, m, n)$ for $y = j + 1, \ldots, m$.

Fix $j < m$ and set $f = f_j^{n-j+1}$, $s = s_j^{n-j+1}$. We will consider three cases.

– All bidders bid 0.
  This happens with probability $P_0 = (V_j(\alpha(j + 1, m, n)))^{n-j+1}$. In this case, the item gets allocated to a random bidder who pays nothing. Set

$$E_0 = E(V_j | f < \alpha(j + 1, m, n)).$$

  We have

$$ES(j, m, n) = E_0, \ ER(j, m, n) = 0, \ EP(j, m, n) = E_0.$$

– Exactly one bidder makes a positive bid.
  The probability of this event is $P_1 = (n - j + 1)(V_j(\alpha(j + 1, m, n)))^{n-j}(1 - V_j(\alpha(j+1, m, n)))$. In this case, the object is allocated to the bidder with a positive bid and the winner pays nothing. Set

$$E_1 = E(f_j^{n-j+1} | s < \alpha(j + 1, m, n) < f).$$

We have

$$ES(j,m,n) = E_1, \ ER(j,m,n) = 0, \ EP(j,m,n) = E_1.$$

- Two or more bidders make a positive bid.
  The probability of this event is $P_{>1} = 1 - P_0 - P_1$. Set

$$E_{>1,s} = E(f|\alpha(j+1,m,n) < s)$$
$$E_{>1,r} = E(s|\alpha(j+1,m,n) < s) - \alpha(j+1,m,n).$$

We have

$$ES(j,m,n) = E_{>1,s}, \ ER(j,m,n) = E_{>1,r}, \ EP(j,m,n) = E_{>1} = E_{>1,s} - E_{>1,r}.$$

By combining these three cases, we obtain

$$EP(j,m,n) = P_0 E_0 + P_1 E_1 + P_{>1} E_{>1}, \tag{3}$$

i.e., given $\alpha(j+1,m,n)$ we can compute $EP(j,m,n)$. Hence, given $\alpha(y,m,n)$ for $y = j+1,\ldots,m$, we can compute $\alpha(j,m,n)$ using formula (1).

Assuming that bidders' valuations are such that in each auction at least two bidders submit a strictly positive bid, i.e., the revenue of each auction is non-zero, this formula can be simplified considerably. Namely, in this case we have

$$ES(j,m,n) = E(f)$$
$$ER(j,m,n) = E(s) - \alpha(j+1,m,n)$$
$$EP(j,m,n) = E(f) - E(s) + \alpha(j+1,m,n),$$

where $f = f_j^{n-j+1}$, $s = s_j^{n-j+1}$. The advantage of this expression is that is does not use conditional expectations. In fact, the only information about the jth distribution that is required is the expectations of the first and second order statistics for $n - j + 1$ bidders. Moreover, for large values of bidders, it is quite likely that each auction has non-zero revenue. Indeed, as the number of bidders increases, the profits from future auctions have to be divided among a higher number of potential winners, reducing α.

4   Choosing the Optimal Agenda

In this section, we consider the problem of choosing the agenda so as to maximize the seller's profit. Our focus here is on those cases where, for each auction, the two highest bids are greater than zero – i.e., all auctions have non-zero profit. As argued above, for a large value of n this scenario is quite likely.

To see how agenda can affect the revenue, consider first a simple example.

Example 1. Suppose that there are 2 items A and B and 3 bidders. The bidders valuation for A are drawn from $U[8,20]$ and the bidders valuations for B are drawn from $U[3,39]$. Suppose we sell these items in the order A, B. Our expected revenue from the second auction is $s_B^2 = 15$ and we have $\alpha(2,2,3) = (f_B^2 - s_B^2)/2 = 6$. Therefore, our expected revenue from the first auction is $s_A^3 - 6 = 8$, and the total revenue is 23. If, on the other hand, we sell these items in the order B, A, our expected revenue from the second auction is $s_A^2 = 12$ and we have $\alpha(2,2,3) = (f_A^2 - s_A^2)/2 = 2$. Therefore, our expected revenue from the first auction is $s_B^3 - 2 = 19$ and the total revenue is 31.

One can see that selecting the wrong agenda can substantially decrease the revenues. This motivates the following question: Given bidder's value distributions for all items, is it possible to select the optimal agenda in time polynomial in n and m? Clearly, if we simply consider all possible agendas and compute the expected revenue for each one using the formulas derived in the previous section, we will identify the optimal agenda, but the running time of this procedure is exponential in m. In what follows, we show how to solve this problem more efficiently.

We start by introducing additional notation. Assume that the objects are numbered from 1 to m; the optimal agenda is then a permutation of $1, \ldots, m$. Let $\delta_1(i, n) = E(s_i^n) - E(s_i^{n-1})$ and $\delta_2(i, n) = E(f_i^n) - E(s_i^n)$. Also, as in this section the number of bidders and objects is fixed, we will write $\beta(y, j)$, $EP(k)$, and $ER(k)$ instead of $\beta(y, j, m, n)$, $EP(k, m, n)$, and $ER(k, m, n)$, respectively.

Proposition 1. *Consider two agendas $A^{(1)}$ and $A^{(2)}$ for the same set of m objects such that $A^{(2)}$ can be obtained from $A^{(1)}$ by changing the order of the first and second auction. Let i and j be the objects sold at the first and second auction in $A^{(1)}$, respectively. Let $R^{(k)}$, $k = 1, 2$, be the seller's expected total revenue from $A^{(k)}$. Then $R^{(1)} > R^{(2)}$ as long as*

$$[\delta_1(i, n) - \delta_1(j, n)] - \beta(2, 2)[\delta_2(i, n - 1) - \delta_2(j, n - 1)] > 0.$$

Proof. Let $\alpha = \alpha(3, m, n)$ be a bidder's expected ex ante profit from the last $m - 2$ auctions; obviously, this number is the same for $A^{(1)}$ and $A^{(2)}$. Also, let $\beta = \beta(2, 2) = 1/(n - 1)$; note that β does not depend on the agenda.

Under agenda $A^{(1)}$, the seller's expected revenue from the second auction is $R_2^{(1)} = E(s_j^{n-1}) - \alpha$, and the winner's expected profit from the second auction is $E(f_j^{n-1}) - E(s_j^{n-1}) + \alpha = \delta_2(j, n - 1) + \alpha$. Therefore, in the first auction a bidder whose value is v is going to bid $v - (\delta_2(j, n - 1) + \alpha)\beta - \sum_{y=3}^m \beta(y, 2)EP(y)$; note that the last term in this expression is independent of the agenda. Finally, the seller's expected revenue from the first auction is

$$R_1^{(1)} = E(s_i^n) - (\delta_2(j, n - 1) + \alpha)\beta - \sum_{y=3}^m \beta(y, 2)EP(y).$$

Similarly, under $A^{(2)}$, the seller's expected revenue from the second auction is $R_2^{(2)} = E(s_i^{n-1}) - \alpha$, and the winner's expected profit from the second auction is $E(f_i^{n-1}) - E(s_i^{n-1}) + \alpha = \delta_2(i, n - 1) + \alpha$. Therefore, in the first auction a bidder whose value is v is going to bid $v - (\delta_2(i, n - 1) + \alpha)\beta - \sum_{y=3}^m \beta(y, 2)EP(y)$. Hence, the seller's expected revenue from the first auction is

$$R_1^{(2)} = E(s_j^n) - (\delta_2(i, n - 1) + \alpha)\beta - \sum_{y=3}^m \beta(y, 2)EP(y).$$

Under both agendas, the seller's expected profit from the last $m - 2$ auctions is the same. Hence, we have $R^{(1)} - R^{(2)} = R_1^{(1)} - R_1^{(2)} + R_2^{(1)} - R_2^{(2)}$. It is easy to see that $R_2^{(1)} - R_2^{(2)} = E(s_j^{n-1}) - E(s_i^{n-1})$. Furthermore, we have

$$R_1^{(1)} - R_1^{(2)} = E(s_i^n) - \beta\delta_2(j, n - 1) - E(s_j^n) + \beta\delta_2(i, n - 1).$$

Hence, we conclude that $R^{(1)} > R^{(2)}$ if and only if

$$\delta_1(i, n) - \delta_1(j, n) + \beta(\delta_2(i, n - 1) - \delta_2(j, n - 1)) > 0.$$

□

Proposition 1 describes the change in the revenue that corresponds to switching the order of the first two auctions on the agenda. If we change the relative order of the $(k - 1)$st and kth auction, we can still use Proposition 1 to compare the revenue from the last $m - k + 2$ auctions under the two agendas. However, to compare the total revenues, we need additional techniques, as the choice of the agenda will influence the bidders' behavior in the first $k - 2$ auctions. Fortunately, it turns out that as long as changing the order of the $(k - 1)$st and kth auction increases the revenue from the last $m - k + 2$ auctions, it increases the total revenue as well.

Proposition 2. *Consider two agendas $A^{(1)}$ and $A^{(2)}$ for the same set of m objects such that $A^{(2)}$ can be obtained from $A^{(1)}$ by changing the order of the $(k - 1)$st and kth auction. Let i and j be the objects sold at the $(k - 1)$st and kth auction in $A^{(1)}$, respectively. Let $R^{(i)}$, $i = 1, 2$, be the seller's expected total revenue from $A^{(i)}$, and let $R^{(i)}_{k-1,k}$, $i = 1, 2$, be the seller's expected revenue from the $(k - 1)$st and kth auction in $A^{(i)}$. Then $R^{(1)} > R^{(2)}$ whenever $R^{(1)}_{k-1,k} > R^{(2)}_{k-1,k}$.*

Proof. For $i = 1, 2$, we have $R^{(i)} = \sum_{j=1}^{m} ER^{(i)}(j)$, where $ER^{(i)}(j)$ is the expected seller's revenue in the jth auction under agenda $A^{(i)}$. Clearly, for $j > k$ we have $ER^{(1)}(j) = ER^{(2)}(j)$, and we assume

$$ER^{(1)}(k - 1) + ER^{(1)}(k) > ER^{(2)}(k - 1) + ER^{(2)}(k).$$

We will now prove that for any $0 < j < k - 1$, if

$$\sum_{t=j+1}^{m} ER^{(1)}(t) > \sum_{t=j+1}^{m} ER^{(2)}(t),$$

then

$$\sum_{t=j}^{m} ER^{(1)}(t) > \sum_{t=j}^{m} ER^{(2)}(t).$$

Applying this result inductively to $j = k - 2, k - 3, \ldots, 1$ completes the proof.

Fix some $j < k - 1$. Let $\alpha^{(1)}(j)$ and $\alpha^{(2)}(j)$ be a bidder's expected ex ante profit from the auctions $j, \ldots, m$ under $A^{(1)}$ and $A^{(2)}$, respectively. For $i = 1, 2$, we have

$$\alpha^{(i)}(j) = \frac{1}{n - j + 1} \sum_{y=j}^{m} EP^{(1)}(y).$$

Under both agendas, the expected total surplus from the last $n - j$ auctions is the same, namely, $\sum_{t=j+1}^{m} E(f_t^{n-t+1})$. Hence, we have

$$\sum_{t=j+1}^{m} [ER^{(1)}(t) + EP^{(1)}(t)] = \sum_{t=j+1}^{m} [ER^{(2)}(t) + EP^{(2)}(t)].$$

Therefore,

$$\sum_{t=j+1}^{m} ER^{(1)}(t) > \sum_{t=j+1}^{m} ER^{(2)}(t)$$

implies

$$\sum_{t=j+1}^{m} EP^{(1)}(t) < \sum_{t=j+1}^{m} EP^{(2)}(t),$$

and consequently $\alpha^{(1)}(j+1) < \alpha^{(2)}(j+1)$. As $ER^{(i)}(j,m,n) = E(s_j^{n-j+1}) - \alpha^{(i)}(j+1)$, it follows that in this case $ER^{(1)}(j) > ER^{(2)}(j)$. Hence,

$$\sum_{t=j}^{m} ER^{(1)}(t) > \sum_{t=j}^{m} ER^{(2)}(t),$$

as required.   □

We summarize our results in the following theorem.

Theorem 2. *For each object $j = 1, \ldots, m$, define $r_j = \delta_1(j,n) - \delta_2(j,n-1)/(n-1)$. Then an optimal agenda can be obtained by ordering the auctions in order of non-increasing r_j.*

Clearly, this means that one can find an optimal agenda in polynomial time. Moreover, the only information about the distributions that is required is their first and second order statistics.

To illustrate Theorem 2, consider the case when the value distributions for two consecutive auctions i and j are $U[a, a+x]$ and $U[b, b+y]$, respectively, and $x > y$. We have $\delta_1(i,n) = x\frac{n-1}{n+1} - x\frac{n-2}{n} = \frac{2x}{n(n+1)}$, $\delta_1(j,n) = y\frac{n-1}{n+1} - y\frac{n-2}{n} = \frac{2y}{n(n+1)}$, $\delta_2(i,n) = \frac{x}{n+1}$, $\delta_2(j,n) = \frac{y}{n+1}$. Consequently, $\delta_1(i,n) - \delta_1(j,n) > 0$ if and only if $x > y$, and also $\delta_2(i,n) - \delta_2(j,n) > 0$ if and only if $x > y$. We conclude that if all values are drawn from uniform distributions the auctions should be run in the order of non-increasing distribution support size (or, equivalently, non-increasing variance), whereas the expected value of each object has no effect on the optimal ordering. This explains why in Example 1 the ordering B, A produced a higher revenue than A, B.

5   Selling a Subset of Items

We have seen that changing the agenda may considerably increase the revenue in a sequential auction. However, in some cases this approach is not feasible, since the objects have to be sold in a fixed order (e.g., they become available one by one and expire shortly after becoming available). In this case, we can try to increase the revenue by selling a subset of all available items. This approach is based on the idea that reducing supply may motivate the bidders to bid more aggressively. In this section, we assume that the agenda is fixed and consider two ways of deciding which auctions to cancel.

5.1 Dynamic Cancellations

As the bidders shade their bids since they expect to profit from the future auctions, it may happen that in some auction in the series there is at most one strictly positive bid. In this case, the seller may be tempted to cancel the auction: he receives no revenue in the current auction anyway, and moreover, by doing so he increases the number of bidders in subsequent auctions (and hence the expected revenue from these auctions). In some cases, doing so may even increase the social welfare: when all bidders bid 0, the object is assigned to a random bidder who may have very little value for it, and there is a chance that if he is not eliminated now, in the future he will have a very high value for another object. However, one has to take into account that changing the auction rules will affect the bidders' behavior. In particular, if canceling auction j increases the bidders' expected profit from the last $m - j + 1$ auctions, the bidders will shade their bids more heavily in the first $j - 1$ auctions, and the net impact on the auction revenue is unclear. We illustrate the changes in the bidders' strategies with the following example.

Example 2. Consider a sequential auction with 2 items and 3 bidders, where the bidders' values for each object are distributed as $U[0, 1]$. It is easy to see that if the second auction has 2 participants, each bidder's ex ante expected profit from this auction is $1/6$, whereas if it has 3 participants, the ex ante expected profit is $1/12$. Hence, under the original rules, in the first auction a bidder with value v will bid $\max\{v - \alpha_1, 0\}$, where $\alpha_1 = 1/6$ is his expected profit from the second auction.

If the seller is allowed to cancel the first auction as long as he gets no profit from it, the bidder will bid $\max\{v - \alpha_2, 0\}$, where α_2 is his expected profit from the second auction under the new rules. We have $\alpha_2 = P_c/12 + (1 - P_c)/6$, where P_c is the probability that the first auction is canceled. The quantity P_c can be expressed as a function of α_2: a bidder bids 0 if his value is at most α_2, so we have $P_c = \alpha_2^3 + 3(1 - \alpha_2)\alpha_2^2$. Combining the expressions for α_2 and P_c, we obtain $2\alpha_2^3 - 3\alpha_2^2 - 12\alpha_2 + 2 = 0$. Solving this numerically and taking into account that $P_c = 2 - 12\alpha_2 \in [0, 1]$, we obtain $\alpha_2 \approx 0.161 < 1/6$. Hence, in this case, by allowing the seller to cancel the first auction, we increase his expected revenue both in the second auction (since there is some chance that it will have three bidders instead of two) and in the first auction (since the bidders expect less profit from the second auction, so they shade less).

The method for computing the bidding strategies described in Example 2 can be generalized to more than two items and general distributions. However, the bidders' computational problem becomes quite complex. Moreover, it is not clear if the inequality $\alpha_1 > \alpha_2$ holds in general. Therefore, it is not necessarily the case that the new format increases the seller's total revenue. Therefore, in practice, the seller may want to pre-compute the expected revenue from both formats and pick the better one rather than assume that canceling non-profitable auctions is always beneficial.

5.2 Static Cancellations

A related, but easier-to-analyze approach is to cancel some auctions in advance based on their value distributions. For example, if the number of items m is equal to the number of bidders n, then the last auction will only have one participant who will therefore get the item for free. Hence, it is clear that in this case the auctioneer should sell at most $n-1$ items. Moreover, even when $n > m$, it may be profitable for the auctioneer to sell less than m items.

Example 3. Consider a sequential auction with 3 bidders and 2 objects, where the values for auction i are drawn from a distribution F_i. Assume for now that in the first auction all bids are positive (the specific distributions we construct later satisfy this property). If both auctions are executed, the seller's expected revenue is $E(s_2^2) + E(s_1^3) - [E(f_2^2) - E(s_2^2)]/2$. If the seller only sells one object, his expected revenue is $E(s_1^3)$. Hence, it is more profitable to sell one object if $3E(s_2^2) < E(f_2^2)$.

Consider the probability distribution on $[0,1]$ whose cumulative density function is given by $V_a(x) = x^a$. It is easy to check that $E(f^2) = \int_0^1 (2ax^{2a})dx = \frac{2a}{2a+1}$, $E(s^2) = \int_0^1 (-2ax^{2a} + 2ax^a)dx = \frac{2a^2}{(a+1)(2a+1)}$.

We have $E(f^2)/E(s^2) = (a+1)/a$, so for $a < 1/2$ we have $3E(s_2^2) < E(f_2^2)$. Fix $a = 1/3$, and shift this probability distribution by 1 i.e., consider the distribution on $[1,2]$ with probability density function $W_{1/3}(x) = V_{1/3}(x-1)$. If the probability distribution for the first object is $W_{1/3}(x)$ and the probability distribution for the second object is $V_{1/3}(x)$, then in the first auction all bids are positive as required, and canceling the second auction increases the total revenue. Note also that in this setting canceling the second auction is more profitable than canceling the first one.

Intuitively, under this distribution, the bidders expect to profit considerably in the second auction, and therefore shade heavily in the first auction, while our own profit from the second auction is relatively small. Therefore, one cannot assume that it is always profitable to sell at least $n-1$ items, where n is the number of bidders.

Consequently, the seller needs to identify the optimal subset of items to sell. Computing the expected revenue for all possible subsets is not feasible, as there are exponentially many of them. While we do not have an exact solution for this problem, in what follows, we sketch an efficient algorithm that finds an approximately optimal subset (i.e., one with almost optimal total revenue). Our algorithm is based on dynamic programming. Set $C = m \max_{i=1,\ldots,m} E(f_i^n)$. Clearly, C is an upper bound on all participants' profit from the entire series. Fix a parameter $\epsilon = 1/N$, which corresponds to the approximation error. For $i = 1,\ldots,n$, $j = 1,\ldots,m$, $k = 0,\ldots,NC$, we fill in the array $TR(K,i,j)$. Intuitively, the values of $TR(K,i,j)$ are approximations to the seller's maximal expected revenue from the last $n-i+1$ auctions, assuming that there are j bidders before the start of the ith auction, and $K\epsilon \leq \sum_{y=i}^m EP(y,m,n) < (K+1)\epsilon$. The values of $TR(K,i,j)$ can be computed inductively starting with $TR(K,n,j)$. In the end, we pick the entry $TR(K,1,j)$ that corresponds to the maximal feasible revenue. For reasonable probability distributions, we can bound the error caused by rounding the winners' profit to the nearest multiple of ϵ. We omit the details due to lack of space.

6   Conclusions and Open Problems

We have studied two methods for increasing the revenue of a sequential auction: choosing an optimal agenda, and, for a fixed agenda, identifying an optimal subset of objects to sell. It would be interesting to see if one can achieve further improvements in total revenue by combining these methods, i.e., choosing the subset of objects and then selecting the optimal ordering in which to sell these objects. Another tool for increasing revenue that should be studied in this context is reserve prices. Also, it would be useful to identify a large class of distributions for which canceling zero revenue auctions is guaranteed to increase the total revenue. An interesting special case of our problem is when all objects have the same value distribution. In this case, the seller simply has to decide how many objects to sell. Currently, we do not know if in this case it is always profitable to sell exactly $\min\{m, n-1\}$ items, or there are value distributions for which the seller may want to sell fewer items.

In many real-life scenarios, some of the assumptions made in this paper may fail to hold. In particular, in the advertisement scheduling problem described in the introduction, the bidders are not necessarily symmetric, i.e., different bidders' valuations for the same slot can differ even ex ante. Also, the auctioneer may not have full control over the ordering of the auctions. For example, in a typical TV show, some episodes have to be screened in a certain order. Unfortunately, as we show in the full version of this paper [4], in this more general setting the problem of selecting the optimal agenda becomes NP-complete. This is the case even if we assume that we know each bidder's value for each item, all bidders are myopic, i.e., they bid truthfully in each auction, and the only restriction on the agenda is that some of the items have expiration times. This hardness result explains why in this paper we chose to focus on the simplified case.

References

1. Bernhardt, D., Scoones, D.: A note on sequential auctions. American Economic Review 84(3), 653–657 (1994)
2. Dasgupta, P., Maskin, E.: Efficient auctions. Quarterly Journal of Economics 115, 341–388 (2000)
3. Edmonds, J.: Optimum branchings. Journal of Research of the National Bureau of Standards (1967)
4. Elkind, E., Fatima, S.: Maximizing Revenue in Sequential Auctions (full version). Available from, http://www.csc.liv.ac.uk/~elkind/agenda.pdf
5. Elmaghraby, W.: The importance of ordering in sequential auctions. Management Science 49(5), 673–682 (2003)
6. Galambos, J.: The asymptotic theory of extreme order statistics. John Wiley and Sons, West Sussex, England (1978)
7. Sandholm, T., Suri, S.: BOB: Improved winner determination in combinatorial auctions and generalizations. Artificial Intelligence 145, 33–58 (2003)
8. Vickrey, W.: Counterspeculation, auctions and competitive sealed tenders. Journal of Finance 16, 8–37 (1961)
9. Wellman, M.P., Walsh, W.E., Wurman, P.R., McKie-Mason, J.K.: Auction protocols for decentralised scheduling. Games and Economic Behavior 35, 271–303 (2001)

Approximate Mechanisms for the Graphical TSP and Other Graph Traversal Problems*

Davide Bilò[1], Luca Forlizzi[2], Luciano Gualà[3], and Guido Proietti[2,4]

[1] Institut für Theoretische Informatik, ETH, Zürich, Switzerland
[2] Dipartimento di Informatica, Università di L'Aquila, Italy
[3] Dipartimento di Matematica, Università di Tor Vergata, Roma, Italy
[4] Istituto di Analisi dei Sistemi ed Informatica, CNR, Roma, Italy
{davide.bilo,forlizzi,guala,proietti}@di.univaq.it

Abstract. Let $G = (V, E)$ be a graph modeling a network where each edge is owned by a selfish agent, which establishes the cost for traversing her edge (i.e., assigns a weight to her edge) by pursuing only her personal utility. In such a setting, we aim at designing approximate *truthful mechanisms* for several NP-hard traversal problems on G, like the *graphical traveling salesman problem*, the *rural postman problem*, and the *mixed Chinese postman problem*, either of which asks for using an edge of G several times, in general. Thus, in game-theoretic terms, these are one-parameter problems, but with a peculiarity: the work load of each agent is a natural number. In this paper we refine the classic notion of monotonicity of an algorithm so as to exactly capture this property, and we then provide a general mechanism design technique that guarantees this monotonicity and that allows to compute efficiently the corresponding payments. In this way, we show that the former two problems and the latter one admit a 3/2- and a 2-approximate truthful mechanism, respectively. Thus, for the first two problems we match the best known approximation ratios holding for their corresponding centralized versions, while for the third one we are only a 4/3-factor away from it.

Keywords: Selfish Agents, Graph Traversal Problems, Algorithmic Mechanism Design, Approximate Truthful Mechanisms.

1 Introduction

Nowadays, physical components of many large communication and transportation networks are often owned by different economic subjects, which, when asked to provide a service, tend to act selfishly and to pursue only their personal goals. On the other hand, from the users' point of view, there is an increasing demand for a rational usage of the network resources, meaning that one should know at each instant – ideally – what is the real marginal contribution that a component

---

* Work partially supported by the Research Project GRID.IT, funded by the Italian Ministry of University and Research. A preliminary version of some the results herein contained was accepted as a short announcement to the *26th Annual ACM Symp. on Principles of Distributed Computing*, Portland, Oregon, August 12-15, 2007.

X. Deng and F.C. Graham (Eds.): WINE 2007, LNCS 4858, pp. 503–514, 2007.

can offer. Traditionally, when a system-wide goal has to be implemented on the network, the problem of reconciling this conflict of interests between owners and users has been exclusively addressed by the subfield of game theory known as *mechanism design*. However, more recently, the consciousness that besides economic factors, computational complexity and distributed computing issues must be taken into proper consideration as well, has led up to an increasing involvement in the playground of the computer science community. This resulted in the emergence of an active research field which is known by today as *computational* (or *algorithmic*) *mechanism design* [12].

Informally speaking, an algorithmic mechanism design problem can be thought as a classic well-formulated optimization problem, but with the additional complication that part of the input is retained by the selfish agents. Hence, it turns out that one has to compute *efficiently* a feasible solution to the given optimization problem, by *incentivizing* the agents, through suitable *payments*, to disclose to the system their secret data. More formally, a *mechanism* is a pair made up of an *algorithm* for computing a solution, and a specification of the *payments* (which is a function of the inputs disclosed by the agents and of the corresponding computed solution) provided to the agents. A mechanism is *truthful* if its payments guarantee that agents are not encouraged to lie.

Since the Internet appears as the ultimate platform where algorithmic mechanism design optimization problems find application, not surprisingly most of the efforts so far concentrated on designing efficient truthful mechanisms for solving several *communication network* problems [8,9,12,14,16]. All these results are either based on the classic *VCG-mechanisms*, which are applicable whenever the underlying problem is *utilitarian*,[1] or they are based on the results of Archer and Tardos [1] for the so-called *one-parameter* problems, where the information held by each agent can be expressed throughout a single value. In particular, in [1] it is shown that the truthfulness of a one-parameter mechanism is related to a property of the underlying algorithm known as *monotonicity*.[2]

1.1 Our Results

In this paper, we aim to extend the horizon to a different category of optimization problems, namely that of *graph traversal problems*. From a purely optimization perspective, such a class of problems has been addressed extensively by many researchers, mainly because of the immediate transportation and logistic applications. Besides, since of the renewed interest in toll roads, either managed by governments or private societies, in the last few years the literature devoted to the so-called *road pricing* got considerably enriched, with contributions from both economists and operation researchers (e.g., see [3] and the papers therein cited).

---

[1] Intuitively, a problem is said to be utilitarian whenever the measure of any feasible solution coincides with the *sum* of all the agents' contributions.

[2] Intuitively, an algorithm is said to be monotone whenever it keeps on using an agent which is part of a solution as soon as her announced cost decreases.

Along this vein of research, in this paper we study, from an algorithmic mechanism design point of view, a set of graph traversal problems in an adversarial setting in which each agent owns a *single* edge of the underlying graph. More formally, let G denote a graph (either directed, undirected, or mixed), with positive real edge weights established by the agents' declarations. A *walk* of length h on G is a non-empty alternating sequence $v_0 e_0 v_1 e_1 \ldots e_{h-1} v_h$ of vertices and edges in G such that edge e_i connects vertices v_i, v_{i+1}, for all $i < h$. The *cost* of a walk is the sum of the weights of the edges belonging to it, as counted with their multiplicity (notice that vertices and edges can be repeated). If $v_0 = v_h$ the walk is *closed* and is called a *tour*. A *path* is a walk where all vertices are distinct. We will consider the following three classic graph traversal problems:

1. The *Graphical Traveling Salesman Problem* (GTSP): assuming G is undirected, find a minimum-cost spanning tour of G;
2. The *Rural Postman Problem* (RPP): assuming G is undirected, and given a subset R of edges of G, find a minimum-cost tour in G which traverses each edge of R *at least* once;
3. The *Mixed Chinese Postman Problem* (MCPP): assuming G is mixed, find a minimum-cost spanning tour of G traversing each edge of G *at least* once.

It is worth noticing that all the above problems can be considered as meaningful variations of the prominent *Traveling Salesman Problem* (TSP), where the input instance is a *complete* graph, and one has to find a minimum-cost *Hamiltonian cycle* of G (i.e., a minimum-cost spanning tour of G where all vertices are distinct, apart from the initial and the ending vertex). Unlike the TSP, however, our selected problems do not require the input graph to be complete, and this is in full accordance with the motivating setting in which each network link must be physically held by a subject – it would be quite unrealistic to assume the existence of a link between each pair of vertices of the graph, indeed.

All the above problems are one-parameter, and they are easily seen to be NP-hard [11,13]. Thus, approximate truthful mechanisms (i.e., approximate monotone algorithms) need to be developed. To this aim, one generally starts by looking at a corresponding approximate algorithm for the canonical centralized version of the problem, trying to check whether it happens to be (or it can easily be transformed to become) monotone. Sometimes, this task is hard to be accomplished, since no general technique is known to establish the monotonicity of an algorithm, or to monotonize it. This is exactly what happens when dealing with our problems. So, in order to devise a uniform approach to face this issue, we focus our attention on a quite large class of one-parameter problems, namely those in which the work load of an agent is an integral number. For these problems, we first of all refine the classic notion of monotonicity used in [1] to that of *step-integral monotonicity* (which conveys the fact that each edge can be used several times). Then, we develop a general algorithm composition technique which is capable to preserve step-integral monotonicity whenever the two composing algorithms satisfy certain easier-to-check monotonicity properties as explained in more detail in Section 3. The usefulness of our technique is twofold:

on one hand we simplify the question of designing monotone algorithms, and on the other hand we provide a way to compute efficiently the payments returned to the agents.

We regard at this as to the main contribution of the paper, since we foresee the application of this general technique to other combinatorial optimization problems whose solution can be constructed in stages. In particular, this technique can actually be used to address our problems, for which we are then able to design efficient (in terms of time complexity and approximation ratio) approximate truthful mechanisms. More precisely, as far as the approximation ratios are concerned, we achieve a factor of 3/2 and 2 for the former two and the latter of the above problems, respectively. Thus, for the first two problems we match the best known approximation ratios holding for their corresponding canonical centralized versions [7], while for the third one we are only a 4/3-factor away from it [17].

This paper is organized as follows. Section 2 recalls some preliminaries from mechanism design, while Section 3 describes the general composition technique which will be used to efficiently solve our problems. Sections 4, 5, 6 describe our mechanisms for GTSP, RPP, and MCPP, respectively. Due to space limitations, some of the proof are postponed to the full version of the paper.

2   Preliminaries: Monotonicity and Truthfulness

Algorithmic mechanism design deals with algorithmic problems in a non-cooperative setting, in which part of the input is owned by selfish agents. As such agents may lie about their parts of input, they are capable of manipulating the algorithm. The main task of mechanism design theory is the study of how to incentivize the agents in order to behave honestly with the algorithm. We will deal with the case in which each agent controls a single link of a network. We provide a simplified formalization below, and we refer the interested reader to [12] for a deeper insight into the topic.

Let $G = (V, E)$ be a graph (either directed, undirected, or mixed). For an edge e of G owned by a selfish agent a_e, we denote by t_e the private information held by a_e. We call t_e the (private) *type* of the agent a_e, and we assume that t_e represents the real cost incurred by a_e for using its link. Each agent has to declare a (public) *bid* $b_e > 0$ to the mechanism. We denote by t the vector of private types, and by b the *bid profile*, namely the vector of all bids. Let b_{-e} denote the vector of all bids besides b_e; the pair (b_{-e}, b_e) will denote the bid profile b (for the sake of simplifying the notation, we will omit the parenthesis whenever (b_{-e}, b_e) appears as the only argument of a function).

For a given optimization problem defined on G, let $\mathcal{F}$ denote the corresponding set of feasible solutions. For each feasible solution $x \in \mathcal{F}$, some measure function $\mu(x, t)$ is defined, which depends on the true types. A *mechanism* is a pair $\mathcal{M} = \langle \mathcal{A}(\mathcal{I}, b), p(b) \rangle$, where $\mathcal{A}(\mathcal{I}, b)$ is an algorithm that, given an instance $\mathcal{I}$ defined on G and given the agents' bids, returns a solution, and $p(b)$ is a scheme which describes the payments provided to the agents. Sometimes, we will simply write $\mathcal{A}(b)$ (resp., $\mathcal{A}$) whenever $\mathcal{I}$ (resp. $\mathcal{I}$ and b) is clear from the context. The *time complexity* of a mechanism corresponds to the time needed to compute $\mathcal{A}$ and p. For each solution x, a_e is supposed to incur in a cost for participating in x, and this is expressed by a valuation function $\nu_e(t_e, x)$. The *utility* of an agent is defined as the difference between the payment provided by the mechanism and its cost w.r.t. the computed solution. Each agent tries to maximize its utility, while an *exact* mechanism aims to compute a solution which extremizes (i.e., either minimize or maximize) $\mu(x, t)$ without knowing t directly. Similarly, if we denote by $\varepsilon(\sigma)$ a positive real function of the input size σ, an $\varepsilon(\sigma)$-*approximation* mechanism returns a solution whose measure comes within a factor $\varepsilon(\sigma)$ from the optimum. In a *truthful* mechanism this tension between the agents and the system is resolved, since each agent maximizes its utility when it declares its type, regardless of what the other agents do.

A mechanism design problem is called *utilitarian* if its measure function satisfies $\mu(x, t) = \sum_{e \in E} \nu(t_e, x)$. For utilitarian problems, Vickrey, Clarke, and Groves discovered a class of truthful mechanisms, i.e., the *VCG-mechanisms*. Basically, VCG-mechanisms handle arbitrary valuation functions, but only utilitarian problems. In [1], Archer and Tardos have shown how to design truthful mechanisms for non-utilitarian problems under the assumption that the problem is *one-parameter*. A problem is said one-parameter if (i) the type of each agent a_e can be expressed as a single parameter $t_e \in \mathbb{R}$, and (ii) each agent's valuation has the form $\nu_e(t_e, x) = t_e \, w_e(x)$, where $w_e(x)$ is called *work load* for agent a_e in x, i.e., some amount of work assigned by the mechanism's algorithm that depends on the computed solution x. A well-studied class of one-parameter problems is that of the so called *binary demand (BD)* problems [10], in which for each agent a_e, its work load can be either 0 or 1. Given a solution x (resp., an algorithm $\mathcal{A}$), we will denote by $w(x)$ (resp., $w(\mathcal{A})$) the *work load vector* associated with x (resp., returned by $\mathcal{A}$). Recall that an algorithm $\mathcal{A}$ is said to be *monotone* if, for all a_e, and any fixed b_{-e}, $w_e(\mathcal{A}(b_{-e}, b_e))$ is a non-increasing function of b_e. We sometimes use $w_e(b_{-e}, b_e)$ instead of $w_e(\mathcal{A}(b_{-e}, b_e))$, when the algorithm is clear from the context. In [1], it is shown that a mechanism for a one-parameter problem is truthful if and only if it makes use of a monotone algorithm, and the payment provided to any agent a_e is equal to

$$p_e(b_{-e}, b_e) = h_e(b_{-e}) + b_e \, w_e(\mathcal{A}(b)) - \int_0^{b_e} w_e(\mathcal{A}(b_{-e}, z)) \, dz, \qquad (1)$$

where $h_e(b_{-e})$ is an arbitrary function independent of b_e.

Moreover, in [1] it is shown that if $\int_0^{+\infty} w_e(b_{-e}, z) \, dz < +\infty$ for all a_e and all b_{-e}, then we can use the following payment scheme to obtain a truthful mechanism guaranteeing that the agents' utilities are always non-negative:

$$p_e(b_{-e}, b_e) = b_e \, w_e(\mathcal{A}(b)) + \int_{b_e}^{+\infty} w_e(\mathcal{A}(b_{-e}, z)) \, dz. \qquad (2)$$

3   The General Composition Scheme

All the algorithms presented in this paper can be naturally decomposed into two simpler ones. In this section we state some general results which will allow us to prove certain properties of a composed algorithm, descending from those of the two composing algorithms. Quite naturally, for all the problems we are going to deal with, we assume that $\mathcal{F} \neq \emptyset$. Moreover, we assume that no agent is *indispensable*, namely that for each agent there always exists a feasible solution not depending on it. These two assumptions will be reflected by the connectivity properties that G needs to satisfy, depending on the specific problem. Finally, for each of the proposed algorithms, we tacitly assume that at each step a suitable tie-breaking rule is applied, if needed, in order to ensure the monotonicity.

Given a solution x, let us assume that the cost incurred by any agent a_e in x is equal to its type t_e times the number of occurrences of e in x. It is easy to see that, under this assumption, our problems fall within the class of the one-parameter problems, since the number of occurrences of e in x is exactly the work load $w_e(x)$, and $w_e(x) = 0$ if e is not part of x. In general, we say that a solution x does not depend on e when $w_e(x) = 0$. However, notice that in the MCPP, for every edge e and any feasible solution x, from the definition of the problem, e must occurs in x at least once. The same happens for every edge $e \in R$ in the RPP. In these cases, we say that a solution x does not depend on e if $w_e(x) = 1$. Moreover, when we compute the integral in (2) for e, to avoid technicalities, we do not count the first occurrence in the work load $w_e(\cdot)$, i.e., we take $w_e(\cdot)$ decremented by 1. This means that we implicity assume that the mechanism does not care about the cost incurred by a_e for the constrained occurrence. Thus, we consider one-parameter, utilitarian problems where the work load of each agent is a natural number.

Definition 1. *An algorithm $\mathcal{A}$ of a one-parameter mechanism is said to be* Step-Integral Monotone *(SIM) if $\mathcal{A}$ is monotone, and the work load of each agent belongs to $\mathbb{N}$.*

For any SIM algorithm $\mathcal{A}$, and any fixed b_{-e}, we define the *thresholds* for a_e w.r.t. $\mathcal{A}$ to be the discontinuity points of the function $f_e(z) := w_e(\mathcal{A}(b_{-e}, z))$, and denote them, sorted in increasing order, by $\theta_1, \theta_2, \ldots, \theta_h$. Notice that computing the integral in (1) and (2) essentially consists in determining the thresholds. Also note that for a BD problem, a monotone algorithm defines a unique threshold, and, for an agent a_e, the payment $p_e(b)$ is exactly that threshold value if a_e owns a selected edge, and 0 otherwise. Basically this threshold defines the supremum value that a_e is allowed to declare to be part of a solution.

We say that $\mathcal{A}$ is a *composition* of algorithms $\mathcal{A}^1$ and $\mathcal{A}^2 := \mathcal{A}^2(\mathcal{I}(\mathcal{A}^1), b)$ (and we will write $\mathcal{A} = \mathcal{A}^2 \circ \mathcal{A}^1$) if $\mathcal{A}$ adheres to the scheme listed in Algorithm 1. Notice that CreateInstance is a generic procedure which uses the output of the first algorithm to generate an instance of the second one. Finally, we say that $\mathcal{A}$ is *stable* if, for any a_e and for any fixed b_{-e}, $\forall x, y \in \mathbb{R}$, we have

$$w_e(\mathcal{A}(b_{-e}, x)) = w_e(\mathcal{A}(b_{-e}, y)) \iff \mathcal{A}(b_{-e}, x) = \mathcal{A}(b_{-e}, y).$$

Algorithm 1. $\mathcal{A} = \mathcal{A}^2 \circ \mathcal{A}^1$

1: let x^1 be the solution returned by $\mathcal{A}^1$;
2: $\mathcal{I}(\mathcal{A}^1) = \texttt{CreateInstance}(x^1)$;
3: let x^2 be the solution returned by $\mathcal{A}^2(\mathcal{I}(\mathcal{A}^1), b)$;
4: let x be a solution built from x^1 and x^2 such that $w_e(x) = w_e(x^1) + w_e(x^2), \forall a_e$;
5: return x.

A first useful consequence of the proposed decomposition scheme, is that the SIM property of the composed algorithm is guaranteed whenever the composing algorithms satisfy suitable properties, as proved in the following theorem.

Theorem 1. *Let $\mathcal{A}^1$ be a stable SIM algorithm for a one-parameter problem, and let $\mathcal{A}^2$ be a monotone algorithm for a BD problem. Then $\mathcal{A} = \mathcal{A}^2 \circ \mathcal{A}^1$ is a SIM algorithm.*

Proof. It is clear that work loads assigned by $\mathcal{A}$ are natural numbers. It remains to prove the monotonicity property. Let b_{-e} be fixed, and let b_e and b'_e be such that $b'_e \geq b_e$. We have to prove that $w_e(\mathcal{A}(b_{-e}, b_e)) \geq w_e(\mathcal{A}(b_{-e}, b'_e))$. Let then $\mathcal{I} := \mathcal{I}(\mathcal{A}_1(b_{-e}, b_e))$ and $\mathcal{I}' := \mathcal{I}(\mathcal{A}_1(b_{-e}, b'_e))$. By definition of $\mathcal{A}$, we have $w_e(\mathcal{A}(b_{-e}, b_e)) = w_e(\mathcal{A}^1(b_{-e}, b_e)) + w_e(\mathcal{A}^2(\mathcal{I}, (b_{-e}, b_e)))$, with $w_e(\mathcal{A}^1(b_{-e}, b_e)) \geq w_e(\mathcal{A}^1(b_{-e}, b'_e))$ holding from the monotonicity of $\mathcal{A}^1$. We have 2 cases:

1. $w_e(\mathcal{A}^1(b_{-e}, b_e)) = w_e(\mathcal{A}^1(b_{-e}, b'_e))$: Then, since $\mathcal{A}^1$ is stable, it is $\mathcal{I} = \mathcal{I}'$, and then from the monotonicity of A_2 we have $w_e(\mathcal{A}^2(\mathcal{I}, (b_{-e}, b_e))) \geq w_e(\mathcal{A}^2(\mathcal{I}', (b_{-e}, b'_e)))$, hence the claim follows.
2. $w_e(\mathcal{A}^1(b_{-e}, b_e)) > w_e(\mathcal{A}^1(b_{-e}, b'_e))$: Then, since $w_e(\mathcal{A}^2(\mathcal{I}', (b_{-e}, b'_e))) \leq 1$, the claim follows.

□

We now concentrate on the computation of payments, and we provide a general method to compute in polynomial-time the thresholds for a certain class of problems.

Theorem 2. *Let $\mathcal{A} = \mathcal{A}^2 \circ \mathcal{A}^1$ be a polynomial-time algorithm of a one-parameter mechanism, where $\mathcal{A}^1$ is a stable SIM algorithm for a one-parameter problem, and $\mathcal{A}^2$ is a monotone algorithm for a BD problem. If there exist polynomial-time algorithms for computing the thresholds w.r.t. $\mathcal{A}^1$ and $\mathcal{A}^2$, respectively, then the thresholds for any agent a_e w.r.t. $\mathcal{A}$ can be computed in $O(T_{p_e^1} + h(T_{CI} + T_{p_e^2}))$ time, where h is the number of thresholds for a_e w.r.t. $\mathcal{A}^1$, T_{CI} is the time required by $\texttt{CreateInstance}$, and $T_{p_e^1}$ and $T_{p_e^2}$ is the time required for computing the thresholds for a_e w.r.t. $\mathcal{A}^1$ and $\mathcal{A}^2$, respectively.*

Proof. We provide a polynomial-time procedure to compute thresholds w.r.t. $\mathcal{A}$. The proof of its correctness is quite simple and we omit it. Let b_{-e} be fixed. Let $\theta_1, \ldots, \theta_h$ be the thresholds for a_e w.r.t. $\mathcal{A}^1$, and let $\theta_0 = 0$, $\theta_{h+1} = \infty$. For $1 \leq i \leq h$, we denote by ω_i the work load assigned by $\mathcal{A}^1$ to a_e, when $\theta_{i-1} < b_e < \theta_i$.

We now show how to compute thresholds of a_e. A *pre-threshold* is a pair (θ, ω), where θ is a threshold value and ω is the corresponding work load value. The following procedure computes a list of pre-thresholds:

1. let L be the list of pairs (θ_i, ω_i), $\forall 1 \leq i \leq h$, ordered according to θ_i's;
2. $\forall 1 \leq i \leq h + 1$:
   (a) let $\mathcal{I}(\mathcal{A}^1)$ be the instance computed by $\texttt{CreateInstance}(\mathcal{A}_1(b_{-e}, z))$, where $\theta_{i-1} < z < \theta_i$ (notice that since $\mathcal{A}^1$ is stable, the same instance will be computed for any z in the interval between θ_{i-1} and θ_i);
   (b) let β_i be the threshold for a_e w.r.t. $\mathcal{A}^2$ on the instance $\mathcal{I}(\mathcal{A}^1)$;
   (c) compare β_i and (θ_{i-1}, θ_i):
       i. case $\beta_i < \theta_{i-1}$: nothing happens;
       ii. case $\theta_{i-1} < \beta_i < \theta_i$: insert $(\beta_i, \omega_i + 1)$ in L (respecting the order);
       iii. case $\theta_i \leq \beta_i$: update (θ_i, ω_i) to $(\theta_i, \omega_i + 1)$.

Notice that L computed as above, is sorted in increasing order w.r.t. the pairs' first value, and in non-increasing order w.r.t. the pairs' second value. Thresholds of $\mathcal{A}$ are then obtained by selecting the maximum threshold value in each set of pre-thresholds having the same work load value. The bound on the running time follows immediately. □

The above result can be enhanced as soon as the algorithm $\mathcal{A}^1$ solves optimally a one-parameter problem which is also utilitarian. Indeed, in this case the following lemma can be proved (details will appear in the full version of the paper):

Lemma 1. *Given a one-parameter and utilitarian problem, solvable in $O(T_{\mathcal{A}})$ polynomial time by a given stable SIM algorithm $\mathcal{A}$, the thresholds $\theta_1, \theta_2, \ldots, \theta_h$ w.r.t. $\mathcal{A}$ of any agent are computable in $O(h\,T_{\mathcal{A}})$ time.*

Finally, combining results of Lemma 1 and Theorem 2, we obtain the following main result:

Theorem 3. *Let $\mathcal{A} = \mathcal{A}^2 \circ \mathcal{A}^1$ be an algorithm of a one-parameter mechanism having $O(T_{\mathcal{A}})$ polynomial running time, where $\mathcal{A}^1$ is a stable SIM algorithm for solving optimally a one-parameter utilitarian problem, and $\mathcal{A}^2$ is a monotone algorithm for a BD problem running in $O(T_{\mathcal{A}^2})$ time. If the threshold of any agent a_e w.r.t. $\mathcal{A}^2$ can be computed in $O(T_{\mathcal{A}^2})$ time, then the thresholds for a_e w.r.t. $\mathcal{A}$ can be computed in $O(h\,T_{\mathcal{A}})$ time, where h is the number of thresholds for a_e w.r.t. $\mathcal{A}^1$.*

4   An Approximate Mechanism for the GTSP

Given an undirected graph $G = (V, E)$, with $n = |V|, m = |E|$, we consider the problem of computing a minimum-cost spanning tour of G. This problem is utilitarian and is equivalent to the classical TSP for the metric instances. Thus we can use for our problem a modified version of Christofides's algorithm [4], where a *path matching* [2] instead of a matching takes place, and where we do not shortcut repeated vertex occurrences. Such modifications allow to prove easily algorithm's monotonicity, and do not change its approximation ratio.

1. Compute a minimum spanning tree (MST) T of G;
2. Let $U \subseteq V$ be the set of odd-degree vertices in T, and let D be the complete graph on U such that, $\forall u, v \in U$, edge $\{u, v\}$ has weight equal to the cost $d_G(u, v)$ of a shortest path in G between u and v;
3. *Path matching (PM) algorithm*: Compute a minimum-cost perfect matching M of D, and let F be the *expansion of* M, i.e., the multiset composed by taking, for each $\{u, v\} \in M$, the edges forming the shortest path in G between u and v;
4. Form an Eulerian multigraph $H = (V, E')$ on G consisting of the edges of T and the edges in F, and compute an Eulerian tour x of it;
5. Return x.

Notice that our algorithm is a composition (as defined in Section 3) of an algorithm for the MST and the PM algorithm. It is easy to prove that it has approximation ratio $3/2$ and that its time complexity is dominated by the $O(n^3)$ time required to compute a minimum-cost perfect matching on a complete graph. It is easy to see that any classic MST algorithm is monotone, BD, and can be made stable through suitable tie-breaking rules. Since the expansion of M forms an edge-disjoint forest in G (see [2]), it is straightforward to see that the PM algorithm is BD (notice that this implies that the work loads will be at most 2). Then to prove the step-integral monotonicity of our algorithm, we use Theorem 1 after showing that PM is a monotone algorithm.

Lemma 2. *The PM algorithm is monotone.*

Proof. Let us fix a graph G and a set of vertices $U \subseteq V$ as the input of the PM algorithm. We denote the cost of a set S of edges of G when the bid profile is b by $c(b, S) = \sum_{e \in S} b_e$. Let us consider a bid profile b given as input to PM, and let F be the corresponding computed solution. Assume that $e \in E \setminus F$ is an edge not selected as part of the output. For $b'_e > b_e$, let F' be the solution computed by PM when the input bid profile is $b' = (b_{-e}, b'_e)$. We have to show that $e \notin F'$.

For the sake of contradiction, assume that $e \in F'$, which implies that $c(b, F') < c(b', F')$. Since PM computes an optimal solution, $c(b, F) \leq c(b, F')$, and since $e \notin F$, it is $c(b', F) = c(b, F)$. Then we have $c(b', F) < c(b', F')$, which is a contradiction since F' is the output of PM when the bid profile is b'. $\square$

Now we show how to compute thresholds w.r.t. the PM algorithm. Given a bid profile b, and $U \subseteq V$, let F be the solution computed by the PM algorithm in b, and assume that $e \in F$ is a selected edge. We denote by $F_{\neg e}$ the solution returned by the PM algorithm in $G - e$. It is easy to see that the threshold for a_e is $c(b, F_{\neg e}) - c(b, F) + b_e$, which is clearly computable with the same asymptotic time bound as PM. Similarly, the thresholds for a_e w.r.t. the MST algorithm can be computed by running the MST algorithm on $G - e$. Then, from Theorem 3, and observing that there are at most $O(n)$ agents in a feasible solution, we have the following:

Theorem 4. *There exists an $O(n^4)$ time $3/2$-approximate truthful mechanism for the GTSP in which each edge is owned by a distinct selfish agent.*

5 An Approximate Mechanism for the RPP

In the RPP, we are given an undirected graph $G = (V, E)$, with $n = |V|, m = |E|$, and a set $R \subseteq E$, with $k = |R|$. We are required to compute a minimum-cost tour in G traversing each edge of R *at least* once.

As observed in [7] this problem has a 3/2-approximation algorithm which is a minor modification of Christofides's one. Similarly, our algorithm for the GTSP can be adapted to this problem, still giving a 3/2-approximation in $O(n^3)$ time. We observe that in this case edge work loads may be greater than 2.

1. Let G' be the complete graph on the vertex set $V' = \{v \in V \mid \exists e \in R \wedge v \in e\}$, where edge $e = \{u, v\}$ has weight equal to b_e if $e \in R$, and to $d_G(u, v)$ otherwise, $\forall u, v \in V'$. Compute a minimum-cost subgraph $C = (V', R')$ of G' such that C is connected and $R \subseteq R'$. Build the multiset of edges x^1 as the union of R and of the edges forming a shortest path in G between u and v, for each $\{u, v\} \in R' \setminus R$;
2. Let $U' \subseteq V'$ be the set of odd-degree vertices in C, and let D be the complete graph on U', where edge $\{u, v\}$ has weight $d_G(u, v)$, $\forall u, v \in U'$;
3. (PM algorithm): Compute a minimum-cost perfect matching M on D. Build the multiset of edges x^2 as the union, $\forall \{u, v\} \in M$, of the edges forming a shortest path in G between u and v;
4. Form the Eulerian multigraph induced by edges in x^1 and x^2, and compute an Eulerian tour x of it;
5. Return x.

To prove that the algorithm is SIM, it suffices to show the following:

Lemma 3. *Step 1 of the above algorithm is a stable SIM algorithm.*

Proof. To prove that Step 1 is a SIM algorithm, it suffices to show that is monotone. We first observe that any agent holding an edge in R has work load 1. Let e be an edge of $E \setminus R$. Then e belongs to some shortest paths in G between pairs of vertices in V'. If a_e increases its bid, Step 1 computes a new solution $\hat{x}^1$ which retains all paths in x^1 not containing e, but where some of the paths of x^1 containing e may be replaced by an equal number of shortest (with respect to the new bid profile) paths. Such new paths do not contain e, otherwise they would be cheaper than the previous ones also with respect to the old bid profile. Then the work load of a_e in $\hat{x}^1$ is not greater than the one in x^1.

If a_e's load in $\hat{x}^1$ is the same as in x^1, then x^1 has the same cost as $\hat{x}^1$ w.r.t. the new profile. Therefore the tie-breaking rules imply the stability of Step 1. □

Then by Lemma 2 and Theorem 1 we have that our algorithm is SIM.

Since we are able to compute the thresholds w.r.t. the PM algorithm (see Section 4), in view of Theorem 2 to compute payments for the complete algorithm we only have to find the thresholds of the algorithm in Step 1. To this aim, we use the method given in Lemma 1. Referring to such algorithm, we observe that for each $e \in R$, the work load of a_e is at least 1. We remind that, for such edges, we implicitly decrease by 1 the work load when computing the integral appearing in the payment scheme (2), in order to guarantee that it has a finite value.

To analyze the time complexity of the mechanism, we first observe that the time complexity of the algorithm is dominated by the PM algorithm on a complete graph with $2k$ vertices, which requires $O(k^3)$ time, and by the computation of G'. The latter requires to compute the all-pairs shortest paths between $2k$ vertices of G, which – depending on k – can be either accomplished in $O(nm \log \alpha(m, n))$ time by computing the all-pairs distances of G [15], or in $O(k(m + n \log n))$ time by k executions of Dijkstra's algorithm. To determine the time complexity of thresholds computation, we then use the result of Theorem 3, by noticing that for each agent a_e it is $w_e(x^1) \leq k$, and that there are at most $O(n + k)$ distinct agents in a feasible solution. Thus, the following theorem summarizes the results of this section:

Theorem 5. *There exists an $O((n+k) k (\min\{nm \log \alpha(m, n), k(m+n \log n)\} + k^3))$ time 3/2-approximate truthful mechanism for the RPP in which each edge is owned by a distinct selfish agent.*

6   An Approximate Mechanism for the MCPP

In the Chinese postman problem, we are given a graph G and we are required to compute a minimum-cost spanning tour of G traversing each edge *at least* once. The problem was shown to be efficiently solvable by Edmonds [5] and by Edmonds and Johnson [6] in the case where the input graph is either undirected or directed, respectively. On the other hand, when a mixed input graph is permitted, we have the MCPP, whose decision version has been shown to be NP-complete by Papadimitriou [13].

In search for an approximate truthful mechanism for the MCPP, we restrict our attention to the algorithm Mixed2, which was originally developed in [7], and for which we can prove its adherence to our scheme, and therefore its monotonicity. This algorithm was shown to have an approximation ratio of 2. Notice that algorithms achieving better approximation ratios are known in the literature (see [7] and [17]), but unfortunately they are provably not monotone. Algorithm Mixed2 takes as input a mixed graph $G = (V, E, A)$, where E is the set of undirected edges, and A is the set of directed edges, with $n = |V|, m = |E| + |A|$. Following a common strategy to attack the MCPP, the algorithm starts by inserting in G a suitable multiset of *additional directed edges*, which are either obtained by duplicating a directed edge of G, or by replacing an undirected edge of G with a directed one. These additional edges can be efficiently found by solving a *minimum-cost flow* (MCF) problem on an *auxiliary network* of n vertices and $\Theta(m)$ edges. The details on the correspondence of Mixed2 to our scheme and the proof of the following result will appear in the full version of the paper:

Theorem 6. *There exists an $O(m|A|(\mathcal{T}_{\mathrm{MCF}} + n^3))$ time 2-approximate truthful mechanism for the MCPP in which each edge is owned by a distinct selfish agent, where $\mathcal{T}_{\mathrm{MCF}} = O(m^2 \log n + mn \log^2 n)$ is the time required to compute a MCF (see [18]) on the auxiliary network.*

Acknowledgements. The authors would like to thank the anonymous referees for their very helpful comments.

References

1. Archer, A., Tardos, É.: Truthful mechanisms for one-parameter agents. In: Archer, A. (ed.) Proc. of the 42nd Annual IEEE Symp. on Foundations of Computer Science (FOCS), pp. 482–491. IEEE Computer Society Press, Los Alamitos (2001)
2. Böckenhauer, H.-J., Hromkovič, J., Klasing, R., Seibert, S., Unger, W.: Towards the notion of stability of approximation for hard optimization tasks and the traveling salesman problem. Theoretical Computer Science 285(1), 3–24 (2002)
3. Brotcorne, L., Labbé, M., Marcotte, P., Savard, G.: A bilevel model for toll optimization on a multicommodity transportation network. Transportation Science 35, 1–14 (2001)
4. Christofides, N.: Worst-case analysis of a new heuristic for the traveling salesman problem. Technical report, GSIA, Carnegy Mellon University (1976)
5. Edmonds, J.: The Chinese postman problem. Operations Research 13, 73–77 (1965)
6. Edmonds, J., Johnson, E.L.: Matching, Euler tours and the chinese postman. Math. Programming 5, 88–124 (1973)
7. Frederickson, G.N.: Approximation algorithms for some postman problems. J. ACM 26(3), 538–554 (1979)
8. Gualà, L., Proietti, G.: Efficient truthful mechanisms for the single-source shortest paths tree problem. In: Cunha, J.C., Medeiros, P.D. (eds.) Euro-Par 2005. LNCS, vol. 3648, pp. 941–951. Springer, Heidelberg (2005)
9. Hershberger, J., Suri, S.: Vickrey prices and shortest paths: what is an edge worth? In: Proc. of the 42nd Annual IEEE Symp. on Foundations of Computer Science (FOCS), pp. 252–259. IEEE Computer Society Press, Los Alamitos (2001)
10. Kao, M.-Y., Li, X.-Y., Wang, W.: Towards truthful mechanisms for binary demand games: A general framework. In: Proc. of the 6th ACM Conf. on Electronic Commerce (EC), ACM Press, New York (2005)
11. Lenstra, J.K., Kan, A.G.H.R.: On general routing problems. Networks 6, 273–280 (1976)
12. Nisan, N., Ronen, A.: Algorithmic mechanism design. Games and Economic Behaviour 35, 166–196 (2001)
13. Papadimitriou, C.: On the complexity of edge traversing. J. ACM 23(3), 544–554 (1976)
14. Penna, P., Proietti, G., Widmayer, P.: Strongly polynomial-time truthful mechanisms in one shot. In: Spirakis, P.G., Mavronicolas, M., Kontogiannis, S.C. (eds.) WINE 2006. LNCS, vol. 4286, pp. 377–388. Springer, Heidelberg (2006)
15. Pettie, S., Ramachandran, V.: Computing shortest paths with comparisons and additions. In: Proc. of the 13th Annual ACM-SIAM Symp. on Discrete Algorithms (SODA), pp. 267–276 (2002)
16. Proietti, G., Widmayer, P.: A truthful mechanism for the non-utilitarian minimum radius spanning tree problem. In: Proc. of the 17th ACM Symp. on Parallel Algorithms and Architectures (SPAA), pp. 195–202. ACM Press, New York (2005)
17. Raghavachari, B., Veerasamy, J.: A 3/2-approximation algorithm for the mixed postman problem. SIAM J. Discrete Math. 12(4), 425–433 (1999)
18. Schrijver, A.: Combinatorial Optimization - Polyhedra and Efficiency. Springer, Heidelberg (2003)

To Be or Not to Be (Served)[*]

Yvonne Bleischwitz[1], Burkhard Monien[1], and Florian Schoppmann[1,2]

[1] Faculty of Computer Science, Electrical Engineering and Mathematics,
University of Paderborn, Fürstenallee 11, 33102 Paderborn, Germany
{yvonneb,bm,fschopp}@uni-paderborn.de
[2] International Graduate School of Dynamic Intelligent Systems

Abstract. A common modeling assumption in the realm of cost sharing is that players persuade each other to jointly submit false bids if none of the members of such a coalition loses utility and at least one gains. In order to counteract this kind of manipulation, the service provider could employ group-strategyproof (GSP) mechanisms that elicit truthful bids. The basically only general technique for the design of GSP mechanisms is due to Moulin. Unfortunately, it has limitations with regard to budget-balance (BB) and economic efficiency (EFF).

In this work, we introduce a slight modification of GSP that we call CGSP, allowing us to achieve vastly better results concerning BB and EFF. In particular, we give new CGSP mechanisms that we call "egalitarian" due to being inspired by Dutta and Ray's (1989) "egalitarian solution". We achieve 1-BB for arbitrary costs and additionally $2H_n$-EFF for the very natural and large class of subadditive costs. Egalitarian mechanisms are also acyclic mechanisms, as introduced by Mehta et al. (2007). Thus far, acyclic was known only to imply weak GSP, yet we show that it is already sufficient for the strictly stronger CGSP.

Finally, we present a framework and applications on how to cope with computational complexity.

1 Introduction and Model

1.1 Motivation

We study *cost-sharing problems* where there is a set of players having (binary) demand for some common service, and the task is to determine which subset S of players to serve and how to distribute the incurred cost $C(S)$. We follow the line of studying this problem from the incentive-compatibility angle, where decisions can solely be based on *valuations* that the players report for the service. This problem is fundamental in economics and has a broad area of applications, e.g., sharing the cost of public infrastructure projects, distributing volume discounts, or allocating development costs of low-volume built-to-order products.

In the standard model, a *service provider* takes the role of offering the common service to the n players and hence has to solve the cost-sharing problem. While

---

[*] This work was partially supported by the IST Program of the European Union under contract number IST-15964 (AEOLUS).

X. Deng and F.C. Graham (Eds.): WINE 2007, LNCS 4858, pp. 515–528, 2007.
© Springer-Verlag Berlin Heidelberg 2007

the valuations reported by the players are binding, they cannot be assumed to be truthful. We refer to them as *bids* in the following. The decision-making of the service provider is governed by a (commonly known) *cost-sharing mechanism* that specifies the set of served players and their respective payments for any combination of bids. The main difficulty lies in achieving *group-strategyproofness*, i.e., designing the mechanism such that players communicate their true valuations out of self-interest, even if they could form coalitions.

Apart from being group-strategyproof, there are many more desirable properties for a cost-sharing mechanism. Most naturally, it has to ensure recovery of the provider's cost as well as competitive prices in that the generated surplus is always relatively small. This constraint is referred to as *budget-balance*. Moreover, there should be a reasonable trade-off between the provider's cost and the valuations of the excluded players, meaning that the mechanism is *economically efficient*. Finally, practical applications demand for polynomial-time computability (in the size of the problem).

The essentially only known general technique for the design of group-strategyproof mechanisms is due to Moulin [15]. Unfortunately, it has severe limitations with respect to the former objectives. The pivotal point of this paper is slightly altering the group-strategyproof requirement to greatly improve performance.

1.2   The Model

Notation. For $n \in \mathbb{N}_0$, let $[n] := \{1,\ldots,n\}$ and $[n]_0 := [n] \cup \{0\}$. Given $\boldsymbol{x}, \boldsymbol{y} \in \mathbb{Q}^n$ and $S \subseteq [n]$, let $\boldsymbol{x}_S := (x_i)_{i \in S} \in \mathbb{Q}^{|S|}$ and $\boldsymbol{x}_{-S} := \boldsymbol{x}_{[n] \setminus S}$. Let $(\boldsymbol{x}_{-S}, \boldsymbol{y}_S) \in \mathbb{Q}^n$ denote the vector where the components in $\boldsymbol{x}$ for S are replaced by the respective ones from $\boldsymbol{y}$. For $k \in [|S|]$, we define $MIN_k\, S$ as the set of k smallest elements in S. Let $H_n = \sum_{i=1}^n \frac{1}{i}$ be the n-th harmonic number. By convention, the vector of the players' true valuations is always $\boldsymbol{v} \in \mathbb{Q}^n$, whereas an actual bid vector is denoted $\boldsymbol{b} \in \mathbb{Q}^n$.

A *cost-sharing problem* is specified by a *cost function* $C : 2^{[n]} \to \mathbb{Q}_{\geq 0}$ mapping each subset of the $n \in \mathbb{N}$ players to the cost of serving them. In the following, we first focus on incentive-compatibility. Afterwards, we relate cost-sharing mechanisms to the cost of serving the selected players.

Definition 1. *A* cost-sharing mechanism $M = (Q \times x) : \mathbb{Q}^n \to 2^{[n]} \times \mathbb{Q}^n$ *is a function where* $Q(\boldsymbol{b}) \in 2^{[n]}$ *is the set of players to be served and* $x(\boldsymbol{b}) \in \mathbb{Q}^n$ *is the vector of cost shares.*

All mechanisms are required to fulfill three standard properties. For all $\boldsymbol{b} \in \mathbb{Q}^n$:

- *No positive transfers* (NPT): Players never get paid, i.e., $x_i(\boldsymbol{b}) \geq 0$.
- *Voluntary participation* (VP): Players never pay more than they bid and are only charged when served, i.e., if $i \in Q(\boldsymbol{b})$ then $x_i(\boldsymbol{b}) \leq b_i$, else $x_i(\boldsymbol{b}) = 0$.
- *Consumer sovereignty* (CS): For any player $i \in [n]$ there is a threshold bid $b_i^+ \in \mathbb{Q}_{\geq 0}$ such that i is served if bidding at least b_i^+, regardless of the other players' bids; i.e., there is a $b_i^+ \in \mathbb{Q}_{\geq 0}$ such that if $b_i \geq b_i^+$ then $i \in Q(\boldsymbol{b})$.

Note that VP and NPT imply that players may opt to not participate (by submitting a negative bid). Together with CS this is referred to as *strict CS*.

We assume players' utilities $u_i : \mathbb{Q}^n \to \mathbb{Q}$ to be *quasi-linear*, i.e., $u_i(\boldsymbol{b}) := v_i - x_i(\boldsymbol{b})$ if $i \in Q(\boldsymbol{b})$ and 0 otherwise. Under this premise and with *rational* players, mechanisms should elicit truthful bids ($\boldsymbol{b} = \boldsymbol{v}$) even if collusion is feasible:

Definition 2. *A mechanism is* group-strategyproof *(GSP) if for all true valuation vectors $\boldsymbol{v} \in \mathbb{Q}^n$ and coalitions $K \subseteq [n]$ there is no bid vector $\boldsymbol{b} \in \mathbb{Q}^n$ with $\boldsymbol{b}_{-K} = \boldsymbol{v}_{-K}$ such that $u_i(\boldsymbol{b}) \geq u_i(\boldsymbol{v})$ for all $i \in K$ and $u_i(\boldsymbol{b}) > u_i(\boldsymbol{v})$ for at least one $i \in K$.*

A mechanism is *weakly GSP* (WGSP) if the inequalities in Definition 2 are required to be strict for all $i \in K$.

Cost shares selected by a GSP mechanism only depend on the set of served players and not on the bids [15]. This gives rise to the following definition:

Definition 3. *A* cost-sharing method *is a function $\xi : 2^{[n]} \to \mathbb{Q}_{\geq 0}^n$ that maps each set of players to a vector of cost shares.*

Clearly, every GSP mechanism $(Q \times x)$ *induces* a unique cost-sharing method ξ, by setting $\xi(S) := x(\boldsymbol{b})$ where $b_i < 0$ if $i \notin S$ and $b_i = b_i^+$ if $i \in S$. A cost-sharing method ξ is *cross-monotonic* if $\xi_i(S \cup T) \leq \xi_i(S)$ for all $S, T \subseteq [n]$ and all $i \in [n]$. In his seminal work [15], Moulin gave the straightforward mechanism *Moulin$_\xi$* that is GSP for any cross-monotonic ξ. *Moulin$_\xi$* repeatedly rejects players whose bids are below their current cost share until all remaining players can afford their payments. For any GSP mechanism M with cross-monotonic cost shares ξ, *Moulin$_\xi$* produces the same utility for each player as M. Thus, we call any GSP mechanism with cross-monotonic cost shares a *Moulin mechanism*.

Avoiding coalitional cheating alone is clearly not sufficient, as it does not yet relate to the cost of serving the selected players. Typically, costs stem from solutions to a combinatorial optimization problem and are defined only implicitly. In this work, $C(S)$ is the value of a minimum-cost solution for the instance induced by the player set $S \subseteq [n]$. There are two major obstacles to recover this cost exactly: First, computing the *optimal cost* $C(S)$ may take exponential time, and the service provider therefore resorts to an approximate solution with *actual cost* $C'(S) \geq C(S)$. Second, already the GSP requirement places restrictions on the possible cost-shares. Nonetheless, the total charge of a mechanism (and, analogously, of a cost-sharing method) should be reasonably bounded.

Definition 4. *A mechanism $M = (Q \times x)$ is β-budget-balanced (β-BB, for $\beta \geq 1$) if for all $\boldsymbol{b} \in \mathbb{Q}^n$: $C'(Q(\boldsymbol{b})) \leq \sum_{i \in Q(\boldsymbol{b})} x_i(\boldsymbol{b}) \leq \beta \cdot C(Q(\boldsymbol{b}))$.*

As a quality measure for the choice of a set of served players, we use *optimal* and *actual social costs* $SC_{\boldsymbol{v}}, SC_{\boldsymbol{v}}' : 2^{[n]} \to \mathbb{Q}_{\geq 0}$, respectively, where $SC_{\boldsymbol{v}}(S) := C(S) + \sum_{i \in [n] \setminus S} \max\{0, v_i\}$ and $SC_{\boldsymbol{v}}'(S) := C'(S) + \sum_{i \in [n] \setminus S} \max\{0, v_i\}$. The cost incurred by the served players and the valuations of the rejected players should be traded off as good as possible:

Definition 5. *A mechanism $M = (Q \times x)$ is γ-efficient (γ-EFF, for $\gamma \geq 1$) if for all true valuations $\boldsymbol{v} \in \mathbb{Q}^n$: $SC_{\boldsymbol{v}}'(Q(\boldsymbol{v})) \leq \gamma \cdot \min_{T \subseteq [n]} \{SC_{\boldsymbol{v}}(T)\}$.*

Often, costs exhibit a special structure that can be exploited. In this work, we focus on *subadditive costs* where for all $S, T \subseteq [n] : C(S) + C(T) \geq C(S \cup T)$.

1.3   Related Work

The essentially only general technique for the design of GSP mechanisms consists of finding a cross-monotonic cost-sharing method ξ for use with $Moulin_\xi$ [15]. Yet, already achieving good BB is challenging for many problems [13].

The notion of social cost is due to Roughgarden and Sundararajan [18], who initiated a sequence of works in which Moulin mechanisms with not just good BB but also reasonable EFF were given [19,3,5,11]. However, cross-monotonic cost shares have limitations that hence no Moulin mechanism can overcome [13,3,18]. Thus, there is great need for alternatives. Acyclic mechanisms, as introduced by Mehta et al. [14], are one alternative framework that performs better with respect to BB and EFF. Yet, acyclic mechanisms are not necessarily GSP but only known to be WGSP. Non-Moulin GSP mechanisms were given by Bleischwitz et al. [2]; yet only for a limited scenario with symmetric costs.

Besides optimizing BB and EFF, several works have put efforts into characterization results that help understanding the fundamentals of cost sharing [15,13,17]. On the negative side, long-standing results [10] imply that, in general, mechanisms cannot fulfill GSP, 1-BB, and 1-EFF all at once. In fact, already for symmetric cost functions, there are in general no GSP, 1-BB mechanisms [2].

For previous results on the makespan cost-sharing problem (costs stem from a schedule for the selected players' jobs) see Table 1.

1.4   Contribution

We introduce the new behavioral assumption that coalitions do *not* form if some member would lose service. Yet, coalitions *do already* form if at least one player wins the service. Being reminded of collectors, we call resistance against collective collusion in the new sense *group-strategyproof against collectors* (CGSP).

- In Section 2, we give the formal definition of CGSP and show that it is strictly stronger than WGSP but incomparable to GSP. Moreover, we prove that – contrary to WGSP – any CGSP mechanism induces unique cost-shares.
- In Section 3, we give an algorithm for computing CGSP mechanisms that we call "egalitarian" due to being inspired by Dutta and Ray's [7] "egalitarian solutions". We achieve 1-BB for arbitrary costs and additionally $2H_n$-EFF for the very natural (and rather large) class of subadditive costs.
- In Section 4, we show that our egalitarian mechanisms are a subclass of acyclic mechanisms and that all acyclic mechanisms are CGSP.
- In Section 5, we present a framework for coping with the computational complexity of egalitarian mechanisms. Besides the use of approximation algorithms, the key idea here are "monotonic" cost functions that must not increase when replacing a player by another one with a smaller number.
- In Section 6, we give applications that underline the power of our new approach. For makespan cost-sharing problems, our results are given in Table 1.

Omitted proofs are given in the extended version of this paper.

Table 1. BB and EFF guarantees of best known polynomial-time mechanisms for makespan cost-sharing problems

Problem	from	GSP mechanisms BB	EFF[1]	CGSP mechanisms BB	EFF
general	[1]	$2d$	$\Omega(\log n)$	2	$4H_n$
identical machines[2]	[1]	$\frac{2m}{m+1}$	$\Omega(n)$	$\left\{\begin{array}{c} 1+\varepsilon \\ \frac{4}{3}-\frac{1}{3m} \end{array}\right.$	$\left.\begin{array}{c} 2(1+\varepsilon)H_n \\ 2(\frac{4}{3}-\frac{1}{3m})H_n \end{array}\right\}$
	[3]	$\frac{2m-1}{m}$	H_n+1		
identical jobs	[2]	$\frac{\sqrt{17}+1}{4}$	$\Omega(\log n)$	1	$2H_n$

n, m, d: number of jobs, machines, and different processing times, respectively

[1] $\Omega(n)$ is due to [3], $\Omega(\log n)$ follows from the instance with n identical jobs and machines where $\boldsymbol{v}=(\frac{1}{i}-\varepsilon)_{i=1}^n$.

[2] CGSP Mechanisms: Upper result based on PTAS with running time exponential in $\frac{1}{\varepsilon}$, lower result achieved with practical algorithm

2   Collectors' Behavior

In the demand for group-strategyproofness lies an implicit modeling assumption that is common to most recent works on cost-sharing mechanisms: First, a player is only willing to be untruthful and join a coalition of false-bidders if this does *not* involve sacrificing her own utility. Second, a coalition always requires an initiating player whose utility *strictly* increases.

Clearly, there are other reasonable behavioral assumptions on coalition formation. We introduce and study the following: First, besides not giving up utility, a player would not sacrifice service, either. (Although her utility is zero both when being served for her valuation and when not being served.) Second, it is sufficient for coalition formation if the initiating player gains *either* utility *or* service. While we consider this behavior very human, it especially reminds us of collectors. We hence denote a mechanism's resistance against coalitions in this new sense as *group-strategyproof against collectors*.

Definition 6. *A mechanism is* group-strategyproof against collectors *(CGSP) if for all* $\boldsymbol{v} \in \mathbb{Q}^n$ *and* $K \subseteq [n]$ *there is no* $\boldsymbol{b} \in \mathbb{Q}^n$ *with* $\boldsymbol{b}_{-K} = \boldsymbol{v}_{-K}$ *such that*

1. $u_i(\boldsymbol{b}) \geq u_i(\boldsymbol{v})$ *and* $i \notin Q(\boldsymbol{v}) \setminus Q(\boldsymbol{b})$ *for all* $i \in K$ *and*
2. $u_i(\boldsymbol{b}) > u_i(\boldsymbol{v})$ *or* $i \in Q(\boldsymbol{b}) \setminus Q(\boldsymbol{v})$ *for at least one* $i \in K$.

We remark that CGSP in a model with quasi-linear utilities is equivalent to GSP in a changed model where a preference of being served for the price of valuation over not being served is internalized in the utilities. To illustrate the interrelation between CGSP and GSP, we introduce a property which is a relaxation of both, called *weakly group-strategyproof against collectors* (WCGSP). Here, (2.) of Definition 6 is replaced by "$u_i(\boldsymbol{b}) > u_i(\boldsymbol{v})$ for at least one $i \in K$".

Lemma 1. *The following implications hold.*

$$GSP \underset{CGSP}{\overset{\displaystyle \Longrightarrow}{\displaystyle \nearrow}} WCGSP \Longrightarrow WGSP$$

We remark that Theorem 5 will imply that $Moulin_\xi$ is both GSP and CGSP. Interestingly, already WCGSP is sufficient for a mechanism to induce unique cost shares:

Theorem 1. *Let $M = (Q \times x)$ be a mechanism that satisfies WCGSP. Then, for any two $b, b' \in Q$ with $Q(b) = Q(b')$, it holds that $x(b) = x(b')$. This result holds even if we restrict our model to non-negative bids and only require CS.*

The proof of Theorem 1 uses ideas from an analogous result in [15]. However, Theorem 1 is stronger since GSP and *strict* CS are relaxed to WCGSP and CS. Conversely, WGSP mechanisms do not always induce (unique) cost-sharing methods, even if we demand 1-BB:

Lemma 2. *For any non-decreasing cost function $C : 2^{[3]} \to \mathbb{Q}_{\geq 0}$, there is a WGSP and 1-BB mechanism $M_C = (Q \times x)$ such that there are bids $b, b' \in \mathbb{Q}_{>0}$ with $Q(b) = Q(b')$, but $x(b) \neq x(b')$.*

3   Egalitarian Mechanisms

Egalitarian mechanisms borrow an algorithmic idea proposed by Dutta and Ray [7] for computing "egalitarian solutions". Given a set of players $Q \subseteq [n]$, cost shares are computed iteratively: Find the *most cost-efficient* subset S of the players that have not been assigned a cost share yet. That is, the quotient of the marginal cost for including S divided by $|S|$ is minimal. Then, assign each player in S this quotient as her cost share. If players remain who have not been assigned a cost share yet, start a new iteration.

Before getting back to most cost-efficient subsets in Section 3.2, we generalize Dutta and Ray's idea by making use of a more general *set selection function* σ and *price function* ρ. Specifically, let $Q \subseteq [n]$ be the set of players to be served. For some fixed iteration, let $N \subsetneq Q$ be the subset of players already assigned a cost-share. Then, $\sigma(Q, N)$ selects the players $S \subseteq Q \setminus N$ who are assigned the cost share $\rho(Q, N)$. We require σ and ρ to be *valid*:

Definition 7. *Set selection and price functions σ and ρ are* valid *if, for all $N \subsetneq Q, Q' \subseteq [n]$:*

1. *$\emptyset \neq \sigma(Q, N) \subseteq Q \setminus N$,*
2. *$Q' \subseteq Q$ and $\sigma(Q, N) \subseteq Q' \Longrightarrow \sigma(Q, N) = \sigma(Q', N)$ and $\rho(Q, N) = \rho(Q', N)$,*
3. *$Q' \subseteq Q \Longrightarrow \rho(Q, N) \leq \rho(Q', N)$,*
4. *$0 \leq \rho(Q, N) \leq \rho(Q, N \cup \sigma(Q, N))$.*

Based on valid σ and ρ, we define $Egal_{\sigma, \rho} : \mathbb{Q}^n \to 2^{[n]} \times \mathbb{Q}_{\geq 0}^n$:

Algorithm 1 (Computing Egalitarian Mechanisms $Egal_{\sigma,\rho}(b)$).
Input: valid set selection and price functions σ, ρ; bid vector $\boldsymbol{b} \in \mathbb{Q}^n$
Output: set of served players $Q \in 2^{[n]}$; cost-share vector $\boldsymbol{x} \in \mathbb{Q}^n_{\geq 0}$

1: $Q := [n]$; $N := \emptyset$; $\boldsymbol{x} := 0$
2: **while** $N \neq Q$ **do**
3:     $S := \sigma(Q, N)$, $a := \rho(Q, N)$
4:     $Q := Q \setminus \{i \in S \mid b_i < a\}$
5:     **if** $S \subseteq Q$ **then** $x_i := a$ for all $i \in S$; $N := N \cup S$

Theorem 2 (Corollary of Theorems 5, 6). *Egalitarian mechanisms are CGSP.*

3.1   Efficiency of Egalitarian Mechanisms

Definition 8. *Let $C : 2^{[n]} \to \mathbb{Q}_{\geq 0}$ be a cost function, ρ be a price function, and $\beta > 0$. Then, ρ is called β-average for C if for all $N \subsetneq Q \subseteq [n]$ and all $\emptyset \neq A \subseteq Q \setminus N$, it holds that $\rho(Q, N) \leq \beta \cdot \frac{C(A)}{|A|}$.*

Lemma 3. *Let $C : 2^{[n]} \to \mathbb{Q}_{\geq 0}$ be a cost function and σ and ρ be valid set selection and price functions such that ρ is β-average for C. Moreover, let $A \subseteq [n]$ and $\boldsymbol{b} \in \mathbb{Q}^n$ be a bid vector with $b_i \geq \beta \cdot \frac{C(A)}{|A|}$ for all $i \in A$. Then, $(Q \times x) := Egal_{\sigma,\rho}$ serves at least one player $i \in A$, i.e., $A \cap Q(\boldsymbol{b}) \neq \emptyset$.*

Theorem 3. *Let $C : 2^{[n]} \to \mathbb{Q}_{\geq 0}$ be a non-decreasing cost function and σ and ρ be valid set selection and price functions such that ρ is β-average for C. Then, if $Egal_{\sigma,\rho}$ always recovers at least the actual cost C', it is $(2\beta \cdot H_n)$-EFF.*

Proof. Let $(Q \times x) := Egal_{\sigma,\rho}$ and $\boldsymbol{v} \in \mathbb{Q}^n$ be the true valuation vector. Denote $Q := Q(\boldsymbol{v})$, $\boldsymbol{x} := x(\boldsymbol{v})$. Moreover, let $P \subseteq [n]$ be a set that minimizes optimal social cost, i.e., $P \in \arg\min_{T \subseteq [n]} \{SC_{\boldsymbol{v}}(T)\}$. W.l.o.g., we may assume that $v_i \geq 0$ for all $i \in [n]$ because C is non-decreasing. We have

$$SC'_{\boldsymbol{v}}(Q) \leq \sum_{i \in Q \cap P} x_i + \sum_{i \in Q \setminus P} \underbrace{x_i}_{\leq v_i} + \sum_{i \in [n] \setminus Q} v_i \leq \sum_{i \in Q \cap P} x_i + \sum_{i \in P \setminus Q} v_i + \sum_{i \in [n] \setminus P} v_i,$$

$$\frac{SC'_{\boldsymbol{v}}(Q)}{SC_{\boldsymbol{v}}(P)} \leq \frac{\sum_{i \in Q \cap P} x_i + \sum_{i \in P \setminus Q} v_i + \sum_{i \in [n] \setminus P} v_i}{C(P) + \sum_{i \in [n] \setminus P} v_i} \leq \frac{\sum_{i \in Q \cap P} x_i + \sum_{i \in P \setminus Q} v_i}{C(P)}.$$

The last inequality holds since the left fraction is at least 1. Now, consider the iteration k when for the first time Algorithm 1 decides to accept a player $i \in Q \cap P$ (line 5). Fix all variables just after line 3 in that iteration k and indicate them with a subscript k. We have $x_i = a_k = \rho(Q_k, N_k) \leq \beta \cdot \frac{C(Q \cap P)}{|Q \cap P|}$, because $Q \cap P \subseteq Q_k \setminus N_k$. With the same arguments, for the second player $i \in Q \cap P$, we can bound her cost-share $x_i \leq \beta \cdot \frac{C(Q \cap P)}{|Q \cap P| - 1}$, and so forth. Finally, $\sum_{i \in Q \cap P} x_i \leq \beta \cdot H_{|Q \cap P|} \cdot C(Q \cap P)$.

On the other hand, in $P \setminus Q$, there is at least one player i with $v_i < \beta \cdot \frac{C(P \setminus Q)}{|P \setminus Q|}$. Otherwise, due to Lemma 3, we would have $(P \setminus Q) \cap Q \neq \emptyset$, a contradiction.

Inductively and by the same lemma, for every $j = 1, \ldots, |P \setminus Q| - 1$, there has to be a player $i \in P \setminus Q$ with $v_i < \beta \cdot \frac{C(P \setminus Q)}{|P \setminus Q| - j}$. Finally, $\sum_{i \in P \setminus Q} v_i \leq \beta \cdot H_{|P \setminus Q|} \cdot C(P \setminus Q)$. Since C is non-decreasing, we get

$$\frac{SC'_v(Q)}{SC_v(P)} \leq \frac{\beta \cdot H_{\max\{|Q \cap P|, |P \setminus Q|\}} \cdot (C(Q \cap P) + C(P \setminus Q))}{C(P)} \leq 2\beta \cdot H_n \, . \quad \square$$

3.2 Most Cost-Efficient Set Selection

Definition 9. *Let $C : 2^{[n]} \to \mathbb{Q}_{\geq 0}$ be a cost function. The most cost-efficient set selection function σ_C and its corresponding price function ρ_C are defined as*

$$\sigma_C(Q, N) := \text{lexicographic max in } \arg\min_{\emptyset \neq T \subseteq Q \setminus N} \left\{ \frac{C(N \cup T) - C(N)}{|T|} \right\},$$

$$\rho_C(Q, N) := \min_{\emptyset \neq T \subseteq Q \setminus N} \left\{ \frac{C(N \cup T) - C(N)}{|T|} \right\}.$$

Lemma 4. *For any cost function $C : 2^{[n]} \to \mathbb{Q}_{\geq 0}$, σ_C and ρ_C are valid. If C is subadditive then ρ_C is also 1-average for C.*

Theorem 4 (Corollary of Theorem 3 and Lemma 4). *For any costs $C : 2^{[n]} \to \mathbb{Q}_{\geq 0}$, $Egal_{\sigma_C, \rho_C}$ is CGSP and 1-BB. If C is both non-decreasing and subadditive, then $Egal_{\sigma_C, \rho_C}$ is also $2H_n$-EFF.*

We remark here that already "sequential stand-alone mechanisms" [15] achieve CGSP and 1-BB for non-decreasing cost. Yet, they are only $\Omega(n)$-EFF in general.

Clearly, evaluating σ_C can take exponentially many steps (in n). Furthermore, evaluating C may be computationally hard. In Section 5 we thus study how to pick "suitable" cost-efficient subsets in polynomial time. We conclude by showing that our EFF bound is tight up to a factor of 2.

Lemma 5. *For the cost function $C : 2^{[n]} \to \mathbb{Q}_{\geq 0}$ with $C(T) = 1$ for all $\emptyset \neq T \subseteq [n]$, the mechanism $Egal_{\sigma_C, \rho_C}$ is no better than H_n-EFF.*

Lemma 6. *For any $\gamma > 1$, there is a non-decreasing cost function $C : 2^{[4]} \to \mathbb{Q}_{\geq 0}$ for which the efficiency of mechanism $Egal_{\sigma_C, \rho_C}$ is no better than γ.*

4 Acyclic Mechanisms and CGSP

By introducing acyclic mechanisms, Mehta et al. [14] gave a framework for constructing WGSP mechanisms. We prove that acyclic mechanisms are in fact CGSP, and thus remarkably stronger. That egalitarian mechanisms are CGSP will follow from the observation that they are acyclic.

An acyclic mechanism $Acyc_{\xi, \tau} : \mathbb{Q}^n \to 2^{[n]} \times \mathbb{Q}_{\geq 0}^n$ makes use of a cost-sharing method ξ and an *offer function* $\tau : 2^{[n]} \to \mathbb{Q}_{\geq 0}^n$ which specifies a non-negative offer time $\tau_i(Q)$ for every subset $Q \subseteq [n]$ and every player $i \in Q$. Mehta et al. [14] showed that if ξ and ρ satisfy a certain validity requirement, $Acyc_{\xi, \tau}$ is WGSP.

Algorithm 2 (Computing Acyclic Mechanisms $Acyc_{\xi,\tau}(\boldsymbol{b})$).
Input: cost-sharing method ξ; valid offer function τ; bid vector $\boldsymbol{b} \in \mathbb{Q}^n$
Output: set of players $Q \in 2^{[n]}$, vector of cost shares $\boldsymbol{x} \in \mathbb{Q}^n_{\geq 0}$
1: $Q := [n]$
2: **while** $\exists i \in Q$ with $b_i < \xi_i(Q)$ **do**
3:    Let $j \in \arg\min_{i \in Q}\{\tau_i(Q) \mid b_i < \xi_i(Q)\}$ (use arbitrary tie breaking rule)
4:    $Q := Q \setminus \{j\}$
5: $\boldsymbol{x} := \xi(Q)$

Theorem 5. *Acyclic mechanisms are CGSP.*

Theorem 6. *Egalitarian mechanisms are acyclic.*

Theorem 6 is based on the fact that Algorithm 2 computes $Egal_{\sigma,\rho}$ when given the cost-sharing method $\xi^{\sigma,\rho}$ and offer function $\tau^{\sigma,\rho}$ as defined by Algorithm 3.

Algorithm 3 (Computing $\xi^{\sigma,\rho}(Q)$ and $\tau^{\sigma,\rho}(Q)$).
Input: valid set selection and price functions σ, ρ; set of players $Q \subseteq [n]$
Output: cost-sharing vector $\boldsymbol{\xi} \in \mathbb{Q}^n_{\geq 0}$; offer-time vector $\boldsymbol{\tau} \in \mathbb{Q}^n_{\geq 0}$
1: $N := \emptyset$; $\boldsymbol{\xi} := 0$; $\boldsymbol{\tau} := 0$
2: **while** $N \neq Q$ **do**
3:    $S := \sigma(Q, N)$, $a := \rho(Q, N)$
4:    $\xi_i := a$ and $\tau_i := 1 + \max_{j \in Q}\{\tau_j\}$ for all $i \in S$; $N := N \cup S$

We remark that the mechanisms given by Devanur et. al. [6] are not just acyclic (see [14]) but also egalitarian. Using the terminology as in [6], they could be computed by Algorithm 1 by letting $\sigma(Q, N)$ be the next set that "goes tight" after all players in N have been "frozen" and all in $[n] \setminus Q$ have been dropped.

5   A Framework for Polynomial Time Computation

In this section, we show how to solve all of the service provider's tasks in polynomial time by using egalitarian mechanisms with a set selection function that picks the most cost-efficient set *w.r.t. costs of approximate solutions*. Formally, a (cost) minimization problem is a tuple $\Pi = (D, \boldsymbol{S} = (S_I)_{I \in D}, \boldsymbol{f} = (f_I)_{I \in D})$, where D is the set of problem instances (domain) such that for any instance $I \in D$, S_I is the set of feasible solutions, and $f_I : S_I \to \mathbb{Q}_{\geq 0}$ is a function mapping any solution to its cost.

We write a cost-sharing problem as $\Phi = (\Pi, \text{INST})$, where $\text{INST} : 2^{[n]} \to D$ denotes the function mapping a subset of the n players to the induced instance of Π. In particular, Φ implicitly defines the optimal cost $C : 2^{[n]} \to \mathbb{Q}_{\geq 0}$ by $C(T) := \min_{Z \in S_{\text{INST}(T)}}\{f(Z)\}$. Moreover, for any algorithm ALG that computes feasible solutions for Π, we define $C_{\text{ALG}} : 2^{[n]} \to \mathbb{Q}_{\geq 0}$, $C_{\text{ALG}}(T) := f(\text{ALG}(\text{INST}(T)))$.

Resorting to approximate solutions does, of course, not yet remedy the need to iterate through all available subsets in order to pick the most cost-efficient one. The basic idea therefore consists of using an (approximation) algorithm ALG that is *monotonic* (see, e.g., [16]): Seemingly favorable changes to the input must not worsen the algorithm's performance. In the problems considered here, every player is endowed with a size (e.g., processing time in the case of scheduling) and reducing a player's size must not increase the cost of the algorithm's solution. We can then simply number the players in the order of their size such that $C_{\mathrm{ALG}}(\min_{|U|} T) \le C_{\mathrm{ALG}}(U)$ for all $U \subseteq T \subseteq [n]$. Finding the most cost-efficient set then only requires iterating through all possible cardinalities.

We generalize this basic idea such that only a (polynomial-time computable) monotonic bound C_{mono} on C_{ALG} is needed whereas ALG itself does not need to be monotonic any more.

Definition 10. *Let $\Phi = (\Pi, \mathrm{INST})$ be a cost-sharing problem. A tuple $R := (\mathrm{ALG}, C_{\mathrm{mono}})$ is a β-relaxation for Φ if ALG is an approximation algorithm for Π and $C_{\mathrm{mono}} : 2^{[n]} \to \mathbb{Q}_{\ge 0}$ is a cost function such that the following holds:*

- *For all $T \subseteq [n]$: $C_{\mathrm{ALG}}(T) \le C_{\mathrm{mono}}(T) \le \beta \cdot C(T)$.*
- *For all $U \subseteq T \subseteq [n]$: $C_{\mathrm{mono}}(\min_{|U|} T) \le C_{\mathrm{mono}}(U)$.*

Note that C_{mono} does not necessarily have to be subadditive (as required for $2H_n$-EFF in Section 3), even if C is. Thus, some additional care is needed.

Given a β-relaxation $R := (\mathrm{ALG}, C_{\mathrm{mono}})$, we define set selection and price functions σ_R and ρ_R recursively as follows. For $N \subsetneq Q \subseteq [n]$, let $\xi^{\sigma_R, \rho_R}(N)$ as computed by Algorithm 3. Furthermore, let

$$k := \max\left\{ \arg\min_{i \in [|Q \setminus N|]} \left\{ \frac{C_{\mathrm{mono}}(N \cup MIN_i(Q \setminus N)) - \sum_{i \in N} \xi_i^{\sigma_R, \rho_R}(N)}{i}, \frac{C_{\mathrm{mono}}(MIN_i(Q \setminus N))}{i} \right\} \right\},$$

and $S := MIN_k(Q \setminus N)$. Then, $\sigma_R(Q, N) := S$ and

$$\rho_R(Q, N) := \min\left\{ \frac{C_{\mathrm{mono}}(N \cup S) - \sum_{i \in N} \xi_i^{\sigma_R, \rho_R}(N)}{k}, \frac{C_{\mathrm{mono}}(S)}{k} \right\}.$$

Note that this recursion is well-defined. Computing $\sigma_R(Q, N)$ and $\rho_R(Q, N)$ requires $\xi^{\sigma_R, \rho_R}(N)$ for which only $\sigma_R(N, \cdot)$ and $\rho_R(N, \cdot)$ is needed (unless $N = \emptyset$). Yet, $N \subsetneq Q$ by assumption.

Lemma 7. *Let $R = (\mathrm{ALG}, C_{\mathrm{mono}})$ be a β-relaxation for some cost-sharing problem Φ. Then σ_R and ρ_R are valid, and ρ_R is β-average for C.*

To also compute a solution for the instance induced by the players selected by $Egal_{\sigma_R, \rho_R}$, we need:

Definition 11. *Let $\Phi = (\Pi, \mathrm{INST})$ with $\Pi = (D, \boldsymbol{S}, \boldsymbol{f})$ be a cost-sharing problem. Then, Φ is called mergable if for all disjoint $T, U \subseteq [n]$, $T \cap U = \emptyset$, and for all $X \in S_{\mathrm{INST}(T)}$ and $Y \in S_{\mathrm{INST}(U)}$, there is a $Z \in S_{\mathrm{INST}(T \cup U)}$ with $f(Z) \le f(X) + f(Y)$. We denote this operation by $Z = X \oplus Y$.*

Based on σ_R and ρ_R, Algorithm 4 solves all of the service provider's tasks, including computing a feasible solution of the underlying optimization problem. We address the running time afterwards.

Algorithm 4 (Computing Egalitarian Mechanisms via β-Relaxations).
Input: β-relaxation $R = (\text{ALG}, C_{\text{mono}})$; bid vector $\boldsymbol{b} \in \mathbb{Q}^n$
Output: player set $Q \in 2^{[n]}$, cost-share vector $\boldsymbol{x} \in \mathbb{Q}_{\geq 0}^n$, solution $Z \in S_{\text{INST}(Q)}$

1:   $\boldsymbol{x} := 0$, $Q := [n]$, $N := \emptyset$, $Z :=$ "empty solution"
2: **while** $N \neq Q$ **do**
3:      $S := \sigma_R(Q, N)$; $a := \rho_R(Q, N)$
4:      $Q := Q \setminus \{i \in S \mid b_i < a\}$
5:      **if** $S \subseteq N$ **then**
6:        $Z := \begin{cases} \text{ALG}(\text{INST}(N \cup S)) & \text{if } C_{\text{mono}}(N \cup S) - \sum_{i \in N} x_i \leq C_{\text{mono}}(S) \\ Z \oplus \text{ALG}(\text{INST}(S)) & \text{otherwise} \end{cases}$
7:        $N := N \cup S$; $x_i := a$ for all $i \in S$

Lemma 8. *Let $R = (\text{ALG}, C_{\text{mono}})$ be a β-relaxation for a mergable cost-sharing problem Φ.*

1. *At the end of each iteration of Algorithm 4, it holds that $\boldsymbol{x} = \xi^{\sigma_R, \rho_R}(N)$.*
2. *Line 3 of Algorithm 4 needs at most $2n$ evaluations of C_{mono}.*
3. *The mechanism computed by Algorithm 4 is β-BB.*

Theorem 7 (Corollary of Lemmata 7, 8). *Let Φ be a mergable cost-sharing problem having a β-relaxation $(\text{ALG}, C_{\text{mono}})$. Then the mechanism computed by Algorithm 4 is CGSP, β-BB, and $(2\beta \cdot H_n)$-EFF. Moreover, Algorithm 4 evaluates C_{mono} for no more than $2n^2$ subsets of $[n]$, makes no more than n (direct) calls to ALG, and the number of merge operations is no more than n.*

6 Applications

We use three approaches for obtaining β-relaxations that are polynomial-time computable in the *succinct representation* of the cost-sharing problem plus the bid vector: Monotonic approximation algorithms (e.g., Theorem 8), a non-monotonic approximation algorithm with a monotonic bound C_{mono} (Theorem 9), and optimal costs that are monotonic and polynomial-time computable (discussed at the end of this section).

A makespan cost-sharing problem is *succinctly represented* by a tuple $(\boldsymbol{p}, \boldsymbol{\varsigma})$ where $\boldsymbol{p} \in \mathbb{N}^n$ contains the processing times $p_1 \leq \cdots \leq p_n$ of the n jobs, and $\boldsymbol{\varsigma} \in \mathbb{N}^m$ contains the speeds of the m machines. If $\boldsymbol{p} = 1$ ($\boldsymbol{\varsigma} = 1$), jobs (machines) are *identical*. Each player owns exactly one job. For any set of served players $S \subseteq [n]$, $C(S)$ is the value of a minimum-makespan schedule for S.

A bin packing cost-sharing problem is succinctly represented by a vector of object sizes $\boldsymbol{s} \in \mathbb{Q}_{\geq 0}^n$ with $s_1 \leq \cdots \leq s_n \leq 1$. The capacity of a single bin is 1. Each player owns exactly one object. For any set of players $S \subseteq [n]$, $C(S)$ is the minimum number of bins needed to serve S.

Note here that we assume that each player is given a unique number $\in [n]$ in advance (outside the scope of Algorithm 4) and that players are sorted according to the respective monotonicity criterion.

526   Y. Bleischwitz, B. Monien, and F. Schoppmann

Lemma 9. *Any bin packing or makespan cost-sharing problem $\Phi = (\Pi, \text{INST})$ is mergable in time $O(n)$. Moreover, INST is computable in linear time (in the size of the succinct representation of Φ).*

First, we consider identical-machine makespan cost-sharing problems. Their succinct representation is $(\boldsymbol{p}, m)$. The LPT (longest processing time first) heuristic [8] is known to be a $\frac{4m-1}{3m}$-approximation algorithm for this problem. It processes the jobs in decreasing order and assigns each job to the machine on which its completion time will be smallest. Its running time is $O(n \cdot \log n)$ for the sorting phase and $O(n \cdot \log m)$ for the job assignment phase. We show that LPT is monotonic w.r.t. processing times:

Lemma 10. *Let $\boldsymbol{p}, \boldsymbol{p}' \in \mathbb{N}^n$, $i \in [n]$, $p_i > p'_i$, and $\boldsymbol{p}_{-i} = \boldsymbol{p}'_{-i}$. Then it holds that $f(\text{LPT}(\boldsymbol{p}, m)) \geq f(\text{LPT}(\boldsymbol{p}', m))$.*

Theorem 8 (Corollary of Lemma 10). *For any identical-machine makespan cost-sharing problem with succinct representation $(\boldsymbol{p}, m)$, where $p_1 \leq \cdots \leq p_n$, it holds that $(\text{LPT}, C_{\text{LPT}})$ is a $\frac{4m-1}{3m}$-relaxation and Algorithm 4 runs in time $O(n^3 \cdot \log m)$.*

Besides the previous result, we show how to adapt the PTAS (for identical machines) by Hochbaum and Shmoys [12]. The approach is different to before: Not the PTAS itself is monotonic but a bound computed inside the algorithm.

The basic idea of the PTAS is a reduction to bin packing: Given processing times $\boldsymbol{p} \in \mathbb{N}^n$, binary search is employed in order to find a makespan d such that the bin packing instance $\frac{\boldsymbol{p}}{d}$ does *not* need more than m bins of size $(1 + \varepsilon)$, whereas the bin packing instance $\frac{\boldsymbol{p}}{d-1}$ *does* need more than m bins. Specifically, the PTAS makes use of an ϵ-dual approximation algorithm BPDUAL$_\varepsilon$ for the bin packing problem (see [12], pp.149–151). BPDUAL$_\varepsilon$ outputs solutions that are *dual feasible*; this means that BPDUAL$_\varepsilon$ may use bins of size $(1 + \epsilon)$.

Now, for any bin packing instance $\boldsymbol{s} \in \mathbb{Q}_{>0}^n$, let $S_{\boldsymbol{s}}^* \supseteq S_{\boldsymbol{s}}$ be the set of all dual-feasible solutions and $f_{\boldsymbol{s}}^* : S_{\boldsymbol{s}}^* \to \mathbb{N}$ be a function mapping each dual-feasible solution to its cost, i.e., the number of used bins. We define $g_{\boldsymbol{s}}^* : S_{\boldsymbol{s}}^* \to \mathbb{N}$, $g_{\boldsymbol{s}}^*(Z) := \max\{f_{\boldsymbol{s}}^*(Z), \lceil \sum_{i \in [n]} s_i \rceil\}$. Hence, the crucial property of g^* is to guarantee that $g_{\boldsymbol{s}}^*$ is never less than the number of bins needed for a feasible optimal solution, i.e., when bins have capacity 1. We show that g^* is monotonic.

Lemma 11. *Let $\boldsymbol{s}, \boldsymbol{s}' \in \mathbb{Q}_{\geq 0}^n$ be two vectors of object sizes, $i \in [n]$, $s_i > s'_i$, and $\boldsymbol{s}_{-i} = \boldsymbol{s}'_{-i}$. Then $b := g_{\boldsymbol{s}}^*(\text{BPDUAL}_\epsilon(\boldsymbol{s})) \geq g_{\boldsymbol{s}'}^*(\text{BPDUAL}_\epsilon(\boldsymbol{s}')) =: b'$.*

Our crucial modification of the PTAS is as follows: Letting $\boldsymbol{s} := \frac{\boldsymbol{p}}{d}$, we use the check $g_{\boldsymbol{s}}^*(\text{BPDUAL}_\varepsilon(\boldsymbol{s})) \leq m$ in the binary search (instead of testing $f_{\boldsymbol{s}}^*$ as in the original PTAS). Moreover, we let $lower_\varepsilon(\boldsymbol{p})$ denote the minimum d for which this check evaluates to true and let HS$_\varepsilon$ denote the adapted PTAS. One can easily verify that $lower_\varepsilon(\boldsymbol{p})$ is a lower bound on the optimal makespan and $(1 + \varepsilon) \cdot lower_\varepsilon(\boldsymbol{p})$ is an upper bound on the schedule found by HS$_\varepsilon$. Moreover, $lower_\varepsilon(\boldsymbol{p})$ is computed within HS$_\varepsilon$ in polynomial time because monotonicity of g^* ensures that indeed the minimum d is found by the binary search.

Theorem 9 (Corollary of Lemma 11). *For any identical-machine makespan cost-sharing problem with succinct representation $(\boldsymbol{p}, m)$, where $p_1 \leq \cdots \leq p_n$, let $C_{\mathrm{mono}}(A) := (1 + \varepsilon) \cdot lower_\varepsilon(\mathrm{INST}(A))$. Then, $(\mathrm{HS}_\epsilon, C_{\mathrm{mono}})$ is a $(1 + \varepsilon)$-relaxation and Algorithm 4 runs in time $O(n^{2 + \frac{1}{\varepsilon^2}} \cdot \log \sum_{i \in [n]} p_i)$.*

Finally, we also obtain 2-relaxations for bin packing and general makespan cost-sharing problems:

Lemma 12. *For any bin packing cost-sharing problem with succinct representation $\boldsymbol{s}$, there is a 2-relaxation for C and Algorithm 4 runs in time $O(n^3 \cdot \log n)$.*

Theorem 10. *For any makespan cost-sharing problem with succinct representation $(\boldsymbol{p}, \varsigma)$, there is a 2-relaxation for C and Algorithm 4 runs in time $O(n^3 \cdot \log m \cdot \log \sum_{i \in [n]} p_i)$.*

There are several mergable scheduling problems for which optimal costs are monotonic and computable in polynomial time. For instance, for any identical-job makespan cost-sharing problem with succinct representation (n, ς), it holds that $(\mathrm{LPT}, C_{\mathrm{LPT}})$ is a 1-relaxation and Algorithm 4 runs in time $O(n^3 \cdot \log m)$. In the following, we give a selection of further problems (taken from [4] and using the classification scheme introduced by Graham et al. [9]). We restrict our attention to the cases in which only one of the properties p_i, w_i (weight), and r_i (release date) is variable and let the others be fixed with $p_i = 1$, $w_i = 1$, and $r_i = 0$. We get that 1-relaxations exist for:

- Variable processing times: $Q|\mathrm{pmtn}|C_{\max}$, $Q||\sum_i C_i$, $Q|\mathrm{pmtn}|\sum_i C_i$
- Variable weights: $P||\sum_i w_i C_i$, $P|\mathrm{pmtn}|\sum_i w_i C_i$
- Variable release dates: $Q|\mathrm{pmtn}|C_{\max}$

The result for $Q||\sum_i C_i$ especially implies 1-BB for $1||\sum_i C_i$. This is a drastic improvement over Moulin mechanisms, since no cross-monotonic cost-sharing method can be better than $\frac{n+1}{2}$-BB [3].

7 Conclusion and Future Work

The pivotal point of this work is our new modeling assumption on coalition formation. We believe that CGSP is a viable replacement for the often too limiting GSP requirement. Besides this novel structural property, we consider the main asset of our work to be threefold: i) Egalitarian mechanisms; showing existence of CGSP, 1-BB, and $2H_n$-EFF mechanisms for any non-decreasing subadditive costs. ii) Our framework for polynomial-time computation that reduces constructing CGSP, $O(1)$-BB, and $O(\log n)$-EFF mechanisms to finding monotonic approximation algorithms. iii) Showing that acyclic mechanisms are CGSP and thus remarkably stronger than was known before.

An immediate issue left often by our work is, of course, to find more applications of our polynomial-time framework. For instance, it is easy to see that (rooted) Steiner tree cost-sharing problems are mergable and their costs non-decreasing and subadditive; but do they allow for a β-relaxation?

References

1. Bleischwitz, Y., Monien, B.: Fair cost-sharing methods for scheduling jobs on parallel machines. In: Calamoneri, T., Finocchi, I., Italiano, G.F. (eds.) CIAC 2006. LNCS, vol. 3998, pp. 175–186. Springer, Heidelberg (2006)
2. Bleischwitz, Y., Monien, B., Schoppmann, F., Tiemann, K.: The power of two prices: Beyond cross-monotonicity. In: Kučera, L., Kučera, A. (eds.) MFCS 2007. LNCS, vol. 4708, pp. 657–668. Springer, Heidelberg (2007)
3. Brenner, J., Schäfer, G.: Cost sharing methods for makespan and completion time scheduling. In: Proc. of the 24th International Symposium on Theoretical Aspects of Computer Science. LNCS, vol. 4393, pp. 670–681 (2007)
4. Bruckner, P.: Scheduling Algorithms. Springer, Heidelberg (1995)
5. Chawla, S., Roughgarden, T., Sundararajan, M.: Optimal cost-sharing mechanisms for Steiner forest problems. In: Spirakis, P.G., Mavronicolas, M., Kontogiannis, S.C. (eds.) WINE 2006. LNCS, vol. 4286, pp. 112–123. Springer, Heidelberg (2006)
6. Devanur, N.R., Mihail, M., Vazirani, V.V.: Strategyproof cost-sharing mechanisms for set cover and facility location games. Decision Support Systems 39(1), 11–22 (2005)
7. Dutta, B., Ray, D.: A concept of egalitarianism under participation constraints. Econometrica 57(3), 615–635 (1989)
8. Graham, R.: Bounds on multiprocessing timing anomalies. SIAM Journal of Applied Mathematics 17(2), 416–429 (1969)
9. Graham, R., Lawler, E., Lenstra, J., Rinnooy Kan, A.: Optimization and approximation in deterministic sequencing and scheduling: A survey. Annals of Discrete Mathematics 5, 287–326 (1979)
10. Green, J., Laffont, J.: Characterizations of satisfactory mechanisms for the revelation of preferences for public goods. Econometrica 45, 427–438 (1977)
11. Gupta, A., Könemann, J., Leonardi, S., Ravi, R., Schäfer, G.: An efficient cost-sharing mechanism for the prize-collecting Steiner forest problem. In: Proc. of the 18th Annual ACM-SIAM Symposium on Discrete Algorithms (2007)
12. Hochbaum, D., Shmoys, D.: Using dual approximation algorithms for scheduling problems: theoretical and practical results. Journal of the ACM 34(1), 144–162 (1987)
13. Immorlica, N., Mahdian, M., Mirrokni, V.: Limitations of cross-monotonic cost sharing schemes. In: Proc. of the 16th Annual ACM-SIAM Symposium on Discrete Algorithms, pp. 602–611 (2005)
14. Mehta, A., Roughgarden, T., Sundararajan, M.: Beyond Moulin mechanisms. In: Proc. of the 8th ACM Conference on Electronic Commerce, pp. 1–10 (2007)
15. Moulin, H.: Incremental cost sharing: Characterization by coalition strategyproofness. Social Choice and Welfare 16(2), 279–320 (1999)
16. Murgolo, F.D.: Anomalous behavior in bin packing algorithms. Discrete Applied Mathematics 21(3), 229–243 (1988)
17. Penna, P., Ventre, C.: The algorithmic structure of group strategyproof budget-balanced cost-sharing mechanisms. In: Durand, B., Thomas, W. (eds.) STACS 2006. LNCS, vol. 3884, pp. 337–348. Springer, Heidelberg (2006)
18. Roughgarden, T., Sundararajan, M.: New trade-offs in cost-sharing mechanisms. In: Proc. of the 38th ACM Symposium on Theory of Computing, pp. 79–88 (2006)
19. Roughgarden, T., Sundararajan, M.: Optimal efficiency guarantees for network design mechanisms. In: Proc. of the 12th Conference on Integer Programming and Combinatorial Optimization, pp. 469–483 (2007)

Ad Auction Design and User Experience

Zoë Abrams[1] and Michael Schwarz[2]

[1] Yahoo!, Inc., 2821 Mission College Blvd., Santa Clara, CA, USA
za@yahoo-inc.com
[2] Yahoo! Research, 1950 University Ave., Berkeley, CA, USA
mschwarz@yahoo-inc.com

Abstract. When users click on poor quality advertisements, there is a hidden cost to the search engine due to the user dissatisfaction (for instance, users are less likely to click on ads in the future). We describe how to incorporate hidden costs into the GSP auction for internet ads such that it is in an advertiser's self interest to create a user experience that maximizes efficiency.

1 Introduction

In sponsored search, the behavior of users in the long run is endogenous: users continue to click on advertisements only if on average the value that a user derives from clicking on ads exceeds the cost of time required to click and to evaluate the contents of the offer. Sometimes, the value of a click to a user may be a large negative number (e.g. an unscrupulous advertiser may mislead an unsuspecting user to infect his computer with spyware).

We consider that a user's future propensity to click on ads is influenced by his experience with past clicks. An ad with disappointing quality of landing page imposes a negative externality on the search engine because the future stream of revenue from a user is reduced by some amount (some of the future clicks are lost since a disappointed user may learn to ignore ads). Of course, the externality may also be positive. A good experience with an ad may train users to pay more attention to other ads. We will refer to this externality as a hidden cost. Obviously, if an ad's hidden cost is greater than its bid, a search engine should never show the ad. How should a search engine incorporate hidden costs into an auction mechanism?

Our main contribution is the design of a mechanism that encourages advertisers to create an experience for users that maximizes efficiency.

A classic method for encouraging or discouraging certain behavior towards the social optimum is the Pigovian tax [12]. Pigovian taxes charge (or subsidize) an agent its *externality* from the transaction (i.e. the effect on agents that occurs outside of the transaction). A Pigovian tax causes an agent to internalize the externality that he imposes by his actions on other agents, creating an incentive for individual agents to take actions that maximize social welfare.

The concept of pricing externalities to encourage social welfare is one of the key insights of economic theory [14,3,2]. For instance, the celebrated VCG mechanism [16,5,8] builds on this idea.

X. Deng and F.C. Graham (Eds.): WINE 2007, LNCS 4858, pp. 529–534, 2007.
© Springer-Verlag Berlin Heidelberg 2007

A relevant example of Pigovian taxation is the market for renting space at a shopping mall. That market has much in common with the virtual "real estate" allocated for ads on a search result page. The shopping mall owner, much like a search engine, tends to allocate space to the stores that value space the most. The auctions for sponsored search considered in the academic literature allocate space based on the advertiser's willingness to pay per click, sometimes adjusted by ad clickabilty (the ads are ranked based on the product of the bid per click and the probability the ad is clicked when it is seen). The current mechanism charges higher prices for ads with low clickability but does not charge a higher price for ads with high hidden cost. No model in the literature that we know of incorporates hidden costs: usually advertisement specific information is the expected clickthrough rate [15,6,1,11,10,13,9]. In the case of shopping malls, reputable stores draw in customer traffic to the shopping mall, thus imposing a long term positive externality on other tenants in the mall. These externalities are huge, as apparent from the contracts between stores and mall operators: the rent paid by premium brand stores may be a few times lower than the rent paid by less reputable tenants [7]. This is because the shopping mall uses pricing to attract tenants that will impose a positive externality on other tenants by creating more traffic. Exactly the same logic applies in sponsored search. To foster efficiency, a search engine should encourage ads that give users a positive experience because it makes users more likely to click on other ads, thus enhancing the value of the virtual real estate. However, at this time, the auctions for sponsored search do not explicitly take into account the hidden costs that are created by advertisers and the literature on sponsored search does not address hidden costs. This causes a large inefficiency if the role of hidden costs in sponsored search is comparable to the role of externalities in an off line retail environment. The experience of shopping malls is not fully transferable to the sponsored search environment, because the rental agreements for shopping mall space are negotiated, while the ad space has to be sold via auction due to fluidity and the high volume of small transactions in this market. Also, the nature and volume of user traffic enables search engines to effectively measure the hidden cost of an advertisement. We show how to incorporate hidden costs in the standard pricing mechanism for ad auctions in a manner that fosters efficiency.

2 Hidden Cost GSP

We begin by describing the environment and then proceed to describe an auction mechanism that incorporate hidden costs into pricing. We assume that an advertiser can make choices about his offerings that influence the value per click for the advertiser and the user experience. For instance, an advertiser may choose to make a misleading offer that leads to poor user experience but higher profit or a more honest offer that may be somewhat less profitable. An advertiser may also choose the price of the product that he sells. The lower the price, the better the user experience. We denote the choice of the landing page for advertiser i by q_i (q_i may belong to a finite set, for instance a binary choice of being explicit or not being explicit about the shipping charges, or it can be a continuous variable such as the price of a good or the cost of shipping).

The search engine allocates positions on a search result page to advertisers. We assume that the number of clicks that an ad receives depends only on its position. The number of clicks in position j is α_j. Ads in higher positions receive more clicks so that $\alpha_k \geq \alpha_{k+1}$. The value that an advertiser derives per click is denoted by s_i. The value per click may depend on the advertiser's choice of q and can be viewed as a function $s_i(q_i)$. The private values per click for each advertiser are denoted with the set s, indexed by value so that $s_k \geq s_{k+1}$. Let r_i be the rank of advertiser i (not necessarily the same as their value index), and K be the total number of positions on the screen, where ads can be displayed. The payoff of an advertiser is the number of clicks that an advertiser receives multiplied by the value per click minus the total cost that an advertiser pays for clicks. That is, *advertiser payoff* $= s_i(q_i)\alpha_{r_i} - payment$.

We assume that an advertiser's choice of q imposes an externality on the search engine's long term health. The hidden cost per click is denoted by $h_i = h(q_i)$. The hidden cost can be thought of as a loss in future revenues due to the user's reduction in propensity to click caused by clicking on an ad of advertiser i. With this interpretation, a search engine can statistically infer a hidden cost of an ad without examining the contents of an advertiser's offer. In light of this, our model assumes that hidden costs are common knowledge for both the advertiser and the search engine. The efficient advertisement quality, that is beneficial to the search engine but gives equal weight to the cost for the advertiser i, is $q_i^* = \arg\max_q s_i(q) - h(q)$. We design a mechanism that (i) for a given vector of offers **q** orders ads efficiently (ii) incentivizes advertisers to make the efficient choice of offerings q_i^*. More formally,

Definition 1. *Efficiency with hidden costs.* *For ranks and qualities $r_i, q_i, \forall i \in I$, efficiency is $\sum_i (s_i(q_i) - h(q_i))\alpha_{r_i}$.*

The generalized second price auction (GSP) is defined in [6,15]. We describe it here for completeness. Given a set of bids b_i and clickabilities c_i, $\forall i \in I$, advertisers are ranked according to their bid times clickability and charged the smallest amount necessary to maintain their position. If all advertisers have identical clickability, i.e. $c_i = c$ for every advertiser, then advertisers are ranked according to their bids and charged the bid of the advertiser ranked immediately below. Note that the GSP design does not penalize advertisers with high hidden costs and thus does not lead to an efficient outcome in an environment with hidden costs. Here we describe a modification of GSP that yields an efficient outcome (in the sense of the above definition). To keep notation as simple as possible we will assume the clickability values are all 1.

Definition 2. *Hidden Cost GSP: Mechanism $\mathcal{M}'$.* *Auction $\mathcal{M}'$ on bids and qualities $b_i, q_i, \forall i \in I$ is as follows:*

1. $\forall i \in I$, $b_i' = b_i - h_i$.
2. *Run the generalized second price (GSP) auction on b_i'.*

3. $\forall i \in I$, add h_i to the price per click of bidder i. Leave the ranking from GSP in Step 2 unchanged.

Mechanism $\mathcal{M}'$ differs from GSP. It subtracts and adds hidden costs before and after (respectively), running GSP. Note that the environment described here is different from the standard models for sponsored search environments [13,10,15,6] because an advertiser controls two input values to the mechanism, b_i and q_i. Despite these differences, $\mathcal{M}'$ maintains many of the attractive properties of the GSP auction, namely there exists an equilibrium solution that has maximum efficiency. Also like in GSP, the bid is a tight upper bound on an advertiser's payment per click in the mechanism $\mathcal{M}'$.

Theorem 1. *Mechanism $\mathcal{M}'$ implements an efficient outcome.*

To prove Theorem 1, we start out by defining VCG and proving some properties of the VCG solution. We then draw conclusions about the GSP auction based on previous work relating it to VCG. Finally, the properties of GSP are used to prove properties of the mechanism $\mathcal{M}'$.

2.1 VCG for Sponsored Search

We denote the total VCG payment for the advertiser ranked k_{th} highest in s with $t_k^{(s,\alpha)}$. Let r be a ranking function such that $r(u,s)$ is the rank of value u if it were to be inserted into the set s. Similarly, $r^{-1}(r,s)$ is the value at rank r in vector s. We prove the following property of the VCG outcome:

Lemma 1. *For any set of values V, $argmax_{v \in V}(v \cdot \alpha_{r(v,s)} - t_{r(v,s)}^{(s+v,\alpha)}) = max_{v \in V} v$. In words, given a choice of values per click, an advertiser's utility in the VCG outcome is highest if they choose the highest value per click.*

Proof. First, we show that for the VCG outcome, the higher an advertiser's value, the larger their utility. By definition, $s_k - s_{k+1} \geq 0$. Multiplying by α_k and adding $s_{k+1}\alpha_{k+1} - t_{k+1}^{s,\alpha}$ to both sides, we see that the utility of the advertiser with the kth largest value is larger than the utility of the advertiser with the $k+1^{th}$ largest value.

Take two potential values, $u > w$ for an advertiser i. Let x be the value of the advertiser at rank $r(w,s)$ in the set of values $s+u$ (this is analogous to taking the value of the advertiser ranked immediately above w in $s+w$). For conciseness, $\Delta_{\alpha_k} = \alpha_k - \alpha_{k-1}$. Using value u gives utility

$$u\alpha_{r(u,s)} - \sum_{k=P+1}^{k=r(u,s)} \Delta_{\alpha_k} r^{-1}(k-1, s+u) \geq x\alpha_{r(w,s)} - \sum_{k=P+1}^{k=r(w,s)} \Delta_{\alpha_k} r^{-1}(k-1, s+u).$$

Since both w and u are ranked higher than any value of k in the summation,

$$\sum_{k=P+1}^{k=r(w,s)} \Delta_{\alpha_k} r^{-1}(k-1, s+u) = \sum_{k=P+1}^{k=r(w,s)} \Delta_{\alpha_k} r^{-1}(k-1, s+w).$$

Because w is ranked lower than x in the set of values $s + w$,

$$x\alpha_{r(w,s)} - \sum_{k=P+1}^{k=r(w,s)} \Delta_{\alpha_k} r^{-1}(k-1, s+u) \geq w\alpha_{r(w,s)} - \sum_{k=P+1}^{k=r(w,s)} \Delta_{\alpha_k} r^{-1}(k-1, s+w).$$

Combining the inequalities, we see that the larger value u brings higher utility in VCG than the lower value w.   □

We define $b(s, \alpha, u)$ to be $\frac{t^{s,\alpha}_{r(u,s-u)}}{\alpha_{r(u,s-u)}}$. The function b relies on the rankings and pricing that VCG outputs (based on s and α).

2.2   Relating VCG to GSP

The following Lemma restates the results from [6], which we will use to prove Theorem 1.

Lemma 2. *All bidders i bidding $b(s, \alpha, s_i)$ is an envy-free bidder optimal equilibrium. Furthermore, the ranking and the price charged to each bidder is equivalent to the ranking and price charged to each bidder in the VCG mechanism.*

Corollary 1. *Since in the bidder optimal equilibrium in GSP advertisers receive the same utility as in VCG, an advertiser with a choice of values per click receives highest utility in the bidder optimal equilibrium by bidding their highest choice of value.*

Although there exist other equilibria, it is reasonable to expect the auction to converge to the bidder optimal equilibrium. The result in [6] describes a generalized English auction that leads to the bidder optimal equilibrium. Also, in [4], it is shown that there exists a simple greedy bidding strategy that leads to the bidder optimal equilibrium. For simplicity, we assume there is only one bidder optimal equilibrium solution, since ties can be broken according to a predetermined ordering.

To show the efficiency of $\mathcal{M}'$, we first prove the efficiency of $\mathcal{M}$.

Definition 3.   Mechanism $\mathcal{M}$. *Auction $\mathcal{M}$ on bids $b_i, \forall i \in I$ is as follows:*

1. *Run the generalized second price (GSP) auction on b_i.*
2. *$\forall i \in I$, add h_i to the ppc of bidder i. Leave the ranking from GSP unchanged.*

Theorem 2. *All bidders $i \in I$ implementing websites with quality q_i^* and submitting bids $b(s(q_i^*) - h(q_i^*), \alpha)$ is an equilibrium point for mechanism $\mathcal{M}$. Furthermore, this equilibrium point has maximum efficiency.*

Proof.   For a fixed quality q_i, the utility of advertiser i in auction $\mathcal{M}$ is $(s(q_i) - h(q_i) - p_i)\alpha_i$, where p_i and α_i are the price and clicks allocated by GSP. By Lemma 2 and the definition of function b, the bid $b(s(q_i) - h(q_i), \alpha)$ must maximize $(s(q_i) - h(q_i) - p_i)\alpha_i$ in the bidder optimal GSP outcome. By Lemmas 1 and 2, the value of q_i that maximizes $(s(q_i) - h(q_i) - p_i)\alpha_i$ is q_i^*. The bidder optimal GSP outcome, since it ranks by $s(q_i^*) - h(q_i^*)$, maximizes $\sum_i \alpha_i(s(q_i^*) - h_{(}q_i^*))$.   □

Corollary 2. *All bidders $i \in I$ implementing websites with quality q_i^* and submitting bids $b(s(q_i^*) - h(q_i^*), \alpha) + h(q_i^*)$ is an equilibrium point for mechanism $\mathcal{M}'$. Furthermore, this equilibrium point has maximum efficiency.*

Since the addition of $h(q_i^*)$ is immediately subtracted in the first step of $\mathcal{M}'$, and the utility of the bidder is unchanged from $\mathcal{M}$, the maximizing behavior of the bidder is unchanged from Theorem 2.

References

1. Abrams, Z., Ghosh, A.: Auctions with revenue guarantees for sponsored search. Workshop on Sponsored Search Auctions (2007)
2. Backmann, M., McGuire, C.B., Winsten, C.B.: Pigouvian pricing and stochastic evolutionary implementation. Studies in the Economics of Transportation (1956)
3. Basker, E.: Job creation or destruction? labor market effects of wal-mart expansion. Review of Economics and Statistics 87(1), 327–353 (1982)
4. Cary, M., Das, A., Edelman, B., Giotis, I., Heimerl, K., Karlin, A., Mathieu, C., Schwarz, M.: Greedy bidding strategies for keyword auctions. In: Conference on Electronic Commerc (EC) (2007)
5. Clarke, E.: Multipart pricing of public goods. Public Choice 11, 17–33 (1971)
6. Edelman, B., Ostrovsky, M., Schwarz, M.: Internet advertising and the generalized second price auction: Selling billions of dollars worth of keywords. American Economic Review 97(1), 242–259 (2007)
7. Gould, E.D., Pashigian, B.P., Prendergast, C.J.: Contracts, externalities, and incentives in shopping malls. Review of Economics and Statistics (2005)
8. Groves, T.: Incentives in teams. Econometrica 41, 617–631 (1973)
9. Immorlica, N., Jain, K., Mahdian, M., Talwar, K.: Click fraud resistant methods for learning click-through rates. Workshop on Internet and Network Economics (2005)
10. Lahaie, S., Pennock, D.M.: Revenue analysis of a family of ranking rules for keyword auctions. ACM Conference on Electronic Commerce (2007)
11. Pandey, S., Olston, C.: Handling advertisements of uknown quality in search advertising. Neural Information Processing Systems Conference (2006)
12. Pigou, A.C.: Wealth and Welfare (1912)
13. Roughgarden, T., Sundararajan, M.: Is efficiency expensive? In: Third Workshop on Sponsored Search Auctions (2007)
14. Sandholm, B.: Negative externalities and evolutionary implementation. Review of Economic Studies 72, 885–915 (2005)
15. Varian, H.R.: Position auctions. International Journal of Industrial Organization (2005)
16. Vickrey, W.: Counterspeculation, auctions, and competitive sealed tenders. Journal of Finance 16, 8–37 (1961)

Personalized Ad Delivery When Ads Fatigue: An Approximation Algorithm

Zoë Abrams[1] and Erik Vee[2]

[1] Yahoo!, Inc., 2821 Mission College Blvd., Santa Clara, CA, USA
[2] Yahoo! Research, 2821 Mission College Blvd., Santa Clara, CA, USA

Abstract. We consider a crucial aspect of displaying advertisements on the internet: the individual user. In particular, we consider *ad fatigue*, where a user tires of an advertisement as it is seen more often. We would like to show advertisements such that, given the impact of ad fatigue, the overall efficiency of the system is optimized. We design an approximation algorithm, for the case that we study, that approaches the optimum as the number of unique ads shown, if there is only one available position, increases.

1 Introduction

Internet advertising is a booming business, and already provides a large portion of search engine revenue. Placing ads strategically is key to optimizing the efficiency of these advertising systems. The current measures used in most academic literature to determine the match between advertisement and user is the estimated clickthrough rate, based on the advertisement, the keyword, and the position on the web page [1,11,5,10,2,6,7]. In practice, landing page information [12] and demographic targeting [9] have been used to better match advertisements to users.

In this paper, we explore another crucial aspect in determining when and where to place ads: the individual user. There are many ways that an individual user's experience may influence how an advertisement is received, including previous positive or negative experiences with advertisements and previous exposure to a company name or logo. We concentrate in this study on how previous experiences viewing an advertisement influence a user's likelihood to click on that advertisement. The setting used is one where ads are embedded in webpages, such as AdSense at Google or Content Match at Yahoo!. An individual user may view the particular site several times in a single day, if the site is a user's homepage or a frequently visited resource, and ads are less likely to be clicked as they are shown more often. This phenomena is referred to as *ad fatigue* [4], since the user tires of the ad after viewing it several times. We study the problem of determining which ads to display where and when in order to maximize efficiency over several displays of the same page. Efficiency is considered to be the expected number of clicks times the value of that click to the advertiser. We design an algorithm that achieves close to optimum efficiency.

X. Deng and F.C. Graham (Eds.): WINE 2007, LNCS 4858, pp. 535–540, 2007.

2   Model

Our model follows that of [8]. We assume the input to the algorithm is:

- The max number of times, T, a particular web page will be viewed by a single user during the course of some time period.
- A vector f of fatigue rates that contains T values. We use f_t to denote the value corresponding to the tth element of the vector f, and $\forall t, 0 \le f_t \le 1$.
- A vector CTR representing the decay in expected clicks due to position on the page, sorted from most to least likely position to be clicked. We use CTR_p to denote the value corresponding to position p. There are $p \in \{1, ..., P\}$ positions total.
- A set of ads, each with a value $v_i, i \in \{1, ..., I\}$. For an ad i, v_i represents the value to the advertiser showing the ad for receiving a click, times the ad dependent component of the click through rate. Although in practice, values are private and known only to the advertiser, there are options for estimating this value based on information observable to the search engine [11].

We use the word *slot* to signify an opening for an advertisement at a particular time and in a particular position. Our results, algorithm and model make the following assumptions:

- Ad values are all a power of some base b.[1]
- Values in f are decreasing, and all of the form $f_t = \frac{1}{b^t}$.
- The expected efficiency of ad i when shown for the kth time in position p is $CTR_p \cdot f_k \cdot v_i$.
- A slot can be left empty.

For every time slot t, position p, and bidder i, let x_{ipt} be an indicator variable for whether bidder i is shown at time t in position p. We require a solution such that, $\forall it, \sum_p x_{ipt} \le 1$ (in words, an ad can only be shown in one position for a given time slot). Let $\forall it, y_{it} = \sum_{k<t,p} x_{ipt}$. In words, y_{it} is the number of times bidder i has already been shown, at time t, in the solution so far. The problem is to decide which advertisement to show in which position and at which time such that we maximize

$$\text{Total Efficiency} = \sum_{ipt} x_{ipt} \cdot CTR_p \cdot f_{y_{it}} \cdot v_i.$$

Motivating Example. We show that the greedy approach of placing the best ad in the best slot currently available is not optimal. Say advertisers A and B have value 1 for placing their ads, C has value $\frac{1}{2}$, the fatigue vector $f = [1, \frac{1}{2}]$, position clickthrough rates are $CTR = [1, \frac{1}{2}]$, and there are two time periods $T = 2$. The greedy placement of ads is shown in Figure 1 (the top left

---

[1] This assumption can be relaxed by rounding ad values down to the nearest number with base b and multiplying the result in Theorem 1 by a factor of $\frac{1}{b}$.

triangle is the advertiser and the bottom right the efficiency they contribute). The total efficiency is 2.25. However, the optimal solution (seen in Figure 2), has a total efficiency of 2.5. In the (extreme and impractical) worst case, the greedy approach can lead to as much as T times less than the optimal efficiency.

	$t = 1$	$t = 2$
Position 1	Ad: A Bid: 1	Ad: A Bid: $\frac{1}{2}$
Position 2	Ad: B Bid: $\frac{1}{2}$	Ad: B Bid: $\frac{1}{4}$

Fig. 1. Greedy Solution

	$t = 1$	$t = 2$
Position 1	Ad: A Bid: 1	Ad: B Bid: 1
Position 2	Ad: C Bid: $\frac{1}{4}$	Ad: A Bid: $\frac{1}{4}$

Fig. 2. Optimal Solution

3   An Approximation Algorithm

We now describe our algorithm and give an approximation guarantee for its performance. The algorithm works in two stages. In the first stage, we generate a "flattened tableau": rather than showing a set of P different ads (placed in positions 1,2,..., P) during each of the T time steps, imagine that we show just one ad during each of $P \cdot T$ time steps. For the first T time steps, we value the ad as though it were shown in position 1. For the next T time steps, we value the ad as though it were shown in position 2, and so on. Ad fatigue is applied normally. We can produce an optimal flattened tableau in a greedy fashion.

Consider "unflattening" the tableau. Take the first T ads and place them all in position 1 (in their respective positions). Take the next T ads and place them all in position 2, and so on. This causes two problems: the first is that ads may appear more than once for a given time step. The second is that the value that we ascribed to an ad in Stage I may no longer be accurate; an ad that appears for the first time in, say, the 2nd position in the flattened tableau, may appear for the first time in the 3rd position in the unflattened tableau. In Stage II, we provide a method for rearranging (and removing) ads so that these problems are resolved. Our rearrangement is provably close to the efficiency for the unflattened tableau, which is more efficient than the optimal solution.

Stage I: Finding an optimal flattened tableau
As we outlined above, Stage I of our algorithm finds the optimal placement of ads in the flattened tableau. Let $\bar{y}_{ipt}$ be the number of times that ad i has appears in slots (p', t') such that either $p' < p$ or $p' = p, t' \leq t$, assuming i is

placed in slot (p,t). In symbols, $\bar{y}_{ipt} = \sum_{p'<p}\sum_t x_{ip't} + \sum_{t'<t} x_{ipt'}$. We seek to maximize $\sum_{ipt} x_{ipt} \cdot CTR_p \cdot f_{\bar{y}_{ipt}} \cdot v_i$. Note that this is the total efficiency, with y_{ipt} replaced with $\bar{y}_{ipt}$. We define $f_{\bar{y}_{ipt}} \cdot v_i$ to be an advertiser's "flattened value". The pseudocode is given below.

STAGE I of ALGORITHM $\mathcal{A}$: FLATTENED TABLEAU

Initialize the "flattened value" of each ad i to be v_i.

For $p = 1$ to P

    For $t = 1$ to T:

1. Place the ad with the largest "flattened value" in slot (p,t). Ties are broken lexicographically.
2. Update the "flattened value" of this ad by dividing by b.

We now show that the efficiency of the flattened tableau (using "flattened values") is better than the efficiency of the optimal solution of the original problem (using the actual values). Let x_{ipt}^A and x_{ipt}^{OPT} be the assignment variables produced by the algorithm of Stage I, and the optimum solution, respectively.

Lemma 1. $\sum_{ipt} x_{ipt}^{OPT} \cdot CTR_p \cdot f_{y_{ipt}} \cdot v_i \leq \sum_{ipt} x_{ipt}^{OPT} \cdot CTR_p \cdot f_{\bar{y}_{ipt}} \cdot v_i \leq \sum_{ipt} x_{ipt}^A \cdot CTR_p \cdot f_{\bar{y}_{ipt}} \cdot v_i$.

Proof. The first two equations differ only in the index for the ad fatigue factor. Consider a single ad i. All variables multiplying the ad fatigue factor remain unchanged. The ad fatigue indices are 1 through the number of occurrences of the ad in both equations. The only thing that changes is the pairing of fatigue values to the other variables. But, the way to pair fatigue values with the other multipliers to maximize efficiency is exactly the pairing created by the $\bar{y}$ variables[2]. It is not hard to verify that algorithm $\mathcal{A}$ produces the flattened tableau with optimal efficiency.   □

Stage II: Reconstructing the flattened tableau

We now use the flattened tableau to construct the final (real) tableau. Stage I produced an assignment of ads to slots. In Stage II, we would like to guarantee that, for each i, all occurrences of ad i in position p appear before any occurrences of ad i in position $p + 1$. We accomplish this by arranging the ads within each position, then shifting ads to the right until our guarantee is met. The algorithm is given below. We show later how to bound the loss in efficiency due to shifting ads to the right.

---

[2] For any two vectors of positive real numbers, the maximum dot product is achieved when both are sorted in ascending (or descending) order.

STAGE II of ALGORITHM $\mathcal{A}$: FEASIBLE TABLEAU
Given the assignment from Stage I, let S_p be the multiset of ads appearing in position p.

1. For each $p \in \{1, ..., P\}$, sort the ads in S_p in ascending order of their v values (breaking ties lexicographically). Place the first ad in slot $(p,1)$, the second ad in slot $(p,2)$, and so on. (Note that S_p is a multiset, so the same ad may appear multiple times, always in a contiguous sequence.)
2. For $p = 2$ to P, shift ads to the right until the last time ad i appears in position $p-1$ is before the first time ad i appears in position p, for all i.

We now prove the approximation ratio for algorithm $\mathcal{A}$. Let $last(j,p)$ and $first(j,p)$ be the last and first, respectively, time at which bidder j is shown in position p. Let Q_{jp} be the set of unique ads shown after ad j (including j) and in position p. Let Q_p be the set of unique ads shown in position p (Q_p is the set version of the multiset S_p). Observe that there could be ads with flattened values in position p that are equal to flattened values in position $p-1$. We ignore this complication and assume flattened values in position p are strictly less than flattened values in position $p-1$. Eliminating this assumption requires Step 2 of Stage II shift ads to the right at most an additional 2 slots. See the full version of this paper for more details.

Lemma 2. *Step 2 of Stage II shifts any row p over by at most an additional $\frac{T}{|Q_{p-1}|}$ time periods after aligning with the row above it.*

Proof. The average number of times an ad is shown in position $p-1$ is $\frac{T}{|Q_{p-1}|}$. For any j, $last(j, p-1)$ is at most $T - |Q_{j,p-1} - 1|\frac{T}{|Q_{p-1}|}$ since every ad shown afterwards is shown at least as often as the average (sorted in increasing order, by number of times shown). $first(j,p)$ is at least $T - |Q_{j,p}|\frac{T}{|Q_{p-1}|} + 1$ since each ad from the previous position is shown (in position p) at most the average number of showings from the previous position $(p-1)$. By definition and Step I of Stage II, $|Q_{j,p-1}| = |Q_{j,p}|$. Clearly, shifting row p over by $\frac{T}{|Q_{p-1}|}$ time units is sufficient to guarantee $last(j, p-1) \leq first(j,p)$. $\square$

Define Avg to be the average efficiency of a bidder in position 1, divided by CTR_1. Precisely, $Avg = \frac{\sum_{ilt} x_{i1t} \cdot f_{y_{it}} \cdot v_i}{|Q_1|}$.

Theorem 1. *Algorithm $\mathcal{A}$ has efficiency at least $OPT - Avg \cdot \sum_{p=2}^{P}(p-1) \cdot CTR_p$.*

Proof. Algorithm $\mathcal{A}$ before step 3 of Stage II finds x_{ipt} that maximizes $E^{\mathcal{A}} = \sum_{ipt} x_{ipt} \cdot CTR_p \cdot f_{\bar{y}_{ipt}} \cdot v_i$. By Lemma 1, optimum efficiency $\leq E^{OPT} \leq E^{\mathcal{A}}$. The efficiency of A after Step 3 is the $E^{\mathcal{A}}$ minus the efficiency in $E^{\mathcal{A}}$ from ads that are removed by the process of shifting over the rows. Since $v_i f_{\bar{y}_{ipt}}$ only decreases as the position increases, by Lemma 2, the efficiency of units shifted off row p is at most $\sum_{k=1}^{p-1} \frac{T}{|Q_k|} \cdot \frac{CTR_p \sum_{i1t} x_{i1t} \cdot f_{yit} \cdot v_i}{T} \leq (p-1) \cdot CTR_p \cdot Avg$. Summing over all positions, at most $Avg \cdot \sum_{p=2}^{P}(p-1) \cdot CTR_p$ is lost.   □

Corollary 1. *Algorithm $\mathcal{A}$ has efficiency at least $OPT \cdot (1 - \frac{P-1}{|Q_1|})$.*

4 Future Work

There are several possible avenues for future work on this problem. First, it would be useful to generalize the result to handle fatigue rates that are not geometrically decreasing. We observe that our algorithm places the most valuable ads latest, so T must be a lower bound on the number of times the page will be shown, to avoid eliminating the most valuable advertisements. There may be other ways to model uncertainty about the number of page showings in the future. There is also the possibility that the ideas presented here will work for personalization in other contexts, such as creating a coordinated advertising campaign targeted at an individual, across multiple domains (i.e. sites for mail, search, etc.) and mediums (i.e. banner ads, studied in [3]). Finally, we do not know the hardness of the problem we study.

References

1. Abrams, Z., Mendelevitch, O., Tomlin, J.: Optimal delivery of sponsored search advertisements subject to budget constraints. ACM Conference on Electronic Commerce (2007)
2. Aggarwal, G., Goel, A., Motwani, R.: Truthful auctions for pricing search keywords. ACM Conference on Electronic Commerce (2006)
3. Chatterjee, P., Hoffman, D.L., Novak, T.P.: Modeling the clickstream: Implications for web-based advertising efforts. Marketing Science 22(4), 520–542 (2003)
4. Davis, H.: Google Advertising Tools (2006)
5. Edelman, B., Ostrovsky, M., Schwarz, M.: Internet advertising and the generalized second price auction: Selling billions of dollars worth of keywords. American Economic Review 97(1), 242–259 (2007)
6. Fain, D., Pedersen, J.: Sponsored search: a brief history. Proceedings of the Second Workshop on Sponsored Search (2006)
7. Feng, J., Bhargava, H.K., Pennock, D.M.: Implementing sponsored search in web search engines: Computational evaluation of alternative mechanisms. Knowledge and Data Management (2005)
8. Gupta, P., Geschwollen, H.: Automatic ad rotation via modeling effects of presentation count on clickthrough rate. Technical report (2006)
9. Kazienko, P., Adamski, M.: Personalized web advertising method. The Third International Conference on Adaptive Hypermedia (2004)
10. Lahaie, S., Pennock, D.M.: Revenue analysis of a family of ranking rules for keyword auctions. ACM Conference on Electronic Commerce (2007)
11. Varian, H.R.: Position auctions. International Journal of Industrial Organization (2005)
12. Zeff, R., Aronson, B.: Advertising on the Internet (1999)

Empirical Price Modeling for Sponsored Search

Kuzman Ganchev, Alex Kulesza, Jinsong Tan, Ryan Gabbard, Qian Liu,
and Michael Kearns

University of Pennsylvania
Philadelphia PA, USA
{kuzman,kulesza,jinsong,gabbard,qianliu,mkearns}@cis.upenn.edu

Abstract. We present a characterization of empirical price data from
sponsored search auctions. We show that simple models drawing bid values independently from a fixed distribution can be tuned to match empirical data on average, but still fail to account for deviations observed
in individual auctions. Hypothesizing that these deviations are due to
strategic bidding, we define measures of "jamming" behavior and show
that actual auctions exhibit significantly more jamming than predicted
by such models. Correspondingly, removing the jamming bids from observed auction data yields a much closer fit. We demonstrate that this
characterization is a revealing tool for analysis, using model parameter values and measures of jamming to summarize the effects of query
modifers on a set of keyword auctions.

1 Introduction

Much of the academic literature on sponsored search to date has been theoretical
in nature [7,4,5,6], characterizing behavior or payoffs under strong assumptions
that may fail in practice—especially when the markets in question are young,
bidders are inexperienced, and relevant pieces of information (such as the exact
rules of the game) are frequently kept secret. To our knowledge there has been
no exploratory study of actual bidding data on a large scale to determine how
real-world auctions can best be analyzed and understood. This paper provides
a simple but needed first look at such questions. We utilize sponsored search
data drawn from a wide array of Overture/Yahoo! auctions and examine how
bids are distributed, what kinds of models of advertiser value can reasonably be
proposed, and the evidence for strategic behavior.

Our analysis serves two immediate purposes. First, a better understanding of
empricial bidding behavior improves the quality of data that can be syntheti-
cally generated for further study. We show that simple models used in practice
fail to account for significant strategic effects, and suggest improvements that
meaningfully enhance the "realism" of such models. Second, our characterization
of sponsored search auctions includes measurable quantities and model parameters that can be used to summarize important features of an auction for further
analysis. To demonstrate the insight provided by such summaries, we show how
groups of query modifiers can influence bidding on a wide array of keyword
auctions. We find, for example, that adding modifiers like "cheap" or "deal" to

X. Deng and F.C. Graham (Eds.): WINE 2007, LNCS 4858, pp. 541–548, 2007.

automobile brand names tends to increase the amount of bid jamming at the first slot of the corresponing sponsored search auctions.

2 Methodology

Our data was obtained from the Overture bidview tool from approximately November 28 to December 2, 2006[1]. We collected bid data for two sets of queries. The first, smaller set includes the keywords used by Rusmevichientong et al [6] and comprises 859 queries related to travel. It is used for aggregate analysis in Section 2.1. The second set, used in the latter sections of the paper, comprises a wide array of 36,900 queries. For the purposes of further analysis (such as that carried out in Section 5), the second set is structured as a cross product of 450 base keywords—e.g., "lawyer"—intended to reflect basic searches that would generate advertiser interest, and 81 modifiers—e.g., "Philadelphia"—intended to capture the ways in which users might further specify searches. The base keywords and modifiers are further structured by placement in groups; there are nine groups of base keywords and six groups of modifiers. Table 1 and Table 2 give some summaries and examples for the groups of keywords in this data set. A complete query in the second set pairs one base keyword with zero or one modifiers (e.g., "lawyer" and "Philadelphia lawyer").

Table 1. Summary of base keyword groups

group	#	examples
cars	41	BMW, Toyota
drugs	62	Xenical, Prozac
electronics	36	laptop, cell phone, camcorder
local-service	55	carpet cleaning, hair dresser
medical	50	anxiety, plastic surgery
non-local-service	27	car insurance, mortgage
software	67	Microsoft Windows, MySQL
subscription	91	cable, magazine
travel	21	cruise, hotel, vacation
total	450	

Table 2. Summary of modifier keyword groups

group	#	examples
action	6	buy, purchase
info	11	information, review
location	40	New York, Ohio, Philadelphia
post	6	support, parts, repair
price	10	cheap, expensive, free, discount
quality	8	best, luxury, new, used
total	81	

Due to resource constraints, we ran each query only once; our data provides no information on dynamic bidding behavior. The data returned by the bidview tool include up to 40 bids, ranked in order from highest to lowest. Advertiser names and ad text are provided, but not used for our analysis. Furthermore, we throw out the first bid in every auction. This is due to the method by which prices are determined: an advertiser pays a price equal to the bid of the next advertiser in bid order, so that the first bid is not relevant to money changing hands except insofar as it is higher than all other bids. For the remainder of the paper we use the term "price" assuming the convention that the kth price is equal to the $(k + 1)^{th}$ bid.

---

[1] http://www.overture.com/; the bidview tool was discontinued shortly after we collected our data.

2.1   Initial Look at the Data

Visualizing the bid books, it is apparent that the data are generally quite noisy. Consequently, we begin by examining the data in aggregate using our smaller, travel domain query set. Figure 1 shows how the price paid by the top bidder is correlated with the total number of bidders in the auction. There is an almost linear relationship between the number of bidders and the mean price of the first position. Figure 2 shows the correspondence between bid position and mean prices. Because prices increase as the number of bidders increases, all the auctions used in computing Figure 2 have at least 19 bids. We normalize the prices so that the first price is 1.0. We find that an exponential decay fits the means surprisingly well, and as a result an exponential model seems a natural choice for fitting individual auctions. We will

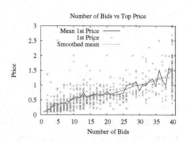

Fig. 1. Correlation between first price and number of bids

see, however, that individual auctions show significantly different behavior than the aggregate. Figure 3 shows the differences between the first and second price, the second and third price and the third and fourth price for auctions with at least 19 bids. We will see in Section 4 that the peak in the small price difference ranges may be due to "jamming" strategies.

3   Independent Bidding Models

Section 2.1 motivates a simple approach to modeling individual auctions under the assumption of bidder independence. If bid averages follow an exponential decay, independent bidders must be drawing from the unique distribution that yields this curve. In particular, bids can be simulated by sampling prices $p(u)$ where continuous function $p(\frac{k-1}{N-1})$ is the expected price of a bidder who is at position k out of N and u is drawn uniformly at random from $[0, 1]$. For example, $p(u) = ae^{-bu}$ yields an exponential curve like that in Figure 2.

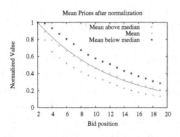

Fig. 2. Correlation between prices and bid position. The curve is an exponential fit to the means.

Fig. 3. Bid differences corresponding to differences in price

Table 3. MSE (*100)

Model	Real	Gauss.	Unif.	Exp.
ab^i	3.8	1.9	3.7	1.7
$ab^i + c$	2.9	1.2	1.3	1.0
linear	14.2	3.2	1.5	7.8
2-linear	1.2	0.6	0.5	0.6

Table 4. Normalized MSE (*100)

Model	Real	Gauss.	Unif.	Exp.
ab^i	9.5	5.7	8.0	7.4
$ab^i + c$	5.9	4.3	3.2	3.0
linear	36.8	15.2	4.2	34.1
2-linear	2.1	1.8	0.9	1.6

Table 5. MAE

Model	Real	Gauss.	Unif.	Exp.
ab^i	0.10	0.08	0.10	0.07
$ab^i + c$	0.06	0.06	0.06	0.05
linear	0.18	0.09	0.07	0.14
2-linear	0.05	0.04	0.04	0.04

While this method faithfully reproduces aggregate price curves, we show here that it does not realistically generate individual bid books. We take measurements using a variety of simple parametric auction models, comparing the quality of each model's best fit to real data and to synthetic data. If the synthetic data are accurate, then the models should fit both data sets equally well. If there is some consistent difference in the quality of fits, then we can conclude that the generative prodecure above is not realistic.

We fit using both exponential and piecewise linear models. Our exponential models have two and three parameters, taking the forms $price[i] = ab^i$ and $price[i] = ab^i + c$, where i is an index of the price positions. Note that the second version allows prices to converge to a nonzero reserve price. We also fit piecewise linear models using dynamic programming. We report only the results for 1 and 2-piece models as MSE drops nearly to zero when 3 or more pieces are used. In all cases, the fits are performed on a per-auction basis to minimize the mean squared error (MSE) of the predicted prices relative to the observed prices. The mean is weighted so that each auction receives equal weight regardless of the number of bids it attracts. We also report normalized MSE (where the highest price in each auction is normzalized to 1.0) and mean absolute error (MAE), computed by averaging the absolute instead of squared differences between predicted and observed prices.

For each auction in our second query set we generated parallel synthetic price data using the sampling technique described above, where $p(\cdot)$ was chosen to be the best exponential fit to the real auction data. Note that the synthetic data is independently sampled from the induced distribution, thus it is not artificially smooth or guaranteed a better fit. We also sampled synthetic bids from Gaussians with mean and variance equal to the empirical prices and from a uniform distribution over the range of empirical prices. These correspond to methods commonly used in practice. Each of the four data sets was fit by each of the four parametric models. The results are presented in Table 3, Table 4, and Table 5.

It is apparent that none of the synthetic methods for generating data displays fit error rates similar to those of real auction data. However, it seems clear that the fits for exponential synthetic data are most similar to those of true auction data, though in magnitude the error measures are much smaller. We conclude, therefore, that the exponential model is the most accurate (as predicted by the aggregate analysis), but that simple, independent-bidder models miss certain key characteristics of sponsored search auctions.

4 Jamming

Figure 4 expands the zero to ten cents region of Figure 3. It is clear that the large number of bid differences below ten cents is due to a peak at differences of one cent or less. We propose that the sharp peak around one cent in the price differences, as well as the non-independence of real auction data, may be due in part to the use of a bidding tactic known as "jamming." Jamming involves bidder A bidding just below bidder B in order to increase B's price while leaving A's price unchanged. This may be an attempt to deplete B's advertising budget or to convince B to drop its bid. This tactic appears to be widely used and is indeed implemented automatically by many bidding packages [3,2].

Of course, jamming is not the only possible explanation for the unusual number of one cent bid gaps. It is possible that bidders choose to play a strategy in which bids are set to one cent *above* the next lowest bidder in an effort to avoid being jammed, that other bidding strategies create the observed effects indirectly, or that collusion is somehow encouraging clumped bidding. Going forward we will continue to use the term "jamming," but we will define it as a purely statistical measure of bid closeness. Further experiments are necessary to draw valid conclusions about bidder intentions.

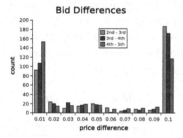

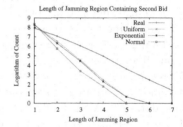

Fig. 4. Bid differences in $0.01 increments. Bars marked "0.1" include all bid differences of $0.10 or greater.

Fig. 5. Counts of the length of the jamming region containing the second bid, on a logarithmic scale

Our definition of jamming is as follows: a bid is a jamming bid if it is one cent or less below the next highest bid. We call a series of consecutive bids each of which (except the first) jams the previous one a "jamming region." To reduce the influence of compression artifacts due to the reserve price, we do not consider bids within two cents of the reserve. By comparing measurements of jamming in real and independent-bidder synthetic data, we seek to tease apart *true* jamming (jamming that results from dependencies between bidders) and apparent jamming due merely to the chance clustering of bids, which may be significant in a market with dozens of bids all less than a dollar.

Figure 5 shows the lengths of the jamming regions starting at the second bid. Intuitively, this corresponds to the number of people jamming the first price point. For real data, the length of the first jamming region is nearly exponentially

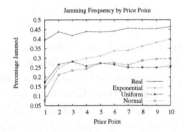

Fig. 6. Frequency of jamming by price position

Fig. 7. Jamming ratios by auction length

distributed, and falls off far more slowly than for the simulated data.[2] Figure 6 shows the frequency of jamming by position. There is a general upward trend for all distributions, probably due to the increasing compression of the range of possible bid values at lower positions creating more chance clusters. However, across a range of price points that there is a strong and statistically significant jamming effect in the real data over and above that seen in the independent-bidder models. Figure 7 shows the jamming ratio, computed as the number of jamming bids over the total number of bids in the auction, versus auction size. As expected, jamming ratios increase gradually for all distributions, due again to chance clustering as more bids are crammed into a small range. Although this data is noisy due to the relatively small number of auctions with certain sizes, the jamming ratio is again significantly higher for real data than exponential data on all auction sizes less than 27 except size 20.

We recomputed our parametric model fits after removing jamming bids from the real auction data. The MSE results are presented in Table 6. Though the gap between synthetic and real data still exists, it has been closed considerably. We hypothesize that further improvements might be obtained by considering other common strategies employed by advertisers. Using similar techniques, it should be possible to formalize and measure the prevalence of such strategies in real-world auction data.

Table 6. MSE results (*100)

Model	Real	Unjam	Exp
ab^i	3.8	2.8	1.7
$ab^i + c$	2.9	1.9	1.0
linear	14.2	13.1	7.8
2-linear	1.2	0.8	0.6

5   Measuring the Effects of Modifiers

Since the queries in our second data set are structured as cross products of keyword/modifier groups, we can visualize interesting trends using the characterization we have developed. We pre-process the data by removing auctions

---

[2] All differences between the real and simulated data here are significant at 95% confidence.

	null	act	info	loc	post	price	quality
cars	0.97	1.09	0.88	1.19	1.55	0.9	0.88
drugs	1.31	1.22	1.11	-	-	0.78	-
electr	1.04	0.85	0.39	1.9	0.7	0.78	0.8
local	1.45	0.94	0.99	3.05	1.36	1.18	1.32
med	1.93	-	2.03	3.66	2.19	0.65	-
n-loc	4.76	2.47	1.98	3.58	1.48	2.67	2.65
soft	0.86	0.48	0.42	-	-	-	0.48
subscr	0.87	0.97	0.59	1.47	1.05	0.9	0.83
travel	0.92	0.54	0.53	0.92	-	0.95	1.3

Fig. 8. First price parameter of the exponential model

	null	act	info	loc	post	price	quality
cars	0.93	0.9	0.87	0.89	0.83	0.88	0.9
drugs	0.86	0.84	0.76	-	-	0.8	-
electr	0.91	0.87	0.88	0.8	0.86	0.88	0.86
local	0.9	0.83	0.82	0.8	0.83	0.86	0.82
med	0.84	-	0.75	0.73	0.81	0.84	-
n-loc	0.9	0.83	0.83	0.89	0.77	0.84	0.86
soft	0.87	0.84	0.88	-	-	-	0.87
subscr	0.88	0.85	0.85	0.8	0.81	0.86	0.86
travel	0.92	0.88	0.9	0.88	-	0.89	0.86

Fig. 9. Decay rate parameter of the exponential model

	null	act	info	loc	post	price	quality
cars	0.19	0.25	0.2	0.26	0.08	0.23	0.2
drugs	0.16	0.16	0.09	-	-	0.08	-
electr	0.11	0.06	0.01	0.09	0.04	0.06	0.05
local	0.15	0.05	0.06	0.11	0.06	0.06	0.07
med	0.09	-	0.07	0.08	0.08	0.07	-
n-loc	0.27	0.12	0.14	0.23	0.04	0.17	0.19
soft	0.03	0.05	0.02	-	-	-	0.0
subscr	0.08	0.08	0.05	0.12	0.03	0.08	0.09
travel	0.11	0.02	0.05	0.12	-	0.11	0.13

Fig. 10. Fraction of jammed bids over 40 cents

	null	act	info	loc	post	price	quality
cars	1.98	2.49	2.34	2.47	1.85	2.65	2.11
drugs	2.23	2.1	1.94	-	-	2.04	-
electr	1.47	1.22	1.56	1.78	1.69	1.41	1.38
local	1.69	1.37	1.6	1.5	1.83	1.53	
med	1.29	-	1.26	1.34	1.83	1.2	-
n-loc	1.52	1.39	1.57	1.61	1.0	1.35	1.43
soft	1.33	2.0	1.4	-	-	-	1.0
subscr	1.65	1.3	1.79	1.68	1.17	1.63	1.64
travel	1.68	1.8	2.06	1.57	-	1.5	1.47

Fig. 11. Length of jamming region starting at first price

with fewer than 11 bids in order to reduce noise, and display quantites of interest in a series of tables. Each row in a table corresponds to a base group of keywords, each column corresponds to a modifier group or an empty ("null") modifier group. (The groups are described in Section 2.) A cell shows the mean of a particular quantity for queries formed from the cross product of the corresponding groups. If a cell is shaded, the mean is statistically different from the "null" entry in the same row; red/bordered cells indicate an increase, and green/unbordered cells indicate a decrease.

Figure 8 shows the effect of keyword modifiers on the first price parameter for the exponential model (a). The table shows that modifiers from the group "location" significantly increase the highest price paid for the four base groups of "local service", "medical", "subscription," and "cars." This seems natural, as all of these groups involve products that frequently depend on local providers. Conversely, "non-local service" keywords have their prices reduced by the addition of a location, as expected. Figure 9 shows the decay rates for the exponential model (b).

We can also visualize interesting trends using the understanding of jamming developed in Section 4. Figure 10 shows that while adding modifiers in general reduces jamming, adding a location or an action word like "buy" can significantly increase the amount of jamming. Figure 11 shows that adding modifiers such as "cheap" to the name of an automobile manufacturer increases the expected length of the jamming region beginning with the second bid.

6 Conclusion

We collected a large set of empirical sponsored search data and performed an exploratory analysis, attempting to characterize and understand real-world search auction data. We found an aggregate exponential decay of prices across many auctions, but showed that this model does not fully describe bidding behavior on a per-auction basis. We showed that jamming is more prevalent in real data than would be predicted by a model of independent bidders, and that removing jamming from empirical data (or, convesely, adding jamming to synthetic data) improves the similarity significantly. Future work will include studying effects other than jamming that contribute to this disparity. Finally, we demonstrated that our model parameters and measures of jamming provide useful summaries of important auction features, revealing trends in the ways modifiers influence the bids for search keywords.

References

1. Animesh, A., Ramachandran, V., Viswanathan, S.: Quality Uncertainty and the Performance of Online Sponsored Search Markets: An Empirical Investigation. SSRN eLibrary (2006)
2. ApexPacific. Overture bid management software & overture bid tool, http://www.apexpacific.com/bidmaximizer/overturebidding.html
3. Atlas. Rules-based bidding for pay-per-click management, http://www.atlasonepoint.com/products/bidmanager/rulesbased
4. Edelman, B., Ostrovsky, M., Schwarz, M.: Internet advertising and the generalized second price auction: Selling billions of dollars worth of keywords. Working Paper (2005), http://rwj.berkeley.edu/schwarz/
5. Lahaie, S.: An analysis of alternative slot auction designs for sponsored search. In: EC 2006 Proceedings of the 7th ACM conference on Electronic commerce, pp. 218–227. ACM Press, New York (2006)
6. Rusmevichientong, P., Williamson, D.P.: An adaptive algorithm for selecting profitable keywords for search-based advertising services. In: Electronic Commerce 2006, pp. 260–269. ACM Press, New York (2006)
7. Varian, H.R.: Position auctions. International Journal of Industrial Organization (2006)

Pay-per-action Model for Online Advertising

Mohammad Mahdian[1] and Kerem Tomak[1]

Yahoo! Research
{mahdian,kerem}@yahoo-inc.com

Abstract. The online advertising industry is currently based on two dominant business models: the pay-per-impression model and the pay-per-click model. With the growth of sponsored search during the last few years, there has been a move toward the pay-per-click model as it decreases the risk to small advertisers. An alternative model, discussed but not widely used in the advertising industry, is pay-per-conversion, or more generally, pay-per-action. In this paper, we discuss various challenges involved in designing mechanisms for the pay-per-action model, and approaches to tackle some of them.

1 Introduction

Online advertising is one of the fastest growing segments in the marketing industry [1]. Currently, there are two main commodities traded in the online advertising market. These are impressions for brand awareness and clicks for traffic. Generally, advertisers is willing to pay for impressions if the aim of the advertising campaign is to increase brand awareness. However, they are more inclined to pay for clicks if the goal is to generate traffic which in turn increases the probability of a sale. In the former case, advertisers pay per impression (PPM) while in the latter they pay per click (PPC). The PPC model currently is based on a rank-by-revenue mechanism in which ads are sorted by their bid per click times click-through-rate (CTR).

With the growth of sponsored search in companies such as Google, Yahoo!, and MSN, the trend in the online advertising market has been to shift more and more of the advertising budgets toward the PPC model. This is mainly due to the fact that the PPC model reduces the risk to advertise to consumers not in the target audience of an advertiser. If this risk is high, advertisers (in particular small advertisers who are more risk averse) tend to choose the PPC model over the PPM model.

As a next step in this direction, the pay per conversion/action (PPA) model links payments to events such as sales, phone calls, or online order directly. An advertiser states his/her willingness to pay for an "action," which can encapsulate anything beyond a click. This includes pay-per-conversion, but also other things. The important distinction is that an "action" needs to be reported by the advertiser, whereas clicks are counted by the ad publisher. For many of the same reasons the PPC model has taken the market over the PPM model, we expect the online advertising market to evolve toward the PPA model in the

X. Deng and F.C. Graham (Eds.): WINE 2007, LNCS 4858, pp. 549–557, 2007.

future. Early signs of such an evolution is evident in Google's announcement of the PPA model in their AdSense platform.

In this paper, we discuss the PPA model, the advantages it offers, and issues that need to be resolved to successfully apply this model. Our focus is on theoretical questions regarding incentive issues facing the advertisers in reporting the true action data. We show how the mechanisms proposed for the PPC model can be adapted to cope with challenges specific to the PPA model.

2   The Pay-per-action Model

The interaction of a user with an ad publisher like Yahoo! or Google starts with the user requesting a page from the publisher that contains ads. This results in an ad *impression* for the ads displayed on the page. The user might then click on an ad, resulting in a *click-through*. Beyond this point, the user leaves the domain of the publisher and enters the advertiser's web site. In her interaction with this web site, the user might perform certain *actions* that are valuable to the advertiser, such as filling out a form, signing up at the web site, calling a phone number listed on the web site, or purchasing a merchandise. In the PPA model, the advertiser can make payments contingent on not only impressions and click-throughs, but also actions. For example, the advertiser can offer to pay 0.1 cents for every impression of their ad, 10 cents every time their ad is clicked on, plus $40 every time the user fills out a credit card application on their web site. The auction mechanism extracts all such bids from the advertisers, decides which ads to show, and how much each advertiser should be charged, depending on whether the ad is clicked on, and whether the advertiser reports that the ad has resulted in an action. A natural generalization of the common *rank-by-revenue* mechanism for the PPC model is to rank the advertisers based on their bid per impression, plus their bid per click times their click-through rate (CTR), plus their bid per action times their action rate.[1]

The major factor that distinguishes the PPA model from the PPC or PPM model is that an action takes place outside the scope of control of the publisher. Therefore, the publisher needs to rely on the advertiser to report the actions that take place (perhaps through an automatic software agent supplied by the ad publisher), whereas click-throughs are counted by the ad publisher. In fact, even the definition of an action can be different from one advertiser to another.

Another distinction between the PPA model and PPC or PPM models is in the *timing* of events. An impression takes place instantaneously after the user requests a page and the publisher decides which ads to display on the page. Also, a click-through often happens shortly after (if at all). However, an action such as buying a merchandise might take place days or even weeks after the user sees the ad. This makes the job of linking a particular action to an ad difficult. There are methods, such as using post-purchase surveys, or using the cookie technology to

---

[1] To completely specify the mechanism, we need to specify a payment scheme as well. The payment scheme we will consider is similar to the generalized second price auction *in expectation*. The details of this issue will be discussed in later sections.

link the two, but the data obtained this way is inherently more noisy than the click-through or impression data.

To discuss the advantages of the PPA model, we need to understand what generates value for an advertiser. In general, there are two factors that the advertisers value:

- *Attention.* Many advertisers, particularly brand advertisers, mainly seek attention from the users. As attention is difficult to measure, various other measures such as impressions, click-throughs, or other actions can be used as proxies for attention.

- *Conversion.* A conversion is defined as any action that directly brings in some revenue. This often means buying a product from the advertiser's web site. However, there can be many other types of conversion, depending on the type of the advertiser. For example, for an ad portal, a click on one of the ads listed on the page can be considered a conversion.

There is a spectrum of advertisers, from purely attention-seeking (such as big brands, e.g., auto manufacturers) to purely conversion-seeking (e.g., small online shops).

Advantages of the PPA model. In the following, we list several advantages the PPA model offers over the more restrictive PPC and PPM models.

- *Trust requirement.* In the PPM model, as in traditional magazine advertisements [2], the advertiser needs to trust the publisher to count the number of impressions of their ad. The situation is better for the PPC model, but still various technical difficulties produce discrepancies between the click statistics on the publisher side and on the advertiser side [4]. In the PPA model, this issue is completely eliminated, as it is the advertiser who counts the number of actions.

- *Expressiveness.* Clearly, the PPA model is a more expressive bidding language than the PPC model. It is not hard to construct examples to show that if an advertiser cannot change her bid too frequently (which is often the case, either because the burden of frequently updating bids is too high for the advertiser, or because of the limits imposed by the publisher), this expressiveness can result in a higher utility for the advertiser.

- *Reducing risk.* In addition to increasing the advertisers' utility, the PPA model can reduce the risk to (some) advertisers.

- *Click fraud.* Click fraud is a phenomenon that has plagued the pay-per-click model for selling online advertisement [5,6]. By definition, a fraudulent click is one that is done without the intention of buying a product. Therefore, an obvious remedy for the click fraud problem (for conversion-seeking advertisers) is to ask the advertisers to report clicks that lead to a conversion, and charge the advertiser only based on those clicks. Given the data about which clicks lead to a conversion, publishers such as Google or Yahoo! can not only eliminate click fraud for the involved advertisers, but also find partner web-sites that are frequent targets of click fraud (perhaps because the fraud is committed by their owners), and discount their value for other advertisers as well.

Challenges of the pay-per-action model. The PPA model assumes that the advertisers voluntarily provide the action data to the publisher. However, there are three main reasons for advertisers not to provide a truthful report of the action data to the publisher:

- *Strategic reasons:* Advertisers might be able to increase their utility by misreporting the actions. For example, if the advertiser is charged a fixed amount per action, she might benefit from not reporting some of the actions.

- *Cost of gathering data:* It might be costly to gather data about which clicks lead to action, especially because an action has a different meaning for each advertiser, many advertisers do not have the software means to track all the actions of their users, and the data is inherently noisy.

- *Cost of disclosing data:* many big advertisers treat the conversion data as confidential information that is valuable to them and their competitors, and therefore might not be willing to share this data with a publisher like Yahoo! or Google.

In the next section, we discuss the strategic factor, and show that in a simple model based on the click-fraud-resistant learning algorithms introduced by Immorlica et al. [3] combined with a participation fee, advertisers cannot gain any significant amount by misreporting the actions.

3   The Incentive Problem

In this section, we discuss the problem of mechanism design in the PPA model with the aim of providing incentive for advertisers to reveal the action data truthfully to the auctioneer (the publisher). A major step toward this goal was taken in the paper of Immorlica et al. [3] on click fraud. We start by briefly explaining their result and its implication for the PPA model, and then move on to a few specific problems in the PPA model.

The model focuses on one advertiser and one ad slot. The advertiser is interested in displaying an ad in the ad slot. In a PPM model with an auction mechanism such as generalized second price, the advertiser wins the slot if his bid per impression is more than a threshold p, and pays p per impression. The value of p is often the bid of the next advertiser or the reserve price. The details of how the mechanism computes p is irrelevant to our discussion; all we need to know is that p is independent of the bid or other characteristics of the advertiser. Similarly, in a PPC model, if the advertiser has a bid b_c per click, and our estimate of the click-through-rate of the advertiser (the probability that an impression of the ad leads to a click) is CTR, then the ad will be shown if $b_c \times CTR \geq p$, and the advertiser will be charged an amount equal to p/CTR if a click occurs.[2] Intuitively, this means that assuming that the estimate CTR is accurate, the advertiser pays an expected amount of p per impression. If this is

---

[2] This mechanism is called a *rank-by-revenue* mechanism since $b_c \times CTR$ is the revenue that auctioneer expects from the impression, and p is the opportunity cost of this impression.

the case, then fraudulent clicks should not be able to increase the average cost per impression to the advertiser. This, however, assumes that the estimate CTR is accurate, which is not a reasonable assumption, especially in a scenario where an adversary injects fraudulent clicks. The main result of Immorlica et al. [3] is that if the algorithm used to learn CTR is from a class of algorithms termed *click-based algorithms*, then the conclusion is indeed true: fraudulent clicks cannot increase the *average* cost per impression to the advertiser by more than a negligible amount.

Immorlica et al. [3] also observe that their result applies to *self-inflicted* fraud as well, i.e., if an advertiser creates fraudulent impressions that lead or not lead to clicks, he cannot change his average cost per impression by any non-negligible amount. This, taken in the context of a PPA model (replacing clicks in the argument by actions), implies that in a PPA model with a payment rule similar to the one for the PPC model and an action-rate learning algorithm from a suitable class of algorithms, the advertiser cannot change his average cost per impression by any non-negligible amount. There are, however, three issues that are left unanswered by this result:

- The payment rule when payments are associated with more than one type of event (impression, click, action): The model studied by Immorlica et al. [3] assumes that the advertiser has a bid b_a per action, AR is the estimated action rate for this advertiser, and p is the price-per-impression of the ad slot. In this setting, the mechanism displays the ad if $b_a \times AR \geq p$, and charges the advertiser an amount equal to p/AR per action. However, in general the advertiser might want to specify a bid per impression b_m, a bid per click b_c, and a bid per action b_a (or perhaps even different bids for different types of action). In this case, the mechanism must display the ad if $b_m + b_c \times CTR + b_a \times AR \geq p$, but it is not clear that in the event of a click or an action, how much the advertiser should be charged. There are many ways this charging scheme can be designed to yield an expected price per impression of p (for example, the bids per impression, click and actions can be discounted by the same or by different factors to make the expected payment equal to p). It is not clear for which, if any, of these rules the result of Immorlica et al. [3] works.
- False-name bidding: The result of Immorlica et al. [3] is asymptotic, in the sense that it shows that if an advertiser stays in the system for long enough the per-impression gain he can derive from misreporting the actions tends to zero. However, one plausible strategy for an advertiser is to stay in the system for a short time and gain from misreporting the actions, and then leave and re-enter the system with a different name.
- Timing of events: In the model studied in [3], the mechanism learns whether an impression has led to an action or not immediately after the impression, and can use this information to update the estimate of the action-rate that will be used for allocating and pricing the next impression. While this is a reasonable model for the PPC model (since most clicks take place almost

immediately after the impression), it is far from being realistic in the PPA model, where an action can take place weeks after the impression.

In the following, we briefly sketch how the above issues can be resolved. The details of the proofs are omitted.

The payment rule. We consider the problem in the case where the advertiser can specify a bid b_m for impressions and a bid b_a for actions. In this case, the ad slot is allocated to the advertiser if $b_m + AR \times b_a \geq p$, where AR is the current estimate of the action rate. Consider the following charging scheme: we define

$$p_m = \min(b_m, p) \quad \text{and} \quad p_a = (p - p_m)/AR. \tag{1}$$

The advertiser is charged p_m for every impression, and p_a every time an action occurs. We can show that with this payment scheme, the result of Immorlica et al. [3] holds with a very similar proof. To explain the intuition, we show this fact for the case that the learning algorithm simply estimates the action rate as 1 divided by the number of impressions since the last impression that lead to an action (this simple algorithm is a canonical case of an *action-based* learning algorithm).

Consider the sequence of impressions, and two consecutive impressions i_1, i_2 in this sequence that have lead to an action (i.e., these two impressions have lead to an action, but none of the impressions between them has). Let $k - 1$ denote the number of impressions between impressions i_1 and i_2. Therefore, at the time of impression i_2, the estimate for AR is equal to $1/k$. Therefore, the advertiser pays a price of $(p - p_m)k$ for the action corresponding to impression i_2. We can re-assign this payment to impressions between i_1 and i_2 (including i_2) by assigning an amount equal to $p - p_m$ to each of those impressions. In addition, each impression is charged an amount equal to p_m. Therefore, with this reassignment of charges, the cost corresponding to each impression will be precisely p.

The above argument can be generalized to more general learning algorithm that are *action-based* (defined analogously to the click-based algorithms of [3]). It is worth noting that other payment rules such as the proportional rule

$$p_m = \frac{b_m p}{b_m + AR \times b_a} \quad \text{and} \quad p_a = \frac{b_a p}{b_m + AR \times b_a}$$

do not yield the same result. Therefore, for the purpose of designing a mechanism that incentivizes the advertisers to reveal the correct action data, it is important to use this particular payment scheme.

False-name bidding. Our approach for tackling this problem is to charge each advertiser a fixed premium for entering the system, and stop displaying ads whose action rate drops below a certain rate. Intuitively, the premium is set at a level so that an advertiser cannot gain by entering the system and not reporting any action, until his action-rate drops below the threshold. The premium is a small one-time fee, so it does not affect honest advertisers who stay in the system for long. Also, all or part of the premium can be refunded to the advertiser upon leaving the system, depending on the advertiser's action rate upon leaving.[3]

The exact value of the premium depends on the threshold for the minimum allowable action rate, the action-rate learning algorithm, and how it initializes the action rate when an advertising campaign starts. For example, in the case where the action-rate learning algorithm estimates the action rate by the average over the last k actions (i.e., AR is equal to k divided by the number of impressions it took to get the last k actions), initializing the AR to 1 (i.e., prepending the history by k impressions all leading to an action), the amount of premium can be calculated to be

$$kp(\frac{1}{\delta} - 1),$$

where δ is the threshold for minimum allowable action rate. Note that (not surprisingly), the amount of premium increases if the threshold δ is decreased, or if the value of k increases, which intuitively corresponds to increasing the robustness of the learning algorithm.

Timing. A simple fix to the timing problem is to use any of the action-based algorithms for learning the action rate using the data available at the moment the estimate is needed, and *re-adjust* previous payments every time a new action is reported (e.g., by refunding part of the charge for a previous action, if the new information reduces the payment for that action). We explain this with the following simple example: assume we use the learning algorithm that estimates the action rate as 1 divided by the number of impressions since the last impression that lead to an action. Also, assume the advertiser has only specified a bid on actions (i.e., no bid on impressions or clicks). With this learning algorithm, every time an action corresponding to an impression i is reported, if i is the latest impression for which an action is reported, then the advertiser will be charged an amount equal to p/AR, where AR is the estimate of the action-rate at the time of impression i. In other words, the charge corresponding to this action will be equal to $p \times k$, where k is the number of impressions before impression i and after the last impression previously reported to lead to an action. If i is not the latest impression for which an action is reported, then this impression should be charged using a similar formula, but in addition, the charge corresponding to the first impression after i for which an action is previously reported should be adjusted. Doing the calculations, it is easy to see that for this particular learning algorithm, this adjustment cancels out the charge for i; in other words, in this case action i will not be charged, since all the charge corresponding to this action are previously paid.

A potential problem with the learning algorithm used in the above example is that it consistently under-estimates the action rate. Even though this is not a problem for charging scheme, it can cause problems in the allocation step (i.e.,

---

[3] In other words, the premium can be thought of as the fee for "buying" an initial high action rate. Upon leaving the system, the advertiser can sell the value of their current action rate back to the auctioneer.

if the action rate gets too low, the advertiser might not even get the slot). To resolve this problem, the learning algorithm should use some of the older data for which most of the actions have already occurred (e.g., it is safe to assume that if no action corresponding to a month-old impression has taken place, the impression will not lead to an action). However, one must be careful not to include the element of time in the formula used for learning, since doing so renders the algorithm *non-action-based*, which causes the fraud-resistance result of Immorlica et al. [3] to fail and opens the door for gaming the system by strategically timing the reports.[4]

The above discussions can be summarized in the following result. The proof of this result is based on the ideas mentioned above, but the details are omitted here.

Theorem 1. *Consider a rank-by-revenue system with a payment rule according to (1) and a payment re-adjustment scheme as above that charges a large enough premium at the sign up (where the value of premium is calculated as described above) and does not show ads whose action rate has drops below a certain threshold. In this system, an advertiser cannot gain more than $o(1)$ per impression by misreporting the actions and/or re-entering the system under other names.*

4   Conclusion

The contribution of this paper is two-fold: to discuss important theoretical questions in the design of incentive-compatible pay-per-action mechanisms for selling online advertisements, and to provide an answer to some of these questions. There are still many directions that remain unexplored. A few particular problems that we would like to emphasize are the following:

Cost of collecting action data. As mentioned earlier, one of the barriers in using the PPA model for selling online advertisements is the difficulty of gathering action (or conversion) data. It would be interesting to model this factor, and design mechanisms where the auctioneer can provide incentive for the advertiser to spend the cost for collecting the data. Notice that collecting the PPA data benefits not only the advertiser, but also the auctioneer, as the auctioneer can detect sources of fraud using this data, and avoid paying any commission to partner web sites that commit fraud.

Cost of disclosing data. Larger advertisers usually have the tools to track and collect the action data, but might not be willing to share this potentially valuable information with the auctioneer. It would be interesting to explore the potential of using privacy-enhancing technologies to reduce this disincentive to use the PPA model.

---

[4] Still, the element of time can be used to compute the initial estimate of the action-rate, but the payments should eventually be adjusted according to an action-based algorithm.

Using action data to improve the PPC model. One of the main reasons click fraud is an issue in online advertising is the obvious incentive of *partner web-sites* (i.e., web sites that are not owned by publishers like Google or Yahoo! but allow these publishers to display ads in return for a commission) to commit click fraud to increase their commission. For this reason, fraud is usually targeted at particular partner web-sites, and not on particular advertisers. This means that even if some percentage of the advertisers use the PPA model to buy ads, the publisher can use the action data that they provide to detect partner web sites that are targets of fraud, and alleviate the fraud problem by discounting the value of a click on such web sites. However, this creates an obvious incentive problem, as the data an advertiser provides is used to change not only his effective bid, but also the effective bid of other advertisers. It would be interesting to explore this tradeoff between incentive compatibility in reporting the action data, and the potential use of the action data in calculating discount rates for partner web sites.

Robustness vs. adaptivity tradeoff. There is a tradeoff between how robust the estimate of the learning algorithm is toward random noises in the data (affected by the length of history the learning algorithm looks at) and how quickly can the algorithm adapt to changes in the action rate caused by changes in the market. The optimal point in this tradeoff should depend on parameters such as the volatility of the market and the amount of noise. Furthermore, by the discussion in the previous section, two other parameters, namely the action-rate threshold below which the ad is dropped and the amount of premium that needs to be charged, also enter this tradeoff. A theoretical analysis of this tradeoff remains open.

References

1. Forrester Research, US Online Marketing Forecast: 2005 to 2010 (May 2, 2005)
2. McCollam, D.: Bad Circulation: How often do newspapers and magazines goose their numbers? Columbia Journalism Review Publication (May 1, 2004)
3. Immorlica, N., Jain, K., Mahdian, M., Talwar, K.: Click Fraud Resistant Methods for Learning Click-Through Rates. In: Deng, X., Ye, Y. (eds.) WINE 2005. LNCS, vol. 3828, pp. 34–45. Springer, Heidelberg (2005)
4. Lockhorn, J.: Cache Busting: Busted? The ClickZ Network (July 11, 2001)
5. Penenberg, A.: Click fraud threatens web. Wired News (October 13, 2004)
6. Stone, B.: When mice attack: Internet scammers steal money with 'click fraud'. Newsweek (January 24, 2005)

Public Advertisement Broker Markets

Atish Das Sarma, Deeparnab Chakrabarty, and Sreenivas Gollapudi

[1] College of Computing, Georgia Institute of Technology, Atlanta, GA 30332–0280
atish;deepc@cc.gatech.edu
[2] Microsoft Search Labs
sreenivas.gollapudi@microsoft.com

Abstract. Motivated by the growth of various networked systems as potential market places, we study market models wherein, owing to the size of the markets, transactions take place between largely unknown agents. In such scenarios, intermediaries or brokers play a significant role in a transaction.

We analyze market behavior in large networks wherein all sellers are not known to the buyers and vice-versa and depend on intermediaries to conduct any transactions. In such markets, we study a specific case where buyers wish to purchase goods from trusted sources at minimal prices. Sellers wish to maximize selling price. Brokers attempt to maximize profit by aiding in trade by acting as intermediaries; brokers have an advertising budget. We show the existence of competitive equilibria in such layered broker markets. We also describe efficient algorithms to compute these equilibria. We give polynomial-time distributed mechanisms to reach the equilibrium for two extreme cases of the brokers' advertising budget constraints.

1 Introduction

The large size and complexity of many markets necessitates the existence of intermediaries or brokers who mediate transactions between buyers and sellers. The large size of a market often results in the development of varying degree of personal relationships between all the players in the market. For example, a buyer can prefer to deal with one broker over another when she chooses to buy a certain commodity from the market. For example, in bilateral search markets (e.g., employment agencies, real estate brokers), the middleman narrows the set of buyers and sellers who search. In such markets, sellers with high selling prices and buyers with small budgets drop out of the search market and instead trade through the middleman [12].

With the growth of technology, in particular the Internet, markets have changed drastically from their traditional bearings,especially in scale, and the need for understanding the role of the middleman in these new settings gains ever more significance. With easy access to information about commodities, scenarios arise wherein multiple brokers often compete to sell the same commodity to the buyer. In such cases, they differentiate themselves not only using pricing

X. Deng and F.C. Graham (Eds.): WINE 2007, LNCS 4858, pp. 558–563, 2007.

discounts but also other value added services to cultivate a longer term relationship with the buyer. Therefore, it is not only important *what* you get, but also *who* you get from. All the factors above lead to a slew of interesting questions like how to model a market, and best behavior strategies in certain models.

In this study, we model various agents being nodes of a directed network. This network is defined for a specific good in the market as the trust network and market behavior depends on the good. Inter-play between dependent goods is a tangential albeit very interesting and important study, that we do not explore in this paper. For any good, each node plays the role of either a buyer, a seller or a broker. Loosely, they correspond to people who need the good and are willing to pay, who have the good and wish to sell, and the intermediaries who make money due to their important role of being a middleman. The model is motivated by the following observations.

- A buyer wishes to maximize his happiness. The happiness not only depends on the good she gets and the price she pays for it, but also depends crucially on who she gets its from.
- A broker wishes to maximize her *profit*. Thus, it is important for her, given her constraints, to decide what to buy, from whom to buy, and for how much, and whom to sell it to.
- A seller wishes to sell at the maximum possible price. These prices depend on the quality of the good and the reputation of the seller.

Our Results

In this paper, we look at networks where buyers and sellers form the extreme layers, with brokers in between. We show that competitive equilibria exist in these networks, and give polynomial time algorithms for computing them. In certain restricted settings, we give efficient mechanisms to reach the equilibrium.

We should point out that our notion of equilibrium differs from the market equilibrium concept of Arrow and Debreu [1]. We consider *indivisible* goods, and not much is known in the Arrow-Debreu setting for indivisible goods, even in the case with no brokers. Our equilibrium notion is that of a competitive equilibrium: buyers get their best goods at the prices, sellers sell at optimum prices, and brokers have no envy or regret in their dealings.

In the case of no brokers, the model above reduces to the market generated by the assignment game of Shapley and Shubik [11], who show the existence of competitive equilibria in these markets. Efficient algorithms for the same are implied by various later works [3], etc.

Related Work. Motivated by the indirect interaction among agents, in their paper, Graphical Economies, Kakade et.al [5] introduce a graph-theoretic generalization of the classical Arrow-Debreu economics. They provide existence results for market equilibria and give algorithms for the same. Rubenstein and Wolinsky [9] study a market model which includes intermediaries and analyzes steady state conditions in such markets. An excellent survey is due to Jackson [4]. Recently, Kleinberg and Raghavan [6] considered query-incentive networks to theoretically study the effect of incentive issues in networks.

Our work was done independent of a recent paper by Blume et. al. [7]. They study a very similar problem of the interaction of buyers and sellers through a layer of intermediaries. In their model, the intermediaries set prices for both sellers and buyers. On the contrary, in our case, sellers *advertise* prices that brokers consume and in turn advertise prices for buyers. Further, the techniques used in their results are LP based which is an alternate way of looking at the initial assignment game of [11]. The techniques in our paper are more algorithmic. We prove the existence of *envy-free* Nash equilibria in our setting, and for certain restricted cases, provide efficient distributed mechanisms to reach the same.

Our model is more general than the ones considered by Babaioff, Walsh [2] and Babaioff, Nisan, Pavlov [8]. The latter paper assumes that the products of the sellers are indistinguishable for the buyers; in contrast our paper allows buyers to have preferences over the sellers and the brokers.

2   Broker Market Games

We model the three kinds of players in our market: buyers, brokers and sellers, as the three layers in a tri-partite network (A, B, C), respectively. Thus we allow interaction between buyers and sellers only via brokers. We assume each seller has one good to sell and each buyer desires only one unit of good. We also assume the same number of buyers and sellers, i.e. $|A| = |C| = n$ and $|B| = m$. Every buyer i has a value u_i associated on obtaining the good. Every seller j has a global reputation r_j. The buyer i to broker j trust weights are denoted by α_{ij}.

We consider the constrained advertisement model for the brokers, that is, we allow each broker j a maximum of N_j advertisements which he can broadcast. For simplicity we assume each $N_j = N$ is the same, and we assume $Nm \geq n$.

We now describe the strategies of the various players and the payoffs they get.

- *Buyers:* The strategy of the buyer is to decide which broker j to trade with, to buy the item from which seller k, when the price the broker offers is p_j. The pay-off is a function $f_i(u_i, \alpha_{ij}, p_j, r_k)$ which is assumed to be continuous, increasing in u_i, α_{ij} and r_k, and decreasing in p_j. We will assume its is linear in the price. The pay-off f_i is called *separable* if there exist functions g_i and h such that

$$f_i(u_i, \alpha_{ij}, p_j, r_k) = g_i(u_i, \alpha_{ij}) + h(r_k) - p_j$$

- *Brokers:* The broker j need to decide which of the N sellers' advertisements should it broadcast and at what prices. The only profit broker makes is $P_{sell} - P_{buy}$, where P_{sell} is the total price he sells goods at and P_{buy} the total money he buys at. For this paper we assume brokers do not make distinctions between which buyers he sells to.
- *Sellers:* The strategy of the seller is to just fix the price at which he sells the good.

Under the assumptions stated above, this game has a Nash equilibrium in pure strategies. We first elaborate what a PSNE looks like in this case.

PSNE (Pure Strategy Nash Equilibrium) of Broker Market Games: A price vector P for sellers, an allocation of some N advertisements for every broker j, and a price vector Q for the mN advertisements by brokers form a Nash equilibrium if the following hold.

- Buyers get the best possible product at the given prices, i.e., at the price vector Q, every buyer i buys a good from seller k advertised by broker j at price Q_j such that it maximizes $f_i(u_i, \alpha_{ij}, Q_j, r_k)$.
- Every good is sold.
- Sellers have no incentive to raise advertised prices, i.e., increase in $p_k = P[k]$ results in seller k's good having zero demand.
- All m brokers have *zero-regret* about the advertisements they chose to broadcast, that is, no broker could have made more profit by broadcasting a different set of N advertisements at some other price.

We further define the following desirable envy-freeness property and then a result on existence of PSNE in broker markets. We defer the proof to the full version [10].

Definition 1. *Envy-freeness of brokers: Broker s will not envy broker t only if every buyer i broker t sold a good to with > 0 profit, is either* happier *buying that good from t than from s, or s did not advertise that good.*

Theorem 1. *For every broker market game with separable pay-off functions for buyers, there exists an envy-free PSNE.*

Our model can be thought off as a generalization of the *assignment game*, defined by Shapley and Shubik [11] which comprised of n buyers and n sellers with each buyer i having a utility u_{ij} for the good sold by j. Their goal was to come up with a price vector P for the goods, such that at this price, every buyer i gets the good maximizing her "happiness" of $u_{ij} - p_j$ and the market clears. Demange et.al. [3] came up with a mechanism to reach these equilibrium prices.

In the next section, we discuss cases where the PSNE can be reached in an efficient fashion via distributed mechanisms.

2.1   Efficient Mechanisms

For certain special cases, we also design efficient mechanisms for computing these envy-free Nash equilibria. Due to lack of space, we only describe one such mechanism.

Theorem 2. *For the extreme cases when $N = n$ (unbounded advertising budget) and $N = 1$ (one advertisement budget), there exist polynomial time distributed mechanisms to compute the Nash equilibria.*

Unbounded Advertising Budget. The mechanism can be thought of as a sequence of two mini-games played one after another until all goods are sold. Both mini-games are similar to the assignment game. We now sketch a continuous version of the mechanism and we leave out the discretization and proof of polynomial time in this abstract.

THE MULTIPLE ROUND MECHANISM
Initialize $P = 0$ for all sellers.
MINI GAME 1

- Sellers pass price-vector P to all brokers.
- Brokers pass P to all buyers they can reach.
- Buyers choose their best advertisement(s) from their options. Draw corresponding $\geq n$ edges.
- As long as there is a subset of buyers, S, such that $N(S)$: the set of brokers they choose as their best option, is smaller in size than S, brokers in $N(S)$ corresponding to a maximal such S increase their selling prices.
- If for all $S \subseteq A$, $|N(S)| \geq |S|$, then by Hall's theorem there is a matching which matches all buyers. Choose such an arbitrary matching and call the matched brokers *active*, and move on to Mini-game 2.

MINI GAME 2

- Draw edges from *active* brokers to sellers that received demand from buyers.
- Consider a maximal subset T of (active) brokers such that the size of its neighborhood $|N(T)| < |T|$, if such a T exists. Repeat this and the following step until no such T exists.
- Sellers in $N(T)$ corresponding to a maximal set T increase their price, modifying P. As soon as some seller's selling price reaches a neighboring broker's selling price, delete the broker-seller edge.
- Brokers advertise this new vector P and a second round of mini-games takes place unless $|N(T)| = |C|$, that is all goods are sold.

---

3   Concluding Remarks

There are several interesting future directions. We prove the envy-freeness property for the specific Nash equilibria we describe. A fundamental question is to give a clean characterization of all possible Nash equilibria in our setting. It is not clear whether one can extend the efficient distributed mechanisms to the intermediate budget constraint cases.

The eventual goal of our study is to prove existence, determine efficient mechanisms, and characterize equilibria in general networks (not necessarily layered). One question about the model that merits attention is that in our case we allow brokers to choose which sellers to advertise. An alternate model could allow sellers to choose which brokers to advertise via; in such a setting, it may make sense to attribute global (perhaps dynamic) reputations on brokers too.

References

1. Arrow, K.J., Debreu, G.: The existence of an equilibrium for a competitive economy. Econometrica 22(3), 265–290 (1954)
2. Babaioff, M., Walsh, W.E.: Incentive-compatible, budget-balanced, yet highle efficient auctions for supply chain formation. Decision Support Systems 39(1), 123–149 (2005)
3. Demange, G., Gale, D., Sotomayor, M.: Multi-item auctions. Journal of Political Economy 94 (1986)
4. Jackson, M.: Network formation. The New Palgrave Dictionary of Economics and the Law
5. Kakade, S., Kearns, M., Ortiz, L.: Graphical economics. In: Shawe-Taylor, J., Singer, Y. (eds.) COLT 2004. LNCS (LNAI), vol. 3120, pp. 17–32. Springer, Heidelberg (2004)
6. Kleinberg, J.M., Raghavan, P.: Query incentive networks. In: Proc. of 46th Annual IEEE Symposium on Foundations of Computer Science, pp. 132–141. IEEE Computer Society Press, Los Alamitos (2005)
7. Kleinberg, J., Tardos, E., Blume, L., Easley, D.: Trading networks with price-setting agents. In: Proceedings of the Eighth ACM Conference on Electronic Commerce (EC 2007), ACM Press, New York (2007)
8. Pavlov, E., Babaioff, M., Nisan, N.: Mechanisms for a spatially distributed market. In: Proceedings of the Fifth ACM Conference on Electronic Commerce (EC 2004), pp. 9–20. ACM Press, New York (2004)
9. Rubenstein, A., Wolinsky, A.: Middlemen. The Quarterly Journal of Economics 102(3), 581–594 (1987)
10. Sarma, A.D., Chakrabarty, D., Gollapudi, S.: Public advertisement broker markets. In (2007), http://www.cc.gatech.edu/~\atish/wine-paper.pdf
11. Shapley, L.S., Shubik, M.: On market games. Journal of Economic Theory 1(1), 9–25 (1969)
12. Yavas, A.: Middlemen in bilateral search markets. Journal of Labor Economics 12(3), 406–429 (1994)

K-NCC: Stability Against Group Deviations in Non-cooperative Computation

Itai Ashlagi, Andrey Klinger, and Moshe Tennenholtz

Technion–Israel Institute of Technology, Haifa 32000, Israel

Abstract. A function is non-cooperative computable [NCC] if honest agents can compute it by reporting truthfully their private inputs, while unilateral deviations by the players are not beneficial: if a deviation from truth revelation can mislead other agents, then the deviator might end up with a wrong result. Previous work provided full characterization of the boolean functions which are non-cooperatively computable. Later work have extended that study in various directions. This paper extends the study of NCC functions to the context of group deviations. A function is K-NCC if deviations by a group of at most K agents is not beneficial: in order to mislead other agents, at least one group member might compute the wrong outcome. A function which is K-NCC for every K is termed *strong-NCC*. In this paper we provide a full characterization of the K-NCC functions, for every K, and of strong-NCC functions in particular. We show that the hierarchy of K-NCC functions is strict. Surprisingly, we also show that an anonymous function is NCC iff it is strong-NCC; that is, an anonymous function which is non-cooperatively computable is stable against deviations by any coalition of the agents. In addition, we show that group deviations are stable: if there exists a deviating coalition of minimal size K, then there is no sub-coalition of it which will benefit by further deviation from the original deviating strategy.

1 Introduction

Non-cooperative computing [NCC], introduced in [7], deals with the desire to compute a function defined on agents' private inputs where the agents might have incentives not to report truthfully. This can be viewed as a task of *informational mechanism design*. While in a classical mechanism design context (see [5] Chapter 23) the essence of the problem is the lack of information about the agents' preferences, in NCC the agents' preferences are known but other information they possess which is needed for the joint activity is private. NCC introduces a game-theoretic version of the problem of multi-party computation.[1].

In order to see the basic idea behind NCC consider for example the situation where each agent's secret is a bit, and the function to be computed is the parity function. If all agents report their bits honestly then the parity can be easily

---

[1] Indeed, the work in [4,1] deals with NCC when there is no center in the system, bridging the gap to the classical assumptions in the cryptographic and distributed computing literature

X. Deng and F.C. Graham (Eds.): WINE 2007, LNCS 4858, pp. 564–569, 2007.

computed. However, if an agent reports 1 (resp. 0) instead of 0 (resp. 1), while all other agents report honestly, then this agent will be able to re-cover the true result by reversing the reported outcome, while misleading the other agents. Hence, the parity function is **not** non-cooperatively computable. On the other hand, if the function is the majority function, then false report might make the deviator unclear about the true result, given that the result of the majority function is computed and reported to the participants using a trusted center based on the information provided by them; this makes this function non-cooperatively computable.

The early results on NCC provided complete characterization of the functions which are non-cooperatively computable. Additional work has been carried out on extending this setting [6], as well as on considering the agents' costs, which lead to other forms of deviations [8].

In this paper we attack a major challenge: deviations by coalitions in the NCC setting. Although it has been already acknowledged that knowing whether a function is stable against deviations by groups of agents is central to the context of non-cooperative computing and rational multi-party computation [1], no analysis has been provided for the characterization of functions which are stable against deviations by coalitions in that context. While NCC is associated with honest computation being in equilibrium, group deviations in that context can be associated with the concept of strong equilibrium as introduced by Aumann [2]; therefore, we refer to a function as strong-NCC if no coalition can mislead in some cases at least one member which is not part of the coalition, without taking the risk this would cause at least one member of the coalition not to know the function value. More generally, we wish to study K-NCC functions, in which deviations of coalition of size at most K are considered. The case of NCC is then associated with 1-NCC functions.

In the NCC model there are n agents, each of which wish to compute an n-ary function w, with each of the agents holding one of the inputs to w. The process of computation is mediated by a center as follows: Each agent declares his input (truthfully or not) to the center, the center performs computation based on those inputs, and reports back to the agents an output. In the setting we deal with, the center applies w to the declared inputs and announces the value to all the agents. Each agent has now to decide on the output he accepts as a result of the computation.[2] We concentrate on agents whose utility function has two components. The main component, termed *correctness*, is the wish to compute the function correctly. The secondary component, termed *exclusivity*, is the wish that other agents do not compute the function correctly. The secondary component - exclusivity - is affecting the agent only if the main component - correctness - is not under risk. The definition of "exclusivity" is rather loose, and allows for many possible variants; for example, it can be more important for an agent to mislead a particular agent than another agent. For the results presented in this paper the exact meaning of exclusivity does not matter; the only

---

[2] In fact, under the famous revelation principle, one can show that the restriction to such mechanisms can be done without loss of generality.

assumption is that the situation in which at least one other agent is mistaken is better than the situation where all other agents are correct, as long as the agent can compute the function correctly.

In the subsequent sections we present sound and complete conditions for a function to be K-NCC, and in particular strong NCC. We prove that an n-ary boolean function is Strong NCC (i.e. resilient to deviation of a coalition of any size) iff it is not dominated and not k-reversible for any $1 \leq k < n$. Our result implies that any anonymous function is strong NCC iff it is NCC. We also show that the hierarchy generated by K-NCC functions is strict and that when a function is not stable against deviation of a minimal coalition of size K, then such a deviation will be stable against further deviations of sub-coalitions. In game-theoretic terms, this result implies that the existence of a coalition-proof equilibrium implies the existence of a strong equilibrium in the NCC setting.

2   Definitions

In this section we define the notion of K-NCC. Given a set of agents $N = \{1, 2, \ldots, n\}$, and a special agent termed "the center", we assume that there exists a private secure communication line between every agent $i \in N$ and the center. The type v_i of agent i is selected from some domain B_i. We concentrate on a Boolean domain, where $B_i = B = \{0, 1\}$

Given a function $w : B^n \to B$, we consider the following protocol:

1. For any instantiated type vector $v \in B^n$, each agent i declares his type $\hat{v}_i$ to the center (truthfully or not; $\hat{v}_i = v_i$ may or may not hold).
2. The center computes the value $w(\hat{v}) = w(\hat{v}_1, \ldots, \hat{v}_n)$ and announces it to all agents.
3. Each agent i computes $w(v)$ based on $w(\hat{v})$ and v_i (his true input).

The protocol defines a strategy space for each agent. A pure strategy for agent i is a pair of functions (f_i, g_i). $f_i : B \to B$, the *declaration function*, determines the input declared to the center based on the agent's true input. The *truthful* declaration function is the identity function $f^t(v) = v$. $g_i : B^2 \to B$, the *interpretation function*, is used by the agent to decide on the value of the function based on the announcement by the center and his true input. The *trusting* interpretation function is the projection function $g^t(v_1, v_2) = v_1$ in which the agent simply accepts the value announced by the center. We will refer to the strategy (f^t, g^t) as the *straightforward* strategy.

Note that the strategy profile consisting only of straightforward strategies results in each agent computing w correctly for all input vectors. We are looking for functions for which such a strategy profile forms an equilibrium, and more generally a (k-)strong equilibrium which is stable against deviations of coalition (of size at most k). We will use the following notations:

Definition 1. *For a set of agents* $C = \{i_1, \ldots, i_k\} \subseteq \{1, \ldots, n\}$, B_C *is defined as* $\prod_{j \in C} B_j$ *and* B_{-C} *is defined as* $\prod_{j \notin C} B_j$. *In the same way,* $v_C \in B_C$ *is a* *tuple of types of agents participating in the set C, and $v_{-C} \in B_{-C}$ is a tuple of types of agents not participating in the set C.*

We can now define K-NCC:

Definition 2. *A function w is called K-NCC if the following holds: For any set of agents $C = \{i_1, \ldots, i_k\}$, $k \leq K$, every tuple of their strategies $((f_{i_1}, g_{i_1}), \ldots, (f_{i_k}, g_{i_k}))$, and every corresponding agent types $v_{i_j} \in B$, $1 \leq j \leq k$, it is the case that:*

- *either $\exists v_{-C} \in B_{-C}, \exists j, i_j \in C$, such that*

$$g_{i_j}(w(f_{i_1}(v_{i_1}), \ldots, f_{i_k}(v_{i_k}), v_{-C}), v_{i_j}) \neq w(v_{i_1}, \ldots, v_{i_k}, v_{-C})$$

- *or $\forall v_{-C} \in B_{-C}$ we have*

$$w(f_{i_1}(v_{i_1}), \ldots, f_{i_k}(v_{i_k}), v_{-C}) = w(v_{i_1}, \ldots, v_{i_k}, v_{-C})$$

In words, each deviating coalition of up to K players will either be mistaken for some types of the non-deviating players or will always produce the same result as if they didn't deviate

The following definition will play a key role in the characterization of functions which are K-NCC:

Definition 3. *A function w is called k-reversible if the following holds: $\exists C = \{i_1, \ldots, i_k\} \subseteq \{1, \ldots, n\}$ such that $\forall v_{-C} \in B_{-C}, \forall j, 1 \leq j \leq k, \forall v_{i_j} \in B_{i_j}$,*

$$w(v_{i_1}, \ldots, v_{i_k}, v_{-C}) = 1 - w(1 - v_{i_1}, \ldots, 1 - v_{i_k}, v_{-C})$$

Note that in this definition, the set C contains exactly k players.

It may worth to notice that the definition of reversible functions discussed in [7] coincides with the definition of 1-reversible functions above.

Another definition, used in previous work on NCC is the following one:

Definition 4. *A function w is called dominated if the following holds: $\exists i \in \{1, \ldots, n\}, v_i \in B$, such that $\forall v_{-\{i\}}, v'_{-\{i\}} \in B_{-\{i\}}$, $w(v_i, v_{-\{i\}}) = w(v_i, v'_{-\{i\}})$, and there is some $v_{-\{i\}} \in B_{-\{i\}}$, for which $w(1 - v_i, v_{-\{i\}}) = 1 - w(1 - v_i, v_{-\{i\}})$.*

If a function is dominated then, for a particular value of a particular agent's type, the agent knows the value of the function, while it can still influence the outcome by his report.

3   A Full Characterization of the K-NCC Functions

Given the previous definitions, the characterization of NCC functions obtained in [7] can now be stated as follows:

A boolean function is 1-NCC iff it is not dominated and is not 1-reversible.

The following theorem establishes the exact conditions under which a function which is $(K - 1)$-NCC is also K-NCC. It will imply necessary and sufficient conditions for a function to be K-NCC, and strong NCC.

Theorem 1. *For* $2 \leq K \leq n-1$ *a boolean function is* K*-NCC iff it is* $(K-1)$*-NCC and not k-reversible for* $k = K$.

Theorem 1 does not deal with the case where $K = n$. As it turns out, this case is immediate:

Theorem 2. *A boolean function is* n*-NCC if it is* $(n\text{-}1)$*-NCC.*

We can now state the following necessary and sufficient conditions for a function to be K-NCC:

Corollary 1. *A boolean function* w *is* K*-NCC iff it is not dominated and not k-reversible for every* $1 \leq k \leq K$. *Therefore, a boolean function is strong NCC iff it is not dominated and not k-reversible for every* $1 \leq k < n$.

3.1   Anonymous Functions

An interesting class of functions are the *anonymous* functions (aka symmetric functions). The value of an anonymous Boolean function depends only on the number of 1's in the input. Many of the functions discussed in the computer science literature, such as parity, majority, consensus, order statistics, etc., are anonymous. As we now show for these functions any NCC function is also Strong NCC. This powerful result is implied by our characterization and the following theorem:

Theorem 3. *Anonymous n-variable functions that are not 1-reversible, are not k-reversible for any* $1 < k < n$.

It now follows:

Corollary 2. *An anonymous n-variable Boolean function is Strong NCC iff it is NCC.*

This follows from Theorem 1 and Theorem 3 for coalitions smaller than n, and from Theorem 2 for coalitions of size n.

4   The K-NCC Hierarchy

The previous section established the characterization of K-NCC functions. We now show that the hierarchy implied by these functions is strict. To show this, we prove the following:

Theorem 4. *For* $n > 2$, $K \leq n$, *there exists a function* w *that is* K*-reversible, but not k-reversible for any* $k < K$

Theorems 1, 2 and 4 imply the strictness of the K-NCC hierarchy:

Corollary 3. *For* $n \geq 2$ *we have:* $n\text{-}NCC = (n\text{-}1)\text{-}NCC \subset (n\text{-}2)\text{-}NCC \subset \ldots \subset 2\text{-}NCC \subset NCC$

5 Stability of Deviations

Stability against deviations by coalitions is typically considered as a very demanding requirement. Nevertheless, we have shown that for anonymous functions a function is stable against deviations by coalitions iff it is stable against unilateral deviations. This can be viewed as a highly positive result. When considering more general situations, it is natural to consider the question of whether the deviations themselves are stable. Indeed, this has led to the introduction of solution concepts, such as coalition-proof equilibrium [3], in which the stability of the deviations is considered. In this section we show that our results remain the same when considering only stable deviations. This will be proven in a very general setup. Namely, we will show that if there exists a deviating coalition, then there exists a stable deviating coalition. Formally, we will consider minimal deviations, and show that any further deviation by a smaller sub-coalition is not beneficial. This implies that in the NCC setting the existence of coalition proof equilibrium [3] coincides with the existence of strong equilibrium [2] (which by itself coincides with the existence of NCC for anonymous functions).

Theorem 5. *Consider a minimal deviation from the straightforward strategy profile, by a coalition C. Then, no further deviation by $C' \subset C$ can be beneficial to C'.*

References

1. Abraham, I., Dolev, D., Gonen, R., Halpern, J.: Distributed computing meets game theory: robust mechanisms for rational secret sharing and multiparty computation. In: PODC 2006: Proceedings of the twenty-fifth annual ACM symposium on Principles of distributed computing, pp. 53–62. ACM Press, New York (2006)
2. Aumann, R.J.: Acceptable points in general cooperative n-person games. In: Tucker, A.W., Luce, R.D. (eds.) Contribution to the Theory of Games. Annals of Mathematics Studies, vol. IV, pp. 287–324 (1959)
3. Bernheim, B.D., Peleg, B., Whinston, M.D.: Coalition-proof nash equilibria i. concepts. Journal of Economic Theory 42(1), 1–12 (1987), available at: http://ideas.repec.org/a/eee/jetheo/v42y1987i1p1-12.html
4. Halpern, J., Teague, V.: Rational secret sharing and multiparty computation: extended abstract. In: Proc. of STOC 2004 (2004)
5. Mas-Colell, A., Whinston, M.D., Green, J.R.: Microeconomic Theory. Oxford University Press, Oxford (1995)
6. McGrew, R., Porter, R., Shoham, Y.: Towards a general theory of non-cooperative computation. In: Proc. of the 9th conference of theoretical aspects of rationality and knowlede (TARK 2003), pp. 59–71 (2003)
7. Shoham, Y., Tennenholtz, M.: Non-cooperative computation: boolean functions with correctness and exclusivity. Theor. Comput. Sci. 343, 97–113 (2005)
8. Smorodinsky, R., Tennenholtz, M.: Overcoming free riding in multi-party computations–the anonymous case. Games and Economic Behavior 55(2), 385–406 (2006), available at: http://ideas.repec.org/a/eee/gamebe/v55y2006i2p385-406.html

Monotone Properties of Randomized Symmetric Incentive Compatible Auctions*

Aries Wei Sun

Department of Computer Science, City University of Hong Kong
sunwei@cs.cityu.edu.hk

Abstract. In this paper, we give the definition of *randomized* symmetric incentive compatible auctions. Then we define three monotone properties of such auctions and study the implication relationships among them. This paper extends our previous work [4] which was focused on *deterministic* symmetric incentive compatible auctions.

1 Introduction

Originally, auctions were used to sell normal items that are in limited supply. Largely because of digital goods of zero marginal cost, new variations of auctions where the supply is unlimited are studied [5,2,1,3]. And several important properties that has not been necessary for many previously well known auction protocols are discovered. Thus a natural question arises: what are the basic principles we have to stick to in economic transactions at the micro level? We are motivated to study this fundamental question to understand the limitation and the possibility in auction protocols.

This paper introduces the concept of *randomzied* symmetric incentive compatible auctions, defines three monotone properties in such auctions, and studies the implication relationships among them. It is an extension to our previous works published in [4], which was focused on *deterministic* symmetric incentive compatible auctions.

§2 introduces the preliminaries, including the model and notations (§2.1), fundamental definitions (§2.2), the definition of symmetric incentive compatible auction (§2.3), and the a discussion on the price function (§2.4).

§3 reviews the definition of deterministic symmetric incentive compatible auction (§3.1), and the implication relationships among them (§3.2). These results have been achieved in our previous works[4].

In parallel, §4 introduces the definition of randomized symmetric incentive compatible auction (§4.1), and studies the implication relationships among them (§4.2). Analyses show that the relationships are similar to the deterministic case studied before.

§5 concludes.

---

* This research is supported by SRG grant (7001989) of City University of Hong Kong.

X. Deng and F.C. Graham (Eds.): WINE 2007, LNCS 4858, pp. 570–575, 2007.

2 Preliminaries

This section introduces the preliminaries. §2.1 introduces the auction model we are studying and its notations. §2.2 reviews some fundamental definitions. §2.3 defines the concepts of deterministic and randomized symmetric incentive compatible auctions and studies their relationship. §2.4 provides a discussion on the price function.

2.1 The Model and Notations

We restrict our attentions to auctions satisfying the following properties:

1. Every bidder wants at most one item.
2. The items sold by the auction are the same.
3. The auction is carried out in a one-round sealed-bid manner.
4. The bidders know the auction protocol.

We use the following notations and terminologies throughout the paper:

n the total number of bidders
$a^{(i)}$ the i-th agent (or bidder) in the auction
$b^{(i)}$ the bid submitted by $a^{(i)}$. $b^{(i)} \geq 0$.
$v^{(i)}$ the *private* valuation on the product of $a^{(i)}$. $v^{(i)} \geq 0$.
$\mathbf{b} = (b^{(1)}, b^{(2)}, \ldots, b^{(n)})$
$\mathbf{b}^{(\sim i)} = (b^{(1)}, b^{(2)}, \ldots, b^{(i-1)}, b^{(i+1)}, \ldots, b^{(n)})$
$w^{(i)}$ The number of items agent $a^{(i)}$ has won from the auction.
$p^{(i)}$ The price agent $a^{(i)}$ should pay for *each unit*. $p^{(i)} \geq 0$. In our model $w^{(i)}$ is
    either 0 or 1.
$u^{(i)}$ The utility of agent $a^{(i)}$. $u^{(i)} = (v^{(i)} - p^{(i)}) \times w^{(i)}$.
Revenue(b) $= \sum_{i=1}^{n} w^{(i)} \times p^{(i)}$. It is the auctioneer's revenue.

The auctions we study in this paper can be viewed as algorithms that take **b** as input, and gives $w^{(i)}$ and $p^{(i)}$, $i = 1, 2, \ldots, n$, as output. $a^{(i)}$ is a *winner* if $w^{(i)} > 0$ and a *loser* otherwise. Notice that if $a^{(i)}$ is a loser, it pays \$0, while $p^{(i)}$ may be a positive number.

Deterministic auctions are those for which $w^{(i)}$ and $p^{(i)}$, $i = 1, 2, \ldots, n$, are completely determined as a function of **b**. Whereas **randomized** auctions are those for which the computation processes of $w^{(i)}$ and $p^{(i)}$ are randomized. [5].

2.2 Fundamental Definitions

Definition 1. *An auction is* individual rational *if* $b^{(i)} < p^{(i)} \Rightarrow w^{(i)} = 0, \forall i$.

Definition 2 ([6]). *A deterministic auction is* incentive compatible *if, for each* $a^{(i)}$ *and any* $\mathbf{b}^{(\sim i)}$, $u^{(i)}$ *is maximized by bidding* $b^{(i)} = v^{(i)}$.

Definition 3 ([5]). *A randomized auction is* incentive compatible *if it can be described as a probability distribution over deterministic incentive compatible auctions.*

2.3 Deterministic and Randomized Symmetric Incentive Compatible Auctions

Definition 4 ([4]). *A **deterministic** auction is symmetric iff for any input:*

1. $b^{(i)} = b^{(j)} \Rightarrow p^{(i)} = p^{(j)}$.
2. $p^{(i)}$ *remains unchanged if two other bidders exchange bids.*

Definition 5. *A **randomized** auction is symmetric iff for any input:*

1. $b^{(i)} = b^{(j)} \Rightarrow \boldsymbol{Pr}\left[p^{(i)} = p\right] = \boldsymbol{Pr}\left[p^{(j)} = p\right], \forall p \in \Re$.
2. $\boldsymbol{Pr}\left[p^{(j)} = p\right]$ *remains unchanged if two other bidders exchange bids,* $\forall p \in \Re$.

Remarks: It is not hard to prove that if an auction satisfies Definition 2, then it also satisfies Definition 3. This result is not used later and is omitted in this short paper submission.

Definition 6 (SIC::D). *An auction* a_d *belongs to the set **SIC::D**, iff:*

1. It is consistent with the model described in §2.1.
*2. It is a **deterministic** symmetric auction.*
3. It is individual rational and incentive compatibe.

Such a_d *is called a "deterministic symmetric incentive compatible auction".*

Definition 7 (SIC::R). *An auction* a_r *belongs to the set **SIC::R**, iff:*

1. It is consistent with the model described in §2.1.
*2. It is a **randomized** symmetric auction.*
3. It is individual rational and incentive compatible.

Such a_r *is called a "randomized symmetric incentive compatible auction".*

Theorem 1
$$SIC::D \subset SIC::R$$

Proof. For any $a_d \in$ **SIC::D**, we can construct a set $\{a_d\} \subset$ **SIC::D**, and view a_d as a probability distribution over $\{a_d\}$. It is easy to check that a_d also satisfies Definition 3 and Definition 5, by which we conclude $a_d \in$ **SIC::R**.

Hence for any $a_d \in$ **SIC::D**, we must also have $a_d \in$ **SIC::R**.   □

2.4 A Discusson on the Price Function

In this subsection, we restrict our attention to auctions in **SIC::R**. The description of allocation policies can be much simplified by a set of price functions, $f_i(\cdot)$, one each for the participating agents. $a^{(i)}$ wins the item if $b^{(i)} > f_i(\cdot)$, loses if $b^{(i)} < f_i(\cdot)$. In the event $b^{(i)} = f_i(\cdot)$, $a^{(i)}$ is either a zero winner or a zero loser depending on whether it is allocated with the item by the auction protocol.

Lemma 1 (Bid Independent Pricing. Folklore, see e.g. [5]). *In an auction, either deterministic or randomized, that is* individual rational *and* incentive compatible, *the pricing function of $a^{(i)}$ does not depend on $b^{(i)}$. In other words, $a^{(i)}$'s price function does not take its bid $b^{(i)}$ as a variable. i.e. $p^{(i)} = f_i(\mathbf{b}^{(\sim i)})$. And for any bidder $a^{(i)}$, if $b^{(i)} > p^{(i)}$, then $a^{(i)}$ is a winner.*

Remarks: Given Lemma 1, $a^{(i)}$'s price function can be expressed as $f_i(\mathbf{b}^{(\sim i)})$.

Lemma 2. *In any auction $a_r \in SIC::R$, every bidder $a^{(i)}$'s price function is independent of its index i.*

Proof. Let $b^{(i)} = b^{(j)}$. By Definition 5,

$$\mathbf{Pr}\left[f_i(\mathbf{b}^{(\sim i)}) = p\right] = \mathbf{Pr}\left[f_j(\mathbf{b}^{(\sim j)}) = p\right], \forall p \in \Re$$

For symmetric auctions, if we sort $\mathbf{b}^{(\sim i)}$ in decreasing order into $\mathbf{b}'^{(\sim i)}$, the distribution of the price function will not change. i.e.,

$$\mathbf{Pr}\left[f_i(\mathbf{b}^{(\sim i)}) = p\right] = \mathbf{Pr}\left[f_i(\mathbf{b}'^{(\sim i)}) = p\right], \forall p \in \Re$$

Similarly, reorder $\mathbf{b}^{(\sim j)}$ into $\mathbf{b}'^{(\sim j)}$, we have

$$\mathbf{Pr}\left[f_j(\mathbf{b}^{(\sim j)}) = p\right] = \mathbf{Pr}\left[f_j(\mathbf{b}'^{(\sim j)}) = p\right], \forall p \in \Re$$

$\mathbf{b}'^{(\sim i)} = \mathbf{b}'^{(\sim j)}$ and $\mathbf{Pr}\left[f_i(\mathbf{b}'^{(\sim i)}) = p\right] = \mathbf{Pr}\left[f_j(\mathbf{b}'^{(\sim j)}) = p\right], \forall p \in \Re$, thus we complete the proof.

Remarks: Given Lemma 2, we can remove the subscript from every bidder $a^{(i)}$'s price function $f_i(\cdot)$, and denote it by $f(\cdot)$. Thus, the output of the auction is indepent of the order of the bidders. In the following parts, we always assume the bid vector is sorted in decreasing order.

3   Deterministic Monotone Properties

This section reviews the results we have achieved in [4], including the definitions of the there deterministic monotone properties (§3.1) and the implication relationships among them (§3.2).

3.1   Definitions

For $d \in$ **SIC::D**, we have defined 3 monotone properties in [4]. Namely, deterministic winner monotone (WM$_D$), deterministic price function monotone (PFM$_D$), and deterministic revenue monotone (RM$_D$), which are defined as follows:

1. **WM$_D$:** $b^{(i)} > b^{(j)} \geq p^{(j)} \Rightarrow b^{(i)} \geq p^{(i)}$.
2. **PFM$_D$:** $\mathbf{b}^{(\sim i)} > \mathbf{b}^{(\sim j)} \Rightarrow f(\mathbf{b}^{(\sim i)}) \geq f(\mathbf{b}^{(\sim j)})$.
3. **RM$_D$:** $\mathbf{b} > \mathbf{b}' \Rightarrow$ Revenue($\mathbf{b}$) $\geq$ Reveune($\mathbf{b}'$).

3.2 Implication Relationships

Theorem 2 ([4]). *For any auction $a_d \in$ **SIC::D**, the implication relationships between any two of the three monotone properties are as follows:*
$PFM_D \Rightarrow WM_D$, $WM_D \nRightarrow PFM_D$; $RM_D \nRightarrow WM_D$, $WM_D \nRightarrow RM_D$; $PFM_D \nRightarrow RM_D$, $RM_D \nRightarrow PFM_D$.

Moreover, the implication relationships from any two to the other one of the three monotone properties are as follows:
PFM_D and $RM_D \Rightarrow WM_D$; WM_D and $RM_D \nRightarrow PFM_D$; WM_D and $PFM_D \nRightarrow RM_D$.

Finally, it is possible that WM_D, PFM_D and RM_D simutaneously exist.

4   Randomized Monotone Propoties

In §4.1 we define radomized monotone properties in parallel to §3.1. In §4.2, we study the implication relationships among them.

4.1   Definitions

For any $a_r \in$ **SIC::R**, we define 3 monotone properties in parallel to §3.1. Namely, randomized winner monotone (WM_R), randomized price function monotone (PFM_R), and randomized revenue monotone (RM_R), which are defined as follows:

1. **WM_R:** $b^{(i)} > b^{(j)} \Rightarrow \mathbf{Pr}\left[b^{(i)} \geq p^{(i)}\right] \geq \mathbf{Pr}\left[b^{(j)} \geq p^{(j)}\right]$.
2. **PFM_R:** $\mathbf{b}^{(\sim j)} > \mathbf{b}^{(\sim i)} \Rightarrow \mathbf{Pr}\left[f(\mathbf{b}^{(\sim j)}) > p\right] \geq \mathbf{Pr}\left[f(\mathbf{b}^{(\sim i)}) > p\right], \forall p \in \Re$.
3. **RM_R:** $\mathbf{b} > \mathbf{b}' \Rightarrow \mathbf{Pr}\left[\text{Revenue}(\mathbf{b}) > y\right] \geq \mathbf{Pr}\left[\text{Revenue}(\mathbf{b}') > y\right], \forall y \in \Re$.

Remarks: It is obvious that the *deterministic* monotone properties are special cases of their *randomized* counterparts. A rigor proof is omitted in this short paper submission to save space and is available upon request.

4.2   Implication Relationships

Lemma 3. $PFM_R \Rightarrow WM_R$

Proof. Suppose $b^{(i)} > b^{(j)}$, then $\mathbf{b}^{(\sim i)} < \mathbf{b}^{(\sim j)}$.
By PFM_R, $\mathbf{Pr}\left[f(\mathbf{b}^{(\sim j)}) > b^{(i)}\right] \geq \mathbf{Pr}\left[f(\mathbf{b}^{(\sim i)}) > b^{(i)}\right]$. i.e.

$$\mathbf{Pr}\left[p^{(j)} > b^{(i)}\right] \geq \mathbf{Pr}\left[p^{(i)} > b^{(i)}\right]$$

And since $\mathbf{Pr}\left[p^{(j)} > b^{(j)}\right] \geq \mathbf{Pr}\left[p^{(j)} > b^{(i)}\right]$, we have:

$$\mathbf{Pr}\left[b^{(j)} \geq p^{(j)}\right] \leq \mathbf{Pr}\left[b^{(i)} \geq p^{(i)}\right]$$

Thus we complete the proof.   □

Theorem 3. *For any auction* $a_r \in \mathbf{SIC::R}$, *the implication relationships between any two of the three monotone properties are as follows:*

$PFM_R \Rightarrow WM_R, WM_R \nRightarrow PFM_R;\ RM_R \nRightarrow WM_R, WM_R \nRightarrow RM_R;\ PFM_R \nRightarrow RM_R, RM_R \nRightarrow PFM_R.$

Moreover, the implication relationships from any two to the other one of the three monotone properties are as follows:

PFM_R *and* $RM_R \Rightarrow WM_R;\ WM_R$ *and* $RM_R \nRightarrow PFM_R;\ WM_R$ *and* $PFM_R \nRightarrow RM_R.$

Finally, it is possible that WM_R, PFM_R *and* RM_R *simultaneously exist.*

Proof. By Lemma 3, we have $PFM_R \Rightarrow WM_R$ and PFM_R and $RM_R \Rightarrow WM_R$. By Theorem 1 and Theorem 2, we know that:

1. $WM_R \nRightarrow PFM_R;\ RM_R \nRightarrow WM_R, WM_R \nRightarrow RM_R;\ PFM_R \nRightarrow RM_R, RM_R \nRightarrow PFM_R.$
2. WM_R and $RM_R \nRightarrow PFM_R;\ WM_R$ and $PFM_R \nRightarrow RM_R.$
3. It is possible that WM_R, PFM_R and RM_R simultaneously exist.

Thus we complete the proof. □

5 Conclusions

In this short paper we have extend our previous works [4] on *deterministic* symmetric incentive compatible auctions to the *randomized* case. At the same time, we have improved notations, presentation, and understandability.

Acknowledgements

I want to thank my supervisor Prof. **Xiaotie Deng** for stimulating discussions and invaluable comments. This paper is done while I am visiting University of California, San Diego. I want to thank Prof. **Fan Chung Graham** for providing me a superb research environment at UCSD.

References

1. Aggarwal, G., Goel, A., Motwani, R.: Truthful auctions for pricing search keywords. In: ACM Conference on Electronic Commerce (EC), ACM Press, New York (2006)
2. Bu, T., Qi, Q., Sun, A.W.: Unconditional competitive auctions with copy and budget constraints. In: Spirakis, P.G., Mavronicolas, M., Kontogiannis, S.C. (eds.) WINE 2006. LNCS, vol. 4286, Springer, Heidelberg (2006)
3. Deng, X., Huang, L., Li, M.: On walrasian price of cpu time. In: Wang, L. (ed.) COCOON 2005. LNCS, vol. 3595, Springer, Heidelberg (2005)
4. Deng, X., Iwama, K., Qi, Q., Sun, A.W., Tasaka, T.: Properties of symmetric incentive compatible auctions. In: The 13th Annual International Computing and Combinatorics Conference (COCOON 2007) (2007)
5. Goldberg, A., Hartline, J., Karlin, A., Saks, M., Wright, A.: Competitive auctions. Games and Economic Behavior 55(2), 242–269 (2006)
6. Vickrey, W.: Counterspeculation, auctions, and competitive sealed tenders. Journal of Finance 16, 8–37 (1961)

Computing Optimal Bundles for Sponsored Search

Arpita Ghosh[1], Hamid Nazerzadeh[2,*], and Mukund Sundararajan[2,**]

[1] Yahoo! Research
arpita@yahoo-inc.com
[2] Stanford University
{hamidnz,mukunds}@stanford.edu

Abstract. A *context* in sponsored search is additional information about a query, such as the user's age, gender or location, that can change an advertisement's relevance or an advertiser's value for that query. Given a set of contexts, advertiser welfare is maximized if the search engine runs a separate auction for each context; however, due to lack of competition within contexts, this can lead to a significant loss in revenue. In general, neither separate auctions nor pure bundling need maximize revenue.

With this motivation, we study the algorithmic question of computing the revenue-maximizing partition of a set of items under a second-price mechanism and additive valuations for bundles. We show that the problem is strongly NP-hard, and present an algorithm that yields a $\frac{1}{2}$-approximation of the revenue from the optimal partition. The algorithm simultaneously yields a $\frac{1}{2}$-approximation of the optimal welfare, thus ensuring that the gain in revenue is not at the cost of welfare. Finally we show that our algorithm can be applied to the sponsored search setting with multiple slots, to obtain a constant factor approximation of the revenue from the optimal partition.

1 Introduction

Sponsored search is a very effective medium for advertising as it allows precise targeting of advertisements to users: a user can be presented with advertisements that are directly related to her search query. However, further targeting is possible by using the *context* of a query and the user associated with the query. A *context* in a sponsored search auction is additional information associated with a particular instance of a query that can change an advertisement's relevance or an advertiser's value for that keyword. For example, zip codes can often be inferred from IP addresses, providing a user location context: for certain queries (say pizza delivery, or dentist) local advertisements might be more relevant to the user than non-local ones. Other examples of contexts are age or gender-related demographic information, or 'search intent' gleaned from other searches by the same user.

---

* Work performed in part while visiting Yahoo! Research.
** Supported by a Stanford Graduate Fellowship.

X. Deng and F.C. Graham (Eds.): WINE 2007, LNCS 4858, pp. 576–583, 2007.
© Springer-Verlag Berlin Heidelberg 2007

The formal study of sponsored search with contexts was recently introduced by Even-Dar et al [10], where the authors showed that splitting a keyword auction into mutiple auctions, one for each context (for example, if the context is location, then having one auction for each location), increases welfare. They also gave examples demonstrating that there is a tradeoff: while welfare increases upon splitting contexts, the search engine's revenue may be larger when the keyword is not split (*i.e.*, all contexts stay combined). (To see why, consider the case when the auction for each context has only one participating advertiser; since the mechanism used is a a variant of second price auctions [16,8], such advertisers face no competition and will generally pay a small reserve. So the revenue to the search engine is very small compared to the situation when contexts are not separated.) However, the search engine's choice is *not limited to the two extreme partitions* of the set of contexts, namely, keeping each context separate (maximizing efficiency) or combining all contexts together (pure bundling): other partitions of the set of contexts may give better points on the revenue-efficiency trade-off curve (in fact, we will show that the revenue from the optimal partition can be arbitrarily larger than the revenue from these two extreme partitions, while losing no more than half the maximum efficiency.)

In this paper, we study the algorithmic problem of optimally partitioning a set of contexts to maximize revenue under a second-price mechanism in the full information setting, *i.e.*, when the matrix of bidder valuations for each context is known (for simplicity, we study the case of a single slot, and later generalize the results to multiple slots). We show that this problem is strongly NP-hard, and then provide a 1/2-approximation algorithm for it. This approximation algorithm also loses no more than 1/2 the maximum possible efficiency (obtained when all contexts are auctioned separately, possibly with great loss in revenue). We emphasize that since the optimal revenue can be arbitrarily larger than the revenue from either selling all contexts separately or combining them all together, the revenue from this algorithm can also be arbitrarily larger than the natural benchmark revenue; the factor 1/2 is with respect to the optimal revenue over *all* partitions, not the larger revenue of the two extreme partitions. Finally we show that our algorithm can be applied to the sponsored search setting with multiple slots to obtain a factor $\frac{(1-q)}{2}$ of the optimal revenue, when slot clickthrough rates decay geometrically [6] as q^j.

We consider the full information setting for the following reason. A search engine making the decision to split contexts might want to compute a partition of contexts into auctions just once (or infrequently), rather than dynamically [1]. In this case the search engine will use observed historical data to compute these partitions. Specifically, consider keywords where the value-per-click remains almost constant across contexts, with only click-through rates varying across context. Search engines usually have reasonable estimates of click-through rates across contexts, and also of valuations of advertisers who bid frequently on a keyword

---

[1] In fact, it is not clear what it means to dynamically compute bundles of contexts in the sponsored search setting, since queries corresponding to all contexts do not appear simultaneously; also advertisers might change their bids asynchronously.

(while the GSP auction is not truthful, techniques from [16] can be used to obtain estimates of values). Further, advertisers' actual valuations for keywords do not vary significantly over time, as these values are typically based on the estimated profit from future conversions. Thus it is reasonable and possible to use a partitioning algorithm based on full information in this setting [2]. A similar reasoning applies to another situation where bundling may be valuable, which is for related keywords with thin markets (for instance, bundling together misspellings of a valuable keyword like insurance, where each misspelling might have bids from only a few advertisers).

Related Work: The study of bundling in the economics literature was started by Palfrey [15], and later extended to various settings [7,5,4]. Recently, Jehiel et. al. [11] proposed a novel framework to study mixed bundling auctions, and proved that under certain distributional assumption over valuations, mixed bundling generates more revenue than both bundling all items together, or selling all items separately. Another related paper in this context is [12], which studies high revenue auctions from the class of virtual valuations combinatorial auctions, and gives an auction which is within a logarithmic factor of the revenue maximizing auction for additive valuations. Bundling has also been studied in the setting of monopoly pricing [1,14,13,3]. Our work differs from all of this literature in that we consider the algorithmic problem of computing the optimal, revenue maximizing partition under a second price mechanism in the full information setting; we give a constant factor approximation for this problem, *along with* an efficiency guarantee.

A different solution for revenue maximization in thin markets is to set a reserve price based on estimates of distributions of advertiser valuations [9]. Bundling is a more robust solution when bidders' values (or distributions of bidder values) change with time, but in a positively correlated fashion, such as temporal or seasonal variations (prominent examples are keywords related to travel, or occasions such as Valentine's day (like flowers)). In such cases the same bundling structure can be maintained as opposed to optimal reserve prices which will need to be updated to maintain high revenues.

2   Model

There is a set I of items numbered $1\ldots k$, and and a set U of agents, $1,\ldots,n$. There is a single copy of each item (we discuss the multiple-slot case in §5). Let v_{ij} be the value that agent i has for item j. We assume that agents valuations for bundles are additive—the value that agent i has for a bundle $B \subseteq I$, v_{iB}, is $\sum_{j\in B} v_{ij}$.

Items, or bundles of items, are sold according to a second-price auction: the winner of a bundle B is the agent with max v_{iB}, and is charged the second highest valuation for that bundle. An allocation partitions I across the bidders. Let S_i

---
[2] Note that once bundles have been computed, the usual equilibrium analysis of a keyword auction can be applied to each bundle [16].

denote the set of items allocated to bidder i. The welfare of the allocation is $\sum_{i \in U} v_{iS_i}$, and the revenue is the sum of the prices paid by each winning agent.

Our problem is the following: Given the matrix of valuations v_{ij}, we want to compute the revenue maximizing partition of items into bundles, when each bundle is awarded to the agent with the highest valuation at a price equal to the second highest valuation for the bundle.

We briefly discuss how the sponsored search setting maps to the above model. Suppose there are n bidders, where bidder i, $1 \leq i \leq n$, has a value per click v_i. Assume that there is just one slot. Suppose there are k different contexts, and the clickthrough rate (CTR) of bidder i for context j is c_{ij}—this is the probability that the advertisement of bidder i will be clicked on when displayed in context j. Further, let f_j denote the number of impressions corresponding to a specific context. The value that advertiser i has for context j is $v_{ij} = v_i f_j c_{ij}$. We assume that valuations are additive, i.e. the valuation for a set of contexts I' is $v_i \cdot \sum_{j \in I'} f_j c_{ij}$. We note that our model is quite general and can also be applied to bundling different keywords together or the case that different context has different values.

3 Characterizing Optimal Bundling

An *optimal bundling* is a partitioning of items into bundles that leads to the largest revenue, when items are allocated to the agent with the highest valuation for the bundle at a price equal to the second-highest valuation. In this section, we characterize the structure of bundles in an optimal bundling, and show that bundling to maximize revenue does not lose much efficiency.

Before we discuss optimal bundling, it is natural to ask whether it is sufficient merely to consider two extreme partitions: sell all items separately, or bundle them all together (in fact, much prior work on bundling restricts itself to these two options). However, the larger of the revenues from these two extreme partitions can be arbitrarily worse than the revenue of the optimal bundling, as the following example shows. The same example shows that the efficiency loss can also be arbitrarily large when we choose the revenue-maximizing bundle from these two extreme partitions.

Example 1. Suppose there are k items and k agents. The valuation of bidder i is 1 for item i, and 0 for all other items. If all items are sold separately, the revenue is 0 (and welfare is k). Bundling them together gives a revenue of 1 (and welfare 1). However, the revenue of optimal bundling is $\frac{k}{2}$, which is obtained by pairing items, *i.e.*, partitioning into $\frac{k}{2}$ bundles; this also has welfare $\frac{k}{2}$. Thus choosing between these two options to maximize revenue can lead to revenue and efficiency that are both arbitrarily worse than the optimal revenue and optimal efficiency.

The following facts follow easily from the above example. (Note that maximum efficiency is always obtained when selling all items separately.)

- An efficiency-maximizing bundling with the highest revenue does not, in the worst case, give a c-approximation of revenue for any constant $c \geq 0$.
- A revenue-maximizing bundle with the highest efficiency does not, in the worst case, yield better than a $\frac{1}{2}$-approximation of welfare.

(Note that the revenue maximizing bundle is not unique, and efficiency can vary across optimal partitions: suppose there are 2 items, and 3 bidders with valuations $(10, 0)$, $(5, 5)$, and $(0, 10)$. Both partitions yield the maximum revenue of 10; however one has welfare 20 and the other has welfare 10.)

We will now show, in Theorem 1, that the statement in the second fact is tight. Let h_j be the highest valuation for item j, i.e. $h_j = \max_i\{v_{ij}\}$, and let s_j be the second highest valuation for item j. We state the following fact without proof. Consider a bundle B in an optimal bundling. If there is an item j that can be removed from B with no decrease in revenue, the new bundling obtained by selling j separately from B is an optimal bundling with weakly greater efficiency. Note that this lemma implies that in any bundle B (in a revenue-optimal bundling with highest efficiency) with two or more items, we can assume that $h_j > s_j$ for $j \in B$. We state the following lemma regarding the structure of the optimal bundling (proof in full version):

Lemma 1. *Consider a bundle B in an optimal bundling with highest efficiency. If bidder i has the highest valuation for item j in bundle B, then i has either the highest valuation or the second highest valuation for bundle B.*

Theorem 1. *An optimal bundling with the highest efficiency also gives a $\frac{1}{2}$-approximation for efficiency.*

Proof. Consider a bundle B in such an optimal bundling, and let i_1 and i_2 be the bidders with the highest and the second highest valuation for the bundle. Since B is allocated to i_1, $v_{i_1 B} \geq (1/2)(\sum_{j \in B} v_{i_1 j} + \sum_{j \in B} v_{i_2 j})$. From Lemma 1, we have $\sum_{j \in B} v_{i_1 j} + \sum_{j \in B} v_{i_2 j} \geq \sum_{j \in B} h_j$. Therefore, summing over all bundles in the optimal bundling, the efficiency of the allocation is at least $\frac{1}{2}\sum_{j=1}^{k} h_j$. The proof follows since the maximum efficiency is $\sum_{j=1}^{k} h_j$.

4   Computing the Optimal Bundling

We now turn to the question of computing a revenue-maximizing bundle.

Theorem 2. *The problem of finding the optimal bundling is strongly NP-Hard.*

Proof. The proof is by reduction from 3-partition, which is strongly NP-hard: given a multiset S of $3n$ positive integers, can $S = \{x_1, x_2, \ldots, x_{3n}\}$ be partitioned into n subsets $S_1, S_2, \ldots, S_n$ such that the sum of the numbers in each subset is equal.

Let $w = \sum_{i=1}^{3n} x_i$. We reduce the problem by constructing an instance of the bundling problem with $n + 1$ bidders and $4n$ items. The instance is given in the table below. Each row corresponds to a bidder and each column represents an item. All empty values are 0.

$\frac{w}{n}$							
	$\frac{w}{n}$						
		$\ddots$					
			$\frac{w}{n}$				
				x_1	x_2	$\cdots$	x_{3n}

It is easy to see that the revenue of the optimal bundling for the instance above is w if and only if there exists a 3-partition.

Approximation Algorithm: Next we present an approximation algorithm for this problem which approximates the optimal revenue by a factor $1/2$; in addition, the efficiency of the bundling is no smaller than $1/2$ of the maximum efficiency. Recall that h_j and s_j are defined as the highest and second highest valuations for item j. Let A_i be the set of items for which agent i has the highest valuation, i.e. $A_i = \{j \mid v_{ij} = h_j\}$, and let $w_i = \sum_{j \in A_i} h_j$. Number agents so that $w_1 \geq w_2 \geq \ldots \geq w_n$. Let $A_{n+1} = \emptyset$, and $w_{n+1} = 0$.

Algorithm $\mathcal{B}$:

$r_1 \leftarrow \sum_{j \in A_1} s_j + \sum_{i=1}^{\lfloor n/2 \rfloor} w_{2i+1}$;
$r_2 \leftarrow \sum_{i=1}^{\lfloor n/2 \rfloor} w_{2i}$;
If $(r_1 \geq r_2)$:
        Sell all items in A_1 separately;
        For $i \leftarrow 1$ to $\lfloor n/2 \rfloor$
            Bundle items in A_{2i} and A_{2i+1};
else
        For $i \leftarrow 1$ to $\lfloor n/2 \rfloor$
            Bundle items A_{2i-1} and A_{2i};

Theorem 3. *Algorithm $\mathcal{B}$ obtains at least half the revenue from an optimal bundling.*

Proof. Let OPT be the optimal revenue. We prove the following inequality.

$$OPT \leq \sum_{j \in A_1} s_j + \sum_{i=2}^{n} w_i = r_1 + r_2. \tag{1}$$

The claim then follows since the revenue of $\mathcal{B}$ is at least $\max\{r_1, r_2\}$.

To prove (1), let B be a bundle in an optimal bundling, and let i and i' be the two agents with highest valuations for B. At least one of these two agents is not agent 1; let i be this agent. Because the mechanism charges the second highest price for each bundle, the revenue of the optimal bundling from B is at most:

$$\sum_{j \in B} v_{ij} = \sum_{j \in B \cap A_1} v_{ij} + \sum_{j \in B - A_1} v_{ij} \leq \sum_{j \in B \cap A_1} s_j + \sum_{j \in B - A_1} h_j$$

Summing over all bundles in the optimal bundling yields (1).

Proposition 1. *The efficiency of algorithm $\mathcal{B}$ is at least half the maximum efficiency.*

Proof. The maximum efficiency is $\sum_j h_j = \sum_{i=1}^n w_i$. The efficiency of $\mathcal{B}$ is at least

$$w_1 + \min\left(\sum_{i=1}^{\lfloor n/2 \rfloor} w_{2i}, \sum_{i=1}^{\lfloor n/2 \rfloor} w_{2i+1}\right) \geq \frac{1}{2}\sum_{i=1}^n w_i,$$

since the algorithm always sells items in A_1 to bidder 1; this gives us the result.

5   Multiple Slots

We finally discuss the case of multiple slots, and show that our algorithm gives a constant factor of the optimal revenue when slot clickthrough rates decrease geometrically, which is realistic for sponsored search auctions [9,6].

Suppose there are m slots numbered $1 \ldots m$. Following [2], assume that the click-through-rate of ad i for context j in slot k is separable into $c_{ij} \cdot \Theta_k$ (*i.e.*, the clickthrough rate can be factored into a term specific to the advertiser-keyword pair and another term specific to the slot). We will show that Algorithm $\mathcal{B}$ continues to give us a constant factor approximation of revenue when the slot-dependent CTR decreases geometrically, i.e. $\Theta_{k+1} = q \cdot \Theta_k$, for some q with $0 < q < 1$.

Fix an instance of the full information, sponsored search problem, *i.e.*, a value per click v_i for each advertiser i, the parameters c_{ij} for each advertiser-context pair, and the slot specific CTRs Θ_j for the slots. Let f_j be the number of impressions from context j. Given any bundling of the keywords, we now define revenue of the generalized second price auction (GSP) [8]. Unlike the second price auction for one slot, this auction is not truthful. We assume that the equilibria of [16,8] are attained. The prices at such an equilibrium is precisely the prices that VCG would charge in each bundle [8,2].

Denote revenue from the revenue maximizing bundling as R^*, and let $\mathcal{P}$ denote the partition of keywords in this bundling. Consider a bundle $B \in \mathcal{P}$. Let $v_{iB} = v_i \cdot \sum_{j \in B} f_j \cdot c_{ij}$. Number bidders in non-increasing sequence of v_{iB}s. The equilibrium from [8] predicts that the first m bidders appear in sequence from slot 1 to slot m, and the revenue from player k is $\left(\sum_{k=i}^m (\Theta_k - \Theta_{k+1})v_{k+1,B}\right)$. Thus the total revenue from all m slots is $R^* = \sum_{B \in \mathcal{P}}\left(\sum_{i=1}^m \sum_{k=i}^m (\Theta_k - \Theta_{k+1})v_{k+1,B}\right)$. The contribution of the first slot to R^*, denoted R_f^*, is $R_f^* = \sum_{B \in \mathcal{P}}\left(\sum_{k=1}^m (\Theta_k - \Theta_{k+1}) \cdot v_{k+1,B}\right)$. Because the number of clicks to the top slot is a $(1-q)$-fraction of all clicks, we can show:

Lemma 2. $R_f^* \geq (1-q) \cdot R^*$.

This allows us to prove the following result (proof in full version):

Theorem 4. *Algorithm $\mathcal{B}$ is $\frac{1-q}{2}$-competitive with the optimal bundling.*

Acknowledgements: We are grateful to Mohammad Mahdian, David Pennock, Amin Saberi and Michael Schwarz for helpful discussions.

References

1. Adams, W., Yellen, J.: Commodity bundling and the burden of monopoly. Quarterly Journal of Economics 90, 475–498 (1976)
2. Aggarwal, G., Goel, A., Motwani, R.: Truthful auctions for pricing search keywords. In: EC 2006: Proceedings of the 7th ACM conference on Electronic commerce, pp. 1–7. ACM Press, New York (2006)
3. Armstrong, M.: Multiproduct nonlinear pricing. Econometrica 6 64, 51–75 (1996)
4. Armstrong, M.: Optimal multi-object auctions. Review of Economic Studies 67, 455–481 (2000)
5. Bakos, Y., Brynjolfsson, E.: Bundling information goods: Pricing, profits, and efficiency. Management Science (1999)
6. Brooks, N.: The Atlas Rank Report: How search engine rank impacts traffic. Atlas Institute (July 2004)
7. Chakraborty, I.: Bundling decisions for selling multiple objects. Economic Theory 13, 723–733 (1999)
8. Edelman, B., Ostrovsky, M., Schwarz, M.: Internet advertising and the generalized second price auction: Selling billions of dollars worth of keywords. Stanford GSB Research Papers: Paper 1917 (2005)
9. Edelman, B., Schwarz, M.: Optimal auction design in a multi-unit environment: the case of sponsored search auctions. Manuscript in preparation (2007)
10. Even-Dar, E., Kearns, M., Wortman, J.: Sponsored search with contexts. Third Workshop on Sponsored Search Auctions (2007)
11. Jehiel, P., Meyer-ter-Vehn, M., Moldovanu, B.: Mixed bundling auctions. Journal of Economic Theory (2007)
12. Likhodedov, A., Sandholm, T.: Approximating revenue-maximixing combinatorial auctions. In: Proceedings of the National Conference on Artificial Intelligence(AAAI) (2005)
13. Manelli, A., Vincent, D.: Bundling as an optimal selling mechanism for a multiple-good monopolist. Discussion paper, Arizona State University (2001)
14. McAfee, P., McMillan, J., Whinston, M.: Multiproduct monopoly, commodity bundling, and correlation of values. The Quarterly Journal of Economics 104, 371–383 (1989)
15. Palfrey, T.: Bundling decisions by a multiproduct monopolist with incomplete information. Econometrica 51, 463–484 (1983)
16. Varian, H.: Position auctions. To appear in International Journal of Industrial Organization (2006)

On the Price of Truthfulness in Path Auctions

Qiqi Yan[*]

Department of Computer Science, Stanford University
contact@qiqiyan.com

Abstract. We study the frugality ratio of truthful mechanisms in path auctions, which measures the extent to which truthful mechanisms "over-pay" compared to non-truthful mechanisms. In particular we consider the fundamental case that the graph is composed of two node-disjoint s-t-paths of length s_1 and s_2 respectively, and prove an optimal $\sqrt{s_1 s_2}$ lower bound (an improvement over $\sqrt{s_1 s_2/2}$). This implies that the $\sqrt{\ }$-mechanism of Karlin et al. for path auctions is 2-competitive (an improvement over $2\sqrt{2}$), and is optimal if the graph is a series-parallel network. Moreover, our results extend to universally truthful randomized mechanisms as well.

1 Introduction

Since the field of algorithmic mechanism design was introduced by Nisan and Ronen [NR99], *path auctions* have been studied extensively. In a path auction, the auctioneer tries to buy an s-t-path from a directed graph, where the edges of the graph are owned by *selfish* agents, and the cost of an edge is known *only* to its owner. *Truthful mechanisms*, the VCG mechanism [MCWG95] in particular, have been applied to path auctions. In such mechanisms, it is of each agent's best interest to simply report their private cost. However, as observed in [AT02, ESS04], every truthful mechanism can be forced to pay a high total amount to the agents. In contrast, the total payment is relatively small in first price non-truthful path auctions [IKNS05, CK07]. Such overpayment of truthful mechanisms compared to non-truthful mechanisms is seen as the *price of truthfulness* [KKT05], which we measure by the notion of *frugality ratio* of Karlin et al. [KKT05]. (The notion was actually proposed for all problems in the general hire-a-team setting [AT01], and Talwar also proposed a notion of frugality ratio with a different benchmark earlier in [Tal03].) Karlin et al. [KKT05] also proposed the $\sqrt{\ }$-mechanism for path auctions, which is $2\sqrt{2}$-competitive, i.e., by a factor of $2\sqrt{2}$ from optimal w.r.t. frugality ratio.

Behind many results on frugality ratio lies the fundamental case that the input graph $\mathcal{G}$ contains exactly two node-disjoint s-t-paths S_1, S_2 of length s_1 and s_2 respectively[1], which we call *1-out-of-2 (S_1, S_2)-auctions*. The VCG mechanism may overpay badly in this case, and has frugality ratio $\max\{s_1, s_2\}$. In

---

[*] Part of this work was done while the author was at the BASICS Laboratory of Shanghai Jiao Tong University.

[1] We use symbols S_i instead of P_i to be consistent with the notations in [KKT05].

X. Deng and F.C. Graham (Eds.): WINE 2007, LNCS 4858, pp. 584–589, 2007.
© Springer-Verlag Berlin Heidelberg 2007

[AT02], a $\frac{2s_1s_2}{s_1+s_2}$ lower bound was proved for the class of min-function (truthful) mechanisms, and later in [ESS04], a weaker $\frac{s_1s_2}{s_1+s_2}$ bound was obtained for all truthful mechanisms. Finally in [KKT05], a truthful mechanism with frugality ratio $\sqrt{s_1s_2}$ was proposed, and an asymptotic $\sqrt{s_1s_2/2}$ lower bound was proved as well, leaving a $\sqrt{2}$ gap open. But it is unlikely that this gap can be closed by previous proof methods, and our understanding of the overpayment issue in even this simple case is not complete.

Our Results. In this paper, we introduce the interesting technique of *mechanism canonicalization*, and close the abovementioned gap by proving the following result, which to our knowledge is the first nontrivial tight lower bound known for frugality ratios. Moreover, this result can be extended to universally truthful randomized mechanisms [NR99] as well.

Theorem 1. *The frugality ratio of 1-out-of-2 (S_1, S_2)-auctions is $\Phi_{s_1,s_2} = \sqrt{s_1s_2}$.*

1-out-of-2 auctions are embedded in not only path auctions, but also many other problems, including vertex cover [EGG07], minimum cost bipartite matching etc. It follows that lower bounds about 1-out-of-2 auctions extend to those problems by reductions. In particular, for path auctions:

Theorem 2. *The $\sqrt{\ }$-mechanism for path auctions is 2-competitive in general, and is optimal if the input graph is a series-parallel network.*

2   The Model

In the setting, $\mathcal{G} = (V, E)$ is a directed graph where V contains two fixed vertices s and t. Each edge e in E represents a *selfish* agent, and has a privately known nonnegative cost $c_e{}^2$, which occurs if the agent is selected. A *path auction* consists of two steps. First each agent e submits a sealed bid b_e to the auctioneer. Then based on the bids, the auctioneer applies a *selection rule* to select an s-t-path P as the winning path, and pays an amount $p_e \geq b_e$ to each agent in P. We say that the agents in P win, and the others lose. The selection rule and payment rule together constitute a *mechanism* for $\mathcal{G}$. We assume that each agent is *rational*, fully knows about $\mathcal{G}$ and the mechanism, and aims at maximizing his own profit, which is $p_e - c_e$ if he wins, and 0 otherwise. As is standard, we assume that $\mathcal{G}$ has no s-t cut edge, otherwise there would be a monopoly.

We say that a mechanism is *truthful*, if each agent e can maximize his profit by bidding his true cost c_e, i.e., $b_e = c_e$, no matter what the others bid. There are two characteristic properties about truthful mechanisms: [AT01, AT02]

The Monotonicity Property. If a mechanism is *truthful*, then the associated selection rule is *monotone*, i.e., a winning agent still wins if he decreases his bid, given fixed bids of the others.

---

[2] For costs, bids, etc., we extend the notation by writing $c(T)$ for $\sum_{e\in T} c_e$, etc.

The Threshold Property. Given a monotone selection rule, there is a *unique* truthful mechanism associated with this selection rule. Moreover, this mechanism pays each agent the *threshold bid*, i.e., the supremum of the amounts that the agent can still win by bidding, given fixed bids of the others.

Let $\mathcal{M}$ be a truthful mechanism for $\mathcal{G}$. Given the cost vector $\mathbf{c}$ (or equivalently, bid vector, since $\mathcal{M}$ is truthful) of the agents, let $p_{\mathcal{M}}(\mathbf{c})$ denote the total payment made by $\mathcal{M}$ to the agents. We use $\nu(\mathbf{c})$ to denote the benchmark for overpayment, whose definition we omit here. But in 1-out-of-2 (S_1, S_2)-auctions, $\nu(\mathbf{c})$ simply equals to the maximum of $c(S_1)$ and $c(S_2)$. The *frugality ratio* $\phi_{\mathcal{M}}$ of a truthful mechanism $\mathcal{M}$ is $\sup_{\mathbf{c} \neq 0} \rho_{\mathcal{M}}(\mathbf{c})$, where $\rho_{\mathcal{M}}(\mathbf{c}) = p_{\mathcal{M}}(\mathbf{c})/\nu(\mathbf{c})$, and the frugality ratio $\Phi_{\mathcal{G}}$ of a graph $\mathcal{G}$, or the path auction on $\mathcal{G}$, is the infimum of $\phi_{\mathcal{M}}$ over all truthful mechanisms for $\mathcal{G}$.

3   1-out-of-2 Auctions

In this section, we show that the frugality ratio Φ_{s_1,s_2} of 1-out-of-2 (S_1, S_2)-auctions is exactly $\sqrt{s_1 s_2}$. For brevity, every mechanism we mention here is a truthful mechanism for 1-out-of-2 (S_1, S_2)-auctions. Consider the mechanism $\mathcal{M}$ such that the S_i with the least value of $\sqrt{s_i} \cdot c(S_i)$ is selected from $i = 1, 2$ with ties broken arbitrarily. One can verify that $\Phi_{\mathcal{M}} \leq \sqrt{s_1 s_2}$. To see this, let the costs of the agents be $\mathbf{c}$, and w.l.o.g. let S_1 wins. Then the threshold bid of each agent $e \in S_1$ is at most $\sqrt{s_2} \cdot c(S_2)/\sqrt{s_1}$. So $\rho_{\mathcal{M}}(\mathbf{c}) \leq p_{\mathcal{M}}(\mathbf{c})/\nu(\mathbf{c}) \leq \sqrt{s_1 s_2} \cdot c(S_2)/\nu(\mathbf{c}) \leq \sqrt{s_1 s_2}$, and hence $\Phi_{s_1,s_2} \leq \sqrt{s_1 s_2}$. We devote the rest of this section to lower bound.

To fix some conventions, we use R_+ to denote the set of nonnegative reals. If $\mathbf{w}$ is a vector in R_+^n, then w_i denotes its ith component. A vector function $\mathbf{t}$: $R_+^m \to R_+^n$ is seen as an n-tuple of functions t_j: $R_+^m \to R_+$ for $1 \leq j \leq n$. We say that vector $\mathbf{w} \in R_+^n$ is *dominated* by vector $\mathbf{w}' \in R_+^n$, or write $\mathbf{w} \preceq \mathbf{w}'$, if $w_i \leq w_i'$ for all i. We let $\mathbf{e}_i$ denote the unit vector with the ith component 1 and others 0. Agents in S_i are numbered from 1 to s_i for $i = 1, 2$. We say that S_i wins at $(\mathbf{u}, \mathbf{v})$ if S_i is selected when the costs $\mathbf{c}$ of the agents are $(\mathbf{u}, \mathbf{v})$, where each u_i is the cost of agent i in S_1, and each v_j is the cost of agent j in S_2. We also assume w.l.o.g. that S_2 wins at $(\mathbf{u}, \mathbf{0})$ if $\mathbf{u} \neq \mathbf{0}$ and S_1 wins at $(\mathbf{0}, \mathbf{v})$ if $\mathbf{v} \neq \mathbf{0}$.

3.1   The $\mathbf{t}^{\mathcal{M}}$ Function

For a mechanism $\mathcal{M}$, function $\mathbf{t}^{\mathcal{M}}$: $R_+^{s_1} \to R_+^{s_2}$ is defined as $t_j^{\mathcal{M}}(\mathbf{u}) = \sup\{y: S_2$ wins at $(\mathbf{u}, y\mathbf{e}_j)\}$, for all $\mathbf{u} \in R_+^{s_1}$ and $1 \leq j \leq s_2$.[3] We find the following way of visualization helpful. Let $s_2 = 2$, and refer to Fig. 1. The solid curve indicates the boundary between the area where S_2 wins and the area where S_1 wins. (If $s_2 > 2$, then the boundary is a surface instead.) By the monotonicity property, loosely speaking, the boundary monotonically decreases. Also by the threshold

---

[3] We may drop the superscript $\mathcal{M}$ when the context is clear.

property, if S_2 wins at $(\mathbf{u}, \mathbf{v})$, the payment to the agents in S_2 is the total length of the two segments crossing at $\mathbf{v}$. With such intuition, it is easy to observe the following properties.

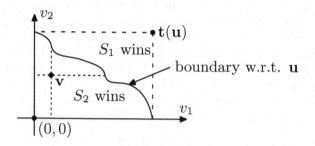

Fig. 1.

Lemma 1. **(i)** *If S_2 wins at $(\mathbf{u}, \mathbf{v})$, then $\mathbf{v} \preceq \mathbf{t}(\mathbf{u})$. In addition, agent j in S_2 is paid at most $t_j(\mathbf{u})$ for all $1 \leq j \leq s_2$.*
(ii) *If $\mathbf{u} \preceq \mathbf{u}'$ then $\mathbf{t}(\mathbf{u}) \preceq \mathbf{t}(\mathbf{u}')$. I.e., $\mathbf{t}$ respects the dominance relation.*
(iii) *For a mechanism $\mathcal{M}$, $\phi_\mathcal{M}$ equals to the maximum of $\sup_{\mathbf{u} \neq \mathbf{0}} \rho_\mathcal{M}(\mathbf{u}, \mathbf{0})$ and $\sup_{\mathbf{v} \neq \mathbf{0}} \rho_\mathcal{M}(\mathbf{0}, \mathbf{v})$. In addition, $\rho_\mathcal{M}(\mathbf{u}, \mathbf{0})$ equals to $\sum_{j=1}^{s_2} t_j(\mathbf{u}) / \sum_{i=1}^{s_1} u_i$ and $\rho_\mathcal{M}(\mathbf{0}, \mathbf{v})$ equals to $\sum_{i=1}^{s_1} \sup\{x \colon S_1 \text{ wins at } (x\mathbf{e}_i, \mathbf{v})\} / \sum_{j=1}^{s_2} v_j$.*

3.2   Mechanism Canonicalization

For each mechanism $\mathcal{M}$, in the following we canonicalize $\mathcal{M}$ into a type-1 mechanism $\mathcal{M}_1$, and then into a type-2 mechanism $\mathcal{M}_2$, and finally into a type-3 mechanism $\mathcal{M}_3$ respectively. In the process, frugality is preserved, i.e., $\phi_\mathcal{M} \geq \phi_{\mathcal{M}_1} \geq \phi_{\mathcal{M}_2} \geq \phi_{\mathcal{M}_3}$. It follows that Φ_{s_1, s_2} can be determined by analyzing the infimum of $\phi_{\mathcal{M}_3}$ over all type-3 mechanism $\mathcal{M}_3$, while the special properties of the class of type-3 mechanisms can be taken advantage of in the analysis. We call such technique as mechanism canonicalization.

Type-1 Mechanisms. For a mechanism $\mathcal{M}$, we first canonicalize it into the mechanism $\mathcal{M}_1$ such that S_2 wins at $(\mathbf{u}, \mathbf{v})$ in $\mathcal{M}_1$ iff $\mathbf{v} \preceq \mathbf{t}^\mathcal{M}(\mathbf{u})$. One can verify that the selection rule of $\mathcal{M}_1$ is monotone, and such canonicalized mechanisms are called *type-1 mechanisms*. In particular, it is guaranteed that $\phi_{\mathcal{M}_1} \leq \phi_\mathcal{M}$. To verify this via Lemma 1(iii), we need to show that $\sup\{x \colon S_1 \text{ wins at } (x\mathbf{e}_i, \mathbf{v}) \text{ in } \mathcal{M}_1\} \leq \sup\{x : S_1 \text{ wins at } (x\mathbf{e}_i, \mathbf{v}) \text{ in } \mathcal{M}\}$. This is true because if S_2 wins at $(x\mathbf{e}_i, \mathbf{v})$ in $\mathcal{M}$ for some $i, x, \mathbf{v}$, then $\mathbf{v} \preceq \mathbf{t}^\mathcal{M}(x\mathbf{e}_i)$ by Lemma 1(i), and then by the definition of $\mathcal{M}_1$, S_2 wins at $(x\mathbf{e}_i, \mathbf{v})$ in $\mathcal{M}_1$ too.

The following follows directly from Lemma 1(iii).

Lemma 2. *Let $\mathcal{M}_1$ be a type-1 mechanism. Then $\phi_{\mathcal{M}_1} \leq r$ if and only if conditions (a) and (b) hold:*

(a) For all $\mathbf{u} \neq \mathbf{0}$, $\rho_{\mathcal{M}_1}(\mathbf{u}, \mathbf{0}) = \sum_j t_j(\mathbf{u}) / \sum_i u_i \leq r$.
(b) For all $\mathbf{v} \neq \mathbf{0}$, $\rho_{\mathcal{M}_1}(\mathbf{0}, \mathbf{v}) = \sum_i \sup\{x : \mathbf{v} \not\preceq \mathbf{t}(x\mathbf{e}_i)\} / \sum_j v_j \leq r$.

Type-2 Mechanisms. Note that each type-1 mechanism $\mathcal{M}_1$ can be determined by its $\mathbf{t}^{\mathcal{M}_1}$ function (denoted by $\mathbf{t}$ for brevity) . Consider the $\hat{\mathbf{t}}$ function such that for all $\mathbf{u}$ in the form of $u_i\mathbf{e}_i$ for some i, $\hat{\mathbf{t}}(u_i\mathbf{e}_i) = \mathbf{t}(u_i\mathbf{e}_i)$, and for all other $\mathbf{u}$, $\hat{\mathbf{t}}(\mathbf{u}) = \sum_i \hat{\mathbf{t}}(u_i\mathbf{e}_i)$. We then canonicalize $\mathcal{M}_1$ into $\mathcal{M}_2$, which is the type-1 mechanism determined by the $\hat{\mathbf{t}}$ function, i.e., $\mathbf{t}^{\mathcal{M}_2} = \hat{\mathbf{t}}$. Each such $\mathcal{M}_2$ is called a *type-2 mechanism*. One can verify that $\hat{\mathbf{t}}$ respects the dominance relation, and therefore the selection rule of $\mathcal{M}_2$ is monotone. Clearly type-2 mechanisms are determined by their $\mathbf{t}(u_i\mathbf{e}_i)$ functions, and it turns out that Lemma 2 can be correspondingly refined to the following.

Lemma 3. *Let $\mathcal{M}_2$ be a type-2 mechanism. Then $\phi_{\mathcal{M}_2} \leq r$ if and only if the following conditions hold:*

(a') *For all $u_i \neq 0$ and i, $\rho_{\mathcal{M}_2}(u_i\mathbf{e}_i, \mathbf{0}) = \sum_j t_j(u_i\mathbf{e}_i)/u_i \leq r$.*
(b') *For all $v_j \neq 0$ and j, $\rho_{\mathcal{M}_2}(\mathbf{0}, v_j\mathbf{e}_j) = \sum_i \sup\{x : t_j(x\mathbf{e}_i) < v_j\}/v_j \leq r$.*

Note that $\mathbf{t}^{\mathcal{M}_2}(u_i\mathbf{e}_i) = \mathbf{t}^{\mathcal{M}_1}(u_i\mathbf{e}_i)$ for all u_i and i, and so by Lemma 3, we have $\phi_{\mathcal{M}_2} = \phi_{\mathcal{M}_1}$.

Type-3 Mechanisms. In a type-2 mechanism $\mathcal{M}_2$, if each $\mathbf{t}^{\mathcal{M}_2}(x\mathbf{e}_i)$ function (denoted by $\mathbf{t}(x\mathbf{e}_i)$ for brevity) is a *curve*, i.e., a continuous mapping from R_+ to $R_+^{s_2}$, we say that it is a *type-3 mechanism*.

Lemma 4. *For each type-2 mechanism $\mathcal{M}_2$, there is a canonicalized type-3 mechanism $\mathcal{M}_3$ such that $\phi_{\mathcal{M}_3} = \phi_{\mathcal{M}_2}$.*

3.3   Determining Φ_{s_1,s_2}

Based on the canonicalization process, $\Phi_{s_1,s_2} \leq r$ is equivalent to that there is a type-3 mechanism $\mathcal{M}_3$ with $\phi_{\mathcal{M}_3} \leq r$. Since a type-3 mechanism is determined by its $\mathbf{t}(x\mathbf{e}_i)$ functions, this equivalence can be rephrased as follows: (with each $\mathbf{t}(x\mathbf{e}_i)$ renamed to $\mathbf{g}^i$)

Theorem 3. *$\Phi_{s_1,s_2} \leq r$ if and only if there exist curves $\mathbf{g}^1, \ldots, \mathbf{g}^{s_1} : R_+ \to R_+^{s_2}$ such that the following conditions are satisfied:*

(i) $\mathbf{g}^i(x) \preceq \mathbf{g}^i(x')$ *for all $1 \leq i \leq s_1$ and $x \leq x'$.*
(ii) $\sum_j g_j^i(x) \leq xr$ *for all $1 \leq i \leq s_1$ and x.*
(iii) $\sum_i \sup\{x : g_j^i(x) \leq y\} \leq yr$ *for all $1 \leq j \leq s_2$ and y.*

So the problem of determining Φ_{s_1,s_2} is converted to an equivalent pure math problem about curves, which can be solved by applying the Young's Inequality.

Proof. (of Theorem 1) First note that one can prove that $\Phi_{s_1,s_2} \leq \sqrt{s_1 s_2}$ via Theorem 3 by setting $r = \sqrt{s_1 s_2}$ and $g_j^i(x) = \sqrt{s_1/s_2} \cdot x$ for all i, j. To prove that $\Phi_{s_1,s_2} \geq \sqrt{s_1 s_2}$, let $\mathbf{g}^1, \ldots, \mathbf{g}^{s_1}$ and r satisfy the conditions in Theorem 3. By (b) of Theorem 3, $\sum_{j'} g_{j'}^i(g_{-j}^i(y))/r \leq g_{-j}^i(y)$ for all i, j. Add a summation over i, and then by (c), $\sum_i \sum_{j'} g_{j'}^i(g_{-j}^i(y))/r \leq \sum_i g_{-j}^i(y) \leq yr$, for all j. Denote $g_{j'}^i(g_{-j}^i(y))$ by $h_{j \to j'}^i(y)$, add another summation over j, and we have $\sum_i \sum_j \sum_{j'} h_{j \to j'}^i(y) \leq s_2 r^2 y$. Note that each $h_{j \to j'}^i(y)$ is increasing, and hence we can define its integral function: $H_{j \to j'}^i(y) = \int_0^y h_{j \to j'}^i(z)dz$, for all i, j, j'. Assume for simplicity that each $h_{j \to j'}^i$ is monotone. Then by applying the Young's Inequality, $H_{j \to j'}^i(y) + H_{j' \to j}^i(y) \geq y^2$ for all i, j, j'. So $\frac{1}{2} s_2 r^2 y^2 \geq \sum_i \sum_j \sum_{j'} H_{j \to j'}^i(y) \geq \frac{1}{2} s_1 s_2^2 y^2$, and thus $r \geq \sqrt{s_1 s_2}$. It follows that $\Phi_{s_1,s_2} \geq \sqrt{s_1 s_2}$ by Theorem 3.

Acknowledgement. I thank Valeriu Anisiu and Li Wu for pointing me to the Young's Inequality, thank Ning Chen for his useful suggestions, and thank Prof. Enshao Shen for his kind support and guidance.

References

[AT01]   Archer, A., Tardos, E.: Truthful mechanisms for One-Parameter agents. In: Proc. of the 42nd IEEE Symposium on Foundations of Computer Science (FOCS 2001), IEEE Computer Society Press, Los Alamitos (2001)

[AT02]   Archer, A., Tardos, E.: Frugal path mechanisms. In: Proc. of the 13th ACM-SIAM Symposium on Discrete Algorithms (SODA 2002), ACM Press, New York (2002)

[CK07]   Chen, N., Karlin, A.R.: Cheap labor can be expensive. In: Proc. of the 18th ACM-SIAM Symposium on Discrete Algorithms (SODA 2007), ACM Press, New York (2007)

[EGG07]   Elkind, E., Goldberg, L.A., Goldberg, P.W.: Frugality ratios and improved truthful mechanisms for vertex cover. In: Proc. of the 8th ACM Conference on Electronic Commerce (EC 2007), ACM Press, New York (2007)

[ESS04]   Elkind, E., Sahai, A., Steiglitz, K.: Frugality in path auctions. In: Proc. of the 15th ACM-SIAM Symposium on Discrete Algorithms (SODA 2004), ACM Press, New York (2004)

[IKNS05]   Immorlica, N., Karger, D., Nikolova, E., Sami, R.: First-price path auctions. In: Proc. of the 6th ACM Conference on Electronic Commerce (EC 2005), ACM Press, New York (2005)

[KKT05]   Karlin, A.R., Kempe, D., Tamir, T.: Beyond VCG: Frugality of truthful mechanisms. In: Proc. of the 46th IEEE Symposium on Foundations of Computer Science (FOCS 2005), IEEE Computer Society Press, Los Alamitos (2005)

[MCWG95]   Mas-Collel, A., Whinston, M., Green, J.: Microeconomic Theory. Oxford University Press, Oxford (1995)

[NR99]   Nisan, N., Ronen, A.: Algorithmic mechanism design (extended abstract). In: Proc. of the 31st ACM Symposium on Theory of Computing (STOC 1999), ACM Press, New York (1999)

[Tal03]   Talwar, K.: The price of truth: Frugality in truthful mechanisms. In: Alt, H., Habib, M. (eds.) STACS 2003. LNCS, vol. 2607, Springer, Heidelberg (2003)

Characterizing Truthful Market Design

Mira Gonen[1], Rica Gonen[2], and Elan Pavlov[3]

[1] Tel-Aviv University, Ramat Aviv 69978, Israel
gonenmir@post.tau.ac.il
[2] Yahoo! Research Labs, 701 First Street, Sunnyvale, CA 94089
gonenr@yahoo-inc.com
[3] Media Lab, MIT, Cambridge MA, 02149
elan@mit.edu

Abstract. This paper characterizes the family of truthful double-sided auctions. Despite the importance of double-sided auctions to market design, to date no characterization of truthful double-sided auctions was made. This paper characterizes truthful mechanisms for double-sided auctions by generalizing Roberts classic result [18], to show that truthful double-sided auctions must "almost" be affine maximizers.

Our main result of characterizing double-sided auctions required the creation of a new set of tools, reductions that preserve economic properties. This paper utilizes two such reductions; a *truth-preserving reduction* and a *non-affine preserving reduction*. The truth-preserving reduction is used to reduce the double-sided auction to a special case of a combinatorial auction to make use of the impossibility result proved in [11]. Intuitively, our proof shows that truthful double-sided auctions are as hard to design as truthful combinatorial auctions.

Two important concepts are developed in addition to the main result. First, the form of reduction used in this paper is of independent interest as it provides a means for comparing mechanism design problems by design difficulty. Second, we define the notion of *extension of payments*; which given a set of payments for some players finds payments for the remaining players. The extension payments maintain the truthful and affine maximization properties.

Introduction. This paper characterizes the class of truthful double-sided auctions. In recent years a large body of research has focused on designing algorithms for environments where the input to the algorithm is distributed among players. Each player attempts to maximize its output function (utility) without considering the environment as a whole. Such environments are increasingly common e.g. the Internet and communication networks. One of the main approaches to designing such auctions is to design *truthful mechanisms* which motivate the players to reveal their true input to the algorithm.

In this paper we look at a double-sided auction which is a market that consists of multiple buyers and sellers who wish to exchange goods. The market's main objective is to produce an allocation of sellers' goods to buyers that maximizes the total gain from trade (i.e., the total value associated with an allocation).

A commonly studied model of participant behavior is taken from the field of economic mechanism design in such papers as e.g., [1,17,15]. In this model each player has a private valuation function that assigns real (non-negative) values to each possible allocation. The auction algorithm uses the payments to the mechanism in order to motivate

X. Deng and F.C. Graham (Eds.): WINE 2007, LNCS 4858, pp. 590–595, 2007.

players to truthfully reveal their functions. Each player is a utility maximizing rational agent, i.e., the player maximizes the difference between his valuation of the algorithm's allocation and his payment. The couplet consisting of an algorithm and a payment is called a mechanism. Mechanisms for which reporting the truth is a dominant strategy for each player are called truthful. Although, truthful mechanisms are the central paradigm of the literature most work has focused on the model consisting of a single seller and multiple buyers[1]. Double-sided auctions remain an important open question.

In a double-sided auction mechanism, there are n sellers each offering a unique good. Each seller s_i, $1 \leq i \leq n$ has a valuation function v_i that assigns a real value $v_i(g_i)$ for his good g_i and each buyer b_j, $1 \leq j \leq m$ has a valuation function v_j that assigns a real value $v_j(g_i)$ for every good g_i, $1 \leq i \leq n$. The goal is to find a match M between buyers and sellers such that the total gain from trade $\sum_{i,j|(s_i,b_j)\in M} v_j(g_i) - v_i(g_i)$ is maximized. The problem of a double-sided auctions where all sellers' goods are identical has been extensively studied in the literature (see e.g. [12]). Relatively little work, e.g., [2] attempts to look at the more general case, where sellers may sell different goods.

Our goal in this paper, is to characterize the set of truthful mechanisms for the double-sided auction. Our proof is partially based on a *truthful preserving reduction* to a special case of a combinatorial auction. In a combinatorial auction, n unique goods are auctioned among m players. Players value bundles of goods in a way that may depend on the combination they win, i.e., each player has a valuation function v_i that assigns a real value $v_i(\lambda)$ for each possible subset of goods. The goal is to find a partition $\lambda_1...\lambda_m$ of the goods that maximizes the total social welfare $\sum_i v_i(\lambda_i)$. The combinatorial auction problem is NP-complete and has been extensively studied as it is an important instance of the interplay between computational difficulty and game theoretic difficulty. A thorough study of combinatorial auctions can be found in e.g., [3,16,8,10].

To better explain the background to the problem of characterizing the class of truthful double-sided auction mechanisms, we formalize the basic model slightly more. Let A denote the range of all mechanism's possible outcomes and let $v_i : A \to \mathbb{R}$ be player i's valuation function that specifies his value $v_i(a)$ for each possible outcome $a \in A$ where v_i is chosen out of a valuations domain V_i. Given the valuations $v = (v_1, ..., v_n)$ the mechanism computes the function $\phi(v)$ that is referred to as the *social choice function*. In the context of double-sided auction mechanisms A is all the possible matchings of buyers and sellers and V_i depends only on a_i (as we assume "no externalities"[2]) The mechanism computes $\phi(v)$ and payments p to the players. We say that a social choice function ϕ is *implementable* if there exists payments supporting ϕ such that the pair (ϕ, p) yields a truthful mechanism. So the basic question is what are the implementable social choice functions?

The well known VCG payment scheme insures the truthfulness of a welfare maximizing social choice function $\phi(v) \in \arg\max_{a\in A} \sum_i v_i(a)$ [20,4][3]. The VCG pay-

---

[1] Or equivalently a single buyer and multiple sellers

[2] For simplicity of the analysis, we make throughout this paper the standard assumption of *free disposal*, i.e., that the functions are monotone non decreasing.

[3] It also insures truthfulness for the welfare maximizing extension for double-sided mechanisms, i.e., the gain from trade social choice function $\phi(v) \in \arg\max_{a\in A} \sum_j v_j(a) - \sum_i v_i(a)$

592 M. Gonen, R. Gonen, and E. Pavlov

ment scheme can be generalized in three ways: (1) The range can be restricted to $A' \subseteq A$; (2) Non-negative weights can be assigned to the players; (3) weights can be added to different outcomes. When applying those generalizations to the VCG payment scheme we obtain an implementation for any social choice function that is an affine maximizer. The formal definition of an affine maximizer social choice function can be found in the full version of the paper [7].

Are there other implementable social choice functions that are not affine maximizers? The answer to that question was given by Roberts [18] in his classic negative result showing that if the players' valuation domain is unrestricted and the outcome range is non-trivial then there does not exist an implementable social choice function that is not an affine maximizer.

Theorem (Roberts, 1979): *If there are at least 3 possible outcomes, and players' valuations are unrestricted ($V_i = R^{|A|}$), then any implementable social choice function is an affine maximizer.*

The requirement for players' valuations domain to be unrestricted is very strong as it implies that players have a value for every possible outcome of the social choice function. In most realistic and practical applications this is not the case. For example for double-sided auctions, players' valuations are restricted by the demand that there are no externalities as mentioned above and for combinatorial auctions, players' valuations are restricted in two ways: free disposal (i's valuation is monotone by inclusion in a_i) and no externalities. On the other hand restrictions on the players' valuation domain sometimes simplify the problem in a way that does not capture problems of interest. For instance in single dimensional valuation spaces (single value), implementable social choice functions do not imply affine maximization. Such is the case with single minded bidders in combinatorial auctions where the valuation function is given by a single positive value v_i which is offered for a single set of items. For instance, [10] present a computationally efficient truthful approximation that is not affine maximizing. Additional mechanisms for the single-minded case were presented e.g., in [14].

However, most interesting problems (computationally and practically) lie somewhere between the two extremes of unrestricted domains and single dimensional domains. This intermediate range includes double-sided auctions with heterogenous goods (which is the model we focus on), a number of single sided auctions (multiple buyers, single seller), non-single-minded combinatorial auctions, and multi-unit (homogeneous) auctions. Little is known about the intermediate range. The only positive example of a non-VCG mechanism for non-single-dimensional domains is for multi-unit combinatorial auctions where each bidder is restricted to demand at most a fraction of the number of units of each type [3][4]. On the negative side [11] showed that for multi-minded bidders a truthful combinatorial auction essentially implies affine maximization.

In all of the mechanisms discussed so far we assume players have quasi-linear utility. Interestingly in the non-quasi-linear case the classic Gibbard-Satterthwaite result [19] shows that no non-trivial social choice function over an unrestricted domain is

---

[4] Other examples are known for relaxations of the deterministic dominant strategy model such as random algorithms and implementations in undominated strategies [5]

implementable. However, for restricted single peaked domains (which is a single dimension domain) [13] implement a non-trivial social choice function.

Our Results. In this paper we characterize the implementable social choice functions of the double-sided auction mechanism over restricted domains in quasi-linear environments. The work follows the initiative of [11] to extend Roberts's impossibility result to multi dimensional but restricted domains. [11]'s work extends Roberts work for multi-minded combinatorial auctions while our work extends Roberts work for double-sided auctions. The double-sided auction is the principle mechanism for many real life markets (such as the stock market) and therefore is fundamental to mechanism design.

To prove their main theorem [11] characterize conditions over the domain in which implementable social choice functions implies affine maximization. The basic conditions require that the domain is an *order based domain* in which valuations over different possible outcomes in the domain can be compared, and that the best outcome for one player is the worst outcome for the other players, i.e. "conflicting preferences". Those domain conditions capture combinatorial auctions and multi-unit auctions. However, since matching problems do not have conflicting preferences [11] left open the question of whether implementable social choice functions implies affine maximization for matching. Our work answers that question positively by showing that the implementable social choice double-sided auctions imply affine maximization.

Our work builds on Roberts results and the results achieved by [11] integrating a classic tool of computer science theory: reductions. Although reduction is a widely used tool in proving the hardness of problems by reducing them to other hard problems this tool has not been used before in the context of mechanism design. Moreover the existing literature does not try to classify the difficulty of different mechanism design problems in terms of game theory but rather classifies difficulty in the context of computational complexity. This work makes use of the negative result in [11] for combinatorial auctions to show the same negative result for double-sided auctions by the means of a reduction. We believe that the use of reduction in the context of mechanism design is of independent interest.

The task of building a reduction between the combinatorial auction and the double-sided auction is not as straightforward as it may sound. Since our main theorem shows that: a mechanism with the property of truthfulness implies affine maximization, we need to construct a reduction that maintains the truthfulness property and the non affine property. In order to use a reduction in the context of mechanism design we define the new concepts of *truth-preserving reduction* and *non-affine preserving reduction*. These new concepts are inspired by the well established concept of gap-preserving reductions [6] which expand the concept of a reduction. The formal definitions can be found in the full version of the paper [7].

Our proof that any implementable double-sided auction's (DSA) social choice function is affine maximizing utilizes the main theorem of [11] for a special case of combinatorial auction which we call the *combinatorial auction product space (CAPS)*[5]. The first stage in our proof is then:

---

[5] Although CAPS is defined as a special case of single-minded combinatorial auction it is no wonder that the following lemma holds as we show later on in the paper that the CAPS problem is equivalent to a special case of multi-minded combinatorial auction.

Lemma: *The social choice function of any truthful CAPS mechanism is an almost affine-maximizer.*

We then utilize a reduction from a special case of DSA (where the sellers all have value zero for their good) which we call *double-sided auction cost 0 problem (DSAC0)* to CAPS. This reduction preserves the truthfulness and the non-affine properties. This reduction will then yield the following theorem:

Lemma: *The social choice function of any truthful DSAC0 mechanism is an almost affine maximizer.*

Once any implementable DSAC0 is shown to be affine maximizing a reduction from DSA to DSAC0 is constructed which again preserves the truthfulness and non-affine properties[6]. As the sellers' values (and therefore the sellers' prices) in the DSAC0 are zero, the reduction DSA $\leq$ DSAC0 preserves the non-max affine property only for the DSA buyers. To prove the max-affine maximizing property for the sellers as well, we define and perform a *price expansion* of the induced buyers' prices and define critical value prices for sellers. The critical prices are shown to be truthful affine-maximizing prices. To complete the structure we prove that the integration of two price vectors that are truthful and affine maximizing is also truthful and affine maximizing.

This then yields our main result:

Main Theorem: *The social choice function of any truthful DSA mechanism is an almost affine maximizer.*

The "almost" in the above theorems is an artifact from the proof of [11]'s main theorem and any improvement in the proof of [11] will benefit our theorem.

[11]'s theorem only shows that the social choice function must be an affine maximizer for large enough input valuations.

Definition ([11]): Almost Affine maximizer: *A social choice function ϕ is an almost affine maximizer if there exists a threshold H s.t. the function is an affine maximizer if $v_z(a) \geq H$ for all a and z.*

[11] believe that this restriction is a technical artifact of their current proof.

Our proof differs significantly from both Roberts' proof and from [11]'s proof. The definitions that we need to get our main result naturally yields the question of whether it is possible to classify mechanism design problems into classes of problems. Such classification can be either into equivalency classes or into a hierarchal relationship. This classification is a refinement of the standard computational complexity classes. For instance, our reduction shows that the double-sided auction is at least *mechanism design hard* as a particular case of combinatorial auction. This despite the fact that from a computational complexity point of view, double-sided auctions can be solved in polynomial time (if the input is given truthfully). This observation emphasizes that the difficulty of mechanism design does not necessarily require us to focus on computationally hard problems but rather, a simple polynomial problem such as the double-sided auction can already capture the essence of the mechanism's design difficulty.

---

[6] Although DSAC0 is a special case of DSA we show that all cases of DSA can be expressed as an instance of DSAC0.

All technical details of the theorems, claims, proofs, and additional references can be found in the full version of the paper at [7].

References

1. Archer, A., Tardos, E.: Truthful Mechanisms for one-parameter agents. In: Proceeding of 42th FOCS 2001 (2001)
2. Bartal, Y., Gonen, R., LaMura, P.: Negotiation-Range Mechanisms:Exploring the Limits of Truthful Efficient Markets. In: Proceeding of 5th EC 2004 (2004)
3. Bartal, Y., Gonen, R., Nisan, N.: Incentive Compatible Multi-Unit Combinatorial Auctions. In: Proc. of TARK 2003, pp. 72–87 (June 2003)
4. Clarke, E.H.: Multipart Pricing of Public Goods. journal Public Choice 2, 17–33 (1971)
5. Dobzinski, S., Nisan, N., Schapira, M.: Truthful Randomized Mechanisms for Combinatorial Auctions. In: Proceeding of 38th STOC 2006 (2006)
6. Feige, U., Goldwasser, S., Lovasz, L., Safra, S., Szegedy, M.: Interactive Proofs and the Hardness of Approximating Cliques. Journal of the ACM 43, 268–292 (1996)
7. Gonen, M., Gonen, R., Pavlov, E.: Characterizing Truthful Market Design. http://www.cs.huji.ac.il/~rgonenor or http://www.ricagonen.com
8. Gonen, R., Lehmann, D.: Optimal Solutions for Multi-Unit Combinatorial Auctions: Branch and Bound Heuristics. In: Proc. of EC 2000, pp. 13–20 (October 2000)
9. Groves, T.: Incentives in teams. journal Econometrica 41, 617–631 (1973)
10. Lehmann, D., O'Callaghan, L.I., Shoham, Y.: Truth Revelation in Approximately Efficient Combinatorial Auctions. Journal of ACM 49(5), 577–602 (2002)
11. Lavi, R., Mu'alem, A., Nisan, N.: Towards a Characterization of Truthful Combinatorial Auctions. In: Proceeding of 44th FOCS 2003 (2003)
12. McAfee, R.: A Dominant Strategy Double Auction. Journal of economic Theory 56, 434–450 (1992)
13. Moulin, H.: The Strategy of Social Choice. North-Holland, Amsterdam (1983)
14. Mu'alem, A., Nisan, N.: Truthful Approximation Mechanisms for Restricted Combinatorial Auctions. In: Proceeding of AAAI 2002 (2002)
15. Nisan, N.: Algorithms for Selfish Agents. In: Meinel, C., Tison, S. (eds.) STACS 99. LNCS, vol. 1563, Springer, Heidelberg (1999)
16. Nisan, N., Ronen, A.: Computationally Feasible VCG mechanisms. In: Proceeding of 2nd EC 2000 and Journal of Games and Economic Behavior, 35, 166-196 (2001)
17. Papadimitriou, C.: Algorithms, Games, and the Internet. In: Proceeding of 33rd STOC 2001 (2001)
18. Roberts, K.: The Characterization of Implementable Choice Rules. In: Laffont, J.-J. (ed.) Aggregation and Revelation Of Preferences. Papers presented at the first European Summer Workshop of the Econometric Society, North-Holland, Amsterdam (1979)
19. Satterthwaite, M.: Strategy-Proofness and Arrow's Conditions: Existence and Correspondence Theorem for Voting Procedures and social Welfare Functions. Journal of Economic Theory 10, 187–217 (1975)
20. Vickrey, W.: Counterspeculation, Auctions and Competitive Sealed Tenders. Journal of Finance 16, 8–37 (1961)

Author Index

Lecture Notes in Computer Science

Sublibrary 3: Information Systems and Application, incl. Internet/Web and HCI

For information about Vols. 1– 4504
please contact your bookseller or Springer

Vol. 4715: J.M. Haake, S.F. Ochoa, A. Cechich (Eds.), Groupware: Design, Implementation, and Use. XIII, 355 pages. 2007.

Vol. 4714: G. Alonso, P. Dadam, M. Rosemann (Eds.), Business Process Management. XIII, 418 pages. 2007.

Vol. 4704: D. Barbosa, A. Bonifati, Z. Bellahsène, E. Hunt, R. Unland (Eds.), Database and XML Technologies. X, 141 pages. 2007.

Vol. 4690: Y. Ioannidis, B. Novikov, B. Rachev (Eds.), Advances in Databases and Information Systems. XIII, 377 pages. 2007.

Vol. 4675: L. Kovács, N. Fuhr, C. Meghini (Eds.), Research and Advanced Technology for Digital Libraries. XVII, 585 pages. 2007.

Vol. 4674: Y. Luo (Ed.), Cooperative Design, Visualization, and Engineering. XIII, 431 pages. 2007.

Vol. 4663: C. Baranauskas, P. Palanque, J. Abascal, S.D.J. Barbosa (Eds.), Human-Computer Interaction – INTERACT 2007, Part II. XXXIII, 735 pages. 2007.

Vol. 4662: C. Baranauskas, P. Palanque, J. Abascal, S.D.J. Barbosa (Eds.), Human-Computer Interaction – INTERACT 2007, Part I. XXXIII, 637 pages. 2007.

Vol. 4658: T. Enokido, L. Barolli, M. Takizawa (Eds.), Network-Based Information Systems. XIII, 544 pages. 2007.

Vol. 4656: M.A. Wimmer, J. Scholl, Å. Grönlund (Eds.), Electronic Government. XIV, 450 pages. 2007.

Vol. 4655: G. Psaila, R. Wagner (Eds.), E-Commerce and Web Technologies. VII, 229 pages. 2007.

Vol. 4654: I.-Y. Song, J. Eder, T.M. Nguyen (Eds.), Data Warehousing and Knowledge Discovery. XVI, 482 pages. 2007.

Vol. 4653: R. Wagner, N. Revell, G. Pernul (Eds.), Database and Expert Systems Applications. XXII, 907 pages. 2007.

Vol. 4636: G. Antoniou, U. Aßmann, C. Baroglio, S. Decker, N. Henze, P.-L. Patranjan, R. Tolksdorf (Eds.), Reasoning Web. IX, 345 pages. 2007.

Vol. 4611: J. Indulska, J. Ma, L.T. Yang, T. Ungerer, J. Cao (Eds.), Ubiquitous Intelligence and Computing. XXIII, 1257 pages. 2007.

Vol. 4607: L. Baresi, P. Fraternali, G.-J. Houben (Eds.), Web Engineering. XVI, 576 pages. 2007.

Vol. 4606: A. Pras, M. van Sinderen (Eds.), Dependable and Adaptable Networks and Services. XIV, 149 pages. 2007.

Vol. 4605: D. Papadias, D. Zhang, G. Kollios (Eds.), Advances in Spatial and Temporal Databases. X, 479 pages. 2007.

Vol. 4602: S. Barker, G.-J. Ahn (Eds.), Data and Applications Security XXI. X, 291 pages. 2007.

Vol. 4601: S. Spaccapietra, P. Atzeni, F. Fages, M.-S. Hacid, M. Kifer, J. Mylopoulos, B. Pernici, P. Shvaiko, J. Trujillo, I. Zaihrayeu (Eds.), Journal on Data Semantics IX. XV, 197 pages. 2007.

Vol. 4592: Z. Kedad, N. Lammari, E. Métais, F. Meziane, Y. Rezgui (Eds.), Natural Language Processing and Information Systems. XIV, 442 pages. 2007.

Vol. 4587: R. Cooper, J. Kennedy (Eds.), Data Management. XIII, 259 pages. 2007.

Vol. 4577: N. Sebe, Y. Liu, Y.-t. Zhuang, T.S. Huang (Eds.), Multimedia Content Analysis and Mining. XIII, 513 pages. 2007.

Vol. 4568: T. Ishida, S. R. Fussell, P. T. J. M. Vossen (Eds.), Intercultural Collaboration. XIII, 395 pages. 2007.

Vol. 4566: M.J. Dainoff (Ed.), Ergonomics and Health Aspects of Work with Computers. XVIII, 390 pages. 2007.

Vol. 4564: D. Schuler (Ed.), Online Communities and Social Computing. XVII, 520 pages. 2007.

Vol. 4563: R. Shumaker (Ed.), Virtual Reality. XXII, 762 pages. 2007.

Vol. 4561: V.G. Duffy (Ed.), Digital Human Modeling. XXIII, 1068 pages. 2007.

Vol. 4560: N. Aykin (Ed.), Usability and Internationalization, Part II. XVIII, 576 pages. 2007.

Vol. 4559: N. Aykin (Ed.), Usability and Internationalization, Part I. XVIII, 661 pages. 2007.

Vol. 4558: M.J. Smith, G. Salvendy (Eds.), Human Interface and the Management of Information, Part II. XXIII, 1162 pages. 2007.

Vol. 4557: M.J. Smith, G. Salvendy (Eds.), Human Interface and the Management of Information, Part I. XXII, 1030 pages. 2007.

Vol. 4541: T. Okadome, T. Yamazaki, M. Makhtari (Eds.), Pervasive Computing for Quality of Life Enhancement. IX, 248 pages. 2007.

Vol. 4537: K.C.-C. Chang, W. Wang, L. Chen, C.A. Ellis, C.-H. Hsu, A.C. Tsoi, H. Wang (Eds.), Advances in Web and Network Technologies, and Information Management. XXIII, 707 pages. 2007.

Vol. 4531: J. Indulska, K. Raymond (Eds.), Distributed Applications and Interoperable Systems. XI, 337 pages. 2007.

Vol. 4526: M. Malek, M. Reitenspieß, A. van Moorsel (Eds.), Service Availability. X, 155 pages. 2007.

Vol. 4524: M. Marchiori, J.Z. Pan, C.d.S. Marie (Eds.), Web Reasoning and Rule Systems. XI, 382 pages. 2007.

Vol. 4519: E. Franconi, M. Kifer, W. May (Eds.), The Semantic Web: Research and Applications. XVIII, 830 pages. 2007.

Vol. 4518: N. Fuhr, M. Lalmas, A. Trotman (Eds.), Comparative Evaluation of XML Information Retrieval Systems. XII, 554 pages. 2007.

Vol. 4508: M.-Y. Kao, X.-Y. Li (Eds.), Algorithmic Aspects in Information and Management. VIII, 428 pages. 2007.

Vol. 4506: D. Zeng, I. Gotham, K. Komatsu, C. Lynch, M. Thurmond, M. Madigan, B. Lober, J. Kvach, H. Chen (Eds.), Intelligence and Security Informatics: Biosurveillance. XI, 234 pages. 2007.

Vol. 4505: G. Dong, X. Lin, W. Wang, Y. Yang, J.X. Yu (Eds.), Advances in Data and Web Management. XXII, 896 pages. 2007.